The Jurisprudence of the FIFA Dispute Resolution Chamber

Asser International Sports Law Series

Editors
Robert C.R. Siekmann and Janwillem Soek

ISSN 1874–6926

T.M.C. ASSER INSTITUUT
ASSER INTERNATIONAL SPORTS LAW CENTRE

THE JURISPRUDENCE OF THE FIFA DISPUTE RESOLUTION CHAMBER

by

Frans DE WEGER

T•M•C•ASSER PRESS

Published by T·M·C·ASSER PRESS
P.O. Box 16163, 2500 BD The Hague, The Netherlands
<www.asserpress.nl>

T·M·C·ASSER PRESS' English language books are distributed exclusively by:

Cambridge University Press, The Edinburgh Building, Shaftesbury Road,
Cambridge CB2 2RU, UK,
or
for customers in the USA, Canada and Mexico:
Cambridge University Press, 100 Brook Hill Drive, West Nyack, NY 10994-2133, USA
<www.cambridge.org>

ISBN 978-90-6704-271-0
ISSN 1874-6926

Cover photograph: Hans Erni, "Fussball – Football", 1995. Tempera on paper, 76 × 57 cm.
© Hans Erni, Lucerne/Switzerland.

T.M.C. Asser Instituut – Institute for Private and Public International Law, International Commercial Arbitration and European Law

Institute Address: R.J. Schimmelpennincklaan 20-22, The Hague, The Netherlands; Mailing Address: P.O. Box 30461, 2500 GL The Hague, The Netherlands; Tel.: +3170 342 0300; Fax: +3170 3420 359; Internet: www.asser.nl.

Over forty years, the T.M.C. Asser Institute has developed into a leading scientific research institute in the field of international law. It covers private international law, public international law, including international humanitarian law, the law of the European Union, the law of international commercial arbitration and increasingly, also, international economic law, the law of international commerce and international sports law.

Conducting scientific research, either fundamental or applied, in the aforementioned domains, is the main activity of the Institute. In addition, the Institute organizes congresses and postgraduate courses, undertakes contract-research and operates its own publishing house.

Because of its inter-university background, the Institute often cooperates with Dutch law faculties as well as with various national and foreign institutions.

SUMMARY OF CONTENTS

FOREWORD

I am very pleased and honoured to write the Foreword to this Book on a subject which has been of professional interest to me for many years. Football – or to be more precise association football to distinguish it from American football – is not only the world's favourite game, but also the world's most lucrative sport. As such, it is not surprising that, on and off the pitch, there is much to play for and disputes of various kinds and complexities, often involving substantial sums of money, are far from uncommon occurrences.

One particular area of contention relates to the international transfer of players from one club to another, in which mega sums are often at stake, particularly where high profile foreign players move to or between famous football clubs. After long discussions with the European Commission, FIFA – the world governing body of football – introduced in 2001 the revised Transfer Rules, with the aim of creating certainty and a 'level playing field'. The same year saw the establishment of the FIFA Dispute Resolution Chamber (DRC). The DRC, together with the Players' Status Committee (a body which deals with problems related to the status of players other than proper transfer or employment disputes), has developed into a major and influential alternative resolution body within FIFA, with an impressive and ever increasing caseload to boot. Sports disputes particularly lend themselves to settlement processes, which in turn give effect to the so-called 'specificity' of sport, an activity with special characteristics and dynamics which distinguish it from other businesses. The DRC also deals with disputes concerning the solidarity contribution and training compensation, which are a special feature and, in practice, also an important element of the international football transfer system.

Not all of the many hundreds of cases handled each year by the DRC are published on the FIFA official website (www. FIFA.com), but only the ones of 'general interest'; and this book contains a selection of 172 of such cases. From these cases, a so-called *Lex Sportiva* is developing and may be discerned, which will help to guide and orientate all those in future with an interest in bringing their disputes to the DRC for resolution. This book, therefore, is not only a useful tool, but an essential resource for players and their clubs and advisers seeking fair play in a legal and sporting sense, as well as all others with a sporting and financial interest in football, including administrators, agents, managers, trainers, researchers and academics.

The author, Frans de Weger, and the publishers deserve to be warmly thanked and congratulated for producing this book, which will, I am sure, prove to be an invaluable work of reference and guidance for all concerned.

Michel ZEN RUFFINEN
Attorney at Law
Former FIFA General Secretary and
Head of the FIFA Legal Division

TABLE OF CONTENTS

LIST OF ABBREVIATIONS

CAS Statutes	Statutes of the Bodies Working for the settlement of sports-related disputes
CAS	Court of Arbitration for Sport
DRC	Dispute Resolution Chamber
EEA	European Economic Area
EU	European Union
FAPL	Football Association Premier League
FFF	French National Association
FIFA Comparison	Comparison of the FIFA regulations version July 2001 and following circular letters with the new FIFA regulations version December 2004
FIFA RSTP	FIFA Regulations for the Status and Transfer of Players
FIFA	Fédération Internationale de Football Association
FIFPro	Fédération International de Footballeurs Professionels
ICAS	International Council of Arbitration for Sport
IFs	International Federations
IOC	International Olympic Committee
IRTS	International Registration Transfer Certificate
ITC	International Transfer Certificate
KNVB	Koninklijke Nederlandse Voetbal Bond
NOC	Nationaal Olympisch Comité
PAR	Players' Agent Regulations
PSC	Players' Status Committee
RSTP	Regulations for the Status and Transfer of Players
TAF	Chamber of the Arbitration Tribunal for Football
UEFA	Union of European Football Associations/Union Européenne de Football Association
WADA	Wereld Anti Doping Agentschap/World Anti Doping Agency

Chapter 1
DISPUTE RESOLUTION CHAMBER

1. Introduction

Needless to say, organised football can only attain uniformity, equality and certainty on a worldwide scale if certain fundamental principles and basic rules apply to all participants in professional football. As the organiser of international football, the Fédération Internationale de Football Association (FIFA) was established in 1904 to achieve these goals. According to its own statutes, FIFA exists to improve the game of football, whereby improvement can be interpreted in the widest sense of the word. Not only improvement with regard to the rules on the field, but also with regard to the rules off the field. During the transfer of a player between national associations, for example, the same rules must apply to all participants concerned. In their quest to establish uniformity, equality and certainty, FIFA started by creating the PSC to decide on all international football disputes. This standing committee had to provide the international football world with legal certainty in relation to matters relating to players' status.[1]

Continuing their search for further professionalism, FIFA set up the Dispute Resolution Chamber (DRC) in 2001. This committee was established to take over certain disputes from the PSC and specifically to resolve disputes regarding the international status and transfer of players. As we will see later on, its competence extends to cases relating to labour disputes with an international dimension but also with respect to disputes concerning training compensation and solidarity contribution. In general, this committee decides on basic issues such as breach of contract, with or without just cause or sporting just cause. Today, the PSC still has a huge influence. The DRC is more or less incorporated in the PSC and one could say that the PSC can be seen as the umbrella organisation of the DRC. The PSC still has general competence on matters relating to players' status that do not lie within the sphere of the DRC.[2]

The DRC is very important to FIFA's aim to achieve the before-mentioned global uniformity, quality and certainty.[3] In that respect one should note that the DRC is not an arbitrational court, such as the Court of Arbitration for Sport (CAS). The decisions of the DRC can only be enforced through the statutes and regulations of FIFA. Nevertheless, the decisions of the DRC are of crucial importance and have a huge impact on the international football world. The members of FIFA, the national associations, must fully comply with all decisions of FIFA, such as decisions of this committee.[4] In turn, the national associations take every precaution to ensure that their own members, the national players and clubs, also fully comply with these decisions.[5] FIFA could therefore have a great influence through the DRC on international football and all its participants. Due to the

1 FIFA Statutes, Art. 34 under m.
2 Id., Art. 47 Para. 2.
3 The DRC is not an official FIFA body like the PSC.
4 FIFA Statutes, Arts. 10 Para. 4 sub a and 13 Para. 1 sub d.
5 Id., Art. 62 Para. 2.

importance and huge influence that the decisions of the DRC could have through its own channels for the football world, more public attention must be given by FIFA and the associations to these decisions.

Although the main emphasis of this book is laid down in Chapter 2, which analyses all the relevant decisions of the DRC and classifies them into different categories, we must start by looking at the most relevant judicial aspects in relation to this Chamber in order to understand these decisions more properly. When taking decisions, the DRC applies the Regulations for the Status and Transfer of Players (RSTP) whilst taking into account all relevant arrangements, laws and/or collective bargaining agreements that exist at national level, as well as the specificity of sport.[6] As we will see later on, the RSTP rules are the main source of law for the DRC when judging a dispute relating to the international transfers of players, their status and their eligibility to participate in organised football.[7] These fundamental rules are compulsory and uniformly applicable all over the world.[8] They aim to regulate international transfer law when judging a dispute between member associations and they also establish basic principles that guarantee uniform and equal treatment of all participants in the football world.[9] In the first part of this chapter, these regulations will be discussed in more detail. In that respect, the history of the RSTP will be briefly discussed followed by a clearly structured survey of the two main important editions, namely the edition of 2001 and the current edition of 2005.

After discussing the judicial field of the RSTP, the sphere within which the DRC has to operate, it is also important to acquire broader knowledge of the relevant procedural aspects relating to this Chamber, such as the course of the proceedings. These procedural rules are outlined in more detail in the Rules Governing the Procedures of the PSC and the DRC (Procedural Rules). Relevant procedural aspects, such as the jurisdiction of the DRC, its composition, jurisdiction and applicable law, procedural aspects such as withdrawal and challenges, the entities which are entitled to lodge a claim before the DRC, the procedural costs and the manner of enforcement of the DRC decisions will be discussed extensively. Finally, the procedure before the Court of Arbitration of Sport (CAS) will be discussed, as the decisions reached by the DRC may be appealed before this panel.

2. Regulations for the Status and Transfer of Players

2.1 Introduction

The most important judicial ground for the judgement of the DRC is the Regulations for the Status and Transfer of Players, also known as the RSTP. As mentioned above, these regulations set up rules regarding the international transfer of players, the status of players, their eligibility to participate in organised football as well as the release of players for association teams and the players' eligibility to play for such teams. In other words, through these rules FIFA provides the international football world with a judicial basis regarding

[6] RSTP, edition 2005, Art. 25 Para. 6.

[7] The RSTP also set up rules regarding the release of players for association teams and the player's eligibility to play for such teams.

[8] FIFA Commentary, explanation Art. 1 Para. 1, p. 8.

[9] Id., explanation Art. 1 Para. 2, p. 8.

the legal status and transfer of players. With respect to the most recent version, the edition of 2005, we must remember that these rules are based on many earlier editions and therefore have a long history. The first regulations were initially adopted in April 1991 and subsequently amended in December 1993, December 1996, May 1997, September 1997 and July 2001 by the FIFA Executive Committee.[10] The last and current version, the edition of 2005 of the RSTP, also known as the reviewed or revised regulations, was officially adopted by the FIFA Executive Committee on 18 December 2004 and finally came into force on 1 July 2005.[11]

2.2 History

In 1982, the first developments took place regarding international transfers for players in Europe. It was the UEFA, the Union of European Football Associations, which produced the first regulations regarding the transfer of players in September 1982, also known as the "Principles of Cooperation between Clubs of different National Associations of the ECC Countries". According to these regulations, football players were only free to conclude a contract with another foreign club after the expiry of their current contract. Subsequently, their former club and the new club could determine transfer compensation. If the clubs were unable to agree on a reasonable transfer sum, then a committee appointed by the UEFA would be competent to determine a reasonable transfer sum. The UEFA regulations were similar to the Dutch transfer regulations at the time. However, the UEFA regulations also provided for a maximum transfer compensation for the player to the amount of CHF 5,000.000.[12]

FIFA followed UEFA and their first transfer regulations were initially adopted in April 1991. In 1992, FIFA subsequently modified these first international regulations and from 1 January 1994, the new FIFA regulations, which were called the "Regulations governing the Status and Transfer of Players 1994", applied to all participants in international football. From then on, the same principle applied to amateurs and non-amateurs: compensation was compulsory in the case of a transfer of a player between clubs from different national associations. FIFA made a distinction between an amateur and a non-amateur. Pursuant to the first five Articles of the Regulations governing the Status and Transfer of Players 1994, the non-amateur was defined as a player registered with a national association who has a written contract and is paid more than the expenses he incurs in return for his football activity. Furthermore, FIFA emphasised for the first time in these regulations that a player was only free to conclude a contract with another club if the employment contract with his present club had expired or would expire within six months.

At this time, FIFA was the only international football organisation which was competent to make the rules and to give decisions in relation to the legal status and transfer of players. Until then, FIFA did not have to take any other organisations into account. It became clear that FIFA was the monopolist that made the rules and their members just had to comply with these rules. However, the European Commission felt that the Regulations

[10] RSTP, edition 2001, Art. 46.

[11] RSTP, edition 2005, Art. 29 Paras. 1 and 2.

[12] H.T. van Staveren, Syllabus 'Sport en Recht' 2003, Vrije Universiteit Amsterdam, Chapter VII, Para. 4.3, p. 226.

governing the Status and Transfer of Players 1994 could not be maintained because of crucial judicial shortcomings.

2.3 *Bosman* case

FIFA's exclusive position of power finally came to an end with the judgment of the European Court of Justice on 15 December 1995, the famous *Bosman* case, which had a huge impact on the international football world.[13] This case can be considered one of the most important sports cases to appear before the Belgian courts, and in relation to European sport law is possibly the most significant case generally.[14] *Bosman* is and always will be a landmark judgment in sports law.[15] By its decision in 1995, the European Court of Justice stressed that sport, just like any other economic activity, is subject to ordinary rules of European Law.[16] In other words, this European decision made it clear that FIFA's transfer system did not function well enough.

The Belgian professional football player Jean-Marc Bosman refused to sign a new contract offered by his club, the first division club RC Liège. In April 1990, the club offered him a new one-year contract at BFR 120,000 a month, the minimum permitted by Belgian rules and a quarter of his previous salary.[17] In turn, Bosman refused the club's proposal and was subsequently placed on the transfer list. Several other clubs were interested in the player and eventually a deal was signed between Bosman, RC Liège and the French second division club Dunkerque. However, RC Liège had some concerns about Dunkerque's financial position and suddenly cancelled the negotiations. Bosman started proceedings against his club RC Liège with the competent Belgian Court in Liege. The Court of Appeal in Liege suspended the case and asked for a preliminary decision of the European Court of Justice. Its main argument was that the transfer system breached European competition law; more specifically it breached the right of free movement of people within the European Union. Bosman claimed that the transfer rules were not suitable to ensure the balance between finances and sporting performance.[18] The European Court of Justice now had to determine the legal status of the transfer regulations concerned. Finally, the European Court decided that professional football, insofar as it constitutes an economic activity, is subject to community law. The football associations are obliged to comply with basic legal principles, including the right of employees within Europe to freedom of movement. It decided that transfer compensation to be paid by a club for a player who

---

[13] Case C-415/93, *Union royale belge des sociétés de football association ASBL v. Jean-Marc Bosman Royal Club liègois SA* v. *Jean-Marc Bosman. SA d'Economic Mixte Sportive de l'Union Sportive du Littoral de Dunkerque, Union Royale Belge des Sociétés de Football Association ASBL, Union des Associations Européennes de Football Union des Association Européennes de Football* v. *Jean-Marc Bosman*, judgement of 15 December 1995, [1991] *ECR* I-4837.

[14] Aaron Wise and Bruce S. Meyer, *International Sports Law and Business*, Vol. 2, The Hague, Kluwer Law International 1997) p. 1104/1105.

[15] Lars Halgreen, 'The European Regulation of Sport', 3/4 ISLJ (2005) p. 47. According to Halgreen there was an unmistakable feeling among sports associations that they were beyond legal control.

[16] Roger Blanpain, 'The fight for player freedom continues, 10 years of Bosman', 1/2 *ISLJ* (2006) p. 116.

[17] Stephen Weatherill, *European Sports Law, Collected Papers*, T.C.M. Asser Press (The Hague, 2007), pp. 90-91.

[18] Roger Blanpain, *De Bosman case*, Reeks Europees Recht, Uitgeverij Peters Leuven (Leuven 1996) p. 332. Blanpain agreed with this point of view of Bosman.

had ended his contractual relationship with his former club was not permitted and was in violation with the free movement of people within the European Union.[19]

2.4 Post-*Bosman* period

Following the decision of the European Court, the football clubs had to respond to the new situation. The clubs wanted to prevent players reaching the end of their contract and running off for free. They therefore started negotiating contracts for longer periods, for over more than five or six years, for example. Clubs were tempted to draft appropriate clauses in the player's contract which allowed the clubs to secure compensation for their loss.[20] Another method invented by the clubs was to insert clauses in the players' contracts whereby the clubs unilaterally reserved the right to extend the agreement, the so-called unilateral extension option. In Chapter 2, the validity of the unilateral extension option will be discussed in view of the DRC. As a result of these important developments, it was no longer efficient to train the players themselves. The clubs now asked extremely high transfer sums if the player wanted to leave his club before his contract expired. Ultimately this created a situation whereby the biggest clubs attracted all the good players, small clubs faced financial difficulties and huge transfer sums were paid. Understandably, these new circumstances after the *Bosman* case had a very negative impact on the international football world.

Since the famous *Bosman* case, at the end of his contract, a professional football player is free to move to any new football club of his choice his new club being obliged to pay a transfer sum to his former club.[21] Therefore, as a result of the imbalance which had arisen in the international football world since the famous *Bosman* case in 1995, FIFA felt obliged to find a solution. FIFA's transfer rules were severely affected by this ruling.[22] FIFA had to react by revising its rules on international transfers in order to align them to the European Court of Justice Rules. FIFA realised that the civil courts were not going to help the international football world. They therefore had to look for a solution through their own rules for the instability that had arisen in the professional football world. Finally, the European Commission started making objections against the transfer rules of FIFA and the UEFA. FIFA started making new regulations to replace the Regulations governing the Status and Transfer of Players 1994 and which had to maintain contractual stability for players, their transfer status and the training facilities. A start was made on the new FIFA RSTP.

In 1997 a new version of the RSTP was sent to the European Commission for judgement. At first, the European Commission did not agree with the content of these regulations, still feeling that these rules did not comply with the European rules. For example, the European Commission had great problems with the fact that the regulations allowed

---

[19] Christian Drolet, 'Extra Time: Are the new FIFA transfer rules doomed?', 1/2 *ISLJ* (2006) p. 66.

[20] Stephen Weatherill, *European Sports Law*, p. 67.

[21] See also Roger Blanpain, *The Legal Status of Sportsmen and Sportswomen under International, European and Belgian National and Regional Law* (2003), p. 98. See also Roger Blanpain, *The Legal Status of Sportsmen and Sportswomen under International, European and Belgian National and Regional Law*, Kluwer Law International (The Hague, London, New York, 2003), p. 98.

[22] Stephen Weatherill, 'Is the pyramid compatible with EC law?', 3/4 *ISLJ* (2005) p. 5. Weatherill is right when he says that there can be no doubt that it is fiendishly difficult to identify what really are rules that belong to the autonomy of sports federations and what are instead rules of a sufficiently commercial character to fall for inspection under the rules of the EC Treaty.

the transfers of players under the age of 18. Neither could it agree with the fact that FIFA excluded proceedings for civil courts. FIFA therefore had to initiate a new plan for RSTP that complied with European legislation.

As a result of all the objections of the European Commission, FIFA started a dialogue with the European Commission to discuss a new concept for transfer rules.[23] The European Commission was of the opinion that the new FIFA Regulations were free to contain provisions with respect to the transfers of players, contractual stability and training compensation for players. However it was crucial that the new regulations complied with the European regulations. The European Commission once more emphasised that the new FIFA regulations could not obstruct the way to the civil courts and that the national laws of the countries concerned had to be obeyed. Finally, as a result of the debate between FIFA and the European Commission, new regulations were drawn up by FIFA. The new regulations were not allowed to rule out civil court proceedings and these rules had to take into account the national legislation concerned.

2.5 **Edition 2001**

In October 2000 FIFA and UEFA sent a joint suggestion for new rules to the European Commission. In 2001, this led to a gentlemen's agreement between FIFA and the European Commission. This became a compromise which was in compliance with the European rules on the one hand while the new rules respected the specificity of sport on the other hand. It was a mixture of the requirements of the European Commission and the special requests of FIFA. After much bargaining and dealing, the new rules were finally adopted by the FIFA Executive Committee on 5 July 2001 and came into force on 1 September 2001. These rules are called the edition 2001. The new Rules were the subject of negotiations with the European Commission. Mario Monti, the commissioner of the European Commission at that time, was assumed to have been personally involved in drafting the transfer rules which became known in the football world as the "Monti-rules".[24]

The new RSTP guaranteed the contractual stability of the players' contracts and regulated the international transfer for players more properly. Even more importantly, the new rules that now replaced the Regulations governing the Status and Transfer of Players 1994 complied with the demands of the European Commission. Three important pillars were inserted to guarantee the above. Contracts had to be for a minimum of one year and a maximum of five years. The main reason for this was that players were now even more inclined to stay with their clubs, particularly now that they were obliged to stay for one entire season. This combined with the main objectives of FIFA, namely to create more certainty. Furthermore, the new regulations introduced two transfer registration periods, i.e., a transfer period during the winter and a transfer period during the summer. Players were only allowed to transfer internationally during these two periods. Finally, FIFA introduced a protection system for the international transfer of minors. As mentioned earlier, minors under the age of 18 from outside the confederation of Europe were not obliged to make a transfer to another association.

---

[23] See for the course of the negotiations: <http://ec.europa.eu/sport/sport-and/markt/bosman/b_bosman_en.html>.

[24] Christian Drolet, 'Extra Time: are the new FIFA transfer rules doomed?', 1/2 *ISLJ* (2006) p. 67.

The RSTP, edition 2001 also created and introduced the DRC, as mentioned earlier.[25] Besides the urgent necessity with regard to the right of any player or club to seek redress before a civil court in disputes between clubs and players, the edition 2001 enabled a dispute resolution and arbitration system to be established. In future, the basic elements, such as whether a contract was breached, with or without just cause or sporting just cause, would have to be decided by this DRC of the FIFA Players' Status Committee. The rules with respect to the procedure before the DRC were laid down in the so-called "Procedural Rules for the FIFA Players' Status Committee and the Rules Governing the Practice and Procedures of the Dispute Resolution Chamber".[26] Furthermore, in relation to the edition 2001 of the RSTP, the rules were provided with the "Regulations Governing the Application of the RSTP". These regulations provided more precise details relating to the legal status and transfer of players.[27] Last but not least, the edition 2001 of the RSTP also contained provisions that regulated the compensation for the training and education of young players.

2.6 **Edition 2005**

At its meeting held in Zurich on 18 and 19 December 2004, the FIFA Executive Committee adopted new regulations, also known as the "Reviewed Regulations for the Status and Transfer of Players". These regulations, also known as edition 2005, replaced the special regulations governing players' eligibility to play for association teams dated 4 December 2003, the RSTP of 5 July 2001, as well as all subsequent amendments, including all relevant circular letters issued before these regulations came into force. The new regulations were officially adopted by the FIFA Executive Committee on 18 December 2004 and the new regulations were finally implemented on 1 July 2005.[28]

The reasons for these amendments were explained by FIFA in its Circular 959. FIFA explained that the new rules had a new layout as well as a more user-friendly structure. According to FIFA, the new rules were meant to improve the old rules. New formal and material elements had been included, such as a list of the most current definitions, a title to every Article and with regard to the jurisdiction, a clear description of the competences of both the PSC and the DRC. Moreover, based on the positive experience with the Single Judge of the PSC, also at the level of the DRC, the so-called DRC Judge was introduced.

Drolet defined the edition 2001 of the RSTP rules and the Application Regulations as "not crystal clear" and "vague". In his opinion, the 2005 rules had to be seen more as an adjustment than a new set of rules. The new rules attempt to fix some of the problems discovered in the 2001 rules.[29] In my opinion, the new rules are certainly clearer and have more structure. However, the new rules were not only given a new layout and more user-friendly structure. As we will see later on, FIFA also implemented new material rules at certain points in the edition 2005.

---

[25] RSTP, edition 2001, Art. 42 Para. 1 under b.

[26] Procedural Rules for the FIFA Players' Status Committee dated 21 February 2003 and the Rules Governing the Practice and Procedures of the Dispute Resolution Chamber dated 28 February 2002.

[27] Regulations Governing the Application of the Regulations for the Status and Transfer of Players Edition 2001.

[28] RSTP, edition 2005, Art. 29 Paras. 1 and 2.

[29] Christian Drolet, 'Extra Time: are the new FIFA transfer rules doomed?', 1/2 *ISLJ* (2006) p. 70.

As we saw earlier, the edition 2005 of the RSTP set up rules regarding international transfers of players, the status of players, their eligibility to participate in organised football, as well as the release of players for association teams and player's eligibility to play for such teams. These fundamental rules are compulsory and uniformly applicable all over the world. These regulations aim to regulate international transfers between member associations and establish basic principles that guarantee the uniform and equal treatment of all participants, also one of the main objectives of FIFA.[30]

In principle, FIFA does not interfere in the day-to-day business of the national associations, as long as there are no severe infringements of the FIFA Statutes or regulations.[31] However, following the FIFA Commentary, the autonomy of the associations is limited by the basic principles of the regulations that have to be observed at all times and in particular by those provisions that are in particular binding at national level and have to be included without modification in the association's regulations.[32] One of the fundamental principles on which the regulations are based is the principle that the associations must provide for appropriate means to protect contractual stability.[33] Finally, the Reviewed Regulations for the Status and Transfer of Players replaced the edition 2001 of the RSTP and were officially adopted by the FIFA Executive Committee on 18 December 2004. They came into force on 1 July 2005.[34] This last version contains the rules which are currently the basis for the judgement of the DRC.

2.7 FIFA Comparison

FIFA compared the FIFA Regulations edition 2001 with the revised and new FIFA Regulations edition 2005, which is called the "Comparison of the FIFA regulations version July 2001 and following circular letters with the new 0fifa regulations version December 2004" (FIFA Comparison). In the FIFA Comparison, the relevant modifications between the two editions are outlined in more detail and included short comments from FIFA.[35] In almost every Article of the RSTP, edition 2005, the changes with the RSTP 2001 have been briefly listed.

In edition 2005, the new definition of the earlier mentioned Non-Amateur now is Professional,[36] the International Registration Transfer Certificate (IRTS) is now called the International Transfer Certificate (ITC), the first registration period was not allowed to exceed 12 weeks and in edition 2005 this has been shortened to 6 weeks. In edition 2001, a minor was allowed to make a transfer if his family moved for reasons not linked to football. In edition 2005, the word "family" has been replaced by "his parents". Furthermore, the minimum working age has been specified.

A relevant difference between the two editions is the sporting just cause. Article 15 of the RSTP 2005 is stated that the examples of sporting just cause in Article 24 of edition

---

[30] FIFA Commentary, explanation Art. 1 Para. 2, p. 9.

[31] Id., explanation Art. 2 Para. 1, p. 9.

[32] Id., explanation Art. 1 Para. 2, p. 9.

[33] Id., explanation Art. 1 Para. 3, p. 9.

[34] RSTP, edition 2005, Art. 29 Paras. 1 and 2.

[35] Comparison of the FIFA Regulations version July 2001 and following circular letters with the new FIFA Regulations version December 2004.

[36] According to the FIFA Commentary, the new terminology is more appropriate as it reflects the evaluation of professionalism in football over the years. FIFA Commentary, explanation Art. 2, p. 10.

2001 have been deleted, such as injury, suspension, player's field position, etc. Only three conditions to apply sporting just cause still remain and have been introduced. The player must be an established professional and have appeared in fewer than 10% of the official matches during the season. In this case, he can terminate the contract in the 15 days following the last official match of the season of the club for which he is registered.

Regarding the protection of minors, the code of conduct provided for in the 2001 edition has been deleted. Article 22 states that the generic term "dispute between players and clubs" has been replaced by disputes between clubs and players in relation to the maintenance of contractual stability if there has been an ITC Request that the employment-related disputes between a club and a player must have an international dimension and that disputes related to training compensation and solidarity mechanism must have arisen between clubs belonging to different associations.

Furthermore with regard to Articles 23 and 24 of the RSTP edition 2005, the four FIFA bodies such as the DRC, the PSC, the DRC Judge and the Single Judge and their competences have been better specified together with their function and jurisdiction. In Annex 4 Article 7 and Annex 5 Article 2 Paragraph 4 now the FIFA Disciplinary Committee and not the PSC is competent to impose disciplinary measures on clubs or players that do not observe the obligations set out in these annexes. As we can see, the FIFA Comparison briefly lists the main changes between the editions RSTP 2001 and RSTP 2005.

2.8 **FIFA Commentary**

In December 2006, FIFA published on its website the so-called "Commentary on the Regulations for the Status and Transfer of Players" (FIFA Commentary).[37] This is an extensive 150 page commentary. Like all FIFA regulations, it is published in the four official languages.[38] With nearly every Article of the edition 2005, a commentary has been given by FIFA in relation to this subject. These explanations are in principle based on the jurisprudence of the competent decision-making bodies of FIFA, such as the PSC and the DRC, including the DRC Judge and the CAS.[39] The FIFA Commentary is therefore a very important document for a better understanding the decisions of the DRC.

Although the FIFA Commentary is meant to be a *commentary* and should therefore be exclusively intended as a clarification and a further explanation of the Articles in the RSTP edition 2005, at some points the FIFA Commentary more or less creates its own kind of law. With respect to the FIFA Commentary, For certain issues, we will see that FIFA gives us more than an explanation based on the jurisprudence of the competent bodies and gives us its own interpretation of the Article concerned.

For example, the so-called "buyout clause". In the event of a buyout clause, the parties may stipulate in the contract the amount that the player will pay to the club as compensation in order to unilaterally terminate his contract. The FIFA Commentary states under

[37] FIFA Commentary on the Regulations for the Status and Transfer of Players. See also Circular 1075 dated 18 January 2007: <http://www.fifa.com/aboutfifa/docuementlibrary/legalmatters.html>. In a decision of the DRC of 22 July 2004, the DRC clarified that circular letters are an administrative instrument, which – as sources of law within the FIFA legal system – are hierarchically subordinated to the FIFA Regulations. Accordingly, the useful and legitimate aim of circular letters is to implement, detail and interpret the FIFA regulations. However, the regulations must remain the main source of law when having to judge a dispute. DRC 22 July 2004, no. 74477.

[38] FIFA Commentary, General Remarks, under 1, p. 4.

[39] Id., General Remarks, under 2, p. 4.

Article 17(3) that if the player terminates the contract on the basis of this buyout clause, then no sporting sanctions may be imposed on the player.[40] However on this point, the FIFA commentary is not in line with the regulations. Here FIFA is following its own line and does not found this on its own regulations or on DRC jurisprudence. FIFA should distinguish the period of termination inside and outside the protected period. In principle, it can be said that when the buyout clause is invoked by the player outside the protected period, then no sporting sanctions may be imposed on the player. When the buyout clause is invoked within the protected period, it may be presumed that sporting sanctions will be imposed on the player. The conclusion of the FIFA Commentary would at this point be against the principle of the maintenance of contractual stability as laid down in Articles 13 to 16. So far, the DRC has never given a decision on this point. However, the FIFA Commentary (i.e., FIFA) explicitly underlines that no sporting sanctions can be imposed as a result of invoking a buyout clause. In other words, the FIFA Commentary prejudges at this point an eventual decision of the DRC.

Another example, is Article 18 Paragraph 3 of the RSTP which states that a club intending to conclude a contract with a professional must inform his current club in writing before entering into negotiations with that professional. According to this Article, the only obligation of a potential new club is to inform the club with which the player is currently contracted in writing. In my opinion, a fax, letter or e-mail may therefore suffice. Following a strict interpretation of this Article, it is irrelevant whether or not the current club agrees with the negotiations between its player and a new club. However, pursuant to Article 18 point 4 of the FIFA Commentary, the club with which the player is contracted explicitly underlines that the current club must agree to the discussion between its player and the prospective new club.[41] Without this agreement, the new club may even be in a situation of inducing the player to breach his contract if it continues negotiations with the player. One can see that the prospective new club following the FIFA Commentary is obliged to have the approval of the current club. Although the DRC has so far never provided us with an answer regarding this issue, nor is the RSTP clear on this point, the FIFA supplies us with the answer through its own commentary.

Notwithstanding the above, the FIFA Commentary is generally very valuable for a better understanding of the various decisions of the DRC which will be discussed in Chapter 2. However, as we have seen before, it is important to be aware that FIFA follows its own line at some points. Sometimes FIFA creates its own kind of law and its opinion may deviate from future decisions of the DRC. One can wonder in all sincerity whether this is justified from a formal point of view.

3. Procedure DRC

3.1 Introduction

The proceedings and deliberations of the DRC, including the DRC Judge which will be discussed later, generally take place at FIFA headquarters in Zurich, Switzerland.[42] As

[40] FIFA Commentary, explanation Art 17, p. 47.

[41] Id., explanation Art 18, p. 54.

[42] Rules Governing the Procedures of the Players' Status Committee and the Dispute Resolution Chamber (DRC), Art. 10.

stated earlier, the DRC was only created by FIFA in 2001 and its first decision was on 22 November 2002.[43] Ever since its first decision of 22 November 2002 until today, the DRC has given many decisions. However, the problem we face is that FIFA does not publish all the decisions of the DRC on its website. Consequently, it is now very difficult to estimate how many decisions have been taken by the DRC. Between 2002 and the end of 2006, exactly 597 decisions by the DRC were published on the official website of FIFA.[44]

As we will see in Chapter 2, all relevant decisions of the DRC are classified into various groups. However, before analysing the most relevant decisions, which will be the main essence of this book, it is crucially important to have broader knowledge of the most relevant procedural aspects in relation to the DRC. Once we know the judicial framework and the limited field and scope within which the DRC has to operate, we have a good foundation and information to understand their decisions more properly. All the relevant procedural aspects will now be discussed, such as the jurisdiction of the DRC, its composition, relevant procedural forms like withdrawal and challenges, the right to representation and furthermore which entities are entitled to lodge a claim with the DRC. It is also very important to know that decisions of the DRC can only be enforced through its own FIFA channels. Finally, another important aspect is that decisions reached by the DRC or the DRC Judge may be appealed before the CAS. All these principles are explicitly laid down in the "Rules Governing the Procedures of the PSC and the Dispute Resolution Chamber (DRC)", also called the Procedural Rules, which will be discussed first.

3.2 **Procedural Rules**

According to Article 25 Paragraph 7 of the RSTP edition 2005, the detailed procedure for the resolution of disputes arising from the application of the RSTP are further explicitly outlined in the FIFA General Procedural Rules.[45] Initially, there were the Procedural Rules of the FIFA PSC dated 21 February 2003 and the Rules Governing the Practice and Procedures of the DRC dated 28 February 2002. These rules were replaced by the new Rules Governing the Procedures of the PSC and the DRC which were approved by the FIFA Executive Committee on 29 June 2005 and which came into force on 1 July 2005.[46] These rules constituted a new set of procedural rules that are now applicable to both the PSC and the DRC.[47]

In each decision, the DRC refers to Article 18 Paragraphs 2 and 3 of the Rules Governing the Procedures of the PSC and the DRC to decide which version of the Procedural Rules is applicable.[48] The current Rules Governing the Procedures of the PSC and the DRC, hereinafter also called the Procedural Rules, are based on Article 31 Paragraph 1 of the FIFA Statutes. Article 18 Paragraph 1 states that the Procedural Rules of July 2005 are applicable to proceedings submitted to FIFA after the date on which these Procedural Rules came into force. In other words, if the case was submitted to FIFA before 1 July 2005, then the Procedural Rules of the FIFA Players' Status Committee dated 21 February

---

43 DRC 22 November 2002, no. 300702.

44 <www.fifa.com/aboutfifa/federation/administration/decision.html>.

45 RSTP, edition 2005, Art. 25 Para. 7.

46 Procedural Rules, Art. 18 Para. 3.

47 As was pronounced in Circular 959 dated 16 March 2005.

48 DRC 17 August 2006, no. 862.

2003 and the Rules Governing the Practice and Procedures of the Dispute Resolution Chamber dated 28 February 2002 are applicable. If the claim was lodged with FIFA after 1 July 2005, then the Procedural Rules of July 2005 are applicable. According to Article 25 Paragraph 1 of the RSTP, the proceedings regarding decisions of the DRC Judge and the DRC will now be governed by the current Procedural Rules.[49]

3.3 Composition

The DRC meets in the form of a panel and adjudicates in principle in the presence of at least three members, including the chairman or the deputy chairman.[50] According to the FIFA Commentary, the composition of the DRC must be based on the fundamental principle of equal representation of players and clubs. Ten members represent the players and are proposed by FIFPro, the international player's union for professional football players, and ten club members are proposed by the national associations and leagues all around the world from amongst their clubs.

The FIFA Executive Committee will then formally appoint the proposed members, together with the chairman and the deputy chairman.[51] In this respect it is furthermore important that the members of the DRC do not perform different functions in the same matter. They will explicitly refrain from attempting to influence other bodies and committees and they must maintain strict confidentiality concerning all information that is brought to their attention in the exercise of their office and not mentioned in the decision. In particular, they are strictly obliged to respect the secrecy of deliberations.[52]

Following the above, it is furthermore important to mention the fact that if the case is of a simpler nature, then it may be handled and decided by one single judge, the so-called DCR Judge. In that event, the members of the DRC will appoint a DRC Judge for the clubs and one for the players from amongst its members.[53] The aspect of the DRC Judge will be reviewed in detail in paragraph 3.4.4.

3.4 Jurisdiction

3.4.1 *Civil court*

Article 61 Paragraph 2 of the FIFA Statutes stipulates that recourse to ordinary courts of law is prohibited unless specifically provided for in the FIFA regulations.[54] To ensure that the association does not address the civil courts, they are obliged to insert a clause in their

[49] In a decision of the DRC of 17 August 2006, the Chamber analysed whether it was competent to deal with the matter at stake. In this respect, it referred to Art. 18 Paras. 2 and 3 of the Rules Governing the Procedures of the Players' Status Committee and the Dispute Resolution Chamber. The present matter was submitted to FIFA on 26 October 2005. As a consequence, the Chamber concluded that the revised Rules Governing Procedures (edition 2005) on matters pending before the decision making bodies of FIFA are applicable on the matter at hand. DRC 17 August 2006, no. 862.

[50] According to the FIFA Statutes, the composition, specific duties and powers of the individual committees, such as the DRC, will be stipulated in special organisation regulations. The composition of the DRC is therefore laid down in the before-mentioned Procedural Rules as well as the RSTP, edition 2005.

[51] FIFA Commentary, explanation Art. 24, p. 72. Procedural Rules, Art. 4.

[52] Procedural Rules, Art. 5 Para. 7.

[53] RSTP, edition 2005, Art. 24 Para. 2.

[54] FIFA Statutes, Art. 60 sub 2.

statutes stipulating that their clubs and members are in turn prohibited from taking a dispute to ordinary courts.[55] However, in general, the national law of many countries provides for the compulsory jurisdiction of ordinary courts in the case of employment-related disputes. Hence, parties can decide to submit a labour dispute to a competent ordinary court, because the choice of judge is a fundamental right that cannot be denied. Players and clubs are therefore entitled to seek redress before a civil court as an exception to the statutory principles of the FIFA Statutes.[56] According to the FIFA Commentary, some national legislation does not even allow labour disputes to be referred to a deciding body other than the civil courts before the dispute has arisen.

Parties may however decide to divert from the choice of judge if there is no compulsory jurisdiction of ordinary courts and instead refer the matter to (national of international) sports arbitration. However, according to the principle of "litispendency", a case pending in front of civil courts cannot be dealt with by sports arbitration.[57] The DRC explicitly forbids a party to address several civil courts and then address FIFA if the decision of the civil court does not satisfy the party concerned, also known as "forum shopping".[58] The DRC is of the opinion that players and clubs are entitled to seek redress before a civil court for employment-related disputes, since for such issues the choice of judge is a fundamental right that cannot be denied. However, parties may decide to divert from the choice of judge and instead refer the matter to sports arbitration. According to the principle of litispendency, a case pending in front of civil courts cannot be dealt with by decision-making bodies of sports arbitration. The DRC deems it of utmost importance to underline that the practice of parties to have their legal cases heard by several decision-making bodies aimed at obtaining the most favourable judgement must be strictly forbidden.

The FIFA Commentary furthermore refers to the fact that despite being entitled to lodge a claim in relation to an employment dispute with an ordinary court of law, parties prefer to refer their litigations to sports-deciding bodies for several reasons. In general, sports arbitration is a fast decision making system. As we will see later on, the DRC will have to adjudicate within 60 days of receipt of the request.[59] Also the knowledge of the sport specialists is a decisive factor in avoiding the civil court and choosing for sports deciding bodies, such as the DRC. One final important aspect, in my opinion the most relevant one, is the possibility for FIFA to enforce the decisions throughout its own FIFA channels.[60] In that respect it must be noted that it is generally difficult to enforce a decision of an ordi-

[55] In a decision of 4 February 2005, a player went straight to the Labour Tribunal Court of the country concerned without having never ever lodged a formal financial complaint with FIFA against the claimant and moreover he never asked for assistance in relation with his ITC. The DRC was of the opinion that "this behaviour contradicts the basic football rules and must be strongly reprimanded". DRC 4 February 2005, no. 25820.

[56] FIFA Commentary, explanation Art. 22, p. 64.

[57] Id., explanation Art. 22, p. 64. In a decision of the DRC of 21 February 2006 with regard to a contractual dispute between a player and a club, the Chamber concluded that it could not protect the player's stance. By referring the question with regard to his registration to a civil court the player had infringed Art. 61 Para. 2 of the FIFA Statutes. With respect to the contractual dispute, the player preferred to revert to the decision-making bodies of the football instances. The DRC however decided that such forum shopping cannot be accepted, in particular in view of the disrespect of the FIFA Statutes. As a consequence, the DRC decided as a result thereof not to enter into the consideration of the player's claim. One can see that the DRC is very rigorous regarding the way to civil courts. DRC 21 February 2006, no. 26267.

[58] DRC 21 November 2006, no. 1161241.

[59] RSTP, edition 2005, Art. 25 Para. 1.

[60] FIFA Commentary, explanation Art. 22, p. 65.

nary court or an arbitration court in another foreign country. According to the Convention on the Recognition and Enforcement of Foreign Arbitral Awards held in New York on 10 June 1958, only 142 countries declared that it applies the Convention to the recognition and enforcement of awards.[61] This means that in certain countries, there is no legal way to enforce an arbitrational decision.[62] FIFA is competent to respond directly to a country that infringes the rules. Parties therefore prefer the DRC as sports deciding bodies.

3.4.2 *PSC*

Without prejudice to the right of any player or club to seek redress before a civil court for employment-related disputes, which was one of the requirements of the European Commission, FIFA is competent regarding cases such as those mentioned in Article 22 of the RSTP, edition 2005. In this light and according to this Article, FIFA makes a distinction between the competence of the PSC as defined in Article 23 RSTP and the DRC as mentioned in Article 24 RSTP.

As mentioned in the introduction, the PSC can be seen as the umbrella organisation of the DRC. This committee, which is officially a standing committee of FIFA, still has an enormous influence on the DRC. Article 23 Paragraph 2 indicates this influence. This Article outlined that in the event of uncertainty as to the jurisdiction of the DRC or the PCS, the chairman of the PSC will then decide which body has jurisdiction. Also the second paragraph of Article 47 of the FIFA Statutes underlines the special relationship between the PSC and the DRC. This Article states that the PSC is responsible for the work of the DRC. Nowadays, the PSC still has general competence on matters relating to players' status that explicitly do not concern disputes related to the competence of the DRC.[63]

Just like the DRC, the PSC will generally adjudicate in the presence of at least three members, including the chairman or the deputy chairman. If the case is of a simpler nature, it may be settled by a single judge. According to Article 23 Paragraph 3 a case that is considered to be urgent, raises no difficult factual or legal issues and in decisions on the issuance of a provisional ITC. Decisions of both the PSC and the Single Judge may be appealed before the CAS. The appeal procedure before the CAS will be furthermore discussed in Paragraph 3.21.

The PSC has general competence with respect to employment-related disputes between a club or an association and a coach which have an international dimension. If there is an independent arbitration tribunal at national level, this committee will be competent to handle the matter concerned. The PSC is furthermore competent with respect to all other disputes between clubs belonging to different associations that do not fall within the explicit remit of the DRC.

Finally, it must be noted that the PSC also decides:

- at the request of a player who wishes to exercise his right to change associations;[64]

---

[61] This Convention will apply to the recognition and enforcement of arbitral awards made in the territory of a state other than the state where the recognition and enforcement of such awards are sought. As of 1 January 2007 142 countries can be entitled as contracting state.

[62] FIFA Commentary, explanation Art. 22, remark 99, p. 65.

[63] FIFA Statutes, Art. 47 Para. 2.

[64] Regulations governing the application of the statutes, 15 Para. 4.

- whether a national association has rejected an applicant for a player's agents' licence fairly;[65]
- on any disputes concerning matters regarding the protection of minors;[66]
- the (withdrawal of a) provisional registration of a player;[67] and
- on issues in relation to the release of players.[68]

For example, in a decision of the DRC of 11 March 2005 regarding an international transfer, the Chamber decided that it was not competent to handle this matter. In this case there was a financial dispute between the parties resulting from the transfer of a Brazilian player. The DRC had decided earlier that the case at hand should be considered as a dispute over the interpretation and execution of a transfer contract that had been signed between the buying and selling clubs. Therefore, the DRC was of the opinion that these disputes did not fall not within their remit and that the PSC was the competent body. The DRC concluded its deliberations by deciding that it was not competent to deal with this claim, which should be forwarded to the next available meeting of the PSC, or, alternatively, the Single Judge of the PSC.[69]

3.4.3 *DRC*

As stated above, the jurisdiction of the DRC is defined in Article 24 of the RSTP. With respect to its jurisdiction, the DRC starts each decision with the following phrase:

> "The DRC will examine its jurisdiction in the light of Articles 22 to 24 of the current version of the Regulations for the Status and Transfer of Players."[70]

According to this and the current version of the RSTP rules, edition 2005, the DRC will therefore adjudicate on all the disputes in accordance with these Articles, Articles 22 to 24, but with the exception of the issue of the ITC.[71] It could be presumed that disputes related to the issue of an ITC will be settled by the PSC. An important basis for this presumption is Article 2 Paragraph 6 of Annex 3 of the RSTP which states that the player and the club have been given the facility to lodge a claim with FIFA in accordance with Article 22 of the RSTP. However, the jurisdiction of the PSC in this respect is not stated in the regulations.

According to Article 22 jo. 24 of the RSTP, the DRC has jurisdiction with regard to:

1. disputes between players and clubs with respect to the maintenance of contractual stability if there has been an ITC request and if there is a claim from an interested

---

[65] Player's Agent Regulations (PAR), Art. 4 Para. 3. Besides that it approves the Player's Agent Regulations of the national associations, according to the preamble of the PAR.

[66] RSTP, edition 2005, Art. 19 Para. 5.

[67] Id., Annex 3, Art. 2 Para. 5.

[68] Id., Annex 1, Art. 6 Para. 2 jo. 3.

[69] DRC 11 March 2005, no. 35671.

[70] See for example DRC 22 July 2004, no. 74557.

[71] RSTP, edition 2005, Art. 24 Para. 1. Although it is not explicitly mentioned in the regulations, disputes related to the *issuance* of an ITC will be settled by the PSC. Following Art. 2 Para. 6 of Annex 3 of the RSTP, the player and the club are entitled to lodge a claim with FIFA in accordance with Art. 22 of the RSTP. FIFA, i.e., the PSC, will then decide on the issuance of the ITC and on sporting sanctions within 60 days.

party in relation to such an ITC request, in particular regarding its issue, regarding sporting sanctions or regarding compensation for breach of contract;
2. employment-related disputes between a player and a club that have an international dimension, unless an independent arbitration tribunal guaranteeing fair proceedings and respecting the principle of equal representation of players and clubs has been established at national level within the framework of the association and/or a collective bargaining agreement; and
3. disputes related to training compensation and solidarity mechanism.[72]

In the following paragraphs, these three special cases that fall within the remit of the DRC will be discussed and reviewed in more detail.

3.4.3.1 ITC request

In the first place the DRC is competent in relation to disputes between clubs and players with respect to the maintenance of contractual stability if there has been an ITC request and if there is a claim from an interested party in relation to such an ITC request regarding sporting sanctions or regarding compensation for breach of contract.[73] In other words, if there is an ITC request from a national association, the DRC automatically has jurisdiction.

A player who is registered for a club that is affiliated to an association will not be eligible to play for a club affiliated to a different association, unless an ITC has been issued by the former association and received by the new association. Until the ITC has been received by the new association, the professional is not eligible to play in official matches for his new club. For example, if a player is transferred from Bayern München to AC Milan, the Italian football association will ask for an ITC from the German football association. Within the following seven days of receiving the ITC request, the German football association will issue the ITC to the Italian football association or inform the Italian football association that the ITC cannot be issued because the contract between Bayern München and the player has not expired or that there has been no mutual agreement regarding its early termination.[74]

In my opinion, the fact that the DRC has jurisdiction in the case of an ITC request and in the event of a claim from an interested party in relation to such ITC request could promote some sort of forum shopping. The only action one party has to take to establish jurisdiction of the DRC is to request an ITC. The possible negative effect can be explained by the following situation. Because decisions of certain national arbitrational court sometimes differ from decisions of the DRC with respect to the same issue, parties will bring their claim to the court where they expect to be most successful. An example is the unilateral extension option. The Dutch national arbitrational court decided that the unilateral extension in the contract of the player Trabelsi with Ajax was valid. If Arsenal, who had shown interest in this player at the time, had informed Ajax that it was interested in the player, then the English Football Association could have requested an ITC from the Dutch

---

[72] RSTP, edition 2005, Art. 22 under a, b and d.

[73] Id., Art. 22 sub a jo. Art. 24.

[74] Id., Annex 3, Administrative Procedure Governing the Transfer of Players between Associations, Para. 2 sub 4.

Football Association. The DRC would then automatically be competent to decide on the same clause, the same unilateral extension option, in the same contract. In line with its jurisprudence, the DRC might then decide that the same unilateral extension option might be invalid. Besides the aspect of forum shopping, this would also lead to an undesirable situation and would also be very contrary to the main purposes of FIFA, namely to create uniformity, equality and certainty for the international football world.

3.4.3.2 Employment-related disputes

In the second place, according to Article 24 sub b of the RSTP rules, edition 2005, the DRC is also competent for employment-related disputes between a club and a player that have an international dimension, unless an independent arbitration tribunal guaranteeing fair proceedings and respecting the principle of equal representation of players and clubs has been established at national level within the framework of the association and/or a collective bargaining agreement.[75]

The DRC is exclusively competent in the event of an employment-related dispute. In a case relating to a training agreement, the DRC concluded that the training agreement did not constitute an employment contract but rather an instrument intended to safeguard and protect the rights of a player in formation.[76] The DRC underlined that its jurisdiction was limited to considering disputes arising from an employment contract concluded between a player and a club affiliated to an association. As a result, the Chamber adjudicated that it was not competent to decide on the consequences of a possible breach of the training agreement or of the non-respect of the formal prerequisites for an early termination of the relevant agreement concluded between the player and the club.[77] Yet, it is important to determine that the dispute is related to an employment agreement, otherwise the DRC will be of the opinion that is not competent.

In the before-mentioned decision of 11 March 2005 with respect to a transfer contract, the DRC also decided in that line, namely that it was not competent due to the fact that this case should be considered as a dispute in relation to the interpretation and execution of a transfer contract that had been signed between the buying and selling clubs. In this case, the DRC was of the opinion that it was not competent in relation to disputes other than employment-related disputes. Here, the PSC was the competent body to decide on the dispute.[78] Officially, this was an issue which did not fall within the remit of the DRC.

As we have seen, two further aspects relating to the employment-related disputes should be considered with respect to the jurisdiction of the DRC, namely (i) whether there is an international dimension, as will be discussed in Paragraph 3.4.3.2.1 and (ii) whether the national association has an independent arbitrational tribunal guaranteeing fair proceedings and respecting the principle of equal representation of players and clubs, as will be analysed in Paragraph 3.4.3.2.2.

[75] RSTP, edition 2005, Art. 22 sub b jo. Art. 24.

[76] Roberto Branco Martins, 'Freedom of movement in relation to sport', 1/2 *ISLJ* (2007) p. 105. Branco Martins refers to the training agreement in the Netherlands, where the agreement is characterised by the fact that the player is obliged to train with the first team.

[77] DRC 26 November 2004, no. 114667-26 and DRC 9 November 2004, no. 114667-09. See also CAS *Roma/FIFA/Mexès*.

[78] DRC 11 March 2005, no. 35671.

3.4.3.2.1 International dimension

With respect to the jurisdiction of the DRC in relation to the employment-related disputes, the first requirement according to Article 24 under b of the RSTP rules, edition 2005, is the presence of the *international dimension* as stated before. The DRC has handed down numerous decisions in which the term "international dimension" came up for consideration.[79] The DRC is competent when a player signs for a club affiliated to *another* association as a result of an employment-related dispute. It is irrelevant whether the player has the nationality of the country where the former club was domiciled. The registration of the player following the termination of the contract determines whether the dispute is national or international. For example, if the player registers for a new club in the same association where his former club is domiciled, the dispute is national. If the player registers for a club in another association and there is an ITC request, the dispute is international. Following the FIFA Commentary, such international disputes are referred to the DRC with respect to the substance of the matter.[80]

In a decision of the DRC of 9 November 2004, the player had concluded "a contrat stagiaire" with a French club, valid from 1 July 2003 until 30 June 2004. After the contract expired, the player signed an employment contract with an English club. On 13 August 2004, the English Football Association asked the French Football Federation to issue the ITC for the player. The French football federation refused to issue the ITC. On 19 August 2004, the English football association asked FIFA to order the French football federation to issue the ITC. On 2 September 2004, FIFA ordered the French football federation to issue the ITC. In the same letter, FIFA authorised the English football association to provisionally register the player. On 14 September 2004, the French club appealed to the CAS and asked for a suspension of the registration and on 6 October 2004 the CAS suspended the registration of the English football association until the final decision of the DRC. The DRC considered that it was competent to judge in this case because of its international dimension.[81] In line with the above, it is clear that the DRC may adjudicate on all cases and disputes where an ITC is involved.

According to several other decisions of the DRC, FIFA bodies such as the DRC are competent to deal with disputes related to the transfer of a player exclusively where there is a so-called *international impact*.[82] In several cases, the DRC refers to its own well established jurisprudence according to which, in employment-related disputes between a club and a player that have an international dimension, the main criterion is that the parties do not belong to the same country. In line with the above, the international dimension is simply represented by the fact that the player concerned is a foreigner in the country concerned. In these cases there is no need for an ITC request. The jurisdiction of FIFA will then be automatically established and the dispute will immediately fall within the remit of the DRC.[83]

---

[79] DRC 1 June 2005, no. 65349, DRC 23 March 2006, no. 631290, DRC 27 April 2006, no. 46610, DRC 17 August 2006, no. 86174, DRC 26 October 2006, no. 1061318.

[80] FIFA Commentary, explanation Art. 22, p. 66.

[81] DRC 9 November 2004, no. 114667-09; see also DRC 26 November 2004, no. 114667-26. The DRC furthermore decided that before it takes a final decision, it will give the parties the possibility to solve their problems amicably. If the parties cannot reach an amicable settlement, then the Chamber will handle the case again on a future meeting.

[82] DRC 26 November 2004, no. 114667-26, DRC 1 June 2005, no. 65349.

[83] FIFA Commentary, explanation Art. 22, p. 66

In a decision of the DRC of 2 November 2005 regarding a financial dispute on the basis of an employment contract, the DRC stressed that the FIFA RSTP (edition 2001) applied to all international disputes between clubs, between players and clubs and between coaches and clubs. The DRC then referred to the preamble of the RSTP and particularly to Paragraphs 2 and 3, according to which some principles are also binding at national level and each association is obliged to draw up its internal regulations. Within the framework of its autonomy, the member association concerned is free to adapt its internal rules to the necessity and the specific situation of the country concerned. Therefore, the competence of FIFA is restricted to international transfers and disputes with an international dimension. The DRC emphasised that a dispute is international when two parties of clearly different nationalities claim against each other. However, when both parties have the same nationality, the dispute will be considered to be national or internal, meaning that the rules and regulations of the member association will be applied to the matter and the deciding bodies in accordance with the relevant provisions are obliged to decide on the issue.

3.4.3.2.2 Independent arbitration tribunal

Furthermore, the second important requirement in relation to employment-related disputes according to Article 24 b of the RSTP rules is that the DRC also has jurisdiction when no independent arbitration tribunal at national level is guaranteed fair proceedings. A further restriction in that respect is that the arbitrational court at national level should respect that the principle of equal representation of players and clubs has been established within the framework of the association and/or a collective bargaining agreement.[84] In other words, an independent arbitration tribunal must be established at national level and it must respect the principles of equal representation of players and clubs with an independent chairman.[85]

Following several other decisions of the DRC, it can be concluded that if the association in which both the player and club are registered has established an arbitration tribunal composed of members chosen in equal numbers by players and clubs with an independent chairman, this tribunal is competent to decide on such disputes.[86] In respect thereof, a clear reference to the competence of the national arbitration tribunal must be included in the employment contract. In particular, the player must be aware at the moment of signing the contract that the parties will be submitting potential disputes related to their employment relationships to this body.[87] The national arbitration tribunals may also be provided for within the framework of a collective bargaining agreement.[88]

In a decision of the DRC of 4 July 2003, a contractual dispute had arisen between a Polish player and a Greek club.[89] The DRC decided that the arbitration body of the Greek League of Football Clubs did not appear to be composed on a parity base. As a result, the DRC decided that it was competent to examine the substance of the matter despite the decision already taken by the national body, provided no other formal element would call the Chamber's jurisdiction into question.

---

84 RSTP, edition 2005, Art. 22 sub b jo. Art. 24.
85 DRC 17 August 2006, no. 861174
86 FIFA Commentary, explanation Art. 22, p. 66.
87 Id., explanation Art. 22, remark 101, p. 66.
88 Id., explanation Art. 22, p. 66.
89 DRC 4 July 2003, no. 730291.

In a decision of the DRC of 10 June 2004, the DRC considered that the disciplinary committee and the arbitration body of a football federation were not based on equal representation of players and clubs.[90] Consequently the DRC stated that the decisions had not been taken in compliance with Article 42 of the before-mentioned regulations and the DRC was therefore entitled to intervene in this matter.

It is even doubtful whether the Dutch KNVB Arbitration Court fulfils the requirements of FIFA. In the strict sense of the DRC, the Dutch Arbitrators are not represented by an equal representation of the judges and are not appointed by the employee and the employer. In the Netherlands there are A and B arbiters who are appointed by the members of the federation meeting and therefore not directly by the employee and the employer.[91] According to the strict requirements of the DRC, it could be presumed that the Dutch national arbitration court is not competent. Until now the competency of the Dutch Arbitration Court has not been challenged. However, if the DRC had to take a decision in this matter, the Chamber might not accept proceedings in the Netherlands for the Dutch national arbitration court because it does not fulfil the requirement with respect to the principle of equal representations of the arbiters.[92]

Although it is not mentioned in Articles 22 to 24 of the RSTP rules, it can be presumed that the DRC also has jurisdiction when the parties have expressed a preference in a written agreement which contains a clause whereby the jurisdiction of another body is appointed. Following several decisions of the DRC, the following case came up for consideration.[93] In a decision of 10 June 2004, the DRC decided that it was also competent to deal with a dispute, "even if written agreements signed between the parties involved in the dispute contain a clause by means of which the jurisdiction of another body is referred to". In addition, it must be mentioned in this respect that neither the player nor the club had invoked the relevant Article in their claim or response to the claim.[94] In a decision of 26 November 2004 with respect to the same issue, the Chamber decided accordingly.[95]

One can even say that the DRC automatically has jurisdiction in the event that the parties do not invoke the clause in which they refer to another competent court. In a case before the DRC on 22 July 2004, neither the player nor the club had invoked the before-mentioned provision in which this preference was made in their claim or response to the claim respectively. Furthermore, according to Appendix2 of the employment contract, the DRC was of the opinion that the "provisions and regulations of FIFA" were then applicable to the employment relationship between the parties. Consequently, the members of the Chamber confirmed that in accordance with Article 42 of the before-mentioned regulations it was competent to deal with the present matter, irrespective of the fact that none of the parties had invoked the relevant clause.

---

[90] DRC 10 June 2004, no. 6400276, DRC 1 June 2005, no. 65349. See also the Dutch extended essay of J.H.E. de Beer, p. 17.

[91] Arbitration Regulations of the Dutch KNVB Arbitration Court, Arts. 4, 5 and 6.

[92] According to O.H.J.M. van Eijndhoven, the Arbitrational Court of the Dutch National Football Association does not fulfil the requirement with respect to the principle of equal representations of the arbiters, in *Sport en Recht* 2007, p. 34.

[93] DRC 11 March 2005, no. 35284, DRC 1 June 2005, no. 65412, DRC 1 June, no. 65414, DRC 17 August 2006, no. 86833.

[94] DRC 10 June 2004, no. 64357

[95] DRC 26 November 2004, no. 114628. See also the Dutch extended essay of J.H.E. de Beer, p. 31.

3.4.3.3 Training compensation and solidarity mechanism

In the third and last place, the DRC has competence with regard to disputes related to training compensation and solidarity mechanism between clubs belonging to different associations.[96] Obviously, when it concerns a dispute between clubs belonging to the same association, the competency of the court will be appointed in the national regulations concerned. The DRC may review disputes concerning the amount of training compensation payable and will have discretion to adjust this amount if it is clearly disproportionate to the case under review.[97]

Hereinafter we will see that with regard to disputes relating to the *calculation* of training compensation and solidarity contribution, the single judge of the DRC, the so-called DRC Judge, is competent to deal with this matter.[98] Chapter 2 discusses the decisions of the DRC in relation to the training compensation and solidarity mechanism and handles relevant aspects relating to this issue.

3.4.4 *DRC Judge*

As a result of the positive experience with the Single Judge of the PSC, a similar figure has been introduced with the DRC since the new regulations of 2005.[99] The single judge of the DRC is officially called the DRC Judge. The identity and jurisdiction of the single judge of the PSC and the DRC Judge is set out in Article 23 Paragraph 3 and Article 24 Paragraph 2 of the RSTP, edition 2005.[100] If the DRC Judge is installed, the members of the DRC will then appoint a DRC Judge for the clubs and a DRC Judge for the players from among its members.

The DRC judge has limited competence and may adjudicate only if the case is related to a dispute with a litigious value of CHF 100,000 and with regard to disputes related to the *calculation* of training compensation and solidarity contribution.[101] The former club as well as the new club may ask the DRC to review disputes concerning the amount of training compensation if they deem that this amount is clearly disproportionate. According to the FIFA Commentary, the term "disproportionate" means that the amount is clearly either too low or too high with respect to the effective training costs incurred in the specific case.[102]

As explained earlier, the DRC generally adjudicates in the presence of three members, but a case of such a nature may be settled by this DRC Judge.[103] But when is the case of

---

[96] RSTP, edition 2005, Art. 22 sub d jo. Art. 24.

[97] Id., Annex 4 Art. 5 Para. 4. Circular 959 dated 16 March 2005.

[98] It is important to emphasise that the Single Judge is competent to decide on the calculation of the amount of solidarity contribution. If the new club paid the entire amount of compensation to the former club without having deducted the 5% solidarity contribution, the claim for recovering the amount paid in excess have to be lodged with the PSC (Art. 22 sub e RSTP, edition 2005). FIFA Commentary, edition 2005, explanation Art. 24, under footnote 108, p. 73.

[99] FIFA Commentary, explanation Art. 24, p. 72. The club alleging the disproportion in the amount of training compensation will submit all necessary evidence substantiating the demand of review. CAS 2004/A/560.

[100] Procedural Rules, Art. 3 Para. 2.

[101] FIFA Commentary, explanation Art. 24 Para. 2, p. 73.

[102] Id., explanation Annex 4, p. 120. The club claiming the disproportion in the amount of training compensation will submit all the necessary evidence in relation thereof to substantiate the demand for review.

[103] RSTP, edition 2005, Art. 24 Para. 2.

"such a nature"? According to the FIFA Commentary, the disputes to be decided by the DRC Judge should be considered "clear-cut cases" in which the facts and figures are clear and unquestionable, but where the player's new club is refusing to make the payment without a valid reason. However, the DRC Judge is obliged to submit fundamental, more difficult cases and issues to the Chamber.[104]

Pursuant to the FIFA Commentary, a fundamental and more difficult issue is the situation that is not covered by existing jurisprudence for which decisions within the Chamber are essential. Furthermore, according to the FIFA Commentary, a fundamental issue can be assumed in a case where existing jurisprudence needs to be extended or amended. Finally, a fundamental case can be defined as a situation that has a major impact on the daily application and interpretation of the RSTP.[105] In all these cases, the DRC Judge will refer the case to the Chamber, because of its level of difficulty. Another important issue according to the FIFA Commentary is that in the event that the new club has paid the entire transfer compensation to the former club without deducting the 5% solidarity contribution, the claim of the new club for recovering the amount paid in excess will be lodged with the PSC, in accordance with the jurisprudence of the DRC.[106]

3.4.5 *Conclusion*

In view of the above, it can be concluded that the DRC is competent with regard to disputes related to: (i) the maintenance of contractual stability if there has been an ITC request, with the important exception of the issuance of an ITC; (ii) employment-related disputes that have an international dimension, unless there is an independent arbitration tribunal at national level according to the standards of the DRC; and (iii) disputes in relation to training compensation or application of the solidarity mechanism, all of which fall under the exclusive jurisdiction of the DRC.

In relation to employment-related disputes, it is also important to know that the jurisdiction of the DRC is excluded where there is an independent arbitration tribunal at national level, which is a requirement, and this court must furthermore respect the principles of equal representation of players and clubs with an independent chairman. Finally, it can be concluded that the DRC also has jurisdiction if the parties have expressed a preference in writing by means of which the jurisdiction of another body is appointed.

With regard to the jurisdiction of the DRC Judge, we have seen that the DRC Judge will only adjudicate if the case is related to a dispute with a litigious value of CHF 100,000. Furthermore the DRC Judge has jurisdiction regarding disputes related to the *calculation* of training compensation and solidarity contribution.

Notwithstanding the above, the PSC still holds general competence on players' status matters that concern all the other disputes.[107] In this respect, it is important to know that if there is doubt with respect to the jurisdiction of the PSC or the DRC, then the chairman of the PSC decides which body has jurisdiction.[108]

---

[104] RSTP, edition 2005, Art. 24 Para. 2.
[105] FIFA Commentary, explanation Art. 24, p. 73.
[106] Id., explanation Art. 24, p. 73.
[107] Id., explanation Art. 23, p. 66.
[108] Idem.

3.5 Applicable law

3.5.1 *National law*

In their application and adjudication of law, the DRC will apply the FIFA statutes and regulations such as the RSTP rules, whilst taking into account all relevant arrangements, laws and/or collective bargaining agreements that exist at national level, as well as the specificity of sport.[109] The DRC will therefore decide on the grounds of the applicable RSTP rules, but the Chamber must also take into account the national law of the country concerned. One is immediately aware of an area of tension between the RSTP rules and the national laws of the countries concerned. An important question is, what law prevails? What happens if the DRC feels that a clause is invalid while according to national law this same clause should be considered as valid? There are many examples when this tension between the RSTP rules and the national laws comes to the surface.

In a case which came before the CAS *AJ Auxerre* v. *Valencia and M. Sissoko*, the CAS decided that in France the football law concerned is not applicable in cases with an international dimension.[110] This is an important decision in relation to the field of tension between national law and the applicable RSTP rules. The CAS decided that the DRC was competent to set aside the French football law and let the applicable RSTP rules prevail. This decision expresses amongst others the importance of the decisions of the DRC and the relevant RSTP rules. Therefore, it might be reasonable to defend the position that certain national laws may be set aside by the DRC in case of inconsistency. In line with the example above, one can say that the RSTP rules sometimes prevail insofar as the national law is not mandatory. In its decision called *PSV/Leandro do Bomfim* which will be discussed in more detail later on, the CAS stated that PSV had not demonstrated that Dutch law or any other law applicable to the contract of 2001 or to the merits of the dispute submitted to FIFA and object of decisions issued by its bodies would prohibit Leandro from being transferred from PSV to a foreign club.[111] In other words, if PSV had been able to underline that according to *mandatory* national law, Leandro should be prohibited from transferring from PSV to a foreign club, then this mandatory national law would prevail.

In another procedure brought before the CAS *Acuña and Cádiz* v. *FIFA and the Asociacion Paraguaya de Futbol*, the court decided that the contested FIFA Rules limiting the international transfer of players under the age of 18 do not violate any mandatory principle of public policy ("ordre public") under Swiss law or any other national or international law, insofar as they pursue a legitimate objective, namely the protection of young players from international transfers which could disrupt their lives, particularly if, as often happens, their football career eventually fails or fails to have the expected success. Accordingly, the court considers that the FIFA rules on the protection of minors are valid.[112] The protection of minors is such a vital point to FIFA that as a result, the DRC feels that the RSTP should apply in this case and overrules the national law.

---

[109] Procedural Rules, Art. 2.

[110] CAS 2003/O/530 *AJ Auxerre* v. *Valencia and M. Sissoko*, decision of 27 August 2004.

[111] CAS 2005/A/835 and 942, *PSV N.V.* v. *FIFA & Federaçao Portuguesa de Futebol* and *PSV N.V.* v. *Leandro do Bomfim & FIFA*, decision of 3 February 2006.

[112] CAS 2005/A/955, *Càdiz C.F., SAD* v. *FIFA and Asociación Paraguaya de Fútbol* and CAS 2005/A/956, *Carlos Javier Acuña Caballero* v. *FIFA and Asociación Paraguaya de Fútbol*.

In general and following the above, it can be assumed that the RSTP is the main ground for the judgement of the DRC. However, within this operational field, the DRC has been limited by the national laws of the countries concerned and the collective bargaining agreements that exist at national level. Therefore, the deciding bodies such as the DRC have been given guidelines by FIFA. These guidelines reflect national particularities such as national law, as well as the specific role played by sport, also known as "the specificity of sport". However, the FIFA Commentary states that the DRC does have a certain amount of discretion as to how the guidelines may be applied to the particular case.[113] In my view and according to the above examples, the RSTP rules sometimes prevail above national law. It is justified that at some points the RSTP rules overrule national law, but this is justified insofar as: (i) national law is not mandatory; and (ii) the RSTP rules pursue a legitimate objective and can be considered as a vital issue, such as the protection of minors. In Chapter 2, we will also see that certain decisions of the DRC contradict certain national laws. It can therefore be concluded that certain decisions of the DRC can be characterised as *Lex Sportiva*. In other words, the DRC then takes into account the specificity of the football sport, at some points to the detriment of the relevant national laws.

Nevertheless, it is also crucial that the decisions of some national associations, such as national arbitrational courts, comply with the decisions of the bodies of FIFA, such as the DRC. Following the above decisions, this area of tension between the RSTP rules and the national laws often comes to the surface. This area of tension more specifically comes to the surface in relation to the unilateral extension option. On the one hand, in June 2004 the Dutch Arbitrational Court decided in the case *AFC Ajax N.V.* against *Hatem Belgacem Trabelsi*, that the unilateral extension option in favour of Ajax according to their national law was valid.[114] On the other hand, as we will discuss in more detail in Chapter 2, the DRC is of the opinion that if the extension option is unilateral in favour of the employer and the player has no say whatsoever in the right of the club to extend the contract or not, such a unilateral extension option is not valid and cannot be binding. This leads to the conclusion that if the unilateral extension option is permitted according to national law, it still risks being deleted and overruled by the opinion of the DRC if this same case is brought before the DRC. In my view, this creates a lack of certainty and uniformity. There is now the situation whereby a national decision can starkly contradict the vision of the DRC. It is therefore crucial that a deciding body of a national arbitrational court, such as the Dutch Arbitrational Court, decides in line with FIFA in order to create more consistency. Obviously, FIFA can only create the above mentioned equality, uniformity and certainty if the same rules apply to all participants in the international professional football world.

3.5.2 *Applicable regulations*

Because of the different versions of the RSTP rules, it is important to establish which version of the RSTP rules applies to the case on which the DRC has to decide. In each decision of the DRC, the Chamber therefore begins by investigating which version applies to the case. To define which version of the regulations applies to the claim in question, the date of the submission of the claim is the most relevant criterion. Therefore, the general

---

[113] FIFA Commentary, explanation Art. 25, p. 76.

[114] Dutch KNVB Court of Arbitration, 4 June 2004, no. 1022.

rule is that any case that has been brought to the DRC before the most recent version of the RSTP rules came into force, namely the edition of 2005, will be assessed according to the previous regulations.[115] In other words, in order to establish which regulations, edition 2001 or edition 2005, apply to a particular case, the date on which the case was brought to FIFA must firstly be determined and is in general the decisive circumstance.[116]

Notwithstanding the above, in 2005 FIFA concluded that according to the above general rule, the date of submission of the claim was the only relevant criterion by which to define which version should apply to the case. FIFA realised that a decision on certain claims thus only depended on their date of submission. This led to the negative result that certain claims should be accepted if they were submitted after 1 July 2005, but the same claims would have had to be rejected if they were submitted before this date. FIFA concluded that the date on which the facts that led to the claim had occurred was not taken into consideration. Therefore, in the view of FIFA, the above situation was clearly in violation with the procedural principles of equality, uniformity and legal certainty, one of the main purposes of FIFA. This resulted in the modification of Article 26 of the RSTP 2005.[117] In its Circular 995, FIFA gave a more detailed explanation regarding the applicable regulations. The submission of the claim is still the most decisive criterion, but FIFA gave three exceptions to this general rule.

Firstly, there is the exception of disputes regarding training compensation. In fact, on the one hand the 2001 edition of the regulations establish that training compensation is calculated by multiplying the training costs of the new club corresponding to the category of the training club by the years of training with the former club.[118] On the other hand, the 2005 edition of the regulations states in Annex 4 Article 5 Paragraph 2 that training compensation is calculated by taking the training costs, and thus only the category of the new club, multiplied by the number of years of training with the former clubs. Secondly, there is the exception of disputes regarding solidarity mechanism. Since the 2005 edition of the regulations came into force, loans are now subject to the same rules that apply to player transfers, including provisions on training compensation and the solidarity mechanism.[119] Thirdly, there is the exception of labour disputes related to contracts signed before 1 September 2001.[120] These contracts, in application of Article 46 Paragraph 3 of the 2001 edition of the regulations, will be governed by the 1997 edition of the regulations.[121]

3.6 Admissibility

Pursuant to Article 6 Paragraph 1 of the Procedural Rules and Article 22 of the RSTP, edition 2005, FIFA intervenes in conflicts involving and between:

- associations;
- clubs;
- players;

[115] RSTP, edition 2005, Art. 26 Para. 1.
[116] FIFA Commentary, explanation Art. 26, p. 79.
[117] Circular 995 dated 23 September 2005.
[118] FIFA Commentary, explanation Art. 25, p. 79.
[119] Id., explanation Art. 25, p. 80.
[120] Id., explanation Art. 25, p. 79.
[121] Id., explanation Art. 25, p. 80.

- coaches; and
- licensed match and players' agent.[122]

As a consequence of this general rule, applications from or against other entities or subjects are not admissible in the light of the before-mentioned regulations. One must draw a distinction between the admissibility of a party before the DRC and the PSC. The before-mentioned association, coach, licensed match and player's agent are not entitled to lodge a claim before the DRC. They are exclusively entitled to bring their claim to the PSC. In other words, for these two entities, the DRC will not be the competent body to deal with the matter concerned. Therefore, with respect to the admissibility of entities before the DRC, one can say that only clubs and players are admissible and entitled to lodge a claim before the DRC.[123]

According to Article 2 Paragraph 1 of the RSTP, edition 2005, players participating in organised football are either amateurs or professionals. It needs no further explanation that a professional is entitled to bring his claim before the DRC. The question now is whether an amateur player is also entitled to lodge a claim before the DRC. As we saw earlier, the DRC is competent if there has been an ITC request. According to Article 3 Paragraph 2 of Annex 3 of the RSTP rules, edition 2005, the issue of an ITC is also compulsory for the transfer of an amateur. Therefore, amateurs as well as professionals are entitled to lodge a claim before the DRC.[124]

The same principle applies to the clubs. Professional football clubs and amateur clubs are entitled to lodge a claim before the DRC. Pursuant to the list of definitions of the RSTP, edition, the former club and the new club are called "the club the player is leaving" and "the club the player is joining", respectively. Obviously both clubs, the former club and the new club, may have the status of amateur club. Consequently, both clubs are entitled to lodge a claim before the DRC, since the RSTP rules, edition 2005, apply to them both. The fact that amateur clubs can bring their claim to the DRC can also be derived from numerous decisions of the DRC in which amateur clubs are entitled as claimants.[125]

In several cases, the DRC refers to cases in which entities were not entitled to lodge a claim, for example, the unlicensed player's agent. Due the fact that the unlicensed players' agent is not entitled to lodge a claim with the DRC, in such cases the DRC will not be competent to decide on the matter. The DRC is not in the position to intervene in such affairs. In a case dated 11 March 2005, the DRC decided that it could not intervene in the refund of the mentioned amount by a non-licensed players' agent, because the person representing the player at the signature of the contract was not a licensed players' agent.[126]

In another case brought before the DRC on 2 November 2005, the Chamber concluded its deliberations by underlining that the present investigation clearly brought to light that the club concerned had used the services of a non licensed players' agent when contracting the services of the player. The DRC decided that it was not competent to decide on the

[122] Procedural Rules, Art. 6 Para. 1.

[123] It is furthermore important to know that a claim will only be dealt with the DRC if there is a legitimate reason for dealing with this claim. Procedural Rules, Art. 5 Para. 4.

[124] DRC 22 July 2004, no. 7481. At the moment the player lodged his claim, he was registered as an amateur. However, the actual dispute was related to his earlier concluded employment contract with a former club.

[125] See for example DRC 28 September 2006, no. 96338. In this case the club transformed from a professional club to an amateur club (at the end of the 2002/03 season).

[126] DRC 11 March 2005, no. 35174.

case. The case was sent to the PSC for consideration and decision on the involvement of the unlicensed agent.[127] One can see that onward transmission to the correct office is effected *ex officio*.[128]

3.7 **Representation**

A party wanting to submit a claim before the DRC may use the services of a representative.[129] However, a written power of attorney is compulsory and will be requested by the DRC from these representatives. Petitions submitted to the DRC must contain the name and address of the legal representative, if applicable, as well as the power of attorney. Following numerous decisions of the DRC, most parties use the services of a representative.[130]

3.8 **Withdrawal and challenges**

The members of the DRC may not exercise their office in any cases in which they have a personal or a direct interest. In such cases, the member in question must withdraw in sufficient time and disclose his or her reasons for the withdrawal.[131]

In this respect, it would normally be advisable that the members of the DRC are of a different nationality than the parties involved in the dispute. It is therefore possible for a party in the conflict to make objections to a member of the DRC.

For example, the chairman of the DRC is currently Mr Slim Aloulou, a Tunisian. In my opinion it would be more than reasonable that if one of the parties was a Tunisian national, the chairman Aloulou would withdraw from the case. Irrespective of the fact of its impartiality, it would in any case remove any possibility of partiality, especially when you consider that DRC members generally adjudicate in the presence of at least three members, including the chairman or the deputy chairman, whereby the chairman has the final vote in case of a tie between the other two members.[132] As a result of a tie between two members, the Tunisian chairman Slim Aloulou would then have the final vote in a dispute involving a Tunisian party.

Another example which underlines the above was given in a decision of the DRC of 4 February 2005 where the DRC took note of the issue raised by a Spanish club with respect to the composition of the DRC Chamber, especially regarding the nationality of two of the members, namely Mario Gallavotti and Michele Colucci, both Italian.[133] In view of such a request, both Mario Gallavotti and Michele Colucci decided of their own volition to leave the Chamber during the course of the debate on the subject of this dispute and consequently did not take part in this judgment. The chairman and the two members of the DRC were then left to pass a decision on this matter, in accordance with Article 1 Para-

---

[127] DRC 2 November 2005, no. 115780.

[128] Procedural Rules, Art. 14 Para. 4. Petitions submitted in time to the wrong FIFA office are deemed to have been submitted within the time limit. Proof of compliance within the time limit is to be provided by the sender.

[129] Procedural Rules, Art. 9.

[130] See for example DRC 12 January 2006, no. 16453. In this case player X was represented by Mr Y.

[131] Procedural Rules, Art. 7 Para. 1.

[132] Id., Art. 13 Para. 1.

[133] DRC 4 February 2005, no. 25960a.

graph 6 of the Rules Governing the Practice and Procedures of the Dispute Resolution Chamber.

Members of the DRC may also be challenged by the parties if there is legitimate doubt as to their independence and impartiality. A challenge must be made under consequence of forfeit within five days of the grounds for the challenge coming to light. These motions must be substantiated and, where possible, supported by evidence. If the member concerned disputes the allegations raised, the DRC will reach a decision on the challenge in the absence of the member concerned.[134] If the DRC is no longer able to function as a consequence of challenges, the Executive Committee will make a final decision on the challenges and, if necessary, appoint an ad-hoc committee to deal with the material facts of the case.[135]

3.9 **Petitions**

Pursuant to Article 9 of the Procedural Rules, petitions must be submitted by the party in one of the four languages via the FIFA general secretariat. From the FIFA general secretariat the submitted petition will be forwarded to the PSC or the DRC. However, petitions submitted to the wrong FIFA office (for example the PSC instead of the PSC), then onward transmission to the correct office (the DRC) will be effected *ex officio* by the wrong FIFA office (the PSC).[136]

According to the before-mentioned article, petitions must contain the following particulars:

- the name and address of the parties;
- the name and address of the legal representative, if applicable, and the power of attorney;[137]
- the motion or the claim;
- a representation of the case, the grounds for the motion or claim and details of the evidence;
- documents of relevance to the dispute such as contracts and previous correspondence with respect to the case in the original version and, if applicable, translated into one of the four official languages (evidence);
- the name and address of other natural and legal persons involved in the case concerned (evidence);
- the amount in dispute, insofar as it is a financial dispute; and
- the date and a valid signature.

If the claimant does not comply with one of the before-mentioned requirements, the petition will be returned to the party concerned with a warning. However, petitions with improper or inadmissible content will be rejected immediately.[138] In that event, the claimant

134 Procedural Rules, Art. 7 Para. 2.

135 Id., Art. 7 Para. 3.

136 Id., Art. 14 Para. 3.

137 As we have seen before (paragraph 3.7), a party who wants to submit a claim before the DRC may use the services of a representative and may appoint one.

138 Procedural Rules, Art. 9 Para. 2.

loses his right to submit his petition to the DRC. In reply to the requested opening of the proceedings, on receipt of the request a written confirmation will then be sent to the claimant.[139]

In general, if there is no reason not to deal with a petition, the petition will be sent to the opposing party of the person affected by the petition, setting a time limit for a statement or reply.[140] If no statement or reply is received before the time limit expires, a decision will then be taken on the basis of the documents on file.[141] We will see later (Paragraph 3.12 renouncement of rights) that if a party does not take a position in the dispute despite having been asked to do so by the FIFA administration, the DRC is of the opinion that the case will be decided only on the basis of the facts and proof as provided by the other party.[142]

3.10 **Evidence**

According to Article 12 of the Procedural Rules, evidence consists of party testimony, witness testimony, documents, expert reports, real evidence and all other pertinent evidence.[143] In this respect, it is important to know that the agreement between the professional and the club must be in written form, as mentioned in Article 2 Paragraph 2 of the RSTP. According to Article 8 of the RSTP, edition 2005, a copy of the player's contract must then be submitted with the national association concerned.[144] In line with this Article and according to numerous decisions of the DRC, the Chamber underlines in that respect that in view of the principle of burden of proof, which principle will be discussed hereinafter, if a player fails to present any evidence for his claim to be entitled to receive a salary, the player's claim cannot be taken into consideration due to lack of evidence.[145] The DRC furthermore refutes that a document signed by the relevant parties is in principle written proof of a valid contract and cannot be declared invalid for a simple allegation.

In a decision of 13 May 2005, the DRC stated that the player's allegation of the rescission of the employment contract by the club was not based on any evidence.[146] In this respect, it is important to remember that evidence consists of party testimony, witness testimony, documents, expert reports, real evidence and all other pertinent evidence.[147] Evidence will furthermore be heard only in respect of facts relevant to the case.[148] In this respect, the DRC may also consider evidence not offered by the parties, which was also contained in a decision of the DRC of 28 September 2006, in which the DRC decided that

[139] Procedural Rules, Art. 6 Para. 3.

[140] According to Art. 6 Para. 3 of the previous Procedural Rules, a statement or reply from the respondent must be received within 15 days.

[141] Procedural Rules, Art. 9 Para. 3. A second exchange of correspondence will only be instituted in special cases.

[142] The procedures before the DRC are in general in writing. Hearings are conducted if circumstances appear to warrant it. FIFA Commentary, explanation Art. 25, under footnote 111, p. 77.

[143] Procedural Rules, Art. 12 Para. 1.

[144] The DRC decided in its decision of 24 March 2004 that the party in this case that claimed that only the contract deposited with the association was applicable contravened in view of the DRC the basic principle of *venire contra factum propia*. DRC 24 March 2004, no. 34325.

[145] DRC 23 March 2006, no. 36882.

[146] DRC 13 May 2005, no. 55359.

[147] Procedural Rules, Art. 12 Para. 1.

[148] Id., Art. 12 Para. 2.

it also considers evidence not offered to the parties.[149] Evidence will be considered subject to discretion, taking into account the conduct of the parties during the proceedings, especially any failure to comply with a personal summons, a refusal to answer questions, the withholding of requested evidence, etc.[150]

In the case of 28 September 2006 mentioned above, the DRC noted that as regards the player's registration period with the club, there is a discrepancy between the statement of the club and the player passport presented by the football federation. The club failed to present documentary evidence in support of its allegation that the player had remained registered with the club until 31 December 1996. Therefore, the DRC concurred that the relevant registration period must be established on the basis of the documentary evidence presented by the football federation, i.e., the player passport. In this context and bearing in mind Article 7 of the RSTP, the DRC pointed out that a player passport commonly constitutes the main documentary evidence pertaining to the period of registration of a player with a club.

In a decision of the DRC of 26 October 2006, the DRC referred to Article 9 Paragraph 3 of the Rules Governing the Procedures of the PSC and the DRC and decided that by not submitting any response to the claim, the club had renounced its right to be heard and had left the statements of the player uncontested. The DRC declared that its considerations and its decision would be based on the information and documentation contained in the file. In other words, the decision would be based on the documents on file.[151]

In a decision of 21 November 2006, a player requested FIFA assistance claiming 3 month's salaries owed by the club. In this respect, the Chamber pointed out that a document signed by the relevant parties is in principle written proof of a valid contract and cannot be declared invalid for a simple allegation. Moreover, the DRC remarked that the party making an allegation has the burden of proof to sustain it reasonably in order to preserve the legal principle of legal security. In view of the foregoing, the members of the Chamber concluded that the player's allegation regarding the invalidity of the termination agreement was not sufficiently proved. Therefore, the DRC decided that the player had not presented any written document substantiating the costs in relation to his medical treatment.[152]

3.11 **Burden of proof**

According to Article 12, the general rule is that any party deriving a right from an alleged fact carries the burden of proof.[153] For example, if the name of a player's agent does not appear in the contract, despite the fact that a licensed player's agent has been involved and therefore the name of the agent should be mentioned in the player's contract (pursuant to Art. 14(f) and Art. 18 Para. 1 of the RSTP), the burden of proof in the event of a dispute will rest with the party claiming that the agent participated in the negotiations.[154] In other words, in accordance with the legal principle of the burden of proof which is a fundamen-

[149] DRC 28 September 2006, no. 96338. Procedural Rules, Art. 12 Para. 4.
[150] Procedural Rules, Art. 12 Para. 6.
[151] DRC 26 October 2006, no. 1061318.
[152] DRC 21 November 2006, no. 116339.
[153] Procedural Rules, Art. 12 Para. 3.
[154] FIFA Commentary, explanation Art. 18, under footnote 88, p. 52.

tal part of every legal system, a party is obliged to prove allegations presented in a legal action if it wishes to use them as the basis for a claim.

In a decision of 13 May 2005, the DRC stated that in accordance with the legal principle of the burden of proof a party must prove allegations presented in a legal action if it wishes to use them as the basis for a claim. In this respect, the Chamber stated that the player's allegation of the rescission of the employment contract by the club at the beginning of July 2003 was not based on any evidence.[155]

In another decision dated 21 November 2006, the DRC referred to Article 12 Paragraph 3 of the Procedural Rules, in accordance with which a party deriving a right from an alleged fact carries the burden of proof.[156] In continuation, the DRC concluded furthermore that no compensation for breach of contract without just cause (conform Art. 17 of the Regulations) is due. In this respect, the DRC referred to Article 12 Paragraph 3 of the Procedural Rules, in accordance with which a party deriving a right from an alleged fact carries the burden of proof.

Furthermore the DRC emphasised in the previous decision of 28 September 2006, that pursuant to the legal principle of the burden of proof which is the basis of every legal system, a party deriving a right from an asserted fact must prove the relevant fact. Therefore, due to the lack of proof with regard to the club's allegations related to the fulfilment of its financial obligations towards the player for the season 2004 and bearing in mind its considerations in connection with the flight ticket, the DRC decided that the club must pay the player with respect to the employment contract for the season 2004.[157]

Another example can be given with respect to the party's offer to substantiate proof of an oral employment agreement. Following numerous decisions of the DRC, it is concluded that all employment contracts must be in writing. If this is not the case, the DRC will decide that verbal agreements will not be taken into consideration and that there is no employment contract. If that is the case, the player is free to leave the club. According to legislation in many countries, the judge will generally give the parties the opportunity to prove that an employment agreement has been concluded between the parties. However, in a case of 23 March 2006, the DRC decided about a party's offer to substantiate proof of an oral agreement. The DRC concluded that it could not accept this. The DRC is very strict in its judgement. The DRC acknowledged in this case that the player had not submitted any agreement signed between him and the club which would lead to the result to the responsibility of the club. One could say that if a party addresses the civil court of his country and requests the court to decide that a legally and binding employment agreement has been concluded between him and the club, most national judges will examine whether there is a valid employment agreement. The national courts will decide on the basis thereof. However, the DRC decides contrarily and one may say that at this point it gives a *Lex Sportiva* which is based on the specificity of professional football.

3.12 **Renouncement of rights**

It is vital to realise that one party may bear the risk of renouncing its rights.[158] In that respect, one can refer to Article 9 Paragraph 3 of the Procedural Rules which states that if

[155] DRC 13 May 2005, no. 55359.

[156] DRC 21 November 2006, no. 116218.

[157] DRC 28 September 2006, no. 961007.

[158] DRC 28 July 2005, no. 75377, DRC 12 January 2006, no. 16716, DRC 27 April 2006, no. 461150, DRC 28 September 2006, no. 96392, DRC 21 November 2006, no. 611814.

there is no reason to deal with a petition, it will be sent to the opposing party or the person affected by the petition, setting a time limit for a statement or reply. If no statement or reply is received before the time limit expires, a decision will be taken on the basis of the documents on file. In that case, the party bears the risk of renouncing his rights, besides special circumstances.

In a case before the DRC of 2 November 2005, the DRC decided on a contractual dispute that had arisen between an Armenian player and a Lebanese club. In this case the club never took a position in the dispute, despite having been asked to do so by the FIFA administration on several occasions. The DRC pointed out that if no reply to the claim is received from the club, the case will be decided only on the basis of the facts and evidence from the player. The DRC reproached the behaviour of the club and underlined that it had now renounced its right to defence and thus accepted the allegations of the player. In this case, the DRC decided in favour of the player due to the lack of action of the club.[159]

3.13 Waiver of rights

If one of the parties waives its rights, then it is not entitled to claim anything from the other party. In a decision of the DRC of 21 November 2006, the player waived his rights and could not claim anything on the basis of the employment agreement. The DRC concluded that the player and the club had agreed to terminate their contractual relationship and that no party could request anything from the other party. The DRC agreed that this document must be considered as a waiver duly signed by the club and the player. Thus, according to the Chamber, by signing the agreement, which explicitly refers to the first contract entered into by the parties, the player waived all rights that he might have towards the club.[160]

3.14 Non ultra petitum

When a player claims a certain amount of damages, the DRC will not adjudicate more than the amount of the claim of the player, also known as the principle of *non ultra petitum*. In such cases, the DRC refers to the *ultra petitum* rule, as a result whereof the Chamber cannot adjudicate more than is claimed.[161]

In a case of 28 July 2005 before the DRC relating to training compensation, the Chamber stated that for the year in which it trained the player, the club would be entitled to training compensation in the amount of EUR 60,000. However, the DRC noted the fact that in its claim submitted to the DRC the club only requested EUR 50,000. Consequently, and with respect to the principle of *non ultra petitum*, the DRC decided that it was not in a position to grant the club the amount EUR 60,000, but only the amount of EUR 50,000.[162]

In another case before the DRC, a player only claimed the amount of USD 300,000. According to the principle of *non ultra petitum*, in this case too the Chamber decided that the club was only required to pay the player the amount of USD 300,000 for salaries, signing-on fees and bonuses.[163]

---

159 DRC 2 November 2005, no. 115334.

160 DRC 21 November 2006, no. 611727.

161 DRC 9 November 2004, nos. 114707, 114708, DRC 2 November 2005, no. 115236, DRC 12 January 2006, no. 16309.

162 DRC 28 July 2005, no. 75231.

163 DRC 2 November 2005, no. 115236.

3.15 Counterclaim

A party can submit a counterclaim during a procedure before the DRC. Following several decisions of the DRC, one can see that this is possible, although not explicitly mentioned in the regulations.[164] The party may then in general respond to this counterclaim. Ultimately, the DRC will give its final decision on both the claim and the counterclaim in one decision. So far no problems have emerged in these kinds of procedures.

In a decision of the DRC of 28 September 2006, a club as respondent and another club entered into a loan agreement under which the player, as the claimant, was loaned to the respondent for a certain period. Following the said employment agreement, which was submitted by the player, a monthly salary of USD 15,000 was agreed for the year 2005. A handwritten note was added to the employment contract for the DRC, stating that the player's monthly salary for 2006 would amount to USD 20,000 In reply to the claimant's claim, the respondent submitted an employment contract that, apart from the financial provisions, was clearly different from the one submitted by the claimant. This employment contract was also signed by both parties. The club as respondent was of the opinion that the claimant did not fulfil the before-mentioned obligations arising from the employment contract as during the 2005 season. For this reason, the respondent deemed that the player had to pay a contractual penalty amounting to USD 50,000 and entered this into a counterclaim. The DRC finally concluded that the claim of the player as claimant, as well as the claim of the player concerned, should be rejected.[165] In this case, one can see that a party may insert a counterclaim and that the DRC will then give its final decision on both the claim and the counterclaim.

3.16 Intervening party

The Procedural Rules do not provide for rules for a party who wishes to intervene in the proceedings before the DRC. However, according to various DRC decisions, a party may intervene if such party has a legitimate right and interest in doing so.[166]

In a decision of the DRC dated 27 April 2006, in 1996 a player was transferred from a national club, acting in this procedure as claimant, to a club B in another country. In 1999 the player transferred to a club C, who acted as the intervening party. On 25 August 2003, a transfer contract for the player was concluded between the latter club and new club D, acting in this procedure as the respondent. The respondent appeared to be prepared to pay the solidarity contribution to the clubs which were entitled to receive it and which were involved in the player's training and education in accordance with the applicable FIFA regulations. On 5 December 2003 and 15 January 2004, the intervening party submitted statements to FIFA regarding the distribution of the solidarity contribution for the player. The intervening party objected to the respondent withholding the solidarity contribution for several reasons. The DRC finally decided that the respondent should pay the claimant

---

164 DRC 26 November 2004, 114628, DRC 28 July 2005, no. 75923, DRC 23 September 2005, no. 95855, DRC 17 August, nos. 861174 and 861307.

165 DRC 28 September 2006, no. 96633.

166 DRC 23 September 2005, no. 95168, DRC 23 March 2005, no. 361290, DRC 27 April 2006, no. 46400, DRC 28 September 2006, no. 96633, DRC 23 March 2006, nos. 361290 and 36446, DRC 21 November 2006, no. 6111183A.

a certain amount as solidarity contribution in relation to the transfer of the player from the intervening party to the respondent. Finally, the members of the Chamber furthermore stated that the intervening party's position should be rejected, since solidarity contribution is an independently existing claim besides training compensation.[167] One can see that a party is entitled to intervene in a procedure. In many decisions with respect to training compensation and solidarity mechanism, an intervening party becomes involved in the procedure. This is logical because the new club is often obliged to pay a solidarity contribution or training compensation to several former clubs involved which take the position that they are entitled to receive a certain amount.

3.17 **Procedural costs**

The general rule is that the costs of proceedings before the DRC and the DRC Judge are free of charge.[168] The DRC is therefore of the opinion that no procedural compensation will be awarded in proceedings of the DRC.[169] In special circumstances, the costs may be assumed by FIFA. Cost will then be borne in consideration of the parties' degree of success in the proceedings. Should a party generate unnecessary costs on account of its conduct, costs may be imposed upon it, irrespective of the outcome of the proceedings.[170] Notwithstanding, the costs before the PSC and the Single Judge are set at a maximum of CFH 25,000. In that case, the deciding body will determine the final amount.[171] The costs will be stated in the decision, which will also mention which party should bear such costs or how they will be shared by the parties. As a general rule and taking into account the outcome of the proceedings, as well as the conduct and financial resources of the parties, the costs will generally be borne by the unsuccessful party.[172]

If a player or a club claims legal fees for the declarations of their legal advisers or lawyers, in all cases the DRC will decide not to grant any legal fees whatsoever. This is reasonable because legal proceedings in the professional football world must not become too expensive. Finally, in a decision of the DRC of 11 March 2005, the DRC also decided that no compensation can be awarded between decisions of the DRC and the civil courts.[173] The DRC considered that with regard to the demand submitted by the party, according to which any amount awarded to the other party in the present matter should be deducted from a debt the relevant club has towards it, the DRC considered that both matters were completely independent and separate from each other and therefore decided to reject any eventual compensation of credits.

In a decision of the DRC of 2 November 2005 regarding legal fees and other expenses, the DRC stated that the player did not quantify or specify these compensations at all, nor did he provide the FIFA administration with any evidence. Consequently, the DRC de-

---

[167] DRC 27 April 2006, no. 46400.

[168] RSTP, edition 2005, Art. 25 Para. 1. Procedural Rules, Art. 15 Para. 2. DRC 24 March 2004, no. 114667, DRC 26 November 2004, no. 114635, DRC 1 June 2005, no. 65723, DRC 23 September 2005, no. 95473, DRC 12 January 2006, no. 16246, DRC 21 February 2006, nos. 26332 and 261043, DRC 23 March 2006, no. 36460, DRC 17 August 2006, no. 86999.

[169] Procedural Rules, Art. 15 Para. 3.

[170] Id., Art. 15 Para. 1.

[171] FIFA Commentary, explanation Art. 25, p. 75.

[172] Idem.

[173] DRC 11 March 2005, no. 35185.

cided not to award these claimed remunerations. Nevertheless, the DRC also considered rejecting the claim with regard to covering any legal or other fees because, in accordance with the well established jurisprudence of the DRC, no procedural compensation would be awarded in proceedings in front of the DRC.[174]

Finally, in a decision of the DRC of 26 October 2006, the Chamber also decided that no procedural compensation would be awarded in proceedings of the DRC and the Chamber made reference to Article 15 Paragraphs 2 and 3 of the Procedural Rules.[175]

3.18 **Provisional measure**

Before answering whether the DRC is competent to decide on the grounds of a provisional measure, one should know that the Single Judge of the PSC is competent to decide on the provisional registration of a player for a club.[176] A provisional registration is the immediate provisional registration in the event that the new association does not receive a response to an ITC request within 30 days from submitting the ITC request.[177] The provisional registration will then become permanent one year after the ITC request. If during this one-year period, the former association presents valid reasons explaining why it did not respond to the ITC request, the PSC may withdraw this provisional registration.[178]

The question now is whether the DRC is also competent to give a provisional decision. This specific competence is not regulated in the applicable rules. Consequently, it can be concluded that neither the DRC nor the Judge, contrary to the competence of the Single Judge of the PSC, is entitled to decide on the basis of a provisional measure. However, it may be possible that in an urgent matter the DRC or the DRC Judge is competent to give a provisional decision if requested to do so by the parties. However, no decisions are known in which the DRC or the DRC Judge declares itself competent to decide on the basis of a provisional measure.

Until now, it has been important to realise that a procedure relating to provisional measures, in particular concerning the provisional registration of the player for the new club, is exclusively, as we have seen above, within the remit of the PSC that in turn has entrusted the Single Judge to deal with these matters. The Single Judge will then be asked to pronounce on the provisional registration for the new club after considering whether the interests of the player from irreparable harm, the likelihood of success of the player on the merits of the claim and whether the interests of the player outweigh those of the opposite party, according to the FIFA Commentary. If these conditions are met, the Single Judge will then authorise the new association to provisionally register the player for the new club. If, as stated in the FIFA Commentary, the conditions will not be met or if the evaluation of the Single Judge does not yet enable the responsibilities to be ascertained in a provisional manner, then the Single Judge will firstly have to pronounce on the substance of the matter. If the claim is also related to an issue which lies within the remit of the DRC,

---

174 DRC 2 November 2005, nos. 6585 and 115999.

175 DRC 26 October 2006, no. 1061318.

176 FIFA Commentary, explanation Art. 22, p. 66.

177 RSTP, edition 2005, Annex 3 Art. 2 Para. 5.

178 Id., Annex 5 Art. 2 Para. 5 and Annex 3, Art. 3 Para. 4. If the case is urgent and in decisions with respect to the issuance of a provisional ITC in accordance with Annex 3 of the RSTP, the chairman or person appointed by him, who must be a member of this committee, may then adjudicate as a Single Judge. RSTP, edition 2005, Art. 23 Para. 3.

for example an issue regarding the employment contract, or as we have seen earlier, the presence of a just cause, then the procedure will be split. Once the DRC has decided on the breach of the contract and consequently on the financial and sporting consequences, the definitive ITC can be issued in favour of the new association.[179]

3.19 Prescription

Pursuant to Article 25 Paragraph 5 of the RSTP, edition 2005, the DRC will not hear any case subject to these Regulations if more than two years have elapsed from the event giving rise to the dispute. In other words, a party waives its right to lodge a claim with the DRC if more than two years have elapsed. The period of limitation in which a claim may be lodged is examined *ex officio* by the DRC while considering the formal aspects.[180] The FIFA Commentary gives the example relating to transfer compensation which is paid in five equal instalments. The FIFA indicates here that the event giving rise to the dispute is the date the last instalment matured.[181]

In a case before the DRC of 28 July 2005, the club stated that the claim was prescript. The DRC turned to the club's argument that the player's claim was already prescript and in this regard, referred to Article 44 of the regulations, edition 2001, in connection with Article 4 of the Procedural Rules, according to which the DRC will not address any dispute if more than two years have elapsed since the facts leading to a dispute arose. Therefore, on account of the before-mentioned provision, the DRC decided that the right to claim for the salary instalments from December 2001 to April 2002 should be considered as prescript and that therefore the DRC was not in a position to handle this part of the claim. As far as the second part of the player's request was concerned, i.e., the payment of the salary of May 2002, the DRC stated that between the origin of this part of the claim on 5 May 2002 and its submission to FIFA on 30 April 2004, two years had not yet elapsed. The DRC stated that, taking into consideration the before-mentioned provision, the right to claim for the salary instalment of May 2002 was not prescript. Therefore, the DRC decided that the club should pay the player a certain amount as salaries for the month of May 2002.[182]

In a case before the DRC of 12 January 2006, the DRC concluded that between the date when the facts leading to the dispute arose, i.e., 30 June 2002 (the date of signing the employment contract between the player and the club) and the submission of the claim to FIFA by the claimant, another club, on 15 March 2005 more than two years had elapsed. On account of the above, the DRC finally concluded that the club's claim against the other club for training compensation of the player concerned should be considered as prescript.[183]

In another case of 27 April 2006 relating to prescription, the DRC referred to Article 4 of the Rules Governing the Practice and Procedures of the DRC in connection with Article 44 of the FIFA Regulations, edition 2001, which stipulates that the DRC does not deal with any litigation if more than two years have elapsed since the facts leading to the dispute arose. Taking into account that the relevant instalments should have been paid on 4 Sep-

179 FIFA Commentary, explanation Annex 3, p. 106.
180 Id., explanation Art. 25, Para. 5, p. 76.
181 Idem.
182 DRC 28 July 2005, no. 75559.
183 DRC 12 January 2006, no. 16432.

tember 2003 and the claim was received on 7 March 2005, the Chamber concurred that the claim with regard to the first instalment in the amount of EUR 28,548 due on 4 September 2002 could not be considered since more than two years had elapsed. In casu, over two years and six months had elapsed. In view of the above, the DRC finally concluded that it could only consider the claim with respect to the second instalment due on 4 September 2003.[184]

In a case for the DRC of 17 August 2006, the DRC unanimously stated that prior to deliberating on the substance of the matter, it is crucial to clarify the date of the submission of the present claim to FIFA in order to establish whether the present action was brought to FIFA in time. In fact, it would be possible for the claim to be considered as forfeited. In this context, the DRC referred to Article 25 Paragraph 5 of the RSTP rules, edition 2005, which, supplementing the general procedural terms outlined in the Procedural Rules, clearly establishes that the decision-making bodies of FIFA will not hear any dispute if more than two years have elapsed since the facts leading to the dispute arose and that the application of the time limit will be examined *ex officio* in each individual case. The DRC established that neither the Rules Governing the Procedures of the PSC and the DRC nor any other current or previous standing orders do or did foresee any exception to the provision of limitation. The DRC stressed that more than 4 years had elapsed between the claimant's possible entitlement to training compensation and the submission of its respective complaint to FIFA. Finally, the DRC concluded that the claimant's complaint against the respondent for training compensation of the player must be considered as prescript.[185]

In view of the above, one can see there are various decisions of the DRC relating to prescription. As we can also see, the Chamber is very strict with respect to this issue. The DRC is determined not to allow any exception to the rule that they will not hear any case subject to the regulations if more than two years have elapsed since the event giving rise to the dispute. The DRC is very stringent to this matter and the Chamber will decide *ex officio* whether the claim is prescript or not.

3.20 **Decision**

3.20.1 *General*

As a general rule, the DRC will adjudicate within 60 days and the DRC Judge will adjudicate within 30 days of receiving a valid request. These proceedings are furthermore outlined and governed by the Procedural Rules.[186] The limit of 60 and 30 days respectively can obviously only be complied with if the parties cooperate in the procedure and are willing to provide comprehensive positions within the granted deadlines.[187] The decisions taken by the DRC are effected by a simple majority vote after secret deliberations.

All members in attendance and the chairman have one vote each. Abstentions are not permitted. In case of a tie, the chairman will cast the final vote. Furthermore it is important to know that decisions may also be taken by way of circulars.[188] The decisions will be

[184] DRC 27 April 2006, no. 46610.
[185] DRC 17 August 2006, no. 86119.
[186] RSTP, edition 2005, Art. 25 Para. 1.
[187] FIFA Commentary, explanation Art. 25, p. 75.
[188] Procedural Rules, Art. 13 Para. 1.

communicated to the parties in writing. In urgent cases, the holding of the decision may be communicated immediately with the result then submitted within the next 20 days.[189] The FIFA General Secretariat is finally entitled to announce the decision in the name of and on behalf of the DRC.[190]

3.20.2 *Form and content*

The written decisions will at least contain the date of the decision, the names of the parties and any representatives. Furthermore, the decision is provided with the names of the members participating in the decision taken by the decision-making body, the claims and/or the motions submitted by the parties and a brief description of the case. The decision must also contain the reasons for the findings, the result of taking evidence and holding the decision.[191] For decisions taken by way of circular, the date of completing the circular process is relevant. With respect to the form and content, it is also important to realise the fact that obvious mistakes in decisions may be corrected by the DRC or the DRC Judge, *ex officio* or on application.[192] In any case, it is important to know that no disadvantage may accrue to any party from an erroneous announcement in a decision of the DRC.

3.20.3 *Service and publication*

Decisions will be sent to the parties directly, with a copy also sent to the respective associations.[193] Decisions which are communicated by fax will be legally binding. Alternatively, decisions may be communicated by registered letter or courier, which will also be legally binding.[194] Decisions, if of general interest, may be published by the General Secretariat in a form determined by the DRC, e.g., condensed in the form of a media release. Due restraint will be exercised when publishing. Following a substantiated request by a party, certain elements of the decision may be excluded from publication.[195]

Bearing in mind all the above, not all decisions of the DRC are published on the official FIFA website. With respect to the decisions that are published on the website, in most cases elements are excluded from the decision. The official decision obviously contains all the relevant information, but unfortunately it is not published in its entirety on the FIFA website. To begin with, FIFA must be advised to publish all the decisions of the DRC on its website. FIFA must present all the decisions to the international football world on its website and not just a selection.

Finally and in line with the above, an important role is laid down here for the national associations regarding the publication of the decisions of the DRC. As we have seen before, the national associations must take every precaution to ensure that the national players and clubs fully comply with important decisions of FIFA.[196] In other words, the national associations must ensure that the national players and clubs are informed of the outcome

---

[189] Procedural Rules, Art. 13 Para.2.
[190] Id., Art. 13 Para. 6.
[191] Id., Art. 13 Para. 4.
[192] Idem.
[193] Procedural Rules, Art. 16 Para. 16.
[194] Id., Art. 16 Para. 3.
[195] Id., Art. 17.
[196] FIFA Statutes, Art. 62 Para. 2 and Art. 13 Para. 1 sub d.

of important decisions taken by the DRC. The national associations could thus help FIFA create more uniformity, certainty and equality for football.

3.20.4 *Enforcement*

As explained earlier, the decisions of the DRC are solely decisions about dispute resolution. The decisions of the DRC are in no way arbitral awards, such as the decisions of the CAS, nor can the decisions of the DRC be described as binding advisories. Consequently, the decisions of the DRC cannot be enforced by the parties through the bailiffs or national civil courts of the various countries. The DRC decisions can only be enforced through FIFA channels, i.e., through disciplinary power.

According to the FIFA Statutes, it comes down to the fact that the confederations, members and leagues, players and clubs indirectly are obliged to agree and comply fully with the decisions passed by the relevant FIFA bodies, such as the DRC. If one of the parties will not abide by the decision of the DRC, the matter will be passed to the FIFA Disciplinary Committee. This committee will then decide which matters will be appropriate to enforce the parties to abide by the decision. In most cases, the party will then immediately abide by this decision of the DRC.

In this respect, it is also important to know that according to the principle of *res iudicata*, the judicial decisions have become definite and can no longer be called into question, which is underlined by the DRC in a decision of 16 August 2006.[197]

In light of the above, enforcement through FIFA's own association law is a very efficient method of enforcement.[198] This method of enforcement can be presumed to be a satisfactory working system. Besides some exceptions, parties are willing to cooperate well in case of a reprimand. As stated above, parties face many problems when enforcing a decision of an ordinary court or an arbitration court in a foreign country. The enforcement of the arbitration awards of the various national courts or the CAS is much more complicated. In some situations, as mentioned earlier, depending on the laws of the country where enforcement of the decision is required, it is not even possible to enforce the decision.

Finally, it is nice to know that parties prefer to refer their litigations to the DRC because its decisions are generally fast, the members of the DRC are specialists in the football world and as mentioned above, FIFA can enforce the decisions through disciplinary power. This all makes the above method of enforcement through its own organisation smooth and effective.

3.21 **Appeal with CAS**

The CAS was established in 1984 in order to settle sports-related disputes through arbitration following the Statutes of the Bodies Working for the Settlement of Sports-related Disputes (CAS Statutes).[199] CAS is placed under the administrative and financial author-

---

[197] DRC 17 August 2006, no. 861307.

[198] In my view this should be an extra reason why more publicity should be given to the decisions of the DRC.

[199] Procedural Rules CAS, S1, A Joint Dispositions.

ity of the International Council of Arbitration for Sport (ICAS).[200] CAS resolves disputes referred to it through ordinary arbitration and it gives non-binding advisory opinions at the request of the IOC, the IFs, the NOCs, WADA, the associations recognised by the IOC and the Olympic Games Organising Committees.[201]

CAS is composed of two divisions: (i) the Ordinary Arbitration Division; and (ii) the Appeal Arbitration Division. The Ordinary Arbitration Division consists of panels whose task is to resolve disputes submitted to the ordinary procedure. The Appeals Arbitration Division consists of panels whose task is to resolve disputes relating to the decisions of sports-related bodies such as the DRC, amongst others. CAS was set up by the International Olympic Committee, which rules on the basis of FIFA rules, the Code of Sports-related Arbitration and, additionally, Swiss law.[202]

Under an agreement between FIFA and the International Council of Arbitration for Sport, the jurisdiction of the Arbitration Tribunal for Football is exercised by the CAS. FIFA has recognised CAS since December 2002 to resolve disputes between FIFA, members, confederations, leagues, clubs, players, officials and licensed match agents and players' agents.[203] In its Circular 827, FIFA outlined that after "intense and very constructive discussions with the International Council of Arbitration for Sport", FIFA finally agreed to recognise the jurisdiction of the CAS. From then on, CAS was ready to act as an appeal committee for decisions taken by the DRC after 11 November 2001.[204] One can say that CAS provides the need for a specialised body to resolve sporting disputes outside the normal court system.[205]

Article 61 Paragraph 1 of the FIFA Statutes explicitly stated that decisions of the DRC could be appealed against before the CAS.[206] This possibility is also mentioned in the decision of the DRC itself.[207] The provisions of the CAS Code of Sports-Related Arbitration will apply to the proceedings and CAS will primarily apply the various regulations of FIFA and additionally, Swiss Law.[208] These provisions apply whenever the parties have agreed to refer a sports-related dispute to CAS. These disputes may arise out of an arbitra-

---

[200] See website of CAS: <www.tas-cas.org/en/present/frmpres.htm>.

[201] Statues of the Bodies Working for the Settlement of Sports-related Disputes (hereinafter 'CAS Statutes') CAS Statutes, S12 sub a and c.

[202] See for a more extended view Matthieu Reeb, 'The Role and Functions of the Court of Arbitration for Sport (CAS)', in *The Court of Arbitration for Sport 1984-2004* (The Hague, T.C.M. Asser Press 2006), p. 31.

[203] FIFA Statutes, Art. 59 Para. 1.

[204] Circular 827 dated 10 December 2002.

[205] Ian S. Blackshaw, Robert C.R. Siekmann, Janwillem Soek (eds.), *The Court of Arbitration for Sport 1984–2004* (The Hague, T.M.C. Asser Institute 2006).

[206] FIFA Statutes, Arts. 60-62, RSTP, edition 2005, Art 24 Para. 2. In Art. 42, Para. 1 under c of the RSTP 2001 FIFA was stated that appeals should be brought before a Chamber of the Arbitration Tribunal for Football (TAF). This Arbitration Tribunal for Football was however never institutionalised. In its place came the appeal on CAS. CAS is not an independent Arbitration Court. The influence of the IOC still exists. Therefore FIFA should yet institutionalise its own appeal possibility to a Top DRC. The Top DRC must not be an Arbitration Court, but a Dispute Resolution Chamber such as the DRC but then for appeals. See also for general information Ian S. Blackshaw, Robert C.R. Siekmann, Janwillem Soek (eds.), *The Court of Arbitration for Sport 1984–2004* (The Hague, T.M.C. Asser Institute 2006), and the article in this book by Christian Krähe, 'The Appeals Procedure before the CAS', pp. 99-104.

[207] Bearing this in mind, it is often said that FIFA then has to decide itself whether a decision of CAS will create a *Lex Sportiva*. Ian S. Blackshaw, Robert C.R. Siekmann, Janwillem Soek (eds.), *The Court of Arbitration for Sport 1984–2004* (The Hague, T.M.C. Asser Institute 2006) and the articles in this book by James A.R. Nafziger, pp. 409-419, Ken Foster, pp. 420-440, Allan Erbsen, pp. 441-454, Darren Kane, pp. 455-477.

[208] FIFA Statutes, Art. 59 Para. 2.

tion clause inserted in a contract or regulations or a later arbitration agreement (ordinary arbitration proceedings) or involve an appeal against a decision rendered by a sports-related dispute, such as the DRC.

The procedure before the CAS comprises written submissions and, if CAS deems it appropriate, an oral hearing.[209] The panel will decide the dispute according to the rules of law chosen by the parties or, in the absence of such a choice, according to Swiss law.[210] CAS has the task of providing for the resolution by arbitration of disputes arising within the field of sport in conformity with the Procedural Rules provide by panels composed of one or three arbitrators.[211]

CAS resolves disputes through the appeals arbitration procedure relating to decisions of sports-related bodies such as the DRC, insofar as the statutes or regulations of the said sports-related bodies or a specific agreement so provide.[212] The arbitrators are appointed by the ICAS according to Article S6, S13 and S14 of the CAS Statutes. ICAS then formally appoints the people to be included on the list of arbitrators and they can also remove them from the list. In establishing the list of CAS arbitrators, the ICAS will call upon people with full legal training, recognised competence with regard to sports law and/or international arbitration, a good knowledge of sport in general and a good command of at least one CAS working language.[213]

Appeals against final decisions passed by FIFA legal bodies and against decisions passed by confederations, members or leagues will be lodged with CAS within 21 days of notification of the decision in question.[214] Each decision of the DRC stipulates that the statement of appeal must be sent to the CAS directly within these 21 days of receipt of notification of this decision and that it will furthermore contain all the elements in accordance with point 2 of the directives issued by the CAS, a copy of which is enclosed with the decision. Within another 10 days following the expiry of the time limit for filing the statement of appeal, the appellant will file a brief stating the facts and legal arguments giving rise to the appeal with the CAS.[215] Within the following 20 days from the receipt of the grounds for the appeal, the respondent will then submit his statement of defence to CAS amongst others.[216]

Finally, it must be noted that recourse may only be made to CAS after all other internal channels have been exhausted.[217] CAS, however, does not deal with appeals arising from: (a) violation of the Laws of the Game; (b) suspensions of up to four matches or up to three months; and (c) decisions against which an appeal to an independent and duly constituted arbitration tribunal recognised under the rules of the association or confederation may be made.[218] Certain decisions passed by the FIFA Appeal Committee may also be appealed against before the CAS.[219] The appeal will not generally have a suspended effect. How-

---

209 Procedural Rules CAS, Art. R44.1.

210 Id., Art. R45.

211 CAS Statutes, S12 junctis Procedural Rules CAS, R40.1.

212 Id., S12 sub b.

213 Id., S14.

214 FIFA Statutes, Art. 60 Para. 1, CAS Procedural Rules, R49.

215 Conform point 4 of the Directives.

216 Procedural Rules CAS, R55.

217 FIFA Statutes, Art. 60 Para. 2.

218 Id., Para. 3.

219 Id., Para. 3 junctis Art. 135 FDC, Art. 60 of the FIFA Statutes, and Art. 81 FDC.

ever, the appropriate FIFA body or, alternatively, CAS may order the appeal to have a suspensive effect.[220]

[220] FIFA Statutes, Art. 60 Para. 4.

Chapter 2
CLASSIFICATION OF DECISIONS

1. Introduction

Having discussed the background of the RSTP rules, its various editions and the most relevant procedural aspects with regard to the DRC, we have enough judicial information regarding this Chamber to enter into the main part of this book, the decisions of the DRC. Since the day of its creation, 597 decisions have been published on the FIFA website.[221] In that respect it should be remembered that FIFA does not publish all the decisions of the DRC on its website. The exact number of decisions taken by the DRC during recent years is therefore difficult to estimate.[222] Furthermore it must be noted that certain elements of the official decisions are excluded from publication.[223] The decision will be published by FIFA "only in case of general interest", the criterion as mentioned in the Procedural Rules.[224] For that reason it is important to know that my conclusions are therefore solely based on the facts as given in these published decisions.

As we will see further in this chapter, with respect to certain important subjects, the DRC creates its own line and sometimes strongly deviates from the opinion of relevant national law in relation to the same subject. Although all decisions of the DRC are based on general principles of labour law, as laid down in the various national laws and treaties, we will see that on some points the DRC makes its own sort of law, which can be characterised as *Lex Sportiva*. In other words, the specificity of the international professional football sport forms an essential principle in the decisions of the DRC. Therefore, in the event that the DRC substantially differs from the point of view of the national laws and their national courts, this will be explicitly outlined and reference will be made to this principle of *Lex Sportiva*. In the conclusion of each subject, it will be mentioned whether one can speak of a *Lex Sportiva* in relation to this specific subject.

All the 597 decisions are analysed and the most relevant ones are classified into various subjects.[225] In this chapter the decisions of the DRC between the years 2002 and 2006 will be discussed. In exceptional circumstances, only if this is crucial and necessary for better comprehension, reference will be made to a case which lies outside this scope. For example, the famous *Webster* case, decided in the year 2007, will also be discussed because of its significant importance for the professional football world. Furthermore, a decision with respect to the unilateral extension option in favour of the club will be discussed,

---

[221] The decisions of the DRC are not easy to find on the official website: <www.fifa.com/aboutfifa/federation/administration/decision.html>.

[222] In the period between 2002 and 2006, my rough estimation is that the DRC has been given approximately 2000 decisions.

[223] Procedural Rules, Art. 17.

[224] Idem.

[225] Because of its significance, some decisions of the DRC will be discussed more extensively. For example the famous *Mexès* case, with respect to the amount of compensation, but also the so-called *Mutu* case, in which the contract of the player was terminated by the club as a result of the player's drug abuse, will be discussed in more detail.

because in this decision the criteria in relation to the validity of the unilateral extension option in favour of the club are mentioned. For the sake of good order, these two cases are the most important cases during the period as from 2007. This book would not be complete without mentioning these two cases. However, the most important decisions of the DRC between the years 2002 and 2006 will be discussed following the classification. In each group, a general view will firstly be given on the subject. Then the most important decisions of the DRC in relation to this subject will be handled. Finally, in the conclusion of each subject, relevant comments will be given with respect to the relevant decisions.

In the first paragraph of this chapter, the difference between amateurs and professionals will be discussed. Attention will be given to the period prior to the parties entering into an employment agreement. Relevant aspects such as the negotiations, medical tests, work permit and the visa will be analysed and the opinion of the DRC in relation thereof will be reviewed. After this period, parties then normally enter into an employment agreement and the most relevant formal aspects such as the specific form and length of the employment contract will be discussed as well as the period of notice and aspects such as salary payments will be handled in line with the opinion of the DRC. Special attention will then be given to the extension option, because of its significant importance and its frequent use in the professional football world. After discussing this important clause, the termination of the employment contract will be reviewed in accordance with the standards of the DRC. The principle that contracts may only be terminated by either party without consequences in case of just cause will be discussed in detail. Specific attention in that respect will be drawn to compensation, amongst others the amount and the sporting sanctions, if the employment agreement comes to an end. The famous *Mexès* case, in which the amount of compensation is outlined in more detail by the DRC, will be analysed. Finally, important subjects such as training compensation and the solidarity mechanism will be discussed. In the final conclusions, the *Lex Sportiva* will emerge.

Before we start to discuss the decisions of the DRC, it must be noted that the decisions of the DRC are very significant for FIFA in order to establish their global uniformity, equality and certainty for the professional football world. It can be said that FIFA should therefore provide us with all the decisions instead of the selection as published on its official website. The national associations should also draw more attention to the decisions of the DRC, because it is their members, the players and clubs that are the most relevant parties.[226] This would also be more in line with the purposes of FIFA in their quest for more uniformity, equality and certainty.

Bearing in mind the above, it is at least remarkable that certain clauses in the employment contracts of players are considered to be valid at national level and are decided by the DRC as invalid at international level. For example, the unilateral extension option which gives the club, as the word says, the right to unilaterally extend the contract with the player. The national arbitrational court of the Dutch Football Association decided that the unilateral extension option is valid, while the DRC is of the opinion that the unilateral extension option which is solely and exclusively in the benefit of the club, must be considered invalid. In line with this important subject, all other sorts of legal issues will be reviewed in this chapter and the football world will be provided with an adequate legal

[226] According to Art. 1 of the RSTP, edition 2005, the Arts. 2-8, 10, 11 and 18 are binding at national level. The other articles "should be considered" or in as stated in the FIFA Commentary they have to be "considered as a strong recommendation". FIFA Commentary, explanation Art. 1, p. 9.

survey of the most relevant legal issues according to the opinion of the DRC, my aim being to contribute and assist FIFA in their quest for more conformity within the professional football world.

To provide the reader with an adequate and complete survey of the legal thoughts of the DRC, it will sometimes be necessary to discuss relevant decisions of the appeal committee of the DRC, the CAS as well as certain relevant decisions from national civil and arbitrational courts. Obviously, only the most relevant elements of these decisions will be highlighted.

2. Amateurs and professionals

2.1 Introduction

The rules about how to decide whether a player is a professional or an amateur are fairly clearly laid down in Article 2 Paragraph 2 of the RSTP, edition 2005. According to this Article, a professional is a player who has a written contract with his club and is paid more than the expenses he effectively incurs in return for his footballing activity. All other players can therefore be considered as amateurs. The difference between a professional and an amateur is important for several reasons. In the event that the player signs his first contract with a new club before the season of his 23rd birthday as a professional, the former clubs may be entitled to receive a training compensation. The difference between an amateur and a professional is also relevant in relation to his transfer status. As we have seen before, if the player is considered to be an amateur, no compensation needs to be paid to his former club.

The first requirement in order to establish whether one can speak of a professional is that the professional must have a written contract with his club. This means that if there is no written contract, the player will be regarded as an amateur. Following several DRC decisions, as we will see in the next paragraph, if the football player does not have a written contract, the Chamber will be of the opinion that the player is free to leave the club and no compensation will be owed. According to the FIFA Commentary, it is compulsory to stipulate a written contract between a club and a player. With regard to oral agreements, irrespective of the fact that national law provides such possibilities, FIFA is of the opinion that these are not in line with the mandatory nature of the conditions of Article 2 Paragraph 2.[227]

The second requirement is that a professional is paid more than the expenses he effectively incurs in return for his footballing activity. However, an amateur is allowed to receive expenses, but these expenses may not exceed the real costs that he has to make in connection with his football activities.[228] Following the FIFA Commentary, the amateur is

[227] FIFA Commentary, explanation Art. 2 Para. 2, p. 11. Semi-professionals should also be considered as professionals if they comply with the requirements. FIFA Commentary, explanation Art. 2, p. 11.

[228] It must be noted that in the daily practice of international football, it is a public secret that many amateurs receive more than the real expenses. This seems to be implicitly allowed. Although nobody objects, besides the fact that this is not correct from an ethical point of view, this will also have a negative impact on professional football. Certain players are more likely to play in the highest amateur league, rather than the lower professional league. Ultimately, this risks creating disequilibrium in international football. See also Roberto Branco Martins, "The representatives of workers' organisations and employers' organisations in the sector of professional football in the Netherlands", report to the European Commission, 31 July 2005 (Draft), p. 17.

a player who pursues sport just for fun or as a hobby without any material gain and who has never received any remuneration other than for the actual expenses incurred. The social aspect of participating in the group life of the club as well as his own health and fitness play a predominant role for an amateur player.[229]

2.2 Difference between amateurs and professionals

In a decision of the DRC of 22 July 2004, the DRC considered that written contracts are unusual for amateur players. The DRC decided that all the parties involved in this case were in agreement about the fact that the "non-professional" contract could not be considered as an employment contract. The remuneration offered to the player did not exceed the actual expenses that the player incurred through football at the club. The DRC was furthermore of the opinion that the denomination non-professional shows that the parties did not consider this an employment contract. As a result thereof, the Chamber concluded that the non-professional contract is a written record of the terms agreed on by the parties with regard to the player's participation at the new club in the capacity of an amateur player. The DRC underlined that written contracts are unusual for amateur players, simply because these players are seen to pursue football as a leisure activity and not as a career. In everyday practice, this means that the professional has an employment contract with his club and the amateur does not. The DRC furthermore emphasises that players who are not old enough to sign an employment contract are also considered amateurs.[230]

In a decision of the DRC of 4 February 2005, the DRC decided in relation to a so-called "aspirant contract". A player was registered for a club, which acted as the claimant, as from the season 2000/01 up to and including the season 2002/03. During the before-mentioned period, the player was registered for the claimant as an amateur. On 17 March 2003, the player and a new club signed an aspirant contract for two sporting seasons valid from August 2003 until July 2005 joining the training centre of the respondent, i.e., the new club of the player. In March 2004, his former club contacted FIFA claiming training compensation from the respondent. The respondent was of the opinion that they were not obliged to pay any training compensation to the former club of the player, due to the fact that the player was transferred from as an amateur player to their club with amateur status. Therefore, the respondent was of the opinion that this contract should be considered a non-amateur contract. The claimant did not accept these arguments and stated that the aspirant contract was a form of scholarship and included the obligation of the new club to pay the player certain amounts of money, therefore it was a non-amateur contract.

The DRC emphasised the following three aspects in this decision:

1. Players who have never received any remuneration other than reimbursement of their actual expenses incurred during the course of their participation in any activity connected with association football are regarded as amateur;
2. Travel and hotel expenses incurred through involvement in a match and the costs of a player's equipment, insurance and training may be reimbursed without jeopardising a player's amateur status; and

[229] FIFA Commentary, explanation Art. 2 Para. 2, p. 12.
[230] DRC 22 July 2004, no. 74557.

3. Any player who has ever received remuneration in excess of the expenses and costs described in paragraph 2 of this Article … will be regarded as a non-amateur …".

In line with the above, the DRC finally concluded that some of the financial obligations assumed by the respondent in the contract with the player were in principle included in Paragraph 3 of the before-mentioned Article 2 of the FIFA Regulations, edition 2001, such as damage compensation for costs incurred by the parents' travel and living costs on the occasions when the player's parents visit him. Therefore, the relationship between the player and the club was regarded as non-amateur. Finally, the DRC was of the opinion that the claimant was indeed entitled to receive compensation for the training and education it provided to the player.[231]

In a decision of the DRC of 28 July 2005, the DRC was of the opinion that the "scholarship agreement" concerned had to be considered an amateur contract. In this case, the two clubs involved were arguing about the nature of the contract in question and the actual question was whether this contract should be considered as a scholarship contract (amateur contract) or an employment contract (non-amateur contract). The player concerned signed a contract with a new club on 1 July 2004 and his former club lodged a claim for training compensation. The player was registered with his former club as an amateur player during the seasons 2001/02 and 2002/03, at the age of 15 and 16. The new club insisted that although they had signed a contract with the player, the latter could keep his amateur status. The club based its statement on the fact that the contract signed was mainly an agreement to educate and train the player, entitling him to compensation for travel and housing expenses. Therefore, they were of the opinion that they were not liable to pay training compensation to his former club. The Chamber pointed out that in disputes concerning training compensation, the nature of a contract between a player and a club is determined by the relevant association. As a principle, the DRC therefore decided that they did not want to enter into the question concerning the status of the player. In such case, the Chamber decided that the autonomy of the association must be respected by the DRC and therefore the status of the registration of such player at the association will be taken into consideration in order to determine whether the conditions stipulating the payment of training compensation have been fulfilled. Finally, the DRC decided that the player in question was, as indicated by the football federation of the club, registered as an amateur player for the new club.[232]

In a decision of 21 February 2006, the DRC decided that no training compensation was owed, due to the fact that the player was not paid more than the expenses he effectively incurred in return for his footballing activity. In this case, the Swedish football association informed FIFA that a non-amateur contract signed between the player involved and the club, valid as from 24 June 2002 until 28 February 2004, was registered with them and that the economic compensation was not fixed as a monthly salary the DRC always uses the word salary, etc. but was related to bonuses only. According to the relevant contract signed between the Swedish club and the player, the latter would receive the bonuses depending on matches played within the Premiership League. On 5 August 2005, the Swedish football association informed FIFA that its affiliated club had never paid any compensation at

[231] DRC 4 February 2005, nos. 25633a en b.
[232] DRC 28 July 2005, no. 75142.

all to the player since the player had never played in any A-team match. Finally, the Swedish football association stressed that although the player had been registered as a non-amateur player, in reality, he was an amateur. Therefore, the DRC concluded that although from a formal point of view the player was registered as a non-amateur and that he had signed a contract, de facto he had to be considered as an amateur since he never received any remuneration at all for his services and it was therefore clear that he did not even receive more than the expenses he effectively incurred in return for his footballing activity.[233]

In a decision of the DRC of 2 November 2005, a player was trained by a German club as an amateur player and this club lodged a claim for training compensation. The German club maintained that the player had appeared for his new club, a Greek club, and was therefore no longer an amateur. In response to an enquiry from FIFA, the Greek club contested the fact that the player had non-amateur status as he was playing for the club's amateur youth team. However, the German club insisted on 11 April 2005 that the player was no longer an amateur, pointing out that although the player may only have been playing in youth and amateur teams, this issue depended exclusively on the status of the player and not on the team for which he appeared. The Greek club stated on 30 June 2005 that, given that the player had moved to Greece without any fee being paid and he had never appeared for a non-amateur team, there were no grounds for the payment of training compensation.

Finally, the DRC unanimously concluded that the player had signed his first contract as a non-amateur and backed the opinion of the German club that this issue depends exclusively on the status of the player and not on the team for which he appeared. The DRC reached the conclusion that the former club was indisputably entitled to receive compensation from the new club for the training and education of the player regarding the timeframe that the latter spent with it, because the contract with his new club had to be considered as a professional players' contract.[234]

In a decision of the DRC of 17 August 2006, the DRC was of the opinion that the scholarship agreement concerned should be considered as a professional contract.[235] The DRC took into consideration the criteria set out in the stated Article 2 of the employment contract and the monies payable to the player on the basis of the scholarship agreement and decided unanimously that the player evidently received remuneration in excess of the expenses and costs described in Paragraph 2 of the said Article and was therefore a professional.[236] The DRC considered it opportune to stress that a player's remuneration as per the criteria set out in the before-mentioned Article 2 of the RSTP constitutes the decisive factor in the determination of the player's status. The Chamber was of the opinion that the legal nature or the determination of the agreement concerned was of no relevance in this regard. This was confirmed by the CAS.[237] In another decision of the CAS, the panel decided accordingly and confirmed that amateur status of a player is not defined by refer-

---

[233] DRC 21 February 2006, no. 26135.

[234] DRC 2 November 2005, no. 115324.

[235] In the earlier mentioned decision of the DRC of 28 July 2005, the Chamber decided that the scholarship agreement concerned had to be seen as amateur contract.

[236] DRC 17 August 2006, no. 86137.

[237] CAS 2005/A/383.

ence to an amateur contract, but by the fact that a player has never received any remuneration other than the actual expenses incurred.[238]

The professional status of the football player in a case from the Dutch football club Top Oss versus the English club Blackpool F.C. was decisive for the admittance of an amount for training compensation and was brought in appeal before the CAS.[239] The CAS considered that in terms of the contract obligations, in the view of the panel it was obvious that there was an employer-employee relationship between the club and the player. From the moment he signed the contract, the player agreed to perform services exclusively for the club. A situation of directional control on the part of the club and subordination on the part of the player was clearly present, in view of the panel. In reward for his services, the player was entitled not only to a weekly salary and appearance bonuses in the events he played, he also enjoyed other rights such as holidays, disability benefits for a limited time and accommodation expenses. Subsequently, all these advantages clearly exceed the category of cost reimbursements described in Article 2 Paragraph 2 of the RSTP rules, edition 2005. In the light of the above, the CAS therefore came to the final conclusion that the player must be considered as a non-amateur while playing for the club.

2.3 **Conclusion**

In everyday practice and subsequent to the above, it can be concluded that the difference between a professional and an amateur is firstly that the professional has a written employment contract with his club and the amateur has not. Secondly, the difference between a professional and an amateur is that the professional is paid more than the expenses he effectively incurs in return for his footballing activity. The amateur can only be considered an amateur if he is paid at most the expenses he effectively incurs in return for his footballing activity.

With regard to the first difference between an amateur and a professional, a professional must have a written contract. The DRC is very strict with regard to this issue. Only professionals have written agreements. The DRC is of the opinion that written contracts are unusual for amateur players, simply because these players are seen to pursue football as a leisure activity and not as a career. At this point the DRC deviates from the opinion of most national courts, because normally an oral agreement does suffice according to legislation in several countries where employee status is concerned. In that respect, one must be aware that FIFA regulations require that the employment contract between the player and the club is registered with their national association. The application to register a professional must be submitted by the new club and will be accompanied by a copy of the contract between the new club and the professional. As long as the association has not received the employment contract, it will not issue the ITC and as a consequence thereof, the player will not be eligible to play for his new club. For the practice of the international football world and for the best organisation of football, it is highly defensible that the DRC differs at this point from most national legislation.

With respect to the second requirement, the fact that an amateur may not get paid more than the expenses he effectively incurs in return for his footballing activity, one can say

[238] CAS 2004/A/691 nos. 76 and 77, FIFA Commentary, explanation Art. 2 Para. 2, p. 12.
[239] CAS 2006/A/1027 *Blackpool F.C.* v. *Club Top Oss*.

that although the amateur is allowed to receive expenses, these expenses may explicitly not exceed the real costs that he has to make in connection with his football activities. Accordingly the DRC emphasises that in this respect a football player will be regarded and considered as a professional if he receives remuneration in excess of the expenses he effectively incurs for his footballing activity.

According to the second requirement, the DRC is not as consistent as it might seem at first sight. In a case of the DRC of 22 July 2004, the DRC concluded that the denomination "non-professional" shows that the parties did not consider this an employment contract. Therefore, the DRC decided that the player should be considered as an amateur.[240] In another decision of 28 July 2005, the DRC decided accordingly. The Chamber also decided that the status of the registration of a player with the association was the decisive factor in order to determine whether the player in question should be considered as an amateur or a professional.[241] In that case, the DRC stressed that the nature of a contract between a player and a club is determined by the relevant association and the Chamber therefore decided that the player in question was, as indicated by the football federation of the club, registered as an amateur player for the new club. However, later on, in the year 2006, we see that the DRC has a more differentiated view in this respect. In its decision of 21 February 2006, the DRC concluded that although in strictly formal terms the player was registered as a non-amateur and that he had signed a contract, in fact he should be considered an amateur as he never received any remuneration for his services and it was therefore clear that he did not even receive more than the expenses he effectively incurred in return for his footballing activity.[242] The DRC confirms the before-mentioned line in its decision of 17 August 2007, in which it says that the legal nature or the determination of the agreement concerned is of no relevance in order to establish the status of the player, which was confirmed by CAS.[243]

Bearing in mind the above and according to the present opinion of the DRC, one can say that a player's amateur status is not defined by reference to an amateur contract, but is exclusively established by the fact that a player has never received any remuneration other than the actual expenses incurred. The DRC is clear; the legal nature or the determination of the agreement is of no relevance with respect to determining whether the player is an amateur of a professional.

3. Negotiations

3.1 Introduction

Before the player and club enter into an employment contract, negotiations are held. Due to the registration periods and their strict time limits, parties often have to act very fast in order to conclude an employment contract. In most cases, medical tests are required, sometimes a work permit or a visa must be arranged and there are always the endless discussions with respect to the salary of the player. The negotiations generally take place in an

[240] DRC 22 July 2004, no. 74557.
[241] DRC 28 July 2005, no. 75142.
[242] DRC 21 February 2006, no. 26135.
[243] DRC 17 August 2006, no. 86137, CAS 2005/A/383 and CAS 2004/A/691 nos. 76 and 77.

international atmosphere, because in international football it is common that a player is transferred to a football club from another country. The enormous pressure involved in the before-mentioned aspects makes it difficult for parties to finalise the deal within the fixed time limits. As a result, this can often lead to cancellation of the negotiations.

In this paragraph, we will see that parties who enter into negotiations could end up paying damages as a result of ending the negotiations without just cause. In such cases, the DRC refers to the principle of *culpa in contrahendo*. However, before we discuss the relevant DRC decisions in relation to this principle, two important elements of Article 18 Paragraph 3 of the RSTP, edition 2005, will be handled. Although there are no DRC decisions in relation to these specific aspects in this Article, it is very important for the clubs and players to be aware of these rules. Firstly, with regard to the period prior to the start of negotiations by the parties and entering into an employment contract, it is very important that, according to Article 18 Paragraph 3 of the RSTP, edition 2005, a club intending to conclude a contact with a professional informs the current club of the player concerned in writing before entering into negotiations with that player (3.2). A second important aspect is that Article 18 Paragraph 3, of the RSTP, edition 2005, states that a professional will only be free to conclude a contract with another club if his contract with his present club has expired or will expire within six months (3.3). Consequently, the player must have the permission from his current club to start negotiations with a prospective new club.

3.2 Informing the current club

An important aspect in relation prior to the period when parties conclude an employment contract, is that, according to Article 18 Paragraph 3 of the RSTP, edition 2005, a club intending to conclude a contact with a professional must inform the current club of the player concerned in writing before entering into negotiations with that player.[244]

The question is now: does the current club have to approve with the negotiations of the potential new club and its player? Or does it suffice that the current club only have to be informed? Although there are no decisions of the DRC regarding this specific issue, as mentioned, the FIFA Commentary does provide us with the answer.

The club with which the player is contracted, the current club, explicitly needs to agree to the discussion between its player and the prospective new club. Obviously, only as far is it concerns a player who has an employment contract with his current club, as stated in the before-mentioned article. Without an agreement between the current club and the potential new club, the latter may even, according to the FIFA Commentary, be in a situation of inducing the player to breach his contract to breach his contract if it continues the negotiations with the player.[245]

3.3 Approach to another club

3.3.1 *Prior written consent*

Article 18 Paragraph 3 of the RSTP, edition 2005, states that a professional will only be free to conclude a contract with another club if his contract with his present club has

[244] According to Art. 1 of the RSTP, edition 2005, this article is binding at national level.
[245] FIFA Commentary, explanation Art. 18 Para. 3, p. 54.

expired or will expire within six months. Any breach of this provision will be subject to appropriate sanctions, which will be discussed later on. A football player who has entered into a written contract of employment with a club is prevented from making an approach to another club with a view to negotiating a contract with this club without the prior written consent of his club. In other words, it is undisputed that a player needs permission from his current club.

In a decision of the DRC of 13 May 2005, the Chamber considered that the player never informed his new club that he was still under contract with his former club.[246] Furthermore, the player even signed the employment contract with his new club, regardless of the fact that he was still contractually bound by another club. In this respect, the DRC pointed out that it is undisputable that the player did not respect the contractual obligations undertaken in the employment contract concluded on 16 January 2003 with his club. Therefore, the Chamber decided that the player must refund to the club the amount of USD 40,000 received as a signing-on fee. The Chamber went on to analyse the sports sanctions to be imposed on the player for having caused the contractual breach without just cause. According to Article 23 Paragraph 1 of the RSTP, edition 2001, a player will be sanctioned by means of a restriction of four months on his eligibility to participate in any official football matches.

For the benefit of the international football world and the required transparency, this seems very defensible. There are no decisions of the DRC in relation to this specific subject. However, because of its significance and its relation to the aspect of negotiations, this issue is important to study. In the following case, also known as the *Cole* case, the beforementioned principle came to the surface. Although this is not a decision of the DRC, the decisions in relation to this subject of the Disciplinary Commission of the Football Association Premier League (FAPL), the FAPL Appeals Committee and the CAS are much too important to be omitted.

3.3.2. Cole *case*

On 27 January 2005 a meeting took place at the Royal Park Hotel in London between amongst others Ashley Cole and representatives from Chelsea Football Club. Arising from that meeting, the Disciplinary Commission of the Football Association Premier League (FAPL) rendered a decision on 1 June 2005, which adjudged Cole to have been in breach of FAPL Rule K5. This rule prevents a player who has entered into a written employment contract with a club from making an approach to another club with a view to negotiating a contract with this club without prior written consent from his club.[247] This rule comes down to Article 18 Paragraph 3 of the RSTP, edition 2005. The Disciplinary Commission of the FAPL imposed a fine of GBP 100,000 on Cole. Cole appealed to the FAPL Appeals Committee. This committee reduced the fine imposed upon him from GBP 100,000 to GBP 75,000.

On 31 August 2005 Cole filed an appeal with CAS against the decision of the FAPL Appeals Committee. However CAS dismissed the appeal and concluded that in order for the CAS to have jurisdiction to rule on an appeal, Article 47 of the procedural rules of the

---

246 DRC 13 May 2005, no. 55484.

247 Roger Welch, 'Player Mobility, the FIFA Transfer Rules and Freedom of Movement', by, 6 *Maxwell's, International Sports Law Review* (2006) no. 4, pp. 83-86.

CAS requires that a direct reference to the CAS must be contained in the statutes or regulations of the body whose decision is being appealed against.

The CAS concluded that the FAPL rules do not provide for a right of appeal to CAS. The FIFA Statutes contain no provision which obliges the FAPL to allow a right of appeal of the decisions to the CAS. If the FAPL was subject to such mandatory provision, no right of appeal to the CAS would exist until the FAPL amended its statutes of regulations to incorporate such a right of appeal. Furthermore, the CAS was of the opinion that there was no specific agreement between the parties to allow the CAS to rule on the merits of this particular dispute. Finally, the CAS decided that they did not have the jurisdiction to rule on the appeal filed by the player Ashley Cole in the present arbitral proceedings.[248]

3.4 *Culpa in contrahendo*

As mentioned earlier, parties who enter into negotiations could end up paying damages as a result of the ending negotiations without just cause. In other countries, however, negotiations may not be stopped abruptly and the party who wishes to do so will be held liable for *culpa in contrahendo*. In this case, a party to a negotiation for an employment contract must compensate causal damages incurred by the other party if it has infringed on its obligation to act in good faith during negotiations and thereby breached the confidence of the other party. By not finalising the contract, the DRC sometimes concludes that one party has breached the other party's confidence.

In a decision of the DRC of 12 January 2006, the DRC decided that the fact that parties enter into negotiations could result in the obligation to pay damages as a result of ending the negotiations without just cause. On 18 June 2004, a club informed a player, apparently with double nationality, in writing about the remuneration payable if an employment contract was signed. After subsequent negotiations, on 3 July 2004 the player and the club signed an employment contract valid from 3 July 2004 to 30 June 2008, stipulating a monthly salary of USD 12,500. Suddenly on 6 July 2004, the sports director of the club informed the player in writing that the player did not have any kind of working contract with his club, as he did not possess an EU passport and that it would be impossible to obtain the necessary working permit in due time before the start of the season. A possible contract could only be negotiated once the player had received his EU passport. Before the DRC, the club emphasised that it was not interested in any player that did not have an EU passport and that the sports director who signed the contract was not entitled to do so. The assessment of the player in question was continued only because he promised to apply for the relevant passport in due course. The club was of the opinion that the document signed on 3 July 2004 was only a draft employment contract, which should allow the player's manager to verify the contents of the contract. They later discovered that the player did not have the relevant passport. It therefore felt misled by the player and sent him with the before-mentioned letter of 6 July 2004. The club was now of the opinion that due to the failure of the player to present a EU passport, the draft contract dated 3 July 2004 was never finalised. The player emphasised before the DRC that the acquisition of said passport was never communicated to him as being an essential condition for the conclusion of the contract. Moreover, the player indicated that the signed contract did not contain an express provision in this respect.

---

[248] CAS 2005/A/952, *Ashley Cole* v. *FAPL*, decision of 24 January 2006.

Taking these circumstances into consideration, the DRC referred to the legal principle of *culpa in contrahendo*, according to which a party to a negotiation for a contract must compensate causal damages incurred by the other party if it has infringed on its obligation to act in good faith during the negotiations and thereby breached the confidence of the other party in the negotiations. In the present case, the player and the club were in negotiations for an employment contract. The behaviour of the sports director of the club, in particular the fact that he signed the reassurance document on 26 June 2004 and the fact that he signed a copy of the employment contract and handed it to the player, although he was not entitled to conclude employment contracts for the club, created a certain confidence for the player, according to which he believed that an employment contract would indeed be concluded. By failing to finalise the employment contract, the club breached the player's confidence. As the contract was probably not finalised because the club was able to contract other players, the player's confidence was breached without any blame assigned to the player and was totally the fault of the club. In this respect, the DRC emphasised that the contract signed by the sports director on 3 July 2004 made no reference to the alleged necessity for the player to hold an EU passport. Neither had club B provided other evidence corroborating its allegation that the player's European nationality would be an essential condition for the conclusion of the contract. Finally, the DRC concluded that the club was liable for breach of the player's confidence. This breach of the player's confidence led to damage for the player, particularly as it meant that the player was unable to negotiate an employment contract with other clubs while negotiating with this club. It was therefore clear to the members of the Chamber that the player had suffered damages. In view of all the above and considering the player's income with clubs following his departure from club, the DRC established that the club should compensate the player for *culpa in contrahendo* to the amount of USD 50,000.[249]

In a decision of the DRC of 26 October 2006, the Chamber concluded that no valid employment contract was concluded between the parties, but the factual relationship should be taken into consideration.[250] The player concerned brought his claim to the DRC, requesting that it be declared that a valid employment contract had been concluded between him and the club concerned. The DRC went on to state that the before-mentioned actual circumstances of the present matter, in particular the participation of the player in three preparatory matches with the club, led to the conclusion that a factual employment relationship should be taken into consideration. Given that a factual employment relationship had been established between the player and the club in which the player had rendered services to the club and given the fact that the player did not bear any responsibility for the actual ending of the before-mentioned factual employment relationship or the non-finalisation of a formal employment contract, the DRC deemed that the player was entitled to receive compensation from the club, despite the fact that no formal and valid written employment contract had been concluded between the parties. The DRC deemed that on account of its stance, the club should be called to account for its responsibilities pertaining to the failure of the envisaged transaction.

[249] DRC 12 January 2006, no. 16830
[250] DRC 26 October 2006, no. 1061318.

3.5 Conclusion

In relation to negotiations between players and clubs, it is decisive and very important that the current club with which the player is contracted, according to the FIFA Commentary, explicitly agrees to discussions between its player and the prospective new club in order to allow the prospective new club to negotiate legitimately with the player of the former club, although this principle, which is rather remarkable, is not explicitly laid down in Article 18 Paragraph 3 of the RSTP rules, edition 2005. In this respect, in order to avoid any misunderstanding and for the sake of completeness, it would be highly advisable to modify Article 18 Paragraph 3 and to provide this Article with the before-mentioned rule that the former club also needs to give its explicit permission to the prospective new club to negotiate with its player. In this respect, it must be noticed that according to the RSTP, edition 2005, the obligation as laid down in Article 18, RSTP, edition 2005, is also a binding principle at national level. Therefore, the impact of this Article may be even more present now that members of a national association are obliged to act accordingly.[251]

Furthermore, in relation to negotiations between the parties and the potential result of concluding a new contract by a player who is contracted by his current club, Paragraph 3 of Article 18 of the RSTP, edition 2005, states that a professional will only be free to conclude a contract with another club if his contract with his present club has expired or will expire within six months. Any breach of this provision will be subject to appropriate sanctions. Cole breached this Article FAPL Rule K5, which rule prevents a player who has entered into a written contract of employment with a club from approaching another club with a view to negotiating a contract with such club without prior written consent from his club. Cole breached this Article, which rule is similar to Article 18 Paragraph 3 of the RSTP, edition 2005, by not informing Arsenal of entering into negotiations with Chelsea. This led to the before-mentioned *Cole* case. Ashley Cole and F.C. Chelsea were initially fined by the English Football Association for breach of Article R.K5, which prevents clubs making an illegal approach to or tapping up a player. The parties appealed to the CAS, but the CAS declined to review the *Cole* case on jurisdictional grounds

Regarding the negotiations and according to the DRC, it can be said that parties who enter into negotiations may end up paying damages as a result of one of the parties ending the negotiations. During the years 2002–2006, the DRC only decided in two cases regarding the principle of *culpa in contrahendo*.[252]

Bearing in mind the above, it is difficult to derive a specific rule from these decisions in order to determine under what circumstances a party has cancelled the negotiations illegitimately. In general, the DRC is of the opinion that a party to a negotiation for a contract must compensate causal damages incurred by the other party if it has infringed on its obligation to act in good faith during the negotiations and thereby breached the confidence of the other party in the negotiations. According to the DRC, the behaviour of one of the parties can create a certain confidence for the other party, according to which the latter could in good faith believe that an employment contract would indeed be concluded. If the contract is not finalised by the parties, a party may be in the position of breaching the other party's confidence. In line with the above and in the opinion of the DRC, it is thus vital that

[251] RSTP, edition 2005, Art. 1 Para. 3 under a.

[252] DRC 12 January 2006, no. 16830 and DRC 12 October 2006, no. 1061118.

the breach of the party's confidence is without any blame to be assigned to the other party.

The Dutch Supreme Court decided that the party which ends the negotiations may be liable for damages as a result of terminating the negotiations by one of the parties. The DRC decides in line with the Dutch Supreme Court. However, in many countries the national courts do not adjudicate damages to the party which ends the negotiations abruptly. Compared to these national laws, the DRC follows its own line, as it is of the opinion that not all cancelled negotiations are legitimate.

4. Medical examination

4.1 Introduction

If a player and a club have an oral agreement with respect to the arrival of the player to this club, the club will usually subject the player to medical tests before signing the employment contract. Everyday practice in the professional football world is that these tests will generally be performed before the contract is signed. Sometimes, however, the club and the player sign an employment contract before the medical tests and subsequently make the positive outcome of the medical test conditional upon the validity of the signed employment contract. Because of the extreme time limits within which players and clubs have to work, they sometimes feel obliged to sign the employment contract before the medical tests. In some countries, this is also valid according to their national laws. The DRC has a different opinion in this respect.

4.2 Information about the player

Before a club is interested in contracting a new player from another club, it is important for the prospective new club to know everything about the physical health of the player concerned. It is therefore common in professional football for a medical test to be performed. However, before a medical test takes place to assess the medical condition of the player, the clubs will gather all the necessary information about the player. As we will see in the decisions of the DRC hereinafter, it is the exclusive responsibility of the new club to be well informed about the player's career.[253] In other words, the new club must inform itself about the player's career, before signing the employment contract.

In a decision of the DRC of 4 February 2005, the Chamber took into consideration the position of a club, according to which the relevant contract signed with the player should not be considered valid as the player did not fulfil the necessary physical, technical or mental conditions necessary to play football, nor did his administrative file allow him to be registered and play for it. In this respect, the Chamber underlined the clause of Article 30 of the RSTP, edition 2001, which stipulates that "the player's prospective new club will be required to make any necessary investigations, studies, tests and/or medical examination or to take any appropriate action before concluding the contract, otherwise it will be liable to pay the amount of the wage due".

---

[253] Following the FIFA Commentary, the player's prospective new club is required to undertake all necessary research and take all appropriate steps before concluding a contract. FIFA Commentary, explanation Art. 18, p. 55.

Consequently, the Chamber rejected the arguments presented by the club and considered the contract valid and binding for both parties.[254]

In another decision of 26 October 2006, the DRC decided that if a club is interested in signing an employment contract with a new player, it is the responsibility of the new club to inform itself about the player's career before signing on the employment contract. Furthermore, the DRC added that the contract concluded between the parties does not contain any clause stipulating the condition that the player had previously played for a first division club. On account of these considerations, the DRC stated that by not verifying the relevant facts about the player, the club had taken the risk of not being accurately informed about the player's career and provided with inaccurate information on the player's former club, but that this did not constitute a valid reason for the unilateral termination of the contract.[255]

4.3 **Medical result**

After gathering all the necessary information about the player, a medical test will generally take place in order to determine the physical fitness of the player. The DRC is of the explicit opinion that the medical test must take place before signing the contract, as we will see in this paragraph. However, due to the extreme time constraints of the registration periods, the club sometimes feels obliged to sign the contract prior to the result of the medical test. Clubs try to resolve this by providing the contract with a provision stating that the validity of the contract depends on the positive result of the medical test. This is not legitimate pursuant to the rules of FIFA and according to the decisions of the DRC.

In a decision of the DRC of 21 November 2003, the DRC decided that the player had not presented any documents corroborating the claimed costs for medical treatment and that therefore the relevant sum could not be awarded to the player.[256] The Chamber had to decide whether the provision stated in the employment contract was valid. According to this provision, the parties agreed that the contract would not come into effect prior to the player successfully passing the medical examination at a hospital appointed by the club. In other words, if the player did not pass the medical examination, the club had the right to unilaterally terminate the contract. The club was claiming that the two agreements concluded on 5 January 2003, namely the employment contract and the "payment agreement", were valid. The DRC was of the opinion that Article 30 of the RSTP, edition 2001, gives clear and unmistakable indications with regard to the relationship between medical examinations and the validity of an employment contract; due to its unambiguous wording, the relevant clause leaves no room for interpretation, the said provision is mandatory and calls for strict application. Therefore, the Chamber decided that the provision in relation to the medical test of the employment contract was null and void, as contrary to the provisions of Article 30 of the regulations, it makes the relevant agreement conditional upon the positive results of a medical examination. The question whether medical examination were carried out prior to the signing of the agreements or not could remain open. The club had to make any necessary medical examination before concluding the agreements in accordance with Article 30 Paragraph 2 of the RSTP, edition 2005.

[254] DRC 4 February 2005, no. 25566.
[255] DRC 26 October 2006, no. 1061118.
[256] DRC 21 November 2003, no. 113291.

In a case of the DRC of 10 June 2004, the Chamber had to decide on the validity of the employment contract if the medical test was made conditional upon the validity of this contract. This also was a decision under the RSTP, edition 2001. Article 30 Paragraph 2 of the RSTP, edition 2001 which stated that the player's prospective new club is required to make any investigation, studies, tests and/or medical examination before concluding the contract, otherwise it will be liable to pay the full amount of the salary due. The DRC explained that according to Article 30 Paragraph 2 RSTP, edition 2001, a club has to wait for the medical results before signing the employment contract. If a club signs a contract before it has received the test results and then dismisses the contract because of negative test results, it must bear the consequences of the signed contract according to the before-mentioned Article 30 Paragraph 2 of the RSTP, edition 2001. The DRC noted that the respective club made the player concerned undergo a medical test before signing the employment contract. Furthermore, it noted that the club did not complete the test phase before signing the employment contract. According to Article 30 Paragraph 2 of the before-mentioned regulations and in the light of the above explanations, the Chamber decided that through its conduct, the club was liable to bear the consequences of the signed contract.[257]

In a decision of the DRC of 17 August 2006, the DRC had to decide about the following facts.[258] On 27 October 2005, a player, the claimant, lodged a claim with FIFA against club B from another country, the respondent, through the football association of his country of origin. The player stated that on 17 June 2005 the parties signed an employment contract for the period from 1 July 2005 to 30 June 2006. The player explained that he had injured himself during training after signing the contract on 1 July 2005. The club had sent him to his country of origin to recover. When the player tried to return to the club, neither he nor the football association of the country of his origin was able to establish contact with the respondent club. The respondent replied that the parties had agreed that the contract would be invalid if the player did not pass all of the medical examinations to its satisfaction. In line with its allegation, the club referred to clause 7 of the employment contract, stating: "It is understood that the player has to pass all medical exams in the satisfaction of the club not later than the 31st of July 2005". In other words, the player was obliged to take all of the medical examinations to the club's satisfaction by 31 July 2005. The club mentioned that, contrary to these requirements, the player had not undergone medical examinations after signing the contract but had gone to the first training session. Before the training had begun, the player had run around the pitch and within five minutes had claimed he had pain in his knee. A visit to the doctor then confirmed that he had serious knee problems. The player had allegedly deceived the club by signing a statement in the player's certificate that he had no health problems before he signed the contract. The DRC decided that Article 18 Paragraph 4 of the RSTP, edition 2005, was applicable to the case at hand. This Article states that the validity of a contract between a professional and a club may not be made subject to a positive medical examination. Therefore, medical examinations will be made by the player's prospective new club prior to concluding the contract. In the case at hand, however, it was a fact that the parties had agreed to the medical examination being conducted prior to the 31 July 2005, which meant that it took place after the parties signed the relevant employment contract. The DRC concluded that

[257] DRC 10 June 2004, no. 6400581.

[258] DRC 17 August 2006, no. 861174.

the before-mentioned clause 7 *in fine* of the employment contract is in violation with Article 18 Paragraph 4 of the RSTP and is therefore not legally binding, respectively null and void. Finally, the DRC deemed that the player had not breached the present employment contract by not undergoing medical examinations after the signing of the contract, but had trained and injured himself instead.

With respect to the above, one notable difference must be noted in relation to the rules of FIFA. The RSTP, edition 2001, was provided with the provision that stated:

> "the player's prospective new club will be required to make any necessary investigations, studies, tests and/or medical examination or to take any appropriate action before concluding the contract, otherwise it will be liable to pay the amount of the wage due".

However, the current RSTP, edition 2005, is provided with the provision that

> "the validity of a contract between a professional and a club may not be made subject to a positive medical examination".

Although it is not explicitly mentioned in the current Article of the edition 2005, to avoid any misunderstanding, it is still the responsibility of the prospective new club to make all the necessary investigations, studies, tests and/or medical examination or any appropriate action before concluding the contract with the player. This can be derived from the recent decision of the DRC of 26 October 2006, in which the edition 2005 was applicable to the matter at hand. In that case the club needed to be accurately informed about the player's career.[259] The prospective new club must acquire all the relevant information about the player. If the club is provided with inaccurate information about the player's former club, this does not constitute a valid reason for the club to unilaterally terminate the contract.

4.4 Conclusion

According to Article 18 Paragraph 4 of the RSTP, edition 2005, the validity of a contract may not be made subject to a positive medical examination. Any such conditions that are included in a contract will not be recognised by the DRC and the contract will still be considered valid without this clause. This means that the new club's failure to respect the contract represents an unconditional breach of contract without just cause.[260] The vision of the DRC with respect to the medical test following the before-mentioned decisions is very clear. The clause in an employment contract stating that the validity of a contract is subject to a positive medical examination is not valid. If after signing the contract the player appears not to be medically fit, the player can hold the club to his employment contract. In that case, the player can claim damages if the club wants to terminate the contract.

It is important to know whether the civil courts of the various countries will also adhere to the FIFA rules or whether they will decide that the FIFA rules are not valid at this point. According to the national labour law of various countries, it is sometimes possible to make the validity of the employment contract conditional upon the positive result of a medical examination of an employee. However, although certain national laws do permit an employer to unilaterally terminate the contract with his employee in case of a negative result

[259] DRC 26 October 2006, no. 1061118.

[260] FIFA Commentary, explanation Art. 18 Para. 4, p. 55.

of the medical test, FIFA at this point rightly differs. International professional football needs to have legal certainty. A player should be protected with respect to his medical state. As far as national courts decide that an employer has the right to unilaterally terminate the contract with his employee in the case of negative medical test results, there is a *Lex Sportiva*, which is justified and will have priority above these national civil laws.

5. Visa and work permit

5.1 **Introduction**

In many countries a foreign player is obliged to have a visa or work permit to be able to play for the club of the country concerned. As we will see hereinafter, the DRC is of the opinion that the responsibility for obtaining the visa or the work permit lies with the club, although in that respect it is important to emphasise that the player must cooperate fully to efforts aimed at obtaining the visa or the work permit.

5.2 **Visa**

In the case of an international transfer, it is sometimes necessary for a foreign player to obtain a visa from the country of his prospective club. The DRC has given various decisions in relation to the obligations of the new club towards the professional player when acquiring a visa for the legitimate residence.

In a case for the DRC of 4 February 2005 about a contractual dispute between a player and a club, the DRC decided explicitly that it is the club's responsibility to arrange the entry visa for the player. In this case, on 29 October 2003 the player received a deportation order issued by the local government, as a result of which he had to leave the territory of the Republic on 31 October 2003 because he had not permit to stay. According to Article 30 Paragraph 2 of the RSTP, edition 2001, the player's new club is required to arrange any necessary work permit for the player. The Chamber pointed out that the club did not undertake any action, or at least not the necessary ones, to prevent the execution of the deportation order, nor had it ever taken any steps to provide the player with the necessary visa by the time the employment contract was concluded.[261]

In a decision of the DRC of 12 January 2006, a player and a club signed an employment contract on 26 February 2003 valid until 25 June 2005. The player informed the DRC that he had played for the club until the end of the 2002/03 season and that, on 24 August 2003, after the club had been eliminated in the UEFA Champions League, the club had informed him that he should start looking for another club. Although he had only played for the club for a very short time, he left the club to find a new club. In September 2003, he returned to the club, but by this time his visa had expired (on 20 September 2003 to be precise). According to the player, he had tried to obtain a visa that would allow him to enter into the country, but at the relevant consulate he had been told that he needed the club's authorisation for this purpose. The player felt that the club had failed to provide the relevant consulate in Portugal with the necessary documents in order for him to obtain the relevant visa. This

[261] DRC 4 February 2005, no. 25488.

meant that not only had he not received any remuneration since the end of the 2002/03 season, but he was also prevented from playing for his club. The player informed the DRC that he had contacted the club several times to solve the problem with his visa. However, the club did not agree with this version. The club was of the opinion that according to the new national legislation, they could not have registered any more foreign players who had no right to work in the country. The DRC finally decided that, according to the player, despite his continuous efforts to contact the club to solve the problem with his visa, the latter had always failed to provide the relevant consulate in Portugal with the necessary documents in order for him to obtain the relevant visa. Finally, the DRC decided that the club had failed to provide FIFA with evidence demonstrating that it had effectively contacted the player to resume duty with it after September 2003 as well as with evidence demonstrating that it had provided the player with a valid visa which would allow him to resume duty with it.[262]

5.3 **Work permit**

In some countries, the foreign employer must have a work permit before he is able to play for the club concerned. The decisions of the DRC indicate that the club as employer is responsible for obtaining the work permit. The decisions of the DRC are always based on the general rule that the employer, in other words the club, must arrange the work permit for the employee, the player. Furthermore, according to Article 18 Paragraph 4 of the RSTP, edition 2005, the validity of a contract may not be made subject to the granting of a work permit.

In a decision before the DRC of 11 March 2005, the club did not provide the player with a work permit. The player claimed that in order to force him to stay to leave the club, the club had not undertaken the necessary steps to provide him with a new visa, not even after he reminded the club to do so. The DRC stated that it is a basic principle of labour law that an employer must provide his employees with a work permit, if necessary. If an employer does not undertake the necessary action to provide his employees with a work permit, and if this forces the player to leave the country in which he is employed and therefore quit his work, this can be considered as an unjustified breach of the employment contract by the employer.[263]

In a decision of the DRC of 1 June 2005, a player and a club signed an employment contract which was valid from 1 June 2002 until 30 July 2007. The player told the DRC that the club had neither paid his salaries nor certain bonuses. However, the club replied that the player's residence and work permit had expired on 30 June 2003. The club thought that this permit could only be extended by the player personally. According to the club, the player did not undertake the necessary steps in order to extend his residence and work permit and therefore the club felt that the player had breached the employment contract. In this case, the DRC stated that it is a basic principle of labour law that an employer must provide his employees with a residence and work permit, if necessary. If an employer does not undertake the necessary actions to provide his employees with a residence and work permit, and if this forces the player to leave the country in which he is employed and

---

[262] DRC 12 January 2006, no. 16107.

[263] DRC 11 March 2005, no. 35131.

therefore quit his work, this can be considered as an unjustified breach of the employment contract by the employer. The Chamber furthermore stated that if an employer maintains that it does not bear any responsibility for the extension of the residence and work permit, it is up to the employer to prove this allegation. If the employer failed to prove this allegation and it therefore had to be presumed that it bore the responsibility for the extension of the residence and work permit.[264]

5.4 Conclusion

In most countries a foreign player must have a visa or work permit to be able to play for the club of that country. In the international professional football world, the DRC is of the opinion that the responsibility for the visa lies with the club. In cases relating to the issue of a visa, the DRC regularly points out that the club must undertake the action, or at least take the necessary ones, to provide the player with the necessary documents by the time the employment contract is concluded. With respect to the work permit, the DRC states that it is a basic principle of labour law that an employer must provide his employees with a residence and work permit, if necessary. If an employer does not undertake the necessary actions to provide his employees with a residence and work permit, and if this forces the player to leave the country where he is employed and therefore quit his work, this can be considered as an unjustified breach of the employment contract by the employer.

For the sake of good order, it is important to know that the player must cooperate fully with efforts to obtain the visa or work permit. Following the FIFA Commentary, the player must put himself at the club's disposal and supply the prospective club with all the necessary information and documents in order to facilitate these tasks. If the player does not apply due diligence when signing a player, it cannot later claim that the failure to fulfil a contract was based on the fact that the player had not received a work permit or a visa.[265] Therefore, the before-mentioned view is justified, since it is reasonable that it is the club's main responsibility to acquire the necessary visa or work permit. It is understandable that this must be done prior to signing the employment contract. The DRC is very rigorous on this point. According to the RSTP, edition 2005, the employment agreement cannot be made conditional upon a work permit or a visa. It is reasonable that the employee is protected in the best possible way at this point. If the club could make the work permit or the visa conditional upon the validity of the contract, this would create too much uncertainty for the professional football player. Ultimately, this could lead to an imbalance which is absolutely not in the benefit of international football.

6. Employment contract

6.1 Introduction

In the professional international football world, all relevant rights and obligations between the players and the clubs are recorded in an employment agreement. However, we will see that the employment agreement between the player and the club varies at some points from

---

264 DRC 1 June 2005, no. 65332 and see also DRC 23 June 2005, no. 65939.

265 FIFA Commentary, explanation Art. 18 Para. 4, p. 55.

the employment agreement following the relevant national laws.[266] By having an employment agreement, the player will be more protected and his rights will be more guaranteed, while the club as employer will be entitled to give the necessary instructions to his employee. Parties sometimes try to avoid entering into an employment agreement by concluding an agreement of command. However, following several decisions, the DRC is of the opinion that the agreement between the professional and the club must be laid down in an employment contract.

This paragraph starts by outlining some relevant formal aspects with regard to the employment contract, such as the form and length of the contract. We will see that the current RSTP rules provide us with various requirements with regard to the employment contract. After the formal elements, the probation period and period of notice will be discussed. Finally, the financial aspects relating to the employment agreement will be handled, such as the salary and the bonuses for the professional. All these issues will be discussed and handled in relation to the opinion of the DRC.

6.2 Protected period

A club and a player who enter into an agreement should in principle respect and honour the contractual obligations during the term of the contract, also known as the principle of *pacta sunt servanda*. FIFA therefore introduced the so-called "protected period", which was meant to safeguard the maintenance of contractual stability. The protected period was the period of three entire seasons or three years, whichever comes first, following the entry into force, if such contract was concluded prior to the 28th birthday of the professional, or to a period of two entire seasons or two years, whichever comes first, following the entry into force of a contract, if such contract was concluded after the 28th birthday of the professional. FIFA was of the opinion that unilateral termination of a contract without a justified reason, especially during this so-called protected period, had to be vehemently discouraged.[267] In other words, during the protected period it was made much more difficult for one of the parties to terminate the contract. We will see in the following Articles that the protected period plays a key role with respect to the amount of compensation in the case of a termination by one of the parties, but also regarding the sporting sanctions to be imposed on of the parties. If the parties agree to extend the employment contract, the protected period will start again.[268] According to the FIFA Commentary, the parties then aim at longer contractual stability.[269]

6.3 Formal aspects

6.3.1 *Form*

In many countries the employment contract is form free and may be concluded orally or in writing. According to the legislation in several countries, despite not having an employ-

[266] Blanpain for example is of the opinion that the legal status of sportsmen and in particular those classed as professionals is clearly different from that of other workers. Roger Blanpain, *The Legal Status of Sportsmen and Sportswomen under International, European and Belgian National and Regional Law* (The Hague, London, New York, Kluwer Law International 2003), p. 141.

[267] FIFA Commentary, explanation Art 13, p. 38.

[268] RSTP, Edition 2005, Art. 17 Para. 3, last sentence.

[269] FIFA Commentary, explanation Art. 17, under footnote 87, p. 50.

ment agreement, parties are deemed to have tacitly entered into an employment agreement. The factual circumstances are decisive. However, notwithstanding the above, FIFA demands a written employment contract at all times. Article 2 Paragraph 2 of the RSTP, edition 2005 explicitly states that the employment agreement must be in writing. As we have seen earlier, this is a prerequisite in order to determine the status of the player. According to numerous DRC decisions, the Chamber decides accordingly and it is clearly indicated that the employment agreement between the professional and the club must be in writing.[270] In view thereof, it can be said that there are no exceptions. Over and over again, the DRC emphasises that the only requirements of the FIFA regulations is the existence of a written contract which is duly registered in the respective federation.[271]

In a decision of the DRC of 22 July 2004, the DRC noted that the last written employment contract between the player and the club expired on 20 November 2003 and that it was only extended until 20 December 2003, when the club ended its participation in the final phase of the second tournament.[272] Moreover, it was noted that the club acknowledged the lack of a written employment contract between the parties for the 2004 season, despite claiming the existence of an oral agreement binding the player to it for such a period. In this respect, the Chamber emphasised that "every player designated as a non-amateur by his national association will have a written employment contract with the club employing him". Consequently, the Chamber concluded that the player stopped being contractually bound to the club on 20 December 2003 and was therefore a free agent.

In another decision of the DRC of 22 July 2004, the DRC deemed it appropriate to declare that it could only decide on the basis of documents duly signed by the parties and that, in accordance with the Procedural Rules, verbal agreements would therefore not be taken into consideration. In the light of the above, the Chamber unanimously concluded that it was not established that the player signed a contract with the club on 1 September 2002 valid until the end of the 2002/03 season and that it therefore had to reject the claim of the Libyan Club concerned.[273]

In a decision of the DRC of 24 October 2004, the DRC was of the opinion that

> "pour le bon ordre, à cet égard, la Chambre a estimé approprié de rappeler que en conformité avec l'Article 2 alinéa 2 du Règlement concernant le Statut et le Transfert des Joueurs (édition 2005), une relation contractuelle entre un joueur et un club doit être toujours basée sur un contrat écrit".[274]

Again, according to this decision, the DRC explicitly underlines that a contract between a player and a club must be in writing.

In a decision of the DRC of 26 October 2006, the DRC decided that no valid employment contract was concluded between the parties because the offer had not been accepted by the player.[275] After examining the two before-mentioned documents, copies of which were remitted to the file, the DRC noted that the two documents had not been signed by the player. Referring to the general principle that every contract requires an offer and the

[270] DRC 24 October 2005, no. 105874(2) and no. 105874.
[271] DRC 4 February 2005, no. 25820.
[272] DRC 22 July 2004, no. 7472A.
[273] DRC 22 July 2004, no. 74165.
[274] DRC 24 October 2005, no. 105874(2).
[275] DRC 26 October 2006, no. 1061318.

acceptance of the offer, the DRC concluded that the offer of the club for employment had not been followed by an acceptance of the offer by the player. Therefore, the DRC decided in this particular case that no valid employment contract had been concluded between the player and the club.

In line with the above, it can be concluded following numerous decisions of the DRC that all employment contracts must be in writing. If this is not the case, the DRC is of the opinion that verbal agreements thereto will not be taken into consideration and the Chamber will conclude that no valid employment contract between the club and the player exist and that the player is therefore free to leave.

6.3.2 *Length*

In the professional football world, employment contracts are concluded for a predetermined period of time. According to Article 18 Paragraph 2 of the RSTP, edition 2005, the minimum length of the employment contract will be from the date of its entry into force until the end of the season, while the maximum length of the contract will be five years. Contracts of any other length will only be permitted when consistent with national laws. According to Article 1 Paragraph 3(a) of the RSTP, edition 2005, this provision is binding at national level and must be included. Players under the age of 18 are not permitted to sign a professional contract for a term longer than three years. Any clause in a contract with a minor referring to a longer period than three years will not be recognised by FIFA under any circumstances.[276]

According to the above, the maximum length of an employment contract is five years. This means that if the club and the player conclude a contract for more than five years, for example for 6 years, the player is entitled to leave the club after the fifth year, without having to pay any compensation or being imposed with any sporting sanctions. However, in this respect it is of crucial importance that contracts that do exceed the five years will only be permitted if consistent with the national law.

Pursuant to Article 18 Paragraph 2, players under the age of 18 may not sign a professional contract for a term longer than three years. Any clause referring to a longer period will not be recognised. Contrary to the normal professional football contract which may be concluded for a maximum of five years, FIFA is of the opinion that minors should be protected by reducing the maximum length of professional contracts with minors to three years. FIFA feels obliged to safeguard the interests of young players and not hinder their progress through an excessive tie to a club. Any clauses signed for a longer period will not be recognised by the football authorities. In the event that the contract is signed for longer than a term of three years, only the first three years of the contract will be considered valid. After the end of the third year, the player is free to leave the club unless he explicitly or de facto accepts the extension.[277] In a case which came before the DRC on 22 July 2004, the Chamber decided that a contract with a minor for a period of five years was invalid.[278]

In a decision of the DRC of 24 October 2005, a club understands that its employment contract with player B is valid and binding for both parties and requests the immediate

[276] RSTP, edition 2005 Para. 2, last two sentences.
[277] FIFA Commentary, explanation Art. 18 Para. 3, p. 53.
[278] DRC 22 July 2004, no. 74234.

intervention of the DRC.[279] In reply, the player claims that the contract that he signed with his club is invalid because it only had a 6 months' duration, which according to him contravenes the rules of FIFA. The Chamber rejected the argument concerning the duration of the player's employment contract with the club which would allegedly imply the contract's nullity, based on Article 4 Paragraph 2 of the RSTP, edition 2005. The DRC was of the opinion that the minimum duration of an employment contract must be seen in connection with Article 5 Paragraph 2 of the RSTP, edition 2001, which allows only one transfer per player in the same sports season in a period of 12 months. The DRC refers to FIFA Circular no. 867, which stated that the wording of the before-mentioned legal ground must be understood to apply only to the sports season rather than to the calendar year. The DRC was of the opinion that a contract signed for the remaining duration of a sports season must therefore be considered as valid. In this decision, the DRC emphasised that Article 18 Paragraph 2 of the new regulation, i.e., edition 2005, explicitly stipulates that the minimum length of a contract will be from the date of its entry into force to the end of the season.

6.3.3 *Signature*

The contract must be signed by both parties. This means that the player and the club must sign the employment contract. Although this is not stated in the FIFA regulations, the DRC is very clear on this point. If one of the parties does not sign the contract, the contract must be held invalid.[280] In the event that one of the parties used a licensed players' agent, then the name of the agent must be mentioned in the employment contract too. This is explicitly stipulated in Article 14 Paragraph 6 of the Players' Agent Regulations and Article 18 Paragraph 1 of the RSTP, edition 2005, in which it states that the players' agent must ensure that his name, signature and the name of his client appear in relevant contracts, such as the employment contract, resulting from every transaction in which he is involved.

Notwithstanding the above and to avoid any misunderstanding, it is irrelevant in relation to the validity of the employment contract whether or not it is signed by his agent. In a case before the DRC of 11 March 2005, the Chamber rejected the argument raised by the player, according to which his contract with the club should be considered as invalid due to the fact that it was not signed by his agent.[281]

The DRC has given various decisions in which the protection of the minor has priority. In a decision of 23 March 2006, the Chamber decided that the contract of a minor must be co-signed by his guardian.[282] In the view of the DRC, the minor should be protected in the best possible way. In the legislation of many countries, the employment contract of a club with a minor must be co-signed by his parents.

The DRC decided in its decision of 12 April 2005 that an employment contract with a minor is void if the contract is not co-signed by his parents. Consequently, the Football Association of the club St.G. was entitled to register him for his affiliated club with immediate effect. Furthermore, the Football Association of the club G should issue the relevant IRTC on behalf of the Football Association of the club St.G. without further delay.[283] The

[279] DRC 11 March 2005, no. 35144 b.
[280] DRC 26 October 2006, no. 106672.
[281] DRC 11 March 2005, no. 35144b.
[282] DRC 23 March 2006, no. 36619.
[283] RSTP, edition 2005, Art. 19 Para. 1, DRC 12 April 2005, no. 45196.

DRC is very strict with respect to co-signing of the guardians, all aimed at providing the minor with maximum protection.

In answer to the question as to who is authorised to bind the club, the DRC decided that it is always the president who is authorised to bind the club, even if the Chamber of Commerce demands the signature of two club officials.[284] This was confirmed in another case.[285] In this regard, the DRC stated that the alleged necessity of three signatures for the validity of an employment contract is a club-internal proxy rule which is not known to third parties and therefore does not have any legal effects on the validity of the present contract unless the contracting partner, in this case the player, is clearly informed about the respective rule. The DRC noted that the club had failed to provide any kind of evidence in order to corroborate its allegation that the player had indeed been informed that the signature of the President of the club was not sufficient for the validity of the contract. The DRC also stated that the player was not obliged to verify whether or not the President of the club was empowered to solely sign a contract. As in the present case where the signature of the club's President is concerned, the player could assume that as the highest possible representative of the club, he is authorised to sign individually. The DRC then turned its attention to the argument of the club that the contract includes three lines, i.e., allegedly space for three signatures. The DRC stated that by simply providing space for three signatures, it could not be concluded that the club had informed the player about the necessity of three signatures from the club. In conclusion of the before-mentioned, the DRC finally stated that the club's argument that the contract is not valid due to the missing of two signatures should be rejected. The DRC was of the opinion that the contract had therefore been duly signed by both parties.

Sometimes it appears that the signature(s) under the contract is/are false. In principle, the national civil judge will conduct a thorough investigation as to whether the signature is false or not. Sometimes it may even come to a criminal procedure when a criminal offence has been committed. In the case of a false signature in the employment contract, the DRC pointed out in several decisions that it is not competent to decide on whether or not a signature is a forgery. Indeed, such a matter will be referred to a criminal court.[286] The DRC follows a very strict rule in this matter and gives the impression that it is not able to investigate whether the signature is false or not. It could be said that the DRC is too strict in case of a false signature. The DRC does not thoroughly investigate the originality of the signature and is too quick to point out that the parties should address the criminal court in their own country. The DRC should conduct a more thorough investigation with regard to the originality of the signature.

6.3.4 *Language*

The four official languages of FIFA are English, French, German and Spanish.[287] The employment contract is usually written in the language of the country of the club. FIFA

---

[284] DRC 26 October 2006, no. 106399.

[285] DRC 26 October 2006, no. 1061097.

[286] DRC 11 March 2005, no. 35239.

[287] FIFA Statutes, Art. 8 Para. 4. English is the official language for minutes, correspondence and announcements. Members are responsible for translations into the language of their country. If there is any divergence in the wording, the English text is always authoritative.

does not provide any rules to the contrary and one may therefore conclude that the parties are free to choose the language of the contract, which is generally English or the language of the country in which the club is domiciled.

In a decision of the DRC of 4 February 2005, the DRC decided that in a contractual dispute between the parties involved, the FIFA regulations do not oblige the parties to sign a contract in one of the official languages.[288] The only requirements stated by the FIFA regulations are the existence of a written contract duly registered in the respective Federation. In this context, on 13 August 2003 the player and the club signed an employment agreement written in Arabic. The DRC was of the opinion that this contract was legally binding between the parties because it fulfilled all the legal requirements under the national law concerned and the FIFA regulations. The player stated that at the time of signing the contract with the club in Arabic, the club had acted in bad faith by not providing him with a copy of the same, duly translated into English, French or Spanish, as required by FIFA. The DRC explicitly underlined that fact and stressed that the regulations do not oblige the parties to sign a contract in one of FIFA's official languages, as claimed by the player in this case. The only requirements stated by FIFA regulations are the existence of a written contract duly registered in the respective Federation.

Finally it is important to know that in its decision of 12 April 2005, the DRC decided that any document that a party wishes to submit in support of its arguments to the DRC must be translated into one of the four official FIFA languages (English, French, German and Spanish) otherwise the document will not be considered.[289]

6.4 **Probation period**

The probation period is the period agreed by both parties in the employment contract in which they may terminate the contract with immediate effect and without being obliged to give any reason to the other party. The probation period is generally a short period, for example two months. During that period, the parties may observe each other and may decide to terminate the agreement promptly without giving any reason. Most national legislations allow a probation period in the employment agreement. However, the DRC has a different opinion with respect to this subject.

The DRC is of the opinion that a probation period is usually not allowed. With regard to the agreed probation period, the DRC recalled that, as a general rule, such clauses are not acceptable as they do not respect the spirit of the regulations.

However, in a case of 11 March 2005, the player accepted the termination of the contractual relationship during the probation period. Consequently, the DRC deemed that, in view of the specificities of the case, the relevant clause could be tolerated.[290] This is a notable decision of the DRC, because one could ask here whether the player's acceptance is relevant.

In a case of the DRC of 27 April 2006, the Chamber again referred to its earlier jurisprudence which stated that a clause that only benefits one party and not the other is a clause with doubtful validity. The clause in the contract is not valid because it creates disequilibrium between the rights and obligations of the player and the club. The proba-

[288] DRC 4 February 2005, no. 25820.

[289] DRC 12 April 2005, no. 3542.

[290] DRC 11 March 2005, no. 35174.

tion clause is not valid and does not justify the unilateral termination of the contract by the club. The DRC concluded that the club breached the contract and had no just cause by unilaterally terminating the contract during the probation period on the grounds that the player did not perform well enough. Therefore, the player may claim compensation. The DRC considered that the club had not paid any salary to the player. The DRC finally concluded that the club should pay compensation to the player equal to the period between the time of the unilateral termination and the moment he played for his new club.[291]

In another case which came before the DRC on 27 August 2006, the DRC decided that after having discussed the issue at length, probation periods in football related employment contracts were unacceptable. Indeed, probation periods usually only favour the employer, i.e., the party that generally has the stronger bargaining power. Furthermore, by nature probation periods tend to contradict one of the main pillars of both the previous and the current version of the RSTP, i.e., the maintenance of contractual stability and the rules related to contractual stability. If clubs and/or players are entitled to end an employment contract invoking a probation period, players in particular may have difficulty in finding other employment in the light of Articles 5 and 6 of the RSTP, edition 2005. In addition, such termination of contract would be in violation of the main principle of Article 13 of the said Regulations. Regardless of the above, in the case at hand the Article relating to the probation period is undoubtedly potestative, the club being the sole party able to terminate the employment contract during the probation period on the basis of the pertinent Article. In the light of the foregoing, the DRC agreed that the probation period inserted in the employment contract cannot justify the early termination of the relevant employment contract.[292]

6.5 Period of notice

According to the decisions of the DRC, parties may agree to a period of notice in the contract. In a decision of 17 August 2006, the DRC was of the opinion that the club had unilaterally terminated the employment contract based on clause 3.4 of the relevant employment contract at the basis of the present dispute.[293] The DRC noted that the before-mentioned clause gives both parties the right to terminate the employment contract upon written notice of one month, that in the event of the contract being terminated by the club, the player could retain the signing-on fee to the amount of USD 140,000 as well as all monthly salary payments to the amount of USD 14,000 that had been made up to that point and that the player would also be entitled to a monthly salary of USD 14,000 for the time covered by the notice period.

The DRC duly analysed clause 3.4 of the relevant employment contract concerning the termination of the contract. In this respect, the members of the DRC noted that the before-mentioned contractual termination clause provides for the right to terminate the relevant contract for both parties. Furthermore, the DRC acknowledged that, in the case of termination of the contract by either party, the before-mentioned clause grants compensation payable to the other party. Finally, the DRC noted that the said clause contains a one month notice period to be respected by the respective terminating party. On account of the above,

[291] DRC 27 April 2006, no. 461021.
[292] DRC 17 August 2006, no. 86833.
[293] DRC 21 November 2006, no. 116218.

the DRC concluded that clause 3.4 of the relevant employment contract should be considered as totally valid and legally binding. Consequently, the DRC decided that the club did not breach the relevant employment contract without just cause but in accordance with clause 3.4 of the relevant contract, which was signed and approved by both parties.

6.6 Payments

6.6.1 *Salaries*

In a decision of the DRC of 11 March 2005, the DRC had to decide about a contractual dispute between a French player and a Turkish club.[294] The DRC decided that the insufficient and poor performance level was no valid reason to pay the player less salaries. The DRC adjudicated compensation to the player. The parties signed an employment contract on 23 August 2004 for the 2004/05 season under the following basic financial terms: a USD 50,000 net cash payment, as well as a monthly remuneration of USD 7,000. The DRC commented that the player's poor performance could have been addressed in several alternative ways, none of which include withholding the basic contractual duties towards the player. According to the DRC, the non-fulfilment of such basic contractual obligations as in the payment of salaries may not be implemented as a tool to sanction a player for disappointing performance levels. Therefore, the DRC decided that the poor performance level was no valid reason to pay the player less salaries.

In another case which came before the DRC on 27 April 2006 in relation to the same issue, the DRC firstly focused on the player's remark regarding the four disciplinary sanctions imposed by the club. In fact, the club established in its relevant list a total amount of USD 3,639 as fines imposed on the player based on low performance of the entire squad. The DRC outlined that, as a general rule, low performance cannot be considered a reason for the club to reduce payments to the player because it is unilaterally determined by the club and based on pure subjective criteria. Therefore, the members of the DRC concluded that this imposition of fines by the club cannot be accepted and thus cannot be deducted from monies payable to the player.[295]

In a decision of 12 January 2006, a player and a club signed an employment contract on 26 February 2003 valid until 25 June 2005.[296] According to the employment contract, the player was entitled to receive a monthly salary of ROL 2,500,000 as well as the following amounts:

- USD 30,000 between 26 February 2003 and 24 June 2003, if he played a minimum of 10 matches in the Romanian championship;
- USD 75,000 during the 2003/04 sporting season, if he played a minimum of 23 official matches; and
- USD 80,000 during the 2004/05 sporting season, if he played a minimum of 23 official matches.

---

[294] DRC 11 March 2005, no. 3542.
[295] DRC 27 April 2006, no. 46290.
[296] DRC 12 January 2006, no. 16107.

According to this agreement, the player only received a salary if he played a certain amount of matches. The player had not received any remuneration since the end of the 2002/03 sporting season because he had not played the required number of matches. The DRC unanimously concluded that the application of such a clause is arbitrary since it is at the club's discretion to decide how many matches the player plays. According to the Chamber, the before-mentioned clause was unacceptable. Therefore, for the season 2003/04 the player was entitled to receive the amount of USD 75,000 plus ROL 30,000,000 and for the sporting season 2004/05 the amount of USD 80,000 plus ROL 30,000,000 independent of the number of matches played.

Furthermore, the parties must explicitly stipulate in the employment contract whether the payments are net or gross. In its deliberations, in its decision of 27 April 2006 the DRC turned to the question as to whether the financial entitlements of the player are payable net or gross. In this regard, the members of the Chamber noted that neither the employment contract signed on 2 August 2004 nor the "private agreement" specify whether the sums payable to the player are net or gross amounts. The DRC departed from the principle that monies must be considered to be payable gross, i.e., the amounts of money being subject to deduction of social insurance and tax, in the absence of a specific clause in the relevant employment contract in accordance with which monies are payable net. Consequently, and the party having substantiated that taxes were deductible from the monies payable to the other party in accordance with the employment contract, the Chamber concluded that the amount of EUR 9,328 was deductible from the before-mentioned amount of EUR 44,000. The DRC therefore concluded that this party was entitled to receive the net amount of EUR 34,672 relating to the four instalments during the first season.[297]

The club is obliged to pay the player a salary. The currency in which the salaries are to be paid is that of the currency stipulated in the contract. In a decision of the DRC of 28 September 2006, the Chamber had to adjudicate in a dispute between a player and a club with relation to amongst others the currency.[298] On 28 September 2001, the player and the club signed an employment contract valid as from the date of the signature until 28 September 2006. The DRC turned its attention to the contradictory positions of the parties in the present dispute with regard to the amount paid to the player in advance, and in particular the currency to which the advance payment refers. The DRC remarked that the player confirmed the receipt of the advance payment in the amount of 325,000 "rubles". In this respect, the members of the Chamber were first and foremost of the unanimous opinion that the decisive and crucial currency to be taken into account is the one to which the relevant employment contract at the basis of the present dispute refers.

6.6.2 *Bonuses*

In the international professional football world, it is usual for players to receive other remunerations such as bonuses on top of their salary. This is very normal in the international professional football world and it is even becoming more popular to work with bonus-related contracts, the so-called "performance-related contracts". To avoid any risks, the club generally gives the player a low salary and sometimes, out of all proportion, extremely high bonuses. These bonuses often have no relation to the low basic salary.

[297] DRC 27 April 2006, no. 46831.

[298] DRC 28 September 2006, no. 96157.

In a case 9 November 2004 before the DRC about the performance of the player and the bonuses payable to him, the Chamber decided that clauses stipulating performance-related pay are common in the employment contracts of footballers. These clauses usually refer to the number of matches in which a player is fielded, often distinguishing between games won and games drawn.[299] Furthermore, these clauses generally refer to the number of matches and not the number of minutes played, since a club is unlikely to risk not fielding a player for reasons relating to a performance-related clause but it may well try and control the total minutes played by a particular player by substituting the latter when it feels that a match is as good as won. Furthermore, it is easier for both parties to establish the number of matches a footballer has played rather than to verify how many minutes a player performed.

In a decision of 1 June 2005, the DRC decided with respect to a contractual dispute between a player and a club regarding outstanding bonuses. The clause that the payment of bonuses would be withheld if the team dropped into the league relegation zone is not valid according to the DRC.

The members of the Chamber discussed the contents of the relevant internal rules, in particular the chapter referring to the bonuses and Article 5 which stipulates:

> "In case that the team falls into the endangered zone on the league table the owner, the managing director or the chief trainer may withhold or withdraw the payment of bonuses".

The DRC concluded that the club's decision to withdraw payment of the contractually agreed bonuses based on the cited Article cannot be supported by FIFA. In this respect, the DRC deemed that the before-mentioned rule is ambiguous and its application arbitrary, since it leads to an unacceptable result based on non-objective criteria. As a result, the DRC finally concluded that the player was entitled to receive the relevant bonuses.[300]

In a case of 26 November 2006, the DRC noted that according to the relevant supplement to the employment contract, the player was entitled to receive a bonus to the amount of USD 5,000 for each goal scored or assisted by him. But the said entitlement was applicable to winning games completed by the club in official matches of the League or the Cup. In this regard, the DRC considered that the official statistics issued by the Football Association, i.e., the player's official "match history 2004/05" constituted the basis for the establishment of the number of goals scored and assists to goals provided by the player in official matches of the before-mentioned competitions. Furthermore, the DRC stated that the player failed to provide FIFA with any adequate documentary evidence regarding the number of goals scored and assisted by him. The DRC acknowledged that in accordance with the applicable statistics issued by the Football Association the player scored five goals in winning games completed by the club in official matches of the relevant competitions.[301]

6.7 Conclusion

One can say that with respect to the formal aspects of the employment agreement, according to various decisions of the DRC, the Chamber is of the explicit opinion that the profes-

---

[299] DRC 9 November 2004, no. 114441.

[300] DRC 1 June 2005, no. 6526.

[301] DRC 26 November 2006, no. 116336.

sional football contract must be in writing. In view thereof, it can be said that there are no exceptions. In this respect, Article 2 Paragraph 2 Annex 3 of the RSTP, edition 2005, states that an application to register a professional must be submitted by the new club to the new association accompanied by a copy of the contract between the new club and the professional. In other words and for the sake of good order, in order to register a professional, it is an absolute requirement that the professional and the club have a written employment agreement.

According to much national legislation, in principle the judge will give the parties the opportunity to prove that an employment agreement was concluded between the parties. If the DRC has to decide about a party's offer to substantiate proof of an oral agreement, the Chamber will not accept such an offer. The DRC is very strict in its decisions and in many cases decided that oral employment agreements are not binding. The national arbitration courts should follow the decisions of the DRC. This will bring more certainty and uniformity within the football world. However, it is remarkable that if a party wishes to submit to the civil court of his country and requests the court to decide that there is a legally and binding employment agreement between them, irrespective of the fact that it is an oral agreement, most national judges may conclude that there is a valid employment agreement. The DRC however decides contrarily and at this point one can speak of a *Lex Sportiva*.

With respect to the length of the contract, it can be said that the minimum length of the employment contract will be from the date of its entry into force until the end of the season, while the maximum length of the contract will be five years. Contracts of any other length will only be permitted when consistent with national laws. As also mentioned earlier, players under the age of 18 are not permitted to sign a professional contract for a term longer than three years. Any clause in a contract with a minor referring to a longer period than three years will not be recognised by FIFA. It is interesting that there are no decisions of the DRC with respect to the maximum length. It would be interesting to find out what the DRC will decide if a player and a club concluded a contract with a length that exceeds the maximum length of five years, especially, when this is permitted by the national law.

Furthermore, the contract must be signed by both parties. Although this is not stated in the regulations, the DRC is also at this point very clear. When one of the parties does not sign the contract, the contract must be held invalid. In this respect, it must be mentioned that it is the President of the club who is authorised to bind the club, even in case the Chamber of Commerce demands the signature of two club officials.

The DRC finds it important to stress that FIFA regulations do not oblige the parties to sign a contract in one of the FIFA official languages. The only requirements are the existence of a written contract which is duly registered in the respective federation. Any documents that a party wishes to submit in support of its arguments to the DRC must be translated into one of the four official FIFA languages, namely English, French, German or Spanish, otherwise the document cannot be considered.

In relation to the probation period, the DRC is also clear. According to various decisions of the DRC, the Chamber is of the opinion that in general a probation period is not allowed. With regard to the agreed probation period, the DRC recalled that, in accordance with its long standing jurisprudence, as a general rule, such clauses are not acceptable as they do not respect the spirit of the regulations. In this respect one may say that the DRC creates its own law at this point, because according to most national laws, a probation period is generally valid. The DRC decided to the contrary. There is a *Lex Sportiva* that will have priority in relation to the national civil law. This is necessary because of the uncertainty for the player with respect to his employment contract. In the professional football world it is not difficult, even easy, to invite the player to come on a trial with the club, which is permitted.

With respect to the issue of the period of notice, one can say that the DRC is of the opinion that the parties may agree to a period of notice in the contract. However, in the daily practice of the professional football world, parties do not provide their employment contracts with a period of notice, as a consequence of which both parties have the right to terminate the employment contract upon a written notice. In case of a period of notice, the club bears the risk that the player, whose star might be on the rise, suddenly terminates his employment contract and becomes a free agent. This is obviously disastrous for the club and therefore the main reason why these provisions are only inserted in the contract in exceptional circumstances.

Finally, with respect to the player's salary, the parties have to explicitly stipulate in the employment contract whether the payments are net or gross. With respect to the bonuses, it is usual practice in the international professional football world that the players receive other remunerations on top of their salary such as bonuses. The DRC is of the opinion that clauses stipulating performance-related pay are indeed common in the employment contracts of footballers and that these clauses usually refer to the number of matches in which a player is fielded for the club.

7. Extension option

7.1 Introduction

The extension option is the right of the player and/or the club to extend the employment contract for a certain period which is stipulated by the parties in the present employment contract. There are many kinds of extension options. We have the reciprocal extension option in favour of the player and the club in which both parties are entitled to prolong the employment contract for a certain predetermined period and there is the unilateral extension option only in favour of one of the parties. In the daily practice of international professional football, we usually find unilateral extension options solely in favour of the club. In order to provide their employments agreements with unilateral extension options in their favour, the clubs try to prevent the situation whereby their professional football player comes to the end of his contract and to leave for free. Most clubs try to keep their player as long as possible when they expect his star to be on the rise. To be sure that the player will stay with the club, the latter sometimes forces the player to extend his contract. Players who do not wish to extend their contract with their club are often excluded from matches and find themselves demoted to the "C" squad. They see their value as a player decline, so they often sign.[302]

According to various national labour laws, the unilateral extension option in favour of the club is generally valid. However, it is certainly a remarkable clause because of its

302 Roger Blanpain, *The Legal Status of Sportsmen and Sportswomen under International, European and Belgian National and Regional Law* (The Hague, London, New York, Kluwer Law International 2003), p. XV.

disputable reputation and the imbalance it creates between the player and the club. As we saw earlier, after the famous *Bosman* case, the clubs invented legal constructions to keep a stronger hold on their players. The clubs therefore inserted these unilateral extension clauses into the players' contracts. Despite its popularity and frequent use in international football, the RSTP, edition 2005, contains no provision governing the validity of the unilateral extension option. Therefore, the opinion of the DRC is even more important in this matter.

This chapter discusses the validity of the unilateral extension option in favour of the club, amongst others in the view of the DRC, as this is the most frequently used unilateral option. In that respect, the famous *Trabelsi* case of the national arbitrational court of the Netherlands will be discussed, in which this court decided that the unilateral extension option for Ajax in the contract of Trabelsi was valid.

Furthermore, a decision of the DRC of 12 January 2007 cannot be left unmentioned, although this decision is outside the scope of this book. However, because of its importance for the validity of the unilateral extension option, this decision should be discussed for the sake of completeness. In line with this decision and based on other relevant DRC decisions, the criteria will be outlined and enumerated with respect to the validity of the unilateral extension clause.

7.2 In favour of the club

If the extension option is in the favour of both the club and the player, the DRC is of the opinion that such a clause in the employment contract is valid. However, and as mentioned above, in most cases parties agree upon a clause in the employment contract which states that the club has the right to unilaterally extend the employment contract for a certain period, for example for two or three years. Following numerous decisions of national courts, such a unilateral extension option in an employment agreement is legitimate. However, according to its constant jurisprudence, the DRC decided that the unilateral extension which is exclusively in favour of the club should be considered as null and void. If the player has no influence whatsoever in the case of the club invoking the unilateral extension option, the unilateral extension option cannot be valid and will not be legally binding.

In a decision of 22 July 2004, a player and a club signed an employment contract valid from 30 July 2003 until 30 June 2004.[303] According to the employment contract, it was valid for the before-mentioned period with a four year unilateral renewal. The player was notified of such via process server with a simultaneous legal notice to the association of football players at least five days before the commencement of the transfer period as prescribed by the professional Players' Regulations. Furthermore, in accordance with the contract, the notification of renewal had to contain the financial terms pertaining to the extended period of time and the form of renewal in order to be valid. In addition, the relevant clause in the contract stipulated that the extension of the contract "will be made every year". In other words, the club had the right to unilaterally extend the contract four times. The Chamber outlined that the player wished to be declared not bound by the unilateral extension option and to be free to sign with another club. The DRC decided that unilateral options are, in general, problematic since they limit the freedom of the party that cannot make use of the option in an excessive manner. According to the DRC, such options are

[303] DRC 22 July 2004, no. 74508.

not based on reciprocity, since the right to extend a contract is left exclusively to the discretion of one party. In the case at hand, the extension option contained in the relevant employment contract is unilateral to the benefit of the club only, i.e., the stronger party in the employment relationship and may be exercised by the club during a period of four footballing seasons. The DRC decided there was no apparent gain for the player, as the conditions of employment remain unaltered. The Chamber finally concurred that the before-mentioned specifics of the unilateral extension option in the case at hand did not fit within the general principles of labour law. Finally, the DRC was of the opinion that the unilateral extension option in the relevant employment contract was not legally binding on the player.

In a decision of 13 May 2005, the DRC decided that the unilateral extension option for the club was not valid either. In this case the parties signed an employment contract on 31 January 2004 for the period from 31 January 2004 until 31 December 2004, providing the club with the possibility to unilaterally extend the contract for another three years, one year at a time. On 21 December 2004, the club announced in writing its unilateral renewal of the contract until 31 December 2005. Nine days later, the player wrote to the club, stating his refusal to accept such unilateral renewal of the contract but declaring that he was prepared to negotiate a renewal under new, mutually acceptable terms. With regard to this provision, the DRC decided that it gave the club the right to unilaterally renew the contract, but also provided that such renewal would not be valid unless the financial conditions of renewal were specified. In its considerations regarding the nature of said provision, the Chamber recalled that a clause which gives one party the right to unilaterally cancel or lengthen it without providing the other party to the contract with similar rights is a clause with disputable validity. It follows that the provision in the contract in question should either have been respected in all of its terms, including the specification of new financial conditions accepted through negotiation by both parties, or else the clause must be considered to be invalid due to its potestative nature. The DRC finally decided that no valid renewal of the contract had taken place. Although the DRC decided in the before-mentioned decision that the unilateral extension option was invalid, it could be presumed that if the unilateral extension option in the contract in question had been respected in all of its terms, including the specification of new financial conditions accepted through negotiation by both parties, the option would have been valid. According to the before-mentioned decision, the renewal will not generally be valid, unless the financial conditions of renewal were specified.

In a decision of 24 October 2005, the DRC decided that a unilateral extension option can be valid in case of special circumstances.[304] In this case the player and the club signed a valid one-year contract with an option that allowed the club to renew the contract on an annual basis for a total of four consecutive years. The contract had been extended for a first year from 1 July 2004 until 30 June 2005. The player acknowledged and accepted this first unilateral renewal of the contract. The DRC again judged that the unilateral extension option in the relevant employment contract is not generally legally binding on the player. In this case however, the DRC deemed that the player had accepted the unilateral extension of the contract and concluded that the club's unilateral extension did become legally binding on the player. Consequently, the Chamber was of the opinion that a valid contract existed between the parties for the 2005/06 season and that the player and the club should

[304] DRC 24 October 2005, no. 105874(2).

therefore respect their relevant obligations. This is a rather remarkable decision with respect to the before-mentioned decisions. In general, we have seen that the DRC, as it referred to in this decision, does not accept a unilateral extension option. However, in this special case the Chamber did agree with the option, because the player had explicitly accepted the unilateral extension option. Therefore, if the player is against the extension of the employment contract, it is wise for him to let the club explicitly know that he does not agree with the prolongation of his employment contract. If the player later agrees with the extension, then the DRC may decide that the extension option of the employment contract is valid.

In a decision of 21 February 2006, a player signed a one-year contract with his new club. Article 2 of the contract provided an option that allowed the club to renew the contract unilaterally on an annual basis for a total of four consecutive years. The contract had been extended for a first year from 1 July 2004 until 30 June 2005 and the player had accepted this first unilateral renewal of the contract. The Chamber then turned to the question whether the clause awarding the club the possibility to unilaterally renew the employment contract was valid or not. The Chamber noted that the player had not signed any document in which he agreed with the unilateral extension of the employment contract for the period from 1 July 2005 until 30 June 2006. In its considerations regarding the nature of Article 2 of the employment contract, which contained the relevant option, the DRC recalled that, in accordance with its established jurisprudence, a clause which gives one party the right to unilaterally cancel or lengthen the contract without providing the counterparty with same rights is a clause with questionable validity. Specifically, a unilateral option in favour of a club cannot generally be considered, since it excessively limits the freedom of the player and creates an unjustified disadvantage of the player's rights towards the club. The DRC came up with the same consideration as mentioned in its decision above of 24 October 2005, in which it said that it follows that Article 2 of the contract in question should either have been respected in all of its terms, including the specification that new financial conditions should be accepted by both parties through negotiation whenever the club wished to make use of the relevant option right, or else the clause would be considered invalid due to its potestative nature. The DRC pointed out that the club's declaration of renewal for the period from 1 July 2005 to 30 June 2006 did not include any separate written agreement in which the new financial conditions were laid out. For the DRC it was crucial that negotiations had not taken place, or in any case had not been brought to a successful conclusion. The extension option contained in the relevant employment contract was exclusively to the benefit of the club, i.e., the normally stronger party in the employment relationship. The exercise of the option by the club to extend the contract for the 2005/06 season did not involve any apparent important gain for the player, as the conditions of employment remain nearly unaltered. The DRC finally concurred that the before-mentioned specifics of the unilateral extension option in the case at hand do not fit in with the general principles of labour law. The DRC finally concluded that the unilateral option in favour of the club in the employment contract at the basis of the present litigation was not legally binding on the player.

In a decision of 23 March 2006, a player and a club concluded on 20 August 2002 an employment contract valid from 20 August 2002 to 30 June 2005.[305] Clause 2 Paragraph 2 of the before-mentioned contract stipulated an option in favour of the club to unilaterally

[305] DRC 23 March 2006, no. 36858.

extend the duration of the contract for the two sporting seasons 2005/06 and 2006/07. On 4 July 2005, the player and another club signed an employment contract valid for the sporting seasons 2005/06, 2006/07, 2007/08 and 2008/09. According to the first club, the option right was legal since it had been previously negotiated and agreed upon by both parties and since the salaries for the future extended contractual duration had already been established in the original contract. The club emphasised that a salary increase had been assured to the player. The club also explained that such an option right was permitted in the national law. According to the club, by signing a new contract with a new club, the player had acted in bad faith. The club felt that the player had violated its contractual obligations and referred to the principle of *in venire contra factum proprium*. The player denied all allegations made by the club and rejected the club's allegation by asking why the club did not notify the execution of the said option right by registered mail or a notary, at least after the alleged unsuccessful personal handing over of the alleged letter. The new club with which the player had signed a contract stated that the option right had to be considered as null and void because it did not correspond to a contractual promise but to a clause which obliged the player to extend his employment relation for two sporting seasons whether he liked it or not. The fact that the employer had decided only and exclusively on the extension of the contractual duration was unacceptable. The former club firmly believed that the option right was legal as it had been previously negotiated and agreed upon by both parties, as the salary increase for the future extended contractual duration had already been established in the original contract, as the stipulated option right corresponded to a labour sportive promise, as the player never invocated the possible nullity of the said option right and as the player can refuse to sign a new contract at any time, provided that he respects the agreed penalty clause. The DRC finally recalled that, in accordance with its established jurisprudence, a clause which gives one party the right to unilaterally cancel or lengthen the contract without providing the player with same rights is a clause with disputable validity. The extension option contained in the relevant employment contract was unilateral to the benefit of the club only, i.e., the stronger party in the employment relationship and may be exercised by the club during the considerable period of two football seasons. This gave the club unequal bargaining power, while there was no apparent gain for the player, even though the conditions of the employment had indeed been improved. The DRC was of the opinion that the increase of the monthly stipulated salary during the said period, if the contract was extended, was lower than EUR 1,000, which confirmed that the before-mentioned extension option did not establish any significant gain for the player. The DRC explicitly emphasised that two years was a significant portion of a footballer's active career. The DRC finally underlined that the said unilateral option in the contract in question excessively curtails the freedom of movement and leaves the player at an unfair disadvantage. The DRC finally concluded that the unilateral option in favour of the club in the employment contract on the basis of the present litigation could not be considered as being legally binding on the player.

7.3 ***Trabelsi*** **case**

The Dutch arbitration court decided in the case of *AFC Ajax N.V.* v. *Hatem Belgacem Trabelsi* that the unilateral extension option was valid.[306] The employment agreement of

[306] Dutch KNVB Court of Arbitration 4 June 2004, no. 1022.

Trabelsi had been concluded for a period of three years, starting on 1 July 2001 and ending on 30 June 2004. The player had granted the club a unilateral irrevocable option right to extend his agreement for a period of two years, starting on 1 July 2004 and ending on 30 June 2004. In this decision, this national arbitration court was of the opinion that the unilateral extension option was valid. Although the DRC had decided in several decisions that the unilateral extension option generally has a potestative nature, the national arbitration court explicitly decided that the unilateral extension option concerned did not have a potestative nature, as claimed by the player Trabelsi. The DRC finally decided that this clause had to be valid.

This decision is very remarkable. Apart from the fact that in my opinion the Dutch arbitration court should have ruled according to the many DRC decisions which clearly state that the unilateral extension option is not valid and legally binding between the parties, even worse, it creates an imbalance between the FIFA and the national arbitrational courts. In creating more uniformity, equality and certainty, it is vital that decisions of national arbitrational courts are in line with the decisions of the DRC. It cannot be denied that it is remarkable that this clause is considered to be valid at national level, while the DRC is generally of the opinion that the unilateral extension option which solely and exclusively benefits the club should be considered as invalid. However, in a decision of the DRC of 17 January 2007, the DRC provides us with the criteria on which to decide whether a unilateral extension option in favour of the club is valid. As mentioned earlier, despite the fact that this decision lies outside the scope of this book, this decision gives us the answer with respect to the validity of a unilateral extension option.

7.4 Criteria validity

The criteria on which to decide that a unilateral extension option is valid are laid down in a decision of the DRC of 12 January 2007.[307] The DRC decided in this case with respect to the validity of the unilateral extension option which was solely in favour of the club. As to the validity of the club's option to unilaterally renew the employment contract, reference was hereby made to two decisions of the CAS of 12 July 2006, which were considered as leading cases within the subject of unilateral options for the extension of employment contracts signed between players and clubs.[308] According to these decisions, the DRC concluded that the system of unilateral renewal of the contract is not generally compatible with the juridical frame which the RSTP, edition 2005, aims to establish. In the mentioned DRC decision, the Chamber referred to the decisions of the CAS in which five crucial elements were established that had to be analysed in order to decide on the validity of a club's option to unilaterally renew the employment contract with its player.

The following criteria were decisive in order to determine whether the unilateral extension option in favour of the club must be considered as being valid:

- The potential maximum duration of the labour relationship will not be excessive.
- The option will be exercised within an acceptable deadline before the expiry of the current contract.

---

[307] DRC 12 January 2007 (not published). It is remarkable that this decision is not published on the official website of FIFA. This is a very important decision of the DRC for professional football in relation to the common used unilateral extension option.

[308] CAS 2005/A/983 and 984, *Penarol* v. *Bueno Suarez, Rodriguez Barrotti and Paris Saint-Germain*, decision of 12 July 2006.

- The salary reward deriving from the option right must be defined in the original contract;
- One party will not be at the mercy of the other party with regard to the contents of the employment contract.
- The option will be clearly established and emphasised in the original contract so that the player is conscious of it at the moment of signing the contract.

The DRC considered all the five elements. In this case the club notified the player within a deadline of five days before the expiry of the contact. In its defence, the club referred to a decision of the CAS in which a unilateral option was declared valid.[309] The DRC decided that a deadline of five days before the expiry of a contract was not acceptable. Furthermore the DRC considered that no party will be at the mercy of the other party with regard to the contents of an employment contract. In this respect, the increase of the salary after the exercise of the option is the most important indication to establish whether a party is at the mercy of the other party with regard to the contractual contents. In view of the above, the DRC finally considered that a party will not be at the mercy of the other party with regard to the contents of the employment contract and decided that the renewal option in the present case had to be considered as invalid. Consequently, the player was no longer contractually bound to the club and the labour relationship between the player and the club was terminated as of 1 July 2006.

7.5 **Conclusion**

Bearing in mind the above and according to the various decisions of the DRC, the Chamber is of the opinion that unilateral options are generally problematic, since they excessively limit the freedom of the party that cannot use the option and lead to an unjustified disadvantage of the players' rights towards the club. A clause which gives one party the right to unilaterally cancel or extend it, without providing the other party to the contract with similar rights, is a clause with disputable validity. In general it can be said that it excessively curtails the freedom of movement and leaves the player at an unfair disadvantage. According to the DRC, unilateral extension options in favour of the club are not based on reciprocity, since the right to extend a contract is left exclusively to the discretion of the club. Therefore as a general rule, a unilateral extension option will be considered to be invalid due to its potestative nature. The DRC repeats again and again that if the extension option is unilateral to the benefit of the club only, i.e., the stronger party in the employment relationship, then there is no apparent gain for the player and as a result thereof the unilateral extension option cannot be valid.

However, the DRC is of the opinion that under very special circumstances, a unilateral extension option in favour of the club can be valid. Over the years, the DRC seems to have reconsidered its position slightly with respect to the validity of the unilateral extension option. Under special circumstances, the Chamber may agree with the option, if the player explicitly accepted the unilateral extension option.

In a decision of 17 January 2007, the DRC gives us an important answer in relation to the validity of the unilateral extension option in favour of the club. Although the DRC had

[309] CAS 2005/A/973, *Panathinaikos FC* v. *Sotirios Kyrgiakos*. According to the DRC, this decision of the CAS was not applicable in this matter.

already stated the circumstances under which this clause could be valid in its earlier mentioned decisions with respect to the unilateral extension option in favour of the club, it now finally enumerates the criteria which are decisive in relation to the validity of the unilateral extension option in favour of the club. In this DRC decision, the Chamber refers to leading decisions of the CAS in respect to this issue.

In the first place, the potential maximal duration of the employment contract may not be excessive. With respect to the maximum duration, the duration of the original contract and the so-called renewal years must be enumerated. According to Article 18 Paragraph 2 of the RSTP, edition 2005, and as we have seen earlier, the maximum length of an employment contract will be five years. This is the decisive element in order to determine whether the maximum duration is excessive. Bearing this in mind, it is also important that the relation between the duration of the original contract is in balance and correctly proportionate with the duration of the contract in the so-called option year(s). For example, the duration of the employment contract is three years and the duration of the invoked option is one year. In that case there will be a justified proportion with respect to the unilateral extension option. On 9 March 2005, the Claimant and the Respondent signed an employment contract valid from 9 March 2005 until 9 June 2005 with an extension option to be exercised in accordance with Article 9 of the same contract. The DRC explicitly emphasised that two years was a significant portion of a footballer's active career.

The second criterion is the fact that the option is exercised within an acceptable deadline before the expiry of the current contract. In the earlier mentioned decision of the DRC 22 July 2004, five days was (indeed) much too short. This is naturally very understandable. The employee cannot be held into a position with too much uncertainty. The option must therefore be exercised early enough to give the player the opportunity to continue his career without interruption at another club should the present club not wish to extend the contract. Some collective bargaining agreements, for example in the Netherlands, state that in the case of an extension of the employment contract, the club must inform the player by registered mail before a certain date of the year in which the contract will end.[310]

Thirdly, the salary reward deriving from the option right must be defined in the original contract. Sometimes the club omits to mention the amount of the salary, simply because it wants to wait and see if the player develops according to their expectations. This must be averted at all times, according to the DRC. The player must be given certainty with respect to his new salary.

In the fourth place, one party will not be at the mercy of the other party with regard to the contents of the employment contract. In this respect, the salary increase after the exercise of the option is the most important indication for establishing whether the party is at the mercy of the other party with regard to the contractual contents. In my opinion, the salary should increase substantially. An increase of 25% in the first option year, i.e., from EUR 58,695 to EUR 73,168, and 100% in the second option year, could be called substantial. In this DRC decision, there was a 9% increase in the first option year and an 8.33% increase in the second option year, which cannot be considered a substantial increase. The DRC is clear in this respect; there must be an apparent financial gain for the player from the unilateral extension. Thus new financial conditions must be accepted through negotiation by both parties.

[310] In the Netherlands before 1 April of the last contracting year. See Art. 6 Para. 4 jo. 7 of the Dutch Collective Bargaining Agreement for professional football players.

The last criterion is that the option will be clearly established and emphasised in the original contract so that the player is aware of it at the moment of signing the contract. The club should explicitly emphasise that a unilateral extension option is stipulated in the contract. In the before-mentioned DRC decision, the clause was mentioned in the middle of the contract. The DRC underlines the fact that the clause must be mentioned at the end and it must be emphasised. This will ensure that the player is fully aware of the unilateral extension option. In turn, in my opinion, the player must explicitly agree with the unilateral extension option. Therefore, if the player is against the extension of the employment contract, he should let the club explicitly know that he does not agree with the prolongation of his employment contract. If the player later agrees with the extension, the DRC may decide that the extension option of the employment contract is valid.

Finally, it must be noted that according to many national employment laws, a unilateral extension option is valid and binding. This was also one of the defences of a club in one of the before-mentioned decisions of the DRC, stating that the option right was permitted in the national law. At this point, therefore, the decisions of the DRC can be characterised as *Lex Sportiva*. In the case of a unilateral extension option which is solely in the favour of the club, there is a lack of parity between the employer and the employee. It can also be stated that the legal power of the club according to the unilateral option may not go so far as to bring about an excessive commitment of the player. This may be considered a breach of public policy.[311]

This inward conflict also emerged with the decision of the Dutch KNVB arbitration court. Apart from the fact, as stated above, that in my opinion the Dutch arbitration court should have ruled according to the many DRC decisions which clearly stated that the unilateral extension option is not valid and legally binding between the parties if it solely benefits the club, it also creates an imbalance between the FIFA line and the opinion of some national arbitrational courts. In their quest for further uniformity, equality and certainty, FIFA could be hindered because some decisions of national arbitrational courts are currently not in line with decisions of the DRC.

8. Termination of the contract

8.1 Introduction

Pursuant to Article 13 of the RSTP rules, edition 2005, the contract between a professional and a club can only be terminated on expiry of the term of the contract or by mutual agreement. The main purpose of this Article is that parties which enter into an agreement should in principle respect and honour the contractual obligations during the term of the contract, also known as the principle of *pacta sunt servanda*. Therefore, FIFA introduced the so-called "protected period", which was meant to safeguard the maintenance of contractual stability. The protected period was, as mentioned before, the period of three entire seasons or three years, whichever comes first, following the entry into force, if such contract was concluded before the 28th birthday of the professional, or to a period of two

[311] Wolfgang Portmann, 'Unilateral Option Clauses in Footballers' Contracts of Employment: an Assessment from the Perspective of International Sports Arbitration', 7 *Sweet & Maxwell International Sports Law Review* (2007) no. 1, pp. 6-16.

entire seasons or two years, whichever comes first, following the entry into force of a contract, if such contract was concluded after the 28th birthday of the professional. FIFA was of the opinion that unilateral termination of a contract without a justified reason, especially during this so-called protected period, had to be vehemently discouraged.[312] In other words, during the protected period it had to be made much more difficult for one of the parties to terminate the contract.

Notwithstanding the above and according to Article 14 of the RSTP rules, the principle of respect of contract is not an absolute one. The situation could occur that it was too much of a strain on the patience of one of the parties to respect the employment contract. FIFA therefore came up with the possibility that in the case of a valid reason for one of the parties, the so-called "just cause", the employment contract may be unilaterally terminated by either party with no consequences of any kind. In other words, there are no consequences in the case of a just cause, which means that the party which terminates the contract for just cause is not obliged to pay any compensation to the other party, nor can sporting sanctions be imposed on him. In that event, the DRC can then take provisional measures in the case of the existence of this just cause for one of the parties, including the most useful provisional measure of allowing the player to register for a new club.[313]

In line with the above, in the case of a just cause for the player, he is free to leave the club. In the case of a just cause for the club, the latter is released from its obligations as laid down in the contract towards its player with immediate effect. This rule is a so-called *lex specialis* of the general rule, which is stated in Article 16 of the RSTP, edition 2005, that a contract cannot be unilaterally terminated during the course of a season.

The obligation to pay compensation and the related sporting sanctions of FIFA will be discussed in the following chapters. It now is interesting to know what can be considered a just cause for the player and the club according to the DRC. As we will see, the definition of the just cause and whether the just cause exists will be established in accordance with the merits of each particular case.[314]

8.2 Mutual agreement

As already mentioned, according to Article 13 of the RSTP, edition 2005, parties may terminate their agreement by mutual consent. This is laid down in an agreement of termination in order to prove such an agreement of termination.

In a decision of 10 June 2004, the DRC was of the opinion that the FIFA RSTP depart from the principle that the parties to an employment contract have entered a contractual obligation for a fixed period of time.[315] This engagement can only be rescinded under the circumstances that justify a unilateral rupture of the contract by one of the parties for just cause or if the parties mutually agree on an early termination of their contractual relationship. A mutual agreement on the early termination of an employment contract is considered admissible since it requires both parties to negotiate the terms on which they are willing to accept a rescission of an otherwise valid contract. Such an agreement must therefore be found when the parties are faced with the circumstances that motivate an

[312] FIFA Commentary, explanation Art. 13, p. 38.
[313] Id., explanation Art. 6, p. 24.
[314] Id., explanation Art. 14, p. 39.
[315] DRC 10 June 2004, no. 64132.

early termination of their engagement. Under particular circumstances, the DRC can admit arrangements whereby the parties have established and agreed on the terms of an early termination of a contract in the employment contract itself. In order to accept such an arrangement, the Chamber must feel that the parties have been able to negotiate these terms in a manner that is not the result of a unilateral command by only one of the parties. Essentially, the rescission clause contained in the employment contract must provide for terms that can be considered acceptable to both the employer as well as the employee. As stated above, in the case at hand, the rescission clause must be considered unilateral and to the benefit of the club only.

In another case for the DRC of 21 November 2006, the parties drew up a termination letter of contract, which was decided to be valid and binding between the parties.[316] One of the parties claimed that the termination agreement was not valid because it was forced upon him. The DRC started by acknowledging that both parties had signed an employment contract on 2 September 2002 expiring on 31 August 2003. Moreover, the DRC noted that on 26 May 2003 both parties concluded a document called "termination letter of contract", with which the relevant parties ended their contractual relationship. The DRC deemed it appropriate to focus on the player's allegation stating that he had signed the termination agreement under pressure from the club. The Chamber pointed out that a document signed by the relevant parties is in principle a written proof of a valid contract and cannot be declared invalid by a simple allegation. The DRC remarked that the party that makes an allegation has the burden of proof to sustain in order to preserve the legal principle of legal security. Finally, the DRC decided that the player's position that the termination agreement was invalid could not be upheld by the DRC. In view of all the above, the DRC concluded that the termination agreement dated 26 May 2003 was legally valid and binding between the relevant parties. Therefore and based on the terms agreed by the player and the club in the referred termination agreement, the player was entitled to receive a certain amount as compensation.

8.3 **Just cause**

8.3.1 *For the club*

If the club wants to unilaterally terminate the contract with the player without any consequences, then a just cause must exist. If the club rescinds the contract because the player does not perform well enough, the DRC will usually decide that such a clause is not valid. Various situations will be discussed below and submitted to the criterion of the just cause.

As mentioned above, it is interesting to know whether a certain rule can be derived from these decisions of the DRC with respect to the just cause for the club. Different situations will be assessed, such as the poor performance of the player, the number of matches played, the number of goals scored, injuries received, absence during training and the drugs abuse of the player.

In the following paragraph, cases of the DRC will be discussed in which a just cause is present. However, decisions will also be discussed where a just cause does not exist in order to try to find a definition for the just cause for the club.

---

[316] DRC 21 November 2006, no. 116338.

8.3.1.1 Performance

In a case which came before the DRC on 26 November 2004, the DRC decided that the clause in an employment contract which stated that the club may terminate the employment contract when the player's performance no longer met the club's requirement cannot be defined as a just cause and is therefore not valid.[317] On 1 November 2003, the parties signed an employment contract valid from 1 November 2003 until 31 October 2005. In line with Article 2.8, the club was entitled to unilaterally terminate the contract after 15 days of notification of the contract termination in writing, for reasons of disciplinary nature or linked to a decline in the player's performance which thus failed to meet the club's requirements. On 1 April 2004, the player was notified in writing of the early termination by the club of his employment contract. According to the relevant document, the player's contract was terminated due to a decline in the player's performance and his inability to meet the club's performance requirements. The DRC finally decided in this case that there was no just cause.

In a decision of the DRC of 1 June 2005, the DRC also decided that a player's lack of performance is not a just cause for a club to unilaterally terminate an employment contract.[318] On 15 February 2004 the player and the club signed an employment contract valid for a period of 4½ months. In this case, the employment contract contained the provision that the club could unilaterally terminate its employment relationship with the player due to his alleged lack of performance. The relevant clause stipulated that the player must follow the training instructions and maintain the performance for which the club had signed him, otherwise this would be considered as a termination of the contract. Subsequently, on 27 February 2004 and based on this Article of the employment contract, the club unilaterally terminated the contract. In his claim, the player denied the alleged lack of performance, but above all underlined that such a reason could not be considered as a just cause for unilaterally terminating an employment contract. The DRC emphasised that, despite the content of the before-mentioned contractual clause, a player's lack of performance cannot and does not constitute just cause for a club to unilaterally terminate an employment contract, as happened in the case at hand. The Chamber deemed that in view of its potestative nature, the before-mentioned contractual clause could not have any effect. After having vehemently rejected the validity of the contractual clause, the Chamber concluded that the club had terminated its employment contract with the player without just cause.

In a case which came before the DRC on 23 June 2005 regarding a contractual dispute between the parties, the DRC decided that a player's lack of performance, lack of commitment and lack of productivity could not be considered a just cause for terminating an employment contract.[319] On 1 March 2003, the player and the club signed an employment contract valid until 1 March 2004. The contract was provided with the clause that the contract could be broken on the initiative of the football club if it deemed that the professional and sports skills of the footballer were inadequate, or in the case of the footballer's non-fulfilment or inappropriate fulfilment of his obligations pursuant to this contract. The club asserted that an amicable settlement had been reached between the parties on 1 June

[317] DRC 26 November 2004, no. 114534.
[318] DRC 28 July 2005, no. 75975.
[319] DRC 23 June 2005, no. 65657.

2003 regarding the termination of the employment contract. However, according to the club, the player refused to sign it at the last minute. As a result, the club decided to unilaterally terminate the employment contract based on the player's alleged lack of commitment and productivity. The club stated that the player's performance was extremely poor and that he made no effort to improve it during training. The DRC finally underlined that a player's lack of performance cannot be considered as just cause for terminating the employment contract.

In a case which came before the DRC on 28 July 2005 regarding a contractual dispute between a player and a club, the DRC decided that a player's lack of performance was not a just cause for a club to unilaterally terminate an employment contract.[320] A contractual clause with a potestative nature is not valid. After having vehemently rejected the validity of the before-mentioned contractual clause, the DRC concluded that the club had terminated its employment contract with the player without just cause.

In a case which came before the DRC on 17 August 2006, the Chamber decided that the clause in the contract relating to the player's inability to fit into the team's playing system could not be considered a valid reason to terminate the employment contract.[321] On 9 March 2005, the player and the club signed an employment contract valid from 9 March 2005 until 9 June 2005. With regard to the player's performance, Article 4 of the contract indicated that the player would be given a performance report according to the guidelines issued by the football association concerned after every game played by him. If his performance was rated poor, he would be given a written warning in the first instance and a final warning in the second instance, after which he would be subject to disciplinary action. On 20 June 2005, the player turned to FIFA maintaining that the club had wrongly terminated his contract after having only played one match. According to the notice of termination of the employment contract, the reason for terminating the contract was that the player did not fit in well to the team's playing system. The DRC concluded that this clause could not be considered a valid reason to terminate an employment contract. The DRC was of the opinion that the club had no just cause to terminate the employment contract.

According to the above decisions and following numerous other decisions of the DRC, one can see that the DRC is of the opinion that a clause in an employment contract which states that the club may terminate the employment contract when the player's performance no longer meets the club's requirement cannot be defined as a just cause and is therefore not valid.[322] The DRC deems that in view of its potestative nature, such contractual clauses could not have any effect.

8.3.1.2 Played matches

In a decision of 4 February 2005, a player from Serbia & Montenegro and a Chinese club signed an employment contract valid from 8 March 2003 until 28 February 2006.[323] On 1 March 2004 the club unilaterally terminated the contract based on Article 8.1 which stated that:

---

[320] DRC 28 July 2005, no. 75975.
[321] DRC 17 August 2006, no. 86833.
[322] DRC 22 July 2004, no. 74653, DRC 12 January 2006, no. 16695, DRC 27 April 2006, no. 46290.
[323] DRC 4 February 2005, no. 25247.

> "If the starting appearance is less than 70% out of the whole CFA League A games (only starting appearance or total appearance time per game no less than 45 minutes can be counted) by his own will, Party A has the right to terminate this agreement and transfer Party B to other football club, except for injuries which should be confirmed by the doctors or hospital appointed by Party A."

According to the club, the statistics of CFA League A games in 2003 showed that B, the player concerned, had a 64% starting appearance rate and that he had only played in 18 of the 23 games of the 2003 season. Consequently, now that the player's starting appearance was less than 70% out of the whole CFA League A games in 2003, the club could rescind the player's contract. The player claimed that he had made appearances in more than 70% of the games because Article 8.1 of the contract clearly mentions "if starting appearance is less than 70% ... *by his own will*". According to the player, this meant that any lack of appearance due to a decision made outside of the player's control, such as a coach's decision to keep him on the bench, should not be considered a non-appearance in the terms of Article 8.1. The DRC concluded that the clause in question was not drafted clearly and therefore left room for interpretation. It was thus necessary, according to the Chamber, to understand what concrete meaning the parties intended this provision to have when the contract was drafted. The members of the DRC unanimously decided that this clause should be found logical and thus acceptable. It was acknowledged that if Article 8.1 could not be invoked by the club at the end of every playing season, the incorporation of this clause in the contract would be pointless. The Chamber could not agree with the player's reasoning regarding the phrase "by his own will", which he used to mean that any non-appearances that may have occurred outside of his scope of influence, such as a decision by the coach not to field him, should not be taken into consideration when calculating his appearance percentage. On the one hand, the DRC was of the opinion that what was particularly objectionable was that the clause offered ample opportunity for the club to misuse its position and unilaterally cancel the contract, simply by preventing the player from participating in over 70% of the season's matches. Its questionability is increased by the fact that this clause did not offer reciprocal opportunities for an early termination of the contract by the player. On the other hand, the DRC was of the opinion that it was also important to consider that Article 8.1 could not be invoked by the club at any arbitrary moment during the season, but is restricted to one point in time after completion of each full playing season. This provided the player with some legal certainty and stability. The DRC emphasised that the contents of Article 8.1 were explicitly accepted by both parties when they signed the contract. Finally, the DRC concluded that the clause was acceptable, despite its beforementioned questionable aspects. The DRC decided that in the case at hand, the club's application of Article 8.1 for the early termination of the employment contract did not amount to an unjust unilateral cancellation of the contract.

Following the decision of the DRC on 4 February 2005, the Chamber was of the opinion that a just cause existed for the club as a result of the fact that the player did not play enough. In my opinion, this decision is rather remarkable because the clause is undisputedly potestative since it is the coach, as an extension of the club, who is entitled to put the player on the bench. The circumstance that the clause could not be invoked during the season is not of such importance to determine that this clause had to be considered as valid. The fact that this was restricted to one point in time after completion of each full season was crucial for the DRC in order to determine that the player was provided with some legal certainty and stability. Furthermore, the DRC emphasised that the contents of the relevant cause were explicitly accepted by both parties when they signed the contract. In my opinion, this could not overrule the fact that this clause is undisputedly invalid. Moreover, on the one hand the DRC is of the opinion that a clause which states that the club is entitled to unilaterally terminate the contract because the player did not play enough matches is valid, while on the other hand, the Chamber is of the opinion that a similar clause is invalid if it is related to the salary, as was outlined in its decision of 27 April 2006. In this decision, the DRC was quite clear and stated that, in principle, poor performance cannot be considered a reason for the club to reduce payments to him, because it is unilaterally determined by the club and based on pure subjective criteria.

In a decision of 28 September 2006, the Chamber decided that a termination clause referring to a number of played matches was not valid.[324] In this case, the DRC unanimously concluded that the application of the provision contained in Article 8 Paragraph 2 of the employment contract concerning the number of matches the player had to play was arbitrary since it was up to the club to decide how many matches the player would have played. Moreover, in this respect the DRC deemed it appropriate to underline that football is played in a team whereby success can only be achieved when the members of a team work together. The obligation imposed on a player in an employment contract that he has to obtain a certain number of goals within one season otherwise his employer may terminate the contract, clearly goes against the spirit of the game and contradicts the fundamental aim of team play. Taking into account the above, the DRC concluded that the above clauses in the employment contract, i.e., Article 8 Paragraph 2 and Article 5 Paragraph 7, are unacceptable and certainly cannot be considered valid reasons to terminate the employment contract.

8.3.1.3 Injury

In a decision of 13 May 2005, the DRC concluded that the club had terminated the employment contract, on account of the fact that the player was injured, without just cause.[325] On 9 January 2003, the player and the club signed an employment contract valid for the 2003 sporting season. The player claimed that he suffered a serious knee injury during a match at the club's service on 5 April 2003 and that, as a result of this injury, the club informed him in front of his team colleagues that it did not count on him any longer. The player subsequently left the club and returned to his country. In order to recover from his injury, the player underwent surgery to his knee on 5 May 2003. The player was now claiming the payment of his salaries for the entire contractual period. The club unilaterally terminated its relevant employment contract with the player based on Article 12 b of the player's contract, according to which a club could release a player at any time prior to the expiry of the contract, without being responsible for any further payments. The DRC emphasised that this cannot and does not constitute just cause for a club to unilaterally terminate its employment contract with a player. The DRC concluded that the player's knee injury was in fact suffered at the club's service and therefore the club was responsible for covering its costs, as well as the costs incurred during the rehabilitation process. As a result, the DRC decided that the club had terminated the contract without just cause.

---

[324] DRC 28 September 2006, no. 96391.
[325] DRC 13 May 2005, no. 55230.

In a decision of 28 July 2005, a player and a club signed an employment contract valid from 1 October 2003 until 31 May 2004.[326] In clause 12 of the contract it was stipulated that the player "will receive free medical treatment according to the system applied in the country of the club Y". On 30 October 2003, the player suffered a knee injury during training with his club's team. Three days later, he travelled to his home country for surgery and medical treatment with the authorisation of the club. The player wrote to the club asking whether he was required to return for the recovery period or whether he could remain in his home country, but received no answer. The knee surgery cost USD 6,620. The club informed the player that pursuant to clause 12 of the employment contract, it was only required to pay to him USD 4,000, as this would be the cost of the same surgery in the country of the club. The DRC decided that as a basic principle in labour law, if an employee gets injured, this does generally constitute a just cause for the employer to terminate the employment contract prematurely and unilaterally and therefore to cancel payment of the player's salaries. Finally, the DRC concluded that the premature and unilateral termination of the employment contract by the club was not justified.

In a decision of the DRC of 12 January 2006, the club indicated that the reason for the early termination of the employment contract was an injury of the player.[327] The DRC stated that according to its constant and persistent jurisprudence, the premature and unilateral termination of an employment contract by a club because of a player's injury was always considered termination of the contract without just cause. The DRC stated that if such a termination was accepted as a termination with just cause, this would create a disproportionate repartition of the rights of the parties to an employment contract, to the detriment of the player. The DRC stated that the fact that a player was injured during the course of an employment contract was clearly not a just cause for the club to prematurely and unilaterally terminate the employment contract. The DRC concluded that the employment contract between the player and the club was terminated by the club in question without just cause.

One can say that following the above decisions, it is usual that according to the constant jurisprudence of the DRC, the premature and unilateral termination of an employment contract by a club because of an injury must be considered as a termination of the contract without just cause. The DRC decides that as a basic principle in labour law, if an employee is injured, in principle this does not constitute a just cause for terminating the employment contract prematurely and unilaterally and therefore to cancel payment of the player's salaries.

8.3.1.4 Absence

In its decision of 22 November 2002, the DRC concluded that the club had terminated the employment contract with the player without just cause. The club and the player concerned signed an employment contract valid from 1 March until 30 November 2002.[328] When the player arrived in the country of his new club, he was immediately given the impression that his new club was no longer interested in his services. Instead of finding an

---

[326] DRC 28 July 2005, no. 75570.

[327] DRC 12 January 2006, no. 16828.

[328] DRC 22 November 2002, no. 300702. This is the only decision which is published during the year 2002 on the official website of the FIFA.

apartment with satellite television, telephone and heating at his disposal, the player had to wait five weeks before being provided with accommodation. The apartment he was eventually given had no heating, causing his wife to become ill. When he returned to his home country for a holiday, he noticed that the club had only provided him with a visa for a duration of two weeks. The player then explained that he had not been paid for the month of June and that he had not received reimbursement for his plane ticket. The player admitted having left his club without the appropriate authorisation to meet up with his wife. The club was of the opinion that it was entitled to impose a disciplinary sanction, which corresponded to a fine of an entire month's salary. Although the Chamber decided that the disciplinary sanction could be accepted, the termination of the contract, on the other hand, was unquestionably disproportionate and could therefore not be accepted. The Chamber was of the unanimous opinion that the club had terminated the employment contract with the player without just cause.

In a decision of 10 June 2004, the DRC came to the conclusion that the restriction imposed on the player concerned to participate in any official football matches for four months was not an appropriate sanction.[329] After the expiry of a loan agreement, the player did not return to his employer club for the last month of his employment contract. The club initiated legal proceedings at its football federation against the player, accusing him of breach of the employment contract. Two days after the expiry of his employment contract, the player signed a new employment contract with a club in another country. Initially, the Disciplinary Committee decided that the player concerned had breached his contract with former club, as he had not returned to it for the remainder of the employment contract. The Committee banned him from playing in official football matches for four months. The player appealed against this decision at the Arbitration Body of the same football federation, but the appeal was rejected and the sanction was upheld. The player lodged a claim before the DRC. The Chamber questioned the proportionality of the restriction imposed. The DRC decided that the condition of proportionality requires that the gravity of a sanction must correspond to the gravity of the conduct leading to the sanction. The DRC emphasised that during the month when the player stayed away from his employer club, no official matches were scheduled in the national league of the federation. Therefore, the absence of the player concerned did not pose a serious problem to the club. Finally, the DRC came to the conclusion that the restriction imposed on the player concerned to participate in any official football matches for four months was not an appropriate sanction. The DRC outlined that it would have been more appropriate in this case if the player had been fined.

In a decision of the DRC of 28 July 2005, the DRC decided that the two day absence of the player from training with the club clearly did not constitute a just cause for the club to terminate the employment contract in question prematurely and unilaterally.[330] On 14 October 2003, a player informed FIFA that his club had terminated his employment contract unilaterally on 26 March 2003 due to an injury, without proving that an injury was the reason of the contract termination. The player informed FIFA that the club had not paid his salaries as from January 2003. The club stated that the employment contract was terminated on 27 March 2003 due to the player's absence without permission from the club's

---

[329] DRC 10 June 2004, no. 6400276.

[330] DRC 28 July 2005, no. 75368.

training on 25 and 26 March 2003. The DRC concluded that if employee is absent for a short period of time from work, the employer should first contact him to remind him of his labour obligations. In general, an absence lasting a few days does not constitute a just cause for the employer to immediately terminate the employment contract, prematurely and unilaterally. The DRC stated that the two day absence of the player from the training with the club clearly did not constitute a just cause for the club to terminate the employment contract in question prematurely and unilaterally. In this respect, the DRC outlined that the club would have been entitled to take sanctions against the player, such as a fine, for not appearing to the training.

In a case of 12 January 2006, the DRC decided in relation to the absence of the player from training. The DRC had to decide whether the player's absence of a week concerned may be a just cause for the club to terminate the employment contract unilaterally.[331] The DRC considered that absence from the team's training can generally constitute just cause for a club to unilaterally terminate the employment contract. The DRC underlined that a player's absence from the team's training sessions for such a short period as one week cannot and does not constitute just cause for a club to unilaterally terminate an employment contract, as happened in the present case. The DRC finally concluded that the club had terminated the employment contract without just cause.

The FIFA Commentary furthermore speaks of a just cause for the club if a player displays an uncooperative attitude ever since his arrival at the club. He does not follow the directives given by the coach; he regularly argues with his team-mates and often fights with them. The player leaves the club and does not appear for training on the following days. After two weeks of unjustified absence from training, the club decides to terminate the contract. The FIFA is of the opinion that this is a just cause for the club to terminate the contract with the player without any consequences.[332]

In a decision of the DRC of 23 March 2006, the Chamber was of the unanimous opinion that the absence of the player concerned was illegitimate for three out of four months of absence. Therefore, the DRC decided that this should be considered a lengthy absence in the sense of the above outlined principle.[333]

The DRC underlined in a decision of 28 September 2006, that as a general rule, lengthy absence of a player from his club without authorisation and without other just cause should be considered an unjustified breach of the employment contract by the player.[334] The club stated that all players in the team had gone on holiday at the end of October 2005 but this player had failed to return. This was the reason why it had wanted to terminate the employment contract with the player. The club informed him accordingly via fax without receiving any feedback from the player. According to the employment contract, all players must return on time after their holidays. Because the player had not returned after the holiday and had already trained on a trial basis with other clubs, the club was of the opinion that the player had breached the employment contract. Finally, the DRC decided that a lengthy absence of a player from his club without authorisation and without other just cause is an unjustified breach of the employment contract by the player.

---

[331] DRC 12 January 2006, no. 16828.

[332] FIFA Commentary, explanation Art. 14, p. 40.

[333] DRC 23 March 206, no. 36460.

[334] DRC 28 September 2006, no. 96391.

According to the above, the DRC is of the opinion that the absence of a player can generally constitute just cause for a club to unilaterally terminate the employment contract. For example, in a decision of 23 March the DRC decided that a three months' absence out of four months should be considered a lengthy absence. However, the DRC underlines that a player's absence from the team's training sessions for a short period, such as a few days or even a week, cannot and does not constitute just cause for a club to unilaterally terminate an employment contract.

8.3.1.5 Drug abuse

In a decision of 21 November 2003, the DRC decided that the positive result of the doping test could have constituted a just cause for the club to unilaterally terminate the employment contract.[335] On 13 January 2003, a player and a club signed an employment contract valid until 30 June 2006. During the 2003/04 season, the player was transferred on a loan basis to another club. On 27 March 2004, the player underwent a doping test and according to the report issued afterwards the player tested positive for banned substances. Towards the end of April 2004, the player and the club prematurely terminated their employment relation, which had nothing to do with the positive result of the test. On 18 June 2004, the relevant body of the football federation decided to suspend the player in question for a period of one year for doping. The FIFA Disciplinary Committee extended the before-mentioned suspension of the player in question on a worldwide basis. On 25 September 2004, the club informed the player in writing that it considered the cancellation agreement null and void, because they found out about the player's 12 months' suspension. The club was of the opinion that the player had obtained the agreement in a fraudulent manner. The club pointed out that if it had been informed of the players' suspension, it would never have concluded the cancellation agreement. In that case, it would rather have terminated the player's contract with just cause. The club informed the player of the termination of his contract as a consequence of his use of banned substances. Finally, the club reiterated that the termination agreement was null and void since it must be considered as an agreement based on a fraudulent action on the part of the player. The DRC finally agreed with the club that the positive result of the doping test could have constituted a just cause for the club to unilaterally terminate the employment contract. The DRC decided finally that the club could not be held liable for the execution of the cancellation agreement into which it had entered with the player.

During the years 2002–2006, the DRC has only decided in the before-mentioned decision with respect to the issue of the use of drugs of a player. As we have seen, the DRC decided that the positive result of the doping test could have constituted a just cause for the club to unilaterally terminate the employment contract. In line with the *Mutu* case described below, one can say that in the case of a player who uses drugs, just cause will be accepted and the club is permitted to unilaterally terminate the contract and to sue the player for compensation.

8.3.1.5.1 *Mutu* case

In 2003 the Romanian national and professional football player Adrian Mutu, born on 8 January 1979, entered into a five year contract with Chelsea Football Club which was to

[335] DRC 21 February 2006, no. 26439.

have run until 30 June 2008. For the release of the player, Chelsea paid EUR 22,500,000 to the player's previous club. Between May and September 2004, Mutu took cocaine on at least four or five occasions. In a letter dated 28 October 2004, Chelsea informed Mutu that the player's contract was terminated for gross misconduct. On 4 November 2004, the FA Disciplinary Commission confirmed the positive result of the player's drug test and suspended him until 18 May 2005. Furthermore, the FA Disciplinary Commission imposed a GBP 20,000 fine on the player. On 12 November 2004, FIFA confirmed the FA Disciplinary Commission's decision and adopted the player's suspension to apply worldwide. Mutu appealed to CAS against the before-mentioned decisions.

The CAS considered that the player had unilaterally breached the contract by taking cocaine and that Chelsea was therefore permitted to terminate the contract unilaterally on the basis of Article 21 of the RSTP, edition 2001.[336] The conclusion is that there is a serious misconduct by the player when using substances forbidden in sport and for that reason the club may terminate the employment contract unilaterally and the player is liable to pay damages and to be imposed with sporting sanctions. On the basis of the decision of the CAS amongst others, Chelsea addressed the DRC to claim compensation from Mutu.[337] The DRC however decided that it was not competent to hear the case as another deciding body, i.e., the Appeal Committee, had already decided about the triggering elements and that it could not therefore partially decide only about the compensation to be paid by Mutu. This dispute should also be decided by the Appeal Committee. The DRC decided that this matter should be considered as having been submitted to FIFA on 4 February 2005 and the DRC subsequently concluded that the previous Procedural Rules (edition 2001) on matters pending before the decision making bodies of FIFA applied to the matter at hand. Once the applicable regulations in respect of the proceedings were established, the DRC focussed on the contents of the club's submissions dated 4 February 2005 and referred to as "Application for an award of compensation". In any case, the DRC is by its own nature unable to consider any partial claim which is the result of an existing decision passed by a different deciding body, such as this claim. In other words, the DRC can call on an enduring jurisdictional tradition in international football-related disputes and cannot confine itself to granting the exequatur to a decision passed by a different (national) body. As a result it was emphasised that, according to a teleological rather than a semantic interpretation of the relevant provisions, in compliance with the general legal principle whereby *electa una via non datur recursus ad alteram,* once the parties have agreed to refer their dispute to a certain decision-making body, this authority will decide on the entire matter. In the current matter, the parties agreed in writing to refer the dispute to the Appeal Committee, which therefore appears to be the body competent to decide every aspect of the dispute. Consequently, the DRC is unable to consider the claim lodged by Chelsea and confirmed by CAS. In conclusion, the DRC decided that it did not have jurisdiction to pass a decision in the dispute between the club Chelsea and the player Adrian Mutu.

8.3.2 *For the player*

Also in the event that the player wants to unilaterally terminate the contract with the club without any consequences, there must be a just cause. For example, if the player has not

[336] CAS 2005/A/876, *Adrian Mutu* v. *Chelsea Football Club*, decision of 15 December 2005.
[337] DRC 26 October 2006, no. 106176.

received his salaries for three months, a just cause exists in the opinion of the DRC. In the following paragraph, this situation will be discussed and submitted to the criterion of the just cause for a player.

8.3.2.1 Outstanding salaries

The DRC is of the opinion that, as a general rule, the persistent failure of a club to pay the salaries of a player without just cause should be considered an unjustified breach of an employment contract by the club. In that case, there is the existence of a just cause for the player, as a result of which he may unilaterally terminate the contract without having to pay any compensation or risking sanctions being imposed on him by FIFA, as we will see in the following chapters.

In a decision of the DRC of 10 June 2004, the DRC noted that on the date of receipt of the player's claim on 16 February 2004, the club had not paid the player's monthly salary for over four months and two of the four instalments pertaining to the signing-on fee remained unpaid.[338] Therefore, the members of the Chamber concurred that the club had seriously neglected its financial obligations towards the player in question. In the light of the above, the club was found to have committed a unilateral breach of the employment contract without just cause.

In a decision of the DRC of 23 March 2006, the DRC decided that in general the persistent failure of a club to pay the salaries of a player without just cause should be considered an unjustified breach of an employment contract by the club. However, the non-payment of one monthly salary is not a just cause for a player to leave his club without permission.[339] On 1 February 2004, a player and a club concluded an employment contract, valid from 1 February 2004 to 1 February 2007, stipulating a monthly salary of USD 10,000. On 10 March 2005, the player notified the club in writing that he had unilaterally terminated the contract, due to the club's non-fulfilment of its financial obligations. On 13 April 2005, he signed a new employment contract with another club. The football association of his new club requested authorisation from FIFA to provisionally register the player in question. The Single Judge of the PSC authorised the football association of the new club to provisionally register the player in order not to hinder his career and thereby stated that any request for compensation and sports sanctions for breach of contract did not hinder the player's provisional registration for his new club. The DRC finally stated that, as a general rule, the persistent failure of a club to pay the salaries of a player without just cause should be considered an unjustified breach of an employment contract by the club. The DRC was of the unanimous opinion that the behaviour of the former club, i.e., the non-payment of the player's salaries as of October 2004, had to be considered as a persistent failure of a club to comply with its financial obligations towards a player. In this respect, the DRC referred to the fact that at the moment of the first unauthorised departure of the player, one month's salary was unpaid. The DRC deliberated whether the non-payment of one monthly salary is a just cause for a player to leave his club without permission and , but came to the conclusion that one outstanding monthly salary does not allow the player to leave his club without authorisation.

---

[338] DRC 10 June 2004, no. 64133.
[339] DRC 23 March 2006, no. 36460.

In a decision of the DRC of 26 October 2006, the Chamber underlined that the persistent failure of a club to pay the salaries of a player for one and a half months does not constitute a just cause for the player to unilaterally terminate his employment contract.[340] In July 2004, the player and the club concluded an employment contract. In addition to this contract, the parties concluded another agreement stipulating the financial conditions. On 10 October 2005, the player lodged a formal complaint with FIFA against the club, claiming that the latter had breached the employment contract. He asserted that salaries to the amount of USD 6,000 net were outstanding for the first season (2004/05) for the following months:

- USD 2,000 for October 2004 (he was paid only USD 2,000);
- USD 2,000 for November 2004 (he was paid only USD 2,000); and
- USD 2,000 for June 2005 (he was paid only USD 2,000).

The DRC added that the alleged outstanding amount of USD 6,000 which is equivalent to one and a half months of the player's salary could not be considered in the present case as substantial enough to justify a premature termination of an employment contract. The DRC concluded that the relevant alleged outstanding salaries did not constitute a just cause for the unilateral termination of the employment contract.

In general, one can say that when the club has omitted to pay the salary to the player in time, in the opinion of the DRC the player is entitled to terminate the employment contract and will consequently be free to leave the club. However, under certain circumstances, only a few weeks' delay in paying the salary of the player by the club would not justify the termination of an employment contract.[341] In that respect, the DRC decided in another case that also a delay of one month or 1½ months does not justify the termination of the employment contract. As we have seen, the DRC is of the explicit opinion that the persistent failure of a club to pay the salaries of a player without just cause for three or four months can be considered a just cause for the player to unilaterally terminate his employment contract.

8.4 Sporting just cause

The contract may also be terminated in the case of a sporting just cause. In Article 15 of the RSTP, edition 2005, we are provided with a definition of the sporting just cause:

> "An established Professional who has, in the course of the season, appeared in less than 10% of the official matches in which his club has been involved may terminate his contract prematurely on the grounds of sporting just cause."

Following the definition of sporting just cause, we immediately see some fundamental differences with the before-mentioned just cause.

In the first place, the sporting just cause is exclusively a possibility for the *player* (not the club) to terminate the contract. Secondly, no sporting sanctions will be imposed on the player as with the just cause, but, contrary to the consequences of a just cause, compensa-

340 DRC 26 October 2006, no. 1061207.

341 FIFA Commentary, explanation under Art. 14, footnote 62, p. 39.

tion may be payable in case of a sporting just cause. As mentioned, compensation *may* be payable but this is in no way definitive. It depends on the merits of the case. The club may lose its entitlement to compensation if the player can prove that the club has completely neglected the player from a sporting point of view, as it was not interested in his services.[342]

8.4.1 *Requirements*

There are three mandatory conditions for a player to be entitled to claim sporting just cause. First of all, the player is recognised as an established player (8.4.1.1) and secondly, he has not played in 10% of the official matches of his club. In this respect, it must be noticed that being entitled to claim sporting just cause in accordance with the above conditions does not automatically mean that sporting just cause has been established (8.4.1.2). This must be done and established by the DRC.[343] Thirdly, it is a strict requirement that the termination on grounds of sporting just cause is only valid if the player terminates his contract in the 15 days following the last official match of the season of the club for which he is registered (8.4.1.3).

8.4.1.1 Established player

In the opinion of FIFA, an established player is a player who has terminated and completed his training period. This established player may have valid sporting reasons, also known as the before-mentioned sporting just cause, for unilaterally terminating his employment contract. In this respect it must be determined whether the player is an established player. The RSTP, edition 2005, do not provide us with a definition of the established player. As a key element, however, the FIFA Commentary mentions that the established player is:

> "a player with a certain level of footballing skill who does not have sufficient opportunities in a club and therefore wishes to leave in order to join a club where he has the opportunity to play on a regular basis".

As mentioned, the player must have terminated and completed his training period. Furthermore the FIFA Commentary emphasises that

> "his level of footballing skill is at least equal to or even superior to those of his team mates who appear regularly. One possible reason for the player in question not playing (regularly) is because his position has already been taken by another player with similar characteristics."

Consequently, this means that the established player cannot be a very young player because of his lack of football experience. Furthermore, it is quite remarkable that the established player should be at least equal, according to the FIFA Commentary, or even superior to those of his team mates. It is difficult to understand why a player who is even superior to his team mates would be held on the bench.

---

342 FIFA Commentary, explanation Art. 15, p. 43.

343 Id., explanation Art. 15 under 2, p. 41

8.4.1.2 Appearance of the professional

The second requirement is that the established professional, as defined in the last paragraph, who has appeared in less than 10% of the official matches in which his club has been involved in the course of the season may terminate his contract prematurely on the grounds of sporting just cause. According to the FIFA Commentary, "appearance" should be understood as being fielded and thus actively taking part in a game. The championship as well as national and international cup matches should be taken into account in order to establish the percentage of games played.[344]

8.4.1.3 15 days term

The third and last requirement is that the termination by the player on the grounds of sporting just cause will only be valid if the player terminates his contract in the 15 days following the last official match of the season of the club for which he is registered. If the player fails to respect this requirement, this will automatically lead to disciplinary sanctions. According to the FIFA Commentary, the closer the termination is to the end of the main registration period, the harder the sanction may be, as the club suffers more in view of the difficulty of finding a replacement for the player who is leaving.[345]

Although the FIFA Commentary states that there have not yet been any DRC decisions with respect to the sporting just cause, which is quite remarkable, there are two decisions in which the sporting just cause has been partially discussed by the Chamber.[346] In a decision of 1 June 2005, a player and a club signed a labour contract on 2 February 2004 valid from 2 February 2004 until 30 June 2005.[347] At the same time, the parties concluded a special agreement which granted the player the right to terminate the employment contract after the last match of the 2003/04 season until 31 May 2004. According to this agreement, the player had the right to terminate the contract and the before-mentioned employment contract would end on 30 June 2004. The DRC decided in general that the fact that a player signs an employment contract with a club does not automatically entitle the player to play. In other words, the DRC was of the opinion that as long as the player is regularly paid his salaries and the club respects all other contractual obligations, a player must accept that he might not be lined up. In this case, the club complied with its financial obligations towards the player. Therefore, the DRC decided that by not fielding the player, the club did not breach the relevant employment contract. Finally, the DRC had to decide and emphasised that according to the signed agreement, the player had chosen to terminate the contractual relationship with the club according to the special agreement dated 2 February 2004. As a result thereof, the DRC was of the opinion that it did not have to consider a contractual termination for sporting just cause by the player in line with Article 24 of the RSTP, edition 2001.

In a decision 23 March 2006, a player did not fulfil amongst others the before-mentioned requirement of the "15 days term". In this decision the player stressed that he had the right to breach the employment contract with his club for sporting just cause according

[344] FIFA Commentary, explanation Art. 15, p. 42.
[345] Id., explanation Art. 15, p. 44.
[346] Id., explanation Art. 15 under footnote 68, p. 43.
[347] DRC 1 June 2005, no. 65850.

to Article 15 of the RSTP, edition 2005, without him being required to pay compensation or to have sporting sanctions applied on him.[348] In response to the player's claim, the club was of the opinion that the player had no basis to invoke the application of sporting just cause in order to terminate the employment contract. The club maintained that in the relevant league, a total of 34 competition matches are played each season and that the player participated in 15 official matches. Finally, the DRC recalled that an established professional may only terminate an employment contract for sporting just cause at the end of the season, more precisely, within 15 days following the last official match of the season of the club for which he is registered. The DRC stressed that the before-mentioned conditions were obviously not fulfilled in this matter and therefore the player could not invoke this reason for terminating his employment contract.

8.5 Conclusion

In the daily practice of the international professional football world, there are clauses in the employment contract which state that the club may terminate the contract when the player does not perform well. The DRC is very clear about these clauses. Most clauses are not valid, because they simply create an imbalance between the rights and obligations of the player and the club. These clauses can be seen as disputable clauses with a potestative nature, according to the DRC. Therefore, a contract which states that the player's performance no longer complies with the club's requirements cannot be defined as a just cause and is therefore not valid.

In line with the above, it can be presumed that clauses with regard to a minimum number of matches to be played by the player can also not be defined as a just cause and can therefore not be considered as a valid reason to terminate the contract. However, in a decision of 4 February 2005 the DRC decided that a provision which stated that the club was entitled to unilaterally terminate the contract if the player played fewer matches could be valid. On the other hand, in a more recent decision of the DRC of 28 September 2006, the Chamber was of the opinion that a termination clause referring to a number of played matches is not valid because it is arbitrary and at the club's sole discretion to decide how many matches the player would have played. Therefore, as a general rule, it can be concluded that the DRC is of the opinion that a provision which states that the club is not entitled to unilaterally terminate the contract if the player did not play enough matches can – although in very special circumstances if there is a provision related to a minimum number of matches to be played – be defined as just cause for the club to terminate the contract.

If a player is injured, there is no discussion. The DRC explicitly underlines that the club does not have the right to unilaterally terminate the contract if the player gets injured, even if such is laid down in the contract. The DRC repeatedly states and explicitly emphasises that the fact that a player is injured or became injured during the course of an employment contract is not a just cause for the club to prematurely and unilaterally terminate the employment contract.

With regard to the absence of a player, the DRC is of the opinion that, as a general rule, a lengthy absence of a player from his club without authorisation and without other just

[348] DRC 23 March 2006, no. 631290.

cause should be considered as an unjustified breach of the employment contract by the player and can be seen as a just cause for the club. However, the DRC also points out that the absence of player from the team's training sessions for a shorter period, such as one week, cannot and does not constitute just cause for a club to unilaterally terminate an employment contract.

Finally, in relation to the use of drugs by a player, the conclusion can be drawn that using banned substances constitutes serious misconduct by the player. For that reason, the DRC concludes that the club may terminate the employment contract unilaterally and that the player is liable to pay damages and may be subjected to sporting sanctions, as will be discussed in the following chapter.

Following the above, in general one can say that if the club has omitted to pay the player's salaries in due time, the DRC is of the opinion that the player is entitled to terminate the employment contract for just cause and will consequently be free to leave the club. However, under certain circumstances, a few weeks' delay in paying or even a delay of 1½ months does not justify the termination of the employment contract.[349] The DRC repeatedly states that as a general rule, the persistent failure of a club to pay a player's salaries without just cause should be considered as an unjustified breach of an employment contract by the club. The DRC is of the opinion that the persistent failure of a club to pay a player's salaries without just cause for three or four months is a just cause for the player to unilaterally terminate his employment contract.[350]

Following the above, an established professional who has appeared in less than 10% of the official matches in which his club has been involved in the course of the season may terminate his contract prematurely on the grounds of the so-called "sporting just cause". Contrary to the consequences of a just cause, compensation may be payable in the case of a sporting just cause. The player must firstly be recognised as an established player, secondly, he may not have played in more than 10% of the official matches of his club and thirdly, termination on the grounds of sporting just cause will only be valid if he terminates his contract in the 15 days following the last official match of the season of his club.

The question is whether this is the only possibility for the player to appeal for a sporting just cause. As we have seen so far, there are only two decisions in which the DRC decided partially regarding the sporting just cause. According to the FIFA Comparison, in which the editions 2001 and 2005 of the RSTP rules are being compared, the given example is the only situation in which FIFA is of the opinion that sporting just cause can exist. However, this is too strict an interpretation with respect to the sporting just cause and it would be reasonable for the player to expect that the sporting just cause has a broader application in order to be entitled to terminate the contract.

For example, the situation with Juventus in the summer of 2006, whereby the club was relegated to the second division as a result of its match-fixing scandal, could be defined as a sporting just cause for a player to leave the club. The existence of a sporting just cause would give the player the possibility to unilaterally terminate the contract and in return a reasonable compensation should be paid by the player to his club. In the former edition 2001, the sporting just cause had a broader application. Former conditions such as injury,

[349] DRC 26 October 2006, no. 1061207.

[350] See also the FIFA Commentary, explanation Art. 14, p. 39. FIFA is of the opinion that the persistent failure to pay the salary of the player for a period of three months, gives the player a just cause to unilaterally terminate his employment contract.

suspension, player field position, etc., are now being deleted and no longer apply to the current situation.

9. Compensation

9.1 Introduction

As we have seen, an employment contract may be unilaterally terminated by either party in the case of a valid reason, the so-called "just cause", without any consequences of any kind. In other words, and to avoid any misunderstanding, a party which terminates the contract for just cause is not obliged to pay any compensation. However, in the event that the contract has been terminated by one of the parties without just cause, i.e., without valid reason, the party in breach is obliged to pay compensation. This is laid down in Article 17 Paragraph 1 of the RSTP, edition 2005. The party which is in breach without just cause is obliged to pay compensation, whether the breach is inside or outside the protected period.[351] Any claims for compensation can be brought before the DRC, which will take into account all relevant arrangements, laws and/or collective bargaining agreements existing at national level, as well as the specificity of sport.[352]

Notwithstanding the above, the difference between the breach within or outside the protected period is that sporting sanctions will only be imposed on the party which breached the contract within the protected period. Unilateral breach without just cause (or sporting just cause) after the protected period will not result in sporting sanctions. The issue related to the sporting sanctions for the players and the club after a termination of the contract will be discussed broadly in the following chapter.

This chapter firstly discusses the criteria with respect to the amount of compensation. The RSPT rules provide us with guidelines in order to determine the amount of compensation. Furthermore, the compensation paid by the club as well as by the player will be discussed in relation to the decisions of the DRC. Regarding the compensation of the player, the disproportionate penalty clause and other important decisions with regard to this issue will be discussed, such as the *N'Zogbia* case, the *Mexès* case and the famous *Webster* case.

9.2 Calculation of the amount

According to Article 17 Paragraph 1, the compensation for breach will be calculated with due consideration for:

- the law of the country concerned;
- the specificity of sport; and
- other "objective criteria".

The objective criteria will include, in particular:

---

[351] FIFA Commentary, explanation Art. 17 RSTP under 1 sub 1, p. 47.
[352] RSTP, edition 2005, Art. 17 Para. 1.

- the remuneration and other benefits due to the player under the existing contract and/or the new contract;
- the time remaining on the existing contract up to a maximum of five years;[353]
- the fees and expenses paid or incurred by the former club (amortised over the term of the contract); and
- whether the contractual breach falls within the protected period.

Claims for compensation can be brought before the DRC. As mentioned in the first chapter, the DRC is competent for disputes between clubs and players in relation to the maintenance of contractual stability if there is a claim from an interested party in relation to compensation for breach of contract.[354]

In addition to the above criteria, the DRC may also take into account all relevant agreements, laws and/or collective bargaining agreements that exist at national level as well as the specificity of sport when establishing the compensation amount due. The laws of the country where the club is domiciled are relevant.[355]

A very important aspect concerning the amount of compensation is whether the contractual breach takes place inside or outside the so-called protected period. As mentioned before, the protected period is the period of three entire seasons or three years, whichever comes first, following the entry into force, if such contract was concluded prior to the 28th birthday of the professional. If the contract with the professional was concluded after his 28th birthday, the protected period was two seasons or two years, whichever comes first, following the entry into force of a contract. FIFA wanted to protect a certain period of the contract by discouraging players and clubs from terminating the contract during this so-called protected period. For example, if a 24 year old player signs his first contract and unilaterally terminates the contract 2½ years later, one can speak of a termination within the protected period. As a result, he will not only be subjected to sporting sanctions, as we will see in the next chapter, but the amount of compensation will also be relatively high. If the player unilaterally terminated his contract 4 years after signing the contract, the amount of compensation will decrease substantially. In the *Mexès* and the *Webster* cases, the before-mentioned relevant elements will be considered in order to establish the amount of compensation.

9.3 **By the club**

In a decision of the DRC of 10 June 2004, the DRC noted that on the date of receiving the player's claim on 16 February 2004, the club had not paid the player's monthly salary for over four months and two of the four instalments pertaining to the signing-on fee were still unpaid.[356] The DRC concurred that the club had seriously neglected its financial obligations towards the player in question and the club was found to have committed a unilateral breach of the employment contract without just cause. With regard to the award of financial compensation in favour of the player, the DRC furthermore took into account that the

[353] It is often presumed by parties that only the so-called "rest value" of the contract is the decisive element in order to determine the exact amount of compensation. As we have seen, this is incorrect.

[354] RSTP, edition 2005, Art. 22 under a.

[355] FIFA Commentary, explanation Art. 17 RSTP under 1, sub 2, p. 47.

[356] DRC 10 June 2004, no. 64133.

relevant employment contract included a clause pertaining to monies payable to either party in the event of the early termination of the employment contract, both parties having duly signed the employment contract and having agreed on such clause, and the relevant clause being reciprocal. The DRC therefore agreed, and this was the decisive factor, that the amount of money stipulated in the contract should be taken into consideration when establishing the financial compensation to be paid by the club to the player.

In a decision of the DRC of 9 November 2004, the DRC was of the opinion that although the player may have committed disciplinary infractions, this could not justify the non-payment of the player's salaries and therefore damage compensation was due for breach of contract by the club.[357] In this respect, the DRC mentioned that the player had repeatedly faced uncertainty as to whether or not he would receive the financial income due to him. This situation could not be tolerated by the player and it constituted a breach of the club's contractual duties, whether it could be excused by financial difficulties or not. The DRC acknowledged that the player may have committed disciplinary infractions during his participation in the matches played for the club and that these acts may be punishable in accordance with the applicable disciplinary rules. Nevertheless, the DRC was clear and decided that this could not justify the non-payment of a player's salaries.

In a decision of the DRC of 2 November 2005, the DRC decided that compensation should be paid by the party who had breached the contract.[358] This concerned a financial dispute on the basis of an employment contract between a player and club. As a result, the DRC established that the player had suffered financial damages due to the early termination of the employment contract signed with the club and therefore the club was liable to pay compensation until the player was able to find a new club within a reasonable timeframe. Finally, in the before-mentioned case the DRC emphasised that taking all of the above into account, the club was liable to pay compensation to the player equivalent to the salaries as from August 2004 until August 2006. The DRC decided that the club had to pay compensation.

In the earlier mentioned decision of 12 January 2006, the DRC decided regarding the absence of a player during training sessions.[359] The DRC had to decide whether a week's absence of the player concerned could be defined as a just cause for the club to terminate the employment contract unilaterally. The DRC considered that the player's absence from the training sessions for a short period of one week could not constitute just cause for a club to unilaterally terminate an employment contract, as happened in the present case. The DRC finally reached the conclusion that the club had terminated the employment contract without just cause. With regard to a compensation for unjustified breach of contract, the DRC stated that the club was liable to pay to the player the contractual salaries for the remainder of the contract, i.e., the net salaries for the months from April 2004 to October 2005, which was USD 93,925 in total. Moreover, the DRC emphasised that the employment contract indicated that the player was entitled to compensation for the rental of an apartment for USD 1,400. The DRC decided that since a fixed amount for the rental was indicated, this amount should also be considered as payment to which the player was entitled from the club. Finally, the DRC concluded that in compensation for breach of contract without just cause, the club had to pay the player USD 1,400 per month for the

[357] DRC 9 November 2004, no. 11417.
[358] DRC 2 November 2005, no. 11522.
[359] DRC 12 January 2006, no. 16828.

remainder of the contract, i.e., for the months from April 2004 to October 2005, which is USD 23,800. Finally, the DRC concluded that the total compensation for breach of contract by the club without just cause amounted to USD 117,725.

Following the above decisions of the DRC, it is difficult to derive a certain rule from the decisions of the DRC with regard to the compensation to be paid by the club. If the club seriously neglects its financial obligations towards the player in question, then the club will be found to have committed a unilateral breach of the employment contract without just cause. The DRC takes into account all the particularities of the case. For instance, in a decision the DRC decided that both parties agreed on a clause which stipulated the amount of money to be paid in the event of a termination. Therefore, this was the decisive element in order to determine the amount of compensation. Furthermore, it is important to know that although the player may have committed disciplinary infractions, the DRC will generally determine that this does not justify the non-payment of the player's salaries. For the sake of clarity, the club may also bear the risk that it has to pay compensation to the player until the player is able to find a new club within a reasonable timeframe.

9.4 By the player

If a player is required to pay compensation, in accordance with Article 17 Paragraph 2 of the RSTP, edition 2005, the professional and his new club will jointly and severally be liable for its payment. To avoid any misunderstanding, the new club will be responsible, according to the FIFA Commentary, for paying the former club of the player in breach, regardless of any involvement or inducement to breach the contract.[360]

9.4.1 *Penalty clause*

In a decision of the DRC of 28 September 2006, the player also referred to specific Articles in the contract stipulating absurdly high compensation payments in case of breach of contract.[361] The DRC was of the opinion that, under such circumstances, the penalty clause appeared to be completely disproportionate and that therefore, the deciding body could legitimately reduce the relevant amount, taking into account the particularities of the specific case. The DRC noted that for the claimant's failure to return in time from his holidays, according to the employment contract, he had to pay a fine of USD 10,000 per day. Moreover, the club pointed out the application of Article 10 Paragraph 5 and Article 17 of the employment contract if the player violated the obligation to resume duty in time. Therefore, the club was of the opinion that it had the right to terminate the contract and demanded compensation from the player to the amount of USD 100,000. In this context, the DRC stressed that with regard to the monthly income of the claimant, i.e., USD 15,000 for the 2005 season and USD 20,000 for the 2006 season respectively, the penalty imposed on the player was completely disproportionate and could not be accepted.

---

360 FIFA Commentary, explanation Art. 17, p. 47.

361 DRC 28 September 2006, no. 96391.

9.4.2 N'Zogbia *case*

On 3 August 2004 the English football club Newcastle concluded an employment contract with the French player Charles N'Zogbia.[362] On 11 August 2004 the English Football Association requested the ITC from the French National Association, the FFF. The FFF refused to issue the international transfer certificate and the parties consequently appealed to FIFA. The PSC decided that N'Zogbia was entitled to play for Newcastle on a provisional registration.

On 9 November 2004, the DRC decided to postpone the case to the meeting of 26 November 2004 to allow the parties to reach an amicable settlement. Because no such settlement was reached, on 26 November 2004 the DRC decided that N'Zogbia no longer had any contractual ties with Le Havre and that he was allowed to play for Newcastle. Finally, the DRC decided that Newcastle had to pay Le Havre training compensation of EUR 300,000.[363]

On 17 December 2004, Le Havre appealed to the CAS against the decision of the DRC. In the case before the CAS between La SASP Le Havre Athletic Club et l'Association Le Havre Athletic Club v/FIFA and Newcastle United FC and M. Charles N' Zogbia, on 27 October 2005 the CAS decided that N'Zogbia was allowed to play for Newcastle, that N'Zogbia had violated his contractual obligations against Le Havre and that Newcastle not only had to pay training compensation, it also had to pay supplementary compensation for the breach of contract of N'Zogbia. The decision of the DRC was partially annulled and the parties were invited to submit their arguments and conclusions regarding compensation amounts.[364]

9.4.3 Mexès *case*

9.4.3.1 Several decisions

Before studying one of the published cases in more detail, it is important to be aware of the fact that the *Mexès* case consists of several cases before the DRC as well as the CAS. To provide the best review of the various decisions, we will look at the relevant decisions in this case:

- DRC 31 August 2004 (not published). In this case, the DRC decided that Mexès unilaterally breached his contract with Auxerre without just cause.
- Mexès appealed to the CAS against the DRC decision of 31 August 2004. Decision of the CAS of 11 March 2005, no. CAS 2004 A/708/709/713.

The CAS confirmed the decision of the DRC of 31 August 2004.

- DRC 13 May 2005, no. 55503. In this case, the DRC ordered Mexès to pay compensation to Auxerre to the amount of EUR 8,000,000.

---

[362] DRC 9 November 2004, no. 114667-09.

[363] DRC 26 November 2004, no. 114667-26.

[364] CAS 2004/A/791, *La SASP Le Havre Athletic Club and l'Association Le Havre Athletic Club* v. *FIFA and Newcastle United and M. Charles N'Zogbia.* DRC 9 November 2004, no. 114667-09 and DRC 26 November 2004, no. 114667-26.

- Mexès appealed to the CAS about the DRC decision of 13 May 2005. Decision of the CAS of 5 December 2005, no. CAS 2005/A/902/903. The CAS found the appeal partially admissible and ordered Mexès to pay Auxerre compensation to the amount of EUR 7,000,000.
- DRC 23 June 2005, no. 65503. The DRC decided that a ban should be imposed on AS Roma for 2 registration periods for the inducement for breach of contract.
- AS Roma appealed to CAS against the decision of the DRC of 23 June 2005, no. 65503. Decision of the CAS of 5 December 2005, no. CAS 2005/A/916. The CAS found the appeal partially admissible and ordered a ban on AS Roma for 1 entire registration period.

9.4.3.2 Condemnation of *Mexès*

The player Philippe Mexès was born on 30 March 1982 in Toulouse in France and started playing for the French Football Club Auxerre at the age of 15. One season later, on 13 May 1998 Mexès signed a youth player's contract with Auxerre for a period of 5 years. On 20 June 2000 the youth player's contract was replaced by a professional football player's contract for a period of 5 years ending at the end of the season 2004/05. On 15 December 2002 Auxerre and Mexès agreed to prolong the contract by 1 season, thus ending at the end of the season 2005/06. On 24 May 2004 the Italian club AS Roma informed Auxerre that it was interested in the player Philippe Mexès and intended to make a transfer bid. On 4 June 2004, AS Roma offered Auxerre EUR 4,500,000 for Mexès by telephone. Auxerre told AS Roma that it did not agree to the transfer of Mexès to AS Roma and that Mexès was still under contract with Auxerre until 30 June 2006. On 11 June 2004, Mexès appealed to FIFA, basing the request on Article 42 of the RSTP, edition 2001. On 12 June 2004, AS Roma and Philippe Mexès signed the employment contract for 4 seasons from the season 2004/05 until the season 2007/08. On 8 July 2004 Auxerre asked FIFA to decide on the dispute.

By decision of the DRC of 13 May 2005, Mexès was ordered to pay Auxerre compensation of EUR 8,000,000 according to Article 22 of the RSTP, edition 2001.[365] However, in this case Auxerre had claimed compensation of EUR 18,000,000. Auxerre stated that Mexès received a much higher salary with AS Roma and the club furthermore stated that it had invested a lot in the player Mexès. In its decision of 13 May 2005, the DRC had examined the objective criteria for calculating the compensation as laid down in Article 22 Paragraph 1 of the RSTP, edition 2001. In the process, the DRC took into account the much higher salary that Mexès was earning at AS Roma, and that Auxerre was famous for training its young players. The DRC referred to the fact that Mexès had been trained by Auxerre for 7 years from the age of 15 until the age of 22. According to the DRC, the remaining value of the contract was EUR 2,403,614 and based on the special circumstances and objective criteria, the DRC finally ordered Mexès to pay Auxerre a total compensation of EUR 8,000,000.

In the appeal, the CAS considered as follows.[366] In its decision of 13 May 2005, the CAS was of the opinion that the DRC had not explicitly motivated and calculated why AS

[365] DRC 23 June 2005, no. 65503.

[366] CAS 2005/A/916, *AS Roma* v. *FIFA*.

Roma should pay compensation of EUR 8,000,000. Therefore, the CAS had to calculate the amount of compensation due. AS Roma offered to pay compensation of EUR 4,500,000. Auxerre refused this offer. At the basis of its calculation was the amount of EUR 2,289,644 for the loss of Auxerre for the period in which Mexès should have played with Auxerre during the 2005/06 season and compensation for not receiving a transfer sum for Mexès fixed at the minimum of EUR 4,500,000. According to the objective criteria, the CAS finally concluded that AS Roma should pay Auxerre a total compensation of EUR 7,000,000.

According to the above decision, both the DRC and the CAS referred to Article 22 Paragraph 1 of the RSTP, edition 2001 (the current Article 17, edition 2005), which mentions the criteria for determining the amount of compensation. In the before-mentioned decision, the DRC took into account the circumstances that the player received a much higher salary from his new club. Furthermore, the DRC felt it was important that the player's former club was famous for training young players and that Mexès had been trained by Auxerre for seven years. The remaining value of the contract also came to the surface in order to determine the amount of compensation. We see that although the RSTP, edition 2005, provide us with the elements that are decisive for determining the amount of compensation, it is still difficult to derive the more specific elements and factors from these decisions to determine the amount of compensation. Regarding the exact amount of compensation, it must be noted that the amount explicitly depends on the merits of the case and its particularities.

With respect to the protected period, it was clear that the player had terminated his contract within the protected period. Due to the prolongation of the contract, as a result of which the protected period starts again as stipulated in Article 17 Paragraph 3 of the RSPT, edition 2005, the player terminated his contract during the so-called protected period. As a consequence, the amount of compensation for the player to be paid to his former club was relatively high. However, it remains difficult to establish the exact amount. As mentioned before, it depends on the specific particularities of the case which should be adjudicated in the light of Article 17 Paragraph 1 of the RSTP, edition 2005. Therefore, the following case of the DRC of 2007, the so-called case *Webster*, in which the player terminated his employment contract outside the protected period, can be used as the best comparative material to determine the amount. The opinion of the DRC with respect to both situations, i.e., a breach within (Webster) and a breach outside (Mexès) the protected period, will give more handholds in order to establish the exact amount of compensation. Although the *Webster* case lies outside the scope of this book (2002–2006), this case is crucially important for a better legal survey of the opinion of the DRC.

9.4.5 Webster *case*

The *Webster* case is a decision of the DRC of 4 April 2007, in which the Chamber adjudicated with respect to the amount of compensation to be paid by the player if he is to leave the club outside the protected period.[367] The Scottish international Andrew Webster was a player with Heart of Midlothian. After a conflict with the club owner Vladimir Romanov in 2006, he was degraded to the bench. That was reason for Webster to terminate his contract. Webster terminated his employment contract outside the protected period and

---

[367] DRC 4 April 2007, no. 47936. See p. 710 for an author's note on the CAS Award of 30 January 2008.

therefore no sporting sanctions would be imposed on him. Following the termination, Webster signed a new contract with Wigan Athletic. However, Heart of Midlothian did not agree with the termination and refused to cooperate with the transfer to Wigan Athletic. As a result, Webster appealed to FIFA and asked for a provisional registration for his new club, which was allowed by the Single Judge of the PSC.

The dispute was now only about the amount of compensation. Heart of Midlothian claimed the market value to the amount of GBP 5,000,000 as compensation. The DRC was of the opinion that the player had terminated his contract outside the protected period and that this was a very important element in order to establish the amount of compensation. The Chamber decided that the unilateral termination undeniably occurred after three seasons, i.e., after the protected period and within 15 days of the last match of the season. The DRC referred to the maintenance of contractual stability, which represents the backbone of the agreement between FIFA/UEFA and the European Commission signed in March 2001, as mentioned earlier. In this decision, the DRC obviously referred to Article 17 Paragraph 1 of the RSPT, edition 2005, which provides us with the key to assessing the amount of compensation due by the player to the club. However, the DRC stated in this respect that this list is not exhaustive and that each request for termination had to be assessed on a case-by-case basis. In other words, the particularities of the case had to be examined.

The remaining value of the employment contract of the player concerned was EUR 199,976. However, the Chamber once again emphasised that the player could not terminate his contract by simply paying his club the remaining value of his contract.[368] Besides his basic salary, the player furthermore received a number of appearance bonuses and the former transfer compensation of EUR 75,000 also had to be taken into consideration as well as the five seasons the player had spent with his club, according to the DRC. The DRC furthermore pointed out that another crucial factor to be taken into account was the way in which his club had contributed to the steady improvement of the player concerned. The before-mentioned considerations led to the conclusion of the DRC that Webster should pay GBP 625,000 to his former club.[369]

There are many similarities with the *Mexès* case. Both players played for their former clubs for many years. Furthermore, it must be noted that the remaining value of their employment contracts did not differ substantially, namely EUR 199,976 for Webster and EUR 2,403,614 for Mexès. Moreover, both former clubs had contributed to the steady improvement of their players Webster and Mexès. However, as said before, the fact that the termination of Webster took place outside the protected period was crucially important for the DRC. The compensation to be paid by Webster was GBP 625,000 while the compensation due by Mexès to his club was EUR 7,000,000. Because of this difference, it obviously is very important whether the termination by the player takes place inside or outside the protected period.

9.4.6 *Buyout clause*

Pursuant to Article 17 RSTP, edition 2005, the contract can include the exact amount of compensation. The parties are entitled to stipulate in the contract the amount that the player

[368] The FIFPro, the worldwide union of players, is of the opinion that the amount of compensation may not be higher than the rest value of the contract.

[369] Andrew Webster did appeal to CAS.

will pay as compensation in order to unilaterally terminate the contract.[370] This is called the so-called "buyout clause".[371] In that respect, it is important to know that on the one hand, the sports legislation of certain countries such as Spain (*Real Decreto* 1006) made it compulsory for a buyout clause to be included in contracts. On the other hand, there are countries that cannot include the buyout clause in their contracts as it is not compatible with mandatory labour law. However, according to FIFA a buyout clause in the employment contract is valid.[372]

The advantage of the buyout clause is that the parties mutually agree on the amount at the very beginning and record this in the player's employment contract. By paying this amount to the club, the player is entitled to unilaterally terminate the employment contract. In other words, with this buyout clause, the club agrees to give the player the opportunity to cancel the contract at any moment and without a valid reason.

9.5 **Conclusion**

In the event that the contract has been terminated by one of the parties without just cause, i.e., without valid reason, the party in breach will pay compensation. This is stated in Article 17 Paragraph 1 of the RSTP, edition 2005. In that respect it can be outlined furthermore that according to this same Article, the compensation for breach will be calculated with due consideration for: (i) the law of the country concerned; (ii) the specificity of sport; and (iii) other objective criteria, such as the remuneration and other benefits due to the player under the existing contract and/or the new contract, the time remaining on the existing contract up to a maximum of five years, the fees and expenses paid or incurred by the former club (amortised over the term of the contract) and whether the contractual breach falls within the protected period. This provides the basis for the DRC to determine and calculate the amount of compensation to be paid by the party in breach. However, the DRC is of the explicit opinion that this list is not exhaustive.

With respect to the club's obligation to pay compensation, the DRC decided in numerous decisions that if the player suffers financial damages due to the early termination of the employment contract by the club without just cause, the latter is liable to pay compensation, sometimes even until the player is able to find a new club within a reasonable timeframe. The DRC is of the opinion that if the club seriously neglects its financial obligations towards the player in question, such as neglecting to pay the player's monthly salary for over four months, the club will be found to have committed a unilateral breach of the employment contract without just cause. The Chamber can refer to the amount of compensation stipulated in the contract that should be taken into consideration when establishing the financial compensation to be paid by the club to the player, both parties having duly signed the employment contract and agreed on such a clause, and the relevant clause being reciprocal. Notwithstanding the above, it is difficult to derive a certain rule with respect to the exact amount of compensation to be paid by the club in breach.

With regard to the player's obligation to pay compensation, it must be mentioned in the first place that the new club is jointly liable for the compensation payable by the player to the respondent club, regardless of any involvement or inducement to breach the contract.

---

370 RSTP, edition 2005, Art. 17 Para. 2.

371 FIFA Commentary, explanation under Art. 17 RSTP under 1 sub 3, p. 47.

372 Id., explanation Art. 17 under footnote 76, p. 47.

Also at this point, it remains difficult to establish the exact amount of compensation to be paid by one of the parties. As mentioned before and as indicated by the DRC, it depends on the specific particularities of the case which are to be adjudicated in the light of Article 17 Paragraph 1 of the RSTP, edition 2005.

In relation to the penalty clause, the DRC is of the opinion that, under circumstances, a penalty clause can be completely disproportionate. For example, a player with a yearly income of USD 15,000 cannot be fined with a disproportionate penalty clause if he violates the obligation to resume duty in time.

As outlined in the *Mexès* and *Webster* cases, it must be noted that a very important element in determining the exact amount of compensation is whether the termination of the contract by the player took place inside or outside the protected period. It will always be difficult to determine the exact amount of compensation. In the *Webster* case, the DRC stated that it would not only deal with the criteria mentioned in Article 17 Paragraph 1, but also with their "specific knowledge of the world of football". Therefore, a specific rule and an exhaustive list for determining the exact amount of compensation can never be provided by FIFA, however advantageous. For the sake of good order, the Chamber repeatedly emphasises that the player cannot terminate his contract by simply paying his club the remaining value of his contract.

As we have seen, the parties may furthermore stipulate in the contract the amount that the player will pay to the club as compensation in order to unilaterally terminate the contract, also known as the buyout clause. In this respect the FIFA Commentary gives us a remarkable comment in relation to this clause. In its FIFA Commentary, FIFA states that if the termination on grounds of the buyout clause has been carried out inside the protected period, no sporting sanctions may be imposed on the player as a result of the premature termination. This may be against the maintenance of contractual stability and therefore contrary to Article 13 of the RSTP rules. Although the DRC has not yet decided with respect to such a specific case, the Chamber may decide that strictly pursuant to Article 17 Paragraph 3, sporting sanctions will be imposed upon him if the player terminates on the grounds of this so-called buyout clause *inside* the protected period. Exclusively the unilateral breach without just cause after the protected period will not result in sporting sanctions, following the RSTP rules. Besides the fact that it may be reasonable that as a result of a buyout clause, (also) no sporting sanctions will follow during the protected period, in strictly legal terms, this is incorrect. It must be noted that at this point, as said before, the FIFA Commentary is therefore making new rules with regard to this issue.

10. Sporting sanctions

10.1 **Introduction**

With respect to the sporting sanctions in relation to a termination by one of the parties without just cause, it is of crucial relevance whether the breach falls inside the earlier mentioned protected period. The difference between the breach inside or outside the protected period is that sporting sanctions will only be imposed on the party which breached the contract inside the protected period. Unilateral breach without just cause (or sporting just cause) after the protected period will not result in sporting sanctions. If the club or player breached the contract without just cause, the FIFA Disciplinary Committee may impose sporting sanctions on the club or the player.

10.2 For the club

According to Article 17 Paragraph 4 of the RSTP, edition 2005, in addition to the obligation to pay compensation, sporting sanctions may be imposed on a club found to be in breach of contract or found to be inducing a breach during the protected period.

According to the second phrase of Article 17 Paragraph 4 of the RSTP, edition 2005, FIFA provides us with the following:

> "it will be presumed, unless established to the contrary, that any club signing a professional who has terminated his contract without just cause has induced that professional to commit a breach".

It is interesting to find out the opinion of the DRC with respect to the so-called buyout clause in relation to the before-mentioned article. However, as mentioned earlier, so far no decisions of the DRC have been published on the official website of FIFA with respect to the buyout clause. Although FIFA is of the opinion that the buyout clause is valid, this could still lead to the situation that sporting sanctions should be imposed on the new club.[373] If a player terminates his contract on grounds of the buyout clause during the protected period, the new club still has to comply with the rule that it has to inform the current club in writing before entering into negotiations with the player.[374] If the new club omits to inform the current club of the player, despite the fact that the employment contract was provided with a buyout clause, this new club could still risk having sporting sanctions imposed by the DRC. So far, however, no DRC decisions regarding this specific issue have been published on the FIFA website. In general, sporting sanctions on a club will consist of being banned from registering new players either nationally or internationally for two registration periods.

10.2.1 *Inducing the player*

On 9 November 2004, the DRC issued a decision on a claim represented by the Polish player Adam Majewski against the Greek club New Panionios, whereby it ordered Panionios to pay an amount of EUR 70,500 to Majewski within 30 days and pronounced a ban on the registration of any new players, either nationally or internationally, until the expiry of the second transfer period following the date on which a breach of contract had been found.[375] It was not disputed that Panionios had not paid the due amounts within the time limit set by the DRC. Therefore, on 14 February 2005, the FIFA Disciplinary Committee issued a decision regarding the failure to comply with a decision passed by a FIFA body.

The Disciplinary Committee was of the opinion that Panionios was guilty of failing to comply with a decision of the DRC of 9 November 2004. It ordered Panionios to pay a fine of EUR 15,000 and granted a final period of grace of 30 days for the payment of the

[373] FIFA Commentary, explanation under Art. 17 RSTP under 1 sub 3, p. 47.
[374] RSTP, edition 2005, Art. 18 Para. 4.
[375] DRC 9 November 2004, no. 11417.

amount due to Majewski. In addition, in this decision the Disciplinary Committee ruled that if payment was not made within this deadline, the creditor club might demand in writing that 6 points be deducted from Panionios' first team in the domestic league championship. Finally, the Disciplinary Committee reminded the Hellenic Football Federation that, as a member of FIFA, it had a duty to implement the decision and that if it failed to do so despite being ordered by FIFA, it would be subject to sanctions. The Greek football club FC Aris Thessaloniki appealed to CAS and the Panel finally decided that it did not have the jurisdiction to hear such a premature appeal and that it could not proceed with the appellant's appeal.[376]

In the earlier mentioned decision of the DRC of 23 June 2005 (the *Mexès* case), the Chamber also decided that the club AS Roma had induced the breach of contract and was therefore banned for two seasons from transferring any new players both nationally and internationally.[377] AS Roma did appeal to the CAS and the Panel subsequently reduced the ban for the club AS Roma to one registration period.[378]

In the before-mentioned decision of the DRC of 23 June 2005, the Chamber emphasised that, with regard to the consequences of inducement to contractual breach, it was irrelevant whether the breach occurred inside or outside the protected period, since according to the FIFA regulations, the inducement to contractual breach is subject to sanctions at any time during the validity of the employment contract. According to the DRC, such a circumstance cannot be considered as a mitigating circumstance. As a consequence, the DRC was left with no other choice than to strictly apply the contents of Article 23 Paragraph 2 of the RSTP, edition 2001, according to which, in case of a club inducing the breach of contract, if the breach occurs at the end of the first or second year of contract, the sanction shall be a ban on registering any new player, either nationally or internationally, for two consecutive transfer periods. Therefore, the Chamber decided that the new club was responsible for inducing a breach of contract and concluded that the new club should be banned from registering any new players, both nationally or internationally, until the end of the second transfer period following the notification of this decision.

In a decision of the DRC of 23 March 2006, the Chamber had to consider and pass a decision on the request made by a club against the new club of the player for sports sanctions for inducement to contractual breach.[379] In this decision the DRC first referred to Article 23 Paragraph 2(c) of the RSTP, edition 2001, according to which a club seeking to register a player who has unilaterally breached a contract during the protected period will be presumed to have induced a breach of contract. The DRC pointed out that as a consequence, it is the new club's responsibility to demonstrate that they should not be held responsible for having induced the breach of contract.[380] The DRC noted that when it signed the employment contract with the player, the new club relied solely on the player's statement that he had a just cause to terminate the contract with his former club, instead of acting with caution and contacting the former club to clarify the situation before signing an employment contract with the player in question. Therefore, the new club had acted

---

[376] CAS 2005/A/899, *FC Aris Thessaloniki* v. *FIFA & New Panionios N.F.C*, decision of 15 July 2005.

[377] DRC 23 June 2005, no. 65503.

[378] CAS 2005/A/916, *AS Roma* v. *FIFA*.

[379] DRC 23 March 2006, no. 36460.

[380] It is just that Janwillem Soek refers to the fact that it is not logical to impose a sanction on the player's new club if it cannot prove that it did not have a hand in the player's transfer (3/4 *ISJL* (2007)).

very negligently. As a consequence, the DRC deemed that in view of the clear circumstances of the matter and the failure of the new club to set aside the presumption contained in Article 23 Paragraph 2(c) of the RSTP, edition 2001, it had to be presumed that the player was induced by the new club to terminate his contract. Finally, the DRC was left with no other choice than to strictly apply the contents of Article 23 Paragraph 2 of the RSTP, edition 2001. According to this article, if a club induces a breach of contract occurring at the end of the first or second year of contract, the sanction will be a ban on registering any new player, either nationally or internationally, for two consecutive transfer periods. Therefore, the new club was banned from registering any new player, either nationally or internationally, until the end of the second transfer period following the notification of this decision.

In a decision of the DRC of 21 November 2006, the Chamber had to decide with respect to a dispute concerning the breach of contract and inducement to breach of contract arising between the parties involved.[381] The DRC had to pass a decision on the request made by the former club against the player's new club, for inducement to breach of contract. The DRC pointed out that, in order to apply possible sanctions on the new club for inducement to breach of contract, as a condition sine qua non, a breach of contract must have actually occurred. However, in this case the DRC was of the opinion that no breach of contract had been committed by any of the parties.

Following the above decisions, the DRC is of the opinion with respect to the sporting sanctions imposed upon a club as consequences of inducement to contractual breach that it is irrelevant whether the breach occurred inside or outside the protected period. However, this is remarkable because the former Article, i.e., Article 23 of the RSTP, edition 2001, implied that only sporting sanctions will be imposed in case of inducement during the protected period. This contradicts the opinion of the DRC, because according to the DRC, the inducement to contractual breach is subject to sanctions *at any time* during the validity of the employment contract. In my opinion the DRC is right, because for legal certainty it should be irrelevant whether the inducement is inside or outside the period. It is also important that, when it signs the employment contract with the player, the new club cannot defend itself by stating that the player felt he had a just cause for terminating the contract with his former club. The club must always contact the former club to clarify the situation before signing an employment contract with the player in question to avoid the risk of being accused of serious negligence. The DRC is also of the opinion that the inducement to breach the contract is a condition sine qua non in order to apply potential possible sanctions on the new club for the inducement.

10.3 For the player

Pursuant to Article 17 Paragraph 3 of the RSTP, edition 2005, sporting sanctions will also be imposed on a player who is found to be in breach of contract during the protected period. This sanction will be a restriction of four months on his eligibility to play in official matches. However, in the case of aggravating circumstances, the restriction for the player will last six months. In all cases, the sporting sanctions will take effect from the start of the following season of the new club. Although unilateral breach without just cause

[381] DRC 21 November 2006, no. 611727.

or sporting just cause after the protected period will not result in sporting sanctions, disciplinary measures may be imposed on the player for failure to give due notice of termination within fifteen days of the last match of the season.[382]

If sporting sanctions have already been imposed on the player, the DRC may decide that sporting sanctions will not be imposed again. In its decision of 28 September 2006, the DRC decided that with regard to sporting sanctions, which apart from in exceptional circumstances should be applied if a player breaches a contract without just cause within the first three respectively two years of his employment contract according to Article 23 Paragraph 1 of the RSTP edition 2001, the Chamber renounced applying such sanctions in view of the fact that sports sanctions had already been imposed on the player in connection with the present dispute.[383]

10.3.1 *Four months rule*

In a decision of the DRC of 15 January 2004, a player and a club had a dispute with respect to their contract which was, according to the club, signed on 2 January 2002 and valid until the end of the 2005/06 sports season. The player stated that he had left the club legitimately, because, at the end of the year 2002, the club had not exercised its option right to extend his employment contract for another season. The player decided to terminate his employment contract with his club in December 2002, based on the before-mentioned fact, namely that the club did not exercise its option right to extend its contractual link for another sports season. Unfortunately for the player, the DRC concluded that there was no just cause for the player to terminate the employment contract with his club. To determine the sporting sanctions, the Chamber took into account that the player was 25 years old by the time the contractual breach occurred and that it took place at the end of the first year of his contract. As a consequence, the Chamber decided to sanction the player with a restriction of four months on his eligibility to participate in any official football matches as from the beginning of the new season of the new club's national championship, as stipulated in Article 23 Paragraph 1 of the RSTP, edition 2001.

In a decision of the DRC of 10 June 2004, the case was initially considered by the Disciplinary Committee of a national football federation.[384] The Disciplinary Committee decided that the player concerned had breached his contract with his club, since he did not return to the latter for the remainder of the employment contract. As a consequence, the Committee banned him from playing in official football matches for four months, starting on the day when the national championship in the league of his new club started. The player appealed to the Arbitration Body of the same football federation against this decision, but the appeal was rejected and the sanction upheld. The player subsequently submitted a claim to FIFA against the disciplinary sanction imposed by his national federation, asking that the sanction preventing him to play for his new team be lifted. Although the player's conduct was considered by the DRC as a breach of contract, the Chamber did question the proportionality of the restriction imposed. According to the DRC, the condition of proportionality requires that the gravity of a sanction must correspond with the gravity of the conduct leading to the sanction. The DRC noted that during the one month

[382] RSTP, edition 2005, Art. 17 Para. 3.

[383] DRC 28 September 2006, no. 96157. See also DRC 17 August 2006, no. 861307.

[384] DRC 10 June 2004, no. 6400276.

when the player stayed away from his employer club, no official matches were scheduled in the national league of his national football federation. Therefore, the absence of the player concerned did not pose a serious problem to the club. As a result thereof, the DRC concluded that the restriction imposed on the player concerned to participate in any official football matches for four months was not an appropriate sanction. The Chamber stated that it would have been more appropriate in this case if the player had been fined. Therefore, the DRC decided that the restriction should be lifted.

In a decision of the DRC of 4 February 2005, the player unilaterally terminated his employment contract without just cause within one year of signing a 5 year contract.[385] Regarding the sporting sanctions, the Chamber took into account the fact that the player was 19 years old at the time of the contractual breach and that it took place within the first year of the contract. As a result, the Chamber decided to sanction the player with a restriction of four months on his eligibility to participate in any official football matches, as stipulated in Article 23 Paragraph 1 of the RSTP, edition 2001.

In the earlier mentioned decision of the DRC of 13 May 2005, the DRC considered that the player had never informed his new club that he was still under contract with the club.[386] The player even signed the employment contract with his new club, despite the fact that he was still contractually bound to another club. The DRC went on to analyse the sports sanctions to be imposed on the player for having caused the contractual breach without just cause. According to Article 23 Paragraph 1 of the RSTP, edition 2001, a player will be sanctioned by means of a restriction of four months on his eligibility to participate in any official football matches.

In its decision of 21 February 2006, with respect to the sporting sanctions on the player, the DRC took into account the fact that the player was 19 years old at the time of the contractual breach and that it took place within the first year of contract.[387] Therefore, the Chamber decided to sanction the player with a restriction of four months on his eligibility to participate in any official football matches, as stipulated in Article 23 Paragraph 1 of the RSTP, edition 2001.

In its decision of 23 March 2006, the DRC underlined that in general a lengthy absence of a player from his club without authorisation and without other just cause justifies the suspension of payment of the players' salaries and that this should be considered as an unjustified breach of the employment contract by the player.[388] The DRC concluded that the player had not presented any evidence that his absence had been authorised except for the vacation period. For that reason, the DRC declared that the player had undoubtedly breached the employment contract without just cause during the protected period. Therefore the DRC was of the opinion that financial and sports sanctions must be imposed on the player. Regarding the sports sanctions, the DRC referred to the basic sanction of four months on the players' eligibility to participate in any official football matches in the case of an unjustified breach of contract by a player. In that respect, the DRC referred to the possibility of taking into consideration exceptional circumstances on the basis of which the sanction could be shortened or extended. Finally, the DRC decided that the player

385 DRC 4 February 2005, no. 25820.
386 DRC 13 May 2005, no. 55484.
387 DRC 21 February 2006, no. 26267.
388 DRC 23 March 2006, no. 36460.

should be sanctioned with a restriction of four months on his eligibility to participate in any official football matches as from the notification of this decision.

According to the above decisions, the DRC generally applies the four months rule as sporting sanction on the player. The DRC then concludes that if the player terminates his employment contract without just cause, the player must be sanctioned with a restriction of four months on his eligibility to participate in any official football matches. However according to the DRC, it is very important that the gravity of the sporting sanction corresponds with the gravity of the conduct leading to the sporting sanction. The DRC refers to important elements in order to determine whether or not sporting sanctions should be imposed on the player. In all decisions of the DRC in which the Chamber decides that the four months rule is applicable, the Chamber refers to the age of the player and the protected period. If the player is relatively young and the contractual breach of the player took place within the first two years of the contract, the DRC seems to be more inclined to apply the four months rule. However, the DRC may take exceptional circumstances into consideration, based on which the sanction could be shortened or extended. In the following case, which has already been referred to, the so-called "six months rule" was imposed on the player as sporting sanction due to the existence of aggravating circumstances, according to the DRC.

10.3.2 *Aggravating circumstances*

As we have seen before, the case *Mexès* consists of several cases before the DRC and its appeal committee the CAS. In the earlier mentioned decisions, the issue concerning the amount of the compensation was highlighted. In this paragraph, the issue concerning the sporting sanctions of six months for the player will be outlined. So far, the case *Mexès* is the only case in which the DRC concluded that there were aggravating circumstances.

On 31 August 2004, the DRC decided that Mexès had unilaterally breached the employment contract with Auxerre without just cause during the protected period. On the basis of Article 23 of the RSTP, edition 2001, the DRC imposed a 6 month suspension on Mexès as from 12 September 2004 as sporting sanction. AS Roma and Mexès appealed to the CAS and in decision of the CAS of 11 March 2005, the Panel confirmed the sporting sanction of 6 months imposed on the player.

As mentioned before, the player Philippe Mexès was not allowed to play for AS Roma for a period of six months, because there were aggravating circumstances. It now is interesting to define the term "aggravating circumstances". Neither the DRC nor FIFA defines this term. It must therefore be presumed that the four months rule is the general rule for the DRC to fine a player if the player terminates his contract without just cause. As mentioned before, important pillars for applying the four months rule are the relatively young age of the player and the fact that the breach took place only one year after the signing of the contract and thus within the protected period. In the case of aggravating circumstances, according to the RSTP, edition 2005 the "six months rule" applies. Mexès was not only a relatively young player who had terminated his contract within the protected period; an important element for determining the existence of aggravating circumstances could be the fact that Mexès was trained by Auxerre for 7 years from the age of 15 until he was 22. According to the DRC, this had to be considered as "a considerably long period of stay with his former club. Apart from his personal talent, the players' positive development must be essentially attributed to the training and education he received from his former club". In that respect, it is a lack of completeness that the decision of the DRC of 31 August 2004 is not published on the website of FIFA, as it was in this case that the DRC decided that Mexès unilaterally breached his contract with Auxerre without just cause. However, according to Article 23 (c) of the RSTP, edition 2001, aggravating circumstances existed in the case of failure to give due notice or recurrent breach of contract. Notwithstanding the above, the considerable length of time spent by the player with his former club can be seen as a special circumstance for establishing the existence of aggravating circumstances.

10.4 **Conclusion**

In relation to the sporting sanctions with respect to a termination by one of the parties without just cause, it is of crucial relevance to establish whether the breach by one of the parties falls within the earlier mentioned protected period. As explicitly stated before, sporting sanctions will only be imposed on the party which breached the contract within the protected period. Unilateral breach without just cause after the protected period of the employment contract will not result in sporting sanctions.

Sporting sanctions may be imposed on the club. In addition to the obligation to pay compensation, sporting sanctions will be imposed on any club found to be in breach of contract or found to be inducing a breach of contract during the protected period. Any club signing a professional who has terminated his contract without just cause may have induced that professional to commit a breach. The club will be banned from registering any new players, either nationally or internationally, for two registration periods. According to the DRC, it is irrelevant whether the breach took place within or outside the protected period. However, as mentioned above, this is rather strange in the light of the current RSTP. At this point, one can say there is a severe contradiction, because the current Article refers to the fact that sporting sanctions will only be imposed in the case of an inducement during the protected period, while according to the decision of the DRC, the inducement to contractual breach per se is subject to sanctions *at any time* during the validity of the employment contract.

In my opinion the DRC is correct and the current Article should be modified, because for legal certainty it should be irrelevant whether the inducement is within or outside the protected period. It would be rather strange not to have the possibility that a new club induced a player to breach the contract with his former club, if he is outside the protected period of his contract. For the sake of good order and to avoid any misunderstanding, it is therefore advisable that the club contacts the former club in order to clarify the situation before signing the contract with the player in question to avoid the risk of being accused of an inducement.

According to Article 17 Paragraph 3, in addition to the obligation to pay compensation, sporting sanctions will also be imposed on any player found to be in breach of contract during the protected period. This sanction will generally be a restriction of four months on his eligibility to play in official matches. In the case of aggravating circumstances, as was the case in the *Mexès* case, this will be six months. However, it is very important according to the DRC that the gravity of the sporting sanction corresponds with the gravity of the conduct leading to the sporting sanction. In all decisions of the DRC in which the Chamber decides that the four months rule is applicable, the Chamber refers to the age of the player and the protected period. If the player is relatively young and the contractual breach of the player took place within the first two years of the contract, the DRC seems to be sooner inclined to apply the four months rule. In order to apply the six months rule, an important factor could be that the player stayed a considerably long period with his former club.

11. Training compensation

11.1 Introduction

The famous *Bosman* case finally led to the abolition of the actual transfer compensation between clubs at the end of the player's employment contract. However, there still were some openings to protect the clubs that had been involved with the training and education of players. FIFA introduced the so-called training compensation for clubs that had been involved in the training and education of players. The RSTP, edition 2001, therefore contained provisions that regulated the compensation for the training and education of young players. According to Circular 769, this system was designed to encourage more and better training of young players and to create solidarity among clubs, by awarding financial compensation to clubs which had invested in the career of its former player.

According to Article 20 of the RSTP, edition 2005, training compensation must be paid to a player's training clubs when a player signs his first contract as a professional before the end the season of his 23rd birthday (11.2.1.) and on each transfer of a professional until the end of the season of his 23rd birthday (11.2.2). The obligation to pay training compensation exists whether the transfer takes place during or at the end of the player's contract.[389] Annex 4 of the RSTP, edition 2005, provides more explicit details regarding training compensation. According to Annex 4, a player's training takes place between the ages of 12 and 23 for training incurred up to the age of 21, unless it is evident that a player has already terminated his training period before the age of 21. For the sake of completeness, no training compensation is due if a player signs his first professional contract or changes clubs at international level after the end of the season of his 23rd birthday.[390]

Before discussing the main aspects relating to training compensation and the opinion of the DRC, it must be noted that the obligation to pay training compensation is without prejudice to any obligation to pay compensation for breach of contract.[391] Furthermore, it is important to distinguish the years relating to the obligation to pay training compensation and the years relating to the *calculation* of the amount of training compensation. Thus training compensation will be payable until the end of the season in which the player reaches the age of 23, although the calculation of the amount payable will be based on the years between 12 and the age when it is established that the player actually completed his training.

Another relevant issue relating to the training compensation is the fact that a former club which claims for training compensation is bound to the restriction to insert his claim within two years. In other words, and as we have seen, a former club waives its rights to

389 As we will see in the chapter hereinafter, the solidarity mechanism only applies in case the player is transferred before the expiry of his contract.

390 This is another difference with the solidarity contribution. The applicability of the solidarity mechanism is not limited to the age of the player.

391 RSTP, edition 2005, Annex 4, Art. 2.

receive training compensation if more than two years have elapsed from the event giving rise to the dispute. Finally, it must be noted that when a player asks for a certain amount of damages, the DRC, as also discussed earlier, will not adjudicate more than the amount of the claim of the club, also known as the principle of *non ultra petitum*. The DRC in these cases refers to the *ultra petitum* rule, as a result of which the Chamber cannot adjudicate more than is claimed by one of the parties, as mentioned in the earlier case of the DRC of 9 November 2004.[392]

11.2 When is training compensation due?

11.2.1 *First professional contract*

In line with the above, when the player signs his first contract as a professional, training compensation is due before the end of the season of his 23rd birthday. In that respect it is important to determine the status of the player. As discussed in Chapter 2, according to the RSTP, edition 2005 and numerous decisions of the DRC, the difference between a professional and an amateur is that the professional has a written employment contract with his club and the amateur does not. Moreover, a professional is paid more than the expenses he effectively incurs in return for his footballing activity. The DRC points out, and this deliberation comes up time and time again, a football player will be regarded and considered as a professional if he receives remuneration in excess of the expenses he effectively incurs for his footballing activity. However, the DRC is clear, the legal nature or the determination of the agreement is of no relevance with respect to the determination whether the player is an amateur of a professional.[393] This means that if the player signs a written employment contract for the first time before the season of his 23rd birthday and if he gets paid more than the expenses he effectively incurs in return for his footballing activity, training compensation is due. Contrarily, this means that if the player signs his first written employment contract and the player does not get paid more than the expenses he effectively incurs in return for his footballing activity, the player must be considered as an amateur and consequently no training compensation is due.

In the earlier mentioned decision of the DRC of 28 July 2005, the DRC was of the opinion that the player in question was, as indicated by the football federation of the club, registered as an amateur player for the new club. No training compensation was therefore due. In this case, two clubs were arguing about the nature of this contract and the relevant question was whether this contract should be considered as a scholarship contract (amateur contract) or an employment contract (non-amateur contract). The player concerned signed a contract with a new club on 1 July 2004 and his former club lodged a claim for training compensation. The player was registered with his former club as an amateur player during the seasons 2001/02 and 2002/03, at the age of 15 and 16. The new club insisted that although they had signed a contract with the player, the latter could keep his amateur status. The club based its statement on the fact that the contract signed was mainly an agreement to educate and train the player, entitling him to a compensation for travel and housing expenses. Therefore, they were of the opinion that the club was not liable to pay

[392] DRC 9 November 2004, no. 114707.

[393] DRC 17 August 2006, no. 86137, CAS 2005/A/383 and CAS 2004/A/691, nos. 76 and 77.

training compensation to his former club. The Chamber pointed out that in disputes concerning training compensation, the nature of a contract between a player and a club is determined by the relevant association. As a principle, the DRC therefore decided that they did not want to enter into the question concerning the status of the player. In this case, the Chamber decided that the autonomy of the association must be respected by the DRC and therefore, the status of the registration of such player at the association will be taken into consideration in order to determine whether the conditions stipulating the payment of training compensation have been fulfilled. Finally, the DRC decided that the player in question was, as indicated by the football federation of the club, registered as an amateur player for the new club.[394] The Chamber came to the final conclusion that the scholarship agreement concerned should be seen as an amateur contract and that as a result, no training compensation was obliged to be paid by the new club.

In a decision of the DRC of 2 November 2005, the Chamber reached the conclusion that the former club was indisputably entitled to receive compensation from the new club for the training and education of the player due to the length of time that the latter had spent with it, because the contract with his new club had to be considered as a professional players' contract. In this case the player was trained by a German club as an amateur player and the club lodged a claim for training compensation. The German club maintained that the player had appeared for his new club, a Greek club, and was therefore no longer an amateur. In response to an enquiry from FIFA, the Greek club contested the fact that the player had non-amateur status as he was playing for the club's amateur youth team. However, the German club insisted on 11 April 2005 that the player was no longer an amateur, pointing out that, while the player may only have been playing in youth and amateur teams at that time, this issue depended exclusively on the status of the player and not on the team for which he appeared. The Greek club stated that, given that the player had moved to Greece without any fee being paid and that he had never appeared for a non-amateur team, there were no grounds for the payment of training compensation. Finally, the DRC unanimously concluded that the player signed his first contract as a non-amateur and backed the opinion of the German club that this issue depended exclusively on the status of the player and not on the team for which he appeared.[395]

11.2.2 *Subsequent transfer*

Besides the obligation to pay compensation if the player signs his first contract as a professional before the end of the season of his 23rd birthday, training compensation is also due if the professional is transferred between clubs of two different associations before the end of his season of his 23rd birthday.[396] In that respect, as said above, it is furthermore irrelevant whether the transfer is during or at the end of his contract.[397] However, if the player is transferred for a second time, training compensation is only due to his former club. To avoid any misunderstanding, the former club is the club where the player played directly

[394] DRC 28 July 2005, no. 75142.

[395] DRC 2 November 2005, no. 115324.

[396] In case the transfer takes place within one association, the national regulations are applicable. In that respect it is important that according to Art. 1 of the RSTP, edition 2005, the national regulations should also foresee a system to reward the clubs investing in the training and education of young players.

[397] RSTP, edition 2005, Annex 4, Art. 1 Para. 2.

prior to his new club (who is entitled to pay the training compensation, if applicable). In other words, in the case of a so-called "subsequent transfer" of the professional, training compensation will only be due to his former club for the time he was effectively trained by that club.[398] This means that in the case of a subsequent transfer, the clubs where the player was registered and trained previously (i.e., the clubs prior to the former club) are not entitled to receive training compensation, since they have already received training compensation in relation to an earlier transfer of the player.

11.3 Responsibility of the new club

According to Article 3 of Annex 4 of the RSPT, edition 2005, it is stipulated that when a player is registered as a professional for the first time, the club for which the player is being registered is responsible for paying training compensation within 30 days of registration to every club for which the player was registered (in accordance with the player's career history as provided for in the player passport) and which has contributed to his training starting from the season in which he had his 12th birthday.[399] Although it is not mentioned in the before-mentioned article whether the "30 days term" also applies to a subsequent transfer, the following paragraph of this Article states that in both cases, the deadline for payment of training compensation is 30 days following the registration of the professional with the new association.[400] It must be noted, as the DRC repeatedly points out and as we will see later on, that it is the responsibility of the new club to calculate the training compensation and the way in which it should be distributed to the clubs for which the player previously played. In that respect, the player passport of the player concerned plays a key role in establishing the entitlement of the clubs to training compensation. The player passport is the document which contains all the relevant details of the player; more specifically, it lists the clubs for which the player has been registered since the season of his 12th birthday up to and including the former club. It is always the registering association which is obliged to provide the club for which the player is registered with this so-called player passport of the player concerned.[401]

In line with the above, it is furthermore important to know that if a link between the professional and any of the clubs that trained him cannot be established, or if those clubs do not make themselves known within 18 months of the player's first registration as a professional, the training compensation will be paid to the association of the country where the professional was trained and will be, according to Article 3 Paragraph 3 of Annex 4 of the RSTP, edition 2005, earmarked for youth football development programmes in the association in question. In that respect it must be noted that the "18 months term" is not equal to the prescription term of two years.

For example, if a club makes itself known in the 19th month after the registration of its former player, it is not too late to be entitled to the training compensation. Following the FIFA Commentary, if an association claims training compensation and an entitled club then appears, the claim of the association will obviously lose all effect. However, in the

---

[398] RSTP, edition 2005, Annex 4, Art. 3 Para. 1 (last sentence). Circular 826 dated 31 October 2002.

[399] Id., Annex 4, Art. 3 Para. 1.

[400] Idem.

[401] RSTP, edition 2005, Art. 7. It is furthermore stipulated that if a birthday falls between seasons, the player will be listed in the player passport for the club for which he was registered in the season following his birthday.

previous edition 2001 of the RSTP, this 18 months term was equal to the prescribed term of 24 months. FIFA modified this Article to prevent a situation where the association had to wait for 24 months, whereupon their claim would be prescript. They now therefore have six months to make themselves known and if, as mentioned above, a club makes itself known after the 18th month after the registration of its former player, the claim of the club will then get priority above the right of the association after all. Finally, it can be noted with respect to this issue that if the association has irrefutable evidence that one of its affiliated clubs which is entitled to training compensation no longer exists (for example as a result of bankruptcy), then the new club should pay training compensation immediately to the association and not only after the 18th month.

In the earlier mentioned decision of the CAS in the case between *Blackpool F.C.* and the Dutch first division club *Top Oss*, the CAS decided that the lack of information provided by the parties involved in the transfer of the player did not release the club from its obligation under the terms of the regulations.[402] On 19 May 2005, Top Oss initiated proceedings with the DRC to order Blackpool to pay to Top Oss the amount of EUR 135,000 as training compensation pursuant to Chapter VII of the FIFA RSTP (edition 2001). The DRC initially concluded that Top Oss was entitled to receive training compensation for the training it provided to the player notably on the following grounds. Regarding the club Top Oss' position, the DRC acknowledged that Top Oss maintains that it was not duly informed by either the player, the agent involved in the transfer, Blackpool, the Netherlands Football Association or the Football Association. The DRC also took note of Top Oss' objection that it had only requested the ITC for the player in order to assess the player's ability. The Chamber duly considered all documentation provided by both parties and unanimously concluded that the argumentation of Top Oss could not be upheld since the relevant provisions in the regulations state that it is the sole responsibility of the new club to calculate the amount of compensation for training and education. In this respect, the DRC emphasised that the player's new club will find out how the training compensation has to be distributed by taking into consideration the player's career history. For this purpose, the new club will, if necessary, request the assistance of the player in order to fulfil this obligation. The DRC pointed out that the lack of information provided by the parties involved in the transfer of the player does not release the club from its obligation under the terms of the regulations.

The DRC awarded training compensation based upon the number of years it considered the player to have been registered with Top Oss and the parameters and indicative amounts laid out in FIFA Circular letter no. 826 dated 31 October 2002 according to which Top Oss falls into category 3 and Blackpool falls in category 2. Consequently, the DRC decided on 23 November 2005 that the claim lodged by Top Oss should be accepted and that Blackpool should pay the total amount of EUR 135,000 to Top Oss within 30 days following the date of the communication of the present decision. In appeal, the CAS decided that Top Oss was entitled to training compensation as stipulated by Chapter VII of the FIFA Regulations. Based on the above, the CAS finally concluded and decided that the training compensation to be awarded to Top Oss was EUR 90,000.[403]

---

402 CAS 2006/A/1027, *Blackpool F.C.* v. *Club Top Oss*.

403 CAS 2003/O/486, *Fulham FC* v. *Olympic Lyonnais*.

11.4 Loan of the player

In a decision of the DRC of 24 March 2004, the DRC decided that no training compensation will be due to the club for the period of time that the player was transferred on a loan basis to another club. In fact, only the club where the player played on a loan basis was entitled to receive training compensation.[404] In the present case, the Chamber outlined that the training period to take into consideration started in the sporting season 1992/93 when the player was 12, until the sporting season 2000/01, at the age of 21. According to the DRC, it was therefore undisputed that the Brazilian club was entitled to receive compensation for the training and education of the player for the ten sporting seasons that the player spent with the Brazilian club. The DRC finally concluded that the Italian club should pay to the Brazilian club the total amount of EUR 570,000, corresponding to EUR 10,000 per season, for the three seasons the player concerned spent with the Brazilian club, plus EUR 90,000 per year of training for the remaining six seasons.[405]

In another decision of the DRC of 23 March 2006, the DRC decided that also the club for which the player played on a loan basis is entitled to receive training compensation.[406] In this case a player who was born on 14 March 1982 was registered with an Italian club during the season 2002/03. During the season 2003/04, the player was registered with the Belgian club. On 6 December 2004, the Italian club turned to FIFA and claimed an amount of EUR 60,000 plus interest as compensation for the training of the player concerned. The player had been registered from 1 July 2002 until 30 June 2003 at the age of 20 and 21 for the Italian club on a loan basis after having been transferred from A.C. Milan. The DRC noted that the player went on loan for the duration of the season 2002/03 to the Italian club, while he was under contract with another club. After the end of the relevant loan period, the player in question duly returned to this club, from which he was transferred to the Belgian club. The Italian club now claimed that it was entitled to receive compensation for the training and education of the player in question for the period of time that he was registered with the club, namely from 1 July 2002 until 30 June 2003, to the amount of EUR 60,000 plus interest. The DRC first had to answer the preliminary question as to whether clubs that accepted a player on loan basis are entitled to receive compensation for the training and education of young players in accordance with Chapter VII of the Regulations and Chapter III of the Regulations governing the Application of the RSTP as well as FIFA Circular no. 826 dated 31 October 2002. The DRC decided that, according to the jurisprudence established by the Chamber, a club is only entitled to receive training compensation for the period of time during which a player was actually trained by the club claiming payment of such compensation. Therefore, the claim for training compensation put forward by the club that had transferred the player on loan basis to another club was dismissed in relation to the period of time that the player in question was registered on a loan basis with another club. However, the claim for training compensation dealt with in the present matter was put forward by a club that accepted the player on a loan basis. The DRC finally concluded that the nature of a player's registration, i.e., on a definite or on a temporary basis, with a club claiming training compensation is in fact irrelevant with respect to the question as to whether such a claimant club would be entitled to receive

[404] DRC 24 March 2004, no. 34368.
[405] DRC 24 March 2004, no. 34432.
[406] DRC 23 March 2006, no. 36928.

training compensation for the period of time that the player was effectively trained by that club. As a result, the DRC concluded that the Italian club was entitled to receive training compensation in the amount of EUR 60,000 within 30 days.

Following the given decisions, the DRC is of the opinion that the club where the player played on a loan basis is entitled to receive training compensation. The nature of a player's registration, i.e., on a definite or on a temporary basis with a club claiming training compensation is irrelevant with respect to the question as to whether such a claimant club is entitled to receive training compensation for the period of time that the player was effectively trained by that club. In other words, it comes down to the point where the player actually played.

11.5 When is training compensation not due?

11.5.1 *Outside EU/EEA*

Besides the fact that training compensation is not due if the transfer takes place between one national association, as a result of which the national regulations of the association concerned are applicable, Annex 4 of the RSTP, edition 2005, provides us with the following. Training compensation is not due if the former club terminates the player's contract without just cause (without the right of the previous clubs).[407] According to the FIFA Commentary, this club should not be rewarded for this behaviour. Furthermore, training compensation is not due if the player is transferred to a category 4 club and finally, training compensation is not due in the event that a professional reacquires amateur status on being transferred. In this respect it is important to know that in the current Article of the RSTP, edition 2005, it is not stated as clearly as it was stipulated in the RSTP, edition 2001, but if an amateur player re-registers as a professional within 30 months of being reinstated as an amateur, then training compensation will be due after all.[408] The edition 2005 of the RSTP is not as clear at this point as the former edition 2001.[409]

11.5.2 *Within EU/EEA*

The above exceptions apply to a matter which concerns an international transfer of a player outside the EU/EEA. However, within the EU/EEA there is an extra exception. If the former club does not offer the player a contract, no training compensation is payable unless the former club can justify that it is entitled to such compensation.[410] Moreover, in line with the before-mentioned, it is a prerequisite that the former club then offers the player a contract in writing via registered mail at least 60 days before the expiry of his current contract.[411] It is important that this offer is at least of an equivalent value to the current contract. In the event that the former club does not offer the player a contract and

[407] If the player breaches his employment contract without just cause, the new club obviously has to pay compensation. FIFA Commentary, explanation Art. 1 Para. 1, p. 112.

[408] According to Art. 3 Para. 2 of the RSTP, edition 2005, a new club will pay training compensation in accordance with Art. 20 of the RSTP, edition 2005.

[409] Art. 5 Para. 3 under a of the Regulations Governing the Application of the Regulations for the Status and Transfer of Player, edition 2001.

[410] According to Circular 769 dated 24 August 2001.

[411] RSTP, edition 2005, Annex 4, Art. 6 Para. 3.

it did not fulfil the before-mentioned requirement with respect to the "60 days term", this leads to the situation where the former club with which the player was registered loses its entitlement to training compensation.[412]

If the former club did not offer the player a contract, it can still be entitled to training compensation, as we have seen before, if the former club can justify that it is entitled to such compensation. However, the justification may be very difficult to prove and limited to extraordinary circumstances to decide on the matter at hand. According to the FIFA Commentary, if a club descends to a lower division in which it is not entitled to register players as professionals, this club will not be in a position to offer an employment contract to young players. As a consequence thereof, it will then not forfeit its entitlement to claim training compensation from the player's new club.[413]

In a decision of the DRC of 11 November 2004, a Norwegian club was of the opinion that it did not owe any training compensation to a Swedish club as the player was allegedly not offered any new contract by the Swedish club, either verbally or in writing, before the expiry of his employment contract.[414] With respect to the Swedish club's claim, the DRC referred to the principle that for transfers which take place within the EU/EEA, the fact that the training club does not offer a player a contract will be taken into account when determining the training compensation payable by the new club. The DRC took into consideration the contents of the FIFA Circular letter no. 769 dated 24 August 2001, which under point 2a, specified that the former club of a player younger than 23, whose contract has come to an end and who has not received a new contract from his club, which is equivalent in remuneration to his previous contract, will be deemed not to have offered a contract to the latter for purposes of calculating training compensation. The Circular letter no. 769 furthermore stated that, as a matter of principle, the player's training club will not be entitled to receive training compensation unless the training club can demonstrate to the DRC that it was entitled to compensation. The DRC finally decided that despite its claim for training compensation, the Swedish club had not offered any documentary evidence that would prove an offer to the player concerned, which needed to correspond to the remuneration of his previous contract with the club. Therefore, the claim of the Swedish club could not be accepted according to the DRC.

In a decision of the DRC of 21 February 2006, the DRC decided that the real reason why the player did not sign an employment contract with his training club, but with the other club, must be seen in the fact that the club did not show enough interest in the player's services as a professional.[415] In this case, the DRC refers to the matter of principle that the player's training club will not be entitled to receive training compensation unless it can demonstrate to the Chamber that it is entitled to compensation in derogation of this principle. The DRC emphasised that the club that claimed to have compensation, by putting an end to the contractual engagement with the player, even though it wanted to enable the player to transfer to another club, failed to meet the requirements of the RSTP rules. According to the DRC, a club willing to transfer a young player to another club is not actually seeking to retain the services of the player and has thus foregone its entitlement to training compensation.

---

412 RSTP, edition 2005, Annex 4, Art. 6 Para. 3.
413 FIFA Commentary, explanation Art. 6 under footnote 176, p. 125.
414 DRC 9 November 2004, no. 114549.
415 DRC 21 February 2006, no. 26595.

In a decision of the DRC of 27 April 2006, the DRC was of the opinion that it could not back the claimant's argument that annex 4 Article 6 Paragraph 3 of the RSTP, edition 2005, was exclusively applicable if the player was already a professional.[416] In fact, according to the DRC, the first sentence of the cited provision clearly stipulated that no training compensation must be paid to the player's former club if the said club does not offer the player a contract, unless the former club can justify its entitlement to such compensation. No reference to a new contract is thus made in this general introduction to the relevant provision. The DRC emphasised and concluded that it is the spirit and purpose of the said provision to penalise clubs which are obviously not interested in the player's services as a professional, no matter whether the club would have to offer the player an employment contract for the first time or a renewal due to the normal expiry of an already existing contract. The former club that was of the opinion that it was entitled to receive training compensation had to make a suitable offer to the player in a written form prior to the beginning of the summer holidays. The DRC concluded that the real reason why the player did not sign an employment contract with his training club, but with the other club, must be seen in the fact that the club did not show enough interest in the player's services as a professional. With such behaviour, following the DRC, the claimant forfeited its entitlement to receive training compensation from the new club.

According to the above decisions, if the former club does not offer the player a contract within the EU/EEA, no training compensation is payable by the new club, unless the former club can justify that it is entitled to such compensation. Such justification is difficult to prove, as we have seen following the decisions of the DRC. If the club does not show enough interest in the player's services as a professional, the consequence of such behaviour is that the claimant forfeits its entitlement to receive training compensation from the new club of its former player. To avoid any misunderstanding and for the sake of clarity, if parties mutually agree to terminate the player's employment contract, the former club obviously cannot justify and prove its entitlement to receive training compensation, since this does not comply with the background of the mentioned provision. It must then be presumed that the club is not sincerely interested in the player.

11.6 **Waiver of rights**

In a decision of the DRC of 9 November 2004, the Chamber decided that despite the existence of a document in which parties agree that no transfer fee would be due in the case of a future acquisition of the player's federative rights after 30 June 2002 and in which no reference is made to the right of the former club to claim the relevant training compensation, the former club is still entitled to receive training compensation.[417] The player concerned was born in 1982 and registered for a club during three sporting seasons, from the 1999/2000 season until the 2001/02 season, between the age of 17 and 20. On 13 August 2002, he signed a non-amateur contract with another club. His former club then claimed training compensation from his new club. The latter is of the opinion that it does not have to pay training compensation for the player concerned to the former club as the latter signed confirmation on 21 June 2002 to the attention of the representative of the player with the following wording:

---

[416] DRC 27 April 2006, no. 461185.
[417] DRC 9 November 2004, no. 114461.

> "We hereby confirm that the contract of … (the player) expires on 30 June 2002 and that no more transfer fees exist."

The former club was of the opinion that because of this confirmation, it did not waive its right for training compensation for the player concerned in accordance to the FIFA regulations, but that it only confirmed that no transfer sum had to be paid in respect to the expiry of the employment contract. The DRC finally concluded that that such document only mentioned that no transfer fee would be due in the case of a future acquisition of the player's federative rights and underlined that no reference was made to the right of the former club to claim training compensation.

However, in the following decision of the DRC of 4 February 2005, we will see that parties are entitled to exclude their entitlement for training compensation by stipulating this in an agreement.[418] The player concerned was born on 22 September 1984 and was registered as an amateur player with a German club for three seasons from 19 July 2000 until 29 June 2003. The German club claimed payment of an amount of money relating to training compensation. The new Turkish club was of the opinion that it only had to pay training compensation to the relevant clubs and submitted a document signed by the German club on 3 January 2004. The DRC concluded that although it is undisputed that the player had been trained and educated at the German club, the document dated 3 January 2004 that had been presented by the Turkish club in its defence, must be seen as a waiver. By having signed such document, which refers to the player in question and states, *inter alia*, that the German club will have no claims against the Turkish club, the German club has waived its right to claim from the new club payment of an amount of money relating to training compensation. However, it must be noted that in this decision, FIFA invited the German club to give its opinion on the relevant document, but the club did not present any comments on the before-mentioned documents.

In a decision of the DRC of 2 November 2005, the Chamber concluded that only the club which is officially entitled to receive training compensation can waive its right to training compensation. This cannot be excluded by an agreement between the player and the new club.[419] The player, who was born on 12 May 1985, was registered with a club as non-amateur for the 2003/04 season between the ages of 18 and 19. In August 2004, the player was registered with another club. His former club now claimed training compensation, but the new club informed FIFA that the player and his agent had given notice to the former club, following which the two parties, the player and the new club had agreed that the player would give up his financial demands against the former club and in return the latter would not ask for any transfer or training compensation. In this respect, the new club provided a player's statement dated 1 February 2005, according to which he affirmed that he had given notice to the former club that he would give up his financial demands and in return the former club would neither ask for any transfer or training compensation nor raise financial demands against him. As a result, the new club was of the opinion that it did not owe any training compensation to the former club. The DRC concluded that the argumentation of the new club could not be upheld since any possible financial settlement

---

418 DRC 4 February 2005, no. 25528a.

419 DRC 2 November 2005, no. 115377. For the sake of good order, the DRC emphasised in this decision that Art. 5 Para. 5 of the FIFA Regulations governing the Application of the FIFA Regulations had not to be taken into consideration in the present matter, since the case at hand did not involve two clubs in the EU/EEA area.

concluded between the former club and the player cannot in any sense abolish the former club's entitlement to receive training compensation. As a consequence thereof, the DRC concluded that the former club was still entitled to receive training compensation for the training and education of the player concerned.

In a decision of the DRC of 18 August 2006, the Chamber concluded that an agreement between the new club and the player does not have legal effect with respect to the entitlement of the former club(s) to claim training compensation.[420] The player concerned was born on 14 January 1983 and was registered for his club from 22 October 1999 until 16 August 2001, the seasons of his 17th to his 18th birthday. In July/August 2005 the player signed his first professional contract with a club from another country, for which he was registered on 30 August 2005. The player also concluded a covenant with his new club by which he completely accepted responsibility for possible claims related to transfer payments or training compensation. The covenant concerned contained a clause which stipulated that neither the player nor the training clubs were entitled to demand payment from the new club. Furthermore, it was agreed by the two parties concerned that no legal action would be taken against the new club. However, on 5 December 2005 his former club lodged a claim with FIFA requesting the payment of training compensation. During this procedure, the new club stated that it was not responsible for paying the requested training compensation on the basis of the before-mentioned covenant. The DRC unanimously concluded that the argumentation of the new club could not be supported since the covenant had been concluded between the new club and the player concerned and thus, according to the DRC, it could not in any sense deprive the former club of its entitlement to receive training compensation.

In another decision of the DRC of 26 October 2006, the DRC concluded and emphasised that only the former club could waive its rights to claim an amount for training compensation.[421] The DRC had to examine a written confirmation, dated 30 January 2004 and signed by the president of the former club at that time, according to which this club waived its right to receive any "financial compensation" from the new club for the player concerned. The DRC took note of the statement of the former club, according to which the waiver only referred to its alleged right to receive transfer compensation for the player in question, whereas the new club was of the opinion that the former club had also renounced any right to receive training compensation. The DRC proceeded to deliberate whether the term financial compensation contained in the waiver of the former club also referred to its possible right to receive training compensation. The Chamber stressed that the notion financial compensation was a general and unspecific term which, in principle, could not be understood to only include transfer compensation. Therefore, the DRC considered amongst others that the term rather encompassed any kind of monetary compensation which, in the case at hand, the former club might have requested from the new club in connection with the player, including training compensation. The DRC finally had to assume that the former club's waiver dated 30 January 2004 also referred to its possible right to receive training compensation.

According to the above decisions, the DRC is of the opinion that only the club which is officially entitled to receive training compensation can waive its right to training compen-

---

[420] DRC 18 August 2006, no. 86130B. It must be noticed that the player did not sign the covenant. However, irrespective of this, the DRC decided that the former club had not waived its right.

[421] DRC 26 October 2006, no. 106574.

sation. The DRC is clear, since any possible financial settlements concluded between the former club or the new club and the player cannot in any sense abolish the former club's entitlement to receive training compensation.

11.7 Calculation of the amount

11.7.1 *Outside EU/EEA*

In order to calculate the compensation due for training and education costs, all associations are instructed by FIFA to divide their clubs into a maximum of four categories in accordance with the clubs' financial investment in training players. The training costs are set for each category and correspond to the amount needed to train one player for one year multiplied by an average so-called "player factor", which is the ratio between the number of players who need to be trained to produce one professional player. The training costs, which are established on a confederation basis for each category, as well as the categorisation of clubs for each association, are published on the official website of FIFA.[422] Through Circular 959, FIFA provided its members (the associations) with a list (see below) of the training costs determined on a confederation basis for each category.[423]

Confederation	Category I	Category II	Category III	Category IV
AFC		USD 40,000	USD 10,000	USD 2,000
CAF		USD 30,000	USD 10,000	USD 2,000
CONCACAF		USD 40,000	USD 10,000	USD 2,000
CONMEBOL	USD 50,000	USD 30,000	USD 10,000	USD 2,000
OFC		USD 30,000	USD 10,000	USD 2,000
UEFA	EUR 90,000	USD 60,000	EUR 30,000	EUR 10,000

To prevent the situation where training compensation for very young players is set at unreasonably high levels, the training costs for players for the seasons between their 12th and 15th birthday (in total four seasons) will be based, according to Article 5 Paragraph 3 of Annex 4 of the RSTP, edition 2005, on the training and education costs for category 4 clubs. As mentioned, FIFA tries to avoid compensation for very young players being set at an unfairly high level, according to the FIFA Commentary.

With respect to the calculation of the amount, it is first important to determine which edition of the RSTP is applicable to the matter at hand, since both editions change in content with respect to the calculation of the amount of training compensation. Therefore, before the DRC can adjudicate with respect to the calculation of the training compensation concerned, it must first establish which version of the RSTP, edition 2001 or edition 2005, is applicable.

---

[422] RSTP, edition 2005, Annex 4, Art. 4 Para. 2. The training costs and the categorisation of clubs are updated at the end of every calendar year.

[423] Circulars 959 and 995a dated 16 March 2005.

11.7.1.1 Edition 2001

According to Article 13 of the RSTP, edition 2001, the calculation of the amount of training compensation will be based on the years between the age of 12 and the age when it is established that the player actually completed his training. When a player signs his first contract as a non-amateur, or when a player moves during the course of a contract before reaching the age of 23, the amount of compensation will be limited to compensation for training and education, calculated in accordance with the parameters set out in the Application Regulations and FIFA Circular 769. According to these regulations and the mentioned circular, for transfers outside the EU/EEA, compensation for training is based on the training and education costs of the country of the new club, but taking into account the category of the club which has effectively trained him.

In a decision of the DRC of 26 November 2004, the Chamber confirmed the beforementioned calculation.[424] The player concerned was born on 21 November 1983 and was registered as a non-amateur player with the German (category 4) club from 1 July 2002 until 28 August 2003. On 29 August 2003, he made a transfer and signed a contract with a Turkish (category 3) club. The German club claimed the amount of EUR 10,000 as compensation for the player's training. The DRC decided that it could be established that the player had been trained and developed by the German club during one sports season, i.e., the 2002/03 season, from the age of 18 up to 19. In that respect the DRC deliberated that the amount due by the Turkish club had to be calculated in accordance with the parameters provided by Circular letter 826 dated 31 October 2002, i.e., with an amount corresponding to EUR 10,000 per year of training (corresponding to the club category 4 of X). Therefore, for the German club as a category 4 club, the amount of training compensation was obtained by multiplying the amount corresponding to the category of the training club for which the player was registered by the number of years of training from 12 to 21 based on the costs of category 4 clubs in Turkey. Finally, the German club was entitled to receive training compensation to a total of EUR 10,000 (1 year × EUR 10,000).

11.7.1.2 Edition 2005

As a general rule, to calculate the training compensation due to a player's former club(s), it is necessary to take the costs that would have been incurred by the new club if it had trained the player itself. Accordingly, the first time a player registers as a professional, the training compensation payable is calculated by taking the training costs of the new club multiplied by the number of years of training in principle from the season of the player's 12th birthday to the season of his 21st birthday. In that respect, it is important to know that the amount payable is calculated on a pro rata basis according to the period of training that the player spent with each club.[425] In the case of a subsequent transfer, training compensation is calculated based on the training costs of the new club multiplied by the number of years of training with the former club.[426] Also at this point, the amount payable is calculated on a pro rata basis according to the period of training that the player spent with each

[424] DRC 26 November 2004, no. 114527.

[425] RSTP, edition 2005, Annex 4, Art. 3 Para. 1, CAS 2004/A/560. FIFA Commentary, explanation Art. 3 Para. 1 under footnote 152, p. 115.

[426] RSTP, edition 2005, Annex 4, Art. 5 Para. 2.

club. As mentioned earlier, training compensation will only be due to the former club. In other words and in line with the above, compensation for training following the edition 2005 of the RSTP, the calculation of the training compensation is based on the training and education costs as well as the category of the country of the new club.

In the earlier mentioned decision of the DRC of 18 August 2006, the Chamber not only concluded that an agreement between the new club and the player does not have any legal effect with respect to the entitlement of the former club(s) to claim training compensation, it also calculated the amount of compensation following the standards as laid down in the RSTP, edition 2005.[427] As mentioned above, the player concerned was born on 14 January 1983 and was registered for his club from 22 October 1999 until 16 August 2001, the seasons of his 17th to his 18th birthday. In July/August 2005, the player signed his first professional contract with a Turkish club, for which he was registered on 30 August 2005. For the sake of good order, the DRC stressed in this respect that Article 6 of annex 4 of the RSTP, edition 2005, concerning special provisions for the EU/EEA, did not apply to the present matter since the case at hand does not involve two clubs inside the territory of the EU/EEA. The DRC stated that in accordance with Article 5 Paragraph 1 of Annex 4 of the RSTP, edition 2005, as a general rule, in order to calculate the training compensation due to the player's former club(s), it is necessary to take the costs that would have been incurred by the new club if it had trained the player itself. For the sake of clarity, the DRC pointed out that the first time a player registers as a professional, the training compensation payable is calculated by taking the training costs of the new club multiplied by the number of years of training in principle from the season of the player's 12th birthday to the season of his 21st birthday. The Turkish club belonged to category IV and, therefore, the corresponding indicative amount for a category IV club belonging to the UEFA is EUR 10,000. This indicative amount mentioned must then be multiplied by the number of years that the player was trained and educated by the former club. The DRC concluded that the total relevant period of time to be taken into consideration corresponded to 1 season and 9 months. Finally, the DRC concluded that the new club had to pay the amount of EUR 17,500 to the former club.

11.7.2 *Within EU/EEA*

Within the EU/EEA there are special provisions relating to training compensation. Not only is there an extra prerequisite in relation to the fact when training compensation is not due to the former club (namely when the former club does not offer the player an employment contract), but also with respect to the amount of compensation, the rules within the EU/EEA differ from before-mentioned rules at international level. However, for the sake of clarity, both editions of the RSTP, edition 2001 and 2005, are equal. For players moving from one association to another association inside the territory of the EU/EEA, the amount of training compensation payable will be established based on the following. If the player moves from a lower to a higher category club, the calculation will be based on the average of the training costs of the two clubs. For example, if a player moves from a category 3 club (EUR 30,000 training costs per year) to a category 1 club (EUR 90,000 training costs per year), the average of cost of training per year will then come down to EUR 60,000. If

[427] DRC 18 August 2006, no. 86130B.

the player moves from a higher to a lower category, the calculation will be based on the training costs of the lower category club.[428]

11.7.3 *Completion of the training*

According to the first Article of Annex 4 of the RSTP, edition 2005, a player's training takes place between the ages of 12 and 23 for training incurred up to the age of 21, unless it is evident that a player has already terminated his training period before the age of 21. In other words and as discussed earlier, training compensation will be payable until the end of the season in which the player reaches the age of 23, although the calculation of the amount will be based on the years between 12 and the age when it is established that the player actually completed his training.[429]

In a decision of the DRC of 22 July 2004, the Chamber considered that as established in Article 13 and Circular letter no. 826 (dated 31 October 2002), training compensation is payable up to the age of 23 for a player's training incurred between the ages of 12 and 21.[430] Notwithstanding the above, due note was taken of the new club's defence according to which the player finished his actual training period by the time he had started the 2001/02 season with his former club. Therefore, the new club was of the opinion that a shorter education period took place as a result of which the training period of the player was completed in a sporting season before that of his 21st birthday. The new club submitted that in the playing season 200/01, the player was fielded on a regular basis (15 times) in the club's "A" team, scoring 3 goals. At that time he had already spent many years as a non-amateur player from an early age and could thus be considered to have been a particularly successful player. The new club's arguments in this respect were accepted by the members of the Chamber. Based on the above, the DRC concluded its deliberations by deciding that in the present case, the 2001/02 training period would not be taken into consideration for calculation purposes. This translated into a reduction of EUR 90,000 over the total amount of EUR 550,000 resulting in a final sum of EUR 460,000 due.

In a decision of the DRC of 9 November 2004, the Chamber decided with respect to the provision that training compensation was owed to the former club of the player unless it was evident that the player had terminated his training period before the age of 21.[431] The DRC remarked in this respect that many clubs and players have erroneously invoked this provision, in cases where it cannot be said that a player had completed his training before the age of 21. The DRC wished to reiterate that it was the understanding of the legislator that such an exemption would only apply in cases of unusually talented young players, which are rarely encountered. This tends to be the case with young players, who at the age of 17 or 18 are globally known for their exceptional talents, who are regulars at club and

[428] During the period 2002–2006 there are no decisions of the DRC published on the FIFA website with respect to training compensation in which the edition 2005 of the RSTP is applicable in relation to a transfer within the EU/EEA. So far there is only one decision of the DRC published on the official website of FIFA, which is related to this issue, but lies without the scope of this book. DRC 27 April 2007, no. 47585.

[429] Following the FIFA Commentary, explanation Art. 1 Para. 1, under footnote 149, p. 112, the CAS decided several times with respect to this issue. CAS 2003/O/527. See also CAS 2004/A/560; FIFA Commentary, explanation Art. 3 Para. 1 under footnote 153, p. 115. See also CAS 2004/A/594.

[430] DRC 22 July 2004, no. 74353, DRC 2 July 2004, no. 74323 (*contrat aspirant*), DRC 22 July 2004, no. 7472 B.

[431] DRC 9 November 2004, no. 114556.

national level and who are frequently the focus of transfer arrangements to the world's top clubs. In such cases, according to the DRC, it would seem rather misplaced to discuss training compensation for these players, who at the age of 17 or 18 are considered absolute world class. The DRC was of the opinion that there were only a very few players with such an exceptional status that they had completed their training and would have gained all the relevant experience before reaching the age of 21. The DRC decided in this case that although the player could display considerable experience at first team level, the Chamber underlined that it is unquestionable that the player was still benefiting from instruction being offered and experience gained in performing for the club. The player only spent one year at the club, i.e., from the age of 18 to 19, and therefore the members of the Chamber were of the unanimous opinion that the club was entitled to receive compensation for the instruction received during this year. The club was entitled to receive training compensation in the amount of EUR 60,000.

In a decision of the DRC of 21 February 2006, the Chamber decided regarding the completion of training of a player.[432] This concerned the question as to whether the player concerned had already completed his training with the former club prior to his 21st birthday. The DRC pointed out that the period of training to be taken into account would only be reduced if it was evident that the player had terminated his training period before the age of 21. In this case the main argument of the new club was that the player had played in numerous matches for the senior team of his former club during the last season. The DRC underlined that, in any case, more than just one indication to the possible earlier termination of the training period must exist in order to justify the application of the relevant exception. Finally, the DRC decided that it was not evident that the player had terminated his training before the age of 21.

According to the above decisions, the DRC is of the opinion with respect to the completion of the training and education period, if it is evident that the player has terminated his training period before the age of 21. The DRC is of the opinion that in any case, more than just one indication to the possible earlier termination of the training period must exist in order to justify the application of the exception.

11.8 **Conclusion**

According to Article 20 of the RSTP, edition 2005, we have seen that training compensation must be paid to a player's training clubs in case the player signs his first employment contract as a professional, but also on each transfer of a professional. With respect to both situations however, the player must sign his employment contract or be transferred to another foreign club before the end the season of his 23rd birthday. Contrary to the solidarity mechanism where compensation is only required if the professional is transferred before the end of his contract, training compensation must be paid irrespective of the fact that the transfer takes place during or at the end of the player's contract.

Following numerous decisions of the DRC, the Chamber decides that only the club where the player played on a loan basis is entitled to receive training compensation. The nature of a players' registration, whether on a definite or on a temporary basis with a club claiming training compensation, is not relevant with regard to the question as to whether

---

[432] DRC 21 February 2006, no. 26562.

such claimant club is entitled to receive training compensation for the period of time that the player was effectively trained by them.

Within the EU/EEA, there is an extra requirement with respect to whether training compensation is due. If the former club does not offer the player a contract within the EU/EEA, no training compensation is payable by the new club unless the former club can justify that it is entitled to such compensation. According to the DRC, it is difficult to prove that this justification exists. Following several decisions, the DRC is of the opinion that if the club does not show enough interest in the player's services as a professional, the consequence of such behaviour is that this club forfeits its entitlement to receive training compensation from the new club of its former player. This means that if parties mutually agree to terminate the player's employment contract, the DRC will be of the opinion that the former club obviously cannot justify and prove its entitlement to receive training compensation and the Chamber will decide that such a club is not sincerely interested in the player.

According to several decisions of the DRC, we have seen that parties often try to exclude the right of the former club(s) to receive training compensation. However, the DRC is very clear on this point. Only the club which is officially entitled to receive training compensation may waive its right to training compensation. Any possible financial settlements concluded between the former club or the new club and the player cannot in any sense establish that the former club(s) loses and therefore waives its right to receive training compensation from the new club.

Finally, regarding the completion of the training and education period, the DRC is of the opinion that if it is evident that the player has terminated his training period before the age of 21, the player may have completed his training. However, the DRC explicitly points out that there must be more than one indication regarding the possible termination of the training period to justify the application of the exception.

12. Solidarity contribution

12.1 Introduction

Each time a professional is transferred before the end of his contract, a so-called solidarity contribution is due by the new club to all the clubs for which the player played between the age of 12 and 23.[433] As with the training compensation, the solidarity mechanism stipulates that the former club that provided the education and training of the player is entitled to receive an amount of solidarity contribution in the event that an international transfer of its former player took place during the course of his employment contract. However, there are some significant differences with training compensation. Training compensation is only applicable when a player moves during his contract as well as after the end of his contract (i.e., if he is transfer free). The solidarity mechanism is solely due if the player moves during the course of his contract. Another important difference is that training compensation is due when the transfer or signing of the contract of the player takes place before the age of 23.[434] The applicability of the solidarity mechanism does not depend on

433 RSTP, edition 2005, Art. 21.
434 Circular 769 dated 24 August 2001.

a certain age level of the player.[435] Annex 5 of the RSTP, edition 2005, shows the details regarding the solidarity mechanism.

An important issue in relation to the solidarity mechanism, as well as regarding the system of training compensation, is that the former club which is claiming the solidarity contribution must also deal with the prescription term of two years. In other words, and as we have seen with the training compensation, a former club waives its rights to receive a solidarity contribution if more than two years have elapsed since the event which gave rise to the dispute. One final remark for the sake of clarity is that both the solidarity mechanism and the system of training compensation is obviously only applicable in the case of an international transfer.[436] The DRC and the FIFA regulations are quite explicit as it is a basic principle regarding the solidarity mechanism that it does not apply to national transfers (i.e., domestic transfers), not even in cases where the club claiming the payment of the relevant contribution is affiliated to another association. The main criterion and key element is, and the DRC confirms this following its own established jurisprudence, that solidarity mechanism applies in cases in which the basis of the claim of the club for solidarity contribution is a transfer of a player between two clubs affiliated to another association.[437]

As we will see in the following paragraphs, the DRC explicitly indicates that it is the responsibility of the new club to calculate the amount of the solidarity contribution and to retain and distribute it in accordance with the player's career history as provided in the player passport. In that respect, it is important to mention that if the new club, as stipulated in Article 2 of Annex 5 of the RSPT, edition 2005, does not fulfil its duty to pay the solidarity contribution to the training club(s) within 30 days after the player's registration or, in case of contingent payments, after the date of such payment, it will be held liable by the DRC to pay an interest payment of 5% to the former clubs.

12.2 Responsibility of the new club

12.2.1 *Calculation*

It is not only the responsibility of the new club to pay, retain and distribute the amount, as we will see below, it is firstly the responsibility of the new club to calculate the amount of the solidarity contribution. The solidarity contribution will generally reflect and indicate the number of years the player was registered with the relevant former clubs between the seasons of his 12th and 23rd birthday.

The calculation, as mentioned in Article 1 of Annex 5 of the RSTP, edition 2005, is as follows:

- season of 12th birthday 5% (i.e., 0.25% of total compensation);
- season of 13th birthday 5% (i.e., 0.25% of total compensation);

---

435 "Solidarity contribution" is the contribution to be paid by the new club. The overarch system is called "solidarity mechanism".

436 Unless the association concerned has included a clear clause in its own regulations, acknowledging the obligation to pay a solidarity contribution as a consequence of domestic transfers. FIFA Commentary, explanation Art. 1, p. 128.

437 DRC 21 November 2006, no. 116132. See several decisions of the DRC: DRC 9 November 2004, nos. 114679, 114678c, 114678b, 114678a, 114677b, 114677a, 114663b, 114663a, 114662, 114407, 114342 and 114465.

- season of 14th birthday 5% (i.e., 0.25% of total compensation);
- season of 15th birthday 5% (i.e., 0.25% of total compensation);
- season of 16th birthday 10% (i.e., 0.5% of total compensation);
- season of 17th birthday 10% (i.e., 0.5% of total compensation);
- season of 18th birthday 10% (i.e., 0.5% of total compensation);
- season of 19th birthday 10% (i.e., 0.5% of total compensation);
- season of 20th birthday 10% (i.e., 0.5% of total compensation);
- season of 21st birthday 10% (i.e., 0.5% of total compensation);
- season of 22nd birthday 10% (i.e., 0.5% of total compensation);
- season of 23rd birthday 10% (i.e., 0.5% of total compensation).[438]

In a decision of the DRC of 21 February 2006, the Chamber had to decide regarding the calculation of the amount.[439] A player who was born on 17 September 1977 was registered with a club from 10 July 1997 until 16 December 1998. The DRC underlined that the new club to which a player is transferred during the course of an employment contract with his previous club, is responsible for the distribution of 5% of the compensation payable to the player's former club to the former club(s) involved in the training and education of the player between the ages of 12 and 23. In the case at hand, the transfer compensation was of the amount of USD 1,800,000. The DRC outlined that the period to be taken into consideration is related to the player's age of 19-20, i.e., the 1997-1998 season, until the player's age of 20-21, i.e., the 1998-1999 season, during which the player was registered until 16 December 1998. The DRC finally concluded that 15% of the 5% solidarity contribution should be apportioned to the former club acting in this procedure as claimant. Now that the Chamber had ascertained that the amount agreed upon by and between the two clubs for the transfer of the player was USD 1,800,000, 15% of the 5% solidarity contribution was USD 13,500. The DRC concluded that the new club was liable to pay the amount of USD 13,500 as solidarity contribution to the former club.

In line with the above, it is important to know that the amount will be calculated pro rata by the new club if the player played less than one year with that former club.[440]

In a decision of the DRC of 28 September 2006, the DRC had to decide with respect to the amount of solidarity contribution to be paid by the new club to the former club for which the player played less than one year.[441] The Chamber referred to Article 1 of Annex 5 of the RSTP, edition 2005, which took into consideration the number of years, calculated pro rata if less than one year, that the player was registered with the club(s) involved in his training and education between the seasons of his 12th and 23rd birthdays. The DRC concluded that the calculation of the solidarity contribution should be made on a pro rata basis of the season of the player's 23rd birthday taking into consideration the registration period as from 22 April 1996 until 6 August 1996. The DRC finally concluded that 2.5% of the 5% solidarity contribution would be apportioned to former club. The amount agreed by and between the two clubs for the transfer of the player was EUR 3,500,000. Therefore, 2.5% of the 5% solidarity contribution was of the amount of EUR 4,375. The DRC finally

---

438 RSTP, edition 2005, Art. 1.

439 DRC 21 February 2006, no. 26866B.

440 RSTP, edition 2005, Art. 1.

441 DRC 28 September 2006, no. 961202B.

decided that the new club was liable to pay an amount of EUR 4,375 as solidarity contribution.

12.2.2 *Distribution*

It is not only the responsibility of the new club to calculate the amount of the solidarity contribution but also to retain and distribute it in accordance with the player's career history as provided in his player passport. We will see that the player passport plays an important role for the club in the allocation of compensation to former clubs. According to Article 1 of Annex 5 of the RSTP, edition 2005, 5% of any compensation paid to the former club should be deducted from the total amount of the transfer compensation and distributed by the new club as a solidarity contribution to the clubs involved in his training and education over the years.[442] The 5% will finally be deducted from the total amount of compensation with the exception of training compensation.[443] In that respect it is important to know that if the player is younger than 23 and he transfers during the term of his contract and a solidarity contribution is payable to his former clubs, the total deduction from the transfer compensation will be less than 5%. For every year that the player is younger than 23, 0.5% will be deducted from 5%.[444]

As we will see in decisions of the DRC, according to Article 2 of Annex 5 of the RSPT, edition 2005, the new club is obliged to pay the solidarity contribution to the training club(s) no later than 30 days after the player's registration, after the date of such payment. Prior to the expiry of this 30-day time limit, training clubs have no legal interest in starting legal action. In other words, the DRC underlines that training clubs may not start legal proceedings relating to the amount due as solidarity contribution in connection with the training and education of a player earlier than 31 days after the player's registration for the new club.[445]

If the player passport is incomplete, it is furthermore very important that the player helps the new club fulfil this obligation by providing his new club with all the relevant documentation.[446] As we have seen earlier, the player passport is the document which contains all the relevant details pertaining to the player; more specifically, it shows which clubs the player has been registered with since the season of his 12th birthday up to and including the former club.

Despite the fact that the player passport plays an important role in allocating the former clubs for the new club, it is good to be aware of the fact that the risk of incompleteness of such a player passport, may be borne by the former club who claims for its part of the solidarity contribution. In the before-mentioned decision of the DRC of 28 September 2006, the player passport was incomplete.[447] According to the player passport provided by the football federation concerned, the player in question was formerly registered with the club, who claimed for solidarity contribution, on loan from 22 April 1996 until 6 August

[442] If the new club paid the entire amount of compensation to the former club without having deducted the 5% solidarity contribution, the claim for recovering the amount paid in excess must be lodged with the PSC (Art. 22. sub e RSTP, edition 2005). FIFA Commentary, edition 2005, explanation Art. 24, under footnote 108, p. 73.

[443] RSTP, edition 2005, Annex 5, Art. 1.

[444] FIFA Commentary, explanation Art. 10 Para. 1, p. 129.

[445] DRC 17 August 2006, no. 861152.

[446] RSPT, edition 2005, Art. 2 Para. 2 Annex 5.

[447] DRC 28 September 2006, no. 961202B.

1996. The DRC noted that as regards the player's registration period with the former club, there was a discrepancy between the statement of this former club and the player passport presented by the football federation of the player concerned. The former club had failed to present documentary evidence in support of its allegation that the player had remained registered with the former club until 31 December 1996. Therefore, the Chamber concurred that the relevant registration period must be established on the basis of the documentary evidence presented by the football federation, in other words the player passport. The DRC finally pointed out that such player passport commonly constitutes the main documentary evidence pertaining to the period of a player's registration with a club.

As well as with training compensation, it is important that no link between the professional and any of the clubs that trained him can be established within 18 months, the solidarity contribution will then be paid to the association of the country where the professional was formerly trained. This solidarity contribution will then be earmarked for youth football development programmes in the association in question.[448] The new club, according to the FIFA Commentary, must contact the player's former clubs to acquire the bank details required to pay the solidarity contribution to which the former clubs in question are entitled.[449]

It is a golden rule following numerous decisions of the DRC that it is only the new club that is entitled to distribute the amount of solidarity compensation to the relevant former clubs of the player. This obligation cannot be transferred to another club.

In a decision of the DRC of 22 July 2004, a player played for a club Z during the period from 1993 until 2000, from the age of 10 until the age of 17.[450] In the year 2000, the player left to club A and in July 2003 the player made a transfer from club A to club B. The latter club had to pay a transfer compensation of EUR 6,000,000.

Clause 4 of the transfer agreement between club A and club B stipulated the following:

> "As to the obligation to pay amounts based on the FIFA Regulations for the Status and Transfer of Players in relation to transfer only, it has been agreed between the parties that such amounts will be for the account of club A."

The DRC finally had to decide with respect to the validity of this clause and whether it was possible to transfer the obligation to pay solidarity contribution to another club, such as the selling party. The Chamber underlined that the new club frequently fails to retain the 5% solidarity contribution payable to the clubs involved in the player's training and education. In such cases, the club that mistakenly paid 100% of the transfer fee agreed with the player's former club will consider itself in the clear regarding the solidarity contribution and will ask the clubs entitled to the solidarity contribution to revert to the former club of the player instead. The Chamber emphasised that it is the task of the new club to calculate the amount owed as a solidarity contribution to the clubs involved in the player's

---

[448] FIFA Commentary, explanation Art. 2 Annex 5, p. 130. As with the training compensation, the association now has six months to make themselves known and if, as mentioned above, a club makes itself known after the 18th month after the registration of its former player, the claim of the club will then get priority above the right of the association after all. Also in this respect, if the association has irrefutable evidence that one of its affiliated clubs which is entitled to solidarity contribution no longer exists, then solidarity contribution should immediately be paid by the new club to the association and not only after the 18th month.

[449] FIFA Commentary, explanation Art. 2 Annex 5, p. 130.

[450] DRC 22 July 2004, no. 74038.

training and to distribute this amount in accordance with the player's career history. The DRC finally concluded that club B should pay the solidarity contribution to the former clubs and was of the opinion that Article 4 of the agreement was not relevant in this respect.

In a decision of the DRC of 26 November 2004, the DRC concluded that the new club was responsible for paying the solidarity contribution to the clubs involved in the player's training, even if it has mistakenly omitted to retain this contribution amount when it paid the federative rights of the player to his previous club.[451] In light of the above, the DRC concluded that the new club was responsible for paying the solidarity contribution to the clubs involved in the player's training, even if it has mistakenly omitted to retain this contribution amount when it paid the federative rights of the player to his previous club. The fact that the new club paid the entire amount agreed on to the selling club had no influence on the claim of a former club, given that the latter was not a party to the transfer agreement signed between both clubs. The DRC decided that the new club should pay the amount of EUR 314,372.50 to the former club within 30 days of notification of the present decision.

In a decision of the DRC of 27 April 2006, the Chamber emphasised that the obligation to pay training compensation can only be an obligation for the new club and not to any other former clubs.[452] The DRC duly noted that the new club had paid the entire amount agreed as transfer compensation to the former, selling club of the player. Furthermore, the selling club agreed with the new club that the selling club would pass on the relevant amount and would be responsible for the payment of any possible third club in connection with the solidarity contribution. In other words, the new club failed to deduct 5% of the relevant transfer compensation relating to the solidarity mechanism, while contractually establishing that the selling club would make the relevant payments. The DRC referred to its well-established jurisprudence applied in similar cases, in accordance with which the player's new club is ordered to remit the relevant proportion of the 5% solidarity contribution to the clubs involved in the player's training. At the same time, the player's former club was ordered to reimburse the same proportion of the 5% of the compensation that it received from the player's new club. The said jurisprudence was based on the fact that there is no contractual link between the training club claiming solidarity contribution and the player's former club. Therefore, the DRC was of the opinion that the relevant claim does not have a contractual basis. The regulations of FIFA clearly establish that the distribution of the solidarity contribution is incumbent on the new club. As a result, the DRC underlined that the regulations only provide a legal basis for the claim of the training club against the new club, but not for a claim against the player's former club.

12.3 Contingent payments

As stated in Article 2 of Annex 4 RSTP, edition 2005, the new club will pay the solidarity contribution to the former clubs also in case of a contingent payment, 30 days after receipt. According to the FIFA Commentary, if the entire solidarity contribution is payable when the clubs involved in the transfer have agreed on a contingent payment, it would represent

---

[451] DRC 26 November 2004, no. 114130.
[452] DRC 27 April 2006, no. 4618.

an undue enrichment of the clubs receiving this contribution, with respect to those instalments that have not yet matured.[453]

In a decision of the DRC of 17 August 2006, the Chamber confirmed that as a result of the fact that the transfer compensation had been paid in three instalments.[454] The DRC was of the opinion and confirmed that in the case of contingent payments, the relevant solidarity contribution should be payable 30 days after the date of such payments.

However, the former club cannot be forced to accept a payment in contingents. In a decision of the DRC of 27 April 2006, the Chamber noted that the former club which was acting as claimant in this procedure for the solidarity contribution did not accept the payment plan offered by the new club and required the new club to pay the claimed amount in full at once.[455] The DRC considered that in view of the above, the members had reached the conclusion that the new club would be required to pay to the claimant the relevant amount pertaining to the solidarity contribution. The DRC finally decided and underlined that the former club was and is not obliged according to the regulations to accept payment of its relevant share of solidarity contribution in instalments and thus the former club may request payment to be made in one single payment.[456]

12.4 **Loan**

According to Article 10 of the RSTP, edition 2005, a loan is subject to the same rules that apply to the transfer of players, including the provisions on solidarity mechanism.[457] If the player is on loan, the club loaning the player is entitled to receive a solidarity contribution.[458] The DRC is of the explicit opinion that every contrary interpretation of the regulations would violate the *ratio legis* of the before-mentioned regulations. In that respect it is also important to know that the club receiving the player on the basis of a loan will retain 5% of the loan fee and distribute it to all clubs that contributed to the training of the player between the ages of 12 and 23.

In a decision of the DRC of 26 October 2006, the DRC decided in a dispute concerning solidarity contribution between two clubs in connection with the transfer of a player.[459] The DRC decided as a general rule that, contrary to the training compensation, the solidarity mechanism is not restricted to the period that the player actually played with that club. Every time a professional is transferred before the end of his contract, the solidarity contribution must be paid by the new club to all the clubs for which the player played between his 12th and 23rd birthday. The DRC decided to reject the club's claim that solidarity contribution was not due since the player concerned had been registered on a loan basis with the claimant. According to the jurisprudence of the DRC, the solidarity contribution is payable to the clubs which effectively trained and educated a player independently of the basis on which the player was registered with a training club, i.e., on a loan or a definitive basis.

---

[453] FIFA Commentary, explanation Art. 2 Annex 5, under footnote 180, p. 180.
[454] DRC 17 August 2006, no. 86558.
[455] DRC 27 April 2006, no. 46557.
[456] DRC 27 April 2006, no. 46557.
[457] RSTP, edition 2005, Art. 10 Para. 1.
[458] FIFA Commentary, explanation Art. 10 Para. 1, p. 32.
[459] DRC 26 October 2006, no. 106419.

In a decision of the DRC of 28 September 2006, the Chamber took into consideration the circumstance that the player was registered with the former club on a loan basis.[460] The DRC referred to Article 10 of the RSTP, edition 2005, in accordance with which the loan of a professional is subject to the same rules as apply to the transfer of players, including the provisions on solidarity mechanism. Taking into account the before-mentioned elements, the DRC concluded that the former club was entitled to receive solidarity contribution in accordance with the regulations.

12.5 Conclusion

In the case of an international transfer of a player which takes place during the course of his employment contract, all his former clubs that have provided the education and training of the player are entitled to receive 5% as a so-called transfer compensation from the new club. In other words, as long as transfer compensation is paid by the new club, a solidarity contribution must be paid to all the former clubs where the player has played. According to the RSTP, edition 2005, it is the responsibility of the new club to calculate the amount of the solidarity contribution and to distribute it in accordance with the player's career history as provided in the player passport.

According to numerous decisions, the DRC explicitly underlines that it is indeed only the new club that is entitled to distribute the amount of solidarity compensation to the relevant former clubs of the player. This obligation cannot be transferred to another club. The new club and the selling club of the player may not include a provision in the transfer agreement stating that the entire transfer compensation will be paid to the selling club and that the latter will instead be responsible for the distribution. The DRC will then order the player's former club to reimburse the same proportion of the 5% of the compensation that it received from the player's new club.

As we have seen, the amount will be calculated pro rata by the new club if the player played less than one year with that former club. If the player passport is incomplete, the player will assist the new club in fulfilling this obligation by providing his new club with all the relevant documentation. Despite the fact that the player passport plays an important role in the allocation of compensation to the former clubs by the new club, the risk of incompleteness of a player passport may be borne by the former club claiming its part of the solidarity contribution from the new club.

It is rather remarkable that a club is charged for a lack of completeness of a player passport, because it is the responsibility of the association concerned to complete the player passport. According to Article 7 of the RSPT, edition 2005, the registering association is obliged to provide the club with which the player is registered with a player passport containing the relevant details of the player. It is reasonable that a club assist the DRC with the indication, but it would be going too far for the former club to bear the risk of incompleteness of the player passport of the player concerned and thus not be entitled to its share of the solidarity contribution.

As stated in Article 2 of Annex 4 RSTP, edition 2005, the new club will pay the solidarity contribution to the former clubs, also in the case of a contingent payment, 30 days after the receipt of this payment. Although the new club may pay the transfer compensation in

[460] DRC 28 September 2006, no. 961202B.

instalments, the DRC is of the opinion and explicitly emphasises that according to the regulations the former club is not obliged to accept payment by the new club of its relevant share of solidarity contribution in instalments. As a result, the former club may request the payment to be made in one single payment.

According to Article 10 of the RSTP, edition 2005, the provisions of loan are subject to the same rules that apply to the transfer of players, including the provisions on solidarity mechanism.[461] If the player is on loan, the loaning club is entitled to receive solidarity contribution.[462] The DRC is of the explicit opinion that any contrary interpretation of the regulations would violate the *ratio legis* of the before-mentioned regulations. In that respect it also important to know that the club receiving the player on the basis of a loan, will retain 5% of the loan fee and distribute it to all clubs that contributed to the player's training between the ages of 12 and 23.

13. Final conclusions

After having analysed and discussed the most relevant decisions of the DRC during the years 2002–2006 following a classification of the most relevant subjects, we can see that in general during the last years, the verdicts of the DRC contain better and more extensive deliberations. During the last years, the DRC refers increasingly to its established jurisprudence and decisions of its appeal committee, the CAS. There seems to be a more consistent line with respect to the most important issues the Chamber has to deal with. Obviously, this is a strongly time-related process, since the DRC has only been in existence since 2001. More-over, it also seems that the DRC is becoming more aware of its position within the international professional football world. As mentioned in the introduction, the decisions of the DRC have a huge impact on the international world of football. All the relevant actors, the national associations, clubs and players are indirectly obliged to comply with the decisions of FIFA, such as decisions of the DRC.

Notwithstanding the above, it still is rather remarkable that the decisions of the DRC are hard to find on the official website of FIFA. Furthermore, it is worth recalling that not all decisions of the DRC are published on the official website of FIFA. On 17 January 2007, the DRC gave a decision relating to the validity of a unilateral extension option in favour of the club. This decision is, without exaggeration, much too important to be omitted from the list of published decisions. Apparently, this decision was not "a case of general interest", the minimum criterion according to the Procedural Rules in order to publish a decision of the DRC on the website of FIFA. In line with this, it also is a lack of completeness that FIFA does not explicitly refer in its so-called FIFA Commentary to the exact number of decisions of the DRC.[463]

The above actions give rise to the suspicion that FIFA is reluctant to provide the football world with the decisions of the DRC. This is noteworthy, since the decisions of the DRC are very important for FIFA in order to establish global uniformity, equality and certainty for the professional football world. FIFA should therefore provide us with all the

[461] RSTP, edition 2005, Art. 10 Para. 1.

[462] FIFA Commentary, explanation Art. 10 Para. 1, p. 32.

[463] Apart from that, it cannot be let unmentioned that the FIFA Commentary is a very useful document for a better understanding of the regulations of FIFA and the decisions of the DRC.

decisions of the DRC, not just the selection as published on its official website. For the sake of transparency and in order to create more uniformity, equality and certainty, the national associations should also draw more attention to the decisions of the DRC.

All decisions of the DRC are based on general principles of labour law, as laid down in the various national laws and treaties. However, we have seen that the DRC sometimes creates its own sort of law, the so-called "specificity of sport", as mentioned in Article 25 of the RSTP, edition 2005, which can also be characterised as *Lex Sportiva*. For example, in the famous *Webster* case, the DRC underlined that it not only had to deal with the regulations and national laws, it also had to deal with "specific knowledge of the world of football". It will always be difficult, not to say impossible, to define the *Lex Sportiva* precisely. However, it is possible, by analysing the decisions of the DRC, to derive a general line with respect to the *Lex Sportiva* in relation to the most important subjects the Chamber has to deal with.

Regarding several issues, the DRC significantly deviates from the opinion of the national laws. According to most national laws, an oral agreement may suffice in order to determine that an employment agreement exists. However, the DRC is quite explicit on this point as it is of the opinion that a professional football player must have a written employment agreement, by default of which the player will be considered as an amateur. Furthermore, with regard to the negotiations, the DRC is of the opinion that not all cancelled negotiations are legitimate and consequently the party in breach will be held liable for compensation. In many countries, the national courts do not adjudicate damages to the party who ends the negotiations abruptly. In the *Webster* case too, we see that the DRC follows its own line, since it decided in this decision that a professional football player cannot terminate his employment contract by simply paying his club the remaining value of his contract.

On some points, it seems very defensible that the DRC creates its own line. Most *Lex Sportiva* finds their justification in the fact that the football world needs to be protected. For that reason, it is sometimes defensible that the DRC differs from the national laws. The probation period is one example which is not valid according to the DRC, because of the uncertainty it creates for the player with respect to his employment contract. Moreover, it plays an important role in that the player can be invited by the club to come on a trial. According to the national labour law of various countries, it is sometimes possible to make the validity of the employment contract conditional upon the positive result of a medical examination of an employee. However, although certain national laws do permit an employer to unilaterally terminate the contract with his employee in the case of a negative result of the medical test, on this point the DRC rightly differs. The DRC is of the opinion that a player should be protected with respect to his medical state.

The protection of minors is another extremely important point for FIFA. As a result, FIFA is of the opinion that the RSTP should have priority above certain national laws. It is defensible that insofar as these rules pursue a legitimate objective, for example the protection of players under the age of 18 from being excluded from making an international transfer as well as the restriction with respect to the maximum length of three years of their employment contracts, that the rules of FIFA prevail above the national laws. According to the above, and as mentioned earlier, on some points the DRC is justified in overruling national law. However, such a deviation is only justified, as we have seen, when national law on that point is not mandatory and when the deviation pursues a legitimate objective and can be considered vital for the international professional football world, such as issues related to the physical state of the professional football player, since he is a special employee who pursues sports at the highest level, but also in relation to the protection of professional players who are under the age of 18.

With regard to certain issues, the *Lex Sportiva* is subject to further discussion. If a clause is valid according to certain national laws, the DRC is sometimes of the opinion that this clause is not valid. One example is the unilateral extension option, as mentioned earlier. In one of the cases submitted to the DRC, the Chamber decided that, despite the fact that one of the parties claimed that the extension option was valid according to their national law, this clause was not valid. Since this issue was not mandatory at national level, the DRC was entitled to decide accordingly, but one may still wonder whether a deviation is justified. As mentioned, opinions are divided in these cases. However, a deviation at this point may be seen as correct, as this clause gives one of the parties the right to unilaterally cancel or lengthen it, without providing the other party with similar rights. This clause excessively restricts the player's freedom of movement and leaves the player at an unfair disadvantage. According to the DRC, unilateral extension options in favour of the club are not based on reciprocity, since the right to extend a contract is left exclusively at the discretion of the club. Therefore, as a general rule, a unilateral extension option will be considered to be invalid due to its potestative nature. However, in very special circumstances, we see that the DRC, in particular following its more recent decisions, may be of the opinion that the unilateral extension option in favour of the club is valid. However, this is still rather remarkable since the right to extend a contract is still left exclusively at the discretion of the club as a result of which the extension option in favour of the club retains its potestative nature.

According to several decisions of the DRC with respect to training compensation and the solidarity contribution, the *Lex Sportiva* is not an important issue. However, it is worth recalling that, with respect to training compensation, parties often try to exclude the right of the former clubs to receive training compensation. The DRC is clear on this point, as it is of the opinion that only the club which is officially entitled to receive training compensation may waive its right to this compensation. Any possible financial settlements concluded between the former club or the new club and the player cannot in any sense establish that the former clubs lose and thus waive their right to receive training compensation from the new club.

In relation to the solidarity contribution, it is important to emphasise that the DRC explicitly underlines that it is only the new club which is entitled to distribute the amount of solidarity compensation to the relevant former clubs. This obligation cannot be transferred to another club, despite the fact that it is common practice to transfer this right. According to numerous decisions of the DRC, the new club and the selling club may not include a provision in the transfer agreement which states that the entire transfer compensation will be paid to the selling club as a result of which the selling club becomes responsible for the payment of the solidarity contribution. The DRC will then order the player's former club to reimburse the same proportion of the 5% of the compensation that it received from the player's new club.

Having discussed the most relevant decisions of the DRC, we still see that in their quest for further uniformity, equality and certainty, FIFA is sometimes hindered because some decisions of national arbitrational courts are not in line with the decisions of the DRC.

Despite the fact, as stated above, that according to the DRC a unilateral extension option in favour of the club should and is sometimes considered as invalid, the Dutch national arbitrational court decided contrarily as it was of the opinion that the unilateral extension option was valid. This creates an imbalance between the line of FIFA and the opinion of some national arbitrational courts. International professional football needs legal certainty with respect to these issues. It is therefore important that the national arbitrational courts decide in accordance with the decisions of FIFA, such as the DRC, although this is very difficult to establish. It cannot be denied that it is rather strange that certain clauses in the employment contracts of players are considered to be valid at national level, while the DRC is of the opinion that this same clause is invalid. This does not benefit international football. FIFA should give more attention to the decisions of the DRC. As a result, better insights into the DRC will ultimately contribute and assist FIFA in their quest for more conformity, equality and certainty in the professional football world.

ANNEXES

REGULATIONS FOR THE STATUS AND TRANSFER OF PLAYERS (2001)*

CHAPTER I – PLAYER REGISTRATION

Article 1 – Registration

1. No player may be registered to play for two different clubs affiliated to the same or to different national associations at any given time. The registration constitutes the licence for a player to play football.
2. Once registration has been effected, the club and the player wilt receive an extract from the register, which will contain, *inter alla,* the details of every club the player has been registered with, or affiliated to, since the age of twelve, the nationality and the date of birth of the player, as well as the date from which the player is eligible to play for his club in competitions organised by the national association to which his club is affiliated.

Article 2 – Registration periods

1. Each national association will decide upon the establishment of two registration periods per year, according to the following principles:
   a) The first registration period will start, at the earliest, when the national championship has ended and finish, at the latest, before the subsequent national championship begins. This period should, in principle, last for no longer than six weeks.
   b) The second registration period will occur approximately in the middle of the season. This period should, in principle, last for no longer than four weeks and should be limited to registrations for strictly sport related reasons, such as technical adjustments to a team or the replacement of injured players, or in exceptional circumstances.
2. The national associations shall notify FIFA of the two periods they have established as registration periods pursuant to par. 1 above.

CHAPTER II – PROTECTION OF MINORS IN THE EU/EEA

Article 3 – Code of conduct for transfers in the EU/EEA

1. FIFA and UEFA shall adopt a Code of Conduct to ensure that the sports training and academic education of minors are guaranteed in the case of transfer in the EU/EEA. The Code of Conduct establishes guidelines which shall be followed by national associations and leagues.
2. The Code of Conduct shall be enforced and applied by the national associations.
3. The national associations shall, in particular, ensure that in every case where a club applies for the registration of a player who is under 18 years of age, the requirements set out in the Code of Conduct are observed.
4. If a club does not comply with the requirements of the Code of Conduct, the national association shall not register the player. Where appropriate, the national association may also impose disciplinary sanctions on the club. Such disciplinary measures may include, but are not limited to:
   – the annulment of wrongful registrations
   – a ban on registering any players under 18 years of age for a given time,
   – fines,
   – deduction of points,
   – exclusion from competitions.
5. In addition, without prejudice to par. 2, the disciplinary measures listed in Art. 23 of the FIFA Regulations for the Status and Transfer of Players may be imposed by the FIFA Players' Status Committee, pursuant to Art. 34 of the FIFA Statutes, whenever a national association has failed to implement the principles set out in the Code of Conduct.
6. National associations may carry out on-the-spot investigations to ensure that any club which has registered a player under 18 years of age continues to comply with the obligations set out in the Code of Conduct. If a club has failed to meet these obligations, disciplinary measures may be imposed, in accordance with the terms of par. 4 above.

---

* See page 182 for an author's note on the amended FIFA Regulations for the Status and Transfer of Players (2008).

7. If third parties, such as agents, have been involved in a registration, or an application for registration, of a ptayer who is under 18 years of age, and have failed to comply with the Code of Conduct, disciplinary measures may be imposed on the agents pursuant to the FIFA Players' Agents Regulations, and on other third parties in accordance with the jurisdiction of the FIFA Players' Status Committee, pursuant to Art. 34 of the FIFA Statutes.
8. Appeals against decisions imposing disciplinary measures pursuant to par. 4, 5, 6 and 7 above can be Lodged to the Arbitration Tribunal for Football (TAF).
9. If in doubt regarding the interpretation of the above-mentioned provisions and of the Code of Conduct, the national association may seek the joint assistance of FIFA and UEFA.

Article 4 – Other Registrations of Minors

1. National associations in the EU/EEA shall refuse the registration of players under 18 years of age who are nationals of countries outside the EU/EEA and who are not moving for family reasons under the terms of Chapter VI of the FIFA Regulations for the Status and Transfer of Players.
2. National associations outside the EU/EEA shall refuse the registration of players under 18 years of age who are nationals of foreign countries and who are not moving for family reasons under the terms of Chapter VI of the FIFA Regulations for the Status and Transfer of Players.
3. Where appropriate, the national association may also impose disciplinary sanctions on the club. Such disciplinary measures may include, but shall not be limited to:
   - the annulment of wrongful registrations
   - a ban on registering any players under 18 years of age for a given time,
   - fines,
   - deduction of points,
   - exclusion from competitions.
4. In addition, the disciplinary measures listed in Art. 23 of the FIFA Regulations for the Status and Transfer of Players may be imposed by the FIFA Players' Status Committee, pursuant to Art. 34 of the FIFA Statutes, whenever a national association has failed to implement the ban on transfers and first registration of players under 18 years of age.
5. If third parties, such as agents, have been involved in the wrongful registration or application for registration of a player who is under 18 years of age, disciplinary measures may be imposed mi the agents pursuant to the FIFA Players' Agents Regulations, and on other third parties in accordance with the jurisdiction of the FIFA Players' Status Committee, pursuant to Art. 34 of the FIFA Statutes.
6. Appeals against decisions imposing disciplinary measures pursuant to par. 3, 4 and 5 above can be lodged to the Arbitration Tribunal for Football (TAF).

CHAPTER III – TRAINING COMPENSATION FOR YOUNG PLAYERS

Article 5 – Principles

1. For the purposes of calculating compensation, the training period starts at the beginning of the season of the player's 12th birthday, or at a Later age, as the case may be, and finishes at the end of the season of his 21st birthday.
2. Compensation for training is due:
   (a) for the first time, when the player acquires non-amateur status according to Art. 1 of the FIFA Regulations for the Status and Transfer of Players
   (b) afterwards, for every transfer up to the age of 23, depending on the player's status, i.e.:
      - from amateur to non-amateur status
      - from non-amateur status to non-amateur status
3. Compensation for training is not due:
   (a) for transfers from amateur status to amateur status or for transfers from non-amateur status to amateur status (reacquisition of amateur status), unless the player (re)acquires non-amateur status within a period of three years
   (b) if a club unilaterally terminates a player's contract without just cause, but without prejudice to the compensation due to the previous training clubs.
4. Payment of compensation for training:
   (a) As a general rule, the amount due shall reflect the costs which were necessary to train the player and shall be paid for the benefit of every club which has contributed to the training of the player in question, starting from the age of 12.

(b) First payment (as mentioned in par. 2 (a)): The amount to be paid is for the benefit of every club which has contributed to the training of the player in question, starting from the age of 12. The money shall be distributed en a pro-rata basis depending on the full years of proper and proven training, and in relation to the category to which the training clubs belong.
(c) In the case of subsequent transfers (as mentioned in par. 2 (b)) from clubs belonging to the third or fourth categories (as defined in Art. 6 par.2), the new club shall pay the former club the costs which it incurred in training the player as well as the training compensation costs which it incurred when registering the player.
(d) In the case of a player moving from a club belonging to the third or fourth categories to a club in a higher category, a cascade principle will apply as defined in Art. 8 below.
(e) In the case of a player moving clubs within the same category, a cascade principle will apply as defined in Art. 8 below.
(f) In the case of a player moving from a club in the first or second category, the amount of training compensation payable shall be the training cost of the previous club.

5. In the EU/EEA, if the training club does not offer the player a contract, this shall betaken into account in determining the training compensation payable by the new club, without prejudice to the rights to compensation of the previous training clubs.

Article 6 – Calculation parameters

1. In order to calculate the compensation for training and education costs, the clubs wilt be categorised in accordance with their financial investments in training players.
2. Four categories shall be established according to the following guidelines:
   (a) Category 1 (top level, e.g. high quality training centre):
   all first-division clubs of national associations investing on average a similar amount in training players. These national associations will be defined based on actual training costs, and this categorisation can be revised on a yearly basis.
   (b) Category 2 (still professional, but at a lower level):
   all second-division clubs of national associations in category 1
   all first-division clubs in all other countries with professional football
   (c) Category 3:
   all third-division clubs of national associations in category 1
   all second-division clubs in all other countries with professional football
   (d) Category 4:
   all fourth- and lower division clubs of the national associations in category 1
   all third- and lower division clubs in all other countries with professional football all clubs in countries with only amateur football.
3. National associations may propose other criteria for categorising the training and education costs incurred by clubs affiliated to them. The training and education costs per category shall be calculated by multiplying the cost of training one player by an average player factor. The player factor determines the ratio between the number of players who need to be trained to produce one professional player.
4. Each year national associations in the EU/EEA shall determine the categories to which their clubs belang, after hearing the views of representatives of players and clubs. The national associations shall notify FIFA of this categorisation at the latest by the mid-season registration period every year and FIFA will publish this information via a circular letter and its internet sites. The categorisation shall be valid for 12 months or two registration periods.
5. National associations in the EU/EEA shall determine the criteria for calculating the training compensation, after hearing the views of representatives of players and clubs. FIFA will acknowledge these criteria, subject to their proportionality. The national associations shall notify FIFA of these criteria at the latest by the mid-season registration period every year and FIFA will publish them via a circular letter and its internet sites. These criteria may be reviewed after a lapse of 24 months or four registration periods.
6. Guidelines on what type of costs may be included in the calculation of training and education costs will be set out in a circular letter from FIFA.

Article 7 – Calculation of compensation for training and education

1. The compensation for training and education shall be obtained by multiplying the amount corresponding to the category of the training club for which the player was registered by the number of years of training from 12 to 21.
2. To ensure that training compensation for very young players is not set at unreasonably high levels, the amount for players aged 12 to 15 shall be based on the training and education costs for category 4.
3. As a general principle, compensation for training is based on the training and education costs of the country in which the new club is located.
4. However, in the EU/EEA area, compensation for training is based en the training and education costs of the country in which the training club wss located. The following rules apply:
   a) the player moves from a lower to a higher category: calculation is the average of the training costs for the two categories;
   b) the player moves from a higher to a lower category: calculation is based on training costs of the lower category club
   c) the player moves from a club in category 1, 2 or 3 to a club in category 4: no compensation for training is payable.
5. In the EU/EEA area, every national association slialt notify FIFA of a ceiling for the training compensation for every club category at the beginning of the sports season, after hearing the views of representatives of players and clubs. FIFA will acknowledge such ceilings, subject to their proportionality. FIFA will publish the ceilings via a circular letter and its internet sites at the latest by the mid-season registration period every year.

Article 8 – Distribution of the compensation payment

The amount paid by the new club as compensation for training and education of the player concerned shall be distributed according to the following principles:

(a) For the transfer of a player from a club in the third or fourth category to a club in a higher category, 75% of the amount exceeding the costs of the category of the former club shall be redistributed on a pro-rata basis to all the clubs that have trained the player from the age of 12 onwards.
(b) For the transfer of a player from a club in the second category to a club in the first category, 50% of the amount exceeding the costs of the category of the former club shall be redistributed on a pro-rata basis to all the clubs that have trained the player from the age of 12 onwards.
(c) For the transfer between two clubs of the same category, 10% of the amount calculated as described under Art. 7, pars. 3 and 4 shall be redistributed on a pro-rata basis to all the clubs that have trained the player from the age of 12 onwards.
(d) If a player's career cannot be traced back to the age of 12, any missing years will be based on category four for the purposes of determining training compensation and the amount will be distributed to the player's national association of origin and be earmarked for training young players.

Article 9 – Payment of compensation

1. The new club shall pay the training clubs the amount due as compensation for training and education pursuant to the above provisions at the latest within 30 days of the signature of the first contract under the terms of Art. 4 of the FIFA Regulations for the Status and Transfer of Players or for any subsequent transfer, within 30 days of the player's new registration.
2. It is the responsibility of the new club to calculate the amount of the compensation for training and education and the way in which it shall be distributed in accordance with the player's career history. The player shall, if necessary, assist the new club in discharging this obligation.
3. The FIFA Players' Status Committee may impose disciplinary measures en clubs or players that do not observe the obligations stipulated in the previous paragraphs. Appeals against these measures may be lodged to the Arbitration Tribunal for Football (TAF).

CHAPTER IV – SOLIDARITY MECHANISM

Article 10 – Principles

If a non-amateur player moves during the course of a contract, a proportion (5%) of any compensation paid to the former club will be redistributed as a solidarity contribution to the clubs involved in the training and education of the player concerned over the years. This solidarity contribution shall be apportioned between the clubs concerned according to the age of the player at the time they provided him with training and education, as follows:

- −12 – 13 years: 5%
- −13 – 14 years: 5%
- −14 – 15 years:10%
- −15 – 16 years:10%
- −16 – 17 years:10%
- −17 – 18 years:10%
- −18 – 19 years:10%
- −19 – 20 years:10%
- −20 – 21 years:10%
- −21 – 22 years:10%
- −22 – 23 years: 10%

Article 11 – Payment of solidarity contribution

1. The new club shall pay the amount due as a solidarity contribution to the training clubs pursuant to the above provisions at the latest within 30 days of the players registration.
2. It is the responsibility of the new club to calculate the amount of the solidarity contribution and the way in which it shall be distributed in accordance with the player's career history. The player shall, if necessary, assist the new club in discharging this obligation.
3. The FIFA Players' Status Committee may impose disciplinary measures on clubs or players that do not observe the obligations stipulated in the previous paragraphs. Appeals against these measures may be lodged to the Arbitration Tribunal for Football (TAF).

CHAPTER V – STABILITY OF CONTRACTS

Article 12

A player is entitled to terminate his contract with his club unilaterally for sporting just cause where he can show at the end of a season that he was fielded in less than 10% of the official matches ptayed by his club. The existence of such sporting just cause shall be established on a case-by-case basis and shall depend on the particular circumstances of the player (including but not limited to injury, suspension, player's field position, position in the team (e.g. reserve goal keeper), player's age, reasonable expectations on the basis of past career, etc).

Article 13

1. A club wishing to engage the services of a player who is at present under contract with another club shall be obliged to inform the club and the player before commencing negotiations with either of them.
2. For any violations of the foregoing obligation, the offending club will be subject to a line of at least CHF 50,000.
3. Such a fine can be imposed by the Dispute Resolution Chamber, pursuant to Art. 42 of the FIFA Regulations for the Status and Transfer of Players. Appeals against any decision to impose a line can be lodged pursuant to the provisions of the same article.

CHAPTER VI – ENFORCEMENT OF COMPENSATION AWARDS

Article 14

1. The party responsible for a breach of contract shall be obliged to pay the sum of compensation determined pursuant to Art. 42 of the FIFA Regulations for the Status and Transfer of Players within one month of notification of the relevant decision of the Dispute Resolution Chamber.
2. If the party responsible for the breach has not paid the sum of compensation within one month, disciplinary measures may be imposed by the FIFA Players' Status Committee, pursuant to Art. 34 of the FIFA Statutes. Appeals against these measures may be lodged to the-Arbitration Tribunal for Football (TAF).
3. If a player is registered for a new club and bas not paid a sum of compensation within the one month time limit referred to above, the new club shall be deemed jointly responsible for payment of the amount of compensation.

4. If the new club has not paid the sum of compensation within one month of having become jointly responsible with the player pursuant to the previous paragraph, disciplinary measures may be imposed by the FIFA Players' Status Committee, pursuant to Art. 34 of the FIFA Statutes. Appeals against these measures may be lodged to the Arbitration Tribunal for Football (TAF).

CHAPTER VII – RULES AND PROCEDURES FOR DISPUTE RESOLUTION

Article 15 – Composition of the Dispute Resolution Chamber

1. The Chairman of the Players' Status Committee shall chair the Dispute Resolution Chamber.
2. The Dispute Resolution Chamber shall be composed of representatives of players and clubs in equal number.
3. The members of the Dispute Resolution Chamber shall be designated by the Executive Committee at the proposal of the President of FIFA based upon nominations from representative players' associations and clubs and/or leagues.

Article 16 – Procedure before the Dispute Resolution Chamber

1. The Dispute Resolution Chamber of the FIFA Players' Status Committee shall review disputes coming under its jurisdiction pursuant to Art. 42 of the FIFA Regulations for the Status and Transfer of Players at the request of one of the parties to the dispute. Failure by one of the parties to appear before the Dispute Resolution Chamber does not impact on the jurisdiction of the Chamber, which shall adjudicate on the dispute based en all the facts known to it.
2. In order to submit a dispute to the Dispute Resolution Chamber, a party shall file a written request with the FIFA general secretariat. Such a request must contain the following elements:
   (a) the complainant's name and other relevant details,
   (b) If the complainant is not a natural person, a copy of its statutes and relevant certificates of incorporation as well as proof that the person filing the request on behalf of the complainant is entitled to represent it in legal proceedings,
   (c) the name and other relevant details of the legal representative assisting the complainant, if any,
   (d) the name and other relevant details of other clubs and/or players involved in the dispute, including e.g. the club accused of having induced a breach of contract.
   (e) a summary presentation of the relevant factual, legal and regulatory considerations.
   (f) ruling of any national arbitration tribunal or national court regarding this dispute.

   In addition, the request shall be accompanied by a copy of all the relevant documents pertaining to the dispute.
3. The FIFA Players' Status Committee shall issue detailed internal rules of procedure for the Dispute Resolution Chamber. These rules of procedure shall ensure that the following principles be observed:
   (a) The Dispute Resolution Chamber shall afford the parties the opportunity to make their views known in full knowledge of the relevant facts of the case.
   (b) Parties shall have the opportunity to make written observations and their oral explanations may be heard, if deemed necessary by the Dispute Resolution Chamber.
   (c) Parties shall be given enough time to prepare their defence, having due regard to the need for a speedy resolution within the deadlines provided for in Art. 42 of the FIFA Regulations for the Status and Transfer of Players.
   (d) Parties will be able to rely on professional legal assistance.
   (e) Hearings before the Dispute Resolution Chamber shall not be open to the public.
   (f) Decisions by the Dispute Resolution Chamber shall be published promptly, in extract or in full.
4. The Dispute Resolution Chamber shall send a copy of alt the relevant documents pertaining to the dispute to the national association which held the registration of the player involved in the dispute when the dispute arose and set a deadline within which the association may send its written observations en the dispute. A copy of these observations shall be forwarded to the parties to the dispute.

Article 17 – Mediation

1. At the request of a party to a dispute, the FIFA general secretariat shall appoint an independent mediator which shall contact the parties to attempt mediation.

2. Mediation attempts shall not suspend the procedure before the Dispute Resolution Chamber, unless all the parties to the dispute agree to such suspension.

CHAPTER VIII – STATISTICS REGISTER

Article 18

National associations shall keep a register of the statistics of the number of registrations they have effected of players coming from other national associations, as well as of the number of international registration transfer certificates they have issued for a player transferring his registration to another national association. This register shall also mention the age and nationality of the player, the country which he is leaving er joining and any information the national association obtains on the reason for the player's transfer of registration (amicable termination, transfer at the end of the contract, or unilateral breach by the player or the club within er outside the period defined under Art. 21, par. 1 of the FIFA Regulations for the Status and Transfer of Players).

CHAPTER IX – FINAL PROVISIONS, ENFORCEMENT

Article 19

Any matter not provided for under these regulations shall be settled by the FIFA Players' Status Committee, subject to review by the Executive Committee.

Article 20

These regulations shall come into force in their present form at the same time as the FIFA Regulations for the Status and Transfer of Players adopted on the same day.

Buenos Aires/Zurich, 5 July 2001
For the FIFA Executive Committee

President	General Secretary
Joseph S. Blatter	Michel Zen-Ruffinen

REGULATIONS GOVERNING THE APPLICATION OF THE REGULATIONS FOR THE STATUS AND TRANSFER OF PLAYERS

CHAPTER I – PLAYER REGISTRATION

Article 1 – Registration

1. No player may be registered to play for two different clubs affiliated to the same or to different national associations at any given time. The registration constitutes the licence for a player to play football.
2. Once registration has been effected, the club and the player will receive an extract from the register, which will contain, inter alia, the details of every club the player has been registered with, or affiliated to, since the age of twelve, the nationality and the date of birth of the player, as well as the date from which the player is eligible to play for his club in competitions organised by the national association to which his club is affiliated.

Article – 2 Registration periods

1. Each national association will decide upon the establishment of two registration periods per year, according to the following principles:
   (a) The first registration period will start, at the earliest, when the national championship has ended and finish, at the latest, before the subsequent national championship begins. This period should, in principle, last for no longer than six weeks.
   (b) The second registration period will occur approximately in the middle of the season. This period should, in principle, last for no longer than four weeks and should be limited to registrations for strictly sport related reasons, such as technical adjustments to a team or the replacement of injured players, or in exceptional circumstances.
2. The national associations shall notify FIFA of the two periods they have established as registration periods pursuant to par. 1 above.

CHAPTER II – PROTECTION OF MINORS IN THE EU/EEA

Article 3 – Code of conduct for transfers in the EU/EEA

1. FIFA and UEFA will adopt a Code of Conduct to ensure that the sports training and academic education of minors are guaranteed in the case of transfer in the EU/EEA. The Code of Conduct establishes guidelines which shall be followed by national associations and leagues.
2. The Code of Conduct shall be enforced and applied by the national associations.
3. The national associations shall, in particular, ensure that in every case where a club applies for the registration of a player who is under 18 years of age, the requirements set out in the Code of Conduct are observed.
4. If a club does not comply with the requirements of the Code of Conduct, the national association shall not register the player. Where appropriate, the national association may also impose disciplinary sanctions on the club. Such disciplinary measures may include, but are not limited to:
   - the annulment of wrongful registrations
   - a ban on registering any players under 18 years of age for a given time
   - fines
   - deduction of points
   - exclusion from competitions.
5. In addition, without prejudice to par. 2, the disciplinary measures listed in Art. 23 of the FIFA Regulations for the Status and Transfer of Players may be imposed by the FIFA Players' Status Committee, pursuant to Art. 34 of the FIFA Statutes, whenever a national association has failed to implement the principles set out in the Code of Conduct.
6. National associations may carry out on-the-spot investigations to ensure that any club which has registered a player under 18 years of age continues to comply with the obligations set out in the Code of Conduct. If a club has failed to meet these obligations, disciplinary measures may be imposed, in accordance with the terms of par. 4 above.
7. If third parties, such as agents, have been involved in a registration, or an application for registration, of a player who is under 18 years of age, and have failed to comply with the Code of Conduct, disciplinary measures may be imposed on the agents pursuant to the FIFA Players' Agents Regulations, and on other third parties in accordance with the jurisdiction of the FIFA Players' Status Committee, pursuant to Art. 34 of the FIFA Statutes.
8. Appeals against decisions imposing disciplinary measures pursuant to par. 4, 5, 6 and 7 above can be lodged to the Arbitration Tribunal for Football (TAF).
9. If in doubt regarding the interpretation of the above-mentioned provisions and of the Code of Conduct, the national association may seek the joint assistance of FIFA and UEFA.

Article 4 – Other Registrations of Minors

1. National associations in the EU/EEA shall refuse the registration of players under 18 years of age who are nationals of countries outside the EU/EEA and who are not moving for family reasons under the terms of Chapter VI of the FIFA Regulations for the Status and Transfer of Players.
2. National associations outside the EU/EEA shall refuse the registration of players under 18 years of age who are nationals of foreign countries and who are not moving for family reasons under the terms of Chapter VI of the FIFA Regulations for the Status and Transfer of Players.
3. Where appropriate, the national association may also impose disciplinary sanctions on the club. Such disciplinary measures may include, but shall not be limited to:
   - the annulment of wrongful registrations
   - a ban on registering any players under 18 years of age for a given time
   - fines
   - deduction of points
   - exclusion from competitions.
4. In addition, the disciplinary measures listed in Art. 23 of the FIFA Regulations for the Status and Transfer of Players may be imposed by the FIFA Players' Status Committee, pursuant to Art. 34 of the FIFA Statutes, whenever a national association has failed to implement the ban on transfers and first registration of players under 18 years of age.
5. If third parties, such as agents, have been involved in the wrongful registration or application for registration of a player who is under 18 years of age, disciplinary measures may be imposed on the agents pursuant to the FIFA Players' Agents Regulations, and on other third parties in accordance with

the jurisdiction of the FIFA Players' Status Committee, pursuant to Art. 34 of the FIFA Statutes.

6. Appeals against decisions imposing disciplinary measures pursuant to par. 3, 4 and 5 above can be lodged to the Arbitration Tribunal for Football (TAF).

CHAPTER III – TRAINING COMPENSATION FOR YOUNG PLAYERS

Article 5 – Principles

1. For the purposes of calculating compensation, the training period starts at the beginning of the season of the player's 12th birthday, or at a later age, as the case may be, and finishes at the end of the season of his 21st birthday.
2. Compensation for training is due:
   (a) for the first time, when the player acquires non-amateur status according to Art. 1 of the FIFA Regulations for the Status and Transfer of Players
   (b) afterwards, for every transfer up to the age of 23, depending on the player's status, i.e.:
      – from amateur to non-amateur status
      – from non-amateur status to non-amateur status
3. Compensation for training is not due:
   (a) for transfers from amateur status to amateur status or for transfers from nonamateur status to amateur status (reacquisition of amateur status), unless the player (re)acquires non-amateur status within a period of three years
   (b) if a club unilaterally terminates a player's contract without just cause, but without prejudice to the compensation due to the previous training clubs.
4. Payment of compensation for training:
   (a) As a general rule, the amount due shall reflect the costs which were necessary to train the player and shall be paid for the benefit of every club which has contributed to the training of the player in question, starting from the age of 12.
   (b) First payment (as mentioned in par. 2 (a)): The amount to be paid is for the benefit of every club which has contributed to the training of the player in question, starting from the age of 12. The money shall be distributed on a pro-rata basis depending on the full years of proper and proven training, and in relation to the category to which the training clubs belong.
   (c) In the case of subsequent transfers (as mentioned in par. 2 (b)) from clubs belonging to the third or fourth categories (as defined in Art. 6 par. 2), the new club shall pay the former club the costs which it incurred in training the player as well as the training compensation costs which it incurred when registering the player.
   (d) In the case of a player moving from a club belonging to the third or fourth categories to a club in a higher category, a cascade principle will apply as defined in Art. 8 below.
   (e) In the case of a player moving clubs within the same category, a cascade principle will apply as defined in Art. 8 below.
   (f) In the case of a player moving from a club in the first or second category, the amount of training compensation payable shall be the training cost of the previous club.
5. In the EU/EEA, if the training club does not offer the player a contract, this shall be taken into account in determining the training compensation payable by the new club, without prejudice to the rights to compensation of the previous training clubs.

Article 6 – Calculation parameters

1. In order to calculate the compensation due for training and education costs, the clubs will be categorised in accordance with their financial investments in training players.
2. Four categories shall be established according to the following guidelines:
   (a) Category 1 (top level, e.g. high quality training centre):
   all first-division clubs of national associations investing on average a similar amount in training players. These national associations will be defined based on actual training costs, and this categorisation can be revised on a yearly basis.
   (b) Category 2 (still professional, but at a lower level):
   all second-division clubs of national associations in category 1 all first-division clubs in all other countries with professional football
   (c) Category 3:
   all third-division clubs of national associations in category 1 all second-division clubs in all other countries with professional football

(d) Category 4:
all fourth- and lower division clubs of the national associations in category 1 all third- and lower division clubs in all other countries with professional football all clubs in countries with only amateur football.

3. National associations may propose other criteria for categorising the training and education costs incurred by clubs affiliated to them. The training and education costs per category shall be calculated by multiplying the cost of training one player by an average player factor. The player factor determines the ratio between the number of players who need to be trained to produce one professional player.
4. Each year national associations in the EU/EEA shall determine the categories to which their clubs belong, after hearing the views of representatives of players and clubs. The national associations shall notify FIFA of this categorisation at the latest by the mid-season registration period every year and FIFA will publish this information via a circular letter and its internet sites. The categorisation shall be valid for 12 months or two registration periods.
5. National associations in the EU/EEA shall determine the criteria for calculating the training compensation, after hearing the views of representatives of players and clubs. FIFA will acknowledge these criteria, subject to their proportionality. The national associations shall notify FIFA of these criteria at the latest by the midseason registration period every year and FIFA will publish them via a circular letter and its internet sites. These criteria may be reviewed after a lapse of 24 months or four registration periods.
6. Guidelines on what type of costs may be included in the calculation of training and education costs will be set out in a circular letter from FIFA.

Article 7 – Calculation of compensation for training and education

1. The compensation for training and education shall be obtained by multiplying the amount corresponding to the category of the training club for which the player was registered by the number of years of training from 12 to 21.
2. To ensure that training compensation for very young players is not set at unreasonably high levels, the amount for players aged 12 to 15 shall be based on the training and education costs for category 4.
3. As a general principle, compensation for training is based on the training and education costs of the country in which the new club is located.
4. However, in the EU/EEA area, compensation for training is based on the training and education costs of the country in which the training club was located. The following rules apply:
   (a) the player moves from a lower to a higher category: calculation is the average of the training costs for the two categories;
   (b) the player moves from a higher to a lower category: calculation is based on training costs of the lower category club
   (c) the player moves from a club in category 1, 2 or 3 to a club in category 4: no compensation for training is payable.
5. In the EU/EEA area, every national association shall notify FIFA of a ceiling for the training compensation for every club category at the beginning of the sports season, after hearing the views of representatives of players and clubs. FIFA will acknowledge such ceilings, subject to their proportionality. FIFA will publish the ceilings via a circular letter and its internet sites at the latest by the mid-season registration period every year.

Article 8 – Distribution of the compensation payment

The amount paid by the new club as compensation for training and education of the player concerned shall be distributed according to the following principles:

(a) For the transfer of a player from a club in the third or fourth category to a club in a higher category, 75% of the amount exceeding the costs of the category of the former club shall be redistributed on a pro-rata basis to all the clubs that have trained the player from the age of 12 onwards.
(b) For the transfer of a player from a club in the second category to a club in the first category, 50% of the amount exceeding the costs of the category of the former club shall be redistributed on a pro-rata basis to all the clubs that have trained the player from the age of 12 onwards.

(c) For the transfer between two clubs of the same category, 10% of the amount calculated as described under Art. 7, pars. 3 and 4 shall be redistributed on a pro-rata basis to all the clubs that have trained the player from the age of 12 onwards.
(d) If a player's career cannot be traced back to the age of 12, any missing years will be based on category four for the purposes of determining training compensation and the amount will be distributed to the player's national association of origin and be earmarked for training young players.

Article 9 – Payment of compensation

1. The new club shall pay the training clubs the amount due as compensation for training and education pursuant to the above provisions at the latest within 30 days of the signature of the first contract under the terms of Art. 4 of the FIFA Regulations for the Status and Transfer of Players or for any subsequent transfer, within 30 days of the player's new registration.
2. It is the responsibility of the new club to calculate the amount of the compensation for training and education and the way in which it shall be distributed in accordance with the player's career history. The player shall, if necessary, assist the new club in discharging this obligation.
3. The FIFA Players' Status Committee may impose disciplinary measures on clubs or players that do not observe the obligations stipulated in the previous paragraphs.
   Appeals against these measures may be lodged to the Arbitration Tribunal for Football (TAF).

CHAPTER IV – SOLIDARITY MECHANISM

Article 10 – Principles

If a non-amateur player moves during the course of a contract, a proportion (5%) of any compensation paid to the former club will be redistributed as a solidarity contribution to the clubs involved in the training and education of the player concerned over the years. This solidarity contribution shall be apportioned between the clubs concerned according to the age of the player at the time they provided him with training and education, as follows:

- 12 – 13 years: 5%
- 13 – 14 years: 5%
- 14 – 15 years: 10%
- 15 – 16 years: 10%
- 16 – 17 years: 10%
- 17 – 18 years: 10 %
- 18 – 19 years: 10 %
- 19 – 20 years: 10 %
- 20 – 21 years: 10 %
- 21 – 22 years: 10%
- 22 – 23 years: 10%

Article 11 – Payment of solidarity contribution

1. The new club shall pay the amount due as a solidarity contribution to the training clubs pursuant to the above provisions at the latest within 30 days of the player's registration.
2. It is the responsibility of the new club to calculate the amount of the solidarity contribution and the way in which it shall be distributed in accordance with the player's career history. The player shall, if necessary, assist the new club in discharging this obligation.
3. The FIFA Players' Status Committee may impose disciplinary measures on clubs or players that do not observe the obligations stipulated in the previous paragraphs.

Appeals against these measures may be lodged to the Arbitration Tribunal for Football (TAF).

CHAPTER V – STABILITY OF CONTRACTS

Article 12

A player is entitled to terminate his contract with his club unilaterally for sporting just cause where he can show at the end of a season that he was fielded in less than 10% of the official matches played by his club. The existence of such sporting just cause shall be established on a case-by-case basis and shall depend on the particular circumstances of the player (including but not limited to injury, suspension, player's field position, position in the team (e.g. reserve goal keeper), player's age, reasonable expectations on the basis of past career, etc.).

Article 13

1. A club wishing to engage the services of a player who is at present under contract with another club is obliged to inform the club and the player before commencing negotiations with either of them.
2. For any violations of the foregoing obligation, the offending club will be subject to a fine of at least CHF 50,000.
3. Such a fine can be imposed by the Dispute Resolution Chamber, pursuant to Art. 42 of the FIFA Regulations for the Status and Transfer of Players. Appeals against any decision to impose a fine can be lodged pursuant to the provisions of the same article.

CHAPTER VI – ENFORCEMENT OF COMPENSATION AWARDS

Article 14

1. The party responsible for a breach of contract is obliged to pay the sum of compensation determined pursuant to Art. 42 of the FIFA Regulations for the Status and Transfer of Players within one month of notification of the relevant decision of the Dispute Resolution Chamber.
2. If the party responsible for the breach has not paid the sum of compensation within one month, disciplinary measures may be imposed by the FIFA Players' Status Committee, pursuant to Art. 34 of the FIFA Statutes. Appeals against these measures may be lodged to the Arbitration Tribunal for Football (TAF).
3. If a player is registered for a new club and has not paid a sum of compensation within the one month time limit referred to above, the new club shall be deemed jointly responsible for payment of the amount of compensation.
4. If the new club has not paid the sum of compensation within one month of having become jointly responsible with the player pursuant to the previous paragraph, disciplinary measures may be imposed by the FIFA Players' Status Committee, pursuant to Art. 34 of the FIFA Statutes. Appeals against these measures may be lodged to the Arbitration Tribunal for Football (TAF).

CHAPTER VII – RULES AND PROCEDURES FOR DISPUTE RESOLUTION

Article 15 – Composition of the Dispute Resolution Chamber

1. The Chairman of the Players' Status Committee shall chair the Dispute Resolution Chamber.
2. The Dispute Resolution Chamber shall be composed of representatives of players and clubs in equal number.
3. The members of the Dispute Resolution Chamber shall be designated by the Executive Committee at the proposal of the President of FIFA based upon nominations from representative players' associations and clubs and/or leagues.

Article 16 – Procedure before the Dispute Resolution Chamber

1. The Dispute Resolution Chamber of the FIFA Players' Status Committee shall review disputes coming under its jurisdiction pursuant to Art. 42 of the FIFA Regulations for the Status and Transfer of Players at the request of one of the parties to the dispute. Failure by one of the parties to appear before the Dispute Resolution Chamber does not impact on the jurisdiction of the Chamber, which shall adjudicate on the dispute based on all the facts known to it.
2. In order to submit a dispute to the Dispute Resolution Chamber, a party shall file a written request with the FIFA general secretariat. Such a request must contain the following elements:
   (a) the complainant's name and other relevant details,
   (b) if the complainant is not a natural person, a copy of its statutes and relevant certificates of incorporation as well as proof that the person filing the request on behalf of the complainant is entitled to represent it in legal proceedings,
   (c) the name and other relevant details of the legal representative assisting the complainant, if any,
   (d) the name and other relevant details of other clubs and/or players involved in the dispute, including e.g. the club accused of having induced a breach of contract.
   (e) a summary presentation of the relevant factual, legal and regulatory considerations.
   (f) ruling of any national arbitration tribunal or national court regarding this dispute.

In addition, the request shall be accompanied by a copy of all the relevant documents pertaining to the dispute.

3. The FIFA Players' Status Committee shall issue detailed internal rules of procedure for the Dispute Resolution Chamber. These rules of procedure shall ensure that the following principles be observed:
   (a) The Dispute Resolution Chamber shall afford the parties the opportunity to make their views known in full knowledge of the relevant facts of the case.
   (b) Parties shall have the opportunity to make written observations and their oral explanations may be heard, if deemed necessary, by the Dispute Resolution Chamber.
   (c) Parties shall be given enough time to prepare their defence, having due regard to the need for a speedy resolution within the deadlines provided for in Art. 42 of the FIFA Regulations for the Status and Transfer of Players.
   (d) Parties will be able to rely on professional legal assistance.
   (e) Hearings before the Dispute Resolution Chamber shall not be open to the public.
   (f) Decisions by the Dispute Resolution Chamber shall be published promptly, in extract or in full.
4. The Dispute Resolution Chamber shall send a copy of all the relevant documents pertaining to the dispute to the national association which held the registration of the player involved in the dispute when the dispute arose and set a deadline within which the association may send its written observations on the dispute. A copy of these observations shall be forwarded to the parties to the dispute.

Article – 17 Mediation

1. At the request of a party to a dispute, the FIFA general secretariat shall appoint an independent mediator which shall contact the parties to attempt mediation.
2. Mediation attempts shall not suspend the procedure before the Dispute Resolution Chamber, unless all the parties to the dispute agree to such suspension.

CHAPTER VIII – STATISTICS REGISTER

Article 18

National associations shall keep a register of the statistics of the number of registrations they have effected of players coming from other national associations, as well as of the number of international registration transfer certificates they have issued for a player transferring his registration to another national association. This register shall also mention the age and nationality of the player, the country which he is leaving or joining and any information the national association obtains on the reason for the player's transfer of registration (amicable termination, transfer at the end of the contract, or unilateral breach by the player or the club within or outside the period defined under Art. 21, par. 1 of the FIFA Regulations for the Status and Transfer of Players).

Chapter IX – Final provisions, enforcement

Article 19

Any matter not provided for under these regulations shall be settled by the FIFA Players' Status Committee, subject to review by the Executive Committee.

Article 20

These regulations shall come into force in their present form at the same time as the FIFA Regulations for the Status and Transfer of Players adopted on the same day.

Buenos Aires/Zurich, 5 July 2001
For the FIFA Executive Committee

President	General Secretary
Joseph S. Blatter	Michel Zen-Ruffinen

REGULATIONS FOR THE STATUS AND TRANSFER OF PLAYERS (2005)

Based on art. 5 of the FIFA Statutes of 19 October 2003, the Executive Committee has issued the following Regulations and its annexes, which form an integral part thereof.

DEFINITIONS

For the purpose of these Regulations, the terms set out below are defined as follows:

1. Former Association: the Association to which the Former Club is affiliated.
2. Former Club: the club that the player is leaving.
3. New Association: the Association to which the New Club is affiliated.
4. New Club: the club that the player is joining.
5. Official Matches: matches played in the framework of Organised Football, such as national league championships, national cups and international championships for clubs, but not including friendly and trial matches.
6. Organised Football: association football organised under the auspices of FIFA, the confederations and the Associations, or authorised by them.
7. Protected Period: a period of three entire Seasons or three years, whichever comes first, following the entry into force of a contract, if such contract was concluded prior to the 28th birthday of the Professional, or to a period of two entire Seasons or two years, whichever comes first, following the entry into force of a contract, if such contract was concluded after the 28th birthday of the Professional.
8. Registration Period: a period fixed by the relevant Association in accordance with Article 6.
9. Season: the period starting with the first Official Match of the relevant national league championship and ending with the last Official Match of the relevant national league championship.
10. Training Compensation: the payments made in accordance with annex 4 to cover the development of young players.

Reference is also made to the "Definitions" section in the FIFA Statutes.

NB: Terms referring to natural persons are applicable to both genders. Any term in the singular applies to the plural and vice-versa.

I. – INTRODUCTORY PROVISION

Article 1 Scope

1. These Regulations establish global and binding rules concerning the status of players, their eligibility to participate in Organised Football, and their transfer between clubs belonging to different Associations.
2. The transfer of players between clubs belonging to the same Association is governed by specific regulations issued by the Association concerned in accordance with Art. 1 par. 3 below, which must be approved by FIFA. Such regulations shall foresee rules for the settlement of disputes between clubs and players, in accordance with the principles stipulated in these Regulations. Such regulations should also foresee a system to reward the clubs investing in the training and education of young players.
3. a) The following provisions are binding at national level and have to be included, without modification, in the Association's regulations:
   Art. 2 – 8, 10, 11 and 18
   b) Each Association shall include in its regulations appropriate means to protect contractual stability, paying due respect to mandatory national law and collective bargaining agreements. In particular, the following principles should be considered:
   – Art. 13: The principle that contracts must be respected;
   – Art. 14: The principle that contracts may be terminated by either party without consequences in case of just cause;
   – Art. 15: The principle that contracts may be terminated by Professionals for sporting just cause;
   – Art. 16: The principle that contracts cannot be terminated during the course of the Season;

* See page 182 for an author's note on the amended FIFA Regulations for the Status and Transfer of Players (2008).

- Art. 17 par. 1 and 2: The principle that in case of termination of contract without just cause, compensation shall be payable and that such compensation may be stipulated in the contract;
- Art. 17 par. 3-5: The principle that in case of termination of contract without just cause, sporting sanctions shall be taken against the party in breach.

4. These Regulations also govern the release of players for Association teams and players' eligibility to play for such teams in accordance with the provisions of annexes 1 and 2 respectively. These provisions are binding for all Associations and clubs.

II. – STATUS OF PLAYERS

Article 2 – Status of Players: Amateur and Professional Players

1. Players participating in Organised Football are either Amateurs or Professionals.
2. A Professional is a player who has a written contract with a club and is paid more than the expenses he effectively incurs in return for his footballing activity. All other players are considered as Amateurs.

Article 3 – Reacquisition of Amateur Status

1. A player registered as a Professional may not re-register as an Amateur until at least 30 days after his last match as a Professional.
2. No compensation is payable upon reacquisition of Amateur status. If a player re-registers as a Professional within 30 months of being reinstated as an Amateur, his New Club shall pay Training Compensation in accordance with Article 20.

Article 4 – Termination of Activity

1. Professionals who end their careers on expiry of their contracts and Amateurs who terminate their activity shall remain registered at the Association of their last club for a period of 30 months.
2. This period begins on the day the player made his last appearance for the club in an Official Match.

III. – REGISTRATION OF PLAYERS

Article 5 – Registration

1. A player must be registered with an Association to play for a club as either a Professional or an Amateur in accordance with the provisions of Art. 2. Only registered players are eligible to participate in Organised Football. By the act of registering, a player agrees to abide by the Statutes and regulations of FIFA, the confederations and the Associations.
2. A player may only be registered for one club at a time.
3. Players may be registered for a maximum of three clubs during the period from 1 July until 30 June of the following year. During this period, the player is only eligible to play in Official Matches for two clubs.

Article 6 – Registration Periods

1. Players may only be registered during one of the two annual Registration Periods fixed by the relevant Association. As an exception to this rule, a Professional whose contract has expired prior to the end of a Registration Period may be registered outside that Registration Period.
   Associations are authorised to register such Professionals provided due consideration is given to the sporting integrity of the relevant competition.
   In case of just cause for termination of a contract, FIFA may take provisional measures in order to avoid abuse and in accordance with Art. 22.
2. The first Registration Period shall begin after the completion of the Season and shall normally end before the new Season starts. This period may not exceed twelve weeks. The second Registration Period shall normally occur in the middle of the Season and may not exceed four weeks. The two Registration Periods for the Season shall be communicated to FIFA at least 12 months before they come into force.
   FIFA shall determine the dates for any Association that fails to communicate them on time.
3. Players may only be registered – subject to the exception as foreseen in Art. 6 par. 1 – if an application from the club is validly submitted to the Association concerned during a Registration Period.

4. The provisions concerning Registration Periods do not apply to competitions in which only Amateurs participate. For such competitions, the relevant Association shall specify the periods when players may be registered, provided that due consideration is given to the sporting integrity of the relevant competition.

Article 7 – Player Passport

The registering Association is obliged to provide the club for which the player is registered with a player passport containing the relevant details of the player. The player passport shall indicate the club(s) for which the player has been registered since the Season of his 12th birthday. If a birthday falls between Seasons, the player shall be listed in the player passport for the club for which he was registered in the Season following his birthday.

Article 8 – Application for Registration

The application for registration of a Professional must be submitted together with a copy of the player's contract. It shall be at the discretion of the relevant decision-making body to take account of any contractual amendments or additional agreements that have not been duly submitted to it.

Article 9 – International Transfer Certificate

1. Players registered with one Association may only be registered with a New Association once the latter has received an International Transfer Certificate (hereinafter: ITC) from the Former Association. The ITC shall be issued free of charge without any conditions or time limitation.
   Any provisions to the contrary shall be null and void. The Association issuing the ITC shall deposit a copy with FIFA. The administrative procedures for issuing the ITC are contained in annex 3 of these Regulations.
2. An ITC is not required for a player under the age of 12 years.

Article 10 – Loan of Professionals

1. A Professional may be loaned to another club on the basis of a written agreement between him and the clubs concerned. Any such loan is subject to the same rules as apply to the transfer of players, including the provisions on training compensation and solidarity mechanism.
2. Subject to Art. 5 par. 3, the minimum period of loan shall be the time between two Registration Periods.
3. The club that has accepted a player on a loan basis is not entitled to transfer him to a third club without the written authorisation of the club that released the player on loan and of the player concerned.

Article 11 – Unregistered Players

If a player who has not been registered with an Association appears for a club in any Official Match, that player will be considered as having played illegitimately. Without prejudice to any measure required to rectify the sporting consequences of such an appearance, sanctions may also be imposed on the player and/or the club. The right to impose such sanctions lies in principle with the Association or the organiser of the competition concerned.

III. – REGISTRATION OF PLAYERS

Article – 12 Enforcement of Disciplinary Suspensions

Any disciplinary suspension imposed on a player prior to a transfer must be enforced or applied by the New Association with which the player is registered. The Former Association is obliged to notify the New Association of any sanction in writing and upon issuing the ITC.

IV. – MAINTENANCE OF CONTRACTUAL STABILITY BETWEEN PROFESSIONALS AND CLUBS

Article 13 – Respect of Contract

A contract between a Professional and a club may only be terminated on expiry of the term of the contract or by mutual agreement.

Article 14 – Terminating a Contract for Just Cause

A contract may be terminated by either party without consequences of any kind (either payment of compensation or imposition of sporting sanctions) in the case of just cause.

Article 15 – Terminating a Contract for Sporting Just Cause

An established Professional who has, in the course of the Season, appeared in less than 10% of the Official Matches in which his club has been involved may terminate his contract prematurely on the grounds of sporting just cause. Due consideration shall be given to the player's circumstances in the appraisal of such cases. The existence of sporting just cause shall be established on a case-by-case basis. In such a case, sporting sanctions shall not be imposed, though compensation may be payable. A Professional may only terminate his contract on this basis in the 15 days following the last Official Match of the Season of the club for which he is registered.

Article 16 – Restriction on Terminating a Contract During the Season

A contract cannot be unilaterally terminated during the course of a Season.

Article 17 – Consequences of Terminating a Contract Without Just Cause

The following provisions apply if a contract is terminated without just cause:

1. In all cases, the party in breach shall pay compensation. Subject to the provisions of Art. 20 and annex 4 in relation to Training Compensation, and unless otherwise provided for in the contract, compensation for breach shall be calculated with due consideration for the law of the country concerned, the specificity of sport, and any other objective criteria. These criteria shall include, in particular, the remuneration and other benefits due to the player under the existing contract and/or the new contract, the time remaining on the existing contract up to a maximum of five years, the fees and expenses paid or incurred by the Former Club (amortised over the term of the contract) and whether the contractual breach falls within a Protected Period.
2. Entitlement to compensation cannot be assigned to a third party. If a Professional is required to pay compensation, the Professional and his New Club shall be jointly and severally liable for its payment. The amount may be stipulated in the contract or agreed between the parties.
3. In addition to the obligation to pay compensation, sporting sanctions shall also be imposed on any player found to be in breach of contract during the Protected Period. This sanction shall be a restriction of four months on his eligibility to play in Official Matches. In the case of aggravating circumstances, the restriction shall last six months. In all cases, these sporting sanctions shall take effect from the start of the following Season of the New Club. Unilateral breach without just cause or sporting just cause after the Protected Period will not result in sporting sanctions. Disciplinary measures may, however, be imposed outside of the Protected Period for failure to give due notice of termination (i.e. within fifteen days following the last match of the Season).
   The Protected Period starts again when, while renewing the contract, the duration of the previous contract is extended.
4. In addition to the obligation to pay compensation, sporting sanctions shall be imposed on any club found to be in breach of contract or found to be inducing a breach of contract during the Protected Period.
   It shall be presumed, unless established to the contrary, that any club signing a Professional who has terminated his contract without just cause has induced that Professional to commit a breach. The club shall be banned from registering any new players, either nationally or internationally, for two Registration Periods.
5. Any person subject to the FIFA Statutes and FIFA regulations (club officials, players' agents, players etc.) who acts in a manner designed to induce a breach of contract between a Professional and a club in order to facilitate the transfer of the player shall be sanctioned.

Article 18 – Special Provisions Relating to Contracts Between Professionals and Clubs

1. If an agent is involved in the negotiation of a contract, he shall be named in that contract.
2. The minimum length of a contract shall be from the date of its entry into force to the end of the Season, while the maximum length of a contract shall be five years. Contracts of any other length shall only be permitted if consistent with national laws. Players under the age of 18 may not sign a professional contract for a term longer than three years. Any clause referring to a longer period shall not be recognised.
3. A club intending to conclude a contract with a Professional must inform his current club in writing before entering into negotiations with that Professional. A Professional shall only be free to conclude a contract with another club if his contract with his present club has expired or will expire within six months. Any breach of this provision shall be subject to appropriate sanctions.

4. The validity of a contract may not be made subject to a positive medical examination and/or the granting of a work permit.
5. If a Professional enters into more than one contract covering the same period, the provisions set forth in Chapter IV shall apply.

V. – INTERNATIONAL TRANSFERS INVOLVING MINORS

Article 19 – Protection of Minors

1. International transfers of players are only permitted if the player is over the age of 18.
2. The following three exceptions to this rule apply:
   a) The player's parents move to the country in which the New Club is located for reasons not linked to football; or
   b) The transfer takes place within the territory of the European Union (EU) or European Economic Area (EEA) and the player is aged between 16 and 18. In this case, the New Club must fulfil the following minimum obligations:
      i. It shall provide the player with an adequate football education and/or training in line with the highest national standards.
      ii. It shall guarantee the player an academic and/or school and/or vocational education and/or training, in addition to his football education and/or training, which will allow the player to pursue a career other than football should he cease playing professional football.
      iii. It shall make all necessary arrangements to ensure that the player is looked after in the best possible way (optimum living standards with a guest family or in club accommodation, appointment of a mentor at the club etc.).
      iv. It shall, on registration of such a player, provide the relevant Association with proof that it is complying with the aforementioned obligations; or
   c) The player lives no further than 50km from a national border, and the club for which the player wishes to be registered in the neighbouring Association is also within 50km of that border. The maximum distance between the player's domicile and the club's quarters shall be 100km. In such cases, the player must continue to live at home and the two Associations concerned must give their explicit consent.
3. The conditions of this article shall also apply to any player who has never previously been registered for a club and is not a national of the country in which he wishes to be registered for the first time.
4. Each Association shall ensure the respect of this provision by its clubs.
5. The Players' Status Committee shall be competent to decide on any dispute arising in relation to these matters and shall impose appropriate sanctions in case of violation of this provision.

VI. – TRAINING COMPENSATION AND SOLIDARITY MECHANISM

Article 20 – Training Compensation

Training Compensation shall be paid to a player's training club(s): (1) when a player signs his first contract as a Professional, and (2) on each transfer of a Professional until the end of the Season of his 23rd birthday. The obligation to pay Training Compensation arises whether the transfer takes place during or at the end of the player's contract.
The provisions concerning Training Compensation are set out in annex 4 of these Regulations.

Article 21 – Solidarity Mechanism

If a Professional is transferred before the expiry of his contract, any club that has contributed to his education and training shall receive a proportion of the compensation paid to his previous club (solidarity contribution). The provisions concerning solidarity contributions are set out in annex 5 of these Regulations.

VII. – JURISDICTION

Article 22 – FIFA Competence

Without prejudice to the right of any player or club to seek redress before a civil court for employment-related disputes, FIFA is competent for:

a) Disputes between clubs and players in relation to the maintenance of contractual stability (Art. 13 – 18) if there has been an ITC Request and if there is a claim from an interested party in relation to such ITC Request, in particular regarding its issuance, regarding sporting sanctions or regarding compensation for breach of contract;

b) Employment-related disputes between a club and a player that have an international dimension, unless an independent arbitration tribunal guaranteeing fair proceedings and respecting the principle of equal representation of players and clubs has been established at national level within the framework of the Association and/or a collective bargaining agreement;
c) Employment-related disputes between a club or an Association and a coach that have an international dimension, unless an independent arbitration tribunal guaranteeing fair proceedings exists at national level;
d) Disputes related to Training Compensation (Art. 20) and Solidarity Mechanism (Art. 21) between clubs belonging to different Associations;
e) Disputes between clubs belonging to different Associations that do not fall within the cases foreseen in a) and d).

VII. – JURISDICTION
Article 23 – Players' Status Committee

1. The Players' Status Committee shall adjudicate on all disputes in accordance with Art. 22 c) and e) as well as on all other disputes arising from the application of these regulations, subject to Art. 24.
2. In case of uncertainty as to the jurisdiction of the Players' Status Committee or the Dispute Resolution Chamber, the chairman of the Players' Status Committee shall decide which body has jurisdiction.
3. The Players' Status Committee shall adjudicate in the presence of at least three members, including the chairman or the deputy chairman, unless the case is of such a nature that it may be settled by a single judge. In cases that are urgent or raise no difficult factual or legal issues, and in decisions on the issuance of a provisional ITC in accordance with annex 3, the chairman or a person appointed by him, who must be a member of the committee, may adjudicate as a single judge. Each party shall be heard once during the proceedings.
   Decisions reached by the single judge or the Players' Status Committee may be appealed before the Court of Arbitration for Sport (CAS).

Article 24 – Dispute Resolution Chamber (DRC)

1. The DRC shall adjudicate on any dispute in accordance with Art. 22 a), b) and d), with the exception of the issuance of the ITC.
2. The DRC shall adjudicate in the presence of at least three members, including the chairman or the deputy chairman, unless the case is of a nature that may be settled by a DRC judge. The members of the DRC shall designate a DRC judge for the clubs and one for the players from among its members. The DRC judge may adjudicate in the following cases:
   i) all disputes up to a litigious value of CHF 100,000;
   ii) disputes relating to the calculation of Training Compensation;
   iii) disputes relating to the calculation of solidarity contributions.
   The DRC judge is compelled to submit fundamental issues to the chamber. The chamber shall consist of equal numbers of club and player representatives, except in those cases that may be settled by a DRC judge. Each party shall be heard once during the proceedings. Decisions reached by the Dispute Resolution Chamber or the DRC judge may be appealed before the Court of Arbitration for Sport (CAS).

VII. – JURISDICTION
Article 25 – Procedural Guidelines

1. As a rule, the single judge and the DRC judge shall adjudicate within 30 days of receipt of a valid request and the Players' Status Committee or the Dispute Resolution Chamber shall adjudicate within 60 days.
   The proceedings shall be governed by the FIFA General Procedural Rules.
2. The maximum cost for proceedings before the Players' Status Committee, including the single judge, shall be set at CHF 25,000 and will normally be paid by the unsuccessful party. The allocation of costs shall be explained in the decision. Proceedings before the DRC and the DRC judge are free of charge.
3. Disciplinary proceedings for violation of these Regulations shall, unless otherwise stipulated herein, conform with the FIFA Disciplinary Code.

4. If there is reason to believe that a case raises a disciplinary issue, the Players' Status Committee, the Dispute Resolution Chamber, the single judge or the DRC judge (as the case may be) shall submit the file to the Disciplinary Committee together with a request for the commencement of disciplinary proceedings, in accordance with the FIFA Disciplinary Code.
5. The Players' Status Committee, the Dispute Resolution Chamber, the single judge or the DRC judge (as the case may be) shall not hear any case subject to these Regulations if more than two years have elapsed from the event giving rise to the dispute. Application of this time limit shall be examined ex officio in each individual case.
6. The Players' Status Committee, the Dispute Resolution Chamber, the single judge or the DRC judge (as the case may be) shall, when taking their decisions, apply these Regulations whilst taking into account all relevant arrangements, laws and/or collective bargaining agreements that exist at national level, as well as the specificity of sport.
7. The detailed procedure for the resolution of disputes arising from the application of these Regulations shall be further outlined in the FIFA General Procedural Rules.

VIII. – FINAL PROVISIONS

Article 26 – Transitional Measures

1. Any case that has been brought to FIFA before these Regulations come into force shall be assessed according to the previous regulations.
2. All other cases shall be assessed according to these Regulations.
3. Member Associations shall amend their regulations in accordance with Art. 1 to ensure that they comply with these Regulations and shall submit them to FIFA for approval by 30 June 2007. Notwithstanding this, each Member Association shall implement Art. 1 par. 3 (a) as from 1 July 2005.

Article 27 – Matters Not Provided for

Matters not prvided for in these regulations and cases of force majeure shall be decided by the FIFA Executive Committee, whose decisions are final.

Article 28 – Official Languages

In the case of any discrepancy in the interpretation of the English, French, Spanish or German texts of these regulations, the English text is authoritative.

Article 29 – Annulment, Enforcement

1. These Regulations shall replace the special regulations governing players' eligibility to play for Association teams dated 4 December 2003 and the Regulations for the Status and Transfer of Players of 5 July 2001 as well as all subsequent amendments, including all relevant circular letters issued before the date of entry into force of these regulations.
2. These Regulations were adopted by the FIFA Executive Committee on 18 December 2004 and come into force on 1 July 2005.

Zurich, December 2004
For the FIFA Executive Committee

Joseph S. Blatter	Urs Linsi
President	General Secretary

ANNEX 1

RELEASE OF PLAYERS FOR ASSOCIATION TEAMS

Article 1 – Principles

1. Clubs are obliged to release their registered players for representative teams of the country for which the player is eligible to play on the basis of his nationality, if he is called up by the Association concerned. Any divergent agreement between a player and a club is prohibited.
2. The release of players under the terms of par. 1 of this article is mandatory for matches on dates listed in the Coordinated International Match Calendar and for all matches for which a duty to release players exists on the basis of a special decision of the FIFA Executive Committee.
3. It is not compulsory to release players for matches scheduled on dates not listed in the Coordinated International Match Calendar.

4. Players must also be released for the period of preparation before the match, which is laid down as follows:
   a) for friendly matches: 48 hours
   b) for qualifying matches for an international tournament: four days (including the day of the match). The release period shall be extended to five days if the match concerned is held in a different confederation to the one in which the player's club is registered.
   c) for qualifying matches for an international tournament that are staged on a date earmarked for friendly matches: 48 hours
   d) for the final competition of an international tournament: 14 days before the first match in the competition.

   Players shall join the Association team no later than 48 hours before kick-off.
5. The players of Associations that have automatically qualified for the final competition of the FIFA World Cup™ or for continental championships for 'A' national teams shall be released for friendly matches on dates earmarked for official qualifying matches in accordance with the directives that would apply for Official Matches staged on these dates.
6. The clubs and Associations concerned may agree a longer period of release.
7. Players complying with a call-up from their Association under the terms of this article shall resume duty with their clubs no later than 24 hours after the end of the match for which they were called up.

   This period shall be extended to 48 hours if the match concerned took place in a different confederation to the one in which the player's club is registered. Clubs shall be informed in writing of a player's outward and return schedule ten days before the match. Associations shall ensure that players are able to return to their clubs on time after the match.
8. If a player does not resume duty with his club by the deadline stipulated in this article, the next time the player is called up by his Association, the period of release shall be shortened as follows:
   a) for a friendly match: to 24 hours
   b) for a qualifying match: to three days
   c) for the final competition of an international tournament: to ten days.
9. Should an Association repeatedly breach these provisions, the FIFA Players' Status Committee may impose appropriate sanctions, which may include but not be limited to:
   – fines
   – reduction of the period of release
   – ban on calling up a player(s) for the subsequent match(es)

Article 2 – Financial Provisions and Insurance

1. Clubs releasing a player in accordance with the provisions of this annex are not entitled to financial compensation.
2. The Association calling up a player shall bear the costs of travel actually incurred by the player as a result of the call-up.
3. The club for which the player concerned is registered shall be responsible for his insurance cover against illness and accident during the entire period of his release. This cover must also extend to any injuries sustained by the player during the international match(es) for which he was released.

Article 3 – Calling up Players

1. As a general rule, every player registered for a club is obliged to respond affirmatively when called up by the Association he is eligible to represent on the basis of his nationality to play for one of its representative teams.
2. Associations wishing to call up a player who is playing abroad must notify the player in writing at least 15 days before the day of the match for which he is required. The player's club shall also be informed in writing at the same time. The club must confirm the release of the player within the following six days.
3. Associations that request FIFA's help to obtain the release of a player playing abroad may only do so under the following two conditions:
   a) The Association with which the player is registered must have been asked to intervene without success.
   b) The case is submitted to FIFA at least five days before the day of the match for which the player is needed.

Article 4 – Injured Players

A player who is unable to comply with a call-up from the Association that he is eligible to represent on the basis of his nationality owing to injury or illness shall, if the Association so requires, agree to undergo a medical examination by a doctor of that Association's choice. If the player so wishes, such medical examination shall take place on the territory of the Association where he is registered.

Article 5 – Restrictions on Playing

A player who has been called up by his Association for one of its representative teams is, unless otherwise agreed by the relevant Association, not entitled to play for the club with which he is registered during the period for which he has been released or should have been released pursuant to the provisions of this annex. This restriction on playing for the club shall, moreover, be prolonged by five days in the event that the player, for whatsoever reason, did not wish to or was unable to comply with the call-up.

Article 6 – Disciplinary Measures

1. Violations of any of the provisions set forth in this annex shall result in the imposition of disciplinary measures.
2. If a club refuses to release a player or neglects to do so despite the provisions of this annex, the FIFA Players' Status Committee shall furthermore request the Association to which the club belongs to declare any match(es) in which the player took part to have been lost by the club concerned. Any points thus gained by the club in question shall be forfeited.
   Any match contested according to the cup system shall be regarded as having been won by the opposing team, irrespective of the score.
3. If a player reports late for duty with his club more than once after being called up by an Association, the FIFA Players' Status Committee may, at the request of the player's club, impose additional sanctions on the player and/or his Association.

ANNEX 2
ELIGIBILITY TO PLAY FOR ASSOCIATION TEAMS FOR PLAYERS WHOSE NATIONALITY ENTITLES THEM TO REPRESENT MORE THAN ONE ASSOCIATION

Article 1 – Conditions

1. A player who, under the terms of Art. 15 of the Regulations Governing the Application of the FIFA Statutes, is eligible to represent more than one Association on account of his nationality, may play in an international match for one of these Associations only if, in addition to having the relevant nationality, he fulfils at least one of the following conditions:
   a) he was born on the territory of the relevant Association;
   b) his biological mother or biological father was born on the territory of the relevant Association;
   c) his grandmother or grandfather was born on the territory of the relevant Association;
   d) he has lived on the territory of the relevant Association for at least two years without interruption.
2. Notwithstanding par. 1 of this article, Associations sharing a common nationality may make an agreement under which item d) of par. 1 of this article is deleted completely or amended to specify a longer time limit. Such agreements must be lodged with and approved by FIFA.

ANNEX 3
ADMINISTRATIVE PROCEDURE GOVERNING THE TRANSFER OF PLAYERS BETWEEN ASSOCIATIONS

Article 1 – Principles

1. Any player who is registered for a club that is affiliated to one Association shall not be eligible to play for a club affiliated to a different Association unless an ITC has been issued by the Former Association and received by the New Association in accordance with the provisions of this annex. Special forms provided by FIFA for this purpose or forms with similar wording shall be used.
2. In the case of Professionals, the Association issuing the ITC shall also attach a copy of the player passport to it.

Article 2 – Issuance of an ITC for a Professional

1. All applications to register a Professional must be submitted by the New Club to the New Association during one of the Registration Periods established by that Association. All applications shall be

accompanied by a copy of the contract between the New Club and the Professional. A Professional is not eligible to play in Official Matches for his New Club until an ITC has been issued by the Former Association and received by the New Association.

2. Upon receipt of the application, the New Association shall immediately request the Former Association to issue an ITC for the Professional (the "ITC Request"). The last date on which the ITC Request can be made is the last day of the Registration Period of the New Association. An Association that receives an unsolicited ITC from another Association is not entitled to register the Professional concerned for one of its clubs.
3. Upon receipt of the ITC Request, the Former Association shall immediately request the Former Club and the Professional to confirm whether the Professional's contract has expired, whether early termination was mutually agreed or whether a contractual dispute exists.
4. Within seven days of receiving the ITC Request, the Former Association shall either:
   a) issue the ITC to the New Association; or,
   b) inform the New Association that the ITC cannot be issued because the contract between the Former Club and the Professional has not expired or that there has been no mutual agreement regarding its early termination.
5. If the New Association does not receive a response to the ITC Request within 30 days of the ITC Request being made, it shall immediately register the Professional with the New Club on a provisional basis ("Provisional Registration"). A Provisional Registration shall become permanent one year after the ITC Request. The Players' Status Committee may withdraw a Provisional Registration, if, during this oneyear period, the Former Association presents valid reasons explaining why it did not respond to the ITC Request.
6. The Former Association shall not issue an ITC if a contractual dispute has arisen between the Former Club and the Professional. In such a case, the Professional, the Former Club and/or the New Club are entitled to lodge a claim with FIFA in accordance with Art. 22. FIFA shall then decide on the issuance of the ITC and on sporting sanctions within 60 days. In any case, the decision on sporting sanctions shall be taken before the issuance of the ITC. The issuance of the ITC shall be without prejudice to compensation for breach of contract. FIFA may take provisional measures in case of exceptional circumstances.
7. The New Association may grant a player temporary eligibility to play on the basis of an ITC sent by fax until the end of the Season that is underway. If the original ITC is not received by that time, the player's eligibility to play shall be considered definitive.
8. Associations are forbidden from requesting the issuance of an ITC in order to allow a player to participate in trial matches.
9. The foregoing rules and procedures also apply for Professionals who, upon moving to their New Club, acquire Amateur status.

Article 3 – Issuance of an ITC for a Amateur

1. All applications to register an Amateur player must be submitted by the New Club to the New Association during one of the Registration Periods established by that Association.
2. Upon receipt of the application, the New Association shall immediately request the Former Association to issue an ITC for the player (the "ITC Request").
3. The Former Association shall, within seven days of receiving the ITC Request, issue the ITC to the New Association.
4. If the New Association does not receive a response to the ITC Request within thirty days, it shall immediately register the Amateur with the New Club on a provisional basis ("Provisional Registration"). A Provisional Registration shall become permanent one year after the ITC Request. The Players' Status Committee may withdraw a Provisional Registration, if, during this one-year period, the Former Association presents valid reasons explaining why it did not respond to the ITC Request.
5. The foregoing rules and procedures also apply for Amateurs who, upon moving to their New Club, acquire Professional status.

Article 4 – Loan of Players

1. The rules set out above also apply to the loan of a Professional from a club affiliated to one Association to a club affiliated to another Association.

2. The terms of the loan agreement shall be enclosed with the ITC Request.
3. On expiry of the period of loan, the ITC shall be returned, upon request, to the Association of the club that released the player on loan.

ANNEX 4
TRAINING COMPENSATION

Article 1 – Objective

1. A player's training and education takes place between the ages of 12 and 23. Training Compensation shall be payable, as a general rule, up to the age of 23 for training incurred up to the age of 21, unless it is evident that a player has already terminated his training period before the age of 21. In the latter case, Training Compensation shall be payable until the end of the Season in which the player reaches the age of 23, but the calculation of the amount payable shall be based on the years between 12 and the age when it is established that the player actually completed his training.
2. The obligation to pay Training Compensation is without prejudice to any obligation to pay compensation for breach of contract.

Article 2 – Payment of Training Compensation

Training Compensation is due:

i) when a player is registered for the first time as a Professional; or,
ii) when a Professional is transferred between clubs of two different Associations (whether during or at the end of his contract) before the end of the Season of his 23rd birthday.

Training Compensation is not due:

i) if the Former Club terminates the player's contract without just cause (without prejudice to the rights of the previous clubs); or
ii) if the player is transferred to a Category 4 club; or
iii) if a Professional reacquires Amateur status on being transferred.

Article 3 – Responsibility to Pay Training Compensation

1. When a player is registering as a Professional for the first time, the club for which the player is being registered is responsible for paying Training Compensation within 30 days of registration to every club for which the player was registered (in accordance with the players' career history as provided for in the player passport) and that has contributed to his training starting from the Season in which he had his 12th birthday. The amount payable is calculated on a pro rata basis according to the period of training that the player spent with each club. In the case of subsequent transfers of the Professional, Training Compensation will only be owed to his Former Club for the time he was effectively trained by that club.
2. In both of the above cases, the deadline for payment of Training Compensation is 30 days following the registration of the Professional with the New Association.
3. If a link between the Professional and any of the clubs that trained him cannot be established, or if those clubs do not make themselves known within 18 months of the player's first registration as a Professional, the Training Compensation shall be paid to the Association(s) of the country (or countries) where the Professional was trained. This compensation shall be earmarked for youth football development programmes in the Association(s) in question.

Article 4 – Training Costs

1. In order to calculate the compensation due for training and education costs, Associations are instructed to divide their clubs into a maximum of four categories in accordance with the clubs' financial investment in training players. The training costs are set for each category and correspond to the amount needed to train one player for one year multiplied by an average "player factor", which is the ratio between the number of players who need to be trained to produce one professional player.
2. The training costs, which are established on a confederation basis for each category of club, as well as the categorisation of clubs for each Association, are published on the FIFA website (www.FIFA.com). They will be updated at the end of every calendar year.

Article 5 – Calculation of Training Compensation

1. As a general rule, to calculate the Training Compensation due to a player's Former Club(s), it is necessary to take the costs that would have been incurred by the New Club if it had trained the player itself.
2. Accordingly, the first time a player registers as a Professional, the Training Compensation payable is calculated by taking the training costs of the New Club multiplied by the number of years of training in principle from the Season of the player's 12th birthday to the Season of his 21st birthday. In the case of subsequent transfers, Training Compensation is calculated based on the training costs of the New Club multiplied by the number of years of training with the Former Club.
3. To ensure that Training Compensation for very young players is not set at unreasonably high levels, the training costs for players for the Seasons between their 12th and 15th birthday (i.e. four Seasons) shall be based on the training and education costs for category 4 clubs.
4. The Dispute Resolution Chamber may review disputes concerning the amount of Training Compensation payable and shall have discretion to adjust this amount if it is clearly disproportionate to the case under review.

Article 6 – Special Provisions for the EU/EEA

1. For players moving from one Association to another inside the territory of the EU/EEA, the amount of Training Compensation payable shall be established based on the following:
   a) If the player moves from a lower to a higher category club, the calculation shall be based on the average of the training costs of the two clubs.
   b) If the player moves from a higher to a lower category, the calculation shall be based on the training costs of the lower category club.
2. Inside the territory of the EU/EEA, the final Season of training may occur before the Season in which the player had his 21st birthday if it is established that the player completed his training before that time.
3. If the Former Club does not offer the player a contract, no Training Compensation is payable unless the Former Club can justify that it is entitled to such compensation. The Former Club must offer the player a contract in writing via registered mail at least 60 days before the expiry of his current contract. Such an offer shall furthermore be at least of an equivalent value to the current contract. This provision is without prejudice to the rights to Training Compensation of the player's previous club(s).

Article 7 – Disciplinary Measures

The FIFA Disciplinary Committee may impose disciplinary measures on clubs or players that do not observe the obligations set out in this annex.

ANNEX 5

SOLIDARITY MECHANISM

Article 1 – Solidarity Contribution

If a Professional moves during the course of a contract, 5% of any compensation, with the exception of Training Compensation, paid to his Former Club shall be deducted from the total amount of this compensation and distributed by the New Club as a solidarity contribution to the club(s) involved in his training and education over the years. This solidarity contribution will refl ect the number of years (calculated pro rata if less than one year) he was registered with the relevant club(s) between the Seasons of his 12th and 23rd birthdays, as follows:

- Season of 12th birthday: 5% (i.e. 0.25% of total compensation)
- Season of 13th birthday: 5% (i.e. 0.25% of total compensation)
- Season of 14th birthday: 5% (i.e. 0.25% of total compensation)
- Season of 15th birthday: 5% (i.e. 0.25% of total compensation)
- Season of 16th birthday: 10% (i.e. 0.5% of total compensation)
- Season of 17th birthday: 10% (i.e. 0.5% of total compensation)
- Season of 18th birthday: 10% (i.e. 0.5% of total compensation)
- Season of 19th birthday: 10% (i.e. 0.5% of total compensation)
- Season of 20th birthday: 10% (i.e. 0.5% of total compensation)
- Season of 21st birthday: 10% (i.e. 0.5% of total compensation)

– Season of 22nd birthday: 10% (i.e. 0.5% of total compensation)
– Season of 23rd birthday: 10% (i.e. 0.5% of total compensation)

Article 2 – Payment Prodedure

1. The New Club shall pay the solidarity contribution to the training club(s) pursuant to the above provisions no later than 30 days after the player's registration or, in case of contingent payments, 30 days after the date of such payments.
2. It is the responsibility of the New Club to calculate the amount of the solidarity contribution and to distribute it in accordance with the player's career history as provided for in the player passport. The player shall, if necessary, assist the New Club in discharging this obligation.
3. If a link between the Professional and any of the clubs that trained him cannot be established within 18 months of his transfer, the solidarity contribution shall be paid to the Association(s) of the country (or countries) where the Professional was trained. This solidarity contribution shall be earmarked for youth football development programmes in the Association(s) in question.
4. The Disciplinary Committee may impose disciplinary measures on clubs that do not observe the obligations set out in this annex.

RULES GOVERNING THE PROCEDURES OF THE PLAYERS' STATUS COMMITTEE AND THE DISPUTE RESOLUTION CHAMBER (DRC)

Based upon Art. 31 par. 1 of the FIFA Statutes, the following Rules have been issued:

Article 1 – Scope

1. The procedures of the Players' Status Committee and the Dispute Resolution Chamber (DRC) shall be in accordance with the Rules laid down here.
2. Any provisions in the FIFA Statutes or other FIFA regulations that deviate from these Rules shall have precedence over the provisions of these Rules.

Article 2 – Applicable material law

In their application and adjudication of law, the Players' Status Committee and the DRC shall apply the FIFA Statutes and regulations, whilst taking into account all relevant arrangements, laws and/or collective bargaining agreements that exist at national level, as well as the specificity of sport.

I. – GENERAL PROVISIONS

Article 3 – Jurisdictions

1. The Players' Status Committee and the DRC shall examine their jurisdiction, in particular in the light of Articles 22 to 24 of the Regulations for the Status and Transfer of Players adopted in December 2004. In the event of any uncertainty as to the jurisdiction of the Players' Status Committee or the DRC, the chairman of the Players' Status Committee shall decide which body has jurisdiction.
2. The identity and jurisdiction of the single judge of the Players' Status Committee and the DRC judge is set out in Art. 23, par. 3 and Art. 24, par. 2 of the Regulations for the Status and Transfer of Players.
3. Subject to other provisions, proceedings before the single judge or the DRC judge shall also be in accordance with these Rules.

Article 4 – Composition

The chairman, deputy chairman and members of the Players' Status Committee and the DRC shall be chosen by the Executive Committee.
The twenty members of the DRC, made up of an equal number of player and club representatives, shall be appointed on the proposal of the players' associations and the clubs or leagues.

Article 5 – General procedural principles

1. The Players' Status Committee and the DRC shall conduct the proceedings and monitor compliance with the procedural regulations.

2. All persons party to legal application and adjudication processes must act in good faith.
3. All persons party to proceedings are obliged to tell the truth to the Players' Status Committee and the DRC.
4. A claim shall be dealt with by the Players' Status Committee and the DRC only if there is a legitimate reason for dealing with the claim.
5. The Players' Status Committee and the DRC shall determine the facts of a case according to their best judgement. All persons party to the proceedings and all persons subject to the regulations of FIFA shall assist in determining the facts of a case.
6. The Players' Status Committee and the DRC shall perform the duties entrusted to them with due expedition.
7. Members of the Players' Status Committee and the DRC may not perform different functions in the same matter. They shall refrain from attempting to infl uence other bodies and committees and must maintain strict confidentiality concerning all information that comes to their attention in the exercising of their office and not mentioned in the decision. They are in particular obliged to respect the secrecy of deliberations.
8. Subject to regulations to the contrary, parties in the proceedings shall be granted the right to be heard, the right to present evidence, the right to inspect evidence leading to a decision, the right to access files and the right to a motivated decision.

Article 6 – Parties

1. Parties are members of FIFA, clubs, players, coaches or licensed match and players' agents.
2. Parties may appoint a representative. A written power of attorney is to be requested from such representatives. If a party is ordered to appear in person, said party must obey the summons.
3. Parties requesting the opening of proceedings shall be sent written confirmation when the request has been received. Parties affected by the opening of proceedings must be notified thereof without delay.

Article 7 – Withdrawal and challenges

1. Members of the Players' Status Committee and the DRC may not exercise their office in any cases in which they have a personal and/or direct interest. The member in question must disclose his or her reasons for withdrawing in sufficient time.
2. Members of the Players' Status Committee and the DRC may be challenged by the parties if there is legitimate doubt as to their independence and impartiality. A challenge must be made under consequence of forfeit within five days of the grounds for the challenge coming to light. Motions must be substantiated and, where possible, supported by evidence. If the member concerned disputes the allegations raised, the Players' Status Committee or the DRC shall reach a decision on the challenge in the absence of the member concerned.
3. If the Players' Status Committee and the DRC are no longer able to function as a consequence of challenges, the Executive Committee shall make a final decision on the challenges and, if necessary, appoint an ad-hoc committee to deal with the material facts of the case.

II. – PROCEDURAL REGULATIONS

Article 8 – Procedural form

As a general rule, proceedings shall be conducted in writing.

Article 9 – Petitions and statements

1. Petitions shall be submitted in one of the four official FIFA languages via the FIFA general secretariat. They must contain the following particulars:
   a) the name and address of the parties;
   b) the name and address of the legal representative, if applicable, and the power of attorney;
   c) the motion or claim;
   d) a representation of the case, the grounds for the motion or claim and details of the evidence;
   e) documents of relevance to the dispute such as contracts and previous correspondence with respect to the case in the original version and, if applicable, translated into one of the official FIFA languages (evidence);
   f) the name and address of other natural and legal persons involved in the case concerned (evidence);

g) the amount in dispute, insofar as it is a financial dispute;
h) the date and a valid signature.

2. Petitions submitted by parties that do not satisfy the aforementioned requirements will be returned for redress along with a warning that the petition will not be dealt with in the event of non-compliance. Petitions with improper or inadmissible content will be rejected immediately.
3. If there is no reason not to deal with a petition, it shall be sent to the opposing party or the person affected by the petition, setting a time limit for a statement or reply. If no statement or reply is received before the time limit expires, a decision shall be taken upon the basis of the documents on file. A second exchange of correspondence will be instituted only in special cases.

Article 10 – Venue

The proceedings and deliberations of the Players' Status Committee (including the single judge) and the DRC (including the DRC judge) shall take place at FIFA headquarters in Zurich, Switzerland, subject to exceptions.

Article 11 – Oral hearing

1. If the circumstances appear to warrant it, the parties may be summoned to attend an oral hearing. A record of the hearing shall be conducted by a person appointed by the chairman. The testimonies from parties, witnesses and experts are to be signed by them.
2. On timely request, an interpreter will be provided by FIFA. The costs for the interpreter are to be borne by the requesting party.

Article 12 – Taking of evidence

1. Evidence consists of party testimony, witness testimony, documents, expert reports, real evidence and all other pertinent evidence.
2. Evidence shall be heard only in respect of facts relevant to the case.
3. Any party deriving a right from an alleged fact shall carry the burden of proof.
4. The Players' Status Committee and the DRC may also consider evidence not offered by the parties.
5. If the hearing of evidence offered is associated with high costs, it may be made dependent upon the party remitting the anticipated costs within a set time limit.
6. Evidence shall be considered with free discretion, taking into account the conduct of the parties during the proceedings, especially a failure to comply with a personal summons, a refusal to answer questions, the withholding of requested evidence etc.

Article 13 – Decisions

1. Decision-making by the Players' Status Committee and the DRC is effected by a simple majority vote after secret deliberations. All members in attendance and the chairman have one vote each. Abstentions are not permitted. In the event of a tie, the chairman shall have the casting vote. Decisions may also be taken by way of circulars.
2. Decisions shall be communicated in writing. In urgent cases, the holding of the decision may be communicated immediately, with the finding then submitted within twenty days.
3. The FIFA General Secretary is entitled to announce the decision in the name of and on behalf of the Players' Status Committee and the DRC.
4. Written decisions shall contain at least the following:
   a) the date of the decision; for decisions taken by way of circular, the date of completion of the circular process;
   b) the names of the parties and any representatives;
   c) the names of the members participating in the decision taken by the decision-making body;
   d) the claims and/or motions submitted by the parties;
   e) a brief description of the case;
   f) the reasons for the findings;
   g) the outcome of the taking of evidence;
   h) the holding of the decision.
5. Obvious mistakes in decisions may be corrected, ex officio or on application, by the body that made the decision.

6. No disadvantage may accrue to any party from the erroneous announcement of a decision.

Article 14 – Time limits

1. Procedural acts must be performed within the time limit prescribed by the Rules or the decision-making body.
2. A time limit is deemed to have been observed if the act is completed before midnight on the final day of the set period.
3. Written petitions and payments must arrive at the designated place or have been paid at a recognised branch of a bank or posted at a recognised post office no later than the final day of the set period. Petitions submitted by e-mail shall have no legal effect, unlike petitions submitted by fax.
4. Petitions and payments submitted in time to the wrong FIFA office are deemed to have been submitted within the time limit. Onward transmission to the correct office shall be effected ex officio.
5. Proof of compliance with the time limit is to be provided by the sender.
6. If these Rules do not specify the consequences of non-compliance with a time limit, they shall be determined by the Players' Status Committee or the DRC. Warnings may not go further than necessary for the due process of the proceedings.
7. The day on which a time limit is instituted and the day on which the payment initiating the time limit is made shall not be counted when calculating the time limit.
8. All time limits shall be suspended in the period from 20 December up to and including 5 January and for a period of five days before and five days after an Ordinary or an Extraordinary Congress. During the FIFA World Cup™ (finals) time limits shall be suspended if so decided, ex officio or on application by a party, by the decision-making body.
9. If the final day of the time limit is an official holiday or a non-working day in the country where the party submitting or receiving a document is domiciled or resident, the time limit shall expire at the end of the next working day.
10. Regulatory time limits may not be extended. Time limits set by the Players' Status Committee and the DRC may be extended, paying due consideration to the principle of expeditious execution of proceedings, if a substantiated request is submitted before the time limit expires.
11. Time limits that are to be set by the Players' Status Committee and the DRC should normally run for no less than ten and no more than twenty days. In urgent cases, time limits may be reduced to twentyfour hours.
12. Should a party or representative be unable to observe a time limit through no fault of its own, the time limit may be re-assigned on substantiated request, although only if the request is made within three days of the hindrance ceasing to exist.
13. The limit for lodging an appeal shall always begin on receipt of the full version of the decision.

Article 15 – Costs

1. Costs in the maximum amount of CHF 25,000 are levied in connection with proceedings of the Players' Status Committee. Costs are to be borne in consideration of the parties' degree of success in the proceedings. In special circumstances, the costs may be assumed by FIFA. Should a party generate unnecessary costs on account of its conduct, costs may be imposed upon it, irrespective of the outcome of the proceedings.
2. DRC proceedings are free of charge.
3. No procedural compensation shall be awarded in proceedings of the Players' Status Committee and the DRC.

Article 16 – Service of decisions

1. Decisions shall be sent to the parties directly, with a copy also sent to the respective associations.
2. Service is deemed to be complete at the moment the decision is received by the party, at least by fax. Service to a representative shall be deemed as service to the party.
3. Decisions communicated by fax shall be legally binding. Alternatively, decisions may be communicated by registered letter or courier, which shall also be legally binding.

Article 17 – Publication

Decisions, should they be of general interest, may be published by the general secretariat in a form determined by the Players' Status Committee or the DRC, e.g. condensed in the form of a media release.

Due restraint shall be exercised when publicising decisions. On substantiated request by a party, certain elements of the decision may be excluded from publication.

III. – FINAL PROVISIONS
Article 18 – Enforcement

1. These Rules were approved by the FIFA Executive Committee on 29 June 2005 and come into force on 1 July 2005.
2. These Rules are applicable to proceedings submitted to FIFA after the date on which these Rules came into force.
3. These Rules replace the Procedural Rules for the FIFA Players' Status Committee dated 21 February 2003 and the Rules Governing the Practice and Procedures of the Dispute Resolution Chamber dated 28 February 2002. In cases submitted to FIFA before these Rules came into force, the old procedural rules shall apply.

Zurich, June 2005
For the FIFA Executive Committee

Joseph S. Blatter	Urs Linsi
President	General Secretary

The costs of the proceedings to be levied in accordance with these Rules are based upon the following:
Amount in dispute Cost of the proceedings
up to CHF 50,000 up to CHF 5,000
up to CHF 100,000 up to CHF 10,000
up to CHF 150,000 up to CHF 15,000
up to CHF 200,000 up to CHF 20,000
from CHF 200,001 up to CHF 25,000

PLAYERS' AGENTS REGULATIONS

At a meeting on 10 December 2000, the FIFA Executive Committee passed the following regulations, in compliance with art. 17, par. 2 of the Regulations governing the Application of the FIFA Statutes:

Preamble

1. These regulations govern the occupation of players' agents who arrange players' transfers within one national association or from one national association to another.
2. Each national association is obliged to draw up its own regulations for players' agents based on the following guidelines. Such regulations must be approved by the FIFA Players' Status Committee and incorporate the principles mentioned below.
3. When drawing up their regulations the national associations shall take the FIFA Statutes and regulations into account as well as their own national legislation and international treaties.

I. General Rules
Article 1

1. Players and clubs are permitted to call upon the services of a players' agent during negotiations with other players or clubs provided the players' agent possesses a licence issued to him by the national association concerned in compliance with art. 2, par. 1 below.
   The players' agent is a natural person who, for a fee, on a regular basis introduces a player to a club with a view to employment or introduces two clubs to one another with a view to concluding a transfer contract, in compliance with the provisions mentioned below.
2. Players and clubs are forbidden from using the services of a non-licensed players' agent (cf. art. 16 and 18).
3. The ban stipulated in par. 2 above does not apply if the agent acting on behalf of a player is a parent, a sibling or the spouse of the player in question or if the agent acting on behalf of the player or club

is legally authorised to practise as a lawyer in compliance with the rules in force in his country of domicile.

II. Issue of a License

Article 2

1. Any natural person wishing to act as a players' agent shall send a written application to the national association of the country of which he is a national or, if he lives elsewhere, to the national association of his country of domicile provided he has lived there constantly for at least two years.
   Within the territory of the EU/EEA the applicant may turn to the national association of the country of his legal domicile, regardless of the duration of his residence.
2. The applicant must have an impeccable reputation otherwise his application will be disregarded. The national association concerned shall decide whether the applicant fulfils the basic requirements in accordance with the national legislation of the country concerned.
3. Only a natural person may apply for a licence. Applications from companies or clubs are not permitted.

Article 3

An applicant may not, under any circumstances, hold a position with FIFA, a confederation, a national association, a club or any organisation connected with these institutions.

Article 4

1. Any national association that receives an application for a licence shall check whether it complies with the prerequisites stipulated in art. 2 and art. 3.
2. If the application is acceptable, the national association shall call the candidate for a written examination.
3. An applicant whose application has officially been rejected by the national association's examining body may send his application to FIFA. The FIFA Players' Status Committee shall decide whether the national association has rejected the applicant unfairly. If the Players' Status Committee also considers the application to be lacking in any form, the applicant may not reapply to the national association concerned for another two years.

Article 5

1. The national associations shall set written examinations twice a year.
2. The examinations shall be held on identical dates throughout the world. FIFA will therefore fix mandatory dates at the beginning of each calendar year in March and September and inform the national associations accordingly.
3. National associations are responsible for arranging the examination in good time and giving the candidates adequate notice to take it.
4. The basic terms and conditions for the examination procedure are defined in Annexe A of these regulations.
5. The national associations may charge an appropriate fee to cover the costs of arranging the examination.

Article 6

1. If a candidate scores the minimum amount of marks required to pass the examination (cf. Annexe A, I. par. 5), the national association shall request him to conclude professional liability insurance with an insurance company in his country.
   Within the territory of the EU/EEA the candidate may conclude the requested insurance policy with an insurance company in any EU/EEA country.
   He shall then send the insurance policy to the national association responsible.
2. The aim of the insurance is to cover any claims for compensation from a player, a club or another players' agent arising from the players' agent's occupation which, in the opinion of the national association and/or FIFA, contravenes the principles of these regulations and/or the national association's regulations. The policy shall therefore be worded in such a way that every possible risk connected with a players' agent's occupation is covered.
3. The maximum amount covered by the insurance policy shall be fixed on the basis of the players' agent's turnover.

4. The professional liability insurance policy shall also cover claims made after expiry of the policy for events that occurred during the duration of the policy.
5. The players' agent is required to renew the insurance policy as soon as it has expired and automatically send the relevant documents to the national association concerned.

Article 7

1. If the players' agent cannot conclude a professional liability insurance policy in compliance with art. 6 above in the country in which he passed the examination, he may deposit a bank guarantee to the amount of CHF 100,000.--. The guarantee shall be issued by a Swiss bank and shall be irrevocable.
2. Only FIFA has access to this bank guarantee. The bank guarantee has the same objective as that of professional liability insurance (cf. art. 6, par. 2). The amount of the guarantee (CHF 100,000.--) does not represent the maximum amount due to any party claiming damages.
3. If the amount of the guarantee is reduced by a payment from the bank in response to a claim for damages against a players' agent, the players' agent's licence will be suspended until the amount of the guarantee has been increased to the initial amount (CHF 100,000.--).

Article 8

1. Every candidate who has passed the examination is required to sign a Code of Professional Conduct (cf. Annexe B) in which he pledges, without fail, to abide by the basic principles described therein when acting as a players' agent.
2. Players' agents who fail to abide by the Code of Professional Conduct during the course of their work are liable to be sanctioned in accordance with art. 15, par. 2.

Article 9

1. Players' associations that are officially recognised by national associations and that wish to provide a job placement service to their member players in accordance with art. 1 above may conclude their own joint professional liability insurance policy with an insurance company in the country where they operate.
2. In such cases, this insurance shall be limited to covering risks for no more than five licences. The licence holders shall, however, be bona fide members of the associations concerned, have passed the written examination in accordance with Annexe A herein and have personally signed the Code of Professional Conduct in accordance with art. 8. The names of the candidates who have received a licence shall also be listed in the insurance policy mentioned in par. 1 of this article.

Article 10

1. After it has received the professional liability insurance policy or the bank guarantee, depending on the situation, and the signed pledge of the Code of Professional Conduct, the national association shall issue the players' agent licence to the candidate. This licence is strictly personal and not transferable. Each national association is required to draw up a list of all of the licensed players' agents on its territory and to send it to FIFA after every examination date.
2. The licence shall be issued for an unlimited period and authorise the players' agent to carry out transactions on a worldwide basis.
3. FIFA will compile a list of every licensed players' agent in the world and publish it on its official website.
4. As soon as the players' agent has received his licence from the national association, he will be entitled to use the following designation in business relations after his name: "Players' agent licensed by [country] national association".

III. Rights & Obligations of Licensed Player's Agents

Article 11

A licensed players' agent has the right:

1. to contact every player who is not, or is no longer, under contract with a club (cf. art. 12 and 13 of the FIFA Regulations for the Status and Transfers of Players);
2. to represent the interests of any player or club that requests him to negotiate and/or conclude contracts on his/its behalf;
3. to take care of the interests of any player who requests him to do so;

4. to take care of the interests of any club which requests him to do so.

Article 12

1. A players' agent may represent or take care of the interests of a player or a club in compliance with art. 11 only if he has concluded a written contract with the player or club.
2. Such a contract shall be limited to a period of two years but may be renewed in writing at the express request of both parties. It may not be tacitly prolonged.
3. The contract shall explicitly mention who is responsible for paying the players' agent's fee, the type of fee and the prerequisite terms for the payment of the fee.
4. Only the client engaging the services of the players' agent, and no other party, may remunerate him.
5. The amount of remuneration due to a players' agent who has been engaged to act on a player's behalf is calculated on the basis of the player's annual basic gross income (i.e. excluding other benefits such as a car, a flat, point premiums and/or any kind of bonus or privilege) that the players' agent has negotiated for him in the employment contract.
6. The players' agent and the player shall decide in advance whether the player will remunerate the players' agent with a lump sum payment at the start of the employment contract that the players' agent has negotiated for the player or whether he will pay annual instalments at the end of a contractual year.
7. If the players' agent and the player do not decide on a lump sum payment and the player's employment contract negotiated by the players' agent on his behalf lasts longer than the representation contract between the players' agent and the player, the players' agent is entitled to annual remuneration even after expiry of the representation contract. This entitlement lasts until the player's employment contract expires or as soon as the player signs a new employment contract without the help of the same players' agent.
8. If the players' agent and the player cannot reach agreement on the amount of remuneration to be paid or if the representation contract does not provide for such remuneration, the players' agent is entitled to payment of compensation amounting to 5% of the basic income described in par. 4 above which the player is due to receive from the employment contract negotiated by the players' agent on his behalf.
9. A players' agent who has been contracted by a club shall be remunerated for his services by payment of a lump sum that has been agreed upon in advance.
10. FIFA will provide its standard representation contract (cf. Annexe C) to the national associations. Every players' agent is required to use this standard contract. The parties to the contract are at liberty to conclude additional agreements and to supplement the standard contract accordingly, providing the relevant public law provisions for arranging employment in the country concerned are observed without fail.
11. The representation contract shall be issued in quadruple and duly signed by both parties. The player or the club shall keep the first copy and the players' agent the second. The players' agent shall send the third and fourth copies to his national association, or the national association to which the player or club belongs, for registration within 30 days of their having been signed. The national associations shall keep a register of the contracts being received. Copies of the contracts shall be sent to FIFA upon request.
12. Minors may not sign a representation contract without the express permission of their legal guardian(s) in compliance with the national law of the country in which the player is domiciled.

Article 13

A players' agent may organise his occupation as a business as long as his employees' work is restricted to administrative duties connected with the business activity of a players' agent. Only the players' agent himself is entitled to represent and promote the interests of players and/or clubs with other players and/ or clubs. The players' agent shall send the national association that issued him the licence a list of his employees at least once a year. Each employee shall have featured on the list for at least three months before being officially confirmed in office. The players' agent shall immediately notify his national association of any elimination from the list. The elimination then takes immediate effect.

Article 14

A licensed players' agent is required:

1. to adhere, without fail, to the statutes and regulations of the national associations, confederations and FIFA;
2. to ensure that every transaction concluded as a result of his involvement complies with the provisions of the aforementioned statutes and regulations;
3. never to approach a player who is under contract with a club with the aim of persuading him to terminate his contract prematurely or to flout the rights and duties stipulated in the contract;
4. to represent only one party when negotiating a transfer;
5. to give, at request, the relevant body at each national association and/or FIFA all of the requisite information and to send in the necessary papers;
6. to ensure that his name, signature and the name of his client appear in the relevant contracts resulting from every transaction in which he is involved;
7. to comply with the relevant public law provisions governing job placement in the country concerned.

Article 15

1. Players' agents who abuse the rights accorded to them or contravene any of the duties stipulated in these regulations are liable to sanctions.
2. The following sanctions may be pronounced:
   1. a caution, censure, or warning;
   2. a fine;
   3. suspension of the licence;
   4. withdrawal of the licence.

   The sanctions may be imposed jointly.
3. The foregoing sanctions may be pronounced only by the national association that issued the licence to the offending players' agent or by FIFA. The delimitations of responsibility are stipulated in art. 22, par. 1 and 2 below.
4. The licence shall be withdrawn if the players' agent fails to fulfil any of the prerequisites for acquiring a licence stipulated under art. 2, 3, 6 and 7 (professional liability insurance or bank guarantee). If this is the case and the omission can be remedied, the appropriate body at the national association shall set him a reasonable deadline in which to reinstate compliance with the rules.
5. In addition to the reasons given under par. 4, the licence shall be withdrawn, in particular if the players' agent repeatedly or seriously infringes the statutes and regulations of the national associations, confederations and/or FIFA.
6. The licence shall be withdrawn by the national association which issued it. FIFA reserves the right to direct a national association to mandatorily withdraw a licence.

IV. Player's Duties

Article 16

1. Players may only call upon the services of a players' agent who holds a licence issued by a national association in compliance with these regulations, subject to the exceptions mentioned in art. 1, par. 3.
2. The players' agent's name and signature shall, without fail, appear in the relevant employment contract(s) in every transaction in which a players' agent represents the players' interests.

   If a player does not use the services of a players' agent, this fact shall also be explicitly stated in the relevant employment contract.

Article 17

If a player engages the services of a non-licensed players' agent, it is left to the discretion of the national association with which the player is registered (in the case of a national transfer) or FIFA (in the case of an international transfer):

1. to take this fact into account when judging a player's situation in any dispute arising as a result of such contracts;
2. to punish the player as follows:

- with a caution, censure or warning;
- with a fine of at least CHF 10,000.--;
- with a disciplinary suspension of up to 12 months.

These sanctions may be imposed jointly.

V. Duties of the clubs

Article 18

1. Clubs which wish to engage the services of a player may only deal either:
   - with the player himself, or
   - with a players' agent who holds a licence issued by a national association in compliance with the provisions of these regulations, subject to the exceptions mentioned in art. 1, par. 3.
2. For every transaction in which a players' agent represents the interests of a club, his name and signature shall, without fail, appear in the relevant transfer and/or employment contract(s).
   If the club does not use the services of a players' agent, this fact shall also be explicitly mentioned in the relevant transfer and/or employment contract(s).
3. A club which pays another club compensation shall pay it directly to the beneficiary club. It is strictly forbidden for the club making the remittance to pay any of the amount, either partially or wholly, to the players' agent, not even as remuneration.

Article 19

1. Any club that infringes any of the bans contained in art. 18 will be liable to the following sanctions:
   1. a caution, censure or warning;
   2. suspension of any or all of its board of directors;
   3. a fine of at least CHF 20,000.--;
   4. a ban on any national and/or international players' transfers for at least three months;
   5. a ban on any kind of national and/or international football activity.

   In addition, any transaction which the club makes in contravention of art. 18 above will be declared null and void.
   The sanctions may be imposed jointly.
2. The sanctions listed above may only be pronounced by the national association to which the club is affiliated (in the case of a national transfer) and by FIFA (in the case of an international transfer).

VI. Special Provisions

Article 20

1. Any players' agent who decides to terminate his activities as such is obliged to return his licence to the national association that issued it. Failure to comply with this provision will incur cancellation of the licence and publication of this decision.
2. The national association shall publish the names of those players' agents who have terminated their activities as such and notify FIFA and the relevant confederation immediately.
3. The players' agent may not cancel his professional liability insurance policy until he has terminated his occupation (the licence has either been returned or withdrawn). The players' agent shall, however, ensure that any claim for compensation made after termination of his occupation, which originates from his former activities as a players' agent, is covered by the insurance (cf. art. 6, par. 4 of these regulations).

Article 21

1. The Players' Status Committee is the supervisory and decision-making body of FIFA responsible for implementing these regulations and for ensuring that players' agents carry out their activities in compliance with the Code of Professional Conduct.
2. Each national association shall designate a supervisory and decision-making body responsible for the activity of players' agents for whom it has issued a licence.

This body shall ensure that the players' agents' activities at national level comply with the principles of the Code of Professional Conduct.

VII. Disputes

Article 22

1. In the event of disputes between a players' agent and a player, a club and/or another players' agent, all of whom are registered with the same national association (national disputes), the national association concerned is responsible. It is obliged to deal with the case and pass a decision, for which service it is entitled to charge an appropriate fee.
2. Any other complaint not covered by par. 1 shall be submitted to the FIFA Players' Status Committee.
3. Complaints about the work of a players' agent shall be directed in writing to the national association concerned or to FIFA within two years of the incident in question and in any case no later than six months after the players' agent concerned has terminated his activities as such.

VIII. Transitional provisions

Article 23

1. Any players' agent who already holds a FIFA licence in accordance with the Regulations governing Players' Agents dated 11 December 1995 may exchange it for a new one at the national association responsible under the terms of art. 2, par. 1 of these regulations within six months of their implementation. These players' agents are not required to take the written examination in compliance with Annexe A of these regulations.
2. Once the transitional period of six months has elapsed, the validity of the former licence will expire. Any players' agents who have not exchanged their FIFA licence by this time will be required to take the written examination to acquire the new licence at the national association concerned.

Article 24

1. Any players' agent who has deposited a bank guarantee with a Swiss bank in compliance with art. 9 of the Regulations governing Players' Agents dated 11 December 1995 may request FIFA to release the bank guarantee upon production of a professional liability insurance policy. The policy shall have been issued by an insurance company that has its headquarters in the country of the national association that is responsible for the players' agents concerned under the terms of art. 2, par. 1.
2. FIFA will notify the national association concerned of the switch and send it the insurance policy.

Article 25

1. Any dispute between a players' agent and a player, a club and/or another players' agent which was submitted to FIFA for settlement by the Players' Status Committee before these regulations came into effect shall be settled in compliance with the Regulations governing Players' Agents dated 11 December 1995.
2. Any dispute submitted for decision after these regulations come into effect shall be settled in compliance with these regulations by those bodies stipulated under art. 22.

IX. Final Provisions

Article 26

The FIFA Executive Committee shall have the final say on any matters not provided for under these regulations.

Article 27

In the event of any discrepancy in the interpretation of the English, French, Spanish or German text of these regulations, the English text is authoritative.

Article 28

These regulations were adopted by the FIFA Executive Committee at its meeting in Rome on 10 December 2000 and come into effect on 1 March 2001.

Rome/Zurich, 10 December 2000

For the FIFA Executive Committee

The President:
Joseph S. Blatter

The General Secretary:
Michel Zen-Ruffinen

Annexe A: Examination Procedure

I.

1. The examination shall be set as a multiple choice test. The candidate will be considered to have passed the examination if he has attained the minimum marks fixed by FIFA (cf. par. 5).
2. Each candidate shall be tested on the following subjects:
    1. familiarity with the current rules of football, especially in connection with transfers (the statutes and regulations of FIFA, the confederations and the national association in whose country the candidate takes the examination),
    2. familiarity with civil law (basic principles of personal rights) and the law of obligations (law of contract).
3. Each examination shall contain twenty questions, fifteen on international regulations and five on national regulations.
4. Each national association shall set its own questions on national subjects whereas FIFA will set the questions on its own statutes and regulations and send the examination papers to be used to the national associations.
5. FIFA will fix the minimum marks required to pass the examination. Each correct answer will be awarded between one to three marks, depending on the degree of difficulty of the question.
6. The national associations shall inform the candidates of the minimum marks to be attained before they take the examination.

II.

1. The examination papers shall be marked immediately after the examination and the candidate informed of the outcome.
2. A candidate who fails to attain the minimum marks may immediately reapply to retake the examination.
3. If a candidate fails to attain the minimum marks after the second try, he may not retake it until the next two examination dates have elapsed. Only then may he apply to take the examination a third time, in which case he may choose to be examined by the national association or by FIFA.
4. Any candidate who fails to attain the minimum marks after the third try may not take the examination again for another two years.

Annexe B: Code of Professional Conduct

I.

The players' agent is required to perform his occupation conscientiously and conduct himself in his profession and other business practices in a manner worthy of respect and befitting his profession.

II.

The players' agent shall adhere to the truth, clarity and objectivity in his dealings with his client, negotiating partners and other parties.

III.

The players' agent shall protect the interests of his client in compliance with the law and a sense of fairness, while creating clear legal relations.

IV.

The players' agent shall, without fail, respect the rights of his negotiating partners and third parties. In particular, he shall respect the contractual relations of his professional colleagues and shall refrain from any action that could entice clients away from other parties.

V.

1. The players' agent shall conduct a minimum of bookkeeping on his business activities. In particular, he shall ensure that he can provide evidence of his activities at any time by means of documents and other records.
2. He shall keep all of the books conscientiously and detail his business activities faithfully in other records.
3. At the request of any authorities conducting an investigation into disciplinary cases and other disputes, the players' agent is required to produce books and records directly connected with the case in point.
4. The players' agent shall produce an invoice showing his fees, expenses and any other charges upon first demand from his client.

AUTHOR'S NOTE

Amended FIFA Regulations for the Status and Transfer of Players

On 1 January 2008 a new edition of the FIFA Regulations for the Status and Transfer of Players entered into force. In addition to purely linguistic alterations the new Regulations also encompass some new provisions. These provisions are primarily a codification of jurisprudence from the FIFA Dispute Resolution Chamber, the Players' Status Committee and the Court of Arbitration for Sports. The FIFA hopes to increase legal certainty by ensuring that the jurisprudence is more strongly represented in the Regulations.
Article 18b of the new Regulations is remarkable. This article regards the prohibition against clubs concluding contracts that enable third parties to exercise influence on the independence of clubs and the decisions taken by the club concerning the transfer of players.
Pursuant to Article 17 paragraph 3 a player who wishes to unilaterally terminate his employment contract outside the protected period should notify his club of this within 15 days following the final official match of the season. Contrary to the 2005 Regulations, in the new Regulations cup competition matches are also deemed to be official matches as provided for in Article 17 paragraph 3. Therefore, if in a specific country the cup final is played after the final competition match, the term of 15 days does not commence until after the cup final.

Finally, in the new Regulations the FIFA Dispute Resolution Chamber is explicitly authorised in respect of disputes concerning a solidarity contribution between two clubs from the same country, if the transfer underlying the dispute is an international transfer (between two clubs from different countries).

CASES

22 NOVEMBER 2002

22-11-2002, 300702
THE DISPUTE RESOLUTION CHAMBER OF THE PLAYERS' STATUS COMMITTEE
convening in Zurich, Switzerland, on 22 November 2002 and comprising:
Slim Aloulou (Tunisia), Chairman
Philippe Piat (France), member
Theo van Seggelen (the Netherlands), member
Maurice Watkins (England), member
Mario Gallavotti (Italy), member
and deliberating in accordance with Article 42 of the FIFA Regulations for the Status and Transfer of Players (edition September 2001) on a claim lodged by the player H., against the club C., regarding a contractual dispute between the player and the club.

TOOK INTO CONSIDERATION
AS TO SUBSTANCE
- the Chamber duly noted that:
- the club C. and the player H. signed an employment contract valid from 1 March until 30 November 2002,
- in accordance with this contract, the player was entitled to receive a monthly salary of USD 10,000 along with match bonuses, furnished accommodation and two round-trip aeroplane tickets to his home country,
- the claimant, the player H., maintains in his claim that:
- when he arrived in the country of his new club C., he was immediately given the impression that the club C. was no longer interested in his services. Instead of finding an apartment with satellite television, telephone and heating at his disposal, he had to wait five weeks before being provided with the mentioned accommodation. Furthermore, the apartment he was eventually given had no heating, causing his wife to become ill,
- subsequently, when he left to his home country for his holidays, he noticed that the club had provided him with a visa for a duration of two weeks only. The club C. had failed to provide him with a work permit. He therefore had to organise a visa himself, in order to return to the club,
- because the club C. had relocated to another city, his wife was left behind. As she felt abandoned, and after having consulted with his contact person, the player returned to collect her,
- upon his return to the club, he was informed that the club had made him redundant,
- according to art. 13 of the employment contract, the club was not entitled to rescind the contract without having consulted him or obtained his approval. As a penalty, the contract foresees the payment of an amount corresponding to three months salary. Finally, the player outlined that he had not been paid for the month of June and that he had not received the reimbursement of his aeroplane ticket, as stated in art. 10 of the contract,
- in response to the claim, the respondent, the club C., maintains that:
- the player H. had displayed a very disagreeable conduct right from the start of his employment. The player would not obey the instructions given by the coach and would only train himself as he liked. On several occasions he refused to attend training,
- the club provided him with all that was foreseen in the employment contract, excepting satellite television, as this was disallowed by the police,
- the club arranged for the necessary visa on 16 April 2002,
- the player failed to pay his telephone expenses,
- finally, the player did not turn up for the training session subsequent to the match of 23 June 2002 since he had left to collect his wife. Therefore, he was fined USD –.– as specified in the employment contract and the employment was terminated. The rules of the club clearly allow the rescission of an employment under such circumstances,
- as a result, the player is not entitled to compensation.

- taking into consideration the above, the Chamber outlined that:
- it shall not enter into the question whether the violations of the contractual arrangements of one party outweighed those committed by the other party,
- clearly, the contractual relationship reigning between both sides was far from satisfactory and appears to have been problematic from the start,
- although the accusations being raised by the parties are significant, there is not a single occurrence that prevails over the other,
- therefore, the question remains whether the dismissal of the player H. was justified,
- the Chamber recognised the admissibility of the employer to impose disciplinary sanctions on an employee if he is failing to comply with his obligations. These sanctions must, however, be in relation to the fault committed by the player,
- in the present case, the parties pre-determined the upper limit of a possible sanction in the employment contact, setting it at a fine of no higher than USD –.–,
- the parties clearly concurred over the adequacy of this sanction,
- the player H. admits having left the club C. without the appropriate authorisation, to meet up with his wife, and consequently, the club C. is entitled to impose a disciplinary sanction,
- the disciplinary sanction corresponding to a fine of USD –.–is the most severe sanction listed in the employment contract and, given that it corresponds to an entire month's salary, certainly not too lenient,
- however, and in light of the circumstances leading to the situation, this disciplinary sanction can be accepted,
- the dismissal of the player, on the other hand, is unquestionably disproportionate and can therefore not be accepted,
- the Chamber was consequently of the unanimous opinion that the club C. terminated the employment contract with the player H. without just cause,
- therefore, the player H. is entitled to claim the penalty listed in art. 13 of the employment contract, amounting to a payment of USD –.–,
- furthermore, the player H. is equally entitled to the payment corresponding to the salary of the month of June 2001, amounting to USD –.–,
- finally, the Chamber concluded that the player must be reimbursed for the expenses related to the aeroplane tickets. The Chamber set the payable amount at USD –.–,
- the fine of USD –.–is, however, admissible and will be deducted from the amounts due to the player,

DECIDED FOR THESE REASONS

1. The claim lodged by Mr. H. is to be partially accepted.
2. The club C. must pay the amount of USD –.–, comprising the penalty for the unilateral breach of contract in the amount of USD –.– and the amount of USD –.– for the compensation of the airfares, to Mr. H., within 30 days of notification of the present decision.
3. This decision may be appealed before the Court of Arbitration for Sport (CAS) within 20 days of receiving notification of this decision by contacting the court directly in writing.

⚽⚽⚽

4 JULY 2003

730291

THE DISPUTE RESOLUTION CHAMBER OF THE PLAYERS' STATUS COMMITTEE

convening in Zurich, Switzerland, on 4 July 2003 and comprising:
Slim Aloulou (Tunisia), Chairman
Philippe Piat (France), member
Theo van Seggelen (Netherlands), member
Mario Gallavotti (Italy), member
Philippe Diallo (France), member
and deliberating in accordance with art. 42 of the FIFA Regulations for the Status and Transfer of Players (edition September 2001; hereinafter: the Regulations) on a claim lodged by the Polish player, X, against the Greek club, Z,

TOOK INTO CONSIDERATION
AS TO SUBSTANCE

- the Chamber duly noted that:
- on 5 August 2002 the player, X, concluded an employment contract with the club, Z, valid for one year, thus expiring on 30 June 2003;
- according to the said contract the player is entitled to a monthly salary of EUR –.–;
- furthermore, a yearly fee of EUR –.– should be paid to the player in 8 equal monthly instalments of EUR –.– starting as from 30 August 2002;
- according to art. 3 of the employment contract, the player is authorised to unilaterally terminate the relevant agreement by written communication to the club, and the club will have to compensate him for all losses, provided that the bills of exchange remitted to the player cannot be cashed on their expiry date;
- yet, the relevant amount to be paid by the club should not be less than the entire remaining value of the contract;
- moreover, under such circumstances, the club shall not be entitled to ask for any compensation from the player's new club;
- on 16 January 2003 the player's lawyer notified the Greek club the unilateral termination of the employment contract by the player, due to the breach of the contractual obligations by the club;
- on 20 January 2003 the club released a document, by means of which they accused the player to have been absent from training without valid reasons since 17 January 2003 and urging the player to immediately rejoin the team;
- on 21 January 2003 the Board of Directors of the Greek club decided to terminate the employment contract with the player, due to the latter's continuing absence;
- furthermore, a complaint against the player was lodged at the competent committee of the Hellenic Football Federation;
- on the same day Mr X asked FIFA to declare that the Greek club is in breach of the employment contract and to be authorised to sign for a new club of his choice;
- on 14 February 2003 the FIFA administration provisionally authorised the player to sign for the club of his choice;
- on 19 February 2003 the Arbitration Body of the Greek League of Football Clubs passed a decision, according to which Z's request for termination of the employment contract was accepted;
- in particular, the deciding body of the Greek League took into account that according to the Greek regulations a player is obliged to respect all clauses of his employment contract;
- if he does not comply with them, the club is at liberty to unilaterally rescind the relevant agreement;
- consequently, it was concluded that the contractual relation between the parties had to be considered as terminated as from 17 January 2003;
- moreover, the deciding body of the Greek League judged that the player had breached the relevant agreement on the same day by leaving the club without any valid reasons;
- in the meantime, the player moved to Poland, where he was engaged by the club, Gornik Zabrze SSA;
- the player, X, maintains in particular in its claim that:
- the club was always late with the payment of his salary and part of it remains still outstanding;
- in particular, he emphasises that the first salary payment was late, the instalment of the yearly fee due in September 2002 was paid in November 2002 and the third instalment was paid in mid December 2002 only;
- moreover, since his lawyer intervened with the club on his behalf, Z has been constantly intimidating, threatening and harassing him;
- until 21 January 2003 he received only three instalments of the yearly fee, i.e. for the months of August, September and October 2002;
- furthermore, the monthly salary of EUR –.– was paid for August, September, October and November 2002, however not for the two subsequent months;
- with regard to the financial part of the dispute, he is demanding the following amounts:
  EUR –.– (outstanding instalments of the yearly fee due respectively on 30 November and 30 December 2002);
  EUR –.– (salary due in December 2002);

EUR –.– (compensation for the breach of the employment contract corresponding to the remaining value of the contract, in accordance with art. 3 of the relevant agreement);
EUR –.– (compensation for losses occurred to him);
EUR –.– Total

- furthermore, he claims a not yet determined sum for bonuses, whereby he estimates that the value of the bonuses due to him during the entire season corresponds to EUR –.–;
- in response to the claim the club, Z, maintains in particular that:
- the player left the club without notice and valid reasons and consequently, did not fulfil his contractual obligations;
- since 17 January 2003 he did not participate to any training session or match;
- by presenting the relevant receipts, it confirms that until February 2003 it has paid only the three instalments of the yearly fee due in August, September and October 2002 to the player;
- remitting copies of the relevant receipts to the FIFA services, it also agrees that it paid four monthly salaries to the player, i.e. for August, September, October and November 2002;
- taking into consideration the above, the Chamber outlined that:
- in view of the fact that the Arbitration Body of the Greek League of Football Clubs had already examined the substance of the present litigation, first of all, it had to be verified whether the Chamber was competent to deal with the case at issue,
- according to art. 42 par. 1 lit. (b) (i) of the Regulations, the Chamber can decide on the triggering elements of the dispute only if the parties have not expressed a preference for a national sports arbitration tribunal composed of members chosen in equal numbers by players and clubs, as well as an independent chairman, in a written agreement, or if this procedure is provided for by collective bargain agreement,
- the aforementioned provision intends to support the parties' freedom to choose to refer their litigations to a national arbitration body, however, it also aims to guarantee that certain fundamental procedural principles are respected by the national instances,
- in particular, the relevant clause expressly requires from the national sports arbitration tribunal a parity composition,
- obviously, although not explicitly stated, the national procedure has to respect the right of the parties to be heard,
- equally, contradictory proceedings as well as a proper and clear motivation of the decision taken, including the enumeration of the members of the deciding body, must be guaranteed and respected,
- on account of all the above, it could be concluded that decisions taken by national sports arbitration tribunals, which do not fulfill all of the aforementioned fundamental procedural principles, cannot be considered as binding for the Chamber and as a consequence, in such cases, the Chamber can reexamine the entire affair de novo,
- the Arbitration Body of the Greek League of Football Clubs does not appear to by composed on a parity base,
- as a result, basically, the Chamber is competent to examine the substance of the matter, despite the decision already taken by the national instance, provided no other formal element would call the Chamber's jurisdiction into question,
- as established in art. 42 par. 1 lit. (b) (i) of the Regulations, it falls within the purview of the Dispute Resolution Chamber to determine whether one of the parties has committed a unilateral breach of contract without just cause,
- if the employment contract was breached by a party, the Dispute Resolution Chamber is responsible to verify whether this party is accountable for outstanding payments and compensation,
- also, the Dispute Resolution Chamber will establish the amount of compensation to be paid and decide whether sports sanctions must be imposed (cf. art. 42 par. 1 (b) (ii) and (iii) in connection with art. 22 and 23 of the Regulations),
- it is uncontested that, until 21 January 2003, the player only received three instalments of the yearly fee, i.e. for the months of August, September and October 2002, as well as the monthly salary for August, September, October and November 2002,
- on account of this fact, it has to be acknowledged that the club admits not having respected its financial obligations,
- in January 2003, the club was in arrears with the payment of the yearly fee and the salary already for two months,

- under these circumstances, art. 3 of the employment contract has to be applied,
- it had to be established that the club had breached the employment contract concluded with the player and as a result, the player had a just cause to unilaterally terminate his engagement on 16 January 2003,
- moreover, this right had explicitly been conferred to the player by means of art. 3 of the employment contract,
- in view of the above, the player, X, is entitled to his salary and the instalments of the yearly fee until December 2002, i.e. EUR –.–,
- in addition, the player is entitled to compensation for the breach of the employment contract by the club, corresponding to the remaining value of the contract, i.e. EUR –.– (instalments of the yearly fee for January until March 2003 in the amount of EUR –.– each; salary for January until June 2003 in the amount of EUR –.– per month),
- since art. 3 of the employment contract clearly provides that the compensation to be paid to the player by the club in case of non-respect of the financial obligations should not be less than the entire remaining value of the contract, the salary received by the player from his new Polish club does not need to be deducted,
- the player had not presented any evidences corroborating additional losses allegedly occurred to him,
- equally, he had not sufficiently substantiated his request for bonuses,
- therefore, no supplementary amounts can be granted to him under these titles,
- for the sake of good order, it should be mentioned that on account of the above considerations and conclusions the club's claim that the player had left the club without valid reasons on 17 January 2003 cannot be backed,
- the player's absence from trainings and matches as from 17 January 2003 is a consequence of his justified written notice sent to the club by his lawyer on 16 January 2003,
- in view of all the above, the decision of the FIFA administration of 14 February 2003 to provisionally authorise the player, X, to sign for the club of his choice must be confirmed,
- finally, in application of art. 3 of the employment contract, the club, Z, is not entitled to ask for any compensation from the player's new club,

DECIDED FOR THESE REASONS

1. The claim lodged by the player, X, is partially accepted.
2. The contractual relation between the player, X, and the club, Z, is terminated as from 16 January 2003.
3. The player, X, is entitled to receive EUR –.– as outstanding salary and yearly fee from the club, Z. The relevant amount has to be paid by the club within 30 days as from notification of the present decision.
4. The club, Z, is directed to pay the player, X, compensation for the breach of the employment contract in the amount of EUR –.– within 30 days of notification of the present decision.
5. If Z fails to comply with the above-mentioned deadlines, an interest rate of 4.50% per year will apply.
6. The club, Z, is not entitled to any compensation from the new club of the player, X.
7. This decision may be appealed before the Court of Arbitration for Sport (CAS) within 20 days of receiving notification of this decision, by contacting the court directly in writing and by following the directions issued by the CAS, copy of which we enclose hereto.

⚽⚽⚽

21 NOVEMBER 2003

113291
THE DISPUTE RESOLUTION CHAMBER OF THE PLAYERS' STATUS COMMITTEE
convening in Zurich, Switzerland, on 21 November 2003 and comprising:
Slim Aloulou (Tunisia), Chairman
Philippe Piat (France), member
Michele Colucci (Italy), member

Mario Gallavotti (Italy), member
Philippe Diallo (France), member
and deliberating in accordance with art. 42 of the FIFA Regulations for the Status and Transfer of Players (edition September 2001; hereinafter: the Regulations) on a claim lodged by the Swiss player, X, against the Chinese club, Y,

TOOK INTO CONSIDERATION
AS TO SUBSTANCE

- the Chamber duly noted that:
- on 5 January 2003 the player, X, and the club, Y, concluded an employment contract valid until 31 December 2003;
- among other things, art. 13 of the relevant agreement provided that in case of unilateral termination of the contract without valid reasons, the fallible party shall compensate the other party with a sum corresponding to three monthly salaries;
- equally, on the same day, a second contract called "Payment Agreement" was concluded;
- after having sent a last warning on 18 April 2003, which remained unanswered, on 24 April 2003 the player informed the club in writing that he rescinded the employment contract with immediate effect, claiming valid reasons, and subsequently, he left the club on the same day;
- in view of the fact that during the course of the investigation into this affair it appeared that both parties considered the contractual relation as being terminated, on 30 July 2003 the FIFA administration provisionally authorised the player to sign for a new club of his choice;
- the player, X, maintains in particular in his claim that:
- he properly fulfilled his contractual obligations, yet, the club did not comply with its financial duties, i.e. payment of salaries, sign-on fee etc.;
- prior to signing the employment contract he had undergone all medical tests required by the club on 5 January 2003, thus on the day when the two agreements were signed, and no reservations were raised with regard to his physical conditions;
- before suffering from an injury in a match played with the Chinese club in mid February 2003, he regularly trained and played for the club without any problems;
- in particular, he participated to the intensive preparation trainings for the new season;
- the medical report presented by the club concerns the examination, which he had to undergo after starting to feel pain at the end of the preparation trainings in February 2003;
- after his injury he was treated by the club's medical staff, and he accepted all the prescribed measures;
- consequently, his recovery mainly depended on the medical treatment he received from the club;
- art. 30 of the Regulations clearly provides that, in any case, the validity of an employment contract between a player and a club cannot be made conditional upon the positive results of a medical examination and moreover, the medical tests need being carried out before concluding the contract, otherwise the club will be liable to pay the full amount of the salary due;
- on 22 April 2003, thus after his last warning sent to the club, he received a not officially signed document indicating that he would have to train with the reserve team;
- based on the employment contract he demands the following amounts:
- Salaries for January to April 2003 (USD –.– / month): USD –.–
- Additional salaries until the end of the originally agreed duration of the employment contract, i.e. December 2003: USD –.–
- Accommodation and meals for eight months (USD –.– per month): USD –.–
  (Note: the employment contract does not contain a precise amount to be paid for accommodation and meals.)
- Costs for ongoing medical treatment as it occurs: at least USD –.–
  Total: USD –.–
- based on the "Payment Agreement" he demands the following amounts:
- Salaries for January to April 2003 (USD –.– / month): USD –.–
- Additional salaries until the end of the originally agreed duration of the employment contract, i.e. December 2003: USD –.–
- Travel expenses: USD –.–
  Total: USD –.–

- in addition, and still on the basis of the "Payment Agreement", he demands for payment of a sign-on fee in the amount of USD –.–;
- to this regard, a mistake occurred when editing the "Payment Agreement", since the clause referring to the "Transfer costs" should actually have read "Transfer costs of USD –.– to be paid by theFootball Club through the Agent to he Player" instead of "… by the Football Club to the Agent";
- for him and his agent, however, it was always clear that the amount was directed to him;
- moreover, the position "Transfer costs" was supposed to be a sign-on fee for him, yet, for some internal reasons unknown to him, the club had explicitly asked to use the wording "Transfer costs";
- in any case, after the "Bosman ruling" no club was entitled to ask for a transfer fee anymore and therefore, the chosen wording could not correspond to what the parties actually intended to stipulate;
- according to the "Payment Agreement" also the larger part of his salary had to be paid through his agent;
- this way of payment had been chosen by him and his agent in order to have a better control over the money transfers made by the club and furthermore, so as to bypass the strict Chinese rules, which considerably limit the export of money;
- referring to the "Payment Agreement" he is also claiming 5% default interest on all outstanding amounts;
- the club's argumentation is inconsistent;
- on the one hand, it pretends that on the basis of art. 11 of the employment contract, the latter is null and void and on the other hand, it states that due to the fact that the player apparently disguised essential information with regard to his physical conditions it had a right to unilaterally terminate the contract;
- he questions how the club can claim that he left Y without authorisation, if the club is of the opinion that no contractual relation existed;
- these aspects clearly show that the Chinese club recognised the validity of the contracts;
- in response to the claim the club, Y, maintains in particular that:
- the player disguised an injury, which he suffered from already before he signed the contract in China and consequently, the relevant agreements should be declared null and void;
- as a result, it refuses to pay the player any salary or other compensation;
- during the negotiations leading to the player's transfer, the player's agent had explained that the player was still under contract with the Swiss club, SR Delémont, and therefore a transfer fee of USD –.– would have to be paid;
- subsequently, it found out that the contract between the player and the Swiss club had expired and consequently, the compensation for the Swiss club had no legal grounds;
- it firmly rejects the claim that it had asked to have the term "sign-on fee" changed with "Transfer costs";
- the player and his agent never asked for the negotiation of a sign-on fee;
- with reference to similar agreements concluded with other players and remitted to the FIFA administration, it could demonstrate that whenever a sign-on fee had been agreed, the relevant contracts explicitly referred to it;
- art. 11 point 3 of the employment contract states that the contract will not come into effect previous to the player successfully passing the medical examination at a hospital appointed by the club;
- when it requested the player to undergo the medical tests, he and his agent found several reasons in order to postpone them;
- in view of the fact that the pre-season preparation had already started on 3 January 2003, the club agreed to have the player joining the team and to have the medical examination made at a later stage;
- the player could not participate to all the preparation trainings due to physical problems;
- when the team returned from the training camp, on 3 February 2003 the player was sent to the club's hospital for a thorough medical examination, which showed that the player had some muscular damages, due to a former hernia surgery, which influenced his capacity to play football at professional level;
- the player did not present any documents giving evidence for medical tests carried out on 5 January 2003;
- as a result, on the basis of art. 11 of the employment contract the club considers the relevant agreements as being null and void;

- only for humanitarian reasons it had continued to provide the player and his family with accommodation and medical treatment, yet, the club's behaviour could not be interpreted as a tacit consent to the validity of the employment contract;
- as long as the player was using the club's infrastructure, it obviously had the right to instruct the player to train with the reserve team;
- it confirms that it actually had instructed the player to train with the reserve team;
- bearing in mind that the player had disguised essential information with regard to his physical conditions it had a right to unilaterally terminate the employment contract;
- for the damage caused to the club, it demands compensation in the amount of USD –.–;
- taking into consideration the above, the Chamber outlined that:
- as established in art. 42 par. 1 lit. (b) (i) of the Regulations, it falls within the purview of the Dispute Resolution Chamber to determine whether one of the parties has committed an unilateral breach of contract without just cause,
- if the employment contract was breached by a party, the Dispute Resolution Chamber is responsible to verify whether this party is accountable for outstanding payments and compensation,
- also, the Dispute Resolution Chamber will establish the amount of compensation to be paid and decide whether sports sanctions must be imposed (cf. art. 42 par. 1 (b) (ii) and (iii) in connection with art. 22 and 23 of the Regulations),
- first it had to be established whether, as the club is claiming, the two agreements concluded on 5 January 2003, i.e. the employment contract and the "Payment Agreement", are null and void,
- art. 30 of the Regulations gives clear and unmistakable indications with regard to the relation between medical examination and the validity of an employment contract,
- due to its unambiguous wording, the relevant clause does not leave space for interpretations,
- the said provision is mandatory and calls for a strict application,
- consequently, art. 11 point 3 of the employment contract is null and void, since, contrary to what art. 30 of the Regulations is requiring, it makes the relevant agreement conditional upon the positive results of a medical examination,
- the question whether medical examination were carried out prior to the signing of the agreements or not could remain open,
- in fact, the club would have had to make any necessary medical examination before concluding the agreements (cf. art. 30 par. 2 of the Regulations),
- therefore, even if, for whatsoever reason, it had decided to have them carried out in February 2003 only, after the training camp, it would have done so at its own risk,
- on account of the foregoing the two agreements concluded between the parties on 5 January 2003 are valid,
- the two agreements, i.e. the employment contract and the "Payment Agreement", are jointly applicable,
- the player left the club on 24 April 2003,
- it is uncontested that the Chinese club did not pay any remuneration to the player for the time he stayed with the club,
- the club did not respect its financial obligations, since it had fallen into arrears with the payment of the salaries of the player for almost four months,
- under these circumstances it had to be established that the club had breached the agreements concluded with the player and as a result, the player had a just cause to unilaterally terminate his engagement on 24 April 2003,
- bearing in mind all the foregoing, the player, X, is entitled to his contractually agreed salary until 24 April 2003, i.e. USD –.– (total salary employment contract and "Payment Agreement" amounting to USD –.– for January until March 2003, plus pro rata of that salary for April 2003 for 24 days),
- according to the "Payment Agreement" the player was entitled to travel money for him and his family in the amount of USD –.– to be paid in cash,
- as a matter of fact, the player and his family travelled to China in order for the player to join the team, and then left again after the early termination of the contract,
- the amount agreed upon in the "Payment Agreement" does not appear to be exaggerated or excessive in order to refund the expenses for those trips,
- therefore, the player is entitled to that amount,
- in accordance with the "Payment Agreement", the player is entitled to 5% default interest per year

on these amounts, starting as from the day on which the employment contract was rescinded, i.e. 24 April 2003,

- with regard to the demanded compensation for accommodation and meals for the months of May to December 2003 it had to be emphasised that the player was not in China anymore and the employment contract had already been terminated,
- as a consequence, the relevant amounts were not due anymore by the club under the employment contract and cannot be awarded to the player,
- following the general legal principle, the burden of proof lies on the party claiming something,
- the player had confirmed that during his stay with the club he had received medical treatment from Y,
- furthermore, Mr X had not presented any documents corroborating the claimed costs for medical treatment,
- therefore, the relevant sum cannot be awarded to the player neither,
- before accepting that the clear and unmistakeable wording of a contract does not correspond to the parties will, the party claiming such fact would have to present substantiated and valid reasons,
- the player's argumentation with regard to the allegedly agreed sign-on fee does not appear to be very convincing,
- in fact, the player is insinuating that two different elements led to a wording, which is not just slightly but completely different from what the parties apparently intended to agree,
- according to the player at first, a mistake occurred with regard to the person entitled to the relevant amount and in continuation, upon the club's request, they had had to disguise the agreement with regard to the payment of a sign-on fee,
- in front of the clear written contract this concatenation of events appears to be somehow weird and therefore, the player's description of the facts cannot be backed,
- the player's agent's confirmation of Mr X' version does not make it more convincing neither, since for obvious reasons, an agent tends to support the position of his client,
- as a result, the player's claim for the payment of a sign-on fee has to be rejected,
- however, the player is entitled to compensation for the breach of the employment contract by the club,
- art. 13 of the employment contract states that in case of unilateral termination of the contract without valid reason, the fallible party shall compensate the other party with a sum corresponding to three of the player's monthly salaries,
- as already explained, the club had breached the contract by not fulfilling its financial obligations and as a consequence had, in the substance, caused the early termination of the relation without just cause,
- when signing the employment contract the parties had agreed to a specific amount of compensation to be paid by the fallible party in such a case,
- as a result, it appears to be appropriate to award the player USD –.–, corresponding to three of his monthly salaries, as compensation for the breach of the contract committed by the Chinese club,
- in conclusion, the Chinese club has to be sanctioned for contractual breach, in application of art. 23 par. 2 lit. (a) of the Regulations, which states that in the case of the club breaching a contract, the sanction shall be a ban on registering any new player, either nationally or internationally, until the expiry of the second transfer period following the date on which the breach became effective, namely on 24 April 2003,
- for the sake of good order, it should be mentioned that on account of the above considerations and conclusions the club's claim that the player had left the club without valid reasons and Y's authorisation on 24 April 2003 cannot be backed,
- as a consequence, the club's demand for compensation in the amount of USD –.– has to be rejected,
- in view of all the above, the decision of the FIFA administration of 30 July 2003 to provisionally authorise the player, X, to sign for the club of his choice must be confirmed,

DECIDED FOR THESE REASONS

1. The claim lodged by the player, X, is partially accepted.
2. The contractual relation between the player, X, and the club, Y, is terminated as from 24 April 2003.

3. The player, X, is entitled to receive USD –.– as outstanding salary as well as USD –.– for travel expenses from the club, Y, plus 5% default interest per year as from 24 April 2003. The relevant amount has to be paid by the club within 30 days as from notification of the present decision.
4. The club, Y, is directed to pay the player, X, compensation for the breach of the employment contract in the amount of USD –.– within 30 days of notification of the present decision.
   If Y fails to comply with the above-mentioned deadline, an interest rate of 4.50% per year will apply.
5. The club, Y, is not entitled to any compensation from the new club of the player, X.
6. A ban is imposed on the Chinese club, Y, from registering any new player, either nationally or internationally, until the expiry of the next transfer period.
7. This decision may be appealed before the Court of Arbitration for Sport (CAS) within 20 days of receiving notification of this decision, by contacting the court directly in writing and by following the directions issued by the CAS, copy of which we enclose hereto.

⚽⚽⚽

24 MARCH 2004

34325
DECISION OF THE DISPUTE RESOLUTION CHAMBER
passed in Zurich, Switzerland, on 24 March 2004,
in the following composition:
Slim Aloulou (Tunisia), Chairman
Theo van Seggelen (Netherlands), member
Michele Colucci (Italy), member
Maurice Watkins (England), member
Jean-Marie Philips (Belgium), member
on the claim presented by
the player, X, as Claimant
against
the club, Y, as Respondent
regarding a contractual dispute between the player and the club,

FACTS OF THE CASE
- On 3 January 2003 the player X and the club Y signed a "private" employment contract valid for the 2002/03 and 2003/04 seasons.
- According to this contract, inter alia, the player is entitled to the following monies:
  - a signing-on fee of USD 60,000 on the date of signature of the contract
  - USD 20,000 in March 2003
  - USD 2,500 per match during 2002/03 season (cf. club's payment regulations)
  - USD 5,000 monthly salary for January, February, March, April and May 2003
  - USD 8,000 monthly salary during 10 months as of July 2003
  - USD 50,000 in August 2003
  - USD 50,000 in December 2003
  - USD 3,000 per match during 2003/04 season (cf. club's payment regulations)
  - In summary: payable in 2003 (January – December)
    lump sums: USD 180,000
    salaries: USD 25,000 (Jan – May at 5,000 /month)
    USD 48,000 (Jul – Dec at 8,000 / month)
    + match bonuses payable in 2004 (January – April)
    salaries: USD 32,000 (Jan – Apr at 8,000 / month)
    + match bonuses
    total amount cf. private agreement (January 2003 – April 2004)
    USD 285,000 + match bonuses

- Furthermore, in accordance with this "private" contract, should any of the payments not be remitted to the player within 45 days of the due date, the player has the right to unilaterally terminate the employment contract without being deprived of his right to receive the outstanding monies up to the date of termination.
- In addition, a "standard" employment contract was signed between the parties valid from 16 January 2003 until 31 May 2004, although the translation of this "standard" contract also indicates a total period of validity of three years.
- This contract does not specify any date of signature.
- According to this "standard" contract, the player is entitled to receive a monthly salary equal to minimum wage as well as the amount of USD 120,000 payable in the following three instalments: USD 20,000 on 15 May 2003, USD 50,000 on 15 August 2004 and USD 50,000 on 15 December 2004.
- On 10 July 2003, the player turned to FIFA claiming that up to that moment the club still owed him a certain amount of money relating to the 2002/03 season and on the basis of the "private" employment agreement.
- Without having provided a detailed breakdown of his financial claim, at first, the player claimed that the total amount of USD 40,000 was outstanding, later on he claimed USD 150,000, which amount he increased at a later stage of the proceedings.
- Mr. X maintains having complied with his contractual obligations at all times.
- According to the player, he was told by the club that Y preferred to sign on younger and cheaper players for the 2003/04 season and that therefore, the club was no longer interested in Mr. X's services.
- Mr. X asserts that by letter dated 3 July 2003, the club authorised the player in writing to find another club until 20 July 2003,
- The relevant letter submitted by the player reads as follows: "the football player X wasgiven permission until the date of July 20, 2003".
- However, the employment contract was not rescinded and the player continues to be employed by Y during the 2003/04 season.
- Only after two reminders from the FIFA administration has Y replied to the player's claim, on 22 January 2004, by referring to the "standard" employment contract and submitting copies of payment vouchers duly signed by the player to the total amount of USD 131,844, which was paid to the player as follows:

Date	USD
27.01.03	40,000
31.01.03	20,000
31.01.03	1,500
10.03.03	20,000
07.05.03	1,303
02.06.03	14,042
29.07.03	2,084
03.10.03	7,154
04.11.03	6,778
08.12.03	6,925
22.12.03	2,091
24.12.03	6,993
15.01.04*	2,975*
TOTAL	131,844

- * No receipt relating to 15.01.04 was submitted by the club, however, one receipt to the amount of USD 6,590, without date and containing the player's signature, was presented.
- After having studied the receipts submitted by the club, the player came to the conclusion that the club still owes him the amount of USD 186,000.
- In spite of repeated and explicit requests made by the FIFA administration, the player has failed to provide a detailed breakdown of his financial claim.
- The player points out that the receipts submitted by Y are solely related to the "standard" contract.
- The player's financial claim is based on the "private" employment agreement. 3
- The player wishes to terminate the employment contract and to transfer to another club.

- Y asserts that the standard contract is the only valid contract in "football law" and that the other contracts are based on civil law.
- Furthermore, given that the contract was concluded in the city of Z, the club considers that the competent body should be the court of law in Z.
- Y has not commented on the player's interpretation of the above-mentioned payment vouchers, in spite of FIFA's explicit request to do so.
- The "standard" contract, written in Y's local language, contains a clause, in item 4 under "contract stipulations", stipulating that the parties accept that "this contract is sole and special document which organise the relation between the parties, there is not any contract with a previous or future date except this contract, and even if it exist we renounce from all of request rights irreversibly basing this contract."
- This clause appears to be a standard clause, printed in red ink.

CONSIDERATIONS OF THE DISPUTE RESOLUTION CHAMBER

The members of the Chamber confirmed that in accordance with Article 42 of the FIFA Regulations for the Status and Transfer of Players (edition September 2001) it is competent to deal with the present matter.

Firstly, the Chamber took into account that the parties have signed two employment contracts for the same period of time. The first contract is referred to as the "standard contract" and the second one as the "private contract".

The members concurred that prior to continuing with the considerations of this case, they needed to address the prejudice question as to which contract shall be taken into account in the case at hand.

On the one hand, the standard contract is the pre-printed model contract provided for by the Y Football Association that must be registered with the said Association. The parties have inserted the basic requirements in the empty positions available for this purpose such as their names, the duration of the employment and the financial terms. In the case at hand, the financial terms of the standard contract differ entirely from those listed in the private contract and are by far inferior. In the present dispute, the standard contract contains the specific pre-printed clause, which excludes the validity of any other contract signed between the player and the club. Both parties signed this agreement.

By means of the private contract, on the other hand, the parties have stipulated additional and different intentions with respect to their employment relationship. In particular, compared to the standard contract, the private contract stipulates greater financial obligations on the part of the club.

The members of the Chamber concurred that by agreeing on a divergent individual understanding in the private contract the parties derogated from the provisions contained in the pre-printed standard contract. The private contract is therefore of full binding value on the parties.

Furthermore, the parties have tacitly complied with the terms of the private contract and, through this action, have implied that their real intentions were stipulated in this agreement.

Therefore, the fact that in the present proceedings Y is claiming that only the contract deposited at the association shall be applicable contravenes the basic principle of "venire contra factum propia".

The issue pertaining to the cessation, at a certain point, of the fulfilment by Y of the financial terms of the private agreement will be addressed in this decision at a later stage.

Taking into consideration the above, the members concluded that an alleged breach of contract must be examined under the provisions of the private agreement.

The members concurred that, in principle, players can be misled into signing two contracts as they are generally not acquainted with administrative practices. They may easily tend to believe that the signing of the standard contract merely constitutes a formality in connection with budgetary purposes and/or in order to comply with the registration requirements of the Regulations of the national association concerned and that, on the other hand, the private contract is the only relevant contract.

In addition to the above circumstances, the Chamber pointed out that in the light of the documentary evidence of payments made by the club to the player, i.e. to the amount of USD 131,844 up to mid-January 2004, which largely exceed the player's financial entitlements according to the standard contract, i.e. USD 20,000 plus 12 months' minimum wage, it is evident that Y has at all moments accepted the validity of the private employment agreement.

For all these reasons, the Chamber decided that the player is entitled to base his claim on the private employment contract and that this contract shall be taken into consideration while making a formal decision.

Departing from the assumption that the monthly salaries fall due at the end of the month and according to the private contract, Y should have paid to the player the amount of USD 253,000 plus match bonuses, if any, up to mid-January 2004. However, the club has paid the amount of USD 131,844 until the said period of time.
Consequently, and taking into account the dates on which monies have been remitted to the player, it can be concluded that Y has failed to respect its financial obligations arising from the private employment contract.
Therefore, the player could have invoked the clause in the private contract entitling him to unilaterally rescind the employment contract, if a payment was not made within 45 days of the due date.
The player not having specified his financial claim amounting to USD 186,000 and given the fact that the player is still rendering his services to the club, the Chamber decided that the player is entitled to receive all monies due to him in accordance with the private employment contract minus the payments already remitted by the club to the player.
Up to the date of the present decision, 24 March 2004, and presuming that the player's salary falls due at the end of the month, in accordance with the private employment contract the player is entitled to receive the amount of USD 269,000 plus match bonuses, if any.
The Respondent having remitted the amount of USD 131,844 to the Claimant, the Dispute Resolution Chamber decided that the Respondent must pay the amount of USD 137,156 plus match bonuses, if any, to the Claimant.
In addition, the Dispute Resolution Chamber decided to order the Claimant to remit the player's financial entitlements relating to the period of time following the date of the present decision in accordance with the said private contract in a timely manner.
In the light of the fact that the player claims that the amount of USD 186,000 remains outstanding, the Chamber considers it opportune to point out that the player's financial entitlements according to the private contract are not in addition to those indicated in the standard contract.

DECISION OF THE DISPUTE RESOLUTION CHAMBER

1. The claim of the Claimant is partially accepted.
2. The Respondent has to pay the amount of USD 137,156 plus match bonuses, if any, to the Claimant.
3. The amount due to the Claimant has to be paid by the Respondent within 30 days as from the date of notification of this decision.
4. In the event that the debt of Y is not paid within the stated deadline, an interest rate of 5% per year will apply as of expiry of the aforementioned deadline.
5. If the sum of USD 137,156 is not paid within the aforementioned deadline, the present matter shall be submitted to the FIFA Disciplinary Committee, so that the necessary disciplinary sanctions may be imposed.
6. In addition, the Respondent is ordered to remit the player's financial entitlements relating to the period of time following the date of the present decision in accordance with the private employment contract in a timely manner.
7. According to art. 60 par. 1 of the FIFA Statutes this decision may be appealed before the Court of Arbitration for Sport (CAS). The statement of appeal must be sent to the CAS directly within 10 days of receiving notification of this decision and has to contain all elements in accordance with point 2 of the directives issued by the CAS, copy of which we enclose hereto. Within another 10 days following the expiry of the time limit for the filing of the statement of appeal, the appellant shall file with the CAS a brief stating the facts and legal arguments giving rise to the appeal (cf. point 4 of the directives).

34368
DECISION OF THE DISPUTE RESOLUTION CHAMBER
passed in Zurich, Switzerland, on 24 March 2004,
in the following composition:
Slim Aloulou (Tunisia), Chairman
Theo van Seggelen (Netherlands), member

Michele Colucci (Italy), member
Maurice Watkins (England), member
Jean-Marie Philips (Belgium), member
on the claim presented by
club X, as Claimant
against
club Y, as Respondent
regarding training compensation in connection with the player, Z,

FACTS OF THE CASE

- The player, Z, was born on 5 May 1980.
- Mr. Z was bound to X by an employment contract valid from 1 July 1997 until 30 June 2002.
- On 1 July 2002, the player signed on with Y.
- X claims compensation for the player's training and education on the basis of the following elements.
- It maintains having trained and educated the player Z as from 1992 until 1998.
- During the 1998/99 – 1999/00 and 2000/01 – 2001/02 seasons the player was transferred on a loan basis by X to A (located in the same country).
- However, according to X during the entire loan period the player was registered as a player of X.
- Consequently, X maintains having trained and educated the player, Z, from the age of 12 to 22 and claims compensation for the ages of 12 to 21 to the amount of EUR –.–.
- The documents submitted by X in respect of the player's registration from 1992 until 1998 and of the loan of the player during the following seasons consist of a written confirmation by the X Football Association.
- In addition, the club submitted a copy of the relevant loan agreements in accordance with which, inter alia, a loan fee of USD –.– per season was payable to X.
- The above-mentioned amount of compensation of EUR –.– was calculated by X on the basis of the following details taking into consideration FIFA circular letter no. 826:
  - X belongs to the 3rd category;
  - Y belongs to the 1st category;
  - Costs are based on country in which player's new club is located (country Y);
  - Ages 12-15: 3 years x EUR –.– = EUR –.– (basis is 4th category);
  - Ages 16-21: 6 years x EUR –.– = EUR –.– (basis is 1st category);
  - Total amount of compensation: EUR –.–
- In addition, on the basis of article 42§1 (iv) of the FIFA Regulations for the status and transfer of players X asks the Dispute Resolution Chamber to increase the above-mentioned amount for the following reasons.
- The player Z and the club X signed an additional agreement on 17 July 1997 in accordance with which the X had the right to sell the player after the expiry of the relevant employment contract.
- Due to the fact that the player signed on with Y on 1 July 2002 without X's involvement, X was allegedly deprived of its right to transfer the player to another club.
- This additional contract having been signed in July 1997, prior to the entering into force of the current transfer regulations, according to X the amount of compensation should also be based on the "market value" and not solely on the basis of the principles of the current transfer Regulations.
- Y acknowledges that it owes training compensation to X.

CONSIDERATIONS OF THE DISPUTE RESOLUTION CHAMBER

It is undisputed that the X is entitled to receive training compensation in accordance with Chapter VII of the FIFA Regulations for the Status and Transfer of Players and Chapter III of the Regulations governing the Application of the Regulations for the Status and Transfer of Players (hereinafter referred to as "Application Regulations") as well as FIFA circular letter no. 826 dated 31 October 2002.

In accordance with the above-mentioned Regulations and circular letter, training compensation is payable up to the age of 23, for training incurred between the ages of 12 and 21.

Firstly, the Chamber turned to the question as to whether training compensation is due for the period of time that a player was transferred on a loan basis to another club, as in the case at hand.

The members of the Chamber unanimously agreed that training compensation in accordance with the

above-mentioned Regulations is solely payable for the period of time during which a player has in actual fact been trained by the club claiming payment of such compensation.
This implies that no training compensation shall be due to X for the period of time that the player was transferred on a loan basis by the Claimant to another club.
Taking into consideration the above, it can be established that the player, Z, has been trained and developed by the X during six sportive seasons, from 1992-1993 to 1997-1998, between the age of 12 and 18.
Furthermore, the amount due by Y is to be calculated in accordance with the parameters provided by circular letter 826 dated 31 October 2002, i.e. with an amount corresponding to EUR –.– per year of training between the ages of 12 to 15 and EUR –.– per year of training between the ages of 16 to 18 (corresponding to the club category 3 of X).
In this respect, the Chamber noticed that X has erroneously based its calculation for the ages over 15 on the club category of Y.
That is, in accordance with article 7.3 of the Application Regulations and the said circular letter the calculation shall be based on the costs of the country in which the new club is located.
Therefore, X being a 3rd category club, the amount of training compensation is obtained by multiplying the amount corresponding to the category of the training club for which the player was registered by the number of years of training from 12 to 21 (cf. art. 7.1 of the Application Regulations) based on the costs of 4th category (ages from 12 to 15) and 3rd category (ages from 16 to 18) clubs in country of Y.
Consequently, X is entitled to receive training compensation to the total amount of EUR –.– (3 years x EUR –.– plus 2 years x EUR –.–).
As regards X's request to adjust the amount of compensation on the basis of article 42§1 (iv) of the FIFA Regulations for the status and transfer of players, the Chamber agreed that the circumstances on the basis of which the claimant considers being entitled to a higher amount of compensation cannot be taken into consideration, as they go against the spirit of the said Regulations and are not related to costs of training in fact incurred by the X in connection with the player in question. Furthermore, X has not submitted relevant evidence to justify a higher amount.
Taking into account all of the above, the Dispute Resolution Chamber decided that the Respondent must pay the amount of EUR –.– to the Claimant.

DECISION OF THE DISPUTE RESOLUTION CHAMBER

1. The claim of the Claimant is partially accepted.
2. The Respondent has to pay the amount of EUR –.– to the Claimant.
3. The amount due to the Claimant has to be paid by the Respondent within 30 days as from the date of notification of this decision.
4. If the sum of EUR –.– is not paid within the aforementioned deadline, the present matter shall be submitted to the FIFA Disciplinary Committee, so that the necessary disciplinary sanctions may be imposed.
5. According to art. 60 par. 1 of the FIFA Statutes this decision may be appealed before the Court of Arbitration for Sport (CAS). The statement of appeal must be sent to the CAS directly within 10 days of receiving notification of this decision and has to contain all elements in accordance with point 2 of the directives issued by the CAS, copy of which we enclose hereto. Within another 10 days following the expiry of the time limit for the filing of the statement of appeal, the appellant shall file with the CAS a brief stating the facts and legal arguments giving rise to the appeal (cf. point 4 of the directives).

34432

DECISION OF THE DISPUTE RESOLUTION CHAMBER

passed in Zurich, Switzerland, on 24 March 2004,
in the following composition:
Slim Aloulou (Tunisia), Chairman
Theo van Seggelen (Netherlands), member
Michele Colucci (Italy), member
Maurice Watkins (England), member
Jean-Marie Philips (Belgium), member

on the claim presented by
Club X, Brazil, as Claimant
against
Club Y, Italy, as Respondent
regarding the training compensation related to the transfer of the federative rights to the player Z, Brazil

FACTS OF THE CASE:

- In August 2002, an employment contract is concluded between the Brazilian player Z and the Italian club Y.
- The player Z, born in 1980, was registered for the Brazilian club from 1991 to 2002, for eleven sporting seasons, between the age of 11 and 22.
- The Brazilian club claims the Training Compensation, in accordance with the Chapter VII of the revised FIFA Regulations for the Status and Transfer of Players.
- As far as the categorisation of clubs is concerned, as provided for by the circular letter 826 dated 31 October 2002, the Brazilian club is a first division club, belonging to the Category 1.
- The amount is to be calculated in accordance with the parameters provided by the circular letter 826 dated 31 October 2002, i.e. with an amount corresponding to EUR 90,000 per year.
- The latter yearly amount represents the indicative amount of Category 1 for Europe, which has to be applied in accordance with the above-mentioned circular letter.

CONSIDERATIONS OF THE DISPUTE RESOLUTION CHAMBER

After a careful study of the facts and allegations outlined above, the Dispute Resolution Chamber commenced its deliberations by referring to the art. 42 par. 1 lit. (b) (iv) of the FIFA Regulations for the Status and Transfer of Players, according to which, it falls within the purview of the Dispute Resolution Chamber to review disputes concerning training compensation fees.

In this sense, as established in Chapter VII of the revised FIFA Regulations for the Transfer and Status of Players, the training compensation is payable for training incurred between the ages of 12 and 21, if the player concludes a non-amateur contract before the age of 23.

In the present case, the Chamber outlined that the training period to take into consideration went from the sporting season 1992/1993 when the player Z was 12, until the sporting season 2000/2001, at the age of 21.

It is therefore undisputed that the Brazilian club is entitled to receive compensation for the training and education of the player Z for the ten sporting seasons the player spent with the Brazilian club.

The amount due by the Italian club Yis to be calculated in accordance with Art. 7 of the Regulations governing the Application of the Regulations for the Status and Transfer of Players, as well as the parameters provided by the Circular letter no. 826 dated 31 October 2002. According to Art. 7 § 3 of the above-mentioned Application Regulations, the relevant amounts are determined by the amounts, which apply in the confederation of the new club. On this basis, according to § 1 of the same article, the specific amount to pay is determined by the category of the player's old club. According to the above-mentioned Circular, the indicative amount of Category 1 for Italy (Europe) is EUR 90,000 per year of training. Also, EUR 10.000 per year are granted to the training club as from the player's age of 12 up to the age of 15.

Taking into account all of the above, the Dispute Resolution Chamber decided that the Italian club Y must pay to the Brazilian club X, the total amount of EUR 570,000, corresponding to EUR 10,000 per season, for the first three seasons the player spent with the Brazilian club, plus EUR 90,000 per year of training, for the remaining six seasons.

DECISION OF THE DISPUTE RESOLUTION CHAMBER

1. The claim of the club X is accepted.
2. The Italian club Y has to pay the amount of EUR 570,000 to the club Y.
3. The amount due to X has to be paid by Y within 30 days as from the date of notification of this decision.
4. If the aforementioned sum is not paid within the aforementioned deadline, the present matter shall be submitted to the FIFA's Disciplinary Committee, so that the necessary disciplinary sanctions may be imposed.
5. According to art. 60 par. 1 of the FIFA Statutes this decision may be appealed before the Court of Arbitration for Sport (CAS). The statement of appeal must be sent to the CAS directly within 10 days

of receiving notification of this decision and has to contain all elements in accordance with point 2 of the directives issued by the CAS, copy of which we enclose hereto. Within another 10 days following the expiry of the time limit for the filing of the statement of appeal, the appellant shall file with the CAS a brief stating the facts and legal arguments giving rise to the appeal (cf. point 4 of the directives).

⚽⚽⚽

10 JUNE 2004

64132
DECISION OF THE DISPUTE RESOLUTION CHAMBER
passed in Zurich, Switzerland, on 10 June 2004,
in the following composition:
Slim Aloulou (Tunisia), Chairman
Theo van Seggelen (Netherlands), member
Philippe Piat (France), member
Mario Gallavotti (Italy), member
Jean-Marie Philips (Belgium), member
on the claim presented by
the player, X, as Claimant
against
the club, Y, as Respondent
regarding a contractual dispute between the player and the club,

FACTS OF THE CASE

- The player X and the club Y signed an employment employment contract valid as from the player's arrival at the club and expiring in 2004.
- No specific period of validity has been specified in the contract, nor does the contract contain any date of signature.
- The player maintains that his contract started on 26 July 2003.
- According to this contract, inter alia, the player is entitled to a monthly salary of USD –.–, bonuses, two flight tickets per season (also for his wife should she register in the country of Y), a car, and accommodation.
- The contract does not indicate any financial details as regards bonuses payable to the player.
- Furthermore, in accordance with clause 2 of this contract the player is entitled to a signing-on fee of USD –.– payable in the following four instalments:
  USD –.– on 15 September 2003
  USD –.– on 15 December 2003
  USD –.– on 15 March 2004
  USD –.– on 15 June 2004
- According to article 11 of the same contract, if the player requests the termination of the contract within its period of validity, he shall pay to the club two months' salary and return the signing-on fee on a pro rata basis.
- On 16 February 2004 the player turned to FIFA claiming that the club Y unilaterally breached the employment contract given that the club had failed to fulfil the following contractual obligations:
  - Salaries for October, November, December 2003 + January 2004
    USD –.–
  - Instalment of signing-on fee due on 15 December 2003
    USD –.–
  - Air ticket for his wife and daughter in order to join him in the country of Y
  - A car
  - Accommodation

    In addition, in the light of the club's breach of the employment contract the player claims payment of the following monies/items:
  - Two months' salary for breach of contract
    USD –.–

  - Air ticket + exit visa in order for the player to leave the country
  - Payment of all his rights until the last day he stays in the country of Y inasmuch he is unable to leave
- The player also asked for FIFA's intervention in order for him to obtain his passport, which according to Mr. X was illegally retained by the club, and to immediately return to his home country.
- On 24 January 2004, the player asked the national association of Y to assist him in this matter.
- On 19 February 2004, the FIFA administration invited the club Y to present its reply to the player's claim within the next 7 days.
- On 9 March 2004, having received no reply from Y and taking into consideration the above information, the FIFA administration authorised the player to return to his home country, as per his wish, and to sign on with the club of his choice.
- In addition, in the light of the player's claim pertaining to his passport and exit visa, the club Y was urged to enable the player to depart from its country.
- On 16 March 2004, the national association of Y informed the FIFA administration that the player did not accept the offer made by its club (no details were provided) and that X decided to stay in the country of Y until the case would have been settled by the DRC.
- In addition, according to the same national association it guarantees the issuance of the player's exit visa and air ticket.
- According to the player, the club only offered him to pay the amount of USD –.–, whereas the club allegedly owes him the amount of USD –.– (6 monthly salaries for October 2003 until March 2004 (USD –.–) + two months' salary for breach of contract (USD –.–) + signing-on fee falling due in December 2003 (USD –.–) and March 2004 (USD –.–).
- No comments have been received from Y in respect of the player's financial claim.
- According to the national association of Y, the player left the country of Y on 24 March 2004 with an exit visa and air ticket provided by the club.

CONSIDERATIONS OF THE DISPUTE RESOLUTION CHAMBER

The members of the Chamber confirmed that in accordance with Article 42 of the FIFA Regulations for the Status and Transfer of Players (edition September 2001) it is competent to deal with the present matter.

As established in Article 42 §1(b) of the Regulations, it is the duty of the Dispute Resolution Chamber to determine whether one of the parties has committed a unilateral breach of contract without just cause.

The members of the Chamber duly noted that the club Y has not presented any comments on the player's financial claim, nor has it submitted any documentary evidence demonstrating that it has paid to the player the monies which according to X remain outstanding.

Consequently, the player's claim not having been refuted by the club, the Chamber agreed that the allegations put forward by X must be considered as confirmed.

The Chamber noted that on the date of receipt of the player's claim, on 16 February 2004, Y had not paid the player's monthly salary for over a four months' period of time and one out of the four instalments pertaining to the signing-on fee remained unpaid. Therefore, the members of the Chamber concurred that Y has seriously neglected its financial obligations towards the player in question.

In the light of the above, the club is found to have committed a unilateral breach of the employment contract without just cause. Consequently, in addition to the monies which have remained unpaid until and including the month in which the player could leave and has left the club, i.e. from October 2003 until and including March 2004, the player is entitled to receive compensation for breach of contract.

As regards the award of financial compensation in favour of the player, the Chamber took into account that the relevant employment contract includes a clause pertaining to monies payable to the club in the event of the player wishing to terminate the employment contract before its expiry. No clause relating to the player receiving compensation from the club in the event that the club would prematurely terminate the contract has been included in the contract. Therefore, the said clause being unilateral and to the benefit of the club only, the Chamber agreed that it is not bound by the termination clause contained in the contract when establishing the amount of compensation owed by the club to the player for breach of contract.

In fact, the Chamber maintained that the FIFA Regulations for the Status and Transfer of Players' depart from the principle that the parties to an employment contract have entered a contractual obligation for a fixed period of time. This engagement can only be rescinded under circumstances that justify a unilateral rupture of the contract by one of the parties for just cause or if the parties mutually agree on an early termination of their contractual relationship. A mutual agreement on the early termination of an employment contract is considered admissible since it requires both parties to negotiate the terms on which they are willing to accept a rescission of an otherwise valid contract. Such an agreement must therefore be found when the parties are faced with the circumstances that motivate an early termination of their engagement.

Under particular circumstances, the Chamber can admit arrangements whereby the parties have foreseen and agreed upon the terms of an early termination of a contract in the employment contract itself. In order to accept such an arrangement, the Chamber must feel that the parties have been able to negotiate these terms in a manner that is not the result of a unilateral command by only one of the parties. Essentially, the rescission clause contained in the employment contract must provide for terms that can be considered acceptable to both the employer as well as the employee. As stated above, in the case at hand, the rescission clause must be considered unilateral and to the benefit of the club only.

The Chamber duly noted that, in the present case, the player has put forward a claim for compensation for breach of contract amounting to two months' salary, i.e. USD –.– . Therefore, the Chamber confirmed the player's claim and decided that X is entitled to receive the amount of USD –.– as compensation for the breach of contract by the club.

In the light of the above, X is entitled to receive the amount of USD –.– in payment of outstanding salaries. Furthermore, the player is entitled to receive the outstanding instalments of the signing-on fee, i.e. December 2003 and March 2004, to the amount of USD –.– . With respect to the amount of compensation owed to the player X, the Chamber maintained that the Y is liable to pay an amount of money equalling 2 months' salary, i.e. USD –.–.

The Chamber decided that the player's claim pertaining to a car and accommodation cannot be taken into consideration. Furthermore, the claim of X relating to air tickets for his family must equally be rejected due to the fact that his family has apparently not joined him during his stay in the country of Y.

Finally, the Chamber confirmed the above-mentioned provisional decision, which was passed by the FIFA administration on 9 March 2004.

DECISION OF THE DISPUTE RESOLUTION CHAMBER

1. The claim of the Claimant is accepted.
2. The Respondent has to pay the amount of USD –.– to the Claimant.
3. The amount due to the Claimant has to be paid by the Respondent within 30 days as from the date of notification of this decision.
4. In the event that the debt of the club Y is not paid within the stated deadline, an interest rate of 5% per year will apply as of expiry of the aforementioned deadline.
5. If the sum of USD –.– is not paid within the aforementioned deadline, the present matter shall be submitted to the FIFA Disciplinary Committee, so that the necessary disciplinary sanctions may be imposed.
6. The provisional decision passed by the FIFA administration on 9 March 2004 is confirmed.
7. According to art. 60 par. 1 of the FIFA Statutes, this decision may be appealed against before the Court of Arbitration for Sport (CAS). The statement of appeal must be sent to the CAS directly within 10 days of receipt of notification of this decision and shall contain all the elements in accordance with point 2 of the directives issued by the CAS, a copy of which we enclose hereto. Within another 10 days following the expiry of the time limit for filing the statement of appeal, the appellant shall file a brief stating the facts and legal arguments giving rise to the appeal with the CAS (cf. point 4 of the directives).

64133
DECISION OF THE DISPUTE RESOLUTION CHAMBER
passed in Zurich, Switzerland, on 10 June 2004,
in the following composition:
Slim Aloulou (Tunisia), Chairman
Theo van Seggelen (Netherlands), member
Philippe Piat (France), member
Mario Gallavotti (Italy), member

Jean-Marie Philips (Belgium), member
on the claim presented by
the player, X, as Claimant
against
the club Y, as Respondent
regarding a contractual dispute between the player and the club,

FACTS OF THE CASE

- The player X and the club Y signed an employment contract valid for the duration of two seasons: 2003/04 and 2004/05.
- According to this contract, inter alia, the player is entitled to a monthly salary of USD –.–, bonuses, one air ticket per season, a car, and accommodation.
- The contract does not indicate any financial details as regards bonuses payable to the player.
- Furthermore, in accordance with clause 3 of this contract the player is entitled to a signing-on fee of USD –.– payable in the following four instalments:
  USD –.– in July 2003
  USD –.– in September 2003
  USD –.– in December 2003
  USD –.– in March 2004
- According to article 12 of the same contract, if the player requests the termination of the contract within its period of validity, he shall pay to the club two months' salary and return the signing-on fee on a pro rata basis.
- Article 13 stipulates that if the club requests the termination of the contract within its period of validity, the club will pay to the player two months' salary.
- On 16 February 2004 the player turned to FIFA claiming that the club Y unilaterally breached the employment contract given that the club had failed to fulfil the following contractual obligations:
  - Salaries for October, November, December 2003 + January 2004
    USD –.–
  - Instalments of the signing-on fee due in September and December 2003
    USD –.–
  - Air ticket for his family in order to join him in the country of Y*
  - A car
  - Accommodation
- *The employment contract does not contain any clause according to which the club would be liable to provide air tickets for the player's family.
- In addition, in the light of the club's breach of the employment contract the player claims payment of the following monies/items:
  - Two months' salary cf. employment contract
    USD –.–
  - Air ticket + exit visa in order for the player to leave the country
  - Payment of all his rights until the last day he stays in the country of Y inasmuch he is unable to leave
- The player also asked for FIFA's intervention in order for him to obtain his passport, which according to Mr. X was illegally retained by the club, and to immediately return to his home country.
- On 24 January 2004, the player asked the national association of club Y to assist him in this matter.
- On 19 February 2004, the FIFA administration invited the club Y to present its reply to the player's claim within the next 7 days.
- On 9 March 2004, having received no reply from the club and taking into consideration the above-mentioned information, the FIFA administration authorised the player to return to his home country, as per his wish, and to sign on with the club of his choice.
- In addition, in the light of the player's claim pertaining to his passport and exit visa, the club Y was urged to enable the player to depart from the country of Y.
- On 16 March 2004, the national association of club Y informed the FIFA administration that the player did not accept the offer made by its club (no details were provided) and that the player X decided to stay in the country of Y until the case would have been settled by the DRC.
- In addition, according to the same association, the issuance of the player's exit visa and air ticket was guaranteed.

- The player asserts that the club only offered him to pay the amount of USD –.–, whereas the club allegedly owes him the amount of USD –.– (6 monthly salaries for October 2003 until March 2004 (USD –.–) + two months' salary for breach of contract (USD –.–) + signing-on fee instalments falling due in September & December 2003 and in March 2004 (USD –.–) and an air ticket (USD –.–).
- No comments and/or documentation have been received from club Y in respect of the player's financial claim.
- According to the national association of club Y, the player left the country of Y on 24 March 2004 with an exit visa and air ticket provided by the club.

CONSIDERATIONS OF THE DISPUTE RESOLUTION CHAMBER

The members of the Chamber confirmed that in accordance with Article 42 of the FIFA Regulations for the Status and Transfer of Players (edition September 2001) it is competent to deal with the present matter.

As established in Article 42 §1(b) of the Regulations, it is the duty of the Dispute Resolution Chamber to determine whether one of the parties has committed a unilateral breach of contract without just cause.

The members of the Chamber duly noted that the club Y has not presented any comments on the player's financial claim, nor has it submitted any documentary evidence demonstrating that it has paid to the player the monies which according to the player X remain outstanding.

Consequently, the player's claim not having been refuted by Y, the Chamber agreed that the allegations put forward by Mr. Cesar dos Santos must be considered as confirmed.

The Chamber noted that on the date of receipt of the player's claim, on 16 February 2004, Y had not paid the player's monthly salary for over a four months' period of time and two out of the four instalments pertaining to the signing-on fee remained unpaid. Therefore, the members of the Chamber concurred that Y has seriously neglected its financial obligations towards the player in question.

In the light of the above, the club is found to have committed a unilateral breach of the employment contract without just cause. Consequently, in addition to the monies which have remained unpaid until and including the month in which the player could leave and has left the club, i.e. from October 2003 until and including March 2004, the player is entitled to receive compensation for breach of contract.

As regards the award of financial compensation in favour of the player, the Chamber took into account that the relevant employment contract includes a clause pertaining to monies payable to either party in the event of the early termination of the employment contract. Both parties having duly signed the employment contract, and thus having agreed on such clause, and the relevant clause being reciprocal, the Chamber agreed that the amount of money stipulated in the contract shall be taken into consideration when establishing the financial compensation to be paid by the club to the player. In addition, in the case at hand, the player explicitly refers to the said contractual clause and the related amount of compensation, i.e. two months' salary.

In the light of the above, X is entitled to receive the amount of USD –.– in payment of outstanding salaries. Furthermore, the player is entitled to receive the outstanding instalments of the signing-on fee, i.e. September 2003, December 2003, and March 2004, to the amount of USD –.–. With respect to the amount of compensation owed to the player X, the Chamber maintained that the club Y is liable to pay an amount of money equalling 2 months' salary, i.e. USD –.–.

The Chamber decided that the player's claim pertaining to a car and accommodation cannot be taken into consideration. Furthermore, X's claim relating to air tickets for his family must equally be rejected due to the lack of a contractual obligation on the part of the club. Furthermore, the club having provided the player with his return ticket to the player's home country, the Chamber also rejected the player's claim for payment of the amount of USD –.– for an air ticket.

Finally, the Chamber confirmed the above-mentioned provisional decision, which was passed by the FIFA administration on 9 March 2004.

DECISION OF THE DISPUTE RESOLUTION CHAMBER

1. The claim of the Claimant is partially accepted.
2. The Respondent has to pay the amount of USD –.– to the Claimant.
3. The amount due to the Claimant has to be paid by the Respondent within 30 days as from the date of notification of this decision.
4. In the event that the debt of the club Y is not paid within the stated deadline, an interest rate of 5% per year will apply as of expiry of the aforementioned deadline.

5. If the sum of USD –.– is not paid within the aforementioned deadline, the present matter shall be submitted to the FIFA Disciplinary Committee, so that the necessary disciplinary sanctions may be imposed.
6. The provisional decision passed by the FIFA administration on 9 March 2004 is confirmed.
7. According to art. 60 par. 1 of the FIFA Statutes, this decision may be appealed against before the Court of Arbitration for Sport (CAS). The statement of appeal must be sent to the CAS directly within 10 days of receipt of notification of this decision and shall contain all the elements in accordance with point 2 of the directives issued by the CAS, a copy of which we enclose hereto. Within another 10 days following the expiry of the time limit for filing the statement of appeal, the appellant shall file a brief stating the facts and legal arguments giving rise to the appeal with the CAS (cf. point 4 of the directives).

⚽⚽⚽

64357
DECISION OF THE DISPUTE RESOLUTION CHAMBER
passed in Zurich, Switzerland, on 10 June 2004,
in the following composition:
Slim Aloulou (Tunisia), Chairman
Theo van Seggelen (Netherlands), member
Philippe Piat (France), member
Mario Gallavotti (Italy), member
Jean-Marie Philips (Belgium), member
on the claim presented by
the player, X, as Claimant
against
the club Y, as Respondent
regarding a contractual dispute between the player and the club,

FACTS OF THE CASE

- On 1 July 2002 the player X and the club Y signed an employment contract valid from 1 July 2002 until 30 June 2005.
- According to this contract the player is entitled to a monthly salary of USD –.–
- Furthermore, in accordance with annexe 1 of this contract (which constitutes article 7 of the employment contract) the player's monthly salary for the 2003/04 season is USD –.– and for the 2004/05 season USD –.–
- In addition, the player is entitled to a signing-on fee of USD –.– for the duration of the contract payable in the following four instalments:
  - USD –.– until 20 September 2002
  - USD –.– until 20 October 2002
  - USD –.– until 15 June 2003
  - USD –.– until 20 October 2004
- Moreover, the player is entitled to USD –.– per month for lodging as well as to four flight tickets per season for himself, his wife and two children.
- Appendix 2 of the employment contract includes a bonus agreement for the 2002/03 season.
- According to article 10 of the employment contract any disputes between the parties shall be resolved amicably or shall be referred to the Football Federation of the club Y and the Professional League.
- None of the parties has invoked this article.
- On 18 July 2003 the player turned to FIFA claiming that the club Y unilaterally breached the employment contract six months after the coming into force of the contract.
- That is, according to the player, in January 2003 the coach told him that he was not included in the coach's programme for the 2003/04 season and that the club had acquired the services of a Brazilian player for his position. In addition, X was allegedly told to go to his home country and the club promised that it would find him another employer and that his salary would be forwarded to him.
- X maintains having returned to his home country on 6 March 2003 with a flight ticket paid for by Y.

- According to the player, since he left he has been in contact with Y to enquire about his employment and he has received no salaries as of February 2003.
- The first deadline set by the FIFA administration in order for Y to present its reply to the player's claim was ignored.
- After having reminded the club to present its reply, the Football Federation of Y conveyed the club's comment that the player repeatedly and deliberately did not fulfil his contractual obligations and that he had left the club without authorisation. In addition, according to the said Federation, Y was in search of another club for the player.
- Later on, Y informed FIFA that it paid the total amount of USD –.– to the player, which amount allegedly includes the first two instalments of the signing-on fee (total USD –.–), the player's monthly salary from July 2002 until and including January 2003 (7 x USD –.–), and bonuses (USD –.–).
- However, Y has omitted to provide the relevant documentary evidence of these payments, in spite of repeated requests from the FIFA administration.
- Y stresses that the player repeatedly had failed to fulfil his contractual obligations, as a result of which the coach decided not to include him in the 2003 season. Furthermore, according to the club, the player left the team at his own will.
- In addition, according to Y, the club has made efforts to find another club for the player, which have remained unsuccessful allegedly due to the "player's character and reputation of a scandalous player".
- The player vehemently rejects the club's accusations and points out that Y has not reported the player's absence to FIFA before he lodged his claim.
- He confirms having received his monthly salary and signing-on fee until January 2003.
- On 2 February 2004, the FIFA administration provisionally authorised the player to sign on with the club of his choice so as to safeguard the player's livelihood and not to hinder his professional career.

CONSIDERATIONS OF THE DISPUTE RESOLUTION CHAMBER

Taking into account article 10 of the relevant employment contract, the Chamber deemed that, firstly, the question as to whether the Chamber has jurisdiction in the present matter must be answered.

In this regard, the members of the Chamber agreed that in the absence of a national sports arbitration tribunal composed of members chosen in equal numbers by players and clubs as well as an independent chairman (cf. Article 42 of the aforementioned Regulations), the Dispute Resolution Chamber of the FIFA Players' Status Committee is competent to deal with a dispute, even if written agreements signed between the parties involved in the dispute contain a clause by means of which the jurisdiction of another body is referred to.

In addition, the player nor the club have invoked the relevant article in their claim or response to the claim, respectively.

Consequently, the members of the Chamber confirmed that in accordance with Article 42 of the FIFA Regulations for the Status and Transfer of Players (edition September 2001) it is competent to deal with the present matter.

As established in Article 42 §1(b) of the Regulations, it is the duty of the Dispute Resolution Chamber to determine whether one of the parties has committed a unilateral breach of contract without just cause.

The Chamber took into account that Y maintains having paid to the player all his dues as from July 2002 until and including January 2003. This statement was confirmed by the player and, therefore, no documentary evidence of payment of these monies is required. However, from the same statement it can be deduced that the club ceased to fulfill its financial obligations arising from the employment contract as from February 2003 in accordance with the player's claim.

The Chamber further took into account that the club has presented a response which merely consists of general allegations against the player, without having provided any details or any relevant documentary evidence in support of its position. Furthermore, Y has acknowledged that it was seeking a new employer for the player, which confirms the player's statements.

Taking into consideration all of the above, the Chamber agreed that Y has unilaterally breached the employment contract without just cause. Consequently, the player is entitled to receive compensation for breach of contract.

In this respect, the Chamber acknowledged that the player has not claimed any amount of money in connection with the breach of contract by the club. Furthermore, it was noted that the relevant employment contract does not contain any rescission clause that could possibly be taken into account.
In fact, the Chamber maintained that the FIFA Regulations for the Status and Transfer of Players depart from the principle that the parties to an employment contract have entered a contractual obligation for a fixed period of time. This engagement can only be rescinded under circumstances that justify a unilateral rupture of the contract by one of the parties for just cause or if the parties mutually agree on an early termination of their contractual relationship. A mutual agreement on the early termination of an employment contract is considered admissible since it requires both parties to negotiate the terms on which they are willing to accept a rescission of an otherwise valid contract. Such an agreement must therefore be found when the parties are faced with the circumstances that motivate an early termination of their engagement.
That is, under particular circumstances, the Chamber can admit arrangements whereby the parties have foreseen and agreed upon the terms of an early termination of a contract in the employment contract itself. In order to accept such an arrangement, the Chamber must feel that the parties have been able to negotiate these terms in a manner that is not the result of a unilateral command by only one of the parties.
The Chamber considered that article 8 of the employment contract in the case at hand, which deals with the early termination of the contract by the club, does not meet these criteria. The said article fails to reflect the fact that a player affected by an early termination of the contractual engagement may be unable to immediately enter into a new employment engagement, especially with regard to art. 5.2 of the FIFA Regulations for the Status and Transfer of Players.
In addition, it does not provide for any compensation payable to the player in the event of an early termination of the contract by the club.
In the light of the above and taking into consideration article 22 of the FIFA Regulations for the Status and Transfer of Players, the Chamber decided that the player is entitled to an amount of compensation for breach of contract equalling the total value of the relevant employment contract (salaries and signing-on fee) minus the amounts that already have been remitted by the club to the player. More precisely, according to the contract, from 1 July 2002 until 30 June 2005 the player was entitled to receive USD –.– in payment of salaries and signing-on fee. X already received USD –.– from the club and therefore, the amount of compensation decided by the Chamber is calculated at USD –.–.
Finally, the Chamber confirmed the above-mentioned provisional decision, which was passed by the FIFA administration on 2 February 2004.

DECISION OF THE DISPUTE RESOLUTION CHAMBER

1. The claim of the Claimant is accepted.
2. The Respondent has to pay the amount of USD –.– to the Claimant.
3. The amount due to the Claimant has to be paid by the Respondent within 30 days as from the date of notification of this decision.
4. In the event that the debt of the club Y is not paid within the stated deadline, an interest rate of 5% per year will apply as of expiry of the aforementioned deadline.
5. If the sum of USD –.– is not paid within the aforementioned deadline, the present matter shall be submitted to the FIFA Disciplinary Committee, so that the necessary disciplinary sanctions may be imposed.
6. The provisional decision passed by the FIFA administration on 2 February 2004 is confirmed.
7. According to art. 60 par. 1 of the FIFA Statutes, this decision may be appealed against before the Court of Arbitration for Sport (CAS). The statement of appeal must be sent to the CAS directly within 10 days of receipt of notification of this decision and shall contain all the elements in accordance with point 2 of the directives issued by the CAS, a copy of which we enclose hereto. Within another 10 days following the expiry of the time limit for filing the statement of appeal, the appellant shall file a brief stating the facts and legal arguments giving rise to the appeal with the CAS (cf. point 4 of the directives).

6400276
DECISION OF THE DISPUTE RESOLUTION CHAMBER
passed in Zurich, Switzerland, on 10 June 2004,
in the following composition:
Slim Aloulou (Tunisia), Chairman
Theo van Seggelen (Netherlands), member
Philippe Piat (France), member
Mario Gallavotti (Italy), member
Jean-Marie Philips (Belgium), member
on the claim presented by
Player X
against
The decision passed by the Arbitration Body of the Football Federation Y

FACTS OF THE CASE
The Player X was under contract for the club Y. During a period of the employment contract he was loaned to club Z. After the expiry of the loan agreement, he did not return to his employer club for the one-month remainder of the employment contract. Two days after the expiry of the employment contract he signed a new employment contract with a club in another country.
In the meantime, the club Y initiated legal proceedings at its Football Federation against the player, accusing him of breach of the employment contract. As the Players' Status Committee of the Football Federation Y was still about to be established, this case was considered by the Disciplinary Committee of the Football Federation Y.
The Disciplinary Committee decided that the player concerned had breached his contract with the club Y since he did not return to the latter for the remainder of the employment contract, and therefore banned him from playing in official football matches for four months, beginning on the day when the national championship in the league of his new club starts.
The player appealed against this decision at the Arbitration Body of the Football Federation Y. The appeal was rejected and the sanction upheld.
The Football Federation Y confirmed to FIFA that the Disciplinary Committee as well as the Arbitration Committee of the Football Federation Y were not composed in accordance with the requirement for equal representation of players and clubs, as required by Article 42 of the FIFA Regulations for the Status and Transfer of Players
On 17 March 2004 the player submitted a claim to FIFA against the disciplinary sanction imposed by the Football Federation Y, asking that the sanction preventing him to play for his new team shall be lifted.
The player pretends that he was dismissed by the club Y before the loan, as it was entered in his player's passport one month before he was loaned to club Z, but that he was never notified about his dismissal. Therefore, he is of the opinion that he did not have the obligation to return to the club Y after the expiry of the loan agreement with the club Z. Moreover, he considers the loan agreement in consequence to his earlier dismissal from the club Y as not valid.
Furthermore, the player is of the opinion that his contract with the club Y was never valid because 1) the date of signature was not indicated in the contract, 2) the date of registration of the contract at the Football Federation Y was not indicated in the contract, and 3) because the salary was indicated in USD, and not in the national currency. Therefore, he is of the opinion that he was not obliged to return to the club Y after the expiry of the loan agreement with the club Z.
The club Y maintains that the entry in the player's passport was made by an oversight and therefore is not valid. This position is based on the fact that the club still fulfilled its contractual obligations towards the player, in particular the salary payments up to the loan period.
Furthermore, club Y is of the opinion that the missing dates and the indication of the salary in USD do not affect the validity of the contract, in particular because during the working relationship between the player and the club, the player never contested the validity of the contract and always received and accepted his salary payments in USD.

CONSIDERATIONS OF THE DISPUTE RESOLUTION CHAMBER
The Dispute Resolution Chamber first examined the case under the light of Article 42 of the FIFA Regulations for the Status and Transfer of Players, according to which disputes between clubs and players

have to be dealt with by a tribunal composed by members chosen in equal numbers by players and clubs.
In this respect, the Dispute Resolution Chamber noticed that the Disciplinary Committee as well as the Arbitration Committee of the Football Federation Y were not composed by equal representation of players and clubs. In consequence, the Dispute Resolution Chamber stated that the decisions were not taken in compliance with Article 42 of the above-mentioned Regulations and that therefore it was entitled to intervene in this matter.
The Dispute Resolution Chamber then turned to the restriction imposed on the player concerned. It noticed that the player, at the expiry of the loan agreement, still was under contract with his employer club Y for one month, but that he did not return to the latter according to the contractual situation. This conduct was considered by the Dispute Resolution Chamber as a breach of contract. In the light of this, the Dispute Resolution Chamber stated that it was correct to sanction the player concerned.
The Dispute Resolution Chamber furthermore noticed that the Football Federation Y, by imposing a restriction of four months on the players eligibility to participate in any official football matches as from the beginning of the new season of the new club's national championship, applied the four-months rule established in Article 23 § 1 of the FIFA Regulations for the Status and Transfer of Players.
However, the Dispute Resolution Chamber questioned the proportionality of the restriction imposed. The condition of proportionality requests that the gravity of a sanction has to correspond to the gravity of the conduct leading to the sanction.
In this regard, the Dispute Resolution Chamber noticed that during the month when the player stayed away from his employer club, no official matches were scheduled in the national league of the Football Federation Y. In the light of this, the absence of the player concerned did not pose a serious problem to the club. Therefore, the Dispute Resolution Chamber came to the conclusion that the restriction imposed on the player concerned to participate in any official football matches during four months was not an appropriate sanction. It stated that it would have been more appropriate in this case if the player would have been fined.
In the light of the above, the Dispute Resolution Chamber decided that the restriction shall be lifted and the player shall immediately be allowed to register for the club of his choice. Therefore, the Football Federation Y is requested to send the ITC to the federation of the club with which the player wishes to register, upon being asked to do so by this federation.

DECISION OF THE DISPUTE RESOLUTION CHAMBER

1. The demand of the player X is accepted.
2. The restriction imposed on the player X by the Football Federation Y is lifted.
3. The player is allowed to be registered immediately for the club of his choice, and to exercise his professional activity as a football player.
4. According to art. 60 par. 1 of the FIFA Statutes, this decision may be appealed against before the Court of Arbitration for Sport (CAS). The statement of appeal must be sent to the CAS directly within 10 days of receipt of notification of this decision and shall contain all the elements in accordance with point 2 of the directives issued by the CAS, a copy of which we enclose hereto. Within another 10 days following the expiry of the time limit for filing the statement of appeal, the appellant shall file a brief stating the facts and legal arguments giving rise to the appeal with the CAS (cf. point 4 of the directives).

⚽⚽⚽

6400581

DECISION OF THE DISPUTE RESOLUTION CHAMBER

passed in Zurich, Switzerland, on 10 June 2004,
in the following composition:
Slim Aloulou (Tunisia), Chairman
Theo van Seggelen (Netherlands), member
Philippe Piat (France), member
Mario Gallavotti (Italy), member
Jean-Marie Philips (Belgium), member
on the claim presented by

Player X, Serbia and Montenegro as Claimant
against
Club Y, Qatar as Respondent

FACTS OF THE CASE

In 2003 the player X, Serbia and Montenegro, signed an employment contract with the club Y, Qatar, valid for the season 2003/04.

According to Attachment 1 of the contract, the player is entitled to a signing on fee of USD 350,000 (the relevant clause does not state a date for the payment), plus a monthly salary of USD 50,000, due the last day of each month. Furthermore, the club shall provide him with a return air ticket for him and his family.

Clause 6.5 of the contract states:

"The player shall pass a medical test with a doctor recommended by the Club. Should theplayer fail to pass the test, this contract shall be invalid. The medical test shall be done oneday after arrival in Qatar. Should the player fail to pass the test, all upfront or prepayments(sign on contract fee) have to be paid back to the Club within 10 days."

The first day after the player's arrival in Qatar he had to undergo a medical test. On the next day, the player and the club signed the above-mentioned employment contract. Twelve days later, the club informed the player of the result of the medical test, according to which he suffers from a cardiologic disease, which could cause his sudden death.

In view of this, the club verbally terminated the employment contract on the same day based on the above-mentioned clause 6.5.

The player therefore left Qatar four days later. Tests he made on his own initiative with doctors in other hospitals showed that he does not suffer from a cardiologic disease potentially causing his sudden death.

The player never received any payment from the club. Until today, he did not officially terminate his employment contract with the Qatari club, nor did he sign a new employment contract with another club.

The player X claims from the club Y the payment of the singing on fee (USD 350,000), the salary pro rata from 27 to 31 August 2003 (5/31 x USD 50,000, i.e. USD 8,064.52), the salaries for September 2003 until June 2004 (USD 500,000), in total USD 858,064.52, as well as EUR 7,965.68 for travel expenses. A copy of a facture proving the aforementioned travel expenses has been provided to the FIFA Administration.

CONSIDERATIONS OF THE DISPUTE RESOLUTION CHAMBER

The Dispute Resolution Chamber examined the case under the light of Article 30 § 2 of the FIFA Regulation for the Status and Transfer of Players, which states that the player's prospective new club is required to make any necessary investigation, studies, tests and/or medical examination before concluding the contract, otherwise it will be liable to pay the full amount of the salary due.

The Dispute Resolution Chamber explained that according to Article 30 § 2 a club has to wait for the medical test results before signing an employment contract, because the results are part of the test itself. If a club signs a contract before it has received the test results, and then dismisses the contract because of negative test results, it has to bear the consequences of the signed contract according to the above-mentioned Article 30 § 2.

The Dispute Resolution Chamber noted that the club Y made the player concerned to undergo a medical test before signing the employment contract. Furthermore, it noticed that the club did not complete the test phase before signing the employment contract by receiving the test results. And finally, the Dispute Resolution Chamber noticed that the respondent club dismissed the employment contract after receipt of the test results, twelve days after the signature, based on the contract clause 6.5.

According to Article 30 § 2 of the above-mentioned Regulations and in the light of the above-made explanations, the Dispute Resolution Chamber decided that by its conduct, the club Y made itself liable to bear the consequences of the signed contract.

Furthermore, the Dispute Resolution Chamber had to consider the clause 6.5 of the employment contract between the parties involved, which says that the employment contract shall not be valid in case of negative test results. In this regard, the Dispute Resolution Chamber referred to Article 30 § 1 of the above-mentioned Regulations, according to which the validity of an employment contract cannot be made conditional upon the positive results of a medical examination. In this respect, the Dispute Resolution Chamber decided that the clause 6.5 of the employment contract does not hinder the validity of the

employment contract and therefore does not release the club from its obligation to bear the consequences of the signed contract according to Article 30 § 2 of the mentioned Regulations.
The Dispute Resolution Chamber therefore decided that the respondent club by his conduct did not fulfill the conditions of the above-mentioned Article 30 § 2. In consequence, in application of this provision, the Dispute Resolution Chamber decided that the club Y has to pay to the player X the singing on fee (USD 350,000), as well as a compensation for the unilateral breach of contract in the amount of USD 500,000, in total USD 850,000, as well as EUR 7,965.68 for travel expenses.

DECISION OF THE DISPUTE RESOLUTION CHAMBER
1. The demand of the player X is accepted.
2. The club Y Sport Club has to pay the amount of USD 850,000 and of EUR 7,965.68 to the player X.
3. The amount due to the player X has to be paid by the club Y within the next 30 days as from the date of notification of this decision.
4. If the aforementioned sum is not paid within the aforementioned deadline, the present matter shall be submitted to FIFA's Disciplinary Committee, so that the necessary disciplinary sanctions may be imposed.
5. According to art. 60 par. 1 of the FIFA Statutes this decision may be appealed before the Court of Arbitration for Sport (CAS). The statement of appeal must be sent to the CAS directly within 10 days of receiving notification of this decision and has to contain all elements in accordance with point 2 of the directives issued by the CAS, copy of which we enclose hereto. Within another 10 days following the expiry of the time limit for the filing of the statement of appeal, the appellant shall file with the CAS a brief stating the facts and legal arguments giving rise to the appeal (cf. point 4 of the directives).

22 JULY 2004

74323
DECISION OF THE DISPUTE RESOLUTION CHAMBER
passed in Zurich, Switzerland, on 22 July 2004,
in the following composition:
Slim Aloulou (Tunisia), chairman
Mario Gallavotti (Italy), member
Jean Marie Philips (Belgium), member
Mario Colucci (Italy), member
Gerardo Movilla (Spain), member
on the claim presented by
X, Greece, as Claimant
against
Y, France, as Respondent
regarding a training compensation dispute concerning the transfer of the player Z

FACTS OF THE CASE:
- The player, born on 08.02.1986, was registered for X from the 1998/1999 season until February 2002, that is, for three and a half (3,5) sporting seasons between the age of 12 and 16.
- A contract was concluded between the player and the French club Y with validity from 1 July 2002 until 1 July 2004.
- X presently claims its right to receive training compensation, in accordance with the Chapter VII of the revised FIFA Regulations for the Status and Transfer of Players.
- As far as the categorisation of clubs is concerned, as provided for by the circular letter 826 dated 31 October 2002, the Claimant is a club belonging to the Category 4 (indicative amount EUR 10,000 per year).
- As far as the categorisation of clubs is concerned, as provided for by the circular letter 826 dated 31 October 2002, the Respondent is a first division club, belonging to the Category 1 (indicative amount EUR 90,000 per year).

- Y deems it is not held to pay any training compensation for the transfer of the player.
- Y motivates its refusal to pay compensation by stating that the player in question signed a 'contrat aspirant' for the 2002/2003 and 2003/2004 seasons with this club and therefore benefited from the training provided to him by its Formation Centre, after which he would be free again to sign a professional contract elsewhere.

CONSIDERATIONS OF THE DISPUTE RESOLUTION CHAMBER

The Dispute Resolution Chamber of the FIFA Players' Status Committee shall review disputes coming under its jurisdiction pursuant to Art. 42 of the FIFA Regulations for the Status and Transfer of Players at the request of one of the parties to the dispute.

According to Art. 42.1(b)(iv) of the FIFA Regulations for the Status and Transfer of Players, the Dispute Resolution Chamber of the FIFA Players' Status Committee shall review disputes concerning training compensation fees and shall have discretion to adjust the training fee if it is clearly disproportionate to the case in review.

Consequently, the Dispute Resolution Chamber is the competent body to decide on the present litigation concerning the training compensation fee claimed by the Greek club.

Once its competence was thus established, the Dispute Resolution Chamber went on to treat the substance of the case.

Firstly, the Chamber affirmed that the player had been trained and developed by the Claimant club during three and a half (3,5) sporting seasons, from 1998 to 2002, between the age of 12 and 16 years.

Furthermore it was stressed that, as of 1 July 2002, Z was bound by a contract to the Respondent for two seasons.

As established in the Circular Letter no. 826 dated 31st October 2002, training compensation is payable up to the age of 23 for a player's training incurred between the ages of 12 and 21.

The Chamber outlined that in the present case the training period taken into consideration goes from the sporting season 1998/1999, when the player was 12, to the month of February of the sporting season 2001/2002, when he had reached the age of 16.

In conclusion, the Chamber established that X is entitled to receive compensation for the training and education it provided to the player Z throughout the timeframe he spent with this club.

The Chamber went on to deliberate on the proper calculation, affirming that the amount due by the Respondent is to be calculated in accordance with the parameters provided in the circular letter 826, dated 31 October 2002.

To begin with, the compensation corresponding to a category 4 club, that is, an amount of EUR 10,000, is granted to the training club per year as from the player's age of 12 up to the age of 15. This results in a total of EUR 30,000.

For the last season that the player was being trained by the Claimant, between the age of 15 and 16 years, the compensation is calculated by taking the average of the indicative amount for Category 1 (EUR 90,000 per year of training) and the indicative amount of Category 2 (EUR 60,000 per year of training). Granted that the player was transferred to Y already in February 2002, this calculation shall only be for half of the sporting season 2001/2002, resulting in an amount of EUR 50,000 divided by two, that is, a total of EUR 25,000.

Taking into account all of the above, the Chamber concluded that the training compensation payable to the Claimant by the Respondent amounts to the total sum of EUR 55,000 (EUR 30,000 + EUR 25,000).

DECISION OF THE DISPUTE RESOLUTION CHAMBER

1. The Respondent shall pay the amount of EUR 55,000 to the Claimant, within 30 days of notification of the present decision.
2. If Respondent fails to comply with the above-mentioned deadline, an interest rate of 5% per year will apply and the case will immediately be presented to the FIFA Disciplinary Committee.
3. According to art. 60 par. 1 of the FIFA Statutes, this decision may be appealed before the Court of Arbitration for Sport (CAS). The statement of appeal must be sent to the CAS directly within 10 days of receiving notification of this decision and has to contain all elements in accordance with point 2 of the directives issued by the CAS, copy of which we enclose hereto. Within another 10 days following the expiry of the time limit for the filing of the statement of appeal, the appellant shall file with the CAS a brief stating the facts and legal arguments giving rise to the appeal (cf. point 4 of the directives).

7472 A
DECISION OF THE DISPUTE RESOLUTION CHAMBER
passed in Zurich, Switzerland, on 22 July 2004,
in the following composition:
Slim Aloulou (Tunisia), Chairman
Gerardo Movilla (Spain), member
Michele Colucci (Italy), member
Jean-Marie Philips (Belgium), member
Mario Gallavotti (Italy), member
on the claim presented by
Club A, as Claimant
against
Player B, as respondent
regarding a contractual dispute and the player's registration with club C.

FACTS OF THE CASE
B was born on 10 February 1983.
On 30 January 2004, B and C signed an employment contract and the player's international registration transfer certificate (IRTC) was therefore requested to club A's Association, which refused to issue it based on an alleged contractual link between A and B.
In light of the above, club C's Association contacted the FIFA Administration for its assistance.
In this respect, the FIFA Administration was provided with a copy of an employment contract signed between A and B dated 19 December 2002, valid between 7 January and 20 November 2003, which would be automatically extended until the date when, in case it would qualify for it, A would end its participation in the final phase of the second tournament, which according to C, happened on 20 December 2003.
Moreover, despite having been requested to do so, A did not provide the FIFA Administration with a copy of an employment contract with B, valid for the season 2004. In this regard, A defended that although it does not have a written employment contract with B, according to its country's Labour Law, the oral agreement that it has with the player constitutes a valid employment contract, with the same force as a written one and therefore, binding for both parties.
On 13 February 2004, and after having carefully analysed the positions and documentation provided by both parties, the FIFA Administration authorized club C's Association to provisionally register B for C until receipt of the original certificate and informed the parties that, with regard to the present matter, the revised FIFA Regulations for the Status and Transfer of Players entitle A to receive training compensation from C.
Despite the aforementioned communication, A insisted for the present matter, in particular, the validity of its contractual link with the player and consequent dispute over the player's federative rights, to be submitted and analysed by FIFA's competent body.
A asserts that, from 9 January 2004, after having been submitted to the club's medical exams, the player was at the club's disposal, participating in its training sessions until 13 January 2004, after which date he decided to leave it, without informing the club.
Moreover, according to A, the player, during his period of stay with it, always recognised the existence of a labour relationship bounding both parties and was therefore included in the club's list of players for the current season.
A provided the FIFA Administration with a document issued by a Labour Court, dated 1 March 2004, attesting that the player has at his disposal the amount of $ 4,949,750 corresponding to salaries, which were paid by A.
Furthermore, the player has a professional health insurance since January 2003, which is still valid by the present date and has also been uninterruptedly registered with the social security system since February 2003, in which A is mentioned as being his employer.
Finally, based on Chapter II of the revised FIFA Regulations for the Status and Transfer of Players, A underlines that FIFA must respect each country's internal legislation and therefore, in the present matter, it should consider as a valid employment contract, the oral agreement, which exists between the relevant parties.
In light of the above, A requested the FIFA Administration to reconsider its aforementioned decision, in particular, to cancel the player's registration for C and consequently declare that B's federative rights belong to it and order the player to return to its country.

Alternatively, A requests to be compensated by C for the transfer of the player's federative rights in the amount of EUR 5,000,000 and to be established an amount as compensation for the player's unlawful breach of contract.
On the other hand, B and C refuse the arguments of A and defend that the latter was unable to provide the FIFA Administration with clear evidence demonstrating the existence of a valid employment contract between it and the player.
In this respect, they underline the content of the Preamble's second paragraph and Chapter II of the revised FIFA Regulations for the Status and Transfer of Players, in particular, Art. 4 Par. 1, according to which "every player designated as non-amateur by his national association shall have a written contract with the club employing him."
As a consequence, B and C assert that, since the player did not sign an employment contract with A for the season 2004, he was no longer contractually bounded to the latter and therefore, in January 2004, he was free to sign for the club of his election without any compensation being due to A, for the acquisition of his federative rights.

CONSIDERATIONS OF THE DISPUTE RESOLUTION CHAMBER
The Dispute Resolution Chamber shall review disputes coming under its jurisdiction pursuant to art. 42 of the revised FIFA Regulations for the Status and Transfer of Players, at the request of one of the parties to the dispute.
In accordance with art. 42 par. 1 lit. (b) of the FIFA Regulations for the Status and Transfer of Players, it falls within the purview of the Dispute Resolution Chamber to determine whether one of the parties has committed a unilateral breach of contract without just cause.
Also, the Dispute Resolution Chamber will establish the amount of compensation to be paid and decide whether sports sanctions must be imposed (cf. art. 42, par. 1, b, ii and iii in connection with art. 22 and 23 of the aforementioned Regulations).
Therefore, the Dispute Resolution Chamber is the competent body to decide on the present litigation concerning the alleged existence of an employment contract between the claimant and the respondent and consequent breach of contract.
Once its competence was thus established, the Dispute Resolution Chamber went on to treat the substance of the case.
The Dispute Resolution Chamber took note that the last written employment contract between B and A expired on 20 November 2003 and moreover, that it was only extended until 20 December 2003, when A ended its participation in the final phase of the second tournament.
Moreover, it was noted that A acknowledges the inexistence of a written employment contract between the parties for the 2004 sporting season, despite claiming the existence of an oral agreement binding the player to it for such period.
In this respect, the Chamber emphasized that, in accordance with art. 4, par. 1 of the revised FIFA Regulations for the Status and Transfer of Players, "every player designated as non-amateur by hs national association shall have a written employment contract with the club employing him".
As a consequence, the Dispute Resolution Chamber concluded that B stopped being contractually bound to A since 20 December 2003 and therefore, was free to sign for the club of his election since then.
In light of all the above, the Dispute Resolution Chamber decided that no compensation is due to A with regard to the transfer of B's federative rights to C.
However, the Dispute Resolution Chamber emphasized the fact that A was entitled to a compensation for training the player, in accordance with Chapter VII of the revised FIFA Regulation for the Status and Transfer of Players. The amount due in this respect would have to be established by separate decision.

DECISION OF THE DISPUTE RESOLUTION CHAMBER
1. The claim lodged by A is rejected.
2. B is considered free to sign for the club of his election without any compensation for the transfer of the federative rights being due to A.
3. A is entitled to a training compensation in accordance with Chapter VII of the revised FIFA Regulation for the Status and Transfer of Players. This amount shall be established by separate decision.
4. This decision may be appealed before the Court of Arbitration for Sport (CAS) in accordance with art. 60 par. 1 of the FIFA Statutes. The statement of appeal must be sent to the CAS directly within 10 days of receiving notification of this decision and has to contain all elements in accordance with

point 2 of the directives issued by the CAS, copy of which we enclose hereto. Within another 10 days following the expiry of the time limit for the filing of the statement of appeal, the appellant shall file with the CAS a brief stating the facts and legal arguments giving rise to the appeal (cf. point 4 of the directives).

⚽⚽⚽

7472 B
DECISION OF THE DISPUTE RESOLUTION CHAMBER
passed in Zurich, Switzerland, on 22 July 2004,
in the following composition:
Slim Aloulou (Tunisia), Chairman
Gerardo Movilla (Spain), member
Michele Colucci (Italy), member
Jean-Marie Philips (Belgium), member
Mario Gallavotti (Italy), member
on the claim presented by
Club A, as Claimant
against
Club B, as respondent
regarding the training compensation for the player C.

FACTS OF THE CASE
C was born on 10 February 1983.
A had a written employment contract with the player dated 19 December 2002, valid between 7 January and 20 November 2003, which was automatically extended until the date when A ended its participation in the final phase of the second tournament, which according to B (this facts were never denied by A), happened on 20 December 2003.
On 30 January 2004, C and B signed an employment contract.
A requests to be compensated by B in the amount of USD 800,000, for the costs in which it incurred with the player's training and education.
B acknowledges that A is entitled to receive training compensation in the present matter.
A's Association informed the FIFA Administration that C has been registered for A from December 1995 until 10 January 2004, with the exception of the period between 1 January and 19 December 2002, during which he wasregistered for D.

CONSIDERATIONS OF THE DISPUTE RESOLUTION CHAMBER
In accordance with Art. 42 par. 1 lit. (b) (iv) of the revised FIFA Regulations for the Status and Transfer of Players, it falls within the purview of the Dispute Resolution Chamber to review disputes concerning training compensation fees.
Consequently, the Dispute Resolution Chamber is the competent body to decide on the present litigation concerning the alleged breach of contract between the claimant and the respondent.
Once its competence was thus established, the Dispute Resolution Chamber went on to treat the substance of the case.
The Chamber acknowledged that C had been trained and developed by A, from December 1995 until 1 January 2002 and from 19 December 2002 until 10 January 2004.
Moreover, as established in Circular letter no. 826, dated 31 October 2002, training compensation is payable for training incurred between the ages of 12 and 21, if the player concludes a non-amateur contract before the age of 23.
Taking into consideration the aforementioned period of stay with the claimant, the Chamber considered that the player's positive development has to be mainly attributed to the training and education that he received from A.
Consequently, it is undisputed that A is entitled to receive from B compensation for the training and education of C with regard to the timeframe that the player spent with it.
However, the Chamber considered that the amount claimed by A was excessive and not motivated and decided to calculate training compensation on the basis of the indicative amounts listed in the aforementioned Circular letter.

Furthermore, according to Art. 5.1 of the Regulations governing the Regulations for the Status and Transfer of Players, for purposes of calculating compensation, the relevant training period starts at the beginning of the season and ends at the end of the season concerned.
In the present matter, the Chamber outlined that the relevant training period to take into consideration went from the sporting season 1996 when the player was 13, until the sporting season 2001, at the age of 18, as well as the sporting season 2003, when the player was 20.
In accordance with the principles for calculation of the training compensation amounts, stipulated in the revised FIFA Regulations for the Status and Transfer of Players and in the aforementioned Circular letter, the category of the former club and the amount corresponding to the same category in the new club's Confederation which is UEFA in the present case, apply.
As a consequence, taking into account the fact that A is a first division club belonging to Category 3 in South America, EUR 10,000 (indicative amount per year, for category 4 in Europe) is granted for each of the first two seasons that the player spent with A and EUR 30,000 (indicative amount per year, for category 3 in Europe) is granted for each of the remaining five seasons.
In view of all the above, the Dispute Resolution Chamber decided that B is liable to pay the total amount of EUR 170,000 to A for the training compensation of C.

DECISION OF THE DISPUTE RESOLUTION CHAMBER

1. B has to pay the amount of EUR 170,000 to A.
2. The amount due to A has to be paid by B within 30 days as from the date of notification of this decision.
3. If B fails to comply with the above-mentioned deadline, an interest rate of 5% per year will apply.
4. Moreover, if the aforementioned sum is not paid within the aforementioned deadline, the present matter shall be submitted to the FIFA's Disciplinary Committee, so that the necessary disciplinary sanctions may be imposed.
5. This decision may be appealed before the Court of Arbitration for Sport (CAS) in accordance with art. 60 par. 1 of the FIFA Statutes. The statement of appeal must be sent to the CAS directly within 10 days of receiving notification of this decision and has to contain all elements in accordance with point 2 of the directives issued by the CAS, copy of which we enclose hereto. Within another 10 days following the expiry of the time limit for the filing of the statement of appeal, the appellant shall file with the CAS a brief stating the facts and legal arguments giving rise to the appeal (cf. point 4 of the directives).

7481

DECISION OF THE DISPUTE RESOLUTION CHAMBER

passed in Zurich, Switzerland, on 22 July 2004,
in the following composition:
Slim Aloulou (Tunisia), Chairman
Mario Gallavotti (Italy), member
Jean-Marie Philips (Belgium), member
Michele Colucci (Italy), member
Gerardo Movilla (Spain), member
on the claim presented by
the player, X, as Claimant
against
the club Y, as Respondent
regarding a contractual dispute between the player and the club,

FACTS OF THE CASE

- On 24 July 2002 the player X and the club Y signed an employment contract valid from 1 July 2002 until 30 June 2004.
- In accordance with appendix 1 of this contract, the player, inter alia, is entitled to a monthly salary of as well as to a signing-on fee of payable in four equal instalments of each falling due on 31 July 2002, 28 February 2003, 31 July 2003 and 28 February 2004.

- In addition, the player is entitled to bonuses as specified in the same appendix and to the amount of per month for lodging.
- According to article 11.3 of the employment contract any disputes between the parties shall be resolved amicably or shall be referred to the relevant labour court.
- None of the parties has invoked this article.
- Appendix 2 of the employment contract contains an enumeration of the regulations and provisions that apply to the contractual relationship between the parties, which includes the "provisions and regulations of FIFA".
- The player submitted a claim in front of the Disciplinary Committee of the Football League of Y's country, as the club had failed to fulfil its contractual obligations.
- The said Disciplinary Committee decided on 12 November 2002 that Y has to pay to the player all his dues up to and including 31 October 2002 within 8 days and submit the relevant documentary evidence of payment.
- The same decision details the sanctions that would be imposed on the club in the event of failure to comply with the decision.
- In addition, according to this disciplinary decision, should the club fail to comply with the decision, the player would be free and able to register with another club owing to a breach of contract.
- On 17 February 2003 the player turned to FIFA claiming that up to 31 October 2002 the club owed him the total amount of –.– for outstanding salaries ( ), signing-on fee ( ), bonuses ( ) and lodging ( ).
- Mr. X maintains that the amount of remains unsettled to date.
- He affirms that he left Y's country on 14 January 2003 in the light of the decision passed by the Disciplinary Committee of the Football League of Y's country and the club's non-fulfilment of this decision.
- Mr. X claims payment of the amount of and wishes to register with another club in order to continue his career.
- After having reminded club Y to submit its response to the player's claim, the Football Federation of Y informed the FIFA administration that the amount owed by the club to the player is in deposit and can be collected by the player at a law firm in Y's country.
- Club Y has failed to reply to the question of the FIFA administration as to whether the Hungarian club would agree with payment of the monies claimed by the player by means of a bank transfer.
- In the meantime, the player was registered as an amateur player with a club in Bosnia and Herzegovina.

CONSIDERATIONS OF THE DISPUTE RESOLUTION CHAMBER

Taking into account article 11.3 of the relevant employment contract, the Chamber deemed that, firstly, the question as to whether the Chamber has jurisdiction in the present matter must be answered.

Neither the player nor the club have invoked the above-mentioned article 11.3 in their claim or response to the claim, respectively. In addition, according to appendix 2 of the employment the "provisions and regulations of FIFA" are applicable to the employment relationship between the parties involved.

Consequently, the members of the Chamber confirmed that in accordance with Article 42 of the aforementioned Regulations it is competent to deal with the present matter.

In this regard, the members of the Chamber agreed that the player cannot be compelled to travel to Y's country in order to collect the amount of., which must be considered far too inconvenient for the player, who is currently living in Bosnia and Herzegovina. In addition, there is no plausible reason for the club not to remit the monies due to the player via a bank transfer.

Therefore, the Chamber concurred that the player is entitled to receive the amount of via a bank transfer. In addition, the members of the Chamber confirmed that the player is entitled to sign on with another club, should he as yet not have proceeded to do so.

DECISION OF THE DISPUTE RESOLUTION CHAMBER

1. The claim of the Claimant is accepted.
2. The Respondent has to pay the amount of to the Claimant via a bank transfer.
3. The Claimant is asked to provide the Respondent with the banking details of his bank account within the next 10 days, with a copy to the FIFA administration.
4. The amount due to the Claimant has to be paid by the Respondent within 30 days as from the date of notification of this decision.

5. In the event that the debt of the club Y is not paid within the stated deadline, an interest rate of 5% per year will apply as of expiry of the aforementioned deadline.
6. If the sum of is not paid within the aforementioned deadline, the present matter shall be submitted to the FIFA Disciplinary Committee, so that the necessary disciplinary sanctions may be imposed.
7. According to art. 60 par. 1 of the FIFA Statutes, this decision may be appealed against before the Court of Arbitration for Sport (CAS). The statement of appeal must be sent to the CAS directly within 10 days of receipt of notification of this decision and shall contain all the elements in accordance with point 2 of the directives issued by the CAS, a copy of which we enclose hereto. Within another 10 days following the expiry of the time limit for filing the statement of appeal, the appellant shall file a brief stating the facts and legal arguments giving rise to the appeal with the CAS (cf. point 4 of the directives).

74038
DECISION OF THE DISPUTE RESOLUTION CHAMBER
passed in Zurich, Switzerland, on 22 July 2004,
in the following composition:
Slim Aloulou (Tunisia), Chairman
Mario Gallavotti (Italy), member
Jean-Marie Philips (Belgium), member
Michele Colucci (Italy), member
Gerardo Movilla (Spain), member
on the claim presented by
Z. as Claimant
against
A. and B. as Respondents
regarding a dispute on the payment of the solidarity contribution in the case of the player C.

FACTS OF THE CASE
- The playerC. was at the club Z. from 1993 until 2000, i.e. from the age of 10 until 17.
- Accordingly, Z. is entitled to 40% of the 5% solidarity contribution owed when the player is transferred during the course of an ongoing employment contract.
- On 1 July 2003, the player transferred from the club A. to the club B. for a fee totalling EUR 6,000,000, payable as follows:
  - EUR 2,000,000 within 25 days
  - EUR 1,000,000 as a bill of exchange dated 31 July 2004 to be handed to the club B. within 25 days
  - EUR 1,500,000 as a bill of exchanged dated 31 July 2004 to be handed to the club B. within 25 days
  - EUR 1,500,000 as a bill of exchange dated 31 July 2005 to be handed to the club B. within 25 days
- Clause 4 of this agreement stipulates the following: 'As to the obligation to pay amounts based on the FIFA Regulations for the Status and Transfer of Players in relation to this transfer only, it has been agreed between the parties that such amounts will be for the account of the club A.'
- Consequently, when asked to remit the solidarity contribution to the club Z., the club B. referred to clause 4 of the transfer agreement and stated that this was of the obligation of the club A.
- In response hereto, the club A. has explained that its own interpretation of clause 4 is as follows: The club B. must check which clubs are entitled to the solidarity contribution, for what amounts and must then proceed with the payments of these obligations. Upon receipt of the evidence of these payments and the underlying documents as to the calculation of the various amounts from the club B., will the club A. reimburse the amounts paid to the club B.
- In this context, FIFA informed the club A. that it could not agree with its interpretation of the clause 4 and that it must pay the total of EUR 120,000 due to the club Z.
- The case regarding the training compensation owed to the club Z. has been decided by the CAS. In this decision, the exact number of years that the player spent with the club Z. were established. Solidarity contribution for the player C.

CONSIDERATIONS OF THE DISPUTE RESOLUTION CHAMBER

The Dispute Resolution Chamber initiated its discussions on this matter by indicating that there has been an augmentation in the cases relating to the non-payment of the solidarity contribution as foreseen in the FIFA Regulations for the Status and Transfer of Players. This is owing to the fact that the clubs acquiring the federative rights to players frequently omit to retain the 5% solidarity contribution payable to the clubs involved in the player's training and education. In such cases, the club that mistakenly paid 100% of the transfer fee agreed upon with the former club of the player will consider itself in the clear regarding the solidarity contribution and will ask the clubs entitled to the solidarity contribution to revert to the former club of the player instead.

The Chamber noted that in the case at hand, the situation is rather similar, in that the clubs A. and B. have agreed to make the club A. responsible for the payment of the solidarity contribution and that this fact has been communicated to the club Z. by the club B.

In this context, the Chamber emphasised that as provided for in art. 11 of the Regulations governing the Application of the FIFA Regulations for the Status and Transfer of Players, it is the task of the new club of the player to calculate the amount owed as a solidarity contribution to the clubs involved in the formation of the player and to distribute this amount in accordance with the player's career history. Moreover, par. 1 of the mentioned article clearly stipulates that the new club of the player must pay the amount due as solidarity contribution to the training clubs within 30 days of the player's registration.

The Chamber underlined that in accordance with the FIFA Regulations for the Status and Transfer of Players, the club B. is responsible for paying the solidarity contribution to the clubs involved in the formation of the player C. The fact that the club B. found a different arrangement with the club A. has no influence on the claim of the club Z., given that Z. was not a party to this agreement.

Consequently, the club B. is liable to pay the amount of EUR 120,000 to the club Z. Furthermore, and in light of the fact that this payment has been due since August 2003, the Chamber established that an interest payment of 5% p.a. must be applied.

Finally, the Chamber maintained that the club B. may turn to FIFA upon paying the amount owed to the club Z., should it encounter any difficulties in recovering the sum paid as solidarity contribution from the club A.

Solidarity contribution for the player C.

DECISION OF THE DISPUTE RESOLUTION CHAMBER

1. The claim of the club Z. is accepted.
1. The respondent, the club B., must pay EUR 120,000 to the club Z. as solidarity contribution. On the aforementioned, amount a default interest payment of 5% p.a. as from 1 August 2003 until the day of the payment is applied.
2. The club B. is directed to pay the amount due to the club Z. within 30 days as from the date of the notification of this decision.
3. According to art. 60 par. 1 of the FIFA Statutes, this decision may be appealed against before the Court of Arbitration for Sport (CAS). The statement of appeal must be sent to the CAS directly within 10 days of receipt of notification of this decision and shall contain all the elements in accordance with point 2 of the directives issued by the CAS, a copy of which we enclose hereto. Within another 10 days following the expiry of the time limit for filing the statement of appeal, the appellant shall file a brief stating the facts and legal arguments giving rise to the appeal with the CAS (cf. point 4 of the directives).

74165

DECISION OF THE DISPUTE RESOLUTION CHAMBER

passed in Zurich, Switzerland, on 22 July 2004,
in the following composition:
Slim Aloulou (Tunisia), Chairman
Mario Gallavotti (Italy), member
Jean-Marie Philips (Belgium), member
Michele Colucci (Italy), member
Gerardo Movilla (Spain), member

on the claim lodged by the club X, Libya, as Claimant
against
the player A, Tunisiaas Respondent
regarding a breach of contract

FACTS OF THE CASE

On 27 February 2004, the football federation of Club Y contacted FIFA to request the international transfer certificate of the player A. The football federation of Club X refused to provide this document, stating that its affiliated club was claiming a payment of LYD 30,000 from the player in question.

On 7 March 2004, following FIFA's intervention, the football federation of Club X sent the certificate to the football federation of Club Y, but also sent FIFA a copy Club X's complaint against the player A.

Club X stated that the player A, having signed a contract with the club on 1 September 2002 until the end of the 2002/2003 season, and having received his full signing-on fee and salary payments, decided to leave the club earlier than agreed, i.e. on 28 January 2003. The club also stated that prior to his departure, the player's behaviour markedly changed and he caused many problems and arguments between his team-mates and the coach. The club also warned the player on a number of occasions, but to no effect.

According to the contract, a copy of which has been provided by the club, the player was entitled to a signing-on fee of –.–, to be paid as follows: –.–: on 1 September 2002 and –.– on 20 November 2002. His monthly salary was –.–.

In view of the player's unilateral decision to break the contract, the club demands:

a) the reimbursement of all the sums received by the player in accordance with article 8 of the contract, which states: "the player shall not refuse to train or participate in friendly or official matches without a valid and legitimate reason. If he violates the terms of this contract, the player will be liable to disciplinary sanctions and the club will have the right to demand that all of the sums paid to the player be reimbursed";
b) compensation for damages;
c) that the player be suspended until he has cleared his debts with the club.

To support its position, Club X has submitted the following documents:

- a copy of a letter addressed to the player on 24 February 2003, stating that the player had one week to rejoin the team and to resolve any problems. Failure to do so would result in a disciplinary matter against the player;
- a copy of a receipt signed on 2 September 2002 by the owner of the apartment let to the player to confirm that he had received from the club X the sum of –.– for the rent of the apartment of the player for the period 1 September 2002 – 30 June 2003;
- a copy of a receipt signed by the player on 6 October 2002 to confirm that he had received his salary for September 2002;
- a copy of a receipt signed by the player on 9 November 2002 to confirm that he had received his salary for October 2002;
- a copy of a receipt signed by the player on 19 November 2002 to confirm that he had received his signing-on fee;
- a copy of a receipt signed by the player on 6 December 2002 to confirm that he had received his salary for November 2002;
- a copy of a receipt signed by the player on 14 January 2003 to confirm that he had received his salary for December 2002;
- i.e. receipts for a total sum of –.–.

On 24 May 2003, the player A outlined his thoughts regarding the complaint lodged by Club X. He confirmed that he signed a one-year employment contract with the club for the period October 2001 – September 2002 and that in August 2002 he reached a verbal agreement with the club's directors. As a result of this agreement, he had to receive a signing-on fee of –.– as well as a monthly salary of –.– and other benefits such as a car, accommodation and a number of match bonuses. In early September, he moved to the country of Club X and, at the start of the 2002/2003 season, he received the sum of –.– as an advance payment on the –.– due to him. While waiting to sign a contract, he continued to play in the team. However, he did not receive the monthly salary payments for July, August, September, October and November 2002.

He only received his salary for December, for which he signed a receipt. In January 2003, he returned to his country having not been able to obtain or sign a contract with Club X. He stressed that due to the behaviour of those in charge at the club, he has lost a year of work and he regards this as an attack on his moral and financial standing.

CONSIDERATIONS OF THE DISPUTE RESOLUTION CHAMBER

After a careful study of the facts and allegations outlined above, the Dispute Resolution Chamber commenced its deliberations by referring to article 42 of the FIFA Regulations for the Status and Transfer of Players, according to which it falls within the purview of the Dispute Resolution Chamber to determine whether one of the parties has committed a unilateral breach of contract without just cause and, in the affirmative, to verify whether this party is accountable for compensation and outstanding payments. Also, and as outlined in the mentioned article, the Dispute Resolution Chamber is responsible to establish the amount of compensation to be paid and decide whether sports sanctions must be imposed.

In the present case, the Dispute Resolution Chamber turned to the question whether the respondent had indeed committed a breach of the employment contract concluded with the claimant or whether it had been the contrary.

In this respect, the Chamber noted that the allegations of the parties concerned were contradictory. On one hand, the claimant maintains that the respondent left the club without permission on 28 January 2003 and, on the other hand, the respondent states that he had to leave because the claimant failed to comply with the financial obligations verbally agreed upon.

After carefully examining the documentary evidence submitted by claimant, the Chamber expressed its astonishment while comparing the signatures on the contract as well as on each receipt contained in the file and affirmed that it was impossible to tell which of them was the real player's signature.

Notwithstanding the fact that claims pertaining to falsification of documents merely fall within the jurisdiction of criminal courts, the Chamber confirmed that, in this specific case, it had to take a decision on whether the parties had actually signed a contract before turning to the question whether this contract had been breached or not.

Given that the signatures on the contract and on the receipts produced by the claimant all differed from one another, the Chamber was not in a position to ascertain that the player had effectively signed the employment contract on which the claim was based.

In this regard, the Chamber deemed it appropriate to declare that it could only decide on the basis of documents duly signed by the parties and that, in accordance with the Rules Governing the Practice and Procedures of the Dispute Resolution Chamber, verbal agreements would therefore not be taken into consideration.

Furthermore, the Chamber considered it rather surprising that the player admits having received the most important amount, i.e. the signing-on fee, but not the amounts relating to the other receipts produced by the claimant. This fact convinced the Chamber of the respondent's good faith and of the plausibility of his allegations.

In light of all the above, the Chamber unanimously concluded that it was not established that the player signed a contract with the club on 1 September 2002 valid until the end of the 2002/2003 season and, therefore, that it had to reject the claim.

DECISION OF THE DISPUTE RESOLUTION CHAMBER

1. The claim of Club X is rejected.
2. According to art. 60 par. 1 of the FIFA Statutes, this decision may be appealed against the Court of Arbitration for Sport (CAS). The statement of appeal must be sent to the CAS directly within 10 days of receipt of notification of this decision and shall contain all the elements in accordance with point 2 of the directives issued by the CAS, copy of which we enclose hereto. Within another 10 days following the expiry of the time limit for filing the statement of appeal, the appellant shall file a brief stating the facts and legal arguments giving rise to the appeal with the CAS (cf. point 4 of the directives).

⚽⚽⚽

74234

DECISION OF THE DISPUTE RESOLUTION CHAMBER

passed in Zurich, Switzerland, on 22 July 2004,
in the following composition:

Slim Aloulou (Tunisia), Chairman
Gerardo Movilla (Spain), member
Michele Colucci (Italy), member
Jean-Marie Philips (Belgium), member
Mario Gallavotti (Italy), member
on the claim presented by
Player A, as Claimant
against
Club B, as respondent
regarding a contractual dispute.

FACTS OF THE CASE

In March 2003, Association C requested the international registration transfer certificate of A to the Association of Club B, which refused to issue it based on the existence of a valid employment contract between A and B.

In view of the above, Association C contacted the FIFA Administration for its assistance.

In this regard, at the request of the FIFA Administration, B forward, via its Association, a copy of an employment contract allegedly signed by the player on 4 December 2001, valid until the end of the 2006 season.

A category denies having signed the relevant contract submitted by B and consequently, does not recognise its validity, which in his opinion appears to be a combination of several documents.

As a consequence, the FIFA Administration requested B to be provided with "a legible copy of the aforementioned employment contract" and later on, with the original copy of the relevant document, but B has never offered any reaction to these requests to date.

A underlined the fact that B has disregarded several deadlines imposed by the FIFA Administration and, in particular, it has failed to provide the original copy of the disputed employment contract.

In light of such behaviour, the player claims to be presently prevented from challenging the authenticity of the relevant document upon which the entire dispute is founded, in country C, since in view of the political situation in club B's country as well as of his refugee status, he cannot file a claim before the courts in club B's country.

Moreover, the player stands that according to the disputed employment contract provided by B, by the date it was allegedly signed, i.e. on 4 December 2001, he was only 16 years old and therefore legally prevented from signing a 5-years' contract.

In fact, the player defends that even if he would have signed the alleged employment contract, in accordance with Art. 35 of the revised FIFA Regulations for the Status and Transfer of Players, he would be prevented from signing a contract for a period longer than three years.

As a consequence, the player asserts that the disputed employment contract provided by B should be considered invalid in its entirety and could not produce any legal effects.

In this respect, A asserts that the effect of the aforementioned Article is to invalidate the entire clause that provides for the duration of the contract and not to amend it to a shorter term. There is no provision in the relevant Regulations for the substitution to a shorter term and to make such a substitution would be to give the relevant Article an entirely different meaning to that provided for in the Regulations.

The player defends that if the relevant Article were given its natural meaning, the present contract would be of an indeterminate length, i.e. without a valid term and therefore should be considered invalid in its entirety.

Furthermore, the player underlines the fact that he was granted political asylum in C country after having left club B's country on 5 February 2002 and, as a consequence, even if a contract were found to exist, it would be frustrated by his refugee status, since it constitutes a serious threat to his life/freedom to return to club B's country. For this reason, the player believes that it is imperative that he is allowed to proceed with his football career abroad.

A copy of the Grant of Status (Asylum) from C country's Home Office, dated 14 August 2002, confirming that A has been granted political asylum, has been provided to the FIFA Administration.

A understands that his refugee status concedes him just cause to unilaterally terminate any employment contract that he would have eventually signed with a club from club B's country before he left to C country in February 2002.

The player also sustains that, even if he would be considered to have breached an employment contract with B, for not complying with his contractual obligations since February 2002, he would have been suspended from his football activity for a maximum period of only 6 months, which is the maximum period that the revised FIFA Regulations for the Status and Transfer of Players allows as a sport sanction for unilateral breach of contract without just cause or sporting just cause, as stipulated in its Art. 23 Par. 1.

The player enhanced the fact that he has been prevented from working/playing since the beginning of 2002 and that it cannot be the purpose of the relevant FIFA Regulations to permit a player's career to be jeopardized to such extend.

Finally, A adds that if the disputed contract would be considered as valid, then B would be in fundamental breach of contract on the grounds that no payment has ever been made to him under the terms of the relevant remuneration clause.

In light of the above, A requests FIFA's competent body to authorize him to proceed with his football career for a club of his election, since his football career has already been severely damaged.

On the other hand, B has always failed to provide the FIFA Administration with a detailed position in the present matter as well as with its final statement.

On 29 January 2004, the FIFA Administration informed both parties that the matter regarding the forgery of A's signature would have to be brought in front of a criminal court, since FIFA is not competent to deal with such charges.

In view of the damages that his personal and professional life is suffering due to his prevention from playing football, A insisted that FIFA's competent body immediately took a decision in the present matter.

CONSIDERATIONS OF THE DISPUTE RESOLUTION CHAMBER

The Dispute Resolution Chamber shall review disputes coming under its jurisdiction pursuant to art. 42 of the revised FIFA Regulations for the Status and Transfer of Players, at the request of one of the parties to the dispute.

In accordance with art. 42 par. 1 lit. (b) of the FIFA Regulations for the Status and Transfer of Players, it falls within the purview of the Dispute Resolution Chamber to determine whether one of the parties has committed a unilateral breach of contract without just cause.

Also, the Dispute Resolution Chamber will establish the amount of compensation to be paid and decide whether sports sanctions must be imposed (cf. art. 42, par. 1, b, ii and iii in connection with art. 22 and 23 of the aforementioned Regulations).

Therefore, the Dispute Resolution Chamber is the competent body to decide upon the present litigation with regard to the validity of the relevant employment contract as well as any eventual breaches of contract that may have occurred.

Once its competence was thus established, the Dispute Resolution Chamber went on to treat the substance of the case.

The Dispute Resolution Chamber took note of the fact that the employment contract signed on 4 December 2001 between A and B is a 5-years' duration contract and that the player was only 16 years old at the time of the contract's signature.

In this respect, the Chamber underlined the content of art. 35 of the revised FIFA Regulations for the Status and Transfer of Players, according to which "a player who has not reached his eighteenth birthday may sign a contract as non-amateur only for a period not exceeding three years. Any clause referring to a longer period shall not be recognised by FIFA or a national sports tribunal".

As a consequence, the Dispute Resolution Chamber concluded that A was not allowed to sign a 5-years contact at the age of 16 years old.

However, the Chamber was of the opinion that the invalidity of the contractual clause that stipulates the contract's duration, does not affect the validity of the entire contract and therefore, decided to reduce its duration to three years, i.e. until 4 December 2004, which is the maximum period for which a minor of eighteen is allowed to sign an employment contract.

With regard to the political asylum granted to A, the Chamber underlined that, the fact that a player possesses a refugee status does not automatically grant him, only by itself, just cause to terminate an employment relationship nor entitles him to be registered elsewhere with a club affiliated to another Association.

Notwithstanding the above, the Chamber acknowledged that B has not only failed to provide the FIFA Administration with the original copy of the relevant employment contract, but also with a detailed position in the present matter as well as with its final statement.
Furthermore, the Dispute Resolution Chamber enhanced the fact that both parties have failed to comply with their respective contractual duties since February 2002 and that their relationship is disrupted to a point that its continuation does not appear possible any longer.
In light of all the above, and since there are only four months left until the relevant employment contract expires, the Dispute Resolution Chamber was of the opinion that the player would be the only jeopardized in case he would be prevented from being immediately registered for another club of his choice.
As a consequence, the Dispute Resolution Chamber decided that A shall be released from his contractual relationship with B and authorized to immediately proceed with his football career and therefore considered free to sign for another club of his election without any compensation being due to B.

DECISION OF THE DISPUTE RESOLUTION CHAMBER

1. The claim lodged by A is accepted.
2. A is considered free to sign for the club of his election without any compensation being due to B.
3. This decision may be appealed before the Court of Arbitration for Sport (CAS) in accordance with art. 60 par. 1 of the FIFA Statutes. The statement of appeal must be sent to the CAS directly within 10 days of receiving notification of this decision and has to contain all elements in accordance with point 2 of the directives issued by the CAS, copy of which we enclose hereto. Within another 10 days following the expiry of the time limit for the filing of the statement of appeal, the appellant shall file with the CAS a brief stating the facts and legal arguments giving rise to the appeal (cf. point 4 of the directives).

74353
DECISION OF THE DISPUTE RESOLUTION CHAMBER
passed in Zurich, Switzerland, on 22 July 2004,
in the following composition:
Slim Aloulou (Tunisia), chairman
Mario Gallavotti (Italy), member
Jean Marie Philips (Belgium), member
Mario Colucci (Italy), member
Gerardo Movilla (Spain), member
on the claim presented by
X, the Netherlands, as Claimant
against
Y, Germany as Respondent
regarding a training compensation dispute concerning the transfer of the player Z

FACTS OF THE CASE:

- The player, born on 06.11.1980, was registered for X, the Claimant, as from the season 1995/1996 up to and including the season 2002/2003, that is, for seven (7) sporting seasons between the age of 14 and 21.
- As from the season 1998/1999 he was registered as a non-amateur player.
- At the beginning of the year 2002 X offered Z a new employment contract that would be valid up until 2005/2006, but these negotiations failed.
- On 01.07.2003, an employment contract was concluded between the player and the Respondent.
- In that same year, before the player's 23rd birthday, X claimed the Training Compensation from the Respondent, in accordance with Chapter VII of the revised FIFA Regulations for the Status and Transfer of Players.
- As far as the categorisation of clubs is concerned, as provided for by the circular letter 826 dated 31 October 2002, both the Claimant as well as the Respondent belong to Category 1 (indicative amount: EUR 90,000 per year).

- X has offered to pay a compensation of no more than EUR 150 000, basing itself on its own interpretations of the applicable FIFA circulars, rules and regulations, as well as on the exception provided for in art. 13 of the FIFA Regulations for the Status and Transfer of Players (hereafter: the Regulations).
- On the basis of art. 13, the Respondent has defended that it is evident that the player had already terminated his training period by the 2001/2002 season, since by then he was a regular player of the Dutch club's "A" team and had been fielded in 15 matches, scoring several goals.
- This submission has not been contradicted by the Claimant.
- The Dispute Resolution Chamber is asked to calculate the training compensation amount due to X.

CONSIDERATIONS OF THE DISPUTE RESOLUTION CHAMBER

The Dispute Resolution Chamber of the FIFA Players' Status Committee shall review disputes coming under its jurisdiction pursuant to Art. 42 of the FIFA Regulations for the Status and Transfer of Players at the request of one of the parties to the dispute.

According to Art. 42.1(b)(iv) of the FIFA Regulations for the Status and Transfer of Players, the Dispute Resolution Chamber of the FIFA Players' Status Committee shall review disputes concerning training compensation fees.

Consequently, the Dispute Resolution Chamber is the competent body to decide on the present litigation concerning the training compensation fee claimed by the Dutch club.

Once its competence was thus established, the Dispute Resolution Chamber went on to treat the substance of the case.

As established in art. 13 and Circular Letter no. 826 (dated 31st October 2002), training compensation is payable up to the age of 23 for a player's training incurred between the ages of 12 and 21.

To begin with, the Chamber affirmed that it remained undisputed that the player had been registered with the X during seven (7) sporting seasons, from 1995 to 2003, between the age of 14 and 21 years, and that the claim for compensation was put forward by the Claimant before the player turned 23 years of age.

Furthermore, it was confirmed that the Claimant had in fact attempted to offer the player Z a new professional contract running up to the 2005/2006 season, without success, after which Z signed instead an employment contract with the Respondent. This precludes the application of the principle found in art. 5.5 of the Regulations governing the Application of the Regulations for the Status and Transfer of Players in the case at hand.

Finally, the rule concerning subsequent transfers as mentioned in point (ii) of the FIFA Circular Letter no. 826, entails that for any transfers after the player's registration with X (such as in the present case his transfer to Y), training compensation shall only be owed to his previous club. This means that compensation shall be payable from Y to X only, and not to any other previous clubs.

In conclusion, the Chamber established that the Claimant is entitled to receive compensation for the training and education it provided to the player. In this respect it should be stressed that whether or not the player signed his first non-amateur contract during his education period with X is irrelevant, as it is not mentioned in any of the FIFA circulars, rules or regulations, that a training club which has benefited from the services of an amateur player turned non-amateur, loses its right to receive the full compensation for his training period as provided for in Chapter VII of the Regulations and Circular Letter no. 826.

Nonetheless, pursuant to art. 13 of the Regulations, the compensating club is reserved the option to defend a shorter education period, that is, that the training period of the player was completed in a sporting season before that of his 21st birthday.

Having thus established the Respondent's obligation to compensate the Claimant, the Chamber went on to deliberate on the proper calculation of this compensation, affirming that the amount due shall be calculated in accordance with the parameters provided in the Circular Letter 826.

It was recalled that, within the EU/EEA area, compensation for training is based on the training and education costs of the country in which the training club of the player is located. In the case at hand, since X belongs to the European Category 1, the indicative amount is of EUR 90,000 per year.

However, for the training of players from the age of 12 up to 15 years of age, the compensation granted shall correspond to the training compensation of a Category 4 club. For Europe that is an indicative amount of EUR 10,000.

In the concrete case this results in the following calculation: an amount of EUR 10,000, corresponding to the first year of the player's training when he was between 14 and 15 years of age, plus a sum in the amount of EUR 540,000, corresponding to the 6 last years of his development between the age of 15 and

21 years, at a rate of EUR 90,000 per year of training. This adds up to a grand total compensation sum of EUR 550,000 that could in principle be payable to the player's developing club.
Due note was taken of the Respondent's arguments according to which the sum payable should be of EUR 150,000 instead of EUR 550,000.
The members observed that whenever particular circumstances are given, the Dispute Resolution Chamber may adjust the amounts for the training compensation so as to reflect the specific situation of a case. Any adjustments to the training fee as mentioned in art. 42.1(b)(iv) of the FIFA Regulations may only be based on criteria established by the applicable rules and regulations and may be proven on the basis of concrete evidentiary documents, such as invoices, costs of training centres, budgets, etcetera.
In view of the foregoing, although the Respondent argues that the player had been offered a part time non-amateur contract by X already in 1998, it was noted that this does not comprise a particular circumstance established in the FIFA rules and regulations that may justify an adjustment of the amounts for the training compensation. For this reason, and in the absence of other evidence as to the real and effective training costs incurred by the Claimant for the formation and the education of the player, it was decided that the indicative amounts mentioned in the Circular 826 shall apply.
Notwithstanding the above, due note was taken of the Respondent's defence according to which the player finished his actual training period by the time he had started the 2001/2002 season with X.
The Respondent submitted that in the playing season 2000/2001 Z was fielded on a regular basis, 15 times, in the Claimant's "A"-team, scoring 3 goals. At that time he had already spent many years as a non-amateur player as from an early age and could thus be considered to have been a particularly successful player.
The Respondent's arguments in this respect were accepted by the members of the Chamber.
Based on the foregoing, the Dispute Resolution Chamber concluded its deliberations by deciding that in the present case the 2001/2002 training period would not be taken into consideration for calculation purposes. This translates into a reduction of EUR 90,000 over the total amount of EUR 550,000 as calculated above, resulting in a final compensation sum of EUR 460,000 due.

DECISION OF THE DISPUTE RESOLUTION CHAMBER

1. The Respondent shall pay the amount of EUR 460,000 to the Claimant within 30 days of notification of the present decision.
2. If Respondent fails to comply with the above-mentioned deadline, an interest rate of 5% per year will apply and the case will immediately be presented to the FIFA Disciplinary Committee.
3. According to art. 60 par. 1 of the FIFA Statutes, this decision may be appealed before the Court of Arbitration for Sport (CAS). The statement of appeal must be sent to the CAS directly within 10 days of receiving notification of this decision and has to contain all elements in accordance with point 2 of the directives issued by the CAS, copy of which we enclose hereto. Within another 10 days following the expiry of the time limit for the filing of the statement of appeal, the appellant shall file with the CAS a brief stating the facts and legal arguments giving rise to the appeal (cf. point 4 of the directives).

74477

DECISION OF THE DISPUTE RESOLUTION CHAMBER

passed in Zurich, Switzerland, on 22 July 2004,
in the following composition:
Slim Aloulou (Tunisia), Chairman
Michele Colucci (Italy), member
Gerardo Movilla (Spain), member
Jean-Marie Philips (Belgium), member
Mario Gallavotti (Italy), member
on the claim presented by
Club A as Claimant
against
Club B as Respondent
regarding the solidarity contribution related to the transfer of the federative rights to the player C

FACTS OF THE CASE:

- In July 2003 the Club Z and the Respondent, both affiliated to the same association, concluded an agreement for the transfer of the federative rights to the player C.
- The player C, born in 1980, was registered for the Claimant for four seasons, from July 1995 to July 1999, between the ages of 15 and 19.
- The Claimant claims the 5% payment established in art. 25 of the FIFA Regulations for the Status and Transfer of Players regarding the contribution to the solidarity mechanism related to the transfer of the federative rights to the player C from the Club Z to the Respondent.
- According to the aforementioned Regulations, the new club concerned is to distribute 5% of this compensatory amount to the club(s) where the player has played between the ages of 12 and 23, in the present case thus between 1992 and 2003.
- According to the Claimant, the amount to be paid by the Respondent for the transfer of the federative rights to the player C is USD 3,000,000.
- The Claimant asks the Dispute Resolution Chamber to sentence the Respondent to start with the distribution of the solidarity contribution of 5% related to the transfer of the federative rights to the player C and to take all the disciplinary measures that the Chamber may deem appropriate against the aforementioned club.
- The Respondent claims that it cannot comply with the demand of the Claimant. Immediately after the transfer of the federative rights to the player C the club communicated to the competent body of its league that it had agreed with the Club Z that the solidarity mechanism should not be applicable to the present case. Any request from clubs, which had trained the player, for solidarity contribution should therefore be addressed to the Club Z. The Respondent is no longer in a position to deduct from the compensation communicated to the competent body of its league any percentage and to distribute it to the training clubs. Apparently, the Club Z acknowledged its obligation to pay any compensation to third clubs if such compensation would be due. No written evidence to this regard was, however, remitted to the FIFA administration.
- Furthermore, the Respondent emphasises that the transfer at the basis of the claimed solidarity contribution was an internal one and that it was executed in accordance with the rules of the relevant association. In fact, FIFA granted to all its member associations the exclusive power to regulate the transfers of players, which occur within the association's territory. The provisions governing the solidarity mechanism of the FIFA Regulations for the Status and Transfer of Players, however, only apply to international transfers. In fact, the Preamble to the aforementioned Regulations does not include art. 25 in the list of those provisions binding at national level. Furthermore, the FIFA circular no. 769 expressly stated that the solidarity mechanism only applies to international transfers.
- According to the Respondent, the amount it had to pay for the transfer of the federative rights to the player C is EUR 1,000,000. This sum was also communicated to the competent body of its league.
- Finally, the Respondent maintains that the player C joined the Club X in early 1999.

CONSIDERATIONS OF THE DISPUTE RESOLUTION CHAMBER

The Dispute Resolution Chamber commenced its deliberations by referring to art. 25 of the FIFA Regulations for the Status and Transfer of Players (hereinafter: the Regulations), according to which it falls within the purview of the Dispute Resolution Chamber to review disputes concerning the distribution of the solidarity contribution. Consequently, the Chamber established that it was competent to deal with the present litigation.

Subsequently, and entering into the substance of the matter, the Chamber acknowledged that, for the case at hand, it was essential to establish whether an internal transfer, this means a move of a player from one club to another, both affiliated to the same association, could be the basis for a claim for solidarity contribution or not. In other words, the Dispute Resolution Chamber recognised that, first of all, it would have to address a matter of principle. If it were to follow the argumentation put forward by the Respondent regarding the application of the Regulations, no solidarity contribution would be due whenever the federative rights to a player are transferred from one club to another both affiliated to the same association. This principle would apply regardless of whether the claiming club is affiliated to a different association or to the same association as that of the two clubs directly involved in the relevant transfer.

The members of the deciding body attending the meeting acknowledged that in previous cases the Dispute Resolution Chamber had decided that the solidarity mechanism applies also to internal transfers, provided a club affiliated to another association is claiming the payment of the relevant contribution.

Furthermore, the Chamber noted that the Respondent is, inter alia, basing its argumentation on the contents of the FIFA circular 769. In this regard, the deciding body clarified that circular letters are an administrative instrument, which – as sources of law within the FIFA legal system – are hierarchically subordinated to the FIFA regulations. Accordingly, the useful and legitimate aim of circular letters is to implement, detail and interpret the FIFA regulations. However, the regulations must remain the main source of law when having to judge a dispute.

Taking into consideration this principle, the Dispute Resolution Chamber referred to the contents of the Regulations and in particular, to their Preamble. Par. 1 of the Preamble establishes that the Regulations deal with the status and eligibility of players, as well as with the rules applicable whenever players move between clubs belonging to different associations. The deciding body lent emphasis to the wording of the last part of the aforementioned clause and concluded that, in fact, the Regulations are not applicable to transfers of the federative rights to a player between two clubs affiliated to the same association. Consequently, the members of the Chamber present at the meeting were of the unanimous opinion that the previous jurisprudence of the Dispute Resolution Chamber needs reviewing and concluded that the principle regarding the solidarity mechanism contained in the Regulations is not applicable to national transfers, not even in cases where the club claiming the payment of the relevant contribution is affiliated to another association.

Moreover, the Chamber pointed out that the principle of the solidarity mechanism is not included in par. 2 of the Preamble of the Regulations and therefore, it is not binding at national level.

On account of all the above, the Dispute Resolution Chamber decided that the claim of the Claimant against the Respondent for payment of solidarity contribution has to be rejected.

DECISION OF THE DISPUTE RESOLUTION CHAMBER

1. The claim of the Club A is rejected.
2. According to art. 60 par. 1 of the FIFA Statutes, this decision may be appealed against before the Court of Arbitration for Sport (CAS). The statement of appeal must be sent to the CAS directly within 10 days of receipt of notification of this decision and shall contain all the elements in accordance with point 2 of the directives issued by the CAS, a copy of which we enclose hereto. Within another 10 days following the expiry of the time limit for filing the statement of appeal, the appellant shall file a brief stating the facts and legal arguments giving rise to the appeal with the CAS (cf. point 4 of the directives).

⚽⚽⚽

74508

DECISION OF THE DISPUTE RESOLUTION CHAMBER

passed in Zurich, Switzerland, on 22 July 2004,
in the following composition:
Slim Aloulou (Tunisia), Chairman
Mario Gallavotti (Italy), member
Jean-Marie Philips (Belgium), member
Michele Colucci (Italy), member
Gerardo Movilla (Spain), member
on the claim presented by
the player, Y, as Claimant
against
the club X, as Respondent
regarding a contractual dispute between the player and the club,

FACTS OF THE CASE

- The player X and the club Y signed an employment contract valid from 30 July 2003 until 30 June 2004 and made out on a standard employment contract form.
- According to this contract, it is valid for the above-mentioned period of time "with a four year unilateral renewal which is announced to the player via process server with a simultaneous legal notice to the Association of Football Players and at least 5 days before the commencement of the transfer period as prescribed by the Professional Players' Regulation".

- The transfer periods in the country of Y are from 1st January until 31st January and from 1st July until 31st July.
- Furthermore, in accordance with the contract, the notification of renewal must contain the financial terms pertaining to the extended period of time and the form of renewal (whether "continuous or interrupted") in order to be valid. In addition, the relevant clause in the contract stipulates that the extension of the contract "will be made every year".
- According to the employment contract, the player is entitled to receive the following monies:
  Monthly salary
  Christmas bonus
  "Passover bonus"
- In addition, in accordance with article 7.2 of the contract, the club is obliged to "deposit" for unilateral renewal payable in 40 unequal instalments (payable in the months of August until March) as from 30 August 2003 until 30 March 2008.
- For each of the 2003/04 and 2004/05 seasons these instalments total –.–. For the following seasons 2005/06, 2006/07 and 2007/08, respectively, the instalments total –.–, and –.–.
- On 24 May 2004, the club notified the player in writing that it exercises its right to unilaterally renew the employment contract from 1 July 2004 until 30 June 2005.
- This document was delivered to the player by a judicial officer.
- Furthermore, the financial terms pertaining to this renewal are equal to the financial benefits of the player in accordance with the above-mentioned employment contract.
- On 7 June 2003, the player turned to FIFA claiming that this automatic and unilateral renewal of the contract by the club cannot be considered valid.
- The player asks the Dispute Resolution Chamber to advise as to whether he can end his employment relation with the club Y.
- The club for its part, maintains that it has fully carried out the terms and conditions of the employment contract.
  Furthermore, it asserts that it has legally renewed the employment contract for the next season.

CONSIDERATIONS OF THE DISPUTE RESOLUTION CHAMBER

Due note was taken of the employment contract which was signed for a pre-determined period of time from 30 July 2003 until 30 June 2004 with a unilateral option for the club to extend such contract.

The Chamber acknowledged that the player wishes to be declared not bound by the unilateral extension option and free to sign on with another club.

Therefore, the Chamber has to consider whether this clause is valid or not.

Unilateral options are, in general, problematic, since they limit the freedom of the party that cannot make use of the option in an excessive manner. Furthermore, such options are not based on reciprocity, since the right to extend a contract is left exclusively at the discretion of one party.

In the case at hand, the extension option contained in the relevant employment contract is unilateral to the benefit of the club only, i.e. the stronger party in the employment relationship, and may be exercised by the club during a period of four footballing seasons. Furthermore, in the present matter, as regards the option being currently exercised by the club to extend the contract with the 2004/05 season and the validity of which is disputed by the player, there is no apparent gain for the player, as the conditions of employment remain unaltered. The Chamber concurred that the afore-mentioned specifics of the unilateral extension option in the case at hand do not fit within the general principles of labour law.

Taking into consideration all of the above, the members of the Chamber agreed that the unilateral extension option in the relevant employment contract is not legally binding on the player, X. Consequently, should the player in question not wish to accept the conditions contained in the notification of the extension of contract by club Y, the relevant employment contract has come to an end at its date of expiry, i.e. 30 June 2004.

DECISION OF THE DISPUTE RESOLUTION CHAMBER

1. The claim of the Claimant is accepted.
2. The employment contract between the Claimant and the Respondent terminated on 30 June 2004.
3. According to art. 60 par. 1 of the FIFA Statutes, this decision may be appealed against before the Court of Arbitration for Sport (CAS). The statement of appeal must be sent to the CAS directly within 10 days of receipt of notification of this decision and shall contain all the elements in accordance

with point 2 of the directives issued by the CAS, a copy of which we enclose hereto. Within another 10 days following the expiry of the time limit for filing the statement of appeal, the appellant shall file a brief stating the facts and legal arguments giving rise to the appeal with the CAS (cf. point 4 of the directives).

74557
DECISION OF THE DISPUTE RESOLUTION CHAMBER
passed in Zurich, Switzerland, on 22 July 2004,
in the following composition:
Slim Aloulou (Tunisia), Chairman
Mario Gallavotti (Italy), member
Jean-Marie Philips (Belgium), member
Michele Colucci (Italy), member
Gerardo Movilla (Spain), member
on the claim presented by
The club B. as Claimant
against
The club A. as Respondent
regarding a dispute on the transfer of the player Z.

FACTS OF THE CASE

- The player Z. signed a 'non-professional' contract and a pre-contract with the club B. on 24 July 2002, at the age of 15. These contracts were deposited at the League on 25 July 2003, i.e. one year later.
- Furthermore, the player signed an employment contract with the club B. that bears no date of signature and that does not mention the starting season.
- All three contracts were signed by the player Z., his parents and the club B.
- The 'non-professional' contract that was signed on 24 July 2002 establishes the intention of the parties for the player Z. to join the amateur teams of the club B. Furthermore, point II. of the preamble to the 'non-professional' contract stipulates that both parties want to establish the terms of a potential integration of the player as a professional in the squad of the club B. by agreeing the conditions for the signing of an employment contract. Point III of the preamble states that the parties had agreed on the terms of this integration and on formalising these in the present contract. Clause 1.1. al. 2 of this contract reiterates that next to integrating the player in a amateur squad of the club B., this contract also sets the terms of the pre-contract that will, subsequently, allow the integration of the player in whichever professional squad of the club.
- The duration of the 'non-professional' contract was to run from 24 July 2002 until 30 June 2008, i.e. for six years, whilst reserving the possibility for this term to be changed for reasons relating to the applicable regulations.
- The contract established that the player is entitled to receive a student grant and compensation for costs incurred through travel to training sessions or matches of the club. During the phase of a cadet player, the grant and the travel compensation was fixed at EUR 1,502 per season.
- Clause 5.1. of the 'non-professional' contract maintains that the rescission of the present agreement, with regard to its main objective, will take place with the expiration of the term agreed upon or if the player enters an employment relationship with another club. In such a case, the club B. would be entitled to receive compensation for the training and education of the player.
- Clause 5.3. stipulates further that if the player were to abandon the club for no fault of the club, he will compensate the club with an amount of EUR 30,000 upon signing with the new club.
- Clause 6 of the 'non-professional' contract states that the parties agree to sign an employment contract and that the agreement to sign such a contract is independent from the validity of the 'non-professional' contract. This engagement will stand, regardless of the duration, validity or extinction of the 'non-professional' contract.
- Clause 6.3 maintains that the parties engage to sign an employment contract once one of the following conditions has materialised:

  - Upon the first request of the club B., provided the player meets the age requirements
  - Once the player has participated in a total of 10 matches for the B team or higher
  - Upon request of the player, if he receives a definite employment offer by another club, which he would have to notify to the club B. at least 3 months before the start of the season of the offer of employment. The player would have to present a signed offer of employment.
  - In any case once the player has reached the age of 18.
- Clause 6.4 states that the extinction of the engagement as a non-professional at the club will not affect the obligation of the parties to sign the employment contract agreed upon.
- Clause 6.6 refers to the to the pre-contract and the employment contract and states that the employment contract does not contain a starting date as it is not yet known.
- The pre-contract outlines in the preamble II. that it is the will of the parties to establish an employment pre-contract that will allow, within a reasonable timeframe, for the club to secure the services of the player Z. as a professional and enable to the player to render his professional services to the club.
- The beginning of this contract was set to commence under the same conditions as drafted in clause 6.3 of the 'non-professional' contract that is mentioned above.
- The duration of the engagement was set at a maximum duration of 5 seasons, with three contractual periods in the same category in which the player will be playing.
- Clause 5 maintains that the club B. retains the right not to sign an employment contract with the player and that the unjustified refusal for not signing a contract will result in the club losing its entitlement to any sort of training compensation. The player, on the other hand, may, provided he does not sign with another club for the next three seasons, leave without having to pay compensation to the club. If he fails to respect this contract because he has signed with another club, the club B. will be entitled to compensation in the amount of EUR 3,000,000. In accordance with the 'Decreto Real 1006/85', the new club of the player may be considered jointly responsible for the payment of this sum, regardless of whether it induced the breach of contract or not. As long as this sum has not been paid, the club B. will remain holder of the federative rights to the player and shall refuse the registration of the player at another club. This payment obligation is independent of the entitlement of the club B. to compensation for the training and formation of the player owed by the club that will sign the player as a professional.
- The employment contract contains no date of signature.
- It makes reference to the pre-contract signed by the parties on 24 July 2002 that is annexed to the present contract.
- The duration of this contract is established at no less than 5 seasons. The employment contract also gives the club the option to extend the contract upon its expiry at the same conditions and for the same duration as offered by a third club.
- The salaries per season for the player (including all other remuneration such as rent, car, travel etc. yet excluding match bonuses), were established as follows:

Season	Youth "C"	Team "B"	First team
200-/-	4.900.- EUR		
200-/-	5.100.- EUR	19.000.- EUR	
200-/-	5.300.- EUR	19.000.- EUR	162.000 EUR
200-/-	7.400.- EUR	23.500.- EUR	162.000 EUR
200-/-		28.000.- EUR	184.000 EUR

- For each match played for the "B" team, the player would be entitled to receive EUR 6,000, which would be increased by EUR 9,000 if the match were played in the "A" team.
- The employment contract also establishes the compensation for image rights and for the right of the coach to line up the player for the most convenient position.
- Clause 8.2.2.4 of the employment contract provides that the anticipated termination of the contract by the player will result in the payment of compensation to the club B. by the player and subsidiarily by the club that has engaged him, in accordance with the 'Real Decreto 1006/85'. This compensation depends on the team in which the player was being registered:
  EUR 30,000,000 if the player was registered in "C" team
  EUR 80,000,000 if the player was registered in "B"
  EUR 150,000,000 if the player was registered in first team
- The player signed an employment contact with the club A. on 1 July 2004.
- The club A. admits owing EUR 220,000 to the club B. as training compensation based on the

FIFA regulations and circular letters but does not recognise the right of the club B. to transfer compensation.

The claimant, the club B., basically maintains that:

- The player Z. must respect the contracts that he signed. Equally, the club A. must respect the contractual relationship that was established by the club B. with the mentioned player and the club A. must acknowledge its entitlement to compensation for the player's federative rights.
- The club B. outlines that although the FIFA Regulations for the Status and Transfer of Players stipulate that employment contracts must be in writing, art. 4.1 of the FIFA Regulations does not rule out that amateur players may also sign binding non-professional contracts.
- Moreover, chapter VIII of the mentioned regulations on the maintenance of contractual stability is applicable to amateur as well as non-amateur players. This is demonstrated in art. 18 of the mentioned regulations, according to which the entitlement of the forming club to compensation for training and education is without prejudice to the entitlement of receiving compensation under the application of art. 22, whenever a player moves during the course of a contract but before reaching the age of 23.
- The compensation that must be paid to the club B. for the breach of contract is specified in art. 22 of the FIFA regulations, which makes particular reference to the applicable national law.
- Consequently, the club A. must be held liable for inducing the breach of the contract existing between the club B. and the player Z.

The respondent, the club A., basically maintains that:

- The player Z. was entitled to leave the club B. because he was an amateur player.
- The provisions of chapter VIII of the FIFA Regulations for the Status and Transfer of Players do not apply to the case at hand.
- The club A. acknowledges that the club B. is entitled to compensation for the training and formation of the player and it is willing to pay the amount of EUR 220,000 to the club B.
- In light of these circumstances, the Football Federation of the club B. must immediately send the international registration transfer certificate of the player to its Football Association in order to facilitate the player's registration at the club A.

CONSIDERATIONS OF THE DISPUTE RESOLUTION CHAMBER

The Dispute Resolution Chamber commenced its deliberations by considering whether the club B. is entitled to claim the payment of compensation for the alleged breach of contract by the player Z. and whether it is entitled to refuse the issuance of the international registration transfer certificate for the player in order to prevent him from registering register with the club A. The Chamber maintained that the requests of the club B. can only be seconded if the player is considered to be contractually bound to it.

The Chamber pointed out that the club B. had turned to FIFA requesting this organisation's intervention in the present case. According to the Chamber, this request demonstrates that the club B. is asking FIFA to rule on the conduct of the club A. based on the Regulations for the Status and Transfer of Players. Consequently, a necessary preliminary examination of the contracts signed by the club B. and the player Z. must be carried out in order to ascertain whether the player committed a breach of contract in accordance with the applicable FIFA regulations. In this regard, the Chamber first examined the 'non-professional' contract and later turned to the pre-contract signed by the parties.

The Dispute Resolution Chamber turned to the 'non-professional' contract that was signed on 24 July 2002 and that lays down the intention of both parties for the player Z. to join the amateur teams of the club B. as well as for the player to eventually become a non-amateur player of the club B. The 'non-professional' contract was to run from 24 July 2002 until 30 June 2008. It was established in this contract that the player is entitled to receive a student grant and compensation for costs incurred through travel to training sessions or matches which, during the cadet phase, were fixed at EUR 1,502 per season.

All the parties involved in this case are in agreement over the fact that the 'non-professional' contract cannot be considered an employment contract as outlined in art. 2.1 of the Regulations for the Status and Transfer of Players. Clearly, the remuneration offered to the player does not exceed the actual expenses that the player incurred through football at the club B. Furthermore, the denomination 'non-professional' shows that the parties did not consider this an employment contract. As a result, the Chamber concluded that the 'non-professional' contract is a written record of the terms, which the parties had agreed upon with regard to the player's participation at the club B. in the quality of an amateur player.

In this context, the Dispute Resolution Chamber underlined that written contracts are unusual when regarding amateur players, simply because these players are seen to pursue football as a leisure activity and not as a career. Players who are not old enough to sign an employment contract are also considered amateurs. Therefore, on the basis of this concept, the FIFA Regulations for the Status and Transfer of Players foresee a number of rules that only apply to non-amateur footballers.

The regulations contain rules on the principle of contractual stability, which are considered paramount for the proper functioning of football. All clubs or players that commit a breach of contract are liable to be sanctioned under the provisions outlined in Chapter VIII of the regulations. In this respect, the Chamber underlined that although not always clearly specified in the Regulations for the Status and Transfer of Players, it is evident from provisions contained in art. 4 of these regulations as well as art. 12 of the Regulations governing the Application that the term 'contract' makes reference to employment contracts and no other contractual agreements. This is highlighted by the contents of the FIFA circular letter no. 769, dated 24 August 2001, which served as a guideline to the revised transfer regulations. Chapter 3 of this circular letter on contractual stability makes reference to the employment laws applicable to the contracts as well as to salaries that are to be considered when determining the compensation payable in the cases of breach of contract. The Chamber added further that the FIFA Regulations for the Status and Transfer of Players do not foresee written contracts for amateur players, as these players are evidently considered free to change clubs without restrictions. Particularly, art. 18 of the transfer regulations does not apply to amateur players.

In consequence, the Chamber rejected the arguments put forward by the club B. according to which the player Z. had a contractual obligation towards its club. Although art. 4.1 of the Regulations for the Status and Transfer of Players does not exclude the right of the parties to establish written contracts that are not employment contracts, the provisions contained in the transfer regulations regarding the stability of contracts only applies to employment contracts and not so-called 'non-professional' contracts.

As a result, the Dispute Resolution Chamber concluded that the 'non-professional' contract signed by the club B. and the player Z. is not subject to the provisions on the maintenance of contractual stability of the Regulations for the Status and Transfer of Players and that consequently, the club B. is not entitled to prevent the issuance of the player's international registration transfer certificate to the benefit of Football Association of the club A. nor can the club B. claim compensation for the breach of contract in accordance with articles 21 and following of the mentioned regulations.

In continuation, the Dispute Resolution Chamber examined the question whether the player Z. should be considered contractually bound to the club B. by the pre-contract signed by the parties also on 24 July 2002.

The Chamber insisted that the existence of the pre-contract did not have any effect on the fact that the player Z. was to be considered an amateur player when he signed the employment contract with the club A. At the moment of his move to the club A., the player was not receiving any remuneration other than the payment of the expenses that he was incurring. Furthermore, the player was not receiving the minimal salary foreseen in the country of the club B. In light of these facts, the Chamber outlined that the rules on the maintenance of contractual stability of the FIFA transfer regulations do not apply in the present case.

Although the Chamber did not wish to pronounce itself on the validity of the contracts signed by the club B. and the player Z., it expressed its discomfort with both the pre-contract and the employment contract. In particular, the Chamber underlined the fact that both contracts do not foresee a starting date of the employment. Although there is an enumeration of conditions that would set-off the validity of the employment contract, the Chamber was of the opinion that the need of an employee regarding the certainty of the employment and the start of this relationship was not being given sufficient consideration. The Chamber underlined that an employee, who is generally considered a weaker party in such contracts, is entitled to more clarity and certainty in such relationships.

Furthermore, the Chamber expressed its surprise at the disparity of the conditions stipulated in the pre-contract. On the one hand, the club B. reserved its right not to sign an employment contract with the player, which entails the sole consequence that the club would not be entitled to claim a possible compensation for the formation of the player. However, by failing to offer the player an employment contract, the club B. would, in any case, not be entitled to compensation for the formation of the player, following art. 5.5 of the Regulations governing the Application of the Regulations for the Status and Transfer of Players in combination with point 2 a) of the circular letter no. 769. On the other hand, the pre-contract foresees that the player Z. would owe EUR 3,000,000 to the club B. if he were to sign a contract with another club. Clearly, the pre-contract grants the club B. the possibility of stepping down from its engagement at no consequence whereas the players would only be able to proceed in such a fashion upon the payment of a penalty sum of EUR 3,000,000. What is more, the Chamber could not discern any substantial benefits awarded to the player in either the 'non-professional' contract or in the pre-contract that would compensate him for the significant restrictions in his freedom to contractually engage with the employer of his choice.

Finally, the Chamber wished to communicate its concern with regard to the contractual construction that the club B. had made use of to secure the services of the player Z. In particular, the Chamber felt troubled with the amounts foreseen as compensation for the club B. in the case of a rescission by the player Z. as well as with the young age of the player. Furthermore, it considered the interdependence of the three contracts problematic, which, despite the lack of any compensation payable to the player, would invariably lead to the employment of the latter.

In light of the aforementioned, and given that the Dispute Resolution Chamber established that the player Z. was an amateur player when he signed with the club A., the Chamber concluded that the club B. is not entitled to claim compensation for the breach of contract by the player in accordance with art. 22 of the FIFA Regulations for the Status and Transfer of Players. Furthermore, and based on art. 6 of the mentioned regulations, the player Z. may be registered for the club A. by this club's Football Association.

The club B. is entitled to compensation for the training and education of the player Z. in accordance with Chapter VII of the Regulations for the Status and Transfer of Players in combination with the FIFA circular letter no. 826. The Chamber accepted the offer of compensation made by the club A. and determined that the club B. is entitled to receive EUR 220,000 from A.

DECISION OF THE DISPUTE RESOLUTION CHAMBER

1. The claim of the club B. regarding compensation for the breach of the contract by the player Z. is rejected. Equally, the club B. is not allowed to prevent the issuance of the player's international registration transfer certificate that is required for his registration at the Football Association of the club A.
2. The club A. is directed to pay EUR 220,000 to the club B. as compensation for the training and education of the player Z.
3. The club A. is directed to pay the amount due the club B. within 30 days as from the date of the notification of this decision.
4. According to art. 60 par. 1 of the FIFA Statutes, this decision may be appealed against before the Court of Arbitration for Sport (CAS). The statement of appeal must be sent to the CAS directly within 10 days of receipt of notification of this decision and shall contain all the elements in accordance with point 2 of the directives issued by the CAS, a copy of which we enclose hereto. Within another 10 days following the expiry of the time limit for filing the statement of appeal, the appellant shall file a brief stating the facts and legal arguments giving rise to the appeal with the CAS (cf. point 4 of the directives).

74653

DECISION OF THE DISPUTE RESOLUTION CHAMBER

passed in Zurich, Switzerland, on 22 July 2004,
in the following composition:
Slim Aloulou (Tunisia), Chairman
Mario Gallavotti (Italy), member
Jean-Marie Philips (Belgium), member
Michele Colucci (Italy), member
Gerardo Movilla (Spain), member
on the claim presented by
The player B. as Claimant
against
The club A. as Respondent
regarding a dispute on contractual relationship established between the parties

FACTS OF THE CASE

- The 32 yrs. old player B. signed an employment contract with the club A. on 18 August 2003 valid for a period of 10 months.

- In the same agreement, it is stated that the services of the player were loaned to the club A. by the club D. and that the loan fee would be of USD 1,200,000.
- The payments listed in the loan contract are as follows:
  USD 60,000 in ten monthly instalments to the player
  USD 300,000 payable to the player
  USD 150,000 payable to the club D. once the player passes the medical test, signs the official contract and the club receives the international registration transfer certificate
  USD 150,000 payable to the club D. 90 days after the payment of the first instalment
- Verbally, the parties arranged that the player would pay USD 150,000 out of his share to the club D. immediately and would, instead, receive the second instalment of USD 150,000 after 90 days of the first payment that would otherwise be payable to the club D.
- Before officially contacting FIFA and requesting its intervention, the player copied a letter to this organisation which he had addressed to the club A. and in which he outlined that he had not yet received a satisfactory reply to his faxes of 19 and 26 November 2003, by means of which he had given the club a deadline to meet its contractual obligations,
- The player maintains that the club A. had not paid the monthly salaries of USD 60,000 due on 18 September, 18 October and 18 November 2003 and that it had failed to pay the second instalment of USD 150,000 of the signing-on fee owed on 18 November 2003.
- Furthermore, the player provided FIFA with a copy of a letter, which the club A. had addressed to his lawyer on 23 November 2003 and in which the club informed the player that the second instalment of the signing-on fee of USD 150,000 was ready to be paid to him but that it would be paid only once the player shows his highest performance.
- According to the player, the second instalment of the signing-on fee was due on 18 November 2003, 90 days after the player signed the official contract and passed the medical test that took place on 18 August 2003.
- In light of these facts, the player announced in his letter of 10 December 2003 that he was herewith terminating the contractual relationship with the club.
- One day later, the player contacted FIFA directly, claiming not only unpaid salaries but also asking FIFA's intervention so as to enable him to obtain a visa required in order to leave the country of the club A.
- The player maintained that the club was using its influence at the local authorities to keep him in the country, thus trying to pressure him into signing a document waiving his claims.
- In light of this situation, the Dispute Resolution Chamber passed a decision on 23 December 2003, ordering the club A. to facilitate the visa for the player within 48 hours and maintaining that a decision on the question regarding the unpaid remuneration would be passed at a later stage.
- The player was thus able to leave the country on 26 December 2003.
- The club A. maintains that on the same date that it received the notification on the rescission of the employment contract, it sent a letter to the player via DHL, asking him to come and see the club so that its Financial Administration could review his entitlement. However, the player refused to receive this letter as well as a second communication also sent by the club via DHL.
- In consequence, the club A. turned to its Football Federation, which invited the player to a meeting. The player was asked to bring his passport to this meeting so that his visa could be arranged, once his due were settled.
- The club insists that it could not have arranged the visa any earlier, since the player had not presented his passport and because, given the immigration rules, the question regarding the payment of the telephone, electricity and other service bills as well as the returning of the house, car and telephone needed to be settled prior to the issuance of the visa.
- Furthermore, the club maintains that instead of settling the dispute with the club, as stipulated in the employment contract, the player turned to the press and then to FIFA.
- With regard to the salary payments, there was some payment delay due to holidays and staff shortage yet, when the player was asked to receive the pay-cheque for September 2003, the latter refused to collect it.
- As per the club's accountancy policy, the cheques for October and November 2003 could not be issued unless the first cheque was received.
- With regard to the signing-on fee, there was no late payment since the due date of payment of the second instalment was 10 December 2003, i.e. 90 days after the first payment of USD 150,000

was made by the club. The club A. has provided FIFA with a copy of the receipt regarding the first payment. Moreover, the club has pointed out that the player rescinded his contract on 16 December 2003.

- The club A. maintains that the player was never able to appreciate living in its country and that therefore he sought to put an end to the relationship.
- The club A. is of the opinion that it is a victim of the conduct of the player and has lodged a counter-claim totalling USD 668,038, corresponding to the following amounts:
  USD 450,000 paid by the club regarding the loan
  USD 10,000 received by the player in cash
  USD 10,038 paid by the club for the airfare of the player's relatives
  USD 36,000 for the leave without pay by the player
  USD 12,000 red card penalty
  USD 500,000 as compensation of losses incurred to the club due to early termination of the contract
  Minus: USD 200,000 + USD 150,000 corresponding to the salaries owed to the player for 3 months and 10 days
  Total: USD 668,038
- The player B. is claiming a total of USD 750,000 corresponding to the following amounts:
  USD 240,000 for the unpaid salaries of September, October and November 2003 plus 10 days in December 2003
  USD 150,000 as the second instalment of the signing-on fee
  USD 360,000 as the remaining amounts due as per the employment contract

CONSIDERATIONS OF THE DISPUTE RESOLUTION CHAMBER

The Dispute Resolution Chamber initiated its discussions by establishing that both the player B. as well as the club A. are claiming that the counter-party committed a breach of contract. The Chamber thus established that it needed to ascertain whether the player B. had acceptable reasons for refusing to reassume work at the club A. or whether A. had valid reasons to justify the late payments of the remuneration owed to the player. The Chamber took into consideration that there are two issues to be addressed, namely the alleged late salary payments and the late payment of the second instalment of the signing-on fee.

Firstly, the Dispute Resolution Chamber turned to the question regarding salary payments. The Chamber acknowledged that neither party debates the fact that the salaries of September, October and November 2003 have not yet been remitted to the player B. According to the club A., there had indeed been some delay in processing the payment caused by staff shortage, yet the pay-cheque for the salary of September 2003 was made available to the player, who, according to the club, refused to collect it. As per the club's accountancy policy, the cheques for October and November 2003 could not be issued before the first cheque was received. In this regard, the Chamber maintained that the club A. was unable to present any proof to underline its allegation that the player had indeed refused to collect the cheque for September 2003. Besides, if the player had indeed refused to receive this payment, the Chamber could not understand why the club A. had not deposited this and the remaining cheques in an escrow account under the name of the player. In addition, the Chamber underlined that the letter of the club A. sent on 23 November 2003 to the lawyer of the player indicated that the non-payment of the club had been motivated by its belief that the player had not been displaying his highest performance. The Chamber therefore concluded that the club A. had indeed committed a breach of contract by failing to pay the salaries of the player B.

In continuation, the Chamber turned to the question of the non-payment of the second instalment of the signing-on fee amounting to USD 150,000. The Chamber took note of the fact that the parties are in disagreement over the actual date on which this instalment should have been paid to the player B. In this context, the Chamber outlined that the first instalment was due on the day that the player passed his medical test, signed the official contract and the international registration transfer certificate was received by the club. According to the information available to the Chamber, this first payment was therefore due on 18 August 2003. Consequently, the second instalment would have been payable 90 days later, i.e. on 18 November 2003. In this context, the Chamber maintained that the assumption of the club A., according to which the second instalment was payable 90 days after it processed the first payment is incorrect, as this would signify that the club A. would have sole influence on determining the deadline of the second payment. Therefore, the Chamber decided that the club A. had failed to proceed with the timely payment of the second instalment of the signing-on fee.

In light of the above, the Chamber concluded that the club A. had committed a breach of the employment contract by failing to pay the salaries and the remaining signing-on fee owed to the player B., without just cause. As a result, the Chamber established that the club A. is liable to compensate the player for the losses incurred through this breach of contract, as foreseen in art. 22 of the FIFA Regulations for the Status and Transfer of Players.
The Chamber calculated that the player in question is entitled to a total of USD 661,340. This amount corresponds to the unpaid salaries of September, October, November and 10 days of December 2003 totalling USD 240,000, the second instalment of the signing-on fee of USD 150,000 and USD 360,000 as the remaining amounts due per the employment contract, which total USD 750,000. From the amount of USD 750,000, the Chamber deducted USD 10,000 that the player had received in cash, USD 10,038 relating to the airfares that the club had paid for the player's relatives and USD 12,000 owed by the player for receiving a red card penalty. Furthermore, the Chamber took into consideration the fact that the player had immediately reassumed work back at home with the club D., where he is receiving a monthly salary of USD 9,437. These salaries received by the player during the otherwise remaining six months of the loan period were also deducted from the amount owed to the player, leaving a total amount due by the club A. of USD 661,340.
Finally, the Chamber re-affirmed that the club A. had committed a breach of contract without just cause and the club is consequently liable to be sanctioned in accordance with art. 21.1. (a) and art. 23.2 (a) of the aforementioned regulations. Therefore, the club A. is banned from registering any new player, either nationally or internationally, until after the next two transfer periods have passed. Although the breach of contract occurred in December 2003, the Chamber established that the ban on registering new players shall apply following the date on which the breach became effective, i.e. the date of the notification of this decision.

DECISION OF THE DISPUTE RESOLUTION CHAMBER

1. The claim of the player B. is partially accepted.
2. The respondent, the club A., must pay an amount of USD 661,340 to Mr. B. as compensation for the unilateral breach of the employment contract without just cause.
3. The club A. is directed to pay the amount due to within 30 days as from the date of the notification of this decision.
4. The club A. is banned from registering any new players, either nationally or internationally, until the expiry of the second transfer period following the date of the notification of this decision.
5. According to art. 60 par. 1 of the FIFA Statutes, this decision may be appealed against before the Court of Arbitration for Sport (CAS). The statement of appeal must be sent to the CAS directly within 10 days of receipt of notification of this decision and shall contain all the elements in accordance with point 2 of the directives issued by the CAS, a copy of which we enclose hereto. Within another 10 days following the expiry of the time limit for filing the statement of appeal, the appellant shall file a brief stating the facts and legal arguments giving rise to the appeal with the CAS (cf. point 4 of the directives).

9 NOVEMBER 2004

11417
DECISION OF THE DISPUTE RESOLUTION CHAMBER
passed in Zurich, Switzerland, on 9 November 2004,
in the following composition:
Slim Aloulou (Tunisia), Chairman
Philippe Piat (France), member
Philippe Diallo (France), member
on the claim presented by
Player X, Poland as Claimant
against
Y , Greece as Respondent
regarding a contractual dispute between the parties involved

FACTS OF THE CASE:

- On 29 May 2003 an employment contract was concluded between the player X and the Greek club Y for 2 years, with an option for real for 1 more year, stipulating the following financial conditions: - a salary of EUR 1,300 net a month; - bonuses for every game, according to internal regulations; - a bonus of EUR 10,000 if the team participates in the UEFA Cup; - a signing-on fee of EUR 120,000 to be paid: EUR 30,000 upon signature, the remaining amount in 5 equal instalments of EUR 18 000 each on 30/9/2003, 30/11/2003, 30/1/2004, 30/03/2004, and 30/4/2004.
- On 05.01.2004 the player approached FIFA claiming several salary payments, as well as an amount of EUR 18,000 (the instalment of the signing-on fee due on 30.11.2003)
- He claimed that the club had approached him, offering EUR 20,000 as a settlement for the cancellation of the contract, but that he refused this offer.
- The player is presently still claiming the following amounts:
  1. His salary (EUR 1,300 per month) for October until December 2003, and January until June 2004, that is a total of EUR 11,700;
  2. The value of his employment contract for the next (2004/2005) season, that is an amount of EUR 130,000;
  3. A total of EUR 72,000 for the instalments of his signing-on fee due up until 30.04.2004;
  4. EUR 10,000 bonus for qualifying for the UEFA Cup;
- Upon being questioned with respect to the player's allegations, Y has presented several arguments:
- Mr. X has committed severe disciplinary offences due to his absences from training sessions in January 2004, as a result of which he was suspended for a period of 2 months from 11.01.2004 until 11.03.2004.
- Although there has been some delay in the payments of the player's salaries, this is due to the financial difficulties faced by the club and does not mean that the club has not been respecting the contract;
- Due to these reasons, the club concludes that it has terminated the contract with just cause and that it does not owe the player any remuneration whatsoever.
- Since the club was unable to present any sort of proof of having paid the player his salaries for the months of October 2003 until December 2003, FIFA provisionally liberated the player from all contractual duties towards Y and was authorized to sign with the club of his election, on 1 March 2004. The player is currently under contract with a Polish club.
- The present case has been dealt with by the Greek League Committee for Resolution of the Financial Disputes, which has decided on 18 March 2004 to terminate the player's contract with the club as of 26 February 2004 through fault of the player. The Appeal Committee of the Greek League then ruled on 6 April 2004 that there was insufficient evidence of any action of the player contrary to his contractual obligations and that therefore it was not proven that he had been responsible for breaches of his contract.
- The Dispute Resolution Chamber is asked to take a formal decision concerning the financial compensation due to be paid to the claimant, if any.

CONSIDERATIONS OF THE DISPUTE RESOLUTION CHAMBER

The Dispute Resolution Chamber of the FIFA Players' Status Committee shall review disputes coming under its jurisdiction pursuant to Art. 42 of the FIFA Regulations for the Status and Transfer of Players (hereafter: FIFA Regulations) at the request of one of the parties to the dispute.

According to Art. 42 of the FIFA Regulations for the Status and Transfer of Players, the triggering elements of the dispute (i.e. whether a contract was breached, with or without just cause, or sporting just cause), will be decided by the Dispute Resolution Chamber of the FIFA Players' Status Committee.

Consequently, the Dispute Resolution Chamber is the competent body to decide on the present litigation concerning the alleged breach of contract between the claimant and the respondent.

The members of the Dispute Resolution Chamber were summoned to pass a decision on this matter by the Chairman pursuant to Art. 1 point 6) of the Rules Governing the Practice and Procedures of the Dispute Resolution Chamber.

Subsequently, and entering into the substance of the matter, the Chamber began its deliberations by analyzing the defence of the respondent.

To begin with, the members pointed out that essentially the dispute revolves around the non-payment of several months of the player's salaries, as well as certain signing-on and bonus fees.

The defence of the respondent is primarily based on three main issues: the financial difficulties faced by the club, the disciplinary offences committed by the player, and the decisions taken by the Greek Athletic Courts.
The defence does not include any documentary or other kind of payment proof regarding the amounts that are yet outstanding, although the respondent has been given several opportunities throughout these procedures to do so.
The Chamber took serious note of the club's argumentation that its financially precarious situation validates the delays concerning some of its contractual obligations towards the claimant.
On the other hand, it was also clear to the members that the claimant has not obtained his dues in accordance with his employment contract, nor within the time schedule foreseen therein.
In this respect the members mentioned that the player had repeatedly faced uncertainty as to whether or not he would be receiving the financial income that he was relying on or got no Player X, Poland / Y, Greece Page 3 of 5
payments at all. This situation need not be tolerated by the player and constitutes a breach of the club's contractual duties, whether it can be excused by financial difficulties or not.
In continuation, the members of the Dispute Resolution Chamber acknowledged that the player may have committed disciplinary infractions during his participation in the matches played for the club, and that these acts may be punishable in accordance with the applicable disciplinary rules and regulations of the club and/or the national association concerned. Nevertheless, this cannot justify the non-payment of a player's salaries without a final and binding decision to this effect by a deciding body with competence to impose such disciplinary sanctions, or without such decision being proportionate to the offence committed. In the case at hand, the Chamber noted, neither of these prerequisites have been met.
Finally, the Dispute Resolution Chamber pointed out that the decisions taken by the Greek Athletic Courts might have been favourable to the respondent in the first instance, but that the main decision to be taken into account should always be the final decision that is no longer open to appeal. In this case that would be the decision taken by the Appeal Committee of the Greek League which ruled on 6 April 2004 that there was insufficient evidence of any action of the player contrary to his contractual obligations and that therefore it was not proven that he had been responsible for breaches of his contract.
In view of all the aforementioned circumstances, the Dispute Resolution Chamber concluded by deciding that the arguments of the respondent could not disprove the allegations put forward by the claimant and that therefore a damage compensation was due for the breach of contract as a result of non-payment of the player's dues.
Considering that the player was authorised to depart from the club on 1 March 2004, the respondent shall pay his outstanding salaries until that date, that is, for the months of October 2003 throughout February 2004, totalling EUR 6,500, as well as the outstanding instalments of the signing-on fees that have fallen due before 1 March 2004 (EUR 54,000), and the UEFA Cup bonus explicitly mentioned in the employment contract (EUR 10,000). Hence, the total amount due amounts to EUR 70,500.
Furthermore, the Chamber emphasised that the Greek club has to be sanctioned for contractual breach, according to Art. 23 par. 2 lit. a) of the Regulations for the Status and Transfer of Players, which states that in the case of the club breaching a contract, the sanction shall be a ban on registering any player, either nationally or internationally, until the expiry of the second transfer period following the date on which the breach became effective. This restriction shall nevertheless not exceed a period of 12 months following the breach or inducement of the breach.

DECISION OF THE DISPUTE RESOLUTION CHAMBER

1. The claim lodged by the Claimant is accepted.
2. The Respondent shall pay the amount of **EUR 70,500** to the Claimant, within 30 days following the date of the communication of the present decision.
3. In the event that the debts of the Respondent are not paid within the stated deadline, an interest rate of 5% per year will apply.
4. In addition to point 3., the sports sanction for unilateral breach of contract will be applied as mentioned in art. 23.2(a) of the FIFA Regulations for the Status and Transfer of Players, that is, a ban on registering any player, either nationally or internationally, until the expiry of the second transfer period following the date on which the breach became effective.
5. According to art. 60 par. 1 of the FIFA Statutes, this decision may be appealed against before the Court of Arbitration for Sport (CAS). The statement of appeal must be sent to the CAS directly within

10 days of receipt of notification of this decision and shall contain all the elements in accordance with point 2 of the directives issued by the CAS, a copy of which we enclose hereto. Within another 10 days following the expiry of the time limit for filing the statement of appeal, the appellant shall file a brief stating the facts and legal arguments giving rise to the appeal with the CAS (cf. point 4 of the directives).

⚽⚽⚽

114342
DECISION OF THE DISPUTE RESOLUTION CHAMBER
passed in Zurich, Switzerland, on 9 November 2004,
in the following composition:
Slim Aloulou (Tunisia), Chairman
Philippe Piat (France), member
Philippe Diallo (France), member
on the claim presented by
the club, X, Uruguay, as Claimant
against
the club, Y, Sweden, as Respondent
regarding solidarity contribution in connection with the player, Z,

FACTS OF THE CASE

- The player, Z, was transferred on a loan basis from A (Uruguay) to Y by means of a loan agreement signed on 31 March 2003.
- A loan fee of EUR 25,000 was agreed upon.
- In addition, according to this loan agreement, Y was given an exclusive option to acquire the player's services on a definite basis. This option had to be exercised in writing prior to 31 July 2003.
- The Swedish Football Federation has confirmed that its member club has not exercised this option.
- Club X (Uruguay), the club with which the player was registered from 21 February 1991 until 29 May 1996 in accordance with the relevant confirmation of the Uruguay FA, claims that it is entitled to receive from Y an amount of money pertaining to solidarity mechanism, even though the fact that the player was transferred on a loan basis only.
- The arguments put forward by X are the following:
  Referring to Article 25 of the Regulations for the Status and Transfer of Players in conjunction with Article 10 of the Application Regulations:
  - The player is a non-amateur player;
  - He moved to another club affiliated to another national association;
  - He moved during the course of his contract;
  - A compensation was paid to his previous club, i.e. a loan fee.

  Referring to section 4 of circular letter nr 769:
  - The loan of a player by one club to another club is dealt with administratively like a transfer;
  - The application of solidarity mechanism arises from "an international transfer during the term of his contract", which has transpired in the present case;
  - His previous club received financial compensation.
- X asks the Dispute Resolution Chamber to determine as to whether the loan of the player, Z, from A to Y generates a right to solidarity contribution in favour of X.

CONSIDERATIONS OF THE DISPUTE RESOLUTION CHAMBER

The members of the Dispute Resolution Chamber were summoned to pass a decision on this matter by the Chairman pursuant to Art. 1 point 6) of the Rules Governing the Practice and Procedures of the Dispute Resolution Chamber.

The members of the Chamber firstly proceeded to confirm that in accordance with Article 42 of the FIFA Regulations for the Status and Transfer of Players the Chamber is competent to deal with the present matter.

The Dispute Resolution Chamber took due note of the argumentation put forward by X. The Chamber agreed that the wording of the Regulations for the Status and Transfer of Players does not specify whether the payment of solidarity contribution is also due in the case of a loan of a player. Indeed, the sole explanation contained in these regulations is that solidarity contribution is owed when a player is transferred during the course of a contract. However, the Chamber underlined that it had never been the intention of the legislator to apply the obligation of the payment of solidarity contribution to the cases of a loan of a player. Essentially, the concept behind the entitlement to solidarity contribution was to share a proportion of a transfer fee among the clubs involved in the training and education of a player. A transfer fee is, however, only owed when a player is transferred on a definite basis and cannot be equated to a loan fee. Therefore, taking into consideration the above and in accordance with its jurisprudence, the Chamber decided to reject the claim of the Uruguayan club.

DECISION OF THE DISPUTE RESOLUTION CHAMBER

1. The claim of the Claimant, X, is rejected.
2. According to art. 60 par. 1 of the FIFA Statutes, this decision may be appealed against before the Court of Arbitration for Sport (CAS). The statement of appeal must be sent to the CAS directly within 10 days of receipt of notification of this decision and shall contain all the elements in accordance with point 2 of the directives issued by the CAS, a copy of which we enclose hereto. Within another 10 days following the expiry of the time limit for filing the statement of appeal, the appellant shall file a brief stating the facts and legal arguments giving rise to the appeal with the CAS (cf. point 4 of the directives).

⚽⚽⚽

114407
DECISION OF THE DISPUTE RESOLUTION CHAMBER
passed in Zurich, Switzerland, on 9 November 2004,
in the following composition:
Slim Aloulou (Tunisia), Chairman
Philippe Diallo (France), member
Philippe Piat (France), member
on the claim presented by
Club M. as Claimant
against
Club T. as Respondent
regarding the solidarity contribution related to the transfer of the federative rights to the player K.

FACTS OF THE CASE:

- In January 2003 the club P. and the club T. concluded an agreement for the transfer of the federative rights to the player K.
- According to the club M., the player K., born on 13 August 1975, was registered for it for 2 seasons, from August 1997 to April 1999, between the ages of 22 and 24.
- The club M. claims the 5% payment established in art. 25 of the FIFA Regulations for the Status and Transfer of Players regarding the contribution to the solidarity mechanism related to the transfer of the federative rights to the player K. from the club P. to the club T.
- According to the aforementioned Regulations, the new club concerned is to distribute 5% of this compensatory amount to the club(s) where the player has played between the ages of 12 and 23, in the present case thus between 1987 and 1998.
- The amount to be paid by the club T. for the transfer of the federative rights to the player K., is USD 2,300,000.
- The club M. asks the Dispute Resolution Chamber to take into account both the seasons in which the player K. was registered for it and, on that basis, to sentence the club T. to start with the distribution of the solidarity contribution of 5% related to the transfer of the federative rights to the player K. as well as to take all the disciplinary measures that the Chamber may deem appropriate against the aforementioned club.
- Contrary to the confirmation from the association with which the club M. is affiliated, which was presented by the claiming club, the club T. maintains that in 1997 the player K. moved from the club M. to the club N., affiliated to the same association, and from there to the club S., which is affiliated

to another association, for the 1997/1998 season. Consequently, during that period of time, he was not registered with the club M. and the latter is not entitled to ask for solidarity contribution.

- Furthermore, the club T. maintains that the transfer agreement concluded between the club T. and the club P. was not yet executed. Apparently, the player K. claims his percentage of the transfer compensation in accordance with the Brazilian regulations from his former club. The club T. is of the opinion that as long as the relevant matter has not been cleared, no solidarity contribution should be paid.
- On 22 July 2004 the Dispute Resolution Chamber already dealt with this case. However, it deem that it was not in a position to take a decision before having the crucial question regarding the club with witch the player K. was registered during the 1997/1998 season fully elucidated. As a result, it temporarily suspended the decision and returned the matter to the FIFA administration with the request to obtain from the association concerned clarification with regard to the registration of the player K. during the 1997/1998 season.
- On 16 August 2004 the association in question confirmed that according to its records the player K. was never registered for any of its affiliated clubs. In particular, he was not registered for the club S. during the 1997/1998 season.

CONSIDERATIONS OF THE DISPUTE RESOLUTION CHAMBER

The members of the Dispute Resolution Chamber were summoned to pass a decision on this matter by the Chairman pursuant to art. 1 point 6) of the Rules Governing the Practice and Procedures of the Dispute Resolution Chamber.

The deciding body commenced its deliberations by referring to art. 25 of the FIFA Regulations for the Status and Transfer of Players (hereinafter: the Regulations), according to which it falls within the purview of the Dispute Resolution Chamber to review disputes concerning the distribution of the solidarity contribution. Consequently, the Chamber established that it was competent to deal with the present litigation.

In continuation, the Chamber entered into the substance of the matter and confirmed the following points of the deliberations of the meeting of 22 July 2004.

In particular, the deciding body indicated that the principle of the solidarity mechanism is governed by art. 25 of the Regulations as well as art. 10 and 11 of the Regulations governing the Application of the Regulations for the Status and Transfer of Players (hereinafter: the Application Regulations). According to art. 25 par. 1 of the Regulations, whenever a non-amateur player moves during the course of an employment contract, a proportion of 5% of any compensation paid to the previous club will be distributed to the club(s) involved in the training and education of the player between the ages of 12 and 23. Moreover, art. 11 par. 1 of the Application Regulations states that the new club concerned is to distribute the relevant proportion to the club(s) involved in the formation of the player.

The Chamber deemed it appropriate to emphasise that, contrary to what the club T. appears to claim, the present affair concerns the possible payment of solidarity contribution and not of training compensation. The complaint filed by the club M. unmistakeably refers to the solidarity mechanism. For the sake of good order, the deciding body made it clear that, in view of the player's age at the time of his move to the club T., i.e. older than 23, the club T. was right in claiming that no training compensation is due. However, as indicated, that is not the substance of the claim submitted by the club M.

In the case at hand, the Dispute Resolution Chamber outlined that the training period to be taken into consideration started with the sporting season 1997/1998, when the player K. was 22, until the end of the said season, when the player concerned reached the age of 23. The 1998/1999 season could in any case not be taken into account, because the solidarity contribution is due only to clubs, which offered the player training and education up to the age of 23 (cf. art. 25 par. 1 of the Regulations and art. 10 of the Application Regulations).

With regard to the distribution of the 5% solidarity contribution, the Chamber explained that this contribution needed to be distributed in accordance with the number of years the player was registered with and effectively trained at and educated by the relevant club(s) between the ages of 12 and 23 (cf. art. 25 par. 1 of the Regulations). Furthermore, art. 10 of the Application Regulations provides the key for the distribution of the solidarity contribution.

The Dispute Resolution Chamber duly considered the information received from the association concerned and acknowledged that, contrary to the allegations of the club T., the player K. had not been registered for the club S. during the 1997/1998 season. Furthermore, it referred to the confirmation remitted by the association of the club M. and established that, in respect to the formation of the player K. the latter had been registered with, and

Solidarity Contribution for the player K. consequently trained and educated by the club M. during the 1997/1998 season, thus between the ages of 22 and 23. Therefore, the claiming club M. is entitled to receive 10% of the 5% proportion related to the transfer of the federative rights to the player K. from the club P. to the club T.
In view of the fact that the club T. did not contest the amount of compensation for the federative rights to the player K. which the club M. claims had to by paid by the club T. to the club P., the Chamber ascertained that the amount to be paid by the club T. for the relevant transfer is USD 2,300,000.
With regard to the club T's allegation that no solidarity contribution has to be paid before the dispute between the player K. and the club P. is settled, the deciding body emphasised that the relevant matter only concerns the two parties to the litigation and does not affect neither the position of the club M. nor the one of club T. In particular, the outcome of the aforementioned dispute will not anyhow influence the amount of compensation, which had to be paid by the club T. for the federative rights to the player K. Therefore, the Chamber concluded that the argumentation of the club T. cannot be backed.
On account of all the above, the Dispute Resolution Chamber decided that the club T. must pay to the club M. 10% of the 5% proportion of the transfer compensation, i.e. USD 11,500.
Finally, the deciding body referred to art. 11 par. 1 of the Application Regulations and stressed that the amount due as a solidarity contribution to the training clubs shall be paid at the latest within 30 days of the player's registration.
In view of the fact that the payment of the solidarity contribution has been due since February 2003, the Chamber established that a default interest payment of 5% p.a. must be applied.

DECISION OF THE DISPUTE RESOLUTION CHAMBER

1. The claim of the club M. is partially accepted.
2. The club T. has to pay the amount of USD 11,500 to the club M.
3. On the aforementioned amount a default interest payment of 5% p.a. as from 1 March 2003 until the day of the payment is applied.
4. The amount due to the club M. has to be paid by the club T. within 30 days as from the date of notification of the present decision.
5. If the relevant sum is not paid within the aforementioned deadline, the present matter shall be submitted to the Disciplinary Committee of FIFA, so that the necessary disciplinary sanctions may be imposed.
6. According to art. 60 par. 1 of the FIFA Statutes, this decision may be appealed against before the Court of Arbitration for Sport (CAS). The statement of appeal must be sent to the CAS directly within 10 days of receipt of notification of this decision and shall contain all the elements in accordance with point 2 of the directives issued by the CAS, a copy of which we enclose hereto. Within another 10 days following the expiry of the time limit for filing the statement of appeal, the appellant shall file a brief stating the facts and legal arguments giving rise to the appeal with the CAS (cf. point 4 of the directives).

114441

DECISION OF THE DISPUTE RESOLUTION CHAMBER

passed in Zurich, Switzerland, on 9 November 2004,
in the following composition:
Slim Aloulou (Tunisia), Chairman
Philippe Piat (France), member
Philippe Diallo (France), member
on the claim presented by
Player A., as Claimant
against
Club C., as Respondent
regarding a dispute on the contractual relationship established between the parties

FACTS OF THE CASE

- The player A. signed an employment contract with the club C. on 15 July 2002, valid from 1 July 2002 until 30 June 2003.

- Clause II 1. c) and d) of this employment contract establish the following:
  c) The 'player' shall receive the following extra bonuses:
     - EUR 30,000 for winning of Championship
     - EUR 15,000 for winning of Cup
  d) All the amounts specified in II. 1 c) shall be paid in case of participation of the 'player' in 70% of the games.
- The player A. maintains that he participated in 21 of a total of 26 matches, which amounts to 80% of the entire number of the league matches.
- Consequently, the player is claiming the payment of EUR 30,000 from the club C., given that the club was league champion in 2002/2003.
- The club C. maintains that the legal interpretation of the expression 'participate in 70% of the games' means that the player should have participated in 70% of the play-time of all the games of the first team. The club has provided FIFA with an official interpretation of the Institute for Language of the Academy of Sciences, which interprets the meaning of this clause in this way.
- Moreover, the club C. has emphasised that the original text of this contract is unambiguous and has been applied without further claims on other footballers contracts.
- If the interpretation of the club C. is followed, the player will have played a 1,194 minutes of a total of 2,250 minutes, corresponding to the duration of all league matches added together, which represents a 53,06% involvement in the league games of the club C.
- The player A. rejects this interpretation, pointing out that the employment contract was established in English and that the clause II 1. c) and d) merely requires the player to take part in more than 70% of all matches, which he clearly fulfilled, given that he was fielded in 21 out of 26 matches of the club C.

CONSIDERATIONS OF THE DISPUTE RESOLUTION CHAMBER

The members of the Dispute Resolution Chamber were summoned to pass a decision on this matter by the Chairman pursuant to Art. 1 point 6) of the Rules Governing the Practice and Procedures of the Dispute Resolution Chamber.

The members of the Dispute Resolution Chamber examined all the documentation put forward by the parties in this litigation and ascertained that the club C. does not deny the allegations of the player A. regarding the number of matches in which he took part as well as the existence of the clause II 1. c) and d) but rather that the club C. disputes the applicability of the mentioned clause in this case.

Therefore, in a first step, the Chamber deliberated over the meaning of the clause II 1. c) and d) contained in the employment contract singed by the club C. and the player A. on 1 July 2002.

In this context, the members of the Chamber recognised that the contents of this clause were somewhat ambiguous, as the interpretation offered by both parties would appear to be applicable. The Chamber therefore established that the true intentions of the parties could only be interpreted by studying the exact wording of the mentioned clause and by questioning how clauses of this nature are usually understood in football.

On the wording of the clause II 1. c) and d), the Chamber noted that the bonuses were to be payable in the case 'of participation of the player in 70% of the games'. The wording contains no mention of actual minutes played but rather of games at such. According to the Chamber, the mere wording of this clause suggests that the relevant criterion was that of the games played rather than the total amount of minutes played.

In continuation, the Chamber proceeded by indicating that clauses stipulating performance-related pay are common in employment contracts of footballers and that these usually make reference to the number of matches in which a player is fielded, often distinguishing between games won and games drawn. These clauses mostly refer to the number of matches and not the number of minutes played, since a club is unlikely to risk not fielding a player for reasons relating to a performance-related clause but it may well try and control the total minutes played by a particular player by substituting the latter when it feels that a match is as good as won. Furthermore, it is easier for both parties to establish how many matches a footballer has played rather than to verify how many minutes a player performed.

In light of these deliberation, the Chamber was of the opinion that performance-related clauses in employment contracts such as clause II 1. c) and d) are generally based on the total matches performed by a player and not on the total number of minutes played. Consequently, the Chamber rejected the explanations contained in the interpretation offered by the Language Institute. Moreover, the Chamber

concluded that if the parties wished to provide for a different approach to the customary one, it is evident that they must foresee it in a very explicit form. The clause II 1. c) and d) of the employment contract signed by the club C. and the player A. does not explicitly mention that the relevant criterion is that of the minutes played rather than the total number of matches and that, as a result, the clause in question must be applied as it is customary and as it could be understood by the player A. himself.
In light of the aforementioned, the Chamber decided to accept the claim of the player A. in the concept of unpaid bonuses amounting to EUR 30,000.

DECISION OF THE DISPUTE RESOLUTION CHAMBER

1. The claim of the player A. is accepted.
2. The respondent, the club C., must pay an amount of EUR 30,000 to the player A.
3. The club C. is directed to pay the amount due to the player A. within 30 days as from the date of the notification of this decision.
4. According to art. 60 par. 1 of the FIFA Statutes, this decision may be appealed against before the Court of Arbitration for Sport (CAS). The statement of appeal must be sent to the CAS directly within 10 days of receipt of notification of this decision and shall contain all the elements in accordance with point 2 of the directives issued by the CAS, a copy of which we enclose hereto. Within another 10 days following the expiry of the time limit for filing the statement of appeal, the appellant shall file a brief stating the facts and legal arguments giving rise to the appeal with the CAS (cf. point 4 of the directives).

114461
DECISION OF THE DISPUTE RESOLUTION CHAMBER
passed in Zurich, Switzerland, on 9 November 2004,
in the following composition:
Slim Aloulou (Tunisia), Chairman
Philippe Piat (France), Member
Philippe Diallo (France), Member
on the claim presented by
Club X, as Claiman
against
Club Y, as Respondent
regarding the training compensation for the player.

FACTS OF THE CASE

The player, born in 1982, was registered for the club X during three sporting seasons, from the season 1999/2000 until the season 2001/2002, between the age of 17 and 20.
On 13 August 2002, he signed a non-amateur contract with club Y.
Club X claims for training compensation from club Y, in accordance with Chapter VII of the FIFA Regulations for the Status and Transfer of Players.
As far as the categorisation of club X is concerned for the season 1999/2000, as provided for by the Circular letter 826 dated 31 October 2002, it belonged to category 1. The indicative amount per year for category 1 in Europe is EUR 90,000.
As far as the categorisation of club X is concerned for the sporting seasons 2000/2001 and 2001/2002, it belonged to category 2. The indicative amount per year for category 2 in Europe is EUR 60,000.
The club X requests the FIFA Dispute Resolution Chamber to pass a decision in the case and to order club Y to pay the training compensation in accordance with the FIFA Regulations.
The club Y is of the opinion that it does not have to pay training compensation for the player concerned to club X as the latter signed a confirmation on 21 June 2002 to the attention of the representative of the player with the following wording:
We hereby confirm that the contract of … (the player) expires on 30 June 2002 and that no more transfer fees exist.
The club X maintains that by means of this confirmation, it did not waive its right for training compensation for the player concerned in accordance to the FIFA Regulations, but that it confirmed only that no transfer sum had to be paid, in respect to the expiry of the employment contract.

Furthermore, according to club X, the person who signed the above-mentioned confirmation is only a member of the administration and would not have been in the position to sign such a confirmation.

CONSIDERATIONS OF THE DISPUTE RESOLUTION CHAMBER

The Dispute Resolution Chamber of the FIFA Players' Status Committee shall review disputes coming under its jurisdiction pursuant to Art. 42 of the FIFA Regulations for the Status and Transfer of Players at the request of one of the parties to the dispute.

In accordance with Art. 42.1 lit. (b) (iv) of the FIFA Regulations for the Status and Transfer of Players, it falls within the purview of the Dispute Resolution Chamber to review disputes concerning training compensation fees.

Consequently, the Dispute Resolution Chamber is the competent body to decide on the present litigation concerning the training compensation fee claimed by club X.

The members of the Dispute Resolution Chamber were summoned to pass a decision on this matter by the Chairman pursuant to Art. 1 point 6) of the Rules Governing the Practice and Procedures of the Dispute Resolution Chamber.

Subsequently, and entering into the substance of the matter, the Dispute Resolution Chamber started by analysing the document dated 21 June 2002, signed on behalf of club X, based on which, the club Y defends that training compensation is not due in the present matter.

In this regard, the members of the Chamber reached the conclusion that such document only mentioned that no transfer fee would be due in case of a future acquisition of the player's federative rights after 30 June 2002 and underlined that no reference was made to the right of the club X to claim the relevant training compensation.

As a consequence, the Chamber decided to address the present claim and acknowledged that the player had been registered with the club X from the sporting season 1999/2000 until the sporting season 2001/2002, i.e. for three sporting seasons, between the age of 17 and 19, and that the present claim for compensation was put forward by the Claimant before the player turned 23 years of age.

Moreover, as established in Circular letter no. 826, dated 31 October 2002, training compensation is payable for training incurred between the ages of 12 and 21, if the player concludes a non-amateur contract before the age of 23.

In light of the above, and particularly taking into consideration the aforementioned period of stay with the Claimant, the Chamber considered that the player's positive development has to be partially attributed to the training and education that he received from the club X.

Consequently, it is undisputed that club X is entitled to receive from club Y compensation for the training and education of the player regarding the timeframe that the latter spent with it.

According to Art. 5.1 of the Regulations governing the Regulations for the Status and Transfer of Players, for purposes of calculating compensation, the relevant training period starts at the beginning of the season and ends at the end of the season concerned.

In the present matter, the Chamber outlined that the relevant training period to take into consideration went from the sporting season 1999/2000 when the player was 17, until the sporting season 2001/2002, when the player was 19.

In accordance with the principles for calculation of the training compensation amounts, stipulated in the FIFA Regulations for the Status and Transfer of Players and particularly, in Art. 7 of the Regulations governing the Application of the Regulations for the Status and Transfer of Players as well as in the aforementioned Circular letter, the category of the former club and the amount corresponding to the same category in the new club's Confederation which is UEFA in the present case, apply.

In view of the above, the Chamber calculated the training compensation amounts based on its well-established jurisprudence and the indicative amounts listed in the aforementioned Circular letter.

In this regard, the Chamber took note that club X belonged to Category 1 in Europe during the sporting season 1999/2000 and to Category 2 during the sporting seasons 2000/2001 and 2001/2002.

As a consequence, EUR 90,000 (indicative amount per year, for category 1 in Europe) is granted for the 1999/2000 sporting season as well as EUR 60,000 (indicative amount per year, for category 2 in Europe) for each of the remaining two seasons that the player spent with the club X.

In conclusion, the Dispute Resolution Chamber decided that club Y is liable to pay the total amount of EUR 210,000 to club X for the training compensation of the player.

DECISION OF THE DISPUTE RESOLUTION CHAMBER

1. The Respondent club Y has to pay the amount of EUR 210,000 to the Claimant club X.
2. The amount due to club X has to be paid by club Y within 30 days as from the date of notification of this decision.
3. If club Y fails to comply with the above-mentioned deadline, an interest rate of 5% per year will apply.
4. This decision may be appealed before the Court of Arbitration for Sport (CAS) in accordance with art. 60 par. 1 of the FIFA Statutes. The statement of appeal must be sent to the CAS directly within 10 days of receiving notification of this decision and has to contain all elements in accordance with point 2 of the directives issued by the CAS, copy of which we enclose hereto. Within another 10 days following the expiry of the time limit for the filing of the statement of appeal, the appellant shall file with the CAS a brief stating the facts and legal arguments giving rise to the appeal (cf. point 4 of the directives).

114465
DECISION OF THE DISPUTE RESOLUTION CHAMBER
passed in Zurich, Switzerland, on 9 November 2004,
in the following composition:
Slim Aloulou (Tunisia), Chairman
Philippe Piat (France), member
Philippe Diallo (France), member
on the claim presented by
Club A., as Claimant
against
Club B., as Respondent 1
and
Club C., as Respondent 2
regarding a dispute on the payment of solidarity contribution relating to the transfers of the player X.

FACTS OF THE CASE

- The player X. was born on 13 October 1976.
- He joined the club A. during the 1991 season, at the age of 14.
- At the age of 21 he was on loan at the club B. for one season.
- On 2 August 2001, the player X. joined the club A.
- On 30 January 2003, the player was transferred from the club Z. to the club B., for a fee of USD 1,200,000.
- Later, on 12 November 2003, the club B. and the club C. agreed on the transfer of the player to the club C. for an amount of EUR 1,751,800, which, however, according to the club C. was later reduced by EUR 70,000 to a total of EUR 1,681,800.
- The club A. is claiming solidarity contribution for both transfers.
- Despite recurring requests, the FIFA Administration received no information from the club B., motivating its non-payment.
- The club C. has indicated that it considers itself not responsible for the payment of the solidarity contribution since it explicitly arranged with the club B. that the latter would take charge of the payment of the solidarity contribution and that this was put down in writing in clause 3 of the annex 1 of the transfer agreement.
- In response hereto, the FIFA Administration informed the club C. of the recent jurisprudence of the Dispute Resolution Chamber which states that the new club of a player remains responsible for the payment of the solidarity contribution even if it has a found agreement contrary to this principle with the former club of the player.
- In such a case, and once the new club has paid the solidarity contribution to the forming club, it can revert to FIFA in order to reclaim the amount paid in lieu of the former club of the player.
- Despite these explanations, the club C. has failed to pay the amount due to the club A.

- The club A. is claiming the full 5% of solidarity contribution for both transfers amounting to USD 60,000 and EUR 87,500.

CONSIDERATIONS OF THE DISPUTE RESOLUTION CHAMBER

The members of the Dispute Resolution Chamber were summoned to pass a decision on these matters by the Chairman pursuant to Art. 1 point 6) of the Rules Governing the Practice and Procedures of the Dispute Resolution Chamber.

As established in Art. 25 §2 of the FIFA Regulations for the Status and Transfer of Players (hereinafter "transfer regulations"), it falls within the purview of the Dispute Resolution Chamber to impose the observance of the obligations deriving from the entitlement to solidarity mechanism.

The members of the Dispute Resolution Chamber commenced their deliberations by indicating that they would first examine the claim of the club A. deriving from the transfer of the player X. from club Z. to the club B. and that, in a second step, they would consider the claim relating to the transfer of the mentioned player from the club B. to the club C.

On the point concerning the transfer of the player X. from the club Z. to the club B., the members of the Chamber underlined that a copy of the transfer agreement established by these club on 28 December 2002, indicating a transfer fee of USD 1,200,000, is in its possession. Furthermore, the Chamber maintained that the Football Association of the club A. had confirmed the taking place of this transfer as well as the fact that the player Z. was registered with its club A. from 1991 until 2001. Taking these facts into consideration, the members of the Chamber established that the requirements of Art. 25 §1 of the transfer regulations had been duly met. Consequently, the club A. is entitled to claim solidarity corresponding to the years which the player Z. spent at its club, between the ages of 12 and 23.

Next, the members of the Chamber turned to Art. 11 §1 of the Regulations governing the Application of the FIFA Regulations for the Status and Transfer of Players, which clearly states that the new club of a player shall pay the amount due as solidarity contribution to the clubs involved in the player's training. Furthermore, this article also establishes that the solidarity contribution is payable within 30 days of the player's new registration. Bearing these provisions in mind, the Chamber concluded that the club B. is responsible to the solidarity contribution deriving from this transfer. As neither the Football Federation of the club B. nor the club B. offered any explanations as to the reasons why the club B.failed to comply with the requirement of paying the solidarity contribution, the Chamber established that the club B. had simply failed to meet the obligation of payment.

The members of the Chamber next turned to the question regarding the proportion of the solidarity contribution payable to the club A. In this context, the Chamber noted that the player Z. joined the club A. at the age of 14 and that, at the age of 21, the player spent one season on loan at the club Q. Bearing these facts in mind, the Chamber concluded that the club A. is not entitled to demand the full 5% solidarity contribution but rather 80% of the 5% solidarity contribution, corresponding to the actual time that the player spent at its club.

In light of the aforementioned, the members of the Chamber decided that the club A. is entitled to receive 80% of the 5% solidarity contribution deriving from the player Z's transfer to the club B. As a result, the club B. must pay USD 48,000 to the club A. On the aforementioned, and given that full amount of solidarity contribution should have been paid by the end of February 2003, a default interest payment of 5% p.a. as from 1 March 2003 until the day of the payment is applied.

In continuation, the Chamber turned to the claim of the club A. originating from the subsequent transfer of the player Z. from the club B. to the club C. In this context, the Chamber took into consideration the explanations offered by the club C., according to which it had contractually arranged with the club B. that the latter would take charge of any payments over solidarity contribution.

On this point, the Dispute Resolution Chamber outlined that there has recently been an augmentation in cases relating to the non-payment of the solidarity contribution, owing to the fact that the clubs acquiring the federative rights to players frequently omit to retain the 5% solidarity contribution payable to the clubs involved in the player's training and education. In such cases, the club that mistakenly paid 100% of the transfer fee agreed upon with the former club of the player will consider itself in the clear regarding the solidarity contribution and will ask the clubs entitled to the solidarity contribution to revert to the former club of the player instead.

The Chamber noted that in the case at hand, the situation is rather similar, in that the clubs B. and C. have agreed to make the club B. responsible for the payment of the solidarity contribution and that this fact was communicated to the club A.

In this context, the Chamber reiterated that according to Art. 11 of the Regulations governing the Application of the FIFA Regulations for the Status and Transfer of Players, it is the task of the new club of the player to calculate the amount owed as solidarity contribution to the clubs involved in the formation of the player and to distribute this amount in accordance with the player's career history. Moreover, § 1 of the mentioned article clearly stipulates that the new club of the player must pay the amount due as solidarity contribution to the training clubs within 30 days of the player's registration.

The Chamber underlined that in accordance with the FIFA Regulations for the Status and Transfer of Players, the club C. is responsible for paying the solidarity contribution to the clubs involved in the formation of the player Z. The fact that the club C. found a different arrangement with the club B. has no influence on the claim of the club A., given that the club A. was not a party to this agreement. Upon paying the amount owed to A., the club C. may revert to FIFA so as to seek the restitution of this amount from the club B.

Consequently, the club C. is liable to pay solidarity contribution to the club A. As indicated earlier, the proportion payable to the club A. is 80% of the 5% solidarity contribution.

In this context, the members of the Chamber noted that the club C. maintains that although the transfer fee agreed upon with the club B. was of EUR 1,751,800, the club B. had granted it a reduction of EUR 70,000, thus reducing the final amount to EUR 1,681,800. On this point, the members of the Chamber insisted that they had not been provided with any documentary evidence corroborating this fact, not even a written statement of the club B. stating that it agreed to this reduction. Therefore, the Chamber could not accept the reduction of the transfer fee as a given fact and established that it would base the claim of the club A. on the transfer fee of EUR 1,751,800. As a result, the club A. is entitled to solidarity in the amount of EUR 70,072. On the aforementioned amount, and given that the full payment of the transfer fee was due by 1 January 2004, a default interest payment of 5% p.a. as from 1 February 2004 until the day of the payment shall apply.

DECISION OF THE DISPUTE RESOLUTION CHAMBER

1. The claims of the club A. are partially accepted.
2. The respondent 1, the club B., must pay an amount of USD 48,000 to the club A. in concept of solidarity contribution. On the aforementioned, amount a default interest payment of 5% p.a., as from 1 March 2003 until the day of the payment, is applied.
3. The respondent 2, the club C., must pay an amount of EUR 70,072 to the club A. in concept of solidarity contribution. On the aforementioned, amount a default interest payment of 5% p.a., as from 1 February 2004 until the day of the payment, is applied.
4. The club B. and the club C. are directed to pay the amounts due to the club A. within 30 days as from the date of the notification of this decision.
5. According to art. 60 par. 1 of the FIFA Statutes, this decision may be appealed against before the Court of Arbitration for Sport (CAS). The statement of appeal must be sent to the CAS directly within 10 days of receipt of notification of this decision and shall contain all the elements in accordance with point 2 of the directives issued by the CAS, a copy of which we enclose hereto. Within another 10 days following the expiry of the time limit for filing the statement of appeal, the appellant shall file a brief stating the facts and legal arguments giving rise to the appeal with the CAS (cf. point 4 of the directives).

114549
DECISION OF THE DISPUTE RESOLUTION CHAMBER

passed in Zurich, Switzerland, on 9 November 2004,
in the following composition:
Slim Aloulou (Tunisia), Chairman
Philippe Piat (France), member
Philippe Diallo (France), member
on the claim presented by
the club, X, Sweden, as Claimant
against

the club, Y, Norway, as Respondent
regarding training compensation in connection with the player, Z,

FACTS OF THE CASE

- The player, Z, born on 2 November 1981, was registered with X, Sweden, as a non-amateur player from 25 January 2002 until 31 October 2002.
- In November or December 2002, the player transferred to Y in Norway as a non-amateur player after the expiry of his employment contract.
- The player having transferred to Y under the age of 23, the Swedish club claims training compensation to the amount of EUR 20,000 maintaining that the amount has to be established taking into consideration the training costs of the new club's category (according to the claimant: Y was category 3 club – EUR 30,000) and of the training club's category (according to the claimant: category 4 – EUR 10,000), which costs allegedly have to be divided. Consequently, the Swedish club maintains being entitled to the amount of EUR 20,000.
- The Swedish club asks that it be awarded compensation to the amount of EUR 20,000 and it asks the Chamber to impose disciplinary measures on the Norwegian club for not having respected the relevant FIFA Regulations.
- The Norwegian club, Y, maintains that it does not owe any training compensation to the Swedish club as the player was allegedly not offered any new contract by the Swedish club, either verbal or in writing, before the expiry of his employment contract.
- To this end, Y has submitted written statements from both the player and his agent confirming that the player and his agent, respectively, were not offered any new contract, either verbal or in writing, before or after the expiry of the player's contract with X.
- In spite of FIFA's invitation to do so, no further comments have been received from the Swedish club.

CONSIDERATIONS OF THE DISPUTE RESOLUTION CHAMBER

The members of the Dispute Resolution Chamber were summoned to pass a decision on this matter by the Chairman pursuant to Art. 1 point 6) of the Rules Governing the Practice and Procedures of the Dispute Resolution Chamber.

As established in art. 42 §1 (b) (iv) of the FIFA Regulations for the Status and Transfer of Players, it falls within the purview of the Dispute Resolution Chamber to decide on disputes concerning the compensation for the training and education of young players and to adjust training compensation fees.

Training compensation is payable by the new club with which a player has signed a contract for training and education that he received from the age of 12 up to 21, payable until he reaches the age of 23.

The present matter involves parties that are established in member states of the European Economic Area (EEA).

With respect to the claim of the club X, the Chamber turned to article 5.5 of the Regulations governing the Application of the Regulations for the Status and Transfer of Players (hereinafter "Application Regulations"), which specifies that for transfers which take place within the EU/EEA, the fact that the training club does not offer a player a contract, will be taken into account when determining the training compensation payable by the new club.

In continuation, the Chamber took in consideration the contents of the FIFA circular letter no. 769 dated 24 August 2001, which under point 2a. specified that the former club of a player younger than 23, whose contract has come to an end and who has not received a new contract from his club, which is equivalent in remuneration to his previous contract, will be deemed not to have offered a contract to the latter for purposes of calculating training compensation. Furthermore, the circular letter no. 769 maintains that, as a matter of principle, the player's training club will not be entitled to receive training compensation unless the training club can demonstrate to the Dispute Resolution Chamber that it is entitled to compensation in derogation of this principle. Moreover, the possibility to derogate is not applicable where national collective bargaining agreements do not envisage it.

The Chamber established in the case regarding the transfer of the player Z that, following the provision contained in art. 5.5 of the Application Regulations and its interpretation contained in the circular letter no. 769, it is the obligation of the Swedish club to demonstrate to the Dispute Resolution Chamber that it offered the player Z an extension to his employment.

Despite its claim for training compensation, X has not offered any documentary evidence that would demonstrate an offer to the player Z, which needed to correspond to the remuneration of his previous contract with the club. On the contrary, the respondent, Y, has provided documentation which demonstrates that the player has not been offered a new contract.
In the light of all of the above, the Dispute Resolution Chamber established that it could not admit the claim of the Swedish club for training compensation in the transfer of the player Z.

DECISION OF THE DISPUTE RESOLUTION CHAMBER

1. The claim of the Claimant, X, is rejected.
2. According to art. 60 par. 1 of the FIFA Statutes, this decision may be appealed against before the Court of Arbitration for Sport (CAS). The statement of appeal must be sent to the CAS directly within 10 days of receipt of notification of this decision and shall contain all the elements in accordance with point 2 of the directives issued by the CAS, a copy of which we enclose hereto. Within another 10 days following the expiry of the time limit for filing the statement of appeal, the appellant shall file a brief stating the facts and legal arguments giving rise to the appeal with the CAS (cf. point 4 of the directives).

⚽⚽⚽

114556
DECISION OF THE DISPUTE RESOLUTION CHAMBER
passed in Zurich, Switzerland, on 9 November 2004,
in the following composition:
Slim Aloulou (Tunisia), Chairman
Philippe Piat (France), member
Philippe Diallo (France), member
on the claim presented by Club A., as Claimant against Club B., as Respondent
regarding a dispute over the transfer of the player W.

FACTS OF THE CASE

- The player W. signed an employment contract with the club A. on 22 July 2002 valid until 30 June 2004. The monthly salaries were established at 3,500 per month. The player also received 2,000 as a signing-on fee as well as a contribution of 1,500 for the rental of an apartment and the payment of a return flight home each year.
- The player left on holidays at the end of the 2002/2003 season and should have returned to the club for training on 11 June 2003, at the latest.
- According to the club A., from that moment on, the player displayed a very unprofessional conduct, much to the damage of the club. Without the authorisation of the club A., the player contacted various agents asking them to find him an employment with a foreign club.
- The circumstances of this case were aggravated through the fact that the club A. was battling financial difficulties in order to obtain the license for the season 2003/2004.
- According to the club A., its financial situation made it very cautious about duly paying the salaries and thus retaining the services of its international quality players at the club. Therefore, the club A. maintains that it was surprised at receiving a communication on the rescission of the employment contract by the player on 8 July 2003, stating that the club had failed to pay two months salaries, yet without specifying which months.
- The club A. reacted by immediately rejecting this accusation in writing on 15 July 2003, informing the player that he had committed grave disciplinary faults.
- On 6 August 2003, the Football Federation of the club B. contacted FIFA on behalf of its club B. so as to obtain the international registration transfer certificate for the player W.
- Both the player and the club B. defended the stance that the player W. was no longer under contract with the club A., given that the latter had unilaterally rescinded his contract without notice and that, as a consequence, the player was no longer contractually bound to the club A. This act of the player was based on the fact that the club A. had omitted to pay two monthly salaries as well as on the fact that the Football Federation of the club A. had withdrawn the license of its club preventing it from playing in the top national league signifying and that the club A. would be relegated.

- The Football Association of the club A., upon the request of the Football Federation of the club B., refused to issue the certificate of the player W., maintaining that the decision to withdraw the club's license was not yet final and that the player was contractually bound to the club A. until 30 June 2004.
- Upon the request of the Football Federation of the club B. on 6 August 2003, FIFA asked the Football Association of the club A. on 13 August 2003 to provide its response to this matter, granting a deadline of 7 days.
- One day later, on 14 August 2003, the club B. and the player W. turned to the Courts of Law in Zurich, asking for an immediate release of the player.
- After negotiations before the Courts in Zurich and after consulting with the Chairman of the Dispute Resolution Chamber, FIFA authorised the Football Federation of the club B. to register the player W. for the club B. on 29 August 2003, underlining however that this decision would have no further effect on a future decision that would be taken in this case.
- The costs of this procedure were borne by the club B.
- In its claim, the club A. acknowledges that it did not pay the salaries due to the player for the months of January and June 2003. On 31 January 2003, the club informed the player that he was being sanctioned with one month's salary for not having presented himself to training. This also occurred in June 2003. The player W. never claimed these outstanding salaries, never contested the fines nor sent a reminder to the club A.
- In this context, it must be pointed out that annex 6 of the employment contract foresees that fines can be inflicted upon the player, yet establishes that the fine for late return from holidays respectively missing training may be up to 1,500.
- In addition, the club A. maintains that the player abandoned the apartment put at his disposal by the club in an appalling manner, leaving damages of up to 8,000, which it has substantiated with several receipts totalling 4,787.05 as well as with photos taken of the apartment.
- The club A. is unwilling to accept the departure of the player without being compensated by the club B., claiming at least 1,000,000 from the club B. for employing a player still under contract respectively for inducing a player to commit a breach of the employment contract. The club A. has underlined that this amount takes into consideration the category of the player, the fact that he is now playing at the highest level in the country of the club B. and that the fact that the club A. contributed decisively in the player's formation.
- In addition, the club A. is asking FIFA to verify whether the player should be sanctioned for his conduct.
- Alternatively, and should the Dispute Resolution Chamber reject the claim for compensation by the club B. for inducing a breach of contract, the club A. claims compensation for the training of the player W.
- The club B., however, rejects the claims of the club A.
- Firstly, the club B. has underlined that the situation of the club A. at the end of the 2002/2003 was more than difficult, given that the license of the club to take part in the 2003/2004 league competition had been withdrawn. This decision was confirmed twice by the appeal body of the Football Association of the club A., following which the club was relegated to the 1. amateur league.
- Given that club was already late in paying two months salaries, the player W. was concerned about his footballing future and therefore sought to register with a new club during the August 2003 transfer period.
- As the season had already commenced and given the urgency brought about by the transfer windows, the club B. and the player W. turned to the Courts of Law in Zurich so as to obtain some clarity regarding the player's employment situation. Indeed, and as stated in the protocol of the Courts of Zurich, the employment relationship between the player and the club A. ceased to exist with the unilateral termination of the contract by the player W.
- With regard to the outstanding salaries, the player maintains that he did not receive any notifications regarding alleged fines that were imposed on him for returning late to the club. Moreover, the player notes that he never signed a receipt for these notifications, which the club B. considers unusual, since such important notifications would normally be sent to the player by registered mail. The club B. is of the opinion that these alleged notifications regarding disciplinary sanctions were only drafted after the player terminated his contract on 8 July 2003. The club B. has pointed out that the club A. does not mention these fines in its correspondence of 15 July 2003, by means of which the club

A. contested the termination of contract by the player. According to the club B., if these sanctions had been the explanation for the outstanding salaries, the club A. would have mentioned this in its reaction to the player.

- In addition, the club B. maintains that the late return of the player in January 2003 was down to his release for national team duty along with the fact that the player sustained an injury during this period of release, which motivated the coach of the club A. to extend the player's leave until 27 January 2003.
- With regard to the salary of the month of June 2003, the club B. has explained that this situation is the same as that of January 2003, given that the player had been released to play with his home team in a tournament. The player returned to the club A. on 25 June 2003. To underline this, the club B. has provided a copy of the summons of the Football Federation of the player W. of 3 June 2003.
- On the claim of the club A. regarding damages caused by the player to the apartment put at his disposal, the club B. maintains that the photos are not conclusive and do not show any damage that would motivate such repairs.
- Furthermore, the club B. questions these allegations, given that it considers it unusual for the owners of the apartment to turn to the club A. on 9 December 2003 when the player had actually moved out in June 2003.
- The club B. also argues that the club A. is claiming damages in the amount of 8,000 although the receipts of the repairs contained in the file amount to 4,787.05.
- Therefore, and considering the contractual violations committed by the club A., the club B. insists that the player W. did not commit a breach of contract.
- The club B. maintains that many players of the club had to endure irregular salary payments. The agents of the player W. turned to the president of the Swiss club on several occasions, yet this was done verbally, as this is the norm in football. Despite the intervention of the player's representatives, the club A. continued to be in default of payment.
- Since the club A. had failed to pay two salaries and given that at the time of the notification of the termination of contract the club A. had been stripped off its license for the 2003/2004 season, the player W. was entitled to breach his contract, given that he could no longer rely on being able to continue his career at the club A. Subsequently, and based on employment law, the player was free to sign a new employment contract with the club of his choice, regardless of whether the club A. agreed with this step or not. Therefore, there cannot be any claim for the breach of the employment contract.
- Furthermore, the club B. maintains that the claim of 1,000,000 is entirely unfounded, given that the player merely earned 42,000 per year, i.e. 84,000 for the duration of the entire employment.
- The contract signed by the parties explicitly mentions that the employment relationship is subject to law the country of the club A. According to the club B., this means that the present litigation must be viewed under the provisions of Articles 319 and following of the Civil Code of the country of the club A. Furthermore, this also means that following Article 337 d) par. 3 of the Civil Code, a party unwilling to accept the termination of an employment contract must contest this termination at the competent courts within 30 of receiving this notification. As the club A. failed to do this, the claim can no longer be taken into consideration.
- With regard to the claim for training compensation, the club B. maintains that this request is unfounded, given that the player W. already completed his training before reaching the age of 23. The club B. bases this allegation on the fact that the player W. completed his training at home and that he was transferred to club Z. as a fully formed player, who was immediately selected to play for the seniors at the club Z. Subsequently, he was transferred to the club A, where he exclusively played for the senior team. The club A. paid no transfer fee to the club Z., which shows that the clubs were in agreement over the fact that the player was no longer in training.
- In response to the arguments raised by the club B., the club A. had underlined that although it is true the club was battling financial problems at the end of the 2002/2003 season, it is untrue that the salaries of the player W. were not paid on time. The non-payment of the two salaries were down to disciplinary sanctions inflicted on the player.
- Furthermore, the club A. maintains that the player W. did not terminate the employment contract at a time when the club A. had been relegated but rather at a time when the decision regarding the withdrawal of the license was not yet final. Consequently, the player had no right to terminate the contract.

- In light of the fact that the player was bound by a valid employment contract to the club A., the club B. was not entitled to contact the player without informing the club A. of its intentions.
- The club B. committed a further violation of the FIFA regulations by referring to the Courts of Law in Zurich in order to obtain the international transfer certificate of the player W.
- The club A. also rejects the arguments put forward by the player regarding his late return to the club. Firstly, it maintains that the former coach of the player can testify that he never authorised the player to stay in his home country in order to cure his injuries. Moreover, the club A. maintains that this notion is absurd, given that it in the case of an injury of the player, the club A. would insist on his return since it has more confidence in the medical care offered here rather than in the home country of the player.
- With regard to the late return of the player in June 2003, the club A. maintains that the player W. had joined the national team without the authorisation of the club and out of his own initiative. Moreover, the club A. maintains it would not have released the player for the tournament since this is not an international competition in the sense of the FIFA regulations foreseeing a mandatory release of players.
- Therefore, it is evident that the player committed a breach of contract on both occasions by failing to reassume work at the club on time.
- The club A. rejects the statement of the club B., according to which it is usual for players to verbally remind a club of unpaid salaries. The club A. maintains that this must always be done in writing and that this is the task of the manager of a player. In the case of the player W., there were never any reminders orally or in writing regarding unpaid salaries.
- With regard to the apartment, the club A. declares that it already received a notification of the owner on 11 June 2003, which did not contain any detailed amounts concerning the damage caused by the player W. The global sum of 8,000 takes into consideration other costs incurred in this context such as the cleaning of the apartment by the owner himself.
- On the argument put forward by the club B. regarding the admissibility of the claim against the player under its law, the club A. maintains that its claim is not directed against the player but rather against the club B. for having employed a player still under contract and for having induced the latter to commit a breach of the employment contract. Moreover, the club A. rejects the notion that it failed to meet the 30 day deadline to react to the termination of contract by the player given that it reacted to the notification of the player by announcing that it does not accept the termination of the contract to its Football Association and by refusing the issuance of the international registration transfer certificate.
- In light of these arguments, the club A. maintains that it suffered from the conduct of the club B. The player was regularly paid by the club A., receiving benefits such as the apartment, car, insurance, food etc. and that, if the club B. were to consider transferring the player W. to another club, it would certainly obtain a transfer fee beyond the 1,000,000 being claimed by the club A. Finally, the club A. is claiming the payment of interests.

CONSIDERATIONS OF THE DISPUTE RESOLUTION CHAMBER

The members of the Dispute Resolution Chamber were summoned to pass a decision on this matter by the Chairman pursuant to Art. 1 point 6) of the Rules Governing the Practice and Procedures of the Dispute Resolution Chamber.

As established in Art. 21 §1 of the FIFA Regulations for the Status and Transfer of Players (hereinafter "transfer regulations"), it falls within the purview of the Dispute Resolution Chamber to determine whether one of the parties involved in a dispute has committed a unilateral breach of contract without just cause. If the employment contract was breached by a party, the Dispute Resolution Chamber is responsible to verify whether this party is accountable for compensation and outstanding payments.

In the case at hand, the members Dispute Resolution Chamber commenced their deliberations by addressing the point raised by the club B., according to which a claim in this case was forfeited, given that the club A. had failed to meet the 30 days deadline provided for in Art. 337 d §3 of its Civil Code. According to the club B., the employment contract signed by the player W. and the representatives of club A. on 22 July 2002 was made subject to the Civil Code of the country of the club A. through article 40 of this contract. Therefore, Art. 337 d §3 of the Civil Code is applicable in the case at hand as well as the deadline mentioned therein.

The members of the Chamber turned to this question first, whereby underlining that article 39 of the employment contract signed by the parties also makes specific reference to the jurisdiction of FIFA as well as the application of its regulations. Furthermore, the FIFA Regulations for the Status and Transfer of Players are an integral part of this employment contract, being included in this agreement as the annexe no. 1. As such, the Chamber established that the employment contract itself provides for the referral of this dispute to the competent body at FIFA.

In continuation, the Chamber emphasised that in the present matter, the claim raised by the club A. is specifically directed against the club B. and not against the player W. Therefore, and without entering into the question of the applicability of Art. 337 d §3 of the Civil Code, the fact remains that the provision of the Civil Code would only affect the admissibility of a claim lodged against the player for the breach of the employment contract, not, however, a claim against the club B. for having induced such a breach. Moreover, the Chamber underlined that a dismissal of the claim on the basis of Art. 337 d §3 of the Civil Code only regards the entitlement to lodge claim as well as the question on the timely presentation of this claim. The provision of Art. 337 d §3 of the Civil Code does not settle the question whether a breach of an employment contract occurred. Consequently, the Chamber concluded that it did not have to decide whether the claim of the club A. is admissible under Art. 337 d §3 of the Civil Code since the claim at hand was not being raised against the player W. Furthermore, and as Art. 44 of the FIFA Regulations for the Status and Transfer of Players provides for a prescription period of two years since the facts leading to the dispute arose, the Chamber considered prescription not to be an issue under the FIFA regulations.

In light of the aforementioned, the members of the Chamber resolved to examine the preliminary question whether the player W. committed a breach of the employment contract signed with the club A. on 22 July 2002 and whether the player's conduct was driven by just cause. Only if it were to find the player W. responsible for having committed a breach of the employment contract without just cause, would the Chamber address the question whether the club B. had induced the player to the breach of contract.

The members of the Chamber thus turned to the explanations offered by the player W. on the reasons why he left the club A. in July 2003. Firstly, the player argued that the Football Federation of the club A. had withdrawn the licence of its club, causing the club's relegation and thus preventing it from playing in the top national league. On this point, the members of the Chamber shared the opinion of the club A., indicating that the decision of the licence-withdrawal had not been final. The members of the Chamber underlined that only a final decision of the sort could, if at all, have an influence on the contractual relationship between player and club. Any other approach would be unsustainable, since one could image a range of different situations which parties may consider reason enough for cancelling a contractual engagement thus putting the principle of contractual stability in doubt.

The second argument of the player W., justifying the premature rescission of the employment contract, stems from the fact that the club A. failed to pay his salary for the months of January and June 2003. This reason was, moreover, stated in the communication sent by the player W. to the club A. on 8 July 2003, by means of which the player announced the termination of the employment.

According to the player, he insists that he never received any notification from the club A. regarding alleged fines that were imposed on him for returning late to the club. The player W. doubts that there are any reasons for the non-payment of the salaries for the months of January and June 2003 other than the financial situation of the club A. The club A., on the other hand, has underlined that the non-payment of the salaries for January and June 2003 are down to the fines inflicted on the player for the late return to the club. Indeed, from the explanations provided by the club A., it appears that the player W. left the country to join his home national team on two occasions: that he was late in returning to the club A. in January 2003, allegedly because he had the oral consent of the club's coach to extend his leave and that, in June 2003, the player joined his national team for a friendly tournament without the consent of the club A.

In this context, the members of the Chamber considered the explanations provided for by the club A. plausible yet the disciplinary sanctions rather questionable with regard to their implementation. Essentially, the Chamber was of the opinion that a decision containing such a strong sanction would indeed require a notification to be counter-signed, confirming receipt by the player. In addition, the Chamber underlined that the sanctions imposed on the player W. on both occasions was disproportionate and that, as such, inadmissible. In this context, the members of the Chamber referred to the annexe 6 of the employment contract, which under point 1 clearly stipulates that inadmissible conduct such as the repeated late return of the player or unjustified absences would be fined with a maximum fine of 1,500. In contrast hereto, the club A. sanctioned the player W with a fine of 3,500 on both occasions, thus evidently exceeding the penalty foreseen in the contract. In light of the fact that the consequence of the player's conduct is contained in the employment contract, it is unacceptable for the club to foresee a different result.

Bearing the aforementioned in mind, the members of the Chamber concluded that the club A. had indeed provoked the breach of the employment contract by considerably exceeding the possible sanctions to be inflicted on the player for the late return to the club. As a result, and based on the provisions of Art. 3 §1 and §2 of the employment contract, the player W. was entitled to declare his engagement at the club A. terminated without further notice.

Furthermore, the members of the Chamber established that the club B. could not be considered liable for having caused the breach of the employment of the player W., given that the player had just cause for terminating his contractual relationship at the club A. Consequently, the Chamber rejected the claim of the club A. regarding compensation for the damages incurred because of the player W.'s unilateral termination of the employment relationship. Equally, the Chamber refused to sanction the club B. for having contacted the player W. without giving prior notice to the club A.

In continuation, the members of the Chamber turned to the claim of the club A. over the amount of 8,000 relating to alleged damages caused by the player W. to the apartment that had been put at his disposal. In particular, the Chamber took note of the fact that the club A. has put forward a number of receipts totalling 4,787.05 as well as photos taken of the apartment in order to substantiate its claim.

In this context, the Chamber turned to the question whether this claim is being addressed against the player W. or the club B. The Chamber considered that it was not clear whether the club A. has directed this claim against the player W., given that in its position of 6 September 2004, the club A. had specified that its claim was being directed against the club B. In such a case, and in light of the fact that the Chamber had found the club B. not responsible for having induced the breach of contract, the Chamber maintained that the club B. could equally not be considered responsible for the alleged damages to the apartment. In addition, the Chamber questioned whether it should rule on the alleged damages to an apartment, given that the courts of law would be better suited to consider such a claim. Notwithstanding this fact, the Chamber determined that the club B. could not be held liable for the alleged damages to the apartment put at the disposal of the player W.

Finally, the Dispute Resolution Chamber turned to the question whether the club A. is entitled to the payment of training compensation for the time which the player W. spent at its club.

On this point, the members of the Chamber commenced their deliberations by explaining the meaning of the final part to the second sentence of Art. 13 of the FIFA transfer regulations. This provision of Art. 13 stipulates that training compensation will be owed to the former club of the player unless it is evident that the player terminated his training period before the age of 21. The members of the Chamber remarked that many clubs and players have erroneously invoked this provision, in cases where it cannot be said that a player has completed his training before the age of 21. In essence, the members of the Chamber wished to reiterate that it was the understanding of the legislator that such an exemption would only apply in cases of unusually talented young players, which are rarely encountered. This tends to be the case of young players who at the age of 17 or 18 are globally known for their exceptional talents, who are regulars on a club and national level and who are frequently the focus of transfer arrangements to the world's top clubs. In such cases, it would seem rather misplaced to discuss the training compensation for these players, who at the age of 17 or 18 are considered absolute world class. Clearly, the very few players with such an exceptional status will have completed their training and will have gained all the relevant experience before reaching the age of 21.

In the case at hand, and although the player W. can show for considerable experience at a first team level, the Chamber underlined that it is unquestionable that the player was still benefiting from formation being offered and experience gained in performing for the club A. Consequently, and bearing in mind that the player W. spent one year at the club A., i.e. from the age of 18 to 19, the members of the Chamber were of the unanimous opinion that the club A. is entitled to receive compensation for the formation received during this year. Basing itself on the FIFA Regulations for the Status and Transfer of Players in conjunction with the circular letter no. 826 and bearing in mind that the club A. is a club belonging to the category II, the Chamber concluded that the club A. is entitled to receive training compensation in the amount of EUR 60,000.

In light of the aforementioned, the Dispute Resolution Chamber rejected the claims of the club A. regarding the inducement to the breach of contract by the club B. as well as compensation for alleged damages to the apartment used by the player W. and accepted the claim of the club A. regarding training compensation, fixing it at an amount of EUR 60,000.

DECISION OF THE DISPUTE RESOLUTION CHAMBER

1. The claim of the club A. against the club B. for compensation over damages caused by an alleged breach of contract of the player W. is rejected.
2. The claim of the club A. against the club B. from compensation over alleged damages to an apartment caused by the player W. is rejected.
3. The claim of the club A. against the club B. for compensation for the training and formation of the player W. is upheld.
4. The respondent, the club B., must pay an amount of EUR 60,000 to the club A.
5. The club B. is directed to pay the amount due to the club A. within 30 days as from the date of the notification of this decision.
6. According to art. 60 par. 1 of the FIFA Statutes, this decision may be appealed against before the Court of Arbitration for Sport (CAS). The statement of appeal must be sent to the CAS directly within 10 days of receipt of notification of this decision and shall contain all the elements in accordance with point 2 of the directives issued by the CAS, a copy of which we enclose hereto. Within another 10 days following the expiry of the time limit for filing the statement of appeal, the appellant shall file a brief stating the facts and legal arguments giving rise to the appeal with the CAS (cf. point 4 of the directives).

⚽⚽⚽

114662 15

DECISION OF THE DISPUTE RESOLUTION CHAMBER

passed in Zurich, Switzerland, on 9 November 2004,
in the following composition:
Slim Aloulou (Tunisia), Chairman
Philippe Piat (France), member
Philippe Diallo (France), member
on the claim presented by
Club A as Claimant
against
Club B as Respondent
regarding the solidarity contribution related to the transfer of the federative rights to the player J

FACTS OF THE CASE:

- By communication dated 23 March 2004 the club A presented FIFA with a claim against the Club B for the 5% payment established in art. 25 of the FIFA Regulations for the Status and Transfer of Players regarding the contribution to the solidarity mechanism.
- This claim was lodged in relation to the transfer, in the season June-July 2003, of the federative rights of the professional player J from Club H to Club B during the course of his contract with H.
- The claimant bases its claim on the assertion that Inter acquired the player for a sum of EUR 4,000,000 and that therefore an amount of EUR 200,000, corresponding to 5% of this sum, should have been distributed among the developing clubs, which included the club A.
- Player J had been registered with Club A during the season 1997/1998, for which this club claims EUR 20,000 (5% of the 5%).
- On 13 August 2004 the FIFA Administration informed the claimant that it is not entitled to any solidarity contribution from the player's new club. This communication was based on a decision taken by the Dispute Resolution Chamber at its meeting held on 22 July 2004, when it had been decided that, since the principle of solidarity mechanism is not included in par. 2 of the Preamble of the Regulations for the Status and Transfer of Players, it is not binding at national level and therefore this principle shall not be applicable to national transfers.
- The claimant has nevertheless insisted on having the case heard by the Dispute Resolution Chamber.
- The claimant deems that the solidarity mechanism is applicable to domestic transfers, stressing in this respect that in the decision of the FIFA Players' Status Committee taken on 12 November 2003, the Chairman determined that the solidarity mechanism applies to domestic transfers in which the claimant club is registered with another national association than that of the club that is due to pay.

- The respondent defends that it is not liable to pay the solidarity contribution to the claimant as the solidarity mechanism system is exclusively applicable to international transfers.

CONSIDERATIONS OF THE DISPUTE RESOLUTION CHAMBER

The Dispute Resolution Chamber of the FIFA Players' Status Committee shall review disputes coming under its jurisdiction pursuant to Art. 42 of the FIFA Regulations for the Status and Transfer of Players (hereinafter: the Regulations) at the request of one of the parties to the dispute.

According to art. 25 of the FIFA Regulations for the Status and Transfer of Players it falls within the purview of the Dispute Resolution Chamber to review disputes concerning the distribution of the solidarity contribution.

Distribution of the Solidarity Contribution for the Player J

Consequently, the Chamber established that it was competent to deal with the present litigation.

The members of the Dispute Resolution Chamber were summoned to pass a decision on this matter by the Chairman pursuant to Art. 1 point 6) of the Rules Governing the Practice and Procedures of the Dispute Resolution Chamber.

Subsequently, and entering into the substance of the matter, the Chamber acknowledged that in its previous meeting on 22 July 2004 it had dealt with a case involving very similar circumstances as those of the present matter. Precisely as in the litigation at hand, a claim had previously been presented by a club from outside of the Italian territory against an Italian club, following a transfer of a player from another Italian club. The members of the Chamber were thus faced with the same question as to whether or not the solidarity mechanism should apply when a player is transferred internally (between clubs affiliated to the same national association).

In the aforementioned previous decision the Chamber had noted that the claimant was, inte alia, basing its argumentation on the contents of the FIFA circular 769. The Chamber then stressed that the FIFA Regulations for the Status and Transfer of Players must remain the main source of law when having to judge a dispute, clarifying that circular letters are an administrative instrument hierarchically subordinated to the FIFA Regulations.

Taking into consideration this principle, the Dispute Resolution Chamber referred to the contents of the Regulations and, in particular, to their Preamble. Paragraph 1 establishes that the Regulations deal with the status and eligibility of players, as well as with the rules applicable whenever players move between clubs belonging to different associations.

The deciding body lent emphasis to the wording of the last part of the aforementioned clause and concluded that, in fact, the Regulations are not applicable to transfers of the federative rights to a player between two clubs affiliated to the same association.

Moreover, the Chamber had also pointed out in this meeting on 22 July 2004 that the principle of the solidarity mechanism is not included in par. 2 of the Preamble of the Regulations and therefore, it is not binding at national level.

Taking into account that in the case at hand no new elements had been introduced regarding the facts, the members of the Dispute Resolution Chamber sufficed in unanimously confirming its recently reviewed jurisprudence that the principle regarding the solidarity mechanism is not applicable to national transfers, not even in cases where the club claiming the payment of the contribution is affiliated to another association. Consequently, the same principles apply in the present case against the respondent and the claim of club A must be rejected.

Distribution of the Solidarity Contribution for the Player J

DECISION OF THE DISPUTE RESOLUTION CHAMBER

1. The claim of the claimant against the respondent, is rejected.
2. According to art. 60 par. 1 of the FIFA Statutes, this decision may be appealed against before the Court of Arbitration for Sport (CAS). The statement of appeal must be sent to the CAS directly within 10 days of receipt of notification of this decision and shall contain all the elements in accordance with point 2 of the directives issued by the CAS, a copy of which we enclose hereto. Within another 10 days following the expiry of the time limit for filing the statement of appeal, the appellant shall file a brief stating the facts and legal arguments giving rise to the appeal with the CAS (cf. point 4 of the directives).

114663 a

DECISION OF THE DISPUTE RESOLUTION CHAMBER

passed in Zurich, Switzerland, on 9 November 2004,
in the following composition:
Slim Aloulou (Tunisia), Chairman
Philippe Piat (France), member
Philippe Diallo (France), member
on the claim presented by
Club A, as Claimant
against
Club B, as Respondent
regarding the solidarity contribution related to the transfer of the federative rights to the player K

FACTS OF THE CASE:

- By communication dated 22 March 2004 the club A presented FIFA with a claim against the Club B for the 5% payment established in art. 25 of the FIFA Regulations for the Status and Transfer of Players regarding the contribution to the solidarity mechanism.
- This claim was lodged in relation to the transfer, in the season June-July 2003, of the federative rights of the professional player K from club M to club B during the course of his contract with M.
- The claimant bases its claim on the assertion that club B acquired the player for a sum of EUR 3,000,000 and that therefore an amount of EUR 150,000, corresponding to 5% of this sum, should have been distributed among the developing clubs, which included the club A.
- K had been registered with the claimant during the season 1990/1991, for which this club claims EUR 7,500 (5% of the 5%).
- On 13 August 2004 the FIFA Administration informed the claimant that it is not entitled to any solidarity contribution from the player's new club. This communication was based on a decision taken by the Dispute Resolution Chamber at its meeting held on 22 July 2004, when it had been decided that, since the principle of solidarity mechanism is not included in par. 2 of the Preamble of the Regulations for the Status and Transfer of Players, it is not binding at national level and therefore this principle shall not be applicable to national transfers.
- The claimant has nevertheless insisted on having the case heard by the Dispute Resolution Chamber.
- The claimant deems that the solidarity mechanism is applicable to domestic transfers, stressing in this respect that in the decision of the FIFA Players' Status Committee taken on 12 November 2003, the Chairman determined that the solidarity mechanism applies to domestic transfers in which the claimant club is registered with another national association than that of the club that is due to pay.
- The respondent defends that it is not liable to pay the solidarity contribution to the claimant as the solidarity mechanism system is exclusively applicable to international transfers.

CONSIDERATIONS OF THE DISPUTE RESOLUTION CHAMBER

The Dispute Resolution Chamber of the FIFA Players' Status Committee shall review disputes coming under its jurisdiction pursuant to Art. 42 of the FIFA Regulations for the Status and Transfer of Players (hereinafter: the Regulations) at the request of one of the parties to the dispute.
According to art. 25 of the FIFA Regulations for the Status and Transfer of Players it falls within the purview of the Dispute Resolution Chamber to review disputes concerning the distribution of the solidarity contribution.
Consequently, the Chamber established that it was competent to deal with the present litigation.
The members of the Dispute Resolution Chamber were summoned to pass a decision on this matter by the Chairman pursuant to Art. 1 point 6) of the Rules Governing the Practice and Procedures of the Dispute Resolution Chamber.
Subsequently, and entering into the substance of the matter, the Chamber acknowledged that in its previous meeting on 22 July 2004 it had dealt with a case involving very similar circumstances as those of the present matter. A claim had previously been presented by a club from outside of the Italian territory against an Italian club, following a transfer of a player from another Italian club. The members of the Chamber were thus faced with the same question as in the present case, regarding whether or not the solidarity mechanism should apply when a player is transferred internally (between clubs affiliated to the same national association).

In the aforementioned previous decision the Chamber had noted that the claimant was, inte alia, basing its argumentation on the contents of the FIFA circular 769. The Chamber then stressed that the FIFA Regulations for the Status and Transfer of Players must remain the main source of law when having to judge a dispute, clarifying that circular letters are an administrative instrument hierarchically subordinated to the FIFA Regulations.

Taking into consideration this principle, the Dispute Resolution Chamber referred to the contents of the Regulations and, in particular, to their Preamble. Paragraph 1 establishes that the Regulations deal with the status and eligibility of players, as well as with the rules applicable whenever players move between clubs belonging to different associations.

The deciding body lent emphasis to the wording of the last part of the aforementioned clause and concluded that, in fact, the Regulations are not applicable to transfers of the federative rights to a player between two clubs affiliated to the same association.

Moreover, the Chamber had also pointed out in this meeting on 22 July 2004 that the principle of the solidarity mechanism is not included in par. 2 of the Preamble of the Regulations and therefore, it is not binding at national level.

Taking into account that in the case at hand no new elements had been introduced regarding the facts, the members of the Dispute Resolution Chamber sufficed in unanimously confirming its recently reviewed jurisprudence that the principle regarding the solidarity mechanism is not applicable to national transfers, not even in cases where the club claiming the payment of the contribution is affiliated to another association. Consequently, the same principles apply in the present case against the respondent and the claim of club A must be rejected.

DECISION OF THE DISPUTE RESOLUTION CHAMBER

1. The claim of the claimant against the respondent, is rejected.
2. According to art. 60 par. 1 of the FIFA Statutes, this decision may be appealed against before the Court of Arbitration for Sport (CAS). The statement of appeal must be sent to the CAS directly within 10 days of receipt of notification of this decision and shall contain all the elements in accordance with point 2 of the directives issued by the CAS, a copy of which we enclose hereto. Within another 10 days following the expiry of the time limit for filing the statement of appeal, the appellant shall file a brief stating the facts and legal arguments giving rise to the appeal with the CAS (cf. point 4 of the directives).

⚽⚽⚽

114663 b

DECISION OF THE DISPUTE RESOLUTION CHAMBER

passed in Zurich, Switzerland, on 9 November 2004,
in the following composition:
Slim Aloulou (Tunisia), Chairman
Philippe Piat (France), member
Philippe Diallo (France), member
on the claim presented by
Club A, as Claimant
against
Club B as Respondent
regarding the solidarity contribution related to the transfer of the federative rights to the player K

FACTS OF THE CASE:

- By communication dated 22 March 2004 the claimant presented FIFA with a claim against the Club B for the 5% payment established in art. 25 of the FIFA Regulations for the Status and Transfer of Players regarding the contribution to the solidarity mechanism.
- This claim was lodged in relation to the transfer, in the season June-July 2003, of the federative rights of the professional player K from club M to club B during the course of his contract with M.
- The claimant bases its claim on the assertion that Club B acquired the player for a sum of EUR 3,000,000 and that therefore an amount of EUR 150,000, corresponding to 5% of this sum, should have been distributed among the developing clubs, which included the club A.

- K had been registered with Club A from 1991/1992 until 1996/97 seasons, for which this club claims EUR 82,500 (55% of the 5%).
- On 13 August 2004 the FIFA Administration informed the claimant that it is not entitled to any solidarity contribution from the player's new club. This communication was based on a decision taken by the Dispute Resolution Chamber at its meeting held on 22 July 2004, when it had been decided that, since the principle of solidarity mechanism is not included in par. 2 of the Preamble of the Regulations for the Status and Transfer of Players, it is not binding at national level and therefore this principle shall not be applicable to national transfers.
- The claimant has nevertheless insisted on having the case heard by the Dispute Resolution Chamber.
- The claimant deems that the solidarity mechanism is applicable to domestic transfers, stressing in this respect that in the decision of the FIFA Players' Status Committee taken on 12 November 2003, the Chairman determined that the solidarity mechanism applies to domestic transfers in which the claimant club is registered with another national association than that of the club that is due to pay.
- The respondent defends that it is not liable to pay the solidarity contribution to the claimant as the solidarity mechanism system is exclusively applicable to international transfers.

CONSIDERATIONS OF THE DISPUTE RESOLUTION CHAMBER

The Dispute Resolution Chamber of the FIFA Players' Status Committee shall review disputes coming under its jurisdiction pursuant to Art. 42 of the FIFA Regulations for the Status and Transfer of Players (hereinafter: the Regulations) at the request of one of the parties to the dispute.

According to art. 25 of the FIFA Regulations for the Status and Transfer of Players it falls within the purview of the Dispute Resolution Chamber to review disputes concerning the distribution of the solidarity contribution.

Consequently, the Chamber established that it was competent to deal with the present litigation.

The members of the Dispute Resolution Chamber were summoned to pass a decision on this matter by the Chairman pursuant to Art. 1 point 6) of the Rules Governing the Practice and Procedures of the Dispute Resolution Chamber.

Subsequently, and entering into the substance of the matter, the Chamber acknowledged that in its previous meeting on 22 July 2004 it had dealt with a case involving very similar circumstances as those of the present matter. A claim had previously been presented by a club from outside of the Italian territory against an Italian club, following a transfer of a player from another Italian club. The members of the Chamber were thus faced with the same question, as in the present case, regarding whether or not the solidarity mechanism should apply when a player is transferred internally (between clubs affiliated to the same national association).

In the aforementioned previous decision the Chamber had noted that the claimant was, inte alia, basing its argumentation on the contents of the FIFA circular 769. The Chamber then stressed that the FIFA Regulations for the Status and Transfer of Players must remain the main source of law when having to judge a dispute, clarifying that circular letters are an administrative instrument hierarchically subordinated to the FIFA Regulations.

Taking into consideration this principle, the Dispute Resolution Chamber referred to the contents of the Regulations and, in particular, to their Preamble. Paragraph 1 establishes that the Regulations deal with the status and eligibility of players, as well as with the rules applicable whenever players move between clubs belonging to different associations.

The deciding body lent emphasis to the wording of the last part of the aforementioned clause and concluded that, in fact, the Regulations are not applicable to transfers of the federative rights to a player between two clubs affiliated to the same association.

Moreover, the Chamber had also pointed out in this meeting on 22 July 2004 that the principle of the solidarity mechanism is not included in par. 2 of the Preamble of the Regulations and therefore, it is not binding at national level.

Taking into account that in the case at hand no new elements had been introduced regarding the facts, the members of the Dispute Resolution Chamber sufficed in unanimously confirming its recently reviewed jurisprudence that the principle regarding the solidarity mechanism is not applicable to national transfers, not even in cases where the club claiming the payment of the contribution is affiliated to another association. Consequently, the same principles apply in the present case against the respondent and the claim of club A must be rejected.

DECISION OF THE DISPUTE RESOLUTION CHAMBER

1. The claim of the claimant against the respondent, is rejected.
2. According to art. 60 par. 1 of the FIFA Statutes, this decision may be appealed against before the Court of Arbitration for Sport (CAS). The statement of appeal must be sent to the CAS directly within 10 days of receipt of notification of this decision and shall contain all the elements in accordance with point 2 of the directives issued by the CAS, a copy of which we enclose hereto. Within another 10 days following the expiry of the time limit for filing the statement of appeal, the appellant shall file a brief stating the facts and legal arguments giving rise to the appeal with the CAS (cf. point 4 of the directives).

114667-09

DÉCISION DE LA CHAMBRE DE RÉSOLUTION DE LITIGES

rendue à Zurich, Suisse, le 9 novembre 2004,
par la composition suivante:
Slim Aloulou (Tunisie), Président
Philippe Piat (France), Membre
Philippe Diallo (France), Membre
dans la procédure opposant Club X, France, Demandeur au Joueur, Défendeur et Club Y, Angleterre, Intervenant

LES FAITS DU CAS

Le joueur a conclu un contrat de joueur aspirant avec le club français X, qui était valide depuis le 1 juillet 2003 jusqu'au 30 juin 2004. Les mêmes parties ont conclu une convention de formation, valide depuis le 1 juillet 2003 jusqu'au 30 juin 2006. Au début du mois d'août 2004, après l'expiration du contrat de joueur aspirant, le joueur a signé un contrat de joueur non-amateur avec le club anglais Y.

Le 13 août 2004, l'Association de Football d'Angleterre a demandé à la Fédération Française de Football d'établir le certificat international de transfert pour le joueur. La Fédération Française de Football n'a pas établi ce certificat international de transfert, suite à l'opposition du club X. Le 19 août 2004, l'Association de Football d'Angleterre a demandé la FIFA à ordonner la Fédération Française de Football d'établir le certificat international de transfert.

Le 2 septembre 2004, la FIFA a ordonné la Fédération Française de Football d'établir immédiatement le certificat international de transfert pour l'Association de Football d'Angleterre, en considérant que la convention de formation qui est valide jusqu'au 30 juin 2006 n'a pas le statut d'un contrat de travail et donc n'empêche pas le joueur concerné de signer un contrat de travail avec un autre club. Par la même lettre, la FIFA a autorisé l'Association de Football d'Angleterre d'enregistrer le joueur jusqu'à la réception du certificat international de transfert officiel.

Le 14 septembre 2004, le club X a déposé un appel devant le Tribunal Arbitral du Sport contre l'autorisation rendue par la FIFA d'enregistrer le joueur en question. Par cet appel, le club X a de même fait une requête d'effet suspensif contre l'autorisation d'enregistrer le joueur. Le 6 octobre 2004, le Tribunal Arbitral du Sport a accordé un effet suspensif à l'appel, et a suspendu la registration du joueur pour le club Y, jusqu'à la décision finale dans l'affaire par la Chambre de Résolution des Litiges de la FIFA.

Suite à l'autorisation d'enregistrer le joueur, le club X a demandé la Chambre de Résolution de Litiges 1) de constater l'existence du lien contractuel entre le club X et le joueur, 2) de décider que le joueur doit signer un contrat de joueur avec le club X, et 3) d'ordonner la suspension du joueur de toute activité de football professionnel, avec effet immédiat, jusqu'à ça réintégration au sein du club X.

A l'avis du club X, le joueur est lié au club X jusqu'au 30 juin 2006 par la convention de formation. Toutefois, le club X avoue dans sa demande que la convention de formation est indépendante d'un contrat de travail éventuellement signé entre le club et le joueur, et n'a pas le statut d'un contrat de travail. Ensuite, le club X explique que la convention de formation prévoit des possibilités de résiliation unilatérale et anticipée. Pourtant, selon le club X, les exigences pour une résiliation n'étaient jamais rempli. En plus, le club X maintient que le contrat de joueur aspirant comportait l'engagement pour les parties de respecter les dispositions sur le statut de joueur aspirant insérées dans la Charte du Football Professionnel de la France (ci-après ; la charte). A l'avis du club X, la charte devrait être applique par la Chambre 2 de Résolution des Litiges de la FIFA lors des transferts internationaux, suite à l'Article 43 du Règlement de

la FIFA concernant le Statut et le Transfert des Joueurs. L'article 261 de la charte statue le suivant :
« A l'expiration normae des contrats apprent et aspirant, le club est en droit d'exige de l'autrepartie la signature d'un nouveau contrat de joueur en formation ou de joueu élite correspondant à l'age du joueur. Le club aura du, le 30 avril au plus tard, prévenir le joueur de ses intenions par lettre recommandée avec accusé de réception, [...].
2. Si le joueur refuse de signer un contrat de joueur en formation [ou] de joueur élite [...], i ne pourra pas, pendant un délai de trois ans, signer dans un autre club de la LFP [...]. »
Le club X maintient que le 1 mars 2004, il a notifié au joueur concerné son intention de conclure avec lui un nouveau contrat stagiaire, et que le joueur ne s'est jamais expressément opposé à la signature du contrat exigé par le club X.
Le joueur et le club Y demandent la Chambre de Résolution des Litiges que la suspension de la registration du joueur pour le club Y soit annulée. Le club Y ne s'oppose pas au payement de l'indemnité de formation pour le joueur concerné.
Ils maintiennent que la convention de formation ne peut pas être considérée comme un contrat de travail, mais seulement comme une convention parallèle au contrat de travail. Le contrat de joueur aspirant entre le joueur et le club X, qui avait le statut d'un contrat de travail, a expiré. A l'avis du joueur et du club Y, aucun contrat existe par lequel le joueur serait lié au club X. En plus, suite à l'article 261 alinéa 2 de la Charte, ils sont d'avis que la Charte seulement limite le joueur d'être transféré en France, mais ne l'empêche pas d'être transféré sur le niveau internationale.

CONSIDÉRATIONS DE LA CHAMBRE DE RÉSOLUTION DES LITIGES

1. Les membres de la Chambre de Résolution des Litiges étaient convoqués de rendre une décision sur le cas présent par le président de la Chambre en application de l'Article 1 al. 6 du Règlement de Procédure de la Chambre de Résolution des Litiges.
2. Ensuite, la Chambre se tournait vers la question de la compétence générale de la FIFA de trancher sur le litige présent. Par principe, la FIFA est compétente de trancher sur tous les litiges de transfert qui ont une portée internationale. Vu que une question dans le cas présent est si le joueur peut être enregistré avec la Fédération d'Angleterre de Football pour le club Y, ou s'il doit rester enregistré avec la Fédération Française de Football pour le club X, la portée internationale existe indubitablement. Par conséquent, la Chambre décidait que la FIFA est compétente de trancher sur ce litige.
3. Après avoir statué sur la compétence de la FIFA, la Chambre examinait la compétence de la Chambre de Règlement des Litiges de trancher sur le présent litige. Selon l'Article 3 al. 2 let. a du Règlement de Procédure de la Chambre de Résolution des Litiges, la Chambre a le pouvoir de décider si un joueur ou un club a rompu un contrat et si cette rupture est intervenue pour une juste cause ou une juste cause sportive. Dans le cas présent, question est si le joueur a rompu son contrat avec le club X et quels en étaient les conséquences. Par conséquent, la Chambre décidait que la Chambre de Résolution des Litiges est l'instance compétente de trancher sur cette affaire.
4. Vu que la compétence de la Chambre de Résolution des Litiges de la FIFA dans ce cas spécifique, la Chambre se tournait vers la substance de l'affaire. Premièrement, la Chambre a constaté que le contrat de joueur aspirant entre le joueur et le club X, s'est terminé le 30 juin 2004. En plus, la Chambre a constaté l'existence d'une convention de formation entre les mêmes parties qui est valide depuis le 1 juillet 2003 jusqu'au 30 juin 2006.
5. Les membres de la Chambre ont constaté que la convention de formation contient la possibilité pour le joueur de résilier unilatéralement et anticipé la convention par voie de lettre recommandée. Pourtant, à cet égard, les membres de la Chambre ont remarqué que le joueur n'a pas fait usage de sa possibilité de résiliation, qu'il n'a jamais notifié au club X par voie de lettre recommandée sa volonté de terminer la convention de formation.
6. Ensuite, la Chambre a pris note du fait que le joueur a signé un nouveau contrat avec le club Y, où il se trouve à présent.
7. Suite à cela, la Chambre a statué que le joueur, en partant à l'étranger avant la terme de la convention de formation et sans résiliation de la même, a violé cette convention.
8. Au lieu de prendre une décision sur les conséquences de la rupture de la convention de formation, la Chambre estimait qu'il serait plus approprié d'accorder un délai aux parties afin de leur rendre possible de résoudre le dispute par accord à l'amiable.
9. Par conséquent, la Chambre décidait d'ajourner la décision sur les conséquences de la rupture de la convention de formation, et de laisser aux parties de l'affaire la possibilité de trouver une solution

à l'amiable. Ensuite, la Chambre décidait que si les parties ne pourraient pas se concilier, le club X devrait indiquer à la Chambre via l'administration de la FIFA jusqu'au 25 novembre 2004 au plus tard le dommage qu'il estime avoir subit par la rupture de la convention de formation par le joueur. Dans le même délai, le joueur devrait indiquer à la Chambre le montant qu'il estime étant approprié pour récompenser le club X pour la rupture de la Convention de Formation.

10. Par conséquent, la Chambre ajournait la décision sur les conséquences de la rupture de la convention de formation à sa prochaine réunion qui aura lieu le 26 novembre 2004. 4
11. Entre temps, pour ne pas préjuger la décision finale que passera la Chambre dans ce cas lors de sa prochaine réunion, la Chambre a décidé de ne pas se prononcer à présent sur la registration du joueur pour le club Y.

DÉCISION DE LA CHAMBRE DE RÉSOLUTION DES LITIGES

1. Le club français X et le joueur sont invité d'entrer en négociation afin de résoudre l'affaire présente par accord à l'amiable, et d'informer la Chambre de Résolution des Litiges d'un éventuel accord jusqu'au 25 novembre 2004 au plus tard, via l'administration de la FIFA, en utilisant le numéro de fax suivant : +41-43/222 72 81.
2. Si l'affaire ne peut pas être résolue par accord à l'amiable, le club X est invité d'indiquer à la Chambre de Résolution des Litiges dans le délai susmentionné le dommage qu'il estime avoir subit par la rupture de la convention de formation par le joueur. Dans le même délai, le joueur devrait indiquer à la Chambre le montant qu'il estime étant approprié pour récompenser le club X pour la rupture de la Convention de Formation. Les parties sont priés de nous faire parvenir leurs positions par le numéro de fax susmentionné.
3. La décision finale dans cette affaire est ajournée jusqu'à la réunion de la Chambre de Résolution des Litiges du 26 novembre 2004. Seulement la décision qui sera prise lors de la réunion de la Chambre de Résolution des Litiges du 26 novembre 2004 pourra faire objet d'appel.

114677 a
DECISION OF THE DISPUTE RESOLUTION CHAMBER
passed in Zurich, Switzerland, on 9 November 2004,
in the following composition:
Slim Aloulou (Tunisia), Chairman
Philippe Piat (France), member
Philippe Diallo (France), member
on the claim presented by
Club A as Claimant
against
Club B as Respondent
regarding the solidarity contribution related to the transfer of the federative rights to the player M

FACTS OF THE CASE:

- By communication dated 25 June 2004 the club A presented FIFA with a claim against the Club B for the 5% payment established in art. 25 of the FIFA Regulations for the Status and Transfer of Players regarding the contribution to the solidarity mechanism.
- This claim was lodged in relation to the transfer, in the season June-July 2002, of the federative rights of the professional player M from Parma to club B during the course of his contract with Parma.
- The claimant bases its claim on the assertion that club B acquired the player for a sum of EUR 10,000,000 and that therefore an amount of EUR 500,000, corresponding to 5% of this sum, should have been distributed among the developing clubs, which included the club A.
- M had been registered with A for three seasons between the age 12 to 15, for which this club claims EUR 100,000 (20% of the 5%).
- On 19 August 2004 the FIFA Administration informed the claimant that it is not entitled to any solidarity contribution from the player's new club. This communication was based on a decision taken by the Dispute Resolution Chamber at its meeting held on 22 July 2004, when it had been decided that, since the principle of solidarity mechanism is not included in par. 2 of the Preamble of

the Regulations for the Status and Transfer of Players, it is not binding at national level and therefore this principle shall not be applicable to national transfers.

- The claimant has nevertheless insisted on having the case heard by the Dispute Resolution Chamber.
- The claimant deems that the solidarity mechanism is applicable to domestic transfers, stressing in this respect that in the decision of the FIFA Players' Status Committee taken on 12 November 2003, the Chairman determined that the solidarity mechanism applies to domestic transfers in which the claimant club is registered with another national association than that of the club that is due to pay.
- The respondent defends that it is not liable to pay the solidarity contribution to the claimant as the solidarity mechanism system is exclusively applicable to international transfers.

CONSIDERATIONS OF THE DISPUTE RESOLUTION CHAMBER

The Dispute Resolution Chamber of the FIFA Players' Status Committee shall review disputes coming under its jurisdiction pursuant to Art. 42 of the FIFA Regulations for the Status and Transfer of Players (hereinafter: the Regulations) at the request of one of the parties to the dispute.

According to art. 25 of the FIFA Regulations for the Status and Transfer of Players it falls within the purview of the Dispute Resolution Chamber to review disputes concerning the distribution of the solidarity contribution.

Consequently, the Chamber established that it was competent to deal with the present litigation.

The members of the Dispute Resolution Chamber were summoned to pass a decision on this matter by the Chairman pursuant to Art. 1 point 6) of the Rules Governing the Practice and Procedures of the Dispute Resolution Chamber.

Subsequently, and entering into the substance of the matter, the Chamber acknowledged that in its previous meeting on 22 July 2004 it had dealt with a case involving very similar circumstances as those of the present matter. Precisely as in the litigation at hand, a claim had previously been presented by a club from outside of the Italian territory against an Italian club, following a transfer of a player from another Italian club. The members of the Chamber were thus faced with the same question as to whether or not the solidarity mechanism should apply when a player is transferred internally (between clubs affiliated to the same national association).

In the aforementioned previous decision the Chamber had noted that the claimant was, inte alia, basing its argumentation on the contents of the FIFA circular 769. The Chamber then stressed that the FIFA Regulations for the Status and Transfer of Players must remain the main source of law when having to judge a dispute, clarifying that circular letters are an administrative instrument hierarchically subordinated to the FIFA Regulations.

Taking into consideration this principle, the Dispute Resolution Chamber referred to the contents of the Regulations and, in particular, to their Preamble. Paragraph 1 establishes that the Regulations deal with the status and eligibility of players, as well as with the rules applicable whenever players move between clubs belonging to different associations.

The deciding body lent emphasis to the wording of the last part of the aforementioned clause and concluded that, in fact, the Regulations are not applicable to transfers of the federative rights to a player between two clubs affiliated to the same association.

Moreover, the Chamber had also pointed out in this meeting on 22 July 2004 that the principle of the solidarity mechanism is not included in par. 2 of the Preamble of the Regulations and therefore, it is not binding at national level.

Taking into account that in the case at hand no new elements had been introduced regarding the facts, the members of the Dispute Resolution Chamber sufficed in unanimously confirming its recently reviewed jurisprudence that the principle regarding the solidarity mechanism is not applicable to national transfers, not even in cases where the club claiming the payment of the contribution is affiliated to another association. Consequently, the same principles apply in the present case against the respondent and the claim of A must be rejected.

DECISION OF THE DISPUTE RESOLUTION CHAMBER

1. The claim of the claimant A against the respondent B, is rejected.
2. According to art. 60 par. 1 of the FIFA Statutes, this decision may be appealed against before the Court of Arbitration for Sport (CAS). The statement of appeal must be sent to the CAS directly within 10 days of receipt of notification of this decision and shall contain all the elements in accordance

with point 2 of the directives issued by the CAS, a copy of which we enclose hereto. Within another 10 days following the expiry of the time limit for filing the statement of appeal, the appellant shall file a brief stating the facts and legal arguments giving rise to the appeal with the CAS (cf. point 4 of the directives).

114677 b
DECISION OF THE DISPUTE RESOLUTION CHAMBER
passed in Zurich, Switzerland, on 9 November 2004,
in the following composition:
Slim Aloulou (Tunisia), Chairman
Philippe Piat (France), member
Philippe Diallo (France), member
on the claim presented by
Club A as Claimant
against
Club B as Respondent
regarding the solidarity contribution related to the transfer of the federative rights to the player M

FACTS OF THE CASE:

- By communication dated 25 June 2004 the club A presented FIFA with a claim against the Club B for the 5% payment established in art. 25 of the FIFA Regulations for the Status and Transfer of Players regarding the contribution to the solidarity mechanism.
- This claim was lodged in relation to the transfer, in the season June-July 2002, of the federative rights of the professional player M from Parma to club B during the course of his contract with Parma.
- The claimant bases its claim on the assertion that B acquired the player for a sum of EUR 10,000,000 and that therefore an amount of EUR 500,000, corresponding to 5% of this sum, should have been distributed among the developing clubs, which included the club A.
- M had been registered with A for eight seasons between the age 15 to 23, for which this club claims EUR 400,000 (80% of the 5%).
- On 19 August 2004 the FIFA Administration informed the claimant that it is not entitled to any solidarity contribution from the player's new club. This communication was based on a decision taken by the Dispute Resolution Chamber at its meeting held on 22 July 2004, when it had been decided that, since the principle of solidarity mechanism is not included in par. 2 of the Preamble of the Regulations for the Status and Transfer of Players, it is not binding at national level and therefore this principle shall not be applicable to national transfers.
- The claimant has nevertheless insisted on having the case heard by the Dispute Resolution Chamber.
- The claimant deems that the solidarity mechanism is applicable to domestic transfers, stressing in this respect that in the decision of the FIFA Players' Status Committee taken on 12 November 2003, the Chairman determined that the solidarity mechanism applies to domestic transfers in which the claimant club is registered with another national association than that of the club that is due to pay.
- The respondent defends that it is not liable to pay the solidarity contribution to the claimant as the solidarity mechanism system is exclusively applicable to international transfers.

CONSIDERATIONS OF THE DISPUTE RESOLUTION CHAMBER

The Dispute Resolution Chamber of the FIFA Players' Status Committee shall review disputes coming under its jurisdiction pursuant to Art. 42 of the FIFA Regulations for the Status and Transfer of Players (hereinafter: the Regulations) at the request of one of the parties to the dispute.

According to art. 25 of the FIFA Regulations for the Status and Transfer of Players it falls within the purview of the Dispute Resolution Chamber to review disputes concerning the distribution of the solidarity contribution.

Consequently, the Chamber established that it was competent to deal with the present litigation.

The members of the Dispute Resolution Chamber were summoned to pass a decision on this matter by the Chairman pursuant to Art. 1 point 6) of the Rules Governing the Practice and Procedures of the Dispute Resolution Chamber.

Subsequently, and entering into the substance of the matter, the Chamber acknowledged that in its previous meeting on 22 July 2004 it had dealt with a case involving very similar circumstances as those of the present matter. Precisely as in the litigation at hand, a claim had previously been presented by a club from outside of the Italian territory against an Italian club, following a transfer of a player from another Italian club. The members of the Chamber were thus faced with the same question as to whether or not the solidarity mechanism should apply when a player is transferred internally (between clubs affiliated to the same national association).

In the aforementioned previous decision the Chamber had noted that the claimant was, inte alia, basing its argumentation on the contents of the FIFA circular 769. The Chamber then stressed that the FIFA Regulations for the Status and Transfer of Players must remain the main source of law when having to judge a dispute, clarifying that circular letters are an administrative instrument hierarchically subordinated to the FIFA Regulations.

Taking into consideration this principle, the Dispute Resolution Chamber referred to the contents of the Regulations and, in particular, to their Preamble. Paragraph 1 establishes that the Regulations deal with the status and eligibility of players, as well as with the rules applicable whenever players move between clubs belonging to different associations.

The deciding body lent emphasis to the wording of the last part of the aforementioned clause and concluded that, in fact, the Regulations are not applicable to transfers of the federative rights to a player between two clubs affiliated to the same association.

Moreover, the Chamber had also pointed out in this meeting on 22 July 2004 that the principle of the solidarity mechanism is not included in par. 2 of the Preamble of the Regulations and therefore, it is not binding at national level.

Taking into account that in the case at hand no new elements had been introduced regarding the facts, the members of the Dispute Resolution Chamber sufficed in unanimously confirming its recently reviewed jurisprudence that the principle regarding the solidarity mechanism is not applicable to national transfers, not even in cases where the club claiming the payment of the contribution is affiliated to another association. Consequently, the same principles apply in the present case against the respondent and the claim of A must be rejected.

DECISION OF THE DISPUTE RESOLUTION CHAMBER

1. The claim of the claimant against the respondent, is rejected.
2. According to art. 60 par. 1 of the FIFA Statutes, this decision may be appealed against before the Court of Arbitration for Sport (CAS). The statement of appeal must be sent to the CAS directly within 10 days of receipt of notification of this decision and shall contain all the elements in accordance with point 2 of the directives issued by the CAS, a copy of which we enclose hereto. Within another 10 days following the expiry of the time limit for filing the statement of appeal, the appellant shall file a brief stating the facts and legal arguments giving rise to the appeal with the CAS (cf. point 4 of the directives).

⚽⚽⚽

114678 a
DECISION OF THE DISPUTE RESOLUTION CHAMBER
passed in Zurich, Switzerland, on 9 November 2004,
in the following composition:
Slim Aloulou (Tunisia), Chairman
Philippe Piat (France), member
Philippe Diallo (France), member
on the claim presented by
Club A as Claimant
against
Club B as Respondent
regarding the solidarity contribution related to the transfer of the federative rights to the player J

FACTS OF THE CASE:

- By communication dated 3 August 2004 the club A presented FIFA with a claim against the Club B for the 5% payment established in art. 25 of the FIFA Regulations for the Status and Transfer of Players regarding the contribution to the solidarity mechanism.
- This claim was lodged in relation to the transfer, in the season June-July 2003, of the federative rights of the professional player J from Club H to Club B during the course of his contract with club H.
- The claimant bases its claim on the assertion that club B acquired the player for a sum of EUR 4,000,000 and that therefore an amount of EUR 200,000, corresponding to 5% of this sum, should have been distributed among the developing clubs, which included the club A.
- J had been registered with Club A during the season 1996/1997, for which this club claims EUR 20,000 (10% of the 5%).
- The claimant asked DRC to recognize the validity of its claim and to oblige the respondent club to pay solidarity contribution.
- The respondent was contacted by FIFA administration and the claimant but never answered the communications
- On 19 August 2004 the FIFA Administration informed the claimant that it is not entitled to any solidarity contribution from the player's new club. This communication was based on a decision taken by the Dispute Resolution Chamber at its meeting held on 22 July 2004, when it had been decided that, since the principle of solidarity mechanism is not included in par. 2 of the Preamble of the Regulations for the Status and Transfer of Players, it is not binding at national level and therefore this principle shall not be applicable to national transfers.

CONSIDERATIONS OF THE DISPUTE RESOLUTION CHAMBER

The Dispute Resolution Chamber of the FIFA Players' Status Committee shall review disputes coming under its jurisdiction pursuant to Art. 42 of the FIFA Regulations for the Status and Transfer of Players (hereinafter: the Regulations) at the request of one of the parties to the dispute.

According to art. 25 of the FIFA Regulations for the Status and Transfer of Players it falls within the purview of the Dispute Resolution Chamber to review disputes concerning the distribution of the solidarity contribution.

Consequently, the Chamber established that it was competent to deal with the present litigation.

The members of the Dispute Resolution Chamber were summoned to pass a decision on this matter by the Chairman pursuant to Art. 1 point 6) of the Rules Governing the Practice and Procedures of the Dispute Resolution Chamber.

Subsequently, and entering into the substance of the matter, the Chamber acknowledged that in its previous meeting on 22 July 2004 it had dealt with a case involving very similar circumstances as those of the present matter. Precisely as in the litigation at hand, a claim had previously been presented by a club from outside of the Italian territory against an Italian club, following a transfer of a player from another Italian club. The members of the Chamber were thus faced with the same question as to whether or not the solidarity mechanism should apply when a player is transferred internally (between clubs affiliated to the same national association).

In the aforementioned previous decision the Chamber had noted that the claimant was, inte alia, basing its argumentation on the contents of the FIFA circular 769. The Chamber then stressed that the FIFA Regulations for the Status and Transfer of Players must remain the main source of law when having to judge a dispute, clarifying that circular letters are an administrative instrument hierarchically subordinated to the FIFA Regulations.

Taking into consideration this principle, the Dispute Resolution Chamber referred to the contents of the Regulations and, in particular, to their Preamble. Paragraph 1 establishes that the Regulations deal with the status and eligibility of players, as well as with the rules applicable whenever players move between clubs belonging to different associations.

The deciding body lent emphasis to the wording of the last part of the aforementioned clause and concluded that, in fact, the Regulations are not applicable to transfers of the federative rights to a player between two clubs affiliated to the same association.

Moreover, the Chamber had also pointed out in this meeting on 22 July 2004 that the principle of the solidarity mechanism is not included in par. 2 of the Preamble of the Regulations and therefore, it is not binding at national level.

Therefore, the members of the Dispute Resolution Chamber confirmed the contents of the FIFA Administration's communication sent to the claimant on 20 August 2004 and reaffirmed its revised jurisprudence according to which the principle regarding the solidarity mechanism is not applicable to national transfers, not even in cases where the club claiming the payment of the contribution is affiliated to another association. Consequently, it was confirmed that the claim of club A must be rejected.

DECISION OF THE DISPUTE RESOLUTION CHAMBER

1. The claim of the claimant against the respondent, is rejected.
2. According to art. 60 par. 1 of the FIFA Statutes, this decision may be appealed against before the Court of Arbitration for Sport (CAS). The statement of appeal must be sent to the CAS directly within 10 days of receipt of notification of this decision and shall contain all the elements in accordance with point 2 of the directives issued by the CAS, a copy of which we enclose hereto. Within another 10 days following the expiry of the time limit for filing the statement of appeal, the appellant shall file a brief stating the facts and legal arguments giving rise to the appeal with the CAS (cf. point 4 of the directives).

114678 b
DECISION OF THE DISPUTE RESOLUTION CHAMBER
passed in Zurich, Switzerland, on 9 November 2004,
Slim Aloulou (Tunisia), Chairman
Philippe Piat (France), member
Philippe Diallo (France), member
on the claim presented by
Club A as Claimant
against
Club B as Respondent
regarding the solidarity contribution related to the transfer of the federative rights to the player J

FACTS OF THE CASE:

- By communication dated 3 August 2004 the club A presented FIFA with a claim against the Club B for the 5% payment established in art. 25 of the FIFA Regulations for the Status and Transfer of Players regarding the contribution to the solidarity mechanism.
- This claim was lodged in relation to the transfer, in the season June-July 2003, of the federative rights of the professional player J from Club H to Club B during the course of his contract with H.
- The claimant bases its claim on the assertion that Inter acquired the player for a sum of EUR 4,000,000 and that therefore an amount of EUR 200,000, corresponding to 5% of this sum, should have been distributed among the developing clubs, which included the club A.
- J had been registered with A from 1993/1994 until 1995/1996 seasons, for which this club claims EUR 60,000 (30% of the 5%).
- The claimant asked DRC to recognize the validity of its claim and to oblige the respondent club to pay solidarity contribution.
- The respondent was contacted by FIFA administration and the claimant but never answered the communications
- On 19 August 2004 the FIFA Administration informed the claimant that it is not entitled to any solidarity contribution from the player's new club. This communication was based on a decision taken by the Dispute Resolution Chamber at its meeting held on 22 July 2004, when it had been decided that, since the principle of solidarity mechanism is not included in par. 2 of the Preamble of the Regulations for the Status and Transfer of Players, it is not binding at national level and therefore this principle shall not be applicable to national transfers.

CONSIDERATIONS OF THE DISPUTE RESOLUTION CHAMBER

The Dispute Resolution Chamber of the FIFA Players' Status Committee shall review disputes coming under its jurisdiction pursuant to Art. 42 of the FIFA Regulations for the Status and Transfer of Players (hereinafter: the Regulations) at the request of one of the parties to the dispute.

According to art. 25 of the FIFA Regulations for the Status and Transfer of Players it falls within the purview of the Dispute Resolution Chamber to review disputes concerning the distribution of the solidarity contribution.

Consequently, the Chamber established that it was competent to deal with the present litigation.

The members of the Dispute Resolution Chamber were summoned to pass a decision on this matter by the Chairman pursuant to Art. 1 point 6) of the Rules Governing the Practice and Procedures of the Dispute Resolution Chamber.

Subsequently, and entering into the substance of the matter, the Chamber acknowledged that in its previous meeting on 22 July 2004 it had dealt with a case involving very similar circumstances as those of the present matter. Precisely as in the litigation at hand, a claim had previously been presented by a club from outside of the Italian territory against an Italian club, following a transfer of a player from another Italian club. The members of the Chamber were thus faced with the same question as to whether or not the solidarity mechanism should apply when a player is transferred internally (between clubs affiliated to the same national association).

In the aforementioned previous decision the Chamber had noted that the claimant was, inte alia, basing its argumentation on the contents of the FIFA circular 769. The Chamber then stressed that the FIFA Regulations for the Status and Transfer of Players must remain the main source of law when having to judge a dispute, clarifying that circular letters are an administrative instrument hierarchically subordinated to the FIFA Regulations.

Taking into consideration this principle, the Dispute Resolution Chamber referred to the contents of the Regulations and, in particular, to their Preamble. Paragraph 1 establishes that the Regulations deal with the status and eligibility of players, as well as with the rules applicable whenever players move between clubs belonging to different associations.

The deciding body lent emphasis to the wording of the last part of the aforementioned clause and concluded that, in fact, the Regulations are not applicable to transfers of the federative rights to a player between two clubs affiliated to the same association.

Moreover, the Chamber had also pointed out in this meeting on 22 July 2004 that the principle of the solidarity mechanism is not included in par. 2 of the Preamble of the Regulations and therefore, it is not binding at national level.

Therefore, the members of the Dispute Resolution Chamber confirmed the contents of the FIFA Administration's communication sent to the claimant on 20 August 2004 and reaffirmed its revised jurisprudence according to which the principle regarding the solidarity mechanism is not applicable to national transfers, not even in cases where the club claiming the payment of the contribution is affiliated to another association. Consequently, it was confirmed that the claim of A must be rejected.

DECISION OF THE DISPUTE RESOLUTION CHAMBER

1. The claim of the claimant against the respondent , is rejected.
2. According to art. 60 par. 1 of the FIFA Statutes, this decision may be appealed against before the Court of Arbitration for Sport (CAS). The statement of appeal must be sent to the CAS directly within 10 days of receipt of notification of this decision and shall contain all the elements in accordance with point 2 of the directives issued by the CAS, a copy of which we enclose hereto. Within another 10 days following the expiry of the time limit for filing the statement of appeal, the appellant shall file a brief stating the facts and legal arguments giving rise to the appeal with the CAS (cf. point 4 of the directives).

114678 c
DECISION OF THE DISPUTE RESOLUTION CHAMBER

passed in Zurich, Switzerland, on 9 November 2004,
in the following composition:
Slim Aloulou (Tunisia), Chairman
Philippe Piat (France), member
Philippe Diallo (France), member
on the claim presented by
Club A as Claimant

against
Club B as Respondent
regarding the solidarity contribution related to the transfer of the federative rights to the player J

FACTS OF THE CASE:

- By communication dated 3 August 2004 the club A presented FIFA with a claim against the Club B for the 5% payment established in art. 25 of the FIFA Regulations for the Status and Transfer of Players regarding the contribution to the solidarity mechanism.
- This claim was lodged in relation to the transfer, in the season June-July 2003, of the federative rights of the professional player J from Club H to Club B during the course of his contract with Club H.
- The claimant bases its claim on the assertion that Club B acquired the player for a sum of EUR 4,000,000 and that therefore an amount of EUR 200,000, corresponding to 5% of this sum, should have been distributed among the developing clubs, which included the club A.
- J had been registered with Club A from 1986/1987 until 1992/1993 seasons, for which this club claims EUR 120,000 (60% of the 5%).
- The claimant asked DRC to recognize the validity of its claim and to oblige the respondent club to pay solidarity contribution.
- The respondent was contacted by FIFA administration and the claimant but never answered the communications
- On 19 August 2004 the FIFA Administration informed the claimant that it is not entitled to any solidarity contribution from the player's new club. This communication was based on a decision taken by the Dispute Resolution Chamber at its meeting held on 22 July 2004, when it had been decided that, since the principle of solidarity mechanism is not included in par. 2 of the Preamble of the Regulations for the Status and Transfer of Players, it is not binding at national level and therefore this principle shall not be applicable to national transfers.

CONSIDERATIONS OF THE DISPUTE RESOLUTION CHAMBER

The Dispute Resolution Chamber of the FIFA Players' Status Committee shall review disputes coming under its jurisdiction pursuant to Art. 42 of the FIFA Regulations for the Status and Transfer of Players (hereinafter: the Regulations) at the request of one of the parties to the dispute.
According to art. 25 of the FIFA Regulations for the Status and Transfer of Players it falls within the purview of the Dispute Resolution Chamber to review disputes concerning the distribution of the solidarity contribution.
Consequently, the Chamber established that it was competent to deal with the present litigation.
The members of the Dispute Resolution Chamber were summoned to pass a decision on this matter by the Chairman pursuant to Art. 1 point 6) of the Rules Governing the Practice and Procedures of the Dispute Resolution Chamber.
Subsequently, and entering into the substance of the matter, the Chamber acknowledged that in its previous meeting on 22 July 2004 it had dealt with a case involving very similar circumstances as those of the present matter. Precisely as in the litigation at hand, a claim had previously been presented by a club from outside of the Italian territory against an Italian club, following a transfer of a player from another Italian club. The members of the Chamber were thus faced with the same question as to whether or not the solidarity mechanism should apply when a player is transferred internally (between clubs affiliated to the same national association).
In the aforementioned previous decision the Chamber had noted that the claimant was, inte alia, basing its argumentation on the contents of the FIFA circular 769. The Chamber then stressed that the FIFA Regulations for the Status and Transfer of Players must remain the main source of law when having to judge a dispute, clarifying that circular letters are an administrative instrument hierarchically subordinated to the FIFA Regulations.
Taking into consideration this principle, the Dispute Resolution Chamber referred to the contents of the Regulations and, in particular, to their Preamble. Paragraph 1 establishes that the Regulations deal with the status and eligibility of players, as well as with the rules applicable whenever players move between clubs belonging to different associations.
The deciding body lent emphasis to the wording of the last part of the aforementioned clause and concluded that, in fact, the Regulations are not applicable to transfers of the federative rights to a player between two clubs affiliated to the same association.

Moreover, the Chamber had also pointed out in this meeting on 22 July 2004 that the principle of the solidarity mechanism is not included in par. 2 of the Preamble of the Regulations and therefore, it is not binding at national level.
Therefore, the members of the Dispute Resolution Chamber confirmed the contents of the FIFA Administration's communication sent to the claimant on 20 August 2004 and reaffirmed its revised jurisprudence according to which the principle regarding the solidarity mechanism is not applicable to national transfers, not even in cases where the club claiming the payment of the contribution is affiliated to another association. Consequently, it was confirmed that the claim of club A must be rejected.

DECISION OF THE DISPUTE RESOLUTION CHAMBER

1. The claim of the claimant against the respondent, is rejected.
2. According to art. 60 par. 1 of the FIFA Statutes, this decision may be appealed against before the Court of Arbitration for Sport (CAS). The statement of appeal must be sent to the CAS directly within 10 days of receipt of notification of this decision and shall contain all the elements in accordance with point 2 of the directives issued by the CAS, a copy of which we enclose hereto. Within another 10 days following the expiry of the time limit for filing the statement of appeal, the appellant shall file a brief stating the facts and legal arguments giving rise to the appeal with the CAS (cf. point 4 of the directives).

5, nr 114679
DECISION OF THE DISPUTE RESOLUTION CHAMBER
passed in Zurich, Switzerland, on 9 November 2004,
in the following composition:
Slim Aloulou (Tunisia), Chairman
Philippe Piat (France), member
Philippe Diallo (France), member
on the claim presented by
X, the Netherlands, as Claimant
against
Y, Italy as Respondent
regarding the solidarity contribution related to the transfer of the federative rights to the player Z

FACTS OF THE CASE:

- In August 2004 the Dutch club X presented FIFA with a claim against the Italian club Y for the 5% payment established in art. 25 of the FIFA Regulations for the Status and Transfer of Players regarding the contribution to the solidarity mechanism.
- This claim was lodged in relation to the transfer, in July 2004, of the federative rights of the Dutch professional player Z from S.S. Lazio Roma to Y during the course of his contract with S.S. Lazio Roma.
- The claimant bases its claim on the assertion that Y acquired the player for a sum of EUR 10,500,000 and that therefore an amount of EUR 525,000, corresponding to 5% of this sum, should have been distributed among the developing clubs, which included the club X.
- Z had been registered with X from the 1984/1985 until 1990/1991 seasons, for which this club claims EUR 315,000 (60% of the 5%).
- On 10 August 2004 the FIFA Administration informed the claimant that it is not entitled to any solidarity contribution from the player's new club. This communication was based on a decision taken by the Dispute Resolution Chamber at its meeting held on 22 July 2004, when it had been decided that, since the principle of solidarity mechanism is not included in par. 2 of the Preamble of the Regulations for the Status and Transfer of Players, it is not binding at national level and therefore this principle shall not be applicable to national transfers.
- The claimant has nevertheless insisted on having the case heard by the Dispute Resolution Chamber.
- The claimant deems that the solidarity mechanism is applicable to domestic transfers, stressing in this respect that in the decision of the FIFA Players' Status Committee taken on 12 November 2003,

the Chairman determined that the solidarity mechanism applies to domestic transfers in which the claimant club is registered with another national association than that of the club that is due to pay.
- The respondent defends that it is not liable to pay the solidarity contribution to the claimant as the solidarity mechanism system is exclusively applicable to international transfers.

CONSIDERATIONS OF THE DISPUTE RESOLUTION CHAMBER

The Dispute Resolution Chamber of the FIFA Players' Status Committee shall review disputes coming under its jurisdiction pursuant to Art. 42 of the FIFA Regulations for the Status and Transfer of Players (hereinafter: the Regulations) at the request of one of the parties to the dispute.
According to art. 25 of the FIFA Regulations for the Status and Transfer of Players it falls within the purview of the Dispute Resolution Chamber to review disputes concerning the distribution of the solidarity contribution.
Consequently, the Chamber established that it was competent to deal with the present litigation.
The members of the Dispute Resolution Chamber were summoned to pass a decision on this matter by the Chairman pursuant to Art. 1 point 6) of the Rules Governing the Practice and Procedures of the Dispute Resolution Chamber.
Subsequently, and entering into the substance of the matter, the Chamber acknowledged that in its previous meeting on 22 July 2004 it had dealt with a case involving very similar circumstances as those of the present matter. Precisely as in the litigation at hand, a claim had previously been presented by a club from outside of the Italian territory against an Italian club, following a transfer of a player from another Italian club. The members of the Chamber were thus faced with the same question as to whether or not the solidarity mechanism should apply when a player is transferred internally (between clubs affiliated to the same national association).
In the aforementioned previous decision the Chamber had noted that the claimant was, inte alia, basing its argumentation on the contents of the FIFA circular 769. The Chamber then stressed that the FIFA Regulations for the Status and Transfer of Players must remain the main source of law when having to judge a dispute, clarifying that circular letters are an administrative instrument hierarchically subordinated to the FIFA Regulations.
Taking into consideration this principle, the Dispute Resolution Chamber referred to the contents of the Regulations and, in particular, to their Preamble. Paragraph 1 establishes that the Regulations deal with the status and eligibility of players, as well as with the rules applicable whenever players move between clubs belonging to different associations.
The deciding body lent emphasis to the wording of the last part of the aforementioned clause and concluded that, in fact, the Regulations are not applicable to transfers of the federative rights to a player between two clubs affiliated to the same association.
Moreover, the Chamber had also pointed out in this meeting on 22 July 2004 that the principle of the solidarity mechanism is not included in par. 2 of the Preamble of the Regulations and therefore, it is not binding at national level.
Taking into account that in the case at hand no new elements had been introduced regarding the facts, the members of the Dispute Resolution Chamber sufficed in unanimously confirming its recently reviewed jurisprudence that the principle regarding the solidarity mechanism is not applicable to national transfers, not even in cases where the club claiming the payment of the contribution is affiliated to another association. Consequently, the same principles apply in the present case against the respondent Y and the claim of X must be rejected.

DECISION OF THE DISPUTE RESOLUTION CHAMBER

1. The claim of the claimant X against the respondent Y, is rejected.
2. According to art. 60 par. 1 of the FIFA Statutes, this decision may be appealed against before the Court of Arbitration for Sport (CAS). The statement of appeal must be sent to the CAS directly within 10 days of receipt of notification of this decision and shall contain all the elements in accordance with point 2 of the directives issued by the CAS, a copy of which we enclose hereto. Within another 10 days following the expiry of the time limit for filing the statement of appeal, the appellant shall file a brief stating the facts and legal arguments giving rise to the appeal with the CAS (cf. point 4 of the directives).

114707
DECISION OF THE DISPUTE RESOLUTION CHAMBER
passed in Zurich, Switzerland, on 9 November 2004,
in the following composition:
Slim Aloulou (Tunisia), Chairman
Philippe Piat (France), member
Philippe Diallo (France), member
on the claim presented by the player, X, Serbia and Montenegro, as Claimant against FC Y, Russia, as Respondent
regarding a contractual dispute between the player and the club,

FACTS OF THE CASE

- After the rescission of the player's contract with his former club, A, an employment contract was signed between X, born on 12 September 1977, and FC Y on 16 July 2004.
- This contract is valid for a three years' period of time as from 15 July 2004, more precisely, until 30 June 2007.
- According to the employment contract, the player X is entitled to receive USD 200,000 upon the signing of the contract as well as the amount of USD 100,000 payable once a year before the start of the new season. Furthermore, the player X is entitled to a monthly payment of USD 21,666 as well as bonuses, lodging, a car, and 4 air tickets per year.
- As regards the aforementioned USD 200,000 payable upon the signing of the contract, it must be noted that the original text of the relevant clause appears to indicate the amount of USD 100,000 but has been amended by hand and now reads USD 200,000, which amendment was countersigned.
- On 27 July 2004 the Russian Football Union requested the issuance of an international registration transfer certificate (IRTC) from the Football Association of Serbia and Montenegro.
- On the same day, the relevant certificate was issued by the said Association on behalf of the Russian Football Union.
- On 3 August 2004, the player contacted the Russian Football Union claiming that FC Y did not respect its contractual obligations.
- On the same day, the player lodged his claim at FIFA.
- According to X, only after 3 to 4 days after having commenced his employment, the coach informed him, without any justification, that he would not be making use of the player's services. In addition, the coach allegedly forbade him to participate in and be present at the team's training.
- The player adds that he has received no written confirmation by the club of the above circumstances.
- X has indicated that he left Russia on 1 August 2004.
- The player wishes that FC Y be ordered to fulfil its contractual obligations.
- Should FC Y refuse to do so, the player claims the unilateral breach of contract by the club without just cause and he wishes to be able to transfer to another club without any compensation being payable.
- In addition, he claims compensation for breach of contract to the total amount of USD 1,079,976 equalling the full value of his employment contract (3 x USD 100,000 and 36 months x USD 21,666).
- As stated above, X's contract indicates that the amount of USD 200,000 is payable upon the signing of the contract, however, in accordance with the player's breakdown of his financial claim, X claims payment of three yearly fees amounting to USD 100,000 each. No reference is made by the player to an amount of USD 200,000.
- On 19 August 2004, the FIFA administration invited FC Y to present its response to the claim lodged by the player.
- In reply, the Russian Football Union maintains that the player in question never signed a contract with FC Y. Allegedly, X refused either to play for or sign a contract with FC Y claiming that the club was not at his level.
- The Russian Football Union further maintains that the player was not registered with the Union.
- The FIFA administration has received no reply from FC Y, either directly or via the Russian Football Union.

CONSIDERATIONS OF THE DISPUTE RESOLUTION CHAMBER

The members of the Dispute Resolution Chamber were summoned to pass a decision on this matter by the Chairman pursuant to Art. 1 point 6) of the Rules Governing the Practice and Procedures of the Dispute Resolution Chamber.

The members of the Chamber firstly proceeded to confirm that in accordance with Article 42 of the FIFA Regulations for the Status and Transfer of Players (edition September 2001) the Chamber is competent to deal with the present matter.

As established in Article 42 §1(b) of the Regulations, it falls within the competence of the Dispute Resolution Chamber to determine whether one of the parties has committed a unilateral breach of contract without just cause.

According to the player, the club failed to fulfil its contractual obligations 3 to 4 days after the commencement of his employment at the Russian club, when the coach informed him that he would not be making use of the player's services and that the player was not allowed to participate in the team's training. X demands that the club be ordered to fulfil its contractual obligations or, should it refuse to do so, that the club be sentenced for having committed a unilateral breach of contract without just cause. In addition, X asks that he be awarded an amount of compensation for breach of contract equalling the full value of his employment contract, i.e. until its date of expiry on 30 June 2007.

In the light of the position put forward by the Russian Football Union, denying the existence of a contractual relation between FC Y and the player X, the members agreed that the Chamber should analyse the document which has been presented by the player as the employment contract that was signed by and between himself and the Russian club. After a thorough analysis, the members of the Chamber concluded that the document presented by Mr. X to this end indeed constitutes an employment contract containing the relevant main elements, such as parties involved, salary, period of validity, position of the player, as well as the parties' signature and the club's stamp.

In this context, the members of the Chamber stressed that the Russian Football Union has requested and received an IRTC from the association of the player's former club, which can be regarded as a clear indication that an employment relationship had been entered into by Mr. X and FC Y.

Taking into consideration the position conveyed to the FIFA administration by the Russian Football Union, in accordance with which FC Y manifestly denies the existence of a contractual relation between the player and the club in question, the Chamber agreed that the player's first request, i.e. to order the club to fulfil its contractual obligations, has become superfluous. Therefore, the Chamber decided to focus on the question as to whether FC Y has committed a breach of contract and, if yes, with or without just cause.

As stated above, the Chamber has concluded that a valid employment contract has been entered into by and between the parties involved in the case at hand. Furthermore, the Chamber deemed that the circumstance whether or not the player was registered with the Russian Football Union must be considered irrelevant, as the registration, in general, does not fall within the scope of a player's responsibilities and obligations. For these reasons, the members unanimously decided that the Chamber has to fully dismiss the arguments put forward in the club's defence.

Taking into account all of the above, the club is found to have committed a unilateral breach of the employment contract without just cause. Consequently, the player is entitled to receive compensation for breach of contract.

In the light of all of the above, articles 21§1(a), 22 and 23§2(a) of the FIFA Regulations for the status and transfer of players are applicable to the present matter.

As regards the award of financial compensation payable to the player in accordance with article 22, the Chamber took into consideration that the relevant employment contract does not contain any clause pertaining to compensation payable to either of the parties in the event of the early termination of the employment relationship. Furthermore, the members agreed that in the light of the fact that the player is free to sign on with the club of his choice, he is able to and has the obligation to mitigate damages. The members of the Chamber took into account that although the relevant employment contract indicates that the amount of USD 200,000 is payable to the player upon the signing of the contract, X has put forward a financial claim based, inter alia, on a fee of USD 100,000. Departing from the principle that the award shall not exceed the claimant's claim, the Chamber agreed that the amount of USD 100,000 shall be taken into consideration when determining the amount of compensation payable to the player. Considering that the breach occurred at the beginning of the contract, only a few days after the arrival of the player, and

taking into account the remuneration that the player was due to receive under the terms of the employment contract, i.e. salary, signing-on fee and bonuses, the Chamber concluded that a compensation amounting to USD 200,000 is adequate.
As regards the player's wish to be able to transfer to another club without any compensation payable to FC Y, the Chamber draws the attention of X to article 20 of the FIFA Regulations for the Status and Transfer of Players, in accordance with which no training compensation shall be payable when a player over the age of 23 changes clubs.
The Chamber further considered that sports sanctions shall be applied in conformity with article 23§2(a) of the aforementioned Regulations. In accordance with the interpretation given by the CAS as body of appeal in a previous decision, the ban shall be set in at the point of time when the decision that a breach occurred has been reached and notified to the parties concerned.

DECISION OF THE DISPUTE RESOLUTION CHAMBER
1. The claim of the Claimant, X, is partially accepted.
2. The Respondent, FC Y, has to pay the amount of USD 200,000 to the Claimant.
3. The amount due to the Claimant has to be paid by the Respondent within 30 days as from the date of notification of this decision.
4. In the event that the debt of the Russian club is not paid within the stated deadline, an interest rate of 5% per year will apply as of expiry of the aforementioned deadline.
5. If the sum of USD 200,000 is not paid within the aforementioned deadline, the present matter shall be submitted to the FIFA Disciplinary Committee, so that the necessary disciplinary sanctions may be imposed.
6. In accordance with article 23§2(a) of the Regulations, the sanction imposed on FC Y is a ban on registering any new player, either nationally or internationally, until the expiry of the second transfer window following the date of notification of the present decision.
7. According to art. 60 par. 1 of the FIFA Statutes, this decision may be appealed against before the Court of Arbitration for Sport (CAS). The statement of appeal must be sent to the CAS directly within 10 days of receipt of notification of this decision and shall contain all the elements in accordance with point 2 of the directives issued by the CAS, a copy of which we enclose hereto. Within another 10 days following the expiry of the time limit for filing the statement of appeal, the appellant shall file a brief stating the facts and legal arguments giving rise to the appeal with the CAS (cf. point 4 of the directives).

⚽⚽⚽

114708
DECISION OF THE DISPUTE RESOLUTION CHAMBER
passed in Zurich, Switzerland, on 9 November 2004,
in the following composition:
Slim Aloulou (Tunisia), Chairman
Philippe Piat (France), member
Philippe Diallo (France), member
on the claim presented by the player, X, Serbia and Montenegro, as Claimant against FC Y, Russia, as Respondent
regarding a contractual dispute between the player and the club,

FACTS OF THE CASE
- After the rescission of the player's contract with his former club, A, an employment contract was signed between X, born on 12 September 1977, and FC Y on 16 July 2004.
- This contract is valid for a three years' period of time as from 15 July 2004, more precisely, until 30 June 2007.
- According to the employment contract, the player X is entitled to receive USD 200,000 upon the signing of the contract as well as the amount of USD 100,000 payable once a year before the start of the new season. Furthermore, the player X is entitled to a monthly payment of USD 21,666 as well as bonuses, lodging, a car, and 4 air tickets per year.

- As regards the aforementioned USD 200,000 payable upon the signing of the contract, it must be noted that the original text of the relevant clause appears to indicate the amount of USD 100,000 but has been amended by hand and now reads USD 200,000, which amendment was countersigned.
- On 27 July 2004 the Russian Football Union requested the issuance of an international registration transfer certificate (IRTC) from the Football Association of Serbia and Montenegro.
- On the same day, the relevant certificate was issued by the said Association on behalf of the Russian Football Union.
- On 3 August 2004, the player contacted the Russian Football Union claiming that FC Y did not respect its contractual obligations.
- On the same day, the player lodged his claim at FIFA.
- According to X, only after 3 to 4 days after having commenced his employment, the coach informed him, without any justification, that he would not be making use of the player's services. In addition, the coach allegedly forbade him to participate in and be present at the team's training.
- The player adds that he has received no written confirmation by the club of the above circumstances.
- X has indicated that he left Russia on 1 August 2004.
- The player wishes that FC Y be ordered to fulfil its contractual obligations.
- Should FC Y refuse to do so, the player claims the unilateral breach of contract by the club without just cause and he wishes to be able to transfer to another club without any compensation being payable.
- In addition, he claims compensation for breach of contract to the total amount of USD 1,079,976 equalling the full value of his employment contract (3 x USD 100,000 and 36 months x USD 21,666).
- As stated above, X's contract indicates that the amount of USD 200,000 is payable upon the signing of the contract, however, in accordance with the player's breakdown of his financial claim, X claims payment of three yearly fees amounting to USD 100,000 each. No reference is made by the player to an amount of USD 200,000.
- On 19 August 2004, the FIFA administration invited FC Y to present its response to the claim lodged by the player.
- In reply, the Russian Football Union maintains that the player in question never signed a contract with FC Y. Allegedly, X refused either to play for or sign a contract with FC Y claiming that the club was not at his level.
- The Russian Football Union further maintains that the player was not registered with the Union.
- The FIFA administration has received no reply from FC Y, either directly or via the Russian Football Union.

CONSIDERATIONS OF THE DISPUTE RESOLUTION CHAMBER

The members of the Dispute Resolution Chamber were summoned to pass a decision on this matter by the Chairman pursuant to Art. 1 point 6) of the Rules Governing the Practice and Procedures of the Dispute Resolution Chamber.

The members of the Chamber firstly proceeded to confirm that in accordance with Article 42 of the FIFA Regulations for the Status and Transfer of Players (edition September 2001) the Chamber is competent to deal with the present matter.

As established in Article 42 §1(b) of the Regulations, it falls within the competence of the Dispute Resolution Chamber to determine whether one of the parties has committed a unilateral breach of contract without just cause.

According to the player, the club failed to fulfil its contractual obligations 3 to 4 days after the commencement of his employment at the Russian club, when the coach informed him that he would not be making use of the player's services and that the player was not allowed to participate in the team's training. X demands that the club be ordered to fulfil its contractual obligations or, should it refuse to do so, that the club be sentenced for having committed a unilateral breach of contract without just cause. In addition, X asks that he be awarded an amount of compensation for breach of contract equalling the full value of his employment contract, i.e. until its date of expiry on 30 June 2007.

In the light of the position put forward by the Russian Football Union, denying the existence of a contractual relation between FC Y and the player X, the members agreed that the Chamber should analyse the document which has been presented by the player as the employment contract that was signed by and

between himself and the Russian club. After a thorough analysis, the members of the Chamber concluded that the document presented by Mr. X to this end indeed constitutes an employment contract containing the relevant main elements, such as parties involved, salary, period of validity, position of the player, as well as the parties' signature and the club's stamp.
In this context, the members of the Chamber stressed that the Russian Football Union has requested and received an IRTC from the association of the player's former club, which can be regarded as a clear indication that an employment relationship had been entered into by Mr. X and FC Y.
Taking into consideration the position conveyed to the FIFA administration by the Russian Football Union, in accordance with which FC Y manifestly denies the existence of a contractual relation between the player and the club in question, the Chamber agreed that the player's first request, i.e. to order the club to fulfil its contractual obligations, has become superfluous. Therefore, the Chamber decided to focus on the question as to whether FC Y has committed a breach of contract and, if yes, with or without just cause.
As stated above, the Chamber has concluded that a valid employment contract has been entered into by and between the parties involved in the case at hand. Furthermore, the Chamber deemed that the circumstance whether or not the player was registered with the Russian Football Union must be considered irrelevant, as the registration, in general, does not fall within the scope of a player's responsibilities and obligations. For these reasons, the members unanimously decided that the Chamber has to fully dismiss the arguments put forward in the club's defence.
Taking into account all of the above, the club is found to have committed a unilateral breach of the employment contract without just cause. Consequently, the player is entitled to receive compensation for breach of contract.
In the light of all of the above, articles 21§1(a), 22 and 23§2(a) of the FIFA Regulations for the status and transfer of players are applicable to the present matter.
As regards the award of financial compensation payable to the player in accordance with article 22, the Chamber took into consideration that the relevant employment contract does not contain any clause pertaining to compensation payable to either of the parties in the event of the early termination of the employment relationship. Furthermore, the members agreed that in the light of the fact that the player is free to sign on with the club of his choice, he is able to and has the obligation to mitigate damages. The members of the Chamber took into account that although the relevant employment contract indicates that the amount of USD 200,000 is payable to the player upon the signing of the contract, X has put forward a financial claim based, inter alia, on a fee of USD 100,000. Departing from the principle that the award shall not exceed the claimant's claim, the Chamber agreed that the amount of USD 100,000 shall be taken into consideration when determining the amount of compensation payable to the player. Considering that the breach occurred at the beginning of the contract, only a few days after the arrival of the player, and taking into account the remuneration that the player was due to receive under the terms of the employment contract, i.e. salary, signing-on fee and bonuses, the Chamber concluded that a compensation amounting to USD 200,000 is adequate.
As regards the player's wish to be able to transfer to another club without any compensation payable to FC Y, the Chamber draws the attention of X to article 20 of the FIFA Regulations for the Status and Transfer of Players, in accordance with which no training compensation shall be payable when a player over the age of 23 changes clubs.
The Chamber further considered that sports sanctions shall be applied in conformity with article 23§2(a) of the aforementioned Regulations. In accordance with the interpretation given by the CAS as body of appeal in a previous decision, the ban shall be set in at the point of time when the decision that a breach occurred has been reached and notified to the parties concerned.

DECISION OF THE DISPUTE RESOLUTION CHAMBER

1. The claim of the Claimant, X, is partially accepted.
2. The Respondent, FC Y, has to pay the amount of USD 200,000 to the Claimant.
3. The amount due to the Claimant has to be paid by the Respondent within 30 days as from the date of notification of this decision.
4. In the event that the debt of the Russian club is not paid within the stated deadline, an interest rate of 5% per year will apply as of expiry of the aforementioned deadline.
5. If the sum of USD 200,000 is not paid within the aforementioned deadline, the present matter shall

be submitted to the FIFA Disciplinary Committee, so that the necessary disciplinary sanctions may be imposed.

6. In accordance with article 23§2(a) of the Regulations, the sanction imposed on FC Y is a ban on registering any new player, either nationally or internationally, until the expiry of the second transfer window following the date of notification of the present decision.
7. According to art. 60 par. 1 of the FIFA Statutes, this decision may be appealed against before the Court of Arbitration for Sport (CAS). The statement of appeal must be sent to the CAS directly within 10 days of receipt of notification of this decision and shall contain all the elements in accordance with point 2 of the directives issued by the CAS, a copy of which we enclose hereto. Within another 10 days following the expiry of the time limit for filing the statement of appeal, the appellant shall file a brief stating the facts and legal arguments giving rise to the appeal with the CAS (cf. point 4 of the directives).

⚽⚽⚽

26 NOVEMBER 2004

114130
DECISION OF THE DISPUTE RESOLUTION CHAMBER
passed in Zurich, Switzerland, on 26 November 2004,
in the following composition:
Slim Aloulou (Tunisia), Chairman
Philippe Piat (France), member
Theo van Seggelen (the Netherlands), member
Jean-Marie Philips (Belgium), member
Mario Gallavotti (Italy), member
on the claim presented by
X, Brazil as Claimant
against
Y, France as Respondent
regarding the solidarity contribution related to the transfer of the federative rights to the player Z

FACTS OF THE CASE:

- In February 2004 the Brazilian club presented FIFA with a complaint against Y regarding payment of the solidarity contribution in respect of the transfer of the player Z.
- Born on 14 November 1974, the player was registered with X from October 1988 until February 1997, that is, for 8 ½ seasons between the ages of 13 and 22 years.
- This complaint was lodged after the transfer of the player Z from the Spanish Club D (hereafter: Club D) to Y in July 2002.
- Y FC affirms having paid an amount of EUR 7,397,000 in full to Club D, without reservation or restriction, for the federative rights of the player. The transfer agreement signed between these two clubs contains no reference to any solidarity contribution payment.
- The FIFA administration put forward a pragmatic solution, ordering Club D to pay the share of the solidarity contribution owed by Y on behalf of this club directly to X FC.
- However, the Spanish club has failed to respond to this injunction and has ignored every letter sent to it.
- Y FC claims it made a payment to Club D that was not due and demands that the Spanish club be compelled to refund the amount that was paid as a solidarity contribution for the federative rights of the player Z.
- The Dispute Resolution Chamber is required to decide on the liability of the different parties and to calculate the amount of the solidarity contribution that may be apportioned, based on a maximum of 5% of EUR 7,397,000, i.e., EUR 369,850.

CONSIDERATIONS OF THE DISPUTE RESOLUTION CHAMBER

The Dispute Resolution Chamber commenced its deliberations by referring to art. 25 of the FIFA Regulations for the Status and Transfer of Players (hereafter: the Regulations), according to which it falls within the purview of the Dispute Resolution Chamber to review disputes concerning the distribution of the solidarity contribution. Consequently, the Chamber established that it was competent to deal with the present litigation.

Subsequently, and entering into the substance of the matter, the members of the Chamber carefully studied the facts outlined above and emphasized that, as further established in the article 25 of the FIFA Regulations, the new club to which a player is transferred during the course of an employment contract with his previous club, is the club responsible for the distribution of 5% of the compensation to the former club(s) where the player has trained between the age of 12 and 23.

The Chamber pointed out that there has been an augmentation in the cases relating to the non-payment of the solidarity contribution as foreseen in the FIFA Regulations. This is owing to the fact that, as in the case at hand, the clubs acquiring the federative rights to players frequently omit to retain the 5% solidarity contribution payable to the clubs involved in the player's training and education. In such cases, the club that mistakenly paid 100% of the transfer fee agreed upon with the former club of the player often considers it is no longer liable regarding the solidarity contribution payment.

However, in this context, the Chamber emphasised that as provided for in art. 11 of the Regulations governing the Application of the FIFA Regulations, it is the task of the new club of the player to calculate the amount owed as a solidarity contribution to the clubs involved in the formation of the player and to distribute this amount in accordance with the player's career history. Moreover, par. 1 of the mentioned article clearly stipulates that the new club of the player must pay the amount due as solidarity contribution to the training clubs within 30 days of the player's registration.

In light of the above, the Chamber concluded that the respondent is responsible for paying the solidarity contribution to the club(s) involved in the formation of the player Z, even if it has mistakenly omitted to retain this contribution amount when it paid the federative rights of the player to his previous club. The fact that the respondent paid the entire amount agreed upon to Club D has no influence on the claim of X FC, given that the latter was not a party to the transfer agreement signed between Y and Club D.

The Chamber subsequently referred to Art. 10 of the Regulations governing the Application of the FIFA Regulations, which provides the figures for the distribution of the solidarity contribution, taking into consideration the time the player was effectively trained by the club concerned.

Considering that the player Z was registered with X FC from October 1988 until February 1997, that is, for 8 ½ seasons between the ages of 13 and 22 years, 85% of the 5% solidarity contribution shall be apportioned to this club.

As it was ascertained that the amount paid by the respondent to Club D for the federative rights of the player Z was EUR 7,397,000, 85% of the 5% solidarity contribution amounts to EUR 314,372.50.

To conclude, the Dispute Resolution Chamber ruled that the Club D shall be held to return the 5% solidarity contribution paid but not due over the sum received from Y FC for the federative rights of the player Z.

DECISION OF THE DISPUTE RESOLUTION CHAMBER

1. The claim of the claimant, X FC, is accepted.
2. The respondent, Y FC, shall pay the amount of **EUR 314,372.50** to the claimant, within 30 days of notification of the present decision.
3. If the respondent fails to comply with the above-mentioned deadline, an interest rate of 5% per year will apply and the case will immediately be presented to the FIFA Disciplinary Committee.
4. Club D is requested to return to Y FC the 5% solidarity contribution that was paid but not due regarding the federative rights of the player Z, within 30 days of notification of the present decision.
5. If Club D fails to comply with the above-mentioned deadline, an interest rate of 5% per year will apply and the case will immediately be presented to the FIFA Disciplinary Committee.
6. According to art. 60 par. 1 of the FIFA Statutes, this decision may be appealed against before the Court of Arbitration for Sport (CAS). The statement of appeal must be sent to the CAS directly within 10 days of receipt of notification of this decision and shall contain all the elements in accordance with point 2 of the directives issued by the CAS, a copy of which we enclose hereto. Within another 10 days following the expiry of the time limit for filing the statement of appeal, the appellant shall file a brief stating the facts and legal arguments giving rise to the appeal with the CAS (cf. point 4 of the directives).

114527
DECISION OF THE DISPUTE RESOLUTION CHAMBER
passed in Zurich, Switzerland, on 26 November 2004,
in the following composition:
Slim Aloulou (Tunisia), Chairman
Jean-Marie Philips (Belgium), member
Mario Gallavotti (Italy), member
Philippe Piat (France), member
Theo van Seggelen (Netherlands), member
on the claim presented by
the club, X, Germany, as Claimant
against
the club Y, Turkey, as Respondent
regarding training compensation in connection with the player Z,

FACTS OF THE CASE

- The player was born on 21 November 1983.
- Z was registered as a non-amateur player with X from 1 July 2002 until 28 August 2003.
- X is category 4 club.
- On 29 August 2003, the DFB issued an international registration transfer certificate on behalf of the Turkish Football Association for the player in question.
- The player was registered with Y as a non-amateur.
- Y is a category 3 club.
- X claims the amount of EUR 10,000 as compensation for the player's training.
- The Turkish club has not presented any response to the claim lodged by the German club.

CONSIDERATIONS OF THE DISPUTE RESOLUTION CHAMBER
As established in art. 42 §1 (b) (iv) of the FIFA Regulations for the Status and Transfer of Players, it falls within the purview of the Dispute Resolution Chamber to decide on disputes concerning the compensation for the training and education of young players and to adjust training compensation fees.
In the light of the above-mentioned facts, it is undisputed that the German club is entitled to receive training compensation in accordance with Chapter VII of the FIFA Regulations for the Status and Transfer of Players and Chapter III of the Regulations governing the Application of the Regulations for the Status and Transfer of Players as well as FIFA circular letter no. 826 dated 31 October 2002.
Training compensation is payable by the new club with which a player has signed a contract for training and education that he received from the age of 12 up to 21, payable until he reaches the age of 23.
It can be established that the player, Z, has been trained and developed by the German club X during one sportive season, during the 2002-2003 season, from the age of 18 up to 19.
Furthermore, the amount due by the Turkish club Y has to be calculated in accordance with the parameters provided by circular letter 826 dated 31 October 2002, i.e. with an amount corresponding to EUR 10,000 per year of training (corresponding to the club category 4 of X).
Therefore, X being a 4th category club, the amount of training compensation is obtained by multiplying the amount corresponding to the category of the training club for which the player was registered by the number of years of training from 12 to 21 (cf. art. 7.1 of the Application Regulations) based on the costs of 4th category clubs in Turkey.
Consequently, X is entitled to receive training compensation to the total amount of EUR 10,000 (1 year x EUR 10,000).

DECISION OF THE DISPUTE RESOLUTION CHAMBER

1. The claim of the Claimant, X, is accepted.
2. The Respondent, Y, has to pay the amount of EUR 10,000 to the Claimant.
3. The amount due to the Claimant has to be paid by the Respondent within 30 days as from the date of notification of this decision.
4. If the sum of EUR 10,000 is not paid within the aforementioned deadline, the present matter shall be submitted to the FIFA Disciplinary Committee, so that the necessary disciplinary sanctions may be imposed.

5. According to art. 60 par. 1 of the FIFA Statutes, this decision may be appealed against before the Court of Arbitration for Sport (CAS). The statement of appeal must be sent to the CAS directly within 10 days of receipt of notification of this decision and shall contain all the elements in accordance with point 2 of the directives issued by the CAS, a copy of which we enclose hereto. Within another 10 days following the expiry of the time limit for filing the statement of appeal, the appellant shall file a brief stating the facts and legal arguments giving rise to the appeal with the CAS (cf. point 4 of the directives).

⚽⚽⚽

114534
DECISION OF THE DISPUTE RESOLUTION CHAMBER
passed in Zurich, Switzerland, on 26 November 2004,
in the following composition:
Slim Aloulou (Tunisia), Chairman
Jean-Marie Philips (Belgium), member
Mario Gallavotti (Italy), member
Philippe Piat (France), member
Theo van Seggelen (Netherlands), member
on the claim presented by the player, X, Nigeria, as Claimant against the club Y, Vietnam, as Respondent regarding a contractual dispute between the player and the club,

FACTS OF THE CASE

- On 1 November 2003, the parties signed an employment contract valid from 1 November 2003 until 31 October 2005.
- According to this contract, the player is entitled to a monthly salary amounting to USD 1,200 payable in two instalments of USD 600 each on the 15th and 30th day of the month.
- In addition, X is entitled to bonuses, lodging and free medical treatments.
- In accordance with article 2.8, the club is entitled to unilaterally terminate the contract "after 15 days of notification of the contract termination in writing", for reasons of disciplinary nature or linked to a decrease in the player's performance, failing to meet the club's requirements.
- After the "ending" of the contract, the club has the obligation to provide the player with a return air ticket.
- On 1 April 2004, the player was notified in writing of the early termination by the club of his contract.
- According to the relevant document, the player's contract was terminated due to a decrease in the player's performance and his inability to meet the club's performance requirements.
- The player turned to FIFA claiming that after the contract termination the club had only given him USD 100 as compensation before he left for Nigeria.
- X asserts that he was paid his salary until (and including) March 2004 and he claims payment of his dues until the expiry date of his contract.
- According to the player, a total of 19 months' salary are to be paid by the Vietnamese club.
- The club, for its part, confirms that it terminated the player's contract for the cause mentioned in the written notification.
- Furthermore, the parties signed a document dated 7 April 2004 in accordance with which the player agreed to receive USD 670 to cover the expenses related to a return air ticket to be bought by X and to leave the city of Y as from 12 April 2004 "without any requirement to Y".
- According to the club, with the same letter the player agreed to receive USD 100 as an allowance.
- For the above reasons, the club rejects the player's claim.
- The player refutes the club's statement as regards the alleged decrease in his performance and stresses that he was lined up in all matches.
- He furthermore points out that he did not ask for the USD 100, but that the club simply gave it to him. He presumes that the club knew that the termination of the contract was not correct.
- No further comments have been received from the Vietnamese club.

CONSIDERATIONS OF THE DISPUTE RESOLUTION CHAMBER

The members of the Chamber firstly proceeded to confirm that in accordance with Article 42 of the FIFA Regulations for the Status and Transfer of Players the Chamber is competent to deal with the present matter.

It was duly noted that according to the player, he is entitled to receive compensation from the Vietnamese club for the early termination of the employment contract. The financial claim put forward by the player covers the value of his contract until the date of its expiry.

The club, for its part, maintains that it has proceeded with the early termination of the employment contract given that the player's performance no longer met the club's requirements. The members of the Chamber noted that according to article 2.8 of the relevant contract, the club has a unilateral right to terminate the contract for such reason. However, in the light of the fact that this clause does not include any compensation to the benefit of the other party in the event of the club exercising this option, the Chamber concluded that such cause cannot be considered valid.

Even so, the members of the Chamber acknowledged that the player has signed an agreement with the Vietnamese club after the termination of his contract, which refers to the termination of the contractual relation between the parties concerned. In accordance with this document, which was duly studied by the Chamber, X confirms that, after having received an amount of money to cover his expenses relating to the purchase of an air ticket, he would return to Nigeria "without any further requirement to Y". The members of the Chamber agreed that this document must be considered as a waiver duly signed by the player.

The player having signed the aforementioned waiver, the Chamber decided that it must reject the claim put forward by the player.

DECISION OF THE DISPUTE RESOLUTION CHAMBER

1. The claim of the Claimant, X, is rejected.
2. According to art. 60 par. 1 of the FIFA Statutes, this decision may be appealed against before the Court of Arbitration for Sport (CAS). The statement of appeal must be sent to the CAS directly within 10 days of receipt of notification of this decision and shall contain all the elements in accordance with point 2 of the directives issued by the CAS, a copy of which we enclose hereto. Within another 10 days following the expiry of the time limit for filing the statement of appeal, the appellant shall file a brief stating the facts and legal arguments giving rise to the appeal with the CAS (cf. point 4 of the directives).

⚽⚽⚽

114628

DECISION OF THE DISPUTE RESOLUTION CHAMBER

passed in Zurich, Switzerland, on 26 November 2004,
in the following composition:
Slim Aloulou (Tunisia), Chairman
Jean-Marie Philips (Belgium), member
Mario Gallavotti (Italy), member
Philippe Piat (France), member
Theo van Seggelen (Netherlands), member
on the claim presented by the player, X, Tunisia, as Claimant against Club Y, Libya, as Respondent and Counterclaimant
regarding a contractual dispute between the player and the club,

FACTS OF THE CASE

- On 14 July 2002 the player X and the club Y signed an employment contract for two sportive seasons.
- According to this contract, during the 2002/03 season the player is entitled to a fee of LYD 60,000 payable as follows:
  - LYD 10,000 on the date of signature of the contract
  - LYD 10,000 at the end of the first part of the championship (i.e. 18.01.03)
  - LYD 10,000 at the half of the second part of the championship (i.e. around 15.04.03)
  - Monthly salary of LYD 3,000, from which amount LYD 500 is payable in Libya and LYD 2,500 in Tunisia

- Moreover, the player is entitled to four air flight tickets Jamahiriya-Tunis-Jamahiriya during the sports season.
- The employment contract also specifies the conditions under which the player shall be entitled to receive bonuses or premiums.
- Article 14 of the employment contract stipulates that the contract is concluded for a period of 2 seasons and that at the end of the first season the parties shall find agreement on the revision of the value of the contract for the second season.
- According to article 16 of the employment contract any disputes between the parties shall fall under the competence of Libyan and Tunisian jurisdiction.
- On 5 November 2003 the player turned to FIFA claiming that after the end of the first season, the club acted in breach of the employment contract without just cause.
- That is, according to the player, after the end of the first season he returned to Tunisia for his holidays, where he has been awaiting a call or a letter from the club in respect of the (contractual) details for the second season (2003/04).
- X affirms that, the club having failed to contact the player, he returned to Libya on 15 August 2003 in order to join the club.
- According to X, he was then verbally informed by the club that it no longer wished to make use of his services.
- Furthermore, he affirms having received, on 21 August 2003, a written attestation issued by the club on the same day "to whom it may concern", by means of which the club confirms that the player is free to register with any other club outside of the Libyan territory. In addition, in the same attestation the club confirms that the document was issued at the player's request and in accordance with the agreement concluded between the parties involved. Finally, according to the same document, the parties have no financial obligations towards each other.
- The player affirms that he did not agree with the contents of this attestation and that he has tried to receive an explanation from the club while the club was on a training camp in Tunisia. In this respect, X submitted a document issued by a Tunisian notary public, by means of which the latter confirms that, on 27 August 2003, the club has refused to receive the player stating that negotiations with the player would take place in Libya.
- X affirms having tried to join the club in Libya a third time on 30 August 2003 in order to fulfil his contractual obligations, but the club again refused to receive him.
- The player asserts having put the club in default of its contractual obligations by registered mail in September 2003.
- X maintains that the contract has been validly concluded for a two years' period of time and could only be terminated by mutual consent or for reasons given by law.
- The player points out that according to the said article 14 the negotiations at the end of the first season would only relate to the revision of the value of the contract for the next season.
- According to the player and referring to the above-mentioned articles 14 and 16 of the employment contract, in accordance with Tunisian law, all conditions have been fulfilled in order to designate the termination of the contract by the club as abusive.
- The player is of the opinion that, in addition to the relevant clauses in the contract and to the FIFA Regulations, he may invoke Tunisian national law.
- He claims that in accordance with Tunisian law he would be entitled to receive compensation equalling the amount of salaries which would have been payable to the player until the expiry of the employment contract at the end of the 2003/04 season (LYD 60,000), plus an amount of money for damages as well as an amount of compensation for "moral prejudice" not less then LYD 30,000.
- The player further maintains that the club has also acted in breach of the relevant FIFA regulations.
- According to the player, he is entitled to submit the present claim to the competent deciding body of FIFA.
- In the light of the above, on the basis of articles 21, 23.2 and 42 of the FIFA regulations for the status and transfer of players, the player claims payment of compensation for breach of contract to the amount of LYD 60,000 (salaries for the 2003/04 season) and compensation for moral damages to the amount of LYD 30,000.
- On 17 December 2003, the player signed an employment contract with a Tunisian club valid until 30 June 2004.

- The club, for its part, maintains that it was agreed between the parties to revise the contract value for the second season at the end of the first sport season. The club is of the opinion that according to article 14, the contract will not be renewed for the second season unless the parties find agreement.
- Furthermore, the club asserts that according to Libyan labour law, contracts concluded for a pre-determined period of time ("duration-limited") automatically expire at the end of the same period of time.
- Finally, the club points out that the employment contract has been terminated at the player's request.
- The Libyan club submitted a copy of a power of attorney, which was signed by the player, apparently in early July 2002, by means of which X authorised Z to act on his behalf in all administrative, legal and financial procedures in Libya during the 2002/03 season.
- Y submitted a copy of a undated addendum to article 9 of the employment contract (which article deals with a financial penalty in the event of a decrease in the player's performance resulting in his non-selection for a match), which specifies under which conditions the club would be entitled to, inter alia, terminate the contract in the event of a continuous decrease in the player's technical and physical performance. This document was signed by the club and the aforementioned Y.
- The club maintains that as early as in May 2003, the player was informed of the decrease in his performances and that the club had decided not to make use of his services for the second season. In this respect, a document signed by the aforementioned Z has been presented by the club.
- However, according to the club, it made an offer to the player, with which he was allegedly not satisfied. Therefore, he allegedly asked the club to end his employment relationship with the club.
- On 23 August 2003 the Libyan club issued a document "to whom it may concern" in which the club states that the player refused to accept the club's offer pertaining to the revision of the contract for the second season corresponding to his performance and that he has been released as from 21 August 2003. This document was signed by the aforementioned Z as the player's attorney.
- Another document dated 27 August 2003 was issued by the club pertaining to the release of the player in question indicating that the player and the club have no administrative or financial claims towards each other. This document was signed by the said Z as the "legal attorney" of the player.
- In the light of the above, the club rejects the claim put forward by the player.
- Referring to article 11 of the relevant employment contract, the club asks that the player pays back all monies that he received from the club in addition to an amount of money as compensation.
- The player asserts that he has been one of the better players of the team throughout the season and to corroborate this fact, he submitted a written statement by the coach, A.
- As regards the aforementioned Z, the player points out that the relevant power of attorney is limited in time, i.e. until the end of the 2002/03 season, and that it has become void as from the moment that the player signed the relevant employment contract with the club, i.e. since 2002. Consequently, according to the player, all documents signed by this Z after the year 2002 must be considered null and void and do not bind the player. The player also points out that he has had no knowledge of the contacts between Z and the Libyan club.
- The player insists that according to article 9 of the employment contract a decrease in his performance would lead to certain consequences, which apparently have not been applied by the club. Furthermore, taking into consideration the contractual clauses, a decrease in the player's performance can be no motive for the rescission of the contract.

CONSIDERATIONS OF THE DISPUTE RESOLUTION CHAMBER

Taking into account article 16 of the relevant employment contract, the members of the Chamber deemed that, firstly, the question as to whether the Chamber has jurisdiction in the present matter must be answered. In this regard, the members of the Chamber agreed that in the absence of a national sports arbitration tribunal composed of members chosen in equal numbers by players and clubs as well as an independent chairman (cf. Article 42 of the aforementioned Regulations), the Dispute Resolution Chamber of the FIFA Players' Status Committee is competent to deal with a dispute, even if written agreements signed between the parties involved in the dispute contain a clause by means of which the jurisdiction of another body is chosen.

Consequently, the members of the Chamber proceeded to confirm that in accordance with Article 42 of the FIFA Regulations for the Status and Transfer of Players the Chamber is competent to deal with the present matter.

It was duly noted that according to the player, the club has acted in breach of the employment contract given that the club has failed to respect the terms of the contract pertaining to the second sportive season. That is, X maintains that after the end of the first sportive season the club verbally informed him that it was no longer interested in making use of his services. Thereafter, on 21 August 2003, the club issued a written attestation confirming that the player was free to sign on with another club outside of the Libyan territory and that the parties do not have any mutual claims. X contests the contents of this document and he has tried to receive an explanation from the club, allegedly in vain. In September 2003, the player put the club in default of the execution of its obligations and he claims compensation for the alleged abusive termination of the employment contract.

Y, for its part, refutes the player's claim asserting that the player was informed in writing as early as in May 2003 of the fact that the club would consider X free from any obligations as from the end of the 2002/03 season. Furthermore, on 23 August 2003, the club issued another document stating, inter alia, that the player was released as from 21 August 2003. These two documents were signed by the player's representative, Z. In addition, according to the Libyan club, the parties agreed to revise the contract value for the second season at the end of the first sporting season. In accordance with the club's interpretation of article 14, the employment contract would not be renewed for the second season unless the parties find agreement.

Y has lodged a counter-claim, in accordance with which the Libyan club asks that the player be obliged to pay back all monies that he received from the club in addition to an amount of money as compensation. In this respect, the club refers to article 11 of the employment contract.

With respect to the counter-claim lodged by the Libyan club, the members of the Chamber duly studied article 11 of the employment contract, in accordance with which the player is obliged to reimburse certain monies to the club in the event of the player having infringed upon the terms of the contract. In the light of the fact that this clause is not mutual, i.e. the club being obliged to compensate the player in the event of the club acting in breach of the contract, the Chamber concluded that such cause cannot be considered valid. Consequently, the Chamber decided to reject the counter-claim lodged by the club, Y.

The Chamber turned to the question as to whether the relevant employment contract can be considered valid for a two years' period of time. That is, the Chamber acknowledged that the employment contract contains all elements required in order for it to be binding on the parties for the first season (e.g. salary, contract duration, parties, etc.). However, the same contract does not include any salary for the subsequent season. The members agreed that the inclusion of the player's salary, payable in compensation for the services rendered, in the contract is a prerequisite in order for the contract to be considered valid and binding upon the parties involved for the specific period of time. Taking into consideration the wording of article 14, the members of the Chamber unanimously agreed that the relevant employment contract must be considered valid and binding upon the parties for the period of one year, with the option for both parties to extend it on condition that a mutual agreement be found. From the above, it can be noted that the Libyan club did not wish to prolong the contractual relation with X. Consequently, the Chamber concurred that the contractual relationship between the parties involved ended at the conclusion of the first sports season.

As regards X's position with respect to above-mentioned Z, the Chamber took note that Z had in fact been authorised by the player to act on his behalf during the 2002/03 sports season. X does not refute having authorised this person to represent him, but according to the player, Z's representation ended after he signed his contract with the Libyan club in 2002. After careful study of the relevant power of attorney, the Chamber decided to reject X's argument in this respect, since the power of attorney does not include any such limitation in time or any other precision in this regard. The player has pointed out that he had no knowledge of the contacts between Z and the Libyan club. In this regard, the Chamber agreed that the Libyan club cannot be held liable for the apparent miscommunication between the player and his representative.

In the light of the above, the Chamber decided to reject the claim lodged by the player, X.

DECISION OF THE DISPUTE RESOLUTION CHAMBER

1. The claim of the Claimant, X, is rejected.
2. The counter-claim of Club Y, is rejected.
3. According to art. 60 par. 1 of the FIFA Statutes, this decision may be appealed against before the Court of Arbitration for Sport (CAS). The statement of appeal must be sent to the CAS directly within 10 days of receipt of notification of this decision and shall contain all the elements in accordance

with point 2 of the directives issued by the CAS, a copy of which we enclose hereto. Within another 10 days following the expiry of the time limit for filing the statement of appeal, the appellant shall file a brief stating the facts and legal arguments giving rise to the appeal with the CAS (cf. point 4 of the directives).

⚽⚽⚽

114635
DECISION OF THE DISPUTE RESOLUTION CHAMBER
passed in Zurich, Switzerland, on 26 November 2004,
in the following composition:
Slim Aloulou (Tunisia), Chairman
Philippe Piat (France), member
Theo van Seggelen (the Netherlands), member
Jean-Marie Philips (Belgium), member
Mario Gallavotti (Italy), member
on the claim presented by
Player X, Cameroon as Claimant
against
Y, Romania as Respondent
regarding a contractual dispute between the parties involved

FACTS OF THE CASE:

- An employment contract was signed between the parties on 07.08.2003, with validity for three years.
- In the month of October 2003 the player was summoned for a tournament by his national team and was allowed to comply with this summons by his club.
- However, upon his return, he encountered problems with his entry visa and was obliged to delay his arrival until 14 November 2003, despite the fact that the tournament for which he had been summoned had already ended on 19 October 2003.
- According to the claimant, ever since his late return from his national team duties, the respondent has stopped paying his salaries and has prevented him from participating in any of the training sessions with the team.
- The claimant therefore contacted FIFA on 26 November 2003, complaining that he was being prevented from playing and he was the only player of the team who had not received the salary for the month of October 2003.
- The club denies all allegations of the player, affirming having paid him USD 15,000 in total between the months of August and October 2003 and having allowed him to train at all times with the rest of the team. The club has submitted copies of documents in order to prove the payment of this amount.
- Of all the payment slips provided by the club, only part of them have been countersigned by the player, and only part of them have been confirmed by the player as having actually been paid to him.
- The claimant confirms having received only USD 8,015 of the USD 20,000 signing-on fee for the 2003/2004 season, leaving an amount of USD 11,985 due.
- Mr. X furthermore claims all of his salaries from October 2003 onwards as well as USD 10,000 corresponding to the advanced payment that was due upon registration of the contract at the professional league, and legal expenses.
- In the meantime, a transfer agreement has been signed between Y and FC A of Switzerland, according to which the player would be loaned as an amateur to FC A between 15.10.2004 and 30.06.2005, free of charge.
- The loan contract has also been signed by Mr. X , who consented to his transfer to FC A and is currently still registered with that club.
- However, the player underlines that he does not wish to return to his Romanian club at the end of the loan period and asks the Dispute Resolution Chamber to declare the termination of his employment

contract with immediate effect, due to the club's breach of contract through non-payment of the player's dues.

CONSIDERATIONS OF THE DISPUTE RESOLUTION CHAMBER

The Dispute Resolution Chamber of the FIFA Players' Status Committee shall review disputes coming under its jurisdiction pursuant to Art. 42 of the FIFA Regulations for the Status and Transfer of Players (hereafter: FIFA Regulations) at the request of one of the parties to the dispute.

According to Art. 42 of the FIFA Regulations for the Status and Transfer of Players, the triggering elements of the dispute (i.e. whether a contract was breached, with or without just cause, or sporting just cause), will be decided by the Dispute Resolution Chamber of the FIFA Players' Status Committee.

Consequently, the Dispute Resolution Chamber is the competent body to decide on the present litigation concerning the alleged breach of contract between the claimant and the respondent.

Subsequently, and entering into the substance of the matter, the Chamber began its deliberations by analyzing the defence of the respondent.

To begin with, the members pointed out that essentially the dispute revolves around the exclusion of the player from training sessions as well as the non-payment of his dues, presumably as a result of his late return from a national team convocation.

The defence of the respondent is primarily based on a denial of all allegations of the claimant and a strong affirmation that all dues have been paid to him, more precisely, a global amount of USD 15,000.

In continuation, the members of the Dispute Resolution Chamber acknowledged that the player, having returned late from his national team duties, might in theory have provoked the imposition of certain sanctions in accordance with the applicable disciplinary rules and regulations of the club and/or the national association concerned.

Even so, such a late return is still no justification for the non-payment of the player's salaries without a final and binding decision to this effect by a deciding body with competence to impose such disciplinary sanctions. Such decision would also have to be proportionate to the offence committed. In the case at hand, the Chamber noted, neither of these prerequisites have been met.

What's more, upon analysis of the payment proofs presented by the club, it became evident that these referred to payments that had allegedly been made to Mr. X throughout the months of August, September, and October 2003, whereas the timeframe for which the player is claiming remuneration regards only the months from October 2003 onwards. Therefore, the Chamber felt that none of the player's financial claims could be considered to have been disproved, except possibly the salary for the month of October 2003. This amounts to a breach of contract as a result of the non-payment of the player's dues.

Hence, the respondent shall pay the claimant all of the remuneration due between the period of November 2003 until the end of the season in which this breach of contract occurred, including the payments due under point G(5) of the employment contract.

In accordance with its established jurisprudence, the Chamber rejected the claims for the legal fees incurred by the player.

In view of the foregoing, the total compensation due to the claimant equals the full nine (9) months of salaries (at ROL 2,500,000 per month) from November 2003 until and including July 2004, plus the remaining USD 11,985 and the USD 10,000 still due in conformity with art. G(5) of the contract.

The totality of the compensation that shall be paid by the respondent is therefore equal to ROL 22,500,000 in concept of salaries, and USD 21,985 in accordance with art. G(5).

Finally, and as a result of the breach of contract through fault of the club, the Chamber accepted the player's request for the immediate termination of the employment contract.

The player's registration with the Swiss club A F.C. shall therefore be deemed to have been concluded on a definite basis and not on a loan.

Mr. X shall be free to sign with the club of his choice once his registration with A F.C. expires, and will not be under any obligation whatsoever to return to Y thereafter.

DECISION OF THE DISPUTE RESOLUTION CHAMBER

1. The claim lodged by the Claimant is accepted.
2. The Respondent shall pay the amount of ROL 22,500,000 as well as USD 21,985 to the Claimant, within 30 days following the date of the communication of the present decision.
3. In the event that the debts of the Respondent are not paid within the stated deadline, an interest rate of 5% per year will apply.

4. According to art. 60 par. 1 of the FIFA Statutes, this decision may be appealed against before the Court of Arbitration for Sport (CAS). The statement of appeal must be sent to the CAS directly within 10 days of receipt of notification of this decision and shall contain all the elements in accordance with point 2 of the directives issued by the CAS, a copy of which we enclose hereto. Within another 10 days following the expiry of the time limit for filing the statement of appeal, the appellant shall file a brief stating the facts and legal arguments giving rise to the appeal with the CAS (cf. point 4 of the directives).

114667-26
DECISION OF THE DISPUTE RESOLUTION CHAMBER
passed in Zurich, Switzerland, on 26 November 2004,
in the following composition:
Slim Aloulou (Tunisia), Chairman
Philippe Piat (France), member
Theo Van Seggelen (Netherlands), member
Jean-Marie Philips (Belgium), member
Mario Gallavotti (Italy), member
on the claim presented by the Club X, France as Claimant against the Player, France as Respondent and the Club Y, England as Intervener
regarding the transfer of the player and the breach of an employment contract

FACTS OF THE CASE:

- The French player signed a youth player's contract (original French denomination: "contrat de joueur aspirant") with the French club X for the period from 1 July 2003 to 30 June 2004.
- The two parties also concluded a training agreement (original French denomination: "convention de formation") for the period from 1 July 2003 to 30 June 2006.
- At the beginning of August 2004, after the youth player's contract had expired, the player signed a professional employment contract with the English club Y.
- On 13 August 2004, The Football Association contacted the French Football Federation to request an International Registration Transfer Certificate (IRTC) for the player.
- The French Football Federation did not issue the IRTC as a result of opposition from the club X.
- On 19 August 2004, The Football Association requested that FIFA order the French Football Federation to issue the IRTC for the player in question.
- On 2 September 2004, the FIFA administration instructed the French Football Federation to immediately issue the IRTC for the player to The Football Association, on the understanding that the training agreement valid until 30 June 2006 did not constitute an employment contract and therefore, did not prevent the player from signing an employment contract with another club of his choice. In the same letter, the FIFA administration authorised The Football Association to register the player until it received the official IRTC from the French Football Federation.
- On 14 September 2004, the club X lodged an appeal with the Court of Arbitration for Sport (CAS) against the authorisation issued by the FIFA administration for the player to be registered with The Football Association. As part of this appeal, the club X, also applied for the stay of execution of the challenged decision.
- On 6 October 2004, the CAS accepted the aforementioned application and suspended the registration of the player in question for the club Y until the Dispute Resolution Chamber had passed a final decision on the case.
- The club X is now asking the Dispute Resolution Chamber:
  - to confirm the existence of contractual ties between the club X and the player;
  - to rule that the player is obliged to sign an employment contract with the club X
  - to order the suspension of the player from all professional football activities, with immediate effect, until he returns to the club X.
- In the opinion of the French club, the player is tied to the club X until 30 June 2006 on account of the training agreement. In its request the club X admits, however, that the training agreement is

independent from any employment contract possibly signed between the player and the club, and it does not have the status of an employment contract.

- Furthermore, the club X explains that the training agreement foresees the possibility of early unilateral termination. However, the French club maintains that the formal conditions for such termination were never fulfilled by the player.
- Moreover, the club X emphasises that the youth player's contract constituted a commitment for the parties to respect the norms regarding the status of youth players' provided for in the French Professional Football Charter (hereinafter: the Charter).
- The French club is of the opinion that, in line with art. 43 of the FIFA Regulations for the Status and Transfer of Players, the Charter must be respected by the Dispute Resolution Chamber also when judging over international transfers.
- Art. 261 of the Charter reads as follows (English translation by the Chamber):
  "Upon normal expiration of apprentice and youth player's contracts, the club has the right to insist that the other party signs a new trainee player or elite playercontract depending on the age of the player.
  ...
  By no later than 30 April, the club must inform the player of its intentions by a registered letter that requires acknowledgement of receipt ... .
  ...
  2. If the player refuses to sign a conract as a trainee player or an elite player ..., he shall not be permitted to sign for another club in the French professional league for a period of three years ... .
  ..."
- The club X maintains that on 1 March 2004 it notified the player of its intention to complete a new trainee contract with him. The club stresses that the player never expressed any opposition to signing the contract in line with its demand.
- The player claims, however, that already in March 2004 he informed the club X of his intention to not accept a further contract from the French club since he was not happy anymore with the way the club treated him. Furthermore, he had come to learn that some of his colleagues had been offered much better contractual conditions.
- The player and the club Y ask the Dispute Resolution Chamber to annul the suspension of the player's registration for the English club.
- The club Y has no objections to paying training compensation for the player in question.
- The English club and the player maintain that the training agreement cannot be viewed as an employment contract, but merely as an agreement that applies in conjunction with an employment contract.
- In the opinion of the player and the club Y, there are no contractual ties between the player and the French club anymore. In particular, they emphasise that the youth player's contract between the player and the club X expired on 30 June 2004.
- Furthermore, in view of art. 261 point 2 of the Charter, the club Y and the player are of the opinion that the Charter only prevents the player from being transferred within France and it does not impose any restriction on transfers at international level.
- On 9 November 2004, the case was submitted for consideration to the Dispute Resolution Chamber, which passed the following decision:
  - the French club and the player are invited to start negotiations in order to amicably settle the present dispute;
  - in case that no amicable agreement can be found, the club X should inform the Dispute Resolution Chamber, by 25 November at the latest, of the damage it assumes having suffered from the alleged breach of the training agreement by the player. Within the same deadline, the player in question should indicate to the Dispute Resolution Chamber the amount he deems to be appropriate in order to compensate the club X for the alleged breach of the training agreement.
- Following the above-mentioned decision, the two clubs and the player involved started negotiations towards a possible amicable settlement. The positions of the opponents were, however, too divergent and no agreement could be found.
- The English club was prepared to immediately pay compensation in the amount of EUR 100,000 to cover any compensation due from the club for the player's training as well as for the player's alleged breach of the regulations.

- The player is of the opinion that the club X is not entitled to any compensation from him personally.
- The French club maintains that, if the player in question agrees to immediately return to the club X, it is entitled to compensation for the damage suffered due to the absence of the player since 1 June 2004, and it claims the amount of at least EUR 1,000,000.
- In the event that the player would not return to the club X, the French club considers that it would, obviously, suffer a much higher damage. Apart from the training compensation of EUR 300,000, calculated on the basis of the general rules currently in force for a player that has been trained by the club since the age of 11, the fact that the player concerned breached the contract and in particular, the general principle of maintenance of contractual stability stipulated in art. 21 of the FIFA Regulations for the Status and Transfer of Players, should also be taken into account. Furthermore, it should be noted that the club Y did not respect art. 13 of the FIFA Regulations for the Status and Transfer of Players, since it did not contact the club X in order to inform the French club of its interest in the player.
- With regard to the amount of the demanded compensation, the French club refers to the transfer of two of its players to anther club for the amount of EUR 4,000,000. In this respect, it emphasises that, after conclusion of the relevant transfer agreement, the players had continued to play for the club X during two seasons and that in case of a future transfer of the players, the French club will participate to the relevant compensation.
- Finally, the club X deems that sportive sanctions should be imposed on the player and the club Y for having induced the player to breach the contract with the French club, in accordance with art. 23 of the FIFA Regulations for the Status and Transfer of Players.

CONSIDERATIONS OF THE DISPUTE RESOLUTION CHAMBER

The members of the Dispute Resolution Chamber were summoned to pass a decision on this matter by the Chairman pursuant to art. 1 point 6) of the Rules Governing the Practice and Procedures of the Dispute Resolution Chamber.

The deciding body started its deliberations by recalling that, as already stated by the Chamber on the occasion of its meeting on 9 November 2004, when it first dealt with the case at hand, as a general rule, the FIFA bodies are competent to deal with disputes related to the transfer of a player exclusively when there is an international impact. The principle question, which the present procedure has to answer is whether the player is authorised to be registered with the English club or whether he has to remain registered with the French club. As a consequence, the existence of an international impact cannot be disputed.

In order to be in a position to properly judge the aforementioned main issue, as a preliminary question, it is essential to examine the relation between the player and the club X. In fact, the question whether the player has a legitimate right to register for a new club of his choice is inevitably linked to the existence or not of contractual ties between the French club and the player.

In this respect, the Chamber indicated that, as established in art. 42 par. 1 lit. (b) (i) of the FIFA Regulations for the Status and Transfer of Players (hereinafter: the Regulations), it falls within the purview of the Dispute Resolution Chamber (DRC) to determine whether one of the parties has committed an unilateral breach of contract without just cause. In the case that the employment contract was breached by a party, the DRC is responsible to verify whether this party is accountable for outstanding payments and compensation. Furthermore, the DRC will establish the amount of compensation to be paid and decide whether sports sanctions must be imposed (cf. art. 42 par. 1 (b) (ii) and (iii) in connection with art. 22 and 23 of the Regulations and art. 3 point 2) of the Rules Governing the Practice and Procedures of the Dispute Resolution Chamber).

In view of the above, the DRC concluded that, fundamentally, it was competent to decide on the present case.

The members present at the meeting then analysed the legal nature of the training agreement concluded between the player and the club X. In this respect, they acknowledged that the French club had admitted that the training agreement is independent from any employment contract possibly signed between the player and the club, and that therefore it does not have the status and the binding effect of an employment contract. Furthermore, the DRC noted that such point of view is clearly confirmed by the French national legislation. In fact, art. 15-4 of the French "Loi du 16 juillet 1984", reviewed by the "Loi no. 99-1124 du 28 décembre 1999", provides that the integration of a player into a formation centre is subject to the conclusion of a training agreement. Such agreement shall specify the duration, the standards and the modalities of the formation period. Furthermore, it foresees that at the end of the formation period an athlete, who intends to practice his sport on a professional level, might be obliged to sign an employment contract with the sportive association, which offered him the formation. The legislation makes thus a clear distinction between the training agreement and an employment contract. Moreover, the standard training agreement agreed upon by the French employers' (clubs) and the employees' (players) representatives states in its art. 9 that in case the beneficiary of the formation (i.e. the player) receives remuneration in exchange for his activity as football player, the financial conditions must be set out in a separate employment contract. Finally, art. 458 of the Charter indicates that also amateur players, who, per definitionem, are not bound to the club by means of an employment contract, may conclude a training agreement.

On account of all the above, the DRC concluded that, undoubtedly, the training agreement does not constitute an employment contract but rather an instrument meant to safeguard and protect the rights of a player in formation. Yet, the Chamber emphasised that its jurisdiction is limited to the consideration of disputes arising on the basis of an employment contract concluded between a player and a club affiliated to an association. As a result, the DRC judged that it was not competent to decide on the consequences of a possible breach of the training agreement, and/or of the non-respect of the formal prerequisites for an early termination of the relevant agreement concluded between the player and the club X for the period from 1 July 2003 to 30 June 2006. That aspect does therefore only affect the French authorities.

In continuation, the deciding body examined whether, apart from the training agreement, other contractual ties possibly existed, which would have bound the player to the French club.

To this regard, at first, the DRC acknowledged that, incontestably, the youth player's contract concluded between the player and the club had come to its natural termination on 30 June 2004. However, it would be necessary to evaluate whether the contents of the relevant contract would have obliged the player to conclude a new contract with X, as it is claimed by the French club.

The deciding body took note of the fact that, by means of the youth player's contract in question, the player had committed himself, in particular, to respect, the provisions regarding the status of youth player's (joueurs aspirants) included in the Charter. According to the first paragraph of the introduction to art. 261 of the Charter, the club has the right to insist that the player signs a new trainee or elite contract, depending on the age of the player, upon normal expiration of the youth player's contract. In case the club intends to make use of that right, it has to inform the player accordingly by means of a registered letter by no later than 30 April prior to the termination of the youth player's contract (third paragraph of the introduction to art. 261 of the Charter). Finally, point 2 of the relevant provision establishes the consequences of the player's refusal to sign a new trainee or elite contract. In such a case, he shall not be permitted to sign for another club in the French professional league for a period of three years.

The DRC agreed that, as claimed by the club X, on the grounds of art. 43 of the Regulations, the Chamber has to take into account the contents of the Charter, provided the relevant provisions are applicable to the case at hand. On the basis of that general consideration, the deciding body evaluated the effect of the reference to the Charter contained in the youth player's contract on the contractual relation between the player and the club X. In this respect, the Chamber was of the unanimous opinion that, by means of the express and unambiguous reference to the Charter, the provisions of the said regulations had become an integral part of the youth player's contract signed by the player and the French club. Consequently, the DRC would have to duly consider the provisions of the Charter, and in particular, its art. 261.

The deciding body acknowledged that the player does not contest the allegation of the French club, that it notified the player in question of its intention to offer him a new trainee contract on 1 March 2004. Moreover, the player maintains that it had informed the club X that he would not accept a further contract in March 2004. In view of these facts, the DRC concluded that the French club had duly fulfilled the formal prerequisites in accordance with the third paragraph of the introduction to art. 261 of the Charter.

In continuation, the Chamber emphasised that the Charter clearly provides for the player's obligation to sign a new trainee contract upon normal expiration of the youth player's contract, provided the club offering him the formation requires him to do so.

As described above, it is established that, within the pertinent deadline, the club X notified the player of its intention to offer him a new trainee contract after normal expiration of the youth player's contract. Equally, it is uncontested, that the player refused the offer and preferred to sign a non-amateur contract with the club Y. The DRC concluded thus that the player did not respect his commitments deriving from the relevant provision of the Charter in connection with the youth player's contract he had concluded with the club X.

The members present at the meeting continued by examining what consequences such conclusion needs to have on the player. In this respect, the deciding body stressed the fact that, on the one hand, art. 261 point 2 of the Charter explicitly foresees the consequence of such a particular disrespect of the Charter and in particular, of the players' duties linked to the status of youth player's. According to the relevant provision, the sanction to be imposed on the player is the interdiction for him to sign for another club in the French professional league for a period of three years. On the other hand, the DRC recalled that the Regulations also provide for a sanctioning system to be applied in case of breach of an employment contract.

The Chamber pointed out that, in casu, the breach of contract committed by the player concerns a particularity of the French sportive legislation. In fact, the Regulations do not provide for an obligations for players to sign a new contract with the club that offered them formation after normal expiry of the prior employment contract. In view of this fact, and considering that the regulations at the basis of the breach, i.e. the Charter, contain a clear sanction for a player's misbehaviour in that specific point (refusal to sign a new trainee contract after normal termination of the youth player's contract), the DRC was of the opinion that there are no reasons, which would justify the application of other norms than those of the Charter when establishing the sanction to be imposed on the player. Yet, as already mentioned, art. 261 point 2 of the Charter limits the sanction to the interdiction for the player to sign for another club in the French professional league for a period of three years.

In particular, it does thus not prevent the player from signing a contract with a new club affiliated to another association than the French Football Federation.

Moreover, the members present at the meeting emphasised that the system drawn up in the Charter obliges the player to sign a new contract after normal termination of the youth player's contract, provided the relevant club offers him one. However, the obligation cannot be qualified as an absolute one. In fact, the Charter explicitly foresees a specific sanction to be imposed on a player refusing to sign the contract for the period after the conclusion of the youth player's contract, but does not stipulate that the player will in any case have to remain with the club that offered him the formation. In other words, despite the general obligation imposed on the players, the Charter leaves them the possibility to refuse the proposed new contract in application of a clearly defined sanction.

For the sake of good order, the DRC stated that a more restrictive line, e.g. an absolute obligation for the player to remain with the club that offered him the formation, would, in all probability, anyway be in conflict with general labour law principles. In this respect, the deciding body took note that on the basis of an opinion formulated by the "Comité National Olympique et Sportif Français" within the scope of a conciliation procedure in a dispute between a French football player and a French club, already the current system provided for by the Charter appears to be questionable with regard to its legality. In particular, the relevant body emphasised the principle that a provision contained in a collective bargaining agreement may not be less favourable to the employee than what is foreseen by the national law. Yet, the deciding body stated that with regard to the present matter, that question may remain open.

On account of all the above, the DRC concluded that, on the basis of the applicable norms, no contractual ties exist anymore between the player and the club X. The Chamber decided that the player in question is thus not obliged to sign a new trainee or employment contract with and to return at the French club. Furthermore, the player cannot be prevented from moving to a club affiliated to an association other than the French Football Federation, since the direct consequences of art. 261 point 2 of the Charter only apply within the territory of the said federation. Finally, no sports sanctions may be applied neither on the player nor on the club Y.

Having come to this conclusion, the deciding body granted the player the authorisation to be registered with the English club and thus confirmed the provisional decision taken by the FIFA administration on 2 September 2004.

In this respect, the DRC took the opportunity to clarify that the decisions of the FIFA administration regarding the registration of a player are provisional and not final ones. As a consequence, they do not fall under art. 60 par. 1 of the FIFA Statutes. Furthermore, the deciding body deemed it appropriate to emphasise that the relevant decisions do not prejudice any further pronouncement that the competent decision-making bodies of FIFA may pass at a later stage in the pertinent affair. In continuation, the DRC recalled that the provisional decisions are limited to and exclusively deal with the registration issue. Therefore, they do neither touch nor affect the economical rights of the parties involved, who are entitled to ask for compensation in the proceedings pending in front of the DRC. In fact, only the DRC is entitled to deal with the substance of a contractual dispute between a player and a club with international impact. According to art. 17 of the Regulations, when a player signs his first contract as non-amateur, or when a player moves as a non-amateur at the end of his contract but before reaching the age of 23, training compensation shall be paid by the player's new club to the club(s) involved in the training and education of the player.

At the time of the conclusion of the employment contract with the club Y, the player was 18 years old and at the end of his youth player's contract with the club X. The DRC established that, under these circumstances, training compensation is due. However, since, as previously established, no contractual ties related to labour law existed anymore between the player in question and the French club, no further compensation will have to be paid neither by the player, nor by the club Y (cf. art. 17 of the Regulations).

With regard to the amount of compensation, the Chamber referred to the FIFA circular no. 826 dated 31 October 2002, which provides for the indicative amounts of compensation to be paid. The relevant figures are subject to review by the DRC. A club is thus entitled to object to the amount of training compensation calculated on the basis of the indicative amounts mentioned in the said circular and to prove that such compensation is clearly disproportionate. Obviously, the burden of proof has to be born by the objecting club. In the absence of sufficient evidence the indicative amounts apply. In this respect, the deciding body stressed in particular, that a club claiming that, in a specific case, the indicative amounts are disproportionate, has to prove that the effective costs incurred by the club for the formation and the education of the player concerned were higher (or lower) than the ones calculated on the basis of the figures mentioned in the circular no. 826. Only concrete evidentiary documents, such as invoices, costs of training centres, budget etc. may used as justification for a possible adjustment. In fact, exclusively economic factors may be taken into account.

The DRC took note that, in its final submissions, the French club referred to the transfer of two of its players to another club and indicated that those players had left the club after having made use of the club's formation facilities for several years. The club X is of the opinion that the position of these players is comparable to the one of the player concerned in the present case. On these grounds, the club deems that compensation of at least EUR 4,000,000 would be reasonable for the transfer of the player. Yet, despite having had the opportunity to do so, the French club did not present any documentary evidence related to economic factors, which would justify such a considerable divergence from the indicative amounts. Consequently, the Chamber decided that there are no reasons for an adjustment of the indicative amounts mentioned in the circular no. 826.

According to the indications contained in the youth player's contract, which was formally accepted by the French Football Federation on 22 July 2003, the player was registered with the club X from the 1997/1998 season. He left the club in summer 2004 and was thus registered with the French club between the ages of 11 and 18. By means of his transfer to the club Y the player moves from a first category club in France to a first category club in England. On the basis of the applicable provisions, i.e. art. 7 of the Regulations governing the Application of the FIFA Regulations for the Status and Transfer of Players (hereinafter: the Application Regulations), and by using the indicative amounts mentioned in the circular no. 826, the DRC established that the English club has to pay the amount of EUR 300,000 as training compensation to the club X. In fact, between the ages of 12 and 15, thus the first three years, the amount is based on the training and education costs for category 4, which in Europe correspond to EUR 10,000 per year (cf. art. 7 par. 2 of the Application Regulations). For the period between the ages of 16 and 18, thus the next three years, the amount is based on the training and education costs for category 1, which in Europe correspond to EUR 90,000 per year (cf. art. 7 par. 4 of the Application Regulations).

DECISION OF THE DISPUTE RESOLUTION CHAMBER

1. It is established that no contractual ties related to labour law exist between the player and the club X.
2. The player is not obliged to return at and to sign a new contract with the club X.
3. The player is entitled to be registered for the English club Y.
4. The club X is entitled to EUR 300,000 as training compensation from the club Y.
5. The amount due to the club X has to be paid by the club Y within 30 days as from the date of notification of the present decision.
6. In the case that the club Y does not respect the above-mentioned deadline, a default interest payment of 5% p.a. shall be applied on the amount of compensation indicated under point 4, as from the day following the expiry of the fixed deadline.

7. If the relevant sum is not paid within the aforementioned deadline, the present matter shall be submitted to the Disciplinary Committee of FIFA, so that the necessary disciplinary sanctions may be imposed.
8. All other claims of the French club X are rejected.
9. According to art. 60 par. 1 of the FIFA Statutes, this decision may be appealed against before the Court of Arbitration for Sport (CAS). The statement of appeal must be sent to the CAS directly within 10 days of receipt of notification of this decision and shall contain all the elements in accordance with point 2 of the directives issued by the CAS, a copy of which we enclose hereto. Within another 10 days following the expiry of the time limit for filing the statement of appeal, the appellant shall file a brief stating the facts and legal arguments giving rise to the appeal with the CAS (cf. point 4 of the directives).

4 FEBRUARY 2005

25247
DECISION OF THE DISPUTE RESOLUTION CHAMBER
passed in Zurich, Switzerland, on 4 February 2005,
in the following composition:
Slim Aloulou (Tunisia), Chairman
Philippe Piat (France), member
Michele Collucci (Italy), member
Maurice Watkins (England), member
Mario Gallavotti (Italy), member
on the claim presented by
Player B, Serbia & Montenegro as Claimant
against
A, China as Respondent
regarding a contractual dispute between the parties involved

FACTS OF THE CASE:
- The parties signed an employment contract valid from 8 March 2003 until 28 February 2006.
- On 1 March 2004 the club addressed the player the unilateral cancellation of the contract, basing itself on art. 8.1 which, according with the English translation contained in the contract itself, states: "If the starting appearance is less than 70% out of the whole CFA League A games (only starting appearance or total appearance time per game no less than 45 minutes can be counted) by his own will, Party A has the right to terminate this agreement and transfer Party B to other football club, except for injuries which should be confirmed by the doctors or hospital appointed by Party A."
- According to the club, the statistics of CFA League A games in 2003 show that B made a 64% starting appearance rate, in that he played in only 18 of the 23 games of the 2003 season. Therefore, the club reasons, the player's starting appearance was less than 70% out of the whole CFA League A games in 2003 and it was possible for the club to rescind B's contract.
- On 5 March 2004 the player B filed a complaint at FIFA regarding this cancellation of his employment contract and claiming a damage compensation sum of USD 2,200,000 from the club.
- Mr. A insists that art. 8.1 may not have been applied already at the end of the first season to justify the cancellation of his contract.
- Moreover, the claimant considers that he made appearances in more than 70% of the games because article 8.1 of the contract clearly mentions "if starting appearance is less than 70%....by his own wil", meaning that any lack of appearance due to a decision made outside of the player's control, such as a coach's decision to keep him on the bench, should not be considered to be a non-appearance in the terms of art. 8.1.
- The Chinese club rejects the players' interpretations entirely, explaining that if his understanding of art. 8.1 were correct, this interpretation would defeat the purpose of having this clause in the contract in the first place.

- The club considers it therefore logical that the 70% appearance requisite applies strictly per playing season.
- In addition, the club points out that it is obvious that only the head coach or main trainer of the first team has the power to decide if a player is selected for appearance or not, it depends on sporting strategies and other purely sportive parameters and is never left to a player's own free will.
- In conclusion, the respondent rejects all of the player's claims to compensation for the early termination of the contract. The arguments put forward by the player in this respect are therefore unrealistic.
- The club's counterclaim for a damage compensation against the player amounts to a total of EUR 55,000.

CONSIDERATIONS OF THE DISPUTE RESOLUTION CHAMBER

The Dispute Resolution Chamber of the FIFA Players' Status Committee shall review disputes coming under its jurisdiction pursuant to Art. 42 of the FIFA Regulations for the Status and Transfer of Players (hereafter: FIFA Regulations) at the request of one of the parties to the dispute.

According to Art. 42 of the FIFA Regulations for the Status and Transfer of Players, the triggering elements of the dispute (i.e. whether a contract was breached, with or without just cause, or sporting just cause), will be decided by the Dispute Resolution Chamber of the FIFA Players' Status Committee.

Consequently, the Dispute Resolution Chamber is the competent body to decide on the present litigation concerning the alleged breach of contract between the claimant and the respondent.

Subsequently, and entering into the substance of the matter, the Chamber began its deliberations by analyzing the allegations of the claimant.

To begin with, it was determined that the principal point of controversy in this litigation relates to the respondent's interpretation and application of art. 8.1 of the contract for the early termination of the employment contract.

It was recalled that the disputed provision reads: "If the starting appearance is less than70% out of the whole CFA League A games (only starting appearance or total appearance time per game no less than 45 minutes can be counted) by his own will, Party A has the right to terminate this agreement and transfer Party B to other footbalclub, except for injuries which should be confirmed by the doctors or hospital appointedby Party A."

The Chamber first remarked that the clause in question was not drafted in a clear manner, leaving room for interpretation. It was thus necessary to understand what concrete meaning the parties intended this provision to have when the contract was drafted.

The claimant's complaint in this respect is primarily based on the fact that his understanding and interpretation of art. 8.1 is that the 70% appearance obligation mentioned therein does not refer to a single season, but rather to the whole of the contract. The 70% appearance condition should therefore be calculated by no earlier than the very last year of the contract, yet the club opted to make its calculation and terminate the contract following the first season already.

This complaint has been extensively refuted by the club.

The Dispute Resolution Chamber took note of the respondent's position, in which it defends that the claimant's interpretation of the disputed clause clearly defeats the purpose of having this clause in the first place.

This point is illustrated by explaining that if the player's reasoning were followed, the club would necessarily lose its right to terminate the contract before its natural end, since the calculation of the percentage of played matches could not take place until it had already expired anyway.

The members of the Dispute Resolution Chamber unanimously voiced their agreement with the club's defence, which they found to be logical and thus acceptable. It was acknowledged that if art. 8.1 could not be invoked by the club at the end of every playing season, the incorporation of this clause into the contract would be pointless.

By virtue of the same logic the Chamber could not agree with the player's reasoning with regard to the phrase "by his own will", which he employs to mean that any non-appearances that may have occurred outside of his scope of influence, such as a decision by the coach not to field him, should not be taken into consideration when calculating his appearance percentage.

This, the Chamber reasoned, would narrow the non-appearance percentage down to comprise only the player's deliberate absences, which would be senseless considering that the club could deal with such

deliberate absenteeism, regardless, by way of disciplinary sanctions or even the unilateral cancellation of the contract with just cause.
Having thus decided that the arguments put forward by the player could not be followed, the Chamber went on to consider whether the clause, as defined in the understanding of the club, should be considered abusive.
Particularly objectionable is that the clause offers ample opportunity for the club to misuse its position and unilaterally cancel the contract, simply by preventing the player from participating in over 70% of the season's matches. The questionability of this is increased by the fact that this clause does not offer reciprocal opportunities for an early termination of the contract by the player.
On the other hand, it was also deemed important to consider that art. 8.1 cannot be invoked by the club at any arbitrary moment during the season, but is restricted to one point in time after completion of each full playing season. This does provide for some legal certainty and stability for the player.
What's more, the contents of art. 8.1 were explicitly accepted by both parties when they signed the contract.
Taking these two factors into consideration, the Dispute Resolution Chamber deemed that the clause was acceptable, despite its aforementioned questionable aspects.
It was furthermore taken into consideration that the club had paid the player all of his financial dues for the season, leaving no room for further discussion regarding ulterior motives for the club's rescission of the contract.
In view of the foregoing, the Dispute Resolution Chamber decided that in the case at hand the club's application of art. 8.1 for the early termination of the employment contract did not amount to an unjust unilateral cancellation of the contract. The claims for damage compensation put forward by Mr. B were therefore rejected.

DECISION OF THE DISPUTE RESOLUTION CHAMBER

1. The claim lodged by the Claimant is rejected.
2. According to art. 60 par. 1 of the FIFA Statutes, this decision may be appealed against before the Court of Arbitration for Sport (CAS). The statement of appeal must be sent to the CAS directly within 10 days of receipt of notification of this decision and shall contain all the elements in accordance with point 2 of the directives issued by the CAS, a copy of which we enclose hereto. Within another 10 days following the expiry of the time limit for filing the statement of appeal, the appellant shall file a brief stating the facts and legal arguments giving rise to the appeal with the CAS (cf. point 4 of the directives).

⚽⚽⚽

25488
DECISION OF THE DISPUTE RESOLUTION CHAMBER
passed in Zurich, Switzerland, on 4 February 2005,
in the following composition:
Slim Aloulou (Tunisia), Chairman
Mario Gallavotti (Italy), member
Maurice Watkins (England), member
Michele Colucci (Italy), member
Philippe Piat (France), member
on the claim presented by
Player X, as Claimant
against
Club Y, as Respondent
regarding a contractual dispute between the player X, and the Club Y,

FACTS OF THE CASE
On 3 July 2003 the player X and the club Y concluded a two-year employment contract, whereby it was agreed that the player would have been entitled to receive 160,000 --- per season according to the following schedule:

- 40,000 --- on 20 August 2003.

- 40,000 --- on 20 October 2003.
- 40,000 --- on 20 February 2004.
- 40,000 --- on 15 July 2004.
- 40,000 --- on 20 August 2004.
- 40,000 --- on 20 October 2004.
- 40,000 --- on 20 February 2005.
- 40,000 --- on 15 April 2005.

On 29 October 2003 the player received a deportation order issued by the local government, in consequence of which, he had to leave the territory of the Republic on 31 October 2003, due to the fact that he did not have any permit to stay.
The club did not undertake any action to prevent the execution of the order, nor had it ever taken any steps in order to provide the player with the necessary visa by the time the employment contract was concluded.
In addition to that, by the time the deportation order was issued, the player was already owed 80,000 ---, which the club failed to pay on 20 August 2003 and on 20 October 2003.
The player is presently still unemployed.
Mr. X asks the Dispute Resolution Chamber to condemn Y to pay him the amount of 320,000 ---, corresponding to the total duration of the employment contract.
Despite being contacted by FIFA several times, the club never replied.

CONSIDERATIONS OF THE DISPUTE RESOLUTION CHAMBER

After a careful study of the facts and allegations outlined above, the Dispute Resolution Chamber commenced its deliberations by referring to the art. 42 par. 1 lit. (b) (i) of the FIFA Regulations for the Status and Transfer of Players (hereinafter, the Regulations), according to which, it falls within the purview of the Dispute Resolution Chamber to determine whether one of the parties has committed a unilateral breach of contract without just cause.
In this sense, if the employment contract was breached by a party, the Dispute Resolution Chamber is responsible to verify whether this party is accountable for outstanding payments and compensation.
Furthermore, the Dispute Resolution Chamber will establish the amount of compensation to be paid and decide whether sports sanctions must be imposed (cf. art. 42 par. 1 (b) (ii) and (iii) in connection with art. 22 and 23 of the Regulations).
Firstly, the Chamber emphasised that, according to Art. 30 §2 of the, the player's new club is required to make any necessary investigations, or to take any appropriate action before concluding the contract in order to legalise the permanence of a player in the country, otherwise it will be liable to pay the full amount of compensation for the amount of salary due.
In this particular case it was in the club's responsibility to provide the entry visa, as well as the necessary working permit to the player. The Chamber further pointed out that the club did not undertake any action, or at least not the necessary ones, in order to prevent the execution of the deportation order, nor had it ever taken any steps in order to provide the player with the necessary visa by the time the employment contract was concluded.
Clearly the club, with its sole behaviour, prevented the above employment contract from being executed and by doing so provoked the breach of the contract.
Furthermore, the club did not respond to the FIFA administration's correspondence, renouncing this way its right to defence and therefore accepting the player's allegations.
Therefore, Mr. X is entitled to compensation for non-execution of the employment contract due to the sole fault of the club.
On account of the above, the Dispute Resolution Chamber deemed that the compensation due to the player shall consist of 80,000 ---, as the outstanding salaries the player was already due on 20 August 2003 and on 20 October 2003, plus the amount of 240,000 ---, corresponding to the salaries the player would have earned until the end of his employment contract, as compensation for contractual breach.
Consequently, the Dispute Resolution Chamber decided that the club has to pay to X the amount 320,000 ---

DECISION OF THE DISPUTE RESOLUTION CHAMBER

1. The claim of Mr. X is accepted.
2. The club Y has to pay to Mr. X the amount 320,000 ---.

3. The amount due to Mr. X has to be paid by Y within 30 days as from the date of notification of this decision.
4. If the aforementioned sum is not paid within the aforementioned deadline, the present matter shall be submitted to FIFA's Disciplinary Committee, so that the necessary disciplinary sanctions may be imposed.
5. According to art. 60 par. 1 of the FIFA Statutes, this decision may be appealed against before the Court of Arbitration for Sport (CAS). The statement of appeal must be sent to the CAS directly within 10 days of receipt of notification of this decision and shall contain all the elements in accordance with point 2 of the directives issued by the CAS, a copy of which we enclose hereto. Within another 10 days following the expiry of the time limit for filing the statement of appeal, the appellant shall file a brief stating the facts and legal arguments giving rise to the appeal with the CAS (cf. point 4 of the directives).

25528 a
DECISION OF THE DISPUTE RESOLUTION CHAMBER
passed in Zurich, Switzerland, on 4 February 2005,
in the following composition:
Slim Aloulou (Tunisia), Chairman
Mario Gallavotti (Italy), member
Maurice Watkins (England), member
Philippe Piat (France), member
Michele Colucci (Italy), member
on the claim presented by
the club, X, Germany, as Claimant
against
the club Y, Turkey, as Respondent
regarding training compensation in connection with the player Q,

FACTS OF THE CASE
- The player was born on 22 September 1984.
- Q was registered as an amateur player with X from 19.07.2000 until 29.06.2003.
- The German club belongs to category 4.
- On 29 June 2003, the DFB issued an IRTC on behalf of the Turkish Football Association for the player in question.
- The player was registered with Y as a non-amateur player.
- Y is a category 4 club.
- The German club claims payment of an amount of money relating to training compensation and it authorised the German Football Federation in writing to receive and distribute the amount.
- The Turkish club maintains that it has paid training compensation to the "relevant clubs" and submitted a document duly signed by X on 3 January 2004.
- In accordance with this document, X declares that it will have no claims against the player, Q, who left the club in July 2003 and that the German club will have no claims against Y.
- In spite of FIFA's invitation to do so, X has not presented any comments on the aforementioned documents.

CONSIDERATIONS OF THE DISPUTE RESOLUTION CHAMBER
As established in art. 42 §1 (b) (iv) of the FIFA Regulations for the Status and Transfer of Players, it falls within the purview of the Dispute Resolution Chamber to decide on disputes concerning the compensation for the training and education of young players and to adjust training compensation fees.
The Chamber turned to the claim presented by the German club X, with which the player, Q, has been registered during 3 sportive seasons. Although it is undisputed that Q has been trained and educated at X, the members of the Chamber agreed that the document dated 3 January 2004 that has been presented by the Turkish club in its defence must be considered as a waiver. By having signed such document, which refers to the player in question and states, inter alia, that X will have no claims against Y, the German club

has waived its right to claim from Y payment of an amount of money relating to training compensation. Consequently, the Chamber decided to reject the claim put forward by X.

DECISION OF THE DISPUTE RESOLUTION CHAMBER

1. The claim of the Claimant, X, is rejected.
2. According to art. 60 par. 1 of the FIFA Statutes, this decision may be appealed against before the Court of Arbitration for Sport (CAS). The statement of appeal must be sent to the CAS directly within 10 days of receipt of notification of this decision and shall contain all the elements in accordance with point 2 of the directives issued by the CAS, a copy of which we enclose hereto. Within another 10 days following the expiry of the time limit for filing the statement of appeal, the appellant shall file a brief stating the facts and legal arguments giving rise to the appeal with the CAS (cf. point 4 of the directives).

25566
DECISION OF THE DISPUTE RESOLUTION CHAMBER

passed in Zurich, Switzerland, on 4 February 2005,
in the following composition:
Slim Aloulou (Tunisia), chairman
Mario Gallavotti (Italy), member
Maurice Watkins (England), member
Michele Colucci (Italy), member
Philippe Piat (France), member
on the claim presented by A as Claimant
against B as Respondent
regarding a contractual dispute

FACTS OF THE CASE

On 24 January 2004, C and B agreed on the loan of A's federative rights and, on 1 February 2004, A and B signed an employment contract valid until 30 June 2004.

According to the relevant employment contract, A was entitled to receive a monthly salary of EUR 3,600, match bonuses and other supplementary allowances in the total amount of EUR 650, per month.

Notwithstanding the above and despite the fact that A has remained in D, at B's disposal, until April 2004, A asserts that B has never complied with its contractual obligations towards him. In fact, A considers that B as simply abandoned him.

In light of the above, A is presently claiming from B, all the amounts that he was entitled to receive during the entire period of their employment contract, as follows:

A - 5 months of Salaries (EUR 18,000);
B - Match Bonuses (the amount was not specified, particularly since A did not play any match for B);
C - 5 monthly allowances (EUR 3250).

Moreover, A is also requesting the Chamber to:

A - Condemn B to pay to him the amount of EUR 20,000, as compensation for professional and moral damages;
B - Impose the necessary disciplinary sanctions on B;
C - Grant him an amount of EUR 5,000 in order to cover his legal expenses;
D - Interests at the rate applicable in Switzerland over the amounts due.

On the other hand, B requests the Chamber to pronounce itself not competent to decide upon the present matter, since it considers the present dispute to be a matter "...of bad treatment and slavery of human beings...".

However, in case the Chamber acknowledges its competence over the present matter, B defends that A did not gather the necessary physical, technical or mental conditions which are necessary in order to play football.

Moreover, B defends that A was not able to sign a valid employment contract under D Law. In this regard, B maintains that A's administrative file did not allow him to be registered or to play for it, but failed to specify the administrative reasons which, according to it, prevented A from signing a valid employment contract.

In this context, B understands that the claimed contract has never entered into force and consequently defends that it should be disregarded. In fact, B is of the opinion that it does not owe any amounts to A, particularly since it has never had any contractual obligations towards him.
In conclusion, B asks the Chamber to reject A's claim in its entirety.
Notwithstanding the above, B underlines that it has provided A with free accommodation and food for a while, whilst his agents were trying to solve his administrative problems. Moreover, despite A's refusal, B authorized him to train with its B team, which clearly shows that it did not abandon him.
Finally, B underlines that the players' agents, E and F, the company G and C were the only responsible for the eventual damages suffered by A, since they were completely aware of his personal situation and consequently, should be the ones to be condemned to pay an eventual compensation which the Chamber may award to A.
In this respect, B is requesting the Chamber to investigate the degree of responsibility of the aforementioned players' agents, company G and C in the present matter and moreover, in case it is condemned to pay any compensation to A, to declare C liable to pay to it an amount of EUR 15,000, which allegedly corresponds to the amount contractually agreed with C in case A would demonstrate to be physically inapt to play football.
Finally, B is requesting the Chamber to:
A – Condemn A to pay to it an amount of EUR 5,000, as compensation for moral damages;
B – Condemn A to pay to it an amount of EUR 5,000, in order to cover its legal expenses.
In response, A defends that its contract with B is valid and binding for both parties and underlines the fact that B should have taken all the necessary measures to prevent the present situation before signing it.
In this context, the player draws the attention of the Chamber to Art. 30 of the FIFA Regulations for the Status and Transfer of Players, which stipulates that "the validity of…an employment contract between a player and a club cannot be made conditional upon the positive results of a medical examination" and that "the player's prospective new club shall be required to make any necessary investigations, studies, tests and / or medical examination or to take any appropriate action before concluding the contract, otherwise it will be lable to pay… the amount of the salary due."
In conclusion, A considers the reasons invoked by B as non-sustainable and consequently requests the Chamber to accept his claim in its entirety.

CONSIDERATIONS OF THE DISPUTE RESOLUTION CHAMBER
The Dispute Resolution Chamber shall review disputes coming under its jurisdiction pursuant to Art. 42 of the FIFA Regulations for the Status and Transfer of Players, at the request of one of the parties to the dispute.
According to Art. 42, par. 1 lit. (b) of the FIFA Regulations for the Status and Transfer of Players, the triggering elements of the dispute (i.e. whether a contract was breached, with or without just cause, or sporting just cause), will be decided by the Dispute Resolution Chamber.
If an employment contract is breached by a party, the Dispute Resolution Chamber is responsible to verify whether a party is accountable for compensation and outstanding payments.
Also, the Dispute Resolution Chamber will establish the amount of compensation to be paid and decide whether sports sanctions must be imposed (cf. Art. 42, par. 1, b, ii and iii in connection with art. 22 and 23 of the aforementioned Regulations).
As a consequence, the Dispute Resolution Chamber is the competent body to decide on the present litigation concerning the alleged breach of contract between the Claimant and the Respondent.
The members of the Dispute Resolution Chamber were summoned to pass a decision on this matter by the Chairman pursuant to Art. 1 point 6) of the Rules Governing the Practice and Procedures of the Dispute Resolution Chamber.
Subsequently, and entering into the substance of the matter, the members of the Chamber started by acknowledging that, as an outcome of B's non-compliance with the contract signed with A on 1 February 2004, the latter filed a claim against B regarding the payment of all the amounts that he was entitled to receive during the entire period of their contract in the total amount of USD 21,250, as well as compensation for damages, interests and legal expenses.
On the other hand, the members of the Chamber also took into consideration the position of B, according to which, the relevant contract signed with A should not be considered valid, since A did not gather the necessary physical, technical or mental conditions necessary in order to play football nor his administrative file allowed him to be registered and play for it.

After analysing all the documentation provided to the FIFA Administration, the members of the Chamber confirmed that the relevant employment contract was duly signed by B.
In this respect, the Chamber underlined the content of Art. 30 of the FIFA Regulations for the Status and Transfer of Players, which stipulates that "the player's prospective new club shall be required to make any necessary investigations, studies, tests and / or medical examination or to take any appropriate action before concluding the contract, otherwise it will be lable to pay…the amount of the salary due."
As a consequence, the Chamber rejected the arguments presented by B and considered the contract valid and binding for both parties.
Moreover, the members of the Chamber reached the conclusion that, despite the club's position, which prevented A from fulfilling his employment contract, the latter did all in his power to comply with it.
In fact, the Chamber concluded that B is the only responsible for the non-fulfilment of the relevant employment contract, having unilaterally breached it without just cause.
In light of all the above, the members of the Chamber decided to partially accept the claim filed by A and to entirely reject the counter claim filed by B in the present matter.
Therefore, the Chamber decided that, since A was contractually entitled to receive a monthly salary of EUR 3,600 and a monthly supplementary allowance of EUR 650, he is entitled to receive the total amount of EUR 21.250 from B, corresponding to EUR 12,750 for the months that he was at the club's disposal and EUR 8,500 as compensation for B's breach of contract.
Furthermore, in accordance with its well-established jurisprudence, the Chamber rejected A's claim concerning the match bonuses, since the latter did not participate in any match for B.
Finally, in view of the present matter's circumstances, the evidence carried to the file and its well-established jurisprudence, the Dispute Resolution Chamber decided to reject all further claims filed by A.

DECISION OF THE DISPUTE RESOLUTION CHAMBER

1. The claim of A is partially accepted.
2. The Respondent, B shall pay the amount of EUR 21,250 to the Claimant, A, within 30 days of notification of the present decision
3. If the Respondent fails to comply with the above-mentioned deadline, an interest rate of 5% per year will apply and the case will immediately be presented to the FIFA Disciplinary Committee.
4. All further claims filed by the parties are rejected.
5. According to art. 60 par. 1 of the FIFA Statutes, this decision may be appealed before the Court of Arbitration for Sport (CAS). The statement of appeal must be sent to the CAS directly within 10 days of receiving notification of this decision and has to contain all elements in accordance with point 2 of the directives issued by the CAS, copy of which we enclose hereto. Within another 10 days following the expiry of the time limit for the filing of the statement of appeal, the appellant shall file with the CAS a brief stating the facts and legal arguments giving rise to the appeal (cf. point 4 of the directives).

25633 a

DECISION OF THE DISPUTE RESOLUTION CHAMBER

passed in Zurich, Switzerland, on 4 February 2005,
in the following composition:
Slim Aloulou (Tunisia), chairman
Mario Gallavotti (Italy), member
Maurice Watkins (England), member
Michele Colucci (Italy), member
Philippe Piat (France), member
on the claim presented by
Club A as Claimant
against
Club B as Respondent
regarding a training compensation dispute concerning the transfer of the player

FACTS OF THE CASE:

- The player C, born on 15 March 1987, was registered for A, the Claimant, for the season 1999/2000 between the age of 13 and 14.
- During the aforementioned period the player was registered for the Claimant as amateur.
- On 17 March 2003 the player C and the Club B signed an "aspirant contract", for 2 sporting seasons valid from August 2003 until July 2005 joining the training centre of the Respondent.
- In March 2004, A contacted FIFA claiming Training Compensation from the Respondent, in accordance with Chapter VII of the revised FIFA Regulations for the Status and Transfer of Players.
- On 27 August 2004 the Respondent informed FIFA Administration that the player left the club for personal reasons and will therefore not take part in the sportive season 2004/2005 of their club.
- As far as the categorisation of clubs is concerned, as provided for by the FIFA Circular letter 826 dated 31 October 2002, the Claimant is assigned to Category 4, whereas the Respondent belongs to Category 1.
- The amount of compensation due is to be calculated in accordance with the parameters provided by the FIFA Regulations for the Status and Transfer of Players (hereafter: FIFA Regulations) and the Article 7 point 2 (players aged 12 to 15) of the Regulations governing the Application of the FIFA Regulations and the Circular letter 826 dated 31 October 2002.
- The Respondent argues that they should not pay any training compensation to the A club, due to the fact that the player was transferred from his previous club as an amateur player to their club with amateur status in accordance with Chapter III, Article 5, third paragraph of the Regulations governing the Application of the Regulations for the Status and Transfer of Players .
- The Claimant does not accept the Respondent's arguments and states that the "aspirant" contract is a form of scholarship and it includes the obligation of Club B to pay to the player certain amounts of money, therefore it is a non-amateur contract.
- The Claimant reaffirmed that it is entitled to receive the training compensation established in Chapter VII of the revised FIFA Regulations based on the fact that the player had actually been transferred from an amateur status to a non-amateur status.
- The Claimant asks the Dispute Resolution Chamber to decide upon the amount of compensation due for the Respondent.
- The Respondent asks the Dispute Resolution Chamber to reject the Claimant's claim.

CONSIDERATIONS OF THE DISPUTE RESOLUTION CHAMBER:

The Dispute Resolution Chamber of the FIFA Players' Status Committee shall review disputes coming under its jurisdiction pursuant to Art. 42 of the FIFA Regulations for the Status and Transfer of Players at the request of one of the parties to the dispute.

According to Art. 42.1(b)(iv) of the FIFA Regulations for the Status and Transfer of Players, the Dispute Resolution Chamber of the FIFA Players' Status Committee shall review disputes concerning training compensation fees.

Consequently, the Dispute Resolution Chamber is the competent body to decide on the present litigation concerning the training compensation fee claimed by the club A.

Once its competence was thus established, the Dispute Resolution Chamber went on to deal with the substance of the case.

Initially, the Chamber affirmed that it is undisputed the Claimant's statements about the "Aspirant" contract between the Player C and the Respondent, particularly when it states that the contract includes several financial obligations to be fulfilled by the Respondent. These obligations are:

- living and educational costs of the player (point 6 of the contract)
- sum of money of EUR 15,240 (point 7 of the contract) as a damage compensation for costs incurred by the parents. This sum of money was paid by the club together with the salary of July 2003 and
- travel and living costs covering visits of the player's parents (point 8 of the contract).

The Chamber mentioned that although it is correct that the Respondent's argument underlines that in Chapter III, Article 5, third paragraph point a) of the Regulations governing the Application of the FIFA Regulations it is an established exception to pay training compensation in case a player is transferred from amateur status to amateur status, however, it is important to carefully analyze the clauses contained in the contract between the player and the club B.

In this respect, the Chamber realized that some of the financial obligations, included in the "Aspirant" contract particularly the sum of money mentioned in point 7 thereof, is a considerable amount and therefore it is not a typical obligation that would normally be present in an amateur relationship.

At this stage, the Chamber considered appropriate to quote verbatim the article 2 of the FIFA Regulations, which states:

"1 Players who have never received any remuneration other than reimbursement of their actual expenses incurred during the course of their participation in any activity connected with association football are regarded as amateur.

2 Travel and hotel expenses incurred through involvement in a match and the costs of a player's equipment, insurance and training may be reimbursed without jeopardising a player's amateur status.

3 Any player who has ever received remuneration in excess of the expenses and costs described in par.2 of this article ... shall be regarded as non amateur ... ."

In light of the above, the Chamber underlined that some of the financial obligations assumed by the Respondent in the contract with the player are in principle included in paragraph 3 of the aforementioned article 2 of the FIFA Regulations, such as, damage compensation for costs incurred by the parents' travel and living costs on the occasions when the player's parents visit him, therefore the relationship between player and club shall be regarded as non- amateur.

In conclusion, the Chamber established that in the present case, the Claimant is entitled to receive compensation for the training and education it provided to the player C.

Having thus established the Respondent's obligation to compensate the Claimant, the Chamber went on to deliberate on the proper calculation of this compensation, affirming that the amount due shall be calculated in accordance with the parameters provided by the FIFA Regulations and Circular No.826.

It was recalled that, within the EU/EEA area, compensation for training is based on the training and education costs of the country in which the training club of the player is located. In the case at hand, since B belongs to the European Category 1, the indicative amount would be EUR 90,000 per year.

However, for the training of players from the age of 12 up to 15 years of age, Article 7 point 2 of the Regulations governing the Application of the FIFA Regulations, states that the compensation granted shall correspond to the training compensation of a Category 4 club. For Europe that is an indicative amount of EUR 10,000.

In this particular case, the calculation is the following: the amount of EUR 10,000 corresponding to the first year of the player's training when he was between the ages of 13 and 14, which, in principle, could be payable to the player's developing club.

Taking all of the foregoing considerations into account, the Dispute Resolution Chamber decided that Club B is liable to pay the total amount of EUR 10,000 to the Claimant as training compensation for the player C.

DECISION OF THE DISPUTE RESOLUTION CHAMBER

1. The Respondent, shall pay the amount of EUR 10,000 to the Claimant, within 30 days of notification of the present decision.
2. If the respondent fails to comply with the above-mentioned deadline, an interest rate of 5% per year will apply and the case will immediately be presented to the FIFA Disciplinary Committee.
3. According to art. 60 par. 1 of the FIFA Statutes, this decision may be appealed before the Court of Arbitration for Sport (CAS). The statement of appeal must be sent to the CAS directly within 10 days of receiving notification of this decision and has to contain all elements in accordance with point 2 of the directives issued by the CAS, copy of which we enclose hereto. Within another 10 days following the expiry of the time limit for the filing of the statement of appeal, the appellant shall file with the CAS a brief stating the facts and legal arguments giving rise to the appeal (cf. point 4 of the directives).

25633 b

DECISION OF THE DISPUTE RESOLUTION CHAMBER

passed in Zurich, Switzerland, on 4 February 2005,
in the following composition:

Slim Aloulou (Tunisia), chairman
Mario Gallavotti (Italy), member
Maurice Watkins (England), member
Michele Colucci (Italy), member
Philippe Piat (France), member
on the claim presented by Club A as Claimant
against
Club B as Respondent
regarding a training compensation dispute concerning the transfer of the player C

FACTS OF THE CASE:

- The player C, born on 15 March 1987, was registered for A, the Claimant, as from the season 2000/2001 up to and including the season 2002/2003, that is, for three (3) sporting seasons between the age of 14 and 16.
- During the aforementioned period the player was registered for the Claimant as amateur.
- On 17 March 2003 the player and the Club B signed an "aspirant contract", for 2 sporting seasons valid from August 2003 until July 2005 joining the training centre of the Respondent.
- In March 2004, Club A contacted FIFA claiming Training Compensation from the Respondent, in accordance with Chapter VII of the revised FIFA Regulations for the Status and Transfer of Players.
- On 27 August 2004 the Respondent informed FIFA Administration that the player left the club for personal reasons and will therefore not take part in the sportive season 2004/2005 of their club.
- As far as the categorisation of clubs is concerned, as provided for by the FIFA Circular letter 826 dated 31 October 2002, the Claimant is assigned to Category 4, whereas the Respondent belongs to Category 1.
- The amount of compensation due is to be calculated in accordance with the parameters provided by the FIFA Regulations for the Status and Transfer of Players (hereafter: FIFA Regulations), the Articles 7 point 2 (players aged 12 to 15) and 7 point 4 a) (transfer from lower to higher category) of the Regulations governing the Application of the FIFA Regulations and the Circular letter 826 dated 31 October 2002.
- The Respondent argues that they should not pay any training compensation to the club A, due to the fact that the player was transferred from A as an amateur player to their club with amateur status in accordance with Chapter III, Article 5, third paragraph of the Regulations governing the Application of the Regulations for the Status and Transfer of Players .
- The Claimant does not accept the Respondent's arguments and states that the "aspirant" contract is a form of scholarship and it includes the obligation of B to pay to the player certain amounts of money, therefore it is a non-amateur contract.
- The Claimant reaffirmed that it is entitled to receive the training compensation established in Chapter VII of the revised FIFA Regulations based on the fact that the player had actually been transferred from an amateur status to a non-amateur status.
- The Claimant asks the Dispute Resolution Chamber to decide upon the amount of compensation due for the Respondent.
- The Respondent asks the Dispute Resolution Chamber to reject the Claimant's claim.

CONSIDERATIONS OF THE DISPUTE RESOLUTION CHAMBER:

The Dispute Resolution Chamber of the FIFA Players' Status Committee shall review disputes coming under its jurisdiction pursuant to Art. 42 of the FIFA Regulations for the Status and Transfer of Players at the request of one of the parties to the dispute.

According to Art. 42.1(b)(iv) of the FIFA Regulations for the Status and Transfer of Players, the Dispute Resolution Chamber of the FIFA Players' Status Committee shall review disputes concerning training compensation fees.

Consequently, the Dispute Resolution Chamber is the competent body to decide on the present litigation concerning the training compensation fee claimed by the club A.

Once its competence was thus established, the Dispute Resolution Chamber went on to deal with the substance of the case.

Initially, the Chamber affirmed that it is undisputed the Claimant's statements about the "Aspirant" contract between the Player C and the Respondent, particularly when it states that the contract includes several financial obligations to be fulfilled by the Respondent. These obligations are:

- living and educational costs of the player (point 6 of the contract)
- sum of money of EUR 15,240 (point 7 of the contract) as a damage compensation for costs incurred by the parents. This sum of money was paid by the club together with the salary of July 2003 and
- travel and living costs covering visits of the player's parents (point 8 of the contract).

The Chamber mentioned that although it is correct that the Respondent's argument underlines that in Chapter III, Article 5, third paragraph point a) of the Regulations governing the Application of the FIFA Regulations it is an established exception to pay training compensation in case a player is transferred from amateur status to amateur status, however, it is important to carefully analyze the clauses contained in the contract between the player and the club B.

In this respect, the Chamber realized that some of the financial obligations, included in the "Aspirant" contract particularly the sum of money mentioned in point 7 thereof, is a considerable amount and therefore it is not a typical obligation that would normally be present in an amateur relationship.

At this stage, the Chamber considered appropriate to quote verbatim the article 2 of the FIFA Regulations, which states:

"1 Players who have never received any remuneration other than reimbursement of their actual expenses incurred during the course of their participation in any activity connected with association football are regarded as amateur.

2 Travel and hotel expenses incurred through involvement in a match and the costs of a player's equipment, insurance and training may be reimbursed without jeopardising a player's amateur status.

3 Any player who has ever received remuneration in excess of the expenses and costs described in par.2 of this article ... shall be regarded as non amateur ... ."

In light of the above, the Chamber underlines that some of the financial obligations assumed by the Respondent in the contract with the player are in principle included in paragraph 3 of the aforementioned article 2 of the FIFA Regulations, such as, damage compensation for costs incurred by the parents' travel and living costs on the occasions when the player's parents visit him, therefore the relationship between player and club shall be regarded as non- amateur.

In conclusion, the Chamber established that in the present case, the Claimant is entitled to receive compensation for the training and education it provided to the player .

Having thus established the Respondent's obligation to compensate the Claimant, the Chamber went on to deliberate on the proper calculation of this compensation, affirming that the amount due shall be calculated in accordance with the parameters provided by the FIFA Regulations and Circular No.826.

It was recalled that, within the EU/EEA area, compensation for training is based on the training and education costs of the country in which the training club of the player is located. In the case at hand, since Club B belongs to the European Category 1, the indicative amount would be EUR 90,000 per year.

However, for the training of players from the age of 12 up to 15 years of age, Article 7 point 2 of the Regulations governing the Application of the FIFA Regulations, states that the compensation granted shall correspond to the training compensation of a Category 4 club. For Europe that is an indicative amount of EUR 10,000.

Moreover, also applicable to this case, is Article 7 point 4 (a) of the Regulations governing the Application of the FIFA Regulations, which establishes that should a player be transferring from a club belonging to a lower category, to a club belonging to a higher category, the calculation of compensation shall be based on the average of the training costs of both categories.

In this particular case, the following calculation would be appropriate: the amount of EUR 20,000 (corresponding to the first and second year of the player's training when he was between the ages of 14 and 15), plus a sum in the amount of EUR 50,000 (corresponding to the year that the player became 16 years of age and in accordance with the aforementioned Article 7 point 4 (a) of the FIFA Regulations). This adds up to a grand total compensation sum of EUR 70,000, which, in principle, could be payable to the player's developing club.

Taking all of the foregoing considerations into account, the Dispute Resolution Chamber decided that Club B is liable to pay the total amount of EUR 70,000 to the Claimant as training compensation for the player C.

DECISION OF THE DISPUTE RESOLUTION CHAMBER

1. The Respondent, shall pay the amount of EUR 70,000 to the Claimant, within 30 days of notification of the present decision.
2. If Club B fails to comply with the above-mentioned deadline, an interest rate of 5% per year will apply and the case will immediately be presented to the FIFA Disciplinary Committee.
3. According to art. 60 par. 1 of the FIFA Statutes, this decision may be appealed before the Court of Arbitration for Sport (CAS). The statement of appeal must be sent to the CAS directly within 10 days of receiving notification of this decision and has to contain all elements in accordance with point 2 of the directives issued by the CAS, copy of which we enclose hereto. Within another 10 days following the expiry of the time limit for the filing of the statement of appeal, the appellant shall file with the CAS a brief stating the facts and legal arguments giving rise to the appeal (cf. point 4 of the directives).

25820
DECISION OF THE DISPUTE RESOLUTION CHAMBER
passed in Zurich, Switzerland, on 4 February 2005,
in the following composition:
Slim Aloulou (Tunisia), chairman
Mario Gallavotti (Italy), member
Maurice Watkins (England), member
Michele Colucci (Italy), member
Philippe Piat (France), member
on the claim presented by Club K as Claimant against Player D and Club A as Respondents
regarding a contractual dispute between the parties involved

FACTS OF THE CASE:

- Player D is a .... citizen, born on 22 February 1981.
- On 13 August 2003, the player and the club K signed a three-season playing contract, valid for a period of three years, from 01.09.2003 to 30.06.2006, with the possibility of automatic renewal. The claimant provided FIFA Administration with a copy of the contract in Arabic language and its respective English translation.
- In accordance with the aforementioned employment contract, Mr. D was entitled to receive a monthly net salary of USD 10,000 and some additional benefits from K, namely accommodation and a car with driver.
- Despite the existing employment contract, the Player did not return for the club's pre-season on 15 August 2004, having been absent from the club since then.
- On 14 September 2004, the player informed FIFA that the reason he had not returned to K was that the club had paid neither an amount of USD 40,000 at the start of the second season, nor an amount of USD 60,000 that had remained outstanding since the signing of the contract; totalizing USD 100,000. The payment of this sum had been specified in the terms of another contract celebrated between the same aforementioned parties in the city of XX in Portuguese-language. The player provide FIFA Administration with a copy of the aforementioned contract.
- The player contends that in the Arabic contract, K had omitted their obligation to pay him USD 60,000 on signing and a further USD 40,000 as an advance at the start of the second season; both of these payments were specified in the Portuguese-language contract.
- Furthermore, the player stated that at the time he had signed the contract with K in Arabic, the club had acted in bad faith by not providing him with a copy of the same, duly translated into English, French or Spanish, as required by FIFA. In addition, the player claims that the terms of the Arabic contract were not identical to those in the Portuguese contract that he had signed in XX city.
- In subsequent correspondence from the player to FIFA, he informed that for the same reasons mentioned earlier, he had not returned to K as he had a valid sporting reason, in accordance with the provisions of Art. 24 of FIFA's "Regulations for the Status and Transfer of Players" [from here on, "the regulations"], based on the fact that he had not received the USD 100,000 from K. The player considered himself as being prevented from playing his trade and thus invested with the legitimate right to rescind the contract which had bound him to the club in question.

- On 18 September 2004, the XX NA informed FIFA that the XX Labour Court had ruled that the player had been registered with the club A (new club) and that, on the authority of the above court order, the XX NA had gone ahead with the registration.
- The player signed an employment contract with Club A for a period of duration of 12 months.
- In light of the aforementioned circumstances the K submitted a formal complaint to FIFA, against the player D and the Club A for breaching unilaterally the terms of his contract without just cause, as well as for the damages suffered.
- On 30 September 2004 the CBF forwarded correspondence to FIFA that they had received from the player's new club. In this letter, the new club announced that they had concluded a contract with the player and that, owing to the imminent closure of the XX NA transfer window on 17 September 2004, the player had taken his case to the XX Labour Court, which had authorised his registration and that consequently, the XX NA had officially respected and authorized the legal ruling.
- K stated that the new club had clearly induced the player to violate the contract binding them and, therefore, calls upon on FIFA to impose disciplinary and financial sanctions on both parties.
- In response to the player's statements, K informed FIFA that the Portuguese language contract is completely false. Firstly the contract is not dated and secondly they never signed it and moreover the person that appearing in this hypothetical contract calls Mr. FCD had not ever been invested with any legal capacity by the club K for signing any contract.
- Moreover, the FIFA administration checked whether the persons that took part in the Portuguese contract, Mr FCD, B or RDS, were licensed FIFA agents, and established that none of them appeared in the database of licensed FIFA agents; neither for FIFA in the past, nor for any its national member associations as they should have to conform to the existing norms.
- Furthermore, K emphasizes that it has made a strong financial investment in the amount of USD 600,000 in order to acquire Player Mr. D's federative rights. A copy of the transfer agreement confirming the aforementioned amount have been provided to the FIFA Administration.
- K reiterate that the player had breached his contract by not returning to K city as agreed and also by having played for another club. Moreover, asserted that they do not owe the player any money at all for season 2003/2004 and that they quite pointedly draw attention to the fact that the player's demand for the USD 60,000 was made one year later, and that he had made no mention of it before.
- Likewise, K reject the argument of the player and his new club, through which they seek the protection of Art. 24 of the FIFA regulations, which rules that a player is legally entitled to terminate his contract if he has a valid sporting reason to do so. K point out that this article is only applicable in cases where the player has taken part in fewer than 10% of the matches in the respective championship; that in the case at hand, the player had played in more than 42 of K's 47 matches during season 2003/2004 and that, for this reason, the "valid sporting reason" does not exist.
- Furthermore, K reject all the defences raised by the player as groundless. The club emphasized that if the player had had a valid sporting reason, in accordance with Art. 24 of the FIFA regulations, he ought to have lodged his complaint with FIFA's Dispute Resolution Chamber (DRC) and not brought it before the XX Courts. K also reject the argument concerning the supposed temporary eligibility that the player was considering taking up, since the IRTC had to be issued by the NA.
- Also, K make reference to the two detrimental effects caused the player's failure to complete his contract, namely the loss of a valuable player from the team and the loss of the opportunity to receive financial compensation through the player's future international transfer.
- K's counterclaim for a damage compensation based on breach of contract against the player amounts to a total of USD 2,752,512 based on the following reasons:
  a) wages (USD 10,000) and benefits (USD 4,432) established in the employment contract articles 4 and 6 respectively, totalizing USD 14,432 per month.
  b) length of time remaining on the existing contract (22 months left) until 30 June 2006, USD 14,432 x 22= USD 317,504.
  c) Transfer fee of USD 600,000 in order to acquire federative rights of the player from MM F.C.
  d) The player is under 28 years old (born on 22/02/1981) and the breach occurred within the first three years of the contract, therefore the breach is included within the definition of Art. 2.1.1 (a) and art. 22 of the FIFA Regulations.
  e) That at the end of the first season in K championship, the player was the top scorer in the Arab League and the three K championships;
  f) That in June 2004 they received an offer of USD 1,35 million from a Mexican club (copy provided to FIFA Administration);

g) That when the new club registered the player with the CBF, a USD 20 million penal clause was included (copy attached);
h) That K received other offers from various clubs;
i) that at the end of the first season in the NEW CLUB championship, the player had taken part in a total of 14 matches for his new club and scored six goals;
j) that K had to sign a replacement player Mr. TY, which cost them USD 300,000 (a copy of the contract is attached);

– The player contends that the Portuguese contract is not, as claimed by K, fraudulent, and that Mr FCD had also been involved in concluding the contracts between K and MM and between K himself.
– The FIFA administration scrutinized both contracts cited by the player, given that K had attached a copy to its correspondence and that, in effect, Mr FCD had participated in the conclusion of the contracts in question, never representing K but always other parties.
– In their letters addressed to FIFA, the player and his new club emphasized that the English version of the contract that the K club had offered as proof, had not been signed and, was, therefore, not legally valid.
– FIFA Administration acknowledges that the Claimant did not provide with an English version of the contract, he provided with an English translation of the contract in Arabic.
– The player's new club explained in different communications to FIFA Administration their reasons for putting the player under contract and registering him. The new club asserted that the judicial decision is not a definitive ruling and, therefore, that it does not imply that the player's contract with K has been rescinded, rather that it represents a means of protecting the player's constitutional right to freedom of employment.
– Moreover, the new club has concluded that the only reason the player now finds himself in contravention of the FIFA regulations is because the deadline for registering transfers in XX was 17 September 2004 and there had not been enough time to request the corresponding International Registration Transfer Certificate (IRTC), in accordance with the normal procedures.
– Besides, the new club stated that they had behaved in complete accordance with FIFA norms, since the contract concluded with the player has a duration of just 12 months and is, therefore, in conformity with the provisions of Art. 7.4 of the FIFA regulations.
– In new club's further correspondence to FIFA, it underlined that the judicial decision does not imply that the player's contract with K has been rescinded, but that it merely had the effect of a temporary cancellation.
– Furthermore, in the same letter the new club emphasized that they had never incited the player to breach his contract with K and that the proof of this lies with the fact that the Labour Court had authorized them to register the player with the club.
– Furthermore, the new club had only registered the player in accordance with the decision taken by the Civil Court, which informed the player that as long as the dispute remained unresolved and was being dealt with by the FIFA judicial bodies, and taking into account his constitutional labour rights, he was eligible to play for a XX club.
– In this point, K maintained that the new club was guilty of a serial violation of FIFA Rules, mentioning in particular the following facts: initiating direct negotiations with a player already under contract; registering and fielding a player without having possession of the relevant International Registration Transfer Certificate; resorting to the courts to seek a solution to an ongoing conflict, instead of submitting to the existing FIFA resolution mechanisms.
– K also made it known to the FIFA administration that the employment contract signed with the player (in Arabic) had been submitted to, and officially stamped by the competent public authorities in K city (a copy of this, complete with the stamp, is attached) and that afterwards, he had been registered with the NA, in accordance with the FIFA regulations. Likewise, the club emphasizes that the hypothetical Portuguese contract was never stamped by the K city public authorities and was never registered with the NA, in accordance with the FIFA regulations.
– Finally, the K club provided FIFA with a good faith declaration made by Mr Z in Portuguese language and its respective official translation into English. This statement was given on 11 November 2004, in the city of XX, in which Mr Z attested the following:

a) Mr Z acted as the player's translator and interpreter during the conclusion and signing of the contract with K in Arabic Language, on 13 August 2003, in K City.
b) Mr Z stated in his declaration that he had proceeded to translate the terms of the contract verbally

into Portuguese for the player and that it had been signed by both parties (player D and K) and that the contract in question was in Arabic language.

c) Mr Z attested that the player understood the terms of the contract with K perfectly well, such as, the time periods, the sums of money, the methods of payment, the termination of the contract.

- Bearing in mind all of the above, and with respect to the player, Club K requested the DRC to pronounce a formal ruling that, without valid reason, the player has breached the terms of, and broken the contract that bound the parties, and that the following sanctions must, therefore, be imposed:
  - financial compensation in favour of K for damages, taking into account the above parameters and values.
  - disciplinary sanctions, prohibiting his transfer, in accordance with Art. 23, paragraph 1 (a) of the FIFA regulations, with a restriction of four months on his eligibility to participate in any official football matches as from the beginning of the new season of the new club's national championship.
  - a fine, in accordance with normal FIFA procedures.
  - taking in consideration two cases law: "Fenerbache vs. Ortega" and "Tigres vs. Enilton Menezes de Miranda".
- Moreover, with respect to the club A, club K sought:
  1. a sanction in accordance with Art. 23, paragraph 2 (a) of the FIFA regulations prohibiting the registration of any new player, national or international, until two transfer periods have expired; fines; deduction of points an exclusion from competitions.
  2. to declare it jointly responsible for ensuring payment of the fine imposed on the player, in accordance with Art. 14, paragraph 3 of the FIFA regulations, in case the player fails to pay within one month.
  3. a disciplinary sanction, taking into account that various provisions of the FIFA regulations were violated, in particular that instead of resolving the dispute through the usual bodies of the International Federation, resort was made to the ordinary courts.
- For his part, the player requested the DRC to reject, comprehensively, the complaint lodged by K that no valid contract exists between the parties and to order the club to pay the sum of USD 2,000,000 representing compensation for having changed the terms of the Arabic version of the contract and failing to comply with the terms of the valid contract concluded between the parties.
- Finally, the club A requested the DRC to reject, comprehensively, the complaint lodged by K.
- FIFA Administration received a communication from the player on the same day (4/02/05) that the Dispute Resolution Chamber met and decided on this case, therefore the content and requests stated on this fax were not taking in consideration. The Respondent's letter did not answer any of FIFA Administration's requests.

CONSIDERATIONS OF THE DISPUTE RESOLUTION CHAMBER:

The Dispute Resolution Chamber of the FIFA Players' Status Committee shall review disputes coming under its jurisdiction pursuant to Art. 42 of the FIFA Regulations for the Status and Transfer of Players (hereafter: FIFA Regulations) at the request of one of the parties to the dispute.

According to Art. 42 of the FIFA Regulations for the Status and Transfer of Players, the triggering elements of the dispute (i.e. whether a contract was breached, with or without just cause, or sporting just cause), will be decided by the Dispute Resolution Chamber of the FIFA Players' Status Committee.

Consequently, the Dispute Resolution Chamber is the competent body to decide on the present litigation concerning the alleged breach of contract between the claimant and the respondents.

If the employment contract was breached by a party, the Dispute Resolution is responsible to verify whether this party is accountable for compensation and outstanding payments.

Moreover, in accordance with the article 21 of the FIFA Regulations, the Dispute Resolution Chamber will establish the amount of compensation to be paid and decide whether sports sanctions must be imposed.

Subsequently, and entering into the substance of the matter, the Chamber began its deliberations by analyzing the allegations of the claimant.

To begin with, the Dispute Resolution Chamber noted that the player D had committed a breach of contract by failing to reassume training with K, after having been on holidays in his country.

The Chamber noted that the player decided to terminate his employment contract with K based on the fact that the Club owed him USD 100,000 based on a second contract apparently signed by both parties in XX in Portuguese language.

In this context the members of the Chamber deemed it was important to underline that the player and K signed an employment contract on 13 August 2003 in K city written in Arabic language and that this contract is legally binding between the parties because it fulfils all the legal requirements under K NA's rules and the FIFA Regulations.

Furthermore, the Chamber considered appropriate and relevant to this case to quote the article 22 of the aforementioned contract " The player acknowledges that he became fully aware of the contract provisions and he knows English in writing and speaking and there is no need for other translation ...". The Chamber therefore acknowledged that through this article the parties renounced to have the contract translated into another language.

Moreover the Chamber focused its attention to the witness's statement provided by the Claimant and in this testimony is clear that Mr. Z acted as interpreter and translator of the player D in occasion of the signing of the contract between the latter and K.

The Chamber concluded that the player D was with the assistance of Mr. Z fully aware about the content of the contract signed on 13 August 2003 in K city with K.

At this stage the members of the Chamber deemed important to remark that the normal and common practice in Arab countries is signing contracts in Arabic language not in a foreign language such as Portuguese. Moreover this contract has to be registered in the respective Federation, therefore the National Association (NA) has to be fully aware about the content of the contracts and this is only possible if it is written in the NA's native language.

With regard to the Contract signed in XX, the Chamber duly noted that K stated that it is not genuine mainly for the three following reasons a) the contract is undated; b) the contract is signed by a person (Mr. FCD) as representative of K who had not been invested with any legal capacity by K and c). it was never stamped by the K city public authorities and never registered with the National Association (NA), in accordance with the FIFA regulations.

The Chamber confirmed the three aforementioned reasons stated by the Claimant, K, as valid and it came to the following additional conclusions:

1) the contract celebrated in XX city was written on the letterhead of Mr. FCD.
2) the terms of the Portuguese contract are different than in the contract signed in K city in Arabic language and particularly the club has additional financial obligations in favour of the player.
3) the contract in Portuguese language is not a faithful translation of the contract in Arabic language.

After stating the aforementioned conclusions the Chamber considered important to focus specifically on the player's statement, according to which, Mr FCD apart from being involved in the Portuguese contract, he had also concluded other contracts with K.

In this point, the Chamber referred to the work of the FIFA Administration scrutinizing both contracts quoted by the player and that, in effect, Mr FCD had participated in the conclusion of the contracts in question but never representing K, always other parties. Specifically, in the contract i) between MM and K for the transfer of the federative rights of the player D, Mr. FCD intervened invested with power of attorney of the Club MM and in the contract ii) between K and the player D, Mr FCD appears in the contract but only mentioned as responsible for insuring the player (Article 5, Contract in Arabic Language) and he did not sign this contract.

Furthermore, the Chamber noted from the file pertaining to this case that the player had not thoroughly justified the status of Mr. FCD as a representative of K. Therefore he could never prove this point.

At this point the Chamber wanted to underline, that it appeared strange that the player after one year from the signature of the contract in K city, began to refer to an undated contract signed in XX city in Portuguese with K club represented by a person without power of attorney.

In view of the above the Chamber acknowledges that there are no evidences at all that can prove the validity of the Contract written in Portuguese language. Therefore, it does not recognized the latter and in fact it recognized the Contract signed in K city on 13 August 2003 in Arabic language as the only valid and enforceable contract between the parties.

Furthermore, the Chamber took note of the relevant fact that K had complied completely with its contractual obligations towards the player D, up until the departure of the player.

On another point the Chamber focused on some letters addressed to FIFA by the player and his new club emphasizing that the English version of the contract that the K club had offered as proof, had not been signed and, was, therefore, not legally valid. At this stage, the Chamber wanted to clarify this issue since the Claimant provided FIFA Administration with an English translation of the contract in Arabic not an English version of the contract. Therefore the contract in Arabic and its respective English translation,

signed by K - player D and official translator respectively are the ones that can be taken into account.
In continuation, the Dispute Resolution Chamber turned its attention to the argument that the player stated "...that at the time he had signed the contract with K in Arabic, the club had acted in bad faith by not providing him with a copy of the same, duly translated into English, French or Spanish, as required by FIFA...". It becomes important to stress that FIFA Regulations does not obliged the parties to sign a contract in one of the FIFA official languages mentioned by the player. The only requirements that FIFA Regulations for the Status and Transfer of Players states in its articles 4 and 5 are the existence of a written contract and duly registered in the respective Federation.
In light of all the above, the Chamber concluded that D committed a breach of contract without just cause during the so-called protected period and was hence damaging K.
The art. 21 of the FIFA Regulations foresees that sports sanctions shall be applied and compensation payable, if a contracting party commits a breach of contract without just cause during the protected period of the employment.
In compliance with the aforementioned article 21, in particular, with its paragraph 1 (a) the Chamber decided to impose sports sanctions for unilateral breach of contract without just cause to Mr. D and to award financial compensation to K.
With respect to the sports sanctions the Chamber stressed that the player was 23 years old by the time when the contractual breach occurred and that it took place at the end of the first year of contract, as a consequence the Chamber decided to sanction Mr. D with a restriction of four months on his eligibility to participate in any official football matches as from the beginning of the new season of the new club's national championship, as stipulated in art. 23 par. 1 (a) of the Regulations, i.e. as from the beginning of the next season of the XX NA championship that is, as of 23 April 2005.
Concerning the financial compensation to be awarded to K Club, the Chamber acknowledged that the player D had committed a grave infraction and that his responsibility weighed heavily on the damages being suffered by the K Club.
Furthermore, the Chamber wanted to underline that not only the player D breached the employment contract in the protected period, i.e. in the first year of its validity, but he also went to the Ordinary Court in order to be released in a severe violation of the FIFA Statutes and Regulations. The player was one year in K city playing for K club and after that he went to XX city (not occasionally before closing the transfer period), he went straight to the XX Labour Tribunal without having never ever lodged a formal financial complaint with FIFA against the claimant and moreover he never asked for assistance in relation with his ITC. This behaviour contradicts the basic football rules and must be strongly reprimanded.
The article 22 of the FIFA Regulations lists the factors that are to be taken into account when establishing the compensation for the breach of contract and in this particular case are the following:

- the player D breached the employment contract in the protected period, i.e. in the first year of its validity and the player was under 28 years old;
- understandably so, this will have had a detrimental impact on the performance and the planning of K.
- moreover the Chamber noted that K paid USD 600,000 in order to acquire the player's federative rights from his former club;
- in the sense of the aforementioned article the Chamber took into consideration that the Player D would have had 2 further seasons remaining on his employment contract with K;
- therefore the transfer compensation amortised over 1 year leads to an amount of USD 400,000 to be taken into account and
- furthermore, K had to sign a replacement player, which cost them USD 300,000.

The Chamber concluded that under consideration of the referred facts, circumstances and art. 22 of the Regulations Mr. D is liable to pay the amount of USD 700,000 to K for damages suffered by the latter.
The further claims put forward by the K Club were rejected.
The counterclaim of the player was completely rejected.
The counterclaim of the Club A was rejected.

DECISION OF THE DISPUTE RESOLUTION CHAMBER:

1. The claim lodged by the Claimant is partially accepted.
2. The player D committed a breach of the employment contract signed with the Club K on 13 August 2003, without just cause.

3. Mr. D is restricted from all football activity worldwide for the period of 4 (four) months, counting from beginning of the next season of the XX NA championship that is, as of 23 April 2005.
4. Mr. D shall pay to the Claimant the total amount of USD 700,000 as compensation for the breach of the employment contract, within 30 days following the date of the communication of the present decision.
5. In the event that the debts of the Respondent are not paid within the stated deadline, an interest rate of 5% per year will apply.
6. The counter claims of the two Respondents are rejected.

.....

8. According to art. 60 par. 1 of the FIFA Statutes, this decision may be appealed against before the Court of Arbitration for Sport (CAS). The statement of appeal must be sent to the CAS directly within 10 days of receipt of notification of this decision and shall contain all the elements in accordance with point 2 of the directives issued by the CAS, a copy of which we enclose hereto. Within another 10 days following the expiry of the time limit for filing the statement of appeal, the appellant shall file a brief stating the facts and legal arguments giving rise to the appeal with the CAS (cf. point 4 of the directives).

25960-a
DECISION OF THE DISPUTE RESOLUTION CHAMBER
passed in Zurich, Switzerland, on 4 February 2005,
in the following composition:
Slim Aloulou (Tunisia), Chairman
Maurice Watkins (England), member
Philippe Piat (France), member
The members Mario Gallavotti (Italy) and Michele Colucci (Italy), did not take part in the judgment
on the claim presented by
X, Italy as Claimant
against
Y, Spain as Respondent
regarding the solidarity contribution related to the transfer of the federative rights to the player A

FACTS OF THE CASE:
The player A, born in 1976, was registered for the Italian club X for two sporting seasons, from 1997 to 1999, from the age of 21 to the age of 23.
On 20 July 2004, an agreement for the transfer of the federative rights to the player A to the Spanish club Y is concluded.
The Italian club X claim the 5 % payment established in article 25 of the FIFA Regulations for the Status and Transfer of Players regarding the contribution to the solidarity mechanism related to the transfer of the federative rights to the A to club Y.
According to the aforementioned Regulations, the new club concerned is to distribute 5% of this compensatory amount to the club(s) where the player has played between the age of 12 and 23. In the present case, between 1997 and 1999.
The amount paid by Yfor the transfer of the federative rights to the player A is EUR 10,500,000.
The Italian club X ask the Dispute Resolution Chamber to sentence the club Y to start with the distribution of proportion of 5% related to the transfer of the federative rights to the player A.

CONSIDERATIONS OF THE DISPUTE RESOLUTION CHAMBER:
Firstly, the Dispute Resolution Chamber took note of the issue raised by the Spanish club Y, with respect to the composition of the Chamber, especially regarding the nationality of two of the members, namely Mr. Mario Gallavotti and Mr. Michele Colucci, both Italians.
In view of such a request, both Mr. Mario Gallavotti and Mr. Michele Colucci decided of their own volition to leave the Chamber during the course of the debate on the subject of this dispute and consequently did not take part in this judgment.

The Chairman and two members of the Dispute Resolution Chamber were then left to pass a decision on this matter, in accordance with Article 1 §6 of the Rules Governing the Practice and Procedures of the Dispute Resolution Chamber.
After a careful study of the facts and allegations outlined above, the Dispute Resolution Chamber commenced its deliberations by referring to article 25 of the revised FIFA Regulations for the Status and Transfer of Players, according to which, it falls within the purview of the Dispute Resolution Chamber to review disputes concerning the distribution of the solidarity contribution.
In this sense, as further established in the article 25 of the revised FIFA Regulations for the Status and Transfer and of Players, the new club concerned is to distribute 5% of any compensation paid to the previous club to the club(s) where the player has played between the age of 12 and 23.
In the present case, the Chamber outlined that the training period to take into consideration went from the sporting season 1997/1998, when the player A was 21, until the sporting season 1998/1999, at the age of 23.
The Chamber made further reference to Art. 10 of the Regulations governing the Application of the Regulations for the Status and Transfer of Players, which provides the figures for the distribution of the solidarity contribution, according to the time the player was effectively trained by the clubs involved.
It is therefore undisputed that the Italian club X is entitled to receive 20% of the 5% related to the transfer of the federative rights to the player A to Y.
Furthermore, the Chamber made reference to Article 11 of the Regulations governing the Application of the Regulations for the Status and Transfer of Players, which reads that the new club shall pay the amount due as a solidarity contribution to the training clubs at the latest within thirty days of the player's registration.
Consequently, in light of the fact that this payment has been due since the thirty-first day after the transfer took place, i.e. 20 July 2004, the Dispute Resolution Chamber established that a default interest payment of 5% p.a. as from the day on which the payment was due, i.e. 20 August 2004, must be applied.
As it was noted that the amount paid by Y for the transfer of the federative rights to the player A was EUR 10,500,000, the Dispute Resolution Chamber decided that the Spanish club Y must pay to the Italian club X 20% of the 5% of the transfer compensation, i.e. EUR 105,000.

DECISION OF THE DISPUTE RESOLUTION CHAMBER

1. The claim of the Italian club X is accepted.
2. The Spanish club Y has to pay the amount of EUR 105,000 to the Italian club X. On the aforementioned amount, a default interest payment of 5% p.a. as from 20 August 2004 is applied.
3. The amount due to the club X has to be paid by Y within 30 days as from the date of notification of this decision.
4. According to art. 60 par. 1 of the FIFA Statutes this decision may be appealed before the Court of Arbitration for Sport (CAS). The statement of appeal must be sent to the CAS directly within 10 days of receiving notification of this decision and has to contain all elements in accordance with point 2 of the directives issued by the CAS, copy of which we enclose hereto. Within another 10 days following the expiry of the time limit for the filing of the statement of appeal, the appellant shall file with the CAS a brief stating the facts and legal arguments giving rise to the appeal (cf. point 4 of the directives).

11 MARCH 2005

3542
DECISION OF THE DISPUTE RESOLUTION CHAMBER
passed in Zurich, Switzerland, on 11 March 2005,
in the following composition:
Slim Aloulou (Tunisia), Chairman
Mr. Gerardo Movilla (Spain), Member
Mr. Jean-Marie Philips (Belgium), Member
Paulo Rogerio Amoretty Souza (Brazil), Member
Philippe Piat (France), Member

on the claim presented by Player B, France *as Claimant* against Club C, Turkey *as Respondent* regarding a contractual dispute between the parties involved

FACTS OF THE CASE:

- The parties signed an employment contract on 23 August 2004 for the 2004/2005 season, under the following basic financial terms: a USD 50,000 net cash payment, as well as a monthly remuneration of USD 7,000 (total payable salaries: USD 70,000).
- B filed a claim with FIFA on 17 December 2004, exposing that he was obliged to rescind his contract with C on 15 December 2004 due to the non-payment of four (4) months of his salaries, from September 2004 until December 2004.
- The player affirms having been working and fully available to the club up until 15 December 2004 when the contract was terminated. He never received any explanations from the club as to why he was not being paid his salaries.
- Before Mr. B formally terminated the employment contract, he sent the club a formal notice with a final payment deadline on 29 November 2004, but the club apparently did not react.
- In response to the player's allegations C has informed FIFA that the player was paid an initial cash amount of USD 50,000 on 25.08.2004, as well as a sum of USD 1,500 on 11.11.2004.
- The club has not submitted any evidence of payment of the player's salaries, explaining that these were not made to him due to his insufficient and poor performance level, which greatly prejudiced the club's position in the Turkish First Super League. In fact, the club felt that the player's bad performance was an abuse of the club's goodwill and was undeserving of its prestigious position, and that the player could therefore not assume that he would be paid his salaries under any conditions.
- Since Mr. B did not participate in the trainings of 20 and 21 December 2004, the Board of Directors of the club held a meeting in which it was decided to impose a fine of YTL 75,000 (USD 50,000).
- Mr. B defends that he did not attend the mentioned training sessions because by that time he had already formally rescinded his contract.
- The player requests the Dispute Resolution Chamber for a confirmation that he has terminated his contract with just cause and is free to register with the club of his choice with immediate effect, and from the respondent he requests a compensation in the amount of all the contractually due salary: USD 70,000.
- The respondent has a counter-claim of USD 100,000 towards the player: it demands the payment of the fine imposed on the player, amounting to USD 50,000 (YTL 75,000), minus the salaries that the club admits owing to the player until December 2004, USD 28,000.
- This leaves an outstanding amount of USD 22,000, to which the club adds the advance payments of USD 50,000 and USD 1,500 already made to the player, totalling USD 72,000, as well as the damages apparently caused to the club by the player's low performance.

CONSIDERATIONS OF THE DISPUTE RESOLUTION CHAMBER

The Dispute Resolution Chamber of the FIFA Players' Status Committee shall review disputes coming under its jurisdiction pursuant to Art. 42 of the FIFA Regulations for the Status and Transfer of Players (hereafter: FIFA Regulations) at the request of one of the parties to the dispute.

According to Art. 42 of the FIFA Regulations for the Status and Transfer of Players, the triggering elements of the dispute (i.e. whether a contract was breached, with or without just cause, or sporting just cause), will be decided by the Dispute Resolution Chamber of the FIFA Players' Status Committee.

Consequently, the Dispute Resolution Chamber is the competent body to decide on the present litigation concerning the alleged breach of contract between the claimant and the respondent.

Subsequently, and entering into the substance of the matter, the Chamber noted that the principle ground on which Mr. B based his termination of the contract with C was the non-payment of his salaries since the day his contract became effective.

The club has not essentially disputed this non-payment of the player's salaries.

Instead, the respondent's arguments are clearly most intent on pointing out that the player's level of performance was poor and has been detrimental to the club's position within its national championship.

Regarding this line of argumentation, the members of the Chamber remarked that the player's bad performance level could have been dealt with in several alternative ways, none of which include withholding the basic contractual duties towards the player. The non-fulfilment of such basic contractual obligations as is the payment of salaries, the Chamber argued, may not be implemented as a tool to sanction a player for disappointing performance levels.

The club has furthermore found it relevant to point out that Mr. B was paid a contractually due sum of USD 50,000, plus an amount of USD 1,500. It is not explained, however, why USD 1,500 was paid instead of the monthly salary stipulated in the contract, USD 7,000, nor why this one payment was made but no others followed.

As to the club's arguments relevant to the fine imposed on the player for his absence to the training sessions of 20 and 21 December 2004, the members of the Chamber unanimously voiced their agreement with the player's defence, which they found to be logical and thus acceptable. It was acknowledged that if he had in fact departed from the club on 15 December 2004 as a result of the long-term nonpayment of his salaries, it was obvious why he had been absent from the training sessions following this date. Hence, having reasonable grounds for his absences on 20 and 21 December 2004, this failure to fulfil his own contractual obligations was justified and should not have been sanctioned by a fine of USD 50,000, nor by any other deductions from the player's dues.

In conclusion, the Dispute Resolution Chamber deemed the allegations put forward by the claimant are credible and unambiguous, particularly in light of the respondent's inability to disprove these statements or to establish a substantiated defence. Consequently, the respondent shall be held responsible for the breach of contract.

In view of the above, the player's claim was partially accepted: it was decided that he would receive the amounts rightfully due to him for the time he spent under contract with the club, up until the termination of the employment relationship, as well as a damage compensation for breach of contract by the club.

The Dispute Resolution Chamber concluded its deliberations with the following calculations: C is held to indemnify Mr. B for the time he was employed with that club, until and including the month of his departure, by paying him the salary from September until December 2004, totalling USD 28,000. Furthermore, the club is liable to pay a compensation for breach of contract in the amount of USD 15,000. The total compensation therefore amounts to USD 43,000. However, since the player has already received a partial salary payment of USD 1,500, this sum shall be subtracted from the total due, leaving an outstanding amount of USD 41,500.

The counter claims of the club are rejected.

Finally, and on account of the above, the Dispute Resolution Chamber decided that the contractual relation between the parties had been terminated on 15 December 2005 (the date of the player's departure) and, as a consequence, the player is authorized to be registered to play with the club of his choice with immediate effect.

In this respect the Dispute Resolution Chamber underlined that upon receipt of the request for the player's international registration transfer certificate from the association of his prospective new club, the Turkish Football Federation is obliged to comply with this request.

DECISION OF THE DISPUTE RESOLUTION CHAMBER

1. The claim lodged by the Claimant is partially accepted and the counterclaims of the Respondent are rejected.
2. The Respondent shall pay the total amount of **USD 41,500** to the Claimant, within 30 days following the date of the communication of the present decision.
3. In the event that the debts of the Respondent are not paid within the stated deadline, an interest rate of 5% per year will apply.
4. The Claimant is authorized to be registered to play with the club of his choice, with immediate effect.
5. The Creditor is directed to inform the Debtor immediately of the bank account number to which the remittance is to be made and to notify the Dispute Resolution Chamber of every payment received.
6. According to art. 60 par. 1 of the FIFA Statutes, this decision may be appealed against before the Court of Arbitration for Sport (CAS). The statement of appeal must be sent to the CAS directly within 10 days of receipt of notification of this decision and shall contain all the elements in accordance with point 2 of the directives issued by the CAS, a copy of which we enclose hereto. Within another 10 days following the expiry of the time limit for filing the statement of appeal, the appellant shall file a brief stating the facts and legal arguments giving rise to the appeal with the CAS (cf. point 4 of the directives).

35131
DECISION OF THE DISPUTE RESOLUTION CHAMBER
passed in Zurich, Switzerland, on 11 March 2005,
in the following composition:
Slim Aloulou (Tunisia), Chairman
Jean-Marie Philips (Belgium), member
Paulo Amoretty Souza (Brazil) , member
Gerardo Movilla (Spain), member
Philippe Piat (France), member
on the claim presented by the Player X, as Claimant
against
Club Y, as Respondent

FACTS OF THE CASE

- On 1 July 2002, the player X and the club Y signed a financial agreement. On 9 July 2002, the same parties signed an employment contract, valid until 30 June 2003.
- The employment contract stipulated, inter alia, a monthly salary of EUR 2,025. The financial agreement stipulated a monthly salary of EUR 529.69, plus, inter alia, a Christmas bonus in the same amount.
- On 7 November 2002, the player's visa allowing him to stay with in the country of his club expired.
- The player pretends that the club Y, with the intention to compel him to leave the club, had not undertaken the necessary steps to provide him with a new visa, even not after he reminded the club to do so on 2 November 2002.
- He pretends that he therefore left the country on 11 December 2002, after he had stayed there illegally during more than one month.
- He claims from the club for a part of the salary of September 2002 (EUR 1554.78), for the salaries for October until December 2002 (three times EUR 2,554.78), as well as for the Christmas bonus (EUR 529.69), therefore in total for EUR 9748.90.
- Whereas, the club Y pretends that on 11 December 2002, an appointment with the player was foreseen, in the occasion of which EUR 1,435.68 would have been paid to the player for salaries for the month of September, October and November. The club pretends that this is the total amount still owed to the player.
- However, the club did not respond to several requests from the FIFA Administration to present payment receipts regarding payments made to the player X.
- The club pretends that the player did not show up on this appointment, but had left the city before without notice.
- For this reason, the board of directors of the club unilaterally terminated the contract with the player on 16 December 2002 and deposed the amount of EUR 1,435.68 in a deposit account for the benefit of the player X.
- The club showed documents according to which it applied for the new visa of the player X on 9 December 2002.
- The player X blames that the modality for the payment via the deposit account is very inconvenient because it is very difficult to cash and the amount will be paid only much later.
- The club denies that it offered the player cheques with complicated modalities.
- On 17 January 2003, FIFA authorised the player X to sign an employment contract with the club of his choice. On 1 August 2003, he signed an employment contract with the club Z.

CONSIDERATIONS OF THE DISPUTE RESOLUTION CHAMBER

1. The members of the Dispute Resolution Chamber were summoned to pass a decision on the present matter by the Chairman pursuant to Art. 1 point 6) of the Rules Governing the Practice and Procedures of the Dispute Resolution Chamber.
2. The deciding body started its deliberations by indicating that, as established in Art. 42 § 1 lit. (b) (i) of the FIFA Regulations for the Status and Transfer of Players, it falls within the purview of the Dispute Resolution Chamber to determine whether one of the parties has committed a unilateral breach of contract without just cause. In the case that the employment contract was breached by

a party, the Dispute Resolution Chamber is responsible to verify and decide whether this party is accountable for outstanding payments and compensation.

3. In view of the above, the Dispute Resolution Chamber concluded that it was competent to decide on the present litigation.
4. The members present at the meeting then entered into the substance of the matter and deemed it appropriate to verify first if the employment contract concluded by the player X and the club Y has been breached by one of them.
5. The Dispute Resolution Chamber first noticed that according to the employment contract, the player was entitled to a total monthly salary of EUR 2,554.69, as well as some specific bonuses. It furthermore noticed that the player X maintained that the club Y has not paid three entire monthly salaries, EUR 1,554.78 of another monthly salary, plus a Christmas bonus of EUR 529.69, and that he therefore claims for the total amount of EUR 9748.90 from the club Y. Finally, the Dispute Resolution Chamber noticed that the club alleged owing the player only the amount of EUR 1,435.68, but had not responded to several requests from the FIFA Administration to present payment receipts regarding payments made to the player X.
6. The Dispute Resolution Chamber stated that the persistent failure of a club to pay the salaries of a player, without just cause, is generally to be considered as a unilateral breach of an employment contract. The club Y did not have a reason justifying the non-payment of the salaries. Furthermore, a delay of three to four months in the payment of salaries has clearly to be considered a "persistent failure".
7. As a result to the above, the behaviour of the club Y has to be considered as a breach of contract without valid reasons.
8. Continuing, the Dispute Resolution Chamber turned to the player's allegation that the club Y did not undertake the necessary to provide him with a visa, and in this regard, took note of the fact that the players visa allowing him to stay with his club expired on 7 November 2002. Furthermore, the Chamber noticed that the club indicated that it had applied for the new visa of the player X on 9 December 2002. Finally, the Chamber noticed that the player left the country concerned on 11 December 2002, after he had stayed there illegally during more than one month.
9. In this regard, the Dispute Resolution Chamber stated that it is a basic principle of labour law that an employer has to provide his employees with a work permit, if need be. If an employer does not undertake the necessary to provide his employees with a work permit, and if this compels the player to leave the country where he is employed, and therefore to quit his work, this is basically to be considered as an unjustified breach of the employment contract by the employer.
10. The Chamber then stated that the visa which allowed the player X to stay in the country concerned, has to be considered as equivalent to his work permit for this country.
11. Furthermore, the chamber stated that, since the club Y let pass more than one month from the expiry of the player X' visa until it made an application for his new visa, and with this behaviour, compelled the player to leave the country concnerned and his club, this has to be seen as a violation of a basic principle of labour law from the side of the club.
12. As a result to the above, the behaviour of the club Y has to be considered as a breach of contract without valid reasons.
13. In consequence to the above, the Dispute Resolution Chamber decided that the player X is entitled to EUR 9748.90 from the club Y for outstanding salaries and bonuses.

DECISION OF THE DISPUTE RESOLUTION CHAMBER

1. The claim of the player X is accepted.
2. The club Y has to pay the amount of EUR 9748.90 to the player X.
3. The amount due to the player X has to be paid by the club Y within the next 30 days as from the date of notification of this decision.
4. In the event that the debts of the Respondent are not paid within the stated deadline, an interest rate of 5% per year will apply as from the first day after the stated deadline.
5. If the aforementioned sum is not paid within the aforementioned deadline, the present matter shall be submitted to FIFA's Disciplinary Committee, so that the necessary disciplinary sanctions may be imposed.
6. The player X is directed to inform the club Y immediately of the account number to which the remittance is to be made, and to notify the Dispute Resolution Chamber of every payment received.

7. According to art. 60 par. 1 of the FIFA Statutes this decision may be appealed before the Court of Arbitration for Sport (CAS). The statement of appeal must be sent to the CAS directly within 10 days of receiving notification of this decision and has to contain all elements in accordance with point 2 of the directives issued by the CAS, copy of which we enclose hereto. Within another 10 days following the expiry of the time limit for the filing of the statement of appeal, the appellant shall file with the CAS a brief stating the facts and legal arguments giving rise to the appeal (cf. point 4 of the directives).

35144 b
DECISION OF THE DISPUTE RESOLUTION CHAMBER
passed in Zurich, Switzerland, on 11 March 2005,
in the following composition:
Slim Aloulou (Tunisia), chairman
Jean-Marie Philips (Belgium), member
Paulo Amoretty Souza (Brazil), member
Gerardo Movilla (Spain), member
Philippe Piat (France), member
on the claim presented by Club A as Claimant
against
Player B as Respondent
regarding a labour dispute

FACTS OF THE CASE
On 19 November 2004, B and A signed an employment contract valid until 30 June 2005, which could be unilaterally extended by A for the 2005/2006 season.
According to such contract, B was entitled to receive the total amount of X
108,400 for the 2004/2005 sporting season and one of the following amounts for the 2005/2006 sporting season:
a. X 400,000 gross amount *"providing A gains at least 25 points in the 2004/2005 season spring round";*
b. X 350,000 gross amount *"providing A gains at least 20 points in the 2004/2005 season spring round";*
c. X 300,000 gross amount *"providing A gains less than 20 points in the 2004/2005 season spring round".*
Since the registration period in Y was closed at the time of the contract's signature, A had to wait until 1 February 2005 to register B.
However, on 1 January 2005, B signed another employment contract with C, valid from that date until 30 June 2007.
In January 2005, after having received the request for B's international registration transfer certificate (hereinafter: IRTC) from the Association D and ignoring the fact that B had signed an employment contract with A, Association D issued the relevant IRTC and B was registered for C.
As a consequence, A is presently claiming compensation from B for his breach of contract, in the amount equivalent to the payments made to the player and the expenses in which it incurred with him, in particular, X 16,945 for salaries, X 4,533 for a flight ticket V-Z-V and X 3,900 for the rent of his apartment.
Moreover, A is also requesting the Chamber to impose the necessary disciplinary sanctions on the player.
In conclusion, A understands that its employment contract with B is valid and binding for both parties and requests the Chamber's immediate intervention.
In response, B defends that the contract that he signed with A is invalid, since it only has a 6 months' duration, which according to him, contravenes the FIFA Regulations for the Status and Transfer of Players.
Moreover, the player requests the Chamber to declare the contract invalid, based on the fact that it was not signed by his agent.

Furthermore, the player accuses A of having threatened him with his deportation back to Z, since he still did not have the necessary legal documents to remain in Y. According to the player, in order not to seriously risk his international career, he was forced to sign the relevant contract with A.
Finally, the player defends that if he would have stayed with A, the compensation that he had to pay to his former club E, in the amount of X 20,000, would have been deducted from his salaries and, as a consequence, he would have not received any remuneration during a long period. In this respect, the player also adds that the C has paid such compensation, without affecting his contractual remuneration.
In conclusion, B asserts that he wishes to comply with his employment contract with C and requests the Chamber to reject A's present claim.

CONSIDERATIONS OF THE DISPUTE RESOLUTION CHAMBER

The members of the Dispute Resolution Chamber were summoned to pass a decision on this matter by the Chairman pursuant to art. 1 point 6) of the Rules Governing the Practice and Procedures of the Dispute Resolution Chamber.
The Dispute Resolution Chamber shall review disputes coming under its jurisdiction pursuant to art. 42 of the FIFA Regulations for the Status and Transfer of Players, at the request of one of the parties to the dispute.
According to art. 42, par. 1 lit. (b) of the FIFA Regulations for the Status and Transfer of Players, the triggering elements of the dispute (i.e. whether a contract was breached, with or without just cause, or sporting just cause), will be decided by the Dispute Resolution Chamber.
If an employment contract is breached by a party, the Dispute Resolution Chamber is responsible to verify whether a party is accountable for compensation and outstanding payments.
Also, the Dispute Resolution Chamber will establish the amount of compensation to be paid and decide whether sports sanctions must be imposed (cf. art. 42, par. 1, b, ii and iii in connection with art. 22 and 23 of the aforementioned Regulations).
Consequently, the Dispute Resolution Chamber is the competent body to decide on the present litigation concerning B's alleged breach of contract and the consequent compensation claimed by A.
Subsequently, and entering into the substance of the matter, the Chamber started by acknowledging that, on 19 November 2004, A and B signed an employment contract valid from 2 November 2004 until 30 June 2005, which could be unilaterally extended by A for the 2005/2006 season, and that, since the registration period in Y was closed in November 2004, A had to wait until the following registration period opened, i.e. February 2005, to register the player with the Association D.
Moreover, the Chamber acknowledged that, on 1 January 2005, and independently of having signed the previously mentioned employment contract with A, B signed another employment contract with C, valid from that date until 30 June 2007, without the consent nor knowledge of A.
In this respect, the members of the Chamber took note that, as an outcome of B's non-fulfilment of his employment contract with A, the latter is presently claiming compensation for breach of contract in the total amount of X 25,378, corresponding to all the payments made to the player, i.e. salaries in the amount of X 16,945, and expenses incurred with him, in particular, a flight ticket V-Z-V in the amount of X 4,533 and the player's accommodation costs X 3,900, as well as the imposition of disciplinary sanctions on him.
The members of the Chamber also noted that A, in support of its allegations, has provided the FIFA Administration with a copy of its employment contract with B, together with copies of receipts concerning the aforementioned payments/expenses.
After having analysing the aforementioned documents, as well as both parties' positions, the members of the Chamber were of the opinion that A has complied with its contractual obligations towards B and particularly, that it has effectively incurred in all the expenses that it is currently claiming from the player.
With respect to the issues raised by the player on his defence, the Chamber started by underlining the fact that B's employment contract with A was duly signed by each of the parties and therefore, is considered valid and binding for both the player and the club.
In this context, the Chamber rejected the argument raised by B, according to which, his contract with A should be considered invalid due to the fact that it was not signed by his agent.
Moreover the members of the Chamber also rejected the argument concerning the duration of the player's employment contract with A, which would allegedly imply the contract's nullity, based on art. 4 par. 2 of the FIFA Regulations for the Status and Transfer of Players (hereinafter: the Regulations). In fact,

the minimum duration of an employment contract has to be seen in connection with art. 5 par. 2 of the Regulations which allows only one transfer per player in the same sports season in a period of 12 months. Yet, by means of the FIFA circular no. 867, it was clarified that the wording of the aforementioned legal ground must be understood to apply only to the sports season, rather than to the calendar years.

A contract signed for the remaining duration of a sports season has therefore, to be considered as valid.

Furthermore, the Chamber emphasized that art. 18 par. 2 of the revised Regulations, which will come into effect on 1 July 2005, explicitly stipulates that understanding ("the minimum length of a contract shall be from the date of its entry into force to the end of the season,...").

With regard to the accusations made by B, according to which, A had threatened him with his deportation back to Z in case he would not sign the employment contract, the Chamber considered these allegations as not sustained, since the player has failed to provide the FIFA Administration with evidence in this regard and consequently decided to reject them.

Finally, the Chamber considered irrelevant and therefore, rejected the arguments raised by the player concerning the financial advantages and disadvantages of his employment contracts with A and C.

In light of all the above, the Dispute Resolution Chamber reached the conclusion that B has clearly breached his employment contract with A, without just cause.

As a consequence, and in compliance with the content of Chapter VIII of the Regulations, in particular, with its art. 21 par. 1 (a), the Chamber decided to impose sports sanctions for unilateral breach of contract without just cause on B.

In this respect, taking into account the fact that B was 25 years old by the time when the contractual breach occurred, i.e. on 1 January 2005, the date when the player signed the relevant employment contract with C, and that it took place within the first year of contract, the Chamber decided to sanction B with a restriction of four months on his eligibility to participate in any official football matches, as stipulated in art. 23 par. 1 (a) of the Regulations.

Furthermore, with regard to the financial claim submitted by A, the Chamber considered B liable to compensate A in the amount equivalent to all the payments made to him by the latter, as well as all the expenses in which it incurred with him, in the total amount of X 25,378.

In conclusion, in view of the present matter's circumstances, the evidence carried to the file and its well-established jurisprudence, the Dispute Resolution Chamber decided to entirely accept the claim filed by A in the present matter.

DECISION OF THE DISPUTE RESOLUTION CHAMBER

1. The claim of A is accepted in its entirety.
2. The Respondent B shall pay the total amount of X 25,378 to the Claimant A, within 30 days of notification of the present decision.
3. If the Respondent fails to comply with the above-mentioned deadline, an interest rate of 5% per year will apply and the case will immediately be presented to the FIFA Disciplinary Committee.
4. The Claimant is directed to inform the Respondent immediately of the account number to which the remittance is to be made and to notify the Dispute Resolution Chamber of every payment received.
5. B is suspended for the period of 4 (four) months from participating in any official football match, as from the date of notification of the present decision.
6. According to art. 60 par. 1 of the FIFA Statutes, this decision may be appealed before the Court of Arbitration for Sport (CAS). The statement of appeal must be sent to the CAS directly within 10 days of receiving notification of this decision and has to contain all elements in accordance with point 2 of the directives issued by the CAS, copy of which we enclose hereto. Within another 10 days following the expiry of the time limit for the filing of the statement of appeal, the appellant shall file with the CAS a brief stating the facts and legal arguments giving rise to the appeal (cf. point 4 of the directives).

35174
DECISION OF THE DISPUTE RESOLUTION CHAMBER

passed in Zurich, Switzerland on 11 March 2005,
in the following composition:
Slim Aloulou (Tunisia), chairman

Jean-Marie Philips (Belgium), member
Paulo Amoretty Souza (Brazil), member
Gerardo Movilla (Spain), member
Philippe Piat (France), member on the claim presented by the player E. L., Brazil, as Claimant against the club FC E., United Arab Emirates, as Respondent,
regarding a contractual dispute.

I. FACTS OF THE CASE

1. On 3 August 2002, the player E. L. and FC E. signed an employment contract for the period as from 1 September 2002 until 31 August 2003. The contract stipulated a monthly salary in the amount of USD –.–. Furthermore, the club was engaged to pay to the agent of the player an amount of USD –.–, amount which had to be returned in case of the cancellation of the contract during the probation period. The probation period was fixed to three months.
2. On 23 November 2002, the club terminated the contract unilaterally. The player signed a receipt of salary and the notice of termination of the contract.
3. On 13 May 2003, FIFA decided that the United Arab Emirates Football Association has to issue the International Registration Transfer Certificate. The issuance was refused until this date due to the fact that the club claimed the amount of USD –.– back from the agent. FIFA stated that the person who represented the player at the signature of the contract was not a licensed players' agent. Therefore, FIFA could not intervene concerning the refund of the amount of USD–.–.
4. On 13 June 2003, the player turned to FIFA and affirmed that after two months and 23 days of being rendering his services to the club, it cancelled the contract. Moreover, he affirmed that as soon as he returned to Brazil, the Brazilian club FC C. hired him, but he could not render his services to the club because the FC E. refused to issue the IRTC. The player emphasised that the refund of the USD –.– paid to the agent is not his problem. The player therefore claimed the following amounts:
   - Salary December 2002 USD –.–
   - Salary January 2003 USD –.–
   - Salary February 2003 USD –.–
   - Salary March 2003 USD –.–
   - Salary April 2003 USD –.–
   - Salary May 2003 USD –.–
   - Salary June 2003 USD –.–
   - Vacation from September 2002 to June 2003 USD –.–
   - contractual penalty for the cancellation of the contract USD –.–

   Total USD –.–
5. On 19 July 2004, the FC E. provided FIFA with its point of view. The club pointed out that the contract was terminated during the probation period and that the player received all amounts due by reason of the contract. However, the club claimed an amount of USD –.– corresponding to the payment made to the players' agent. Therefore, the club lodged a counterclaim because it was of the opinion that both, the player and the agent, were jointly responsible for the refund of this amount.
6. The player admitted that he received the salary from September 2002 until 29 November 2002. He reiterated that only the players' agent was beneficiary of the amount of USD –.– Furthermore, he never received the contractual penalty in the amount of USD –.–. As he could not play in Brazil due to the fact that the United Arab Emirates Football Association refused to issue the IRTC, he claimed the salaries for the period he was prevented to play.

II. CONSIDERATIONS OF THE DISPUTE RESOLUTION CHAMBER

1. The Dispute Resolution Chamber of the FIFA Players' Status Committee shall review disputes coming under its jurisdiction pursuant to art. 42 of the FIFA Regulations for the Status and Transfer of Players at the request of one of the parties to the dispute.
2. Therefore, the members of the Dispute Resolution Chamber at first confirmed to be competent to pass a decision in this matter. In addition, the Committee acknowledged the above-mentioned facts, as well as the further documentation contained in the file.
3. The Chamber carefully considered the contents of the contract concluded between the parties on 3 August 2002. In particular, it noted that the parties had agreed on a probation period of three months.

4. In continuation, the Chamber duly considered that, prior to the end of the probation period, the player signed the receipt of the salary in the amount of USD –.– for the end of service as well as a notice of cancellation of the contract. Therefore, the Chamber stated that the player cannot allege that the contract has been terminated unilaterally. The Chamber considered the signature of the player on the payment receipt "end of service" and on the notice of cancellation of his contract as an acceptance of the termination of the contract. Therefore, the Chamber concluded that the player cannot claim the execution of a contract that had been terminated on mutual consent.
5. With regard to the agreed probation period, the Chamber recalled that, in accordance with its long standing jurisprudence, as a general rule, such clauses are not acceptable, since they do not respect the spirit of the regulations. In the case at hand, however, the player had accepted the termination of the contractual relationship during the probation period. As a consequence, the Chamber deemed that, in view of the specificities of the case, the relevant clause could be tolerated.
6. Furthermore, the Chamber outlined that, if the player had problems with the issuance of the IRTC, he should have lodged an adequate claim with FIFA for his provisional registration in due course and not lodged a complaint for execution of the contract more than half a year after its termination.
7. Concerning the counterclaim lodged by the club, the Chamber stated that, according to the contract, the amount was paid to the agent directly and that the contract does not stipulate that this amount should be refunded by the player to the club. In particular, the agreement does not foresee that the player should be jointly liable for the refund of that sum. Therefore, the club has to claim this amount to the agent directly and the player cannot be declared responsible for the refund of the amount of USD –.–. Hence, the counterclaim has to be rejected.
8. Taking into account all of the above, the Dispute Resolution Chamber decided that both, claim and counterclaim, are rejected.

III. DECISION OF THE PLAYERS' STATUS COMMITTEE

1. The claim of the player E. L. is rejected.
2. The counterclaim of the FC E. is rejected.
3. According to art. 60 par. 1 of the FIFA Statutes this decision may be appealed before the Court of Arbitration for Sport (CAS). The statement of appeal must be sent to the CAS directly within 10 days of receiving notification of this decision and has to contain all elements in accordance with point 2 of the directives issued by the CAS, copy of which we enclose hereto. Within another 10 days following the expiry of the time limit for the filing of the statement of appeal, the appellant shall file with the CAS a brief stating the facts and legal arguments giving rise to the appeal (cf. point 4 of the directives).

⚽⚽⚽

35185

DECISION OF THE DISPUTE RESOLUTION CHAMBER

passed in Zurich, Switzerland, on 11 March 2005,
in the following composition:
Slim Aloulou (Tunisia), chairman
Jean-Marie Philips (Belgium), member
Paulo Amoretty Souza (Brazil), member
Gerardo Movilla (Spain), member
Philippe Piat (France), member
on the claim presented by A as Claimant
against
B as Respondent
regarding the solidarity contribution related to the transfer of the player C

FACTS OF THE CASE

In summer 2004, club D and B concluded an agreement for the transfer of the player C.
The Association E informed the FIFA Administration that C was born on 19 May 1979 and registered for A on 4 March 1998 until 22 January 2002, for the 1998, 1999, 2000 and 2001 sporting seasons, between the ages of 19 and 22.

A is claiming the implementation of the principles stipulated in art. 25 of the FIFA Regulations for the Status and Transfer of Players (hereinafter: the Regulations) regarding the contribution for the solidarity mechanism related to the transfer of C to B.
The total amount paid by B for the relevant transfer of C was EUR 2,000,000.
According to the Regulations, the new club concerned is to distribute 5% of this compensatory amount to the club(s) where the player has played between the ages of 12 and 23.
As a consequence, A is presently claiming the payment of EUR 40,000 from B, which corresponds to 40% of 5% of EUR 2,000,000.
In response, and with regard to the distribution of the solidarity contribution for the present transfer of C's federative rights, B asserts that it has already complied with its obligations towards all the other clubs that were entitled to receive such contribution.
However, with regard to A's claim, B defends that it should not pay any amount to it, since the latter owes it the amount of Y 87,523, as a result of a decision taken by the Civil Court X, in 2001.
In fact, B draw's the attention of the Chamber to A's bad faith and defends that the amount due as solidarity contribution in the present matter, should be deducted from the aforementioned amount, by means of a compensation of credits, via the aforementioned Civil Court.
A defends that the aforementioned proposal of B should be rejected since the credits at stake emerge from separate matters and should therefore, be treated separately.

CONSIDERATIONS OF THE DISPUTE RESOLUTION CHAMBER

The members of the Dispute Resolution Chamber were summoned to pass a decision on this matter by the Chairman pursuant to art. 1 point 6) of the Rules Governing the Practice and Procedures of the Dispute Resolution Chamber.
After a careful analysis of the facts and allegations outlined above, the Dispute Resolution Chamber commenced its deliberations by referring to art. 25 of the Regulations, according to which it falls within the purview of the Dispute Resolution Chamber to review disputes concerning the distribution of the solidarity contribution.
Consequently, the Dispute Resolution Chamber established that it was the competent body to decide on the present litigation concerning the solidarity contribution claimed by A.
Once its competence was thus established, the Dispute Resolution Chamber went on to deal with the substance of the case.
The members of the Chamber carefully studied the facts outlined above and emphasized that, as further established in the art. 25 of the Regulations, the new club to which a player is transferred during the course of an employment contract with his previous club, is the club responsible for the distribution of 5% of the compensation to the former club(s) where the player has trained between the age of 12 and 23.
The Chamber subsequently referred to art. 10 of the Regulations governing the Application of the FIFA Regulations, which provides the figures for the distribution of the solidarity contribution, taking into consideration the time the player was effectively trained by the club concerned.
Considering that the player C was registered with A from 4 March 1998 until 22 January 2002, that is, between the ages of 19 and 22 years, for 4 sport seasons, 40% of the 5% solidarity contribution shall be apportioned to this club.
As it was ascertained that the amount paid by the respondent to D for the federative rights of C was EUR 2,000,000, 40% of the 5% solidarity contribution amounts to EUR 40,000.
In light of the above, the Chamber reached the conclusion that B is liable to pay the amount of EUR 40,000 to A.
Finally, with regard to the demand submitted by B, according to which, any amount awarded to A in the present matter should be deducted from a debt that the relevant club has towards it, the Chamber considered that both matters are completely independent and separate from each other and therefore, decided to reject any eventual compensation of credits.

DECISION OF THE DISPUTE RESOLUTION CHAMBER

1. The claim of A is accepted.
2. The Respondent, B, shall pay the amount of EUR 40,000 to the Claimant, A, within 30 days of notification of the present decision.
3. If the Respondent fails to comply with the above-mentioned deadline, an interest rate of 5% per year will apply and the case will immediately be presented to the FIFA Disciplinary Committee.

4. The demand of the Respondent is rejected.
5. The Claimant is directed to inform the Respondent immediately of the account number to which the remittance is to be made and to notify the Dispute Resolution Chamber of every payment received.
6. According to art. 60 par. 1 of the FIFA Statutes, this decision may be appealed before the Court of Arbitration for Sport (CAS). The statement of appeal must be sent to the CAS directly within 10 days of receiving notification of this decision and has to contain all elements in accordance with point 2 of the directives issued by the CAS, copy of which we enclose hereto. Within another 10 days following the expiry of the time limit for the filing of the statement of appeal, the appellant shall file with the CAS a brief stating the facts and legal arguments giving rise to the appeal (cf. point 4 of the directives).

35239
DECISION OF THE DISPUTE RESOLUTION CHAMBER
passed in Zurich, Switzerland, on 11 March 2005,
in the following composition:
Slim Aloulou (Tunisia), Chairman
Jean-Marie Philips (Belgium), member
Paulo Amoretty Souza (Brazil), member
Philippe Piat (France), member
Gerardo Movilla (Spain), member
on the claim presented by the club, X as Claimant against the player, Y and the club, Z as Respondents regarding a contractual dispute between the player and the club X in connection with the player's international clearance,

FACTS OF THE CASE

- The player, Y, signed an employment contract with Z on 10 January 2005.
- On 3 February 2005, the Football Federation of Z's country turned to FIFA with a request relating to the player's international clearance for its member club, Z, as the Football Association of X's country (hereinafter also referred to as "FA Xc") did not issue the international registration transfer certificate maintaining that the player is still contractually bound to its member club, X.
- On 18 February 2005, the Single Judge of the Players' Status Committee considered that the contractual situation of the player first needs to be verified before being able to consider the matter concerning the player's registration.
- Consequently, the Single Judge deemed that the present case has to be considered as to the substance by the Dispute Resolution Chamber and decided that the request of the Football Federation of Z dated 3 February 2005 for the provisional registration of the player Y for its affiliate, Z, is to be rejected.
- Y maintains having been registered with X as an amateur player, which fact he allegedly had verified and which was confirmed to him prior to having signed an employment contract with the above-mentioned club Z.
- Z asserts that it signed an employment contract with the player in question after having ascertained that Y was not contractually bound to another club.
- According to the Z, this was confirmed in writing by the player and his agent.
- In this context, Z submitted the player's written confirmation dated 10 January 2005.
- Moreover, Z points out that the confirmation that the player had no contractual obligations towards another club was a condition in order for the club to enter into a contractual relation with the player, as it is not in the position to pay a "transfer fee".
- X, on the other hand, maintains that the player is bound to the club by contract valid until the 2005-06 season.
- In support of its position, the club submitted a copy of a signed contract dated 17 May 2003 as well as documents pertaining to payments allegedly made by the club to the player.
- The FA Xc approved and registered the said contract on 3 February 2005.
- FA Xc has explained that it received the player's contract on 12 June 2003 for approval in conformity with its circular letter nr. 4 dated 5 June 2003, but that the contract was not approved at that time

because it was not "notarised" by the relevant branch. On 2 February 2005 the contract was duly notarised by this branch and subsequently approved by FA Xc on 3 February 2005.

- The contract with X indicates the following:
  - a period of validity of 3 seasons, until the 2005-06 season
  - monies payable to the player:
    150,000 for 3 seasons / 50,000 per season
    125,000 payable on 01.08.03, 01.10.03, 01.01.04, and 01.03.04 : 1st season
    125,000 payable on 01.08.04, 01.10.04, 01.01.05, and 01.03.05: 2nd season
    Monthly salary: 1,500
  - The receipts submitted by the X indicate the following:
    - payment of 16,399 on 21.03.04
    - payment of 1,421, salary for September 2004
    - 18,582 as a bonus
- According to the X, the player duly received all contractual payments relating to the 2003-04 season and he signed the receipts.
- The members of the Chamber noticed that it is rather difficult to distinguish a pertinent signature on these documents.
- In addition, the club has submitted a copy of correspondence to the player dated 01.10.04 and 25.11.04, in which the player is asked to pick up a cheque to the amount of 20,499 as 50% of contract value for the 2004-05 season.
- X also maintains that, in contradiction to Z's statement, Z was fully aware of the fact that the player was under contract with X.
- In this respect, the X presented a fax dated 7 December 2004 that it received from Z offering a fee of EUR 350,000 for the transfer of 2 players including the player in question during the registration period of January 2005.
- In the light of the above, X claims that the player has acted in breach of the relevant FIFA Regulations and his employment contract.
- The player, for his part, vehemently denies having signed the contract presented by X, of which he allegedly never received a copy.
- In addition, he denies having received the monies indicated on the receipts submitted by the club.
- Y furthermore asserts that he has not received the payments that he would be entitled to receive in accordance with the disputed contract.
- He acknowledges having received from the club the total amount of 17,000 plus monthly sums for "private circumstances".
- The player was surprised to receive another reminder from X, dated 5 February 2005, to pick up the above-mentioned cheque amounting to 20,499.
- According to the player, he was registered as an amateur player.
- Prior to his departure for Z's country, he allegedly received the confirmation that there was no approved contract and that all registrations stated that he was an amateur player.
- No documents have been presented by the player in this respect.
- The player refutes the validity of the contract presented by X for the following reasons: of the contract dated 17 May 2003 was registered by the FA Xc on 3 February 2005 only. In accordance with the "draft law of players' affairs" contracts are not valid unless registered in the FA Xc. Therefore, the contract was certainly not valid on 10 January 2005 when he signed on with Z;
  - he has not signed the disputed contract;
  - the signature of the player on the contract is a falsification;
  - on 17 May 2003, he was a minor and therefore, his parent(s) should have signed the same contract. Instead, his brother signed the contract.
- No documents have been presented by the player in support of this position.
- According to the player, X is trying to secure a transfer payment by maintaining that he is contractually bound to it.

CONSIDERATIONS OF THE DISPUTE RESOLUTION CHAMBER

The members of the Chamber firstly proceeded to confirm that in accordance with Article 42 of the FIFA Regulations for the Status and Transfer of Players the Chamber is competent to deal with the present matter. In this respect, the Chamber stressed that the facts leading to the present dispute between Y and X,

who share the same nationality, regarding their employment relationship, i.e. the player having signed an employment contract with Z that is affiliated to another association, internationalise the case at hand.
The Chamber duly noted that the player maintains that he was not contractually bound to X and that therefore, he was entitled to sign an employment contract with Z on 10 January 2005. Z, for its part, stresses that this was a condition in order to engage the player in question by means of a written agreement. In this respect, it was taken into consideration that Z proceeded to sign on the player on the basis of the information provided by the player and his agent. The members of the Chamber took into account that Y has not presented any documentation in support of his allegation that he received confirmation that he was not contractually bound to X prior to having signed an employment contract with Z.
X, however, contests the player's allegations and asserts that Y is contractually bound to it until the 2005-06 season. In support of its position, the X has presented a signed employment contract dated 17 May 2003 which indicates a period of validity of 3 seasons, i.e. until the 2005-06 season. The two signatures on this contract relating to Y are indicated as being from Y himself as well as from a person "for parents for less than 18 years". In addition, the club has presented documents pertaining to payments allegedly made to the player on the basis of the same contract. The members of the Chamber, however, were unable to distinguish a pertinent signature on these documents and therefore these were not taken into consideration.
The player, on the other hand, contests the validity of the contract presented by the club for various reasons which have not been corroborated with relevant documentary evidence. In addition, Y denies having received the monies that are indicated on the receipts submitted by the club and he stresses that he has received no monies that he would have been entitled to according to the contract presented by X.
The Chamber duly noted that the player acknowledges having received from the club the total amount of 17,000 plus monthly sums for "private circumstances". As regards Y's position pertaining to the signatures on the contract, the Chamber acknowledged that the player confirms that his brother did sign the contract in question, but that his alleged signature is a falsification. In this regard, the Chamber pointed out that it is not competent to decide on whether or not a signature is a forgery. Indeed, such a matter shall be referred to a criminal court.
The Chamber took into consideration that by fax dated 7 December 2004 addressed to X, Z confirmed its interest "to transfer" two players, including Y, during the registration period of January 2005. In this respect, Z also refers to the meeting it had with X in the city of X.
According to the said fax, Z offered the total sum of EUR 350,000 for the two players payable in instalments until 30 December 2005. In addition, X would be entitled to receive 15% of the total amount that Z would receive for a future transfer of the players in question.
On the basis of the above-mentioned offer to pay a transfer compensation, the members of the Chamber concurred that Z must have been aware that Y was contractually bound to X in contradiction to the statements that it has made throughout the proceedings in the case at hand.
Taking into account all of the above, the Chamber decided that the player in question is bound to X by means of the above-mentioned contract dated 17 May 2003. Y having signed an employment contract with Z on 10 January 2005 whilst being contractually bound to X during the same period of time as indicated in the employment contract with Z, the Chamber decided that Y is found to have committed a unilateral breach of contract without just cause within the so-called protected period. Consequently, articles 21§1(a), 22 and 23§1(a) of the Regulations for the Status and Transfer of Players are applicable to the present matter.
On account of the above, the Chamber decided that the player is liable to pay compensation for breach of contract to X. With respect to the calculation of the amount of compensation in accordance with the said article 22, the Chamber took into consideration that the length of time remaining on the existing contract with X amounts to 1,5 year. In accordance with this contract, the player was entitled to receive 50,000 per season as well as 4 payments of 125,000 each per season and a monthly salary of 1,500. These amounts in relation to the remaining period of time on the contract total 852,000. Furthermore, the members of the Chamber noted that according to the contract that he signed with Z, Y is entitled to receive the approximate amount of EUR 338,333 per season.
It was also taken into consideration that the unilateral breach of contract has occurred during the first 3 years of the contract and that such breach has caused X to look for a replacement of the player in question, who left his club during the course of the season. In the light of all of these elements, the Chamber decided that the amount of compensation of USD 250,000 is appropriate and justified.
The Chamber went further on analysing the sports sanctions to be imposed on the player for having

caused the contractual breach. According to article 23 par. 1(a) of the said Regulations, basically, a player shall be sanctioned by means of a restriction of four months on his eligibility to participate in any official football matches. In application of this article, the Chamber decided to suspend the player from any official football matches as of the date of notification of the present decision.
Finally, taking into account that there has been a breach of the employment contract, the contractual relation between the player, Y, and the club, X, is considered terminated.
Consequently, the player is authorised to register with Z.

DECISION OF THE DISPUTE RESOLUTION CHAMBER

1. The claim of the Claimant, X, is accepted.
2. The player, Y, has committed a unilateral breach of the employment contract without just cause.
3. The player must pay the amount USD 250,000 as compensation for breach of contract to X within 30 days of notification of the present decision.
4. The amount due to the Claimant, X, has to be paid by the player, Y, within 30 days as from the date of notification of this decision.
5. In the event that the debt of the player is not paid within the stated deadline, an interest rate of 5% per year will apply as of expiry of the aforementioned deadline.
6. If the sum of USD 250,000 is not paid within the aforementioned deadline, the new club, Z, shall be deemed jointly responsible for payment of the amount of compensation (cf. article 14 par. 3 of the Regulations governing the Application of the aforementioned Regulations).
7. If the sum of USD 250,000 is not paid within one month of the club having become jointly responsible with the player, the present matter shall be submitted to the FIFA Disciplinary Committee
8. The Claimant, X, is directed to inform the player, Y, immediately of the account number to which the remittance is to be made and to notify the Dispute Resolution Chamber of every payment received.
9. The player, Y, is authorised to register with Z.
10. The player is not eligible to participate in any official football matches during a four months' period of time as of the date of notification of the present decision.
11. According to art. 60 par. 1 of the FIFA Statutes, this decision may be appealed against before the Court of Arbitration for Sport (CAS). The statement of appeal must be sent to the CAS directly within 10 days of receipt of notification of this decision and shall contain all the elements in accordance with point 2 of the directives issued by the CAS, a copy of which we enclose hereto. Within another 10 days following the expiry of the time limit for filing the statement of appeal, the appellant shall file a brief stating the facts and legal arguments giving rise to the appeal with the CAS (cf. point 4 of the directives).

35284
DECISION OF THE DISPUTE RESOLUTION CHAMBER
passed in Zurich, Switzerland, on 11 March 2005,
in the following composition:
Slim Aloulou (Tunisia), Chairman
Gerardo Movilla (Spain), Member
Philippe Piat (France), Member
Jean-Marie Philips (Belgium), Member
Paulo Rogerio Amoretty Souza (Brazil), Member
on the claim presented by
Player R, Moldova as Claimant
against
F.C. X , Ukraine as Respondent
regarding a contractual dispute between the parties involved

FACTS OF THE CASE:

- The parties signed an employment contract on 1 March 2002 for the period from 1 March 2002 until 31 December 2006, under the following basic financial terms:

- art. 4.1:"...an individual monthly payment which consists of an official salary in accordance with the staff list, paid in UAH (Ukraine Hryvnia), in the amount equivalent to 150 CMU (conventional monetary units)."
- art. 4.2: additional payments, raises and salary supplements.
- clause 1.1 of the Appendix, under the title Basic Payments: "The parties come to the agreement that the player receives monthly additional payments in the form of premium ....at the rate of 850 - 1850 CMU."
- clause 1.2 of the Appendix, under the title Basic Payments: "The parties come to agreement that the player has the right to receive a personal annual premium in the sum of 10,000 USD, in addition to the payment stipulated in point 1.1. After the contract is signed, the player obtains an advance sum of 15,000 USD..."
- clause 1.5 of the Appendix, under the title Basic Payments: "If the player receives a professional injury, he gets additional payment in full range, in terms confirmed by team doctor."
- The Ukrainian Trade Union, on behalf of the player, filed a claim with FIFA in March 2004, exposing that the players of the club were not insured, despite the fact that art. 3.3.10 of the contract obliges the club to assure social and life insurance of the football players: "*For the validity period of the contract the player shall be granted all types of social insurance envisaged by the Ukrainian Legislature, as well as the obligatory health and life insurance, at the expense of the club. The latter shall render the obligatory social and health insurance to the player in compliance with the legislation in force.*"
- Moreover, according to art. 3.3.8 the club "*Undertakes to organize medical care for the player, including diagnostics, treatment, medicine and vitamins supply, and finance treatment and operation, if necessary, as well as recovery under supervision of professional doctors.*"
- The player alleges never having received a copy of his individual insurance policy.
- Furthermore, he complains that in his contract the wages are indicated in the sum of "150 conventional monetary units", without specifying a concrete currency, by means of which the player claims that the club has intentionally profited from his ignorance of the Ukrainian language, so that the order and conditions of payment would not be known to him. He believes that the confusion created regarding the amounts that are properly due to him has led to the non-payment of all that is rightfully due to him.
- Mr. R has been on loan to Football Club "Nikolaev" Ukraine, from 01.03.2004 until 30.06.2004, and afterwards to "Zakarpatje" Ushgorod, Ukraine.
- However, he has been unemployed since the end of November 2004 and is still without employment.
- Mr. R asks the Dispute Resolution Chamber for the confirmation of the termination of the contract by fault of the club for non-payment of his wages and due to negligence to insure the player in accordance with legal and contractual obligations.
- He also claims the following amounts from the club:
  USD 10,000 annual bonus for 2003 as per the annexe of the contract.
  USD 12,600 for 7 months of salary at USD 1,800 p/month from June-December 2003.
  Total amount claimed: USD 22,600
- F.C. X categorically denies all allegations put forward by the player, stressing that they have already been analysed and decided upon at the club Council meeting on 22.02.2003, at the Professional Football League of Ukraine Bureau Session on 11.11.2003, and at the meeting of the Control and Disciplinary Committee of the Ukrainian Football Federation, all of which apparently confirmed in their decisions, the groundlessness of the player's claims. Copies of the minutes of these meetings and their decisions have been provided.
- Moreover, the club has provided spread sheets signed by all the players of the club, including R, confirming that they have each been insured for an amount of 950,000 (currency not specified) by an insurance company called "Lemma", which also signed and stamped this document.
- According to the Ukrainian Trade Union, however, this document is a fraud since art. 23 of the Ukrainian insurance law stipulates that it is only possible to be insured on an individual basis, not collectively, and each person is therefore required to obtain an individual insurance policy.
- F.C. X has nevertheless not been able to provide the FIFA Administration with copies of an individual insurance policy, despite repeated requests.
- F.C. X has presented documents pertaining to the payment of the player's salaries throughout the period from January 2003 until September 2003. The club has also presented documents entitled

"Expense Cash Orders" for payments of salaries from October 2003 until February 2004, as well as a premium in the amount of USD 5,000, but none of these Expense Cash Orders have been signed by the player, nor have they been certified by any other authority than the accountant of the club.

CONSIDERATIONS OF THE DISPUTE RESOLUTION CHAMBER

The Dispute Resolution Chamber of the FIFA Players' Status Committee shall review disputes coming under its jurisdiction pursuant to Art. 42 of the FIFA Regulations for the Status and Transfer of Players (hereafter: FIFA Regulations) at the request of one of the parties to the dispute.

According to Art. 42 of the FIFA Regulations for the Status and Transfer of Players, the triggering elements of the dispute (i.e. whether a contract was breached, with or without just cause, or sporting just cause), will be decided by the Dispute Resolution Chamber of the FIFA Players' Status Committee.

Consequently, the Dispute Resolution Chamber is the competent body to decide on the present litigation concerning the alleged breach of contract between the claimant and the respondent.

Subsequently, and entering into the substance of the matter, the Chamber noted that two of the principle complaints of the claimant against F.C. X relate to the issue of remuneration. In the first place, the ambiguity in the contract regarding the terms of payment.

To assess this point, the members of the Dispute Resolution Chamber proceeded to analyse the employment contract at its disposal, including the annexe thereto, in order to determine the ease of understanding of the provisions regarding the player's monthly remuneration. In particular they focused their attention on Chapter 4 of the contract, entitled '*Remuneration of Labor, Rest Period, Social Welfare'*.

It was observed that art. 4.1 stipulates that the official salary of the player will be paid in UAH (*Ukraine Hryvnia)* currency, and that the individual monthly payment is equal to 150 "conventional monetary units", without providing further indications or numbers that could conclusively reveal what this monthly salary concretely amounts to. It was furthermore established that no additional explanations were included in the contract or its annexe to officially define the term "conventional monetary units", nor were there any indications as to how much 150 conventional monetary units are worth in UAH, or whether this amount is meant to be gross or net.

The club has not essentially defended the aforementioned ambiguity in the employment contract, nor has it offered any helpful clarifications in this regard.

In view of the foregoing, the Dispute Resolution Chamber was unable to determine the official monthly remuneration of the player from the contents of the contract or its annexe. It follows that the arguments presented by the player in this regard were considered admissible, particularly in view of the missing contestation from the club's side.

As a result, the Chamber established that in accordance with the player's claim, the monthly salary due to him corresponds to USD 1,800, an amount which does not appear to be disproportional.

In continuance, the members focused on the complaint regarding the non-payment of the player's salaries and the USD 10,000 annual bonus for 2003.

To investigate this issue, it was necessary to closely analyse the various documents submitted by F.C. X as evidence of the payments effectuated in favour of the player, including documents entitled "Expense Cash Orders" for payments of salaries from October 2003 until February 2004, as well as a single payment of USD 5,000.

In this sense, it was noted that the expense cash orders submitted were signed and certified only by members of the club, namely the club's chief and chief accountant, but not by the recipient himself, nor by any other third objective party such as a bank or similar institution. The documents in question could therefore not be accepted by the Dispute Resolution Chamber as valid and irrefutable proof of having paid the player the amounts claimed.

As to the club's defence relevant to the various administrative and arbitration decisions apparently already taken in connection to the player's financial claims by bodies such as the Club Council, the Bureau of the Professional Football League, and the Control and Disciplinary Committee of the Ukrainian Football Federation, the Dispute Resolution Chamber underlined the following.

It has not been ascertained that each of these deciding instances is an official arbitration tribunal composed of representatives chosen in equal numbers by players and by clubs with an independent chairman, both crucial prerequisites outlined in art. 42.1 (b)(i) of the FIFA Regulations for the Status and Transfer of Players. The contents of these decisions could therefore not be considered as decisive factors in the Dispute Resolution Chamber's deliberations on the case.

Finally, the members turned their attention to the important issue of the player's insurance. As evidenced by the various articles regarding this subject matter in the employment contract, the club was undoubtedly held to insure the player and to provide him with all necessary medical treatment and expenses incurred in connection to the eventuality of a professional injury.
Although the club has provided FIFA with a spreadsheet on which all its players have signed in apparent recognition of their insurance through a company called 'Lemma', it remains doubtful why the individual insurance policy of the player in question could not be produced, all the more when such individual insurance papers were directly being requested in the claim of the player.
It was therefore in the interest of the respondent to make all the necessary arrangements to ensure that the claimant's individual insurance policy documents were made available to the FIFA Administration during the course of the investigation proceedings.
Hence, since the principle document being requested by both the player and the FIFA Administration in particular, has not been produced by the respondent, the Dispute Resolution Chamber deemed that the allegations put forward by the claimant with respect to the insurance are credible and acceptable.
Consequently, having thus analysed each of the various aspects of the player's claim, as well as all of the club's defence statements in response, the Dispute Resolution Chamber concluded its deliberations by announcing that the player's claims were admissible on all counts.
In conclusion, the respondent shall be held responsible for the breach of the employment contract between the parties and shall indemnify the player in accordance with his present claim.
Finally, and on account of the above, the Dispute Resolution Chamber decided that the contractual relation between the parties is terminated with immediate effect and, as a consequence, the player is authorized to sign with the club of his choice.
In this respect the Dispute Resolution Chamber underlined that upon receipt of a possible request for the player's international registration transfer certificate from the association of a prospective new club, the Football Federation of Ukraine is asked to comply with this request, so as not to hinder the player's career.

DECISION OF THE DISPUTE RESOLUTION CHAMBER

1. The claim lodged by the Claimant is accepted.
2. The Respondent shall pay the total amount of USD 22,600 to the Claimant, within 30 days following the date of the communication of the present decision.
3. In the event that the debts of the Respondent are not paid within the stated deadline, an interest rate of 5% per year will apply.
4. The employment contract between the parties is terminated and the player authorized to sign with the club of his choice, with immediate effect.
5. If the relevant sum is not paid within the aforementioned deadline the present matter shall be submitted to the FIFA Disciplinary Committee so that the necessary disciplinary sanctions may be imposed.
6. The Claimant is directed to inform the Respondent immediately of the bank account number to which the remittance is to be made and to notify the Dispute Resolution Chamber of every payment received.
7. According to art. 60 par. 1 of the FIFA Statutes, this decision may be appealed against before the Court of Arbitration for Sport (CAS). The statement of appeal must be sent to the CAS directly within 10 days of receipt of notification of this decision and shall contain all the elements in accordance with point 2 of the directives issued by the CAS, a copy of which we enclose hereto. Within another 10 days following the expiry of the time limit for filing the statement of appeal, the appellant shall file a brief stating the facts and legal arguments giving rise to the appeal with the CAS (cf. point 4 of the directives).

35671
DECISION OF THE DISPUTE RESOLUTION CHAMBER
passed in Zurich, Switzerland, on 11 March 2005,
in the following composition:
Slim Aloulou (Tunisia), Chairman

Gerardo Movilla (Spain), Member
Philippe Piat (France), Member
Jean-Marie Philips (Belgium), Member
Paulo Rogerio Amoretty Souza (Brazil), Member
on the claim presented by M, Russia
against
C, Brazil
regarding the financial dispute between the parties resulting from the transfer of the player **G**, Brazil

FACTS OF THE CASE

- The player G was transferred from C, the selling club, to M, the buying club, for a net amount of USD 2,000,000. The transfer contract signed between the parties on 1 August 2003 makes no mention of the solidarity contribution.
- M paid the entire sum of USD 2,000,000 to C, without retaining the 5% reserved for solidarity contribution payments to the player's former developing club(s).
- On 16 June 2004 one of the developing clubs, B, came forward with a claim to its USD 60,000 proportion of the 5% solidarity contribution.
- FIFA advised M that in accordance with the established jurisprudence of the Dispute Resolution Chamber, such payment was the responsibility of the buying club, and that M was thus held to compensate B despite having neglected to retain the 5% solidarity compensation when it paid C the amount of USD 2,000,000.
- M thus paid B the requested solidarity contribution of USD 60,000.
- M is now demanding reimbursement from C, but the latter refuses to do so. C defends that according to clause 2 of their transfer contract, M had the obligation to pay C a compensation amount of USD 2 million *net*, meaning free of any and all taxes, costs and expenses. Therefore, the club reasons, there may not be further deductions from this sum.

CONSIDERATIONS OF THE DISPUTE RESOLUTION CHAMBER

The Dispute Resolution Chamber commenced its deliberations by referring to art. 25 of the FIFA Regulations for the Status and Transfer of Players (hereinafter: the Regulations), according to which it falls within the purview of the Dispute Resolution Chamber to review disputes concerning the distribution of the solidarity contribution.
Subsequently, the Chamber noted that from the FACTS OF THE CASE it could be observed that the solidarity contribution due to at least one of the player's developing clubs, i.e. B, had been duly paid and that, consequently, the litigation at hand did not involve a dispute concerning the distribution of the solidarity contribution, nor any other issue directly pertaining to the provisions in the FIFA Regulations regarding the solidarity mechanism.
The fact that the claimant was not one of the player's former developing clubs, lends emphasis to the above.
The Chamber continued by identifying the case at hand as a dispute over the interpretation and execution of the transfer contract that had been signed between the buying and selling clubs involved in the transfer of the player G.
Considering that such disputes are not of the competence of the Dispute Resolution Chamber, but rather of the Players' Status Committee, the Chamber concluded its deliberations by deciding that it was not competent to deal with this claim, which should be forwarded to next available meeting of the Players' Status Committee or, alternatively, of the Single Judge of the Players' Status Committee.

DECISION OF THE DISPUTE RESOLUTION CHAMBER

The Dispute Resolution Chamber is not competent to deal with the present claim of the Claimant. The claim shall be referred to the competent body, the Players' Status Committee, for consideration and decision.

12 APRIL 2005

45196
DECISION OF THE DISPUTE RESOLUTION CHAMBER
passed in Zurich, Switzerland, on 12 April 2005,
in the following composition:
Slim Aloulou (Tunisia), Chairman
Michele Colucci (Italy), member
Theo van Seggelen (Netherlands), member
Philippe Diallo (France), member
Jean-Marie Philips (Belgium), member
on the claim presented by
Club G. as Claimant
against
Player G.F. as Respondent 1
and
Club St.G. as Respondent 2
regarding the transfer of the player, G.F., and the breach of an employment contract

FACTS OF THE CASE

- The present matter has been referred by the Single Judge of the Players' Status Committee to the Dispute Resolution Chamber (DRC) in the context of the request for the international clearance of the player, G.F., for the club, St.G. Such request was denied by the Single Judge in the light of the contractual dispute between the player and the club G.
- In January 2005 the player, G.F., and the club G., signed an employment contract valid as from 29 January 2005 until 29 January 2009. The relevant contract does not indicate the precise date of its conclusion. It was, however, deposited at the Football Association of the club G. on 28 January 2005.
- According to the contract, the player was entitled to the minimum legal salary. Despite various requests from the FIFA administration the Football Association of the club G. did not indicate to what amount this corresponds.
- On 20/21 January 2005 the player, G.F., signed an employment contract with the club, St.G., valid from 1 February 2005 to 30 June 2009. The contract was co-signed by the player's parents.
- By means of an undated letter addressed to the club, G., the player, G.F., declared his irrevocable will to rescind the professional football player's contract he had concluded with the said entity. The club, St.G., confirmed in writing towards the Football Association of the club St.G. that fact.
- On 17 February 2005 the Single Judge of the Players' Status Committee rejected the request of the Football Association of the club St.G. to be authorised to provisionally register the player, G.F., for its affiliated club, St.G..

Position of the club, G.:

- The player has been registered for the club since 29 January 2002.
- On 26 April 2004 a contract was concluded between the club and the parents of the player, G.F., acting as legal representatives of the player. By means of the relevant agreement the parties confirmed the registration of the player for the club G., and the latter agreed to pay the amount of USD 10,000 to the player's parents. Furthermore, it was agreed that in case of a transfer of the player, the club would be entitled to 80% of the compensation received, while the player's parents would collect the other 20%. Finally, it was agreed that the player would sign an employment contract with the club when he would be reaching his majority. On 15 November 2004 a second agreement was signed by the same parties, by means of which the parents of the player consented to sell to G. the remaining 20% of the financial rights to the player for [currency] 40,000,000 (approx. USD 6,500). The second contract was signed also by the player personally. Copies of both contracts have been remitted to the attention of the FIFA administration.
- Since then the club is holding 100% of the federative rights to the player, G.F.
- Around the 13 of January 2005 an employment contract was signed with the player, G.F.. The space for the date of conclusion was left open with the aim to complete it after the player's return from his

trip with the U-20 national team. This way of proceeding had been chosen in view of the fact that the player would celebrate his 18 birthday on 28 January 2005.

- The club G. confirms that, as a general rule, according to the applicable national legislation, all persons that have reached the age of 18 may exercise their legal rights alone, without needing the assistance of a representative. Furthermore, it explains that the capacity to validly conclude an employment contract coincides with the legal majority. However, the club G. emphasises that the national civil legislation provides that, as long as it has not been declared null and void by a formal sentence of the competent judicial body, a contract concluded between the parties is valid and raises its legal effects. Since the player, G.F., did not contest the validity of the employment contract he signed with G., the relevant agreement is valid and binding. Finally, the club G. evokes the principle of good faith and states that no party may use its own unskilfulness in order to derivate rights in its favour.
- On 27 January 2005 the player returned from his stage with the U-20 national team. However, he did not even leave the airport and, accompanied by his father, he left for the country of the club St.G.
- On 28 January 2005 the employment contract was deposited at the Football Association of the club G.
- The St.G. never informed G. that it was negotiating with the player a possible engagement.
- The club, G., maintains that the player, G.F., has a valid contract with the club G., which he has to respect. The club G. maintains that, on the basis of the relevant employment contract, the player is entitled to an average monthly remuneration (salaries and bonuses) of [currency] 6,500,000 (approx. USD 1,000).
- During the course of the procedure at FIFA, the club G. offered to release the player and to amicable settle the matter in case the club, St.G., would pay the amount of USD 1,100,000 as compensation.

Position of the player, G.F.:

- The player claims that until he decided to sign the employment contract with the club, St.G., he had been registered as amateur player with the club G. By means of an attestation issued on 21 January 2005 the Football Association of the club G. had confirmed that no employment contract between the player and G. had been deposited at the association and that the player was registered with the relevant club as an amateur. Furthermore, the player emphasised that in its letter of 27 January 2005 the club, G., had expressly stated that, to that date, the player, G.F., was registered as an amateur player with the club. Therefore, the player deems that the club had admitted that on 27 January 2005 no valid contract existed between the parties.
- Despite the above, on 28 January 2005 the club, G., deposited an employment contract concluded between the player and the club G. for registration. Yet, on that day, the player, G.F., was not even in the relevant country. The player concludes that, in view of all the above, the club's position appears to be contradictory.
- Furthermore, the player considers the employment contract apparently concluded between him and the club, G., as not valid. It is evident that the club, G., confirmed that on 27 January 2005 no contract existed. Furthermore, it is proven that the player was not in the relevant country on 28 January 2005. Since the contract deposited at the Football Association of the club G. does not contain any date of conclusion, in accordance with the national legislation, it has to be assumed that it was concluded on the day of the registration, which is not possible.
- Taking into account that only the date of the registration of the contract can be considered as the date of the conclusion of the contract, the player emphasises that the contract with G. would in any case have been concluded after him having signed the contract with the St.G. on 20/21 January 2005.
- Furthermore, the player explains that if, as claimed by the club G., the employment contract between Mr G.F. and G. would have been signed around 13 January 2005, it would not be valid for another reason. In fact, at that time, the player was not yet 18 years old. Consequently, in accordance with the relevant national law, his parents should have co-signed the document, which evidently was not the case.
- In this respect, the player refers to the relevant national labour law and exposes that only persons that have reached the age of 18 may conclude a valid employment contract without the need of the authorisation of anybody else. Persons between the ages of 12 and 18 may sign employment contracts only with the express authorisation of their legal representative. This principle is confirmed

also in the national Code regarding Childhood and Youth, in particular in the section dealing with the protection of young workers.

- With regard to the validity of the employment contract, the player finally claims that according to the applicable regulations of the Football Association of the club G. only players who have reached the age of 18 may sign a valid employment contract with a club. Since the contract between him and G. was in any case signed prior to his 18 birthday, it is invalid also on the basis of the regulations of the Football Association of the club G.
- Moreover, the player stresses that G. maintains having signed the contract with him on 13 January 2005. Yet, on that day, he was not in that country but already in C. with the U-20 national team.
- Mr G.F. explains that, assuming a valid employment contract would actually exist between him and the club, G., the latter would have had to comply with a series of administrative prerequisites in accordance with the relevant national legislation. Yet, this was not the case. In particular, assuming the contract had been concluded on 13 January 2005, the club should have informed the competent authorities that it had signed a contract with a minor. Assuming that the contract was concluded on 28 January 2005, the club should have registered the player at the Ministry for Justice and Labour as well as with the body for social security. However, none of these actions were taken.
- The player maintains that his termination notice sent to the club G. did not refer to the employment contract but to the financial agreements concluded between his parents and the relevant club. As a result, the said notice cannot be considered recognition of the existence of an employment contract.
- Finally, the player emphasises that the negative decision of the Single Judge excessively penalises him. In fact, he is currently not in a position to pursue his career neither in the country of the club G. nor in the one of the club St.G. Therefore, his right to work is being disrespected. Furthermore, he is of the opinion that, on account of all the above, no contractual dispute in the sense of art. 6 par. 5 of the FIFA Regulations for the Status and Transfer of Players exists between him and the club, G.. He deems that the DRC should therefore only decide whether he has to compensate the club G. for a possible breach of an employment contract and, in the affirmative, decide on the relevant amount. However, he cannot be prevented from playing with the St.G.
- The player supports the position of the club, St.G., according to which the club G., is only entitled to training compensation in the amount of EUR 90,000.
- Just for the case that the DRC should come to the conclusion that the player breached the employment contract with the club, G., Mr G.F. deems that the club G. should be entitled to compensation amounting to USD 7,456.20 on the basis of art. 22 of the Regulations for the Status and Transfer of Players. In particular, the player points out that according to the applicable national legislation, the club would be entitled to compensation corresponding to the remaining value of the contract. In other words, the club would be entitled to the total amount of the salaries, which would have been due to the player if the contract had been duly fulfilled. The player explains that currently, the minimum legal salary in the country of the club G. corresponds to [currency] 972.413 (approximately USD 155).
- Finally, the player is of the opinion that no sports sanctions should be applied. In this respect, he maintains that he signed the employment contract with the club, St.G., in good faith on the basis of the attestation issued by the Football Association of the club G. confirming that no employment contract had been deposited regarding Mr G.F.

Position of the club, St.G.:

- The club St.G. contests the existence of an employment contract binding the player, G.F., to the club, G.
- The St.G. emphasises that in its justification for its refusal to authorise the issuing of the international registration transfer certificate (IRTC) for the player in question, on 27 January 2005 the club G. had indicated that it was the holder of 100% of the federative rights to the player. However, in the same letter the club, G., had stated that the player was registered as an amateur and that he had not yet signed any employment contract with it.
- Furthermore, the club St.G. refers to the attestation from the Football Association of the club G. dated 21 January 2005 according to which, to that date, no employment contract concluded between the player, G.F., and the club, G., had been deposited and that the player was registered for the said club as an amateur. Moreover, it points out that it signed the employment contract with the player

on the day the Football Association of the club G. issued the said attestation and that it applied for a work permit for the player in question on 24 January 2005.

- The St.G. emphasises that on 28 January 2005 the player was in the country of the club St.G. and not in the one of the club G. Notwithstanding this fact, on that day, the club, G., deposited an undated employment contract at the Football Association of the club G., which, according to the club, had been signed by the player already 15 days earlier. On the basis of that act, on 1 February 2005 the Football Association of the club G. denied the issuance of the IRTC for the player, G.F.. The club St.G. wonders: if on 27 January 2005 no employment contract existed and on 28 January 2005 the player was not in the country of the club G., when was the deposited contract signed?
- The club St.G. considers that the employment contract apparently concluded between the player, G.F., and the club, G., is not valid. Since the relevant contract does not contain any date of conclusion, in accordance with the national legislation, it has to be assumed that it was concluded on the day of the registration, i.e. on 28 January 2005. Yet, due to the player's absence from the country of the club G., this is not possible. The club G. did not offer any evidences corroborating its allegation that the contract had been signed 15 days earlier, i.e. around 13 January 2005. Furthermore, at that date the player was still under 18. Consequently, the contract should have been signed by his parents, what evidently did not happen.
- Moreover, the St.G. emphasises that if, as claimed by G., the contract had been signed on 13 January 2005 and the parties had agree to include a different date of conclusion, i.e. 28 January 2005, such proceedings would constitute simulation of legal acts and therefore, the contract could not be considered as valid.
- With regard to the validity of the employment contract, the club St.G. finally claims that according to the applicable regulations of the Football Association of the club G. only players who have reached the age of 18 may sign a valid employment contract with a club. Since the contract between Mr G.F. and G. was in any case signed prior to the player's 18 birthday, it is invalid also on the basis of the regulations of the Football Association of the club G.
- In line with the player's position, the club St.G. maintains that the termination notice, which the player had addressed to the club G., did not refer to the employment contract but to the two financial agreements concluded between the player's parents and the relevant club. The wrong denomination used in the relevant letter is due to the insufficient legal knowledge of the player and his parents. As a result, the said notice cannot be considered recognition of the existence of an employment contract. For the sake of good order, the club St.G. explains that the said letter was not even forwarded to the club G.
- The St.G. is of the opinion that, on account of all the above, no contractual dispute in the sense of art. 6 par. 5 of the FIFA Regulations for the Status and Transfer of Players exists between the player, G.F., and the club, G.. It deems that the DRC should therefore only decide whether the player has to compensate the club G. for a possible breach of an employment contract and, in the affirmative, decide on the relevant amount. However, the player cannot be prevented from playing with the St.G.. According to the club St.G., the decision of the Single Judge, who had rejected the request of the Football Association of the club St.G. to provisionally register the player for its club, excessively penalises the player. In fact, he is currently not in a position to pursue his career neither in the country of the club G. nor in the one of the club St.G. Therefore, the player's right to work is being disrespected.
- The St.G. cannot exclude that, by misusing the young age and the little experience of the player, the club, G., had obtained the player's signature on an employment contract. However, such action would certainly have taken place much earlier and not only 15 days prior to the player's 18 birthday, so as to have the document ready in case of necessity. Such abuse of the dominant position of the club cannot be protected. In this respect, the club St.G. emphasises that on 13 January 2005, the day of the alleged signature of the employment contract between the player and the club G., the player was not in the country of the club G. but already in C. with the U-20 national team.
- Finally, the club St.G. emphasises that the club G. did not specify any compensation it deems appropriate for the player to pay in case a breach of the employment contract is established. In fact, G. only demanded transfer compensation from the club St.G.
- The St.G. acknowledges that it will have to pay training compensation, and it expressed its willingness to pay EUR 90,000 in accordance with the FIFA Regulations for the Status and Transfer of Players and the circular no. 826.

– In the case that the Dispute Resolution Chamber decided that the player breached the contract with the club, G., without valid reasons, the St.G. points out that, in that respect, any compensation would have to be paid by the player.

CONSIDERATIONS OF THE DISPUTE RESOLUTION CHAMBER

The members of the Dispute Resolution Chamber were summoned to pass a decision on this matter by the Chairman pursuant to art. 1 point 6) of the Rules Governing the Practice and Procedures of the Dispute Resolution Chamber.

The deciding body started its deliberations by indicating that, as established in art. 42 par. 1 lit. (b) (i) of the FIFA Regulations for the Status and Transfer of Players (hereinafter: the Regulations), it falls within the purview of the Dispute Resolution Chamber (DRC) to determine whether one of the parties has committed an unilateral breach of contract without just cause. In the case that the employment contract was breached by a party, the DRC is responsible to verify whether this party is accountable for outstanding payments and compensation. Furthermore, the DRC will establish the amount of compensation to be paid and decide whether sports sanctions must be imposed (cf. art. 42 par. 1 (b) (ii) and (iii) in connection with art. 22 and 23 of the Regulations).

In view of the above, the DRC concluded that it was competent to decide on the present litigation.

Subsequently, and entering into the substance of the matter, the Chamber acknowledged that the central issue of the case at hand would be to establish whether the contract concluded between the player, G.F., and the club, G., is valid and legally binding or not.

In this respect, it was emphasised that the exact date of the signature of the relevant contract cannot be established. In fact, the club G. maintains that it was signed around the 13 January 2005. Yet, on that day, the player was not in the country of the club G. but in C. with the U-20 national team. However, the deciding body took note of the fact that, in any case, the employment contract between the player and G. was signed prior to the player's 18 birthday, i.e. before 28 January 2005. This fact is not being contested by neither of the parties and in particular, not by the club G.

Furthermore, the members of the Chamber present at the meeting acknowledged that the relevant employment contract had been signed by the player and the representatives of G. only. The document in question does, however, not bear the signature of the player's parents.

At this stage, the deciding body referred to the general legal principle according to which only a person that has reached his/her majority enjoys the legal capacity to act. Prior to having reached the relevant age limit, a person needs the explicit authorisation of his/her legal representative in order to validly sign legal acts that bind him/her. Moreover, the Chamber took into account that the relevant national labour law reports that principle. In particular, it states that persons between the ages of 12 and 18 may sign an employment contract only with the express authorisation of their legal representatives.

In view of the above, the deciding body concluded that the employment contract signed between the player, G.F., and the club, G., cannot be considered as valid, since it was not co-signed by the player's parents.

In this respect, the Chamber emphasised the fact that the club G. indirectly admitted that the conclusion reached corresponds to the actual legal reality. In fact, G. explicitly explained that, on the day the relevant agreement was signed, they had deliberately chosen not to include the date of conclusion in the contract in view of the fact that the player would celebrate his 18 birthday only at a later stage, i.e. on 28 January 2005. The club G. thus admitted that it had tried to find a way in order to circumvent the existing legal basis. That point of view is even corroborated by the fact that the contract was deposited with the Football Association of the club G. on 28 January 2005, thus exactly on the day of the player's 18 birthday.

In continuation, the deciding body pointed out that, apart from the relevant national legislation, also the application of the pertinent regulations of the Football Association of the club G. would lead to the conclusion that the employment contract signed between the player, G.F., and the club, G., is not valid. The relevant provisions appear to permit only to players who have reached the age of 18 to sign a valid employment contract with a club.

On account of all the above, the DRC decided that the contract signed between the player, G.F., and the club, G., is not valid and can therefore not raise any legal effects. Yet, the Chamber deemed it appropriate to state that the player should nevertheless be censured for having signed the relevant document. At the same time, the deciding body stressed, however, that the previously evoked legal principle has been introduced precisely in order to protect young and inexperienced people from entering into contractual obligations without having first duly considered all possible consequences.

The DRC stated that, on account of the reached conclusions, the breach of contract does not produce the consequences as provided for in art. 21 and 23 of the Regulations, i.e. that neither compensation nor sporting sanctions are applicable. Yet, the club G. is entitled to claim training compensation from the club St.G. for the period of time it has contributed to the player's training and formation. In its position, the club, St.G., already signalised its willingness to pay the relevant compensation. In this respect, the deciding body recalled that, should a dispute arise with regard to the relevant training compensation payment, the club G. would be at liberty to refer the matter to the Dispute Resolution Chamber for consideration and a formal decision.

In conclusion, the deciding body referred to the contract the player signed with the club, St.G., on 20/21 January 2005, and emphasised that the club had decided to sign the player, G.F., only after having received the attestation issued by the Football Association of the club G. on 21 January 2005 and confirming that, to that date, no employment contract signed between the player in question and the club, G., had been deposited and that the player was registered for the said club as an amateur. As a consequence, the club St.G. was deemed to have acted in good faith. Moreover, the Chamber pointed out that, contrary to the contract with G., the agreement with the St.G. was duly co-signed by the player's parents. As a consequence, the relevant contract is valid and legally binding for both the parties concerned. As a result, the Chamber established that at the time when the void contract with the club G. was registered with the Football Association of the club G., i.e. on 28 January 2005, a valid employment contract with the club St.G. already existed.

In view of the above considerations, the DRC decided that, currently, the player, G.F., is contractually bound exclusively to the club, St.G.. As a consequence, the Football Association of the club St.G. is entitled to register him for its affiliated club with immediate effect. Furthermore, the Football Association of the club G. should issue the relevant IRTC on behalf of the Football Association of the club St.G. without further delay.

DECISION OF THE DISPUTE RESOLUTION CHAMBER

1. The claim of the club G. is rejected.
2. The Football Association of the club St.G. is authorised to register the player, G.F., for its affiliated club, St.G., with immediate effect after notification of the present decision.
3. The Football Association of the club G. is instructed to issue the international registration transfer certificate for the player, G.F., on behalf of the Football Association of the club, St.G.
4. According to art. 60 par. 1 of the FIFA Statutes, this decision may be appealed against before the Court of Arbitration for Sport (CAS). The statement of appeal must be sent to the CAS directly within 10 days of receipt of notification of this decision and shall contain all the elements in accordance with point 2 of the directives issued by the CAS, a copy of which we enclose hereto. Within another 10 days following the expiry of the time limit for filing the statement of appeal, the appellant shall file a brief stating the facts and legal arguments giving rise to the appeal with the CAS (cf. point 4 of the directives).

13 MAY 2005

55230
DECISION OF THE DISPUTE RESOLUTION CHAMBER
passed in Zurich, Switzerland, on 13 May 2005,
in the following composition:
Slim Aloulou (Tunisia), chairman
Maurice Watkins (England), member
Paulo Amoretty Souza (Brazil), member
Gerardo Movilla (Spain), member
Theo van Seggelen (Netherlands), member
on the claim presented by
A as Claimant
against
B as Respondent
regarding a labour dispute

FACTS OF THE CASE

On 9 January 2003, A and B signed an employment contract valid for the 2003 sporting season, starting in March.

According to such contract, A was entitled to receive a monthly salary of USD 3,000 and a monthly accommodation allowance in the amount of USD 750, amongst other financial privileges.

A asserts that he suffered a serious knee injury during a match at B's service on 5 April 2003 and that, as a consequence of such injury, B informed him in front of his team colleagues, that it did not count with him any longer.

Consequently, A left B and returned to country X on 18 April 2003. Before leaving country Y, A asserts that B has paid him the amount of USD 1,227.69.

Finally, in order to recover from his aforementioned injury, A undertook a surgery to his knee on 5 May 2003.

In light of the above, A is presently claiming the payment of USD 26,000, corresponding to his salaries for the entire season (7 salaries of USD 3,000 each in the total amount of USD 21,000) and the costs in which he incurred in order to recover from his knee injury, in particular, the surgery he undertook and respective rehabilitation process (USD 5,000). In this respect, A has provided the FIFA Administration with several documents in order to support his position in the matter.

In response, B provided the FIFA Administration with the following statement, via the Association C: "We did sign A to a contract in 2003. After a pre-season weekin late March and five days in April, we decided to release him on April 5th 2003 as our contract permits".

In fact, with regard to the player's present claim, in particular, the club's alleged contractual termination without just cause and a possible compensation to be allocated to the player, B defends that art. 12 b) of the player's Standard Z contract allows clubs to "releae players at any time prior to July 1, unless the contract is guaranteed" and that A's contract was not. As a consequence, the club stated "we terminated this player in accordance with Section 12 Clause B of the standard Z Players' contract" and therefore defends that its contractual termination was legally supported and therefore should be considered as valid.

Requested by the FIFA Administration to clarify the meaning of a guaranteed contract, B explained that "In addendum B of A's contract, the word guaranteed does not appear. Contracts that are guaranteed contain the following language in addendum B Section 1-A: club shall pay to payer for services rendered the following salary: 2003 season, USD –.– per month guaranteed".

Art. 12 b) of the relevant employment contract ("Termination by the Club") stipulates that, "Unless this contract is guaranteed in addendum B, the club may terminate the contract of any player prior to July 1st of the contract year by written notice to player and the League. Notice shall not be effective unless delivered in hand to player or sent via certified mail, return receipt request. After termination,the club shall be under no further obligation to player for payment of future contract payments. All players contracts are guaranteed by the club for the remainder of the season should this contract be in effect on July 1st. Any team releasing a player afer the date set forth by the League shall be responsible for the compensation of that player per Addendum B through the team's final regular season or playoff match (whichever is later)."

Finally, B defends that its trainer "has no records of A being injured while he was there. The club paid for his flight to country X and paid him for hs services until he was released".

CONSIDERATIONS OF THE DISPUTE RESOLUTION CHAMBER

The members of the Dispute Resolution Chamber were summoned to pass a decision on this matter by the Chairman pursuant to art. 1 point 6) of the Rules Governing the Practice and Procedures of the Dispute Resolution Chamber.

The Dispute Resolution Chamber shall review disputes coming under its jurisdiction pursuant to art. 42 of the FIFA Regulations for the Status and Transfer of Players, at the request of one of the parties to the dispute.

According to art. 42, par. 1 lit. (b) of the FIFA Regulations for the Status and Transfer of Players, the triggering elements of the dispute (i.e. whether a contract was breached, with or without just cause, or sporting just cause), will be decided by the Dispute Resolution Chamber.

If an employment contract is breached by a party, the Dispute Resolution Chamber is responsible to verify whether a party is accountable for compensation and outstanding payments.

Also, the Dispute Resolution Chamber will establish the amount of compensation to be paid and decide whether sports sanctions must be imposed (cf. art. 42, par. 1, b, ii and iii in connection with art. 22 and 23 of the aforementioned Regulations).

Consequently, the Dispute Resolution Chamber is the competent body to decide on the present litigation concerning the alleged breach of contract between the Claimant and the Respondent.

Subsequently, and entering into the substance of the matter, the Chamber acknowledged that A is claiming the payment of his salaries for the entire contractual period, i.e. for the 2003 sporting season, which corresponds to 7 (seven) months, in the total amount of USD 21,000. The Chamber took into consideration the fact that the player, in support of his allegations, has provided the FIFA Administration with a copy of his employment contract with B as well as of the contract's addendum B.

In this respect, the members of the Chamber took note that the player was contractually entitled to receive a monthly salary of USD 3,000 together with other financial privileges and that B has never disputed such amounts.

The Dispute Resolution Chamber also noted that, on 5 April 2003, B unilaterally terminated its relevant employment contract with A, based on art. 12 b) of the player's Standard Z contract, according to which, a club can release a player at any time prior to 1 July, without being responsible for any further payments, if his contract is not guaranteed in addendum B, i.e. if such addendum does not state that the player's salary is guaranteed.

In view of the above, the Chamber underlined that, the fact that the addendum of a player's employment contract does not expressly mention that his salary is guaranteed, cannot and does not constitute just cause for a club to unilaterally terminate its employment contract with a player, like it happened in the present case, and even less to be "under no further obligation to player for payment of future contract payments". In fact, the Chamber deemed that in view of its potestative nature, the aforementioned contractual clause shall not have any effect.

After having vehemently rejected the validity of the aforementioned contractual clause, the members of the Chamber reached the conclusion that B has terminated its employment contract with A without just cause.

As a consequence, the Chamber considered B liable to pay all the salaries due for the 2003 sporting season, in accordance with its employment contract with A, in the total amount of USD 21,000.

Moreover, the Chamber also concluded that the amount of USD 1,227.69, received from B and acknowledged by A, had the nature of accommodation allowances and/or other financial privileges stipulated in their employment contract.

Furthermore, the Dispute Resolution Chamber took note that A is also claiming the reimbursement of all the expenses in which he incurred in order to recover from a knee injury allegedly suffered on 5 April 2003 at the club's service, in the total amount of USD 5,000. In this respect, the Chamber took into consideration the fact that A, in support of his allegations, has provided the FIFA Administration with copies of the respective payment receipts, confirming the costs of the relevant surgery and the following rehabilitation process.

In this regard, the members of the Chamber took into consideration the evidence carried to the file by A, in particular, a medical exam signed by F, dated 21 April 2003, attesting that A was suffering from the claimed knee injury and a hospital document stamped by G, confirming that A has effectively undertaken the claimed surgery on 5 May 2003.

In light of the aforementioned evidence, the player's claim and the fact that A has left B on 5 April 2003, i.e. only one month before the relevant surgery took place, the Dispute Resolution Chamber concluded that the player's knee injury was in fact suffered at the club's service and therefore, that the latter is responsible to cover its costs, as well as the ones incurred with the rehabilitation process.

In light of all the above, the Chamber decided that B is responsible for the non-fulfilment of its relevant employment contract with A and is consequently liable to pay to the player the total amount of USD 26,000, corresponding to USD 21,000 for the player's aforementioned outstanding salaries and USD 5,000 for the expenses incurred with his relevant knee surgery and the consequent rehabilitation process.

In conclusion, the members of the Chamber decided to accept A's claim and to condemn B to pay to him the total amount of USD 26,000.

DECISION OF THE DISPUTE RESOLUTION CHAMBER

1. The claim of A is accepted.
2. The Respondent B shall pay the total amount of USD 26,000 to A, within 30 days of notification of the present decision.
3. If the Respondent fails to comply with the above-mentioned deadline, an interest rate of 5% per year will apply and the case will immediately be presented to the FIFA Disciplinary Committee.

4. The Claimant is directed to inform the Respondent immediately of the account number to which the remittance is to be made and to notify the Dispute Resolution Chamber of every payment received.
5. According to art. 60 par. 1 of the FIFA Statutes, this decision may be appealed before the Court of Arbitration for Sport (CAS). The statement of appeal must be sent to the CAS directly within 10 days of receiving notification of this decision and has to contain all elements in accordance with point 2 of the directives issued by the CAS, copy of which we enclose hereto. Within another 10 days following the expiry of the time limit for the filing of the statement of appeal, the appellant shall file with the CAS a brief stating the facts and legal arguments giving rise to the appeal (cf. point 4 of the directives).

55359
DECISION OF THE DISPUTE RESOLUTION CHAMBER
passed in Zurich, Switzerland, on 13 May 2005,
in the following composition:
Slim Aloulou (Tunisia), Chairman
Maurice Watkins (England), member
Paulo Amoretty Souza (Brazil) , member
Gerardo Movilla (Spain), member
Theo Van Seggelen (Netherlands), member
on the claim presented by Player A, as Claimant
against
Club B, as Respondent
regarding a labour dispute between the above-mentioned parties

FACTS OF THE CASE
On 29 April 2003, the player A and the club B signed an employment contract for the period from 15 July 2003 to 15 May 2004. The employment contract stated that the player would receive a monthly salary of USD 18,000. Article 1 par. 2 of the contract read as follows:
This contract comes into force once the player has passed a medical examination. After a trial period of three months, the club will decide whether i t is satisfied with the player's performance. If not, the contract will be terminated without compensation.
The player says that the club B never summoned him after he had signed the contract and then informed him verbally at the beginning of July 2003 that it would not be fulfilling or proceeding with the contract, yet did not give any reason for the decision. On 12 August 2003, the player gave the club formal notice to pay the salary payments owing to him in their entirety, a total amount of USD 180,000. On 3 October 2003, the player asked FIFA to order the club B to pay him the amount of USD 180,000, and to impose sports and financial sanctions upon the club, in accordance with FIFA regulations. On 12 January 2004, the player A signed an employment contract with the club C, under which he would receive a monthly salary of EUR 2,500.
The club B says that the player A contacted the club on his own initiative before the contract was completed and the club never invited the player to come to the club to sign a contract. After signing the contract on 29 April 2003, the club maintains that it had no further contact with the player until 12 August 2003, the date on which the player issued the club with formal notice in writing. As it did not have any contact details for the player, the club itself was not able to contact the player. Moreover, the club says that it did not inform the player that it would not be fulfilling or proceeding with the contract on 29 April 2003. Given that the contract commenced on 15 July 2003, the club considered that the player's absence rendered the contract, which had been signed on 29 April 2003, null and void due to the player's negligence.
The club B also feels that the provisions of article 1 par. 2 of the contract dated 29 April 2003 mean that the contract is not valid because the player did not pass the club's medical examination. Furthermore, with regard to the conditions relating to the trial period, the club feels that it was in a position not to proceed with the contract because the player did not make his services available to the club from 15 July 2003.
In response, the player stressed that the initiative to sign him had originated from the club and he produced documentary evidence to this effect that he had received from the club, dated 10 April 2003, inviting him

to take part in an international tournament it was organising. It could therefore not be true that the club did not have his contact details. The player insists that he made several attempts to contact the president of the club by telephone, without ever getting a reply.

CONSIDERATIONS OF THE DISPUTE RESOLUTION CHAMBER

1. The members of the Dispute Resolution Chamber were summoned to pass a decision on the present matter by the Chairman pursuant to Art. 1 point 6) of the Rules Governing the Practice and Procedures of the Dispute Resolution Chamber.
2. The deciding body started its deliberations by indicating that, as established in Art. 42 § 1 lit. (b) (i) of the FIFA Regulations for the Status and Transfer of Players, it falls within the purview of the Dispute Resolution Chamber to determine whether one of the parties has committed a unilateral breach of contract without just cause. In the case that the employment contract was breached by a party, the Dispute Resolution Chamber is responsible to verify and decide whether this party is accountable for outstanding payments and compensation.
3. In view of the above, the Dispute Resolution Chamber concluded that it was competent to decide on the present litigation.
4. The members present at the meeting then entered into the substance of the matter and first noticed that the parties involved in this matter had signed an employment contract on 29 April 2003, with a validity from 15 July 2003 to 15 May 2004. Furthermore, the Chamber took note of the player's allegation that the contract was verbally and unilaterally rescinded by the club B via phone in the beginning of July 2003. Finally, the Chamber noticed that the player A did not present himself at the club's facilities on 15 July 2003 in accordance with the relevant employment contract.
5. With regard to the rescission of the contract, the Chamber noticed in particular that besides the alleged phone call, the player A did not present any evidence that the club B rescinded the employment contract unilaterally in the beginning of July 2003. Moreover, the club B never acknowledged having rescinded the employment contract as alleged by the player, but on the contrary, accuses the player A of having breached the employment contract by not presenting him at the club's facilities at the beginning of the contract on 15 July 2003.
6. The Chamber then stated that in accordance with the legal principle of the burden of proof, which is a fundamental part of every legal system, a party is obliged to prove allegations presented in a legal action if it wishes to use them as the basis for a claim.
7. In this respect, the Chamber stated that the player's allegation of the rescission of the employment contract by the club in the beginning of July 2003 is not based on any evidence. Therefore, at that time, the contract had to be seen as not rescinded, and therefore executable for both parties involved.
8. In consequence, the Chamber stated that it was the player's obligation to comply with the contract, i.e. present himself at the club's facilities on 15 July 2003.
9. However, since the player A never presented himself at the club's facilities, and therefore never participated to the club's activities, he is not in the position to claim for any payment from club B.
10. In consequence, the Dispute Resolution Chamber decided that the claim of the player A is to be rejected, due to lack of evidence of the rescission of the employment contract.

DECISION OF THE DISPUTE RESOLUTION CHAMBER

1. The claim of the player A is rejected.
2. According to art. 60 par. 1 of the FIFA Statutes, this decision may be appealed against before the Court of Arbitration for Sport (CAS). The statement of appeal must be sent to the CAS directly within 10 days of receipt of notification of this decision and shall contain all the elements in accordance with point 2 of the directives issued by the CAS, a copy of which we enclose hereto. Within another 10 days following the expiry of the time limit for filing the statement of appeal, the appellant shall file a brief stating the facts and legal arguments giving rise to the appeal with the CAS (cf. point 4 of the directives).

55484

DECISION OF THE DISPUTE RESOLUTION CHAMBER

passed in Zurich, Switzerland, on 13 May 2005,
in the following composition:
Mr Slim Aloulou (Tunisia), Chairman
Mr Maurice Watkins (England), Member
Mr Paulo Amoretty Souza (Brazil), Member
Mr Gerardo Movilla (Spain), Member
Mr Theo van Seggelen (Netherlands), Member
on the claim presented by Club X as Claimant against Player Y as Respondent
regarding a contractual dispute between the Club X and the player Y

FACTS OF THE CASE:

On 16 January 2003 the player Y and the club X concluded a one-year employment contract whereby the club committed itself to pay to the player USD 40,000 as a signing-on fee and USD 60,000 as a total yearly salary.

The amount of USD 40,000 due as a signing-on fee was duly paid by the club.

Requested by the X Football Association to issue the player's International Registration Transfer Certificate, on 24 January 2003 the Y Football Association replied that they were not in a position to issue the document requested, as Mr Y was still under contract with their affiliated club Z.

After several, yet fruitless attempts to contact the aforementioned club in order to negotiate the player's transfer to X, on 22 February 2003 X agreed in writing that the player would be sent back to his country for four days, in order for him to try and settle the matter directly with the club.

Not only the player failed to go back to X but, what is more, he carried on with his football career with the club Z.

Subsequently, on 3 April 2003 X communicated to Y that the employment contract signed on 16 January 2003 was terminated due to his sole fault and intimated the player to refund the amount of USD 40,000 he had received as a signing-on fee.

The player maintains in his position that on 22 February 2003, after having waited a long time for his IRTC to be issued, he left for his country only because the club X allowed him to do so and that after his departure he had not heard from the club X any longer.

The player further states that he cannot be deemed responsible for the contractual breach and that, on the contrary, the club X should have been aware in advance of the fact that they were signing a player, who was already under contract with another club.

The club X asks the Dispute Resolution Chamber to condemn Y to refund the amount of USD 40,000 received as a signing-on fee and to take against him all the sanctions the Chamber may deem appropriate.

CONSIDERATIONS OF THE DISPUTE RESOLUTION CHAMBER:

After a careful study of the facts and allegations outlined above, the Dispute Resolution Chamber commenced its deliberations by referring to the art. 42 par. 1 lit. (b) (i) of the FIFA Regulations for the Status and Transfer of Players (hereinafter, the Regulations), according to which, it falls within the purview of the Dispute Resolution Chamber to determine whether one of the parties has committed an unilateral breach of contract without just cause.

In this sense, if the employment contract was breached by a party, the Dispute Resolution Chamber is responsible to verify whether this party is accountable for outstanding payments and compensation.

Furthermore, the Dispute Resolution Chamber will establish the amount of compensation to be paid and decide whether sports sanctions must be imposed (cf. art. 42 par. 1 (b) (ii) and (iii) in connection with art. 22 and 23 of the Regulations).

In view of the above, the Chamber concluded that it has jurisdiction to pass a decision on this matter.

Firstly, after a thorough analysis of the relevant documentation, the Chamber took note of the fact that the one-year employment contract the player Y and the club X concluded on 16 January 2003 is a valid one.

The Chamber further noted that the amount of USD 40,000 the club committed itself to pay to the player as a signing-on fee was duly paid.

Furthermore, the Chamber considered that Y never informed his new club that he was still under contract with the club Z.

What is more, the player even signed an employment contract with X, regardless of the fact that he was still contractually bound to another club.
In point of fact, by the time Y signed the employment contract with the club X, i.e. on 16 January 2003, he was under contract with two clubs at the same time.
In addition to that, after Y was allowed to go back to his country for four days, in order to try and settle the matter directly with the club he was originally under contract with, he plainly decided to remain in his country and carry on his professional career with Z.
In this respect, the Chamber pointed out that it is undisputable that the player did not respect the contractual obligations undertaken in the employment contract concluded on 16 January 2003 with the club X.
Therefore, the Chamber decided that Y must refund to the club X the amount of USD 40,000 received as a signing-on fee.
The Chamber went further on analysing the sports sanctions to be imposed on the player for having caused the contractual breach without just cause. According to Art. 23 §1 of the Regulations, a player shall be sanctioned by means of a restriction of four months on his eligibility to participate in any official football matches.
In light of the above, the Chamber decided that Y is not eligible to participate in any official football matches for a period of four months as from the date of notification of this decision.

DECISION OF THE DISPUTE RESOLUTION CHAMBER

1. The claim of the club X is accepted.
2. Y has to pay the amount of USD 40,000 to the club X.
3. The amount due to X has to be paid by Y within 30 days as from the date of notification of this decision.
4. If the aforementioned sum is not paid within the aforementioned deadline, a 5% default interest rate per annum will apply and the present matter will be submitted to FIFA's Disciplinary Committee, so that the necessary disciplinary sanctions may be imposed.
5. X is directed to inform Y immediately of the account number to which the remittance is to be made and to notify the Dispute Resolution Chamber of every payment received.
6. Y is not eligible to participate in any official football matches for a period of four months as from the date of notification of this decision.
7. According to art. 60 par. 1 of the FIFA Statutes this decision may be appealed before the Court of Arbitration for Sport (CAS). The statement of appeal must be sent to the CAS directly within 10 days of receiving notification of this decision and has to contain all elements in accordance with point 2 of the directives issued by the CAS, copy of which we enclose hereto. Within another 10 days following the expiry of the time limit for the filing of the statement of appeal, the appellant shall file with the CAS a brief stating the facts and legal arguments giving rise to the appeal (cf. point 4 of the directives).

⚽⚽⚽

55503
DECISION OF THE DISPUTE RESOLUTION CHAMBER
passed in Zurich, Switzerland, on 13 May 2005,
in the following composition:
Mr Slim Aloulou (Tunisia), Chairman
Mr Maurice Watkins (England), Member
Mr Paulo Amoretty Souza (Brazil), Member
Mr Gerardo Movilla (Spain), Member
Mr Theo van Seggelen (Netherlands), Member
on the claim presented by Club X as Claimant
against
Player Y as Respondent
regarding compensation for contractual breach

FACTS OF THE CASE:
On 31 August 2004 the Dispute Resolution Chamber passed a decision on the contractual litigation between Y and X.

The Chamber decided that, due to the fact that Y unilaterally breached the employment contract with X without just cause, he would not be eligible to participate in any official football matches for a period of six weeks as from the beginning of the championship.
On the same day, following its meeting, the Dispute Resolution Chamber disclosed the holding of the decision to the parties involved.
At the same time, the Bureau of the Players' Status Committee authorised the registration of the player in favour of Z, however, with reference to the sporting sanctions imposed by the Dispute Resolution Chamber.
The decision of the Dispute Resolution Chamber was appealed before the Court of Arbitration for Sport by Y and Z on 3 September 2004.
On 10 September 2004 X lodged an appeal before the Court of Arbitration for Sport against Y and Z. All the proceedings were merged together.
On 16 February 2005 the Court of Arbitration for Sport communicated the holding of the decision to all parties involved.
The reasoning of this award was notified on 11 March 2005. This award upheld the decision reached on 31 August 2004 by the Dispute Resolution Chamber.
In particular, the Court of Arbitration for Sport confirmed that Y unilaterally breached the employment contract with X without just cause during the so-called protected period as provided for in Art. 23 §1 lit. (a) of the Regulations for the Status and Transfer of Players (hereafter, the Regulations).
As a consequence, the question regarding the financial compensation due for breach of contract can be addressed, in accordance with point 4 of decision passed on 31 August 2004 by the Dispute Resolution Chamber.
The Dispute Resolution Chamber had also directed X to provide FIFA with its request for compensation, emphasising that such a request should give details on the way this amount should be calculated.
Likewise, Y was granted a deadline to file its position with respect to Xs request for compensation.
Moreover, in accordance with Art. 23 §2 lit. (c) of the Regulations, the Dispute Resolution Chamber sustained that Z is presumed to have induced the unilateral breach of Ys contract with X.
The Chamber stated that such inducement to the breach of contract and its consequences would be established in a separate proceedings and instructed Z to provide FIFA with its position with respect to such a charge.
The dispute between Y and X relating to the amount of compensation due for contractual breach and the investigation concerning the inducement to the breach of contract against Z were merged together in these proceedings, consistently with the principle of procedural economy.
In light of the above, Y, X and Z provided the each member of the Dispute Resolution Chamber with their respective concluding positions, which are hereafter summarised.

Position of X:
X maintains in its position that, in light of the award rendered by the Court of Arbitration for Sport on 16 February 2005, it is evident that it has to receive compensation for the unilateral breach of contract, that occurred without just cause and during the so-called protected period.
Such compensation is meant to repair the damage incurred by X, that was deprived without just cause of the services of a player, Y, who was still bound by an employment contract for two more years.
Therefore, X refers to the objective criteria, which must be taken into account by the Dispute Resolution Chamber in the calculation of the amount of compensation due as provided for by Article 22 of the Regulations.
In compliance with the above criteria, X asks the Dispute Resolution Chamber to place particular emphasis on the increased amount, both in salaries and benefits, the player has obtained by his new club, Z.
The X is also eager to highlight the significant financial investment it had sustained in the scope of the extension of Mr Ys contract in August 2003, as well as the damage it suffered after the players departure, essentially in view of the amount the club could have earned in case the transfer had taken place under the normal market conditions.
All the above criteria, as well as a list of the most high-priced transfers occurred during the summer transfer period in 2004, are reported in a table X provided the Chamber with.
In light of the above, X asks the Dispute Resolution Chamber to condemn Y to pay the amount of EUR –.– as compensation for contractual breach, accompanied by first-class bank guarantees undertaken by Z.
With respect to the responsibility of Z, X maintains that the club, by signing Mr Y while he was still

under contract with his club, undeniably excluded X from the regular transfer operations and must pay compensation for the damages caused.
In addition to that, X points out that any possible attenuating circumstance, which could be taken into account when considering the players behaviour, should not be applied at all to the stance of Z.
X further maintains that, had Z not induced the player to breach the contract with his club, X would have never suffered all the losses it is seeking compensation for.
In view of the above, X asks the Dispute Resolution Chamber to condemn Z jointly with Y to pay the amount of EUR –.– as compensation for contractual breach accompanied by first-class bank guarantees undertaken by Z itself.
In addition to that, X asks the Dispute Resolution Chamber to apply against Z the sanctions provided for by Article 23 §2 a) of the Regulations.

Position of Y:
Y maintains in his position that, by means of its award rendered on 16 February 2005, the Court of Arbitration for Sport pointed out that, in compliance with the principle of the maintenance of contractual stability, the only damage X is entitled to claim is the fact that Y failed to perform the last two years of contract.
According to the player, the club cannot be entitled to any other damage, let alone the frustrated expectation of a transfer fee.
In particular, the players agent, pointed out that Y is nothing more than a mid-level player, who only happened to make a five-minute appearance with his national team and actually contributed to the poor performances of the defence of Z.
According to the agent, X cannot claim any prejudice under the sporting point of view, especially as the performances of the X improved after the players transfer to Z.
As far as the alleged financial prejudice is concerned, the players agent deems that the X has caused to itself such a loss due to its non-cooperative attitude towards the player, as outlined by the Court of Arbitration for Sport in its decision.
The agent further points out that the amount paid by X for the transfer of another player, W, who apparently replaced Y, is EUR –.–.
According to the agent, W is a much more experienced and valuable player than Y.
The players agent further provided the Chamber with some calculations, according to which, the value of the two last years of Ys employment contract with X would not exceed the amount of EUR –.–.
In view of the above, Y asks the Dispute Resolution Chamber to establish in favour of X an amount of compensation between EUR –.– and EUR –.–.

Position of Z:
Z maintains in its position that in its decision the Court of Arbitration for Sport took into account the exceptional circumstances surrounding the contractual dispute between Y and X.
The club maintains that, amongst the exceptional circumstances, the Court of Arbitration for Sport considered that the player remained with the X for seven years, as from the age of 15. Therefore, the contractual relationship between the player and the club had an actual stability for seven years.
Z is also emphasising the players good faith, that clashed against Xs non-cooperative attitude towards him, as outlined by the Court of Arbitration for Sport in its decision.
Z further acknowledges that, although the player could have been sanctioned by means of a restriction of four months on his eligibility to participate in any official football matches as from the beginning of the new season of the new clubs national championship, in view of the above-mentioned circumstances, his sanction has been considerably reduced.
Consequently, Z maintains that the above-mentioned attenuating circumstances should apply as well to the club, whose behaviour always showed good faith, yet collided with Xs non-cooperative attitude.
Z points out that it actually never incited the player to breach his employment contract with X.
In view of the above, Z asks the Dispute Resolution Chamber to establish in favour of X an amount of compensation, which is proportionate and consistent with the conclusions reached by the Chamber itself and by the Court of Arbitration for Sport with respect to the players sanction.
With respect to the possible sporting sanctions it may incur in, Z requests the Dispute Resolution Chamber to take into account all the exceptional circumstances surrounding the case in hand, as well as the clubs constant good faith.

CONSIDERATIONS OF THE DISPUTE RESOLUTION CHAMBER:

After a careful study of the facts and allegations outlined above, the Dispute Resolution Chamber commenced its deliberations by referring to Article 42 §1 (b) (ii) and (iii) in connection with Articles 22 and 23 of the Regulations according to which, if the employment contract was breached by a party, the Dispute Resolution Chamber is responsible to verify whether this party is accountable for compensation and decide whether sports sanctions must be imposed.

All the parties had been duly informed that this case would have been submitted, for decision, to the Dispute Resolution Chamber on 13 May 2005 and that a hearing of the three parties involved would have taken place.

However, the Chamber acknowledged the fact that, while X and Y were present at the hearing, the representatives of Z were not able to attend due to the fact that the flight to Zurich was cancelled at short notice, circumstance which was duly ascertained by an official document.

In view of these circumstances, the Chamber deemed that the matter relating to the compensation for contractual breach between X and Y and the investigation against Z for inducement to contractual breach, merged together in this process consistently with the principle of procedural economy, have to be considered and decided disjointedly.

Therefore, the Chamber decided to consider and pass a decision on the dispute for contractual breach between X and Y, in accordance with Articles 22 and 23 §1 of the Regulations. In this respect, the Chamber concluded that it has jurisdiction to pass a decision on this matter.

The investigation carried out by FIFA against Z for inducement to contractual breach will be considered in a separate proceedings and notified through a different decision by the Dispute Resolution Chamber, in accordance with Articles 22 and 23 §2 of the Regulations.

Having established this, the Chamber started to consider the substance of the matter in order to establish the compensation due for contractual breach.

Preliminarily, the Chamber took note of the fact that the Court of Arbitration for Sport confirmed that Y unilaterally breached the employment contract with X without just cause during the so-called protected period as provided for in Art. 23 §1 lit. (a) of the Regulations.

The Chamber then focussed its analysis on the amount of compensation due by the player to the club for breach of contract.

Therefore, the Chamber examined the objective criteria listed in Article 22 of the Regulations, in order to verify their relevance in the case at stake.

The first factor taken into consideration was the remuneration and other benefits under the existing contract and under the new contract.

The Chamber noted that, in accordance with the contract concluded between X and Y on 15 December 2002, but deposited at the Football League on 18 July 2003, the player would have earned EUR –.– gross per month in the season 2002/2003, EUR –.– gross per month in the following season, whereas he would have earned EUR –.– gross per month and EUR –.– gross per month respectively in the last two seasons of his contract. In addition to that, the player would have received the amount of EUR –.– gross as outstanding salaries for the period July to December 2002, as well as an amount of EUR –.– gross in three instalments to be paid in January and July 2003 and July 2004.

Also, X paid to the players agent a commission amounting to EUR 239,200.

The Chamber thus ascertained that X made an investment amounting to EUR –.– gross (EUR –.– including social security contribution, as reported by X) in the scope of the contract concluded with Y on 15 December 2002 and deposited at the Football League on 18 July 2003.

Above all, the Chamber considered that the remaining value of the employment contract between X and Y was of EUR –.–.

As regards the financial conditions of the employment contract concluded between Y and Z, the Chamber acknowledged the fact that the player would receive EUR –.– gross per year in the season 2004/2005, EUR –.– gross per year in the season 2005/2006, EUR –.– gross per year in the season 2006/2007, and EUR –.– gross per year in the season 2007/2008.

The Chamber concluded its analysis of the objective criteria listed in Article 22 of the Regulations, by acknowledging that the player, by the time when the contractual breach occurred, was still bound to X by two further years of contract.

Subsequently, the Chamber stated that it falls under its responsibility to estimate the prejudice suffered by X, not only in accordance with the above-stated criteria, but also with its specific knowledge of the world of football, as well as with the experience the Chamber itself has gained throughout the years.

The Chamber outlined that, in the football environment, X is renowned worldwide as a club formateur, i.e. a club whose key activity is to train and educate young talented players and whose main source of income is represented by the transfer of such players.
In this respect, the notion of training and education includes all actions, of physical and technical nature, which contribute to ensure that a certain player receives an appropriate training allowing him to successfully proceed with his professional career.
The Chamber concluded in the sense that such a description fully applies to Y, who has become a rather skilful and internationally well-known player.
It was observed that Y was 15 years old when he first registered with X and that X played a fundamental role in the players training and education. In actual fact, it is not contested that the player has been trained and developed by X during seven years, i.e. between the ages of 15 and 22.
Taking into account the considerably long period of stay with X, it is evident that, apart from his personal talent, the players positive development has to be essentially attributed to the training and education he received from the X.
According to the Chambers position, any decision which disregarded this last circumstance, would end up jeopardising not only Xs organisation, but possibly even affect all the clubs involved in the training and education of young players.
Moreover, it is imperative to recall that X showed their very high consideration for the player, by offering him a new contract at considerably high financial conditions, especially taking into account the players young age.
Subsequently the Chamber placed emphasis on that part of the decision it had reached on 31 August 2004, whereby it had stated that any sanction against Y should have taken into consideration the exceptional circumstances surrounding the contractual dispute between him and X.
In this respect, the Chamber was eager to point out that the object of the present decision does not relate to the extent of the players responsibility, but to the unquestionable prejudice suffered by X, which remains unaffected by the mitigating circumstances the Chamber applied to the players sporting sanction in the decision reached on 31 August 2004.
In particular, the Chamber deemed that, in the assessment of such prejudice, the starting factor to be taken into account is the remaining value of the employment contract between X and Y, i.e. EUR –.–.
In addition to that, amongst the criteria applied to determine the amount of compensation due by the player to the club for breach of contract, the circumstance that Y unilaterally terminated the employment contract with X only after the first season of the new contract must be taken into paramount consideration.
Furthermore, the fact that X did not acquire the rights of an already established player, but registered the player in a young age and trained him in order to bring him to a good level, represents an added value per se.
As a matter of fact, the clubs that promote the training and education of young players shall not be penalised by the fact that, in accordance with Article 22 point 3 of the Regulations, they have not paid any transfer fee to the players' former club, circumstance which could have been taken into account in order to establish the amount of compensation due for contractual breach.
As a consequence, the seven years Y spent with X shall play a chief role in determining the amount of compensation due for contractual breach.
In this respect, it is worth emphasising that, while when Y was first registered with X the investment of the latter was in first line made so as to train and develop the players skills, it became evident with the time that these investments were made in order to maintain and even increase the value of the player. X definitely succeeded in this task.
In light of all the above circumstances, the Chamber decided that Y must pay the amount of EUR –.– to X.
The arguments put forward by Y could therefore not be followed.
If the aforementioned sum is not paid within 30 days as from the date of notification of this decision, Z is jointly responsible for such a payment, in accordance with Article 14 §3 of the Regulations governing the Applications of the Regulations.
The Chamber finally pointed out that Zs joint liability does not in any way affect the investigation carried out by FIFA against Z for inducement to contractual breach, which is object of separate proceedings.

DECISION OF THE DISPUTE RESOLUTION CHAMBER

1. The claim of X is partially accepted.
2. Y has to pay the amount of EUR –.– to X.
3. The amount due to X has to be paid by Y within 30 days as from the date of notification of this decision.
4. If the aforementioned sum is not paid within the aforementioned deadline, a 5% default interest rate per annum will apply and the present matter will be submitted to FIFAs Disciplinary Committee, so that the necessary disciplinary sanctions may be imposed.
5. If the aforementioned sum is not paid within 30 days as from the date of notification of this decision, Z is jointly responsible for the payment.
6. The claimant is directed to inform the respondent immediately of the account number to which the remittance is to be made and to notify the Dispute Resolution Chamber of every payment received.
7. According to art. 60 par. 1 of the FIFA Statutes this decision may be appealed before the Court of Arbitration for Sport (CAS). The statement of appeal must be sent to the CAS directly within 10 days of receiving notification of this decision and has to contain all elements in accordance with point 2 of the directives issued by the CAS, copy of which we enclose hereto. Within another 10 days following the expiry of the time limit for the filing of the statement of appeal, the appellant shall file with the CAS a brief stating the facts and legal arguments giving rise to the appeal (cf. point 4 of the directives).

1 JUNE 2005

6526
DECISION OF THE DISPUTE RESOLUTION CHAMBER

passed in Zurich, Switzerland, on 1 June 2005,
in the following composition:
Slim Aloulou (Tunisia), Chairman
Jean-Marie Philips (Belgium) member
Philippe Diallo (France) member
Michele Colucci (Italy) member
Philippe Piat (France) member
on the claim presented by
Player X, as Claimant
against
Club Y, as Respondent
regarding a contractual dispute in connection with outstanding bonuses

I. FACTS OF THE CASE:

1. The player X from Z, Claimant, and the club Y from W, Respondent signed an employment contract valid as from 15 February 2003 until 31 December 2003.
2. Apart from the salary, article V(1) of the employment contract stipulates that, if the Claimant comes out on the pitch to play on a championship match, he is paid the amount of EUR 10 per minute, as bonus.
3. On 25 October 2004, the Claimant contacted the FIFA administration and affirmed that he had played during 1050 minutes for the club and that in accordance with article V(1) of the relevant contract he is entitled to receive the amount of EUR 10,500. However, the Respondent had refused to pay him the requested bonuses.
4. On 1 February 2005, the Respondent contested the Claimant's entitlement to receive any bonuses. Moreover, the Respondent pointed out that the Claimant had not supplied evidence concerning the period of time, based on which he calculated his request.
5. The Respondent pointed out that according to article I(5) of the employment contract the Claimant confirmed that he understood the in-house rules, that according to article II(1) he declared that he is

aware of the regulations and accepts them in view of his scope of duties and that according to article III(8) he agreed to carry out his duties in accordance with the regulations issued by the club.

6. Furthermore, the Respondent stressed that article V(2) of the relevant contract stipulates that the bonus determined by the club's remuneration policy and the club's regulations issued in view of sanctions are integral part of the Claimant's remuneration.
7. In order to sustain its position, the Respondent provided a copy of the Bonus and Sanctions Regulations being in force for the period as from 1 July 2003 until 30 June 2004 for the players involved in the 1 League of the Adult National Football Championship (the internal rules). According to the aforementioned internal rules the Respondent has the right to impose sanctions, such as suspension or cancellation of the bonus, namely, in case that the team falls into the zone endangered by drop out on the table. In this respect, the Respondent pointed out that in July, August, September, October and November 2003 the team continuously was in the endangered zone and therefore, the management of the Respondent decided to cancel all bonus during the period between July and November 2003.
8. The Respondent provided copies of the imposed sanction for each relevant month and affirmed that the sanctions were communicated among the players and that the decision was handed by the skipper in writing. However, the Respondent did not provide any evidence that the Claimant was personally informed about the relevant sanctions.
9. As a result, the Respondent is of the opinion that the Claimant is not entitled to receive the claimed bonuses.
10. On 17 February 2005, the Claimant stressed that the internal rules, to which the Respondent referred in its answer to his claim, came into force after he concluded the employment contract and that he never received a copy of the relevant rules. Furthermore, the Claimant provided copies of the match statistics, downloaded from the Respondent's official website, according to which he spent exactly 970 minutes on the field during the period starting as from 26 July 2003 until 29 November 2003.
11. As a result, the Claimant rectified his claim and requests the amount of EUR 9,700 from the Respondent.
12. On 11 March 2005, the Respondent once again pointed out that according to article I(5) of the employment contract the Claimant confirmed that he understood and accepted the in-house rules. Furthermore, the Respondent provided a copy of the same internal rules concerning bonus and sanctions being in force for the period as from 1 July 2002 until 30 June 2003, i.e. at the time the employment contract was concluded, wherein the exact same rule is established as in the rules being in force during the period of time of the requested bonuses.
13. Therefore, the Respondent once again stressed that the Claimant is not entitled to receive any bonus, since he confirmed in the employment contract that he accepted and knew the club's internal rules, namely, the rules concerning sanctions and bonus.

II. CONSIDERATIONS OF THE DISPUTE RESOLUTION CHAMBER

14. The Dispute Resolution Chamber of the FIFA Players' Status Committee shall review disputes coming under its jurisdiction pursuant to Art. 42 of the FIFA Regulations for the Status and Transfer of Players at the request of one of the parties to the dispute.
15. Consequently, the Dispute Resolution Chamber is the competent body to decide on the present litigation concerning the outstanding bonuses allegedly owed by the Respondent to the Claimant.
16. Subsequently, and entering into the substance of the matter, the Chamber carefully considered the contents of the duly signed employment contract as well as of the relevant articles of the Respondent's internal rules.
17. On the one hand, the Chamber acknowledged that according to the employment contract the Claimant was entitled to receive, among other remunerations, the amount of EUR 10 per each minute he would spend on the field on a championship match, as bonus.
18. On the other hand, the Chamber took due note that according to the internal rules of the club, the Respondent has the right to impose sanctions, such as suspension or cancellation of the bonus, namely, in case that the team falls into the zone endangered by drop out on the table.
19. Turning its attention to the demand of the Claimant, the members of the Chamber acknowledged that the present dispute concerns only the allegedly outstanding bonuses. In this respect, the members noted that the Claimant provided copies of the match statistics, downloaded from the Respondent's official website, according to which he spent exactly 970 minutes on the field during the period starting as from 26 July 2003 until 29 November 2003. Furthermore, the Chamber pointed out that

the Respondent did not provide any evidence in order to abrogate the Claimant's affirmations with regard to the time based on which he is calculating the requested bonuses.

20. As a result, the Chamber concluded that it is undisputed that the Claimant spent 970 minutes on the field during the period starting as from 26 July 2003 until 29 November 2003.
21. Subsequently, the Chamber analysed the internal rules, based on which the Respondent cancelled the contractually agreed bonuses and is presently denying the Claimant's entitlement to receive the relevant bonuses.
22. The members of the Chamber discussed the contents of the relevant internal rules, in particular, the chapter referring to the bonuses and article 5, which stipulates: " In case that the team falls into the endangered zone on the league table the owner, the managing director or the chief trainer may withhold or withdraw the payment of bonuses." and concluded that the Respondent's decision to withdraw the payment of the contractually agreed bonuses, based on the cited article cannot be supported by FIFA.
23. In this respect, the Chamber deemed that the above-mentioned rule is ambiguous and its application is arbitrary, since it leads to an unacceptable result based on non-objective criteria.
24. The Chamber, emphasised that the lack of objective criteria by the application of the relevant rule leads to an unjustified disadvantage of the Claimant's financial rights.
25. In the light of the foregoing, the members of the Chamber unanimously concluded that the decision of the Respondent to withdraw the contractually agreed bonuses cannot be endorsed.
26. As a result, the Chamber concluded that the Claimant is entitled to receive the relevant bonuses.
27. Taking into account all of the above, the Dispute Resolution Chamber decided that the Respondent has to pay to the Claimant the outstanding bonuses amounting to EUR 9,700.

III. DECISION OF THE DISPUTE RESOLUTION CHAMBER

1. The claim lodged by the Claimant, Mr X, is accepted.
2. The Respondent, Y, shall pay the total amount of EUR 9,700 to the Claimant, within 30 days following the date of the communication of the present decision.
3. In the event that the above-mentioned amount is not paid within the stated deadline, an interest rate of 5% per year will apply and the present matter shall be submitted to FIFA's Disciplinary Committee, so that the necessary disciplinary sanctions may be imposed.
4. The Claimant is directed to inform the Respondent directly and immediately of the account number to which the remittance is to be made and to notify the Dispute Resolution Chamber of every payment received.
5. According to art. 60 par. 1 of the FIFA Statutes, this decision may be appealed against before the Court of Arbitration for Sport (CAS). The statement of appeal must be sent to the CAS directly within 10 days of receipt of notification of this decision and shall contain all the elements in accordance with point 2 of the directives issued by the CAS, a copy of which we enclose hereto. Within another 10 days following the expiry of the time limit for filing the statement of appeal, the appellant shall file a brief stating the facts and legal arguments giving rise to the appeal with the CAS (cf. point 4 of the directives).

⚽⚽⚽

65332

DECISION OF THE DISPUTE RESOLUTION CHAMBER

passed in Zurich, Switzerland, on 1 June 2005,
in the following composition:
Slim Aloulou (Tunisia), Chairman
Philippe Piat (France), member
Michele Colucci (Italy) , member
Jean-Marie Philips (Belgium), member
Philippe Diallo (Netherlands), member
on the claim presented by
Player A, as Claimant
against
Club B, as Respondent
regarding a labour dispute between the above-mentioned parties.

FACTS OF THE CASE

- The player A and the club B signed an employment contract which is valid from 1 June 2002 until 30 July 2007. The contract stipulates a monthly salary of EUR 3,000 and following bonus payments:
  - 24 July 2002 EUR 30,000
  - 1 July 2003 EUR 10,000
  - 1 July 2004 EUR 15,000
  - 1 July 2005 EUR 20,000
  - 1 July 2006 EUR 25,000
- The player A maintains that the club did neither pay his salaries for April, May and June 2003, nor the bonus payable on 1 July 2003, and so unilaterally breached the contract.
- Therefore, he claims for the salaries from April 2003 until June 2007, i.e. EUR 153,000, and unpaid bonuses in the amount of EUR 70,000, therefore in total for EUR 223,000.
- Since July 2003, the player is unemployed.
- The club B maintains that the player's residence and work permit expired on 30 June 2003. The extension of this permit allegedly can only be arranged personally by the player. According to the club, the player did not undertake the necessary steps in order to extend his residence and work permit. In consequence, the club is of the opinion that the player has breached the employment contract.
- The club provided the FIFA administration with a record of its financial department, according to which the salaries for the player A from April to June 2003 had been paid. This record is not signed by the player.
- Moreover, the club presented a payment slip dated 24 April 2003, stating the amount of HUF 3,618,000 (EUR 15,000), and signed by the player. This payment slip does not indicate the legal grounds of the respective payment.
- Besides that, the club refers to clause 11 of the employment contract, which stipulates a minimal price of the player's federative rights in the amount of EUR 400,000.
- As a result to the above, the club makes a counterclaim against the player for:
  - the difference between the amount paid to the player on 24 April 2003 (HUF 3,618,000, i.e. EUR 15,000) and the three monthly salaries claimed by the player (EUR 9,000), i.e. for HUF 1,186,207, and
  - EUR 400,000 based on clause 11 of the employment contract.
- The Player in his answer on the counterclaim contests being liable for the lack of residence and work permit as from 1 July 2003.

CONSIDERATIONS OF THE DISPUTE RESOLUTION CHAMBER

1. The members of the Dispute Resolution Chamber were summoned to pass a decision on the present matter by the Chairman pursuant to Art. 1 point 6) of the Rules Governing the Practice and Procedures of the Dispute Resolution Chamber.
2. The deciding body started its deliberations by indicating that, as established in Art. 42 § 1 lit. (b) (i) of the FIFA Regulations for the Status and Transfer of Players (hereinafter: the Regulations), it falls within the purview of the Dispute Resolution Chamber to determine whether one of the parties has committed a unilateral breach of contract without just cause. In the case that the employment contract was breached by a party, the Dispute Resolution Chamber is responsible to verify and decide whether this party is accountable for outstanding payments and compensation.
3. In view of the above, the Dispute Resolution Chamber concluded that it was competent to decide on the present litigation.
4. The members present at the meeting then entered into the substance of the matter and first noticed that the player A maintains neither having been paid by the club B for the months of April, May and June 2003 in the total amount of EUR 9,000, nor having received the bonus of 1 July 2003 in the amount of EUR 10,000. Furthermore, the Chamber took note of a record of the club's financial department, which is not signed by the player, but according to which the salaries for the player A from April to June 2003 had been paid. Finally, the Chamber noticed that the player's residence and work permit expired on 30 June 2003, and that both parties accuse each other for being responsible for the extension of these permits.
5. The Dispute Resolution Chamber then stated that the persistent failure of a club to pay the salaries of a player, without just cause, is generally to be considered as a unilateral breach of an employment contract.

6. In this regard, the Dispute Resolution Chamber stated that the club B did not present any considerable written evidence proving that the salaries and the bonus claimed by the player were paid. The documentation presented by the club is not reliable, since it does not contain the players signature, proving the receipt of the amounts concerned. Therefore, the Chamber stated that it has to be presumed that the amounts in question, claimed by the player, were not paid. This has clearly to be considered a "persistent failure".
7. In continuation, the Chamber stated that the club B did not have any reason justifying the non-payment of three salaries and one bonus payment in the total amount of EUR 19,000.
8. As a result to the above, the Dispute Resolution Chamber stated that the behaviour of the club B has to be considered as a breach of contract without just cause.
9. The Dispute Resolution Chamber then turned to the mutual accusation between the player and the club for not having undertaken the necessary to extend the player's residence and work permit, and in this regard, took note of the fact that the players visa allowing him to stay with and work for his club expired on 30 June 2003. Moreover, the Chamber noticed that the club B maintained that the extension of these permits can only be arranged personally by the player. Finally, the Chamber noticed that the club did not provide any written evidence proving that the extension of the mentioned permits indeed can only be arranged by the player.
10. The Dispute Resolution Chamber then stated that it is a basic principle of labour law that an employer has to provide his employees with a residence and work permit, if need be. If an employer does not undertake the necessary to provide his employees with a residence and work permit, and if this compels the player to leave the country where he is employed, and therefore to quit his work, this is basically to be considered as an unjustified breach of the employment contract by the employer.
11. Moreover, the Chamber stated that if an employer maintains that it does not bear any responsibility for the extension of the residence and work permit, it is up to the employer to prove this allegation. In case that the employer fails to prove this allegation, it has to be presumed that it bears the responsibility for the extension of the residence and work permit.
12. Since the club B did not present written evidence proving that it does not bear any responsibility for the extension of the residence and work permit of the player, and since these permits expired on 30 June 2003, i.e. four years and one month before the expiration of the employment contract, without that the club B undertook the necessary steps for their extension, the Dispute Resolution Chamber stated that this behaviour of the club B again has to be considered as a breach of contract without just cause.
13. In consequence to all the above, in application of Art. 42 § 1 lit. (b) (i) of the Regulations, the Dispute Resolution Chamber had to deliberate whether the club B is accountable for outstanding payments and compensation towards the player A.
14. As far as the responsibility of the club B for outstanding payments is concerned, the Dispute Resolution Chamber stated that the club has to pay to the player in question the salaries for April, May and June 2003 in the total amount of EUR 9,000 and the bonus of 1 July 2003 in the amount of EUR 10,000 .
15. As far as compensation for breach of contract is concerned, the Chamber decided that the club has to compensate the player with an amount corresponding to one years salaries, i.e. EUR 36,000, plus the bonus payable on 1 July 2004, i.e. EUR 15,000, therefore in total EUR 51,000.
16. In conclusion, the Dispute Resolution Chamber decided that the club B has to pay to the player A the amount of EUR 19,000 for outstanding remuneration, and the amount of EUR 51,000 for compensation for breach of contract. Therefore, in total, the club B has to pay to the player A the amount of EUR 70,000.

DECISION OF THE DISPUTE RESOLUTION CHAMBER

1. The claim of the player A is partially accepted .
2. The club B has to pay the amount of EUR 70,000 to the player A.
3. The amount due to the player A has to be paid by the club B within the next 30 days as from the date of notification of this decision.
4. In the event that the debts of the Respondent are not paid within the stated deadline, an interest rate of 5% per year will apply as from the first day after the stated deadline.
5. If the aforementioned sum is not paid within the aforementioned deadline, the present matter shall be submitted to FIFA's Disciplinary Committee, so that the necessary disciplinary sanctions may be imposed.

6. The player A is directed to inform the club B immediately of the account number to which the remittance is to be made, and to notify the Dispute Resolution Chamber of every payment received.
7. According to art. 60 par. 1 of the FIFA Statutes this decision may be appealed before the Court of Arbitration for Sport (CAS). The statement of appeal must be sent to the CAS directly within 10 days of receiving notification of this decision and has to contain all elements in accordance with point 2 of the directives issued by the CAS, copy of which we enclose hereto. Within another 10 days following the expiry of the time limit for the filing of the statement of appeal, the appellant shall file with the CAS a brief stating the facts and legal arguments giving rise to the appeal (cf. point 4 of the directives).

65349
DECISION OF THE DISPUTE RESOLUTION CHAMBER
passed in Zurich, Switzerland, on 1 June 2005,
in the following composition:
Slim Aloulou (Tunisia), Chairman
Philippe Piat (France), member
Michele Colucci (Italy), member
Jean-Marie Philips (Belgium), member
Philippe Diallo (Netherlands), member
on the claim presented by Player A, as Claimant against Club B, as Respondent
regarding a labour dispute between the above-mentioned parties.

FACTS OF THE CASE
- The player A and the club B signed a contract valid from 1 January 2003 until 31 December 2005.
- For the year 2004, the contract stipulates a monthly salary of USD 25,000, payable on the 15 of every month, plus a thirteenth wage in the same amount. For 2005, the contract stipulates a monthly salary and thirteenth wage of USD 29,153.
- In November 2004, after his last game with the team of club B, the player returned to his home-country for holidays.
- The club B did not pay the player's salary for December 2004 and the thirteenth wage on time. The club tried to pay these amounts on 21 January 2005, but failed, according to its opinion due to a mistake of the player's bank. According to the player, the club did not indicate the player's banking details in the money transfer documents.
- On 31 January 2005 the player would have had to report back from holidays at his club.
- However, the club did not provide him with a ticket, which, according to the player would have been its obligation in application of Article 2 § 3 c. of the contract, which states that
  "Party A (the club) shall provide Party B (the player) four economic class return tickets Home-Club."
- Moreover, in the interim, besides the salary of December and the thirteenth salary of 2004, the salary of January 2005 was outstanding, in total an amount of USD 79,153.
- Therefore, the player did not report back at his club.
- On 21 February 2005, the player reminded the club of its duties to pay his salaries and to provide him with a ticket to return to the club's country.
- On 4 March 2005, the player contacted FIFA, claiming for the above-mentioned amount plus the salary of February 2005, which became due in the interim, therefore for a total in the amount of USD 108,306. Furthermore, he claims for his immediate release in order to sign for a new club, and in this regard, claims for the entire amount of salaries until the expiry of the contract, the amount of USD 291,530 (salaries March until December 2005).
- the same day, the player informed the club that he terminates the employment contract with just cause.
- On 7 March 2005, a second try of the club to transfer the amount of USD 56,831 to the player was successful.
- Confronted with the player's claim, the club does not contest not having paid a part of the salaries as from January 2005, and the salary of December 2004 and the thirteenth wage of 2004 only late.

- As far as the airplane ticket is concerned, the club maintains that it was not its duty to pay a ticket to the player in advance. Usually, the players would only be refunded their travel expenses upon return to the club.
- The club requests the player to report back at the club immediately, and states that it would then pay the outstanding amounts to the player.
- Furthermore, the club quotes Article 3 § 5 of the employment contract, which states that
  "This contract shall be governed by the laws of the club's country, any notation between the parties, or lack of agreement in arbitration must be demitted to the Football Association of the club, if it can not arbitrate, the negotiation must be admitted to FIFA for final decision."
  In consequence, the club B is of the opinion that FIFA shall not have jurisdiction to decide upon the case. According to club B, the case must be referred to its Football Association.
- Finally, the club states that if the player would not return to the club, he would have to pay to the club the amount of three monthly salaries, in application of Article 3 § 1 of the employment contract, which states that
  "Neither party may cancel or repudiate the contract without the consultation or permission of the other party. The defaulting party as penalty payment must pay the total amount of the (Player's) three months salary."

CONSIDERATIONS OF THE DISPUTE RESOLUTION CHAMBER

1. The members of the Dispute Resolution Chamber were summoned to pass a decision on the present matter by the Chairman pursuant to Art. 1 point 6) of the Rules Governing the Practice and Procedures of the Dispute Resolution Chamber.
2. First of all, the members of the Dispute Resolution Chamber referred to the argument of the Respondent according to which the latter disputed the competence of FIFA, since Article 3 § 5 of the employment contract stipulates that any contractual dispute should be dealt with by the club's Football Association.
3. In this respect, the Chamber referred to the well established jurisprudence of the Dispute Resolution Chamber according to which, in general, in employment-related disputes between a club and a player that have an international dimension, i.e. the parties do not belong to the same country, both parties were entitled to refer the dispute to FIFA's bodies, unless an independent arbitration tribunal respecting the principle of equal representation of players and clubs with an independent chairman has been established at national level.
4. The members of the Chamber acknowledged that the Respondent was unable to prove that an independent arbitration tribunal in compliance with the requirements of the FIFA's regulations has been established in the club's country. As a consequence, the Dispute Resolution Chamber established that the Respondent's objection to the competence of FIFA to deal with the matter has to be rejected and that the matter can be considered as to the substance.
5. The deciding body then indicated that, as established in Art. 42 § 1 lit. (b) (i) of the FIFA Regulations for the Status and Transfer of Players (hereinafter: the Regulations), it falls within the purview of the Dispute Resolution Chamber to determine whether one of the parties has committed an unilateral breach of contract without just cause. In the case that the employment contract was breached by a party, the Dispute Resolution Chamber is responsible to verify and decide whether this party is accountable for outstanding payments and compensation.
6. In view of the above, the Dispute Resolution Chamber concluded that it was competent to decide on the present litigation.
7. The members present at the meeting then entered into the substance of the matter and first noticed that the salaries due by the club B for December 2004 and January 2005 were due on the fifteenth day of the relevant month, but were only paid on 7 March 2005, and only partially. Furthermore, the Chamber took note that the thirteenth wage for 2004 was due on the last day of 2004, but was also paid only on 7 March 2005. Finally, the Chamber noticed that the player A reminded the club of the above-mentioned outstanding payments on 21 February 2005.
8. The Dispute Resolution Chamber then stated that the persistent failure of a club to pay the salaries of a player, without just cause, is generally to be considered as a unilateral breach of an employment contract. The club B did not have any reason justifying the non-payment of a part of the salary of January 2005 and the delay of almost three months in the payment of the salary of December 2004 as well as of more than two months for the thirteenth wage for 2004. Moreover, the club did

not have any reason justifying that at the end of January 2005, three contractual payments (i.e. December 2004, thirteenth wage 2004, January 2005) were outstanding. These facts have clearly to be considered a "persistent failure".

9. As a result to the above, the Dispute Resolution Chamber stated that the behaviour of the club B has to be considered as a breach of contract without just cause. The employment contract between the parties was breached by the club by the end of January 2005.
10. In consequence, in application of Art. 42 § 1 lit. (b) (iii) of the Regulations, the Dispute Resolution Chamber had to deliberate whether the club B is accountable for outstanding payments and compensation towards the player A.
11. As far as the responsibility of the club B for outstanding payments is concerned, the Dispute Resolution Chamber stated that the club has to pay to the player in question the salaries for December 2004, the thirteenth wage of 2004, and for January 2005, in the total amount of USD 79,153, and in this regard, took into consideration that the amount of USD 56,831 was already paid by the club on 7 March 2005.
12. Therefore, the Dispute Resolution Chamber decided that the club B has to pay to the player A for outstanding salaries the amount of USD 22,322.
13. As far as compensation for breach of contract is concerned, the Chamber took into consideration Article 3 § 1 of the employment contract, which states that in case of breach of contract, the responsible party has to pay the total amount of three months salaries as penalty payment.
14. Therefore, the Chamber decided that the club has to compensate the player with an amount corresponding to three monthly salaries. Moreover, since the contract was breached in 2005, the Chamber decided that the salary stipulated for 2005 has to be taken into consideration, i.e. USD 29,153. Therefore, the compensation for breach of contract payable from the club B to the player A amounts to USD 87,459.
15. In conclusion, the Dispute Resolution Chamber decided that the club B has to pay to the player A the amount of USD 22,322 for outstanding salaries, and the amount of USD 87,459 for compensation for breach of contract without just cause. In total, the club B has to pay to the player A the amount of USD 109,781.
16. Furthermore, in view of the above, the Dispute Resolution Chamber established that the contractual relation between the parties had to be considered as terminated. In this respect, the Chamber underlined that, should the player enter into a new contractual relationship with a club and should the Association of this club ask for the issuance of the International Transfer Certificate from the club's Football Association, the club B is asked not to hinder the players' career and therefore to permit the issuance of the International Transfer Certificate.

DECISION OF THE DISPUTE RESOLUTION CHAMBER

1. The claim of the player A is partially accepted.
2. The employment contract between the club B and the player A is terminated as of 31 January 2005.
3. The club B has to pay the amount of USD 109,781 to the player A.
4. The amount due to the player A has to be paid by the club B within the next 30 days as from the date of notification of this decision.
5. In the event that the debts of the Respondent are not paid within the stated deadline, an interest rate of 5% per year will apply as from the first day after the stated deadline.
6. If the aforementioned sum is not paid within the aforementioned deadline, the present matter shall be submitted to FIFA's Disciplinary Committee, so that the necessary disciplinary sanctions may be imposed.
7. The player A is directed to inform the club B immediately of the account number to which the remittance is to be made, and to notify the Dispute Resolution Chamber of every payment received.
8. According to art. 60 par. 1 of the FIFA Statutes this decision may be appealed before the Court of Arbitration for Sport (CAS). The statement of appeal must be sent to the CAS directly within 10 days of receiving notification of this decision and has to contain all elements in accordance with point 2 of the directives issued by the CAS, copy of which we enclose hereto. Within another 10 days following the expiry of the time limit for the filing of the statement of appeal, the appellant shall file with the CAS a brief stating the facts and legal arguments giving rise to the appeal (cf. point 4 of the directives).

65412
DECISION OF THE DISPUTE RESOLUTION CHAMBER
passed in Zurich, Switzerland, on 1 June 2005,
in the following composition:
Slim Aloulou (Tunisia), Chairman
Jean-Marie Philips (Belgium), member
Philippe Diallo (France), member
Philippe Piat (France), member
Michele Colucci (Italy), member
on the claim presented by
the player, X, Belgium, as Claimant
against
the club, Y, Cyprus as Respondent
regarding a contractual dispute between the player and the club,

FACTS OF THE CASE

- On 28 January 2003, the parties signed an employment contract valid for a fixed period of 17 months from 28 January 2003 to 30 June 2004.
- In accordance with this contract, the player is entitled to receive, inter alia, the total amount of EUR 145,000 (free of taxes) payable as follows: a lump sum of EUR 21,750 upon receipt of the player's proof that he is able to fulfil his transfer; EUR 123,250 in 17 monthly instalments of EUR 7,250 each.
- In addition, the player is entitled to receive bonuses (free of taxes) for matches won in accordance with the internal club regulations.
- No copy of these internal club regulations has been made available to FIFA.
- Article 10 of this contract stipulates that the club shall pay the player's emoluments with a grace period of 60 days.
- According to article 8, a financial dispute between the parties shall be subject to arbitration before the competent authority of the Cyprus Football Association (CFA) pursuant to the provisions governing financial disputes applicable by the CFA.
- Article 12, which covers the reasons for the termination or suspension of the contract, (f) specifies that "the club has the right to terminate (the player agrees) the current agreement without any financial commitment to the player for the remaining said contract if the club notifies in writing the player prior to 01.06.2003."
- According to article 15, the parties agree to "submit to the exclusive jurisdiction of the competent sporting organs and/or authorities of Cyprus setting aside and/or otherwise waiving the provisions of any labour law and/or labour related tribunal as well as the jurisdiction of any civil courts."
- On 24 March 2004, the player turned to FIFA claiming that the club had omitted to pay the following amounts:
- Salaries from February 03 to June 03*
  EUR 24,895
- Remainder of lump sum (see above)
  EUR 13,276
- Bonuses
  CYP 3,250
  TOTAL
  CYP 3,250 and
  EUR 38,171
  * the player allegedly only received EUR 11,355 out of the EUR 36,250 due to him for the said period of time.
- With respect to his claim for bonuses, X has failed to present supporting documentation.
- In reply, the club affirms that according to article 12(f) it was entitled to terminate the contract with the player without any financial commitment to the player for the remaining period of the contract if the notification was made prior to 1 June 2003.
- According to the club, it exercised this right.
- To this end, the club submitted a copy of a document without date addressed to the player, by means

of which it terminated the contract referring to its clause 12. In addition, the club submitted a copy of an envelop addressed to the player and stamped 31 May 2003, which was returned to the club as the player had left the address indicated on the said envelop.
- In addition, the club is surprised to receive a financial claim from the player almost one year after the termination of the contract and it asserts that it has paid what he was entitled to and it denies that it would owe any monies to the player.
- No documents have been presented by the club in this regard.
- The club adds that the player had never before complained or asked for money.
- According to Y, the player did not contribute or offer his services to the club at the expected standards.
- Furthermore, the club maintains that the player was injured and did not participate in almost 80% of the matches.
- Y claims that the Dispute Resolution Chamber has no jurisdiction in the present matter referring to articles 8 and 15 of the employment contract.
- The player has presented further comments to the club's reply stating that he never received any letter of termination from the club and he points out that the document presented by the club does not bear any date.
- He furthermore points out that he does not claim any monies beyond the period of time that he effectively was rendering his services to the club, i.e. until June 2003.
- X rejects all of the allegations made by the Cypriot club.
- As regards the jurisdiction of the Dispute Resolution Chamber in the present matter, the player asserts that there was no intention of the parties to exclude FIFA's jurisdiction, which is why article 13 imposes an obligation on the club to copy the CFA and/or UEFA-FIFA on any notice of termination of the contract by the club.
- For this and other reasons, X denies that FIFA has no jurisdiction to decide on this case.

CONSIDERATIONS OF THE DISPUTE RESOLUTION CHAMBER

The members of the Chamber considered that, in principle, in accordance with Article 42 of the FIFA Regulations for the Status and Transfer of Players the Chamber is competent to deal with matters as the case at hand. However, taking into account articles 8 and 15 of the relevant employment contract, which are being invoked by the Respondent in its motivation, the Chamber deemed that the question as to whether it has jurisdiction in the present matter must be answered. Article 15, which deals with exclusive jurisdiction, stipulates that exclusive jurisdiction is assigned to "competent sporting organs and/or authorities of Cyprus ..." The Chamber concurred that this ambiguous phrase can be interpreted in such a way that it would include the Dispute Resolution Chamber, which indeed is a competent sporting organisation.

In addition, the members of the Chamber agreed that in the absence of a national sports arbitration tribunal composed of members chosen in equal numbers by players and clubs as well as an independent chairman (cf. article 42 par. 1 (b)(i) of the Regulations for the Status and Transfer of Players [hereinafter referred to as the "Regulations"]), at the request of a party, the Dispute Resolution Chamber of the FIFA Players' Status Committee is competent to deal with an employment-related dispute between a player and a club that has an international dimension, i.e. the parties involved do not belong to the same country.

The Chamber acknowledged that the Respondent was unable to prove that an independent arbitration tribunal in compliance with the requirements of the Regulations has been established in Cyprus. As a consequence, the members of the Chamber established that the Respondent's objection to the competence of FIFA to deal with the matter has to be rejected and that the matter can be considered as to the substance.

The Chamber noted that X terminated the employment contract invoking article 12 f) of the relevant contract. In spite of the fact that the player's claim is limited to payment of the monies that he considers being due to him for the period of time that he rendered his services to the club, the Chamber pointed out that the said article is potestative and, therefore, not acceptable.

Y maintains that it has paid to the player all monies that he was entitled to receive. However, it has failed to present any supporting documentation in this regard. The club also points out that the player's performance did not meet the club's expectations and standards.

The members of the Chamber presumed that the club has made such statement in an attempt to justify its assertion that the player has received all monies that he was entitled to receive, as the club may have deemed that X was entitled to a lower salary and to only part of the aforementioned lump sum of EUR 21,750 in the light of his allegedly disappointing performance.

The Chamber then turned in greater detail to the player's financial claim that, in addition to outstanding salaries and the remainder of the lump sum, also contains allegedly outstanding bonuses for the 2002-03 season to the amount of CYP 3,250. In reply to the player's claim, the Cypriot club asserts that it has paid to the player all his dues. However, as stated above, it failed to present pertinent documentary evidence in support of its position. On the other hand, the player, X, has plainly produced an enumeration of the matches on the basis of which he maintains being entitled to bonuses without having presented any pertinent documentary evidence in this regard. Consequently, the Chamber agreed to accept the player's claim for bonuses to 50% only.

All in all, the Chamber concluded that Y has failed to substantiate its assertion that it has paid to the player all monies that he was entitled to receive during the period of time that the employment contract was in force. In addition, the members of the Chamber agreed that the Cypriot club has not presented any valid reasons which would justify non-payment of the monies included in the player's claim.

In the light of all of the above, the Chamber decided that X is entitled to receive the outstanding salaries and the remainder of the lump sum to a total sum of EUR 38,171 and the amount of CYP 1,625 for outstanding bonuses.

DECISION OF THE DISPUTE RESOLUTION CHAMBER

1. The claim of the Claimant, X, is partially accepted.
2. The Respondent, Y, has to pay the amounts of EUR 38,171 and CYP 1,625 to the Claimant.
3. The amount due to the Claimant has to be paid by the Respondent within 30 days as from the date of notification of this decision.
4. In the event that the debt of the Cypriot club is not paid within the stated deadline, an interest rate of 5% per year will apply as of expiry of the aforementioned deadline.
5. If the sums of EUR 38,171 and CYP 1,625 are not paid within the aforementioned deadline, the present matter shall be submitted to the FIFA Disciplinary Committee, so that the necessary disciplinary sanctions may be imposed.
6. The Claimant is directed to inform the Respondent immediately of the account number to which the remittance is to be made and to notify the Dispute Resolution Chamber of every payment received.
7. According to art. 60 par. 1 of the FIFA Statutes, this decision may be appealed against before the Court of Arbitration for Sport (CAS). The statement of appeal must be sent to the CAS directly within 10 days of receipt of notification of this decision and shall contain all the elements in accordance with point 2 of the directives issued by the CAS, a copy of which we enclose hereto. Within another 10 days following the expiry of the time limit for filing the statement of appeal, the appellant shall file a brief stating the facts and legal arguments giving rise to the appeal with the CAS (cf. point 4 of the directives).

65414
DECISION OF THE DISPUTE RESOLUTION CHAMBER
passed in Zurich, Switzerland, on 1 June 2005,
in the following composition:
Slim Aloulou (Tunisia), Chairman
Jean-Marie Philips (Belgium), member
Philippe Diallo (France), member
Philippe Piat (France), member
Michele Colucci (Italy), member
on the claim presented by
the player, X, Bosnia and Herzegovina, as Claimant
against
the club, Y, Cyprus as Respondent
regarding a contractual dispute between the player and the club,

FACTS OF THE CASE

- On 11 January 2003, the parties signed an employment contract valid for a fixed period of 18 months from 11 January 2003 to 30 June 2004.
- In accordance with this contract, the player is entitled to receive, inter alia, the total amount of EUR 140,000 (free of taxes) payable as follows: EUR 28,000 upon receipt of the player's proof that he is able to fulfil his transfer; EUR 112,000 in 18 monthly instalments.
- In addition, the player is entitled to receive bonuses (free of taxes) for matches won in accordance with the internal club regulations.
- No copy of these internal club regulations has been made available to FIFA.
- Article 10 of this contract stipulates that the club shall pay the player's emoluments with a grace period of 60 days.
- According to article 8, a financial dispute between the parties shall be subject to arbitration before the competent authority of the Cyprus Football Association (CFA) pursuant to the provisions governing financial disputes applicable by the CFA.
- According to article 15, the parties agree to "submit to the exclusive jurisdiction of the competent sporting organs and/or authorities of Cyprus setting aside and/or otherwise waiving the provisions of any labour law and/or labour related tribunal as well as the jurisdiction of any civil courts."
- On 15 January 2004, the parties signed an agreement in accordance with which the club was obliged to pay to X the amount of EUR 32,000 on or before 29 February 2004 in full settlement of all outstanding monies in connection with his employment.
- Furthermore, should this deadline be met, the player would withdraw any claim against the Cypriot club.
- On the other hand, according to clause 3, should the said deadline be ignored by the club, the player would reserve all claims in connection with his employment contract.
- The said agreement also stipulates that the club undertakes to notify the Cyprus Football Association to issue the international registration transfer certificate.
- On 23 March 2004, the player turned to FIFA claiming that the club failed to pay any amount of money and therefore, X claims payment of the following monies invoking the above-mentioned clause 3 of the settlement agreement:
  a) 50% of January 2003 salary
     EUR 3,111
  b) Balance for salaries March – July 2003
     EUR 1,000
  c) Salaries from August – December 2003
     EUR 31,110
  d) Bonuses for the 2002-03 season
     CYP 9,250 (EUR 15,725 acc. to player)
  e) Reimbursement of air ticket costs
     EUR 1,000
  f) School fees for player's child
     EUR 350
     TOTAL
     CYP 9,250 and
     EUR 36,571
- As regards point f) it must be noted that the employment contract includes a pertinent clause, however, no receipts have been presented by the player.
- As regards points e) and f) it must be noted that the player withdrew these items in reaction to the club's response.
- With respect to point d) regarding match bonuses no supporting documentation has been presented by the player.
- In reply, the club confirms that items a) and c) above are outstanding.
- The club strongly denies that items b), d), e), and f) above are due to the player maintaining that these claims are unfounded.
- No supporting documentation has been presented by the club in this regard.
- However, Y claims that the Dispute Resolution Chamber has no jurisdiction in the present matter referring to articles 8 and 15 of the employment contract.

- Therefore, according to the club, X's claim should be rejected.
- In reply to the club's response, the player has specified the matches in relation with which he claims being entitled to bonuses. Furthermore, he withdrew his claim relating to air ticket costs and school fees.
- As regards the jurisdiction of the Dispute Resolution Chamber in the present matter, the player asserts that his claim is based on the agreement dated 15 January 2004 by means of which the employment contract was terminated. As a result, the club cannot invoke the above-mentioned provisions regarding jurisdiction.
- For this and other reasons, X denies that FIFA has no jurisdiction to decide on this case.

CONSIDERATIONS OF THE DISPUTE RESOLUTION CHAMBER

The members of the Chamber considered that, in principle, in accordance with Article 42 of the FIFA Regulations for the Status and Transfer of Players the Chamber is competent to deal with matters as the case at hand. However, taking into account articles 8 and 15 of the relevant employment contract, which are being invoked by the Respondent in its motivation, the Chamber deemed that the question as to whether it has jurisdiction in the present matter must be answered. Article 15, which deals with exclusive jurisdiction, stipulates that exclusive jurisdiction is assigned to "competent sporting organs and/or authorities of Cyprus …" The Chamber concurred that this ambiguous phrase can be interpreted in such a way that it would include the Dispute Resolution Chamber, which indeed is a competent sporting organisation.

In addition, the members of the Chamber agreed that in the absence of a national sports arbitration tribunal composed of members chosen in equal numbers by players and clubs as well as an independent chairman (cf. article 42 par. 1 (b)(i) of the Regulations for the Status and Transfer of Players [hereinafter referred to as the "Regulations"]), at the request of a party, the Dispute Resolution Chamber of the FIFA Players' Status Committee is competent to deal with an employment-related dispute between a player and a club that has an international dimension, i.e. the parties involved do not belong to the same country.

The Chamber acknowledged that the Respondent was unable to prove that an independent arbitration tribunal in compliance with the requirements of the Regulations has been established in Cyprus. As a consequence, the members of the Chamber established that the Respondent's objection to the competence of FIFA to deal with the matter has to be rejected and that the matter can be considered as to the substance.

The Chamber noted that approximately one year after the commencement of the player's employment at Y, on 15 January 2004, the parties signed an agreement in accordance with which the club was obliged to pay to X the amount of EUR 32,000 on or prior to 29 February 2004 in full settlement of all outstanding monies. According to clause 3, should this time limit not be respected by the Cypriot club, the player would reserve all his rights in accordance with the employment contract that was signed between the parties on 11 January 2003.

From the claim lodged by the player in March 2004, it can be noted that the aforementioned time limit was not respected by the Cypriot club and, therefore, X, invoking clause 3 of the above-mentioned settlement agreement, claims payment of certain monies on the basis of the employment contract.

In its response to this claim, Y acknowledges that it owes 50% of X's salary for January 2003 (EUR 3,111) as well as salaries as from August 2003 until December 2003 (EUR 31,110) to the total amount of EUR 34,221. This amount surpasses the amount of EUR 32,000 contained in the settlement agreement. Subsequently, the members of the Chamber concluded that Y implicitly accepts the validity of the aforementioned clause 3 of the settlement agreement.

The Chamber then turned in greater detail to the player's financial claim that also contains allegedly outstanding bonuses for the 2002-03 season to the amount of CYP 9,250. According to the Cypriot club, the player's claim for bonuses is "unfounded". However, it failed to present pertinent documentary evidence in support of its position. On the other hand, the player, X, has plainly produced an enumeration of the matches on the basis of which he maintains being entitled to bonuses without having presented any pertinent documentary evidence in this regard. Consequently, the Chamber agreed to accept the player's claim for bonuses to 50% only. Finally, the Chamber duly noted that the club, Y, has not presented any written evidence pertaining to payment of the claimed balance for salaries due for March to July 2003. As a consequence, the Chamber decided that the relevant amount of EUR 1,000 must also be awarded to the player, X.

In the light of all of the above, the Chamber decided that Mr. X is entitled to receive the amounts of EUR 35,221 and CYP 4,625.

DECISION OF THE DISPUTE RESOLUTION CHAMBER

1. The claim of the Claimant, X, is partially accepted.
2. The Respondent, Y, has to pay the amounts of EUR 35,221 and CYP 4,625 to the Claimant.
3. The amount due to the Claimant has to be paid by the Respondent within 30 days as from the date of notification of this decision.
4. In the event that the debt of the Cypriot club is not paid within the stated deadline, an interest rate of 5% per year will apply as of expiry of the aforementioned deadline.
5. If the sums of EUR 35,221 and CYP 4,625 are not paid within the aforementioned deadline, the present matter shall be submitted to the FIFA Disciplinary Committee, so that the necessary disciplinary sanctions may be imposed.
6. The Claimant is directed to inform the Respondent immediately of the account number to which the remittance is to be made and to notify the Dispute Resolution Chamber of every payment received.
7. According to art. 60 par. 1 of the FIFA Statutes, this decision may be appealed against before the Court of Arbitration for Sport (CAS). The statement of appeal must be sent to the CAS directly within 10 days of receipt of notification of this decision and shall contain all the elements in accordance with point 2 of the directives issued by the CAS, a copy of which we enclose hereto. Within another 10 days following the expiry of the time limit for filing the statement of appeal, the appellant shall file a brief stating the facts and legal arguments giving rise to the appeal with the CAS (cf. point 4 of the directives).

65723

DECISION OF THE DISPUTE RESOLUTION CHAMBER

passed in Zurich, Switzerland, on 1 June 2005,
in the following composition:
Slim Aloulou (Tunisia), chairman
Jean Marie Philips (Belgium), member
Philippe Diallo (France), member
Michele Colucci (Italy), member
Philippe Piat (France), member
on the claim presented by
Player G as Claimant
against
Club Ch as Respondent
regarding a contractual dispute between the parties involved

FACTS OF THE CASE:

- On 10 September 2001, the player G signed a contract with Ch for two seasons until 30 June 2003.
- Art. 3 of the contract between the player and the club stipulated a monthly salary of BGL 400 (Bulgarian Leva). Art. 4 of the contract provided for an annexe to be signed in which remuneration and other amounts were stipulated. The player sent a copy of both documents to the FIFA administration. The relevant annexe was dated 1 August 2002.
- On 2 June 2004, the player sent the FIFA administration a formal claim for USD 20,018 plus interest, comprising the following:
- Second instalment of the bonus
  upon signing the contract USD 5,000
- Instalment 9 of extra salary USD 2,509
- Instalment 10 of extra salary USD 2,509
- Rewards USD 10,000
  Total: USD 20,018
- The FIFA administration forwarded the player's claim to Ch club, requesting it to comment.
- The club replied to FIFA as follows:

1) the club had fulfilled all of its obligations towards the player in compliance with the contract signed on 10 September 2001;
2) the player had given FIFA only part of the employment contract he had concluded with the club;
3) the club attached a full copy of the contract in question and pointed out that art. 3 stipulated the player's monthly salary as BGL 400;
4) there was neither any truth or proof to the player's claim that other remuneration had been provided for in an annexe to the contract and he could not prove it conclusively;
5) art. 4 of the contract was clear, the English translation of which was:
"... (2) The additional agreement (the annex) under par. 2, which is bound to bear the number and the date of this employment contract, shall be deposited at the BFU [Bulgarian Football Union], sealed in an envelope, which is to be stamped with the stamps of the relevant PFC [club] and BFU, and opened before the BFU Arbitration Committee only in case disputes arise between the PFC and the EMPLOYEE [football player] ...";
6) the club was obliged only to pay the player the monthly salary described in article 3 of the employment contract and not to pay any extra remuneration, the proof of this being that the spaces to be filled in with figures in the contract were empty;
7) there was no annexe to the employment contract signed on 10 September 2001 and neither had it been submitted to the BFU for registration;
8) it admitted that the club had signed a project for an annexe on 10 September 2001 but it was invalid and neither party was under any obligation as it had not been submitted or registered with the BFU. A copy of this alleged draft annexe, with a complete different content than the one submitted by the player, was remitted by the club to the FIFA Administration. Moreover, the club remarked that an employment contract with a foreign footballer must be registered and endorsed by the National Labour Office, as could be seen in the stamp on the employment contract signed on 10 September 2001;
9) the argument that the annexe in question was only a draft and not a final contract reflects the fact that it had been signed in Sofia on the same day of the employment contract, which itself had been signed in Varna, which is six hours away from Sofia.
10) moreover, the draft annexe was valid for two years and the currency was expressed in German marks and not dollars;
11) finally, the club criticised the statements of Mr G's legal representative, arguing that according to Bulgarian law a legal representative must be a lawyer and have passed the examinations necessary to practise as such.

- On 21 October 2004, the player replied to the club's statements, categorically rejecting them and pointing out:
  1) that the annexe signed by both parties, agreeing to extra remuneration, was signed on 1 August 2002, i.e. twelve months after the employment contract, and he was given a pay rise, to take account of G's good performance;
  2) that the club had generally complied with the agreements reached but had not paid some amounts which were part of the player's remuneration, as mentioned above; despite repeated reminders to the club, these amounts were not paid;
  3) that the contract sent to the FIFA administration was the entire document and not part of it, as the club claimed;
  4) that his earnings exceeded BGL 400 and that a professional player such as G would clearly never have signed a contract for that amount; as evidence, the salary he was currently earning with a Russian club amounted to a six-figure salary in US dollars;
  5) that, for some months, the club had paid the extra remuneration mentioned in the annexe whose validity they dispute and that it was much more than BGL 400;
  6) that with regard to the claim that it was only a draft annexe, the club was completely confused and contradicted itself in stating that the club and the player had signed the annexe and then that it had been signed in Sofia, which is six hours away from Varna, as though it was physically impossible to be in both places at the same time.
  7) that the club had signed and officially stamped the contract and the annexe;
  8) that although the annexe had not been submitted to and registered with the BFU, it did not exempt the club from its obligations to pay in accordance with a perfectly valid contract signed by the parties concerned;

9) that it was incumbent upon the club to register contracts and annexes and not the duty of the player to go to the association to carry out such administrative work, especially in the case of a foreign footballer who did not master the local language;
10) The player sent the FIFA administration an official declaration from Mr D, deputy chairman of K club. Mr D had personally attended the signing of the employment contract on 10 September 2001 and the annexe on 1 August 2002. Moreover, Mr D co-signed the latter document.
11) In his official statement dated 19 October 2004, Mr. D declared:

- that he had been deputy chairman of K club since January 2000,
- that before playing for Ch club, the player, G, had played for K;
- that on 6 September 2001, the player had been transferred from his club to Ch;
- that both clubs had therefore concluded contracts in connection with the transfer and K had acquired some rights yielding future income for his club;
- that he had attended the signing of the employment contract between Ch and the player on 10 September 2001;
- that as the transfer contract between the clubs contained pending obligations on the part of Ch, K club had needed to keep an eye on the player with the Ch club;
- that during the first twelve months, the player had performed well with the club, becoming one of the top members of the team. Towards the end of the 2001-2002 season, the player had had negotiations with Ch club to arrange for an increase of remuneration. K had supervised the negotiations;
- that as a result, Mr. D had gone to Bulgaria in August 2002 and attended the signing of the annexe, which included terms and conditions agreed upon by both parties. The annexe signed on 1 August 2002 had been declared an integral part of the employment contract dated 10 September 2001 by the parties. Mr D was a witness to the signing of that agreement and, as such, signed each page of the relevant annexe. In fact the original document contains Mr D signature.
- that Ch club had failed to fulfil its obligations with K by not paying instalments due from the transfer contract, proof of which can be seen in the formal complaint that his club had been required to make to FIFA and for which proceedings have already been initiated under reference che 04-T0349.
- The club replied to the player's arguments claiming:
  a. that to corroborate its claims, it was attaching a declaration from the BFU signed by its General Secretary, stating that the only document registered in the association was the contract signed between the parties in September 2001 to which no annexe had been attached;
  b. that the player's statements were unfounded and confused and that the official declaration was inadmissible;
  c. that the documents submitted by the player were incomplete and not clear;
  d. that the club had paid the player a salary of BGL 400 in addition to food and accommodation and bonuses for performance, which is common practice in Bulgarian clubs, besides which Ch could not afford higher salaries for players.
  e. that, finally, according to art. 16 of the BFU statutes, every contract must show signatures certified by a notary but that, in the case at hand, the relevant employment contract did not comply with this condition.
- The player is requesting the assistance of the Dispute Resolution Chamber in order to establish an interest applicable on the amount of USD 20,018 owed by the Club Ch.
- Besides, the player G is demanding that the club Ch repays him the legal costs that he had to incur in order to lodge the present claim.
- Finally the player sent a fax to the FIFA administration on 12 January 2005, stating that the club had made completely confused and contradictory allegations with regard to the fact that it had provided the player with accommodation. This obligation to provide accommodation was actually, not provided for in the contract of 10 September 2001 but in the annexe only, which the very same club had declared invalid. It had therefore indirectly admitted the existence and validity of the annexe.
- The player is requesting the Dispute Resolution Chamber to demand that Ch club pay the amount of USD 20,018 as salary, bonuses and remuneration in addition to interest due.
- The club is requesting the Dispute Resolution Chamber to reject the player's claim entirely.

CONSIDERATIONS OF THE DISPUTE RESOLUTION CHAMBER:

The members of the Dispute Resolution Chamber were summoned to pass a decision on this matter by the Chairman pursuant to Art. 1 point 6) of the Rules Governing the Practice and Procedures of the Dispute Resolution Chamber.

The Dispute Resolution Chamber shall review disputes coming under its jurisdiction pursuant to Art. 42 of the FIFA Regulations for the Status and Transfer of Players, edition September 2001(hereafter: FIFA Regulations) at the request of one of the parties to the dispute.
According to Art. 42, paragraph 1 (b) (i) of the FIFA Regulations, the triggering elements of the dispute (i.e. whether a contract was breached, with or without just cause, or sporting just cause), will be decided by the Dispute Resolution Chamber.
If the employment contract was breached by a party, the Dispute Resolution Chamber is responsible to verify whether this party is accountable for compensation and outstanding payments.
Consequently, the Dispute Resolution Chamber is the competent body to decide on the present litigation concerning the alleged non respect of the contract.
Subsequently, and entering into the substance of the matter, the Chamber began its deliberations by analyzing the allegations of the Claimant.
To begin with, the Dispute Resolution Chamber noted that the player G stated clearly all the facts and circumstances on which he based his claim and gave evidence to justify them.
The Chamber pointed out that the player was claiming an amount of USD 20,018 as salary, bonuses and remuneration plus the relevant interest. All these items were established in an annexe to the employment contract signed by the player G and the Club Ch on 1 August 2002.
The player G had provided a copy of the relevant annexe. In this respect, the Chamber acknowledged in particular that, with regard to the player's claim the said document stated:

- Second instalment of the bonus upon signing the contract, due on 15 January 2003 USD 5,000
- Instalment 9 of extra salary, due on 5 April 2003 USD 2,509
- Instalment 10 of extra salary, due on 5 May 2003 USD 2,509
- Rewards, due at the end of the season June-July 2003 USD 10,000

Furthermore, the Chamber took note of the relevant fact stated by the player G in his claim that Ch had complied completely with its contractual obligations towards him including those stipulated in the relevant annexe, except for this amount of USD 20,018 plus due interest that he is claiming.
On the other hand, the club Ch rejected the claim of the player basing their objections on the fact that there had been no written agreement to pay other remunerations except for the BGL 400 established in the employment contract celebrated between the parties in the city of Varna on 10 September 2001.
The Chamber underlined that the parties involved in the present affair agreed totally on the terms of the employment contract signed by them on 10 September 2001 in the city of Varna. However that they totally disagreed about the legal existence and contents of the annexe to the aforementioned contract on which the player's demands were based.
In continuation, the Chamber deemed it appropriate to make an in-depth analysis of the allegations of the Respondent. In this sense, the deciding body pointed out that the club Ch was not consistent and clear enough in its allegations in the present affair. In fact the Chamber outlined that each time that the club Ch had had the possibility to exercise its right of defence and express its position and comments, these had not been uniform and had always contained additional new facts and elements without being well founded.
In this sense, the Chamber noted that the main defence presented by Ch could be summarized as follows:

1. there was no annexe to the employment contract signed on 10 September 2001, nor had such an annexe been submitted to the BFU for registration;
2. the club had signed the draft of an annexe on 10 September 2001 but this was not legally binding between the parties as it had not been submitted or registered with the BFU;
3. the annexe in question was only a draft and not a final contract and proof of this was that it had been signed in Sofia on the same day as the employment contract had been signed in Varna, which is six hours away from Sofia;
4. according to art 16 of the BFU´s statutes every contract must show signatures certified by a notary but that, in this case, the employment contract did not comply with this condition;
5. the club does not recognize the existence or at least the validity of the annexe dated 1 August 2002, which was submitted by the player.

In continuation, the deciding body pointed out that the annexe dated 1 August 2002 remitted by the player contains the signature of both parties concerned i.e. the player G as well as the club Ch. Therefore, the Chamber stated that as a general rule the relevant annexe has to be considered as valid and legally binding between the parties. Yet, the Respondent appears to be contesting its validity for formal reasons.

The Chamber remarked that the Respondent's arguments in respect of the lack of registration of the annexe with the respective Federation and the observation of the BFU internal rules are not valid reasons since they do not justify Ch's non fulfilment of its financial commitments towards the player G. In this respect, the deciding body explained that, generally, players are not acquainted with administrative practices. Also it recalled that, as a general rule, it is the club´s reasonability to deposit the contract and any possible annexes at the relevant association. Therefore, if these formal requisites had not been complied with, this falls into the responsibility of the club and the player cannot suffer disadvantages or be denied his rights because of the lapse of the club.
In addition, the Chamber duly noted that the club Ch tacitly admitted the existence of the annexe dated 1 August 2002 when it stated that it had paid the player the salary of BGL 400 (agreed in the employment contract) plus food; accommodation and bonuses for performance. In fact, as emphasized in the response of the player G, these items (food, accommodation and bonuses for performance) were obligations not established in the employment contract but in the annexe, which the very same club had declared invalid. Equally, according to the player, the club had complied with the financial obligations stipulated in the relevant annexe over a certain period of time, in particular by paying:

- the first instalment and 70 % (approx.) of the second instalment of the bonus upon signing the contract and
- the first eight instalments of the extra salary.

In view of the aforementioned, the Chamber duly noted that the Respondent had not been able to justify such stance.
In continuation, the Chamber focused its attention on the witness's statement presented by the player G. In this testimony, Mr. D, Deputy Chairman of the player's former club K, unambiguously confirmed the celebration and the signature of the annexe on 1 August 2002 between the player G and the club Ch. In this respect, the Chamber remarked that the purpose of Mr. D´s assistance in the celebration of the employment contract and its annexe had been clear, reasonable and justifiable.
In summary, the Chamber concluded from the exchanges of correspondence, documents and evidences submitted by the parties to the FIFA Administration that the parties involved in this case signed an employment contract on 10 September 2001 and after almost one year, the player and the representative of the club Ch had signed an annexe on 1 August 2002 which was formally declared to be an integral part of the employment contract. Therefore the content of the annexe signed by the parties on 1 August 2002 is legally binding between the player G and the club Ch.
In view of all the above, the Chamber acknowledges that the reasons stated by the Claimant are valid and justified.
Concerning the claimed interests by the player G, the Chamber took note that no default interest clause had been included in the relevant annexe. As a consequence, the deciding body rejected the relevant claim to that regard.
Finally, and referring to its well established jurisprudence, the Chamber did not award any amount as contribution for his legal expenses to the player.
In light of all of the foregoing, the Chamber decided that under consideration of the referred facts and circumstances the club Ch is liable to pay the total amount of USD 20,018 to the player G.

DECISION OF THE DISPUTE RESOLUTION CHAMBER

1. The claim lodged by the Claimant is partially accepted.
2. The Respondent shall pay to the Claimant the total amount of USD 20,018, within 30 days following the date of the communication of the present decision.
3. Any other claim of the Claimant is rejected.
4. In the event that the debts of the Respondent are not paid within the stated deadline, an interest rate of 5% per year will apply. Furthermore, the FIFA Administration will be entitled to submit the file to the Disciplinary Committee.
5. The Claimant is directed to inform the Respondent immediately of the account number to which the remittance is to be made and to notify the Dispute Resolution Chamber of every payment received.
6. According to art. 60 par. 1 of the FIFA Statutes, this decision may be appealed against before the Court of Arbitration for Sport (CAS). The statement of appeal must be sent to the CAS directly within 10 days of receipt of notification of this decision and shall contain all the elements in accordance with point 2 of the directives issued by the CAS, a copy of which we enclose hereto. Within another 10 days following the expiry of the time limit for filing the statement of appeal, the appellant shall

file a brief stating the facts and legal arguments giving rise to the appeal with the CAS (cf. point 4 of the directives).

⚽⚽⚽

65850
DECISION OF THE DISPUTE RESOLUTION CHAMBER
passed in Zurich, Switzerland, on 1 June 2005, in the following composition:
Slim Aloulou (Tunisia), chairman
Jean-Marie Philips (Belgium), member
Philippe Diallo (France), member
Philippe Piat (France), member
Michele Colucci (Italy), member
on the claim presented by the player A, Portugal, as Claimant
against the club H, Germany, as Respondent,
regarding a contractual dispute arisen between the parties.

I. FACTS OF THE CASE

1. On 2 February 2004, the player A and the German club, H, concluded a labour contract with validity from 2 February 2004 until 30 June 2005. The contract stipulated a basic monthly salary of EUR 68,000 (gross) and an appearance and performance bonus of EUR 3,000 (gross) per point (at least 45 minutes, otherwise 50%).
2. At the same time, the parties concluded a special agreement, which granted the right to the player to terminate the employment contract after the last match of the season 2003/2004 until 31 May 2004. This agreement stipulated that in case the player would make use of that right, the above mentioned employment contract would end on 30 June 2004.
3. On 26 May 2004, H submitted to the player an agreement for the mutual termination of the contract. According to this agreement, the player should receive the monthly salaries of May and June 2004 and renounce to further claims against the club. However, this agreement has never been signed.
4. On 27 May 2004, the player turned to FIFA and filed his claim. By means of a copy of his claim against the club, the player apparently notified the club in written that according to the special agreement signed on 2 February 2004 he wished to terminate the employment contract. In this demand, the player claimed according to art. 24 of the Regulations for the Status and Transfer of Players compensation in the amount of EUR 408,000 (6 monthly salaries). Furthermore, the player claimed the uncontested monthly salaries of May and June 2004.
5. The player based his claim on the fact that, after the management of the club engaged a new coach, he has not been lined up with the first team. Prior to this banishment from the first team, the Federação Portuguesa de Futebol announced an observer in order to reintegrate the player in the National Team of Portugal. Informed about the banishment of the player from the first team of H, the Federação Portuguesa de Futebol renounced to reintegrate the player in its National Team. However, the player considers himself as an absolutely professional player with a perfect attitude. This has been certified by the two team captains of H. The player also annexed to his claim a document signed by the physical trainer of the team, which certified that the player was in an excellent form. The player alleged that he concluded his employment contract with H only because of the fact that he wanted to play as a "key player" and to recommend himself for the National Team of Portugal. Therefore, he accepted a lower salary. The player is of the opinion that he suffered an important damage because he lost his chance to play for a more illustrious club and the National Team of Portugal only because of the arbitrariness of his new coach.
6. In its response dated 25 October 2004 to the player's claim, the club alleged that the player's attitude was not at all professional and that he was not in the physical condition to play in the "Bundesliga". The club stated that the player could not satisfy the requirements of the former coach as well as the one of the new coach of the first team and has therefore not been constantly lined up. The club underlined the fact that the player left the club on 23 May 2004, without leaving a message. The club emphasised that the player's lawyer called in June 2004 the club and informed it that the player wanted to terminate the contract. This dismissal has been confirmed by the club on 4 June 2004. Furthermore, the club alleged that the player's lawyer proposed compensation of one monthly

salary but the club did not accept. As several attempts to contact the player or the lawyer to reach an amicable solution were unsuccessful, the club had no other choice then to cancel on 8 July 2004 the contract without notice. The club confirmed that it paid the player's salaries until May 2004 as the player left the club on 23 May 2004. Finally, the club referred to § 12 par. 6 of the employment contract according to which claims arising from the contract must be filed in writing by the parties within six months after they fall due, however in the case of termination of the contract within three months after such termination. In this context, the club stated that the claim is dated 27 May 2004 but that it never received the claim directly and that it was only informed by FIFA of the existence of this claim. Considering the above-mentioned, the club is of the opinion that it did not commit a breach of contract and that therefore no compensation is due to the player.

7. On 8 November 2004, the player answered that the club paid the salary of May 2004, however, not on the account indicated by his lawyer. Therefore, this salary cannot be presumed as being settled. Furthermore, the player reiterated his conclusions concerning the June salary and requested the immediate payment of both salaries. In addition, the player emphasised that the claim was sent to FIFA on 27 May 2004 and that the club received a copy of the claim on the same day. Finally, the player insisted on his other conclusions.
8. The club alleged on 18 November 2004 that it received on 27 May 2004 only a draft of the claim, whose content and background the player's lawyer wanted to elucidate. An explicit and written assertion of the claim was therefore not made. Furthermore, the club underlined the fact that the payment of the May salary had been transacted to the same account of the player as all previous salaries on the same day as the player's lawyer notified his draft of the claim. As a result, the relevant amount could be drawn by the player at any time. In addition, the club reiterated that the player left the club without message and traceless and that therefore, the player committed a massive violation of the contract. Finally and concerning the claim for compensation, the club accentuated that for the condemnation to pay compensation according to art. 24 of the Regulations for the Status and Transfer of Players, a default of the club is preconditioned.
9. On 30 November 2004, the player alleged that the club had been informed that he would leave H for Belgium in order to discuss his situation with his Belgian lawyers. Therefore, he did not leave the club traceless.

II. CONSIDERATIONS OF THE DISPUTE RESOLUTION CHAMBER

1. The Dispute Resolution Chamber of the FIFA Players' Status Committee shall review disputes coming under its jurisdiction pursuant to art. 42 of the FIFA Regulations for the Status and Transfer of Players (edition September 2001) at the request of one of the parties to the dispute.
2. According to Art. 42, par. 1 lit. (b) (i) of the FIFA Regulations for the Status and Transfer of Players (edition September 2001), the triggering elements of the dispute (i.e. whether a contract was breached, with or without just cause, or sporting just cause), will be decided by the Dispute Resolution Chamber.
3. If an employment contract is breached by a party, the Dispute Resolution Chamber is responsible to verify whether a party is accountable for compensation and outstanding payments.
4. Therefore, the members of the Dispute Resolution Chamber at first confirmed to be competent to pass a decision in this matter. In addition, the Chamber acknowledged the above-mentioned facts, as well as the further documentation contained in the file.
5. Subsequently, and entering into the substance of the matter, the Chamber considered that the player A and the club H signed on 2 February 2004 a valid employment contract according to which the parties agreed on a basic monthly salary in the amount of EUR 68,000 (gross) and an appearance and performance bonus of EUR 3,000 (gross) per point.
6. Furthermore, the Chamber acknowledged that on the same day, the parties concluded a special agreement according to which the player could terminate the employment contract after the last match of the season 2003/2004 until 31 May 2004. In this case, the employment of the player would end on 30 June 2004.
7. Subsequently, the Chamber acknowledged that, uncontestedly, the player left the club on 23 May 2004 and that as of that date, the player rendered no more his services to the German club. The player stated that by means of a copy of his claim against the club addressed to FIFA he notified the club in written his wish to terminate the employment contract according to the special agreement signed on 2 February 2004. The dismissal has been confirmed by the club on 4 June 2004.

8. In this respect, the Chamber referred to the contents of the special agreement signed on 2 February 2004, which granted the right to the player to prematurely terminate the employment contract unilaterally by informing the club accordingly in the period of time between the last match of the season 2003/2004 and 31 May 2004.
9. To that regard, the deciding body emphasised that in its claim filed with FIFA, the player had explicitly explained that by means of a copy of his claim he had notified the club in written that he wished to terminate the employment contract on the basis of the special agreement signed on 2 February 2004. On 4 June 2004, the club then confirmed the relevant dismissal.
10. On account of the foregoing, the Chamber concluded that the player had made use of his right to unilaterally terminate the contract in accordance with the special agreement concluded between the parties, and that the club had accepted the early termination of the relevant relationship. As a consequence, the deciding body deemed that the contractual relationship between the parties ended on 30 June 2004.
11. In continuation, the Chamber stated that based on the above-mentioned conclusions, the parties had to comply with their contractual obligations until 30 June 2004.
12. In this respect, the deciding body acknowledged that, on the one hand, it is undisputed that the club regularly paid all salaries due to the player until April 2004. Furthermore, it is not contested that the salary for May 2004 was also paid. However, the player is of the opinion that since the relevant amount had not been paid into the bank account indicated by his lawyer, it could not be considered as having been properly received.
13. The Chamber could not back the player's position to that regard. In fact, the club had transferred the salary of May 2004 into the bank account of the player, like all previous ones, and the player could thus dispose of the relevant sum. As a consequence, the Chamber concluded that the club has complied with the payment of the May salary and the player's claim has to be rejected as to this point.
14. With regard to the salary for June 2004, the Chamber acknowledged that the club stated that since 23 May 2004, the player was not present at the training sessions and that therefore, he has no right to claim the amount due for June 2004. Furthermore, it was taken note that the player did not contest having left the club at the end of May 2004.
15. The deciding body recalled that, as previously explained, the player had made use of his right to early terminate the contract in accordance with the special agreement by 30 June 2004. Equally, the Chamber pointed out that the club had fully complied with its financial obligations towards the player until May 2004. Under these circumstances, the deciding body concluded that the player would have had to remain at the club's disposal until the termination of the contract on 30 June 2004. Yet, he left the club earlier and could not provide evidence for an authorization received by the club or any other justification. As a consequence, the Chamber decided that the player is not entitled to any salary for the month of June 2004.
16. The Chamber then turned to the question, if any compensation is payable to the player and if so, to what amount. The player alleged that he has not been lined up with the first team and that therefore, the Federação Portuguesa de Futebol renounced to reintegrate him in its National Team. In this respect, the player considered himself as a professional player with a perfect attitude and an excellent form who should have been regularly fielded.
17. With regard to the player's position, the Chamber stated that the fact that a player signs an employment contract with a club does not content automatically the entitlement to play. In other words, as long as he is regularly paid his salaries and the club respects all other contractual obligations, a player has to accept that he might not be lined up.
18. As established before, the club complied with its financial obligations towards the player. Therefore, the Chamber concluded that by not fielding the player, the club did not breach the relevant employment contract. As a result, it was decided that no compensation is due.
19. Finally, the Chamber emphasised once again that according to his statements in the case at hand, the player had chosen to terminate the contractual relationship with the club according to the special agreement dated 2 February 2004. Therefore, the Chamber was of the opinion that it did not have to consider a contractual termination for sporting just cause in accordance with art. 24 of the Regulations for the Status and Transfer of Players (edition September 2001).
20. Taking into account all of the above, the Chamber decided that the claim of the player A has to be rejected.

III. DECISION OF THE DISPUTE RESOLUTION CHAMBER

1. The claim of the player A is rejected.
2. According to art. 60 par. 1 of the FIFA Statutes this decision may be appealed before the Court of Arbitration for Sport (CAS). The statement of appeal must be sent to the CAS directly within 10 days of receiving notification of this decision and has to contain all elements in accordance with point 2 of the directives issued by the CAS, copy of which we enclose hereto. Within another 10 days following the expiry of the time limit for the filing of the statement of appeal, the appellant shall file with the CAS a brief stating the facts and legal arguments giving rise to the appeal (cf. point 4 of the directives).

⚽⚽⚽

23 JUNE 2005

65503
DECISION OF THE DISPUTE RESOLUTION CHAMBER
passed in Zurich, Switzerland, on 23 June 2005,
in the following composition:
Mr Slim Aloulou (Tunisia), Chairman
Mr Maurice Watkins (England), Member
Mr Theo van Seggelen (Netherlands), Member
on the claim presented by Club X as Claimant against Player Y
Club Z as Respondents
regarding contractual breach and instigation to contractual breach

FACTS OF THE CASE:

On 31 August 2004 the Dispute Resolution Chamber passed a decision on the contractual litigation between the player Y and the club X.

The Chamber decided that, due to the fact that Mr Y unilaterally breached the employment contract with X without just cause, he would not be eligible to participate in any official football matches for Z for a period of six weeks as from the beginning of the championship.

On the same day, following its meeting, the Dispute Resolution Chamber disclosed the holding of the decision to the parties involved.

At the same time, the Bureau of the Players' Status Committee authorised the registration of the player in favour of Z, however, with the reference to the sporting sanctions imposed by the Dispute Resolution Chamber.

The Decision of the Dispute Resolution Chamber was appealed before the Court of Arbitration for Sport by Mr Y and Z on 3 September 2004.

On 10 September 2004 the club X lodged an appeal before the Court of Arbitration for Sport against Mr Y and Z. All the proceedings were merged together.

On 16 February 2005 the Court of Arbitration for Sport communicated the holding of the decision to all parties involved.

The reasoning of this award was notified on 11 March 2005. This award upheld the decision reached on 31 August 2004 by the Dispute Resolution Chamber.

In particular, the Court of Arbitration for Sport confirmed that Mr Y unilaterally breached the employment contract with X without just cause during the so-called protected period as provided for in Art. 23 §1 lit. (a) of the Regulations for the Status and Transfer of Players (hereafter, *the Regulations*).

As a consequence, the question regarding the financial compensation due for breach of contract can be addressed, in accordance with point 4 of decision passed on 31 August 2004 by the Dispute Resolution Chamber.

The Dispute Resolution Chamber had also directed X to provide FIFA with its request for compensation, emphasising that such a request should give details on the way this amount should be calculated.

Likewise, Mr Y was granted a deadline to file its position with respect to the club's request for compensation.

Moreover, in accordance with Art. 23 §2 lit. (c) of the Regulations, the Dispute Resolution Chamber sustained that Z is presumed to have induced the unilateral breach of Mr. Y's contract with X.

The Chamber stated that such inducement to the breach of contract and its consequences would be established in a separate proceedings and instructed Z to provide FIFA with its position with respect to such a charge.
The dispute between Mr Y and X relating to the amount of compensation due for contractual breach and the investigation concerning the inducement to the breach of contract against Z were merged together in these proceedings, consistently with the principle of procedural economy.
In light of the above, Mr Y, X and Z provided the each member of the Dispute Resolution Chamber with their respective concluding positions, which are hereafter summarised.

Position of X:
The club X maintains in its position that, in light of the award rendered by the Court of Arbitration for Sport on 16 February 2005, it is evident that it has to receive compensation for the unilateral breach of contract, that occurred without just cause and during the so-called protected period.
Such compensation is meant to repair the damage incurred by X, that was deprived without just cause of the services of a player, Mr Y, who was still bound by an employment contract for two more years.
Therefore, X refers to the objective criteria, which must be taken into account by the Dispute Resolution Chamber in the calculation of the amount of compensation due as provided for by Article 22 of the Regulations.
In compliance with the above criteria, X asks the Dispute Resolution Chamber to place particular emphasis on the increased amount, both in salaries and benefits, the player has obtained by his new club, Z.
The club is also eager to highlight the significant financial investment it had sustained in the scope of the extension of Mr Y's contract in August 2003, as well as the damage it suffered after the player's departure, essentially in view of the amount the club could have earned in case the transfer had taken place under the normal market conditions.
All the above criteria, as well as a list of the most high-priced transfers occurred during the summer transfer period in 2004, are reported in a table X provided the Chamber with.
In light of the above, X asks the Dispute Resolution Chamber to condemn Mr Y to pay the amount of EUR –.– as compensation for contractual breach, accompanied by firstclass bank guarantees undertaken by Z.
With respect to the responsibility of Z, X maintains that the club, by signing Y while he was still under contract with his club, undeniably excluded X from the regular transfer operations and must pay compensation for the damages caused.
In addition to that, X points out that any possible attenuating circumstance, which could be taken into account when considering the player's behaviour, should not be applied at all to the stance of Z.
The club further maintains that, had Z not induced the player to breach the contract with his club, X would have never suffered all the losses it is seeking compensation for.
In view of the above, X asks the Dispute Resolution Chamber to condemn Z jointly with Mr Y to pay the amount of EUR –.– as compensation for contractual breach accompanied by first-class bank guarantees undertaken by Z itself.
In addition to that, X asks the Dispute Resolution Chamber to apply against Z the sanctions provided for by Article 23 §2 a) of the Regulations.

Position of Mr Y:
Mr Y maintains in his position that, by means of its award rendered on 16 February 2005, the Court of Arbitration for Sport pointed out that, in compliance with the principle of the maintenance of contractual stability, the only damage X is entitled to claim is the fact that Mr Y failed to perform the last two years of contract.
According to the player, the club cannot be entitled to any other damage, let alone the frustrated expectation of a transfer fee.
In particular, the player's agent pointed out that Y is nothing more than a mid-level player, who only happened to make a five-minute appearance with the national team and actually contributed to the poor performances of the defence of Z.
According to the agent, X cannot claim any prejudice under the sporting point of view, especially as the performances of the club improved after the player's transfer to Z.
As far as the alleged financial prejudice is concerned, the player's agent deems that the club has caused to itself such a loss due to its non-cooperative attitude towards the player, as outlined by the Court of Arbitration for Sport in its decision.

The agent further points out that the amount paid by X for the transfer of W, who apparently replaced Y, is EUR –.–
According to the agent, W is a much more experienced and valuable player than Y.
The player's agent further provided the Chamber with some calculations, according to which, the value of the two last years of Y's employment contract with the club would not exceed the amount of EUR –.–.
In view of the above, Mr Y asks the Dispute Resolution Chamber to establish in favour of X an amount of compensation between EUR –.– and EUR –.–.

Position of Z:
Z maintains in its position that in its decision the Court of Arbitration for Sport took into account the exceptional circumstances surrounding the contractual dispute between Y and X.
The club maintains that, amongst the exceptional circumstances, the Court of Arbitration for Sport considered that the player remained with the club for seven years, as from the age of 15. Therefore, the contractual relationship between the player and the club had an actual stability for seven years.
Z is also emphasising the player's good faith, that clashed against X's non-cooperative attitude towards him, as outlined by the Court of Arbitration for Sport in its decision.
Z further acknowledges that, although the player could have been sanctioned by means of a restriction of four months on his eligibility to participate in any official football matches as from the beginning of the new season of the new club's national championship, in view of the above-mentioned circumstances, his sanction has been considerably reduced.
Consequently, Z maintains that the above-mentioned attenuating circumstances should apply as well to the club, whose behaviour always showed good faith, yet collided with X's non-cooperative attitude.
Z points out that it actually never incited the player to breach his employment contract with X.
In view of the above, Z asks the Dispute Resolution Chamber to establish in favour of X an amount of compensation, which is proportionate and consistent with the conclusions reached by the Chamber itself and by the Court of Arbitration for Sport with respect to the player's sanction.
With respect to the possible sporting sanctions it may incur in, Z requests the Dispute Resolution Chamber to take into account all the exceptional circumstances surrounding the case in hand, as well as the club's constant good faith.

CONSIDERATIONS OF THE DISPUTE RESOLUTION CHAMBER:
The members of the Dispute Resolution Chamber were summoned to pass a decision on this matter by the Chairman pursuant to Article 1 point 6) of the Rules Governing the Practice and Procedures of the Dispute Resolution Chamber.
After a careful study of the facts and allegations outlined above, the Dispute Resolution Chamber commenced its deliberations by referring to Article 42 §1 (b) (ii) and (iii) in connection with Articles 22 and 23 of the Regulations according to which, if the employment contract was breached by a party, the Dispute Resolution Chamber is responsible to verify whether this party is accountable for compensation and decide whether sports sanctions must be imposed. Furthermore, the Chamber shall decide any other issues relating to a contractual breach, thus including the question related a possible inducement to the breach.
All the parties had been duly informed that this case would have been submitted, for decision, to the Dispute Resolution Chamber on 13 May 2005 and that a hearing of the three parties involved would have taken place.
However, the Chamber acknowledged the fact that, while X and Mr Y were present at that hearing, the representatives of Z were not able to attend due to the fact that the flight to Zurich was cancelled at short notice, circumstance which was duly ascertained by an official document.
In view of these circumstances, the Chamber deemed that the matter relating to the compensation for contractual breach between X and Mr Y and the investigation against Z for inducement to contractual breach, merged together in this process consistently with the principle of procedural economy, had to be considered and decided disjointedly.
Therefore, on 13 May 2005, the Chamber considered and passed a decision on the dispute for contractual breach between X and Mr Y, in accordance with Articles 22 and 23 §1 of the Regulations. This decision was duly notified to the parties involved on 9 June 2005.
Subsequently, Z was granted the opportunity to be heard by the Dispute Resolution Chamber in a subsequent hearing on 23 June 2005, in view of the fact that they were unable to attend on 13 May 2005.

X was also invited to attend this hearing to present their position on the responsibility of Z in this dispute.
Consequently, the Chamber acknowledged the fact that both the representatives of Z, and those of X were present at the hearing.
In view of the above, the Dispute Resolution Chamber concluded that it was finally in a position to consider and pass a decision on the investigation carried out by FIFA against Z for inducement to contractual breach, in accordance with Articles 22 and 23 §2 (c) of the Regulations. In this respect, the Chamber concluded that it has jurisdiction to pass a decision on this matter.
Having established this, the Chamber started to consider the substance of the matter in order to establish the alleged responsibility of Z for inducement to contractual breach.
Preliminarily, the Chamber deemed it appropriate to recall some of the key events in the contractual breach between Mr Y and X. In particular, it was recalled that, by letter dated 11 June 2004, the player communicated to X his willingness to leave the club.
Subsequently, on 12 June 2004 Mr Y and the club, Z, signed a four-year employment contract that was registered with the Football League the same day.
It is worth lending emphasis to the fact that twenty-four hours after having breached the contract with X without any valid reason, the player already entered into a new contract with Z.
In order to be able to sign an employment contract, negotiations between the parties are necessary. These negotiations are usually long lasting. It therefore appears very clear that the player was negotiating with Z already for a long time and that the signature on 12 June 2004 was a mere formalisation of the agreement that was already found between Y and Z. The player was therefore already contravening his employment contract with X by negotiating, and afterwards signing an employment contract with Z.
Therefore, the Chamber took note of the fact that the Chamber first and the Court of Arbitration for Sport afterwards, confirmed that Mr Y unilaterally breached the employment contract with X without just cause during the so-called protected period as provided for in Article 23 §1 lit. (a) of the Regulations.
The Chamber then focussed its analysis on the accountability of Z for inducement to the contractual breach between Mr Y and X.
In particular, the Chamber first referred to lit. (c) of Article 23 §2 of the Regulations, according to which, a club seeking to register a player who has unilaterally breached a contract during the protected period will be presumed to have induced a breach of contract.
As a consequence, it falls under Z's responsibility to demonstrate that they should not be held responsible for having induced the breach of contract.
The Chamber examined the position of Z, according to which, the mitigating circumstances the Chamber applied to the player's sporting sanction in the decision reached on 31 August 2004 should apply as well to the club, who always acted in good faith, yet collided with X's non-cooperative attitude.
The Chamber took further note of Z's statement, whereby an adequate sanction in case the club was found responsible for inducement to contractual breach would be a fine.
In this respect, the Chamber deemed it appropriate to evoke the extraordinary, if not unique circumstances under which the sanction decided against the player by means of the decision reached on 31 August 2004 had been rather lenient.
Amongst the exceptional circumstances, the Chamber had considered that the player remained with the club for seven years, as from the age of 15.
Therefore, the contractual relationship between the player and the club had an actual stability for seven years.
The Chamber had taken further note of the good relationship between Y and X, which deteriorated only after having signed the new contract on 15 December 2002.
Moreover, this contract was deposited with the Professional Football League only on 4 August 2003, *i.e.* eight months after its actual signature.
The Chamber had further noted the fact that the player trusted he was behaving correctly when he breached the contract with his club, and that such wrongful interpretation misled him in his actions.
In the light of these circumstances, the Chamber was eager to emphasise that such mitigating circumstances could Y and X and could not be extended to the behaviour of the club Z.
According to the Chamber, Z could not provide any evidence corroborating their request for exceptional circumstances to be applied in their favour.
In fact, the Chamber outlined that documental evidence established that Z had shown interest in the player already long time before signing him, so that the club seemed to be well aware of Y's contractual situation with X.

Throughout the development of the entire affair, Z has never left the Chamber with the impression that they were unconscious of the prospective danger linked with their behaviour.
Furthermore, the Chamber was eager to point out that the club did not confine itself to a mere inducement, but played a chief role in the contractual breach occurred between Y and X by provoking it.
In this respect, it is crucial to bear in mind that Z first made contact with, then signed a player, Y, who was still bound by an employment contract to another club.
The Chamber then referred to Z's assertion, whereby, by the time when they concluded the employment contract with Y, it was unclear whether or not the player's contract with X was within the so-called protected period. According to the club this fact should also be considered as a mitigating circumstance.
In response to the above, the Chamber emphasised that, with regard to the consequences of inducement to contractual breach, it was irrelevant whether the breach occurred within or outside the protected period, since according to the FIFA Regulations, the inducement to contractual breach *per se* is subject to sanctions at any time during the validity of the employment contract. Consequently, such a position cannot be considered as a mitigating circumstance.
Z, it was further noted, is a club of such international standing that is certainly conscious of the applicable regulations and of the potential consequences in case of infringement.
Without fail, the Chamber went further on analysing the sports sanctions that could be imposed on the club Z for having induced the contractual breach.
In this respect, the Chamber pointed out that if it accepted the club's demand for a fine as an adequate sanction, the entire system of rules governing the maintenance of contractual stability would be put into serious danger.
According to the Chamber's position, if clubs inducing the breach of contract were sanctioned only by means of a fine, a perilous precedent would be set, whereby it would even be possible for any club illicitly approaching a player already under contract with another club, to calculate *a priori* the amount to be paid as a sanction for inducement to contractual breach.
The Chamber was eager to emphasise that such an undesired consequence would definitely not serve as a deterrent against clubs that are determined to provoke breaches of contract.
Therefore, the Chamber deemed that it was left with no other choice than to strictly apply the contents of Article 23 §2 of the Regulations, according to which, in case of a club inducing the breach of contract, if the breach occurs at the end of the first or second year of contract, the sanction shall be a ban on registering any new player, either nationally or internationally, for two consecutive transfer periods.
In light of all the above circumstances, the Chamber decided that the club Z is responsible for inducement to breach of contract and concluded that a ban is imposed on Z from registering any new player, either nationally or internationally, until the expiry of the second transfer period following the notification of this decision.

DECISION OF THE DISPUTE RESOLUTION CHAMBER

1. The club Z is responsible for inducement to breach of contract.
2. A ban is imposed on Z from registering any new player, either nationally or internationally, until the expiry of the second transfer period following the notification of this decision.
3. According to Article 60 par. 1 of the FIFA Statutes this decision may be appealed before the Court of Arbitration for Sport (CAS). The statement of appeal must be sent to the CAS directly within 10 days of receiving notification of this decision and has to contain all elements in accordance with point 2 of the directives issued by the CAS, copy of which we enclose hereto. Within another 10 days following the expiry of the time limit for the filing of the statement of appeal, the appellant shall file with the CAS a brief stating the facts and legal arguments giving rise to the appeal (cf. point 4 of the directives).

⚽⚽⚽

65657
DECISION OF THE DISPUTE RESOLUTION CHAMBER
passed in Zurich, Switzerland, on 23 June 2005,
in the following composition:
Slim Aloulou (Tunisia), chairman
Maurice Watkins (England), member

Theo van Seggelen (The Netherlands), member
on the claim presented by
A as Claimant
against
B as Respondent
regarding a contractual dispute arisen between the parties

FACTS OF THE CASE

On 1 March 2003, A and B signed an employment contract valid until 1 March 2004.

The aforementioned contract does not precise the player's salaries nor any other financial privileges that he would be entitled to receive from the club. In fact, the contract only stipulates that "the main salary is determined according to the payroll of the club".

B asserts that, on 1 June 2003, an amicable settlement was reached between the parties in order to terminate their employment contract. However, according to B, A refused to sign it at the last minute.

As a result, B decided to unilaterally terminate their employment contract based on the player's alleged lack of commitment and productivity and draws the attention of the Chamber to Art. 6.3.1 of the relevant contract, which stipulates the following:

"the contract can be broken under the initiative of the football club in case of: discovery of the inadequacy of the professional and sports skills of the footballer; in case of the footballer's non-fulfilment or inappropriate fulfilment of his obligationsconditioned by this contract, ...".

In fact, B defends that A did not fulfil his contractual obligations, particularly with regard to his level of preparation and skills. B maintains that the player's performance was extremely poor and that he did not make the necessary efforts during the training sessions in order to improve it. In this regard, the club adds that during the period between 1 March and 31 May 2003, out of 12 matches, A only participated in three, playing a total of 104 minutes.

A confirms having agreed with the club's proposal regarding the early termination of their contract, under the condition that he would receive the amount of USD 12,000. However, the player has informed the FIFA Administration that during the entire period that he remained with the club, i.e. three months, he was only paid the amount of USD 1,000.

In light of the above, A is presently claiming the amount of USD 11,000 from B.

In response, B maintains that it has complied with all its financial obligations towards A until the date of the contract's termination.

Moreover, B underlines the inexistence of any documents supporting A's claim, in particular, proving that he is entitled to receive any further amounts from it and consequently requests the Chamber to reject the player's claim for lack of sustainability.

In this respect, the FIFA Administration was provided with a copy of an amicable settlement, not signed by A. However, such agreement also failed to mention any amount to be paid to the player, as compensation for the contract's early termination.

Moreover, the FIFA Administration received a copy of a letter signed by the agent representing the player, addressed to B, confirming A's concordance with the amicable settlement proposed by the club in the present matter, but stating that he would only sign such agreement after having received his contractual outstanding amounts, which were not specified.

Despite having been several times requested to provide the FIFA Administration with evidence confirming that he is entitled to receive the claimed amounts from B, A has failed to do so.

The present file was submitted to the Dispute Resolution Chamber for consideration and decision at its meeting on 13 May 2005. However, the Chamber was of the opinion that it needed to obtain some additional information in order to decide upon the matter.

In this respect, the FIFA Administration asked A, once gain, to clarify which was his monthly salary with B and what other amounts he was entitled to receive, as well as to provide any written evidence supporting his position.

In reply, the player, via C Association, informed the FIFA Administration that the salary agreed between the parties was of USD 3,000 per month, but that he only received USD 1,000 for the entire period that he remained with the club. Moreover, the player re-asserted that the amount agreed in order to terminate their employment contract was USD 12,000, from which the total amount of USD 11,000 is still outstanding. Furthermore, A asserted that he was not entitled to any other financial privileges (e.g. signing-on fees, match bonuses, etc).

Notwithstanding all the above, the player did not provide the FIFA Administration with any evidence confirming that he was entitled to receive a monthly salary of USD 3,000 or that B had agreed to pay him the total amount of USD 12,000, as compensation for the early termination of their employment contract.
On the other hand, the FIFA Administration asked B about the payments that it made to A and their respective nature, as well as to be provided with the respective payment receipts in order to support its position. Furthermore, B was also requested to inform the FIFA Administration about its payroll for the 2003/2004 sporting season, as mentioned in art. 4 par. 1 of the parties' employment contract ("The main salary is determined according to the payroll of the club").
In reply, B informed the FIFA Administration that A was paid the salaries of March, April and May 2003 in the total amount of approximately USD 193 (approximately USD 64 per month) and a compensation for contractual termination, in the total amount of more or less USD 1,000, that the player acknowledges having received from it.
Moreover, B informed that according to its payroll for 2003, each foreign player was entitled to receive the amount of approximately USD 49 net per month and provided the FIFA Administration with evidence supporting such statement.
Finally, the FIFA Administration was informed by the Association D that the minimum salary in E in 2003, was of approximately USD 37.

CONSIDERATIONS OF THE DISPUTE RESOLUTION CHAMBER

The members of the Dispute Resolution Chamber were summoned to pass a decision on this matter by the Chairman pursuant to art. 1 point 6) of the Rules Governing the Practice and Procedures of the Dispute Resolution Chamber.
The Dispute Resolution Chamber shall review disputes coming under its jurisdiction pursuant to art. 42 of the FIFA Regulations for the Status and Transfer of Players (edition September 2001), at the request of one of the parties to the dispute.
According to art. 42, par. 1 lit. (b) (i) of the FIFA Regulations for the Status and Transfer of Players (edition September 2001), the triggering elements of the dispute (i.e. whether a contract was breached, with or without just cause, or sporting just cause), will be decided by the Dispute Resolution Chamber.
If an employment contract is breached by a party, the Dispute Resolution Chamber is responsible to verify whether a party is accountable for compensation and outstanding payments.
Also, the Dispute Resolution Chamber will establish the amount of compensation to be paid (cf. art. 42, par. 1, (b), (iii) in connection with art. 22 of the aforementioned Regulations).
Consequently, the Dispute Resolution Chamber is the competent body to decide on the present litigation concerning the alleged non-respect of contract between the Claimant and the Respondent.
Subsequently, and entering into the substance of the matter, the members of the Chamber started by underlining the fact that a player's lack of performance does not and cannot be considered as just cause to terminate an employment contract.
Notwithstanding the above, the Chamber acknowledged that A claims having reached an amicable agreement with B for the early termination of their employment contract, according to which he would receive from B the total amount of USD 12,000. However, according to the player, he has only received the amount of USD 1,000 from B and is therefore, presently claiming the outstanding amount of USD 11,000.
In this regard, the members of the Chamber emphasized the fact that A has failed to provided the FIFA Administration with any kind of evidence confirming that B has agreed to pay to him the amount of USD 12,000, in order to terminate their contractual relationship.
On the other hand, the members of the Chamber took into consideration the position of B, according to which, it has fully complied with its contractual obligations towards the player until the date of his departure, in particular, that it has paid to A, his salaries of March, April and May 2003 in the net amount of approximately USD 49 per month, as well as a compensation for the termination of their employment contract, in the total net amount of approximately USD 1053.
In this respect, after having analysed the relevant employment contract signed between the parties, the members of the Chamber took note that such document fails to determine A's salaries and remits such issue to the club's payroll.
In fact, the Chamber took note that, in support of its allegations, B has provided the FIFA Administration with a copy of its 2003 payroll, in which it is stipulated that each player was entitled to receive a monthly gross salary of approximately USD 64.

Moreover, the Chamber noted that B has also provided the FIFA Administration with a copy of its May's pay sheet, in which it is clearly mentioned that A was paid the net amount of approximately USD 49.
In light of the above, the members of the Chamber emphasized that the aforementioned amount claimed by the club, as having been paid to the player, basically corresponds to the amount acknowledged by the player, as having been received from the club.
Furthermore, the Chamber took into consideration the fact that the aforementioned player's salary, duly stipulated in the club's payroll, is higher than the 2003 minimum salary in E, which confirms its legality.
In view of all the aforementioned, as well as all the documentation contained in the file, the members of the Chamber reached the conclusion that A has failed to provide the FIFA Administration with evidence supporting his allegations in the present matter, in particular, with concrete documentation which would confirm his entitlement to receive the claimed amounts.
As a consequence, the Chamber considered that B is not liable to pay any amounts to A in the matter at hand and decided to reject the player's present claim.

DECISION OF THE DISPUTE RESOLUTION CHAMBER

1. The claim of A is rejected in its entirety.
2. According to art. 60 par. 1 of the FIFA Statutes, this decision may be appealed before the Court of Arbitration for Sport (CAS). The statement of appeal must be sent to the CAS directly within 10 days of receiving notification of this decision and has to contain all elements in accordance with point 2 of the directives issued by the CAS, copy of which we enclose hereto. Within another 10 days following the expiry of the time limit for the filing of the statement of appeal, the appellant shall file with the CAS a brief stating the facts and legal arguments giving rise to the appeal (cf. point 4 of the directives).

⚽⚽⚽

65939
DECISION OF THE DISPUTE RESOLUTION CHAMBER
passed in Zurich, Switzerland, on 23 June 2005,
in the following composition:
Slim Aloulou (Tunisia), chairman
Maurice Watkins (England), member
Theo van Seggelen (The Netherlands), member
on the claim presented by
A as Claimant
against
B as Respondent
regarding a labour dispute arisen between the parties

FACTS OF THE CASE

On 7 January 2004, A and B signed an employment contract valid until 1 February 2007, according to which, the player was entitled to receive a basic monthly salary of approximately USD 99.
Moreover, an addendum to the aforementioned contract, also dated 7 January 2004, stipulated that the player was entitled to receive signing-on fees in the amount of USD 20,000 gross, per year, in accordance with the following payment plan:

USD 5,000 on 7 January 2004, 2005 and 2006;
USD 5,000 on 1 May 2004, 2005 and 2006;
USD 5,000 on 1 August 2004, 2005 and 2006;
USD 5,000 on 1 November 2004, 2005 and 2006.

Copies of the aforementioned contract and addendum have been provided to the FIFA Administration.
In October 2004, the player contacted FIFA with regard to a dispute which had arisen on the basis of the employment contract concluded between the parties. In this respect, A asserts that B has failed to comply with its contractual obligations towards him, in particular, that it did not cancel the signing-on fees which were scheduled to be paid on 7 January and 1 May 2004, in the total amount of USD 10,000.
Moreover, the player asserts that his visa expired on 13 July 2004 and that the club failed to provide him with a new one. In fact, the player underlines that he was warned by the embassy of C in X and by the

D customs when he returned from holidays in July 2004, that in case he would stay in D without a visa, he could be arrested. As a consequence, the player left D on 10 July 2004 and is presently claiming the amount of USD 10,000 from B.
B underlines that, on 22 July 2004, it suspended A for the period of two years, for having hit a team mate and a coach, as well as having missed some training sessions. Such decision was confirmed by the Disciplinary Committee of the Association D on 4 August 2004. The suspension is thus effective until 4 August 2006.
A copy of the aforementioned decision has been provided to the FIFA Administration.
With regard to A's financial claim, B asserts that it has always complied with its contractual obligations towards him, in particular, it has cancelled the amounts that are currently claimed by the player.
However, B defends that the player did not sign the respective payment receipts.
Furthermore, concerning the visa issue, B defends that the player failed to provide it with the necessary personal documents (e.g. criminal record from his homeland and school records) in order to get it, after arriving from holidays, on 5 July 2004.
In light of all the above, on 19 November 2004, FIFA reached the conclusion that the labour relationship between the parties had ceased to exist and, in order to avoid jeopardizing A's future career, considered the latter, free to sign for another club of his election.
Notwithstanding the above, B insisted that its labour relationship with A had not ceased to exist with the aforementioned disciplinary sanction and currently asks to be compensated for the investment made on the player (no concrete amounts have been claimed in this respect).
In response, the player asserts that he has never hit any of his colleagues nor the coach and that those facts were entirely fabricated by B.
Moreover, the player maintains that he has never received the amounts that he is presently claiming, otherwise he would have been obliged to sign the respective payment receipts.
On the other hand, B asserts that A has appointed a lawyer to represent him in the relevant disciplinary procedures which led to the aforementioned player's suspension, but the player denies it, stating that neither him nor any lawyer acting on his behalf, has ever participated in such procedures.
On 4 April 2005, the player's international registration transfer certificate was issued by the Association D in favour of the Association C, under the condition that the previously mentioned disciplinary sanction would be respected, in accordance with art. 9 of the FIFA Regulations for the Status and Transfer of Players.
After having been requested to provide the FIFA Administration with more detailed information concerning the relevant disciplinary procedure, which ended with the player's suspension for the period of two years, the Association D stated that it started by deciding upon the request made by A to be declared a free player, in which the latter was represented by his attorney. However, due to a request submitted by B in order for the D Disciplinary Committee to ratify the aforementioned disciplinary sanction taken by the club on 22 July 2004, the analysis of the player's initial request was suspended until a decision was taken in that regard. Finally, the Association D informed the FIFA Administration that, as a consequence of the decision taken by the D Disciplinary Committee, confirming the aforementioned disciplinary sanction imposed by the club, the player's initial request was no longer analysed by the Players' Status Committee of Association D.
In reply, A asserted that the Association D has never informed him about the relevant disciplinary procedure. Therefore, he was prevented from submitting his defence in the matter and moreover, from appealing from the relevant decision, since he was only informed of it on 6 September 2004, via his Association.
As a consequence, A and the Association E ask FIFA to force the Association D to cancel its relevant disciplinary decision, based on "rough breach of procedure", in order for him to be authorized to proceed with his football career.
Furthermore, the FIFA Administration was provided with the minutes of the meeting of the Association D's Body of Appeal, dated 19 August 2004, in which the appeal lodged by the player was dealt with. According to the aforementioned Association, and despite the fact that A's legal representative was absent, the appeal proves that the player was aware of the first instance decision. Finally, the Body of Appeal confirmed the decision taken by the first instance.

CONSIDERATIONS OF THE DISPUTE RESOLUTION CHAMBER

The members of the Dispute Resolution Chamber were summoned to pass a decision on this matter by the Chairman pursuant to art. 1 point 6) of the Rules Governing the Practice and Procedures of the Dispute Resolution Chamber.

The Dispute Resolution Chamber shall review disputes coming under its jurisdiction pursuant to art. 42 of the FIFA Regulations for the Status and Transfer of Players (edition September 2001), at the request of one of the parties to the dispute.

According to art. 42, par. 1 lit. (b) (i) of the FIFA Regulations for the Status and Transfer of Players (edition September 2001), the triggering elements of the dispute (i.e. whether a contract was breached, with or without just cause, or sporting just cause), will be decided by the Dispute Resolution Chamber.

If an employment contract is breached by a party, the Dispute Resolution Chamber is responsible to verify whether a party is accountable for compensation and outstanding payments.

Also, the Dispute Resolution Chamber will establish the amount of compensation to be paid (cf. art. 42, par. 1, (b), (iii) in connection with art. 22 of the aforementioned Regulations).

Consequently, the Dispute Resolution Chamber is the competent body to decide on the present litigation, concerning the alleged breach of contract between A and B.

However, before entering into the substance of the matter, the members of the Chamber took note of the relevant disciplinary procedure which took place against the player in front of the disciplinary bodies of the Association D, and which mainly concern alleged aggressions of the player towards the coach and a team mate. In this respect, the Chamber underlined that disciplinary matters are of the competence of the FIFA Disciplinary Committee and therefore, decided to abstain from taking any decision in that regard and to remit the file to the aforementioned disciplinary body, for consideration.

Subsequently, and entering into the substance of the present labour dispute, the Chamber started by acknowledging that, on 7 January 2004, A and B signed an employment contract valid until 1 February 2007, according to which the player was entitled to receive a monthly salary of approximately USD 99 and signing-on fees in the gross amount of USD 20,000 per year.

The Chamber also acknowledged that A is presently claiming from B, the payment of some outstanding amounts under their employment contract which were due during the period of time he actually played for the club, in particular, the signing-on fees that he was contractually entitled to receive on 7 January and 1 May 2004, in the total amount of USD 10,000.

The Dispute Resolution Chamber took into account that A, in support of his allegations, has provided the FIFA Administration with a copy of his employment contract with B. In this regard, the Chamber concluded that the amounts claimed by the player are effectively stipulated in the relevant employment contract.

Furthermore, the Chamber acknowledged that the payments due to the player as signing-on fees, actually constituted the main remuneration for the player, since in comparison, the amount due as salary is relatively low.

In this respect, the members of the Chamber also took into consideration the fact that, although B defends that it has cancelled the amounts claimed by A, it has failed to provide the FIFA Administration with evidence supporting such position.

Referring to the alleged visa problems, the deciding body recalled that, as a general rule and without evidence to the contrary, it is the club's responsibility to ensure that the player is provided with all the necessary permits in order to stay and work in the club's country. The Chamber took note that despite the reasons submitted by B in that regard, B has also failed to provide the player with the necessary visa, which was indispensable for him to fulfil his employment contract. In particular, it could not corroborate its allegation that the player had refused to offer his assistance.

Furthermore, the Dispute Resolution Chamber noted that, as a consequence of all the above, A has left D on 10 July 2004

In light of all the above, the Dispute Resolution Chamber reached the conclusion that B has breached its employment contract with A, mainly, by failing to comply with its principle financial obligations towards the player, in particular, to cancel his signing-on fees which were contractually due on 7 January and 1 May 2004, in the total amount of USD 10,000 and also by failing to provide him with a valid visa.

In conclusion, in view of the present matter's circumstances and the evidence carried to the file, the Dispute Resolution Chamber considered B responsible for the non-fulfilment of its employment contract with A and decided to acept the claim filed by the latter, condemning B to pay to him the claimed amount of USD10,000

Finally, the Dispute Resolution Chamber confirmed the termination of the working relationship between A and B as from July 2004.

DECISION OF THE DISPUTE RESOLUTION CHAMBER

1. The claim of A is accepted
2. The Respondent B shall pay the amount of USD 10,000 to the Claimant A, within 30 days of notification of the present decision
3. If the Respondent fails to comply with the above-mentioned deadline, an interest rate of 5% per year will apply and the case will immediately be presented to the FIFA Disciplinary Committee
4. The Claimant is directed to inform the Respondent immediately of the account number to which the remittance is to be made and to notify the Dispute Resolution Chamber of every payment received
5. The contractual relation between the Claimant and the Respondent is terminated as of July 2004
6. The relevant disciplinary matter between the parties will be submitted to the FIFA Disciplinary Committee, for consideration
7. According to art. 60 par. 1 of the FIFA Statutes, this decision may be appealed before the Court of Arbitration for Sport (CAS). The statement of appeal must be sent to the CAS directly within 10 days of receiving notification of this decision and has to contain all elements in accordance with point 2 of the directives issued by the CAS, copy of which we enclose hereto. Within another 10 days following the expiry of the time limit for the filing of the statement of appeal, the appellant shall file with the CAS a brief stating the facts and legal arguments giving rise to the appeal (cf. point 4 of the directives).

28 JULY 2005

75142
DECISION OF THE DISPUTE RESOLUTION CHAMBER
passed in Zurich, Switzerland, on 28 July 2005,
in the following composition:
Slim Aloulou (Tunisia), Chairman
Jean-Marie Philips (Belgium), Member
Philippe Diallo (France), Member
Gerardo Movilla (Spain), Member
Philippe Piat (France), Member
on the claim presented by
Club A, as Claimant
against
Club B, as Respondent
regarding Training Compensation for the player X

I. FACTS OF THE CASE

1. The player X, born in August 1986, signed a contract with the club B on 1 July 2004.
2. The club A, that contributed to the training of the player in question, has lodged a claim for training compensation as described in chapter VII of the FIFA Regulations for the Status and Transfer of Players, edition September 2001 (hereinafter; the Regulations).
3. The player X was registered with the club A as an amateur player during the seasons 2001/02 and 2002/03, at the age of 15 and 16.
4. According to the classification of clubs outlined in circular 826 dated 31 October 2002, the club A belongs to category 4 (indicative amount of EUR 10,000 per year), the club B belongs to category 1 (indicative amount of EUR 90,000 per year).
5. The club B insists that although they signed a contract with the player, the latter was able to keep his amateur status. The club based its statement on the fact that the contract signed was mainly an agreement to educate and train the player, entitling him to a compensation for travel and housing expenses. Therefore, the club B deems that it is not liable to pay training compensation to the club A.

6. The club A is of the opinion that the following clauses of the contract show that had lost his amateur status in accordance with the FIFA Regulations:
Section 5 – Housing:
The club pays the cost of the player's housing, if the player has to move to the club's immediate vicinity in relation to the training
Section 6 – Travel and living expenses
In case the club does not ferry the player to and from the educationactivities and if the single travel distance exceeds 30 kilometres, the player is entitled to compensation of travel and living expenses that are paid by the player for the education.
Section 7 – Consequences in case the training agreement is not fulfilled
7.1 If one of the parties does not fulfil this agreement, that party s obliged to pay damages.
7.2 In case the player does not observe this agreement, the player also owes the club the training expenses that have been made. The training expenses amount to EUR 11,345 per year of training.
7. The Dispute Resolution Chamber is invited to determine the amount owed by the club B to the club A.
8. Upon request, the Football Federation of the club B provided FIFA with an excerpt of its registers, according to which the player in question is registered for the club B as an amateur player.
9. However, in a letter dated 8 July 2004, the Football Federation of the club B informed the Football Federation of the club A that the player is a non-amateur player of its club B.

II. CONSIDERATIONS OF THE DISPUTE RESOLUTION CHAMBER

1. The members of the Dispute Resolution Chamber were summoned to pass a decision on the present matter by the Chairman pursuant to Art. 1 point 6) of the Rules Governing the Practice and Procedures of the Dispute Resolution Chamber.
2. The Dispute Resolution Chamber of the FIFA Players' Status Committee reviews disputes coming under its jurisdiction pursuant to Art. 42 of the Regulations, at the request of one of the parties to the dispute.
3. In accordance with Art. 42.1 lit. (b) (iv) of the Regulations, it falls within the purview of the Dispute Resolution Chamber to review disputes concerning training compensation fees.
4. Consequently, the Dispute Resolution Chamber is the competent body to decide on the present claim for training compensation.
5. Entering into the substance of the matter, the Chamber acknowledged the documentation contained in the file, and in this respect noted that the player X signed a contract with the club B on 1 July 2004, at the age of 18. Moreover, the members of the Chamber acknowledged that the two clubs involved in this matter are arguing over the nature of the contract in question, i.e. whether it is to be considered as a scholarship contract (amateur contract) or an employment contract (non-amateur contract). And finally, the Chamber took into account that the player in question was registered at the Football Federation of the club B as an amateur player.
6. The Chamber then stated that, as established in Chapter VII of the Regulations, training compensation is payable for training incurred between the ages of 12 and 21, if the player concerned concludes a non-amateur contract before the age of 23.
7. In continuation, the Chamber pointed out that in disputes concerning training compensation, the nature of a contract between a player and a club is determined by the relevant association. As a principle, the Chamber will not enter into the question concerning the status of the player. In such case, the autonomy of the Association must be respected by the Dispute Resolution Chamber, and therefore, the status of the registration of such player at the Association shall be taken into consideration in order to determine whether the conditions stipulating the payment of training compensation have been fulfilled.
8. In the present case, the player in question was, as indicated by the Football Federation of the club B, registered as an amateur player for the club B at the said Association.
9. Therefore, the above-mentioned conditions for training compensation to become due are not fulfilled.
10. On account of the above the members of the chamber decided that the club B is not liable to pay training compensation to the club A for the training of the player X.
11. Finally, the Chamber stated that the club A still is entitled to claim for training compensation for the training of the player X, should the player reach non-amateur status before his age of 23.

12. In conclusion, the Dispute Resolution Chamber decided that the claim of the club A against the club B for the training of the player X is to be rejected.

III. DECISION OF THE DISPUTE RESOLUTION CHAMBER

1. The claim of the club A is rejected.
2. According to art. 60 par. 1 of the FIFA Statutes this decision may be appealed before the Court of Arbitration for Sport (CAS). The statement of appeal must be sent to the CAS directly within 10 days of receiving notification of this decision and has to contain all elements in accordance with point 2 of the directives issued by the CAS, copy of which we enclose hereto. Within another 10 days following the expiry of the time limit for the filing of the statement of appeal, the appellant shall file with the CAS a brief stating the facts and legal arguments giving rise to the appeal (cf. point 4 of the directives).

75231

DECISION OF THE DISPUTE RESOLUTION CHAMBER

passed in Zurich, Switzerland, on 28 July 2005,
in the following composition:
Slim Aloulou (Tunisia), Chairman
Jean-Marie Philips (Belgium), Member
Philippe Diallo (France), Member
Gerardo Movilla (Spain), Member
Philippe Piat (France), Member
on the claim presented by
Club A, as Claimant
against
Club B as Respondent
regarding Training Compensation for the player X

I. FACTS OF THE CASE

1. The player X, born in February 1983, signed a non-amateur contract with the club B on 22 July 2004
2. The club A, that contributed to the training of the player in question, has lodged a claim for training compensation as described in chapter VII of the FIFA Regulations for the Status and Transfer of Players, edition September 2001 (hereinafter; the Regulations)
3. The player X was registered with the club A from 1 September 2003 to 30 June 2004, at his age of 20 and 21
4. According to the classification of clubs outlined in circular 826 dated 31 October 2002, the club A belongs to category 2 (indicative amount of EUR 60,000 per year)
5. Since the player spent only ten months with the club A, the claimant specifies its claim against the club B for the training Compensation for the player X to the amount of EUR 50,000
6. The club B never provided FIFA with its position towards the claim of the club A
7. The Dispute Resolution Chamber is invited to determine the amount owed by the club B to the club A

II. CONSIDERATIONS OF THE DISPUTE RESOLUTION CHAMBER

1. The members of the Dispute Resolution Chamber were summoned to pass a decision on the present matter by the Chairman pursuant to Art. 1 point 6) of the Rules Governing the Practice and Procedures of the Dispute Resolution Chamber
2. The Dispute Resolution Chamber of the FIFA Players' Status Committee shall review disputes coming under its jurisdiction pursuant to Art. 42 of the Regulations, at the request of one of the parties to the dispute
3. In accordance with Art. 42.1 lit. (b) (iv) of the Regulations, it falls within the purview of the Dispute Resolution Chamber to review disputes concerning training compensation fees
4. Consequently, the Dispute Resolution Chamber is the competent body to decide on the present claim for training compensation

5. Entering into the substance of the matter, the Chamber outlined that the training period to take into consideration went from 1 September 2003 to 30 June 2004, at the player's age of 20 and 21. Furthermore, the chamber took into consideration that the player concluded his first non-amateur contract at the age of 21, with the club B
6. Continuing, the Chamber stated that, as established in Chapter VII of the Regulations, the training compensation is payable for training incurred between the ages of 12 and 21, if the player concerned concludes a non-amateur contract before the age of 23
7. It is therefore undisputed that the club A is entitled to receive compensation from the club B for the training and education of the player X for the sporting season 2003/04, which the player spent with this club
8. The amount due by the club B is to be calculated in accordance with the Regulations and the FIFA Circular letter no. 826 dated 31 October 2002. As far as the categorisation of the club A is concerned, as provided for by the Circular letter 826, it belongs to the Category 2. According to the mentioned Circular letter, the indicative amount for the club A, belonging to Category 2, is EUR 60,000 per year of training
9. As a result to the above, the Chamber stated that for the year of training of the player X, the club A would be entitled to training compensation in the amount of EUR 60,000. In this regard, the Chamber took note however of the fact that the club A in its claim submitted to the FIFA Dispute Resolution Chamber only asked for the amount of EUR 50,000
10. In consequence, and with respect to the principle ultra petitum, the Chamber stated that it is not in a position to grant to the claimant, the club A, the amount of EUR 60,000, but only the amount of EUR 50,000, i.e. the amount which the club A actually claimed for from the club B for the training of the player X
11. In view of the above, the Chamber decided that the club B has to pay to the club A EUR 50,000 for the training of the player X

III. DECISION OF THE DISPUTE RESOLUTION CHAMBER

1. The claim of the club A is accepted
2. The club B has to pay the amount of EUR 50,000 to the club A
3. The amount due to the club A has to be paid by the club B within the next 30 days as from the date of notification of this decision
4. If the aforementioned sum is not paid within the aforementioned deadline, the present matter shall be submitted to FIFA's Disciplinary Committee, so that the necessary disciplinary sanctions may be imposed
5. If the aforementioned sum is not paid within the aforementioned deadline, an interest rate of 5% per year will apply as from the first day after the aforementioned deadline
6. The club A is directed to inform the club B immediately of the account number to which the remittance is to be made and to notify the Dispute Resolution Chamber of every payment received
7. According to art. 60 par. 1 of the FIFA Statutes this decision may be appealed before the Court of Arbitration for Sport (CAS). The statement of appeal must be sent to the CAS directly within 10 days of receiving notification of this decision and has to contain all elements in accordance with point 2 of the directives issued by the CAS, copy of which we enclose hereto. Within another 10 days following the expiry of the time limit for the filing of the statement of appeal, the appellant shall file with the CAS a brief stating the facts and legal arguments giving rise to the appeal (cf. point 4 of the directives).

⚽⚽⚽

75368

DECISION OF THE DISPUTE RESOLUTION CHAMBER

passed in Zurich, Switzerland, on 28 July 2005,
in the following composition:
Slim Aloulou (Tunisia), Chairman
Jean-Marie Philips (Belgium), Member
Philippe Diallo (France), Member
Gerardo Movilla (Spain), Member

Philippe Piat (France), Member
on the claim presented by
Player A, as Claimant
against
Club B, as Respondent

I. FACTS OF THE CASE

1. The player A and the club B signed an employment contract valid from 11 July 2002 until 30 June 2003.
2. The employment contract stipulates that the player is entitled to a monthly salary according to the club's regular payment schedule. The contract does not stipulate an exact amount as the player's monthly salary.
3. According to the club's regular payment schedule, the monthly salary of the club's football players is USD 220.
4. On 14 October 2003, the player informed FIFA that the club had terminated his employment contract unilaterally on 26 March 2003 due to an injury, without that it proved that an injury was the reason of the contract termination.
5. Moreover he informed FIFA that the club had not paid his salaries as from January 2003. In this regard, the player maintained that the monthly salary agreed upon was USD 5,000, without presenting any written evidence proving this amount.
6. In consequence, the player claims from the club the amount of USD 50,000, for his salaries from January 2003 to 26 March 2003, and as compensation for the breach of contract by the club. Between 26 March and 30 June 2003, he did not sign any employment contract with another club.
7. Moreover, the player asks that sanctions for breach of contract in accordance with the Articles 21 to 23 of the FIFA Regulation for the Status and Transfer of Players are applied against the club.
8. Confronted with the player's claim, the club stated that the employment contract was terminated on 27 March 2003 due to the player's absence without permission from the club's training on 25 and 26 March 2003.
9. As far as the player's claim for outstanding salaries is concerned, the club stated that the players monthly salary was USD 170.
10. In this respect, the club presented payment receipts signed by the player in question, according to which all the salaries were paid pro rata until 27 March 2003.
11. In conclusion, the club asks that the player's claims are rejected.

II. CONSIDERATIONS OF THE DISPUTE RESOLUTION CHAMBER

1. The members of the Dispute Resolution Chamber were summoned to pass a decision on the present matter by the Chairman pursuant to Art. 1 point 6) of the Rules Governing the Practice and Procedures of the Dispute Resolution Chamber.
2. The deciding body started its deliberations by indicating that, as established in Art. 42 § 1 lit. (b) (i) of the FIFA Regulations for the Status and Transfer of Players (hereinafter: the Regulations), it falls within the purview of the Dispute Resolution Chamber to determine whether one of the parties has committed a unilateral breach of contract without just cause. In the case that the employment contract was breached by a party, the Dispute Resolution Chamber is responsible to verify and decide whether this party is accountable for outstanding payments and compensation.
3. In view of the above, the Dispute Resolution Chamber concluded that it was competent to decide on the present litigation.
4. The Chamber then acknowledged the documentation contained in the file and took note in particular of the fact that according to the club B, the employment contract was prematurely terminated on 27 March 2003 due to the player's absence without permission from the club's training on 25 and 26 March 2003.
5. Entering into the deliberations, the Chamber first outlined that in case an employee (player) is absent during a short period of time from work, the employer (club) should first contact him to remind him of his labour obligations. Moreover, in general, an absence during a few days does not constitute for the employer (club) a just cause to immediately terminate the employment contract, prematurely and unilaterally.

6. Taking into account the above-mentioned facts of the present matter, the members of the chamber stated that the absence of the player A during two days from the training with the club clearly did not constitute a just cause for the club B to terminate the employment contract in question prematurely and unilaterally. The club would however have been entitled to take appropriate sanctions against the player, like for instance a fine, for not appearing to the training.
7. Therefore, the members of the Chamber came to the conclusion that the premature and unilateral termination of the employment contract in question by the club B was not justified.
8. In consequence, the Dispute Resolution Chamber was asked to verify and decide whether the club B is accountable for outstanding payments and compensation towards the player A.
9. In this regard, the Chamber took note in particular that the player claimed for his salaries from January to March 2003, and that the club B presented written evidence that the player's salaries up to the date of termination of the employment contract were paid.
10. Moreover, the Chamber noticed that the player maintained that his monthly salary was USD 5,000, and not only USD 220.
11. And finally, the Chamber acknowledged that the player asked for USD 50,000 as compensation for the breach of contract by the club.
12. As far as the player's claim for the salaries from January to March 2003 is concerned, the Chamber stated first that the player did not present any written evidence that the monthly salary was USD 5,000 instead of USD 220, which is indicated in the club's regular payment schedule. Moreover, the Chamber acknowledged that the club B presented written evidence that the player's salaries up to the date of termination of the employment contract were paid.
13. Therefore, the Chamber came to the conclusion that on account of salaries up to the date of termination of the contract, obviously no payments were outstanding.
14. The Chamber then turned to the question of compensation for unjustified breach of contract, and in this respect first of all decided that the club had to pay to the player the salaries for the three months period from the unilateral termination on 27 March 2003 to the expiry date stipulated in the contract on 30 June 2003, i.e. USD 660.
15. In this regard, the Chamber stated that the player A was entitled to USD 660 from the club B.
16. In continuation, the Chamber stated that on account of compensation for damages, the player shall be entitled to an additional amount of USD 10,000, being a reasonable amount to compensate the player for the unjustified breach of contract committed by the club B.
17. In conclusion, the Dispute Resolution Chamber decided that the club B has to pay to the player A on account of all of the above the amount of USD 10,660.

III. DECISION OF THE DISPUTE RESOLUTION CHAMBER

1. The claim of the player A is partially accepted.
2. The club B has to pay the amount of USD 10,660 to the player A.
3. The amount due to the player A has to be paid by the club B within the next 30 days as from the date of notification of this decision.
4. All further claims of the player A against the club B are rejected.
5. In the event that the debts of the Respondent are not paid within the stated deadline, an interest rate of 5% per year will apply as from the first day after the stated deadline.
6. If the aforementioned sum is not paid within the aforementioned deadline, the present matter shall be submitted to FIFA's Disciplinary Committee, so that the necessary disciplinary sanctions may be imposed.
7. The player A is directed to inform the club B immediately of the account number to which the remittance is to be made, and to notify the Dispute Resolution Chamber of every payment received.
8. According to art. 60 par. 1 of the FIFA Statutes this decision may be appealed before the Court of Arbitration for Sport (CAS). The statement of appeal must be sent to the CAS directly within 10 days of receiving notification of this decision and has to contain all elements in accordance with point 2 of the directives issued by the CAS, copy of which we enclose hereto. Within another 10 days following the expiry of the time limit for the filing of the statement of appeal, the appellant shall file with the CAS a brief stating the facts and legal arguments giving rise to the appeal (cf. point 4 of the directives).

75377
DECISION OF THE DISPUTE RESOLUTION CHAMBER
passed in Zurich, Switzerland, on 28 July 2005,
in the following composition:
Slim Aloulou (Tunisia), Chairman
Jean-Marie Philips (Belgium), Member
Philippe Diallo (France), Member
Gerardo Movilla (Spain), Member
Philippe Piat (France), Member
on the claim presented by Player X, as Claimant
against
Club Y, as Respondent

I. FACTS OF THE CASE

1. The player X signed a contract with the club Y, valid from 8 July 2002 until 31 July 2003.
2. The contract stipulates the payment of ten monthly salaries of EUR 3,000 each.
3. On 21 January 2004, the player reminded the club that he had not yet received the salaries for March, April and May 2003 in the total amount of EUR 9,000.
4. On 16 March 2004, the player lodged a claim against the club Y before FIFA, claiming for the amount of EUR 9,000.
5. Despite several requests, the club Y failed to provide FIFA with its position concerning the claim of the player X.
6. On 21 April 2005, the player informed us that the outstanding amount had been reduced to EUR 6,000.

II. CONSIDERATIONS OF THE DISPUTE RESOLUTION CHAMBER

1. The members of the Dispute Resolution Chamber were summoned to pass a decision on the present matter by the Chairman pursuant to Art. 1 point 6) of the Rules Governing the Practice and Procedures of the Dispute Resolution Chamber.
2. The Dispute Resolution Chamber of the FIFA Players' Status Committee shall review disputes coming under its jurisdiction pursuant to Art. 42 of the Regulations, at the request of one of the parties to the dispute.
3. Consequently, the Dispute Resolution Chamber is the competent body to decide on the present claim for training compensation.
4. Entering into the substance of the matter, the Chamber acknowledged the documentation contained in the file and took note of the fact that the player X and the club Y had signed an employment contract valid from 8 July 2002 until 31 July 2003, stipulating ten monthly salaries of EUR 3,000 each. Moreover, the members of the Chamber noticed that according to the player X, the due amount of EUR 6,000 has not been paid. And finally, the Chamber took note of the fact that the club Y never issued its position in the matter, despite having been asked to do so by the FIFA administration on several occasions.
5. The Chamber then stated that as a general principle of procedure before the Dispute Resolution Chamber, if a respondent does not reply to the claim, the case shall be decided by the Dispute Resolution Chamber only on the basis of the facts and proof provided by the claimant, since with its conduct, the respondent renounces to its right of defence and thus accepts the allegations of the claimant.
6. On account of the above, the Chamber stated that because the respondent, the club Y, never took position in the dispute, the Dispute Resolution Chamber must pass a decision based only on the facts and evidence provided by the player X.
7. In this regard, the Chamber underlined that the player X is claiming for two monthly salaries from Y, which amounts to EUR 6,000.
8. In conclusion to the above, the Dispute Resolution Chamber decided that the club Y must pay the amount of EUR 6,000 to the player X.

III. DECISION OF THE DISPUTE RESOLUTION CHAMBER

1. The claim of the player X is accepted.

2. The club Y has to pay the amount of EUR 6,000 to the player X.
3. The amount due to the player X has to be paid by the club Y within the next 30 days as from the date of notification of this decision.
4. In the event that the debts of the Respondent are not paid within the stated deadline, an interest rate of 5% per year will apply as from the first day after the stated deadline.
5. If the aforementioned sum is not paid within the aforementioned deadline, the present matter shall be submitted to FIFA's Disciplinary Committee, so that the necessary disciplinary sanctions may be imposed.
6. The player X is directed to inform the club Y immediately of the account number to which the remittance is to be made, and to notify the Dispute Resolution Chamber of every payment received.
7. According to art. 60 par. 1 of the FIFA Statutes this decision may be appealed before the Court of Arbitration for Sport (CAS). The statement of appeal must be sent to the CAS directly within 10 days of receiving notification of this decision and has to contain all elements in accordance with point 2 of the directives issued by the CAS, copy of which we enclose hereto. Within another 10 days following the expiry of the time limit for the filing of the statement of appeal, the appellant shall file with the CAS a brief stating the facts and legal arguments giving rise to the appeal (cf. point 4 of the directives).

75559
DECISION OF THE DISPUTE RESOLUTION CHAMBER
passed in Zurich, Switzerland, on 28 July 2005,
in the following composition:
Slim Aloulou (Tunisia), Chairman
Jean-Marie Philips (Belgium), Member
Philippe Diallo (France), Member
Gerardo Movilla (Spain), Member
Philippe Piat (France), Member
on the claim presented by
Player X, as Claimant
against
Club B, as Respondent

I. FACTS OF THE CASE

1. The player X and the club Y concluded an employment contract valid from 1 November 2001 until 31 May 2002
2. The contract stipulates a monthly salary of USD 4,650 payable between the first and the fifth day from November 2001 to May 2002
3. On 30 April 2004, the player lodged a claim before FIFA against the club Y
4. Several unsuccessful efforts to resolve the matter by amicable agreement preceded this action
5. The player maintains only having received the salary for the month of November 2001, and therefore claims for the payment of six monthly salaries (December 2001 until May 2002) in the total amount of USD 27,900
6. The club Y is of the opinion that, in accordance with the FIFA Regulations, the right of the player to claim for outstanding salaries from the club has already prescript
7. Moreover, the club Y presents payment receipts signed by the player in the total amount of USD 5,000, and in addition of USD 3,625. Besides these, the club Y presents payment receipts in the amount of USD 8,000, which are not signed by the player, but a third person
8. All of the payment receipts presented are dated 4 April 2002 or earlier
9. Besides that, the club alleges having paid to the player on 24 April 2004 the amount of USD 1,160

II. CONSIDERATIONS OF THE DISPUTE RESOLUTION CHAMBER

1. The members of the Dispute Resolution Chamber were summoned to pass a decision on the present matter by the Chairman pursuant to Art. 1 point 6) of the Rules Governing the Practice and Procedures of the Dispute Resolution Chamber (hereinafter: Procedural Rules)

2. The Dispute Resolution Chamber of the FIFA Players' Status Committee shall review disputes coming under its jurisdiction pursuant to Art. 42 of the Regulations, at the request of one of the parties to the dispute
3. In view of the above, the Dispute Resolution Chamber concluded that it was competent to decide on the present litigation
4. Entering into the substance of the matter, the Chamber acknowledged the documentation contained in the file and in this respect, took note in particular that the player claimed for salary payments in the amount of USD 4,650 per month from December 2001 until May 2002, therefore for the total amount of USD 27,900
5. Moreover, the members of the Chamber noticed that the entire amount the player was entitled to in accordance with the employment contract was USD 41,850, and that the club maintained having paid to the player approximately USD 17,785
6. And finally, the Chamber took note of the fact that the salary instalments claimed by the player were due between the first and the fifth day of every month from December 2001 to May 2002, and that the player's claim was submitted to FIFA on 30 April 2004
7. The Chamber then turned to the defendant's argument that the player's claim was already prescript, and in this regard, referred to Article 44 of the Regulations in connection with Article 4 of the Procedural Rules, according to which the Dispute Resolution Chamber shall not address any dispute if more than two years have elapsed since the facts leading to a dispute arose
8. In this regard, the Chamber noted that in the present case, between the origin of the first part of the claim, i.e. the due dates of the claimed salary installments from December 2001 to April 2002, and the submission of the claim to FIFA on 30 April 2004, more than two years have elapsed
9. Therefore, on account of the above-mentioned provision, the Dispute Resolution Chamber decided that the right to claim for the salary installments from December 2001 to April 2002 is to be considered as prescript, and that therefore, the Chamber is not in a position to deal with this part of the claim
10. As far as the second part of the player's request was concerned, i.e. the payment of the salary of May 2002, the Chamber stated that, between the origin of this part of the claim on 5 May 2002 and its submission to FIFA on 30 April 2004, two years had not elapsed yet
11. Therefore, the Chamber stated that, taking into consideration the above-mentioned provision, the right to claim for the salary installment of May 2002 is not prescript
12. In continuation, the Chamber took into consideration that the entire amount the player was entitled to from the club in accordance with the employment contract was USD 41,850, and that the club had stated that it had paid to the player only approximately USD 17,785 so far. Therefore, the Chamber stated that the salary for May 2002 in the amount of USD 4,650 was undoubtedly still outstanding
13. On account of this, the Dispute Resolution Chamber decided that the club Y had to pay to the player X the amount of USD 4,650 as salary for the month of May 2002.

III. DECISION OF THE DISPUTE RESOLUTION CHAMBER

1. The claim of the player X is partially accepted
2. The club Y has to pay the amount of USD 4,650 to the player X
3. The amount due to the player X has to be paid by the club Y within the next 30 days as from the date of notification of this decision
4. In the event that the debts of the Respondent are not paid within the stated deadline, an interest rate of 5% per year will apply as from the first day after the stated deadline
5. All further claims of the player X against the club Y are rejected
6. If the aforementioned sum is not paid within the aforementioned deadline, the present matter shall be submitted to FIFA's Disciplinary Committee, so that the necessary disciplinary sanctions may be imposed
7. The player X is directed to inform the club Y immediately of the account number to which the remittance is to be made, and to notify the Dispute Resolution Chamber of every payment received
8. According to art. 60 par. 1 of the FIFA Statutes this decision may be appealed before the Court of Arbitration for Sport (CAS). The statement of appeal must be sent to the CAS directly within 10 days of receiving notification of this decision and has to contain all elements in accordance with point 2 of the directives issued by the CAS, copy of which we enclose hereto. Within another 10 days following the expiry of the time limit for the filing of the statement of appeal, the appellant shall file

with the CAS a brief stating the facts and legal arguments giving rise to the appeal (cf. point 4 of the directives).

⚽⚽⚽

75570
DECISION OF THE DISPUTE RESOLUTION CHAMBER
passed in Zurich, Switzerland, on 28 July 2005,
in the following composition:
Slim Aloulou (Tunisia), Chairman
Jean-Marie Philips (Belgium), Member
Philippe Diallo (France), Member
Gerardo Movilla (Spain), Member
Philippe Piat (France), Member
on the claim presented by
Player X, as Claimant
against
Club Y, as Respondent

I. FACTS OF THE CASE

1. The player X and the club Y signed an employment contract valid from 1 October 2003 until 31 May 2004.
2. The contract stipulates a monthly salary of USD 10,000, as well as two bonuses of USD 95,000 each, one payable on 2 October 2003, and the other on 1 January 2004.
3. Furthermore, clause 12 of the contract stipulates that the player
"shall receive free of charge medical treatment according to the system applied in the country of the club Y".
4. On 30 October 2003, the player suffered an injury on his knee during the training with the team of club Y.
5. On 2 November 2003, he travelled to his home country for the surgery and medical treatment, with the authorisation of the club Y.
6. Clarifications in his home country showed that the surgery of the players knee will cost USD 6,620.
7. This was communicated to the club Y on 11 November 2003.
8. On 12 November 2003, the player underwent surgery.
9. On 13 November 2003, the club Y informed the player that in application of clause 12 of the employment contract, it will only pay him USD 4,000, since this would be the price for the same surgery in the country of the club Y.
10. On 22 December 2003, 13 January and 16 March 2004, the player asked the club in written if he was required to return for the recovery period, or if he shall remain in his home country, but did not receive any answer.
11. In the interim, his salaries as from October 2003, as well as the bonus payable on 1 January 2004 became due, but stayed unpaid.
12. On 25 March 2004, the player informed the club Y in written that he terminates the contract.
13. Between 25 March 2004 and the expiry date of the contract (31 May 2004), the player did not conclude an employment contract with another club.
14. On 14 April 2004, he lodged a claim before FIFA against the club Y for the following amounts:
USD 60,000 Salaries from October 2003 to March 2004
USD 95,000 Bonus payable on 1 January 2004
USD 6,620 Expenses for surgery passed on 12 November 2003 (the player presents receipts for his payments in the amount of USD 3,246)
USD 161,620 Total
15. The club Y estimates that since the player got injured on 30 October 2003, the employment contract was prematurely terminated, and therefore the salaries did not become due.
16. Furthermore, the club in question maintains that it has authorized the player to undergo surgery in his home country only if it would cost not more than USD 4,000, since this would be the price for the relevant surgery in the country of the club Y.

17. Finally, the club estimates that the employment contract only grants the player free of charge medical treatment in the country of the club Y, but does not stipulate that the club has to reimburse expenses of the player for medical treatment he received in other countries.

II. CONSIDERATIONS OF THE DISPUTE RESOLUTION CHAMBER

1. The members of the Dispute Resolution Chamber were summoned to pass a decision on the present matter by the Chairman pursuant to Art. 1 point 6) of the Rules Governing the Practice and Procedures of the Dispute Resolution Chamber.
2. The deciding body started its deliberations by indicating that, as established in Art. 42 § 1 lit. (b) (i) of the FIFA Regulations for the Status and Transfer of Players (hereinafter: the Regulations), it falls within the purview of the Dispute Resolution Chamber to determine whether one of the parties has committed a unilateral breach of contract without just cause. In the case that the employment contract was breached by a party, the Dispute Resolution Chamber is responsible to verify and decide whether this party is accountable for outstanding payments and compensation.
3. In view of the above, the Dispute Resolution Chamber concluded that it was competent to decide on the present litigation.
4. The Chamber then acknowledged the documentation contained in the file and took note in particular of the fact that according to the club Y, the employment contract was prematurely terminated because the player X got injured on 30 October 2003, and that therefore the player's salaries and bonuses were not paid anymore.
5. Entering into the deliberations, the Chamber first outlined that as a basic principle in labour law, in case an employee (player) gets injured, this does in general not constitute for the employer (club) a just cause to terminate the employment contract prematurely and unilaterally, and therefore to cancel the payment of the player's salaries.
6. Taking into account the above-mentioned facts of the present matter as well as the outlined principle of labour law, the members of the Chamber stated that the injury the player X incurred on 30 October 2003 clearly did not constitute a just cause for the club Y to terminate the employment contract in question prematurely and unilaterally, and therefore to cancel the payment of Mr. X' salaries.
7. Therefore, the members of the Chamber came to the conclusion that the premature and unilateral termination of the employment contract in question by the club Y was not justified.
8. In consequence, the Dispute Resolution Chamber was asked to verify and decide whether the club Y is accountable for outstanding payments and compensation towards the player X.
9. In this regard, the chamber took note in particular that the player X requested from the club Y the payment of salaries in the total amount of USD 60,000, i.e. from October 2003 to March 2004, when he accepted the termination of the relevant employment contract, plus the bonus payable on 1 January 2004 in the amount of USD 95,000.
10. Moreover, the Chamber noticed that the player requested from the club Y the reimbursement of USD 6,620 on account of expenses for a surgery passed on 12 November 2003.
11. As far as the player's claim for salaries and the bonus payable on 1 January 2004 are concerned, the Chamber acknowledged that the club Y did not deny not having paid the relevant amounts, because it deemed not being obliged to do so. However, in consequence to the above conclusion that the termination of the employment contract by the club Y was not justified, the Chamber stated that the relevant salaries and the bonus were to be paid to the player.
12. Therefore, the Chamber decided that the club Y has to pay to the player X, on account of salaries from October 2003 to March 2004, the amount of USD 60,000, as well as the bonus of 1 January 2004 in the amount of USD 95,000.
13. As far as the player's claim for reimbursement of the expenses incurred with the surgery in the amount of USD 6,620 is concerned, the Chamber took note of the payment receipts presented by the player for the relevant surgery in the amount of USD 3,246, and moreover, noticed that the club Y agreed to pay the amount of USD 4,000 for the relevant surgery.
14. Since the player did not provide written evidence that he had expenses with the surgery in the amount of USD 6,620, but only presented payment receipts over the amount of USD 3,246, the Chamber could not take into consideration any amount claimed for reimbursement of the surgery expenses beyond USD 3,246.
15. The reimbursement of the said amount was however not refused by the club Y, since the same had stated that it would agree to pay the amount of USD 4,000 for the relevant surgery.

16. Therefore, the Chamber decided that the club Y has to pay to the player X on account of reimbursement of surgery expenses the amount of USD 3,246.
17. In conclusion, the Dispute Resolution Chamber decided that the club Y has to pay to the player X on account of all of the above the amount of USD 158,246.

III. DECISION OF THE DISPUTE RESOLUTION CHAMBER

1. The claim of the player X is partially accepted.
2. The club Y has to pay the amount of USD 158,246 to the player X.
3. The amount due to the player X has to be paid by the club Y within the next 30 days as from the date of notification of this decision.
4. All further claims of the player X against the club Y are rejected.
5. In the event that the debts of the Respondent are not paid within the stated deadline, an interest rate of 5% per year will apply as from the first day after the stated deadline.
6. If the aforementioned sum is not paid within the aforementioned deadline, the present matter shall be submitted to FIFA's Disciplinary Committee, so that the necessary disciplinary sanctions may be imposed.
7. The player X is directed to inform the club Y immediately of the account number to which the remittance is to be made, and to notify the Dispute Resolution Chamber of every payment received.
8. According to art. 60 par. 1 of the FIFA Statutes this decision may be appealed before the Court of Arbitration for Sport (CAS). The statement of appeal must be sent to the CAS directly within 10 days of receiving notification of this decision and has to contain all elements in accordance with point 2 of the directives issued by the CAS, copy of which we enclose hereto. Within another 10 days following the expiry of the time limit for the filing of the statement of appeal, the appellant shall file with the CAS a brief stating the facts and legal arguments giving rise to the appeal (cf. point 4 of the directives).

75923
DECISION OF THE DISPUTE RESOLUTION CHAMBER
passed in Zurich, Switzerland, on 28 July 2005,
in the following composition:
Slim Aloulou (Tunisia), Chairman
Philippe Piat (France), member
Jean-Marie Philips (Belgium), member
Gerardo Movilla (Spain), member
Philippe Diallo (France), member
on the claim presented by the player
A, Serbia and Montenegro, as Claimant
against the club
K, Cyprus, as Respondent,
regarding a contractual dispute arisen between the parties.

I. FACTS OF THE CASE

1. On 15 January 2003, the player A and the club K signed an employment contract with validity until 31 May 2003. The parties stipulated a total salary of CYP 5,000, i.e. CYP 1,000 per month.
2. On 20 October 2004, the player turned to FIFA and alleged that the club had only paid him only an amount of CYP 450. Therefore, the remainder of the debt amounted to CYP 4,550 and was never cancelled despite several interventions of the Football Association of Serbia and Montenegro. The player provided FIFA with a copy of the signed employment contract dated 15 January 2003.
3. On 23 February 2005 as well as on 9 and 16 March 2005, the club alleged that the parties had signed a new contract on 1 February 2003, modifying the original contract dated 15 January 2003. The club provided FIFA with a copy of this signed contract. This new employment contract stipulated a total salary of CYP 1,600, i.e. CYP 400 per month, instead of a total salary of CYP 5,000. The club alleged that it paid the latter amount. The club counterclaimed an amount of CYP 3,540, which it had

been asked to pay for 118 overnight stays of the player at the hotel. The club provided FIFA with a confirmation made out in the name of the player.

4. The player filed his position on 8 April 2005. He underlined that he only ever signed the contract dated 15 January 2003. He alleged that the club changed the first two pages of the contract with the stipulated amounts and the date of the contract and that therefore, the document dated 1 February 2005 is a falsification.
   Furthermore, concerning the counterclaim of the club the player referred to the contract, according to which the club had the obligation to allocate him a flat.
5. Despite the express warranty that the club had paid the player an amount of CYP 1,600 for which it would provide FIFA with evidence, the club failed to submit such proof.
6. The Cyprus Football Association provided FIFA with a certified copy of the employment contract deposited at the Association. This contract stipulates the total salary of CYP 5,000 and is dated 15 January 2003. The Cyprus Football Association confirmed that this is the only contract that had been deposited.

II. CONSIDERATIONS OF THE DISPUTE RESOLUTION CHAMBER

1. The Dispute Resolution Chamber of the FIFA Players' Status Committee shall review disputes coming under its jurisdiction pursuant to art. 42 of the FIFA Regulations for the Status and Transfer of Players (edition September 2001) at the request of one of the parties to the dispute.
2. According to art. 42 par. 1 lit. (b) (i) of the Regulations for the Status and Transfer of Players (edition September 2001), the triggering elements of the dispute (i.e. whether a contract was breached, with or without just cause, or sporting just cause), will be decided by the Dispute Resolution Chamber.
3. If an employment contract is breached by a party, the Dispute Resolution Chamber is responsible to verify whether a party is accountable for compensation and outstanding payments.
4. At first, the members of the Dispute Resolution Chamber confirmed to be competent to pass a decision in this matter. In addition, the Chamber acknowledged the above-mentioned facts as well as the further documentation contained in the file.
5. Subsequently, and entering into the substance of the matter, the Chamber considered that the player A and the club K signed a valid employment contract dated 15 January 2003 according to which the parties agreed on a total salary in the amount of CYP 5,000. Only this contract has been deposited, as it confirmed the Cyprus Football Association, and therefore, only this contract deploys a legal effect in front of the Dispute Resolution Chamber.
6. The Chamber then emphasised that the club did not provide FIFA with the promised evidence concerning the payment of CYP 1,600. Therefore, the Chamber considered that the remainder due to the player amounts to CYP 4,550, as alleged by him.
7. However, with respect to the counterclaimed amount of CYP 3,540, the Chamber could not back the player's position, according to which the club should have allocated him with a flat in accordance with the employment contract and that its failure to do so justified the payment of the hotel costs by the club. In none of the contracts provided to FIFA was it stipulated that the club would bear the costs for the accommodation of the player. Therefore, the Chamber decided to accept the counterclaim in the amount of CYP 3,450.
8. Consequently, having thus analysed the various aspects of the player's claim as well as of the club's defence statement, the Dispute Resolution Chamber concluded its deliberations by announcing that the player's claims were partially admissible and that the counterclaim is accepted.
9. Taking into account all of the above, the Chamber decided that the club K must pay the amount of CYP 1,010 to the player A.

III. DECISION OF THE DISPUTE RESOLUTION CHAMBER

1. The claim of the player A is partially accepted.
2. The counterclaim of the club K is accepted.
3. The club K has to pay the amount of CYP 1,010 to the player A within the next 30 days as from the date of notification of this decision.
4. Any further financial claims lodged by the player A are rejected.
5. In the event that the above-mentioned amount is not paid within the stated deadline, an interest rate of 5% per year will apply and the present matter shall be submitted to FIFA's Disciplinary Committee, so that the necessary disciplinary sanctions may be imposed.

6. The player A is instructed to inform K immediately and directly of the account number to which the remittance is to be made and to notify the Dispute Resolution Chamber of every payment received.
7. According to art. 60 par. 1 of the FIFA Statutes this decision may be appealed before the Court of Arbitration for Sport (CAS). The statement of appeal must be sent to the CAS directly within 10 days of receiving notification of this decision and has to contain all elements in accordance with point 2 of the directives issued by the CAS, copy of which we enclose hereto. Within another 10 days following the expiry of the time limit for the filing of the statement of appeal, the appellant shall file with the CAS a brief stating the facts and legal arguments giving rise to the appeal (cf. point 4 of the directives).

75975
DECISION OF THE DISPUTE RESOLUTION CHAMBER
passed in Zurich, Switzerland, on 28 July 2005,
in the following composition:
Slim Aloulou (Tunisia), chairman
Jean-Marie Philips (Belgium), member
Philippe Diallo (France), member
Gerardo Movilla (Spain), member
Philippe Piat (France), member
on the claim presented by A as Claimant
against
B as Respondent
regarding a contractual dispute arisen between the parties

I. FACTS OF THE CASE

1. On 15 February 2004, A and B signed an employment contract valid for a period of 4 ½ months, "starting from the date of passing the medical test, receiving the international certificate and signing all official documents in the X Assocation".
2. According to the relevant contract, A was entitled to receive the total amount of USD 120,000, to be paid as follows:
   a. USD 40,000 as signing-on fee, to be paid "after 15 days of passing the medical test, receiving the international certificate and signing all official documents in the X Association";
   b. Four monthly salaries of USD 20,000 each, to be paid during the period of the contract.
3. Amongst other financial privileges, A was also entitled to receive two economy flight tickets (Y/Z and return).
4. A claims that he underwent the relevant medical tests, that his international transfer certificate was received and that he signed all the official documents at the X Association.
5. Moreover, A asserts that he participated in two official matches for B.
6. On 27 February 2004, and based on Art. 3 of their employment contract, B decided to unilaterally terminate its employment relationship with A, due to his alleged lack of performance.
7. Art. 3 of the relevant employment contract stipulates that "A has to follow the instructions of training, camping and to keep his known performance upon which B signed the contract with him, otherwise this will be consider a termination of the contract by A and then FIFA regulations should be applied".
8. As a consequence, A left B in the end of February 2004.
9. In his claim, A denies the claimed lack of performance, but above all, underlines that such reason cannot be considered as just cause to unilaterally terminate an employment contract.
10. Moreover, A asserts that, during the period that he remained at B's disposal, he was not paid any amount.
11. In light of all the above, A is presently requesting the Chamber to consider that B has terminated their employment contract without just cause and to consequently condemn B to cancel to him all the sums that are stipulated in their employment contract, in the total amount of USD 120,000, as well as the amount of EUR 761 (approximately USD 926) which he paid for a return flight ticket (Y/Z) and which he was contractually entitled to receive.

12. In conclusion, A is presently claiming the payment of USD 120,926 from B.
13. On the other hand, B, via the X Association, informed the FIFA Administration that it has unilaterally terminated its employment contract with A, due to his poor performance, in accordance with Art. 3 of such contract. In fact, B asserts that "the contract has been terminated by A depending on Article 3 of the signed contract as he shown very poor technical level and unable to perform his duties..."
14. Furthermore, B defends that it has offered to pay to A, the amounts corresponding to the time that he remained with it, i.e. 10 days. However, A has refused to collect such amount and left the country.
15. Finally, according to B, A has orally promised not to claim any further amounts with respect to the present matter.
16. In response, A asserts that in order to leave the country, he had to sign a letter in which he stated "I have received my passport for my wsh to leavebecause my contract is now terminated". However, he underlines that it is absolutely false that he has ever orally promised not to claim any further amounts from B, in the present matter.

II. CONSIDERATIONS OF THE DISPUTE RESOLUTION CHAMBER

1. The FIFA Regulations for the Status and Transfer of Players (edition September 2001) are the applicable Regulations to the present procedure, since the case has been brought to FIFA before the coming into force of the current version of the said Regulations on 1 July 2005. Furthermore, the contractual dispute at hand has its basis on the employment contract signed between the parties on 15 February 2004.
.2. In light of the above, the Dispute Resolution Chamber shall review disputes coming under its jurisdiction pursuant to art. 42 of the FIFA Regulations for the Status and Transfer of Players (edition September 2001), at the request of one of the parties to the dispute.
3. According to art. 42, par. 1 lit. (b) (i) of the FIFA Regulations for the Status and Transfer of Players (edition September 2001), the triggering elements of the dispute (i.e. whether a contract was breached, with or without just cause, or sporting just cause), will be decided by the Dispute Resolution Chamber.
4. If an employment contract is breached by a party, the Dispute Resolution Chamber is responsible to verify whether a party is accountable for compensation and outstanding payments.
5. Consequently, the Dispute Resolution Chamber is the competent body to decide on the present litigation concerning the alleged non-respect of the contract concluded between the Claimant and the Respondent.
6. Subsequently, and entering into the substance of the present labour dispute, the Chamber started by acknowledging that, on 15 February 2004, A and B signed an employment contract valid for a period of 4 ½ months, "starting from the date of passing the medical test, receiving the international certificate and signing all official documents in the X Association".
7. The members of the Chamber also acknowledged that, by letter dated 27 February 2004, B unilaterally terminated its employment contract with A, due to the latter's alleged lack of performance and based on Art. 3 of the aforementioned contract which stipulates that "The player has to follow the instruction of training, camping and to keep his known performance upon which B signed the contract with him, otherwise this will be consider a termination of the contract by A and then FIFA regulations should be applied".
8. On the other hand, the Chamber noted that A considers that the aforementioned contractual termination was unilaterally operated by B without just cause and is presently claiming the payment of all the outstanding amounts under his employment contract with B, until its end, in the total amount of USD 120,000.
9. Moreover, the Chamber noted that A is also claiming the reimbursement of the expenses in which he incurred concerning flight tickets, in particular, the amount of EUR 761 (approximately USD 926) that he paid for a return flight ticket (Y/Z).
10. Furthermore, the Chamber took into consideration the fact that A, in support of his allegations, has provided the FIFA Administration with a copy of his employment contract with B, which clearly stipulates that he was contractually entitled to receive the aforementioned claimed amounts. In this context, the Chamber took into account that A also provided the FIFA Administration with a copy of the claimed flight tickets, confirming the amount claimed in this regard.
11. In view of all the above, the Chamber underlined that, despite the content of the aforementioned contractual clause, a player's lack of performance cannot and does not constitute just cause for a club

to unilaterally terminate an employment contract, like it happened in the case at hand. In fact, the Chamber deemed that in view of its potestative nature, the aforementioned contractual clause shall not have any effect.

12. After having vehemently rejected the validity of the aforementioned contractual clause, the members of the Chamber reached the conclusion that B has terminated its employment contract with A without just cause.
13. As a consequence of B's unlawful breach of contract, the Chamber considered the latter responsible for the non-fulfilment of its relevant employment contract with A and therefore, liable to pay to A all the amounts that are outstanding under their employment contract until its end, in the total amount of USD 120,000, as well as the amount of EUR 761 (approximately 926), which A paid for the relevant flight tickets.
14. In conclusion, the members of the Chamber decided to accept A's claim and to condemn B to pay to him the total amount of USD 120,926.

III. DECISION OF THE DISPUTE RESOLUTION CHAMBER

1. The claim of A is accepted in its entirety.
2. The Respondent B has to pay the amount of USD 120,926 to the Claimant A.
3. The amount due to A has to be paid by B within 30 days as from the date of notification of the present decision.
4. If the Respondent fails to comply with the above-mentioned deadline, an interest rate of 5% per year will apply and the case will immediately be presented to the FIFA Disciplinary Committee.
5. The Claimant is directed to inform the Respondent immediately of the account number to which the remittance is to be made and to notify the Dispute Resolution Chamber of every payment received.
6. According to art. 60 par. 1 of the FIFA Statutes, this decision may be appealed before the Court of Arbitration for Sport (CAS). The statement of appeal must be sent to the CAS directly within 10 days of receiving notification of this decision and has to contain all elements in accordance with point 2 of the directives issued by the CAS, copy of which we enclose hereto. Within another 10 days following the expiry of the time limit for the filing of the statement of appeal, the appellant shall file with the CAS a brief stating the facts and legal arguments giving rise to the appeal (cf. point 4 of the directives).

23 SEPTEMBER 2005

95168
DECISION OF THE DISPUTE RESOLUTION CHAMBER
passed in Zurich, Switzerland, on 23 September 2005,
in the following composition:
Slim Aloulou (Tunisia), Chairman
Theo van Seggelen (Netherlands), member
Michele Colucci (Italy), member
David Mayebi (Cameroon), member
John Didulica (Australia), member
Philippe Diallo (France), member
Paulo Rogerio Amoretty Souza (Brazil), member
Eissa M. Selah Al-Housaini (U.A.E.), member
Peter Friend (Australia), member
on the claim presented by the club, X as Claimant
against
the club, Y as Respondent
with
the club, Z as Intervening party
regarding the distribution of solidarity contribution in connection with the player, A

I. FACTS OF THE CASE

1. The player, A, was born on 14 September 1979.
2. A was registered as an amateur player with X from 25 March 1991 until 31 March 1995.
3. In the summer registration period of 2003 the player was transferred from Z to Y.
4. According to the corresponding transfer agreement signed between Z and Y on 27 July 2003, Y was obliged to pay to Z EUR 5,000,000 via the bank account indicated by the latter.
5. The player, A, having been registered with X from the age of 12 (on 14 September 1991) until the age of 15,5 (on 31 March 1995), X maintains being entitled to receive from Y 30% of the 5% solidarity payment in accordance with the FIFA Regulations for the Status and Transfer of Players (edition September 2001), i.e. the amount of EUR 75,000.
6. A copy of the player's passport outlining the player's football career at X has been presented by the Football Federation of X.
7. Y asserts having paid 100% of the transfer amount to Z and points out that X should turn to Z in order to collect the amount it claims.
8. The FIFA administration suggested to the parties that Y distributes the relevant proportion relating to the 5% solidarity contribution of the transfer compensation to X and that Z reimburses to Y the same proportion relating to the 5% solidarity contribution of the amount of compensation agreed upon with Y.
9. The parties have not been able to settle the matter in accordance with FIFA's suggestion.
10. Z has intervened in this matter and explains that it does not consider itself obliged to participate in the payment of solidarity contribution in connection with the transfer of the player, A, to Y.
11. Furthermore, Z considers that the transfer amount agreed upon between the clubs serves as the basis for the calculation of the relevant amount payable by the new club and excludes the 5% relating to solidarity mechanism, unless the parties inserted a clause in the agreement indicating that the 5% solidarity mechanism is included in the transfer amount.

II. CONSIDERATIONS OF THE DISPUTE RESOLUTION CHAMBER

1. The present dispute having been lodged in front of the Dispute Resolution Chamber (hereinafter referred to as "DRC" or "Chamber") in October 2004, the members of the DRC firstly proceeded to confirm that the September 2001 edition of the FIFA Regulations for the Status and Transfers of Players (hereinafter referred to as "the Regulations") applies to the case at hand.
2. The DRC commenced its deliberations by referring to art. 25 of the Regulations, according to which it falls within the purview of the Dispute Resolution Chamber to decide upon disputes concerning the distribution of the solidarity contribution. Consequently, the DRC established that it was the competent body to decide on the present litigation concerning the solidarity contribution claimed by X.
3. Once its competence was thus established, the DRC went on to deal with the substance of the case. The members of the Chamber carefully studied the facts outlined above, which show that the player, A, was transferred from Z to Y on a definitive basis in the summer registration period of 2003.
4. To this end, Z and Y signed a transfer agreement in accordance with which Y was obliged to pay to Z a transfer compensation to the amount of EUR 5,000,000.
5. At this point, the Chamber recalled that, as established in article 10 in conjunction with article 11 of the Regulations governing the Application of the Regulations (edition September 2001), the new club to which a player is transferred during the course of an employment contract with his previous club is responsible for the distribution of 5% of the compensation payable to the player's former club to the club(s) involved in the training and education of the player between the ages of 12 and 23.
6. The Chamber took into account that the Respondent, i.e. the player's new club, rejects the claim put forward by X maintaining that X should turn to Z, i.e. the player's former club, in order to obtain its proportion of the 5% solidarity contribution payment, given that Y remitted 100% of the transfer compensation to Z.
7. In this respect, the Chamber once more referred to paragraph 1 of the above-mentioned article 11 of the Regulations governing the Application of the Regulations (edition September 2001) which clearly states that the new club shall pay the amount due as a solidarity contribution to the training clubs.
8. In addition, the members of the Chamber stressed that FIFA circular letter nr. 826 dated 31 October 2002, which deals with the interpretation of the FIFA Regulations for the Status and Transfer of

Players (edition September 2001), elucidates that the 5% solidarity contribution is to be deducted from the amount payable to the player's former club.

9. Furthermore, the deciding body recalled its well established jurisprudence, in accordance with which, in cases like the one at hand, it was established that the player's new club is ordered to remit the 5 % solidarity contribution to the club(s) involved in the player's training in strict application of the said article 11 of the Regulations governing the Application of the Regulations (edition September 2001). At the same time, the player's new club may request the player's former club to reimburse 5 % of the compensation that it received from the player's new club.
10. In light of all the above, the Chamber concluded that on the basis of its jurisprudence and in particular of the strict application of article 11 of the Regulations Governing the Application of the Regulations (edition September 2001) it is the responsibility of the new club, i.e. Y, to pay the relevant proportion of the solidarity contribution to the club(s) involved in the player's training, i.e. X.
11. In addition, taking into account all of the above and, in particular, the aforementioned well-established jurisprudence of the Chamber, the members of the Chamber deemed that the arguments put forward by the intervening party, Z, cannot be accepted.
12. Therefore, Z, having unduly received the amount of money pertaining to solidarity contribution, is to be held liable for the reimbursement to the Respondent of the relevant proportion(s) of the solidarity contribution payable by the Respondent, Y, to the player's former training club(s).

    Having established that the transfer of the player in question was on a definitive basis and that a transfer compensation was agreed upon between the player's former club and new club, the Chamber then turned to the calculation of the relevant proportion due to X on the basis of the period of time that the player was effectively trained by X.
14. The Chamber subsequently referred to art. 10 of the Regulations governing the Application of the Regulations, which provides the figures for the distribution of the solidarity contribution.
15. Considering that the player, A, was registered with X from the age of 12 (on 14 September 1991) until the age of 15,5 (on 31 March 1995) 25% of the 5% solidarity contribution shall be apportioned to this club.
16. Having ascertained that the amount agreed upon by and between the Respondent and Z for the transfer of the player, A, is EUR 5,000,000, 25% of the 5% solidarity contribution amounts to EUR 62,500.
17. Consequently, the Chamber decided that Y is liable to pay the amount of EUR 62,500 as solidarity contribution to X.
18. Furthermore, in line with the above, the intervening party, Z, is liable to reimburse to Y the same amount of EUR 62,500.

III. DECISION OF THE DISPUTE RESOLUTION CHAMBER

1. The claim lodged by the Claimant, X, is partially accepted.
2. The Respondent, Y, has to pay the amount of EUR 62,500 to the Claimant, X, within 30 days as from the date of notification of this decision.
3. The Intervening Party, Z, has to reimburse to the Respondent, Y, the amount of EUR 62,500 within 30 days as from the date of notification of this decision.
4. If the sum of EUR 62,500 is not paid within the aforementioned deadline by Y and/or Z, an interest rate of 5% per year will apply and the matter shall be submitted to the FIFA Disciplinary Committee, so that the necessary disciplinary sanctions may be imposed.
5. The Claimant is directed to inform the Respondent immediately of the account number to which the remittance is to be made and to notify the Dispute Resolution Chamber of every payment received.
6. The Respondent is directed to inform the Intervening Party immediately of the account number to which the reimbursement is to be made and to notify the Dispute Resolution Chamber of every payment received.
7. According to art. 60 par. 1 of the FIFA Statutes, this decision may be appealed against before the Court of Arbitration for Sport (CAS). The statement of appeal must be sent to the CAS directly within 10 days of receipt of notification of this decision and shall contain all the elements in accordance with point 2 of the directives issued by the CAS, a copy of which we enclose hereto. Within another 10 days following the expiry of the time limit for filing the statement of appeal, the appellant shall file a brief stating the facts and legal arguments giving rise to the appeal with the CAS (cf. point 4 of the directives).

95473
DECISION OF THE DISPUTE RESOLUTION CHAMBER
passed in Zurich, Switzerland, on 23 September 2005,
in the following composition:
Slim Aloulou (Tunisia), Chairman
Theo Van Seggelen (Netherlands), member
Michele Colucci (Italy), member
David Mayebi (Cameroon), member
John Didulica (Australia), member
Philippe Diallo (France), member
Paulo Rogerio Amoretty Souza (Brazil), member
Eissa M. Selah Al-Housaini (U.A.E.), member
Peter Friend (Australia), member
on the claim presented by Player L as Claimant
against
Club K as Respondent
regarding a contractual dispute between the parties involved

FACTS OF THE CASE:

- On 1 July 2002, the player, L and K Club signed an employment contract valid until 30 June 2004. The two parties signed an annexe to the contract on the same date, in which the club agreed to pay the player USD 50,000 upon signing, monthly instalments of USD 5,833 from 1/7/02 to 30/6/03 and of USD 10,000 from 1/7/03 to 30/6/04. On 25 July 2003, the parties signed another agreement to the employment contract, stipulating that as from 1/8/03 the player's monthly salary would amount to USD 15,000.
- The player L was born on 8 August 1973.
- On 31 May 2004, the football association A sent FIFA a claim from the player regarding the club K. The player stated that after the holidays in January 2004, the club did not call him back or send him a return ticket to join the team for pre-season training. The player therefore sent the club a telegram on 19 January 2004, requesting it to settle the debt it owed him in the form of salary for September, October, November and December 2003 and to send him a plane ticket from his home to where the team was training. It was not until 18 February 2004 that the club notified him that he would be moved to another team on the R league (X FC) for the pre-season period. The player complied accordingly, paying for his trip himself as a token of his willingness to honour his contract. His transfer on loan to X FC did not materialise after the pre-season period for financial reasons. X FC then apparently told him to return to his country to await a decision and gave him his return fare to the city B of A. The player states that, despite repeated attempts, he did not manage to contact officials at K to clarify the situation and he was therefore obliged to return to A on 11 March 2004, using the plane ticket that X FC had given him.
- The player is claiming payment of his entire salary and bonuses since September 2003 up to the termination of the contract (USD 150,000 as salary and USD 10,500 as prize money for actual appearances in matches). He is also requesting payment of USD 7,620 for incidental expenses, USD 16,800 for fees due to his legal representative and an amount of interest to be decided. TOTAL: USD 184,920.
- When approached by the FIFA administration, the club claimed that it was the player who had broken the contract by not returning from the loan period with X FC. K explained that the player had not accepted the return fare it had reserved for him to return to the team and that he had requested X FC officials to give him his return fare to A. When it noticed his absence in early March, the K club initiated disciplinary proceedings against the player and sent news of this action to the player's residence in R. As a result of the player's breach of contract, the club terminated it on 25 March 2004, backdated to 9 March 2004 (the date on which the player should have returned to the club), in compliance with the R football association's regulations.
- The club admits that it owes L his salary from September 2003 to 9 March 2004, minus tax due under R law, i.e. USD 63,785. The club maintains that this amount is awaiting the player in the national currency in the club's finance department and the player is requested to collect the money personally or send a legal representative officially authorised to collect it on his behalf.

- The player categorically refutes the club's allegations, reiterating that it did not allow him to rejoin the team, and now it was claiming breach of contract. The player points out that further proof of his firm resolve to comply with his contract is that he waited for the deadline to expire before accepting an offer of work from another club. He also maintains that the facts confirm that the K club initiated disciplinary proceedings after the dates shown so as to justify its position to FIFA. Furthermore, he explains that the salary the club used as a basis to calculate the debt owed to him is not the amount stated in the last agreement signed on 25/7/03. Finally, the player requests the club to pay him the amount owed in US dollars, as stipulated in the contract, via FIFA and without deducting any taxes whatsoever, as in the past.
- In October, K club and the player tried to find an amicable solution to the dispute but in vain, as the club offered to pay him the amount of USD 59,812 in 10 monthly instalments, and the player had accepted a reduction in his initial request of USD 184,920 to the final amount of USD 150,000. Given the considerable difference in the amounts proposed by each party, L did not accept the offer from the K club and the FIFA administration continued to investigate the case. The FIFA administration then twice requested K club to comment on the case but in vain. Consequently the case will be submitted to the Dispute Resolution Chamber (DRC) for an official decision on the matter.
- The player is requesting the DRC to demand that the club pay the amount of USD 184,920 in the form of outstanding salary up to the end of the contract, prizes, incidental expenses and fees for his legal representative. The player also requests the DRC to determine the amount of interest owed.
- The club requests the Dispute Resolution Chamber to reject the player's claim and to recognise only the amount of USD 63,785 as the amount owed for outstanding salary.

CONSIDERATIONS OF THE DISPUTE RESOLUTION CHAMBER

The members of the Dispute Resolution Chamber were summoned to pass a decision on this matter by the Chairman pursuant to Art. 1 point 6) of the Rules Governing the Practice and Procedures of the Dispute Resolution Chamber.

The Dispute Resolution Chamber of the FIFA Players' Status Committee shall review disputes coming under its jurisdiction pursuant to Art. 42 of the FIFA Regulations for the Status and Transfer of Players, edition September 2001, (hereinafter: the Regulations) at the request of one of the parties to the dispute.

According to Art. 42 of the Regulations, the triggering elements of the dispute (i.e. whether a contract was breached, with or without just cause, or sporting just cause), will be decided by the Dispute Resolution Chamber of the FIFA Players' Status Committee.

Consequently, the Dispute Resolution Chamber (DRC) is the competent body to decide on the present litigation concerning the alleged breach of contract.

If the employment contract was breached by a party, the Dispute Resolution is responsible to verify whether this party is accountable for compensation and outstanding payments.

Moreover and in accordance with the articles 22 and 23 of the Regulations, the DRC will establish the amount of compensation that it has to be paid by the responsible of the breach and if sporting sanctions would apply or not.

Subsequently, and entering into the substance of the matter, the Chamber began its deliberations by analyzing the allegations of the claimant.

To begin with, the DRC noted that the player L claims the entire salary and bonuses since September 2003 up to the termination of the contract (9 March 2004) based on the contract signed with the respondent on 1 July 2002 and the two annexes. The first annex signed on the same date as the employment contract, i.e. 1 July 2002, and the second one on 25 July 2003. Besides, the player claims incidental expenses, fees due to his legal representative and an amount of interest to be decided.

In this point, the DRC considered appropriate to analyze the amounts claimed by the player L and also the explanations provided by the respondent in this regard.

The Chamber noted that the positions of the parties were in line with each other only in two points i.e. that they signed a valid employment contract and its annex on 1 July 2002 and that the club owes salaries to the player since September 2003.

In this context the members of the Chamber deemed it important to underline that the player and the respondent signed a second annex to the employment contract on 25 July 2003 and that the player provided evidences to the FIFA administration that this document is legally binding between them. Particularly, the Chamber remarked that the most relevant fact is that the player received from the club the payment of two months salaries for an amount of USD 15,000 (in accordance with the annex dated 25/07/03) corresponding to July and August 2003. This fact was not questioned by the respondent and moreover it expressly recognized that it owes salaries to the player L since September 2003.

In continuation, the DRC analyzed the statement of the club regarding the deduction of taxes from the salaries mandatory under the R Law. In this point the player L emphatically refused this statement mainly because he received his salaries since 1 July 2002 until August 2003 (last payment received from K) always in dollars (never in national currency) and without any deduction.

The Chamber remarked that in the employment contract article 3.4 states within the club's obligations, "The Club shall bear other obligations provided for in the present contract, the guidance documents of FIFA , UEFA , the R Football Association and the R Football Premier League, labour legislation of the R Federation".

At this stage the members of the Chamber focused on the statement of the player in which he explained the usual procedure every month to collect his salary from the respondent.

As the claimant stated the usual and common practice during the 13 months that he received his salary and also the bonuses from the club K was that, the foreign players had special treatment by the club since they received the monies "in cash" and in dollars without signing any receipt. The foreign players received the money in the headquarters of the club (where the team usually trains) after that, during the week all of them (L from A, B from C, and three T players G, L and J), together with Mr. S (K's official) went to an office in the centre of the city of U where each foreign player transmitted the relevant amount to their bank accounts. In the case of L he transmitted each month the relevant amount to his bank account in the P Bank of N. Moreover, the player remitted to the FIFA Administration statements of the aforementioned bank account showing evidence of this practice.

In view of the above, the Chamber concluded that the practice developed by the parties during 13 months (i.e. the club paid in cash in dollars without any deduction) and the provisions in the contract in the chapter that establish the club's obligations, give enough evidence that the player received his salary net, directly from the club's officials and in cash.

Therefore the Chamber concluded that the annex signed between the player L and the club K on 25 July 2003 was enforceable between them and that the club owes to the player salaries from September 2003 until 9 March 2004 (date of termination) i.e. 6 months plus 9 days of salaries (USD 15,000 per month) amounting to USD 90,000 plus USD 4356, and without any deduction.

After reaching the aforementioned conclusion the Chamber considered important to focus specifically on the point of the breach of the contract alleged by both parties against each other.

According to the player's statements, the club K is the sole responsible for the breach of the employment contract celebrated between the parties based in particular on the following reasons:

1) after the holidays in January 2004, the club did not call him back or send him a return ticket to join the team for the pre-season training. Consequently the player sent a telegram on 19 January 2004 asking for the ticket to join the team and asking for the relevant outstanding salaries (4 months at that moment);
2) the player paid by himself the flight ticket to join, FC X on loan following the express orders of K;
3) once the period of loan with FC X finished, the respondent did not contact the player and therefore the player returned to A on 11 March 2004 with a flight ticket suddenly provided by the FC X;
4) even though the player wanted to join the respondent's team, K did not provide any clear or concrete instructions to the player in order to do so;
5) he never received a flight ticket from K to go from K (headquarters of the FC X) to U (headquarters of the respondent).

On the other hand, the respondent stated that the player was responsible for the breach of contract based on his behaviour because:

1) the player L did not come back to the respondent's club after he finished his loan period in the FC X;
2) the player had not accepted the return fare that K had reserved for him to return to the team and that he had requested X FC officials to give him his return fare to A;
3) the player was not planning to come back to R.

The Chamber referred to the documents submitted by the parties and in this regard outlined the fact that the legal representative of the player maintained contact with the Vice President of K in several occasions and each time, the legal representative of the player asked to the Vice President of K a flight ticket for the player L to join the team and to fulfil the contract. Moreover, once the team was in S in pre-seasonal training the legal representative of the player offered the Vice President of K to pay the ticket for the claimant in order to join the team. The Vice President of K's answer was "please tell the player, L not to return to the club because he will not be well received either in the first or in the second team, he has to wait".

The Chamber pointed out that there are strong elements that show the good faith of the player, for instance, that he paid the ticket by himself to join FC X (giving evidence of that) ; that he sent a telegram on 19 January 2004 to K, that was never answered by the respondent, asking for 4 months of outstanding salaries and the flight ticket to join the team. Moreover, the Chamber specifically remarked that even though the player L was in A since March 2004 (when he came back from city K), he did not play for any other club because he did not want to breach his contract with K. Once the player stated publicly that his contract with the respondent had expired (30/06/04) he started to play for an A club becoming the captain of the team.

The Chamber noted that the respondent did not provide evidence to its main defence consisting in that the player had not accepted the return fare that K had reserved for him to return to the team and therefore was refusing to come back to join the team and the claimant provided several elements about the opposite.

In addition the Chamber noted that the player provided enough evidence of his willingness to return to U in order to play for K.

Furthermore, the Chamber analyzed the statement of the respondent in which its directives noticed the absence of the player L in early March and as a consequence the K club initiated disciplinary proceedings against the player and notified him in his private address in R. As a result of the player's breach of contract, the club terminated it on 25 March 2004, backdated to 9 March 2004 (the date on which the player should have returned to the club), in compliance with the R football association's regulations.

In this respect, the Chamber deemed that the location where the respondent notified the player L about the decision of its Disciplinary Committee (in its address in R) even though the management of the respondent were aware of the departure of the player from the city K to A is at least contradictory.

An additional important point that the DRC remarked was the way in which the club FC X gave the player the ticket to travel to A. In this respect, the Chamber stated that in cases of loan it is the responsibility of the club where the player is on loan (once the period of loan is finished) to assure that the player return to his club of origin. Therefore, in this specific case it was not clear for the Chamber why the FC X would provide a flight ticket to A instead of to U (R), surprisingly almost immediately upon L's request and without the authorization of the respondent.

At this stage, the Chamber took note of the allegations of the claimant according to which it would have been sufficient for the respondent to show its cooperation with only one positive action from K of this three: a) by sending a flight ticket to the player at the beginning of the season; b) by answering the telegram sent by the player on 19 January 2005 or c) by providing him with a flight ticket to U when he was in the city of K playing for FC X. The player L remarked that the respondent did not comply with one single action of these.

In light of all the above, the Chamber concluded that the club K committed a breach of contract without just cause during the so-called protected period.

Article 21 of the FIFA Regulations foresees that sports sanctions shall be applied and compensation payable, if a contracting party commits a breach of contract without just cause during the protected period of the employment contract.

In compliance with the aforementioned article 21, in particular, with its paragraph 1 (b) the Chamber decided to award financial compensation to the player L.

With respect to the financial compensation to be awarded to the Claimant, the Chamber acknowledged that the Respondent had committed a grave infraction and that his responsibility weighted heavily on the damages being suffered by the player L.

Furthermore, the Chamber wanted to underline that not only the respondent breached the employment contract in the protected period, i.e. in the second year of its validity, but it also claimed damages from the player without having never ever lodged a formal financial complaint with FIFA against the claimant and moreover it never asked for assistance in relation with the alleged breach made by the player.

Article 22 of the FIFA Regulations lists the criteria that are to be taken into account when establishing the compensation for the breach of contract, which are in this particular case the following:

- the club K breached the employment contract when the player was older than 28 years old and before the expiry of the second year of the contract;
- the monthly salary since August 2003 was USD 15,000;

- in the sense of the aforementioned article the Chamber took into consideration that the player L would have had 3 further months remaining on his employment contract with the respondent and
- the date of the termination was 9 March 2004 and the original date of expiry of the contract was 30 June 2004.

The Chamber concluded that under consideration of the referred facts, circumstances and art. 22 of the Regulations the club K is liable to pay the amount of USD 47,178 to the player L for damages suffered by the latter.

With regard to the bonus claimed by the player, the Chamber noted that the amount of USD 10,500 even though it appears from the allegations of the player that was agreed between the parties, the deciding body has not strong evidence how this amount was composed. Particularly, the Chamber mentioned that the player provided the FIFA Administration with a list of matches but without any specification of dates and therefore the DRC considered that this point was not exhaustively proved by the player. As a consequence, the Chamber rejected the claim to this regard.

Concerning the interests claimed by the player L, the Chamber took note that no default interest clause had been included neither in the contract dated 1 July 2002 nor in the two annexes. As a consequence, the deciding body rejected the relevant claim to that regard.

Finally, and referring to its well established jurisprudence, the Chamber did not award any amount as contribution for his legal expenses or another incidental expenses to the player.

The Chamber , in view of the above partially accepted the claim of the player.

At the same time, the counterclaim of K was rejected.

DECISION OF THE DISPUTE RESOLUTION CHAMBER

1. The claim of the player L is partially accepted.
2. The Respondent K has to pay the amount of USD 141,534 to the Claimant.
3. The amount due to the Claimant has to be paid by the Respondent within 30 days as from the date of notification of this decision.
4. In the event that the debt of the Respondent is not paid within the stated deadline an interest rate of 5% per year will apply. Furthermore, the FIFA Administration will be entitled to submit the file to the Disciplinary Committee.
5. The Claimant is directed to inform the Respondent immediately of the account number to which the remittance is to be made and to notify the Dispute Resolution Chamber of every payment received.
6. According to art. 60 par. 1 of the FIFA Statutes this decision may be appealed before the Court of Arbitration for Sport (CAS). The statement of appeal must be sent to the CAS directly within 10 days of receiving notification of this decision and has to contain all elements in accordance with point 2 of the directives issued by the CAS, copy of which we enclose hereto. Within another 10 days following the expiry of the time limit for the filing of the statement of appeal, the appellant shall file with the CAS a brief stating the facts and legal arguments giving rise to the appeal (cf. point 4 of the directives).

⚽⚽⚽

95855

DECISION OF THE DISPUTE RESOLUTION CHAMBER

passed in Zurich, Switzerland, on 23 September 2005,
in the following composition:
Slim Aloulou (Tunisia), Chairman
Theo van Seggelen (Netherlands), member
Michele Colucci (Italy), member
David Mayebi (Cameroon), member
John Didulica (Australia), member (did not participate in the hearing of this dispute)
Philippe Diallo (France), member
Paulo Rogerio Amoretty Souza (Brazil), member
Eissa M. Selah Al-Housaini (U.A.E.), member
Peter Friend (Australia), member
on the claim presented by the player, X as Claimant
against

the club, Y as Respondent and Counter-Claimant
regarding a contractual dispute between the player and the club,

I. FACTS OF THE CASE

1. X was born on 10 July 1977.
2. On 16 August 2002 the parties signed an employment contract valid from 1 July 2002 until 30 June 2007.
3. According to this contract, the player is entitled to receive the following emoluments:
   - Monthly salary: EUR 3,000 converted into …
   - "Reward for preparation and incentive" payable as follows (all amounts converted into …):
   - Total of EUR 60,000 for the preparation: EUR 30,000 until 24 July 2002 & EUR 30,000 until 1 March 2003
   - Total of EUR 100,000 as an incentive:
     - EUR 10,000 until 24 July 2002 (period from 01.07.02 – 30.06.03)
     - EUR 15,000 until 1 July 2003 (period from 01.07.03 – 30.06.04)
     - EUR 20,000 until 1 July 2004 (period from 01.07.04 – 30.06.05)
     - EUR 25,000 until 1 July 2005 (period from 01.07.05 – 30.06.06)
     - EUR 30,000 until 1 July 2006 (period from 01.07.06 – 30.06.07)
   - Various bonuses specified in the contract
4. According to article V.3 if the contract is terminated for any reasons prior to the date of expiry, the player shall only be entitled to that part of the "incentive remuneration" relating to the shorter period of time. Should the club have paid in excess of the amount due to the player, it shall be entitled to reimbursement.
5. In accordance with article XI of the contract, the parties, inter alia, agreed upon the lowest price of the player's "playing right" amounting to EUR 400,000 until 30 January 2004.
6. In July 2004, the player turned to FIFA claiming that the club unilaterally terminated the employment contract without reason on 30 June 2003.
7. In this regard, the player has presented a document dated 16 June 2003 according to which X was released from his duties by the club while the contract was still considered to be valid. This document further indicates that the parties would have a discussion on future developments concerning the contract on 30 June 2003.
8. Another document dated 2 July 2003 was presented by the player in accordance with which the club released the player from his duties until 7 July 2003.
9. In addition, the player submitted a copy of a letter dated 22 July 2003 which was addressed by the club to the player, in accordance with which the contract terminated as of 30 June 2003 pursuant to Art. 79 par. 5 and Art. 8 par. 1 of the Labour Act.
10. The notice of termination further refers to the player's failure to obtain the residence permit as well as a confirmation of tax payments in order for the prolongation of the work permit to be valid, after having been reminded by the club to do so.
11. According to the player, the club failed to remit his salary for the months of April, May, and June 2003 to the total amount of EUR 9,000.
12. Furthermore, the player claims payment of all monies due to him until the expiry date of the contract, i.e., according to the player, the additional amount of EUR 240,000 on the basis of a fix amount of EUR 60,000 per year.
13. Therefore, the player claims payment of the total amount of EUR 249,000.
14. The club, for its part, maintains that it did not unilaterally terminate the contract, but that the contract terminated in terms of law on 30 June 2003.
15. No articles of law have been presented.
16. In fact, according to the club, the player failed to obtain his residence permit as well as a tax payment confirmation due to the fact that he has not taken the necessary action in this regard. The club asserts that it has reminded the player to make the required efforts in order to obtain the said documents in a timely manner.
17. The club stresses that the work permit was arranged for and issued, but that it has not become valid due to the player's omission to make the necessary efforts in order to obtain the above-mentioned documents.
18. In this regard, the club submitted a copy of the decision passed by the legal department of the "job

centre" in the city of Y on 13 June 2003 granting a work permit to X valid from 1 July 2003 until 30 June 2004 stating, inter alia, that such work permit is valid together with a visa and a residence permit and that the work permit does not exempt anybody of obtaining any other permit needed to establish a legal relationship for employment or to perform a job.

19. Y asserts that the player received the notice of termination of the employment contract without any objection and that he registered with another club.
20. The club stresses that it fails to understand the legal ground of the player's claim given that the labour agreement had come to an end due to the player's fault and he was able to sign on with another club for the period following the termination of the contract.
21. Y claims that the player must reimburse to the club the amount of … 2,167,952 that it allegedly paid to the player in excess of his entitlements taking into consideration net and gross salaries and the relevant tax rules.
22. In reply, the player refutes the club's allegations as regards his failure to obtain the necessary permits. He stresses that the club had released him from his duties in accordance with the above-mentioned documents.
23. At a later stage in the proceedings, Y presented a second counter-claim in accordance with which it claims payment of the amount of EUR 400,000 as compensation for the damages that it allegedly suffered due to "defaulting behaviour" of and the subsequent breach of contract by the player. In this regard, the club refers to the above-mentioned article XI of the employment contract regarding the "lowest price for the player's playing right".
24. It furthermore insists that the player reimburses the above-mentioned amount of … 2,167,952 that it allegedly paid to the player in excess of his entitlements.
25. This amount was calculated by the club after a financial audit carried out in December 2004.
26. The club has presented a translation of a document dated 30 December 2002 in accordance with which the player declares that he has no claims against Y. However, Y has failed to present the original version of this document bearing the player's signature.
27. The following calculation relating to the period as from 1 January 2003 until 30 June 2003 has been presented by the club:

Gross salary	4,499,040
Match bonus	100,000
Total gross remuneration	4,609,040
Tax deduction	2,167,952
Net remuneration	2,441,088

25. The club has presented a payment voucher duly signed by the player in accordance with which it paid … 4,758,000 to the player on 30 April 2003.
26. The player having failed to arrange for and obtain the necessary residence permit, the club maintains being obliged to pay the related taxes. Therefore, as stated above, the club claims reimbursement of the amount of … 2,167,952 relating to taxes.
27. In reply to the club's counter-claim, the player has reiterated his claim and he insists that the club has committed a unilateral breach of the employment contract.
28. He furthermore points out that he has always acted as a true professional throughout his career and that he currently is registered with a club in Singapore.
29. In spite of having been requested to do so, the player has failed to provide the FIFA administration with information on his footballing activities as from the termination of the employment contract.

II. CONSIDERATIONS OF THE DISPUTE RESOLUTION CHAMBER

1. The present dispute having been lodged in front of the Dispute Resolution Chamber (hereinafter referred to as "DRC" or "Chamber") in July 2004, the members of the DRC firstly proceeded to confirm that the September 2001 edition of the FIFA Regulations for the Status and Transfers of Players (hereinafter referred to as "the Regulations") applies to the case at hand.
2. As established in Article 42§1(b) of the Regulations, it falls within the competence of the Dispute Resolution Chamber to determine whether one of the parties has committed a unilateral breach of contract without just cause.
3. The Chamber noted that Y protested against the participation of Mr. John Didulica in the hearing of the present dispute. Therefore, Mr. John Didulica withdrew from the hearing and the subsequent decision-taking in the case at hand.

4. Once its competence was thus established, the DRC went on to deal with the substance of the case. The members of the Chamber carefully studied the facts outlined above, which show that only in July 2004 did X lodge the present claim against Y on the basis of facts that occurred in June and July 2003.
5. According to X, the club terminated the employment contract without any valid reasons on 30 June 2003.
6. Y, on the other hand, asserts that it has not rescinded the employment contract, but that the contract merely ended in terms of national law on 30 June 2003, in the light of the fact that X failed to present to the club a valid residence permit and confirmation of tax payments.
7. The Chamber recalled that the club has not presented any relevant articles of law in its support, but the club's assertion in this respect appears to be confirmed by the job centre of the city of Y in its decision dated 13 June 2003 regarding the issuance of the work permit.
8. The members of the Chamber noted that the player, X, refutes the club's allegation with respect to his residence permit. However, it was taken into account that X has not presented any written evidence in support of his defence, in order to show that he has at least attempted to acquire the relevant residence permit.
9. In his defence, the player merely relies on the club's written notifications dated 16 June and 2 July 2003 in accordance with which the club released him from his duties.
10. The Chamber deemed that the club may have released the player from his duties in the light of the fact that the work permit was not yet validated awaiting the residence permit and tax payment confirmation to be provided by the player.
11. On account of the above, the Chamber concurred that the player's claim for breach of contract is to be dismissed.
12. Y, for its part, has lodged a counter-claim against X. Subsequently, the DRC entered into the substance of such counter-claim.
13. Y considers that the player has brought about the early termination of the employment contract due to his "defaulting behaviour", as a result of which Y claims having sustained a loss in the form of "unrealised benefits" to the amount of EUR 400,000 relating to the "playing rights" to the player as indicated in the employment contract.
14. The club has not specified any further its claim in this respect.
15. In addition, referring to the difference between gross and net remuneration, Y considers that it has paid … 2,167,952 in excess of the player's financial entitlements covering the period as from 1 January 2003 until 30 June 2003. Consequently, the club maintains that the player shall reimburse this amount to the club.
16. The Chamber first turned to the club's claim for compensation.
17. The financial loss that the club asserts having sustained appears to based on article XI of the employment contract, that sets forth the price of the player's "playing rights".
18. In this regard, the DRC deemed that such article was inserted into the contract to indicate the amount payable to Y by the player's potential new club for the acquisition of the player's services.
19. The Chamber agreed that such article cannot be considered binding on the player or even on the player's potential new club that is no party to the relevant contract between the player and the club.
20. Therefore, any compensation payable for the acquisition of X's services would have been subject to negotiation between the player's potential new club and Y. Consequently, the Chamber concurred that the club has no legal ground for its claim for compensation to the amount EUR 400,000, which is merely based on speculation.
21. In conclusion, the Chamber established that Y has failed to present documentary evidence in support of its assertion that it has sustained a financial loss to the amount of EUR 400,000.
22. As regards the claim for reimbursement of the amount of … 2,167,952 that Y maintains having paid in excess of the player's financial entitlements for the period as of 1 January 2003 until 30 June 2003, the Chamber closely examined the calculation presented by Y as well as the payment voucher that was presented by Y.
23. The Chamber noticed that in accordance with the payment voucher dated 30 April 2003, which refers to an advance payment, the amount of … 4,758,000 was remitted to the player.
24. The employment contract does not stipulate whether the player's financial entitlements are payable net or gross. On the basis of the calculation presented by the club, the Chamber noticed that the club deducted approximately 46% in order to arrive at net amounts.

25. However, Y has failed to produce any written evidence showing, firstly, that taxes were to be deducted from the amounts payable to the player and, secondly, that 46% would be the applicable rate.
26. Consequently, the Chamber concurred that the club's counter-claim is not substantiated and, therefore, must be rejected.
27. In this context, the Chamber recalled that according to the player his salary for the months of April, May and June 2003, amounting to the total sum of EUR 9,000, remains unpaid. X has not included the payment of EUR 30,000 that fell due on 1 March 2003 in his claim. Therefore, the Chamber departed from the assumption that this amount was duly received by the player.
28. In accordance with the relevant employment contract, the player was entitled to receive a monthly salary of EUR 3,000. Therefore, for the period as from 1 January 2003 until 30 June 2003, X was entitled to receive salaries to the amount of EUR 18,000. This Euro amount approximately represents 4,450,890 ....
29. As established above, on 30 April 2003, X received ... 4,758,000 from Y as an advance payment, which amount appears to include a match bonus to the amount of ... 110,000 in accordance the calculation presented by the club.
30. On account of the above, the Chamber concluded that X has fully received his salary for the period as from 1 January 2003 until 30 June 2003 and that, therefore, the player's claim for payment of his salary for the months of April, May, and June 2003 must be rejected.

III. DECISION OF THE DISPUTE RESOLUTION CHAMBER

1. The claim of the Claimant, X, is rejected.
2. The counter-claim of Y is rejected.
3. According to art. 60 par. 1 of the FIFA Statutes, this decision may be appealed against before the Court of Arbitration for Sport (CAS). The statement of appeal must be sent to the CAS directly within 10 days of receipt of notification of this decision and shall contain all the elements in accordance with point 2 of the directives issued by the CAS, a copy of which we enclose hereto. Within another 10 days following the expiry of the time limit for filing the statement of appeal, the appellant shall file a brief stating the facts and legal arguments giving rise to the appeal with the CAS (cf. point 4 of the directives).

24 OCTOBER 2005

105874

DÉCISION DE LA CHAMBRE DE RÉSOLUTION DES LITIGES

ayant siégé le 24 octobre 2005, à Zurich, Suisse
dans la composition suivante:
Slim Aloulou (Tunisie), Président
Theo Van Seggelen (Pays-Bas), membre
Mario Gallavotti (Italie), membre
au sujet d'une plainte soumise par le Joueur X, ci-après, le demandeur et le Club Z, ci-après, la partie intervenante à l'encontre du Club Y, ci-après, le défendeur
concernant un litige contractuel survenu entre le demandeur et le défendeur.

I. EN FAIT

1. En date du 9 février 2004, le demandeur, né le 30 septembre 1985, a signé un contrat de travail avec le défendeur. Ce contrat entrait en vigueur rétroactivement le 1er janvier 2004 et finalisait le 31 décembre 2004. Ce contrat de travail prévoyait une rémunération brute de environ EUR 3,200 au taux de change.
2. Les 3, 6, et 9 janvier 2005, selon un document transmis par l'Association du club défendeur en date du 1er septembre 2005, le joueur en question a pris part à 3 matches officiels avec le club défendeur.
3. Le 10 février 2005, le demandeur a disputé un matche avec le club défendeur contre un club tiers dans le cadre d'un championnat continental.

4. Le 8 mars 2005, le défendeur déclare le joueur en « rébellion » et ce en application du Statut du Joueur de Football national, qui est une convention collective.
5. Le 14 mars 2005, le demandeur a réclamé les salaires du 1er février au 8 mars 2005 par l'intervention d'un notaire et ils se sont rendus auprès de l'Association du défendeur tout d'abord. Le même jour et suite au nom dépôt des créances dues auprès de l'Association., le joueur ainsi que le notaire se sont rendus au syndicat des joueurs de football professionnels afin de notifier cet état de fait.
6. Les 16 et 17 mars 2005, le club défendeur envoie deux lettres adressées au syndicat. Dans ces lettres, le club défendeur informe le syndicat susmentionné qu'il a payé le mois de janvier 2005 au joueur en question et que comme ce dernier n'a pas signé de nouveau contrat, le paiement du mois de février 2005 est encore à l'étude et il requière un arbitrage du syndicat à ce sujet.
7. De mars à juin 2005, le demandeur s'entraîne seul ou avec un entraîneur personnel, selon un certificat du syndicat daté du 2 septembre 2005, qui mentionne que dès le 9 mars 2005, le joueur s'est vu interdire de s'entraîner avec le reste de l'équipe ainsi que d'utiliser les installations du club.
8. Le 8 juin 2005, selon la confirmation transmise le 1er septembre 2005 par l'Association du défendeur, le demandeur réclame une seconde fois, son salaire du mois de mars 2005 à ladite Association.
9. En date du 19 juillet 2005, le demandeur a signé un contrat de travail de durée déterminée en qualité de joueur professionnel avec le Club Z. Ce contrat prenait effet au 1er juillet 2005 et arrive à terme à la fin de la saison 2008/2009.
10. Le 4 août 2005, la Fédération à laquelle appartient la partie intervenante s'est adressée à la FIFA afin d'obtenir son assistance dans la délivrance du Certificat International de Transfert du joueur en question et ce en raison du refus de l'Association à laquelle appartient le défendeur de délivrer ledit certificat.
11. Le 18 août 2005, le Juge Unique de la Commission du Statut du Joueur a émis une décision autorisant l'enregistrement provisoire du joueur par la Fédération de la partie intervenante en faveur de son club affilié Z.
12. Les 18 et 26 août 2005, selon la communication datée du 29 septembre 2005 émise par l'Association du club défendeur et transmise par le demandeur, le défendeur dépose les sommes des salaires des mois de février et mars 2005 du demandeur, ainsi qu'une somme correspondant au 14 jours d'une grève de l'année 2004 auprès de l'Association du défendeur. Finalement, le 31 août 2005, le défendeur dépose auprès de l'Association l'augmentation concernant l'indice des prix à la consommation pour le salaire de janvier 2005 du demandeur.
13. Le 1er septembre 2005, le Juge Unique de la Commission du Statut du Joueur a émis une décision incidente à la demande en reconsidération déposée par le défendeur le 31 août 2005, décision qui suspendait avec effet immédiat l'autorisation d'enregistrement provisoire du joueur et ce au vu des nouveaux éléments présentés.
14. En date du 23 septembre 2005, le Juge Unique de la Commission du Statut du Joueur a rendu une décision en reconsidération concernant l'enregistrement provisoire du demandeur. Cette décision refusait à la Fédération de la partie intervenante, pour son club affilié, le droit de procéder à l'enregistrement provisoire du demandeur, dans l'attente d'une décision concernant le litige contractuel entre le joueur et le défendeur.
15. Par fax daté du 28 septembre 2005, et pour donner suite à la décision en reconsidération susmentionnée, la FIFA a transmis aux parties une notification dans laquelle il était mentionné que le litige opposant le demandeur au défendeur serait soumis pour décision quant au litige contractuel, à la prochaine séance de la Chambre de Résolution des Litiges, le 24 octobre 2005. Il était également imparti au demandeur, ainsi qu'à la partie intervenante, un délai de 5 jours ouvrables afin de déposer auprès de la Chambre une requête formelle complète et précise pour le premier, respectivement sa position pour la partie intervenante.
16. Le 3 octobre 2005, le demandeur, a transmis la requête concernant cette affaire. Dans ce mémoire le joueur mentionne, dans l'exposé des faits, que le contrat liant le joueur au défendeur, à son article 4 prévoyait que si le club participait en janvier 2005 à une compétition officielle, ce contrat serait prorogé jusqu'au 31 janvier 2005 et que par conséquent ceci s'est produit étant donné que la compétition officielle de l'année 2004 a été retardée en raison d'une grève qui s'est produite entre juin et juillet 2004. Cet article 4 du contrat de travail dispose textuellement que le joueur accepte si non que le contrat se prolonge jusqu'au 31 janvier suivant, si l'institution participe a un tournoi officiel qui se joue en ce moment. Dans cette requête, le demandeur annexe également deux certificats du syndicat des joueurs. Ces certificats, datés du 2 et 5 septembre 2005, affirment que les matches joués par le

défendeur dans la Ligue entre le 3 janvier et le 19 janvier 2005 correspondaient à la saison 2004 et que ce retard était dû à une grève des joueurs professionnels, grève survenue entre le 24 juin et le 13 août 2004. De plus, les certificats mentionnent littéralement que les matches joués par le demandeur en février 2005 contre un club tiers ont été joués avec un contrat enregistré en 2004. Au vu de ces éléments, le demandeur met donc en avant le fait qu'il était contractuellement libre car le fait qu'il ait disputé des matches après décembre 2004 ne signifie pas qu'il a accepté le renouvellement de son contrat et qu'il ne s'agit en fait que du report des engagements courants jusqu'au 31 décembre 2004 et que par conséquent, les sommes versées en janvier 2005 correspondaient à la période de report et ce en application de l'article 4 du contrat de travail.

17. Dans sa requête, le demandeur affirme qu'entre février et début mars 2005, il a participé à des matches avec le défendeur car il croyait que des négociations allaient aboutir à la signature d'un nouveau contrat et que par la suite dû à l'échec de ces négociations il a été déclaré en « rébellion » par le défendeur.

18. L'article 37 du Statut du Joueur de Football national, article qui règlemente le mécanisme de la rébellion, mentionne textuellement que le joueur qui se nie à contracter selon ce qui est dit dans ce Statut ou qui se nie à accomplir avec ses obligations sera lié au club si ce dernier le déclare en rébellion et si le club a respecté les préceptes réglementaires. Ainsi le joueur restera lié au club tant que ce club le maintiendra en « rébellion ». De plus cet article dispose que durant le lapse de temps pendant lequel le joueur sera déclaré en rébellion, le club sera relevée de toutes ses obligations contractuelles.

19. En outre, et pour contesté le bien fondé de cet état de « rébellion » qui lui a été appliqué par le défendeur, le demandeur met en avant que, le 14 mars 2005, lors de sa réclamation de salaire, constatée par acte notarié, devant, selon ses dires le club défendeur, les salaires n'ont pas été payés par le club ce qui selon le demandeur ne permet pas d'instaurer le mécanisme de « rébellion » prévu dans le Statut susmentionné.

20. En effet, le joueur affirme que pour instaurer ce mécanisme le club devait être au courant de ses obligations réglementaires, ce qui n'est pas le cas selon lui, car l'obligation de paiement des salaires dues jusqu'à la déclaration de rébellion, le 8 mars 2005, n'était pas remplie en ce qui concernait le versement des salaires de février et mars 2005.

21. En effet, le demandeur argumente que ce n'est que quand l'enregistrement provisoire a été autorisé, le 18 août 2005, que le club défendeur a déposé les sommes réclamées par le joueur auprès de l'Association, ce qui selon le joueur signifie que le club n'avait pas remplis ses obligations de paiement des salaires jusqu'à la déclaration de rébellion et qu'ainsi la rébellion a été déclarée sans base juridique, donc en contradiction avec l'article 37 du Statut susmentionné, et que par conséquent ladite « rébellion » était nulle. Il annexe un document de l'Association du défendeur daté du 29 septembre 2005, qui mentionne que les dépôts des sommes dues par le club, auprès de l'Association ont été accomplis à partir du 18 août 2005.

22. Le joueur fait une constatation concernant le Statut du Joueur de Football national et plus particulièrement concernant la prolongation unilatérale des contrats par un club. Il mentionne que les contrats liant les joueurs au défendeur sont des contrats de durée déterminée et qu'ils ne peuvent être prolongés de façon unilatérale que par le club lui-même et ceci selon le Statut susmentionné, sans que les joueurs puissent s'y opposer. Par conséquent, il insiste sur le fait que de telles dispositions statutaires constituent des atteintes à des principes du droit tels que la Liberté contractuelle et la Liberté du travail et ce sans aucune justification, en prévoyant simplement une augmentation salariale correspondant à l'augmentation de l'indice des prix de l'année antérieure.

23. L'article 18 du Statut du Joueur de Football national, un des articles qui réglemente l'augmentation automatique du salaire des joueurs ainsi que la prorogation unilatérale, prévoit d'une part qu'à partir de chaque mois de janvier suivant la date de souscription du contrat, le salaire du joueur sera automatiquement augmenté selon la variation de l'indice des prix à la consommation. D'autre part, cet article mentionne que les joueurs avec un contrat arrivé à terme et qui ont fêté leur 24ème anniversaire la saison antérieur devront tout de suite après conclure un contrat avec leur club pour 2 ans. Il mentionne également que remplis le contrat ou après la fin de la rébellion, le joueur sera libre mais que cependant le club pourra retenir le joueur de façon unilatérale et automatique, une saison de plus en augmentant la masse salariale de 1,5 par rapport à l'augmentation de l'indice des prix. Cet article mentionne aussi que la finalisation des contrats des joueurs de moins de 24 ans n'est pas une cause de déliement envers le club.

24. L'article 19 du même Statut ne fait que mentionner que le club peut renoncer à cette augmentation automatique salariale et dispose que les clubs pourront renoncer à l'augmentation automatique prévue à l'article précédent via communication à l'Association et le joueur sera ainsi considéré libre.
25. Par conséquent et au vu des éléments susmentionnés, le demandeur insiste sur le fait que la FIFA en s'appuyant sur l'article 25 alinéa 6 du Règlement de la FIFA concernant le Statut et le Transfert des Joueurs, ne doit pas tenir compte ni des clauses des contrats de travail ni de la Réglementation du Statut du Joueur de Football national susmentionnée.
26. En second lieu et subsidiairement, le demandeur fait remarquer que même en admettant que le droit contractuel et statutaire s'applique, il devait quand même être considéré comme libre car tout contrat de travail ainsi que sa reconduction exige la forme écrite et ce en application du Règlement de la FIFA susmentionné.
27. De plus, le demandeur insiste sur le fait qu'il aurait pu se considérer comme contractuellement libre en imputant au défendeur la rupture du contrat car ce dernier se trouvait en demeure dans le versement des salaires déjà réclamés une première fois en mars 2005, comme l'indique l'acte notarié cité plus haut, et une deuxième fois le 8 juin 2005 pour le demandeur. Cette dernière réclamation ressort également du document transmis par l'Association et daté du 1er septembre 2005 cité plus haut.
28. Concernant le dépôt par le club défendeur, auprès de l'Association, des sommes réclamées, le joueur mentionne que l'Association, dans le document daté du 1er septembre 2005, voulait faire croire que les salaires avaient été mis à la disposition de ladite Association, par le club défendeur le 27 juillet 2005. Le joueur maintient donc que ceci est faux et contredit un autre document de l'Association daté du 29 septembre 2005 qui mentionne que les dates de dépôt des salaires et primes ont été accomplis par le club défendeur les 18, 26 et 31 août 2005.
29. Concernant le dépôt des salaires, le demandeur met également en avant un article de journal dont la date n'est pas mentionnée mais que ce dernier affirme être du 17 mars 2005. Le joueur mentionne que dans cet article, le Président du club défendeur annonçait que certaines primes de contrat du demandeur étaient disponibles au club et ce depuis le 8 mars 2005. Ainsi, le demandeur conteste ce fait car le 14 mars 2005 par l'intermédiaire d'un notaire, il s'est rendu, selon lui, au club défendeur pour réclamer les sommes dues et ces dernières n'y étaient pas.
30. Par conséquent le demandeur maintient que pendant le mois de février et mars 2005, il a tenté de faire aboutir des négociations avec le club défendeur et a même joué un matche au mois de février 2005 avec ce club. Finalement aucun accord n'est intervenu et donc le club n'a pas utilisé l'option de l'article 18 susmentionné qui était de retenir le joueur pour une saison de plus, par prorogation unilatérale du contrat, mais a opté pour la « rébellion » car selon les dire du demandeur le club voulait un contrat de plus longue durée et non une simple prolongation et ainsi pouvoir faire pression sur le joueur.
31. Finalement, le joueur mentionne comme argumentation que même si, contrairement à ce qu'il affirme antérieurement, un contrat de travail avait existé au mois de février et jusqu'au 8 mars 2005, celui-ci serait basé sur le Statut du Joueur de Football national, donc sur l'option unilatérale de proroger par le défendeur le contrat antérieur. Mais si cela était ainsi alors pourquoi avoir déclaré le joueur en « rébellion », ce qui, selon le demandeur, ne peut se faire que si un joueur ne veut pas contracter selon ce qui est prévu dans le Statut susmentionné.
32. Le demandeur demande à la Chambre de Résolution des Litiges :
    - qu'il soit établis l'inexistence d'un lien contractuel liant le demandeur au défendeur ;
    - qu'il puisse être enregistré par la Fédération à laquelle appartient la partie intervenante en faveur de cette dernière;
    - d'établir la somme de l'indemnité qui est due au demandeur en raison des conséquences économiques et sportives subies par celui-ci en raison du refus de l'enregistrement provisoire.
33. Par fax daté du 5 octobre 2005, la Fédération de la partie intervenante a transmis la position de son club affilié, partie intervenante à la présente procédure, au sujet du litige en question.
34. La partie intervenante signale en premier lieu que ces observations font suite au mémoire déjà déposé le 12 septembre 2005. Mentionnons que les points mis en avant par le club dans ce mémoire se retrouvent dans le mémoire du demandeur.
35. Dans sa position et en premier lieu, la partie intervenante mentionne, tout comme l'a fait le joueur auparavant, que la reconduction automatique et unilatérale du contrat du joueur par le club défendeur

est une atteinte grave au principe de la Liberté contractuelle et au principe de la Liberté du travail et que l'article 20 du Statut du Joueur de Football national n'indique pas la durée de reconduction d'office du contrat ce qui serait contraire à la Réglementation de la FIFA. De plus, il affirme que le défendeur lie l'article 20 à l'article 15 du Statut susmentionné, lequel ne crée qu'une possibilité de conclure un contrat pour deux ans, sans autre précision.

36. Au vu du paragraphe susmentionné, il est à préciser que l'article 15 du Statut du Joueur de Football national dispose que les contrats conclus entre un joueur et un club pourront se prolonger jusqu'au deuxième 31 décembre de la date de la finalisation du contrat et que par la suite le joueur sera libre. L'article 20 du même Statut parle de prorogation automatique et dispose que dans les cas où les clubs ne communiquent pas le renoncement aux prorogations désirées, comme prévu à l'article 19, dans les délais, comme ceci est précisé à l'article 18, alors le contrat sera considéré comme automatiquement prolongé.

37. D'autre part la partie intervenante ajoute que si le demandeur a joué au mois de février s'était en vue d'une négociation d'un nouveau contrat qui n'a pas aboutis.

38. La partie intervenante argumente également contre la validité du mécanisme de la « rébellion » du Statut du Joueur de Football national susmentionné qui empêche un joueur de s'entraîner avec le club et d'exercer sa profession tant que le litige n'est pas résolu et qui de plus, libère le club de toute obligation, notamment celle du versement du salaire. Il affirme donc que ce mécanisme porte atteinte aux principes du droit mentionnés plus haut, et que par conséquent ces faits constituent une rupture du contrat par le défendeur.

39. Finalement, la partie intervenante affirme sa bonne foi et insiste surtout sur le fait qu'il n'a nullement incité le joueur à rompre le contrat car il croyait que ledit joueur était libre de tout engagement contractuel précédent. En effet il affirme que le joueur s'est présenté comme étant libre et qu'il a vérifié son ancien contrat auparavant. Il affirme également que le fait que le joueur soit libre est mentionné dans le contrat de travail que ce dernier a signé avec la partie intervenante.

40. La partie intervenante demande :
   – que soit délivré à titre définitif le Certificat International de Transfert permettant à sa Fédération d'enregistrer le joueur ;
   – que le défendeur soit condamné à lui rembourser tous les frais engagés dans cette procédure.

41. Par fax daté du 11 octobre 2005, le défendeur a transmis sa position concernant le litige en question.

42. En premier lieu, le défendeur mentionne que le contrat, signés par le joueur avec ce club, finalisait le 31 décembre 2004 mais, en janvier 2005, ce contrat, en application du Statut du Joueur de Football national, convention collective et texte de droit public non modifiable par les parties, s'est prorogé automatiquement et ce jusqu'au 31 décembre 2006. Cette prorogation automatique prévoyait une augmentation salariale correspondant à la variation de l'indice des prix à la consommation de l'année 2004.

43. Dans sa position, le défendeur insiste sur le fait que ce Statut du Joueur de Football national susmentionné est une convention collective, adoptée grâce et suite aux insistances du propre syndicat des joueurs, qui reconnaît lui-même, dans une lettre annexée, la validité dudit Statut. Le défendeur affirme de plus que cette convention collective est une règle de droit public et impérative et ceci en conformité avec la loi nationale sur les licences annuelles ainsi que la loi sur l'activité sportive. Ces lois en effet élève au rang de droit impératif les normes qui règlemente l'activité sportive rémunérée, selon lecture desdites lois.

44. Par la suite le défendeur détaille les articles dudit Statut qui ont été appliqués dans le cas présent. En effet, selon ses dires, les contrats qui arrivent à leur terme contractuel se prolongent automatiquement pour deux ans (art. 15 et 20 du Statut), en augmentant les salaires selon la variation de l'indice des prix à la consommation (art. 18), à moins que le club renonce à cette prorogation (art. 19). Le club ajoute qu'à l'échéance des deux ans de prorogation le joueur est libre. Cet état de droit est confirmé par une note transmise par l'Association du défendeur et datée du 21 septembre 2005.

45. L'article 15 dudit Statut dispose textuellement que les contrats souscrits pourront se proroger jusqu'au deuxième 31 décembre suivant la date de leur validité. A la fin de cette prorogation le joueur sera libre. Concernant le texte des articles 18 et 19, il est renvoyé à la partie concernant la requête déposée par le joueur. L'article 20 mentionne quant à lui que en cas de ne pas accomplir les communications prévues précédemment (donc les communications prévues dans les articles précédents), le contrat sera considéré automatiquement prorogé avec l'augmentation (salariale) prévue à l'article 18.

46. Le défendeur mentionne également qu'il n'y a pas eu violation à l'obligation de forme écrite du contrat car cette prorogation automatique reposait sur un contrat de travail écrit signé en 2004.
47. Le défendeur mentionne que depuis août 2004, l'agent du joueur négociait avec le club défendeur l'acquisition des droits fédératifs du demandeur et ce jusqu'en juillet 2005. Le club annexe des articles de journaux, certains non datés qui détaillent cette négociation et son échec.
48. Le défendeur ne contredit pas le fait que le joueur ait été déclaré en « rébellion » le 8 mars 2005, il annexe la notification y relative adressée à l'Association en question. Il mentionne que cette sanction a été appliquée en raison du non respect du Statut du Joueur de Football national susmentionné. Le club précise que le joueur n'a jamais recouru contre cette décision de « rébellion », alors que cette possibilité lui était offerte selon l'article 27 du Statut susmentionné.
49. Concernant la réclamation du demandeur de son salaire de mars 2005, effectuée le 8 juin 2005 à travers le syndicat, le défendeur annexe une lettre datée du 15 juin 2005 dans laquelle en réponse à la réclamation il affirme et répète que cet argent se trouve à la trésorerie du club. De plus, le club mentionne qu'après cette lettre, le joueur n'est quand même pas venus recouvrer l'argent et que donc le club a dû déposer cette somme auprès de l'Association. A ce jour, la somme s'y trouve toujours selon confirmation de ladite Association datée du 7 octobre 2005.
50. Concernant cette fois la reconnaissance par le demandeur lui-même, le défendeur affirme que le joueur a reconnu, pendant l'année 2005, de façon tacite et expresse la validité du contrat écrit et que par conséquent il a accepté la reconduite automatique de ce dernier. En effet, il appuie son argumentation en se basant sur les matches joués par le joueur en 2005 pour le compte du club défendeur.
51. Le défendeur affirme ainsi que le joueur a acquiescé à la reconduite du contrat sans la nier, ni accomplir des actes qui démontreraient sa négation à cette reconduite. Ainsi, comme l'annonce le défendeur, pour que des joueurs puissent participer à des matches officiels, ils doivent être sous contrat de travail. Il annexe un document de son Association, daté du 21 septembre 2005, qui mentionne que des joueurs ne peuvent participer à un championnat continental sans contrat de travail valable et en vigueur. Cette précision par l'Association vient du fait que le défendeur avait communiqué à ladite Association la liste des joueurs qui participeraient à cette compétition, liste dans laquelle figuraient le demandeur. Cette liste a elle-même été communiquée à la Confédération du continent en question.
52. De plus, le défendeur insiste sur le fait que si le joueur désire être libre après la déclaration de « rébellion », selon une demande accomplie par le joueur au syndicat en juillet 2005, en raison du non accomplissement par le club de ses obligations salariales, comme ceci est précisé dans un article de journal de juillet 2005, publié sur Internet, ceci démontrerait que le joueur se considérait lié par un contrat après 2004.
53. A l'argument selon lequel la « rébellion » était nulle en raison du retard dans les salaires de février et mars 2005, le défendeur maintient que ceci est faux en raison du fait que l'échéance pour le paiement du mois de février 2005 était le 10 mars 2005, en application de l'article 23 du Statut du Joueur de Football national, donc après la déclaration de « rébellion » prononcée le 8 mars 2005, et que par conséquent le défendeur n'avait aucune obligation pendante au moment de ladite « rébellion ». Il est important de mentionner que les salaires correspondant à un mois peuvent être payés par le club jusqu'au 10 du mois suivant. Ce fait est confirmé par le document de l'Association daté du 21 septembre 2005. Concernant les salaires, le club affirme la mauvaises fois du joueur, en mentionnant que le 14 mars 2005, il s'est rendu à l'Association afin de réclamer ces salaires alors que ces derniers ont toujours été versés au sein des installations du club. Le défendeur annexe des quittances anciennes signées par le joueur, mais ces dernières ne mentionnent nullement le lieu du paiement.
54. Concernant les certificats transmis les 2 et 5 septembre 2005 par le syndicat, dont il est fait mention dans la partie consacrée à la requête du joueur, le défendeur fait référence au document transmis par l'Association, le 21 septembre 2005, et ayant pour but de rectifier ces certificats. En effet, conformément à ce qu'affirmait le syndicat comme quoi les matches de février 2005 joués par le joueur l'avaient été en fonction d'un contrat enregistré en 2004, l'Association précise qu'au mois de février 2005 le joueur avait un contrat en vigueur pour 2005.
55. A titre subsidiaire, le défendeur met en doute l'authenticité des certificats des 2 et 5 septembre 2005 susmentionnés émis par le syndicat des joueurs et annexés par le joueur à la présente procédure et ceci en raison du fait que sur le sommet des pages figure la mention de la société de l'agent du joueur.

56. Le défendeur présente également une demande reconventionnelle et mentionne qu'étant donné que le contrat avec son club est en vigueur jusqu'en décembre 2006 et que le joueur a signé un nouveau contrat avec la partie intervenante, le demandeur a ainsi signé plus d'un contrat pour la même période. Ce qui rentre selon lui sous l'application de l'article 18 alinéa 5 du Règlement concernant le Statut et le Transfert des Joueurs.
57. Par conséquent, le défendeur demande une indemnisation de la part du joueur et affirme que la partie intervenante doit être solidairement responsable du paiement de cette indemnisation. De plus, le défendeur exige des sanctions sportives à l'égard de la partie intervenante qui aurait incité à une rupture de contrat. En effet le club défendeur affirme que la partie intervenante a contacté le joueur directement ou par l'intermédiaire de son agent et ensuite a signé le contrat, le tout sans avoir au préalable ni consulté ni pris contact avec le défendeur, ni avec l'Association de ce dernier. Pour étayer ce point le défendeur précise que la partie intervenante n'a jamais répondu à une lettre envoyée par le défendeur le prévenant de cette situation et datée du 20 juillet 2005.
58. Ainsi, concernant le demandeur, le défendeur tient en compte que ce dernier n'a que 20 ans et note qu'avec le contrat le liant à la partie intervenante, ce club aurait dû versé le salaire de USD 5,856,000 durant la durée du contrat.
59. Par conséquent le défendeur réclame une indemnisation de USD 5,500,000 pour rupture du contrat par le demandeur.
60. Le défendeur réclame une indemnisation au titre de pertes patrimoniales et tort moral en raison d'une perte au niveau sportif du club, perte qui lui a oté la possibilité d'engendrer des bénéfices dû en cas de réussite. Il réclame également une indemnisation au titre de perte patrimoniale et tort moral en raison de la nuisance à l'image sportive ainsi qu'une indemnité pour tort moral en raison du tort fait à l'image du club défendeur. Finalement, le défendeur demande également une indemnisation englobant tous les frais engendrés dans la présente procédure et la procédure concernant l'enregistrement provisoire. En conclusion, au titre de ces indemnisations additionnelles, le défendeur réclame la somme de USD 2,750,000 de la part du demandeur.
61. Par conséquent le défendeur réclame :
    - que l'enregistrement du joueur ne soit pas autorisé et ce jusqu'au paiement de l'indemnité réclamée ;
    - USD 8,250,000 au titre d'indemnisation par le demandeur ;
    - que la partie intervenante soit considérée comme solidairement responsable de l'indemnité à payer par le joueur ;
    - des sanctions sportives à l'encontre de la partie intervenante.

II. CONSIDÉRATIONS DE LA CHAMBRE DE RÉSOLUTION DES LITIGES

1. En premier lieu, la Chambre de Résolution des Litiges établit que sur la base de l'article 22 lit. a et de l'article 24 alinéa 1 du Règlement concernant le Statut et le Transfert des Joueurs (édition 2005), sa compétence à traiter ce cas et à rendre une décision formelle concernant ce litige contractuel opposant le demandeur au défendeur est donnée.
2. La Chambre de Résolution des Litiges prend note du fait que le contrat de travail liant le joueur au club défendeur était un contrat de travail écrit de durée déterminée, signé le 9 février 2004, qui aurait dû arriver à échéance le 31 décembre 2004 avec une option unilatérale en faveur du club de proroger cette durée. Cette option est basée sur le Statut du Joueur de Football national.
3. En premier lieu la Chambre note que l'article 15 du Statut du Joueur de Football national dispose, au conditionnel, que, à la finalisation des contrats de travail, ces derniers pourront s'étendre jusqu'au deuxième 31 décembre suivant leur finalisation. La Chambre souligne le caractère conditionnel de cette clause et l'interprétation littérale qui en ressort permettant de conclure qu'un consentement mutuel est nécessaire à la reconduction du contrat initial pour deux ans.
4. Cependant la Chambre constate qu'en application des articles 18, 19 et 20 du Statut susmentionné, les contrats peuvent uniquement être prorogés de façon unilatérale et automatique par le club et ce en prévoyant une simple augmentation salariale conforme à la variation de l'indice des prix à la consommation. Il est pris note du fait que cette combinaison des articles susmentionnés peut permettre au club de retenir le joueur de façon unilatérale et ce jusqu'à ses 27 ans.
5. En effet, la Chambre fait ressortir le caractère strictement unilatéral des articles 18 et 19 du Statut susmentionné dans le sens que cet article 18 oblige le joueur de 24 ans, dont le contrat serait arrivé à échéance, à conclure un nouveau contrat d'une durée de deux ans, simplement en prévoyant une

augmentation salariale basée sur la variation de l'indice des prix à la consommation. De plus à l'échéance de ce nouveau contrat, le club possède l'option unilatérale de proroger pour une année supplémentaire ledit contrat de travail.

6. En outre, l'article 18 du Statut du Joueur de Football national mentionne également que la finalisation des contrats des joueurs de moins de 24 ans n'est pas une cause de déliement envers le club.

7. Par la suite, la Chambre fait ressortir le caractère unilatéral d'une telle clause en se basant sur l'article 19 du Statut susmentionné, qui dispose que le club uniquement pourra renoncer à la reconduction du contrat et ce via notification d'un préavis. Il est également tenu compte de l'article 20 dudit Statut qui reconduit de façon automatique et unilatérale les contrats de travail si le club ne fait pas recours à ce préavis.

8. Par conséquent la Chambre établit que de telles clauses sont tout à fait potestatives et rendent donc impossible une quelconque application de l'article 15 du Statut du Joueur de Football national. Il s'ensuit que la Chambre de Résolution des Litiges note que de telles clauses autorisant une reconduction unilatérale du contrat par le club, constituent des clauses abusives et contraires aux principes de la Liberté contractuelle et de la Liberté du travail, principes juridiques reconnus par le Droit International Public et surtout contraires également à l'article 13 du Règlement de la FIFA concernant le Statut et le Transfert des Joueurs (édition 2005) qui dispose qu'à l'échéance contractuelle prévue d'un commun accord, le contrat est considéré comme ne déployant plus d'effets et le joueur sera considéré libre de tout engagement.

9. De plus, la Chambre fait également référence à la jurisprudence du Tribunal Arbitral du Sport et plus particulièrement à la décision rendue le 27 août 2004 dans la procédure opposant AJ Auxerre à Valencia CF et M. Mohamed Lamine Sissoko. Dans cette décision à son considérant 47, la Formation a écarté l'application d'une Charte du Football Professionnel en vigueur en France en considérant que de telles chartes sont de portée nationale et ne sauraient prétendre déployer leurs effets dans un autre état et qu'il appartient par conséquent à la Chambre de tenir compte ou non de tous les arrangements, lois et/ou accords de conventions collectives pertinents existant au niveau national. Ce conformément à l'article 25 alinéa 6 du Règlement concernant le Statut et le Transfert des Joueurs (édition 2005).

10. Par conséquent et au vu des éléments susmentionnés, la Chambre établis qu'elle ne peut pas tenir compte du Statut du Joueur de Football national en relation avec l'extension unilatérale d'un contrat de travail et que ce dernier ne saurait déployer ses effets dans une situation comportant des éléments d'extranéité.

11. La Chambre de Résolution des Litiges conclut également que les 3 matches joués par le demandeur en janvier 2005, entrent sous l'application du contrat de travail de février 2004 et plus particulièrement de son article 4. En effet, sur la base des éléments présentés lors la présente procédure, il ressort que les matches joués en janvier 2005 l'ont été en raison d'une grève survenue en 2004 et que par conséquent ces matches correspondent à la saison 2004.

12. La Chambre note par la même que le matche joué en février 2005 par le demandeur en question, n'a nullement constitué une reconduction tacite du contrat de travail de février 2004 et ne saurait par conséquent être considéré comme une relation contractuelle de fait faisant suite au précédent contrat. En effet, la Chambre conclut que le matche joué en février 2005, entrait dans la phase négociatrice que le joueur avait entamé dans le but de conclure un nouveau contrat de travail et ne constituait pas une quelconque intentionnalité de la part du joueur d'accepter tacitement un nouveau contrat de travail. La Chambre appuie cet élément sur le fait que le joueur n'a participé que jusqu'au 10 février 2005 aux rencontres avec le club défendeur, et ne voyant pas ces négociations aboutir il a cessé de disputer d'autres matches. Dans ce sens, la Chambre cite sa jurisprudence établie lors d'une décision n°55161 rendue le 13 mai 2005, concernant un litige contractuel, dans laquelle cet organe décisionnel a établis que le fait pour un joueur de participer aux activités du club après l'échéance contractuellement prévue n'implique nullement une acceptation tacite de la part du joueur à la reconduction du contrat, si ce dernier a participé auxdites activités de bonne foie dans le but de démontrer ces bonnes intentions dans le cadre d'une négociation d'un nouveau contrat.

13. A titre subsidiaire, la Chambre doit aussi noter que même en considérant une très hypothétique relation contractuelle de fait liant le joueur au club après le 31 janvier 2005, ce lien contractuel aurait pris fin et ceci en application de l'article 41 du Statut du Joueur de Football national. Cet article dispose que les salaires seront payés dans les 10 jours suivants l'échéance mensuelle et dans le cas où le salaire ne serait pas versé dans ce délai, le joueur pourra se présenter à l'Association afin de

réclamer lesdites créances. Cet article mentionne également que le joueur aura la possibilité de se départir du contrat si 90 jours se sont écoulés dès la réclamation auprès de l'Association et si les salaires n'y sont toujours pas déposés.

14. En effet, la Chambre constate que la première réclamation de la part du demandeur auprès de l'Association a eu lieu le 14 mars 2005 et que les créances dues n'ont été déposées par le club qu'à partir du 18 août 2005 auprès de l'Association, donc après 90 jours à partir de la première réclamation. La Chambre conclut donc que même en prenant en considération l'existence d'une relation contractuelle à partir de février 2005, celle-ci aurait pris fin le 13 juin 2005 et ce en application de l'article 41 susmentionné. Ce joueur a fait communication de son choix de se départir du contrat en signant le nouveau contrat avec la partie intervenante le 19 juillet 2005.
15. Pour le bon ordre, à cet égard, la Chambre a estimé approprié de rappeler que en continuité avec l'article 2 alinéa 2 du Règlement concernant le Statut et le Transfert des Joueurs (édition 2005), une relation contractuelle entre un joueur et un club doit être toujours basée sur un contrat écrit.
16. La Chambre de Résolution des Litiges prend également note du fait que le mécanisme de la « rébellion », tel qu'il est prévu à l'article 37 du Statut du Joueur de Football national, et notifié au joueur le 8 mars 2005, constitue une atteinte grave au principe de la Liberté personnelle du joueur ainsi qu'au principe de la Liberté contractuelle et contrevient à toutes normes reconnues du droit du travail.
17. En effet, l'organe décisionnel constate que ce mécanisme de la « rébellion » prive le joueur de toute rémunération, de toute participation aux activités du club et de plus enferme ce dernier dans une situation juridique le liant au club de façon impérative et l'empêchant ainsi d'exercer une activité lucrative, principe fondamental reconnu par le Droit International Public.
18. La Chambre constate également que contrairement à ce qu'affirme le défendeur, ce mécanisme de la « rébellion » tel qu'il a été notifié le 8 mars 2005, ne saurait empêcher le club défendeur de se conformer au paiement des salaires contractuellement prévus et échus au moment de ladite notification. Ce mécanisme permet de suspendre le paiement des salaires futurs et non des salaires échus. En effet, comme le dispose l'article 41 et l'article 23 du Statut du Joueur de Football susmentionné, les créances salariales dues aux joueurs peuvent être payées jusqu'au 10ème jour suivant le mois échu. La Chambre insiste sur l'interprétation littérale qu'il convient de donner à cet article et mentionne que d'aucune manière on ne saurait interpréter lesdits articles d'une manière contraire à la bonne foi devant être observée dans le droit des contrats.
19. Ainsi, selon la Chambre, cette application des articles 41 et 23 susmentionnés ne peut permettre au club de suspendre ledit paiement par l'utilisation du mécanisme de la « rébellion » deux jours avant l'échéance mentionnée et ce uniquement dans le but d'éviter le paiement des salaires dus au joueur pour le mois de février et mars 2005, en raison de l'échec des négociations pour la conclusion d'un nouveau contrat de travail. Ceci constitue aux yeux de la Chambre une atteinte à la bonne foie devant être observée dans le droit contractuel.
20. La Chambre constate également que le paiement des salaires susmentionnés a été effectué par le club défendeur le 18 août 2005 auprès de l'Association, donc le même jour auquel le Juge Unique de la Commission du Statut du Joueur a rendu sa première décision autorisant l'enregistrement provisoire du joueur en question, ce qui selon la Chambre dénote une attitude contradictoire de la part du défendeur, étant donné que comme l'affirme cette institution le mécanisme de la « rébellion » suspend toutes les obligations du club et démontre ainsi un comportement contraire au principe de la bonne foi généralement reconnu en droit contractuel.
21. La Chambre de Résolution des Litiges met également en avant le fait que la notion de droits fédératifs d'un joueur, tel que le mentionne le défendeur, n'est plus d'actualité mais a laissé place, avec l'entrée en vigueur du Règlement FIFA concernant le Statut et le Transfert des Joueurs (édition 2001), à la règle mentionnant qu'un contrat entre un joueur professionnel et un club finalise à l'échéance prévue contractuellement ou d'un commun accord, ce qui laisse le joueur libre de tout engagement après cette finalisation (cf. article 13 du Règlement FIFA concernant le Statut et le Transfert des Joueurs, édition 2005).
22. Par conséquent et au vu des éléments susmentionnés, la Chambre de Résolution des Litiges a admis partiellement la demande présentée par le demandeur et a décidé qu'il n'existe aucun lien contractuel liant le joueur au défendeur et que par conséquent le joueur est autorisé à jouer pour la partie intervenante et la Fédération de ce dernier est autorisée a procéder à l'enregistrement du demandeur pour son club affilié. Il s'ensuit que le présent organe rejette dans sa totalité la demande

reconventionnelle présentée par le défendeur et établis que ce dernier serait éventuellement simplement titulaire d'un droit à une indemnité de formation pour ce joueur, droit qui cependant doit faire l'objet d'une demande séparée.

23. La Chambre de Résolution des Litiges rejette la demande financière présentée par le demandeur en raison du caractère international des relations contractuelles dans le domaine footballistique et plus particulièrement en raison de la complexité juridique connue et admise par le joueur que peuvent engendrer des relations contractuelles entre parties soumises à différents ordres juridiques.
24. Sur la base de l'article 15 alinéa 3 du Règlement de la Commission du Statut du Joueur et de la Chambre de Résolution des Litiges (édition 2005), lequel dispose que les procédures devant la Chambre ne donnent lieu à aucune indemnité de procédure, la Chambre rejette la même demande d'indemnisation présentée par la partie intervenante, pour le remboursement des frais encourus.

III. DÉCISION DE LA CHAMBRE DE RÉSOLUTION DES LITIGES

1. La demande du demandeur est partiellement admise.
2. L'existence d'une relation contractuelle entre le demandeur et le défendeur est rejetée.
3. La Fédération à laquelle appartient la partie intervenante est autorisée à enregistrer le joueur en question pour son club affilié.
4. Aucune indemnité n'est accordée au demandeur.
5. La demande reconventionnelle présentée par le défendeur est rejetée dans sa totalité.
6. Selon l'article 60 alinéa 1 des Statuts de la FIFA, cette décision peut faire l'objet d'un appel devant le Tribunal Arbitral du Sport (TAS). La déclaration d'appel doit être soumise directement au TAS dans les dix jours après notification de cette décision et doit contenir tous les éléments conformément au point 2 des directives émises par le TAS, dont copie est annexée. Dans les dix jours suivant l'expiration du délai d'appel, l'appelant doit soumettre au TAS un mémoire contenant une description des faits et des moyens de droit fondant l'appel (cf. point 4 des directives).

105874(2)
DÉCISION DE LA CHAMBRE DE RÉSOLUTION DES LITIGES
ayant siégé le 24 octobre 2005, à Zurich, Suisse
dans la composition suivante:
Slim Aloulou (Tunisie), Président
Theo Van Seggelen (Pays-Bas), membre
Mario Gallavotti (Italie), membre
au sujet d'une plainte soumise par le
Joueur X, ci-après, le demandeur
et le Club Z, ci-après, la partie intervenante
à l'encontre du Club Y, ci-après, le défendeur
concernant un litige contractuel survenu entre le demandeur et le défendeur.

I. EN FAIT

1. En date du 5 février 2004, le demandeur, né le 10 mai 1980, a signé un contrat de travail avec le défendeur. Ce contrat entrait en vigueur rétroactivement le 1er janvier 2004 et finalisait le 31 décembre 2004. Ce contrat de travail prévoyait une rémunération brute de environ EUR 3,530 au taux de change.
2. Les 3, 6, 12, 16 et 19 janvier 2005, selon un document transmis par l'Association du club défendeur en date du 1er septembre 2005, le demandeur a pris part à 5 matches officiels avec le club défendeur.
3. Les 3 et 10 février 2005, le demandeur a disputé deux matches avec le club défendeur contre un club tiers dans le cadre d'un championnat continental.
4. Le 8 mars 2005, le défendeur déclare le demandeur en « rébellion » et ce en application du Statut du Joueur de Football national, qui est une convention collective.
5. Le 14 mars 2005, le demandeur a réclamé les salaires du 1er février au 8 mars 2005 par l'intervention d'un notaire et ils se sont rendus auprès de l'Association du club défendeur (ci-après l'Association) tout d'abord. Le même jour et suite au nom dépôt des créances dues auprès de l'Association, le demandeur ainsi que le notaire se sont rendus au syndicat des joueurs de football professionnels afin de notifier cet état de fait.

6. Les 16 et 17 mars 2005, le défendeur envoie deux lettres adressées au syndicat susmentionné. Dans ces lettres, le défendeur informe le syndicat susmentionné qu'il a payé le mois de janvier 2005 au demandeur et que comme ce dernier n'a pas signé de nouveau contrat, le paiement du mois de février 2005 est encore à l'étude et il requière un arbitrage du syndicat à ce sujet.
7. De mars à juin 2005, le demandeur s'entraîne seul ou avec un entraîneur personnel, selon un certificat du syndicat daté du 2 septembre 2005, qui mentionne que dès le 9 mars 2005, le demandeur s'est vu interdire de s'entraîner avec le reste de l'équipe ainsi que d'utiliser les installations du club.
8. En date du 19 juillet 2005, le demandeur a signé un contrat de travail de durée déterminée en qualité de joueur professionnel avec la partie intervenante. Ce contrat prenait effet au 1er juillet 2005 et arrive à terme à la fin de la saison 2008/2009.
9. Le 26 juillet 2005, selon la confirmation transmise par l'Association du défendeur en date du 1er septembre 2005, le demandeur réclame une seconde fois son salaire du mois de mars 2005 à l'Association susmentionnée.
10. Le 4 août 2005, la Fédération à laquelle appartient la partie intervenante s'est adressée à la FIFA afin d'obtenir son assistance dans la délivrance du Certificat International de Transfert du demandeur et ce en raison du refus de l'Association à laquelle appartient le défendeur de délivrer ledit certificat.
11. Le 18 août 2005, le Juge Unique de la Commission du Statut du Joueur a émis une décision autorisant l'enregistrement provisoire du demandeur par la Fédération de la partie intervenante en faveur de son club affilié.
12. Les 18 et 26 août 2005, selon la communication datée du 29 septembre 2005 émise par l'Association du défendeur et transmise par le demandeur, le défendeur dépose les sommes des salaires du mois de février 2005 du demandeur, ainsi qu'une somme correspondant au 14 jours d'une grève de l'année 2004 auprès de ladite Association. Finalement, le 31 août 2005, le défendeur dépose auprès de l'Association le salaire du mois de mars 2005 du demandeur ainsi que l'augmentation concernant l'indice des prix à la consommation pour le salaire de janvier 2005 du demandeur.
13. Le 1er septembre 2005, le Juge Unique de la Commission du Statut du Joueur a émis une décision incidente à la demande en reconsidération déposée par le défendeur le 31 août 2005, décision qui suspendait avec effet immédiat l'autorisation d'enregistrement provisoire du demandeur et ce au vu des nouveaux éléments présentés.
14. En date du 23 septembre 2005, le Juge Unique de la Commission du Statut du Joueur a rendu une décision en reconsidération concernant l'enregistrement provisoire du demandeur. Cette décision refusait à la Fédération de la partie intervenante, pour son club affilié, le droit de procéder à l'enregistrement provisoire du demandeur, dans l'attente d'une décision concernant le litige contractuel entre le demandeur et le défendeur.
15. Par fax daté du 28 septembre 2005, et pour donner suite à la décision en reconsidération susmentionnée, la FIFA a transmis aux parties une notification dans laquelle il était mentionné que le litige opposant le demandeur au défendeur serait soumis pour décision quant au litige contractuel, à la prochaine séance de la Chambre de Résolution des Litiges, le 24 octobre 2005. Il était également imparti au demandeur, ainsi qu'à la partie intervenante, un délai de 5 jours ouvrables afin de déposer auprès de la Chambre une requête formelle complète et précise pour le premier, respectivement sa position pour la partie intervenante.
16. Le 3 octobre 2005, le demandeur, a transmis la requête concernant cette affaire. Dans ce mémoire le demandeur mentionne, dans l'exposé des faits, que le contrat liant le demandeur au défendeur, à son article 4 prévoyait que si le club participait en janvier 2005 à une compétition officielle, ce contrat serait prorogé jusqu'au 31 janvier 2005 et que par conséquent ceci s'est produit étant donné que la compétition officielle de l'année 2004 a été retardée en raison d'une grève qui s'est produite entre juin et juillet 2004. Cet article 4 du contrat de travail dispose textuellement que le joueur accepte si non que le contrat se prolonge jusqu'au 31 janvier suivant, si l'institution participe a un tournoi officiel qui se joue en ce moment. Dans cette requête, le demandeur annexe également deux certificats du syndicat des joueurs. Ces certificats, datés du 2 et 5 septembre 2005, affirment que les matches joués par le défendeur dans la Ligue entre le 3 janvier et le 19 janvier 2005 correspondaient à la saison 2004 et que ce retard était dû à une grève des joueurs professionnels, grève survenue entre le 24 juin et le 13 août 2004. De plus, les certificats mentionnent littéralement que les matches joués par le joueur en février 2005 contre un club tiers dans le cadre d'un championnat continental ont été joués avec un contrat enregistré en 2004. Au vu de ces éléments, le demandeur met donc en avant le fait qu'il était contractuellement libre car le fait qu'il ait disputé des matches après décembre 2004

ne signifie pas qu'il a accepté le renouvellement de son contrat et qu'il ne s'agit en fait que du report des engagements courants jusqu'au 31 décembre 2004 et que par conséquent, les sommes versées en janvier 2005 correspondaient à la période de report et ce en application de l'article 4 du contrat de travail.

17. Dans sa requête, le demandeur affirme qu'entre février et début mars 2005, il a participé à des matches avec le défendeur car il croyait que des négociations allaient aboutir à la signature d'un nouveau contrat et que par la suite dû à l'échec de ces négociations il a été déclaré en « rébellion » par le défendeur.

18. L'article 37 du Statut du Joueur de Football national, article qui règlemente le mécanisme de la rébellion, mentionne textuellement que le joueur qui se nie à contracter selon ce qui est dit dans ce Statut ou qui se nie à accomplir avec ses obligations sera lié au club si ce dernier le déclare en rébellion et si le club a respecté les préceptes réglementaires. Ainsi le joueur restera lié au club tant que ce club le maintiendra en « rébellion ». De plus cet article dispose que durant le lapse de temps pendant lequel le joueur sera déclaré en rébellion, le club sera relevée de toutes ses obligations contractuelles.

19. En outre, et pour contesté le bien fondé de cet état de « rébellion » qui lui a été appliqué par le défendeur, le demandeur met en avant que, le 14 mars 2005, lors de sa réclamation de salaire, constatée par acte notarié, devant, selon ses dires le club défendeur, les salaires n'ont pas été payés par le défendeur ce qui selon le demandeur ne permet pas d'instaurer le mécanisme de « rébellion » prévu dans le Statut du Joueur de Football national susmentionné. En effet, il affirme que pour instaurer ce mécanisme le défendeur devait être au courant de ses obligations réglementaires, ce qui n'est pas le cas selon lui, car l'obligation de paiement des salaires dues jusqu'à la déclaration de rébellion, le 8 mars 2005, n'était pas remplie en ce qui concernait le versement des salaires de février et mars 2005.

20. En effet, le demandeur argumente que ce n'est que quand l'enregistrement provisoire a été autorisé, le 18 août 2005, que le club défendeur a déposé les sommes réclamées par le joueur auprès de l'Association du club défendeur, ce qui selon le joueur signifie que le défendeur n'avait pas remplis ses obligations de paiement des salaires jusqu'à la déclaration de rébellion et qu'ainsi la rébellion a été déclarée sans base juridique, donc en contradiction avec l'article 37 du Statut susmentionné, et que par conséquent ladite « rébellion » était nulle. Il annexe un document de l'Association daté du 29 septembre 2005, qui mentionne que les dépôts des sommes dues par le défendeur, auprès de l'Association ont été accomplis à partir du 18 août 2005.

21. Le joueur fait une constatation concernant le Statut du Joueur de Football national et plus particulièrement concernant la prolongation unilatérale des contrats par un club. Il mentionne que les contrats liant les joueurs au club sont des contrats de durée déterminée et qu'ils ne peuvent être prolongés de façon unilatérale que par le club lui-même et ceci selon le Statut susmentionné, sans que les joueurs puissent s'y opposer. Par conséquent, il insiste sur le fait que de telles dispositions statutaires constituent des atteintes à des principes du droit tels que la Liberté contractuelle et la Liberté du travail et ce sans aucune justification, en prévoyant simplement une augmentation salariale correspondant à l'augmentation de l'indice des prix de l'année antérieure.

22. L'article 18 du Statut du Joueur de Football national, un des articles qui réglemente l'augmentation automatique du salaire des joueurs ainsi que la prorogation unilatérale, prévoit d'une part qu'à partir de chaque mois de janvier suivant la date de souscription du contrat, le salaire du joueur sera automatiquement augmenté selon la variation de l'indice des prix à la consommation. D'autre part, cet article mentionne que les joueurs avec un contrat arrivé à terme et qui ont fêté leur 24ème anniversaire la saison antérieur devront tout de suite après conclure un contrat avec leur club pour 2 ans. Il mentionne également que remplis le contrat ou après la fin de la rébellion, le joueur sera libre mais que cependant le club pourra retenir le joueur de façon unilatérale et automatique, une saison de plus en augmentant la masse salariale de 1,5 par rapport à l'augmentation de l'indice des prix. Cet article mentionne aussi que la finalisation des contrats des joueurs de moins de 24 ans n'est pas une cause de déliement envers le club.

23. L'article 19 du même Statut ne fait que mentionner que le club peut renoncer à cette augmentation automatique salariale et dispose que les clubs pourront renoncer à l'augmentation automatique prévue à l'article précédent via communication à l'Association et le joueur sera ainsi considéré libre.

24. Par conséquent et au vu des éléments susmentionnés, le demandeur insiste sur le fait que la FIFA en s'appuyant sur l'article 25 alinéa 6 du Règlement de la FIFA concernant le Statut et le Transfert des Joueurs, ne doit pas tenir compte ni des clauses des contrats de travail ni de la Réglementation du Statut du Joueur de Football national susmentionnée.
25. En second lieu et subsidiairement, le demandeur fait remarquer que même en admettant que le droit contractuel et statutaire susmentionné s'applique, il devait quand même être considéré comme libre car tout contrat de travail ainsi que sa reconduction exige la forme écrite et ce en application du Règlement de la FIFA susmentionné.
26. De plus, le demandeur insiste sur le fait qu'il aurait pu se considérer comme contractuellement libre en imputant au défendeur la rupture du contrat car ce dernier se trouvait en demeure dans le versement des salaires déjà réclamés une première fois en mars 2005, comme l'indique l'acte notarié cité plus haut, et une deuxième fois le 26 juillet 2005 pour le demandeur. Cette dernière réclamation ressort également du document transmis par l'Association et daté du 1er septembre 2005 cité plus haut et annexé au présent dossier.
27. Concernant le dépôt par le club défendeur, auprès de son Association, des sommes réclamées, le demandeur mentionne que ladite Association, dans le document daté du 1er septembre 2005, voulait faire croire que les salaires avaient été mis à la disposition de ladite Association, par le défendeur le 27 juillet 2005. Le demandeur maintient donc que ceci est faux et contredit un autre document de l'Association daté du 29 septembre 2005 qui mentionne que les dates de dépôt des salaires et primes ont été accomplis par le club défendeur les 18, 26 et 31 août 2005.
28. Par conséquent le demandeur maintient que pendant le mois de février et mars 2005, il a tenté de faire aboutir des négociations avec le défendeur et a même joué deux matches au mois de février 2005 avec ce club. Finalement aucun accord n'est intervenu et donc le défendeur n'a pas utilisé l'option de l'article 18 susmentionné qui était de retenir le joueur pour une saison de plus, par prorogation unilatérale du contrat, mais a opté pour la « rébellion » car selon les dire du demandeur le défendeur voulait un contrat de plus longue durée et non une simple prolongation et ainsi pouvoir faire pression sur le joueur.
29. Finalement, le demandeur mentionne comme argumentation que même si, contrairement à ce qu'il affirme antérieurement, un contrat de travail avait existé au mois de février et jusqu'au 8 mars 2005, celui-ci serait basé sur le Statut du Joueur de Football national, donc sur l'option unilatérale de proroger par le défendeur le contrat antérieur. Mais si cela était ainsi alors pourquoi avoir déclaré le joueur en « rébellion », ce qui, selon le demandeur, ne peut se faire que si un joueur ne veut pas contracter selon ce qui est prévu dans le Statut susmentionné.
30. Le demandeur demande à la Chambre de Résolution des Litiges :
    - qu'il soit établis l'inexistence d'un lien contractuel liant le demandeur au défendeur ;
    - qu'il puisse être enregistré par la Fédération de la partie intervenante au profit de son club affilié ;
    - d'établir la somme de l'indemnité qui est due au demandeur en raison des conséquences économiques et sportives subies par celui-ci en raison du refus de l'enregistrement provisoire.
31. Par fax daté du 5 octobre 2005, la Fédération à laquelle appartient la partie intervenante a transmis la position de la partie intervenante à la présente procédure, au sujet du litige en question.
32. La partie intervenante signale en premier lieu que ces observations font suite au mémoire déjà déposé le 12 septembre 2005. Mentionnons que les points mis en avant par le club dans ce mémoire se retrouvent dans le mémoire du demandeur.
33. Dans sa position et en premier lieu, la partie intervenante mentionne, tout comme l'a fait le demandeur auparavant, que la reconduction automatique et unilatérale du contrat du joueur par le défendeur est une atteinte grave au principe de la Liberté contractuelle et au principe de la Liberté du travail et que l'article 20 du Statut du Joueur de Football national n'indique pas la durée de reconduction d'office du contrat ce qui serait contraire à la Réglementation de la FIFA. De plus, il affirme que le défendeur lie l'article 20 à l'article 15 du Statut susmentionné, lequel ne crée qu'une possibilité de conclure un contrat pour deux ans, sans autre précision.
34. Au vu du paragraphe susmentionné, il est à préciser que l'article 15 du Statut du Joueur de Football national dispose que les contrats conclus entre un joueur et un club pourront se prolonger jusqu'au deuxième 31 décembre de la date de la finalisation du contrat et que par la suite le joueur sera libre. L'article 20 du même Statut parle de prorogation automatique et dispose que dans les cas où les clubs ne communiquent pas le renoncement aux prorogations désirées, comme prévu à l'article 19, dans les

délais, comme ceci est précisé à l'article 18, alors le contrat sera considéré comme automatiquement prolongé.

35. D'autre part la partie intervenante ajoute que si le demandeur a joué au mois de février s'était en vue d'une négociation d'un nouveau contrat qui n'a pas aboutis.
36. La partie intervenante argumente également contre la validité du mécanisme de la « rébellion » du Statut du Joueur de Football national qui empêche un joueur de s'entraîner avec le club et d'exercer sa profession tant que le litige n'est pas résolu et qui de plus, libère le club de toute obligation, notamment celle du versement du salaire. Il affirme donc que ce mécanisme porte atteinte aux principes du droit mentionnés plus haut, et que par conséquent ces faits constituent une rupture du contrat par le défendeur.
37. Finalement, la partie intervenante affirme sa bonne foi et insiste surtout sur le fait qu'il n'a nullement incité le joueur à rompre le contrat car il croyait que ledit joueur était libre de tout engagement contractuel précédent. En effet il affirme que le demandeur s'est présenté comme étant libre et que la partie intervenante a vérifié son contrat auparavant. Il affirme également que le fait que le demandeur soit libre est mentionné dans le contrat de travail que ce dernier a signé avec la partie intervenante.
38. La partie intervenante demande :
    - que soit délivré à titre définitif le Certificat International de Transfert permettant à sa Fédération d'enregistrer le demandeur ;
    - que le défendeur soit condamné à lui rembourser tous les frais engagés dans cette procédure.
39. Par fax daté du 11 octobre 2005, le défendeur a transmis sa position concernant le litige en question.
40. En premier lieu, le défendeur mentionne que le contrat, signés par le demandeur avec le défendeur, finalisait le 31 décembre 2004 mais, en janvier 2005, ce contrat, en application du Statut du Joueur de Football national, convention collective et texte de droit public non modifiable par les parties, s'est prorogé automatiquement et ce jusqu'au 31 décembre 2006. Cette prorogation automatique prévoyait une augmentation salariale correspondant à la variation de l'indice des prix à la consommation de l'année 2004.
41. Dans sa position, le défendeur insiste sur le fait que ce Statut du Joueur de Football national est une convention collective, adoptée grâce et suite aux insistances du propre syndicat des joueurs, qui reconnaît lui-même, dans une lettre annexée, la validité dudit Statut. Le défendeur affirme de plus que cette convention collective est une règle de droit public et impérative et ceci en conformité avec la loi nationale sur les licences annuelles ainsi que la loi sur l'activité sportive. Ces lois en effet élève au rang de droit impératif les normes qui règlemente l'activité sportive rémunérée, selon lecture desdites lois.
42. Par la suite le défendeur détaille les articles dudit Statut qui ont été appliqués dans le cas présent. En effet, selon ses dires, les contrats qui arrivent à leur terme contractuel se prolongent automatiquement pour deux ans (art. 15 et 20 du Statut), en augmentant les salaires selon la variation de l'indice des prix à la consommation (art. 18), à moins que le club renonce à cette prorogation (art. 19). Le club ajoute qu'à l'échéance des deux ans de prorogation le joueur est libre. Cet état de droit est confirmé par une note transmise par l'Association du club défendeur et datée du 21 septembre 2005.
43. L'article 15 dudit Statut dispose textuellement que les contrats souscrits pourront se proroger jusqu'au deuxième 31 décembre suivant la date de leur validité. A la fin de cette prorogation le joueur sera libre. Concernant le texte des articles 18 et 19, il est renvoyé à la partie concernant la requête déposée par le demandeur. L'article 20 mentionne quant à lui que en cas de ne pas accomplir les communications prévues précédemment (donc les communications prévues dans les articles précédents), le contrat sera considéré automatiquement prorogé avec l'augmentation (salariale) prévue à l'article 18.
44. Le défendeur mentionne également qu'il n'y a pas eu violation à l'obligation de forme écrite du contrat car cette prorogation automatique reposait sur un contrat de travail écrit signé en 2004.
45. Le défendeur mentionne que depuis août 2004, l'agent du joueur négociait avec le club défendeur l'acquisition des droits fédératifs du demandeur et ce jusqu'en juillet 2005. Le défendeur annexe des articles de journaux, certains non datés qui détaillent cette négociation et son échec.
46. Le club ne contredit pas le fait que le demandeur ait été déclaré en « rébellion » le 8 mars 2005, il annexe la notification y relative adressée à l'Association. Il mentionne que cette sanction a été appliquée en raison du non respect du Statut du Joueur de Football national susmentionné. Le club précise que le joueur n'a jamais recouru contre cette décision de « rébellion », alors que cette possibilité lui était offerte selon l'article 27 dudit Statut.

47. Concernant la réclamation du demandeur de son salaire de mars 2005, effectuée le 26 juillet 2005 à travers le syndicat, le défendeur annexe une lettre datée du 27 juillet 2005 dans laquelle en réponse à la réclamation il affirme et répète que cet argent se trouve à la trésorerie du club. De plus, le club mentionne qu'après cette lettre, le demandeur n'est quand même pas venus recouvrer l'argent et que donc le club a dû déposer cette somme auprès de l'Association. A ce jour, la somme s'y trouve toujours selon confirmation de l'Association datée du 7 octobre 2005.
48. Concernant cette fois la reconnaissance par le demandeur lui-même, le défendeur affirme que le joueur a reconnu, pendant l'année 2005, de façon tacite et expresse la validité du contrat écrit et que par conséquent il a accepté la reconduite automatique de ce dernier. En effet, il appuie son argumentation en se basant sur les matches joués par le joueur en 2005 pour le compte du club défendeur. Il s'ensuit qu'ainsi le joueur a acquiescé à la reconduite du contrat sans la nier, ni accomplir des actes qui démontreraient sa négation à cette reconduite. Ainsi, comme l'annonce le défendeur, pour que des joueurs puissent participer à des matches officiels, ils doivent être sous contrat de travail. Il annexe un document de l'Association, daté du 21 septembre 2005, qui mentionne que des joueurs ne peuvent participer à un championnat continental sans contrat de travail valable et en vigueur. Cette précision par l'Association vient du fait que le défendeur avait communiqué à l'Association la liste des joueurs qui participeraient à cette compétition, liste dans laquelle figuraient le joueur en question. Cette liste a elle-même été communiquée à la Confédération du continent en question.
49. De plus, le défendeur insiste sur le fait que si le joueur désire être libre après la déclaration de « rébellion », selon une demande accomplie par le demandeur au syndicat en juillet 2005, en raison du non accomplissement par le club de ses obligations salariales, comme ceci est précisé dans un article de journal de juillet 2005, publié sur Internet, ceci démontrerait que le joueur se considérait lié par un contrat après 2004.
50. A l'argument selon lequel la « rébellion » était nulle en raison du retard dans les salaires de février et mars 2005, le défendeur maintient que ceci est faux en raison du fait que l'échéance pour le paiement du mois de février 2005 était le 10 mars 2005, en application de l'article 23 du Statut du Joueur de Football national, donc après la déclaration de « rébellion » prononcée le 8 mars 2005, et que par conséquent le club n'avait aucune obligation pendante au moment de ladite « rébellion ». Il est important de mentionner que les salaires correspondant à un mois peuvent être payés par le club jusqu'au 10 du mois suivant. Ce fait est confirmé par le document de l'Association daté du 21 septembre 2005. Concernant les salaires, le club affirme la mauvaises fois du joueur, en mentionnant que le 14 mars 2005, il s'est rendu à l'Association afin de réclamer ces salaires alors que ces derniers ont toujours été versés au sein des installations du club. Le club annexe des quittances anciennes signées par le joueur, mais ces dernières ne mentionnent nullement le lieu du paiement.
51. Concernant les certificats transmis les 2 et 5 septembre 2005 par le syndicat, dont il est fait mention dans la partie consacrée à la requête du joueur, le club fait référence au document transmis par l'Association, le 21 septembre 2005, et ayant pour but de rectifier ces certificats. En effet, conformément à ce qu'affirmait le syndicat comme quoi les matches de février 2005 joués par le joueur l'avaient été en fonction d'un contrat enregistré en 2004, l'Association précise qu'au mois de février 2005 le joueur avait un contrat en vigueur pour 2005.
52. A titre subsidiaire, le défendeur met en doute l'authenticité des certificats des 2 et 5 septembre 2005 susmentionnés émis par le syndicat des joueurs et annexés par le joueur à la présente procédure et ceci en raison du fait que sur le sommet des pages figure la mention de la société de l'agent du joueur.
53. Le défendeur présente également une demande reconventionnelle et mentionne qu'étant donné que le contrat avec le défendeur est en vigueur jusqu'en décembre 2006 et que le joueur a signé un nouveau contrat avec la partie intervenante, le joueur a ainsi signé plus d'un contrat pour la même période. Ce qui rentre selon lui sous l'application de l'article 18 alinéa 5 du Règlement concernant le Statut et le Transfert des Joueurs.
54. Par conséquent, le défendeur demande une indemnisation de la part du demandeur et affirme que la partie intervenante doit être solidairement responsable du paiement de cette indemnisation. De plus, le défendeur exige des sanctions sportives à l'égard de la partie intervenante qui aurait incité à une rupture de contrat. En effet le défendeur affirme que la partie intervenante a contacté le joueur directement ou par l'intermédiaire de son agent et ensuite a signé le contrat, le tout sans avoir au préalable ni consulté ni pris contact avec le défendeur, ni avec l'Association. Pour étayer ce point le défendeur précise que la partie intervenante n'a jamais répondu à une lettre envoyée par le défendeur le prévenant de cette situation et datée du 20 juillet 2005.

55. Ainsi, concernant le demandeur, le défendeur note qu'avec le contrat le liant à la partie intervenante, ce club aurait dû versé le salaire de USD 5,856,000 durant la durée du contrat. De plus il prend en considération, entre autres, une offre émise par un autre club pour ce joueur, qui s'élevait à la somme de USD 3,050,000.
56. Par conséquent le défendeur réclame une indemnisation de USD 4,500,000 pour rupture du contrat par le demandeur.
57. Le défendeur réclame une indemnisation au titre de pertes patrimoniales et tort moral en raison d'une perte au niveau sportif du club, perte qui lui a oté la possibilité d'engendrer des bénéfices dû en cas de réussite. Il réclame également une indemnisation au titre de perte patrimoniale et tort moral en raison de la nuisance à l'image sportive ainsi qu'une indemnité pour tort moral en raison du tort fait à l'image du défendeur. Finalement, le club demande également une indemnisation englobant tous les frais engendrés dans la présente procédure et la procédure concernant l'enregistrement provisoire. En conclusion, au titre de ces indemnisations additionnelles le club réclame la somme de USD 2,250,000 de la part du demandeur.
58. Par conséquent le défendeur réclame :
    - que l'enregistrement du demandeur ne soit pas autorisé et ce jusqu'au paiement de l'indemnité réclamée ;
    - USD 6,750,000 au titre d'indemnisation par le demandeur ;que la partie intervenante soit considérée comme solidairement responsable de l'indemnité à payer par le demandeur ;
    - des sanctions sportives à l'encontre de la partie intervenante.

II. CONSIDÉRATIONS DE LA CHAMBRE DE RÉSOLUTION DES LITIGES

1. En premier lieu, la Chambre de Résolution des Litiges établit que sur la base de l'article 22 lit. a et de l'article 24 alinéa 1 du Règlement concernant le Statut et le Transfert des Joueurs (édition 2005), sa compétence à traiter ce cas et à rendre une décision formelle concernant ce litige contractuel opposant le demandeur au défendeur est donnée.
2. La Chambre de Résolution des Litiges prend note du fait que le contrat de travail liant le demandeur au défendeur était un contrat de travail écrit de durée déterminée, signé le 5 février 2004, qui aurait dû arriver à échéance le 31 décembre 2004 avec une option unilatérale en faveur du club de proroger cette durée. Cette option est basée sur le Statut du Joueur de Football national.
3. En premier lieu la Chambre note que l'article 15 du Statut du Joueur de Football national dispose, au conditionnel, que, à la finalisation des contrats de travail, ces derniers pourront s'étendre jusqu'au deuxième 31 décembre suivant leur finalisation. La Chambre souligne le caractère conditionnel de cette clause et l'interprétation littérale qui en ressort permettant de conclure qu'un consentement mutuel est nécessaire à la reconduction du contrat initial pour deux ans.
4. Cependant la Chambre constate qu'en application des articles 18, 19 et 20 du Statut du Joueur de Football national, les contrats peuvent uniquement être prorogés de façon unilatérale et automatique par le club et ce en prévoyant une simple augmentation salariale conforme à la variation de l'indice des prix à la consommation. Il est pris note du fait que cette combinaison des articles susmentionnés peut permettre au club de retenir le joueur de façon unilatérale et ce jusqu'à ses 27 ans.
5. En effet, la Chambre fait ressortir le caractère strictement unilatéral des articles 18 et 19 du Statut susmentionné dans le sens que cet article 18 oblige le joueur de 24 ans, dont le contrat serait arrivé à échéance, à conclure un nouveau contrat d'une durée de deux ans, simplement en prévoyant une augmentation salariale basée sur la variation de l'indice des prix à la consommation. De plus à l'échéance de ce nouveau contrat, le club possède l'option unilatérale de proroger pour une année supplémentaire ledit contrat de travail.
6. Par la suite, la Chambre fait ressortir le caractère unilatéral d'une telle clause en se basant sur l'article 19 du Statut susmentionné, qui dispose que le club uniquement pourra renoncer à la reconduction du contrat et ce via notification d'un préavis. Il est également tenu compte de l'article 20 dudit Statut qui reconduit de façon automatique et unilatérale les contrats de travail si le club ne fait pas recours à ce préavis.
7. Par conséquent la Chambre établit que de telles clauses sont tout à fait potestatives, et rendent donc impossible une quelconque application de l'article 15 du Statut du Joueur de Football national. Il s'ensuit que la Chambre de Résolution des Litiges note que de telles clauses autorisant une reconduction unilatérale du contrat par le club, constituent des clauses abusives et contraires aux principes de la Liberté contractuelle et de la Liberté du travail, principes juridiques reconnus

par le Droit International Public et surtout contraires également à l'article 13 du Règlement de la FIFA concernant le Statut et le Transfert des Joueurs (édition 2005) qui dispose qu'à l'échéance contractuelle prévue d'un commun accord, le contrat est considéré comme ne déployant plus d'effets et le joueur sera considéré libre de tout engagement.

8. De plus, la Chambre fait également référence à la jurisprudence du Tribunal Arbitral du Sport et plus particulièrement à la décision rendue le 27 août 2004 dans la procédure opposant AJ Auxerre à Valencia CF et M. Mohamed Lamine Sissoko. Dans cette décision à son considérant 47, la Formation a écarté l'application d'une Charte du Football Professionnel en vigueur en France en considérant que de telles chartes sont de portée nationale et ne sauraient prétendre déployer leurs effets dans un autre état et qu'il appartient par conséquent à la Chambre de tenir compte ou non de tous les arrangements, lois et/ou accords de conventions collectives pertinents existant au niveau national. Ce conformément à l'article 25 alinéa 6 du Règlement concernant le Statut et le Transfert des Joueurs (édition 2005).
9. Par conséquent et au vu des éléments susmentionnés, la Chambre établis qu'elle ne peut pas tenir compte du Statut du Joueur de Football national en relation avec l'extension unilatérale d'un contrat de travail et que ce dernier ne saurait déployer ses effets dans une situation comportant des éléments d'extranéité.
10. La Chambre de Résolution des Litiges conclut également que les 5 matches joués par le demandeur en janvier 2005, entrent sous l'application du contrat de travail de février 2004 et plus particulièrement de son article 4. En effet, sur la base des éléments présentés lors la présente procédure, il ressort que les matches joués en janvier 2005 l'ont été en raison d'une grève survenue en 2004 et que par conséquent ces matches correspondent à la saison 2004.
11. La Chambre note par la même que les deux matches joués en février 2005 par le demandeur, n'ont nullement constitué une reconduction tacite du contrat de travail de février 2004 et ne sauraient par conséquent être considérés comme une relation contractuelle de fait faisant suite au précédent contrat. En effet, la Chambre conclut que les matches joués en février 2005, entraient dans la phase négociatrice que le joueur avait entamé dans le but de conclure un nouveau contrat de travail et ne constituaient pas une quelconque intentionnalité de la part du joueur d'accepter tacitement un nouveau contrat de travail. La Chambre appuie cet élément sur le fait que le joueur n'a participé que jusqu'au 10 février 2005 aux rencontres avec le club défendeur, et ne voyant pas ces négociations aboutir il a cessé de disputer d'autres matches. Dans ce sens, la Chambre cite sa jurisprudence établie lors d'une décision n°55161 rendue le 13 mai 2005, concernant un litige contractuel, dans laquelle cet organe décisionnel a établis que le fait pour un joueur de participer aux activités du club après l'échéance contractuellement prévue n'implique nullement une acceptation tacite de la part du joueur à la reconduction du contrat, si ce dernier a participé auxdites activités de bonne foie dans le but de démontrer ces bonnes intentions dans le cadre d'une négociation d'un nouveau contrat.
12. A titre subsidiaire, la Chambre doit aussi noter que même en considérant une très hypothétique relation contractuelle de fait liant le demandeur au défendeur après le 31 janvier 2005, ce lien contractuel aurait pris fin et ceci en application de l'article 41 du Statut du Joueur de Football national. Cet article dispose que les salaires seront payés dans les 10 jours suivants l'échéance mensuelle et dans le cas où le salaire ne serait pas versé dans ce délai, le joueur pourra se présenter à l'Association afin de réclamer lesdites créances. Cet article mentionne également que le joueur aura la possibilité de se départir du contrat si 90 jours se sont écoulés dès la réclamation auprès de l'Association et si les salaires n'y sont toujours pas déposés.
13. En effet, la Chambre constate que la première réclamation de la part du demandeur auprès de l'Association a eu lieu le 14 mars 2005 et que les créances dues n'ont été déposées par le défendeur qu'à partir du 18 août 2005 auprès de l'Association, donc après 90 jours à partir de la première réclamation. La Chambre conclut donc que même en prenant en considération l'existence d'une relation contractuelle à partir de février 2005, celle-ci aurait pris fin le 13 juin 2005 et ce en application de l'article 41 susmentionné. Le joueur a fait communication de son choix de se départir du contrat en signant le nouveau contrat avec la partie intervenante le 19 juillet 2005.
14. Pour le bon ordre, à cet égard, la Chambre a estimé approprié de rappeler que en conformité avec l'article 2 alinéa 2 du Règlement concernant le Statut et le Transfert des Joueurs (édition 2005), une relation contractuelle entre un joueur et un club doit être toujours basée sur un contrat écrit.
15. La Chambre de Résolution des Litiges prend également note du fait que le mécanisme de la « rébellion », tel qu'il est prévu à l'article 37 du Statut du Joueur de Football national, et notifié au

joueur le 8 mars 2005, constitue une atteinte grave au principe de la Liberté personnelle du joueur ainsi qu'au principe de la Liberté contractuelle et contrevient à toutes normes reconnues du droit du travail.

16. En effet, l'organe décisionnel constate que ce mécanisme de la « rébellion » prive le joueur de toute rémunération, de toute participation aux activités du club et de plus enferme ce dernier dans une situation juridique le liant au club de façon impérative et l'empêchant ainsi d'exercer une activité lucrative, principe fondamental reconnu par le Droit International Public.
17. La Chambre constate également que contrairement à ce qu'affirme le défendeur, ce mécanisme de la « rébellion » tel qu'il a été notifié le 8 mars 2005, ne saurait empêcher le club défendeur de se conformer au paiement des salaires contractuellement prévus et échus au moment de ladite notification. Ce mécanisme permet de suspendre le paiement des salaires futurs et non des salaires échus. En effet, comme le dispose l'article 41 et l'article 23 du Statut du Joueur de Football national, les créances salariales dues aux joueurs peuvent être payées jusqu'au 10ème jour suivant le mois échu.
18. La Chambre insiste sur l'interprétation littérale qu'il convient de donner à cet article et mentionne que d'aucune manière on ne saurait interpréter lesdits articles d'une manière contraire à la bonne foi devant être observée dans le droit des contrats. Ainsi cette application des articles 41 et 23 susmentionnés ne peut permettre au club de suspendre ledit paiement par l'utilisation du mécanisme de la « rébellion » deux jours avant l'échéance mentionnée et ce uniquement dans le but d'éviter le paiement des salaires dus au joueur pour le mois de février et mars 2005, en raison de l'échec des négociations pour la conclusion d'un nouveau contrat de travail. Ceci constitue aux yeux de la Chambre une atteinte à la bonne foie devant être observée dans le droit contractuel.
19. La Chambre constate également que le paiement des salaires susmentionnés a été effectué par le défendeur le 18 août 2005 auprès de l'Association, donc le même jour auquel le Juge Unique de la Commission du Statut du Joueur a rendu sa première décision autorisant l'enregistrement provisoire du demandeur, ce qui selon la Chambre dénote une attitude contradictoire de la part du club défendeur, étant donné que comme l'affirme cette institution le mécanisme de la « rébellion » suspend toutes les obligations du club et démontre ainsi un comportement contraire au principe de la bonne foi généralement reconnu en droit contractuel.
20. La Chambre de Résolution des Litiges met également en avant le fait que la notion de droits fédératifs d'un joueur, tel que le mentionne le défendeur, n'est plus d'actualité mais a laissé place, avec l'entrée en vigueur du Règlement FIFA concernant le Statut et le Transfert des Joueurs (édition 2001), à la règle mentionnant qu'un contrat entre un joueur professionnel et un club finalise à l'échéance prévue contractuellement ou d'un commun accord, ce qui laisse le joueur libre de tout engagement après cette finalisation (cf. article 13 du Règlement FIFA concernant le Statut et le Transfert des Joueurs, édition 2005).
21. Par conséquent et au vu des éléments susmentionnés, la Chambre de Résolution des Litiges a admis partiellement la demande présentée par le demandeur et a décidé qu'il n'existe aucun lien contractuel liant le demandeur au défendeur et que par conséquent le joueur est autorisé à jouer pour la partie intervenante et la Fédération à laquelle appartient la partie intervenante est autorisée a procéder à l'enregistrement du joueur pour son club affilié. Il s'ensuit que le présent organe rejette dans sa totalité la demande reconventionnelle présentée par le défendeur.
22. La Chambre de Résolution des Litiges rejette la demande financière présentée par le demandeur en raison du caractère international des relations contractuelles dans le domaine footballistique et plus particulièrement en raison de la complexité juridique connue et admise par le joueur que peuvent engendrer des relations contractuelles entre parties soumises à différents ordres juridiques.
23. Sur la base de l'article 15 alinéa 3 du Règlement de la Commission du Statut du Joueur et de la Chambre de Résolution des Litiges (édition 2005), lequel dispose que les procédures devant la Chambre ne donnent lieu à aucune indemnité de procédure, la Chambre rejette la même demande d'indemnisation présentée par la partie intervenante, pour le remboursement des frais encourus.

III. DÉCISION DE LA CHAMBRE DE RÉSOLUTION DES LITIGES

1. La demande du demandeur est partiellement admise.
2. L'existence d'une relation contractuelle entre le demandeur et le défendeur est rejetée.
3. La Fédération à laquelle appartient la partie intervenante est autorisée à enregistrer le joueur en question pour son club affilié.

4. Aucune indemnité n'est accordée au demandeur.
5. La demande reconventionnelle présentée par le défendeur est rejetée dans sa totalité.
6. Selon l'article 60 alinéa 1 des Statuts de la FIFA, cette décision peut faire l'objet d'un appel devant le Tribunal Arbitral du Sport (TAS). La déclaration d'appel doit être soumise directement au TAS dans les dix jours après notification de cette décision et doit contenir tous les éléments conformément au point 2 des directives émises par le TAS, dont copie est annexée. Dans les dix jours suivant l'expiration du délai d'appel, l'appelant doit soumettre au TAS un mémoire contenant une description des faits et des moyens de droit fondant l'appel (cf. point 4 des directives).

2 NOVEMBER 2005

6585
DECISION OF THE DISPUTE RESOLUTION CHAMBER
passed in Zurich, Switzerland, on 1 June 2005,
in the following composition:
Slim Aloulou (Tunisia), Chairman
Jean-Marie Philips (Belgium) member
Philippe Diallo (France) member
Michele Colucci (Italy) member
Philippe Piat (France) member
on the claim presented by the Player X, as Claimant
against
Club Y, as Respondent
regarding outstanding remuneration on the basis of an employment contract

I. FACTS OF THE CASE
1. On 15 July 2004, the player X from Z, Claimant, and the club Y, Respondent, signed an employment contract valid as from 1 July 2004 until 30 June 2005.
2. According to clause 5c. and 5d. the Respondent agreed to pay to the Claimant a monthly salary amounting to EUR 1,500, as well as two monthly salaries in advance for the months of May and June 2005, under the condition that the Claimant is registered with the Respondent. Furthermore, according to the relevant contract the Claimant is entitled to receive, during the period of the contract and based on invoices, premium and award in accordance with the Rule Book of the Respondent.
3. However, after signing the contract the Respondent terminated the contract, allegedly, affirming that the contract was signed for the purpose of acquiring the Claimant's International Registration Transfer Certificate (IRTC) and that the relevant IRTC was received too late.
4. The Board for the Status of Players of Association of the First XXX Soccer Division decided on 19 October 2004 that the Respondent had unilaterally violated the contract and that therefore the contractual obligations shall not be cancelled by the unilateral termination of the contract. An appeal against this decision was possible within 8 days. However, the FIFA administration was never informed that any party lodged an appeal.
5. On 29 November 2004, the Claimant contacted the FIFA administration requesting that the Respondent should pay him the amount of EUR 18,000 equivalent to all salaries as per the relevant employment contract.
6. On 15 February 2005, the Respondent affirmed that the parties had terminated the contract on 16 August 2004 and that it paid the travel expenses amounting to EUR 1,000 to the Claimant. The Respondent provided a document in the Slovenian language as well as a translation of the document, according to which both parties confirmed that the Respondent unilaterally terminated the employment contract as from 16 August 2004 and that the Claimant received the amount of SIT 240,000 as compensation for the "costs of entering and leaving" the Respondent. However, the Respondent did not refer at all to the decision passed on 19 October 2004 by the Board for the Status of Players of Association of the First XXX Soccer Division.
7. On 15 March 2005, the Claimant informed the FIFA administration that according to the decision of the Board for the Status of Players of Association of the First XXX Soccer Division dated 19 October

2004, the club has to fulfil its contractual obligations and therefore he claims the amount of EUR 18,000 plus all premiums and bonuses and procedural costs. Moreover, the Claimant explained that the document provided by the Respondent only refers to the travel expenses paid to him. Furthermore, the Claimant pointed out that he is rendering his services to the club xxx since March 2005.

8. Upon FIFA's request the Football Federation of R provided a copy of the employment contract signed between its affiliate and the Claimant valid as from 17 January 2005 until 20 June 2005, according to which the Claimant is entitled to receive a transfer indemnity amounting to EUR 11,000. However, no other financial remuneration is established by the contract and the Claimant's International Registration Transfer Certificate was issued on 15 February 2005.

II. CONSIDERATIONS OF THE DISPUTE RESOLUTION CHAMBER

1. The Dispute Resolution Chamber shall review disputes coming under its jurisdiction pursuant to Art. 42 of the FIFA Regulations for the Status and Transfer of Players, at the request of one of the parties to the dispute.
2. According to Art. 42, par. 1 lit. (b) of the FIFA Regulations for the Status and Transfer of Players, the triggering elements of the dispute (i.e. whether a contract was breached, with or without just cause, or sporting just cause), will be decided by the Dispute Resolution Chamber.
3. If an employment contract is breached by a party, the Dispute Resolution Chamber is responsible to verify whether a party is accountable for compensation and outstanding payments.
4. As a consequence, the Dispute Resolution Chamber is the competent body to decide on the present litigation involving a club and a player from Z.
5. The members of the Dispute Resolution Chamber were summoned to pass a decision on this matter by the Chairman pursuant to Art. 1 point 6) of the Rules Governing the Practice and Procedures of the Dispute Resolution Chamber.
6. Subsequently, and entering into the substance of the matter, the members of the Chamber started by acknowledging that, after signing the relevant employment contract on 15 July 2004, according to which the Respondent agreed to pay to the Claimant a monthly salary amounting to EUR 1,500, the Respondent terminated the contract on 16 August 2004.
7. The Chamber also noted that the Board for the Status of Players of Association of the First XXX Soccer Division decided on 19 October 2004 that the Respondent had unilaterally violated the contract and that therefore the contractual obligations shall not be cancelled by the unilateral termination of the contract.
8. In continuation, the Chamber noted that the Claimant requests the amount of EUR 18,000 plus all premiums and bonuses and procedural costs from the Respondent, due for the unilateral breach of the employment contract. Moreover, the Chamber acknowledged that the Claimant signed an employment contract with the club xxx valid as from 17 January 2005 until 20 June 2005, according to which he is entitled to receive the total remuneration amounting to EUR 11,000 for the contractual time-frame.
9. Turning its attention to the position of the Respondent, concerning the termination of the employment contract, the members of the Chamber acknowledged that the Respondent only explained that it had terminated the contract on 16 August 2004 and that it paid the travel expenses amounting to EUR 1,000 to the Claimant. In this respect, the Respondent provided a document in Slovenian language as well as a translation of the document, which states that the Claimant received the amount of SIT 240,000 as compensation for the "costs ofentering and leaving" the Respondent. However, the Respondent never referred to the grounds based on which it had actually terminated the relevant employment contract nor to the decision passed by the competent bodies of the S Football Federation.
10. Taking into account the above the Chamber pointed out that the Respondent, by not addressing the charges raised against it, renounced to its right to defence with respect to the allegations of the Claimant regarding the unjustified breach of the contract, even confirmed by the competent bodies of the S Football Federation, and thus accepts the allegations of the Claimant with regards that it had terminated the contract without any reason.
11. As a result, the Chamber concluded that the Respondent terminated the employment contract duly signed with the Claimant on 15 July 2004 without just cause and should therefore be liable to pay compensation to the Claimant.
12. When establishing the amount of compensation that the Respondent would have to pay to the Claimant, the Chamber took into account that, on the one hand, the Claimant requested, inter alia, the

amount of EUR 18,000 corresponding to all monthly salaries during the validity term of the relevant employment contract as from 1 July 2004 until 30 June 2005. On the other hand, the Chamber took into account that, the Claimant would receive from his new club the total amount of USD 11,000 during the period of time as from 17 January 2005 until 20 June 2005.

13. Furthermore, the Chamber considered that, the fact that the Claimant concluded a new employment contract as from 17 January 2005, clearly attenuated the financial damages suffered by him.
14. On account of the above, the Dispute Resolution Chamber decided that the Respondent is liable to pay compensation to the Claimant, in an amount equivalent to the difference between the remuneration stipulated on the Claimant's employment contracts with the Respondent and the club xxx, until the date when the Claimant's contractual link with the Respondent would end, i.e. 30 June 2005. As a result, the Claimant is entitled to receive the amount of USD 7,000 (USD 18,000 - USD 11,000). Furthermore, the Chamber emphasized that the Respondent's behavior has to be considered when fixing the amount of compensation due to the Claimant. In particular, the fact that the Respondent clearly failed to fulfil its financial obligations towards the player and evidently ignored the decision passed by the competent bodies of the S Football Federation. In the light of these considerations, the Chamber deemed that an additional compensation in the amount of USD 3,000 is justified and appropriate in the case at state.
15. On the other hand, in view of the lack of evidence carried to the file the Dispute Resolution Chamber decided to reject the Claimant's claim concerning the premiums and bonuses. Furthermore, the Dispute Resolution Chamber rejected the Claimant's claim regarding the procedural costs based on its well-established jurisprudence.
16. Taking into account all of the above, the Dispute Resolution Chamber decided that the Respondent has to pay the amount of USD 10,000 to the Claimant.

III. DECISION OF THE DISPUTE RESOLUTION CHAMBER

1. The claim lodged by the Claimant, Mr X, is partially accepted.
2. The Respondent, Y, shall pay the total amount of USD 10,000 to the Claimant, within 30 days following the date of the communication of the present decision.
3. Any further claims lodged by the Claimant are rejected.
4. In the event that the above-mentioned amount is not paid within the stated deadline, an interest rate of 5% per year will apply.
5. If the aforementioned sum is not paid within the aforementioned deadline the present matter shall be submitted to FIFA's Disciplinary Committee, so that the necessary disciplinary sanctions may be imposed.
6. The Claimant is directed to inform the Respondent directly and immediately of the account number to which the remittance is to be made and to notify the Dispute Resolution Chamber of every payment received.
7. According to art. 60 par. 1 of the FIFA Statutes, this decision may be appealed against before the Court of Arbitration for Sport (CAS). The statement of appeal must be sent to the CAS directly within 10 days of receipt of notification of this decision and shall contain all the elements in accordance with point 2 of the directives issued by the CAS, a copy of which we enclose hereto. Within another 10 days following the expiry of the time limit for filing the statement of appeal, the appellant shall file a brief stating the facts and legal arguments giving rise to the appeal with the CAS (cf. point 4 of the directives).

11522
DECISION OF THE DISPUTE RESOLUTION CHAMBER

passed in Zurich, Switzerland, on 2 November 2005,
in the following composition:
Slim Aloulou (Tunisia), Chairman
Jean-Marie Philips (Belgium) member
Ivan Gazidis (USA) member
Philippe Piat (France) member
Mick McGuire (England) member

on the claim presented by the Player X,
represented by A as *Claimant*
against the Club Y, as *Respondent*
regarding a financial dispute on the basis of an employment contract

I. FACTS OF THE CASE

1. The player X, Claimant, and the club Y, Respondent, signed an employment contract on 21 February 2004 valid as from 1 February 2004 until 31 December 2006. According to art. 1 of the relevant employment contract the Respondent agreed to pay to the Claimant the total amount of PLN 490,000 for the entire period of the contractual relation, i.e. PLN 14,000 each month. Furthermore, in accordance with art. 4.4. of the relevant employment contract the Respondent agreed to pay to the Claimant accommodation amounting to PLN 1,500 monthly.
2. The Claimant lodged a complaint in front of the P Football Association and on 4 January 2005, the P Football Association passed a decision in which it concluded that the Respondent's termination of the contract on 31 August 2004 is ineffective and caused no legal effects, since it was unilateral. An appeal against the decision was possible within 2 weeks.
3. On 1 November 2004, the Claimant contacted FIFA affirming that the Respondent terminated the relevant employment contract without valid reason on 31 August 2004. Moreover, the Claimant emphasised that he was hindered to find a new club, since the Respondent terminated the employment contract on the date on which the registration periods ended. Therefore, he is claiming all salaries as from August 2004 until December 2006. Furthermore, the Claimant affirmed that since the termination of the employment contract the Respondent stopped paying his accommodation and therefore he was forced to leave the country. Finally, the Claimant explained that he got injured on 28 May 2004, but that he rendered his services to the Respondent until 2 June 2004.
4. On 14 March 2005, the Respondent informed FIFA that the employment contract was signed 6 days before the expiry date of the transfer periods set by the P Football Association and that therefore it was not able to inspect the Claimant's football skills. Therefore, the parties included art. 5 in the employment contract which stipulates that: "*While during the contract the club at the end of each championship round, that is in terms from February 1st to February 28th and from July 1st to August 31st has a right to dissolve this contract with the competitor by delivering in writing a suitable declaration. Handing over that declaration to the competitor means that with that day it comes to a termination of contract on principle of the agreement of the parties*".
5. Moreover, the Respondent pointed out that in June 2004 the Claimant suffered a slight injury and that the latter refused to practice in July and August 2004 disregarding the club's doctor recommendation. This caused further decrease of his professional skills. In spite of the fact that the Claimant did not train with the Respondent's team in July and August 2004 the Respondent affirmed that it paid him his salaries for the mentioned two months.
6. The Respondent explained that it notified the Claimant's agent that it will make use of its right established in art. 5 of the relevant employment contract and the contract was mutually terminated on 31 August 2004. The Respondent pointed out that it acted in accordance with the duly signed contract and also paid to the Claimant all dues until the end of August 2004. The Respondent provided a copy of the termination letter addressed to the Claimant dated 31 August 2004.
7. On 28 April 2005, the Claimant contested the Respondent's position and pointed out that if the Respondent had not been aware of his skills it would not have signed an agreement valid until 2006. Furthermore, the Claimant pointed out that the Respondent saw his skills on several videos. Moreover, the Claimant underlined that the contract was written in the Polish language and that he never agreed that the Respondent could terminate the contract unilaterally.
8. Finally, the Claimant once again requested all outstanding salaries as from August 2004 until December 2006, i.e. 29 monthly salaries amounting in total to PLN 406,000, since according to the decision of the P Football Association the unilateral termination of the contract was illegal and therefore he was still contractually bound to the Respondent.
9. On 24 June 2005, the Appeal Commission of P Football Association confirmed the decision passed by the P Football Association on 4 January 2005.
10. Upon FIFA's request the Respondent informed again that in its opinion it had the right to terminate the employment relation with the Claimant on 31 August 2004 in accordance with art. 5 of the relevant employment contract. Furthermore, the Respondent stressed that the Claimant never offered

his services after the decisions taken by the instances of the P Football Association.

11. In this respect, the Claimant provided copies of correspondences sent on 20 December 2004 and 14 July 2005, by means of which he offered his services and also requested the outstanding salaries.
12. On 2 August 2005, in view of this situation, FIFA advised the parties involved in this matter to consider their employment relationship as terminated and to focus on the financial aspects of the dispute.
13. On 25 August 2005, the Respondent once again pointed out that in its opinion it had the right to terminate the contract. Furthermore, the Respondent pointed out that it never forced the Claimant to leave the country, as affirmed by him, but he left on his own initiative. Moreover, the Respondent denied that it ever forbid the Claimant from rendering his services and that the Claimant left as from the date of the termination of the employment relation. The Respondent is of the opinion that the Claimant being convinced that he still should receive remuneration under the terminated contract, has made no attempts to execute the contract. Finally, the Respondent underlined that the last statement of the player regarding his alleged readiness to play for the club aims to improve his image in the present process.
14. As a result, the Respondent is of the opinion that the employment contract was properly terminated in accordance with art. 5 of the said contract and that the Claimant accepted it due to his lack of readiness to render his services. The Respondent deems that the Claimant only intends to get remuneration.
15. The Claimant explained that based on the decisions of the P Football Association he has always understood that he was still under contract with the Respondent and therefore hindered to sign a contract with a new club until 22 August 2005, when he finally was informed by his lawyer that under the given circumstances of the present matter FIFA had advised the parties to consider their employment relation as terminated. In this respect, the Claimant explained that as from 22 August 2005, he has been trying very hard to find a new club, but without success since the clubs are in the middle of the league championship.
16. The Respondent again referred to all its previous submissions and stressed that the Claimant never offered his services and that the letter dated 14 July 2005, was only made in order to sustain the Claimant's claim. Finally, the Respondent provided a statement of the club's trainer confirming that the Claimant has never offered his services or presented himself at the club.

II. CONSIDERATIONS OF THE DISPUTE RESOLUTION CHAMBER

1. The Dispute Resolution Chamber reviews disputes coming under its jurisdiction pursuant to Art. 42 of the FIFA Regulations for the Status and Transfer of Players (edition 2001), at the request of one of the parties to the dispute.
2. In continuation, the members of the Chamber first of all, emphasised that the competent deciding bodies have already established that the relevant employment contract at the basis of the present dispute has been breached by the Respondent without justification. As a result, the members will not pronounce themselves in that respect, since the matter has been finally decided by the relevant competent bodies. However, the members of the Chamber acknowledged that the relevant decisions do not establish any financial consequences, in particular whether a party is accountable for compensation for breach of contract.
3. Taking into account the above and in accordance with Art. 42 par. 1 lit. (b) (iii) of the FIFA Regulations for the Status and Transfer of Players (edition 2001), the Dispute Resolution Chamber is responsible to verify whether a party is accountable for compensation for breach of contract.
4. As a consequence, the Dispute Resolution Chamber is the competent body to decide on the present litigation.
5. Subsequently, and entering into the substance of the matter, the members of the Chamber started by acknowledging that according to the relevant employment contract the Respondent agreed to pay to the Claimant the total amount of PLN 490,000 for the entire period of the contractual relation, i.e. PLN 14,000 each month.
6. In continuation, the Chamber acknowledged that the Claimant requested compensation equivalent to all salaries as from August 2004 until December 2006 in a total amount of in total to PLN 406,000, i.e. 29 monthly salaries amounting each to PLN 14,000.
7. Moreover, the Chamber took due note that based on the decisions of the P Football Association the Claimant has always understood that he was still under contract with the Respondent and therefore

hindered to sign a contract with a new club until August 2005, when he was informed that under the given circumstances of the present matter FIFA had advised the parties to consider their employment relation as terminated.

8. Finally, the Chamber took into consideration that the Claimant explained that as from August 2005, he has been trying very hard to find a new club, but without success since the clubs are in the middle of the league championship.
9. Turning its attention to the Respondent's position, the Chamber acknowledged that, on the one hand, the Respondent affirmed that it paid to the Claimant all salaries until August 2004 and, on the other hand, the Respondent considers that it was entitled to terminate the employment contract and therefore contests any further financial obligation towards the Claimant.
10. In this respect, the Chamber observed that the Respondent did not provide any documentation in order to corroborate its allegations that it actually paid the salary for the month of August 2004, which is also claimed by the Claimant.
11. As a result and due to the lack of evidence, the Chamber has to conclude that the Claimant did not receive his salary as from August 2004.
12. For the sake of clarity, the Chamber emphasised that the Respondent is liable to pay compensation to the Claimant, in an amount equivalent to the difference between the amounts stipulated on the Claimant's employment contract with the Respondent and the new income of the player until the date on which the contractual link with the Respondent would have ended, i.e. in December 2006.
13. The Chamber took into account all of the above when establishing the compensation due by the Respondent to the Claimant. Moreover, the Chamber took into consideration that during the period in which the dispute was pending in front of the deciding bodies, i.e. until it had been finally decided that the Respondent breached the contract, the Claimant was hindered to find a new club, which, according to the members, would have clearly attenuated the financial damages that he suffered. Furthermore, the Chamber took into account that as from the time when the Claimant was in a position to find a new club, he has been trying to attenuated the financial damages, but without success.
14. As a result, the Chamber established that the Claimant did suffer financial damages due to the early termination of the employment contract signed with the Respondent and therefore, the Respondent is liable to pay compensation until the Claimant will be able to find a new club within a reasonable timeframe.
15. Therefore, the Chamber emphasised that taking into account all of the above the Respondent is liable to pay compensation to the Claimant equivalent to the salaries as from August 2004 until August 2006.
16. Taking into account all of the above, the Dispute Resolution Chamber established that the Respondent has to pay compensation to the Claimant in the amount of PLN 336,000.

III. DECISION OF THE DISPUTE RESOLUTION CHAMBER

1. The claim lodged by the Claimant, Mr X, is partially accepted.
2. The Respondent, Y, shall pay the total amount of PLN 336,000 to the Claimant, **within 30 days** following the date of the communication of the present decision.
3. In the event that the above-mentioned amount is not paid within the stated deadline, an interest rate of 5% per year will apply and the present matter shall be submitted to FIFA's Disciplinary Committee, so that the necessary disciplinary sanctions may be imposed.
4. Any further claims lodged by the Claimant are rejected.
5. The Claimant is instructed to inform the Respondent directly and immediately of the account number to which the remittance is to be made and to notify the Dispute Resolution Chamber of every payment received.
6. According to art. 60 par. 1 of the FIFA Statutes, this decision may be appealed against before the Court of Arbitration for Sport (CAS). The statement of appeal must be sent to the CAS directly within 10 days of receipt of notification of this decision and shall contain all the elements in accordance with point 2 of the directives issued by the CAS, a copy of which we enclose hereto. Within another 10 days following the expiry of the time limit for filing the statement of appeal, the appellant shall file a brief stating the facts and legal arguments giving rise to the appeal with the CAS (cf. point 4 of the directives).

115236
DECISION OF THE DISPUTE RESOLUTION CHAMBER
passed in Zurich, Switzerland, on 2 November 2005,
in the following composition:
Slim Aloulou (Tunisia), Chairman
Jean-Marie Philips (Belgium), Member
Ivan Gazidis (United States), Member
Mick McGuire (England), Member
Philippe Piat (France), Member
on the claim presented by Player A, as Claimant
against
Club B, as Respondent
regarding a dispute about the employment contract concluded between the parties

I. FACTS OF THE CASE

1. On 1 July 2004, the player A and the club B signed an employment contract valid from 1 July 2004 to 31 December 2004, stipulating a monthly salary of USD 15,000 (hereinafter; contract A).
2. On the same date, the same parties signed a second employment contract with the same duration, stipulating a monthly salary of USD 20,000, as well as a signing on fee of USD 100,000 due on 15 July 2004 and of USD 30,000 due on 15 August 2004 (hereinafter; contract B).
3. On 10 January 2005, the player submitted the following claim to FIFA against the club:
   - Salaries from July to December 2004 (USD 35,000/month) USD 210,000
   - Signing on fee USD 130,000
   - Match bonus for match on 22 August 2004 USD 5,000
   - Total USD 345,000
   - Received so far from the club USD 45,000
   - Claim USD 300,000
4. On 16 March 2005, in reply to the player's claim, the club stated that the player was paid the salaries from 1 July to 15 September 2004 in the total amount of USD 37,500.
5. The club also stated that the salaries from 16 September to 31 December 2004 in the total amount of USD 52,500 were still due.
6. The club enclosed only a copy of the contract A to its statement.
7. On 2 June 2005, after a change in the managing board of the club, the club clarified its position. In this regard, the club in particular acknowledged that the player's monthly salary was USD 35,000, and that he was entitled to a signing on fee in the amount of USD 130,000.
8. Moreover, the club enclosed payrolls signed by the player, according to which he was paid the total amount of USD 210,000.
9. Finally, the club stated that the signing on fee of USD 130,000 was paid to the player's representative, Mr. X.
10. On 13 July 2005, in response to the club's new position, the player first stated that the club obviously acknowledged his right to a monthly salary in the total amount of USD 35,000 and a signing on fee of USD 130,000.
11. Moreover, the player stated that the club did not contest his claim for a match bonus in the amount of USD 5,000.
12. With regard to the payrolls, the player agrees having signed the payrolls dated 11 and 19 August 2004 over the total amount of USD 37,500. With regard to the signatures on the other payrolls over the total amount of USD 172,500, he maintains that these signatures are falsifications, and reiterates that he did not receive the relevant amounts.
13. With regard to the payment of the signing on fee to Mr. X, the player states that he never gave instructions to the club to make payments to this person Moreover, the player claims never having had any relationship of agency or otherwise with Mr. X and never having received money from him.
14. On 11 August 2005, asked for its final position, the club did not contest the player's statements.
15. Moreover, despite having been requested to do so by the FIFA-Administration, the club did not submit the originals of the mentioned payrolls, and declared that it was not in a position to submit them,

since it was forbidden by its national law to submit original documents to judicial committees. The club instead sent the documents to its interior ministry for a verification of the player's signatures.

16. Since then, and despite having been asked once again by the FIFA Administration to remit the relevant original documents, no further information was received from the club with regard to the originals of the payrolls.

II. CONSIDERATIONS OF THE DISPUTE RESOLUTION CHAMBER

1. The members of the Dispute Resolution Chamber were summoned by the Chairman to pass a decision on the present matter pursuant to Art. 1 point 6) of the Rules Governing the Practice and Procedures of the Dispute Resolution Chamber.
2. The deciding body started its deliberations by indicating that, as established in Art. 42 § 1 lit. (b) (i) of the FIFA Regulations for the Status and Transfer of Players (hereinafter: the Regulations), it falls within the purview of the Dispute Resolution Chamber to determine whether one of the parties has committed a unilateral breach of contract without just cause. In the case that the employment contract was breached by a party, the Dispute Resolution Chamber is responsible to verify and decide whether this party is accountable for outstanding payments and compensation.
3. In view of the above, the Dispute Resolution Chamber concluded that it was competent to decide on the present litigation.
4. The Chamber then acknowledged the documentation contained in the file and took note in particular of the financial obligations stipulated in the two contracts signed by the parties. In this respect, the Chamber noted that in accordance with contract A, the player was entitled to USD 90,000 in total on account of salaries. Cumulating the two contracts, the player would have been entitled to USD 340,000 on account of salaries. Moreover, the Chamber noted that the player indicates having received from the club so far the amount of USD 45,000.
5. As far as the club's answer to this claim is concerned, the Chamber noticed first of all that the two submissions of the club dated 16 March 2005 and 2 June 2005 were contradictory. On 16 March 2005, the respondent declared that the player was paid the amount of USD 37,500, that therefore the amount of USD 52,500 was still outstanding. By this, the club implied that only contract A was to be considered.
6. On 2 June 2005 however, the club stated that the player was paid the amount of USD 340,000, that therefore the club had respected the two contracts and that no payment was outstanding. The Chamber took note as well of the payment receipts submitted by the club, which should corroborate the club's position.
7. On account of this, the Chamber noticed that the player agreed having signed the payment receipts presented over the total amount of USD 37,500. With regard to the signatures on the other payment receipts over the total amount of USD 172,500, the Chamber noticed the player's position that these signatures were falsifications and that he did not receive the relevant amounts. Moreover, the Chamber noted that the player stated with regard to the payment of the signing on fee to Mr. X, that he never gave instructions to the club to make payments to this person, never had any relationship of agency or otherwise with Mr. X and never received money from him.
8. Finally, the Chamber acknowledged that the club never provided FIFA with the originals of the relevant payment receipts, despite having been expressly requested to do so several times.
9. On account of the above, the Chamber stated that as a general rule, in application of the legal principle *pacta sunt servanda*, clubs have to pay the players' contractual salaries and signing on fees.
10. In this regard, the Chamber stated that the player's claim for USD 340,000 was based on the salary clause of the two employment contracts concluded with the club, as well as the clause for the signing on fee in the contract B.
11. The members of the Chamber then concurred that prior to continuing with the considerations of this case, they needed to address the prejudice question as to which contract shall be taken into account in the case at hand, and in consequence, which is the salary the player was entitled to from the club.
12. In this regard, the members of the Chamber referred to the fact that in the club's submission dated 2 June 2005, the club stated that the player was paid the amount of USD 340,000, that therefore the club had respected the two contracts.
13. In view of this, the Chamber stated that in accordance with the club's position, in the present case, both employment contracts had to be applied cumulatively.

14. Therefore, the player's salaries for the entire duration of the contract was USD 210,000, and the signing on fee was USD 130,000.
15. In continuation, the Chamber stated that that the respondent had not forwarded sufficient evidence that it had duly respected its financial obligations towards the player and paid the amount claimed by the player.
16. In particular, the authenticity of some payment receipts, by means of which the player allegedly acknowledged the receipt of USD 172,500 from the club on account of salaries, was challenged by the player. In this regard, the respondent did not submit the necessary originals of these documents to counter this challenge.
17. Hence, the Chamber concluded that the amount of USD 172,500 to be paid by the club to the player on account of salaries is to be considered as not paid.
18. With regard to the clubs position that the signing on fee in the amount of USD 130,000 was paid to Mr. X, who allegedly was entitled to receive this amount for the claimant, the Chamber stated that the respondent did not provide any evidence that the player gave instructions to the club to make payments to this person or that the player had any relationship of agency or otherwise with Mr X.
19. Therefore, the Chamber stated that the amount of USD 130,000 on account of the signing on fee was never paid to the player. Should it be true that the amount in question was indeed paid to Mr. X for player A, the Chamber stated that there was no legal basis which allowed to the club to fulfil its financial obligations towards the player by paying a third person, would it be Mr. X or any other third person.
20. Therefore, the Chamber concluded that the amount of USD 130,000 claimed by the player from the club on account of the signing on fee is to be considered as not paid as well.
21. Finally, the Chamber addressed the player's claim for USD 5,000 on account of a match bonus for match on 22 August 2004, and in this regard, took note of the fact that the club has never contested such claim.
22. Therefore, this amount is to be considered still due by the club to the player as well.
23. Before coming to its final conclusion, the Chamber stated that the club had not presented any reason justifying the non-payment of the amounts in question to the player.
24. Therefore, in application of the legal principle *pacta sunt servanda*, the Chamber decided that the club B is owing to player A on account of outstanding salaries, signing on fees and bonuses the total amount of USD 307,500.
25. Since the player claimed in front of FIFA only for the amount of USD 300,000, and in application of the principle *no ultra petita*, the Chamber decided that the club B has to pay to the player A the amount of USD 300,000 on account of salaries, signing on fees and bonuses.

III. DECISION OF THE DISPUTE RESOLUTION CHAMBER

1. The claim of the player A is accepted.
2. The club B has to pay the amount of USD 300,000 to the player A.
3. The amount due to the player A has to be paid by the club B within the next 30 days as from the date of notification of this decision.
4. If the aforementioned amount is not paid within the stated deadline, an interest rate of 5% per year shall apply.
5. If the aforementioned amount is not paid within the aforementioned deadline, the present matter shall be submitted to FIFA's Disciplinary Committee, so that the necessary disciplinary sanctions may be imposed.
6. The player A is directed to inform the club B immediately of the account number to which the remittance is to be made, and to notify the Dispute Resolution Chamber of every payment received.
7. According to art. 60 par. 1 of the FIFA Statutes this decision may be appealed before the Court of Arbitration for Sport (CAS). The statement of appeal must be sent to the CAS directly within 10 days of receiving notification of this decision and has to contain all elements in accordance with point 2 of the directives issued by the CAS, copy of which we enclose hereto. Within another 10 days following the expiry of the time limit for the filing of the statement of appeal, the appellant shall file with the CAS a brief stating the facts and legal arguments giving rise to the appeal (cf. point 4 of the directives).

115324
DECISION OF THE DISPUTE RESOLUTION CHAMBER
passed in Zurich, Switzerland, on 2 November 2005,
in the following composition:
Slim Aloulou (Tunisia), Chairman
Jean-Marie Philips (Belgium), member
Ivan Gazidis (USA), member
Mick Mc Guire (England), member
Philippe Piat (France), member
on the claim presented by the club
H., Germany, represented by D., Germany as Claimant
against the club K., Greece, as Respondent,
regarding the training compensation related to the transfer of the federative rights of the player G.

I. FACTS OF THE CASE

1. The player G. was born on 6 July 1987. The player was trained by H. as an amateur player from 1 July 2003 until 30 June 2004.
2. On 1 July 2004, the player was transferred to the Greek club K.
3. On 28 January 2004, H. established contact with FIFA to lodge a claim for training compensation totalling EUR 30,000. The German club maintained that the player had appeared for the Greek club and therefore was no longer an amateur.
4. In response to an enquiry from FIFA, the Greek club contested the fact that the player had non-amateur status as he was playing for the club's amateur youth team.
5. However, the German club insisted on 11 April 2005 that the player was no longer an amateur, pointing out that, while the player may at that time have been playing only in youth and amateur teams, this issue depended exclusively on the status of the player and not on the team for which he appeared.
6. The Greek club stated on 30 June 2005 that, given that the player had moved to Greece without any fee being paid and he had never appeared for a non-amateur team, there were no grounds for the payment of training compensation.
7. On 11 July 2005, the Hellenic Football Federation informed FIFA that, although the player had never appeared for a non-amateur team, he was actually registered as a non-amateur player. Furthermore, his contract with the club was a professional player's contract.

II. CONSIDERATIONS OF THE DISPUTE RESOLUTION CHAMBER

1. Since the claim at hand had been lodged prior to 1 July 2005 and since the player was transferred to K. on 1 July 2004, the September 2001 edition of the Regulations for the Status and Transfer of Players (hereinafter the Regulations) shall apply (cf. art. 26 par. 1 and 2 of the July 2005 Regulations).
2. The Dispute Resolution Chamber of the FIFA Players' Status Committee shall review disputes coming under its jurisdiction pursuant to art. 42 of the Regulations at the request of one of the parties to the dispute.
3. In accordance with art. 42 par. 1 lit. (b) (iv) of the Regulations, it falls within the purview of the Dispute Resolution Chamber to review disputes concerning training compensation fees.
4. Consequently, the Dispute Resolution Chamber is the competent body to decide on the present litigation concerning the training compensation fee claimed by H.
5. Therefore, the members of the Dispute Resolution Chamber at first confirmed to be competent to pass a decision in this matter. In addition, the Chamber acknowledged the above-mentioned facts as well as the further documentation contained in the file.
6. Subsequently, and entering into the substance of the matter, the Chamber acknowledged that the player was registered with H. from 1 July 2003 until 30 June 2004, i.e. for the sporting season 2003/2004, between the ages of 16 and 17, and that the present claim was put forward by H. before the player turned 23 years of age.
7. Continuing, the chamber stated that, as established in Chapter VII of the Regulations and in Circular letter no. 826, dated 31 October 2002, training compensation is payable for training incurred between the ages of 12 and 21, if the player concludes a non-amateur contract before the age of 23.
8. It is therefore undisputed that the club H. is entitled to receive compensation for the training and

education of the player G. for the sporting season 2003/2004, during which the player rendered his services to H. if the player concluded a nonamateur contract with K.

9. However, the Greek club based its argumentation on the fact that the player had never appeared for a non-amateur team and that therefore, there were no grounds for the payment of training compensation.
8. In this respect, the Chamber took note that the Hellenic Football Federation informed FIFA that, although the player had never appeared for a non-amateur team, he was actually registered as a non-amateur player. Furthermore, the Chamber stated that his contract with the club was a professional player's contract.
9. As a result, the Chamber unanimously concluded that the player G. signed his first contract as a non-amateur and backed the opinion of the German club that this issue depends exclusively on the status of the player and not on the team for which he appeared.
10. As a consequence, the Chamber reached the conclusion that H. is undisputably entitled to receive from K. compensation for the training and education of the player G. regarding the timeframe that the latter spent with it.
11. Consequently, having thus analysed the various aspects of the player's claim, as well as the club's defence statement and referring to art. 13 of the Regulations, art. 5 et seqq. of the Regulations governing the Application of the Regulations for the Status and Transfer of Players (edition 2001) and Circular letter no. 826, the Chamber decided that K. is liable to pay the amount of EUR 30,000 to H., for the training compensation of the player G.

III. DECISION OF THE DISPUTE RESOLUTION CHAMBER

1. The claim of the club H. is accepted.
2. The club K. has to pay the amount of EUR 30,000 to H. within next 30 days as from the date of notification of the present decision.
3. In the event that the above-mentioned amount is not paid within the stated deadline, an interest rate of 5% per year will apply and the present matter shall be submitted to FIFA's Disciplinary Committee, so that the necessary disciplinary sanctions may be imposed.
4. H. is instructed to inform K. immediately and directly of the account number to which the remittance is to be made and to notify the Dispute Resolution Chamber of every payment received.
5. According to art. 60 par. 1 of the FIFA Statutes this decision may be appealed before the Court of Arbitration for Sport (CAS). The statement of appeal must be sent to the CAS directly within 10 days of receiving notification of this decision and has to contain all elements in accordance with point 2 of the directives issued by the CAS, copy of which we enclose hereto. Within another 10 days following the expiry of the time limit for the filing of the statement of appeal, the appellant shall file with the CAS a brief stating the facts and legal arguments giving rise to the appeal (cf. point 4 of the directives).

115334

DECISION OF THE DISPUTE RESOLUTION CHAMBER

passed in Zurich, Switzerland, on 2 November 2005,
in the following composition:
Slim Aloulou (Tunisia), Chairman
Jean-Marie Philips (Belgium), member
Ivan Gazidis (USA), member
Mick Mc Guire (England), member
Philippe Piat (France), member
on the claim presented by the player
A., Armenia, as Claimant
against the club H., Lebanon, as Respondent,
regarding a contractual dispute arisen between the parties

I. FACTS OF THE CASE

1. On 25 September 2003, the player A. and the Lebanese club H. signed an employment contract valid until the end of the Lebanese Football Federation season of 2003/2004. According to the relevant employment contract the club agreed to pay a yearly salary amounting to USD 15,000 [recte: USD 14,000] to the player, payable as follows:
   - USD 3,500 on 30 October 2003;
   - USD 3,500 on 30 December 2003;
   - USD 3,500 on 29 February 2004;
   - USD 3,500 at the end of season 2003/2004.
2. On 23 December 2004, the player contacted FIFA and claimed the amount of USD 7,000 from the club. The player provided a document entitled "Statement of Account" dated 11 June 2004 and duly signed by the club's president and general secretary. According to the mentioned document, the club confirmed that it owed the amount of USD 7,000 to the player.
3. Despite several invitations from FIFA, the club renounced to its right to forward its answer to the claim to FIFA.

II. CONSIDERATIONS OF THE DISPUTE RESOLUTION CHAMBER

1. Since the claim at hand had been lodged prior to 1 July 2005 and concerns an employment contract concluded on 25 September 2003, the September 2001 edition of the Regulations for the Status and Transfer of Players (hereinafter the Regulations) shall apply (cf. art. 26 par. 1 of the July 2005 Regulations).
2. The Dispute Resolution Chamber of the FIFA Players' Status Committee shall review disputes coming under its jurisdiction pursuant to art. 42 of the Regulations at the request of one of the parties to the dispute.
3. According to art. 42 par. 1 lit. (b) (i) of the Regulations, the triggering elements of the dispute (i.e. whether a contract was breached, with or without just cause, or sporting just cause), will be decided by the Dispute Resolution Chamber.
4. As a consequence, the Dispute Resolution Chamber is the competent body to decide on the present litigation involving a club from Lebanon and a player from Armenia and regarding outstanding remuneration in connection with an employment contract signed between the parties.
5. Therefore, the members of the Dispute Resolution Chamber at first confirmed to be competent to pass a decision in this matter. In addition, the Chamber acknowledged the above-mentioned facts as well as the further documentation contained in the file.
6. Subsequently, and entering into the substance of the matter, the Chamber considered that the player A. and the Lebanese club H. signed a valid employment contract on 25 September 2003, according to which the player rendered his services until the end of the Lebanese Football Federation season 2003/2004.
7. The Chamber also noted that according to a document entitled "Statement of Account" duly signed by its president and general secretary dated 11 June 2004, the Respondent acknowledged that it still owed the amount of USD 7,000 to the player.
8. In continuation, the Chamber noted that the player requests the amount of USD 7,000 based on the aforementioned duly signed document dated 11 June 2004.
9. The Chamber observed that the club H. never took position in the dispute, despite having been asked to do so by the FIFA administration on several occasions.
10. Furthermore, the Chamber pointed out that if no reply is received from the club H to the claim, the case shall be decided only on the basis of the facts and proofs provided by the player A.
11. In this respect, the Chamber reproached the behaviour of the club H. and underlined that it renounced to its right to defence and thus accepts the allegations of the player A.
12. Taking into account all of the above, the Chamber decided that H. must pay the amount of USD 7,000 to the player A.

III. DECISION OF THE DISPUTE RESOLUTION CHAMBER

1. The claim of the player A. is accepted.
2. The club H. has to pay the amount of USD 7,000 to the player A. **within the next 30 days** as from the date of notification of this decision.

3. In the event that the above-mentioned amount is not paid within the stated deadline, an interest rate of 5% per year will apply and the present matter shall be submitted to FIFA's Disciplinary Committee, so that the necessary disciplinary sanctions may be imposed.
4. The player A. is instructed to inform H. immediately and directly of the account number to which the remittance is to be made and to notify the Dispute Resolution Chamber of every payment received.
5. According to art. 60 par. 1 of the FIFA Statutes this decision may be appealed before the Court of Arbitration for Sport (CAS). The statement of appeal must be sent to the CAS directly within 10 days of receiving notification of this decision and has to contain all elements in accordance with point 2 of the directives issued by the CAS, copy of which we enclose hereto. Within another 10 days following the expiry of the time limit for the filing of the statement of appeal, the appellant shall file with the CAS a brief stating the facts and legal arguments giving rise to the appeal (cf. point 4 of the directives).

115377
DECISION OF THE DISPUTE RESOLUTION CHAMBER
passed in Zurich, Switzerland, on 2 November 2005,
in the following composition:
Slim Aloulou (Tunisia), Chairman
Jean-Marie Philips (Belgium) member
Ivan Gazidis (USA) member
Philippe Piat (France) member
Mick McGuire (England) member
on the claim presented by the club X, Turkey as Claimant
against the
Y, Hungary as Respondent
regarding training compensation for the player A

I. FACTS OF THE CASE

1. The player A, born on 12 May 1985, was registered with X, Claimant, for the season 2003/04 between the ages of 18 and 19 as non-amateur.
2. In August 2004, the aforementioned player was registered with the club, Y, Respondent.
3. The Claimant, claims training compensation in accordance with Chapter VII of the FIFA Regulations for the Status and Transfer of Players (edition 2001).
4. According to the FIFA circular no. 826 dated 31 October 2002, which regards the categorisation of clubs, the Claimant is a 1 division club, belonging to category 2 (indicative amount EUR 60,000 per year) and the Respondent is also a 1 division club, belonging to category 2.
5. The amount of compensation is to be calculated in accordance with the parameters provided for by art. 7 par. 3 of the Regulations governing the Application of the Regulations for the Status and Transfer of Players (edition 2001), i.e. based on the training and education costs of the country in which the new club is located.
6. The Claimant is requesting the payment of training compensation from the Respondent in the amount of EUR 90,000.
7. The Respondent informed FIFA that the player and his agent gave notice to the Claimant, following which the two parties, the player and the Claimant, agreed that the player would give up his financial demands against the Claimant and in return the latter would not ask for any transfer or training compensation. In this respect, the Respondent provided a player's statement dated 1 February 2005, according to which he affirmed that he gave notice to the Claimant that he would give up his financial demands and in return the Claimant would neither ask for any transfer or training compensation nor raise financial demands against him. As a result, the Respondent is of the opinion that it does not owe any training compensation to the Claimant.
8. On 20 May 2005, the Claimant pointed out that there was neither a verbal nor a written agreement regarding the alleged remuneration to the training compensation signed between both clubs. Finally, the Claimant stressed that if the Respondent does not want to fulfil its obligations it has to provide enough evidence, i.e. it should provide a contract in this respect.

9. On 2 June 2005, the Respondent provided a copy of a duly signed letter dated 7 June 2004, according to which the senior Vice President of the Claimant, Mr xxxxxx, explained to the player's agent that: "*X would like to propose an agreement, if accepted, concludes our contract with player A. To release the player, we do not want to pay the remainder of his salary for the previous year. The debt remainder from the transfer fee will be paid immediately. If this agreement is accepted, the player will be free and out of contract. Regarding the player, our decision is like this at the moment and we will be very glad to finalize this subject in a meeting with you in xxxxx*".
10. In respect to the aforementioned letter, the Respondent understood that it would not have to pay any transfer or training compensation, in return to the favour the player did for the Claimant by renouncing to claim his outstanding salaries. As a result, the Respondent is of the opinion that it assisted the Claimant in achieving its intention of not having to pay the remaining salaries to the player. Therefore, the Respondent stressed that it is not a sportive behaviour to demand compensation from the party that helped the Claimant to save money. Finally, the Respondent explained that it was the responsibility of the Claimant to conclude a written agreement in this respect and provide it.
11. On 14 June 2005, the Claimant contested the arguments of the Respondent and explained that in the letter dated 7 June 2004 its senior Vice President informed the player's agent that the player would be free and out of contract, but never that the club would give up its rights to training compensation. Furthermore, the Claimant provided a copy of the quittance letter signed by the player on 29 July 2004, by means of which he confirmed that all debts were settled.
12. Finally, the Claimant pointed out that the fact that player waived his remaining remuneration does not annul the club's entitlement to receive compensation for training and education of the player in accordance with art. 17 of the FIFA Regulations for the Status and Transfer of Players (edition 2001).
13. On 22 June 2005, the Respondent referred to its previous submission.

II. CONSIDERATIONS OF THE DISPUTE RESOLUTION CHAMBER

1. The Dispute Resolution Chamber reviews disputes coming under its jurisdiction pursuant to Art. 42 of the FIFA Regulations for the Status and Transfer of Players (edition 2001), at the request of one of the parties to the dispute.
2. According to Art. 42 par. 1(b)(iv) of the FIFA Regulations for the Status and Transfer of Players (edition 2001), the Dispute Resolution Chamber of the FIFA Players' Status Committee shall review disputes concerning training compensation.
3. Consequently, the Dispute Resolution Chamber is the competent body to decide on the present litigation concerning the training compensation claimed by the Claimant.
4. Entering into the substance of the matter, the Chamber maintained that as established in chapter VII of the FIFA Regulations for the Status and Transfer of Players (edition 2001) training compensation for a player's training and education is payable by the new club either when the player signs his first contract as a nonamateur or each time a player changes from one club to another up to the time his training and education is complete, which, as a general rule, occurs when the player reaches 23 years of age.
5. In accordance with art. 5 of the FIFA Regulations governing the Application of the FIFA Regulations, the training period to take into account for the calculation of the training compensation, starts at the beginning of the season of the player's 12th birthday, or at a later age, as the case may be, and finishes at the end of the season of the player's 21st birthday.
6. In this respect, the Chamber emphasised that in the present case the period to take into account is as from the season 1997 until 2006. Moreover, the Chamber acknowledged that the player, born on 12 May 1985, was registered with the Claimant for the season 2003/04 between the ages of 18 and 19 as non-amateur.
7. Subsequently, the Chamber considered that, on the one hand, the Claimant requested training compensation in the amount of EUR 90,000 and, on the other hand, that the Respondent contested the Claimant's entitlement to receive any training compensation.
8. In particular, the Chamber acknowledged that according to the Respondent the player and his agent gave notice to the Claimant, following which the player and the Claimant agreed that the player would give up his financial demands against the Claimant and in return the latter would not ask for any transfer or training compensation.

9. Turning its attention to the Claimant's position, the Chamber took due note that the Claimant contested the arguments of the Respondent and explained that in the relevant letter dated 7 June 2004, to which the Respondent referred, the player's agent was informed that the player would be free and out of contract, but never that the club would give up its rights in connection with the training compensation.
10. The Chamber duly considered all documentation provided by both parties and unanimously concluded that the argumentation of the Respondent cannot be upheld since any possible financial settlement concluded between the Claimant and the player and in particular, the letter dated 7 June 2004 cannot in any sense abolish the Claimant's entitlement to receive training compensation.
11. As a result, the Chamber concluded that the Claimant is entitled to receive training compensation for the training and education of the player A as established in chapter VII of the FIFA Regulations.
12. For the sake of good order, the Chamber emphasised that art. 5 par. 5 of the FIFA Regulations governing the Application of the FIFA Regulations must not be taken into account in the present matter, since the case at hand does not involve two clubs in the EU/EEA area.
13. The Chamber does consequently rectify the assertion made by the Claimant with respect to the category to which it belongs. In fact, all clubs affiliated to the Turkish Football Association are allocated as from category 2. The Claimant does therefore belong to category 2. Then, the Chamber observed that with regard to the categorisation of clubs, the Claimant is a 1 division club, belonging to category 2 (indicative amount EUR 60,000 per year) and the Respondent is also a 1 division club, belonging to category 2.
14. In this respect, the Chamber explained that the amount of compensation must be calculated in accordance with art. 7 of the FIFA Regulations governing the Application of the FIFA Regulations, applying the parameters established by the FIFA circular no. 826 dated from the 31 of October of 2002.
15. In accordance with art. 7 par. 3 of the FIFA Regulations governing the Application of the FIFA Regulations, as a general principle, the compensation for training is based on the training and education costs of the country in which the new club is located. In this respect, and in order to clarify the sense of the mentioned clause, the Chamber referred to the point 2b(ii) of the FIFA circular n. 769 dated 24 of August of 2001 and maintained that, for the transfer of a player from a country outside the area of the EU or the EEA to a country outside the area of the EU or the EEA, as long as training compensation is owed, the compensation should be calculated based on the costs of the country of the new club applying the category of the club which effectively has formed and educated the player. Article 7 par. 1 of the said FIFA Regulations confirms the mentioned principle ("*the compensation for training and education shall be obtained by multiplying the amount corresponding to the category of the training club for which the player was registered by the number of years of training from 12 to 21*").
16. Therefore and in compliance with the above-mentioned the amount owed as training compensation is obtained by multiplying the sum corresponding to the category of the Claimant, i.e. EUR 60,000.
17. Consequently, in application of article 7 par. 1 of the FIFA Regulations governing the Application of the FIFA Regulations the indicative amount mentioned in the previous point must be multiplied by the number of years of training of the player in case.
18. Taking into account all of the above, the Chamber concluded that the Respondent has to pay the amount of EUR 60,000 to the Claimant as training compensation for the training and education of the player A.

III. DECISION OF THE DISPUTE RESOLUTION CHAMBER

1. The claim lodged by the Claimant, X, is partially accepted.
2. The Respondent, Y, shall pay the total amount of EUR 60,000 to the Claimant, within 30 days following the date of the communication of the present decision.
3. Any further claims lodged by the Claimant are rejected.
4. In the event that the above-mentioned amount is not paid within the stated deadline, an interest rate of 5% per year will apply and the present matter shall be submitted to FIFA's Disciplinary Committee, so that the necessary disciplinary sanctions may be imposed.
5. The Claimant is instructed to inform the Respondent directly and immediately of the account number to which the remittance is to be made and to notify the Dispute Resolution Chamber of every payment received.

6. According to art. 60 par. 1 of the FIFA Statutes, this decision may be appealed against before the Court of Arbitration for Sport (CAS). The statement of appeal must be sent to the CAS directly within 10 days of receipt of notification of this decision and shall contain all the elements in accordance with point 2 of the directives issued by the CAS, a copy of which we enclose hereto. Within another 10 days following the expiry of the time limit for filing the statement of appeal, the appellant shall file a brief stating the facts and legal arguments giving rise to the appeal with the CAS (cf. point 4 of the directives).

⚽⚽⚽

115780
DECISION OF THE DISPUTE RESOLUTION CHAMBER
passed in Zurich, Switzerland, on 2 November 2005,
in the following composition:
Slim Aloulou (Tunisia), Chairman
Jean-Marie Philips (Belgium), member
Ivan Gazidis (USA), member
Mick Mc Guire (England), member
Philippe Piat (France), member
on the claim presented by the
Player X, represented by A as Claimant
against
Club Y, as Respondent
regarding compensation for contractual breach

I. FACTS OF THE CASE

1. On 26 August 2004, the player X (date of birth: Z) turned to FIFA requesting the examination of his contractual situation with the club Y. In this regard, the player asked FIFA to confirm by decision of the Dispute Resolution Chamber that his employment contract signed on 28 August 2003 with club Y terminated on 27 August 2004 and he was therefore free to sign a new employment contract with any club of his choice.
2. Essentially, at first, the player maintained that the four-years employment contract which had been presented to him by the club Y was forged and that on the basis of the true contract signed on 28 August 2003, with a validity of one year only, he had to be considered free from all contractual engagement as from 27 August 2004. In this regard, the player provided the FIFA administration with copies of the two aforementioned versions of the employment contract, one of which foresaw a four years duration and one with a one year duration only. The player underlined that he would never have accepted the employment contract with the duration of four years, since the remuneration sharply decreased after the first year.
3. Upon request of the FIFA administration and in order for the club to demonstrate that the employment contract with the four years duration contained the authentic signature of the player, the club Y provided FIFA with the original copy of the relevant employment contract signed by the parties involved on each single page. The document even bore the finger print of the player at the last page.
4. This four-years employment contract was signed on 28 August 2003. According to this contract, the club Y committed to pay to the player X a salary of USD 100,000 in the first year of employment, payable in 10 instalments. The player was also granted bonuses of USD 10,000 per championship won. Additionally, the parties agreed on the payment of a signing-on fee to the player of USD 170,000. Finally, for the remaining years of the employment, the club committed itself to pay to the player the amount of USD 60,000 per year.
5. According to art. 20 of the said employment contract, the club Y reserved its right to rescind the employment contract at any time by sending a letter to the player and by giving him a one month's notice. In such a case, the player would have no entitlement to compensation or to the remaining salaries.
6. According to art. 4 of this employment contract, the player would not be entitled to the right of unilaterally terminating the contract. In the case of an early termination, the player would be held

liable to reimburse the transfer compensation and other costs incurred by the club with regard to his employment as well as to compensate the club for damages.

7. According to the player X, he had always departed from the assumption that the employment would run until 27 August 2004, i.e. for one year only.
8. Furthermore, the player pointed out that the contract greatly favours the club Y by awarding it the right to rescind the engagement at any time and without consequences. Here too, the player affirmed that he would never have accepted such a provision.
9. The legal representative of the player X has also indicated that if the player indeed signed this disputed employment contract, he would have done so without being represented by an advisor and without having sufficient knowledge of the English language to recognise the extent of this engagement. It would escape all logic if the player should have accepted such a contract under normal conditions.
10. In this regard, the player highlighted the involvement of a certain Mr. B, agent mandated by the club Y, who, however, assisted the player X in this transaction (Note: Mr. B has no players' agent license).
11. According to the player X, the day after signing the employment contract, he went accompanied by Mr. B and an employee of club Y to the bank. In this context, the player affirmed having encashed the signing-on fee check in the amount of USD 170,000 and given the amount forthwith to the employee of the club. The player affirmed that he was told by Mr. B to do so. Furthermore, he has knowledge of the fact that Mr. B was due to receive USD 250,000 from another club C for an envisaged loan of the player.
12. Furthermore, the player X asked the FIFA administration to examine the case of the player D who had also signed a one-year employment contract with the club Y and who is now being confronted with a four-years engagement as well.
13. The FIFA administration rejected this request, outlining that such an investigation would only take place if either club Y or the player D presented a claim before FIFA's deciding bodies.
14. The player X also explained that he left the country of club Y for the summer break with the instructions of club Y to remain in contact with the club's director, so as to discuss a new engagement. However, when he did revert to the club during the summer holidays, he was unable to reach any of the responsible staff and, therefore, assumed that there was no more interest of the club. He then affirmed having departed to another country, to join the club C. The player insists that this shows that neither party had considered his employment to run for more than one year.
15. On the other hand, according to club Y, the player X had signed an employment contract with a duration of four years, starting on 28 August 2003 and running until 27 August 2007. Therefore, the club Y maintained that the player X unilaterally broke the employment contract by disappearing after only one year and that, in this context, he should be held liable to compensate the club.
16. In accordance with the four-years employment contract, the player received on 28 August 2003 the amount of USD 170,000 as a signing-on fee (receipt provided is signed by the player), the amount of USD 100,000 as salary for the first year (receipts provided are signed by the player) and USD 40,000 for winning championships (receipts provided are signed by the player). Thus, it appears that the player received the total amount of USD 310,000 from club Y. (Note: The player himself confirmed having been paid correctly during that year in question and did not contest any above-mentioned payment).
17. The employment contract was issued in four copies, which all bear the stamp of the public authority for youth and sports.
18. Based on the fact that the player X disputed the validity of the four-years employment contract and rejected to return to the country of club Y, and that, on the other hand, the club Y did not ask for the player's return but for financial compensation, FIFA, on 16 September 2004, provisionally authorised the player's registration with the club of his choice. The player was, however, made aware of the possible financial consequences of this premature termination of contract as well as the fact that the Dispute Resolution Chamber may judge the case at hand under the terms of the articles 21 and following of the Regulations for the Status and Transfer of Players (edition September 2001).
19. On 13 December 2004, club Y specified its claim and claimed the total amount of USD 1,265,465 from the player X. The claim was composed of the following amounts: USD 170,000 as signing-on fee, USD 100,000 as salaries, USD 40,000 as winning rewards, USD 70,000 as commission for the agent, USD 17,758 as hotel accommodation, USD 3,342 as the annual fee for car rental

(annual contract), USD 9,405 as apartment rent (two-years contract), USD 120,000 for contracting another player, USD 14,560 for air tickets, USD 70,400 for losing the chance to qualify for a specific tournament, USD 500,000 for affecting the reputation of the club Y and finally USD 150,000 for losing the chance to transfer the player.

20. On 15 July 2005, the FIFA administration asked the player to provide its final statement to the dispute, in particular, to take position on the receipts provided by the club and to provide the original version of the employment contract with the duration of one year.
21. On 26 August 2005, changing his point of view, the player informed the FIFA administration that, at that time, he was deceived by the club Y and on 28 August 2003 signed a "*document*" in which the period of duration was four years, thinking that he was signing a one-year employment relationship only. In order to corroborate this alleged fraud committed by the club, the player explained that the contract was signed before 08:00 o'clock in the morning at the Marriot Hotel in the country of club Y, the club's representative being in a hurry and the player himself without knowledge of the English or the country of club Y's language. In addition, the player maintained that the disorder of the articles stipulated in the four-years contract had the only purpose to mislead him. In fact, the said contract mixed up clauses, in particular the ones referring to the remuneration of the player, without following a logical structure. Finally, in clear contradiction to his previous position, the player maintained that he never signed the one-year contract, but the four-years contract only. Yet, according to the player, the oneyear employment contract had been set up subsequently by the club by using the signatures of the original four years employment contract. According to the player, shortly after, a copy of the falsified one-year employment contract, which he rejects having signed, was given to him by club Y. Taking the above-mentioned into account, the player did not provide the FIFA administration with the original one year employment contract.
22. Attached to the above-mentioned statement, the player X provided the FIFA administration with an expertise ordered in Brazil. Therein, the expert affirmed that the employment contract with a validity of one year was, with no doubt, a forgery. With regard to the question concerning the authorship of the forgery, the expert affirmed that all evidences indicated that both contracts had been printed in the same print machine, however, it was "*not possible to give a categoric answer to that question.*"
23. In the same statement, the player X refused the claim put forward by club Y in the amount of USD 1,265,465, particularly refusing the payment of any allowance fees, car rent fees and hotel expenses. Moreover, the player himself specified his financial claim by requesting the payment of USD 1,250,000 plus reimbursement of additional expenses in connection with the present proceeding (amount to be determined by FIFA) from club Y. The amount was composed by 30 months salaries of USD 28,000 each, bonuses in the amount of USD 160,000 as well as the compensation for moral damages in the amount of USD 250,000.
24. In addition, the player X requested the production of the following proofs: to force the club Y to present the other three original versions of the four years contract; to be allowed the deposition of witnesses in the persons of other players with a similar legal dispute, i.e. Mr. D and E; to force the club Y to present the original contracts signed with the aforementioned players; to allow a technical exam to confirm the veracity of the facts alleged in relation to the elaboration of the forged employment contract with a duration of one year, and finally; to be heard in an inquiry procedure before the Dispute Resolution Chamber.
25. On 16 September 2005, the parties to the dispute were duly informed by the FIFA Administration that the present case was going to be submitted to the Dispute Resolution Chamber for a formal decision on 23 September 2005.
26. On 19 October 2005, the parties to the dispute were duly informed by the FIFA Administration that the Dispute Resolution Chamber dealt with the present matter at its meeting held on 23 September 2005. However, on the occasion of the said reunion the members of the Dispute Resolution Chamber concluded that some important aspects of the case should be further investigated and therefore referred the matter back to the FIFA Administration.
27. After having obtained specific further information mainly related to the player's career history as from him joining the club Y until the day of the decision, the FIFA Administration informed the parties to the dispute that the case at hand would once again be submitted to the Dispute Resolution Chamber for consideration and a formal decision on 2 November 2005.

II. CONSIDERATIONS OF THE DISPUTE RESOLUTION CHAMBER

1. The members of the Dispute Resolution Chamber were summoned to pass a decision on this matter by the Chairman pursuant to art. 1 point 6) of the Rules Governing the Practice and Procedures of the Dispute Resolution Chamber (edition February 2002).
2. The Dispute Resolution Chamber of the FIFA Players' Status Committee indicated that, as established in art. 42 § 1 lit. (b) (i), (ii) and (iii) in connection with art. 21 and following of the FIFA Regulations for the Status and Transfer of Players (edition September 2001) (hereinafter: *the Regulations*), it falls within the purview of the Dispute Resolution Chamber to determine whether one of the parties has committed an unilateral breach of contract with or without just cause and if so, to verify whether this party is accountable for outstanding payments and whether sport sanctions must be imposed.
3. Consequently, the Dispute Resolution Chamber is the competent body to decide on the dispute for breach of contract between the player X and club Y.
4. Having established this, the Chamber took note that on 16 September 2005, both parties involved were duly informed by the FIFA administration that the present case was going to be submitted to the Dispute Resolution Chamber for a formal decision on 23 September 2005.
5. However, the Chamber took note of the last correspondence received from the player one day before the first meeting, i.e. on 22 September 2005, stating that the present case had to be withdrawn from the list of cases to be decided in order to proceed to further examine the facts of the case through additional technical reports. The player demanded that FIFA appoint an expert.
6. In view of these circumstances, after having carefully studied the facts of the case and even postponed the decision to the next meeting of the Dispute Resolution Chamber in order to further clarify specific aspects of the case, the members of the Chamber were of the opinion that the investigation of the case at hand had now been fully completed and that there were no reasons to further delay a decision.
7. Subsequently, and entering into the substance of the matter, the Chamber took note of the fact that, the player X, apparently confronted with two employment contracts with different periods of validity, approached FIFA on 26 August 2004 in order to have his contractual situation with club Y clarified. In this context, the members of the Dispute Resolution Chamber observed that at that time, the player strongly maintained having signed an employment contract with club Y with a period of validity of one year only. Since club Y challenged the validity of that contract by presenting a four-years employment contract, the latter insisted that FIFA should confirm that his employment contract with club Y had expired and he was free to sign with any club of his choice.
8. Thereupon, the Chamber acknowledged that, although being in possession of the original employment contract with a period of validity of four years, i.e. running until 27 August 2007, FIFA, due to the fact that the player strongly refused to return to club Y and that the club itself had not explicitly asked for the players' return, provisionally authorised the player on 16 September 2004 to register with the club of his choice. In this context, the members of the Dispute Resolution Chamber pointed out that the player was informed that the original employment contract with a validity of four years did not give rise to the assumption that there had been a forgery on that document. Therefore, FIFA, at that time, had warned the player that the case at hand may be judged once under the terms of the articles 21 and following of the Regulations.
9. Then, the members of the Chamber pointed out that the player had obviously changed his point of view during the course of the investigation and maintained having signed a four-years employment contract only but having been deceived by club Y in this respect. In this regard, the members took note that the player maintained having signed the four-years employment contract thinking that it was a one-year employment contract only. Moreover, the Chamber acknowledged that according to the player, he signed the said contract before 08:00 o'clock in the morning in country of club Y, apparently without being able to read and/or speak neither the English language nor the country of club Y's language. In addition, the representative of club Y was, according to the player, in a hurry.
10. Thereupon, the members of the Chamber took note of the contents of the expertise provided by the player to the FIFA administration. In this context, after carefully studying the said document, the members observed that the expert declared the four-years employment contract signed by the parties involved to be genuine and the one-year employment contract to be a forgery. Moreover, the Chamber acknowledged the fact that according to the expertise, the question concerning the authorship of the forged one-year employment contract remained unclear and subject to speculation.
11. Taking into account all of the above, the members of the Dispute Resolution Chamber affirmed that the employment contract signed by the parties involved on 28 August 2003, with a validity of four

years, had to be qualified genuine and therefore legally binding upon both parties involved. The members underlined that the player himself admitted, at the end of the investigation, having signed the four-years employment contract. However, the members also took into consideration the claims of the player that he had been deceived by club Y and its agent, Mr. B. Nevertheless, the Chamber pointed out that the player X acted highly negligently by signing an employment contract without having apparently understood its content and far reaching consequences.

12. As a result, the members of the Chamber rejected the player's financial claim and unanimously decided that the player X had unilaterally breached the employment contract signed with club Y on 28 August 2003 by leaving the club after only one season, i.e. on August 2004. In this context, the members pointed out that the player had breached the employment contract without just cause during the socalled protected period as provided for in art. 21 §1 lit. (a) of the Regulations.
13. The Chamber then focussed its analysis on the amount of compensation due by the player to the club for the breach of contract, in accordance with art. 21§1 lit. (a) of the Regulations, as well as on the sport sanctions to be imposed on the player in accordance with art. 23§1 lit. (a) of the Regulations. The Chamber decided to start by establishing the compensation amount.
14. Therefore, the Chamber examined the objective criteria listed in art. 22 of the Regulations, in order to verify their relevance in the case at stake. For the sake of good order it is recalled that the list of criteria is not exhaustive and that the deciding body is entrusted to analyze and consider supplementary criteria while deciding on the dispute.
15. The first factor taken into consideration was the remuneration and other benefits under the employment contract signed by the player with club Y.
16. The Chamber noted that, in accordance with the duly signed and legally valid four-years employment contract concluded with club Y on 28 August 2003, the player X received, in his first year, the amount of USD 170,000 as a signing-on fee, the amount of USD 100,000 as salary and USD 40,000 for winning championships. With regard to the three remaining years of the contract, the Chamber took note that the player would have been entitled to receive the amount of USD 60,000 per year, adding up to USD 180,000.
17. The second and third factor taken into consideration was the length of time remaining on the existing contract as well as any amount or fee paid by the club to the player to be amortised over the length of the contract.
18. In this context, the Chamber observed that at the time the breach of contract took place, the employment contract was still to run for three more years and the remaining value of the same was of USD 180,000, i.e. the remuneration for three seasons of USD 60,000 each.
19. Taking the fourth factor listed in art. 22 of the Regulations into account, the Chamber affirmed that the player broke the four-years employment contract after the first year, i.e. during the protected period stipulated in art. 21 of the Regulations.
20. Subsequently, the Chamber stated that it falls under its responsibility to estimate the damage suffered by club Y, not only in accordance with the above-stated criteria, but also with the specificity of football.
21. The Chamber has furthermore analyzed the stance of the two parties involved. On one hand, the club has complied with all terms of the contract signed, particularly with the financial terms. On the contrary, the attitude of the player can be judged as particularly reproachable. In fact, the player signed a four-year contract with a signing-on fee and favourable financial conditions in the first years, and he left exactly after the end of the first season, when his yearly salary decreased to USD 60,000. The damage caused by the player is not only of a financial nature, but also a sporting one, since the club, in good faith, could rely on the services of the player for further three years and had to find a replacement for the player by investing in a new one, for which a transfer compensation was paid.
22. The Chamber therefore concluded that when deciding on the compensation to be paid by the player to his former club, the aforementioned considerations should duly be taken into account.
23. Taking the above-mentioned into account, the Chamber decided that the player X must pay the amount of USD 615,000 to club Y.
24. The reasoning put forward by the player X could not be followed and the claim lodged by the player therefore had to be rejected.
25. Subsequently, the Chamber focussed its analysis on the sports sanctions to be imposed on the player in accordance with art. 23 § 1 lit. (a) of the Regulations. In this context, the members of the Dispute

Resolution Chamber deviated from the four months suspension stipulated in the relevant provision for several reasons. The Chamber was of the opinion that the apparent sparse communication between club Y and the player during the summer break after the season 2003/2004 had an impact on the developments in this case. Moreover, taking into account the obvious unequal disposition of rights and duties in the employment contract, the Chamber was convinced that the club Y abused of the ignorance of the player as well as its bigger bargaining power at the moment of signing the said document. Furthermore, the Chamber considered that the player remained without being registered for a new club during a considerable amount of time, and therefore concluded that it could deviate from the sanction provided for in the Regulations. The consideration of these exceptional circumstances, has however no prejudice effect on other cases, since every single case has to be decided on its merits. Furthermore, a sanction imposed for a shorter timeframe would allow to the player to resume playing faster and thus enable him to pay off the compensation due to the club Y with the money earned.

26. Therefore, the Chamber decided that under consideration of the exceptional circumstances the player X had to be sanctioned with a restriction of 6 weeks on his eligibility to participate in any official football matches as from the notification of this decision.
27. The Chamber concluded its deliberations by underlining that the present investigation clearly brought to light that, club Y had used the services of a not licensed agent, i.e. Mr. B, when contracting the services of the player X. However, since not the Dispute Resolution Chamber but the Players' Status Committee is competent to judge this aspect of the case, this part will be the object of a separate proceeding and the case shall be sent to the Players' Status Committee for consideration and decision on the involvement of the unlicensed agent.

III. DECISION OF THE DISPUTE RESOLUTION CHAMBER

1. The claim of the player X is rejected.
2. The counter-claim of club Y is partially accepted.
3. The eligibility of the player X to participate in any official football matches shall be restricted for 6 weeks as from the notification of this decision.
4. The player X has to pay the amount of USD 615,000 to club Y within the next 30 days as from the date of notification of this decision.
5. Any further claims lodged by club Y are rejected.
6. If the aforementioned sum is not paid within the aforementioned deadline, a 5% default interest rate per annum will apply and the present matter will be submitted to FIFA's Disciplinary Committee, so that the necessary disciplinary sanctions may be imposed.
7. Club Y is directed to inform the player X immediately of the account number to which the remittance is to be made and to notify the Dispute Resolution Chamber of every payment received.
8. The file shall be remitted to the Players' Status Committee for a decision regarding club Y's use of a non-licensed agent.
9. According to art. 60 par. 1 of the FIFA Statutes this decision may be appealed before the Court of Arbitration for Sport (CAS). The statement of appeal must be sent to the CAS directly within 10 days of receiving notification of this decision and has to contain all elements in accordance with point 2 of the directives issued by the CAS, copy of which we enclose hereto. Within another 10 days following the expiry of the time limit for the filing of the statement of appeal, the appellant shall file with the CAS a brief stating the facts and legal arguments giving rise to the appeal (cf. point 4 of the directives).

115999

DECISION OF THE DISPUTE RESOLUTION CHAMBER

passed in Zurich, Switzerland, on 2 November 2005,
in the following composition:
Slim Aloulou (Tunisia), Chairman
Jean-Marie Philips (Belgium), member
Ivan Gazidis (USA), member
Mick McGuire (England), member

Philippe Piat (France), member
on the claim presented by
the player, M represented by Mr T, Attorney at Law, as Claimant
against the club, O as Respondent
regarding a contractual dispute between the player and the club,

FACTS OF THE CASE

1. On 2 October 2001 the player M, Claimant, and the club O, Respondent, signed an employment contract initially valid from 1 December 2001 until 15 May 2002. Subsequently, the duration of the contract was extended for the 2002/2003 season.
2. According to the relevant employment contract, for the period between 1 December 2001 and 30 May 2002 the Claimant was entitled to receive the following emoluments:
   - 23,000 due on 1 December 2001 and
   - 42,000 payable in six equal monthly instalments of 7,000, the first of which due in January 2002.
3. For the 2002/2003 season the Claimant was entitled to receive the following remunerations:
   - 43,000 due on 1 July 2002 and
   - 100,000 payable in 10 equal monthly instalment of 10,000, the first of which due on 1 August 2002.
4. On 7 January 2004, the player turned to FIFA claiming that after leaving the club, at the end of the 2002/2003 season, the Respondent still owed him 10,000. The Respondent issued two checks, of 5,000 each, in his favour. The Claimant maintains, however, that he could not cash them.
5. In addition, the Claimant maintains that it is not possible for him to indicate to what specific months the claimed amount refers, since the Respondent paid him very irregularly.
6. Therefore, the Claimant demands immediate payment of the sum of 10,000 plus an amount, which the deciding body deems appropriate to cover his legal fees and other expenses.
7. On 19 January 2005, FIFA invited the Respondent to present its response to the player's claim by 8 February 2005. No reply was received. A second invitation dated 10 March 2005 to the Respondent to submit its response by no later than 21 March 2005 also remained unanswered.
8. On 8 July 2005 the Claimant confirms that he gave the two checks back to the Respondent.

CONSIDERATIONS OF THE DISPUTE RESOLUTION CHAMBER

1. The Dispute Resolution Chamber started its deliberations by indicating that the matter at stake was submitted to FIFA before 1 July 2005. Therefore, and in accordance with Article 26 Para. 1 of the revised Regulations for the Status and Transfer of Players (edition 2005), the Chamber stated that not the revised Regulations, but the previous Regulations for the Status and Transfer of Players (edition 2001, hereinafter referred to as; the Regulations) do apply on the matter at hand.
2. The Dispute Resolution Chamber then asserted that the matter at stake concerns a dispute between a player and a club regarding the fulfilment of a financial obligation resulting from an employment contract.
3. According to Article 42 of the Regulations the Dispute Resolution Chamber is competent to deal with matters with an international dimension which concern employment related contractual disputes between players and clubs. As a result, the Dispute Resolution Chamber is competent to deal with disputes resulting from the non-fulfilment of an employment contract.
4. On account of the above, the Dispute Resolution Chamber concluded that it is competent to decide upon the matter at hand.
5. Entering into the substance of the matter, the Chamber acknowledged the documentation contained in the file and took note of the fact that the Claimant and the Respondent had signed an employment contract valid from 1 December 2001 until the end of the season 2002/2003, stipulating as salaries for the season 2002/2003 43,000 and ten monthly instalments of 10,000 each. Moreover, the members of the Chamber noticed that according to the Claimant, the due amount of 10,000 has not been paid. Furthermore, the Chamber took into consideration that the claimed amount could not be specified to what months it refers by the Claimant, since the Respondent paid the Claimant very irregularly. Also the Chamber paid attention to the fact that the Claimant gave the two checks in the amount of 10,000 back to the Respondent because he could not cash them. And finally, the Chamber took note of the

fact that the Respondent never issued its position in the matter, despite having been asked to do so by the FIFA administration on several occasions.

6. In continuation, the Chamber then stated that as a general principle of procedure before the Dispute Resolution Chamber, if a Respondent does not reply to the claim, the case shall be decided by the Dispute Resolution Chamber only on the basis of the facts and proof provided by the Claimant, since with its conduct, the Respondent renounces to its right of defence and thus accepts the allegations of the claimant.
7. On account of the above, the Chamber stated that because the Respondent never took position in the dispute, the Dispute Resolution Chamber has to pass a decision based only on the facts and evidence provided by the Claimant.
8. In this regard, the Chamber underlined that the Claimant is claiming outstanding remunerations from the Respondent, which amounts to 10,000.
9. In conclusion to the above, since this demand has remained uncontested by the Respondent, the Dispute Resolution Chamber decided that the Respondent has to pay the amount of 10,000 to the Claimant.
10. As regards the claimed amount to cover legal fees and other expenses, the Chamber stated hat the Claimant did not quantify or specify these compensations at all, nor provided the FIFA administration with any proving document. Consequently, the Chamber decided to not award these claimed remunerations. Notwithstanding the aforementioned, the Chamber also considered to reject the claim with regard to the covering of any legal or other fees because in accordance with the well established jurisprudence of the Dispute Resolution Chamber no procedural compensation shall be awarded in proceedings in front of the Dispute Resolution Chamber.
11. In the light of all of the above, the Chamber decided that the Claimant is entitled to receive the amount of 10,000 from the Respondent.

DECISION OF THE DISPUTE RESOLUTION CHAMBER

1. The claim of the Claimant is partially accepted.
2. The Respondent has to pay the amount of 10,000 to the Claimant.
3. The amount due to the Claimant has to be paid by the Respondent within the next 30 days as from the date of notification of this decision.
4. In the event that the debt of the Respondent is not paid within the stated deadline, an interest rate of 5% per year will apply as of expiry of the aforementioned deadline.
5. If the sum of 10,000 is not paid within the aforementioned deadline, the present matter shall be submitted to the FIFA Disciplinary Committee, so that the necessary disciplinary sanctions may be imposed.
6. The Claimant is directed to inform the Respondent immediately of the account number to which the remittance is to be made and to notify the Dispute Resolution Chamber of every payment received.
7. Any further claims submitted by the Claimant are rejected.
8. According to art. 60 par. 1 of the FIFA Statutes, this decision may be appealed against before the Court of Arbitration for Sport (CAS). The statement of appeal must be sent to the CAS directly within 10 days of receipt of notification of this decision and shall contain all the elements in accordance with point 2 of the directives issued by the CAS, a copy of which we enclose hereto. Within another 10 days following the expiry of the time limit for filing the statement of appeal, the appellant shall file a brief stating the facts and legal arguments giving rise to the appeal with the CAS (cf. point 4 of the directives).

12 JANUARY 2006

16107

DECISION OF THE DISPUTE RESOLUTION CHAMBER

passed in Zurich, Switzerland, on 12 January 2006,
in the following composition:
Mr Slim Aloulou (Tunisia), chairman
Mr Jean-Marie Philips (Belgium), member

Mr Zola Malvern Percival Majavu (South Africa), member
Mr Rinaldo Martorelli (Brazil), member
Mr Theo van Seggelen (Netherlands), member
on the claim presented by Mr X Represented by as Claimant
against
Y as Respondent
regarding a contractual dispute arisen between the parties

I. FACTS OF THE CASE

1. On 26 February 2003, the player X and the club Y signed an employment contract valid until 25 June 2005. The Claimant has provided FIFA with a copy of the aforementioned employment contract.
2. According to the aforementioned employment contract, the player was entitled to receive a monthly salary of ROL 2,500,000, as well as the following amounts:
   A. USD 30,000 between 26 February 2003 and 24 June 2003, if he would play a minimum of 10 matches in the Romanian championship;
   B. USD 75,000 during the 2003/2004 sporting season, if he would play a minimum of 23 official matches;
   C. USD 80,000 during the 2004/2005 sporting season, if he would play a minimum of 23 official matches.
3. Moreover, if the player plays during the period of the validity of the contract he will receive bonuses as stipulated in the Internal Regulations. Furthermore, the player was also entitled to receive two return flight tickets (Bucharest - Lisbon – Bucharest).
4. The player asserts that he played for the club until the end of the 2002/2003 sporting season and that, on 24 August 2003, after the club had been eliminated in the second preliminary round of the UEFA Champions League, the club's president informed him that he should start looking for another club.
5. As a consequence, and despite the short period left in order to find a new club, the player claims to have gone abroad with that purpose. By the time he returned, in September 2003, his visa had already expired (on 20 September 2003). According to the player, he tried to get a visa that would allow him to enter into the country, but he was told at the relevant consulate in Portugal that he needed the club's authorization for that effect.
6. Moreover, according to the player, the club failed to provide the relevant consulate in Portugal with the necessary documents in order for him to obtain the relevant visa and, as a consequence, not only had he not received any remuneration since the end of the 2002/2003 sporting season, but he was also prevented from playing/working.
7. In this regard, the player asserts that he has contacted the club for several times in order to solve the problem with his visa. Copies of some letters and phone receipts confirming the aforementioned position were provided to FIFA.
8. In light of the above, the player is presently requesting the Chamber to consider that the club has terminated their employment contract without just cause and to consequently condemn the club to pay to him the amount of USD 167,500. In particular, the player is requesting the amount of USD 12,500 for winning the Romanian championship in the 2002/2003 sporting season (half the bonus for winning the Romanian championship, since he played only half season), the amount of USD 75,000 as salaries for the 2003/2004 sporting season, the amount of USD 80,000 as salaries for the 2004/2005 sporting season, as well as the procedural costs which he incurred in the present procedure.
9. In reply, the club confirmed that it has paid to the player all the amounts that the player was contractually entitled to receive during the 2002/2003 sporting season.
10. With regard to the 2003/2004 sporting season, the club asserts that the player in question signed a document, according to which, he renounced to the amounts that he was entitled to receive during such period. The Respondent has provided FIFA with a copy of the aforementioned declaration.
11. Such document, dated 8 September 2003, and signed by the player, states the following:
    "I, X, footballer with Y declare today that, in any event I secure a contract with any club of my choice in the season 2003-2004, I declare that I renounce the total sum of 75,000 USD I have in contract with Y for season 2003-2004. It is agreed today between me and the club that, I will be transfer free if I secure any team interested in my service for season 2003-2004".

12. Moreover, the club defends that, on 21 August 2003, both parties signed an appendix to their employment contract, decreasing the amounts that the player was entitled to receive in accordance with their original employment contract, with regard to the 2004/2005 sporting season. The Respondent has provided FIFA with a copy of the aforementioned appendix.
13. Y also informed FIFA that, in January 2004, it has reached an agreement with the Saudi Arabian club xxxxxxx for the loan of the player on a free basis until May 2004, which was accepted by the player and that subsequently, his international transfer certificate (hereinafter: ITC) was issued in favour of the Saudi Arabian Football Federation. The Respondent has provided FIFA with a copy of the aforementioned agreement.
14. In response, the player asserts that, with regard to the 2003/2004 sporting season, and according to the aforementioned declaration, he would only waive his right to receive the amounts that are contractually established in his employment contract, in case he would find a club with which he would sign an employment contract for that period.
15. However, the player emphasizes that he spent 7 days only with xxxxx in January 2004, but that he did not sign any employment contract with the relevant Saudi Arabian club because of the latter's financial crisis.
16. Moreover, the player asserts that, on 30 January 2004, he finally managed to sign an employment contract valid until 30 June 2004 with xxxxxxx, a club participating in the second league of Portugal, with a gross monthly salary of EUR 1,600. The Claimant has provided FIFA with a copy of the aforementioned employment contract.
17. Notwithstanding all the above, the player defends that he did not sign the aforementioned appendix presented by Y nor the relevant declaration dated 8 September 2003 and claims that his signature in such documents was forged. However, the player did not provide any evidence in this respect in order to corroborate his allegations.
18. In reply, the Romanian club confirmed the amount of the bonus for winning the Romanian championship in the 2002/2003 sporting season, but asserted that such bonus would be paid within the following conditions:

    A. USD 10,000 at the end of the championship;

    B. USD 5,000 once the club had passed the 2nd preliminary round of the UEFA Champions League;

    C. USD 10,000 once the club qualified to the group stage of the UEFA Champions League.
19. However, according to the club's internal regulations, each player would receive such bonus in proportion to the amount of matches played. Therefore, in the specific case of Mr X, he would be entitled to receive the sole amount of USD 2,000 as *pro rata* payment of the USD 10,000 bonus that was scheduled to be paid at the end of the championship. With regard to the remaining amount of USD 15,000, the player is not entitled to receive any of it, since the club was eliminated in the second preliminary round of the UEFA Champions League.
20. On the other hand, the club defends that the player left in September 2003 at his request, without having been subjected to any threats, in order to leave for one year on a free loan basis. Moreover, Y asserts that during a long period it was not contacted by the player nor had his personal contacts.
22. Finally, the club defends that, with regard to the player's visa, according to the new national legislation, the club could not have registered any more foreign players who had no right to work in the country.
23. In light of the above, FIFA requested Y, twice, to inform whether it has contacted the player to resume duty with it after September 2003 or not and, if so, when. In the affirmative, the club should provide evidence supporting such disputed position. Y was also requested to provide a copy of its internal regulations for the 2002/2003 sporting season, duly translated into one of the FIFA official languages, as well as the original of the disputed declaration dated 8 September 2003, apparently signed by the player (doc. no. 598/08.09.2003) and of the disputed annex to the parties' employment contract (doc. no. 535/21.08.2003), allegedly also signed by the player. Finally, the club was requested to provide a copy of a visa for the player in question, valid from September 2003 onwards. However, to date, Y has not provided FIFA with any reply towards the aforementioned requests.
24. On the other hand, FIFA requested the Saudi Arabian Football Federation to be informed whether the player in question has ever been registered with its affiliated club xxxxxx and in the affirmative, to be provided with a copy of the parties employment contract and respective period of registration.

Moreover, the aforementioned Association was also requested to inform whether the player's ITC was actually issued by the Romanian Football Federation or not.

25. In reply, the Saudi Arabian Football Federation informed FIFA that the player was effectively registered with xxxxxx for the period from 15 January 2004 until 15 June 2004, but the contract was early terminated per mutual consent on 22 January 2004. In this regard, and at the request of FIFA, the player informed that he has received the amount of USD 400 from the relevant Saudi Arabian club, corresponding to the period of 7 days that he effectively remained with the Saudi club.
26. Moreover, at the request of FIFA, the player informed that, in the meantime, he has been registered for the Egyptian club xxxxx from September until December 2004 and for the Cypriot club xxxxx from February until May 2005, but that he has no copies of the relevant employment contracts at his disposal.
27. As a consequence, FIFA requested the Egyptian Football Association and the Cypriot Football Association to be provided with a copy of the player's aforementioned employment contracts.
28. In reply, the Egyptian Football Association provided FIFA with a copy of the player's employment contract with xxxxx. According to such contract, valid from 1 September until 31 December 2004, the player was entitled to receive a total amount of USD 30,000.
29. The Cypriot Football Association, for its part, also provided FIFA with a copy of the player's employment contract with xxxxxx. According to such contract, valid from 17 January 2005 until 31 May 2005, the player was entitled to receive a monthly salary of CYP 2,200 in the total amount of CYP 11,000 (5 months), plus a signing-on fee of CYP 6,000.

II. CONSIDERATIONS OF THE DISPUTE RESOLUTION CHAMBER

1. The FIFA Regulations for the Status and Transfer of Players (edition September 2001) are the applicable Regulations to the present procedure, since the case has been brought to FIFA before the coming into force of the current version of the said Regulations on 1 July 2005. Furthermore, the contractual dispute at hand has its basis on the employment contract signed between the parties on 26 February 2003.
2. In light of the above, the Dispute Resolution Chamber shall review disputes coming under its jurisdiction pursuant to Art. 42 of the FIFA Regulations for the Status and Transfer of Players (edition September 2001), at the request of one of the parties to the dispute.
3. According to Art. 42, par. 1 lit. (b) (i) of the FIFA Regulations for the Status and Transfer of Players (edition September 2001), the triggering elements of the dispute (i.e. whether a contract was breached, with or without just cause, or sporting just cause), will be decided by the Dispute Resolution Chamber.
4. If an employment contract is breached by a party, the Dispute Resolution Chamber is responsible to verify whether a party is accountable for compensation and outstanding payments. Consequently, the Dispute Resolution Chamber is the competent body to decide on the present litigation concerning the alleged non-respect of the contract concluded between the Claimant and the Respondent.
5. Subsequently, and entering into the substance of the present labour dispute, the Chamber started by acknowledging that, on 26 February 2003, the player X and the club Y signed an employment contract valid until 25 June 2005.
6. The Chamber also acknowledged that according to the relevant employment contract the club agreed to pay to the player during the sporting season 2003/2004 a monthly salary amounting to ROL 2,500,000 as well as the amount of USD 75,000, if he would play a minimum of 23 official matches and for the season 2004/2005 a monthly salary amounting to ROL 2,500,000 as well as the amount of USD 80,000, if he would play a minimum of 23 official matches.
7. In this respect, the Chamber came to the conclusion that the monthly payment of ROL 2,500,000, approximate USD 82, cannot be considered as the solely component of the player's salary since the said amount is unreasonably low. As a result, the Chamber decided that the additional payment of USD 75,000 for the season 2003/2004 and USD 80,000 for the season 2004/2005 must be considered as an essential part of the player's yearly remuneration.
8. Then, the Chamber turned its attention to the fact that according to the contract USD 75,000 would only be paid to the player depending on a relevant amount of matches played.
9. In this respect, the Chamber unanimously concluded that the application of such a clause is arbitrary since it is at the club's discretion to decide how many matches the player would have played. Taking

into consideration the foregoing clause is unacceptable, in this sense, the Chamber concurred that, in principle, the player would be entitled to receive for the season 2003/2004 the amount of USD 75,000 plus ROL 30,000,000 and for the sporting season 2004/2005 the amount of USD 80,000 plus ROL 30,000,000, independently from the number of matches he would have played.

10. In view of the above, the Chamber concluded that the player's salary for the season 2003/2004 was USD 75,000, i.e. USD 6,250 monthly plus ROL 2,500,000 per month.
11. Then, the Chamber took due note that, according to the player, the club has failed to comply with its contractual obligations towards him since the beginning of the 2003/2004 sporting season. The player asserts that the club committed a unilateral breach of contract and consequently asks to be awarded the amount of USD 75,000 due for the 2003/2004 sporting season, the amount of USD 80,000 due for the 2004/2005 sporting season, as well as the amount of USD 12,500 for winning the Romanian championship.
12. In this respect, the members of the Chamber considered that Y has failed to provide any evidence corroborating that it complied with its financial contractual obligations towards the player as from the beginning of the 2003/2004 season, in particular, to pay to him USD 6,250 and ROL 2,500,000 per month.
13. Moreover, the members of the Chamber acknowledged that, according to the player, on 24 August 2003, the president of Y informed him that he should start looking for another club, which allegedly led him to leave the country. Then, apparently by the time he returned, in September 2003, his visa had already expired on 20 September 2003 and he tried to get one that would allow him to enter. However, he was allegedly told, at the relevant consulate in Portugal, that he needed the club's authorization for that effect.
14. In this respect, the Chamber noted that, according to the player, despite his continuous efforts to contact Y in order to solve the problem with his visa, the club has always failed to provide the relevant consulate in Portugal with the necessary documents in order for him to obtain the relevant visa. In support of his position, the player has provided FIFA with a copy of some letters addressed to the Respondent, as well as phone receipts concerning calls allegedly made to the latter in order to solve his visa problem.
15. On the other hand, the Dispute Resolution Chamber noted that, Y defends that the player left in September 2003 at his own request, without having been subjected to any threats, in order to be loaned on a free basis, during the 2003/2004 sporting season. However, the Chamber duly noted that the loan transpired in January 2004 only.
16. In continuation, the Chamber took special attention to the fact that, despite having been requested to do so, Y has failed to provide FIFA with evidence demonstrating that it has effectively contacted the player to resume duty with it after September 2003 as well as with evidence demonstrating that it provided the player with a valid visa which would allow him to resume duty with it.
17. In light of all the above, the members of the Chamber agreed that the club has acted in breach of the employment contract without just cause.
18. Then, the Chamber took note that the Romanian club defends that, according to a document dated 8 September 2003, a copy of which it has provided to FIFA, the player has allegedly renounced to the amounts that he was entitled to receive from the Respondent during the season 2003/2004.
19. However, and although Y has particularly failed to provide FIFA with the original of the declaration dated 8 September 2003 (doc. no. 598/08.09.2003), which validity is disputed by the player, the members of the Chamber underlined the content of the correspondence that has been remitted to FIFA by the player's legal representative on 2 May 2005, in which the latter clearly states that: "*The declaration made by the applicant said that if he found a club he would renounce the amount of 75,000USD for season 2003/2004 and that if he did not find a team he would come back to xxxxxx and his contract would remain valid. This last sentence has been taken from the declaration*".
20. In this context, the members of the Chamber reached the conclusion that the previously mentioned position of the player's legal representative fully coincides with the content of the document dated 8 September 2003, i.e. that the player would renounce to receive from the club the total sum of USD 75,000 which he was entitled to receive from it during the 2003/2004 sporting season, in case he would secure an employment contract with any other club of his choice during that same sporting season.
21. Moreover, the Chamber took into account, that the player did not provide any evidence in order to support his allegations with regard that his signature has been forged in the declaration dated 8 September 2003.

22. In view of the above, the Chamber established that it could not uphold the player's position with regard to the alleged fake signature due to lack of evidence in this respect. Finally, the Chamber emphasised that it does not fall under its competence to decide on the authenticity of a document and/or signature.
23. The members of the Chamber were also of the opinion that, according to the aforementioned declaration, in case the player would not sign an employment contract with another club during the 2003/2004 sporting season, the club would be liable to pay to him all the amounts that are established in their employment contract.
24. However, taking into account the fact that the player has effectively signed two consecutive employment contracts during the 2003/2004 sporting season, both in January 2004, respectively with xxxx and xxxxx, the members of the Chamber reached the conclusion that the player in question is not entitled to claim from Y any amounts concerning that sporting season, since he has voluntarily waived such right by means of the relevant declaration.
25. Yet, the Chamber emphasised that the declaration dated 8 September 2003 has no retroactive effect on the time during which the player had not found another club, i.e. first half of the season 2003/2004 as from July 2003 until January 2004. In this sense, the Chamber concluded that the club did not fulfil its financial obligations towards the player during the afore-mentioned time period and taking into consideration the above breached the employment contract without just cause.
26. In view of all of the above and based on all documentation at its disposal, the Chamber concluded that the club is obliged to pay compensation to the player due to the breach of contract.
27. However, and for the sake of good order, the Chamber underlined that due to the declaration dated 8 September 2003, the sporting season 2003/2004, respectively the remuneration for the mentioned season, cannot be taken into account for the relevant calculation of the due compensation for breach of contract.
28. Consequently, the Chamber rejected the player's claim regarding the amount of USD 75,000 for the season 2003/2004.
29. Subsequently, the Chamber turned its attention to the calculation of the relevant compensation and started by enhancing the fact that Y has failed to provide FIFA with the original of the disputed annex to the parties' employment contract, according to which, apparently, both parties had agreed to decrease the amounts that the player was contractually entitled to receive during such period.
30. As a consequence, the Chamber established that the remuneration due for the 2004/2005 sporting season in the total amount of USD 80,000 on the basis of the employment contract signed on 26 February 2003 must be taking into account in order to establish the compensation due to the player.
31. In this respect, the Chamber underlined that the compensation corresponds to an amount equivalent to the difference between the amounts stipulated on the player's employment contract with the Respondent, i.e. USD 80,000 and the amounts earned by the player rendering his services to other clubs during the 2004/2005 sporting season.
32. In this sense, the Chamber considered that, from the total amount of USD 80,000 that the player was entitled to receive from Y during the 2004/2005 sporting season, should be deducted the amount of USD 30,000 that the player has received from xxxx from 1 September until 31 December 2004 and EUR 29,689 (USD 35,975), corresponding to 5 salaries and signing-on fees that he has received from xxxx, between 17 January and 31 May 2005.
33. For the sake of good order, the Chamber emphasises that the remuneration earned by the player due to his services to the Portuguese club xxxx must not be taken into account for the calculation of the relevant compensation, since the player rendered his services to the said Portuguese club during the sporting season 2003/2004.
34. In view of the above, the Chamber established that the club has to pay to the player compensation in the amount of USD 14,025.
35. Turning its attention to the claimed bonuses in the amount of USD 12,500, the Chamber took into account, on the one hand, the fact that the player did not provide any evidence in order to sustain his request in this respect.
36. On the other hand, the Chamber took into account that the Respondent explained that according to the internal regulations, each player would receive such bonus in proportion to the amount of matches played. In this sense, the club acknowledged that the player would be entitled to receive the amount of USD 2,000 at the end of the championship.

37. In view of the above, the Chamber partially rejected the player's claim regarding the match bonuses in the total amount of USD 12,500 for winning the Romanian championship in the 2002/2003 sporting season based on lack of evidence and to grant him the amount of USD 2,000 which was acknowledged to be owed by the club.
38. Finally, and with regard to the reimbursement of the procedural costs claimed by the player, the Chamber referred to its well established jurisprudence and rejected the player's claim in this respect.
39. In conclusion, the members of the Chamber decided to partially accept Mr X claim and to condemn Y to pay to him the total amount of USD 16,025.

III. DECISION OF THE DISPUTE RESOLUTION CHAMBER

1. The claim of Mr X is partially accepted.
2. The Respondent Y shall pay the total amount of USD 16,025 to the Claimant Mr X within 30 days as from the date of notification of the present decision.
3. If the Respondent fails to comply with the above-mentioned deadline, an interest rate of 5% per year will apply and the case will immediately be presented to the FIFA Disciplinary Committee.
4. Any further claims lodged by the player are rejected.
5. The Claimant is directed to inform the Respondent immediately of the account number to which the remittance is to be made and to notify the Dispute Resolution Chamber of every payment received.
6. According to art. 60 par. 1 of the FIFA Statutes, this decision may be appealed before the Court of Arbitration for Sport (CAS). The statement of appeal must be sent to the CAS directly within 21 days of receiving notification of this decision and has to contain all elements in accordance with point 2 of the directives issued by the CAS, copy of which we enclose hereto. Within another 20 days following the expiry of the time limit for the filing of the statement of appeal, the appellant shall file with the CAS a brief stating the facts and legal arguments giving rise to the appeal (cf. point 4 of the directives).

16246

DECISION OF THE DISPUTE RESOLUTION CHAMBER

passed in Zurich, Switzerland, on 12 January 2006, in the following composition:
Slim Aloulou (Tunisia), Chairman
Jean-Marie Philips (Belgium), member
Zola Malvern Percival Majavu (South Africa), member
Rinaldo Martorelli (Brazil), member
Theo van Seggelen (The Netherlands), member
on the claim presented by the player W., Costa Rica, as Claimant
against the club S., Russia, as Respondent,
regarding a contractual dispute arisen between the parties.

I. FACTS OF THE CASE

1. On 19 February 2003, the player W. signed a contract with Russian club S. for the period from 1 March 2003 to 15 December 2005. The two parties agreed that the player would receive a monthly wage of USD 8,000. According to the payment details given in annex to the contract, the player's annual salary would be USD 150,000, with wages of USD 8,000 being paid every month and the remainder of the annual salary being paid in November each year.
2. On 23 March 2004, the player's representative informed FIFA that the player had not been paid since December 2003. One of the player's Brazilian team-mates who was in the same situation had been summoned to a meeting with the club a few days earlier and, in an attempt to intimidate him, requested in the presence of a uniformed police office, the club's lawyers and a cameraman to terminate his contract.
3. On 26 March 2004, FIFA confronted the club with these claims and asked the club to submit a statement, which the club failed to do.
4. On 13 May 2004, the player contacted FIFA again to report that he had been paid in full up until November 2003. However, he had not been paid from December 2003 up until the date he had

submitted his complaint. In March 2004, the club had suggested that he plays for a club in the Russian second division. The player had unsuccessfully asked for a guarantee of the other Russian club's ability to pay him. Had he received a positive response, he would have agreed to this move. On 11 March 2004, the club informed him that it could no longer provide him with accommodation at the club's facilities (however, a copy of this letter that was submitted to FIFA is dated 11 May 2004). Furthermore, it was proposed in the same letter that he and his Brazilian team-mate could seek accommodation at the sanatorium and the club would cover all costs. However, this sentence was crossed out and the chief executive of the Russian club has signed below. Furthermore, the player says that at the end of March 2004 he had, just like the other Brazilian player a few days earlier, been summoned for a meeting with the club and, in an attempt to intimidate him, he was asked to terminate his contract in the presence of a uniformed police office, the club's lawyers and a cameraman. On 6 April 2004, he had left Russia. The player therefore requested two years' salary totalling USD 300,000, compensation of USD 40,000 for missed bonuses (in 2003, he had received USD 18,000 in bonuses) and compensation for legal costs and expenses incurred due to the club's actions amounting to USD 7,500. Furthermore, the player demanded that a transfer ban be imposed on the club and that its international licence for UEFA matches be revoked.

5. FIFA wrote to the club on 14 June 2004 and 3 July 2004 about the player's complaint and requested that it submit a statement.
6. On 22 July 2004, S. informed FIFA that the player had failed to report for a training camp on 25 February 2004. The player had informed the club that he was not prepared to play in the reserve team. In addition, he had also refused to attend a training camp on 8 March 2004. Documents drafted by the club, which were said to attest to the player's failure to attend the training camps in question, were submitted to FIFA.
7. The club had subsequently initiated disciplinary proceedings against the player. On 25 March 2004, the club terminated the contract as of 7 March 2004. This letter was submitted to FIFA. Given the player's repeated failure to attend training and his failure to submit any statement, the contract had been terminated legitimately in line with Russian law. Moreover, the club stated that the player had last been paid in February 2004.
8. The club also submitted expert statements from the Legal Committee of the Football Union of Russia, the Dispute Resolution Chamber of the Football Union of Russia and the Ministry of Health and Social Politics of the Russian Federation, all of which support the club's position.
9. On 23 July 2004, the Football Union of Russia informed FIFA that the club had prepared a comprehensive file and sent it to the arbitration body of the Players' Status Committee of the Football Union of Russia. That was why it was requested that the deadline be extended to 9 August 2004.
10. FIFA subsequently asked the Football Union of Russia whether the aforementioned arbitration body had passed a decision and how the arbitration body was composed. It did not receive any reply.
11. In the meantime, the Costa Rican football association asked FIFA to intervene in connection with the issue of an international registration transfer certificate for the player W. In a letter dated 20 August 2004, FIFA authorised the Costa Rican football association to provisionally register the player for his club.
12. On 24 January 2005, the player made a statement to the effect that the club's comments had been received by FIFA after the relevant deadline. He also contested the fact that he had not taken part in training camps. To this effect, the player also submitted copies of plane tickets for him and his interpreter as proof that the player had attended the training camps (though the tickets were dated 11 February 2004). He emphasised that he had not been paid since November 2003. The payment in February 2004 shown in the above-mentioned receipt had been made to reimburse a plane ticket. He disputed the fact that he had ever been informed of the pending disciplinary proceedings. While it was possible that such proceedings are permitted under Russian law, the legal principles of FIFA also had to be taken into account. For these reasons, the player felt that the comments from the club should be disregarded. The player expressed his consent to the club's payment of the outstanding amount in instalments. This proposal was declined by the club.

II. CONSIDERATIONS OF THE DISPUTE RESOLUTION CHAMBER

1. Since the claim at hand had been lodged prior to 1 July 2005 and concerns an employment contract concluded on 19 February 2003, the September 2001 edition of the Regulations for the Status and Transfer of Players (hereinafter the Regulations) shall apply (cf. art. 26 par. 1 of the July 2005 Regulations).

2. The Dispute Resolution Chamber of the FIFA Players' Status Committee shall review disputes coming under its jurisdiction pursuant to art. 42 of the Regulations at the request of one of the parties to the dispute.
3. According to art. 42 par. 1 lit. (b) (i) of the Regulations, the triggering elements of the dispute (i.e. whether a contract was breached, with or without just cause, or sporting just cause), will be decided by the Dispute Resolution Chamber.
4. As a consequence, the Dispute Resolution Chamber is the competent body to decide on the present litigation involving a club from Russia and a player from Costa Rica and regarding outstanding remuneration in connection with an employment contract signed between the parties.
5. Therefore, the members of the Dispute Resolution Chamber at first confirmed to be competent to pass a decision in this matter. In addition, the Chamber acknowledged the above-mentioned facts as well as the further documentation contained in the file.
6. Subsequently, and entering into the substance of the matter, the Chamber considered that the player W. and the club S. signed a valid employment contract on 19 February 2003 valid from 1 March 2003 until 15 December 2005 and that the parties concluded an annual salary in the amount of USD 150,000, with wages of USD 8,000 being paid every month and the remainder of the annual salary being paid in November each year.
7. The Chamber observed that the player obtained all the salaries until November 2003 and claimed an amount of USD 300,000 corresponding to two annual salaries. Equally, the Chamber noted that the player claimed compensation of USD 40,000 for missed bonuses and compensation for legal costs and expenses amounting to USD 7,500.
8. The Chamber took note that the player rendered his services uncontestedly until the month of March 2004 and that he left Russia on 6 April 2004. The club alleged that the player had last been paid in February 2004. The Chamber took note that payment receipts were submitted to FIFA, however, the file contains only one receipt for the period from December 2003 to February 2004, which confirms a payment of approximately USD 1,280 and is dated 8 February 2004. Therefore, the Chamber could not back the club's position that all salaries until the termination of the contract had been paid and that therefore, the monthly salaries from 15 December 2003 to 15 March 2004 had not been paid. Therefore, the Chamber concluded that the player is entitled to claim until the termination of the contract three monthly salaries in the total amount of USD 24,000.
9. Having taken into consideration all the above, the Chamber concluded that by stopping to pay the player's salary in December 2003 and trying to dissolve the contract in March 2004, the Russian club had breached the relevant employment contract without valid reasons. The Chamber backed therefore the player's position and took into consideration that the player lodged his complaint already on 23 March 2004 and that the club decided on 25 March 2004 to terminate the contract on 25 March 2004 as of 7 March 2004.
10. Furthermore, the Chamber took note that the club based his answer to the claim and the letter of termination of the employment contract on the fact that the player had failed to report for a training camp on 25 February 2004 and that he informed the club that he was not prepared to play in the reserve team. Then, the Chamber took note that the club based his answer to the claim and the letter of termination of the employment contract on the fact that the player had been asked to attend the training sessions and that the club provided FIFA with reports of the player's absences.
11. In continuation, the Chamber referred to the amount of compensation to which the player should be entitled to for the unjustified breach of the employment contract. To that regard, the Chamber considered the remaining duration of the contract at the time of its breach and the financial terms of the contract. Furthermore, the Chamber took note of the fact that the Russian club provided FIFA with some evidence concerning the disciplinary proceedings initiated against the player. In this respect, a copy of a letter summoning the player to a meeting and the termination letter were submitted to FIFA. Finally, the expert statements from the Legal Committee of the Football Union of Russia, the Dispute Resolution Chamber of the Football Union of Russia and the Ministry of Health and Social Politics of the Russian Federation do somehow assist the position of the club. In fact, the Chamber acknowledged that the player did not participate and defense himself at the disciplinary proceedings initiated against him. The Chamber concluded that, although the club did not fully respect its contractual obligations, the behaviour of the club does not justify the player's departure. As a consequence, the player has to bear some responsibility for the course of actions.

12. Taking into account the foregoing, as well as the remaining duration of the contract at the time of its breach and the financial terms of the contract and considering that the player has a new contract as of August 2004, the Chamber deemed that a lump sum of USD 75,000 appears to be an adequate and appropriate compensation to be paid by S. to the player W.
13. Subsequently, the Chamber turned to the question of the claimed missed bonuses in the amount of USD 40,000 and compensation for legal costs and expenses incurred due to the club's actions amounting to USD 7,500. In that regard, the Chamber took note that the player alleged that he had received an amount of USD 18,000 during the year 2003 but that no documentary evidence of this was submitted to FIFA. However, the Chamber retained that the player did no more render his services as from March 2004 and cannot claim any bonuses for matches he did not play for the Russian team. Concerning the claim of the reimbursement of the legal costs the Chamber referred to its jurisprudence, according to which it never awarded such demands. Finally, the Chamber took note that the costs for flights and the telephone costs are not mentioned in the employment contract and that therefore, this claim cannot be considered. Therefore, the Chamber decided to reject this claim.
14. Consequently, having thus analysed the various aspects of the player's claim, as well as the club's defence statement, the Dispute Resolution Chamber concluded its deliberations by announcing that the player's claims were partially accepted.
15. Taking into account all of the above, the Dispute Resolution Chamber decided that S. must pay the amount of USD 99,000 (USD 24,000 corresponding to three monthly salaries and USD 75,000 as lump sum for breach of contract) to the player W.

III. DECISION OF THE DISPUTE RESOLUTION CHAMBER

1. The claim of the player W. is partially accepted.
2. The club S. has to pay the amount of USD 99,000 to the player W. within the next 30 days as from the date of notification of this decision.
3. Any further financial claims lodged by the player W. are rejected.
4. In the event that the above-mentioned amount is not paid within the stated deadline, an interest rate of 5% per year will apply and the present matter shall be submitted to FIFA's Disciplinary Committee, so that the necessary disciplinary sanctions may be imposed.
5. The player W. is instructed to inform S. immediately and directly of the account number to which the remittance is to be made and to notify the Dispute Resolution Chamber of every payment received.
6. According to art. 60 par. 1 of the FIFA Statutes this decision may be appealed before the Court of Arbitration for Sport (CAS). The statement of appeal must be sent to the CAS directly within 21 days of receiving notification of this decision and has to contain all elements in accordance with point 2 of the directives issued by the CAS, copy of which we enclose hereto. Within another 10 days following the expiry of the time limit for the filing of the statement of appeal, the appellant shall file with the CAS a brief stating the facts and legal arguments giving rise to the appeal (cf. point 4 of the directives).

16309
DECISION OF THE DISPUTE RESOLUTION CHAMBER
passed in Zurich, Switzerland, on 12 January 2006,
in the following composition:
Slim Aloulou (Tunisia), Chairman
Jean-Marie Philips (Belgium), Member
Zola Malvern Percival Majavu (South Africa), Member Rinaldo Martorelli (Brazil), Member Theo van Seggelen (Netherlands), Member
Player A, on the claim presented by against regarding a dispute about the employment contract concluded between the parties. as as Claimant Club B, Respondent

I. FACTS OF THE CASE

1. On 1 January 2002, the player A and the club B concluded an employment contract valid until 1 January 2005, stipulating the following financial rights of the player:o monthly salary for the year 2002 USD 12,500

- monthly salary for the year 2003 USD 14,500
- monthly salary for the year 2004 USD 16,500
- 1 flight ticket from X to Y per year for the player and his closest relatives
- rental of a car

2. Moreover, on 3 March 2002, the parties concluded the following bonus agreement:
   - for each goal scored in the Championship USD 1,000
   - if the player scores more than ten goals, for each goal USD 1,500
   - if the player scores more than 15 goals, for each goal USD 2,000
   - for every assist USD 500
   - if the player is top scorer of the Championship USD 25,000
3. According to the player, the following amounts were not paid to him by the club during the course of the contract:
   - salary October 2003
   - salary November 2003
   - salary December 2003
   - salary January 2004
   - salary February 2004
   - pro rata salary until 23 March 2004
   - reimbursement of flight ticket
   - rental of a car
   - bonus for two goals scored (on 8 May 2003 in match against P, and on 9 July 2003 in match against T)
   - other bonuses for the sports season 2003

   Total
4. Therefore, the player reminded the club in written to pay to him the abovementioned outstanding amounts on 12, 17, and 18 March 2004.
5. The reminders were without success, therefore, he unilaterally terminated the employment contract on 23 March 2004.
6. On 1 April 2004, the player submitted a claim to FIFA against the club B, asking for the payment of the above-mentioned amount of USD 112,950, plus the salaries until the expiry of the contract, i.e. the salaries for April to December 2004, in the total amount of USD 148,500.
   USD 14,500 USD 14,500 USD 14,500 USD 16,500 USD 16,500
   USD 12,650 USD 3,800
   USD 8,000 USD 2,000
   USD 10,000 USD 112,950
7. As far as the expenses for the flight ticket are concerned, the player presented the bills for a flight ticket from X to Y in the amount of USD 4,840.
8. The player did not present any written evidence proving the amounts claimed for the rental of a car.
9. The player did not present any legal basis entitling him to the bonuses in the amount of USD 10,000 for the sports season 2003.
10. On 5 May 2004, the player entered into a new contract with a third club, valid until 31 December 2004, and stipulating a monthly salary of USD 6,420.
11. On 12 October 2004, the club B submitted its position on the claim of the player, by means of which it alleged that the player was absent from the club without permission during 18 days, in particular from 8 to 11 March 2004. The other dates of the alleged absence were not specified. Therefore, the club terminated the contract on 23 March 2004, as of 7 March 2004.
12. According to the club, all the salaries of the player were paid, except the pro rata salary from 1 to 7 March 2005, which the player could collect at the club's office.
13. By means of such submission, the club also provided FIFA with payment receipts regarding its payments to the player. According to these payment receipts, the last salary which was paid to the player was the salary for August 2003.
14. In continuation, the parties tried to reach an agreement in order to settle the matter amicably. However, such attempts were in vain.
15. On 26 September 2005, the club B submitted a further position regarding the matter at stake, by means of which it specified the dates of the absence of the player. The player allegedly was absent to

a training camp from 5 to 18 January 2004. Moreover, he was absent from two pre-season training sessions, as of 25 February 2004 and as of 8 until 25 March 2004.

16. Moreover, the club stated that a part of the salaries claimed by the player, i.e. the salaries for October 2003, March 2004 and a part of the salary of February 2004 (USD 1,350) were paid. However, the club did not present any written evidence thereto.
17. On account of this, the club is of the opinion that the player breached the contract without just cause, and therefore makes a counterclaim against the player, claiming for the reimbursement of all the payments made to the player during the course of the contract, without providing a proper breakdown of this counterclaim. Moreover, the club requests an interest of 15% on the amount claimed. Finally, the club asks for the reimbursement of the legal costs it incurred through the present procedure.
18. On 25 October 2005, the player submitted to FIFA his position towards the answer of the club on his claim, and his answer towards the counterclaim.
19. In this respect, he maintained his claim against the club B for outstanding payments in the amount of USD 112,950, plus a compensation for breach of contract in the amount of USD 148,500, being the salaries until the expiry of the contract.
20. With regard to the counterclaim, the player stated that this claim is totally unfounded and therefore should not be taken into consideration.
21. On 16 December 2005, the club submitted its final position on the matter, reiterating that the club was entitled to dismiss the player due to his unexcused absences (cf. point 15).
22. Moreover, the club stated that the player shall be put to proof that the salaries he claims were not paid to him.
23. In continuation, the club accused the player for not having mitigated his loss caused by the early termination of the contract.
24. With respect to the player's claim for the reimbursement of the expenses for the rental of a car in the amount of USD 8,000, the respondent stated that the player did not submit any written evidence for these expenses.
25. As far as the bonuses in the amount of USD 10,000 claimed by the player are concerned, the club stated that the player does not have any legal basis for such a claim.
26. With regard to the bonus of USD 1,000 claimed for a goal scored on 8 May 2003 in a match against P, the responding club stated that on that date, the club did not play a match against P, nor did it play any match on that date. With regard to the bonus of USD 1,000 claimed for a goal scored on 9 July 2003 in a match against T, the responding club stated that it did not play a match on that date against T.
27. Finally, the club stated that the amounts which were due to the player on the date of the contract termination were to be collected by the player at the club's offices. The amount due to the player was USD 54,571 (salaries from November 2003 to February 2004, plus USD 4,217.44 for miscellaneous expenses, less the pro-rata salaries for the time periods during which the player was absent from the club, less the amount of USD 1,350, which was already paid to the player).
28. The mentioned amount was however never collected by the player.
29. Note: The Club played a match against R on 4 May 2003, where the player in question scored one goal. On 9 August 2003, the player scored one goal in a match the club played against T.

II. CONSIDERATIONS OF THE DISPUTE RESOLUTION CHAMBER

1. The matter at stake was submitted to FIFA before 1 July 2005. Therefore, and in accordance with Article 18 Para. 2 and 3 of the revised Rules Governing the Procedures of the Players' ' Status Committee and the Dispute Resolution Chamber (edition 2005), not the revised Rules, but the previous Rules Governing the Practice and Procedures of the Dispute Resolution Chamber (edition 2002, hereinafter referred to as; the Procedural Rules) do apply on the matter at hand as procedural rules.
2. Moreover, in accordance with Article 26 Para. 1 and 2 of the revised Regulations for the Status and Transfer of Players (edition 2005), not the revised Regulations, but the previous Regulations for the Status and Transfer of Players (edition 2001, hereinafter referred to as; the Regulations) do apply on the dispute at stake as far as the substance of the matter is concerned.
3. The members of the Dispute Resolution Chamber of the FIFA Players' Status Committee were

summoned to pass a decision on the matter at stake by the Chairman of the Dispute Resolution Chamber pursuant to Art. 1 point 6) of the Procedural Rules.

4. The members of the Chamber started their deliberations asserting that the matter at stake concerns a dispute about the unilateral termination of an employment contract concluded between a player and a club, a request of the player for compensation in view of such unilateral termination, and a counterclaim of the club for compensation for non-respect of the employment contract by the player.
5. In accordance with Art. 42 Para. 1 lit. (b) of the Regulations, and in particular let. (b) (i) of the said provision, it falls within the purview of the Dispute Resolution Chamber to determine whether one of the parties has committed a unilateral breach of contract without just cause. In case the employment contract was breached by a party, the Dispute Resolution Chamber is responsible to verify and decide whether this party is accountable for outstanding payments and compensation.
6. In view of the above, the Dispute Resolution Chamber concluded that it was competent to decide on the present litigation.
7. Entering into the substance of the matter, the Chamber acknowledged the FACTS OF THE CASE as well as the documentation contained in the file, and in view of the circumstances of the matter, turned to the question whether the club has committed a unilateral breach of the employment contract without just cause, and if so, to verify and decide whether the club is accountable for outstanding payments and compensation.
8. With regard to the question whether the club has committed a unilateral breach of the employment contract without just cause, the Chamber first of all took note that according to the documentation submitted by the club, in particular the payment receipts, the last salary which was paid to the player was the salary for August 2003. The respondent's allegation that parts of the salaries after August 2003 were paid to the player could not be taken into consideration by the Chamber, since the club failed to prove that it had done so.
9. In this regard, the Chamber clarified that in contrary to the respondent's argumentation, the claimant does not have the burden of proof regarding the non-payment of the salaries in question. Basically, according to the principle of burden of proof, every party to a dispute has to prove the facts upon which its position is based. It would, however, be absurd to expect from a party to prove that a certain fact did not occur, e.g. a payment was not made. In such a situation, the party insisting that the fact actually occurred, i.e. that the payment was made, has as well to prove such position.
10. Moreover, the Chamber noted that allegedly, the player was partly absent without permission from the club between January and March 2004. This allegation as well lacks of proof.
11. And finally, the Chamber acknowledged that the employment contract was terminated unilaterally by both parties on 23 March 2004.
12. The Dispute Resolution Chamber then stated that the persistent failure of a club to pay the salaries of a player, without just cause, is generally to be considered as a unilateral breach of an employment contract.
13. On account of the above, the Dispute Resolution Chamber stated that the behaviour of the club B, i.e. the non-payment of the player's salaries for morethan half a year has to be considered as a breach of contract without just cause.
14. The Chamber emphasised in particular that the club B did not have any reason justifying the non-payment of the salaries as of September 2003. The unexcused absence of the player, if it really occurred, took place only as of 5 January 2004, i.e. after four months the player's salaries were not paid. In this regard, the Chamber mentioned that, as a general rule, the non-payment of a player's salaries during four months has to be considered as a persistent failure of the club to respect its financial obligations towards a player, and therefore is to be considered as a breach of contract without just cause. Therefore, the Chamber as well stated that if the player was indeed partly absent without permission as of January 2004, this could not be considered as a breach of contract by the player.
15. In conclusion, the Chamber stated that the employment contract between the player A and the club B was terminated by the club in question without just cause.
16. In consequence, the Dispute Resolution Chamber had to verify and decide whether the club B is accountable for outstanding payments and compensation towards the player A.
17. With regard to outstanding payments, the Chamber referred to the aforementioned fact that according to the payment receipts submitted by the club, the last salary which was paid to the player was the

salary for August 2003. Therefore, as a general rule, the club would have to pay to the player the salaries as of September 2003.

18. In this regard, the Chamber took note however of the fact that the player A in his claim submitted to the FIFA Dispute Resolution Chamber, inter alia, only asked for the payment of the salaries as of October 2003, until 23 March 2004, but did not ask for the payment of the salary of September 2003.
19. In consequence, and with respect to the principle ultra petitam, the Chamber stated that it is not in a position to grant to the claimant the salaries as of September 2003, but only as of October 2003, for which the player Aactually claimed from the club B on account of outstanding salaries.
20. The salaries from October 2003 to 23 March 2004 amount to USD 89,150 (USD 14,500 per month from October to December 2003, USD 16,500 per month for January and February 2004, plus USD 12,650 pro rata from 1 to 23 March 2004).
21. Moreover, according to the employment contract, the player was entitled to a flight ticket X – Y. In this regard, the player presented the bills for a flight from Sao Paulo to Samara amounting to USD 4,840, but claims for the reimbursement of USD 3,800 only.
22. Again with respect to the principle ultra petitam, the Chamber is not in a position to grant to the claimant the reimbursement of USD 4,840, but of USD 3,800 only.
23. In addition, the player claimed for USD 2,000 on account of bonus for two goals scored on 8 May and 9 July 2003 in matches against P and T.
24. With regard to the bonus of USD 1,000 claimed for a goal scored on 8 May 2003 in a match against P, the responding club stated that on that date, the club did not play a match against P, nor did it play any match on that date. The club however played a match against R on 4 May 2003, where the player scored one goal, and therefore is entitled to the bonus of USD 1,000.
25. With regard to the bonus of USD 1,000 claimed for a goal scored on 9 July 2003 in a match against T, the responding club stated that it did not play a match on that date against T. The club however played a match against T on 9 August 2003, where the player scored one goal, and therefore is as well entitled to the bonus of USD 1,000.
26. With respect to the player's claim for reimbursement of USD 8,000 for the rental of a car, the Chamber stated that the player failed to provide any written evidence entitling him to the reimbursement of the claimed amount. Therefore, this request is to be dismissed.
27. And finally, regarding the player's claim for USD 10,000 for other bonuses for the sports season 2003, the Chamber stated that the player did not provide any legal basis based on which he would be entitled to claim such bonus. Therefore, the Chamber stated that this request is to be dismissed as well.
28. In conclusion, the player is entitled on account of outstanding salaries (USD 89,150), reimbursement of expenses (USD 3,800) and bonuses (USD 2,000) to the total amount of USD 94,950.
29. With regard to a compensation for unjustified breach of contract, the Chamber stated that according to Art. 22 of the Regulations, the club B has to pay to the player A on account of compensation for breach of contract without just cause the contractual salaries for the remainder of the contract, i.e. the net salaries for the months from April to December 2004 which is USD 148,500 in total (USD 16,500 per month).
30. With respect to the obligation of the parties to mitigate a loss, the Chamber decided that the salaries which the player earned between the early termination of the employment contract and its expiry had to come in deduction from the above-mentioned compensation.
31. In this respect, the Chamber noted that the player in question signed a new employment contract valid from 5 May to 31 December 2004 with a third club, stipulating a monthly salary of USD 6,420. The player therefore earned with the third club the amount of USD 51,360. The compensation is to be reduced by this amount.
32. Therefore, the total compensation for breach of contract without just cause amounts to USD 97,140.
33. In view of the above, the Chamber decided that the club B from has to pay to the player A the amount of USD 192,090 (USD 94,950 on account of outstanding salaries, bonuses and reimbursement of expenses plus USD 97,140 as compensation for unjustified breach of contract).
34. Finally, the Dispute Resolution Chamber decided that on account of the above, the counterclaim of the club B is to be dismissed entirely.

III. DECISION OF THE DISPUTE RESOLUTION CHAMBER

1. The claim of the player A is partially accepted.
2. The counterclaim of the club B is to be dismissed entirely.
3. The club B has to pay the amount of USD 192,090 to the player A.
4. The amount due to the club player A has to be paid by the club B within the next 30 days as from the date of notification of this decision.
5. If the aforementioned sum is not paid within the aforementioned deadline, the present matter shall be submitted to FIFA's Disciplinary Committee, so that the necessary disciplinary sanctions may be imposed.
6. If the aforementioned sum is not paid within the aforementioned deadline, an interest rate of 5% per year will apply as from the first day after the aforementioned deadline.
7. Any further request by the player A is rejected.
8. The player A is directed to inform the club B immediately of the account number to which the remittance is to be made and to notify the Dispute Resolution Chamber of every payment received.
9. According to art. 60 par. 1 of the FIFA Statutes this decision may be appealed before the Court of Arbitration for Sport (CAS). The statement of appeal must be sent to the CAS directly within 21 days of receiving notification of this decision and has to contain all elements in accordance with point 2 of the directives issued by the CAS, copy of which we enclose hereto. Within another 10 days following the expiry of the time limit for the filing of the statement of appeal, the appellant shall file with the CAS a brief stating the facts and legal arguments giving rise to the appeal (cf. point 4 of the directives).

⚽⚽⚽

16432

DECISION OF THE DISPUTE RESOLUTION CHAMBER

passed in Zurich, Switzerland, on 12 January 2006,
in the following composition:
Slim Aloulou (Tunisia), Chairman
Jean-Marie Philips (Belgium), Member
Zola Malvern Percival Majavu (South Africa), Member
Rinaldo Martorelli (Brazil), Member
Theo van Seggelen (Netherlands), Member
on the claim presented by Club A, as Claimant
against
Club B, as Respondent
regarding a dispute about training compensation for the player X.

I. FACTS OF THE CASE

1. On 30 June 2002, the player X, born in July 1981, signed a non-amateur contract with the club B, at the age of 20.
2. On 15 March 2005, the club A that contributed to the training of the player in question, lodged a claim against the club B for training compensation as described in chapter VII of the FIFA Regulations for the Status and Transfer of Players, edition 2001.
3. On 29 August 2005, the club B provided its position to the claim lodged by the club A, stating that the claim must be rejected due to prescription.
4. After having been referred by FIFA to the possibility that the present claim could be prescribed in application of Article 44 of the above mentioned Regulations, the claimant referred to a claim for training compensation lodged at FIFA by the club C on 2 January 2003 against the club B for the training of the same player, and stated that it had lodged the present claim together with club C already at that time, and in the same correspondence.
5. The above-mentioned submission dated 2 January 2003 was made by the Association of club A and C and contains a list of the clubs, which contributed to the training of the player in question. The list does also contain the club A.
6. In continuation, attached to the relevant correspondence from the Association is a letter from the club C, by means of which this club expressly claims for the training compensation for the training of the player X.

7. The said correspondence, however, does not contain an express claim from the club A. In particular, it does neither comprise any petition from the said club nor a power of attorney authorising the Association to act on its behalf in the present matter.
8. On 15 January 2004, the Dispute Resolution Chamber decided about the claim for training compensation lodged by the club C. The club A, like the other clubs mentioned in the list of the Association presented on 2 January 2003, was not taken into consideration, since as previously mentioned, no express claim was submitted to FIFA by the club in question.

II. CONSIDERATIONS OF THE DISPUTE RESOLUTION CHAMBER

1. The matter at stake was submitted to FIFA before 1 July 2005. Therefore, and in accordance with Article 18 Para. 2 and 3 of the Rules Governing the Procedures of the Players' Status Committee and the Dispute Resolution Chamber (edition 2005), the previous Rules Governing the Practice and Procedures of the Dispute Resolution Chamber (edition 2002, hereinafter referred to as; *the Procedural Rules*) apply to the matter at hand as procedural rules.
2. Moreover, in accordance with Article 26 Para. 1 and 2 of the Regulations for the Status and Transfer of Players (edition 2005), the previous Regulations for the Status and Transfer of Players (edition 2001, hereinafter referred to as; *the Regulations*) do apply to the dispute at stake as far as the substance of the matter is concerned.
3. The members of the Dispute Resolution Chamber were summoned to pass a decision on the matter at stake by the Chairman of the Dispute Resolution Chamber pursuant to Art. 1 point 6) of the Procedural Rules.
4. The members of the Chamber started their deliberations asserting that the present matter concerns a dispute between two clubs regarding training compensation, based on Chapter VII of the Regulations.
5. In accordance with Art. 42 Para. 1 lit. (b) of the Regulations, and in particular Para. (vi) of the said provision, it falls within the purview of the Dispute Resolution Chamber to review disputes concerning training compensation fees, at the request of one of the parties to the dispute.
6. In view of the above, the Dispute Resolution Chamber concluded that it was competent to decide on the present litigation.
7. The Chamber then acknowledged the FACTS OF THE CASE as well as the documentation contained in the file.
8. On account of the circumstances of the matter, the Chamber stated that prior to deliberating on the substance of the matter, it is crucial to clarify the date of the submission of the present claim to FIFA, in order to establish if the present claim for training compensation is prescript.
9. In this respect, the Chamber acknowledged that as the date of submission of the present claim, two dates come into question, i.e. 2 January 2003 or 15 March 2005.
10. On 2 January 2003, the Association submitted to FIFA a claim for training compensation by the club C against the club B for the training of the player X. This submission contained a list of the clubs that contributed to the training of the player in question, including the club A.
11. Attached to the relevant correspondence from the Association was a letter from the club C, by means of which this club expressly claimed for the training compensation for the period of time it trained the player X. The said correspondence, however, did neither contain a letter, an express claim or any petition from the club A nor a power of attorney authorising the Association to act on behalf of the club A in the present matter.
12. On 15 March 2005, the club A submitted to FIFA an individual and formal claim against the club B for training compensation for the player X.
13. In view of these facts, the members of the Chamber stated that a clear distinction has to be made between a proper claim of a club for training compensation and a list of the club's included in the player's career history, which includes a specific club xy, and which is attached to the claim for training compensation of another club included in this list. The mere indication of club xy on such a list, without the express request of the club xy to claim for training compensation cannot be considered as an official claim for training compensation of the club xy.
14. On account of the above, the members of the Chamber were of the unanimous opinion that on 2 January 2003 no official claim by the club A against the club B for training compensation of the player X was submitted to FIFA.

15. In consequence, the claim of the club A against the club B for training compensation of the player X is to be considered as formally submitted to FIFA on 15 March 2005.
16. In continuation, the members of the Chamber acknowledged that the player X and the club B signed the employment contract, which is at the basis of the present claim, on 30 June 2002.
17. According to Article 44 of the Regulations in connection with Article 4 of the Procedural Rules, the Dispute Resolution Chamber shall not address any dispute if more than two years have elapsed since the facts leading to the dispute arose.
18. In the present case, between the date when the facts leading to the dispute arose, i.e. 30 June 2002 (the date of the signature of the employment contract between the player X and the club B) and the submission of the claim to FIFA by the claimant, the club A, on 15 March 2005, more than two years had elapsed.
19. On account of the above, the Dispute Resolution Chamber concluded that the claim of the club A against the club B for training compensation of the player X is to be considered as prescript.
20. Consequently, the Chamber decided that it shall not enter into the substance of this matter.
21. In the light of the above, the Dispute Resolution Chamber decided that the claim of the club A against the club B for training compensation in connection with the player X is to be rejected.

III. DECISION OF THE DISPUTE RESOLUTION CHAMBER

1. The claim of the club of the club A against the club B for the training compensation of the player X is rejected.
2. According to art. 60 par. 1 of the FIFA Statutes this decision may be appealed before the Court of Arbitration for Sport (CAS). The statement of appeal must be sent to the CAS directly within 21 days of receiving notification of this decision and has to contain all elements in accordance with point 2 of the directives issued by the CAS, copy of which we enclose hereto. Within another 10 days following the expiry of the time limit for the filing of the statement of appeal, the appellant shall file with the CAS a brief stating the facts and legal arguments giving rise to the appeal (cf. point 4 of the directives).

16453

DECISION OF THE DISPUTE RESOLUTION CHAMBER

passed in Zurich, Switzerland, on 12 January 2006,
in the following composition:
Mr Slim Aloulou (Tunisia), chairman
Mr Jean-Marie Philips (Belgium), member
Mr Zola Malvern Percival Majavu (South Africa), member
Mr Rinaldo Martorelli (Brazil), member
Mr Theo van Seggelen (Netherlands), member
on the claim presented by
the player, Mr X,
Represented by Mr A as Claimant
against
the club, Y, as Respondent
regarding a contractual dispute arisen between the parties

I. FACTS OF THE CASE

1. On 27 January 2003, the player, X, the club, Y and a company called Z signed an agreement that stipulated the conditions of an employment contract between the player and the club. The Claimant has provided FIFA with a copy of the aforementioned agreement.
2. Moreover, such agreement also stipulated that Y would pay the amount of EUR 75,000 to the aforementioned company for the transfer of the player.
3. According to the aforementioned agreement, valid from 1 February 2003 until 30 June 2006, Mr X was entitled to the following remuneration:
   From 01.02.03 - 30.06.03 - Monthly net salary of EUR 2,200;
   From 01.07.03 - 30.06.05 - Monthly net salary of EUR 2,500;

From 01.07.05 - 30.06.06 - Monthly net salary of	EUR 2,800;
Within 01.09.03 – Net signing-on fees in the amount of	EUR 10,000;
Within 01.09.04 – Net signing-on fees in the amount of	EUR 10,000;
Within 01.09.05 – Net signing-on fees in the amount of	EUR 10,000;

Free accommodation and 2 return tickets country of Y – country of X, amongst other benefits.

4. On 3 October 2003, the player turned to FIFA claiming that, on 12 June 2003, Y informed him by letter of its decision to release him from the training sessions. However, the club also informed the player that he should be ready to resume duty at any time, as long as he would be informed of it 48 hours in advance. In support of his allegations, the player has provided FIFA with a copy of the relevant letter.
5. Moreover, Mr X asserts that Y has failed to comply with its contractual obligations towards him since May 2003. In this respect, the player also asserts that he has received salaries in the total amount of EUR 6,600, relating to the months of February, March and April 2003.
6. Furthermore, the player claims that, from the end of June 2003 until 22 August 2003, the date of his departure from the country of Y, he trained with the club's Junior team. According to the player, such situation, together with the non-payment of his salary, provoked health problems which forced him to go back home. In this respect, the player provided FIFA with a medical report, dated 22 September 2003, which diagnostic stated that the player was suffering from "*anxious and depressive reactive disturbance*".
7. In light of the above, Mr X is presently claiming from Y the total amount of EUR 93,600 corresponding to all the salaries as from July 2003 until the end of the contractual period of time, i.e. June 2006, and signing-on fees to the amount of EUR 30,000.
8. Y defends that the presented employment contract was only a draft agreement, since it mentions the transfer compensation which would have had to be paid for the acquisition of the player's services and the relevant payment plan. In fact, the club asserts that, due to the fact that such transfer compensation was requested to be paid to a singular person, it wanted to "*clear up the status of the player, and after that they would have contracted*". The club underlines that such agreement was only a draft and that the parties were aware of it.
9. Notwithstanding the above, Y asserts that the player remained with it and at a certain point, it stated that "*Irrespectively of the above the player could get his salary for 3 months in the checkout of the club, but the player did not feel inclined to do so. The opinion of our club is that the player wish to enforce the breach of contract of the club in this way*".
10. However, Y underlines that, although the amounts claimed as salaries by the player correspond to the ones established in the aforementioned draft agreement, they are not the salaries established in the employment contract signed between them on 1 February 2003.
11. In this regard, in July 2005, the Football Federation of Y provided FIFA with a copy of the aforementioned employment contract that was registered with the Football League of the country of Y, valid from 1 February 2003 until 30 June 2006, and according to which Mr X was entitled to receive a monthly salary of EUR 1,000.
12. Moreover, Y does not only deny that the player in question has ever received a monthly salary of EUR 2,200, but it also asserts that during the entire period that Mr X rendered his services to the club, he has only received salaries from February until April 2003 in the total amount of EUR 3,000 and match bonuses in the amount of 164,000 currency Y.
13. Finally, Y has provided FIFA with a payment receipt duly signed by the player in question pertaining to February 2003 and indicating the amount of 243,330 currency of Y.
14. As a consequence, Mr. X was invited to provide his comments with respect to the latest position of Y and particularly with regard to the aforementioned employment contract. The player has failed to do so.
15. The Football Federation of Y informed FIFA that Mr X was registered for its affiliated club Y from 3 March 2003 until 13 March 2004.
16. In March 2004, FIFA authorised the Football Federation of X to register the player with its member club W on a provisional basis.
17. The present matter was submitted to the Dispute Resolution Chamber on 2 November 2005, which decided to refer the matter back to the FIFA administration in order to proceed with the investigation and clarify a few aspects.

18. In this respect, on 3 November 2005, the player was again asked to provide FIFA with any documentation pertaining to the salaries that he received for the months of February, March and April 2003.
19. In addition, the player was once more requested to provide FIFA with his comments on the contents of Y's correspondence that was remitted via the Football Federation of Y in July 2005, in particular with respect to the employment contract dated 1 February 2003 that Y claims to be valid.
20. Finally, the player was requested to inform FIFA about all the clubs, starting with W, for which he has been registered from March 2004 onwards and to provide copies of the employment contracts that he signed with such clubs.
21. In reply, the player insists that the agreement dated 27 January 2003 is not a draft, but a valid contract. Moreover, he asserts that he has not received from Y any document or payment receipt regarding his salaries of February, March and April 2003.
22. As a consequence, on 23 November 2005, FIFA asked the player and the Football Federation of X and W to present a copy of the player's employment contract with W.
23. In reply, the aforementioned Federation informed FIFA that Mr X was registered with W as an amateur player as from 10 February 2004 until 30 June 2004 and that he was registered with its other affiliated club V from 5 July 2004 until 23 June 2005. Finally, the Football Federation of X, W, and V pointed out that the player in question was subsequently transferred to another country (U).
24. At the request of FIFA, a copy of the player's employment contract with V has been provided by the Football Federation of of X, W, and V. According to such contract, valid from 5 August 2004 until 5 August 2006, the player was entitled to receive a monthly salary of 1,200 currency of V.
25. At the request of FIFA, a copy of the player's employment contract with the U club R has been provided by the Football Association of R. According to such contract, valid from 4 July 2005 until 30 June 2006, the player was entitled to receive a monthly salary of 4,000 currency of U and R. In the meantime, the parties have amicably terminated their employment contract on 2 December 2005 with the notice period ending on 31 December 2005.

II. CONSIDERATIONS OF THE DISPUTE RESOLUTION CHAMBER

1. The Dispute Resolution Chamber first established that the 2001 edition of the FIFA Regulations for the Status and Transfer of Players are applicable to the present case (hereinafter referred to as the "Regulations"), since the case has been brought to FIFA before the coming into force of the current version of the said Regulations on 1 July 2005.
2. The Dispute Resolution Chamber shall review disputes coming under its jurisdiction pursuant to Art. 42 of the Regulations at the request of one of the parties to the dispute.
3. According to Art. 42, par. 1 lit. (b) (i) of the Regulations the triggering elements of the dispute (i.e. whether a contract was breached, with or without just cause, or sporting just cause), will be decided by the Dispute Resolution Chamber.
4. If an employment contract is breached by a party, the Dispute Resolution Chamber is responsible to verify whether a party is accountable for compensation and outstanding payments.
5. Consequently, the Dispute Resolution Chamber is the competent body to decide on the present litigation concerning the alleged non-respect of the contract concluded between the Claimant and the Respondent.
6. Subsequently, and entering into the substance of the present labour dispute, the Chamber started by acknowledging that, on 27 January 2003, Mr X, Y and a company called Z signed an agreement that stipulated the conditions of an employment contract between the player and the club, valid from 1 February 2003 until 30 June 2006.
7. The Chamber also acknowledged that according to Mr X Y has failed to comply with its contractual obligations since May 2003 asserting that Y has only paid him his salaries of February, March and April 2003 to the total amount of EUR 6,600 during the entire period that he rendered his services to the club. This would correspond to a monthly salary of EUR 2,200.
8. Moreover, the members of the Chamber acknowledged that according to X, by letter dated 12 June 2003, Y informed him of its decision to release him from the training sessions. However, simultaneously the club informed the player that he should be ready to resume duty at any time as long as he would be informed of it 48 hours in advance.
9. Furthermore, the Chamber acknowledged that Mr X claims that, from the end of June 2003 until 22 August 2003, the date of his departure from the country of Y, he trained with the club's Junior team,

which according to him, together with the non-payment of his salaries, caused him health problems that led to his departure back home.

10. In this respect, the Chamber noted that the Claimant has provided FIFA with a copy of the aforementioned agreement dated 27 January 2003, of the letter dated 12 June 2003 and of the medical report dated 22 September 2003 attesting that he was suffering from "*anxious and depressive reactive disturbance*".
11. The Chamber took note that, as a consequence of the above and on the basis of the contract signed on 27 January 2003, Mr X claims payment by Y of the amounts stipulated in the agreement, i.e. EUR 93,600, corresponding to all his salaries from July 2003 until the end of the contractual period of time, i.e. June 2006, as well as signing-on fees in the amount of EUR 30,000.
12. The Dispute Resolution Chamber acknowledged that Y, for its part, defends that the employment contract dated 27 January 2003 was only a draft agreement and that the parties were aware of it, since it mentions the transfer compensation, which would have had to be paid for the acquisition of the player's services, and the respective payment plan.
13. The Chamber also took into consideration the fact that, notwithstanding the above, Y asserts that the player could have received his salary for 3 months when he left, but that he did not feel inclined to do so since he wished to enforce a breach of contract by the club.
14. It was noted that no documentary evidence of such allegation has been presented by Y.
15. Moreover, the members of the Chamber paid particular attention to the fact that, according to Y, although the amounts claimed as salaries by X correspond to the ones established in the aforementioned agreement, they do not correspond to the ones established in the employment contract signed between the parties on 1 February 2003, valid from 1 February 2003 until 30 June 2006.
16. In fact, Y denies that X has ever received a monthly salary of EUR 2,200 and it asserts that during the entire period that the player rendered his services to the club, he has received his salaries from February until April 2003 to the total amount of EUR 3,000, i.e. a monthly salary of EUR 1,000 per month, and match bonuses in the amount of 164,000 currency of Y.
17. In this context, the members took into consideration that, in July 2005, the Football Federation of Y informed FIFA that the employment contract dated 1 February 2003, which is being invoked by the Respondent, was registered with the Football League of the country of Y and that according to this contract Mr X was entitled to receive a monthly salary of EUR 1,000.
18. Moreover, the members took into consideration the fact that Y has provided FIFA with the payment receipt pertaining to February 2003, signed by X, in which the amount of 243,330 currency of Y (approximately EUR 1,000) is mentioned.
19. Furthermore, the Chamber took into account that x has failed to provide FIFA with his comments on the latest position of y, particularly with regard to the employment contract dated 1 February 2003, and with documentary evidence in support of his allegation that his monthly salary amounted to EUR 2,200.
20. Taking into account the relevant payment receipt provided by Y and the fact that the employment contract being invoked by the Respondent was the contract registered with the Football League of the country of Y, the members of the Chamber concurred that the employment contract dated 1 February 2003 should be the contract to be taken into consideration by the Chamber in its examination of this matter.
21. The members of the Chamber concurred that it is undisputed that the club has ceased to remit the player's salaries as from May 2003.
22. On account of the above, and in particular of the circumstance that Y failed to pay the player's salaries as from May 2003, the Chamber reached the conclusion that Y has acted in breach of the employment contract without just cause.
23. Having established that the club has committed a unilateral breach of contract without just cause, the Chamber decided that the club is liable to pay compensation for breach of contract to X in accordance with article 22 of the Regulations.
24. The Chamber took into consideration that the relevant employment contract dated 1 February 2003 does not contain any clause pertaining to compensation payable to either of the parties in the event of the early termination of the employment relationship.
25. With respect to the determination of the amount of compensation in accordance with the said article 22, the Chamber took into consideration that the length of time remaining on the contract with Y amounted to 36 months, i.e. from July 2003 until June 2006.

26. In accordance with this employment contract, the player was entitled to receive a monthly salary of EUR 1,000. The relevant employment contract dated 1 February 2003 does not include any signing-on fee payable to the player. Consequently, in relation to the remaining period of time on the contract the aforementioned adds up to EUR 36,000.
27. The Chamber took into consideration that the player was employed by and received 11 monthly salaries from V between August 2004 and June 2005 to the total amount of EUR 6,748.50. In addition, the player received 6 monthly salaries between July and December 2005 from the U club R to the total amount of EUR 6,234. Consequently, the Chamber decided that the amount of EUR 12,982.50 must be deducted from the above-mentioned amount of EUR 36,000 in order to establish the amount of compensation payable to the player.
28. In conclusion, the members of the Chamber decided to partially accept X's claim and to condemn Y to pay to him the total amount of EUR 23,017.50.

III. DECISION OF THE DISPUTE RESOLUTION CHAMBER

1. The claim of the Claimant, X, is partially accepted.
2. The Respondent, Y, shall pay the total amount of EUR 23,017.50 to the Claimant, X, within 30 days as from the date of notification of the present decision.
3. If the Respondent fails to comply with the above-mentioned deadline, an interest rate of 5% per year will apply as of expiry of the aforementioned deadline and the case will immediately be presented to the FIFA Disciplinary Committee.
4. The Claimant is directed to inform the Respondent immediately of the account number to which the remittance is to be made and to notify the Dispute Resolution Chamber of every payment received.
5. According to art. 60 par. 1 of the FIFA Statutes, this decision may be appealed before the Court of Arbitration for Sport (CAS). The statement of appeal must be sent to the CAS directly within 21 days of receiving notification of this decision and has to contain all elements in accordance with point 2 of the directives issued by the CAS, copy of which we enclose hereto. Within another 10 days following the expiry of the time limit for the filing of the statement of appeal, the appellant shall file with the CAS a brief stating the facts and legal arguments giving rise to the appeal (cf.

16695

DECISION OF THE DISPUTE RESOLUTION CHAMBER

passed in Zurich, Switzerland, on 12 January 2006,
in the following composition:
Slim Aloulou (Tunisia), Chairman
Jean-Marie Philips (Belgium), member
Zola Malvern Percival Majavu (South Africa), member
Rinaldo Martorelli (Brazil), member
Theo van Seggelen (Netherlands), member
on the claim presented by
the player M represented by B as Claimant
against
the club H represented by J as Respondent
regarding a contractual dispute between the player and the club,

I. FACTS OF THE CASE

1. On 2 October 2004, the player H, Claimant, and the club H, Respondent, signed an employment contract valid for the period of ten months from 1 October 2004 to 31 July 2005.
2. According to the above-mentioned employment contract, the player was entitled to receive the following remuneration:

- USD 5,000 as a monthly salary (cf. clause 2, lit. A of the contract) and
- USD 30,000 in the case that the player plays against the club A on 8 October 2004 to the full satisfaction of the club, upon receipt of the International Transfer Certificate and if the result of the medical exams is positive (cf. clause 2, lit. F of the contract).

3. Clause 14 of the aforementioned employment contract states that if the club terminates the contract with the player within the first ten days of the contractual duration, the player has no claiming rights.
4. On 26 April 2005, the player turned to FIFA claiming that after having passed all the formalities of the transfer and the medical exams, which turned out positive and after having scored a goal in the match on 8 October 2004, which ended 2:1 for the adversary, the club did not pay him the contractually agreed amount of USD 30,000.
5. The Claimant maintains that the club terminated the contract with the explanation that it allegedly had not liked his performance.
6. In addition, the player points out that the club had retained his passport, in order to make him sign a unilateral termination of the employment contract ("declaration"), drafted in two languages that he does not master. In this respect, the player presented to FIFA a copy of the said "declaration".
7. The above-mentioned "declaration" signed by the player stipulates the following:
"*Declaration. It is on the day Wednesday 10/11/2004. I, the player, H. Enrolled in H club (...) has received all my financial dues until 10-11. Thus, the club (...) has totally acquitted from any financial obligation related to me in accordance to the contract that was signed between us on the date 1-20-2004. This declaration is issued by myself without any pressure or coercion from anyone.*"
8. Furthermore, the player claims that after 37 days of anguish, he signed the aforementioned "declaration" and the club paid him USD 3,200 as compensation for accommodation and his return to X. The player amplifies that he wrote to the respondent's Football Association that he did not agree with the declaration he signed and asked them several times for mediation, but without success. In this respect, the player presented to FIFA a copy of the aforementioned letter addressed to the said Football Association.
9. On account of the above, the player is claiming compensation of USD 80,000 in connection with the remaining value of the employment contract including the above-mentioned outstanding USD 30,000, based on the unilateral breach of contract by the club without just cause. Furthermore, the Claimant requests sporting sanctions to be imposed on the club.
10. On 12 October 2004, well before the player had lodged a claim in front of FIFA, the respondent's Football Association informed FIFA that the player and its affiliate had reached an agreement in accordance with the above-mentioned clause 14 of the employment contract. A copy of the said agreement was presented to FIFA.
11. On 22 August 2005, in response to the player's claim, the club confirmed the information provided by the above-mentioned Football Association to FIFA on 12 October 2004, emphasising that the "declaration" signed by the player is binding, because it was signed in front of impartial witnesses and without any coercion. Therefore, it would owe him nothing. The Respondent explains that after the player's failure to impress the board of the directors in the match against A on 8 October 2004 due to his poor performance, the club fulfilled all of its financial obligations towards the player for the first ten days pursuant to clause 14 and to clause 2 par. F of the employment contract (cf. above). Therefore, the club categorically rejects the claim put forward by the player.
12. In reply hereto, the player adheres to his position. He adds that due to the fact that the club did not hand him out the employment contract in a known language as stipulated in art. 2 par. A of the employment contract, he had no knowledge of the contents of art. 14, on which the club bases the termination of the contract. Furthermore, the player explains that he remained at the club's disposal until 10 November 2004, when he signed the "declaration" under coercion. Therefore, he deems the club has released him only by this moment.
13. The club on its part responds that the contract had been concluded at the presence of the player's representative Mr. Q (same nationality as Claimant), who also signed the contract as witness and who translated and explained the contents of the contract to the player. Furthermore, the club provided FIFA with a copy of a report dated 9 October 2004, by means of which the club's coach informed the president of the club about the player's weak performance and the recommendation to release him. The club insists that the player refused twice (on 9 and on 10 October 2004) to receive its notice of termination of the employment contract, in order to let the 10 days deadline mentioned in clause 14 pass. Furthermore, the club asserts that it paid to the player 12,022 in cash plus 4,467 as compensation for phone calls and daily expenses. The club explains that, as a consequence of the aforementioned, the player agreed to sign the declaration letter.

14. Upon request, the player informed FIFA that since having left the respondent he did not sign any new employment contract. With regard to the list of expenses presented by the club he maintains that he did not receive any payment and that the phone calls to the Football Federation of his origin were not made by him. Furthermore, he points out that Mr. Q was neither his representative, nor had he been present at the moment of the termination of the contract.

II. CONSIDERATIONS OF THE DISPUTE RESOLUTION CHAMBER

1. The Dispute Resolution Chamber (DRC) started its deliberations by indicating that the matter at stake was submitted to FIFA before 1 July 2005. Therefore, and in accordance with Article 26 Para. 1 of the Regulations for the Status and Transfer of Players (edition 2005), the Chamber stated that the previous Regulations for the Status and Transfer of Players (edition 2001, hereinafter referred to as; the Regulations) apply to the matter at hand.
2. The Dispute Resolution Chamber then asserted that the matter at stake concerns a dispute between a player and a club regarding the fulfilment of a financial obligation resulting from an employment contract.
3. According to Article 42 of the Regulations the Dispute Resolution Chamber is competent to deal with matters with an international dimension which concern employment related contractual disputes between players and clubs. As a result, the DRC is competent to deal with disputes resulting from the non-fulfilment of an employment contract.
4. On account of the above, the Dispute Resolution Chamber concluded that it is competent to decide upon the matter at hand.
5. Once its competence was thus established, the members of the Chamber went on to deal with the substance of the case starting by acknowledging that the parties to the present contractual dispute provided a copy of the employment contract duly signed between the player and the club dated 2 October 2004 as well as a copy of the above-mentioned "declaration" and the agreement dated 9 November 2004 (hereinafter; "waiver"). With regard to the aforementioned "declaration" and "waiver" the DRC noted that they were both signed by the player and the club and that both documents contain a declaration of the player having received all his dues and entitlements from the club according to the contract and waiving, therefore, any further claim.
6. In continuation, and analysing all the submitted documents, the Chamber noted that the positions of the litigating parties are contradictory. On the one hand, the Claimant is of the opinion that the termination of the contract was made by the club without a just cause, and that therefore the club owes him a compensation of USD 80,000 including the contractually agreed USD 30,000 after the match played against A on 8 October 2004 and that the "declaration" and the "waiver" were signed by him under pressure from the club only, in order to leave the country. Whereas, on the other hand, the Respondent is of the firm opinion that it terminated the contract with just cause based on clause 14 of the employment contract, that the amount of USD 30,000 is not owed to the player based on clause 2, lit. F of the employment contract, i.e. the failure to impress the board of the club playing the match against A on 8 October 2004 and that, finally, the "declaration" and the "waiver" were signed by the player without any type of coercion.
7. To start with, the Chamber turned its attention to clause 14 of the employment contract, according to which the club has the right to unilaterally terminate the contract within the first ten days of the contractual duration excluding all claiming rights of the player.
8. After extended deliberations, the Chamber considered that such clause creates a disequilibrium between the rights and the obligations of the player and the club. Even more, since the right to terminate the contract is left exclusively at the discretion and the subjective criteria of the club, i.e. the stronger party in the employment relationship. Furthermore, the DRC stated that according to the jurisprudence of the Players' Status Committee, a probation period of a player is not admissible in employment contracts of football players. As a consequence, the DRC decided that such clause has to be qualified as not admissible, respectively, null and void.
9. In continuation, the Chamber analysed the Respondent's allegations and noted that they do not contain any reference to a precise or concrete behaviour of the player, which would establish and prove a just cause for the club to terminate the employment contract unilaterally and prematurely. In addition, the Chamber deemed that the allegedly bad performance of a player during a match can be no valid reason for the termination of en employment contract.

10. Taking into consideration the above, the DRC decided that the Respondent terminated the employment contract without just cause.
11. With regard to a possible compensation in favour of the player due to the breach of contract without just cause of the club, and under this point, the question of the admissibility of the contractual clause 2 lit. F, the members of the Chamber considered that these issues do not have to be answered in the present dispute due to the following reasons:
12. The DRC acknowledged that the player has signed a "waiver" on 9 November 2004 and a "declaration" on 10 November 2004 with the club H, which refers to the termination of the contractual relation between the parties concerned. In accordance with these documents, which were duly studied by the Chamber, the player M confirms that, after having received all his financial dues and entitlements from the respondent, he has no further or pending claims or matters against the club. The members of the Chamber agreed that these documents must be considered as waivers duly signed by the player.
13. In continuation, and after studying carefully all the submitted documents, the DRC stated that the player failed to present documentary evidence in support of his allegation that he had been forced to sign the above-mentioned "declaration" and "waiver", as for example documentary evidence of a pending penal procedure against the club. Consequently, the DRC decided that the Respondent's allegations in this regard cannot be considered.
14. In the light of all of the above, and in particular bearing in mind the fact that the player signed the aforementioned waivers, the Dispute Resolution Chamber decided that it must reject the claim put forward by the player.

III. DECISION OF THE DISPUTE RESOLUTION CHAMBER

1. The claim submitted by the Claimant is rejected.
2. According to art. 60 par. 1 of the FIFA Statutes, this decision may be appealed against before the Court of Arbitration for Sport (CAS). The statement of appeal must be sent to the CAS directly within 21 days of receipt of notification of this decision and shall contain all the elements in accordance with point 2 of the directives issued by the CAS, a copy of which we enclose hereto. Within another 10 days following the expiry of the time limit for filing the statement of appeal, the appellant shall file a brief stating the facts and legal arguments giving rise to the appeal with the CAS (cf. point 4 of the directives).

16716

DECISION OF THE DISPUTE RESOLUTION CHAMBER

passed in Zurich, Switzerland, on 12 January 2006,
in the following composition:
Slim Aloulou (Tunisia), Chairman
Jean-Marie Philips (Belgium), member
Zola Malvern Percival Majavu (South Africa), member
Rinaldo Martorelli (Brazil), member
Theo van Seggelen (Netherlands), member
on the claim presented by
the player V as Claimant
against
the club G as Respondent
regarding a dispute between the player and the club,

I. FACTS OF THE CASE

1. The player V, Claimant, and the club G, Respondent, signed an employment contract for the sporting season 2004.
2. On 29 November 2004, the club acknowledged a debt in the amount of USD 13,500 towards the player relating to outstanding salary and bonus and payable to the player by 15 January 2005.
3. On 19 May 2005, the player C lodged a claim against the club in front of FIFA, demanding the sum of USD 13,500 from the club in accordance with the above-mentioned acknowledgement of

indebtedness, which allegedly remained unpaid. The player presented to FIFA copies of the relevant employment contract and of the relevant debt acknowledgment.

4. On 29 June 2005, FIFA invited the Respondent to present its response to the player's claim by 13 July 2005. No reply was received. Further invitations dated 22 and 29 July and 7 and 20 September 2005 to the Respondent to submit its response also remained unanswered.

II. CONSIDERATIONS OF THE DISPUTE RESOLUTION CHAMBER

1. The Dispute Resolution Chamber started its deliberations by indicating that the matter at stake was submitted to FIFA before the coming into force of the current Regulations for the Status and Transfer of Players on 1 July 2005. Therefore, and in accordance with Article 26 Para. 1 of the Regulations for the Status and Transfer of Players (edition July 2005), the Chamber stated that the previous Regulations for the Status and Transfer of Players (edition 2001, hereinafter referred to as "the Regulations") do apply to the matter at hand.
2. The Dispute Resolution Chamber then asserted that the matter at stake concerns a dispute between a player and a club regarding the fulfilment of a financial obligation resulting from an employment contract.
3. According to Article 42 of the Regulations the Dispute Resolution Chamber is competent to deal with matters with an international dimension which concern employment related contractual disputes between players and clubs. As a result, the Dispute Resolution Chamber is competent to deal with disputes resulting from the non-fulfilment of an employment contract.
4. On account of the above, the Dispute Resolution Chamber concluded that it is competent to decide upon the matter at hand.
5. Entering into the substance of the matter, the Chamber acknowledged the documentation contained in the file and took note of the fact that the Claimant and the Respondent had signed an employment contract valid for the sporting season 2004. Moreover, the members of the Chamber noticed that the litigating parties entered into an agreement on 29 November 2004, according to which the club committed to pay to the player the amount of USD 13,500 in connection with outstanding salary and bonus by 15 January 2005.
6. Furthermore, the Chamber took into consideration that according to the Claimant the aforementioned amount of USD 13,500 remains unpaid.
7. Finally, the Chamber took note of the fact that the Respondent never presented its position in the matter, despite having been asked to do so by FIFA on several occasions.
8. In continuation, the Chamber then stated that as a general principle of procedure before the Dispute Resolution Chamber, if a Respondent does not reply to the claim, the case shall be decided by the Dispute Resolution Chamber only on the basis of the facts and proof provided by the Claimant, since with its conduct, the Respondent renounces to its right of defence and thus accepts the allegations of the claimant.
9. On account of the above, the members of the Chamber agreed that because the Respondent never took position in the dispute, the Dispute Resolution Chamber shall pass a decision based only on the facts and evidence provided by the Claimant.
10. In this regard, the Chamber underlined that the Claimant is claiming outstanding remuneration from the Respondent according to the above-mentioned debt acknowledgement in the amount of USD 13,500. The Chamber concurred that the Claimant has substantiated his claim.
11. Taking into consideration the above, the Dispute Resolution Chamber decided that the Respondent has to pay the amount of USD 13,500 to the Claimant.

III. DECISION OF THE DISPUTE RESOLUTION CHAMBER

1. The claim of the Claimant is accepted.
2. The Respondent has to pay the amount of USD 13,500 to the Claimant.
3. The amount due to the Claimant has to be paid by the Respondent within 30 days as from the date of notification of this decision.
4. In the event that the debt of the Respondent is not paid within the stated deadline, an interest rate of 5% per year will apply as of expiry of the aforementioned deadline.
5. If the sum of USD 13,500 is not paid within the aforementioned deadline, the present matter shall be submitted to the FIFA Disciplinary Committee, so that the necessary disciplinary sanctions may be imposed.

6. The Claimant is directed to inform the Respondent immediately of the account number to which the remittance is to be made and to notify the Dispute Resolution Chamber of every payment received.
7. According to art. 60 par. 1 of the FIFA Statutes, this decision may be appealed against before the Court of Arbitration for Sport (CAS). The statement of appeal must be sent to the CAS directly within 21 days of receipt of notification of this decision and shall contain all the elements in accordance with point 2 of the directives issued by the CAS, a copy of which we enclose hereto. Within another 10 days following the expiry of the time limit for filing the statement of appeal, the appellant shall file a brief stating the facts and legal arguments giving rise to the appeal with the CAS (cf. point 4 of the directives).

16828
DECISION OF THE DISPUTE RESOLUTION CHAMBER
passed in Zurich, Switzerland, on 12 January 2006,
in the following composition:
Slim Aloulou (Tunisia), Chairman
Jean-Marie Philips (Belgium), Member
Zola Malvern Percival Majavu (South Africa), Member
Rinaldo Martorelli (Brazil), Member
Theo van Seggelen (Netherlands), Member
on the claim presented by
Player A, as Claimant
against
Club B, as Respondent
regarding a dispute about the employment contract concluded between the parties.

I. FACTS OF THE CASE

1. The player A and the club B concluded an employment contract valid from January 2004 until October 2005, stipulating a gross monthly salary of USD 6,500 (net USD 5,525), rental of an apartment for USD 1,400, and the payment of one flight ticket from X to Y per year for the player and his family.
2. On 15 May 2004, the club notified the player that it unilaterally terminated the employment contract due to the player's injury, and paid the player a compensation of two monthly salaries.
3. On 9 July 2004, the player A submitted a claim to FIFA against the club B, maintaining that the club had no just cause to unilaterally terminate the contract and should therefore be condemned to pay compensation.
4. In this respect, the player claims for USD 97,500, being the salaries from 1 June 2004 to 31 October 2005, less the compensation of two monthly salaries, which the club had already paid to the player.
5. Moreover, the player claims for USD 23,800, being the amount related to the apartment rentals from 1 June 2004 to 31 October 2005.
6. On 3 February 2005, the club B replied to the claim of the player by presenting a cheque signed by the player for the receipt of USD 11,050, being the two months compensation for the early termination of the contract.
7. The club is of the opinion that by signing this cheque, the player agreed on the premature termination of the contract.
8. Note: Since the termination of the player's contract with club B, the player did not enter into a labour relationship with any other club.

II. CONSIDERATIONS OF THE DISPUTE RESOLUTION CHAMBER

1. The matter at stake was submitted to FIFA before 1 July 2005. Therefore, and in accordance with Article 18 Para. 2 and 3 of the revised Rules Governing the Procedures of the Players' Status Committee and the Dispute Resolution Chamber (edition 2005), not the revised Rules, but the previous Rules Governing the Practice and Procedures of the Dispute Resolution Chamber (edition 2002, hereinafter referred to as; *the Procedural Rules*) do apply on the matter at hand as procedural rules.

2. Moreover, in accordance with Article 26 Para. 1 and 2 of the revised Regulations for the Status and Transfer of Players (edition 2005), not the revised Regulations, but the previous Regulations for the Status and Transfer of Players(edition 2001, hereinafter referred to as; *the Regulations*) do apply on the dispute at stake as far as the substance of the matter is concerned.
3. The members of the Dispute Resolution Chamber of the FIFA Players' Status Committee were summoned to pass a decision on the matter at stake by the Chairman of the Dispute Resolution Chamber pursuant to Art. 1 point 6) of the Procedural Rules.
4. The members of the Chamber started its deliberations asserting that the matter at stake concerns a dispute about the unilateral termination of an employment contract concluded between a player and a club, and a request for compensation in view of such unilateral termination.
5. In accordance with Art. 42 § 1 lit. (b) of the Regulations, and in particular Para. (i) of the said provision, it falls within the purview of the Dispute Resolution Chamber to determine whether one of the parties has committed a unilateral breach of contract without just cause. In the case that the employment contract was breached by a party, the Dispute Resolution Chamber is responsible to verify and decide whether this party is accountable for outstanding payments and compensation.
6. In view of the above, the Dispute Resolution Chamber concluded that it was competent to decide on the present litigation.
7. Entering into the substance of the matter, the Chamber acknowledged the facts of the case as well as the documentation contained in the file, and in view of the circumstances of the matter, turned to the question whether the club has committed a unilateral breach of the employment contract without just cause, and if so, to verify and decide whether the club is accountable for outstanding payments and compensation.
8. With regard to the question whether the club has committed a unilateral breach of the employment contract without just cause, the Chamber took note that the club indicated as reason for the early termination of the employment contract an injury of the player.
9. In this regard, the Chamber had to deliberate if this was a just cause for the club to terminate the contract.
10. The Chamber stated that according to its constant and persistent jurisprudence, the premature and unilateral termination of an employment contract by a club because of an injury of the player was always considered as an abusive termination of the contract without just cause.
11. Moreover, the Chamber stated that if such a termination would be accepted as a termination with just cause, this would create a disproportionate repartition of the rights of the parties to an employment contract, to the strong detriment of the player.
12. Therefore, the Dispute Resolution Chamber stated that the fact that a player is injured during the course of an employment contract is clearly not a just cause for the club to prematurely and unilaterally terminate the employment contract.
13. On account of the above, the Chamber concluded that the employment contract between the player A and the club B was terminated by the club in question without just cause.
14. In consequence, the Dispute Resolution Chamber had to verify and decide whether the club B is accountable for outstanding payments and compensation towards the player A.
15. With regard to a compensation for unjustified breach of contract, the Chamber stated that according to Art. 22 of the Regulations, the club B has to pay to the player A on account of compensation for breach of contract without just cause the contractual salaries for the remainder of the contract, i.e. the net salaries for the months from April 2004 to October 2005, which is USD 93,925 in total.
16. Moreover, the Chamber noted that the employment contract indicated that the player was entitled to the rental of an apartment for USD 1,400. The Chamber decided that since a fix amount for the rental was indicated, this amount was also to be considered as a salary the player was entitled to from the club.
17. Therefore, the Chamber stated that in addition to the above, the club has to pay to the player on account of compensation for breach of contract without just cause USD 1,400 per month for the remainder of the contract, i.e. for the months from April 2004 to October 2005, which is USD 23,800.
18. Therefore, the total compensation for breach of contract without just cause amounts to USD 117,725.
19. With regard to the position of the club that by signing a cheque in the amount of two monthly salaries, the player agreed on the premature termination of the contract and renounced to any further

compensation, the Chamber stated that the player indeed received the relevant payment, but never declared accepting this amount in settlement of all debts. Moreover, the player expressly contested such position of the club. As a result, and due to the lack of evidence in this respect, the Chamber could not uphold the club's position.

20. The Chamber however noted that the club already paid the player a compensation for the early termination of the contract in the amount of USD 11,050, amount which therefore is to be deducted from the compensation.
21. Therefore, the total compensation for breach of contract amounts to USD 106,675.
22. In view of the above, the Chamber decided that the club B has to pay to the player A the amount of USD 106,675.

III. DECISION OF THE DISPUTE RESOLUTION CHAMBER

1. The claim of the player A is partially accepted.
2. The club B from has to pay the amount of USD 106,675 to the player A.
3. The amount due to the player A has to be paid by the club B within the next 30 days as from the date of notification of this decision.
4. If the aforementioned sum is not paid within the aforementioned deadline, the present matter shall be submitted to FIFA's Disciplinary Committee, so that the necessary disciplinary sanctions may be imposed.
5. If the aforementioned sum is not paid within the aforementioned deadline, an interest rate of 5% per year will apply as from the first day after the aforementioned deadline.
6. Any further request made by the player A is rejected.
7. The player A is directed to inform the club B immediately of the account number to which the remittance is to be made and to notify the Dispute Resolution Chamber of every payment received.
8. According to art. 60 par. 1 of the FIFA Statutes this decision may be appealed before the Court of Arbitration for Sport (CAS). The statement of appeal must be sent to the CAS directly within 21 days of receiving notification of this decision and has to contain all elements in accordance with point 2 of the directives issued by the CAS, copy of which we enclose hereto. Within another 10 days following the expiry of the time limit for the filing of the statement of appeal, the appellant shall file with the CAS a brief stating the facts and legal arguments giving rise to the appeal (cf. point 4 of the directives).

16830
DECISION OF THE DISPUTE RESOLUTION CHAMBER

passed in Zurich, Switzerland, on 12 January 2006,
in the following composition:
Slim Aloulou (Tunisia), Chairman
Jean-Marie Philips (Belgium), Member
Zola Malvern Percival Majavu (South Africa), Member Rinaldo Martorelli (Brazil), Member Theo van Seggelen (Netherlands), Member
Player A, on the claim presented by against regarding a contractual dispute arisen between the parties. as Claimant Club B, as Respondent

I. FACTS OF THE CASE

1. On 18 June 2004, the club B informed the player A, apparently with double nationality, X and Y, in writing about the remuneration payable in case of conclusion of an employment contract.
2. On 26 June 2004, prior to a test match with the team of the club A, the player sought a reassurance from the club in case he would get injured in that match. Therefore, the sport director of the club signed a document according to which the club could not withdraw the offer made on 18 June 2004 in the event that the player would get injured in that test match.
3. On 3 July 2004, the player and the sport director of the club signed an employment contract, valid from 3 July 2004 to 30 June 2008, stipulating a monthly salary of USD 12,500. The space where the sport director of the club signed was designated as "second signature, if necessary". The space above the sport director's signature, designated as "Signature of the employer" stayed empty.

4. On 6 July 2004, the sport director informed the player in writing that the club "confmmfs] that player A does not have any kind of working contract with club B. As the player is not in possession of an EU passport, there is no possibility to obtain the necessary working permit in due time before the start of the season. A possible contract could be negotiated only when the player has received his EU passport."
5. After having insisted in writing on the validity of the contract dated 3 July 2004 with the club B without success, the player signed another contract with the club C, where he earned USD 41,000 in total from August to December 2004. In continuation, from March 2005 to February 2008, he signed a contract with a club D, according to which he earns in total USD 353,000.
6. On 21 July 2004, the player A submitted to FIFA a claim against the club B, requesting the payment of the entire amount of the salaries stipulated in the contract, i.e. the amount of USD 600,000, less the amount he would earn during the stipulated duration of the contract with the club B with other clubs (USD 41,000 with the club C and USD 353,000 with the club D).
7. The player stated that he was convinced that the sport director had the authority to conclude binding contracts for the club, since the same person also signed the reassurance document on 26 June 2004.
8. Moreover, the player stated that according to the FIFA Regulations, the acquisition of a work permit is the sole risk and responsibility of the club.
9. On 11 April 2005, the club B provided FIFA with its reply to the claim at stake, emphasizing that in June/July 2004, it was not interested in any player that did not have an EU-passport. The assessment of the player in question was continued only because he promised to file in his relevant passport in due course.
10. Moreover, according to the excerpt from the commercial register, the sport director was not authorized to conclude binding contracts for the club.
11. In this respect, the club maintained that before having the reassurance document being signed on 26 June 2005, the player was verbally informed that the sport director was not authorized to conclude contracts for the club. The reassurance document was only signed by the sport director since the player insisted on it and would not have played the test match without such document.
12. The document signed on 3 July 2004 was only a draft of an employment contract, which should allow the player's manager to verify the contents of the contract. Also before signing this document, it was reiterated verbally that the sport director was not authorized to conclude binding contracts for the club. The person who was authorized to conclude binding contracts for the club did not sign the relevant document.
13. Allegedly, after receipt of the draft of the employment contract on 3 July 2004, the player added his signature and the following note: "player has applied for relevant Citizenship, and is eligible".
14. Later, the club B found out that the player did not have the respective passport. In this respect, it felt deceived by the player and therefore provided him with the above-mentioned letter dated 6 July 2004.
15. The club is of the opinion that due to the failure of the player to present his respective passport, the draft of the contract dated 3 July 2004 was never finalized.
16. It is also of the opinion that the question in the present matter is not the acquisition of a work permit, but the fact that the player's EU-nationality was an essential condition for the conclusion of an employment contract.
17. On 10 May 2005, the player provided FIFA with his position towards the answer of the club, emphasizing that the acquisition of the respective passport was never communicated to him as being an essential condition for the conclusion of the contract. Moreover, the signed contract would not contain an express provision in this regard.
18. In this respect, the player is of the opinion that the status of his nationality was subsequently used by the club to avoid its obligations under the contract.
19. On 31 October 2005, the club B provided FIFA with its final position on the matter, stating that it was clearly communicated to the player that his respective citizenship was an essential condition for the conclusion of a contract.
20. In this regard, the club refers on the one hand to alleged oral information of the player, and on the other hand to a letter dated 15 July 2005 from a person called Mr X in which this person stated that he was aware that the club B was looking only for a player with EU-citizenship. According to the club, Mr X was the agent of the player A. Therefore, Mr A presumably had been informed accordingly.

21. Moreover, the club emphasized that at that time, its quota for non EU-players was already exhausted. Therefore, the player's nationality was not used by the club to avoid its obligations under the contract, but rather the reason for not concluding a contract with the player at all.
22. In continuation, the club stated that on 3 July 2004, only one exemplar of the contract draft was signed. However, according to Art. 36 of the draft of the contract, three copies would have had to be signed, one handed out to both parties and one registered at the National League, in order to become legally binding. Since only one exemplar of the draft contract was signed, the contract could not become legally binding anyway.
23. Furthermore, the club emphasised that on 3 July 2004, only the sport director signed the draft contract, the player did not sign it. It was allegedly only in the correspondence exchanged with regard to the present dispute, when the club saw for the first time the contract signed by the player as well, and amended with the above-mentioned note 'player has applied for respective Citizenship, and is eligible'.
24. On account of the above, the club B is of the opinion that in July 2004, no contract was concluded between the parties in question.
25. However, in case it should be considered that a contract was concluded, the club B is of the opinion that such contract was not valid, since the club was deceived by the player about his nationality and therefore had no will to conclude this contract.
26. Finally, in case it should be considered that a valid contract was concluded between the parties, the club B maintains that the player violated his obligation to mitigate his damage, since he had no contract during certain periods of the duration of the contract with club B.

II. CONSIDERATIONS OF THE DISPUTE RESOLUTION CHAMBER

1. The matter at stake was submitted to HFA before 1 July 2005. Therefore, and in accordance with Article 18 Para. 2 and 3 of the revised Rules Governing the Procedures of the Players' ' Status Committee and the Dispute Resolution Chamber (edition 2005), not the revised Rules, but the previous Rules Governing the Practice and Procedures of the Dispute Resolution Chamber (edition 2002, hereinafter referred to as; the Procedural Rules) do apply on the matter at hand as procedural rules.
2. Moreover, in accordance with Article 26 Para. 1 and 2 of the revised Regulations for the Status and Transfer of Players (edition 2005), not the revised Regulations, but the previous Regulations for the Status and Transfer of Players (edition 2001, hereinafter referred to as; the Regulations) do apply on the dispute at stake as far as the substance of the matter is concerned.
3. The members of the Dispute Resolution Chamber were summoned to pass a decision on the matter at stake by the Chairman of the Dispute Resolution Chamber pursuant to Article 1 point 6) of the Procedural Rules.
4. The members of the Chamber started their deliberations asserting that the matter at stake concerns a dispute about the conclusion of an employment contract between a player and a club as well as a request of the player for compensation for unjustified unilateral termination of such contract.
5. In accordance with Article 42 Para. 1 lit. (b) of the Regulations, and in particular Para. (i) of the said provision, it falls within the purview of the Dispute Resolution Chamber to determine whether one of the parties has committed a unilateral breach of contract without just cause. In case the employment contract was breached by a party, the Dispute Resolution Chamber is responsible to verify and decide whether this party is accountable for outstanding payments and compensation (cf. Article 42 Para. 1 lit. (b) (iii) of the Regulations).
6. In view of the above, the Dispute Resolution Chamber concluded that it was competent to decide on the present litigation.
7. Entering into the substance of the matter, the Chamber acknowledged the FACTS OF THE CASE as well as the documentation contained in the file, and in view of the circumstances of the matter, emphasized that it was of prior and crucial importance to provide an answer to the question whether an employment contract was validly concluded between the parties to the dispute at stake, the player A and the club B.
8. In this regard, the Chamber stated that for the valid conclusion of a contract, the congruent expression of the will of the parties or their legal representatives to conclude such contract is required. The signature of a party or its legal representative is considered as an expression of its will to conclude a contract.

9. In view of the above outlined principle, the Chamber acknowledged that on 3 July 2004, the player B and the sport director of the club B put their signature under an employment contract. In this respect, the Chamber pointed out that the club B had not provided any evidence for its allegation that the player had signed the document only at a later stage. Moreover, the Chamber noticed in particular that the space where the sport director signed the contract was designated as 'second signature, if necessary', and that the space above the sport director's signature, designated as 'signature of the employer', was not signed.
10. On account of the above, the members of the Chamber stated that since the space on the contract designated 'signature of the employer' was not signed, the employer, the club B, had not expressed its will to conclude the relevant employment contract.
11. Therefore, no contract was concluded between the employee, the player A, and the employer, the club B.
12. However, the Chamber emphasized that the sport director, with his signature on the space designated as 'second signature, if necessary', may have validly concluded an employment contract for the club, without that the signature of the employer was necessary.
13. In this regard, the Chamber first of all acknowledged that according to the excerpt of the commercial register regarding the club B, the sport director was not authorized to conclude binding contracts for the club.
14. Therefore, the Chamber stated that since in accordance with the commercial register, the sport director does not have the power to conclude binding contracts for the club B, as a general rule, he could not validly conclude an employment contract for the club B with the player A.
15. In continuation, the Chamber analysed if the player could in good faith trust that the sport director of the club was entitled to conclude binding contracts for the club. Under such circumstances, the contract in question would have to be considered after all as validly concluded between the player and the club.
16. In this regard, the members of the Chamber acknowledged that on 24 June 2004, the sport director of the club signed a document according to which the club could not withdraw its contract offer made towards the player in the event that the player would get injured in the upcoming test match. Moreover, the Chamber acknowledged that on 3 July 2004, the sport director signed the employment contract in question on the space designated 'signature, if necessary'.
17. On account of the above, the Chamber stated that the fact that the sport director signed the document dated 18 June 2004 could indeed possibly be interpreted in a way that the player could in good faith believe that the sport director was duly authorised by the club to conclude binding contracts for it, such as to sign an employment contract.
18. The Chamber was of the opinion that such good faith can, however, not be maintained with regard to the signing of the employment contract dated 3 July 2004. On this contract, the sport director did not sign on the space designated 'signature of the employer', but on the space which was clearly designated 'second signature, if necessary'. It is obvious that if the sport director would have been entitled to conclude an employment contract for the club, he would have signed at the space designated as 'signature of the employer'. Since he signed at the space designated 'second signature, if necessary', it was clear that he was not entitled to conclude an employment contract for the club, or at least not him alone. Moreover, it was clear that the conclusion of such a contract, besides the sport director's signature, requires the signature of another person, the 'signature of the employer', in order that an employment contract is validly concluded.
19. Therefore, the Chamber concluded that the player could not in good faith believe that the sport director was a legal representative of the club with the power to conclude the employment contract in question.
20. The player as well cannot argue that he could not understand the designations on the contract, since they were in a language the player did not master. It was the player's responsibility to translate the contract in English, or at least to ask for a translation of the contract, before signing it. By signing the presented version of the contract, the player accepted the contract and thereby implied understanding this version. The Chamber remarked, however, that the player is not evoking such argumentation.
21. On account of the above, the Chamber came to the conclusion that between the parties to the present dispute, no valid employment contract was concluded.
22. The Chamber then turned to the circumstances of the negotiations for the employment contract in question between the parties involved, and thereby acknowledged that with his behaviour, the sport

director of the club gave the strong impression to the player that an employment contract would be concluded with him. The Chamber particularly referred to the fact that the player was provided with an offer on 18 June 2004, received an assurance confirmation signed by the sport director on 26 June 2004 in case he would get injured in a test match, was given a copy of the contract dated 3 July 2004, signed by the sport director, and finally, on 6 July 2004, was informed that no contract would be concluded with him.

23. In view of these facts, it appeared to the members of the Chamber that the club arranged to keep the player during the registration period as a reserve, for the event that it could not take under contract other preferred players. Once it was then clarified that some other players could be contracted, the player A was abandoned. Would it not have been possible to contract the preferred players, the contract with the player A could still have been finalised.
24. On account of the above outlined circumstances, the Chamber referred to the legal principle of culpa in contrahendo, according to which a party to a negotiation for a contract has to compensate causal damages incurred by the other party, if it has infringed on its own fault its obligation to act in good faith during the negotiations and thereby breached the confidence of the other party in the negotiations.
25. In the present case, the player A and the club B were in negotiations for an employment contract. The behaviour of the sport director, in particular the fact that he signed the reassurance document on 26 June 2004, in connection with the fact that he signed a copy of the employment contract and handed it to the player, although he was not entitled to conclude employment contracts for the club, created a certain confidence for the player, according to which he could in good faith believe that an employment contract would indeed be concluded.
26. By not finalising the employment contract, the club breached the player's confidence. Since most probably, the contract was not finalised because the club could contract other player's, the breach of the player's confidence was done without any blame to be assigned to the player, but only by the club's fault. In this respect, the Chamber emphasised that the contract signed by the sport director on 3 July 2004 did not refer at all to the alleged necessity for the player to hold an EU-passport. Neither had the club B provided other evidences corroborating its allegation that the player's European nationality would be an essential condition for the conclusion of the contract. On account of this, the Chamber concluded that the club is liable for the breach of the confidence of the player.
27. The breach of the player's confidence has led to a damage for the player, in particular since the player was not able to negotiate for an employment with other clubs during the time of negotiations with the club B. Moreover, in order not to be without a club after having been disappointed by the club B, the player had to find new employment in a very short time, which did not allow him to carefully negotiate the financial aspects of the new contract. It was therefore clear for the members of the Chamber that the player had suffered damages. In view of all the above, and considering the player's income with the clubs following his departure from club B, the Chamber established that the club B has to compensate the player for culpa in contrahendo with the amount of USD 50,000.
28. Finally, the Dispute Resolution Chamber stated that it is clear that negotiations for the conclusion of an employment contract can last for a longer time. In this regard, the Chamber emphasized that there is nothing illegal if such negotiations take some time. The Chamber, however, stressed that the practice applied by the club B in the present case, i.e. the holding of a player at the reserve by providing him with an employment contract which is signed by a person which is not authorised by the club to conclude contracts for the club, is not acceptable and tolerable and therefore has to lead to a compensation of the damaged player.
29. In view of the above, the Chamber decided that the club B has to pay to the player A the amount of USD 50,000 on account of culpa in contrahendo.

III. DECISION OF THE DISPUTE RESOLUTION CHAMBER

1. The claim of the player A is partially accepted.
2. The club B has to pay the amount of USD 50,000 to the player A.
3. The amount due to the player A has to be paid by the club B within the next 30 days as from the date of notification of this decision.
4. If the aforementioned sum is not paid within the aforementioned deadline, an interest rate of 5% per year will apply as from the first day after the aforementioned deadline.

5. If the aforementioned sum is not paid within the aforementioned deadline, the present matter shall be submitted to FIFA's Disciplinary Committee, so that the necessary disciplinary sanctions may be imposed.
6. Any further request by the player A is rejected.
7. The player A is directed to inform the club B directly and immediately of the account number to which the remittance is to be made and to notify the Dispute Resolution Chamber of every payment received.
8. According to art. 60 par. 1 of the FIFA Statutes this decision may be appealed before the Court of Arbitration for Sport (CAS). The statement of appeal must be sent to the CAS directly within 21 days of receiving notification of this decision and has to contain all elements in accordance with point 2 of the directives issued by the CAS, copy of which we enclose hereto. Within another 10 days following the expiry of the time limit for the filing of the statement of appeal, the appellant shall file with the CAS a brief stating the facts and legal arguments giving rise to the appeal (cf. point 4 of the directives).

21 FEBRUARY 2006

26135
DECISION OF THE DISPUTE RESOLUTION CHAMBER
passed in Zurich, Switzerland, on 21 February 2006,
in the following composition:
Slim Aloulou (Tunisia), Chairman
Joaquim Evangelista (Portugal), member
Michele Colucci (Italy) member
Philippe Diallo (France) member
Mohamed Mecherara (Algeria) member
on the claim presented by the club
X, Sweden as Claimant
against the club Y, Netherlands as Respondent
regarding training compensation for the player Z

I. FACTS OF THE CASE

1. The Swedish Football Association confirmed that the player Z, born on 1 March 1986, was registered with the Swedish club X, Claimant, from 1992 until December 2000, i.e. for 8 years, between the ages of 6 until 15.
2. In December 2000 the player was transferred from the Claimant to the Swedish club xxxxxx and in July 2004 the player was transferred from the aforementioned the Swedish club to the Dutch club Y, the Respondent.
3. The Claimant claims training compensation in accordance with Chapter VII of the FIFA Regulations for the Status and Transfer of Players (edition 2001) payable by the Dutch club Y.
4. In particular, the Claimant claims training compensation amounting to EUR 150,000. Furthermore, the Claimant explains that the player was transferred to the club xxxxxxx in December 2000 where he signed a contract according to which he was not entitled to any salary or compensation, i.e. he was still an amateur.
5. On 7 October 2004, the Respondent contested the position of the Claimant affirming that it already paid training compensation to the club xxxxxx and that the player had signed an non-amateur contract with the aforementioned club.
   Therefore, the Respondent is of the opinion that the transfer at the basis of the present dispute is a "subsequent transfer" and that consequently, no compensation is due.
6. Finally, the Respondent pointed out that in the unlikely event that the deciding body would conclude that training compensation is due to the Claimant the compensation could never be higher than the amount of category 4 (indicative amount of EUR 10,000 per year), the category of the Claimant and is only due for the period during which the player was between the ages of 12 and 15, meaning that the amount of training compensation would be EUR 30,000.

7. On 2 May 2005, the Swedish Football Association informed FIFA that a non-amateur contract signed between the player involved and the club xxxxxx, valid as from 24 June 2002 until 28 February 2004, was registered within the association.
Furthermore, the Swedish Football Association explained that the economic compensation was not fixed as a monthly salary but related to bonuses only.
8. According to the relevant contract signed between the Swedish club xxxxxx and the player, the latter would receive the bonuses depending on played matches within the Super One League or Premiership League in the A-team: 1-9 matches SK 2000 or SEK 3000, 10-14 matches SEK 4,000 or SEK 6,000, 15-20 matches SEK 6,000 or SEK 8,000, 21-30 matches SEK 8,000 or SEK 10,000, over 31 matches SEK 12,000 or SEK 14,000.
9. On 5 August 2005, the Swedish Football Association informed FIFA that its affiliated club, xxxxx, never paid any compensation at all to the player since the player never played in any A-team match.
10. Finally, the Swedish Football Association stressed that although the player had been registered as a non-amateur player, in reality, he was an amateur.
11. On 22 August 2005, the Respondent pointed out that the player involved was transferred from the Claimant to the Swedish club xxxxx, where he was registered as a non-amateur, and therefore his transfer from xxxxx to the Respondent needs to be considered as a subsequent transfer. In this respect, the Respondent underlined that in case of a subsequent transfer the training compensation is only due to the former club, and since it already paid training compensation to xxxxx it is not obliged to pay any training compensation to Claimant.

II. CONSIDERATIONS OF THE DISPUTE RESOLUTION CHAMBER

1. First of all, the Chamber analysed whether it was competent to deal with the matter at stake. In this respect, it referred to art. 18 par. 2 and 3 of the Rules Governing the Procedures of the Players' Status Committee and the Dispute Resolution Chamber. The present matter was submitted to FIFA on 15 September 2004, as a consequence the Chamber concluded that the previous Procedural Rules (edition 2001) on matters pending before the decision making bodies of FIFA are applicable on the matter at hand.
2. With regard to the competence of the Chamber, art. 42 par. 1 lit. (b) (iv) of the FIFA Regulations for the Status and Transfer of Players (edition 2001) establishes that, disputes concerning training compensation, will be decided by the Dispute Resolution Chamber.
3. As a consequence, the Dispute Resolution Chamber is the competent body to decide on the present litigation concerning the training compensation claimed by the Claimant for the training and education of the player Z.
4. Subsequently, the members of the Chamber analyzed which edition of the Regulations for the Status and Transfer of Players should be applicable as to the substance of the matter. In this respect, the Chamber referred to art. 26 par. 1 and 2 of the Regulations for the Status and Transfer of Players (edition 2005) in the modified version in accordance with the FIFA circular no. 995 dated 23 September 2005. Furthermore, it acknowledged that the professional had been registered for his new club in July 2004. Equally the Chamber took note that the claim was lodged at FIFA in September 2004. In view of the aforementioned, the Chamber concluded that the former FIFA Regulations for the Status and Transfer of Players (edition 2001, hereafter: the Regulations) are applicable on the case at hand as to the substance.
5. In continuation, and entering into the substance of the matter, the members of the Chamber maintained that as established in chapter VII of the FIFA Regulations training compensation for a players training and education is payable by the new club either when the player signs his first contract as a non-amateur or each time a player changes from one club to another up to the time his training and education is complete, which, as a general rule, occurs when the player reaches 23 years of age.
6. In accordance with art. 5 of the FIFA Regulations governing the Application of the FIFA Regulations, the training period to take into account for the calculation of the training compensation, starts at the beginning of the season of the players 12th birthday, or at a later age, as the case may be, and finishes at the end of the season of the players 21st birthday.
7. In this respect, the Chamber emphasised that in the present case the period to take into account is as from the beginning of the season of the players 12th birthday, i.e. the season 1998/99 until December 2000.

8. Subsequently, the Chamber considered that, on the one hand, the Claimant requested training compensation in the amount of EUR 150,000 and, on the other hand, that the Respondent contested the Claimants entitlement to receive any training compensation arguing that the transfer at the basis of the present dispute is a "subsequent transfer" and consequently, no compensation is due to the Claimant since the player had already a non-amateur status with his former club.
9. Then, the Chamber clarified that in accordance with the FIFA circular no. 826 dated 31 October 2002 the rule remains that training compensation will be payable to all clubs that have trained a player between the ages of 12 and 21 once the player acquires non-amateur status (i.e., by signing a non-amateur contract with the club for which he has been playing as an amateur, or by signing a non-amateur contract with another club to which he transfers). Moreover, in case of subsequent transfers of young players, training compensation will only be payable to the previous training club, and not to any other training club.
10. In view of the above, the Chamber needed to address the question whether the player concerned had signed an employment contract with the club xxxx and whether, in the affirmative, the transfer of player from xxxx to the Respondent should be considered as a subsequent transfer.
11. To this regard, the Chamber emphasised that a player shall be regarded as non-amateur if he has a written employment contract based on which he receives remuneration in excess of the expenses effectively incurred for his football activity.
12. The Chamber took into account that according to the contract signed between the player involved and the club xxxx, valid as from 24 June 2002 until 28 February 2004, the economic compensation was not fixed as a monthly salary but related to bonuses depending on played matches within the Super One League or Premiership League in the A-team. In particular, for participating in 1-9 matches SK 2000 or SEK 3000, 10-14 matches SEK 4,000 or SEK 6,000, 15-20 matches SEK 6,000 or SEK 8,000, 21-30 matches SEK 8,000 or SEK 10,000, over 31 matches SEK 12,000 or SEK 14,000. However, the Chamber duly considered that the Swedish Football Association informed FIFA that its affiliate, club xxxx, never paid any compensation at all to the players since the player never played in any A-team match.
13. In this respect, the Chamber took into account, that the player never received any salary at all from the club xxxx during the time he spent with the said club as confirmed by the Swedish Football Association.
14. As a result, the Chamber concluded that although from a formal point of view the player was registered as non-amateur and had signed a contract, de facto he has to be considered as an amateur since he never received any remuneration at all for his services and therefore it is clear that he did not even receive more than the expenses he effectively incurred in return for his footballing activity.
15. In view of all of the above, the Chamber unanimously decided that the transfer of the player from xxxx to Y cannot be considered a subsequent transfer.
16. Consequently, the Chamber decided that the position of the Respondent that no compensation would be due to the Claimant since the transfer at the basis of the dispute should be considered as a subsequent transfer cannot be upheld.
17. As a result, the Chamber concluded that the Claimant is entitled to receive training compensation for the training and education of the player Z from the Respondent as established in chapter VII of the FIFA Regulations, since the said player is considered to have signed his first employment contract with the Respondent in July 2004.
18. In this respect, the Chamber explained that the amount of compensation must be calculated in accordance with art. 7 of the FIFA Regulations governing the Application of the FIFA Regulations, applying the parameters established by the FIFA circular no. 826 dated 31 October 2002.
19. Then, the Chamber observed that with regard to the categorisation of clubs, the Claimant belongs to category 4 and the Respondent is a 1 division club, belonging to category 1.
20. In accordance with art. 7 par. 2 and 4 of the FIFA Regulations governing the Application of the FIFA Regulations, in order to ensure that training compensation for very young players is not set at unreasonably high levels, the amount for players aged 12 to 15 shall be based on the training and education costs for category 4 of the country in which the training club was located. In the present case the amount corresponding to the category 4 within Sweden is EUR 10,000.
21. The Chamber took into consideration the figures under point II. 7. Consequently, in application of article 7 par. 1 of the FIFA Regulations governing the Application of the FIFA Regulations the indicative amount of EUR 10,000 must be multiplied by the number of years of training of the player

in case. In the present case 2 ½ years corresponding to the time as from the beginning of the season of the players 12th birthday, i.e. the season 1998/99 until December 2000.

22. Taking into account all of the above, the Chamber concluded that the Respondent has to pay the amount of EUR 25,000 to the Claimant as training compensation for the training and education of the player Z.

III. DECISION OF THE DISPUTE RESOLUTION CHAMBER

1. The claim lodged by the Claimant, X, is partially accepted.
2. The Respondent, Y, shall pay the total amount of EUR 25,000 to the Claimant, within 30 days following the date of the notification of the present decision.
3. Any further financial claim from the Claimant is rejected.
4. In the event that the above-mentioned amount is not paid within the stated deadline, an interest rate of 5% per year will apply as of expiring of the fixed time limit and the present matter shall be submitted to FIFAs Disciplinary Committee, so that the necessary disciplinary sanctions may be imposed.
5. The Claimant X is instructed to inform the Respondent Y directly and immediately of the account number to which the remittance is to be made and to notify the Dispute Resolution Chamber of every payment received.
6. According to art. 60 par. 1 of the FIFA Statutes, this decision may be appealed against before the Court of Arbitration for Sport (CAS). The statement of appeal must be sent to the CAS directly within 21 days of receipt of notification of this decision and shall contain all the elements in accordance with point 2 of the directives issued by the CAS, a copy of which we enclose hereto. Within another 10 days following the expiry of the time limit for filing the statement of appeal, the appellant shall file a brief stating the facts and legal arguments giving rise to the appeal with the CAS (cf. point 4 of the directives).

⚽⚽⚽

26267

DECISION OF THE DISPUTE RESOLUTION CHAMBER

passed in Zurich, Switzerland, on 21 February 2006,
in the following composition:
Mr Slim Aloulou (Tunisia), chairman
Mr Philippe Diallo (France), member Mr Ivan Gazidis (USA), member
Mr Joaquim Evangelista (country y), member Mr Michele Colucci (Italy), member
Mr X, .., represented by Mr O on the claim presented by against the as Claimant Clube Y, represented by Mrs U as Respondent
regarding a contractual dispute arisen between the parties

I. FACTS OF THE CASE

1. On 1 July 2004, the player X and Clube Y signed an employment contract valid from that date until 30 June 2009. Both parties have provided FIFA with a copy of the aforementioned employment contract.
2. On 25 February 2005, Mr informed FIFA that Clube Y had failed to provide him with a working visa, which was necessary for him to fulfil his employment contract. As a consequence, the player was prevented from entering into country y when he returned from country x, in January 2005. In this respect, the player provided the FIFA Administration with a copy of a document issued by the Y authorities, confirming that he was not allowed to enter the country due to the lack of a valid visa.
3. In light of the above and taking into account the alleged fact that he had also not received his salaries since September 2004, Mr X requested the Chamber to consider his employment contract with Clube Y as terminated and declare the latter liable for having breached the contract without just cause. In the meantime, the player informed FIFA that he had requested the Civil Courts in country x to authorize him to proceed with his career on a provisional basis.
4. Moreover, the player requested the Dispute Resolution Chamber to condemn Clube Y to pay him the outstanding amounts that were due to him under their employment contract, i.e. his salaries from

September 2004 until February 2005, in the total amount of EUR 5,990.88 (EUR 998,48 per month) and to be considered free to sign for another club of his choice.

5. On 28 February 2005, FIFA asked the player to confirm if he had already requested a country x an Civil Court to authorize him to be registered for a new club in country x. Moreover, FIFA warned the player that players are forbidden from submitting matters connected with their registration to Civil Courts.
6. In reply, the player confirmed that in case FIFA would not take a decision regarding the possibility for him to proceed with his career with another club within a deadline of 2 (two) days, he would go before the Civil Courts in country x for that purpose.
7. On 10 March 2005, the country x an Football Confederation informed FIFA that a country x Civil Court had authorized Mr Xs registration for its affiliated club, Clube Q.
8. On 8 April 2005, the Y Football Federation forwarded to the attention of FIFA, a copy of the aforementioned decision taken by the country xian Civil Court, dated 2 March 2005. Furthermore, the said Federation stated that Clube Y had a valid employment contract with Mr X until 30 June 2009. Moreover, from the content of the relevant decision, it can be noted that the player in question signed an employment contract with Clube Q on 23 February 2005.
9. Apart from the above, Clube Y, a club participating in the third national division in country y, added that Mr X left for country x in December 2004, without its necessary authorization or knowledge and never returned to the club. According to the .. club, the player was informed several times that he should immediately return in order to comply with their employment contract. The Y club failed, however, to provide any evidence in this regard.
10. Moreover, the Y club asserts that the player has always avoided to comply with the necessary legal procedures in order to obtain a working visa. In this respect, the club draws the Chambers attention to the fact that, even without a proper working visa, Mr could have entered into country y with his country xian passport, like he had previously done.
11. In response, Mr X asserts that, in December 2004, he had the clubs authorization to leave the country. The player failed, however, to provide any evidence in this regard. Furthermore, he underlines that the club waited a long time before complaining to FIFA about his alleged breach of contract.
12. Moreover, the player maintains that he could not have remained without an income for much longer and that his recourse to a country xian Civil Court was absolutely necessary in order to guarantee his subsistence.
13. On the other hand, the player insists that he was prevented from entering into country y in January 2005, due to the fact that the club had failed to provide him with a valid visa, which would have allowed him to work in country y. In order to support his position in this regard, the player provided FIFA with a copy of his passport bearing the Y customs' stamp and denying his entrance in country y, based on the fact that he had no valid working visa to enter into the country.
14. As a consequence, the player defends that he was prevented from fulfilling his employment contract with Clube Y, entirely due to the clubs fault.
15. In addition to the above, the player asserts that he waited almost two months for the Y club to solve his visa problem, without any success. As a consequence, and since he had already been without any remuneration for six months, he had to find another club to work.
16. Finally, the player draws the Chambers attention to the fact that the Y club only reported his alleged contractual breach to FIFA in April 2005, which according to him, not only demonstrates that the club was aware of his departure to country x, but also proves its negligence in order to get him a valid visa to work in country y.
17. In response, Clube Y asserts that it has always been in contact with the player in January 2005 until the moment when the player stopped answering its phone calls.
18. Moreover, the Y club underlines that the passport provided by the player to FIFA in May 2005 is not the passport that allows him to enter into country y. In this respect, the club provided FIFA with a copy of a valid passport of the player.
19. In this context, FIFA asked the Y Football Federation to inform it under which circumstances a country xian citizen may enter into country y, in particular, if such a citizen needs any kind of visa or if his passport would be sufficient. In reply, the aforementioned Federation asserted that "[...] the entrance of country xian citizens is free of visa if they come to country y for cultural, journalistic, tourist or business purposes. In this case, the country xian citizen can stay in country y up to 180 days. Any other enter requests (working permit, residence, etc) needs visa.

20. In light of the above, Clube Y explains that it has incurred into the following expenses with regard to the engagement of Mr X and, as a counterclaim, is consequently demanding the following amounts from the player:
    A. EUR 3,175 for the players international transfer and registration in country y. The Respondent has provided FIFA with a copy of the relevant registration document with the Y Football Federation confirming the claimed amount.
    B. EUR 8,987.30 as costs incurred with regard to the players personal accident insurance. The Respondent has provided FIFA with a copy of an insurance policy against working accidents for 20 players, including Mr X, regarding the 2004/2005 sporting season, in the amount of EUR 4,301.50 and payment receipts in the total amount of EUR 9,889.72.
    C. EUR 6,900 regarding an accommodation contract allegedly concluded for the player in the amount of EUR 575 per month. The Respondent has provided FIFA with a copy of the aforementioned contract and respective payment receipts from August 2004 until June 2005, in the total amount of EUR 6,900 (these include two receipts for August 2004).
    D. EUR 49,924 corresponding to all the salaries due to the player until the end of their employment contract, i.e. from May 2005 to 30 June 2009.
21. In conclusion, Clube Y is claiming the total amount of EUR 68,986.30 from Mr X, as well as the imposition of the adequate disciplinary measures on the player.
22. Finally, the Y club provided FIFA with copies of salary receipts not signed by the player in the total amount of EUR 4,773.77, regarding the months from July until November 2004, as well as cheques issued in favour of the player in the total amount of EUR 2,840.
23. In reply, Mr X acknowledges having received the amounts claimed by the Y club as salaries and match bonuses, but reaffirms that he has not received his salaries of December 2004, as well as January and February 2005.
24. As a consequence, the country xian player is requesting the Chamber to condemn the Y club to pay to him his salaries of December 2004, as well as January and February 2005, plus compensation corresponding to half of the amounts that are stipulated in the parties' employment contract until its end, in accordance with country xian Law (amounts were not specified).
25. Moreover, the player asserts that the fact that he used a new passport when he tried to return to country y in January 2005 is due to the fact that he had lost his original one (the one claimed by the club).
26. In reply, the club defends that it did not pay the players salary of December 2004 because the latter was absent in country x on 8 January 2005, i.e. the date when the salary was effectively due. Moreover, it understands that the players salaries of January and February 2005 are not due since he was not at the clubs disposal any longer.
27. At the request of FIFA, the player informed that, in the meantime, and since his departure from the Y club, he has been registered for the country xian clubs Clube Q (contract valid from 23 February 2005 until 23 February 2008, with a monthly salary of BRL 5,000, UUU from 15 March until 30 June 2005 (monthly salary of BRL 5,000) and OOO FC since 10 August 2005 (contract valid until 31 December 2005, with a monthly salary of BRL 8,000). The Claimant has provided FIFA with copies of the aforementioned employment contracts.
28. The present matter was already submitted to the Dispute Resolution Chamber for consideration and formal decision on 12 January 2006, which decided to refer the matter back to the FIFA administration in order to proceed with the investigation and clarify certain aspects.
29. In this respect, the Y Football Federation was requested to inform FIFA whether Mr X was registered for Clube Y or not and if the player in question has actually represented the Y club in any official matches during the 2004/2005 sporting season.
30. In reply, the Y Football Federation informed FIFA that Mr X has effectively been registered with Clube Y during the sporting season 2004/2005 and that he has represented such club in 14 official matches, from September until December 2004.
31. Furthermore, on 13 and 27 January 2006, Clube Y and the Y Football Federation were respectively asked to inform FIFA whether Mr X had a valid work permit enabling him to work in country y during the sporting season 2004/2005 or not and, if so, to provide FIFA with a copy of it. The Y Football Federation was also asked to inform FIFA about who would be entitled to apply for such permit, in particular, if the Y club could have done it by itself or if such application should have been made by the player. Finally, the aforementioned Federation was asked to inform FIFA about

the reasons why it had proceeded to register Mr X with Clube Y, in case he was not holding the aforementioned work permit.

32. In reply, Clube Y only stated that "all the necessary procedures were done for his inscription at the Y Football Federation".
33. On the other hand, the Y Football Federation informed FIFA that it was not possible for it to check whether the player in question had a valid work permit for the relevant sporting season. Moreover, it underlined that, "... only theplayer may obtain his working visa [...]".
34. Finally, the Y Football Federation clarified that it had registered the players contract with Clube Y due to the fact that "the documents submitted together with the registration request contained sufficient elements for the acquisition of working visa ...".

II. CONSIDERATIONS OF THE DISPUTE RESOLUTION CHAMBER

1. First of all, the Chamber analysed whether it was competent to deal with the matter at stake. In this respect, it referred to art. 18 par. 2 and 3 of the Rules Governing the Procedures of the Players' Status Committee and the Dispute Resolution Chamber. The present matter was submitted to FIFA on 25 February 2005, as a consequence the Chamber concluded that the previous Procedural Rules (edition 2001) on matters pending before the decision making bodies of FIFA are applicable to the matter at hand.
2. With regard to the competence of the Chamber, art. 42 par. 1 lit. (b) (i) of the FIFA Regulations for the Status and Transfer of Players (edition 2001) establishes that, the triggering elements of the employment-related dispute (i.e. whether a contract was breached, with or without just cause, or sporting just cause), will be decided by the Dispute Resolution Chamber.
3. If an employment contract is breached by a party, the Dispute Resolution Chamber is also responsible to verify whether the party is accountable for outstanding payments and/or compensation. Equally, the Chamber shall decide whether sports sanctions shall be imposed.
4. As a consequence, the Dispute Resolution Chamber is the competent body to decide on the present litigation involving a Y club and a country xian player regarding a dispute in connection with an employment contract concluded between the parties.
5. Subsequently, the members of the Chamber analyzed which edition of the Regulations for the Status and Transfer of Players should be applicable as to the substance of the matter. In this respect, the Chamber referred, on the one hand, to art. 26 par. 1 and 2 of the Regulations for the Status and Transfer of Players (edition 2005) and, on the other hand, to the fact that the relevant contract at the basis of the present dispute was signed on 1 July 2004 and the claim was lodged at FIFA on 25 February 2005. In view of the aforementioned, the Chamber concluded that the former FIFA Regulations for the Status and Transfer of Players (edition 2001, hereinafter: the Regulations) are applicable on the case at hand as to the substance.
6. In continuation, and entering into the substance of the present labour dispute, the Chamber started by acknowledging that, on 1 July 2004, Mr X and Clube Y signed an employment contract valid until 30 June 2009.
7. On the basis of that contract, the player lodged a claim with FIFA asking in particular, for the confirmation that the Y club has breached the relevant contract, that the contractual relationship is terminated and that he is to be considered free from any contractual obligation towards the said club. Furthermore, the player demands for the payment of outstanding salaries for the months of December 2004 until February 2005 and an unspecified amount as compensation.
8. In this respect, the members of the Chamber duly noted that Mr X had requested a country xian Civil Court to authorize him to be registered for a new club in country x, in particular, Clube Q, and, moreover, that FIFA had warned him that players are forbidden from referring matters connected with their registration to Civil Courts.
9. The Chamber also noted that, despite of the above, on 10 March 2005, the country xian Football Confederation informed FIFA that a country xian Civil Court had authorized Mr Xs registration for its affiliated club, Clube Q.
10. In view of the above, the Chamber concluded that it could not protect the players stance. In fact, by referring the question of his registration to a Civil Court he had violated art. 61 par. 2 of the FIFA Statutes. Yet, with regard to his contractual dispute, he preferred to revert to the decision-making bodies of the football instances. The Chamber was of the unanimous opinion that such

forum shopping cannot be accepted, in particular in view of the disrespect of the FIFA Statutes. As a consequence, it decided not to enter into the consideration of the players claim.

11. In continuation, the deciding body turned to the counterclaim lodged by the Y club. The members of the Chamber noted that Clube Y defends that, by signing a new employment contract with Clube Q on 23 February 2005, Mr X has breached their employment contract without just cause and is consequently claiming from the player, compensation in the total amount of EUR 68,986.30, corresponding to EUR 3,175 for the players international transfer and registration in country y, EUR 8,987.30 as costs incurred with regard to the players personal accident insurance, EUR 6,900 regarding an accommodation contract allegedly concluded for the player in the amount of EUR 575 per month and EUR 49,924 corresponding to all the amount due to the player until the original end of their employment contract, i.e. from May 2005 to 30 June 2009.
12. The members of the Chamber acknowledged that, in support of its aforementioned financial claim, the Y club has provided FIFA with a copy of the players registration document with the Y Football Federation, confirming the claimed amount, a copy of an insurance policy against working accidents for 20 players, including Mr X, regarding the 2004/2005 sporting season in the amount of EUR 4,301.50 and payment receipts in the total amount of EUR 9,889.72 as well as a copy of the aforementioned contract for accommodation and respective payment receipts form August 2004 until June 2005, in the total amount of EUR 6,900, whereby the relevant receipts include two receipts for August 2004.
13. Furthermore, the Chamber noted that, in support of its claim, the Y club explains that the player, X left the club without authorisation in December 2004. Furthermore, the Y club defends that, not only it has paid to Mr X all his salaries until and including November 2004 and that Decembers salary was only payable in January 2005, but also that the player had always avoided to comply with the necessary legal procedures in order to obtain a working visa.
14. On the other hand, the Chamber acknowledged that, according to the player, at the time of his claim, he had already been without any remuneration for six months, i.e. from September 2004 until February 2005. Mr X defends that under such circumstances, he had no alternative than to find another club to work, which was allegedly the reason why he signed a new employment contract with Clube Q, on 23 February 2005.
15. In this regard, the Chamber emphasized the fact that, throughout the present procedure, the Claimant has contradicted himself regarding his outstanding salaries. In particular, contrary to his initial claim, in which he claimed the aforementioned six months of outstanding salaries, in his final statements, after the Y club having provided FIFA with copies of the relevant salary receipts, Mr X has confirmed having received his salaries up to and including November 2004.
16. Moreover, the Chamber considered that Mr X asserts that Clube Y has failed to provide him with a working visa, which was necessary for him to fulfil his employment contract and that, as a consequence, in January 2005, after having left to country x on holidays, he was prevented from entering into country y again. In this respect, the Chamber noted that, in support of his position, the player has provided FIFA with a copy of his passport bearing the Y customs stamp, denying his entrance in country y, based on the fact that he had no valid working visa to enter into the country.
17. In this respect, the Chamber in particular took into consideration that the player claims that he was prevented from fulfilling his employment contract with Clube Y, entirely due to the clubs fault. The player stresses that he had waited a long time for the Y club to solve his visa problem, without any success.
18. To that regard, the deciding body noted that the Y club defends that, even without a proper working visa, Mr X could have entered into country y with his country xian passport, like he had previously done.
19. With regard to the central issue of the working visa, the members of the Chamber also took into consideration the information provided by the Y Football Federation, at the request of FIFA, according to which, "[...] the entrance of country xian citizens is free of visa if they come to country y for cultural, journalistic, tourist or business purposes. In this case, the country xian citizen can stay in country y up to 180 days. Any other enter request (working permit, residence, etc) needs visa.
20. Moreover, the Chamber noted that Mr X was effectively registered with Clube Y during the sporting season 2004/2005 and that he represented such club in 14 official matches, from September until December 2004.

21. In this context, at the request of FIFA, and regarding the fact whether Mr X had or not a valid work permit enabling him to work in country y during the sporting season 2004/2005, Clube Y informed that "all the necessary procedures were done for his (the players) inscription at the Y Football Federation".
22. Furthermore, the Chamber took into account that, with regard to the question whether anyone would be entitled to apply for such permit, in particular, if the Y club could have done it by itself or if such application should have been made by the player himself, the Y Football Federation informed FIFA that "[...] only the player may obtain his working visa ..." and that it was not possible for it to check whether the player in question had a valid work permit for the relevant sporting season.
23. With respect to the question related to the reasons why it would have had proceeded to register Mr X with Clube Y in case the player did not have the aforementioned work permit, the Y Football Federation clarified that it had registered the players contract with Clube Y due to the fact that "the documents submitted together with the registration request contained sufficient elements for the acquisition of working visa ...".
24. In light of the above, the members of the Chamber reached the conclusion that, once Mr X signed a valid employment contract with Clube Y, he should have done everything in order to obtain his working permit, in particular, taking into account that he was the only person entitled to do so. As a consequence, he should have offered all his assistance in this respect to the Y club.
25. Furthermore, the members of the deciding body concluded that, in view of the statements of the Y Football Federation, Clube Y appears to have prepared all documents and taken all measures, which were in its power, in order for the player to obtain the relevant working visa. In other words, a possible nonissuance of a working visa was not to be attributed to its negligence. As a consequence, it cannot be blamed for any misconduct in this respect.
26. Equally, the members of the Chamber were of the opinion that, being a country xian citizen, even if he was not in possession of a working permit, Mr X could have entered into country y with a valid passport, as he appears to have done earlier, e.g. for the first half of the 2004/2005 season.
27. Furthermore, and taking into account the fact that, Mr X has effectively been registered with Clube Y during the sporting season 2004/2005 and that he represented such club in 14 official matches, from September until December 2004, the Chamber rejected the arguments raised by the player, according to which, he was prevented from fulfilling his employment contract with the Y club due to the lack of a valid visa/working permit.
28. With regard to the financial aspect, the members of the Chamber concluded that Clube Y has complied with its financial obligations towards Mr X, in particular, that, as recognized by the player, it has paid to Mr X all his salaries until November 2004, i.e. until the date of his departure from country y. The salary for December 2004 became only due in January 2005, thus after the players departure. As a consequence, when the player left, no salaries remained unpaid to him.
29. In addition, the Chamber emphasised that the player had lodged his claim with FIFA on 25 February 2005, thus two days after having already signed a new contract with the country xian Clube Q on 23 February 2005, which guaranteed him a significantly higher salary than in country y. From the Chambers point of view, such stance does not speak in favour of the players good faith either.
30. Finally, the deciding body pointed out that there were no evident interests for the Y Clube Y for a contractual breach. From a financial point of view, as exposed before, it had complied with its obligations towards the player and invested - for a club of its seize and importance (a club of the third national division in country y) - a considerable amount of money for the acquisition of the players services. On the other hand, in view of the considerable higher salary agreed upon with the country xian Clube Q, the player had an obvious reason for an early termination of the contract with the Y club.
31. In light of all the above, the Dispute Resolution Chamber concluded that Mr X has breached his employment contract with Clube Y without just cause. Furthermore, the deciding body stated that since the breach occurred during the first season of a 5 years contract, the relevant infringement happened during the so-called protected period (cf. art. 21 par. 1 (a) of the Regulations).
32. As a consequence, and in compliance with the content of Chapter VIII of the Regulations, in particular, with its art. 21 par. 1 (a), the Chamber decided that the player is liable for the payment of compensation and to impose sports sanctions for unilateral breach of contract without just cause during the socalled protected period on Mr X.

33. With regard to the amount of compensation to be paid, the Chamber referred on the one hand to the financial claim submitted by Clube Y. Furthermore, and on the other hand, the deciding body recalled that according to art. 22 of the Regulations, compensation for breach of contract shall be calculated with due respect to all objective criteria which may be relevant to the case, such as remuneration under the existing contract and/or the new contract, length of time remaining on the existing contract, amount of any fee or expense paid or incurred by the former club, amortised over the length of the contract and whether the breach occurred during the so-called protected periods.
34. In this respect, the members of the Chamber at first acknowledged that the rest value of the contract concluded between the parties to the dispute is of EUR 49,924, corresponding to the salaries due to the player from May 2005 until 30 June 2009, date of the ordinary end of the relevant employment contract. Furthermore, the Chamber noted that the contractual breach occurred after six months only of a 5 years employment contract. Equally, the deciding body emphasised that the players salary with his new country xian club corresponds to double the amount he earned with the Y club.
35. In continuation, the Chamber took note of the fact that the Y club had presented written evidence with regard to the costs it incurred with regard to the players international transfer and registration in country y, i.e. EUR 3,175. The deciding body was of the opinion that this amount should in any case be refunded to Clube Y. Yet, the members of the Chamber deemed that the costs claimed by the Y club with regard to the players personal accident insurance had not been sufficiently accredited by the club. The same goes for the costs allegedly related to the accommodation contract, which, according to the Y club, had been concluded on behalf of the player.
36. As a result of these considerations, as well as in view of the Y clubs claim for compensation, the Chamber deemed it appropriate to award an amount of EUR 53,099 to Clube Y as compensation for the unjustified breach of the employment contract.
37. Finally, and taking into account the fact that Mr X was 19 years old at the time when the contractual breach occurred, and that it took place within the first year of contract, the Chamber decided to sanction Mr X with a restriction of four months on his eligibility to participate in any official football matches, as stipulated in art. 23 par. 1 (a) of the Regulations.

III. DECISION OF THE DISPUTE RESOLUTION CHAMBER

1. The claim filed by the Claimant, Mr X, shall not be considered.
2. The counter-claim of the Respondent, Clube Y, is partially accepted.
3. The Claimant, Mr X, shall pay the total amount of EUR 53,099 to the Respondent, Clube Y, within 30 days of notification of the present decision.
4. If the Claimant, Mr X, fails to comply with the above-mentioned deadline, an interest rate of 5% per year will apply and the case will immediately be presented to the FIFA Disciplinary Committee.
5. Any other financial claim of the Respondent, Clube Y, is rejected.
6. The Respondent, Clube Y, is directed to inform the Claimant, Mr X, immediately of the account number to which the remittance is to be made and to notify the Dispute Resolution Chamber of every payment received.
7. The Claimant, Mr X, is suspended for the period of 4 (four) months from participating in any official football match, as from the date of notification of the present decision.
8. According to art. 60 par. 1 of the FIFA Statutes this decision may be appealed before the Court of Arbitration for Sport (CAS). The statement of appeal must be sent to the CAS directly within 21 days of receiving notification of this decision and has to contain all elements in accordance with point 2 of the directives issued by the CAS, copy of which we enclose hereto. Within another 10 days following the expiry of the time limit for the filing of the statement of appeal, the appellant shall file with the CAS a brief stating the facts and legal arguments giving rise to the appeal (cf. point 4 of the directives).

26332
DECISION OF THE DISPUTE RESOLUTION CHAMBER
passed in Zurich, Switzerland, on 21 February 2006,
in the following composition:
Slim Aloulou (Tunisia), Chairman

Michele Colucci (Italy), member
Joaquim Evangelista (Portugal), member
Philippe Diallo (France), member
Mohamed Mecherara (Algeria), member
on the claim presented by the Player X, Slovakia Represented by Mr XXXXXX as Claimant
against the club Y, Cyprus Represented by Mr XXXXXX
as Respondent
regarding outstanding remuneration on the basis of an employment contract

I. FACTS OF THE CASE

1. On 6 August 2003, the player X from Slovakia, Claimant, and the Cyprus club Y, Respondent, signed an employment contract valid as from August 2003 until 31 May 2004 with an extension option for another year as from 1 June 2004 until 31 May 2005.
2. According to art. 4B of the relevant employment contract the Respondent agreed to pay to the Claimant for the second year the amount of CYP 19,000 (payable in 10 instalments of CYP 1,900 each) plus 20% increment provided that the Claimant participates at least in 20 official games in the season 2003/2004. Furthermore, in accordance with art. 5C of the relevant employment contract the Respondent agreed to pay to the Claimant CYP 200 per month for accommodation.
3. On 2 December 2004, the Claimant contacted FIFA claiming that the Respondent terminated the contractual relationship on 17 November 2004, i.e. during the second year, without just cause.
4. As a result, the Claimant demanded the amount of CYP 3,800 as salaries for the period as from 1 October until 17 November 2004, the amount of CYP 11,400 corresponding to all remaining salaries until 31 May 2005, the amount of CYP 3,040 as bonuses in accordance with art. 4B of the relevant employment contract and the legal expenses.
5. On 6 May 2005, the Respondent contested the Claimants allegations. The Respondent explained that on 17 November 2004 it unilaterally, but with just cause, terminated the employment relationship with the Claimant. The Respondent explained that the Claimant was injured and was therefore instructed to present himself to the clubs doctor as established in art. 2 of the relevant employment contract. However, the Claimant left Cyprus and went to Slovakia. As a result, the Respondent is of the opinion that the Claimant breached the employment contract by leaving the country unauthorised and therefore the Respondent was entitled to terminate the employment contract.
6. Furthermore, the Respondent maintained that by the time the employment contract was terminated it only owed to the Claimant the amount CYP 2,280 and not CYP 3,800 as claimed by the Claimant. In this respect, the Respondent explained that it sent a cheque amounting to CYP 2,280 to the Cyprus Football Federation in order to be forwarded to the Claimant.
7. Finally, the Respondent stated that in accordance with the Regulations of the Cyprus Football Association any party has the right to terminate an employment contract and since the Claimant failed to appeal the clubs decision to terminate the relevant employment contract within 30 days, the termination had become legal and effective. Furthermore, the Respondent maintained that the Claimant immediately after the termination signed a new employment contract with the Slovakian club XXXXXXX.
8. On 27 May 2005, the Claimant contested the Respondents position with regard to the outstanding amount until the termination of the contract. In particular, the Claimant stated that the Respondent still owes him the amount of CYP 3,800 as salaries for the period as from 1 October until 17 November 2004 and that he never received any cheque. Furthermore, the Claimant affirmed that he went to Slovakia on 17 October 2004 with the clubs permission. However, the Claimant did not provide any documentation in order to corroborate his affirmation. The Claimant also maintained that the Regulations of the Cyprus Football Association, stating that he should have appealed the clubs decision to terminate the contract, are not applicable since he is from Slovakia and therefore the FIFA Regulations are applicable.
9. Finally, the Claimant provided a copy of the new employment contract signed with the Slovakian club, valid for one year and starting on 30 January 2005. According to the mentioned employment contract he was entitled to receive the amount of SKK 13,000.
10. As a result, the Claimant claims 2 ½ months' salary amounting to CYP 4,750 as compensation for the 2 ½ months he was unemployed as from the date of the unilateral termination 17 November 2004 until the date on which he found a new club on 30 January 2005, plus the difference between both

salaries for the period of 4 months amounting to CYP 6,828 (CYP 1,900 - CYP 193 (new monthly salary) = CYP 1,707 x 4).

11. In summary, the Claimant claims a total compensation amounting to CYP 11,578 plus outstanding salaries, interest, damage and legal costs.
12. On 4 August 2005, the Respondent referred to its earlier statement and once again pointed out that it terminated the employment contract unilaterally but with justification. The Respondent stressed that the Claimant never provided any medical certificate from his doctor and that as from the time he left he always refused to render his services. Moreover, the Respondent pointed out that the cheque amounting to CYP 2,280 was collected by the Claimant. As a result, the Respondent is of the opinion that it does not owe any amount to the Claimant.
13. On 22 August 2005, the Claimant referred to his previous statement and pointed out that he never received any cheque and that the Respondent never provided any evidence in this respect. The Respondent did not provide any further statement.

II. CONSIDERATIONS OF THE DISPUTE RESOLUTION CHAMBER

1. First of all, the Chamber analysed whether it was competent to deal with the matter at stake. In this respect, it referred to art. 18 par. 2 and 3 of the Rules Governing the Procedures of the Players' Status Committee and the Dispute Resolution Chamber. The present matter was submitted to FIFA on 2 December 2004, as a consequence the Chamber concluded that the previous Procedural Rules (edition 2001) on matters pending before the decision making bodies of FIFA are applicable on the matter at hand.
2. With regard to the competence of the Chamber, art. 42 par. 1 lit. (b) (i) of the FIFA Regulations for the Status and Transfer of Players (edition 2001) establishes that, the triggering elements of the employment-related dispute (i.e. whether a contract was breached, with or without just cause, or sporting just cause), will be decided by the Dispute Resolution Chamber.
3. If an employment contract is breached by a party, the Dispute Resolution Chamber is also responsible to verify whether a party is accountable for outstanding payments and/or compensation.
4. As a consequence, the Dispute Resolution Chamber is the competent body to decide on the present litigation involving a club from Cyprus and a Slovakian player regarding a claim concerning outstanding remuneration in connection with an employment contract.
5. Subsequently, the members of the Chamber analyzed which edition of the Regulations for the Status and Transfer of Players should be applicable as to the substance of the matter. In this respect, the Chamber referred, on the one hand, to art. 26 par. 1 and 2 of the Regulations for the Status and Transfer of Players (edition 2005) and, on the other hand, to the fact that the relevant contract at the basis of the present dispute was signed on 6 August 2003 and the claim was lodged at FIFA on 2 December 2004. In view of the aforementioned, the Chamber concluded that the former FIFA Regulations for the Status and Transfer of Players (edition 2001, hereafter: the Regulations) are applicable to the case at hand as to the substance.
6. In continuation, and entering into the substance of the matter, the members of the Chamber started by acknowledging that on 6 August 2003 the Claimant and the Respondent signed an employment contract valid until 31 May 2004 with an extension option for another year as from 1 June 2004 until 31 May 2005.
7. In continuation, the Chamber took note that it is undisputed by the parties that the employment contract was prematurely terminated on 17 November 2004 and that the Claimant left Cyprus on the said date.
8. Nevertheless, the Chamber duly noted that, on the one hand, the Claimant is of the opinion that the Respondent breached the employment contract and is therefore requesting outstanding salaries amounting to CYP 3,800, compensation amounting to CYP 11,578 plus interest, damage and legal costs. On the other hand, the Chamber took due note, that the Respondent argued that the Claimant breached the employment contract by leaving the country unauthorised, and not complying with art. 2 of the employment contract, refusing to consult the clubs doctor after being injured, and therefore the Respondent was entitled to terminate the employment contract.
9. The Chamber noted that according to the Claimant he left Cyprus with the authorization of the club. However, the Claimant has failed to corroborate this assertion with documentary evidence.
10. Moreover, the Chamber acknowledged that it is not disputed that the Claimant signed a new employment contract valid as from 30 January 2005. Finally, the Chamber took due note that the

Claimant affirmed that it paid the amount of CYP 2,280 corresponding to the salaries until 17 November 2004 by means of a cheque via the Cyprus Football Association and that the Claimant contested that he ever received any amount for the claimed salaries.

11. Turning its attention to the question whether the Respondent has committed a unilateral breach of the employment contract without just cause, the Chamber took note that the Respondent indicated as reason for the early termination of the employment contract that the player left the country and refused to consult the clubs doctor after being injured.
12. In this regard, the Chamber had to deliberate if this was a just cause for the Respondent to prematurely terminate the employment contract.
13. The Chamber started by maintaining that according to its constant jurisprudence the premature and unilateral termination of an employment contract by a club because of an injury or its closest consequences must be considered as a termination of the contract without just cause.
14. In the present case, it can be established that the Claimant was injured and preferred to be treated at home rather than abroad and since he left, apparently, without the Respondents authorization, the Respondent terminated the employment contract on 17 November 2004.
15. In continuation, the Chamber stated that if such a termination would be accepted as a termination with just cause, this would create a disproportionate repartition of the rights of the parties to an employment contract, to the strong detriment of the player.
16. In the light of the above, the Chamber reached the conclusion that the Respondent breached the employment contract signed with the Claimant without just cause.
17. As a consequence, the Dispute Resolution Chamber had to verify and decide whether the Respondent is accountable for outstanding payments and/or compensation towards the Claimant.
18. In continuation, the Chamber concluded that the Respondent is liable to cancel all outstanding amounts under the employment contract until the date when the employment relation was terminated, i.e. until 17 November 2004.
19. In this respect, the Chamber emphasised that, on the one hand, the Claimant claims the amount of CYP 3,800 as salaries for the period as from 1 October until 17 November 2004. On the other hand, the Respondent contested the outstanding amount and affirmed that it sent a cheque amounting to CYP 2,280 to the Cyprus Football Federation in order to be forwarded to the Claimant. However, the Respondent did not provide any evidence in order to corroborate its affirmation.
20. In this context, the Chamber emphasized that in accordance with the legal principle of the burden of proof, which is a basic principle in every legal system, a party asserting a fact has the obligation to prove the same. Therefore, due to the lack of proof of the Respondents allegations, and in application of the aforementioned principle, the Dispute Resolution Chamber decided that the Respondent has to pay to the Claimant the outstanding salaries for the period as from 1 October until 17 November 2004.
21. As a result, the Chamber concluded that the Respondent has to pay the amount of CYP 2,976 corresponding to the salaries for the period as from 1 October until 17 November 2004.
22. In continuation, the Chamber established that the Respondent is also liable to pay compensation to the Claimant, for its breach of the contract. However, the Chamber took into consideration the contributory negligence of the Claimant which led to the early termination of the employment contract at the basis of the present dispute.
23. In this respect, and after long deliberations taking into account all submissions made by both parties, the Chamber came to the conclusion that the Claimants behaviour, in particular, that he left without the authorization of the Respondent and without consulting the clubs doctor must be taken into account for the calculation of the compensation.
24. The Chamber pointed out that in spite the circumstances that the player may have had valid reasons to leave Cyprus for Slovakia, i.e. for medical treatment, he should have acquired the clubs written consent to do so prior to having left Cyprus.
25. In view of all of the above, the Chamber rejected the Claimants claim with regard to the requested compensation in the amount of CYP 11,578 plus interest as well as damage and concluded that the Respondent must pay compensation for the breach of the contract in the amount of CYP 4,000 to the Claimant.
26. Finally, and with regard to the claimed legal expenses, the Chamber referred to its well-established jurisprudence in this respect and rejected the claim with regard to the reimbursement of the legal expenses of the Claimant.

27. Taking into account all of the above, the Chamber decided that the Respondent must pay the amount of CYP 6,976 to the Claimant.

III. DECISION OF THE DISPUTE RESOLUTION CHAMBER

1. The claim lodged by the Claimant, Mr X, is partially accepted.
2. The Respondent, club Y, must pay the total amount of CYP 6,976 to the Claimant within 30 days as from the date of notification of this decision.
3. Any further claims lodged by the Claimant are rejected.
4. If the aforementioned sum is not paid within the aforementioned deadline an interest rate of 5% per year will apply and the present matter shall be submitted to FIFAs Disciplinary Committee, so that the necessary disciplinary sanctions may be imposed.
5. The Claimant Mr X is directed to inform the Respondent directly and immediately of the account number to which the remittance is to be made and to notify the Dispute Resolution Chamber of every payment received.
6. According to art. 60 par. 1 of the FIFA Statutes, this decision may be appealed against before the Court of Arbitration for Sport (CAS). The statement of appeal must be sent to the CAS directly within 21 days of receipt of notification of this decision and shall contain all the elements in accordance with point 2 of the directives issued by the CAS, a copy of which we enclose hereto. Within another 10 days following the expiry of the time limit for filing the statement of appeal, the appellant shall file a brief stating the facts and legal arguments giving rise to the appeal with the CAS (cf. point 4 of the directives).

⚽⚽⚽

26439

DECISION OF THE DISPUTE RESOLUTION CHAMBER

passed in Zurich, Switzerland, on 21 February 2006,
in the following composition:
Slim Aloulou (Tunisia), Chairman
Michele Colucci (Italy), member
Joaquim Evangelista (Portugal), member
Philippe Diallo (France), member
Mohamed Mecherara (Algeria), member
on the claim presented by the player, X, represented by Mr. W as Claimant
against
the club, Y, as Respondent
regarding a contractual dispute between the player and the club

I. FACTS OF THE CASE

1. On 13 January 2003, the player, X, the Claimant, and Y, the Respondent, signed an employment contract valid as from the date of its signature until 30 June 2006.
2. During the 2003-04 season the player was transferred on a loan basis to Z.
3. On 27 March 2004, X underwent a doping test.
4. On 30 April 2004, a report was issued confirming the positive result on the appearance of banned substances.
5. Towards the end of April 2004, the player and the Z apparently prematurely terminated their employment relation.
6. On 18 June 2004, the relevant body of the Football Federation of Z decided to suspend the player in question for the period of one year for cause of doping on the basis of the test carried out on 27 March 2004.
7. On 17 July 2004, the player and Y signed a cancellation agreement whereby the club committed itself to pay to the player, "unconditionally" and "irrevocably", the total net amount of EUR 550,000, payable as follows: EUR 110,000 on 30 September 2004, EUR 110,000 on 30 November 2004, EUR 110,000 on 30 January 2005, EUR 110,000 on 30 March 2005 and EUR 110,000 on 30 May 2005.
8. In addition, the parties agreed that an interest rate of 15% p.a. would be applicable in the event of non-payment by the club.
9. Subsequent to the conclusion of the cancellation agreement, the player transferred to V.

10. On 4 August 2004, the FIFA Disciplinary Committee extended the above- mentioned suspension of the player in question on a worldwide basis.
11. On 25 September 2004, Y informed the player in writing that it considers the cancellation agreement null and void. According to the club, the player has concealed his 12 months' suspension and therefore he has obtained the clubs agreement in a fraudulent manner. The club adds that had it been informed of the players suspension, it would never have concluded the said cancellation agreement, but it would rather have terminated the players contract with just cause.
12. Furthermore, the club maintains that according to art. 31 b) of the relevant Regulations of the Football Association of Y, a club has the right to unilaterally terminate any employment contract with a player in the event that a player is suspended for more than 6 months.
13. In the same correspondence, "for the sake of good order" Y informed the player of the termination of his contract as a consequence of his wrongful behaviour, i.e. the use of banned substances.
14. On 29 December 2004, the player lodged a claim against Y in front of FIFA maintaining that in accordance with the agreement dated 17 July 2004 Y owes him the total amount of EUR 550,000 plus 15% interest rate p.a. as from 18 November 2004, date on which he put the club in default.
15. X explains that the notification of the decision by the doping commission of the Football Federation of Z was sent to his former address in a city in the country of Z, which he had already left in the light of the early termination of his contractual relation with Z. Therefore, X asserts that he was not in the position to take knowledge of this decision whereby he was suspended for the period of one year.
16. On 10 August 2004, X asked the Football Federation of Z to re-open the relevant proceedings due to the fact that his right to defence was allegedly violated given that he was allegedly only informed of his suspension on 5 August 2004 in the context of his international transfer V.
17. The player maintains that the doping commission of the Football Federation of Z affirmed that the player could not have had knowledge of the decision passed on 18 June 2004 and therefore re-opened the case. The player submitted a copy of the relevant decision by the said doping commission dated 3 September 2004.
18. On 19 November 2004, the deciding body of the Federation of Z decided that the players suspension runs as from 18 June 2004 until 19 January 2005.
19. In the light of the above, the player asserts that he had no knowledge of his one year suspension by the doping commission of the Football Federation of Z when he concluded the above-mentioned cancellation agreement with Y on 17 July 2004. X affirms that he was informed of his suspension on 5 August 2004.
20. According to the player, the club will have to prove that he has acted in a fraudulent manner as stated in the clubs letter dated 25 September 2004.
21. Y, for its part, rejects the claim put forward by the player for the following reasons.
22. The player having used prohibited drugs, Y asserts that he must have been aware of the upcoming positive result of the doping test carried out in March 2004 and the legal consequences of such result.
23. According to Y, the players allegation that he was not duly notified of the above-mentioned decision passed by the medical committee of the Football Federation of Z on 18 June 2004 is not relevant, as this is to be considered as an internal issue between the player and the Football Federation of Z and Y was not a party to the notification of the said decision.
24. Y insists that the player has acted in a fraudulent manner by concealing the fact that he had been through a doping test which would render "unpleasant results" and inducing the club into signing the above-mentioned cancellation agreement with a compensation of EUR 550,000 for the early termination of the employment contract.
25. According to the club, as per the established principles of law, in particular art. 28 of the Swiss Code of Obligations and art. 28 of the Code of Obligations of the country of Y, an agreement which is based on illegal grounds is null and void, since it can never represent the true intention of the parties to that agreement.
26. In the light of the above, Y rejects the claim put forward by the player. In addition, it asks that the player be ordered to pay for all costs incurred by the club relating to the present dispute resolution.
27. In reaction to the clubs response, the player points out that there is no proof that he voluntarily used banned substances, which issue is emphasised by Y. The fact that banned substances are discovered in the athletes organism does not proof that the athlete voluntarily used such substances.
28. X stresses that he was playing in the B-team of Z when the doping test was carried out, as the coach allegedly considered his performance insufficient.

Being active in the B-team only, the player points out that he had no reason to use banned substances.

29. He asserts that he wished to prematurely put an end to his employment relation with Z, as he believed that he had no future Z.
30. He stresses that it can be noted from the file that the result of the doping test came to his knowledge on 5 August 2004 only and that, therefore, he was unaware of the sanction that was pronounced against him on 18 June 2004 during the negotiations with Y in July 2004.
31. In conclusion, the player affirms that Y has not proven that he acted in a fraudulent manner as stated above.
32. In its final submission, Y points out that in its second decision the relevant deciding body of the Football Federation of Z has not altered the findings that the Claimant had used prohibited drugs.
33. Y rejects the players assertion that Y will have to prove that he voluntarily used banned substances. In this respect, the club points out that once prohibited drugs have been found it is the burden of the player and his legal representative to demonstrate that there is a just reason for the appearance of drugs in the samples. It adds that this should have been done during the proceedings related to the use of doping in front of the competent deciding body of the Football Federation of Z.
34. The club points out that in its second decision, the deciding body of the Football Federation of Z solely altered the period of time relating to the players suspension and that the player has refrained from making any explanations in respect of the doping test result.
35. Y asserts that at the time of the conclusion of the "termination agreement" the player was solely not aware of the specific sanction imposed upon him, but he was well aware of the fact that he had used banned substances and that he had undergone a doping test on 27 March 2004.
36. Finally, referring to the above-mentioned articles 28, the club reiterates that the "termination agreement" is null and void since it must be considered as an agreement based on a fraudulent action on the part of the player.

II. CONSIDERATIONS OF THE DISPUTE RESOLUTION CHAMBER

1. The members of the Dispute Resolution Chamber (hereinafter also referred to as "DRC" or "Chamber") firstly proceeded to examine whether the DRC is competent to deal with the case at hand.
2. Article 18.2 of the Rules Governing the Procedures of the Dispute Resolution (edition July 2005, hereinafter referred to as "Procedural Rules") stipulates that "These Rules are applicable to proceedings submitted to FIFA after the date on which these Rules came into force".
3. Article 18.1 of the Procedural Rules stipulates that these rules come into force on 1 July 2005.
4. According to Article 18.3 of the Procedural Rules cases submitted to FIFA before such date shall be governed by the former procedural rules.
5. The present matter having been submitted to FIFA on 29 December 2004, the Chamber concluded that the previous Procedural Rules on matters pending before the decision making bodies of FIFA are applicable to the matter at hand.
6. With regard to the competence of the Chamber, art. 42 par. 1 lit. (b) (i) of the FIFA Regulations for the Status and Transfer of Players (edition 2001) establishes that the triggering elements of the employment-related dispute will be decided by the Dispute Resolution Chamber.
7. As a consequence, the Dispute Resolution Chamber is the competent body to decide on the present litigation involving a club from the country of Y and a player from the country of X regarding an agreement in connection with the early termination of an employment contract.
8. Having confirmed its competence to deal with the case at hand on the basis of the relevant facts in the file, the Chamber proceeded to establish the Rules and Regulations applicable to the substance of the case.
9. According to Article 26.1 of the Regulations for the Status and Transfer of Players (edition 2005) "any case that has been brought to FIFA before these Regulations came into force shall be assessed according to the previous Regulations".
10. As stated above, the present matter was referred to FIFA on 29 December 2004, thus prior to the coming into effect of the current version of the Regulations.
11. In the light of these circumstances the Chamber confirmed that the previous version of the Regulations, i.e. the Regulations for the Status and Transfer of Players, edition September 2001 (hereinafter referred to as the "Regulations") is applicable to the matter at stake as to the substance.

12. The Chamber then entered into the substance of the matter acknowledging the above-mentioned Facts of the Case, from which it can be noted that the Claimant was contractually bound to the Respondent as from 13 January 2003 until 30 June 2006.
13. Within this contractual period of time, the Claimant was transferred on a loan basis to Z during the 2003-04 season. According to the player, his employment contract with Z was prematurely terminated by mutual consent towards the end of April 2004.
14. On 27 March 2004, while still being on loan at Z, the player underwent a doping test.
15. On 17 July 2004, the Claimant and the Respondent signed an agreement aiming at the early termination of their contractual relationship whereby the Respondent committed itself to pay to the Claimant, "unconditionally" and "irrevocably", the total net amount of EUR 550,000, payable as follows: EUR 110,000 on 30 September 2004, EUR 110,000 on 30 November 2004, EUR 110,000 on 30 January 2005, EUR 110,000 on 30 March 2005 and EUR 110,000 on 30 May 2005.
16. Y does not consider itself obliged to execute this agreement on the basis of the fact that on the moment of signing the agreement with the player, on 17 July 2004, the player had concealed the fact that he had undergone a doping test and that he was suspended by the deciding body of the Football Federation of Z on the basis of the positive outcome of such test.
17. The Chamber agreed with Y that the positive result of the doping test could possibly have constituted a just cause for the club to unilaterally terminate the employment contract.
18. The player, for his part, insists on the execution of the relevant cancellation agreement by Y and asserts that on 17 July 2004 he could not have been aware of his suspension given that the notification of the decision by the doping commission of the Football Federation of Z was sent to his former address in a city of the country of Z, which he had already left in the light of the early termination of his contractual relation with Z.
19. The Chamber pointed out that under these circumstances, on 17 July 2004, the day on which he entered into the agreement to prematurely rescind his employment contract with Y, the player may indeed not have been informed of the fact that he was suspended by the deciding body of the Football Federation of Z as a result of the outcome of the doping test carried out on 27 March 2004.
20. However, the members of the Chamber pointed out that from the documentation in its possession, which includes the dossier of the FIFA Disciplinary Committee relating to the worldwide suspension of the player in question, it can be noted that the player has had a crucial influence on the appearance of such circumstance.
21. Indeed, the correspondence from the Football Federation of Z to the player, X, in connection with the result of the doping test and the related disciplinary proceedings was sent to the players address in a city of the country of Z that was indicated on the Doping Control Form dated 27 March 2004, which was duly signed by the player in question.
22. The player has confirmed that he had left his former address in a city of the country of Z subsequent to the early termination of his employment relation with Z, which he indicates as the reason why he could not have had knowledge of the result of the doping test and his suspension.
23. The Chamber, however, was of the unanimous opinion that the player had the responsibility to inform the relevant bodies of the Football Federation of Z of his change of address in the light of the proceedings relating to the doping test that he had undergone. It is not arguable that the player was aware that such procedure was pending.
24. What is more, the Chamber had difficulty to accept that the Claimant would not have been interested in the result of the doping test that had been carried out.
    That is, from the file in its possession and in the light of the fact that the player changed his address subsequent to the doping test, the Chamber could not find any indication that the player has tried to obtain knowledge of the result of the relevant doping test during a considerable period of time, i.e. between 27 March 2004, date on which the doping test was made, and 5 August 2004, date on which the player claims having learned about his suspension within the scope of his transfer to the country of V.
25. Taking into account the above considerations, the Chamber agreed that the players reasoning why he was not or could not have been aware of his suspension must be considered too simple and superficial. The Chamber concurred that the player must be held responsible for the circumstance that on 17 July 2004 he might not have been aware of his suspension which was communicated by letter dated 18 June 2004 to his former address in a city of the country of Z.

26. Equally important, the Chamber noted that the player has not even informed Y, club to which he was still contractually bound, of the fact that he had undergone this doping test.
27. In this regard, the Chamber concurred that, as a general rule, a player having undergone a doping test is obliged to inform his employer of such fact without delay.
28. The doping test was carried out on X on 27 March 2004, i.e. well in advance of the date on which he signed the disputed agreement with Y, i.e. 17 July 2004. In this context, the Chamber also pointed out that within such period of time the result of a doping test generally is delivered.
29. The Chamber agreed that the player should have informed Y of the fact that he had undergone the doping test. By failing to do so, the player has withheld an important fact from the knowledge of Y during the negotiations relating to the premature rescission of their employment relation, a fact which presumably would have caused an other outcome of such negotiations. In this regard, the Chamber recalled its findings under point II.17.
30. In the event of the player having informed his employer, Y, of the mere fact that he underwent a doping test, Y would at least have been in the position to postpone negotiations with the player until the result of the doping test would have come to its knowledge.
31. Taking into consideration the above, the Chamber felt confirmed in its believe that the behaviour of the player was in anticipation of possible events related to the doping test that he had undergone on 27 March 2004 in the near future and that X has induced the club into entering into the disputed agreement with the player in accordance with which the club agreed to pay "unconditionally" and "irrevocably" EUR 550,000 to the player in the light of the early termination of the relevant employment contract by mutual consent.
32. The Chamber also felt confirmed in its conclusions by the fact that in spite of repeated requests by FIFA, the player failed to present documentary evidence of the termination by mutual consent of the players contract with Z. Yet, the player had stated that the employment contract with Z was prematurely terminated by mutual consent towards the end of April 2004.
33. The members of the Chamber deemed that, even though the exact date of the contractual termination was not known to it, on the basis of the players statement it was most probably after having undergone the doping test that the players employment contract with Z was terminated by mutual consent.
34. In this regard, the Chamber reckoned that it is not of common practice to prematurely rescind employment contracts that have been concluded in the context of a loan, especially such a short period of time prior to the expiry of the relevant contract. In fact, without the agreement of the club of origin the player would not be in a position to prematurely return to that club or find employment at a third club. Therefore, he would run the risk to remain without employment for the remaining period of time of the loan. In addition, the interest of a third club would be limited being aware that the player would have to return to his club of origin in the near future.
35. In the light of the above, the Chamber considered that it could, at least, not be excluded that the early termination of the contractual relationship with Z was somehow related to the doping test carried out on the player on 27 March 2004.
36. The Chamber concluded that, in its opinion, through his behaviour, the player had deceived Y. When signing the cancellation agreement, Y was subject to an error. Had the Respondent known about the factual circumstances on 17 July 2004, it would not have concluded a cancellation agreement with such contents with the Claimant.
37. Finally, the Chamber concurred with Y that it would have been the players task to demonstrate that there were valid reasons justifying the presence of banned substances in his organism and this within the doping related procedure in front of the competent deciding bodies of the country of Z.
38. On account of the above, the Chamber decided that the Respondent, Y, cannot be held liable for the execution of the cancellation agreement that it entered into with the player, X, on 17 July 2004. Consequently, the Chamber decided to fully reject Xs claim.
39. Furthermore, in line with its constant jurisprudence, the Chamber decided to reject the Respondents counter-claim relating to reimbursement by X of the costs that it allegedly incurred in connection with the present proceedings.

III. DECISION OF THE DISPUTE RESOLUTION CHAMBER

1. The claim of the Claimant, X, is rejected.
2. The counter-claim of the Respondent, Y, is rejected.

3. According to art. 60 par. 1 of the FIFA Statutes, this decision may be appealed against before the Court of Arbitration for Sport (CAS). The statement of appeal must be sent to the CAS directly within 21 days of receipt of notification of this decision and shall contain all the elements in accordance with point 2 of the directives issued by the CAS, a copy of which we enclose hereto. Within another 10 days following the expiry of the time limit for filing the statement of appeal, the appellant shall file a brief stating the facts and legal arguments giving rise to the appeal with the CAS (cf. point 4 of the directives).

⚽⚽⚽

26562
DECISION OF THE DISPUTE RESOLUTION CHAMBER
passed in Zurich, Switzerland, on 21 February 2006,
in the following composition:
Slim Aloulou (Tunisia), Chairman
Joaquim Evangelista (Portugal), member
Michele Colucci (Italy), member
Philippe Diallo (France), member
Mohamed Mecherara (Algeria), member
on the claim presented by the club, X, as Claimant
against
the club, Y, as Respondent
regarding a training compensation dispute related to the transfer of the player A

I. **FACTS OF THE CASE**
1. The player, A, was born on 24 March 1981, and was, according to the official confirmation from the XXX Football Federation (player passport) registered with the club X as an amateur from 6 October 1998 until 21 October 1999 for one season, between the ages of 17 and 18 before he turned non-amateur with the same club. Within this period of time, the player was on loan at ZZZ for the time between 29 June 1999 and 29 September 1999. The player signed his first contract as a non-amateur with X and was registered as a non-amateur with the latter from 22 October 1999 until 30 June 2003, for 4 seasons between the ages of 18 and 22.
During this period of time, the player was again on loan at ZZZ club for the time between 9 June 2000 until 12 October 2000.
2. On 1 July 2003 the player signed a two years contract with the club, Y, aged 22 ½.
3. On 12 April 2005, X lodged a claim against Y for training compensation in accordance with Chapter VII of the FIFA Regulations for the Status and Transfer of Players (edition September 2001).
4. Given that the compensation for the players training was not paid within 30 days from the registration of the player with Y, in addition X seeks for penalty interest over the last 24 months on the due amount.
5. Before signing the employment contract with Y on 1 July 2003 for two years, the player initially signed a new contract offer of re-employment with X on 23 March 2003 for 1 year (season 2003/2004), on the same terms as the last year of his previous 3 years contract he had signed with X.
6. Y, by referring to art. 5.5 of the Regulations governing the Application of the Regulations for the Status and Transfer of Players (edition 2001), states that it does not consider training compensation to be appropriate, because X failed to offer the player an improved or equivalent contract to his existing one. This opinion is based on the fact that the annual payments proposed to the player by X in the new contract correspond to the ones of his former contract, but the newly offered contract should have been concluded for one year only instead of 3 years like the old one. This opinion is based on a written statement provided by the OOO Professional Footballers' Association. Moreover, the respondent maintains that, prior to signing the contract with the player, they established that the player was a "Free Agent" in terms of his status as a player.
7. X in reply thereto remains of the conviction to be entitled to training compensation for the player A. In particular, it maintains that the transfer of Mr. A did not take place within the EU / EEA and therefore art. 5.5 of the Regulations governing the Application of the Regulations for the Status and Transfer of Players (edition 2001) is not applicable. Furthermore, the ... club maintains that the

new contract offer to the player was on the basis of the equivalent remuneration that the player was receiving on his existing contract since 29 October 2001.
Additionally, it leads that the opinion provided by the .. Professional Footballers' Association is non-binding and non-authoritative on this matter and at best represents a view of the ....

8. In response thereto, Y, inter alia, stated that if, however, training compensation would be granted to X by the Dispute Resolution Chamber, it should be calculated on the basis of verifiable information concerning the players history at the ... club.
In particular, it affirms that X made divergent specifications in its correspondence regarding the players career.
9. Additionally, the ... club asserts that the player had no fewer than 25 appearances with the A-Team of X in the season 2000/2001 and a greater number in subsequent seasons. Therefore, it deems that the player has accomplished his training with X already on his 21 birthday, i.e. 24 March 2002. Therefore, the period of time for which, if any, training compensation should be calculated is from July 1999 until 24 March 2002.
10. Moreover, the ... club deems that the provisions of art. 5.5 of the Regulations governing the Application of the Regulations for the Status and Transfer of Players (edition 2001) and the terms of the circular no. 769, are intended to ensure that FIFAs rules relating to training compensation are compatible with the rights of EU nationals under EU law, particularly in relation to free movement of employees. The .. club considers that the protection which these provisions confer are necessary to ensure free movement of EU nationals whether or not those nationals are moving to an EU/EEA state from another member state or from outside the EU (remark: the player in question is EU national on heritage grounds).
11. Finally, Y, by referring to art. 6.1 of the Rules Governing the Practice and Procedures of the Dispute Resolution Chamber (edition February 2002), deems that the .. club did not make its claim for training compensation in time. When the claim for compensation was made towards the ... club in January 2004 and rejected at that time, X took no further steps to initiate proceedings before the Dispute Resolution Chamber until it raised its claim in April 2005. Given this delay in taking steps in front of FIFA, the ... club deems that the ... club should not be entitled to request training compensation.
12. In its reply, the ... club, inter alia, emphasized that the Dispute Resolution Chamber should not give any consideration to the players status as a EU national, since the move of the player cannot be classified as a "within EU/EEA transfer". Only the players club registration status is relevant, i.e. that he was transferred from an ... club to a ... club.
13. Furthermore, the ... club provided the player passport, in order to have verifiable information regarding the players history with the clubs within the Football Federation XX....
14. Regarding the players appearances with the senior team of X, the ... club affirmed that the player was still trained by them when he was transferred to the ... club.
The ... club pointed out that the player in fact had only three seasons as a non- amateur player in XX. In this respect, the ... club admitted that the player was lucky in the season 2000/2001 having a lot of appearances with the first team because of other senior players' injuries / suspensions and so he enjoyed an extended run in the senior squad ahead of the clubs expectations for the player. But contrary to the assertion of Y, the player actually made less senior appearances in subsequent seasons. In this respect, it provided copies of the ... National Soccer League Official Season Guide for the seasons 2001/2002 and 2002/2003, according to which the player had 25 appearances in the season 2001/2002 and 19 games played in the season 2002/2003. Furthermore, it stressed that it was also admitted by the ... club that it acquired the services of the player as a squad player since he was a young and inexperienced ... footballer.
15. Finally, the ... club alleges that it was actually the ... club which has caused the delay of the present matter by not performing its obligation to pay the training compensation due to X immediately. Moreover, it explains that the club has been distracted with its own internal issues due to the reform of their association in 2004 and the revamp of the national league landscape in the country.
16. In its final submission, the ... club stressed that the fact that X allegedly was distracted by internal issues does not excuse the delay of 15 months between Ys rejection to Xs claim and the latters initiation of proceedings before the Dispute Resolution Chamber.
17. Moreover, it pointed out that the period of time where the player was on loan at ZZZ cannot be taken into account when calculating the amount of training compensation. With regard to the appropriate

training period, it added that the player concluded his training by the beginning of the season 2000/2001 during which season he had 25 senior team appearances for the ... club.

II. CONSIDERATIONS OF THE DISPUTE RESOLUTION CHAMBER

1. First of all, the Chamber analysed whether it was competent to deal with the matter at stake. In this respect, it referred to art. 18 par. 2 and 3 of the Rules Governing the Procedures of the Players' Status Committee and the Dispute Resolution Chamber. The present matter was submitted to FIFA on 12 April 2005, as a consequence the Chamber concluded that the previous Procedural Rules (edition 2001) on matters pending before the decision making bodies of FIFA are applicable on the matter at hand.
2. With regard to the competence of the Chamber, art. 42 par. 1 lit. (b) (iv) of the FIFA Regulations for the Status and Transfer of Players (edition 2001) establishes that, disputes concerning training compensation, will be decided by the Dispute Resolution Chamber.
3. As a consequence, the Dispute Resolution Chamber is the competent body to decide on the present litigation concerning the training compensation claimed by the Claimant for the training and education of the player A.
4. Subsequently, the members of the Chamber analyzed which edition of the Regulations for the Status and Transfer of Players should be applicable as to the substance of the matter. In this respect, the Chamber referred to art. 26 par. 1 and 2 of the Regulations for the Status and Transfer of Players (edition 2005) in the modified version in accordance with the FIFA circular no. 995 dated 23 September 2005. Furthermore, it acknowledged that the player had been registered for his new club on 1 July 2003. Equally the Chamber took note that the claim was lodged at FIFA on 12 April 2005. In view of the aforementioned, the Chamber concluded that the former FIFA Regulations for the Status and Transfer of Players (edition 2001, hereafter: the Regulations) are applicable on the case at hand as to the substance.
5. In continuation, the members took note of the Respondents objection that the Claimant did not make its claim in time and thus is not entitled to demand for training compensation.
6. In this regard, the members underlined that it is actually the responsibility of the new club to calculate the amount of compensation for training and education and the way in which it shall be distributed in accordance with the players career history. For that purpose, the new club may ask the player for his assistance in order to help in discharging its obligation (cf. art. 9.1 of the Regulations governing the Application of the Regulations, hereinafter; the Application Regulations). The Chamber stated that the delay of the Claimant in reclaiming the outstanding amount of training compensation from the Respondent did not release the Respondent from the aforementioned obligation.
7. Furthermore, the Chamber referred to art. 44 of the Regulations in connection with art. 4 of the Rules Governing the Practice and Procedures of the Dispute Resolution Chamber which state that the Chamber will not hear any case if more than two years have elapsed since the facts leading to the dispute arose. Yet, in the case at hand, the relevant transfer took place in July 2003, whereas the Claimant lodged its complaint in April 2005.
8. In view of these considerations, the members of the Chamber concluded that the claim of the X club is receivable.
9. In continuation, the members of the Chamber acknowledged that on the one hand, the Claimant requested training compensation based on the number of years the player spent training with the Claimant and, on the other hand, by referring to art. 5.5 of the Application Regulations, the Respondent invoked that the Claimant is not entitled to receiving any training compensation by means of not having offered to the player an improved or equivalent contract to his existing one.
10. In this respect, the members of the Chamber emphasized that the art. 5.5 of the Application Regulations, to which the Respondent referred, is not applicable on the case at hand, since it does not involve two clubs situated in the EU/EEA. The members pointed out that the nationality of the player concerned is not relevant in this regard. In fact, neither the aforementioned provision nor the circular no. 769 indicate that the players nationality should also be taken into consideration.
11. The Dispute Resolution Chamber then referred to art. 13 of the Regulations and emphasized that, as a general rule, training compensation is payable up to the players age of 23. In this respect, it was noted that at the time of his move to Y, the player A was 22 ½ years old.
12. As a result of all the above, and after having duly considered all the documentation provided by both parties, the members unanimously concluded that the Claimant is entitled to receive training

compensation for the training and education of the player A as established in Chapter VII of the Regulations.

13. After having established the Respondents obligation to compensate the Claimant for the training of the player in question, the members went on to deliberate on the proper calculation of this compensation, affirming that the amount due shall be calculated in accordance with the parameters provided for by the Regulations and the FIFA circular no. 826.
14. In accordance with art. 5.1 of the Application Regulations, the training period to be taken into account for the calculation of the training compensation, starts at the beginning of the season of the players 12th birthday and finishes at the end of the season of the players 21st birthday.
15. In this respect, the Chamber emphasised that in the present case the period to be taken into account is from the season 1993/1994 until the season 2001/2002.
    Moreover, the Chamber acknowledged that, according to the relevant player passport, the player A, born on 24 March 1981, was registered with the Claimant as an amateur in the season 1998/1999 and subsequently as a non-amateur from the season 1999/2000 until the season 2002/2003.
16. In this respect, the members of the Chamber expressed themselves concerning the allegation of the Respondent that it was not provided by the Claimant with accurate and verifiable information concerning the players career history.
17. The members noted that the Football Federation XX provided the relevant player passport, based on which the career of the player can accurately be established.
18. Therefore, the members stated that the objection of the Respondent has to be rejected as unfounded.
19. In continuation, the Chamber turned to the question as to whether training compensation is due to the Claimant for the period of time during which the player A was transferred on a loan basis to another club, in casu ZZZ club.
20. In this respect, the members referred to the well-established jurisprudence of the Dispute Resolution Chamber, which has been confirmed by the Court of Arbitration for Sport (CAS), according to which a club is only entitled to receive training compensation for the period of time during which a player has in fact been trained by the club claiming payment of such compensation. This implies that no training compensation shall be due to the Claimant for the period of time during which the player A was transferred on a loan basis to ZZZ.
21. Taking into consideration the above, the request for training compensation put forward by the Claimant with respect to the period of time during which the player in question was registered on a loan basis with the aforementioned ... club, ZZZ, has to be dismissed.
22. Subsequently, the Chamber continued by deliberating the question as to whether the player A had completed his training with the Claimant already prior to his 21st birthday, i.e. at the beginning of the season 2000/2001 at the very latest as asserted by the Respondent.
23. In this respect, the deciding body pointed out that the period of training to be taken into account shall only be reduced if it is evident that the player has terminated his training period before the age of 21 (cf. art. 13 of the Regulations).
    Furthermore, the Chamber stated that the Respondent carries the burden of proof to that regard.
24. The Dispute Resolution Chamber acknowledged that the main argument put forward by the Respondent is the fact that the player A played in a considerable amount of matches for the senior team of the Claimant during the 2000/2001 season. On the other hand, the Claimant had stated that this was due to exceptional circumstances, e.g. injuries and suspensions of established players.
    Moreover, the Respondent had explicitly stated that it aimed to acquire the services of a young inexperienced player.
25. The Chamber emphasized that, in any case, more than just one indication to the possible earlier termination of the training period needs to exist in order to justify the application of the relevant exception. The members of the Chamber where thus of the opinion that it is not evident that the player A terminated his training before reaching the age of 21.
26. On account of all the above, the Chamber concluded that the allegation of the Respondent, according to which the player A had completed his training with the Claimant before having reached his 21st birthday, could not be backed.
27. In continuation, the Chamber referred to the Respondents argument according to which training compensation would in any case only be due until the day of the players 21st birthday, i.e. 24 March 2002. In this respect, the members referred to art. 5.1 of the Application Regulations and emphasized

that the entire season of the players 21st birthday needs to be taken into consideration.

28. In light of all of the above, the Chamber decided that the Claimant is entitled to training compensation for the period of 3 and a half seasons (season 98/99 minus 3 months loan at ZZZ, season 99/00, season 00/01 minus 3 months loan at ZZZ and season 01/02).
29. In continuation, the members stated that in accordance with art. 7.3 of the Application Regulations, as a general principle, compensation for training is based on the training and education costs of the country in which the new club is located. In this respect, and in order to clarify the sense of the mentioned clause, the Chamber referred to the point 2b(i) of the FIFA circular no. 769 dated 24 of August of 2001 and stated that, for the transfer of a player from a country outside the EU or the EEA to a country inside the EU or the EEA, whenever training compensation is owed, the compensation should be calculated based on the costs of the country of the new club applying the category of the club which effectively has formed and educated the player. Article 7.1 of the Application Regulations confirms the mentioned principle ("the compensation for training and education shall be obtained by multiplying the amount corresponding to the category of the training club for which the player was registered by the number of years of training from 12 to 21" [it is us who emphasize]).
30. According to the FIFA circular no. 826 dated 31 October 2002, which regards the categorisation of clubs, the ... club, X, belongs to category 3, thus the corresponding indicative amount for a third category club in Europe is EUR 30000.00.
31. Consequently, in application of art. 7.1 and 7.3 of the Application Regulations, the indicative amount mentioned in the previous point must be multiplied by the number of years the player spent training with the Claimant. The total relevant period of time to be taken into consideration equates to 3 and half seasons between the ages of 17 and 21. The relevant period of time the player spent on a loan basis with another club, cannot, as explained above, be taken into account.
32. Based on all the foregoing considerations, the Chamber concluded that the Respondent has to pay the amount of EUR 105.000.00 to the Claimant as training compensation for the training and education of the player A.
33. Finally, the members of the Chamber made reference to art. 9.1 of the Application Regulations, which reads, inter alia, that the new club shall pay the training clubs the amount due as compensation for training and education pursuant to the above provisions at the latest within 30 days of the players new registration.
34. Consequently, in light of the fact that this payment is due since the thirty-first day after the registration of the player A with the association of his new club, i.e. 1 July 2003, the Chamber established that a default interest payment of 5% p.a. as from 1 August 2003 must be applied on the due amount.

III. DECISION OF THE DISPUTE RESOLUTION CHAMBER

1. The claim lodged by the Claimant, X, is partially accepted.
2. The Respondent, Y, shall pay the amount of EUR 105000.00 to the Claimant, X, within 30 days following the date of the communication of the present decision.
3. On the aforementioned amount, a default interest payment of 5% p.a. as from 1 August 2003 until the date of the payment is applied.
4. Any further claims lodged by the Claimant, X, are rejected.
5. In the event that the above-mentioned amount is not paid within the stated deadline, the present matter shall be submitted to FIFAs Disciplinary Committee, so that the necessary disciplinary sanctions may be imposed.
6. The Claimant, X, is instructed to inform the Respondent, Y, directly and immediately of the account number to which the remittance is to be made and to notify the Dispute Resolution Chamber of every payment received.
7. According to art. 60 par. 1 of the FIFA Statutes, this decision may be appealed against before the Court of Arbitration for Sport (CAS). The statement of appeal must be sent to the CAS directly within 21 days of receipt of notification of this decision and shall contain all the elements in accordance with point 2 of the directives issued by the CAS, a copy of which we enclose hereto. Within another 10 days following the expiry of the time limit for filing the statement of appeal, the appellant shall file a brief stating the facts and legal arguments giving rise to the appeal with the CAS (cf. point 4 of the directives).

26595

DECISION OF THE DISPUTE RESOLUTION CHAMBER

passed in Zurich, Switzerland, on 21 February 2006,
in the following composition:
Slim Aloulou (Tunisia), Chairman
Joaquim Evangelista (Portugal), member
Michele Colucci (Italy), member
Philippe Diallo (France), member
Mohamed Mecherara (Algeria), member
on the claim presented by the club, X, ... as Claimant
against
the club, Y, ... as Respondent
regarding a training compensation dispute related to the transfer of the player Z

I. FACTS OF THE CASE

1. The player, Z, was born on 25 March 1982 and was registered, according to the ... Football Federation, with X from 19 March 1999 until 30 June 2004.
2. On 1 August 2004, the aforementioned player was transferred to the ... club, Y, and signed with the latter an employment contract.
3. On 20 April 2005, the ... club, X, lodged a formal complaint in front of FIFA for the payment of training compensation for the player Z in accordance with the provisions contained in Chapter VII of the Regulations for the Status and Transfer of Players (edition September 2001).
4. The ... club, X, is claiming the amount of EUR 320000.00 taking into consideration the aforementioned period of registration.
5. In reply to the claim of the club, the club maintains that X confirmed in its letter dated 12 July 2004 that the player was given the opportunity to change clubs until 31 August 2004 without having to pay any compensation payments by the players potential future club.
6. Furthermore, the club stresses that on the occasion of the issuance of the international transfer certificate by the Football Federation for the transfer of the player, no remarks or reservations have been made with regard to the financial aspects of the transfer of the player in question.
7. Additionally and with reference to the FIFA Regulations, the club asserts that training compensation is due only in case the player was under a valid contract before his transfer to another club or in case the employment contract with the former club has expired and the former club has offered a new contract to the player. In this respect, the club alleges that since the employment contract between X and the player Z was terminated by mutual agreement, the situation corresponds to the one where the player is not offered a new contract by X.
8. In reply thereto, the club contests the position of the club and states that the letter in question dated 12 July 2004 only indicates that it has no objections regarding the transfer of the player to another club and at the same time the club agrees to the mutual termination of the employment contract without any transfer compensation payments to be imposed on the potential future club.
9. Furthermore, the club states that the player had a valid employment contract until 30 August 2005 at the time of the termination of the relevant employment contract.
10. In its final position, the club reiterates its position and remains of the opinion that it is not obliged to pay training compensation to the club.

II. CONSIDERATIONS OF THE DISPUTE RESOLUTION CHAMBER

1. First of all, the Chamber analysed whether it was competent to deal with the matter at stake. In this respect, it referred to art. 18 par. 2 and 3 of the Rules Governing the Procedures of the Players' Status Committee and the Dispute Resolution Chamber. The present matter was submitted to FIFA on 20 April 2005, as a consequence the Chamber concluded that the previous Procedural Rules (edition 2001) on matters pending before the decision making bodies of FIFA are applicable on the matter at hand.
2. With regard to the competence of the Chamber, art. 42 par. 1 lit. (b) (iv) of the FIFA Regulations for the Status and Transfer of Players (edition 2001) establishes that, disputes concerning training compensation, will be decided by the Dispute Resolution Chamber.

3. As a consequence, the Dispute Resolution Chamber is the competent body to decide on the present litigation concerning the training compensation claimed by the Claimant for the training and education of the player Z.
4. Subsequently, the members of the Chamber analyzed which edition of the Regulations for the Status and Transfer of Players should be applicable as to the substance of the matter. In this respect, the Chamber referred to art. 26 par. 1 and 2 of the Regulations for the Status and Transfer of Players (edition 2005) in the modified version in accordance with the FIFA circular no. 995 dated 23 September 2005. Furthermore, it acknowledged that the professional had been registered for his new club on 1 August 2004. Equally the Chamber took note that the claim was lodged at FIFA on 20 April 2005. In view of the aforementioned, the Chamber concluded that the former FIFA Regulations for the Status and Transfer of Players (edition 2001, hereafter: the Regulations) are applicable to the case at hand as to the substance.
5. In continuation, and entering into the substance of the matter, the members of the Chamber started by acknowledging that on the one hand, the Claimant requests training compensation based on the number of years that the player was trained and educated by the Claimant and, on the other hand, the Respondent contests the Claimants entitlement to receive any training compensation.
6. The Chamber noted the Respondents position that the Claimant did not offer the player an employment contract and that therefore the Claimant should have no entitlement to training compensation from the Respondent.
7. In this respect, the members of the Chamber pointed out that the present matter involves parties which are situated in member states of the European Union (EU).
   Consequently, the Chamber wished to underline that transfers within the EU/EEA are subject to particular norms put in place so as to safeguard the free movement of workers within the EU members states. Such a norm is contained in art. 5 par. 5 of the Regulations governing the Application of the FIFA Regulations for the Status and Transfer of Players (hereinafter: Application Regulations). This provision specifies that in case of transfers which take place within the EU/EEA, the fact that the training club seeking training compensation does not offer a player a contract will be taken into account when determining the training compensation payable by the new club.
8. In continuation, the members of the Chamber pointed out that the meaning of the aforementioned art. 5 par. 5 of the application regulations is clarified in the FIFA Circular No. 769 dated 24 August 2001, which, under point 2a specifies that the former club of a player younger than 23, whose contract has come to and end and who has not received a new contract from his club, equivalent in remuneration to his previous contract, will be deemed not to have offered a contract to the latter for purposes of calculating training compensation.
   Furthermore, the said FIFA Circular maintains that, as a matter of principle, the players training club will not be entitled to receive training compensation unless it can demonstrate to the Dispute Resolution Chamber that it is entitled to compensation in derogation of this principle. The members of the Chamber emphasized in this respect that this approach corresponds to the constant jurisprudence of the Dispute Resolution Chamber.
9. The deciding body then turned to the claim of the Claimant, which is based on the transfer of the player Z from the Claimant to the Respondent. As such and taking into consideration the above, the Chamber confirmed that the transfer of the player in question is subject to the particular provisions provided for in the Application Regulations for transfers within the EU/EEA.
10. In this context, the members of the Chamber emphasized that, so as to transfer the player in question to the Respondent, the Claimant terminated the employment contract with the player by mutual agreement. This fact has even been confirmed by the Claimant in its correspondence dated 18 July 2005.
11. The members of the Chamber underlined that the Claimant, by putting an end to the contractual engagement with the player, even though it wanted to enable the player to transfer to another club, failed to meet the requirements of art. 5 par. 5 of the Application Regulations. In essence, the deciding body maintained that a club wiling to transfer a young player to another club is not actually seeking to retain the services of the player and has thus foregone its entitlement to training compensation, as specified under the aforementioned art. 5 par. 5 of the Application Regulations.
12. The Chamber emphasized that the jurisprudence developed with respect to art. 5 par. 5 of the Application Regulations and the aforementioned FIFA Circular No. 769 dated 24 August 2001, clearly directly applies to the case at hand.

13. In light of all the above, the Dispute Resolution Chamber established that it could not admit the claim of the Claimant for training compensation pertaining to the transfer of the player Z to the Respondent.

III. DECISION OF THE DISPUTE RESOLUTION CHAMBER

1. The claim lodged by the Claimant, X, is rejected.
2. According to art. 60 par. 1 of the FIFA Statutes, this decision may be appealed against before the Court of Arbitration for Sport (CAS). The statement of appeal must be sent to the CAS directly within 21 days of receipt of notification of this decision and shall contain all the elements in accordance with point 2 of the directives issued by the CAS, a copy of which we enclose hereto. Within another 10 days following the expiry of the time limit for filing the statement of appeal, the appellant shall file a brief stating the facts and legal arguments giving rise to the appeal with the CAS (cf. point 4 of the directives).

26866B

DECISION OF THE DISPUTE RESOLUTION CHAMBER

passed in Zurich, Switzerland, on 21 February 2006,
in the following composition:
Slim Aloulou (Tunisia), Chairman
Michele Colucci (Italy), member
Joaquim Evangelista (Portugal), member
Philippe Diallo (France), member
Mohamed Mecherara (Algeria), member
on the claim presented by the club, X, represented by Mr. W, lawyer as Claimant
against
the club, Y, as Respondent
regarding solidarity contribution related to the transfer of the player

I. FACTS OF THE CASE

1. The player, X, was born on 17 September 1977.
2. The player was registered with X as from 10 July 1997 until 16 December 1998.
3. This registration period has been confirmed in writing by the Football Association of X.
4. In July 2004, the player was definitively transferred from V to Y.
5. In accordance with the transfer agreement concluded between V and Y, the transfer compensation for the player Z amounts to USD 1,800,000.
6. FIFA is in possession of a copy of the relevant transfer agreement.
7. On 9 November 2004, the Dispute Resolution Chamber passed a formal decision in the labour dispute between the player in question, Z, and Y.
8. On 8 December 2004, the Single Judge of the Players' Status Committee passed a formal decision in the contractual dispute between V and Y relating to the transfer of the player in question, Z.
9. These decisions have become final and binding and, in the meantime, Y appears to have executed these formal decisions.
10. On 14 April 2005, X turned to FIFA maintaining that in accordance with article 25 of the former Regulations for the Status and Transfer of Players (edition September 2001) and articles 10 and 11 of the Regulations governing the Application of the aforementioned Regulations, it is entitled to receive a proportion of the solidarity contribution taking into consideration the above- mentioned registration period.
11. In addition, the Claimant asks for payment of interest at a rate of 5%.
12. By fax dated 19 September 2005, the Football Federation of Y conveyed the position of its member club rejecting the claim put forward by X alleging that a) no labour contract was concluded between the player, Z, and Y and that b) the player was not registered with the Football Federation of Y.
13. Consequently, Y deems that the claim for payment of the relevant proportion of the solidarity contribution is unjustified.

14. By fax dated 16 February 2006, i.e. after the closure of the investigation into the present matter and shortly prior to the hearing by the DRC, the Football Federation of Y conveyed the request of Y asking to be allowed to present "the evidence necessary for making an objective decision".
15. By fax dated 20 February 2006, FIFA informed Y that the investigation into this matter had been closed referring to FIFAs fax dated 19 December 2005.

II. CONSIDERATIONS OF THE DISPUTE RESOLUTION CHAMBER

1. The present dispute having been lodged in front of the Dispute Resolution Chamber (hereinafter referred to as "DRC" or "Chamber") prior to the coming into force of the current Regulations for the Status and Transfer of Players on 1 July 2005, the members of the DRC firstly proceeded to confirm that the September 2001 edition of the FIFA Regulations for the Status and Transfers of Players (hereinafter referred to as the "Regulations") applies to the case at hand.
2. The Dispute Resolution Chamber commenced its deliberations by referring to art. 25 of the Regulations, according to which it falls within the purview of the Dispute Resolution Chamber to decide upon disputes concerning the distribution of the solidarity contribution. Consequently, the DRC established that it was competent to decide on the present litigation concerning the solidarity contribution claimed by X.
3. Once its competence was thus established, the DRC went on to deal with the substance of the case.
4. The members of the Chamber duly noted that X claims payment of solidarity contribution for the period from 10 July 1997 until 16 December 1998 on the basis of the transfer of the player, Z, from V to Y.
5. Y, for its part, rejects the claim put forward by X maintaining that a) no labour contract was concluded between the player, Z, and Y and that b) the player was not registered with the Football Federation of Y.
6. The DRC noted that Y has not presented any documentary evidence to substantiate its allegations.
7. In this context, the members of the Chamber duly analysed the decisions that were passed by the DRC on 9 November 2004 in the labour dispute between the player, Z, and Y and by the Single Judge of the Players' Status Committee on 8 December 2004 in the contractual dispute between V and Y.
8. From the decision passed by the DRC, it can be noted that Y invoked the same arguments as indicated under point 5 above and that these arguments were dismissed by the Chamber. That is, the DRC found that a valid employment contract had been concluded between the player, Z, and Y.
9. Furthermore, according to the Single Judge of the Players' Status Committee a legally binding transfer agreement had been concluded between V and Y dismissing Ys allegation that the said agreement was forged.
10. What is more, the said decisions have in the meantime been executed by Y. To be more precise, inter alia, V has confirmed having received the relevant transfer compensation from Y.
11. Having ascertained that the transfer of the player to Y was definitive, the Chamber emphasized that, as established in article 25 of the Regulations, the new club to which a player is transferred during the course of an employment contract with his previous club is responsible for the distribution of 5% of the compensation payable to the players former club to the former club(s) involved in the training and education of the player between the ages of 12 and 23. In the case at hand, in accordance with the relevant agreement, the transfer compensation amounts to USD 1,800,000.
12. The Chamber subsequently referred to art. 10 of the Regulations governing the Application of the aforementioned Regulations, which provides the figures for the distribution of the solidarity contribution, taking into consideration the period of time that the player was effectively trained by the club concerned.
13. In the present case, the Chamber outlined that the period to be taken into consideration is related to the players age of 19-20, i.e. the 1997-98 season, until the players age of 20-21, i.e. the 1998-99 season, during which the player was registered until 16 December 1998.
14. In view of the above, the Chamber concluded that 15% of the 5% solidarity contribution shall be apportioned to X.
15. Having ascertained that the amount agreed upon by and between the Respondent and V for the transfer of Z is USD 1,800,000, 15% of the 5% solidarity contribution amounts to USD 13,500.
16. In light of the above, the Chamber decided that Y is liable to pay the amount of USD 13,500 as solidarity contribution to X.

17. Furthermore, the Chamber made reference to article 11 of the Regulations governing the Application of the aforementioned Regulations, which reads that the new club shall pay the amount due as solidarity contribution to the training club(s) at the latest within 30 days of the players registration with the new club.
18. Consequently, taking into consideration the claim of the Claimant and in the light of the fact that the solidarity contribution payment has been due since the 31st day of the registration of the player with Y, club to which the player was transferred in July 2004, the Chamber established that a default interest payment of 5% per year as from the day as of which the relevant payment was due, i.e. on 1 September 2004, must be applied.

III. DECISION OF THE DISPUTE RESOLUTION CHAMBER

1. The claim of the Claimant, X, is accepted.
2. The Respondent, Y, shall pay the amount of USD 13,500 to the Claimant, X, within 30 days of notification of the present decision.
3. The Respondent has to pay default interest at the rate of 5% p.a. on the amount of USD 13,500 as from 1 September 2004 until the day of the execution of the present decision.
4. If the Respondent fails to comply with the above-mentioned deadline, the case will immediately be presented to the FIFA Disciplinary Committee.
5. The Claimant is directed to inform the Respondent immediately of the account number to which the remittance is to be made and to notify the Dispute Resolution Chamber of every payment received.
6. According to art. 60 par. 1 of the FIFA Statutes, this decision may be appealed against before the Court of Arbitration for Sport (CAS). The statement of appeal must be sent to the CAS directly within 21 days of receipt of notification of this decision and shall contain all the elements in accordance with point 2 of the directives issued by the CAS, a copy of which we enclose hereto. Within another 10 days following the expiry of the time limit for filing the statement of appeal, the appellant shall file a brief stating the facts and legal arguments giving rise to the appeal with the CAS (cf. point 4 of the directives).

261043
DECISION OF THE DISPUTE RESOLUTION CHAMBER
passed in Zurich, Switzerland, on 21 February 2006,
in the following composition:
Slim Aloulou (Tunisia), Chairman
Michele Colucci (Italy), member
Joaquim Evangelista (Portugal), member
Philippe Diallo (France), member
Mohamed Mecherara (Algeria), member
on the claim presented by Player B as Claimant
against
Club H as Respondent
regarding a contractual dispute between the parties involve

I. FACTS OF THE CASE

1. The player B was born on 9 November 1971.
2. On 21 February 2004, the player B signed an employment contract with the club H valid until 31 November 2004 (date of the end of the football season in China).
3. Article 7, point 2 of the employment contract stipulates a monthly salary of USD 20,000.
4. The claimant states that, in respect of the salary for the month of June 2004, the respondent only paid the sum of USD 16,500. The player B claims the sum of USD 103,500 from the respondent in respect of unpaid salary, as follows:
   Reminder of salary for June USD 3,500 Salary from July to November USD 100,000 (USD 20,000 per month) Total: USD 103,500.
5. The claimant considers that, due to the failure to pay his salaries, the respondent has breached the terms of the contract between them.

6. The respondent club informed FIFA that the player had provided the club with his services from 21 March 2004 to 27 November 2004. The club stated that in accordance with Chinese legislation it could not deposit the sums corresponding to player's salary in a foreign bank account and requested that the claimant provide details of his bank account in China so that the payments could be made. Furthermore, the respondent stated that in accordance with Chinese legislation, the player was due to pay taxes in China amounting to USD 65,380.12. As a consequence, the respondent only owed the player the sum of USD 38,844.87.
7. Article 7, points 2 and 4 (5) of the employment contract stipulates that the club will deduct amounts corresponding to the payment of income tax from the salary and bonuses to which the player is entitled, to be forwarded by the club to the Chinese tax authorities.
8. The player's response to the club's reasoning was that payments previously made by the respondent had never been subject to deductions for tax and furthermore this was a matter between the player and the Chinese tax authorities to which the club was not a party. The claimant considers that the respondent was merely putting forward excuses to defend its non-fulfilment, given that a deduction of 70% of salary for tax could not be justified. Finally, the player declared that the matter of a Chinese bank account was also an excuse as the club had previously made payments to the claimant's bank account in Spain.
9. In subsequent communications, the claimant informed FIFA that the respondent had made partial payments by means of deposits to his Spanish bank account, leaving a final outstanding balance of USD 40,000.
10. FIFA sent three communications to the respondent on 7 July, 14 September and 13 December 2005, but did not receive any further response from the club H.
11. The player B requests the Dispute Resolution Chamber to order the club H to pay the sum of USD 40,000 as well as lawyer's fees (no specific amount indicated).

II. CONSIDERATIONS OF THE DISPUTE RESOLUTION CHAMBER

1. First of all, the Chamber analysed whether it was competent to deal with the matter at stake. In this respect, it referred to art. 18 par. 2 and 3 of the Rules Governing the Procedures of the Players' Status Committee and the Dispute Resolution Chamber. The present matter was submitted to FIFA before 1 July 2005, as a consequence the Chamber concluded that the previous Procedural Rules (edition 2001) on matter pending before the decision making bodies of FIFA are applicable on the matter at hand.
2. With regard to the competence of the Chamber, art. 42 par. 1 lit. (b) (i) of the FIFA Regulations for the Status and Transfer of Players (edition 2001) establishes that, the triggering elements of the employment-related dispute (i.e. whether a contract was breached, with or without just cause, or sporting just cause), will be decided by the Dispute Resolution Chamber.
3. If an employment contract is breached by a party, the Dispute Resolution Chamber (DRC) is also responsible to verify whether a party is accountable for outstanding payments and/or compensation.
4. As a consequence, the Dispute Resolution Chamber is the competent body to decide on the present litigation involving a Chinese club and a Serbia and Montenegro player regarding outstanding salaries claimed by the player B in connection with an employment contract.
5. Subsequently, the members of the Chamber analyzed which edition of the Regulations for the Status and Transfer of Players should be applicable as to the substance of the matter. In this respect, the Chamber referred, on the one hand, to art. 26 par. 1 and 2 of the Regulations for the Status and Transfer of Players (edition 2005) and, on the other hand, to the fact that the relevant contract at the basis of the present dispute was signed on 21 February 2004 and the claim was lodged at FIFA before 1 July 2005. In view of the aforementioned, the Chamber concluded that the former FIFA Regulations for the Status and Transfer of Players (edition 2001, hereafter: the Regulations) are applicable on the case at hand as to the substance.
6. In continuation, and entering into the substance of the matter, the members of the Chamber started by acknowledging that both parties signed an employment contract on 21 February 2004 expiring on 31 November 2004. Moreover, the Chamber noted that the respondent confirmed that the player played his last match on 27 November 2004 , therefore the contract was fulfilled by the claimant.
7. At this stage, the DRC considered appropriate to analyze the amounts claimed by the player B and the explanations provided by the respondent in this regard. The player B claimed outsanting salaries (USD 103,500) and the club H presented two main defences: a) the Chinese club cannot make

deposit of salaries outside China and b) the club has to retain taxes from the salary of the player in accordance with the national law.

8. In view of the aforementioned, the Chamber deemed important to analyze the attitude of the respondent. In particular, "a posteriori" the claim was notified to the respondent, the club started to do partial payments (USD 63,500) to the player B in his Spanish bank account. As a consequence, the DRC interpreted this behaviour of the respondent as a tacit recognition of the validity of claim of the player B.
9. In continuation, the Chamber considered appropriate to point it out that as a general rule when a club states that in accordance with national law they are obliged to deduct taxes directly from the salary of the players, the burden of proof belongs to the club. Therefore it is an exclusive obligation of the club to provide with sufficient and accurate evidence (such as copy of the relevant law, examples of taxes deduction, etc.). In this specific case the Chamber took note that the respondent did not provide enough evidence in this respect.
10. Moreover the Chamber noted, that even though the employment contract concluded between the parties on 21 February 2004 established in its article 7 points 2 and 4 (5) that the club will deduct from the salary and bonus the relevant taxes it looks excessive the relevant amount as tax. The fact that the respondent made partial payments to the claimant (USD 63,500) and the lack of response to the FIFA communications (three) shows clearly that the player' B B claim is acceptedby the respondent and valid.
11. In view of all the above, the Chamber concluded that the claim of the player B was reasonable and implicitly recognized by the respondent, therefore the DRC considered that the respondent has to pay USD 40,000 to the claimant.
12. Finally, and referring to its well established jurisprudence, the Chamber did not award any amount as contribution for his legal expenses to the player.
13. The Chamber, in view of the above partially accepted the claim of the player.

III. DECISION OF THE DISPUTE RESOLUTION CHAMBER

1. The claim of the player B is partially accepted.
2. The Respondent H has to pay the amount of USD 40,000 to the Claimant.
3. The amount due to the Claimant has to be paid by the Respondent within 30 days as from the date of notification of this decision.
4. In the event that the debt of the Respondent is not paid within the stated deadline an interest rate of 5% per year will apply. Furthermore, the FIFA will be entitled to submit the file to the Disciplinary Committee.
5. The Claimant is directed to inform the Respondent immediately of the account number to which the remittance is to be made and to notify the Dispute Resolution Chamber of every payment received.
6. According to art. 60 par. 1 of the FIFA Statutes this decision may be appealed before the Court of Arbitration for Sport (CAS). The statement of appeal must be sent to the CAS directly within 21 days of receiving notification of this decision and has to contain all elements in accordance with point 2 of the directives issued by the CAS, copy of which we enclose hereto. Within another 10 days following the expiry of the time limit for the filing of the statement of appeal, the appellant shall file with the CAS a brief stating the facts and legal arguments giving rise to the appeal (cf. point 4 of the directives).

23 MARCH 2006

36446
DECISION OF THE DISPUTE RESOLUTION CHAMBER
passed in Zurich, Switzerland, on 23 March 2006,
in the following composition:
Slim Aloulou (Tunisia), Chairman
Mario Gallavotti (Italy), member
Peter Friend (Australia), member
Gerardo Movilla (Spain), member

Mick Mc Guire (England), member
on an matter between
B., Serbia,
and
L., France,
and
C., Serbia, as Intervening party,
regarding the solidarity contribution related to the transfer of the player, V.

I. FACTS OF THE CASE

1. The player V. was born on 16 May 1977 and was registered during 8 seasons with B. (season 89/90 until 96/97).
2. On 29 March, the Serbian club turned to FIFA and informed that the player had been transferred from the Serbian club C. to the French club L. for an amount of EUR 307,500. Therefore, B. stressed that it is entitled to receive an amount of EUR 10,762.50 plus interest from L., amount which corresponds to 70% of the 5% solidarity contribution. B. emphasised that the French club, however, refuses to pay this amount to B. as it was agreed in the transfer agreement that C. would pay the solidarity contribution to the training clubs.
3. On 18 May 2005, FIFA referred to the constant jurisprudence of the Dispute Resolution Chamber in such cases and invited the French club to pay the relevant proportion relating to the 5% solidarity contribution of the transfer compensation to B. and invited C. to reimburse to L. this amount.
4. On 2 June 2005, the French club answered that it would pay the amount as soon as it receives the reimbursement from C.
5. On 10 June 2005, B. informed FIFA that the amount had not been paid yet.
6. On 21 June and on 6 July 2005, FIFA invited the parties once again to act according to its letter dated 18 May 2005 in order to avoid unnecessary proceedings.
7. Thereupon, the French club invited on 15 July 2005 C. to pay directly the amount to B.
8. On 21 July 2005, C. informed the French club, that it would be in contact with B. and that it would pay the amount directly to this club.
9. On 22 August 2005, B. informed FIFA that it neither received any amount from C. nor from L.
10. On 19 September 2005, FIFA invited the parties for the last time to settle the matter. However, the matter remained unsettled and therefore, the Dispute Resolution Chamber is asked to pass a formal decision on the matter.

II. CONSIDERATIONS OF THE DISPUTE RESOLUTION CHAMBER

1. First of all, the Chamber analysed whether it was competent to deal with the matter at stake. In this respect, it referred to art. 18 par. 2 and 3 of the Rules Governing the Procedures of the Players' Status Committee and the Dispute Resolution Chamber. The present matter was submitted to FIFA on 29 March 2005, as a consequence the Chamber concluded that the previous Procedural Rules (edition 2001) on matters pending before the decision making bodies of FIFA are applicable on the matter at hand.
2. With regard to the competence of the Chamber, art. 25 par. 2 of the FIFA Regulations for the Status and Transfer of Players (edition 2001) establishes that, it falls within the purview of the Dispute Resolution Chamber to review disputes concerning the distribution of the solidarity contribution.
3. As a consequence, the Dispute Resolution Chamber is the competent body to decide on the present litigation concerning the distribution of the solidarity contribution claimed by the Claimant in connection with the transfer of the professional V. during the course of a contract.
4. Subsequently, the members of the Chamber analyzed which edition of the Regulations for the Status and Transfer of Players should be applicable as to the substance of the matter. In this respect, the Chamber referred to art. 26 par. 1 and 2 of the Regulations for the Status and Transfer of Players (edition 2005) in the modified version in accordance with the FIFA circular no. 995 dated 23 September 2005. Furthermore, it acknowledged that the professional had been registered for his new club in August 2004. Equally the Chamber took note that the claim was lodged at FIFA on 29 March 2005. In view of the aforementioned, the Chamber concluded that the former FIFA Regulations for the Status and Transfer of Players (edition 2001, hereafter: the Regulations) are applicable on the case at hand as to the substance.

5. In continuation, and entering into the substance of the matter, the members of the Chamber started by acknowledging that the player was registered with B. during 8 seasons at the age of 12 until 20 years and was transferred in August 2004 from C. to L. on a definitive basis.
6. To this end, C. and L. signed a transfer agreement in accordance with which the French club was obliged to pay to C. a transfer compensation to the amount of EUR 307,500.
7. L. has remitted the total amount of EUR 307,500 to C. in accordance with the transfer agreement.
8. At this point, the Chamber recalled that, as established in art. 10 in conjunction with art. 11 of the Regulations governing the Application of the Regulations for the Status and Transfer of Players, the new club to which a player is transferred during the course of an employment contract with his previous club is responsible for the distribution of 5% of the compensation payable to the players former club to the club(s) involved in the training and education of the player between the ages of 12 and 23.
9. The Chamber took into account that L., i.e. the players new club, rejects the claim put forward by B. maintaining that it remitted 100% of the transfer compensation to C.
10. In this respect, the Chamber once more referred to par. 1 of the above-mentioned art. 11 of the Regulations governing the Application of the Regulations for the Status and Transfer of Players which clearly states that the new club shall pay the amount due as a solidarity contribution to the training clubs.
11. In addition, the members of the Chamber stressed that FIFA circular letter no. 826 dated 31 October 2002, which deals with the interpretation of the Regulations for the Status and Transfer of Players elucidates that the 5% solidarity contribution is to be deducted from the amount payable to the players former club.
12. Furthermore, the deciding body recalled its well established jurisprudence, in accordance with which, in cases like the one at hand, it was established that the players new club is ordered to remit the 5% solidarity contribution to the club(s) involved in the players training in strict application of the said article 11 of the Regulations governing the Application of the Regulations (edition September 2001).
13. At the same time, the players new club may request the players former club to reimburse the same proportion(s) of the 5% of the compensation that it received from the players new club.
14. In light of all the above, the Chamber concluded that on the basis of its jurisprudence and in particular of the strict application of article 11 of the Regulations Governing the Application of the Regulations (edition September 2001) it is the responsibility of the new club, i.e. L., to pay the relevant proportion of the solidarity contribution to the club(s) involved in the players training, i.e. B.
15. In addition, taking into account all of the above and, in particular, the aforementioned well-established jurisprudence of the Chamber, the members of the Chamber deemed that the arguments put forward by the intervening party, C., cannot be accepted.
16. Therefore, C., having unduly received the amount of money pertaining to solidarity contribution, is to be held liable for the reimbursement to the Respondent of the relevant proportion(s) of the solidarity contribution payable by the Respondent, L., to the players former training club(s).
17. Having established that the transfer of the player in question was on a definitive basis and that a transfer compensation was agreed upon between the players former club and new club, the Chamber then turned to the calculation of the relevant proportion due to B. on the basis of the period of time that the player was effectively trained by B.
18. In this regard, the Chamber took into account that according to the player passport of V., he was registered with B. during 8 seasons, from the age of 12 until 20 years. The Chamber subsequently referred to art. 10 of the Regulations governing the Application of the Regulations, which provides the figures for the distribution of the solidarity contribution. Consequently, 70% of the 5% solidarity contribution shall be apportioned to this club.
19. Having ascertained that the amount agreed upon by and between the L. and C. for the transfer of the player, V., is EUR 307,500, 70% of the 5% solidarity contribution amounts to EUR 10,762.50.
20. Consequently, the Chamber decided that L. is liable to pay to B. the amount of EUR 10,762.50 as solidarity contribution.
21. The DRC took into account that the B. asks for payment of 5% interest p.a. due to unjustified delay in payment of the solidarity contribution. In this sense, the Chamber referred to art. 11 par. 1 of the Regulations Governing the Application of the Regulations, which stipulates that the amount due as a solidarity contribution should be paid at the latest within 30 days of the players registration. Such

claim having been put forward, in addition to the aforementioned amount of EUR 10,762.50, the DRC decided that L. is liable to pay 5% interest over the said amount as from the 31st day of the players registration at L.

22. Furthermore, in line with the above, the intervening party, C., is liable to reimburse to L. the aforementioned amount of EUR 10,762.50.

III. DECISION OF THE DISPUTE RESOLUTION CHAMBER

1. The claim of B. is accepted.
2. L. has to pay to B. the amount of EUR 10,762.50 increased with 5% interest p.a. as from the 31st day of the players registration at L. within the next 30 days as from the date of notification of this decision.
3. C. has to reimburse L. the amount of EUR 10,762.50 within the next 30 days as from the date of notification of this decision.
4. In the event that the above-mentioned amount is not paid by L. to B. within the stated deadline, the present matter shall be submitted to FIFAs Disciplinary Committee, so that the necessary disciplinary sanctions may be imposed.
5. In the event that the above-mentioned amount is not reimbursed by C. to L. within the stated deadline, an interest rate of 5% per year will apply as from the 31st day of notification of this decision and the present matter shall be submitted to FIFAs Disciplinary Committee, so that the necessary disciplinary sanctions may be imposed.
6. B. is instructed to inform L. immediately and directly of the account number to which the remittance is to be made and to notify the Dispute Resolution Chamber of every payment received.
7. L. is instructed to inform C. immediately and directly of the account number to which the reimbursement is to be made and to notify the Dispute Resolution Chamber of every payment received.
8. According to art. 60 par. 1 of the FIFA Statutes, this decision may be appealed against before the Court of Arbitration for Sport (CAS). The statement of appeal must be sent to the CAS directly within 21 days of receipt of notification of this decision and shall contain all the elements in accordance with point 2 of the directives issued by the CAS, a copy of which we enclose hereto. Within another 10 days following the expiry of the time limit for filing the statement of appeal, the appellant shall file a brief stating the facts and legal arguments giving rise to the appeal with the CAS (cf. point 4 of the directives).

⚽⚽⚽

36460

DECISION OF THE DISPUTE RESOLUTION CHAMBER

passed in Zurich, Switzerland, on 23 March 2006,
in the following composition:
Slim Aloulou (Tunisia), Chairman Mario Gallavotti (Italy), Member Peter Friend (Australia), Member Mick McGuire (England), Member Gerardo Movilla (Spain), Member
Club A,
on the claim presented by
against
and as Claimant
Player B,
as first Respondent
Club C,
as second Respondent
regarding a dispute about the breach of an employment contract and the inducement to breach an employment contract.

I. FACTS OF THE CASE

1. On 1 February 2004, the player A (hereinafter; the player) and the club B concluded an employment contract, valid from 1 February 2004 to 1 February 2007, stipulating a monthly salary of USD 10,000.

2. On 4 February 2004, the same parties signed an agreement, stipulating a signingon fee in the amount of USD 200,000, payable on 4 February 2004, and a signing-on fee of USD 50,000, payable on 31 July 2004. Furthermore, the agreement stipulates a monthly salary of USD 30,000.
3. On 10 March 2005, the player notified the club in writing that he unilaterally terminated the contract, due to the clubs non-fulfilment of its financial obligations.
4. On 13 April 2005, he signed a new employment contract with the club C.
5. On 9 May 2005, the Football Association of club C requested FIFA to be authorised to provisionally register the player in question.
6. On 20 May 2005, club A provided its answer to the above-mentioned request.
7. On 26 May 2005, the Single Judge of the Players' Status Committee authorised the Football Association of club C to provisionally register the player in order not to hinder his career and thereby stated that any request for compensation and sports sanctions for breach of contract does not hinder the players provisional registration for club C, but will be decided at a later stage of the procedure by the Dispute Resolution Chamber (DRC). The decision of the Single Judge emphasised that it would not prejudice any decision as to the substance of the matter.

Position of club A

8. On 20 May 2005, with its answer to the request of the Football Association of club C to be authorised to provisionally register the player for club C, club A accused the player of breach of contract without just cause, and club C of inducement to breach of contract.
9. Therefore club A requested FIFAs intervention and claimed for compensation from the player and/or club C in the amount of

– the transfer compensation paid for the player	USD 1,800,000
– reimbursement of all paid salaries	USD 574,100
– reimbursement of costs for the player (e.g. accommodation, transport)	USD 4,500
– sports prejudice caused to the club	USD 2,000,000
total	USD 4,738,600

10. In this respect, club A asked for an interest rate of 15% on the compensation to be awarded, as of the date when the breach of contract occurred.
11. Moreover, it requested the imposition of sports sanctions on the player and club C, in accordance with the applicable Regulations of FIFA.
12. Finally, club A asked that the respondents be ordered to pay the legal costs it incurred through the present procedure.
13. Besides the above, club A requested the imposition of sanctions on the players' agent involved in the players engagement for club C. This request makes part of a different procedure, which is pending before the FIFA Players' Status Committee.
14. Club As requests are based on the following argumentation:
15. The player left club A without permission on 18 October 2004.
16. Until that date, club A had fulfilled all its financial obligations towards the player, except the salaries for September and October 2004.
17. On 4 November 2004, the player returned to club A.
18. On the one hand, in order to preserve a good image of the player, it was announced on club As official website that the player was absent due to family reasons. But on the other hand, due to the unexcused absence, club A imposed a fine on the player, equal to the salary for the period of absence.
19. On 8 November 2004, the player left club A again without permission, and only returned on 16 February 2005. The player failed in particular to report to the pre-season training camps, which took place as of 15 December 2004.
20. In this regard, club A declared that the period from 18 November to 15 December 2004 was considered as the players vacation. Therefore, only the absence from 8 to 18 November 2004 and from 15 December 2004 to 16 February 2005 was unexcused.
21. When the player returned in February 2005, club A paid him USD 30,000, being the salary for September 2004. According to club A, this amount could not have been paid before, since the national law allegedly does not allow to transfer money abroad.
22. On 7 March 2005, on the players request to return to his home country for family reasons, club A allowed the player to leave again, under the condition that he had to return in two days.
23. The player never again returned to club A.

24. On account of the above, club A is of the opinion that the player terminated the employment contract without just cause.

Position of the player

25. On 22 June 2005, the player provided FIFA with his answer, requesting that the claim of the club A shall be dismissed and that all due amounts shall be paid to him, since he terminated the contract with just cause.
26. In this regard, he stated that club A paid the salary of September 2004 only in March 2005, and never paid the salaries from October 2004 to February 2005.
27. With regard to his absence from 18 October to 4 November 2004, he first of all stated that he already returned to club A on 3 November 2004, and not only on 4 November 2004, as indicated by club A.
28. Moreover, he maintained that he was duly authorized by club A to travel home, because his mother was very ill. In this respect, he referred to the relevant statements of club A on its website, announcing that he was absent due to family reasons.
29. In order to prove this, he presented phone bills showing that he received several phone calls from his home country until 11 October 2004, whereby he was allegedly informed by his brother about the aggravation of their mothers health state. In continuation, he several times called a different number in his home country, whereby he informed his relatives of when he would be able to arrive there.
30. With regard to his absence from 8 November 2004 to 16 February 2005, he first of all stated that he returned on 17 February 2005, and not, as indicated by club A, on 16 February 2005.
31. Moreover, he maintained that he could not return for the pre-season, since club A did not provide him with a ticket to return from his home country.
32. In this regard, he stated that he had informed club A verbally that he would not return if he had not been provided with a flight ticket, and if the outstanding salary had not been paid to him.
33. On 17 February 2005, due to the verbal promise of club A that all the outstanding salaries would be paid upon his arrival, he returned to club A with a flight ticket which he bought himself. In continuation, club A, however, only paid the salary for September 2004 but neither the other outstanding salaries nor the ticket.
34. The player also stated that he was not aware of any disciplinary procedure against him by club A, which led to the fine club A mentioned.
35. On account of the above, the player concluded that he terminated the employment contract with just cause.

Position of the club C

36. On 16 June 2005, club C provided FIFA with its answer to the claim of club A, and requested that the claim shall be dismissed, since the player terminated the employment contract with club A with just cause.
37. Therefore, club C is of the opinion that it did not infringe the FIFA Regulations for the Status and Transfer of Players when it signed an employment contract with the player in question.
38. In this regard, club C maintained that before it signed the employment contract with the player concerned, the player presented the termination notice, which he sent to club A on 10 March 2005, whereby he had stated that the contract was terminated with just cause since the monthly salaries for the last five months were outstanding. Moreover, at that time the player had stated that he was not bound to any club and could be hired by any club.
39. Finally, club C stated that if it should be considered that the player had no just cause to terminate the employment contract with club A, club C would not have acted illicitly, since it would be the players responsibility to have induced the club into such error.

II. CONSIDERATIONS OF THE DISPUTE RESOLUTION CHAMBER

As to the competence of the Dispute Resolution Chamber

1. First of all, the Dispute Resolution Chamber (DRC) analysed whether it was competent to deal with the matter at stake. In this respect, it referred to art. 18 par. 2 and 3 of the Rules Governing the Procedures of the Players' Status Committee and the Dispute Resolution Chamber. The present matter was submitted to FIFA on 20 May 2005, as a consequence the DRC concluded that the previous Procedural Rules (edition 2001) on matters pending before the decision making bodies of FIFA are applicable on the matter at hand.

2. Furthermore, the DRC analyzed which edition of the Regulations for the Status and Transfer of Players should be applicable as to the substance of the matter. In this respect, the Chamber referred, on the one hand, to art. 26 par. 1 and 2 of the Regulations for the Status and Transfer of Players (edition 2005) and, on the other hand, to the fact that the claim was lodged at FIFA on 20 May 2005. In view of the aforementioned, the DRC concluded that the former FIFA Regulations for the Status and Transfer of Players (edition 2001, hereinafter: the Regulations) are applicable on the case at hand as to the substance.
3. With regard to its competence, the DRC indicated that, as established in art. 42 par. 1 lit. (b) (i), (ii) and (iii) in combination with art. 21 and following of the Regulations, it falls within the purview of the DRC to determine whether one of the parties has committed an unilateral breach of contract with or without just cause and if so, to verify whether this party is accountable for outstanding payments and whether financial or sport sanctions must be imposed.
4. As a consequence, the DRC is the competent body to decide on the present litigation involving a club on one side and a player as well as a club on the other side with different nationalities regarding a dispute in connection with an employment contract.

As to the substance

5. Entering into the substance of the matter, the DRC acknowledged the documentation contained in the file, and in view of the circumstances of the case, focused on the question whether an unjustified breach of the employment contract between the player and club A occurred and which party is responsible for such breach of contract, whether inducement to breach of contract occurred, and to verify and decide if sanctions for breach of contract and inducement to breach of contract have to be applied.

Responsibility for the breach of contract

6. As far as the question of the responsibility for the breach of contract is concerned, the DRC first of all acknowledged that the players salaries until August 2004 were duly paid. Furthermore, the DRC took note of the fact that the salary for September 2004 was paid by club A only in March 2005, and that the salaries as of October 2004 were not paid at all.
7. In view of the above, the DRC stated that, as a general rule, the persistent failure of a club to pay the salaries of a player without just cause is to be considered as an unjustified breach of an employment contract by the club.
8. In the issue at stake, the DRC was of the unanimous opinion that the behaviour of club A, i.e. the non-payment of the players salaries as of October 2004, has to be considered as a persistent failure of a club to comply with its financial obligations towards a player.
9. Consequently, the DRC had to analyse if the club had any reason justifying the non-payment of the salaries in question.
10. In this regard, the DRC took note of the fact that the player was absent from the club from 18 October 2004 to 17 February 2005, with the exception of a few days from 3 or 4 November to 8 November 2004.
11. In view of this, the DRC underlined that, as a general rule, a long-lasting absence of a player from his club without authorisation and without other just cause is a justifying reason for the suspension of the payment of the players salaries and moreover is to be considered as an unjustified breach of the employment contract by the player.
12. In this respect, the DRC had to deliberate whether the player was authorised or had any other just cause to temporarily leave the club.
13. First of all, with regard to the period from 18 November to 15 December 2004, the DRC acknowledged that this period was undisputedly considered as the players vacation.
14. With regard to the other absences, the DRC had to analyse the evidence submitted by the player, according to which his absence should have been authorised, i.e. the list of phone calls and an extract from club As official website.
15. With regard to the list of phone calls, the DRC took note of the fact that the said list contained some phone numbers. In view of this, the DRC had to declare, however, that from this fact as such could not be derived that 1) the players mother, as alleged by the player, was indeed in a bad state of health, and that 2) the club authorised the players absence for the period of time in question.
16. As far as the extracts from club As official website are concerned, the DRC took note of the fact that it is undisputed that club A declared on its website that the player had left the club for family

reasons. The DRC, however, took note as well of club As position that such statement was made only to preserve a good image of the player, but that it did not correspond with the reality. In this regard, the DRC concluded that the reason of the players absence was not established. Moreover, even presuming that family reasons were at the basis of the players absence, club A did not state on its website that the players absence was authorised.

17. In view of the above, the DRC came to the conclusion that the player had not presented any evidence that his absence should have been authorised except for the vacation period.
18. The DRC then had to analyse if the player had any other just cause to temporarily leave his club.
19. In this respect, the DRC referred to the fact that at the moment of the first unauthorised departure of the player, one months salary was unpaid. In view of this, the DRC deliberated whether the non-payment of one monthly salary is a just cause for a player to leave his club without permission, but came to the conclusion that one outstanding monthly salary does not allow the player to leave his club without authorisation.
20. Moreover, the DRC declared that family reasons, i.e. the mothers bad health state, is also not to be considered to be a just cause for a player to leave his club without permission.
21. Finally, with respect to the players complaint that club A, in violation of its contractual obligations, did not provide him with a flight ticket to return to club A, the DRC had to declare that the player did not submit any written evidence regarding such obligation of club A. Therefore, in application of the principle of the burden of proof, the DRC emphasized that the alleged failure of club A to provide the player with the necessary flight ticket cannot be considered as a just cause for the player not to return to club A.
22. As a result, the DRC came to the conclusion that the player had no just cause to leave his club.
23. On account of the above, the DRC concluded that the player had neither an authorisation nor a just cause to be absent from the club except for his vacation. Therefore, his absence from club A was illegitimate from 18 October 2004 to 17 February 2005 with the exception of four to five days in November 2004 and the vacation of 28 days from 18 November to 15 December 2004.
24. In conclusion, his absence was illegitimate during three out of four months of absence. In view of this duration of absence, the DRC was of the unanimous opinion that the absence of the player from club A is to be considered a long lasting absence in the sense of the above outlined principle (cf. pt.11).
25. In consequence, the club had a justifying reason for the suspension of the payment of the players salaries. Moreover, the players absence without authorisation or just cause is to be considered as an unjustified breach of the employment contract by the player.

Consequences of the unjustified breach of contract against the player

26. On account of the above-mentioned conclusion, the DRC had to address the issue of possible sanctions against the player for unjustified breach of contract, in accordance with article 21 and following of the Regulations.
27. In this context, the DRC first of all pointed out that the employment contract in question was signed on 1 February 2004. Moreover, the DRC stated that the date to be considered as the date of the breach of the employment contract by the player is 10 March 2005, the day when the player notified the club that he unilaterally terminates the contract.
28. In view of this, the DRC declared that the player had breached the employment contract without just cause undoubtedly during the so-called protected period as provided for in article 21 par. 1 of the Regulations. Therefore, according to the afore-mentioned provision, financial and sports sanctions shall be imposed on the player.
29. The DRC first focussed its analysis on the amount of compensation for the unjustified breach of contract due by the player to club A and examined the objective criteria listed in article 22 of the Regulations.
30. The first criteria the DRC took into consideration was the amount of transfer compensation paid by club A to the former club of the player amortised over the length of the breached employment contract (article 22 (3) of the Regulations).
31. The employment contract was signed on 1 February 2004, valid until 1 February 2007 (36 months), and not any-longer respected by the player as of mid October 2004, i.e. after 9 months of its validity. Therefore, the transfer compensation paid by club A to the former club of the player, i.e. the amount of USD 1,800,000 was amortised to ¼, i.e. USD 450,000. The non-amortised part of the transfer compensation amounts to USD 1,350,000.

32. In this respect, the Chamber explained that, as a general rule, the amortisation of a transfer compensation is determined by the period of effective execution of the employment contract, in the present case from the signature of the employment contract to the first unexcused absence of the player in mid October 2004. Moreover, the Chamber emphasised that the end of the effective execution of an employment contract does not have to coincide with the date of the breach of contract.
33. The second criteria the DRC took into consideration was the remuneration under the employment contract between the player and club A, and the length of time remaining on the said contract, i.e. the rest value of the employment contract (art 22 (1) and (2) of the Regulations). In this regard, the DRC firstly stated that despite the fact that the player and club A signed two employment contracts stipulating different amounts of salaries (USD 10,000, resp. USD 30,000), a tacit agreement apparently existed that only the salary of USD 30,000 was actually applied, since the salary payment of USD 30,000 (for September 2004) was undisputedly considered by both parties as the entire monthly salary. Secondly, the DRC took note of the fact that the player would have been entitled to receive from March 2005 to January 2007 on account of salaries the amount of USD 690,000 (USD 30,000 per month).
34. On account of the above, the DRC calculated the amount of compensation for breach of contract as follows:
    - non- amortised transfer compensation USD 1,350,000
    - plus remaining value of contract USD 690,000

    total USD 2,040,000
35. The DRC furthermore analysed the stances of the player and club A, in order to consider if there were any exceptional circumstances mitigating or aggravating the amount of compensation.
36. In this respect, the DRC acknowledged that on the one hand, club A had not complied with all terms of the contract signed, particularly with its obligation to pay the players salary for September 2004 without delay. This could have a mitigating effect on the amount of the financial compensation to be paid by the player to club A.
37. On the other hand, the DRC stated that the attitude of the player could be judged as particularly reproachable. In fact, the player was absent from club A without authorisation or just cause during three months. The damage caused by the player is not only of a financial nature, but also a sporting one, since club A could not rely on the services of the player during the period of absence. This could have an aggravating effect on the amount of the financial compensation to be paid by the player to club A.
38. In view of the fact that the stances of the player and club A have on the one hand a mitigating effect and on the other hand an aggravating effect, the DRC concluded that the exceptional circumstances derived from the stances of the parties compensate each other. Therefore, the compensation for breach of contract to be paid by the player to club A is USD 2,040,000.
39. Furthermore, the DRC decided that in accordance with article 14 par. 3 of the Regulations governing the Application of the Regulations for the Status and Transfer of Players, the new club of the player, i.e. club C, shall be deemed jointly responsible for the payment of the amount of compensation the player has to pay, if the afore-mentioned amount is not paid to club A within one month of notification of the present decision.
40. The DRC then turned to the question of the sports sanctions to be imposed on the player in accordance with article 23 par. 1 of the Regulations.
41. In this respect, the DRC referred to the basic sanction of four months on the players eligibility to participate in any official football matches in case of an unjustified breach of contract by a player. Moreover, the DRC referred to the possibility of taking into consideration exceptional circumstances based on which the sanction could be shortened or extended.
42. The DRC then stated that the player was fully responsible for the breach of contract, since he was absent from the club for a long lasting period of time without any permission from the side of the club. Besides that, the DRC stated that the same mitigating and aggravating circumstances which were taken into consideration when the amount of compensation for breach of contract was fixed, had to be taken into consideration as well when the sports sanction is to be determined, but in this respect as well compensate each other, and therefore, have no effect on the duration of the players sports sanction.
43. Therefore, the DRC decided that the player had to be sanctioned with a restriction of four months on his eligibility to participate in any official football matches as from the notification of this decision.

Consequences against the club for inducement to unjustified breach of contract

44. In continuation, the DRC had to consider and pass a decision on the request made by club A against club C for sports sanctions for inducement to contractual breach, in accordance with the articles 22 and 23 par. 2 (c) of the Regulations.
45. Considering the substance of the matter in order to establish the alleged responsibility of club C for inducement to contractual breach, the DRC preliminarily deemed it appropriate to recall some of the key events in the contractual breach between the player and club A. In particular, it was recalled that, by letter dated 10 March 2005, the player communicated to club A, without any valid reason, that he terminated the contract. Subsequently, on 13 April 2005, the player and club C signed a new employment contract, which was registered with the Football Association of club C on 26 May 2005.
46. The DRC then focussed its analysis on the accountability of club C for inducement to the contractual breach between the player and club A.
47. In particular, the DRC first referred to lit. (c) of art. 23 par. 2 of the Regulations, according to which, a club seeking to register a player who has unilaterally breached a contract during the protected period will be presumed to have induced a breach of contract.
48. As a consequence, it falls under club Cs responsibility to demonstrate that they should not be held responsible for having induced the breach of contract.
49. In this respect the DRC examined the position of club C and thereby noted that club C, when it signed the employment contract with the player, based itself only on the players statement that he had a just cause to terminate the contract with club A, instead of acting with the advised caution and to contact club A in order to clarify the situation before signing an employment contract with the player in question.
50. In view of this, the DRC declared that on the one hand, it appears that club C has acted with very serious negligence. On the other hand, the DRC concluded that club C did not provide any crucial position or evidence setting aside the presumption contained in article 23 par. 2 lit. (c) of the Regulations and corroborating its request to dismiss the claim for sports sanction against it.
51. Without fail, the DRC went further on analysing the sports sanctions that could be imposed on club C for having induced the contractual breach.
52. The DRC deemed that it in view of the clear circumstances of the matter and the failure of club C to set aside the presumption contained in article 23 par. 2 lit. (c) of the Regulations, it has to be presumed that the player was induced by club C to terminate his contract. Therefore, it was left with no other choice than to strictly apply the contents of art. 23 par. 2 of the Regulations, according to which, in case of a club inducing the breach of contract, if the breach occurs during the protected period, the sanction shall be a ban on registering any new player, either nationally or internationally, for two consecutive transfer periods.
53. In light of all the above circumstances, the DRC concluded that club C is responsible for inducement to breach of contract and decided that a ban is imposed on club C to register any new player, either nationally or internationally, until the expiry of the second transfer period following the notification of this decision.

Further requests

54. The request of club A for interest on the financial compensation at a rate of 15 % as of the date of the breach of contract was dismissed since it was excessive. Instead, an interest rate of 5% per year was adjudicated in case of non-payment of the fixed compensation within 30 days of notification of the present decision, as of expiry of this deadline.
55. Moreover, the request of club A for reimbursement of its legal costs was rejected in compliance with the constant and continuous jurisprudence of the DRC with regard to such requests.
56. Finally, and obviously, the DRC rejected all counterclaims from the player against club A.

III. DECISION OF THE DISPUTE RESOLUTION CHAMBER

1. The claim of the club A is partially accepted.
2. The player is ordered to pay USD 2,040,000 to the club A within 30 days as of notification of the present decision.
3. The club C is jointly responsible for the payment of the above-mentioned amount if the same is not paid within one month of notification of the present decision.

4. If the aforementioned amount is not paid within the stated deadline, an interest rate of 5% per year shall apply, as from expiry of the stated deadline.
5. A restriction of four months on his eligibility to play in official matches is imposed on the player. This sanction shall take effect from the start of the first season of the players current club following the notification of the present decision.
6. The club C is banned from registering any new player, either nationally or internationally, until the expiry of the second transfer period following the notification of this decision.
7. In the event that the player or the club C do not comply with the present decision, the matter shall be submitted to FIFAs Disciplinary Committee, so that the necessary disciplinary sanctions may be imposed.
8. Any further request of the club A is rejected.
9. All requests of the player against the club A are rejected.
10. The club A is directed to inform the player and the club immediately of the account number to which the remittance is to be made, and to notify the Dispute Resolution Chamber about the receipt of the payment.
11. According to art. 60 par. 1 of the FIFA Statutes this decision may be appealed before the Court of Arbitration for Sport (CAS). The statement of appeal must be sent to the CAS directly within 21 days of receiving notification of this decision and has to contain all elements in accordance with point 2 of the directives issued by the CAS, copy of which we enclose hereto. Within another 10 days following the expiry of the time limit for the filing of the statement of appeal, the appellant shall file with the CAS a brief stating the facts and legal arguments giving rise to the appeal (cf. point 4 of the directives).

36619
DECISION OF THE DISPUTE RESOLUTION CHAMBER
passed in Zurich, Switzerland, on 23 March 2006,
in the following composition:
Slim Aloulou (Tunisia), Chairman Mario Gallavotti (Italy), Member Peter Friend (Australia), Member Mick McGuire (England), Member Gerardo Movilla (Spain), Member
on the claim presented by
Club A, as Claimant
against
Player B, as Respondent
regarding a dispute about the employment contract concluded between the parties.

I. FACTS OF THE CASE

1. The player B (hereinafter; the player), born on 8 April 1987, concluded an employment contract with the club A (hereinafter; the club) on 6 December 2004, valid as of 1 December 2004 until 31 December 2006.
2. Annex 2 to the contract stipulates a monthly salary of USD 3,000.
3. Due to the players minor age at that time, the contract and all annexes were faxed to his guardian, who co-signed them.
4. In May 2005, the player joined his U-20 association team for a preparation camp for the U-20 World Cup in the Netherlands.
5. On 27 May 2005, the players Association had to hand to the organisation committee of the U-20 World Cup the official final list of players of its squad. The player in question was not included in the list.
6. On 7 June 2005, the club requested FIFAs intervention, since the player in question did not resume duty after it was announced that he was not in the official final list of players of the squad of his Associations representative U-20 team.
7. The player did not respect the request to return to the club, but on 2 July 2005, contacted FIFA, maintaining that he had been deceived by the CEO of the club to sign the above-mentioned employment contract.
8. On 1 August 2005, the player completed his former submission, requesting the annulment of the employment contract and disciplinary sanctions against the club.

9. First of all, the player complained that the contract does not stipulate any obligation of the club to provide him with the basic requirements, such as accommodation, feeding and educational support.
10. Moreover, he stated that a third club X was responsible for his training and education, and that therefore the club could not have signed an employment contract with him. The player did not submit any agreement signed by him and the club X.
11. Finally, the player accused the club A of non respect of the FIFA regulations regarding the protection of minors, because the relevant contract was signed when he still was a minor. In this regard, the player also complained that the contract was signed without contacting his agent beforehand, but sent to his guardian for signature.
12. The player furthermore submitted a statement of his guardian, by means of which the latter confirmed having co-signed the contract in question. The guardian, however, alleges that as far as annex 2 of the contract is concerned, only the signature sheet was sent to him, therefore he was not aware of the contractual salary.
13. On 15 August 2005, the club answered to the players accusations by stating that the player was not deceived into signing the relevant employment contract, but that he signed the contract in free will.
14. Besides the above, the club refrained from making any further statements, as it appeared that the situation could be resolved amicably between the parties, since according to media reports, the player was about to return to the club.
15. On 22 August 2005, the player contested that he would be about to return to the club.
16. On 26 August 2005, the club stated that the player was bound by an employment contract to the club and that he therefore had to resume duty immediately. The club, however, was still of the opinion that the matter could be solved amicably.
17. In contradiction to the afore described circumstances, the club now stated that the player and the club had signed a contract on 8 April 2005 (instead of 6 December 2004).
18. On 6 September 2005, the player stated that an amicable settlement of the matter was not likely.
19. The player was still of the opinion that he was deceived by the club when he signed the employment contract.
20. Moreover, the player denied having signed an employment contract with the club on 8 April 2005, the date when he turned 18 years of age.
21. On 30 September 2005, the club informed FIFA that the player had resumed duty on 5 September 2005.
22. Moreover, the club stated that the player had a work permit valid until 31 December 2006, and that all his salaries were paid so far, despite his absence.
23. In continuation, the club reserved its right to make a claim against the player for his unexcused absence from 27 May to 5 September 2005, but for the time being, refrained from submitting an official claim, since the player apparently acted under high pressure of his counsels.
24. Finally, the submission contained a copy of the employment contract between the parties concerned, dated 8 April 2005, and valid as of 8 April 2005 until 31 December 2006.
25. On 25 October 2005, the player informed FIFA that he insisted on a formal decision to be taken by the Dispute Resolution Chamber.
26. First of all, the player confirmed having resumed duty with the club on 5 September 2005, and in this regard, also confirmed that the club respected its financial obligations towards him.
27. In continuation, he insisted that he and his guardian did not sign any contract with the club on 8 April 2005. He instead alleged that the CEO of the club altered the date on the initial contract dated 6 December 2004. In this regard, he furthermore stated that on 8 April 2005, the signature of his guardian would anyway not have been necessary, since on that date, he turned 18 years of age.
28. Finally, he stated that he was illegally registered for the club, since his former Association allegedly never sent his International Transfer Certificate to the new Association.
29. On 7 December 2005, the club informed FIFA that the player in question again left the club without permission on 28 November 2005, and therefore requested FIFA to intervene so that the player would immediately return to the club.
30. On 11 December 2005, the club provided FIFA with its final position on the matter, and thereby made, inter alia, the following statement:
"The contract [dated 8 April 2005] seems to be co-signed by the player's guardian, but that was because of an administrative error made by an official of the club some of the pages from an earlier option contract was delivered to the Association, which recognised it and issued a professional player's licence."

31. Moreover, the club stated that the employment contract with the player was valid, since the player accepted the contract by acting accordingly.
32. On 15 February 2006, the player submitted his answer to the clubs request for immediate return, and thereby maintained that he was absent from the club due to his participation with his Association team in an international tournament. In continuation, he stated that on 16 February 2006, he allegedly had to attend to an award ceremony. Finally, he stated that he planed to rejoin the club upon conclusion of the activities connected with such ceremony.
33. Besides the above, he still maintained that the employment contract binding him to the club was not valid, since he was deceived into signing the said contract.
34. NB: Through investigations carried out by FIFA, it was established that the players new Association requested the issuance of the players International Transfer Certificate from the players former Association on 20 August 2004. In reply to such request, the latter issued the players International Transfer Certificate on 23 August 2004.

II. CONSIDERATIONS OF THE DISPUTE RESOLUTION CHAMBER

1. First of all, the Dispute Resolution Chamber (DRC) analysed whether it was competent to deal with the matter at stake. In this respect, it referred to art. 18 par. 2 and 3 of the Rules Governing the Procedures of the Players' Status Committee and the Dispute Resolution Chamber. The present matter was submitted to FIFA on 7 June 2005, as a consequence the Chamber concluded that the previous Procedural Rules (edition 2001) on matters pending before the decision making bodies of FIFA are applicable on the matter at hand.
2. With regard to the competence of the DRC, art. 42 par. 1 lit. (b) (i) of the FIFA Regulations for the Status and Transfer of Players (edition 2001) establishes that, the triggering elements of an employment-related dispute (i.e. whether a contract was breached, with or without just cause, or sporting just cause) will be decided by the Dispute Resolution Chamber.
3. As a consequence, the Dispute Resolution Chamber is the competent body to decide on the present litigation involving a club and a player with different nationalities regarding a dispute in connection with an employment contract.
4. Subsequently, the members of the Chamber analyzed which edition of the Regulations for the Status and Transfer of Players should be applicable as to the substance of the matter. In this respect, the Chamber referred, on the one hand, to art. 26 par. 1 and 2 of the Regulations for the Status and Transfer of Players (edition 2005) and, on the other hand, to the fact that the relevant contract at the basis of the present dispute was signed on 6 December 2004 and the claim was lodged at FIFA on 7 June 2005. In view of the aforementioned, the Chamber concluded that the former FIFA Regulations for the Status and Transfer of Players (edition 2001, hereafter: the Regulations) are applicable on the case at hand as to the substance.
5. Entering into the substance of the matter, the DRC acknowledged the documentation contained in the file, and in view of the circumstances of the case, focused on the question whether the employment contract between the club and the player was to be considered as null and void or if the player had to resume duty with the club.
6. In this respect, the DRC had, in particular, to analyse the following argumentations (in italics) forwarded by the player, according to which the said employment contract, from the players point of view, should be declared null and void.
7. 1) The player had been deceived by the CEO of the club to sign the abovementioned employment contract.
8. The DRC acknowledged that the player alleged that he had been deceived to sign the employment contract in question, but that he had neither outlined how this should have happened, nor submitted any clear evidence corroborating such allegation.
9. Therefore, in application of the principle of the burden of proof, and due to lack of evidence, the DRC had to reject the first argument of the player.
10. 2) The employment contract does not stipulate any obligation of the club to provide the player with the basic requirements, such as accommodation, feeding and educational support.
11. The DRC deliberated if clubs are obliged, according to the Regulations, to provide their players with basic requirements, such as accommodation, feeding and educational support.
12. In this respect, the DRC could only refer to art. 12 par. 1 b) of the Regulations, based on which an international transfer of a minor within the EU/EEA shall only be permitted in case the player

concerned has reached the minimum working age in the new training clubs country, and if suitable arrangements are guaranteed for the players sports training and academic education by the new training club.

13. The DRC had to clarify, however, that the above-mentioned provision 1) does not concern the validity of an employment contract, but only the possibility of an international transfer of a minor, and 2) does apply only to transfers of players between two clubs affiliated to Associations in the EU/EEA.
14. In the present case, the player challenged the validity of the employment contract, but not the validity of his international transfer.
15. Moreover, the international transfer of the player did obviously not occur between two clubs affiliated to Associations in the EU/EEA. Therefore, the above-mentioned provision does not apply to the matter at stake
16. In conclusion, the DRC had to reject such argumentation of the player.
17. 3) The club X was responsible for the players training and education, therefore the club could not have signed an employment contract with the player.
18. The DRC acknowledged that the player had not submitted any agreement signed between him and club X, according to which club X would be responsible for his training and education.
19. Therefore, in application of the principle of the burden of proof, and due to lack of evidence, the DRC had as well to reject the third argument of the player.
20. 4) The club had not respected the FIFA regulations regarding the protection of minors, because the relevant contract was signed when he still was a minor.
21. With regard to this argument, the DRC emphasized that the FIFA regulations regarding the protection of minors (i.e. art. 12 of the Regulations) do not bar the conclusion of an employment contract between a minor player and a club, but only the international transfer of such player, i.e. the issuance of the players International Transfer Certificate.
22. In view of the players request that the employment contract in question shall be declared invalid, the DRC had to state that the provision invoked by the player does not have any effect on the validity of the relevant employment contract, and therefore had to reject argument 4 of the player.
23. The DRC, however, took note of the fact that the players International Transfer Certificate was requested by the players new Association and issued by the players former Association before the player had reached the age of 18. Therefore, the DRC decided, ex officio, that the questions related to the issuance of the players International Transfer Certificate shall be referred to the FIFA Players Status Committee, for consideration and possible measures.
24. 5) The contract was signed without contacting the players agent beforehand, but sent to his guardian for signature.
25. The DRC underlined that if a minor player signs an employment contract, the same must be co-signed by the players legal representative/guardian in order to be valid. There is, however, no obligation contained in the applicable Regulations of FIFA preventing a minor player from signing an employment contract with a club without contacting his agent beforehand. The same applies for a club entering into a contract with a minor player. Such club has no obligation to contact the players agent before the conclusion of an employment contract.
26. Therefore, and in view of the fact that the minor players legal representative/guardian undisputedly had co-signed the employment contract, also from this point of view the DRC considered the said contract as having been concluded validly, and hence had to reject argument 5 of the player.
27. 6) As far as annex 2 of the contract is concerned, only the signature sheet was sent to the guardian, therefore he was not aware of the contractual salary.
28. The DRC duly acknowledged this argument of the player, but once again had to take note of the fact that no evidence at all was presented in order to corroborate such position. Equally, the DRC emphasised that if indeed only the signature sheet had been forwarded to the players guardian, which was not proven, it would have been the guardians responsibility to insist on receiving the entire annex prior to signing it.
29. Therefore, in application of the principle of the burden of proof, and due to lack of evidence, the DRC had as well to reject this argument of the player.
30. Moreover, the DRC declared that signing a contract without knowing the contracts content, and without insisting to be provided with or informed about the relevant content is a negligence by the signatory which cannot have consequences on the contractual partner.

31. Assuming the guardian of the player was indeed not aware of the entire contents of annex 2 when he signed it, it was negligent of him to sign it nevertheless, instead of insisting to be provided with the entire document. The consequences of such negligence by the players guardian could not be imposed on the club.
32. 7) The player denied having signed an employment contract with the club on 8 April 2005; the CEO of the club altered the date on the initial contract dated 6 December 2004.
33. The DRC emphasised that since the contract dated 8 April 2005 did neither modify the rights and obligations of the parties resulting from the contract dated 6 December 2004 nor the expiry date of the contractual relationship between the parties concerned, an annulment of the contract dated 8 April 2005 would not have any effect on the validity of the contract dated 6 December 2004.
34. Moreover, the DRC stated that in the past, it had, on several occasions, to deal with cases concerning the alleged forgery of signatures and documents. In such cases, the DRC continuously established that FIFA is not competent to decide upon matters of criminal law, such as signature or document forgery, but that such affairs fall into the jurisdiction of the competent national criminal authority.
35. As long as the possible forgery of the contract dated 8 April 2005 is not established, the DRC has to base its conclusion and decision on the presumption that the contract in question is authentic. All the more, as the player did not present any indication at all which would at least suggest that his allegation could be correct.
36. 8) The player was illegally registered for the club, since his former Association allegedly never sent his International Transfer Certificate to his new Association.
37. In view of the investigations carried out by FIFA, by means of which it was established that the players International Transfer Certificate was requested and issued by the competent Associations, the last argument of the player was declared by the DRC as being wrong.
38. In view of all the above, the DRC concluded that the invalidity of the employment contract in question, i.e. the contract dated 6 December 2004, was not established by the claimant. Therefore, in application of the principle of pacta sunt servanda, which is a basic principle to every legal system in the world, the DRC decided that the player had to resume duty with the club immediately.
39. Finally, the DRC also pointed out that the player had explicitly recognised that the club had fully complied with the payment of his salary and thus had always adhered to its contractual obligations.

III. DECISION OF THE DISPUTE RESOLUTION CHAMBER

1. The claim of the club is accepted.
2. The counterclaim of the player is rejected.
3. The player has to resume duty with the club immediately.
4. In the event that the player does not comply with the present decision, the matter shall be submitted to FIFAs Disciplinary Committee, so that the necessary disciplinary sanctions may be imposed.
5. The present file shall be forwarded to the Players' Status Committee for consideration regarding the circumstances of the issuance of the International Transfer Certificate for the player.
6. According to art. 60 par. 1 of the FIFA Statutes this decision may be appealed before the Court of Arbitration for Sport (CAS). The statement of appeal must be sent to the CAS directly within 21 days of receiving notification of this decision and has to contain all elements in accordance with point 2 of the directives issued by the CAS, copy of which we enclose hereto. Within another 10 days following the expiry of the time limit for the filing of the statement of appeal, the appellant shall file with the CAS a brief stating the facts and legal arguments giving rise to the appeal (cf. point 4 of the directives).

36858

DECISION OF THE DISPUTE RESOLUTION CHAMBER

passed in Zurich, Switzerland, on 23 March 2006,
in the following composition:
Slim Aloulou (Tunisia), Chairman Mario Gallavotti (Italy), member Peter Friend (Australia), member Mick McGuire (England), member Gerardo Movilla (Spain), member
on the claim presented by the player
H, G, as Claimant/Counter-Respondent
against the club

O, P as Respondent/Counter-Claimant
and involving the club D, S as Counter-Co-Respondent
regarding a contractual dispute between the player and the club and the players new club.

I. FACTS OF THE CASE

1. The player H, Claimant, and the club O, Respondent, concluded on 20 August 2002 an employment contract valid from 20 August 2002 to 30 June 2005.
2. Clause 2 par. 2 of the aforementioned contract stipulates an option in favour of the club to "irrecusably, ineludibly" and unilaterally extend the duration of the contract for the two sporting seasons 2005/06 and 2006/07, exercisable until 30 June 2005 by means of a registered letter with notice of receipt sent to the player's domicile or by means of personal handing over.
3. Clause 4 par. 5 of the relevant employment contract stipulates a penalty clause according to which the player has to pay to the club the amount of EUR 2,000,000 in the following cases:
   - if the player terminates the contract unilaterally and without just cause,
   - in the case that a contract is concluded with a new club during the course of the contract,
   - if the aforementioned option right (note: clause 2 par. 2) is violated,
   - by denying the establishing of the contract agreed in the relevant extension clause (note: clause 2 par. 2)
   - or by not complying with the establishing of the contract without just cause, when required.
4. On 4 July 2005, the player and the club D, signed an employment contract valid for the sporting seasons 2005/06, 2006/07, 2007/08 and 2008/09.
5. On 2 August 2005, the Football Federation of the club D contacted FIFA asking for its assistance in obtaining the International Transfer Certificate (ITC) from the Football Federation of the club O for the player A.
6. In the meantime, FIFA was informed that a contractual dispute had arisen between the player and the club O, since the player was of the opinion that he was free to register with the club D. In fact, the player emphasised that the unilaterally option in favour of the club O, to extend the duration of the contract, firstly, had not been exercised by the club, because the club communicated such an intention neither by registered letter, nor by personal handing over as stipulated in the employment contract, and secondly, because the option clause itself is not valid. Thus, the player deemed to be free to enter into a new contract with another football club. A corresponding claim to determine this alleged right has been submitted by the player in front of FIFA on 3 August 2005.
7. The club O, on its part, asserts having executed the option right in time. As a consequence, the club is of the opinion that the duration of the employment contract with the player has been extended for the sporting seasons 2005/06 and 2006/07.
8. On 18 August 2005, the Single Judge of the Players' Status Committee decided that under the given circumstances the Football Federation of the club D could be authorized to provisionally register the player A with its affiliated club D with immediate effect, pending the outcome of the contractual dispute between the player and the club O.
9. With regard to the substance of the contractual dispute, the club O presented FIFA on 24 August 2005 its position on the players claim and lodged a counter-claim against the player A, Claimant/Counter-Respondent, and the club D, Counter-CoRespondent. According to O, Respondent/Counter-Claimant, the above-mentioned option right to unilaterally extend the duration of the employment contract with the player was an indispensable condition for it to conclude the contract.
10. Furthermore, the club is of the opinion that it duly executed the option right. It maintains that it delivered a respective letter to the player A, contents of which were read by the player, but the player refused to sign the relevant delivery bond. In this respect, the club presented a copy of the delivery bond not signed by the player and a witness statement of the players alleged refusing to sign the said delivery bond on 12 May 2005. Moreover, the club explains that the player had been expressly called up to go to the X Notary Office for this purpose on 19 May 2005.
11. According to the Respondent/Counter-Claimant, the option right is legal, since it was previously negotiated and agreed upon by both parties and since the salaries for the future extended contractual duration had already been established in the original contract. In this respect, the club emphasised that a salary increase had been assured to the player.
12. O further explains that the stipulated option right corresponds by all legal effects to a labour sportive promise, since it does not contain an automatically renewal, but a contractual obligation

to sign another employment contract, i.e. a contract for the 2005/06 and 2006/07 sporting seasons. Furthermore, the option right is legal in the clubs point of view, since the player can refuse to sign a new contract anytime, provided that he respects the agreed penalty clause (cf. above). Also, the club O explains that such option right is foreseen in the national law. According to O, the employment contract concluded with the player fulfils all the requirements of the national law: a written promise, the will and obligation to sign the definitive and pledged contract in a irrefutable and unquestionable way, the date of the beginning and the ending of the pledged contract and the indication of the remuneration.

13. Furthermore, the club O alleges that during the three passed sporting seasons the player never invocated the possible nullity of the option right. Consequently, the player recognized the option right and considered it always as valid and effective. The club further maintains that the aforementioned behaviour of the player created the belief that he would always respect that option right and would sign the pledged contract. Also, the said behaviour made the club decide not to contract other players for the position of Mr. A.
14. O explained that by signing a new contract with the Counter-Co-Respondent the player acted with bad faith, "in venire contra factum proprium" and violated contractual obligations. As a consequence, the club O is of the opinion that the player has to pay the amount of EUR 2,000,000 agreed between the parties according to the penalty clause (cf. above). The club maintains that this compensation paid is fair and adequate considering the transfer compensation for the player of EUR 344,172, the amount payable to the player for a further transfer (the parties agreed on the participation of the player to 15 % of any future compensation paid to O), the salaries paid and to be paid to the player during 5 sporting seasons (EUR 513,764) and the international nature of the transfer.
15. Finally, the club O maintains that the club D is co-responsible for the payment of the aforementioned compensation, because it induced the player to the non-compliance of his contract.
16. In reply hereto, the player A adheres to his position and denies all allegations made by the club O. He insists that the employment contract with O expired on 30 June 2005 and that he, therefore, was free to sign with D. He further reiterates that the illegal option right had not been executed by the club. In this respect, he denies the veracity of the witness statement, since it was drafted by employees of O. The player ascertains that he never received any kind of letter regarding the extension of the contract. Consequently, he could not have refused to sign such letter. The player rejects the clubs allegation by asking: Why did the club not notify the execution of the said option right by registered mail or a notary, at least after the alleged unsuccessful personal handing over of the alleged letter?
17. Furthermore, the Claimant/Counter-Respondent explains that the option right is null and void because it does not correspond to a contractual promise, but to a clause, which obliges the player to extend his employment relation for two sporting seasons, whether he likes it or not. The fact that the employer decides only and exclusively on the extension of the contractual duration is - according to the player - unacceptable. The player further insists that the overall excessive penalty clause of EUR 2,000,000 definitively violates the principle of contractual freedom, and such a clause would be, therefore, "nulla ab initio" without the possibility of validation.
18. The club D, Counter-Co-Respondent, denies all the allegations made by the club O and rejects the claim. The club D ascertains that it did not induce the player to a breach of contract, since at the time of signing the contract with the player, there was no contractual link between the club O and the player any longer as the relevant contract expired on 30 June 2005. Furthermore, the club D shares the opinion of the player, according to which the stipulated option right is null and void.
19. In reply hereto, the club O insists that it executed the option right, because it delivered the letter to the player A personally, by means of which it formally exercised the aforementioned option right on 12 May 2005. In this respect, the club enumerates four witnesses, who can allegedly testify the aforementioned allegation. The club further insists that the option right was freely negotiated, i.e. not imposed on the player, and for its inclusion into the contract the player has received the amounts and benefits fixed in the contract. Finally, the club explains that any juridical promise is, by nature, irrefutable and unquestionable by one or both parties.
20. With regard to the alleged inducement of D to a breach of contract, the club O states that the co-responsibility does not depend only on the practice of any illicit fact, but results and is presumed following the mere fact of signing a contract with a player still under contract with another club, in case the player has the obligation to pay compensation to his previous club.
21. In reply hereto, the player and the club D adhere to their previously submitted positions.

II. CONSIDERATIONS OF THE DISPUTE RESOLUTION CHAMBER

1. First of all, the Chamber analysed whether it was competent to deal with the matter at stake. In this respect, it referred to art. 18 par. 2 and 3 of the Rules Governing the Procedures of the Players' Status Committee and the Dispute Resolution Chamber. The present matter was submitted to FIFA on 3 August 2005, as a consequence the Chamber concluded that the revised Rules Governing Procedures (edition 2005) on matters pending before the decision making bodies of FIFA are applicable to the matter at hand.
2. With regard to the competence of the Chamber, art. 3 par. 1 of the abovementioned Rules states that the Dispute Resolution Chamber shall examine its jurisdiction in the light of articles 22 to 24 of the current version of the Regulations for the Status and Transfer of Players (edition 2005). In accordance with art. 24 par. 1 in connection with art. 22 (b) of the aforementioned Regulations, the Dispute Resolution Chamber shall adjudicate on employment-related disputes between a club and a player that have an international dimension.
3. As a consequence, the Dispute Resolution Chamber is the competent body to decide on the present litigation involving a club from the country P and a player from the country G and a club from the country S regarding a dispute in connection with an employment contract.
4. Subsequently, the members of the Chamber analyzed which edition of the Regulations for the Status and Transfer of Players should be applicable as to the substance of the matter. In this respect, the Chamber referred, on the one hand, to art. 26 par. 1 and 2 of the Regulations for the Status and Transfer of Players (edition 2005) and, on the other hand, to the fact that the relevant contract at the basis of the present dispute was signed on 20 August 2002 and the claim was lodged at FIFA on 3 August 2005. In view of the aforementioned, the Chamber concluded that the current FIFA Regulations for the Status and Transfer of Players (edition 2005, hereafter: the Regulations) are applicable on the case at hand as to the substance.
5. In continuation, and entering into the substance of the matter, the members of the Chamber acknowledged the above-mentioned facts as well as all the further documentation contained in the file.
6. To that regard, the members acknowledged that the player A and the club O signed an employment contract on 20 August 2002 for the pre-determined period of time from 20 August 2002 to 30 June 2005 with an option in favour of the club to unilaterally extend the contract for the two sporting seasons 2005/06 and 2006/07, exercisable until 30 June 2005 by means of a registered letter with notice of receipt sent to the players domicile or by means of personal handing over.
7. In this respect, the members took due note that the player demands for the clause regarding the unilateral option to be declared invalid. Furthermore, he requests that it shall be established that he is not bound to the club O any longer and was free to sign with the club D, since, firstly, the option right had not been exercised in accordance with the condition stipulated in the relevant employment contract and, secondly, the exercise of the said option right itself cannot be accepted.
8. On the other hand, the members acknowledged that the club is in particular convinced of having validly exercised its right to extend the duration of the contract for another two sporting seasons and hence is of the opinion that the player is still bound by the employment contract he signed with it on 20 August 2002, until the end of the sporting season 2006/2007. Furthermore, the club is of the firm opinion that the option right is legal, since it was previously negotiated and agreed upon by both parties, since the increasing salaries for the future extended contractual duration had already been established in the original contract, since the stipulated option right corresponds to a labour sportive promise, since the player never invocated the possible nullity of the said option right and since the player can refuse to sign a new contract anytime, provided that he respects the agreed penalty clause.
9. In consideration of these positions, the members started their deliberations by verifying whether the relevant clause in the employment contract, which awards the club the possibility to unilaterally renew the employment contract is valid or not.
10. In this respect, the Chamber firstly took note, in particular, that the player did not sign any document different from the original employment contract according to which he acknowledges and agrees explicitly with the unilateral extension of the employment contract for the sporting seasons 2005/06 and 2006/07.
11. Furthermore, and with regard to the stipulated option right in clause 2 par. 2 of the relevant employment contract, the Chamber recalled that, in accordance with its established jurisprudence,

a clause which gives one party the right to unilaterally cancel or lengthen the contract, without providing the counter-party with same rights, is a clause with disputable validity.

12. In the case at hand, the extension option contained in the relevant employment contract is unilateral to the benefit of the club only, i.e. the stronger party in the employment relationship, and may be exercised by the club during the considerable period of two football seasons. This gives the club unequal bargaining power whereas there is no apparent gain for the player, even though the conditions of the employment indeed have been increased.
13. To that specific aspect, the members noted that at the time the parties signed the employment contract, they already stipulated the wages the player would receive throughout the validity of the contract, including the period of time covered by the contract only in case the contract would be unilaterally extended by the club. In this respect, the members acknowledged particularly that the increase of the monthly stipulated salary during the said period of time in case the contract would be extended, is lower than EUR 1,000, which confirms definitively that the abovementioned extension option does not establish any significant gain for the player.
14. To that regard in this specific case, the members of the Chamber emphasised that although the financial terms had been specified in advance, they necessarily cannot take into account, neither by the player nor the club, the possible enhancement of the players value, and hence earning power, over a two year period, in particular if he could propel his football career during that time by an international transfer to the club D.
15. Furthermore, the members pointed out that two years are a significant portion of a footballers active career.
16. In continuation, the Chamber emphasised that the unilateral option in the contract in question curtails the freedom of movement in an excessive way and leaves the player at an unfair disadvantage.
17. Subsequently, the Chamber rejected all the remaining allegations of the Respondent after having them analysed carefully, since they do not constitute a reason, in order to possibly affirm the validity of the multi-named option clause.
18. Taking into consideration all of the above, the members of the Chamber concluded that the unilateral option in favour of the club in the employment contract at the basis of the present litigation cannot be considered as being legally binding on the player A.
19. Notwithstanding the above, and for the sake of completeness, the Chamber emphasized that even if it would have admitted the present option clause, the said clause would not have been legally binding on the player, since the Respondent was not able to provide FIFA with the sufficient evidences, i.e. the necessary discharge of having duly executed the said clause.
20. In addition, the Chamber stated that the clarification, as to whether the present penal clause is valid or not, can remain unanswered following the aforementioned considerations.
21. On account of the foregoing, the members of the Chamber decided that the contract signed between the parties on 20 August 2002 has come to an end on 30 June 2005.
22. As a result, the Dispute Resolution Chamber decided that the player A is not contractually bound to O any longer and therefore, he was free to sign with the club D. Consequently, the members fully accepted the players claim and rejected the counter-claim of the club P.

III. DECISION OF THE DISPUTE RESOLUTION CHAMBER

1. The claim submitted by the Claimant/Counter-Respondent, Mr A, is fully accepted.
2. The contract concluded between the Claimant/Counter-Respondent and the Respondent/Counter-Claimant, on 20 August 2002, expired on 30 June 2005.
3. The counterclaim submitted by the Respondent/Counter-Claimant, club O, is rejected.
4. According to art. 60 par. 1 of the FIFA Statutes, this decision may be appealed against before the Court of Arbitration for Sport (CAS). The statement of appeal must be sent to the CAS directly within 21 days of receipt of notification of this decision and shall contain all the elements in accordance with point 2 of the directives issued by the CAS, a copy of which we enclose hereto. Within another 10 days following the expiry of the time limit for filing the statement of appeal, the appellant shall file a brief stating the facts and legal arguments giving rise to the appeal with the CAS (cf. point 4 of the directives).

36882
DECISION OF THE DISPUTE RESOLUTION CHAMBER
passed in Zurich, Switzerland, on 23 March 2006,
in the following composition:
Slim Aloulou (Tunisia), Chairman Mario Gallavotti (Italy), Member Peter Friend (Australia), Member Mick McGuire (England), Member Gerardo Movilla (Spain), Member
on the claim presented by
Player A, as Claimant
against
Club B, as Respondent
regarding a dispute about the employment contract concluded between the parties.

I. FACTS OF THE CASE

1. The player A (hereinafter; the player), born on 1 June 1986, concluded an employment contract with the club B (hereinafter; the club) on 6 December 2004, valid as of 1 December 2004 until 31 December 2007. In annex 2 to the contract, a monthly salary of USD 3,000 is stipulated.
2. In May 2005, the player joined the U-20 representative team of his Association for the U-20 World Cup in the Netherlands.
3. On 18 August 2005, the player contacted FIFA, maintaining that he had been deceived by the CEO of the club to sign the above-mentioned employment contract.
4. On 9 September 2005, the player completed his former submission, requesting the annulment of the employment contract and disciplinary sanctions against the club.
5. First of all, the player complained that the contract does not stipulate any obligation of the club to provide him with the basic requirements, such as accommodation, feeding and educational support. The stipulated salary would not cover the players expenses, therefore he should be considered de facto as an amateur.
6. Moreover, he stated that the club X sponsored and was responsible for his training and education, and that therefore the club could not have signed an employment contract with him. The player did not submit any agreement signed by him and club X.
7. Furthermore, the player complained that since he was 18 years old at the time of the conclusion of the relevant contract, the signing of a professional contract was in violation of article 13 of the FIFA Regulations for the Status and Transfer of Players (edition 2001), which states that the training and education of a player has to take place between the ages of 12 and 23.
8. Finally, the player also complained that the contract was signed without his agent having been contacted before, and that the agents name was not included in the contract.
9. On 30 September 2005, the club answered to the players accusations.
10. In this respect, the club first of all informed FIFA that the player had resumed duty after the U-20 World Cup in the Netherlands only on 5 September 2005.
11. In continuation, the club stated that the player was not deceived into signing the relevant employment contract, but that he signed the contract in free will. Therefore, he must respect the contract and fulfil his contractual obligations.
12. Moreover, the club stated that all the players salaries were paid so far, despite his long and unexcused absence. Besides that, the club stated that the agreed salary was adequate for the player in question and more than sufficient to cover his needs. In this regard, the club also stated that the player had free board and lodging, and moreover, was provided with a new car.
13. Finally, the club reserved its right to make a claim against the player for his unexcused absence from the end of the U-20 World Cup in the Netherlands on 2 July 2005 until 5 September 2005, but for the time being, refrained from submitting an official claim, since the player apparently acted under high pressure of his counsels.
14. On 25 October 2005, the player informed FIFA that he insisted on a formal decision to be taken by the Dispute Resolution Chamber, since he was still of the opinion that he had been deceived by the club when he signed the employment contract.
15. In this regard, the player confirmed having resumed duty with the club on 5 September 2005, and in this regard, also confirmed that the club respected its financial obligations towards him.
16. Moreover, he stated that he was illegally registered, since his former Association allegedly never sent his International Transfer Certificate to his new Association.

17. On 7 December 2005, the club informed FIFA that the player in question again left the club without permission on 28 November 2005, and therefore requested FIFA to intervene so that the player would immediately return to the club.
18. On 11 December 2005, the club provided FIFA with its final position in the matter, stating that a valid employment contract had been concluded between the parties, that the club always had respected all its contractual obligations towards the player, and that therefore, the player also must respect his contractual obligations.
19. On 15 February 2006, the player submitted his answer to the clubs request for immediate return, and thereby maintained that he was absent from the club due to his participation with his Association team to an international tournament. In continuation, he stated that on 16 February 2006, he allegedly had to attend to an award ceremony. Finally, he stated that he planed to rejoin the club as soon as all activities connected with the said ceremony were concluded.
20. Besides the above, he was still of the opinion that the employment contract binding him to the club was not valid, since he was deceived into signing the said contract.

II. CONSIDERATIONS OF THE DISPUTE RESOLUTION CHAMBER

1. First of all, the Dispute Resolution Chamber (DRC) analysed whether it was competent to deal with the matter at stake. In this respect, it referred to art. 18 par. 2 and 3 of the Rules Governing the Procedures of the Players' Status Committee and the Dispute Resolution Chamber. The present matter was submitted to FIFA on 18 August 2005, as a consequence the Chamber concluded that the revised Rules Governing Procedures (edition 2005) on matters pending before the decision making bodies of FIFA are applicable on the matter at hand.
2. With regard to the competence of the Chamber, art. 3 par. 1 of the abovementioned Rules states that the Dispute Resolution Chamber shall examine its jurisdiction in the light of articles 22 to 24 of the current version of the Regulations for the Status and Transfer of Players (edition 2005). In accordance with art. 24 par. 1 in connection with art. 22 (b) of the aforementioned Regulations, the Dispute Resolution Chamber shall adjudicate on employment-related disputes between a club and a player that have an international dimension.
3. As a consequence, the Dispute Resolution Chamber is the competent body to decide on the present litigation involving a club and a player with different nationalities regarding a dispute in connection with an employment contract.
4. Subsequently, the members of the Chamber analyzed which edition of the Regulations for the Status and Transfer of Players should be applicable as to the substance of the matter. In this respect, the Chamber referred, on the one hand, to art. 26 par. 1 and 2 of the Regulations for the Status and Transfer of Players (edition 2005) and, on the other hand, to the fact that the relevant contract at the basis of the present dispute was signed on 6 December 2004 and the claim was lodged at FIFA on 18 August 2005. In view of the aforementioned, the Chamber concluded that the current FIFA Regulations for the Status and Transfer of Players (edition 2005, hereafter: the Regulations) are applicable on the case at hand as to the substance.
5. Entering into the substance of the matter, the DRC acknowledged the documentation contained in the file, and in view of the circumstances of the case, focused on the question whether the employment contract between the club and the player was to be considered as null and void or if the player had to resume duty with the club.
6. In this respect, the DRC had, in particular, to analyse the following argumentations (in italics) forwarded by the player, according to which the said employment contract, from the players point of view should be declared null and void.
7. 1) The player had been deceived by the CEO of the club to sign the abovementioned employment contract.
8. The DRC acknowledged that the player alleged that he had been deceived to sign the employment contract in question, but that he had neither outlined how this should have happened, nor submitted any clear evidence corroborating such allegation.
9. Therefore, in application of the principle of the burden of proof, and due to lack of evidence, the DRC had to reject the first argument of the player.
10. 2) The employment contract does not stipulate any obligation of the club to provide the player with the basic requirements, such as accommodation, feeding and educational support.

11. The DRC deliberated if clubs are obliged, according to the Regulations, to provide their players with basic requirements, such as accommodation, feeding and educational support.
12. In this respect, the DRC could only refer to art. 19 par. 9 b) of the Regulations, based on which an international transfer of a minor within the EU/EEA shall only be permitted in case the player concerned is aged between 16 and 18, and if suitable arrangements are guaranteed for the players sports training, academic education and care by the new training club.
13. The DRC had to clarify, however, that the above-mentioned provision 1) does not concern the validity of an employment contract, but only the possibility of an international transfer of a minor, and 2) does apply only to transfers of players between two clubs affiliated to Associations in the EU/EEA.
14. In the present case, the player challenged the validity of the employment contract, but not the validity of his international transfer.
15. Moreover, the international transfer of the player did not occur between two clubs affiliated to Associations in the EU/EEA. Therefore, the above-mentioned provision does not apply to the matter at stake
16. Finally, the DRC emphasized that at the time of the relevant transfer, the player was already older than 18.
17. In conclusion, the DRC had to reject such argumentation of the player.
18. For the sake of good order, the DRC also referred to article 2 par. 2 of the Regulations and deemed that a monthly salary of approximately USD 3,000 has to be considered a higher remuneration as just refund of expenses incurred by the player in return for his footballing activity. As a consequence, the DRC rejected also the players claim that he should be, de facto, considered an amateur.
19. 3) The club X was responsible for the players training and education, therefore the club could not have signed an employment contract with the player.
20. The DRC acknowledged that the player had not submitted any agreement signed between him and the club X, according to which the club X would be responsible for his training and education.
21. Therefore, in application of the principle of the burden of proof, and due to lack of evidence, the DRC had as well to reject the third argument of the player.
22. 4) The signing of a professional contract was in violation of article 13 of the FIFA Regulations for the Status and Transfer of Players (edition 2001), which states that the training and education of a player has to take place between the ages of 12 and 23, since the player was only 18 years old at the time of the conclusion of the relevant contract.
23. The DRC emphasized that the duration of the period of training and education of a player provided in art. 13 of the afore-mentioned Regulations is relevant only for the entitlement to and the calculation of the amount of training compensation for young players. The provision in question does, however, not prevent players and clubs from concluding an employment contract before the players age of 23.
24. In this respect, the DRC clarified that clubs and players can conclude employment contracts without the same having to be co-signed by the players legal representative/guardian as soon as the player, in accordance with the national law applicable, has attained majority.
25. Therefore, and in view of the fact that the player was already at the age of 18 when he signed the employment contract in question, the DRC came to the conclusion that, under this aspect, the said contract was concluded validly.
26. 5) The contract was signed without contacting the players agent beforehand, and the agents name was not included in the contract.
27. The DRC underlined that there is no obligation contained in the applicable Regulations of FIFA preventing a player and a club from signing an employment contract without contacting the players agent beforehand. Furthermore, in case the agent of a player is not involved in the conclusion of an employment contract, his name, in consequence, is not to be mentioned in that contract.
28. In view of the above, also from this point of view, the DRC considered the employment contract in question as having been concluded validly, and hence rejected argument 5 of the player.
29. 6) The player was illegally registered, since the players former Association allegedly never sent his International Transfer Certificate to the players new Association.
30. In view of the investigations carried out by FIFA, by means of which it was established that the players International Transfer Certificate was requested and issued by the competent Associations, the last argument of the player was declared by the DRC as being wrong.

31. Finally, the DRC also pointed out that the player had explicitly recognised that the club had fully complied with the payment of his salary and thus had always adhered to its contractual obligations.
32. In view of all the above, the DRC concluded that the invalidity of the employment contract in question was not established by the claimant. Therefore, in application of the principle of pacta sunt servanda, which is a basic principle to every legal system in the world, the DRC decided that the player had to resume duty with the club immediately.

III. DECISION OF THE DISPUTE RESOLUTION CHAMBER

1. The claim of the player is rejected.
2. The counterclaim of the club is accepted.
3. The player has to resume duty with the club immediately.
4. In the event that the player does not comply with the present decision, the matter shall be submitted to FIFAs Disciplinary Committee, so that the necessary disciplinary sanctions may be imposed.
5. According to art. 60 par. 1 of the FIFA Statutes this decision may be appealed before the Court of Arbitration for Sport (CAS). The statement of appeal must be sent to the CAS directly within 21 days of receiving notification of this decision and has to contain all elements in accordance with point 2 of the directives issued by the CAS, copy of which we enclose hereto. Within another 10 days following the expiry of the time limit for the filing of the statement of appeal, the appellant shall file with the CAS a brief stating the facts and legal arguments giving rise to the appeal (cf. point 4 of the directives).

36928
DECISION OF THE DISPUTE RESOLUTION CHAMBER
passed in Zurich, Switzerland, on 23 March 2006,
in the following composition:
Slim Aloulou (Tunisia), Chairman
Mario Gallavotti (Italy), member
Peter Friend (Australia), member
Gerardo Movilla (Spain), member
Mick Mc Guire (England), member
on the claim presented by the club
A., Italy, as Claimant,
against the club S., Belgium, as Respondent,
regarding training compensation related to the transfer of the player D.

I. FACTS OF THE CASE

1. The player D. was born on 14 March 1982 and was registered with A. during the season 2002/2003. During the season 2003/2004, the player was registered with the Belgian club S.
2. On 6 December 2004, the Italian club turned to FIFA and claimed an amount of EUR 60,000 plus interests as compensation for the training of the player D. The player had been registered from 1 July 2002 until 30 June 2003 at the age of 20 and 21 for A. on a loan basis after having been transferred from A.C. Milan.
3. On 10 December 2004, the Belgian club answered and referred to a letter from S. to the Union Royale Belge des Sociétés de Football Association dated 29 September 2004, indicating that the player had been transferred from M. The Belgian club underlined that in terms of FIFA circular no. 826, M. is the last club of the player. Therefore, the Belgian club was of the opinion that A. is not entitled to claim any training compensation.
4. On 15 April 2005, the Belgian club provided FIFA with a specified answer to the claim and estimated that the Players' Status Committee is not competent for the case at hand as it concerns training compensation and such matters have to be submitted exclusively to the Dispute Resolution Chamber. Furthermore, the Belgian club stressed that the Italian club did not provide FIFA with any proof of payment of the administrative costs so that the claim cannot be considered. As to the substance, the Belgian club emphasised that the player had been under contract with M. and played during the season 2000/2001 for club B. in the Italian Serie B as a regular player. During the season 2001/2002,

the player got injured and could therefore not play for M. Therefore and considering the jurisprudence of the Dispute Resolution Chamber, the Belgian club was of the opinion that the period of training of the player has to be considered terminated before the season 2002/2003. Notwithstanding the above, the Belgian club underlined that M. is the last club of the player as the transfer was concluded between this club and itself.

5. On 11 November 2005, A. underlined that it lodged its complaint with the Dispute Resolution Chamber and reminded that the procedure in front of this Chamber is free of charge. The Italian club contested that the player already terminated his training period, as he was transferred to A. in order to get experience and to be lined up repeatedly. A. rejects that the player was lined up regularly with club B.
   Furthermore, A. referred to FIFA circular no. 826 and emphasised that training compensation is due only to the last club which effectively trained the player.
   Therefore, the Italian club considered its complaint as justified.
6. The Italian club belongs today to the first category in Italy but was in the second category during the season 2002/2003 before being promoted to Serie A at the end of this season 2002/2003. The Belgian club belongs to category 2.

II. CONSIDERATIONS OF THE DISPUTE RESOLUTION CHAMBER

1. First of all, the Chamber analysed whether it was competent to deal with the matter at stake. In this respect, it referred to art. 18 par. 2 and 3 of the Rules Governing the Procedures of the Players' Status Committee and the Dispute Resolution Chamber. The present matter was submitted to FIFA on 6 December 2004, as a consequence the Chamber concluded that the previous Procedural Rules (edition 2001) on matters pending before the decision making bodies of FIFA are applicable to the matter at hand.
2. With regard to the competence of the Chamber, art. 42 par. 1 lit. (b) (iv) of the FIFA Regulations for the Status and Transfer of Players (edition 2001) establishes that disputes concerning training compensation will be decided by the Dispute Resolution Chamber.
3. As a consequence, the Dispute Resolution Chamber is the competent body to decide on the present litigation concerning the training compensation claimed by A. for the training and education of the player D.
4. Subsequently, the members of the Chamber analysed which edition of the Regulations for the Status and Transfer of Players should be applicable as to the substance of the matter. In this respect, the Chamber referred to art. 26 par. 1 and 2 of the Regulations for the Status and Transfer of Players (edition 2005) in the modified version in accordance with the FIFA circular no. 995 dated 23 September 2005. Furthermore, it acknowledged that the player has been registered for his new club as from July 2003. Equally, the Chamber took note that the claim was lodged on 6 December 2004. In view of the aforementioned, the Chamber concluded that the former FIFA Regulations for the Status and Transfer of Players (edition 2001, hereafter: the Regulations) are applicable to the case at hand as to the substance.
5. In continuation, and entering into the substance of the matter, the members of the Chamber started by acknowledging that the player was registered with A. as from 1 July 2002 until 30 June 2003. The Chamber noted that the player was during this season under contract with M. and went on loan for the duration of the season 2002/2003 to A.
6. After the end of the relevant loan period, the player in question duly returned to M., from which he was transferred on 24 July 2003 to S. A. claims that it is entitled to receive compensation for the training and education of the player in question for the period of time that he was registered with the club, i.e. from 1 July 2002 until 30 June 2003 to the amount of EUR 60,000 plus interest. The Respondent, S., however, categorically denies that any training compensation would be due to A. in the light of the fact that the player was last registered with M., which club did not claim or wish to receive any training compensation.
7. The Chamber first turned to the preliminary question as to whether clubs that accepted a player on loan basis are entitled to receive compensation for the training and education of young players in accordance with Chapter VII of the Regulations and Chapter III of the Regulations governing the Application of the Regulations for the Status and Transfer of Players as well as FIFA circular no. 826 dated 31 October 2002.

8. Art. 13 of the Regulations stipulates that "Training compensation shall be payable, as a general rule, up to the age of 23 for training incurred up to the age of 21, unless it is evident that a player has already terminated his training period before the age of 21. In the latter case, ..., the calculation of the amount of compensation shall be based on the years between 12 and the age when it is established that the player actually completed his training."
9. According to art. 15 of the Regulations, "Compensation shall be paid each time a player changes from one club to another up to the time his training and education is complete, which, as a general rule, occurs when the player reaches 23 years of age.
10. According to the jurisprudence established by the Dispute Resolution Chamber, a club is only entitled to receive training compensation for the period of time during which a player has in actual fact been trained by the club claiming payment of such compensation. Therefore, the claim for training compensation put forward by the club that had transferred the player on loan basis to another club was dismissed with respect to the period of time that the player in question was registered on a loan basis with another club.
11. The claim for training compensation dealt with in the present matter, however, was put forward by a club that accepted the player on a loan basis.
12. The Chamber agreed that the nature of a players registration, i.e. on a definite or on a temporary basis, with a club claiming training compensation is in fact irrelevant with respect to the question as to whether such claimant club would be entitled to receive training compensation for the period of time that the player was effectively trained by that club.
13. The Chamber concluded that the relevant and above-mentioned provisions of the Regulations pertaining to training compensation basically also apply to clubs that accepted a player on a loan basis provided that the player in question has in actual fact been trained by that club.
14. As stated above, the player in question transferred to A. on a loan basis at the age of 20, where he was registered from 1 July 2002 until 30 June 2003.
15. Furthermore, in the case at hand, art. 13 of the Regulations has been invoked by S. The Belgian club is of the opinion that the player has already terminated his training period before the age of 21. However, A. underlines that the player was not fielded on a regular basis in the Italian Serie A, but was fielded only in the Italian Serie B and therefore could not be considered to have been a particularly successful player. A. emphasises that the player was transferred on loan by M. to A. in order to get more experience in an inferior league. Therefore, the Claimant is of the opinion that the jurisprudence of the Dispute Resolution Chamber related to art. 13 of the Regulations cannot be applied. Finally, the Chamber took note that no documentary evidence concerning the alleged termination of the training period was presented by S.
16. The Chamber considered the fact that the player had been transferred on loan from M., which is a Serie A club in Italy, to A., which was at the time of the loan period a Serie B club. The Chamber emphasised that exactly this fact proves that the player did not terminate yet his training and education as the player was sent on loan to a smaller club in Italy in order to get experience and to be lined up repeatedly.
17. S., however, does contest that A. would be entitled to receive training compensation, in the light of the fact that the player was last registered with M. According to S., M. did not claim or wish to receive any training compensation.
18. In this respect, the Chamber took into account that should the players last training club waive any right to training compensation, such waiver would be without prejudice to the right to training compensation of the other clubs that were involved in the training of the player until the age of 21. For the sake of good order, the Chamber pointed out that the same goes for last training clubs that do not offer the player a contract (see art. 5 par. 5 of the Regulations governing the Application of the Regulations for the Status and Transfer of Players [edition 2001, hereafter: the Application Regulations]).
19. On account of the above considerations, the Chamber concluded that the argumentation of S. cannot be considered valid. Furthermore, the Chamber concluded that A. is entitled to receive training compensation from S. in accordance with Chapter VII of the Regulations and Chapter III of the Regulations governing the Application of the Regulations as well as FIFA circular letter no. 826 dated 31 October 2002.
20. At the time of the players move to the Belgian club, both A. and S. were category 2 clubs. The amount due by the Belgian club has to be calculated in accordance with the parameters provided by

FIFA circular no. 826 dated 31 October 2002, i.e. with an amount corresponding to EUR 60,000 per year of training (corresponding to club category 2 of UEFA).

21. Consequently, taking into account the above-mentioned elements, A. is entitled to receive training compensation from S. to the amount of EUR 60,000.
22. Furthermore, the Chamber made reference to art. 11 of the Application Regulations, which reads that the new club shall pay the amount due as solidarity contribution to the training club(s) at the latest within 30 days of the players registration with the new club.
23. Consequently, taking into consideration the claim of the Claimant and in the light of the fact that the solidarity contribution payment has been due since the 31st day of the registration of the player with S., club to which the player was transferred in July 2004, the Chamber established that a default interest payment of 5% per year as from the day as of which the relevant payment was due, i.e. on 1 September 2003, must be applied.

III. DECISION OF THE DISPUTE RESOLUTION CHAMBER

1. The claim of A. is accepted.
2. S. has to pay the amount of EUR 60,000 to A. within 30 days as from the date of notification of this decision.
3. S. has to pay default interest at the rate of 5% p.a. on the amount of EUR 60,000 as from 1 September 2003 until the day of the execution of the present decision.
4. In the event that the above-mentioned amount is not paid within the stated deadline, the present matter shall be submitted to FIFAs Disciplinary Committee, so that the necessary disciplinary sanctions may be imposed.
5. A. is instructed to inform S. immediately and directly of the account number to which the remittance is to be made and to notify the Dispute Resolution Chamber of every payment received.
6. According to art. 60 par. 1 of the FIFA Statutes, this decision may be appealed against before the Court of Arbitration for Sport (CAS). The statement of appeal must be sent to the CAS directly within 21 days of receipt of notification of this decision and shall contain all the elements in accordance with point 2 of the directives issued by the CAS, a copy of which we enclose hereto. Within another 10 days following the expiry of the time limit for filing the statement of appeal, the appellant shall file a brief stating the facts and legal arguments giving rise to the appeal with the CAS (cf. point 4 of the directives).

23-03-2006, 631290
DECISION OF THE DISPUTE RESOLUTION CHAMBER
passed in Zurich, Switzerland, on 23 March 2006,
in the following com position:
Slim Aloulou (Tunisia), Chairman
Mario Gallavotti (Italy), member
Peter Friend (Australia), member
Mick McGuire (England), member
Gerardo Movilla (Spain), member
on the claim presented by the
Player X, B, represented by Mr U, attorney at law as Claimant
against
Clube D, P, as Respondent
regarding a contractual dispute arisen between the parties involved.

Facts of the case

1. The B player X, the Claimant, had signed an employment contract on 1 July 2004 with the P club, D, the Respondent, with the term from 1 July 2004 until the end of the season 2007/2008, i.e. 30 June 2008.
2. According to the employment contract, the Claimant was entitled to receive for the season 2004/2005, 12 monthly instalments of EUR 2,664.29 each, the first on 1 July 2004 and the last on 30 June 2005. For the season 2005/2006, it was stipulated that if the club will be part of the League of ..., the

Claimant should receive 12 monthly instalments of EUR 3,142.85 each beginning on 1 July 2005 and terminating on 30 June 2006. Provided that the club will be part of the League of ..., it was stipulated for the seasons 2006/2007 and 2007/2008 that the Claimant would receive 12 monthly instalments of EUR 3,571.42 each (from 1 July 2006 until 30 June 2007, respectively 1 July 2007 until 30 June 2008). Should the club participate to the Super League in the seasons 2006/2007 and 2007/2008, the Claimant would be entitled to receive in both seasons 12 monthly instalments of EUR 4,464.28.

3. In the course of the contractual duration, the Claimant was loaned for the period of time from 14 April 2005 until 31 December 2005 to the club, XXX. The relevant ban agreement was signed by both the involved clubs as well as by the Claimant. Furthermore, the said ban contract stated that the club, XXX, assumes the payment of the salaries of the Claimant from 15 April to 31 December 2005.
4. On 20 September 2005, the said ban agreement was prematurely terminated by mutual consent of the two clubs concerned with immediate effect. The Claimant co-signed also the termination agreement.
5. On the same day, i.e. 20 September 2005, the Respondent concluded a further ban agreement with another B ian club, P, in order to ban the Claimant to the said B ian club until the end of the year, i.e. 31 December 2005. This ban agreement was again co-signed by the Claimant. However, the Claimant could not be registered for P Club at the B ian Football Federation. The responsibility for this non-registration is in dispute between the Claimant and the Respondent. The respective positions of the parties are stated below.

Formal claim of the Claimant

6. With correspondence dated 8 November and 13 December 2005, the Claimant submitted a claim in front of FIFA against the Respondent and maintained that he is being kept under contract by the club, without, however, being allowed to practise his profession and to participate in matches or trainings. In this connection, the Claimant stated that the Respondent delayed the procedure concerning the issuance of the International Transfer Certificate (ITC) to the B ian Football Federation. Consequently, he could not be registered for the B ian club, P Club.
7. The Claimant stressed that he has the right to breach the employment contract with the Respondent for sporting just cause according to article 15 of the Regulations for the Status and Transfer of Players, without compensation to be paid by or sporting sanctions to be applied on him. Moreover, he maintained that a breach of the employment contract without just cause has been committed by the Respondent by obstructing him of playing matches or participating in trainings.
8. Based on his allegations, the Claimant requests the following:
   - his immediate release in order to sign on with any other club
   - declare the breach of the employment contract by the sole responsibility of the Respondent
   - condemn the Respondent to pay compensation (pecuniary and moral) in the amount of EUR 187,714.00 (amount not further specified) plus attorney fees of EUR 18,771.00

Position of the Respondent

9. In reply to the claim of the player, the club D informed FIFA that the player's reasoning to invoke the application of art. 15 of the Regulations for the Status and Transfer of Players in order to terminate the employment contract for sporting just cause has no basis. In particular, the club maintained that in the P II League, there are a total of 34 competition matches per season to play. In this respect, the club submitted a letter issued by the "Liga P de ... Professional", according to which the Claimant in question participated in 15 official matches in the season 2004/2005 for the Respondent.
10. Furthermore, the club asserts having paid to the Claimant all the financial dues fixed in the employment contract and in this respect submitted a confirmation from "Banco Comercial Dos Açores", according to which it made several payments towards the Claimant until July 2005. With regard to the alleged non-payment of the Claimant's salaries as from July 2005, the Respondent referred to the ban agreements it signed with the respective B ian clubs. It emphasized in particular that, according to the ban agreement it concluded with P Club, the batter was responsible for the payments of the Claimant's salaries for September until December 2005 (point 4 a of the relevant contract). This obligation of P Club remained although it could not register the Claimant for its team

with the B ian Football Federation.

11. Moreover and with regard to the circumstances of the non-registration of the Claimant with the B ian Football Federation for its affiliate, P Club, the Respondent stated that it made all the necessary in order to respect the interests of the Claimant, who had requested to remain in B after the early termination of the ban with XXX. In particular, it maintained having sent the termination-agreement of the ban with XXX as well as the new ban agreement with P Club to the P Football Federation on the same day it received the relevant request from the batter.
12. According to the Respondent, it came to beam that the Claimant apparently could not be registered for P Club at the B ian Football Federation only in December 2005. Therefore, it immediately tried to reach the Claimant in order to find out his objectives for the rest of the season. Thereupon and in accordance with the Claimant's wish, it concluded a ban agreement with another B ian club, R, for the ban of the Claimant to the batter until 30 November 2006 for the amount of EUR 20,000.00. A copy of the relevant agreement was remitted to the file. However, the Respondent asserted that the Claimant refused to sign the employment contract with R.
13. On account of the above, the Respondent emphasized that, as a matter of fact, the Claimant is still under a valid employment contract with it until 30 June 2008.
14. Finally, the Respondent argued that FIFA, i.e. the Dispute Resolution Chamber, is not competent to deal with this matter, since, based on the employment contract and the P sports law, there is an instance in the P League which deals with this kind of disputes and which respects the principle of equal representation of players and clubs with an independent chairman.

Request for registration of the Claimant

15. In the meantime, on 2 January 2006, the Claimant signed a new employment contract with the B ian club, Z, for the period until 30 April 2006. According to the employment contract, the Claimant is entitled to receive a monthly wage of ....
16. Following the refusal of the P Football Federation to issue the relevant ITC, the B ian Football Federation asked for FIFA's intervention.
17. On 23 February 2006, the Single Judge of the Players' Status Committee decided that under the given circumstances the B ian Football Federation could not be authorized to provisionally register the Claimant for its affiliated club, Z, pending the outcome of the contractual dispute between the Claimant and the Respondent.

Second position of the Claimant

18. In his second submission, the Claimant, inter alia, mentioned that for the purpose of his registration with the B ian club, P Club, the B ian Football Federation sent the request for the issuance of the ITC to the Respondent through the P Football Federation, but the Respondent obstructed his registration.
19. In this respect, the Claimant stated that the deadline for him to be registered with the B ian Football Federation for P Club, expired on 23 September 2005.
20. According to the Claimant, the Respondent did not undertake the necessary actions to assure his registration with the B ian Football Federation. In this respect, he refers to a fax issued by the P Football Federation dated 23 September 2005 (copy in the file), in which the batter asked the Respondent to terminate first the ban agreement with XXX in order for them to give permission to the issuance of the ITC in favour of the Claimant to the B ian Football Federation. The Claimant maintained that the said letter of the P Football Federation does not mention that the termination of the former ban contract had to be done previously, i.e. before the permission of the issuance of the ITC could be granted.
21. Furthermore, he maintained that the Respondent did not pay him his salaries since September 2005, i.e. more than three months.
22. Moreover, he reiterated having sporting just cause to terminate the employment contract with the Respondent. In this respect, he added that since September 2005, the date of the termination of the ban agreement with XXX, he did not participate in any official match with the Respondent although the batter would have had the possibility to register him according to the Regulations of the P Championship.
23. Finally, the Claimant pointed out that he has just cause to terminate the employment contract with the Respondent given that the batter obstructed his right to work by not undertaking the necessary actions for the completion of his registration with the B ian Football Federation for P Club.

Final position of the Respondent

24. The Respondent denied any relation between the termination of the ban agreement it signed with XXX on 20 September 2005 and an alleged and never proved intention from its part to hinder the Claimant from playing in its team.
25. With regard to the non-registration of the Claimant for P Club, the Respondent emphasized that it did not, at any moment, deny the issuance of the relevant ITC for the Claimant. In this respect, it stated that it received on 23 September 2005 a fax from the P Football Federation, referring to the urgency to issue the ITC in favour of the Claimant for the B ian Football Federation. According to the said fax of the P Football Federation, it was required that the Respondent first terminates the ban contract with XXX. Therefore, it sent on the same day, i.e. 23 September 2005, the requested document to the P Football Federation (termination of the ban agreement with XXX and the new ban contract it concluded with P Club).
26. Finally, it reiterated that it was not responsible for the player's salary payments as from September 2005.

Position of Z

27. The B ian club, Z, for which the player signed an employment contract on 2 January 2006, was kindly invited by FIFA to participate as an intervening party to the procedure concerning the contractual dispute between the Claimant and the Respondent and in this capacity it was asked to provide its founded statement. However, the said B ian club did not provide any statement at all.

II. CONSIDERATIONS OF THE DISPUTE RESOLUTION CHAMBER

1. First of all, the Chamber analysed whether it was competent to deal with the matter at stake. In this respect, it referred to art. 18 par. 2 and 3 of the Rubes Governing the Procedures of the Players' Status Committee and the Dispute Resolution Chamber. The present matter was submitted to FIFA on 8 November and 13 December 2005, as a consequence the Chamber concluded that the revised Rubes Governing Procedures (edition 2005) on matters pending before the decision making bodies of FIFA are applicable on the matter at hand.
2. With regard to the competence of the Chamber, art. 3 par. 1 of the abovementioned Rubes states that the Dispute Resolution Chamber shall examine its jurisdiction in the light of articles 22 to 24 of the current version of the Regulations for the Status and Transfer of Players (edition 2005). In accordance with art. 24 par. 1 in connection with art. 22 (b) of the aforementioned Regulations, the Dispute Resolution Chamber shall adjudicate on employment-rebated disputes between a club and a player that have an international dimension.
3. As a consequence, the Dispute Resolution Chamber is the competent body to decide on the present litigation involving a P club and a B ian player regarding the breach of contract and outstanding compensation in connection with an employment contract.
4. Subsequently, the members of the Chamber analyzed which edition of the Regulations for the Status and Transfer of Players should be applicable as to the substance of the matter. In this respect, the Chamber referred, on the one hand, to art. 26 par. 1 and 2 of the Regulations for the Status and Transfer of Players (edition 2005) and, on the other hand, to the fact that the relevant contract at the basis of the present dispute was signed on 1 July 2004 and the claim was lodged at FIFA on 8 November and 13 December 2005. In view of the aforementioned, the Chamber concluded that the current FIFA Regulations for the Status and Transfer of Players (edition 2005; hereafter; the Regulations) are applicable on the case at hand as to the substance.
5. In continuation, the members of the Chamber referred to the argument of the Respondent by means of which the batter disputed the competence of the Dispute Resolution Chamber to deal with this affair since there is an instance functioning in the P Club, which deals with employment rebated disputes as in the case at hand.
6. In this respect, the members referred to the well established jurisprudence of the Dispute Resolution Chamber according to which, in general, in employment-rebated disputes between a club and a player that have an international dimension, i.e. the parties do not belong to the same country, both parties were entitled to refer the dispute to FIFA's bodies, unless an independent arbitration tribunal respecting the principle of equal representation of players and clubs with an independent chairman has been established at national bevel.

7. The members acknowledged that, the Respondent was unable to prove that an independent arbitration tribunal in compliance with the requirements of the FIFA's regulations has been established in P. As a consequence, the members established that the Respondent's objection to the competence of FIFA to deal with the matter has to be rejected and that the matter can be considered as to the substance.
8. In continuation, and entering into the substance of the matter, the members of the Chamber started by acknowledging that the Claimant and the Respondent signed on 1 July 2004 an employment contract valid until the end of the season 2007/2008, i.e. 30 June 2008.
9. Furthermore, the members took note that the Respondent, with the express consent of the Claimant, initially concluded a ban agreement with a first B ian club, XXX, for the period of time from 14 April 2005 until 31 December 2005, which was, however, prematurely terminated on 20 September 2005 by mutual agreement of the parties concerned. The Chamber noted that the player had explicitly accepted the termination by co-signing also that agreement.
10. Moreover, the members acknowledged that subsequently, the Respondent, again with the express consent of the Claimant, signed a further ban agreement with a second B ian club, P Club, in order to ban the Claimant to the batter until the end of the year, i.e. 31 December 2005.
11. In this respect, the members of the Chamber noticed the Claimant's allegation that the Respondent failed to accomplish with the necessary release prerequisites in order for the Claimant to be registered for the second B ian club, P Club, with the B ian Football Federation.
12. In this connection, the members of the Chamber examined the documentary evidences submitted by the parties involved and determined that the Claimant, by means of his signature, in fact expressly agreed to the two ban agreements the Respondent concluded with the two above-mentioned B ian clubs.
13. Moreover and based on the submitted documents, the Chamber stated that no evidence was provided by the Claimant for the allegation that the Respondent delayed the procedure concerning the issuance of the ITC for the Claimant in order for the batter to be registered for the B ian club, P Club, with the B ian Football Federation, and therefore, as accused by the Claimant, abusively prevented the Claimant from practising his professional activity. On the contrary, the members acknowledged that the Respondent received on 23 September 2005 correspondence from the P Football Federation whereby it was informed about an urgent ITC request made by the B ian Football Federation in order to register the Claimant for one of the batter's affiliated clubs. In this respect, the members noted that the Respondent replied to the P Football Federation on the same day it received the relevant request and provided the P Football Federation with the termination agreement of the ban it concluded with XXX as well as with the new ban agreement it signed with the player's new club, P Club.
14. Considering the aforementioned explanations, the members first concluded that the Respondent cannot be hold responsible for the non-registration of the player for P Club with the B ian Football Federation.
15. Furthermore, the deciding body acknowledged that the Respondent affirmed having had no knowledge about the Claimant's situation and residence as from 23 September 2005, when it last was contacted about the Claimant's registration with P Club, until December 2005, when it was notified by FIFA of the claim lodged at FIFA by the Claimant. In other words, the Respondent maintains that prior to having been contacted by FIFA with regard to the present litigation, it did not have knowledge of the unsuccessful registration of the Claimant with P Club. In this respect, the Chamber stated that the Claimant had not provided any valid argument to rebut the Respondent's allegation. Furthermore, it was emphasized that following the failure of the registration, it would have been the Claimant's obligation to revert to his club of origin, the Respondent, in order to immediately offer his services. Yet, no indications for such action are contained in the file. As a consequence, the Chamber concluded that until December 2005, when it was informed of the present claim, the Respondent could in good faith assume that the player had been registered with P Club.
16. In continuation, the members took note that the Respondent, after having gained knowledge in December 2005 that the Claimant could not be registered for P Club, tried to find a new club for the player, again on a ban basis. The Respondent provided in this respect a document dated 12 December 2005, in which R made a proposal towards the Respondent regarding the amount it was prepared to pay to the Respondent for the ban of the Claimant until 30 November 2006. Given this approach of the Respondent to negotiate with another club a further ban of the player, the members of the Chamber considered that the Respondent expressed its willingness to continue the contractual relationship with the Claimant.

17. In this connection, the Respondent alleged that the Claimant refused to sign the employment contract with R. To that regard and for the sake of good order, the members underlined that the Claimant did not have the obligation to sign an employment contract with the aforementioned B ian club and agree to the relevant ban since the ban of a professional, which necessarily takes place during the validity of an employment contract with his club of origin, is also subject to the express agreement of the player.
18. Subsequently, the Chamber underlined that the ban contract the Respondent signed with P Club, and which was co-signed by the Claimant, would have, in any case, expired on 31 December 2005. Therefore, the members pointed out that the Claimant should have offered his services to the Claimant on 1 January 2006 at the latest. In this respect, the members referred to the employment contract the Claimant concluded with the B ian club, Z, on 2 January 2006. By acting this way, the Claimant manifested having not fulfilled its contractual obligation towards the Respondent by not offering his services to the employer after the ban period with another club expired.
19. In continuation, the members turned their attention to the Claimant's allegation that the Respondent did not pay him his salaries since July 2005.
20. With regard to the Claimant's salary until September 2005, the Chamber referred to the ban contract between the Respondent and XXX dated 14 April 2005, which had been co-signed by the Claimant. In accordance with the said ban contract, the members observed that the bending club, XXX, assumed the payment of the Claimant's salaries for the ban period, i.e. from 14 April until 31 December 2005. Consequently, taking into account that the aforementioned ban agreement was prematurely terminated by mutual agreement between the clubs concerned as well as with the consent of the Claimant on 20 September 2005, the members concluded that the payment of the Claimant's salary until the end of September 2005 was the obligation of the bending club, XXX.
21. Concerning the salary payments for the months of October and November 2005, the Chamber recalled that, as previously explained, the Respondent could, in good faith, assume that the player was regularly registered with P Club. In particular, it was emphasized that the Claimant did not render, nor even offer, his services to the Respondent. Therefore, the members concluded that the Respondent was not responsible for the payment of the Claimant's salaries for this period of time.
22. In view of the foregoing, the Chamber concluded that by the end of December 2005, only the payment of the Claimant's salary for one month, i.e. December 2005, was outstanding.
23. Given the history and the relevant circumstances of the case at hand, the members underlined that the non-payment of one monthly salary is no valid reason for the Claimant to unilaterally terminate the employment contract with the Respondent for just cause.
24. On account of all the above, the members of the Chamber concluded that a valid employment contract between the Claimant and the Respondent still exists, which has to be respected by both involved parties throughout its validity.
25. Finally, the members proceeded by acknowledging that the Claimant deems having sporting just cause for the termination of the employment contract he concluded with the Respondent.
26. For the sake of good order, the members recalled that an established professional may only terminate an employment contract for sporting just cause at the end of the season, more precisely, within 15 days following the last official match of the season of the club for which he is registered. The members stressed that the aforementioned conditions are obviously not fulfilled in the present matter and therefore this reason invoked by the Claimant does not apply to the case at hand anyway.

III. DECISION OF THE DISPUTE RESOLUTION CHAMBER

1. The claim of the Claimant, Player X, is rejected.
2. It is established that a valid employment contract still exists between the Claimant, Player X, and the Respondent, D.
3. According to art. 60 par. 1 of the FIFA Statutes this decision may be appealed before the Court of Arbitration for Sport (CAS). The statement of appeal must be sent to the CAS directly within 21 days of receiving notification of this decision and has to contain all elements in accordance with point 2 of the directives issued by the CAS, copy of which we enclose hereto. Within another 10 days following the expiry of the time limit for the filing of the statement of appeal, the appellant shall file with the CAS a brief stating the facts and legal arguments giving rise to the appeal (cf. point 4 of the directives).

27 APRIL 2006

4618
DECISION OF THE DISPUTE RESOLUTION CHAMBER
passed in Zurich, Switzerland, on 27 April 2006,
in the following composition:
Slim Aloulou (Tunisia), Chairman
Jean-Marie Philips (Belgium), member
Wilfried Straub (Germany), member
Carlos Soto (Chile), member
Philippe Piat (France), member
on a matter between
the club, X, represented by xxxxx
and
the club, Y, represented by xxxxx
and
the club, Z, represented by xxxxxx as Intervening party
regarding the solidarity contribution related to the transfer of the player A

I. FACTS OF THE CASE

1. The player A, born on 19 June 1979, was transferred from Z to the club Y on 24 July 2004 for the amount of 5,000,000. A copy of the relevant transfer contract was submitted to FIFA.
2. On 24 July 2004, the club, X, sent a complaint against the club Y to FIFA regarding the payment of solidarity contribution and/or training compensation in respect of the player, A.
3. On 19 August 2004, Y informed FIFA that the player had been transferred to them on 24 July 2003 from the club, Z, for the sum of 5,000,000. Taking into account that at the time the player was 24 years old no training compensation is due. With regard to the claim for solidarity contribution Y referred to the articles 5, 6 and 13 of the relevant transfer agreement and pointed out that it already paid the amount of 75,000 to Z, on behalf of O, as solidarity contribution.
   Article 5 of the transfer agreement stipulates: "Z confirms and warrants to Y that since the 3 June 1995 the Player has been registered solely with Z and O and no other football clubs and/or teams and that since the 3 June 1995 no other football clubs and/or teams are entitled to any compensation in respect of the Players registration with Y hereunder including but without limitation pursuant to the FIFA Regulations." Article 6 of the transfer agreement stipulates: "Z confirms and warrants to Y that it will within 21 days of receipt of the sum payable under clause 3 [5,000,000] hereof pay to O the sum of £75,000 (Seventy five thousand pounds sterling) in full and final satisfaction of Os claim for solidarity payment under Chapter IX of the FIFA Regulations." Article 13 of the transfer agreement stipulates: "Z shall indemnity Y on demand in respect of any claims with any other football clubs and/or teams may have and/or may bring against Y arising out of Zs breach of the warranties set out in clause 5 and 6 in respect of the Players registration with Y hereunder for a solidarity payment pursuant to Chapter IX of the FIFA Regulations."
4. Furthermore, Y stressed that it has at no stage attempted to avoid its obligation as the "new club" to deal with the solidarity contribution under the FIFA Regulations. On the contrary, Y in fact distributed the solidarity payment within 30 days of the players registration in accordance with art. 25 of the FIFA Regulations for the Status and Transfer of Players, however, as it seems to be, not to the legitimate players training club(s).
5. As a result, Y requested FIFA to invite the xxx Football Association to clarify the situation and in case that it is established that any solidarity contribution should have been paid to Z instead of O, Y deems that Z should deal with the matter, i.e. reimburse the amount of 75,000 paid to them as solidarity contribution on behalf of O.
6. Subsequently, X renounced to further pursue its claim for training compensation.
7. On 15 March 2005, FIFA invited Z to provide its statement to the mater, in particular regarding the position of Y that it should reimburse the amount of 75,000. In this respect, Z affirmed that X is no longer registered within the xxx and therefore it shall not be entitled to claim anything.
8. On 27 September 2005, FIFA informed the clubs concerned by the present procedure the well-established jurisprudence of the Dispute Resolution Chamber applied in cases in which the new

club omitted to deduct the relevant proportion(s) of the 5% solidarity contribution, from the paid compensation, and invited them to consider it accordingly.

9. Upon FIFAs request, the xxx confirmed that X had been registered within its association as from 1994 until now. Moreover, the xxx confirmed that the player A had been registered with X as from 15 March 1996 to 9 April 1997 and as from 11 July 1997 to 14 July 1998.
10. On 10 October 2005, Z contested the period of time during which the player in question had been registered with X. According to Z the player had only been registered with X from 15 March 1996 until April 1997. As a result, Z is of the opinion that only 10.83% of 5% of the transfer compensation paid by Y is due to X as solidarity contribution, i.e. the amount of 27,080.
11. Y once again underlined its willingness to solve the present affair, but requested the intervention of FIFA in order to properly clarify the matter taking into account particularly the contradictory information with regard to the players career history.
12. On 12 October 2005, X contested the arguments of Z and referred to the official confirmation issued by the xxxx regarding the period of registration of the player, A, with X.
13. In November 2005, the xxx re-examined the matter and amended the period of time during which the player had been registered with its affiliated club X, i.e. the xxx confirmed that the player A had been registered with X as from April 1996 until May 1997 only, that is, for a bit more than one season between the ages of 16 and 17.

II. CONSIDERATIONS OF THE DISPUTE RESOLUTION CHAMBER

1. First of all, the Chamber analysed whether it was competent to deal with the matter at stake. In this respect, it referred to art. 18 par. 2 and 3 of the Rules Governing the Procedures of the Players' Status Committee and the Dispute Resolution Chamber. The present matter was submitted to FIFA on 24 July 2004, as a consequence the Chamber concluded that the previous Procedural Rules (edition 2001) on matters pending before the decision making bodies of FIFA are applicable on the matter at hand.
2. With regard to the competence of the Chamber, art. 25 par. 2 of the FIFA Regulations for the Status and Transfer of Players (edition 2001) establishes that, it falls within the purview of the Dispute Resolution Chamber to review disputes concerning the distribution of the solidarity contribution.
3. As a consequence, the Dispute Resolution Chamber is the competent body to decide on the present litigation concerning the distribution of the solidarity contribution claimed by the club X in connection with the transfer of the professional player A during the course of a contract.
4. Subsequently, the members of the Chamber analyzed which edition of the Regulations for the Status and Transfer of Players should be applicable as to the substance of the matter. In this respect, the Chamber referred to art. 26 par. 1 and 2 of the Regulations for the Status and Transfer of Players (edition 2005) in the modified version in accordance with the FIFA circular no. 995 dated 23 September 2005. Furthermore, it acknowledged that the professional had been registered for his new club in July 2003. Equally the Chamber took note that the claim was lodged at FIFA in July 2004. In view of the aforementioned, the Chamber concluded that the former FIFA Regulations for the Status and Transfer of Players (edition 2001, hereafter: the Regulations) are applicable on the case at hand as to the substance.
5. In continuation, and entering into the substance of the matter, the members of the Chamber started by acknowledging that, as established in the art. 25 par.1 of the Regulations in connection with art. 11 par.1 of the Regulations governing the Application of the Regulations , the new club of the player is to distribute 5% of any compensation paid to the previous club to the club(s) involved in the training and education of the player in proportion to the number of years the player has been registered with the relevant clubs between the ages of 12 and 23.
6. In the present case, the Chamber outlined that the entire period to be taken into consideration with regard to the solidarity contribution would run from the sporting season 1992, when the player was 12, until the sporting season 2002, at the age of 23.
7. In continuation, the Chamber duly noted that Y (the players new club) asserts having paid the entire amount of 5,000,000, agree upon as transfer compensation, to Z (the players previous club). Furthermore, it agreed with the said club, on the one hand, that the amount of 75,000 corresponds to the solidarity contribution due to O and that Z would therefore pass on the relevant amount to the said club, and on the other hand, that Z would be responsible for the payment of any possible

third club in connection with solidarity contribution. In other words, Y omitted to deduct 5% of the relevant transfer compensation relating to the solidarity mechanism, while contractually establishing that Z would make the relevant payments.

8. Furthermore, the Chamber observed that in view of what had been contractually agreed between Y and Z, the club deemed that X should thus turn to Z in order to collect the amount relating to its part of the 5% solidarity contribution.
9. In this respect, the Chamber referred to its well-established jurisprudence applied in similar cases, in accordance with which the players new club is ordered to remit the relevant proportion(s) of the 5% solidarity contribution to the club(s) involved in the players training in strict application of art. 11 of the Regulations governing the Application of the Regulations. At the same time, the players former club is ordered to reimburse the same proportion(s) of the 5% of the compensation that it received from the players new club.
10. The said jurisprudence is based on the fact that there is no contractual link between the training club claiming for solidarity contribution and the players former club. Therefore, the relevant claim does not find a contractual basis. Yet, the Regulations clearly establish that the distribution of the solidarity contribution is incumbent on the new club. As a consequence, the Regulations provide for a legal basis for the claim of the training club against the new club, yet not for a claim against the players former club. Finally, the new club and the previous club are bound by a contractual agreement, which needs to be respected.
11. The Chamber then referred to art. 10 of the Regulations, which provides the figures for the distribution of the solidarity contribution, according to the time the player was effectively trained by the clubs involved.
12. In the present case, the Chamber outlined that according to the amended confirmation of the xxx the period to be taken into consideration (period of registration of the player with the club X) went from April 1996 until May 1997, when the player was between the age of 16 and 17. In this respect, the Chamber concluded that the period of effective training to be taken into account corresponds to 1 season and 2 months.
13. Therefore, the Chamber established that, in accordance with the breakdown provided for in art. 10 of the Regulations governing the Application of the Regulations, X is entitled to receive 11.7% of the 5% of the compensation paid in relation to the transfer of the player A from Z to Y.
14. The Chamber noted that according to the transfer contract remitted to the file the player A was transferred for the amount of 5,000,000.
15. Based on all of the above, the Dispute Resolution Chamber decided that Y must pay to X 11.7% of the 5% of the transfer compensation paid in relation to the transfer of the player A, i.e. 29,250 and that Z must reimburse the amount of 29,250 to Y.

III. DECISION OF THE DISPUTE RESOLUTION CHAMBER

1. The claim of X is accepted.
2. The club Y has to pay the amount of 29,250 to X within 30 days as from the date of notification of this decision.
3. If the aforementioned sum is not paid within the aforementioned deadline an interest rate of 5% per year will apply as of expiry of the fixed time limit and the present matter shall be submitted to FIFAs Disciplinary Committee, so that the necessary disciplinary sanctions may be imposed.
4. X is directed to inform Y directly and immediately of the account number to which the remittance is to be made and to notify the Dispute Resolution Chamber of every payment received.
5. Z has to reimburse the amount of 29,250 to Y within 30 days of notification of the present decision.
6. If the aforementioned sum is not paid within the aforementioned deadline an interest rate of 5% per year will apply as of expiring of the fixed time limit and the present matter shall be submitted to FIFAs Disciplinary Committee, so that the necessary disciplinary sanctions may be imposed.
7. Y is directed to inform Z directly and immediately of the account number to which the remittance is to be made and to notify the Dispute Resolution Chamber of every payment received.
8. According to art. 60 par. 1 of the FIFA Statutes, this decision may be appealed against before the Court of Arbitration for Sport (CAS). The statement of appeal must be sent to the CAS directly within 21 days of receipt of notification of this decision and shall contain all the elements in accordance with point 2 of the directives issued by the CAS, a copy of which we enclose hereto. Within another

10 days following the expiry of the time limit for filing the statement of appeal, the appellant shall file a brief stating the facts and legal arguments giving rise to the appeal with the CAS (cf. point 4 of the directives).

⚽⚽⚽

46290
DECISION OF THE DISPUTE RESOLUTION CHAMBER
passed in Zurich, Switzerland, on 27 April 2006,
in the following composition:
Mr. Slim Aloulou (Tunisia), Chairman
Mr. Carlos Soto (Chile), Member Mr. Philippe Piat (France), Member
Mr. Jean-Marie Philips (Belgium), Member Mr. Wilfried Straub (Germany), Member
On the claim presented by Player T, as Claimant against Club A, as Respondent
regarding a contractual dispute between the parties involved

I. FACTS OF THE CASE

1. On 19 June 2002, the player T and the club A signed an employment contract valid for the season 2002/2003 expiring on 30 June 2003.
2. The employment contract established in its clause III all the payments that the player T had to receive from the club A as well as the relevant conditions as follows:
   a) Guaranteed Payments: Total USD 85,000 payable in three instalments 1)USD 25,000 (day of signing in cash); 2) USD 30,000 (until 23 August 2002) and 3) USD 30,000 (until 31 December 2002).
   b) Appearance Fee: USD 3,000 for the games he plays in the Turkish League, Turkish Cup and European Cup under following conditions: -if the player is on the first 11, he receives 100% of USD 3,000; -if the player is on the bench, he receives 50 % i.e. USD 1,500 and -if the player is on the bench as substitute and takes part in the game he receives 75%, i.e. USD 2,250.
   c) Injuries: after playing three games as starter player (first 11), in case of injury during the game, the player will receive 100% of the agreed appearance fee for the next three games and furthermore 50 % of the Appearance Fee for the next three games.
   d) All above mentioned payments are net (state taxes and fees regarding above mentioned payments will be paid by the club).
   e) The club will pay USD 5,000 until 1 August 2002 and USD 2,500 until 1st October 2002 for accommodation, car, etc. to the player.
3. On 16 January 2004 the player T communicated directly in writing to the club that it breached the employment contract due to non-payment of USD 32,750 as appearance fees and he enclosed a copy of an account statement specifying games and monies.
4. On 4 January 2005 the player lodged a formal complaint against the club A at FIFA.
5. The player claims the payment of the following amounts:
   a. 8 matches USD 24,000 (100%, USD 3,000 per match)
   b. 1 match USD 2,250 (75 %)
   c. 5 matches USD 7,500 (50%, USD 1,500 per match)
   d. 3 matches injured USD 9,000 (USD 3,000 per match)
   e. check for TRL 15,000 millions. The club gave to the player this check payable on 26 September 2003 however it allegedly remains unpaid.
6. The Club A states that they paid all the monies that they were obliged to based on the contract and submitted a list of payments due and a list of payments allegedly done for an amount of USD 163,933 and another list of payments such as for the house and the car for an amount of TRL 17,675,000,000. The club concluded that they paid to the player T the total amount of USD 175,198 some in cash and some through bank account and the club has presented receipts to FIFA.
7. In his reply the player states that:
   a) the position of the club is not clear and accurate;
   b) in the list of payments allegedly done the club mentioned 4 disciplinary sanctions (fines), that the player was never informed of and therefore does not accept, amounting USD 3,645;
   c) the club maintains that they paid everything to the player but they could not prove accurately this circumstance;

d) the club did not mention 3 matches in which the player was injured and based on point III c) of the contract was entitled to USD 9,000 (USD 3,000 per match);
e) he totally refuses the clubs argument stating that the player had the habit to be injured. The player states that if this had been the case the club could have applied a disciplinary sanction on him but this was not the case. Furthermore, the medical report, provided by the club, states that the player had pain in his feet and if he had to play he would have to take analgesics;
f) the club mixed up different payments such as house, car, flight tickets, etc.;
g) the club gave to the player a check for TRL 15,000 millions on 26 September 2003, i.e. after the expiry of the contract in payment of monies owed but the check could not be cashed. The player provided a copy of the check;

8. In its final position the club A added that
   a) regarding the 4 fines imposed on the player T, the club used to impose fines on all the players of the squad when they did not play successfully and they applied premiums when they were successful. For this reason the player T received the relevant fines; and
   b) regarding the check of TRL 15,000 millions, they paid the relevant amount to a team-mate of the Claimant named M L in cash. However, the player T did not return the original check to the club.
9. The player T asks the DRC to order the club A to pay the amount of USD 42,750.

II. CONSIDERATIONS OF THE DISPUTE RESOLUTION CHAMBER

1. First of all, the Chamber analysed whether it was competent to deal with the matter at stake. In this respect, it referred to art. 18 par. 2 and 3 of the Rules Governing the Procedures of the Players' Status Committee and the Dispute Resolution Chamber. The present matter was submitted to FIFA before 1 July 2005, more specifically on 4 January 2005, as a consequence the Chamber concluded that the previous Procedural Rules (edition 2001) on matters pending before the decision making bodies of FIFA are applicable to the matter at hand.
2. With regard to the competence of the Chamber, art. 42 par. 1 lit. (b) (i) of the FIFA Regulations for the Status and Transfer of Players (edition 2001) establishes that the triggering elements of the employment-related dispute will be decided by the Dispute Resolution Chamber.
3. If an employment contract is breached by a party, the Dispute Resolution Chamber (DRC) is also responsible to verify whether a party is accountable for outstanding payments and/or compensation.
4. As a consequence, the DRC is the competent body to decide on the present litigation involving a player and a club regarding outstanding monies claimed by the player T in connection with an employment contract.
5. Subsequently, the members of the Chamber analyzed which edition of the Regulations for the Status and Transfer of Players should be applicable as to the substance of the matter. In this respect, the Chamber referred, on the one hand, to art. 26 par. 1 and 2 of the Regulations for the Status and Transfer of Players (edition 2005) and, on the other hand, to the fact that the relevant contract at the basis of the present dispute was signed on 19 June 2002 and the claim was lodged at FIFA on 4 January 2005. In view of the aforementioned, the Chamber concluded that the former FIFA Regulations for the Status and Transfer of Players (edition 2001, hereinafter: the Regulations) are applicable to the case at hand as to the substance.
6. In continuation, and entering into the substance of the matter, the members of the Chamber started by acknowledging that both parties signed an employment contract on 19 June 2002 expiring on 30 June 2003. Moreover, the Chamber noted that in the relevant contract the Respondent assumed the obligation to pay to the Claimant certain amounts, such as, guaranteed payments, match bonuses and expenses.
7. At this stage, the DRC pointed out that the parties in the present matter have a contradictory position with respect to the determination of the relevant amounts supposedly owed to the player. On one hand, the player T claims that the amount of USD 42,750 remains unpaid by the Respondent, and on the other hand the club A considered that they already paid all the amounts to the player based on the obligations assumed in the relevant contract.
8. The DRC noted that the players claim solely pertain to outstanding monies. Therefore, the Chamber considered it appropriate to focus on the amounts claimed by the player T, the Respondents allegation regarding the amounts already paid and the documentary evidence submitted by both parties.
9. The members of the Chamber particularly focused on the analysis of the lists of payments submitted by the Respondent to FIFA.

10. First of all, the Chamber focused on the players remark with respect to the four (4) disciplinary sanctions imposed by the Respondent. In fact, the club established in its relevant list the total amount of USD 3,639 as fines imposed on the Claimant based on low performance of the entire squad. In this respect, the DRC outlined that, as a general rule, low performance cannot be considered a reason for the club to reduce payments to the player, because it is unilaterally determined by the club and based on pure subjective criteria. Therefore, the members of the DRC concluded that this imposition of fines by the Respondent cannot be accepted and thus cannot be deducted from monies payable to the player.
11. Secondly, the DRC identified one receipt dated 23 August 2002 for an amount of USD 30,000 in which the beneficiary of the bank deposit is not the Claimant. The Chamber analyzed all the payments made by bank deposit provided by the Respondent and concluded that there are six payments made in this way. In all of them it clearly appears that the player T was the beneficiary except the one made on 23 August 2002, in which a beneficiary called H is referred to. As a consequence, the DRC deemed that this receipt relating to the alleged payment of USD 30,000 cannot be accepted as documentary evidence.
12. In continuation, the Chamber focused its attention to the Claimants allegation with respect the check issued by the Respondent in the amount of USD 10,987 (payable on 26/09/2003), which according to the player appeared not covered with necessary funds. In this respect the members of the DRC remarked that this allegation was not contested by the Respondent. In this regard, the Respondent informed FIFA that the Claimant authorized a team mate to receive on his behalf the relevant amount of USD 10,987 (TRL 15,000,000,000) in cash. The DRC deemed that the Respondent failed to substantiate this allegation with documentary evidence and that it had to reject this argument.
13. The members of the DRC concluded that the remainder of the payments indicated by the Respondent are valid and therefore shall be admitted. Consequently the DRC concluded that the Respondent failed to prove payment to the Claimant of the total amount of USD 44,626 (i.e. disciplinary sanctions, receipt dated 23/08/2002 and amount indicated on check).
14. In continuation, the Chamber pointed out that the player T claims the amount of USD 42,750.
15. Departing from the principle that the amount to be awarded shall not exceed the amount claimed, the Chamber decided that the Respondent has to pay the amount of USD 42,750 to the Claimant.
16. Finally, the Chamber decided that the Claimant has to return the original check to the Respondent.

III. DECISION OF THE DISPUTE RESOLUTION CHAMBER

1. The claim of the Claimant, the player T, is accepted.
2. The Respondent, Club A, has to pay the amount of USD 42,750 to the Claimant.
3. The amount due to the Claimant has to be paid by the Respondent within 30 days as from the date of notification of this decision.
4. The player T is instructed to return the check to Club A.
5. In the event that the debt of the Respondent is not paid within the stated deadline an interest rate of 5% per year will apply as of expiry of the said time limit and the file will be submitted to the Disciplinary Committee.
6. The Claimant is directed to inform the Respondent immediately of the account number to which the remittance is to be made and to notify the Dispute Resolution Chamber of every payment received.
7. According to art. 60 par. 1 of the FIFA Statutes this decision may be appealed before the Court of Arbitration for Sport (CAS). The statement of appeal must be sent to the CAS directly within 21 days of receiving notification of this decision and has to contain all elements in accordance with point 2 of the directives issued by the CAS, copy of which we enclose hereto. Within another 10 days following the expiry of the time limit for the filing of the statement of appeal, the appellant shall file with the CAS a brief stating the facts and legal arguments giving rise to the appeal (cf. point 4 of the directives).

46400
DECISION OF THE DISPUTE RESOLUTION CHAMBER
passed in Zurich, Switzerland, on 27 April 2006,
in the following composition:
Slim Aloulou (Tunisia), Chairman

Carlos Soto (Chile), member
Philippe Piat (France), member
Jean-Marie Philips (Belgium), member
Wilfried Straub (Germany), member
on the claim presented by the club X, A, as Claimant
against the club Y, B as Respondent
with the club Z, C as intervening party
regarding the solidarity contribution related to the transfer of the player D.

I. **FACTS OF THE CASE**

1. According to a written letter of confirmation from the claimant Football Association, the player D, born 4 August 1974, was registered for the following national clubs between the ages of 9 and 22:
   - from 08.04.1984 to 05.03.1985: club G,
   - from 05.03.1985 to 08.04.1990: club E,
   - from 08.04.1990 to 11.08.1995: club F and
   - from 11.08.1995 to 29.08.1996: club X.
2. In August 1996, the player D was transferred from the national club X, the Claimant, to the club H in country C apparently for the amount of USD –.– and in August 1999 to the club Z in C apparently for the approximate amount of USD –.–.
3. On 25 August 2003, a transfer contract for the player D was concluded between the club Z, the intervening party, and the club Y of country B, the Respondent, for the net sum of EUR –.– (approximately USD –.–).
4. The Respondent appeared to be prepared to pay the solidarity contribution to the clubs of the country A involved in the players training and education in accordance with the applicable FIFA regulations, as it deducted the corresponding amount from the transfer compensation and kept it in reserve for the clubs in A.
5. On 5 December 2003 and 15 January 2004, the intervening party submitted statements to FIFA regarding the distribution of the solidarity contribution for the player D. The intervening party objects to the Respondent withholding the solidarity contribution for the following reasons (5.1-5.7):
   5.1. As part of the relevant transfer compensation, each training club in country A has already received an amount towards the player's training at the time of the relevant transfers, and this payment exceeded the 5% due as a solidarity contribution. Furthermore, the club G does not have any right to claim solidarity contribution. However, the intervening party does not know whether the club E received compensation at the time of the player's transfer to F.
   5.2. Art. 25 of the FIFA Regulations for the Status and Transfer of Players (edition 2001, hereinafter referred to as; the Regulations 2001) only came into effect after all transfers involving the training clubs in country A had been completed, and as such, this provision cannot be applied retrospectively to this matter. As this provision cannot be applied retrospectively, and in the interests of legal security, the training clubs cannot have any right to compensation in the sense of the solidarity mechanism.
   5.3. Not until FIFA circular 826 dated 31 October 2002 was it made clear that the transfer compensation agreed between the players new, i.e. the Respondent, and the players former club, i.e. the intervening party, must be 100%. Once again, this could not be applied retrospectively. In other words, the circular could not be applied to transfers that took place before the circular was issued.
   5.4. If retrospective application were to be allowed, the 5% solidarity contribution would have to be taken into account also in earlier transfer compensations. In this respect, the intervening party provided several day-by-day calculations, showing that it was the only club that had received less compensation for the players transfer than it had actually paid to his former club.
   5.5. According to art. 20 of the Regulations 2001, training compensation is not payable for any player over the age of 23. Solidarity contributions cannot be irrespective of age, as claimed in circular 769.
   5.6. By analysing the solidarity mechanism in terms of its etymology, teleology and stages of conception, it is clear that solidarity contribution is only due if at the time of the players

transfer between two clubs the clubs involved did not reach any agreement on compensation. Therefore, if a club received compensation when a player left the club, no solidarity contribution is due in case of future transfers.

5.7. The Respondent provided a bank guarantee for the exact net amount of the transfer compensation agreed upon with the intervening party. Therefore, it is clear that when the Respondent signed the transfer contract, it did not make it clear that it intended to deduct 5%. "Net" means "after deduction of 5% for a solidarity contribution. It is not possible to make a retrospective deduction.

Furthermore, in the transfer contract, the Respondent explicitly agreed to bear all costs.

6. Finally, the intervening party demanded that the Football Association of country A should hand out the transfer agreement between the club F and the X, the Claimant.

7. On 19 April 2004, the Football Association of country A lodged a claim with FIFA against the Respondent on behalf of its affiliated club, F, for the payment of the corresponding amount in accordance with the relevant proportion of the 5% solidarity contribution.

8. In response to the aforementioned position of the intervening party, the club F refuted the allegations made. F believes that the intervening party, on the one hand, is incorrectly comparing the claims for training compensation with claims made on the basis of the solidarity mechanism, and thereby creating significant confusion and drawing incorrect conclusions, and on the other hand, is failing to recognise the existence of the solidarity mechanism.

9. In its response, the intervening party adhered to its position. In particular, it stated as follows:

9.1. That the above-mentioned club F had only disputed a few minor points in its statement, and that as a result, it had accepted the other arguments. For example, and in particular club F had therefore admitted to have received the sum of USD –.– for the players transfer to X, the Claimant.

9.2. The intervening party further stated that the principle of solidarity is to ensure that compensation reaches the clubs which did not receive payments at the start.
Consequently, the training club should only be compensated if there is no agreement on and payment of compensation at the time of the player's transfer from the training to a new club. F received compensation when the player was transferred to X, the Claimant, which is why the club does not have the right to be compensated again for the same training.

9.3. In addition, there is no compensation due because when the original transfer compensation was agreed upon by F and the Claimant, the clubs did not know that as of September 2001, i.e. as of the coming into effect of the Regulations 2001, another 5% of any compensation paid within the scope of a further transfer would be due.

10. Finally, the intervening party demanded once again that the Football Association of country A hands out the transfer agreement concluded between the club F and the claimant club.

11. In continuation, the Respondent reasoned as follows:

11.1. The Respondent informed FIFA that the transfer agreement with the intervening party stipulated a total transfer compensation of EUR –.–, payable as follows:
- 1st instalment of EUR –.– within 24 hours of receipt of the International Transfer Certificate,
- 2nd instalment of EUR –.– by 20 September 2003 at the latest, and
- 3rd instalment of EUR –.– by 20 July 2004 at the latest.

11.2. The Respondent explained that the first two instalments were paid on time and without any deductions. Furthermore, the Respondent maintained that before the 3rd instalment was due, it informed the intervening party that it would withhold the corresponding solidarity contribution of EUR –.– in order to distribute this money to the training clubs.

11.3. With regard to the agreed net payment of the transfer compensation, the Respondent explained that it had only been agreed that it would cover the costs of administration and registration, but that it had never been agreed that the Respondent would also pay the solidarity contribution. Such an agreement would have had to be defined explicitly, in other words, with "solidarity contribution" mentioned in the relevant transfer contract. With this in mind, the respondent club referred to the wording of the contract, which states: "exempt from any other costs".

11.4. According to the FIFA circulars 769 and 826, the new club is responsible for paying the 5% solidarity contribution, and it is therefore allowed to subtract the relevant amount from the transfer compensation. With regard to the solidarity contribution, contrary to the intervening partys opinion, it is not the training work itself but the simple fact that the club was involved in training the player that gives rise to the claim. Training compensation and compensation regarding solidarity mechanism are two completely different rights or claims that exist independently of each other.

11.5. The Respondent also refutes the intervening party's argument that a a bban guarantee for the entire transfer compensation is incompatible with a later deduction of the 5% solidarity contribution from the final instalment, as the Respondent would still have to pay the full amount anyway, but to various clubs instead of to the intervening party only.

11.6. Finally, the respondent club stated that it was happy to wait for the Dispute Resolution Chamber to reach a decision before making the necessary payment.

12. In response, the intervening party submitted numerous statements.

12.1. It repeated that the club F, having received a transfer compensation of USD –.– from X, the Claimant, had received much more than a solidarity contribution for its training, and that it had even made a considerable profit (sic: in its previous submission, the intervening party had referred to a compensation of USD –.–).

12.2. The intervening party also reiterated that the Respondent should have explicitly excluded the solidarity contribution from the transfer contract if it wanted to proceed this way. The opposite, however, was in fact true. It is clear that the Respondent, from the outset, knew that it would have to cover the solidarity contribution itself. Otherwise, the Respondent would not have paid the first two instalments without subtracting 5%. The note regarding the 30-day payment 5 deadline in art. 11 of the Regulations governing the Application of the Regulations 2001 also supports this.

12.3. Furthermore, the intervening party once again stressed that a club could not be compensated twice for the same right.

12.4. Finally, the intervening party insisted that the Football Association of country A should hand out the transfer agreement between the club F and the claimant club.

13. In its submissions dated 18 May and 29 July 2004, the Football Association of country A informed FIFA that its club and the Respondent held the same viewpoints in this dispute, and therefore asked for a decision that reflected this.

14. On 6 July 2004, without prejudice to any decision which might have to be taken by the competent body at a later stage, FIFA drew the parties' attention to the general principle that legal provisions and regulations are only open to interpretation if their wording is not clear and precise. FIFA stated that the provisions in the FIFA Regulations regarding the solidarity mechanism and its application are clear and precise, and therefore leave no room for interpretation.
FIFA invited the parties to duly consider this fact and to proceed accordingly.

15. In response, the intervening party stated that it would be standing by its position, whereas the Football Association of country A demanded that the parties act in accordance with FIFAs instructions.

16. The Respondent then informed FIFA that its bank, i.e. where the bank guarantee had been placed, had received a request from the intervening party, i.e. the recipient of the guarantee, for a partial payment of the guarantee in the amount of EUR –.– and that the bank had approved this request. The Respondent therefore stated that the club F should make direct contact with the intervening party regarding the solidarity contribution. FIFA should also order the intervening party to pay the EUR –.– which it had obtained illegally, to the club F.

17. The Football Association of country A then once again called upon the parties involved to act in accordance with FIFAs letter dated 6 July 2004, and demanded that the relevant proportions of the solidarity contribution are paid to the clubs that had been involved in the players training. Furthermore, in response to a request from FIFA for clarification, the Football Association of country A submitted copies of the complaints for payment of solidarity contribution from the clubs E and X, the Claimant. Finally, the Football Association of country A submitted another letter in which it once again demanded that the solidarity contribution is to be paid to its clubs, while also claiming the relevant interests.

18. In their final submissions dated 6 March 2006, the clubs X, E and F stood by their complaints and opinions (i.e. backed the former submissions of F), and demanded that the interest is to be paid as well as appropriate disciplinary measures are to be imposed.

19. The intervening party disputed its involvement and its capacity to be made a respondent in this whole dispute. The intervening party stated that the only question to be answered was whether the new club,

i.e. the Respondent, had paid a solidarity contribution in accordance with the FIFA regulations and circular as well as in accordance with FIFA jurisdiction. Consequently, other questions regarding contractual relationships with other clubs were not to be examined.

With regard to its previous submissions, the intervening party stated that these had only been made in order to learn about FIFAs interpretation of the new system that had been introduced at the start of proceedings. Furthermore, the intervening party stated that, in any case, it was the responsibility of the Respondent to pay the solidarity contribution. In addition, any claim submitted by the Respondent for repayment would have to be considered in separate proceedings at a later date. Furthermore, the intervening party is of the opinion that, contrary to the statements submitted by the clubs X, E and F, the FIFA letter dated 6 July 2004 had only contained directives for the respondent club, not any orders directed to the intervening party. Finally, the intervening party stressed that the delay in this proceedings could only be attributed to the Respondents actions.

II. CONSIDERATIONS OF THE DISPUTE RESOLUTION CHAMBER

1. First of all, the Chamber analysed whether it was competent to deal with the matter at stake. In this respect, it referred to art. 18 par. 2 and 3 of the Rules Governing the Procedures of the Players' Status Committee and the Dispute Resolution Chamber. The present matter was submitted to FIFA on 19 April 2004, as a consequence the Chamber concluded that the previous Procedural Rules (edition 2001) on matters pending before the decision making bodies of FIFA are applicable on the matter at hand.
2. With regard to the competence of the Chamber, art. 25 par. 2 of the FIFA Regulations for the Status and Transfer of Players (edition 2001) establishes that, it falls within the purview of the Dispute Resolution Chamber to review disputes concerning the distribution of the solidarity contribution.
3. As a consequence, the Dispute Resolution Chamber is the competent body to decide on the present litigation concerning the distribution of the solidarity contribution claimed by the Claimant in connection with the transfer of the professional player D during the course of a contract.
4. Subsequently, the members of the Chamber analyzed which edition of the Regulations for the Status and Transfer of Players should be applicable as to the substance of the matter. In this respect, the Chamber referred to art. 26 par. 1 and 2 of the Regulations for the Status and Transfer of Players (edition 2005) in the modified version in accordance with the FIFA circular no. 995 dated 23 September 2005. Furthermore, it acknowledged that the professional player in question had been registered for his new club in August 2003. Equally the Chamber took note that the claim was lodged at FIFA on 19 April 2004. In view of the aforementioned, the Chamber concluded that the former FIFA Regulations for the Status and Transfer of Players (edition 2001, hereafter: the Regulations) are applicable on the case at hand as to the substance.
5. In continuation, and entering into the substance of the matter, the members of the Chamber started by acknowledging that as established in art. 25 of the Regulations in connection with art. 11 par. 1 of the Regulations governing the Application of the Regulations 2001 (hereinafter: Application Regulations), the new club concerned is to distribute 5% of any compensation paid to the previous club of the player to the club(s) where the player had played between the ages of 12 and 23.
6. In the present case, the Chamber outlined that the entire period to be taken into consideration for the calculation and distribution of the solidarity contribution ran from the sporting season 1987, at the beginning of which the player was 12, until the sporting season 1997, at the end of which the player was 23.
7. The Chamber made further reference to art. 10 of the Application Regulations, which provides the figures for the distribution of the solidarity contribution, in accordance with the time the player was effectively trained by the clubs involved.
8. In the case at hand, the Chamber observed that Football Association of country A confirmed that the player D had been registered for the Claimant from 11 August 1995 until 29 August 1996.
9. Consequently, the Chamber concluded that the period of effective training to be taken into account for the solidarity contribution due to the Claimant corresponds to one year, from 11 August 1995, at the time when the player was 20 years old until 29 August 1996.
10. Therefore, the Chamber established that, in accordance with the breakdown provided for in art. 10 of the Application Regulations, the Claimant is in principle entitled to receive 10% of the 5% of the compensation paid in relation to the transfer of the player from the intervening party to the Respondent.

11. In continuation, the Chamber turned its attention to the Respondents position.
The Chamber acknowledged, in particular, that the Respondent had intended to withhold 5% of the transfer compensation it had agreed upon with the intervening party in order to distribute the relevant amount to the players training clubs. Yet, after having the bank, where the bank guarantee for the intervening party had been placed, upon request of the intervening party, transferred the amount of EUR –.– (the amount which the Respondent had withheld in order to distribute to the training clubs) to the intervening party, the Respondent contests its obligation to pay any compensation to the Claimant.
12. The Chamber noted that the Respondent asserts having now paid 100% of the transfer compensation. Moreover, the Respondent argues that it agreed with the intervening party that the transfer compensation was paid exempt from any other costs. From the Respondents point of view, this did, however, not mean that it would have to pay solidarity contribution to the training clubs in addition to the transfer compensation to the intervening party. The relevant provision only committed the Respondent to cover all costs of administration and registration.
The Chamber observed that the Respondent is of the opinion that the Claimant should therefore turn to the intervening party directly in order to receive the relevant proportion of solidarity contribution.
13. Taking the above into account, the Chamber outlined that it could not upheld the position of the Respondent with regard to its obligation to pay solidarity compensation to the Claimant. The Chamber emphasised that the relevant provisions contained in the Regulations as well as in the Application Regulations on the duty of the new club to distribute 5% of any compensation paid to the previous club(s) where the player had played between the ages of 12 and 23 are clear and precise and do not leave room for interpretation. Moreover, the Chamber deemed it important to clarify that besides the aforementioned, the Claimants rights could not be forgone by a contractual clause, such as the above- mentioned wording “exempt from any other costs”, agreed between two other parties.
14. In this respect, the Chamber referred to its well-established jurisprudence in similar cases, according to which the players new club is ordered to remit the relevant proportion(s) of the 5% solidarity contribution to the club(s) involved in the players training in strict application of art. 11 of the Application Regulations.
Moreover, and in applying the said jurisprudence, the Chamber underlined that the Respondent, in turn, will have the right to claim the reimbursement of the same proportion(s) of the 5% in relation to solidarity mechanism from the players former club.
15. The said jurisprudence is based on the fact that there is no contractual link between the training club claiming for solidarity contribution and the players former club. Therefore, the relevant claim does not find a contractual basis. Yet, the Regulations clearly establish that the distribution of the solidarity contribution is incumbent on the new club. As a consequence, the Regulations provide for a legal basis for the claim of the training club against the new club, yet not for a claim against the players former club. Finally, the new club and the previous club are bound by a contractual agreement, which needs to be respected.
16. The Chamber noted that in accordance with the transfer contract regarding the player D signed on 25 August 2003, the Respondent agreed to pay the amount of EUR to the club Z. Furthermore, the Chamber recalled that, as clarified in the FIFA circular 826, the 5% solidarity contribution is to be deducted from the amount payable to the players former club.
17. Taking into account the above, the Chamber decided that the Respondent must pay the Claimant 10% of the 5% of the transfer compensation it paid in relation to the transfer of the player in question from the intervening party to the Respondent, i.e. EUR –.– .
18. In continuation, the Chamber referred to the Claimants demand for default interest. In this respect and with regard to the mode of payment, the members of the Chamber referred to the well-established jurisprudence of the Dispute Resolution Chamber, according to which in case of contingent payments the new club shall pay the solidarity contribution to the training club(s) 30 days after the date of such payments. It is in fact on the basis of this jurisprudence that the revised Regulations (edition 2005) explicitly provide for this rule (cf. art. 2 par. 1 of Annex 5 to the revised Regulations).
19. Consequently, in light of the fact that from the relevant payment of transfer compensation ¼ (i.e. EUR –.–) had been due within 24 hours of receipt of the International Transfer Certificate, ¼ (EUR –.–) on 20 September 2003 and ½ (EUR –.–) on 20 July 2004, the Dispute Resolution Chamber established that a default interest payment of 5% p.a. according to the agreed contingent payments must be applied, as follows:

default interest of 5% p.a. on EUR –.–, i.e. ¼ of the above-decided solidarity contribution due to the Claimant, as from the day on which the 1st instalment was due, i.e. 25 August 2003, default interest of 5% p.a. on EUR –.–, i.e. ¼ of the above-decided solidarity contribution due to the Claimant, as from the day on which the 2nd instalment was due, i.e. 20 September 2003 and default interest of 5% p.a. on EUR –.–, i.e. ½ of the above-decided solidarity contribution due to the Claimant, as from the day on which the 3rd instalment was due, i.e. 20 July 2004.

20. Taking into account all of the above, the Dispute Resolution Chamber decided that the Respondent must pay the Claimant EUR –.– as solidarity contribution in relation to the transfer of the player D from the intervening party to the Respondent, plus 5% default interest per year on EUR –.– starting on 25 August 2003, on EUR –.– starting on 20 September 2003 and on EUR –.– starting on 20 July 2004, all applicable until the effective date of payment to the Claimant.

21. Finally, notwithstanding the above and for the sake of completeness, the Chamber turned its attention to the intervening party's position. The Chamber acknowledged that from the very beginning and even prior to the present claim being lodged the intervening party contested before FIFA its obligation to accept a deduction from the transfer compensation that it had agreed upon with the Respondent, on the basis of payment of solidarity contribution for the transfer of the player in question. In particular, the intervening party argues that at the time of the players transfer from a training club as part of the relevant transfer compensation, each training club has already received an amount towards the players training, and therefore has no right to be compensated again for the same training. Furthermore, the Chamber acknowledged that the intervening party is of the opinion that solidarity contribution is only due if the parties involved in the transfer of the player from a training club did not reach an agreement on compensation. Therefore, if a training club already received compensation when a player left the club, no solidarity contribution should be due.

22. In this respect, the Chamber outlined that it could not upheld the position of the intervening party, since training compensation, transfer compensation and solidarity contribution are three completely different rights or claims that exist independently of each other. The Chamber was eager to emphasise that it is one of the essential aims of the FIFA Regulations for the Status and Transfer of Players to encourage the work of training clubs by trying to ensure appropriate compensation for their efforts made within the scope of training and educating players. Therefore not only the principle of training compensation for young players but also the pillar of the solidarity contribution was included as a central principle of the Regulations. A training club should thus not only be compensated for its work at the moment when the player leaves it (training compensation), but throughout the duration of the players career, whenever another club receives financial contribution for the player (solidarity contribution).

23. Moreover, the Chamber duly noted that the intervening party asserts that art. 25 of the Regulations and the FIFA circular 826 only came into effect after all transfers involving the training clubs had been completed, and as such, these provisions cannot be applied retrospectively to this matter.

24. To that regard, the Chamber pointed out that the facts that give rise to the claim, i.e. the transfer of the player to the respondent club and its registration date, occurred in August 2003, thus after the coming into force of art. 25 of the Regulations (1 September 2001) and after the issuance of the FIFA circular 826 (31 October 2002). As a consequence, the Chamber stated that, as a matter of principle, no retrospective application of the aforementioned provisions appears to be existent. The relevant rules are being applied on a transfer that clearly took place after their coming into effect. The Chamber was of the unanimous opinion that under such circumstances also those clubs that trained the player prior to the coming into effect of the applicable Regulations and the implementation of the principle of the solidarity mechanism, have to be entitled to participate to such contribution. Any other approach would constitute an illegitimate discrimination of certain training clubs and go against the aim of encouraging training of young players. Finally, the Chamber stressed that the principle of legal security is safeguarded since any club transferring a player after 1 September 2001 needs and can be aware of that institution. Equally, the Chamber stressed that the Regulations are not limiting in time the training clubs entitled to claim solidarity contribution but simply refer to "the club(s) involved in the training and education of the player" (cf. art. 25 par. 1 of the Regulations).

25. In continuation, the Chamber took note of the intervening party's assertionaccording to which solidarity contribution cannot be irrespective of age analogue to training compensation. Therefore, no solidarity contribution should be due in the case at hand.

26. In this context, the members of the Chamber again stated that the intervening partys position has to be rejected, since - as outlined above - solidarity contribution is an independently existing claim beside training compensation. The two claims have two different aims and therefore the provisions need different requirements to be met. In particular, as already exposed, the solidarity mechanism shall make sure that a training club can financially profit from its training work throughout the entire career of a player it contributed to train and educate. The FIFA circular 769 therefore rightly states that solidarity contribution is due irrespective of the players age. Furthermore, the Chamber emphasised that neither art. 25 of the Regulations nor art. 10 and 11 of the Application Regulations anyhow refer to a possible age limitation.
27. With regard to the intervening partys remark that only the FIFA circular 826 dated 31 October 2002 made clear that the transfer compensation agreed between the former and the new club is 100% and that therefore, the 5% solidarity contribution is to be deducted from the amount payable to the player's formerclub, the Chamber again recalled that the transfer at the basis of the present dispute took place after the issuing of the relevant circular, i.e. in August 2003.
Therefore, again, it is not appropriate to speak of a retrospective application.
Equally, the Chamber deemed it important to explain that, in any case, the relevant circular only clarified the understanding of the relevant provision, yet it did not create any new rule.
28. Finally, the Chamber turned its attention to the intervening partys allegation according to which the Respondent should have explicitly excluded the solidarity contribution from the transfer contract if it wanted to proceed this way, i.e. to deduct the 5% related to the solidarity mechanism from the transfer compensation.
29. In this respect, the Dispute Resolution Chamber outlined that it could once again not upheld the position of the intervening party. As previously shown, the FIFA circular 826 unmistakably clarified that the 5% solidarity contribution is to be deducted from the amount payable to the players former club. Therefore, it is not necessary to explicitly report this fact in the relevant agreement. Equally, the Chamber deemed that the agreement on a net amount cannot affect this principle but only refer to tax and other (administrative) costs. The circular had already been issued at the time of the relevant transfer agreement.

III. DECISION OF THE DISPUTE RESOLUTION CHAMBER

1. The claim of the Claimant, X, is accepted.
2. The Respondent, Y, has to pay the amount of EUR –.– to the Claimant.
3. The Respondent, Y, has to pay default interest of 5% p.a. until the effective date of payment to the Claimant, as follows:
   3.1. on EUR –.–, as from 25 August 2003,
   3.2. on EUR –.–, as from 20 September 2003 and
   3.3. on EUR –.–, as from on 20 July 2004.
4. The amount due to the Claimant, X, has to be paid by the Respondent, Y, within 30 days as from the date of notification of this decision.
5. If the aforementioned sums according to the above-stated points 2 and 3 are not paid within the aforementioned deadline the present matter shall be submitted to FIFAs Disciplinary Committee, so that the necessary disciplinary sanctions may be imposed.
6. The Claimant, X, is directed to inform the Respondent, Y, directly and immediately of the account number to which the remittance is to be made and to notify the Dispute Resolution Chamber of every payment received.
7. According to art. 60 par. 1 of the FIFA Statutes, this decision may be appealed against before the Court of Arbitration for Sport (CAS). The statement of appeal must be sent to the CAS directly within 21 days of receipt of notification of this decision and shall contain all the elements in accordance with point 2 of the directives issued by the CAS, a copy of which we enclose hereto. Within another 10 days following the expiry of the time limit for filing the statement of appeal, the appellant shall file a brief stating the facts and legal arguments giving rise to the appeal with the CAS (cf. point 4 of the directives).

46557
DECISION OF THE DISPUTE RESOLUTION CHAMBER
passed in Zurich, Switzerland, on 27 April 2006,
in the following composition:
Slim Aloulou (Tunisia), Chairman
Carlos Soto (Chile), member
Philippe Piat (France), member
Jean-Marie Philips (Belgium), member
Wilfried Straub (Germany), member
on the claim presented by the club,
A, X, as Claimant
against the club, B, Y,
represented by Ms U, attorney at law, as Respondent
regarding the solidarity contribution related to the transfer of the player Z

I. FACTS OF THE CASE:

1. The player Z, born on 8 July 1981, was registered with A from summer 1998 until summer 2001 that is, for 3 seasons between the ages of 17 and 20.
2. The player was transferred from K to B in summer 2004 for the amount of 3000000.00.
3. On 16 March 2005, A lodged its claim against B and requested its portion of the solidarity contribution amounting to 30% of 5%, i.e. 1.5% of the transfer compensation.
4. On 2 June 2005, B informed FIFA that it is not denying being liable to pay the solidarity contribution to the X club, but requested to pay off the amount of 45000.00 in six equal monthly installments of ...7500.00 each, starting on 30 October 2005.
5. On 15 September 2005, the X Football Association informed FIFA on behalf of its affiliate, A, that the latter is not interested in a payment plan but demands to be paid in full at once.
6. Although FIFA has twice requested a statement from B (on 1 November and 23 November 2005), to this day, the Y club has failed to respond.

II. CONSIDERATIONS OF THE DISPUTE RESOLUTION CHAMBER:

1. First of all, the Chamber analysed whether it was competent to deal with the matter at stake. In this respect, it referred to art. 18 par. 2 and 3 of the Rules Governing the Procedures of the Players' Status Committee and the Dispute Resolution Chamber. The present matter was submitted to FIFA on 16 March 2005, as a consequence the Chamber concluded that the previous Procedural Rules (edition 2001) on matters pending before the decision making bodies of FIFA are applicable on the matter at hand.
2. With regard to the competence of the Chamber, art. 25 par. 2 of the FIFA Regulations for the Status and Transfer of Players (edition 2001) establishes that, it falls within the purview of the Dispute Resolution Chamber to review disputes concerning the distribution of the solidarity contribution.
3. As a consequence, the Dispute Resolution Chamber is the competent body to decide on the present litigation concerning the distribution of the solidarity contribution claimed by the Claimant in connection with the transfer of the professional Z during the course of a contract.
4. Subsequently, the members of the Chamber analyzed which edition of the Regulations for the Status and Transfer of Players should be applicable as to the substance of the matter. In this respect, the Chamber referred to art. 26 par. 1 and 2 of the Regulations for the Status and Transfer of Players (edition 2005) in the modified version in accordance with the FIFA circular no. 995 dated 23 September 2005. Furthermore, it acknowledged that the professional had been registered for his new club in the summer 2004. Equally the Chamber took note that the claim was lodged at FIFA on 16 March 2005. In view of the aforementioned, the Chamber concluded that the former Regulations for the Status and Transfer of Players (edition 2001, hereafter: the Regulations) are applicable on the case at hand as to the substance.
5. In continuation, and entering into the substance of the matter, the members of the Chamber started by acknowledging that the club, A, the Claimant, requested from the club, B, the Respondent, the payment of ... 45000.00, representing its share related to the solidarity mechanism in relation to the transfer of the player in question to the Respondent.

6. Turning its attention to the Respondents position, the deciding body took note that it did not contest owing the claimed amount to the Claimant, but wished to pay off its debt towards the Claimant in various instalments and therefore proposed a payment plan in accordance with which it would pay the total amount of ... 45000.00 to the Claimant in six equal instalments of ... 7500.00 each, starting on 30 October 2005.
7. On account of the above and for the sake of good order, the members determined that the Respondent recognized owing the amount of ... 45000.00 to the Claimant and thus is liable to cancel its debt towards the Claimant.
8. In continuation, the Chamber observed that the Claimant did not accept the payment plan offered by the Respondent but requested thereupon that the Respondent had to pay the claimed amount of ... 45000.00 in full at once.
9. In this respect, the deciding body expressed its regret that the parties did not come to an agreement for a payment plan in order to settle the present matter, and that it had to be submitted to the Dispute Resolution Chamber for a formal decision.
10. Furthermore, the members of the Chamber mentioned that the amount in dispute is not very high, but rather appears to be payable by the Respondent at once.
11. Moreover, the deciding body underlined that according to art. 11 of the Regulations governing the Application of the Regulations for the Status and Transfer of Players, the new club, in the case at hand the Respondent, ... shall pay the amount due as solidarity contribution to the training clubs pursuant to the above provisions at the latest within 30 days of the players registration ...".
12. In view of the above, the members reached the conclusion that the Respondent would have anyway had the obligation to pay to the Claimant the relevant claimed amount pertaining to the solidarity contribution. Yet, the Claimant was and is not obliged according to the Regulations to accept the payment of its relevant proportion as solidarity contribution in instalment and thus can ask the payment to be done in one single payment.
13. On account of all the above, the Dispute Resolution Chamber decided that the Respondent has to pay to the Claimant the amount of ... 45000.00 t at once.

III. DECISION OF THE DISPUTE RESOLUTION CHAMBER

1. The claim of the Claimant, A, is accepted.
2. The Respondent, B, has to pay the amount of ... 45000.00 to the Claimant, A.
3. The amount due to the Claimant has to be paid by the Respondent within 30 days as from the date of notification of this decision.
4. If the aforementioned sum is not paid within the aforementioned deadline the present matter shall be submitted to FIFAs Disciplinary Committee, so that the necessary disciplinary sanctions may be imposed.
5. The Claimant, A, is instructed to inform the Respondent, B, immediately and directly of the account number to which the remittance is to be made and to notify the Dispute Resolution Chamber of every payment received.
6. According to art. 60 par. 1 of the FIFA Statutes this decision may be appealed before the Court of Arbitration for Sport (CAS). The statement of appeal must be sent to the CAS directly within 21 days of receiving notification of this decision and has to contain all elements in accordance with point 2 of the directives issued by the CAS, copy of which we enclose hereto. Within another 10 days following the expiry of the time limit for the filing of the statement of appeal, the appellant shall file with the CAS a brief stating the facts and legal arguments giving rise to the appeal (cf. point 4 of the directives).

⚽⚽⚽

46610

DECISION OF THE DISPUTE RESOLUTION CHAMBER

passed in Zurich, Switzerland, on 27 April 2006,
in the following composition:
Slim Aloulou (Tunisia), Chairman Jean-Marie Philips (Belgium), member Wilfried Straub (Germany), member Carlos Soto (Chile), member Philippe Piat (France), member
on the claim presented by the

Player X, as Claimant
against the club Y, as Respondent
regarding outstanding remuneration on the basis of an employment contract

I. FACTS OF THE CASE

1. The player X, Claimant, and the club Y, Respondent, signed an employment contract on 22 March 2000 valid until the end of the season 2003/2004.
2. On 29 July 2002, the Claimant and the Respondent signed a termination agreement, according to which the Respondent agreed to pay to the Claimant the amount of EUR 28,548 on 4 September 2002 and the amount of EUR 48,080 on 4 September 2003.
3. On 7 March 2005, the Claimant contacted FIFA claiming that the Respondent never paid him any amount as agreed on 29 July 2002. The Claimant provided a duly signed copy of the relevant termination agreement dated 29 July 2002.
4. The Respondent is disputing the competence of the FIFA Dispute Resolution Chamber since article 4 of the relevant settlement agreement dated 29 July 2002 stipulates that any dispute regarding the fulfillment of the settlement agreement should be dealt with by the "Liga Nacional de Futbol Profesional" (LNFP). However, the Respondent never provided its position with regard to the substance of the matter although it was duly informed by FIFA that the competent body would deal with the question of its competence and in the affirmative also with the substance of the present matter on the occasion of the same meeting.
5. The Claimant requested the submission of the matter for a formal decision.

II. CONSIDERATIONS OF THE DISPUTE RESOLUTION CHAMBER

1. First of all, the Chamber analysed whether it was competent to deal with the matter at stake. In this respect, it referred to art. 18 par. 2 and 3 of the Rules Governing the Procedures of the Players' Status Committee and the Dispute Resolution Chamber. The present matter was submitted to FIFA on 7 March 2005, as a consequence the Chamber concluded that the previous Procedural Rules (edition 2001) on matters pending before the decision making bodies of FIFA are applicable on the matter at hand.
2. With regard to the competence of the Chamber, art. 42 par. 1 lit. (b) (i) of the FIFA Regulations for the Status and Transfer of Players (edition 2001) establishes that, the triggering elements of the employment-related dispute (i.e. whether a contract was breached, with or without just cause, or sporting just cause), will be decided by the Dispute Resolution Chamber.
3. If an employment contract is breached by a party, the Dispute Resolution Chamber is also responsible to verify whether a party is accountable for outstanding payments.
4. As a consequence, the Dispute Resolution Chamber is the competent body to decide on the present litigation involving a Spanish club and a Croatian player regarding outstanding remuneration in connection with an employment contract.
5. Subsequently, the members of the Chamber analyzed which edition of the Regulations for the Status and Transfer of Players should be applicable as to the substance of the matter. In this respect, the Chamber referred, on the one hand, to art. 26 par. 1 and 2 of the Regulations for the Status and Transfer of Players (edition 2005) and, on the other hand, to the fact that the relevant termination agreement at the basis of the present dispute was signed in July 2002 and the claim was lodged at FIFA on 7 March 2005. In view of the aforementioned, the Chamber concluded that the former FIFA Regulations for the Status and Transfer of Players (edition 2001, hereafter: the Regulations) are applicable on the case at hand as to the substance.
6. In continuation, the Chamber referred to the argument of the Respondent according to which the latter disputed the competence of the Dispute Resolution Chamber arguing that article 4 of the relevant settlement agreement stipulates that any dispute regarding the fulfilment of the settlement agreement should be dealt with by the "Liga Nacional de Futbol Profesional" (LNFP).
7. In this respect, the Chamber referred to its well-established jurisprudence according to which, in general, in employment-related disputes between a club and a player that have an international dimension, i.e. the parties do not belong to the same country, both parties are entitled to refer the dispute to the FIFA's decision making bodies, unless an independent arbitration tribunal respecting the principle of equal representation of players and clubs with an independent chairman has been established at national level.

8. The Chamber acknowledged that the Respondent was unable to prove that the "Liga Nacional de Futbol Profesional" complies with the requirements of the FIFAs regulations and is composed of an equal number of player and club representatives and has an independent chairman. As a consequence, the Chamber established that the Respondents objection to the competence of FIFA to deal with the present matter has to be rejected and that the matter can be considered as to the substance.
9. In continuation, and entering into the substance of the matter, the members of the Chamber started by acknowledging that the Claimant and the Respondent signed a termination agreement on 29 July 2002, according to which the Respondent agreed to pay to the Claimant the amount of EUR 28,548 on 4 September 2002 and the amount of EUR 48,080 on 4 September 2003.
10. In particular, the Chamber noted that the Claimant argued that the Respondent neither paid him the amount of EUR 28,548 due on 4 September 2002 nor the amount of EUR 48,080 due on 4 September 2003.
11. In this respect, the Chamber referred to art. 4 of the Rules Governing the Practice and Procedures of the Dispute Resolution Chamber in connection with art. 44 of the FIFA Regulations, which stipulates that the Dispute Resolution Chamber does not deal with any litigation if more than two years have elapsed since the facts leading to the dispute arose. Taking into account that the relevant instalments should have been paid on 4 September 2002 and on 4 September 2003 and the claim was received on 7 March 2005 the Chamber concurred that the claim with regard to the first instalment in the amount of EUR 28,548 due on 4 September 2002 cannot be considered, since more than two years have elapsed. In casu, over 2 years and 6 months have elapsed.
12. In view of the above, the Chamber concluded that it could only consider the Claimants claim regarding the second instalment amounting to EUR 48,080 and due on 4 September 2003.
13. Turning its attention to the Respondent, the Chamber took due note that the Respondent never took position in the dispute as to the substance, despite having been informed by FIFA that the competent deciding body would deal with the question of its competence and in the affirmative also with the substance of the present matter on the occasion of the same meeting.
14. In this way the Respondent renounced to its right to defence and accepted the allegations of the Claimant with respect that the second instalment amounting to EUR 48,080 has not been paid.
15. In view of all of the above, the Chamber came to the conclusion that the Respondent must pay to the Claimant the amount of EUR 48,080.

III. DECISION OF THE DISPUTE RESOLUTION CHAMBER

1. The claim lodged by the Claimant, X, is partially accepted.
2. The Respondent, club Y, shall pay the total amount of EUR 48,080 to the Claimant, within 30 days following the date of the communication of the present decision.
3. Any further claims lodged by the Claimant are rejected.
4. In the event that the above-mentioned amount is not paid within the stated deadline, an interest rate of 5% per year will apply as of expiring of the fixed time limit and the present matter shall be submitted to FIFAs Disciplinary Committee, so that the necessary disciplinary sanctions may be imposed.
5. The Claimant is instructed to inform the Respondent directly and immediately of the account number to which the remittance is to be made and to notify the Dispute Resolution Chamber of every payment received.
6. According to art. 60 par. 1 of the FIFA Statutes, this decision may be appealed against before the Court of Arbitration for Sport (CAS). The statement of appeal must be sent to the CAS directly within 21 days of receipt of notification of this decision and shall contain all the elements in accordance with point 2 of the directives issued by the CAS, a copy of which we enclose hereto. Within another 10 days following the expiry of the time limit for filing the statement of appeal, the appellant shall file a brief stating the facts and legal arguments giving rise to the appeal with the CAS (cf. point 4 of the directives).

46831
DECISION OF THE DISPUTE RESOLUTION CHAMBER
passed in Zurich, Switzerland, on 27 April 2006,
in the following composition:
Slim Aloulou (Tunisia), Chairman Philippe Piat (France), member Carlos Soto (Chile), member Jean-Marie Philips (Belgium), member Wilfried Straub (Germany), member
on the claim presented by
the player, X, as Claimant
against
the club, Y as Respondent
regarding a contractual dispute between the player and the club,

I. FACTS OF THE CASE

1. On 2 August 2004, an employment contract was concluded between the player X and the club Y valid until 30 June 2005 with an option for renewal for one more year.
2. This employment contract was drawn up by using a standard employment contract issued by the Association of Y.
3. In accordance with this contract, the player was entitled to receive, inter alia, a monthly salary of EUR 605.54 (12 months plus Christmas bonus), monthly accommodation compensation to the amount of EUR 300 and various instalments ranging from EUR 15,000 to EUR 21,000, the first one amounting to EUR 20,000 falling due on 9 August 2004.
4. On 24 June 2005, the player turned to FIFA maintaining that the club had breached its financial obligations stipulated in the relevant employment contract by failing to remit the following monies:
   - EUR 1,000 relating to the second instalment of 30 October 2004
   - EUR 15,000 relating to the third instalment of 30 December 2004
   - EUR 21,000 relating to the fourth instalment of 30 March 2005

   EUR 37,000 total
5. Therefore, the player asks that the club be ordered to pay to him the outstanding amount of EUR 37,000.
6. In response to the players claim, the club asserts that on 9 February 2005 the parties concluded a "private agreement for the amendment of contract" (hereinafter also referred to as the "private agreement"), which was ratified by the Football League of the country of Y on 15 February 2005.
7. According to the club, the aforementioned private agreement amended the instalments agreed upon in the initial contract, which agreement was accepted and signed by the player due to his serious injury that prevented him playing football for no less than three months (from September until December 2004).
8. The club explains that by signing the private agreement the player accepted to receive EUR 3,000 gross instead of the full first instalment to the amount of EUR 20,000 (falling due on 09.08.04) and he accepted to receive EUR 5,000 gross instead of the full second instalment (falling due on 30.10.04) to the amount of EUR 15,000.
9. Consequently, according to the club, the player accepted to reduce the instalments for the first season of his contract (which amounted to the total of EUR 71,000) with the amount of EUR 27,000. Therefore, he accepted to receive the total gross amount of EUR 44,000 for the first four instalments.
10. Y maintains that from this gross amount tax at a rate of 21.2% (EUR 9,328) must be deducted and, therefore, the total net amount to be received by the player in accordance with the "private agreement for the amendment of contract" is EUR 34,672.
11. Y maintains having paid the amount of EUR 30,000 to X and, taking into account the aforementioned, it acknowledges that it still owes the amount of EUR 4,672 to the player.
12. Y has presented a copy of the private agreement along with documents relating to the alleged payment of the amount of EUR 30,000 to the player.
13. According to clause 3 of this private agreement, except for the 2 instalments mentioned under number I.8, the terms included in the employment contract concluded on 2 August 2004 shall be applicable.
14. The various documents pertaining to the alleged payment of EUR 30,000 indicate the following:
   - EUR 10,000 on 11.08.04
   - EUR 5,000 on 15.11.04

- EUR 2,000 on 23.12.05
- EUR 6,000 without indication of date
- EUR 1,000 on 15.02.05
- EUR 1,500 on 26.02.05
- EUR 2,500 on 02.03.05
- EUR 1,500 on 06.04.05
- EUR 500 on 05.05.05

15. In reaction, the player does not comment on the private agreement, but he maintains that the club duly paid to him the first instalment of EUR 20,000 and he acknowledges that he agreed to receive EUR 5,000 instead of EUR 15,000 for the second instalment. However, according to X, the club only paid EUR 4,000 out of the EUR 5,000. In addition, he insists on his claim pertaining to payment of the third and fourth instalments of EUR 15,000 and 21,000, respectively.
16. No comments have been received from the player with regard to the financial documents presented by the club.
17. On 21 February 2006, the Dispute Resolution Chamber considered this matter on the basis of the above-mentioned facts and concluded that Y should present a certified and full translation of the aforementioned financial documents as well as documentary evidence pertaining to the clubs allegation that taxes at the rate of 21,2% must be deducted from the players financial entitlements.
18. In reply to FIFAs request dated 27 February 2006, Y presented a written statement dated 2 March 2006 issued by the Association of Professional Football Clubs in accordance with which, inter alia, certain articles of law (the articles are specified) provide that the "quoted amounts as a bonus of the contract are paid to the footballer after deducting a tax of 21,2% which is rendered by the club to the competent tax service.
19. In addition, the club presented a "certificate of awareness for debt to the state" dated 16 January 2006 issued by the Tax office of the city of Y.
20. The certification of all the documents presented appears to have been made by an attorney at law of the country of Y.
21. As regards the said financial documents, the club presented print-outs made by the Bank (name related to country of Y) (containing the stamp and signatures of the bank) along with a translation.
22. The player has not presented any comments on these documents.

II. CONSIDERATIONS OF THE DISPUTE RESOLUTION CHAMBER

1. First of all, the Chamber analysed whether it was competent to deal with the matter at stake. In this respect, it referred to art. 18 par. 2 and 3 of the Rules Governing the Procedures of the Players' Status Committee and the Dispute Resolution Chamber. The present matter was submitted to FIFA on 24 June 2005, as a consequence the Chamber concluded that the previous Procedural Rules (edition 2001) on matters pending before the decision making bodies of FIFA are applicable to the matter at hand.
2. With regard to the competence of the Chamber, art. 42 par. 1 lit. (b) (i) of the FIFA Regulations for the Status and Transfer of Players (edition 2001) establishes that the triggering elements of the employment-related dispute will be decided by the Dispute Resolution Chamber.
3. As a consequence, the Dispute Resolution Chamber is the competent body to decide on the present litigation involving a club from the country of Y and a player from the country of X regarding a dispute in connection with an employment contract.
4. Subsequently, the members of the Chamber analyzed which edition of the Regulations for the Status and Transfer of Players should be applicable as to the substance of the matter. In this respect, the Chamber referred, on the one hand, to art. 26 par. 1 and 2 of the Regulations for the Status and Transfer of Players (edition 2005) and, on the other hand, to the fact that the claim was lodged at FIFA on 24 June 2005. In view of the aforementioned, the Chamber concluded that the former FIFA Regulations for the Status and Transfer of Players (edition 2001, hereafter: the Regulations) are applicable to the case at hand as to the substance.
5. Once its competence was thus established, the Dispute Resolution Chamber went on to deal with the substance of the case acknowledging the abovementioned FACTS OF THE CASE, from which it can be noted that the Claimant was contractually bound to the Respondent as from August 2004 until at least 30 June 2005.

6. During the contractual term, on 9 February 2005, the parties signed the "private agreement for amendment of contract" whereby they agreed that the financial entitlements of the player set out in the employment contract dated 2 August 2004 would be amended in the light of the injury sustained by the player in September 2004.
7. More precisely, the said private agreement sets forth that the first and second instalment payable to the player were reduced to EUR 3,000 and EUR 5,000, respectively, and that the remaining conditions of the employment contract dated 2 August 2004 would stay in force.
8. The Claimant maintains that the Respondent has not fully respected its contractual obligations by failing to pay to him the total amount of EUR 37,000 relating to the second, third, and fourth instalments.
9. The Chamber noted that the players claim does not include any monthly salaries or bonuses.
10. The Respondent, on the other hand, refers to the private agreement in accordance with which the player accepted to amend his financial entitlements for the first season to the amount of EUR 44,000.
11. After a careful study of the two relevant contracts, the Chamber confirmed that by signing the private agreement the player accepted and agreed that his financial entitlements relating to the four instalments payable to the player during the first season would amount to EUR 44,000 instead of EUR 71,000.
12. The members of the Chamber then turned to the analysis of the documentation submitted by the Respondent in support of its position that it duly paid EUR 30,000 to the Claimant and noted that the pertinent documentation consists of print outs of accounting documents without the Claimants signature relating to the total amount of EUR 16,500 and payment vouchers duly signed by the Claimant to the total amount of EUR 13,500.
13. Furthermore, the Chamber noted that the financial documents presented by the Respondent subsequent to FIFAs request 27 February 2006 consist of print-outs apparently made by the Bank along with a translation. These documents, however, differ from the documents that were presented by the Respondent at an earlier stage of the proceedings. According to the translation of the newly presented documents payments to the total amount of EUR 16,500 were made to the Claimant. The Chamber noticed that the translation indicates the name of the Claimant, whereas the original documents do not seem to bear the Claimants name, except for one document representing the amount of EUR 5,000.
14. In addition and in the context of the apparent discrepancy found in relation to the aforementioned documents, the Chamber took into account that the translation of the aforementioned documents was not certified in spite of the specific request having been made by FIFA.
15. Consequently, the Chamber concurred that it could only accept the vouchers bearing the Claimants signature as documentary evidence relating to payment of the amount of EUR 13,500.
16. However, the members of the Chamber took into account that the Claimant acknowledges having received from the Respondent payment of the amounts of EUR 20,000 and EUR 4,000 allegedly relating to the first and second instalment, respectively, of the employment contract dated 2 August 2004 (cf. I.15).
17. Consequently, the Chamber concluded that notwithstanding the findings under point II.15 the club at least remitted EUR 24,000 to the player in connection with the instalments due to the player in accordance with the relevant employment contract.
18. Taking into consideration the Respondents position, the Chamber then turned to the question as to whether the financial entitlements of the player are payable net or gross. In this regard, the members of the Chamber noted that neither the employment contract signed on 2 August 2004 nor the "private agreement" specify whether the sums payable to the player are net or gross amounts.
19. The Chamber departed from the principle that monies must be considered to be payable gross, i.e. the amounts of money being subject to deduction of, for example, social charges and tax, in the absence of a specific clause in the relevant employment contract in accordance with which monies are payable net.
20. Consequently, and the Respondent having substantiated that taxes at a rate of 21,2% are deductible from the monies payable to the Claimant in accordance with the employment contract, the Chamber concluded that the amount of EUR 9,328 is deductible from the above-mentioned amount of EUR 44,000 (cf. point II.11). Therefore, and taking into consideration the above-mentioned point II.11, the Chamber concluded that the Claimant is entitled to receive the net amount of EUR 34,672 relating to the four instalments during the first season.

21. The Claimant having acknowledged receipt of the total amount of EUR 24,000 (cf. I.16), the Chamber decided that the Respondent is liable to pay the remainder of EUR 10,672 to the Claimant.

III. DECISION OF THE DISPUTE RESOLUTION CHAMBER

1. The claim of the Claimant, X, is partially accepted.
2. The Respondent, Y, shall pay the amount of EUR 10,672 to the Claimant, X, within 30 days of notification of the present decision.
3. Any further claims from the Claimant are rejected.
4. In the event that the amount of EUR 10,672 is not paid within the stated deadline, an interest rate of 5% per year will apply as of expiry of the aforementioned deadline and the case will immediately be presented to the FIFA Disciplinary Committee.
5. The Claimant is directed to inform the Respondent immediately of the account number to which the remittance is to be made and to notify the Dispute Resolution Chamber of every payment received.
6. According to art. 60 par. 1 of the FIFA Statutes, this decision may be appealed against before the Court of Arbitration for Sport (CAS). The statement of appeal must be sent to the CAS directly within 21 days of receipt of notification of this decision and shall contain all the elements in accordance with point 2 of the directives issued by the CAS, a copy of which we enclose hereto. Within another 10 days following the expiry of the time limit for filing the statement of appeal, the appellant shall file a brief stating the facts and legal arguments giving rise to the appeal with the CAS (cf. point 4 of the directives).

461021

DECISION DE LA CAMARA DE RESOLUCION DE DISPUTAS

reunida en Zurich, Suiza, el 27 de abril de 2006,
e integrada por:
Sr. Slim Aloulou (Tunez), Presidente
Sr. Carlos Soto (Chile), Miembro
Sr. Philippe Piat (Francia), Miembro
Sr. Jean-Marie Philips (Belgica), Miembro Sr. Wilfried Straub (Alemania), Miembro
conocio de la controversia planteada por el jugador
F,
contra el club
Ll,
en adelante, "el Demandante" en adelante, "el Demandado"
en relacion con la ruptura del contrato laboral que los vinculaba

I. HECHOS

1. El 17 de agosto de 2004, el jugador F y el club Ll firmaron un contrato laboral valido por el periodo del Torneo de ascenso 2da. division, Apertura y clausura 2004 - 2005. El contrato laboral empezaba el 17 de agosto de 2004 y terminaba el 31 de mayo de 2005. El salario mensual acordado en dicho contrato era de USD 1,000. El contrato laboral incluia la siguiente clausula:
   "Los primeros 45 dias de este contrato se consideran a prueba y durante este termino EL LL podra darlo por terminado sin previo aviso, sin indemnizacion alguna. "
2. Segun las copias presentadas a la FIFA, el club rescindio unilateralmente el contrato antes mencionado mediante una carta enviada al jugador el 30 de agosto de 2004. En ella, el club se referia a la clausula antes mencionada y senalaba que el jugador no habia demostrado el rendimiento requerido durante el periodo de prueba.
3. Segun las copias enviadas a la FIFA, el jugador informo por escrito al club el 23 de septiembre de 2004 acerca de su objecion a la rescision unilateral del contrato. El jugador expreso que el club baso su decision en una clausula que no es reconocida por la FIFA ni por la FVF. Asimismo, el jugador declaro que un atleta profesional no puede estar sometido a un periodo de prueba y al mismo tiempo participar activamente y estar alineado en los partidos oficiales de liga.
4. El 15 de noviembre de 2004, el jugador se dirigio a la FIFA y presento una demanda en la que reclamaba todos los salarios desde agosto de 2004 hasta mayo de 2005 (10 meses). En base a un salario mensual de USD 1,000, el jugador reclama el monto total de USD 10,000 de parte del Ll.

5. El 31 de mayo de 2005, el Ll FC reconocio haber firmado el 17 de agosto de 2004 un contrato laboral con el jugador F valido para la temporada 2004/2005. Segun el club, al cabo de solo 13 dias se notifico al jugador que su rendimiento no era suficiente. Por otro lado, el club declaro que, desafortunadamente, el jugador no se acostumbro a la vida alli y extranaba a su familia, la cual se habia quedado en su pals de origen.
6. El club informo a la FIFA que estaba dispuesto a pagar el salario del jugador por los 13 dias (del 17 al 30 de agosto de 2004) que el jugador estuvo en el club. Sin embargo, el club se nego a pagar los salarios del jugador por un monto de USD 10,000.
7. Nota: El 19 de octubre de 2004, el jugador F firmo un contrato laboral con el club Chimaltengo. El contrato empezo el dia de la firma y termino cuando finalizo el Torneo de clausura. Se acordo el salario mensual de GTQ 3,000, lo que equivale a USD 394.

II. CONSIDERACIONES DE LA CAMARA DE RESOLUCION DE DISPUTAS

1. En primer lugar, la Camara de Resolucion de Disputas analizo si era competente para tratar el presente asunto. A este respecto, hizo referencia al art. 18 par. 2 y 3 del Reglamento de procedimiento de la Comisi6n del Estatuto del Jugador y de la Camara de Resolucion de Disputas de la FIFA. El presente asunto fue sometido a la FIFA el 15 de noviembre de 2004 por lo tanto la Camara concluyo que las reglas de procedimiento anteriores (edicion 2001) en cuestiones pendientes ante los organos decisorios de la FIFA son aplicables al presente asunto.
2. En consecuencia y analizando la competencia de la Camara, el art. 42 par. 1 lit (b) (i) del Reglamento FIFA sobre el estatuto y la transferencia de jugadores (edicion 2001) establece que, le compete a la Camara de Resolucion de Disputas decidir sobre los elementos desencadenantes de la disputa laboral (es decir si se ha producido un incumplimiento de contrato con o sin causa justificada o causa deportiva justificada).
3. Si un contrato laboral es incumplido por una de las partes, la Camara de Resolucion de Diputas tambien es competente para verificar si una parte debera pagar remuneracion adeudada y/o una indemnizacion.
4. Por consiguiente, la Camara de Resolucion de Disputas es el organo competente para decidir sobre la presente disputa entre un jugador y un club referente a la ruptura de un contrato laboral.
5. Posteriormente, la Camara analizo cual es la edicion del Reglamento sobre el estatuto y la transferencia de jugadores que debe ser aplicado al fondo del presente asunto. A este respecto, la Camara hizo referencia al art. 26. par. 1 y 2 del Reglamento sobre el estatuto y la transferencia de jugadores (edicion 2005) en su version revisada en conformidad con la circular FIFA Nº 995 con fecha del 23 de septiembre de 2005. Ademas, la Camara tomo en cuenta que el relevante contrato laboral fue firmado entre las partes el 17 de agosto de 2004 y que la demanda fue sometida a FIFA el 15 de noviembre de 2004. En vista de lo antedicho la Camara concluyo que el anterior Reglamento FIFA sobre el estatuto y la transferencia de jugadores (edicion 2001, en adelante el Reglamento) es aplicable al fondo del presente caso.
6. A continuacion, la Camara de Resolucion de Disputas (CRD) procedio a examinar el litigio en cuanto al fondo. A este respecto, los miembros de la Camara revisaron todos los documentos que figuran en el expediente y observaron que las posiciones eran antagonicas, por cuanto, por una parte, el demandante afirma que el demandado terming el contrato laboral anticipadamente sin motivo justificado y, por otra, el demandado sostiene que rescindio la relacion laboral basado en la clausula decimo primera del contrato relevante.
7. A este respecto, la CRD tomo nota que el demandante y el demandado celebraron un contrato laboral el 17 de agosto de 2004 valido desde ese dia hasta el 31 de mayo de 2005. Asimismo, la Camara constato que el club demandado rescindio unilateralmente el contrato mediante una carta enviada al jugador el 30 de agosto de 2004, es decir, 13 dias despues de la firma del contrato de trabajo.
8. Los miembros de la Camara consideraron pertinente analizar las razones argumentadas por el demandado en cuanto a la causa de la rescision laboral, en consecuencia la Camara procedio a analizar la clausula 11 del contrato laboral que estipula lo siguiente:
   "Los primeros 45 dias de este contrato se consideran a prueba y durante este termino EL LL F.C. podra darlo por terminado sin previo aviso, sin indemnizacion alguna."
9. A este respecto, la Camara recordo que de acuerdo con su jurisprudencia establecida y reiterada, una clausula que otorga a una parte el derecho de terminar unilateralmente el contrato sin proveer a la contraparte el mismo derecho, es, en principio, una clausula con una validez disputable. En

particular, la referida disposicion ha de ser calificada como no admisible, es decir nula, si crea un desequilibrio ostensible e injustificado entre los derechos y las obligaciones del demandante y del demandado.

10. Con respecto al presente caso y particularmente a la referencia que hace la clausula contractual 11 al periodo de prueba (primeros 45 dias del contrato), la Camara concluyo que aunque se trate de la etapa probatoria, dicho extremo no constituye razon valida suficiente para justificar una terminacion unilateral sin causa alguna y en consecuencia dicha alegacion del demandado debe ser rechazada.
11. Asimismo, los miembros de la CRD concluyeron que como regla general en toda relacion laboral y en particular en este caso entre un jugador y un club es requisito primordial que impere la seguridad juridica. Ello implicaria que ambas partes estuvieran adecuadamente informadas de sus derechos y obligaciones asi como tambien de la configuracion y posibles consecuencias que acarrearia una conducta impropia o irregular de cualquiera de las partes. Lo contrario privaria segun la Camara a ambas partes a su derecho a defenderse y/o a recurrir la decision, lo cual contraviene principios juridicos elementales.
12. A continuacion la Camara puntualizo, que el argumento presentado por el demandado en cuanto que el jugador extranaba a su familia que por dicha razon tenia bajo rendimiento no constituye en si ni podia ser interpretados como un motivo justificado de despido, maxime cuando los criterios para determinarlo son puramente subjetivos y dependen exclusivamente del juicio de una sola parte. Asimismo, los miembros de la Camara manifestaron que de todas maneras el demandado no habia proporcionado pruebas contundentes que corroboraran sus afirmaciones, ya que no existia en el expediente elemento alguno que demostrara el supuesto bajo rendimiento del jugador y ademas que el hecho que solo hubieran transcurrido 13 dias de relacion laboral era un indicio significativo que demostraba que el club demandado habia tenido un obrar intempestivo y poco diligente.
13. Por todo lo expuesto, la Camara de Resolucion de Disputas decidio unanimemente que el demandado habia rescindido unilateralmente su relacion contractual con el demandante sin causa justificada y que, consecuentemente, el demandante tiene derecho a una indemnizacion por la ruptura injustificada del contrato de trabajo.
14. En primer lugar, la CRD destaco que el demandante presto sus servicios como jugador de futbol durante el mes de agosto de 2004 y que el demandado no abono ningun salario al jugador, en consecuencia la Camara decidio que el periodo efectivamente trabajado por el jugador correspondiente al mes de agosto quedaba indiscutiblemente por liquidar por parte del demandado. La clausula segunda del presente contrato laboral estipula un salario mensual de USD 1000. En virtud de lo expuesto, la Camara estimo que el demandado ha de pagar al demandante la suma de USD 1,000 en concepto de salario adeudado por el tiempo trabajado, es decir por el mes de agosto de 2004.
15. En segundo lugar la CRD se refirio a la indemnizacion por ruptura injustificada del contrato laboral, la Camara resalto que el demandado debera pagar una compensacion equivalente a los meses en que el jugador estuvo desempleado y por lo que estuvo empleado en su nuevo club, deberia abonar la diferencia entre la cantidad estipulada en el contrato laboral celebrado entre el demandado y demandante y el contrato celebrado con entre el demandante y su nuevo club (guatemalteco), hasta el 31 de mayo de 2005 (fecha en la cual la relacion contractual con el demandado vencia).
16. En este contexto la Camara destaco que la FNFG confirmo que el demandante celebro contrato laboral con uno de sus afiliados (Deportivo Chimaltengo) desde el 19 de octubre de 2004 hasta el 1 de mayo de 2005 (fecha de finalizacion del torneo clausura) estipulando un salario mensual de GTQ 3000 lo que equivale a USD 394.
17. Teniendo en cuenta lo antedicho, la Camara subrayo que durante el mes de septiembre de 2004 el jugador estuvo desempleado y que desde el mes de octubre de 2004 hasta el mes de mayo de 2005 sufrio una perdida mensual equivalente a USD 606 correspondiente a la diferencia de salario.
18. Por lo tanto, la Camara considero que teniendo en cuenta los elementos del presente caso, y en particular los periodos en que el jugador estuvo desempleado, asi como la remuneracion que el demandante recibio segun su nuevo contrato hasta el 1 de mayo de 2005, el demandante tiene derecho a recibir en concepto de indemnizacion por terminacion unilateral de contrato la cantidad de USD 5848. Es decir el valor restante del contrato de trabajo menos el valor de los salarios percibidos por el demandante con su nuevo club.
19. Por todo lo expuesto precedentemente, la Camara de Resolucion de Disputas acepto la reclamacion del demandante parcialmente y decidio que el demandado debera pagarle al demandante la cantidad de USD 1,000 en concepto de salario adeudado por el periodo trabajado en el mes de agosto de 2004

mas USD 5,848 como indemnizacion por la ruptura injustificada del contrato de trabajo, arribando a la suma total de USD 6848.

III. DECISION DE LA CAMARA DE RESOLUCION DE DISPUTAS

1. Aceptar parcialmente la reclamacion del demandante, Sr. F.
2. Requerir al demandado, club Ll FC, que abone al Sr. F la suma de USD 6848 en un plazo de 30 dias a contar desde la notificacion de la presente decision.
3. Advertir al club Ll FC que, en caso de no respetar el plazo establecido en el punto anterior, a la cantidad de USD 6848 se aplicaran intereses moratorios del 5% per annum. Ademas, el caso podra ser trasladado a la Comisi6n Disciplinaria de la FIFA, la cual podra imponer las sanciones disciplinarias necesarias.
4. El jugador F se compromete a comunicar al Club Ll el numero de cuenta en la que debera abonarse la suma adeudada directamente, asi como informar a la Camara de Resolucion de Disputas sobre los pagos efectuados por el Club Ll FC.
5. De acuerdo con lo previsto por el articulo 60, apartado 1, de los Estatutos de la FIFA, esta decision podra recurrirse ante el Tribunal de Arbitraje Deportivo (CAS, en sus siglas en ingles) El recurso debera interponerse en un plazo de 21 dias tras la notificacion de la decision, en conformidad con el punto nº 2 de las normas procesales publicadas por el CAS, cuya copia adjuntamos a la presente. El demandante dispone de 10 dias adicionales a partir del vencimiento del plazo para recurrir a fin de presentar su escrito de alegaciones con la descripcion de los hechos y los argumentos legales sobre los cuales basa su recurso (vease el punto nº 4 de las normas procesales adjuntas).

461150
DECISION OF THE DISPUTE RESOLUTION CHAMBER
passed in Zurich, Switzerland, on 27 April 2006,
in the following composition:
Slim Aloulou (Tunisia), Chairman
Carlos Soto (Chile), member
Philippe Piat (France), member
Jean-Marie Philips (Belgium), member
Wilfried Straub (Germany), member
on the claim presented by the
Player A, X, represented by Mr O, attorney at lawas Claimant
against the club B, Y as Respondent
regarding a contractual dispute between the parties involved

I. FACTS OF THE CASE

1. On 27 January 2005, the Y club, and the player A, concluded a duly signed agreement, according to which the “parties agree and accept that the player shall sign a contract which will remain in force until the 30th of March 2005”.
2. It was also stipulated in point 2 of the said agreement that the player is entitled to receive a remuneration of ... 2000.00 per month, which was to be paid six times, the first one on 31 January 2005 and the last one on 31 June 2005.
3. Moreover, it was agreed that the player shall receive all the bonuses set out in the internal regulations of the club. According to the player, the club never signed the internal regulations but promised orally to the players, that in case the club finishes on the 4th or 5th place of the Y Championship, it will pay the amount of ... 3000.00 as primes and/or bonuses. In this respect, the player maintains that the club finished the season 2004/2005 on the 5th place of the Y Championship.
4. On 29 September 2005, the player lodged a formal complaint in front of FIFA and maintained that he signed a valid employment contract with the Y club for a predetermined period of six months, thus from 27 January 2005 to 30 May 2005 which provided for a salary of ... 2000.00 per month, payable in 6 equal monthly instalments. The player claimed ... 7500.00, representing unpaid salaries/instalments for the months March (partly), April, May and June 2005 as well as ... 3000.00, representing unpaid bonuses.

5. Furthermore, the player informed that the Y club, after the Y Championship had finished, sent a letter dated 7 May 2005 to the Y Football Association, informing the latter that by a clubs letter dated 30 May 2005 it would terminate the contract with the player. According to the player, the said termination of the contract was unjustified. As a consequence, the player requested damages for the unjustified unilateral termination of the contract.
6. Although FIFA has twice requested a statement from Y (on 4 November and 7 December 2005), to this day, the Y club has failed to respond.

II. CONSIDERATIONS OF THE DISPUTE RESOLUTION CHAMBER

1. First of all, the Chamber analysed whether it was competent to deal with the matter at stake. In this respect, it referred to art. 18 par. 2 and 3 of the Rules Governing the Procedures of the Players' Status Committee and the Dispute Resolution Chamber. The present matter was submitted to FIFA on 29 September 2005, as a consequence the Chamber concluded that the revised Rules Governing Procedures (edition 2005) on matters pending before the decision making bodies of FIFA are applicable to the matter at hand.
2. With regard to the competence of the Chamber, art. 3 par. 1 of the above- mentioned Rules states that the Dispute Resolution Chamber shall examine its jurisdiction in the light of articles 22 to 24 of the current version of the Regulations for the Status and Transfer of Players (edition 2005). In accordance with art. 24 par. 1 in combination with art. 22 (b) of the aforementioned Regulations, the Dispute Resolution Chamber shall adjudicate on employment- related disputes between a club and a player that have an international dimension.
3. As a consequence, the Dispute Resolution Chamber is the competent body to decide on the present litigation involving a Y club and a X player regarding allegedly outstanding payments of salaries and compensation for breach of contract in connection with an employment contract.
4. Subsequently, the members of the Chamber analyzed which edition of the Regulations for the Status and Transfer of Players should be applicable as to the substance of the matter. In this respect, the Chamber referred, on the one hand, to art. 26 par. 1 and 2 of the Regulations for the Status and Transfer of Players (edition 2005) and, on the other hand, to the fact that the relevant contract at the basis of the present dispute was signed on 27 January 2005 and the claim was lodged at FIFA on 29 September 2005. In view of the aforementioned, the Chamber concluded that the current FIFA Regulations for the Status and Transfer of Players (edition 2005, hereafter; the Regulations) are applicable on the case at hand as to the substance.
5. In continuation, and entering into the substance of the matter, the members of the Chamber started by acknowledging the above-mentioned facts and documentation contained in the file and took note that the player A, the Claimant, and the Y club, the Respondent, signed an agreement dated 27 January 2005 in order to enter into an employment contract and to determine their respective rights and duties for the relevant period of time of their contractual relationship.
6. Subsequently, the members noted that on the basis of the aforementioned agreement, the Claimant requested, on the one hand, the payment of outstanding salaries for the months of March (partly), April, May and June 2005 in the total amount of ... 7500.00 and, on the other hand, unpaid bonuses in the amount of ... 3000.00.
7. With regard to the claimed outstanding salaries, the members observed that although the agreement foresaw only a duration of the employment relation until 30 March 2005, the Claimant stated that the employment contract was concluded for the predetermined period as from January 2005 until 30 May 2005.
8. Moreover, the Chamber noted that the Claimant was, according to the terms of the agreement, entitled to receive a remuneration of ... 2000.00 per month, which had to be paid six times, the first one on 31 January 2005 and the last one on 31 June 2005. The members took note that the Respondent did not pay to the Claimant the salaries as from March 2005.
9. In continuation, the Chamber acknowledged that the Claimant claimed bonuses in the amount of ... 3000.00 in line with the clubs internal regulations, which, however, were apparently not signed by the Respondent neither did the Claimant provide for a copy of the said internal regulations.
10. Turning its attention to the Respondent, the members of the Chamber took note of the fact that the Respondent never provided FIFA with its position in the present proceeding, despite having been asked by FIFA to do so on several occasions.

11. In continuation, the Chamber then stated that as a general principle of procedure before the Dispute Resolution Chamber, if a Respondent does not reply to the claim of the Claimant, the case shall be decided by the Dispute Resolution Chamber only on the basis of the facts and proof provided by the Claimant, since with its conduct, the Respondent renounced to its right of defence and thus accepts the allegations of the Claimant.
12. On account of the above, the deciding body stated that due to the Respondents failure to reply to the claim of the Claimant, it has to pass a decision only on the facts and evidences provided by the Claimant.
13. Consequently, the Chamber concluded that the Respondent, due to its failure to respond to the claim of the Claimant, confirmed the allegation of the Claimant that the duration of the agreement ran until the end of May 2006.
14. The members then stated that the Respondent, by not providing its position in the present matter, also admitted the accusation of the Claimant for having failed to pay to the latter the salaries since March 2005. The Chamber emphasized in this respect that the persistent failure of the Respondent to pay the salaries and bonuses to the Claimant without just cause, is generally to be considered as a unilateral breach of an employment contract. The Respondent did not have any reason justifying the non-payment of the salaries since March 2005, or did not, at least, provide for any reasons which might have given reason not to pay the salaries to the Claimant.
15. As a result of the above, the Dispute Resolution Chamber stated that the behaviour of the Respondent has to be considered as a breach of contract without just cause.
16. In consequence, in application of Art. 17 of the Regulations, the members had to deliberate whether the Respondent is accountable for outstanding payments and compensation towards the Claimant.
17. As far as the responsibility of the Respondent for outstanding salary payments is concerned, the Dispute Resolution Chamber stated that the Respondent has to pay to the Claimant the salaries for March (partly; ... 1500.00), April (... 2000.00) and May 2005 (... 2000.00), i.e. until the end of the duration of the agreement between the Claimant and the Respondent.
18. Therefore, the members of the Dispute Resolution Chamber decided that the Respondent has to pay to the Claimant for outstanding salaries the amount of ... 5500.00.
19. Moreover, it was determined by the deciding body that the Respondent is liable to pay to the Claimant the claimed bonuses in the amount of ... 3000.00. In this respect, the Chamber deemed it important to clarify that although the exact amount of bonuses is not stipulated in the relevant agreement and the internal regulations of the Respondent which govern the calculation of bonuses were not provided by the Claimant, the latters affirmation with regard to the amount of the claimed bonuses were not contested by the Respondent either. For the sake of good order, the deciding body confirmed having received an official confirmation from the Y Football Association, according to which the Respondent finished on the 4th place of the Y Championship in the season 2004/2005, and thus, according to the statement of the Claimant, the latter would have been entitled to receive the alleged orally promised bonuses.
20. As far as compensation for breach of contract is concerned, the deciding body deemed it appropriate to compensate the Claimant with the amount of ... 2000.00, representing the rest value of the agreement signed between the parties to the dispute, i.e. the instalment for June 2005.
21. In conclusion, the Dispute Resolution Chamber decided that the Respondent has to pay to the Claimant the amount of ... 5500.00 for outstanding salaries, the amount of ... 2000.00 for compensation for breach of contract without just cause and ... 3000.00, representing unpaid bonuses. In total, the Respondent has to pay to the Claimant the amount of ... 10500.00.

III. DECISION OF THE DISPUTE RESOLUTION CHAMBER

1. The claim of the Claimant, player A, is accepted.
2. The Respondent, B, has to pay the amount of ... 10500.00 to the Claimant, player A, within the next 30 days as from the date of notification of this decision.
3. In the event that the due amount is not paid within the stated deadline, an interest rate of 5% p.a. will apply as of expiring of the fixed time limit.
4. If the aforementioned sum is not paid within the aforementioned deadline, the present matter shall be submitted to FIFAs Disciplinary Committee, so that the necessary disciplinary sanctions may be imposed.

5. The Claimant, player A, is directed to inform the Respondent, B, immediately of the account number to which the remittance is to be made and to notify the Dispute Resolution Chamber of every payment received.
6. According to art. 60 par. 1 of the FIFA Statutes this decision may be appealed before the Court of Arbitration for Sport (CAS). The statement of appeal must be sent to the CAS directly within 21 days of receiving notification of this decision and has to contain all elements in accordance with point 2 of the directives issued by the CAS, copy of which we enclose hereto. Within another 10 days following the expiry of the time limit for the filing of the statement of appeal, the appellant shall file with the CAS a brief stating the facts and legal arguments giving rise to the appeal (cf. point 4 of the directives).

⚽⚽⚽

461185
DECISION OF THE DISPUTE RESOLUTION CHAMBER
passed in Zurich, Switzerland, on 27 April 2006,
in the following composition:
Slim Aloulou (Tunisia), Chairman
Carlos Soto (Chile), member
Philippe Piat (France), member
Jean-Marie Philips (Belgium), member
Wilfried Straub (Germany), member
on the claim presented by
Club X, as Claimant
against
Club Y, as Respondent
regarding a dispute about training compensation for the player Z

I. FACTS OF THE CASE

1. The player Z was born on 4 April 1988 and according to the information provided by the Football Association of the club X was registered with the Claimant as from 1 August 1996 until 30 June 2005, that is for 9 seasons, between the ages of 8 and 17 as an amateur.
2. On 18 July 2005, the player Z signed an employment contract as professional football player with the Respondent and afterwards, on 11 August 2005, he was registered for the Respondent.
3. The Claimant lodged a formal complaint with FIFA for the payment of training compensation in the amount of EUR 220,000 for the player Z, in accordance with article 20 of the FIFA Regulations for the Status and Transfer of Players (edition 2005).
4. The Respondent stated that from its point of view there is no training compensation to be paid to the Claimant. In particular, the Respondent emphasised that the Claimant did not offer a new contract to the player Z which is the reason why, by taking into account the wording of annex 4 art. 6 par. 3 of the FIFA Regulations for the Status and Transfer of Players (edition 2005), no training compensation is due to the Claimant. The cited article reads:
   "If the Former Club does not offer the player a contract, no Training Compensation is payable unless the Former Club can justify that it is entitled to such compensation. The Former Club must offer the player a contract in writing via registered mail at least 60 days before the expiry of his current contract. Such an offer shall furthermore be at least of an equivalent value to the current contract. This provision is without prejudice to the rights to Training Compensation of the players previous club(s)."
5. In reply thereto, the Claimant exposed that from its point of view the aforementioned article is only applicable if the player was already a professional at his former club. In fact, the Claimant emphasised that the wording of the relevant article in the second sentence clearly states that:
   "The Former Club must offer the player a contract in writing via registered mail at least 60 days before the expiry of his current contract."
6. In this respect, the Claimant explained that for the application of annex 4 art. 6 par. 3 of the said Regulations, the player must have already had a contract with the Claimant, which was not the case with the player Z who was registered for the Claimant as an amateur. In addition, the Claimant

underlined that in May/June 2005 a proposal for a contract had been discussed with the player Z and that the parties involved had agreed that the negotiations would be continued after the summer holidays. However, after the summer holidays, the Claimant was allegedly informed that the player in question was going to play for the Respondent.

7. In reply thereto, the Respondent pointed out once again that from its point of view no training compensation must be paid to the Claimant. With regard to the Claimants allegation that there was a discussion about a formal proposal for an employment contract in May/June 2005, the Respondent argued that the player never received a formal offer from the Claimant.

II. CONSIDERATIONS OF THE DISPUTE RESOLUTION CHAMBER

1. First of all, the Chamber analysed whether it was competent to deal with the matter at stake. In this respect, it referred to art. 18 par. 2 and 3 of the Rules Governing the Procedures of the Players' Status Committee and the Dispute Resolution Chamber. The present matter was submitted to FIFA on 15 September 2005. As a consequence, the Chamber concluded that the revised Rules Governing Procedures (edition 2005) on matters pending before the decision making bodies of FIFA are applicable on the matter at hand.
2. With regard to the competence of the Chamber, art. 3 par. 1 of the above-mentioned Rules states that the Dispute Resolution Chamber shall examine its jurisdiction in the light of articles 22 to 24 of the current version of the Regulations for the Status and Transfer of Players (edition 2005). In accordance with art. 24 par. 1 in connection with art. 22 (d) of the aforementioned Regulations, the Dispute Resolution Chamber shall adjudicate on disputes between two clubs belonging to different Associations related to training compensation.
3. As a consequence, the Dispute Resolution Chamber is the competent body to decide on the present litigation concerning the training compensation claimed by the Claimant for the training and education of the player Z.
4. Subsequently, the members of the Chamber analyzed which edition of the Regulations for the Status and Transfer of Players should be applicable as to the substance of the matter. In this respect, the Chamber referred to art. 26 par. 1 and 2 of the Regulations for the Status and Transfer of Players (edition 2005) in the modified version in accordance with the FIFA circular no. 995 dated 23 September 2005. Furthermore, it acknowledged that the player had been registered for the first time as a professional on 11 August 2005. Equally, the Chamber took note that the claim was lodged at FIFA on 15 September 2005. In view of the aforementioned, the Chamber concluded that the current FIFA Regulations for the Status and Transfer of Players (edition 2005, hereinafter: the Regulations) are applicable on the case at hand as to the substance.
5. In continuation, and entering into the substance of the matter, the members of the Chamber started by acknowledging that on the one hand, the Claimant requests training compensation based on the number of years that the player Z spent training at the Claimant as from his 12th birthday. On the other hand, the Chamber took note that the Respondent contests the Claimants entitlement to training compensation by referring to annex 4 art. 6 par. 3 of the Regulations.
6. Turning its attention to the documents presented by the parties in dispute, the Chamber took note that the player was registered for the Claimant as an amateur until 30 June 2005. Furthermore, the Chamber acknowledged that the Claimant is a first division club, belonging to category 1 in terms of the FIFA circular no. 959 dated 16 March 2005. In addition to that, the Chamber took note of the fact that the Respondent is also a first division club belonging to category 1.
7. Regarding the Respondents position, the Chamber acknowledged in particular its statement that the Claimant, situated in the EU, like the Respondent too, did not formally offer the player an employment contract and, therefore, should not be entitled to training compensation.
8. The Chamber established that since the move of the player from the Claimant to the Respondent took effectively place between two clubs belonging to different Associations inside the territory of the EU, the special provisions of annex 4 art. 6 of the Regulations need to be taken into account.
9. In view of the positions exposed by the parties, the Chamber deemed that first of all it would have to establish whether, as maintained by the Claimant, the terms of annex 4 art. 6 par. 3 of the Regulations only apply to cases in which the player already had a contract with his former club.
10. In this respect, the Chamber was of the opinion that it could not back the Claimants argument that annex 4 art. 6 par. 3 of the Regulations is exclusively applicable if the player was already a professional. In fact, the first sentence of the cited provision clearly stipulates that no training compensation must be

paid to the players former club if the said club did not offer the player a contract unless it can justify its entitlement to such compensation. No reference to a new contract is thus made in this general introduction to the relevant provision. In this respect, the Chamber emphasised that it is the spirit and purpose of the said provision to penalise clubs which are obviously not interested in the players services as a professional, no matter if the club would have to offer the player for the first time an employment contract or a renewal due to the ordinary expiration of an already existing contract. On the basis of this general approach, the Chamber exposed that the sentence of the relevant provision, to which the Claimant is referring, intends to indicate a time limit for the club that already has a contract with the player, until when the new offer must be made. Yet, it cannot be the intention of that sentence to limit the application of the provision as such.

11. On account of the foregoing the Chamber concluded that annex 4 art. 6 par. 3 of the Regulations is applicable also to cases, like to the one at hand, in which the player was registered as an amateur with his former club.
12. In continuation, the Chamber turned to the question about the offering of a contract by the Claimant to the player Z. In this respect, the Chamber emphasised that the Claimant itself expressly exposed having discussed with the player Z in May/June 2005 a proposal for a contract, stressing that it would have agreed with the player concerned to continue the negotiations after the summer holidays. In other words, confessedly, the Claimant only discussed a possible employment contract without, however, making a formal and concrete offer in a written form to the player in question, whereas the Respondent must have presented the player a formal and serious offer since, in the end, the player signed an employment contract with the Respondent on 18 July 2005. In this context, the Chamber particularly pointed out that vague discussions about a possible employment contract do not correspond to an offer in terms of the first sentence of annex 4 art. 6 par. 3 of the Regulations, since the second sentence of the said provision clearly establishes that such an offer must be made in a written form.
13. Subsequently, the Chamber scrutinised whether the Claimant presented sufficient justification for its entitlement to training compensation even though it did not formally offer the player an employment contract.
14. In this context, first of all, the Chamber congruently argued that the Claimant, as a first division club belonging to category 1, would have been able to seriously offer the player an employment contract at anytime if it had been really interested in having the player working as a professional in its squad.
15. Furthermore, due to the fact that the player and the Respondent, also a first division team belonging to category 1, signed an employment contract on 18 July 2005, the Chamber draw the conclusion that the player, at his age of 17, must have already achieved a sufficient level to be integrated in a team of professional football players of that level. Nevertheless, the Claimant refrained from offering an employment contract in a written form to the player at that time.
16. In light of all of the above, the Chamber concluded that the Claimants decision to refrain from making an adequate and concrete offer to the player must have been motivated by its low interest at the end of the season 2004/2005 in having him in its squad as a professional with effect from the following season, i.e. the season 2005/2006. Otherwise, the Claimant would have made a suitable offer to the player in a written form prior to the beginning of the summer holidays.
17. Recapitulatory, the Chamber was of the opinion that the real reason why the player did not sign an employment contract with his training club, the Claimant, but with the Respondent, must be seen in the fact that the Claimant did not show enough interest in the players services as a professional. With such behaviour, so the Chamber, the Claimant forfeited its entitlement to receive training compensation from the Respondent.
18. As a consequence of all of the above, the Chamber decided that the Respondent is not liable to pay training compensation to the Claimant for the training and education of the player Z.

III. DECISION OF THE DISPUTE RESOLUTION CHAMBER

1. The claim of the club X is rejected.
2. According to art. 60 par. 1 of the FIFA Statutes, this decision may be appealed against before the Court of Arbitration for Sport (CAS). The statement of appeal must be sent to the CAS directly within 21 days of receipt of notification of this decision and shall contain all the elements in accordance with point 2 of the directives issued by the CAS, a copy of which we enclose hereto. Within another

10 days following the expiry of the time limit for filing the statement of appeal, the appellant shall file a brief stating the facts and legal arguments giving rise to the appeal with the CAS (cf. point 4 of the directives).

⚽⚽⚽

17 AUGUST 2006

862
DECISION OF THE DISPUTE RESOLUTION CHAMBER
passed in Zurich, Switzerland, on 17 August 2006,
in the following composition:
Slim Aloulou (Tunisia), Chairman Jean-Marie Philips (Belgium), member Zola Majavu (South Africa), member Rinaldo Martorelli (Brazil), member Mick Mc Guire (England), member
on the claim presented by the player
X, as Claimant
against the club
Y, as Respondent
regarding a contractual dispute arisen between the parties.

I. FACTS OF THE CASE

1. In January 2005, the Claimant signed an employment contract for the period up until 31 October 2005 with the Respondent. In annexe I, paragraph a of this contract, the parties agreed that the player would receive a gross monthly salary of ... 5,100. In addition, the parties agreed that the club would provide the player with suitable, furnished accommodation for a monthly rent of no more than ... 1,400. Annexe III explains in general terms the potential medical costs that the club would cover and which medical costs it would not cover. Moreover, on 20 January 2005, the parties signed an "Addendum to ... League Player's Contract" in which they agreed the following in a section entitled "CCompensation: "The club refrains the right to determine the Contract during any of the transfer windows and compensation shall be limited to two (2) months of the players monthly salary".
2. On 26 October 2005, the Claimant submitted a complaint to FIFA, saying that the Respondent had unilaterally terminated his contract in June 2005 due to a knee injury that he had suffered in May 2005 while employed by the club. He said that, as a result of the injury, he had not been able to work again until the termination of his contract. He had remained in the country of the club Y until July 2005 for medical treatment and had required additional medical care after leaving the country. In view of the termination of his contract, he had received two months' salary from the club in compensation. The player stressed that he had never relinquished any of his other rights in relation to the contract. As a result, he lodged a claim for compensation of ... 30,300 for breach of contract. This compensation was broken down into the following amounts: a) ... 10,200 in compensation for breach of contract, b) ... 8,400 for rent for his accommodation that he had not received for the months from January to June 2005, c) ... 5,600 for rent for his accommodation that he would have been paid for the period up until the contracts original date of expiry, d) ... 1,000 as a refund for an unwarranted deduction from his salary for the month of June due to medical costs incurred (inconsistent with annexe III), e) ... 4,000 to reimburse ongoing medical costs in line with annexe III.
3. On 6 February 2006, the Respondent submitted its comments to the player's complaint. It said that the contractual relationship with the player had been terminated by mutual consent because, due to injury and also for personal reasons, the player was not in a position to play for the club. The Respondent asserted that, based on an agreement that the two parties had made, it was entitled to terminate the players contract during any of the transfer windows upon payment of compensation equal to two months' salary. The Respondent had simply exercised this right. Moreover, the Respondent had, contrary to the player's claims, not made unauthorised deductions for the player's medical bills. At the player's request, the club had made an additional payment to him equal to 23 days of his monthly salary (... 3,910) in addition to the compensation payment of two months' salary and it had also allowed him to stay in his accommodation until 30 June 2005. All of these arrangements had been part of the agreement that had been reached with the player. To substantiate its statement, the Respondent submitted a receipt that had been signed by the Claimant and was dated

28 June 2005 indicating that the Respondent had paid the Claimant ... 11,993.50. On this receipt, the following words are written above the player's signature: Received ... 11,993.50 Cash being Full + Final settlement of amount due to me, as per Notice of Termination dated 7th June 2005.

4. On 2 March 2006, the Claimant submitted his reply. He disputed the fact that the contract had been terminated by mutual consent. He also said that it was his injury alone that had prevented him from playing for the club and not any personal problems. According to the Claimant, the Respondent had unilaterally terminated the contract on 7 June 2005 by invoking an illegal clause of the contract that allowed it to terminate the player's contract upon payment of compensation equal to two months' salary. The Claimant maintains that he had had no choice but to accept this unauthorised termination of the contract and the club had ultimately informed him that, because of the injury he had suffered, it would neither continue to pay his salary in line with the terms of his contract nor would it continue to cover his medical costs. Furthermore, he said that the club had told him that it would no longer provide him with accommodation. The Claimant is of the opinion that the actions of the club, specifically terminating his contract upon payment of compensation equal to two months' salary, contravened article 13 of the Regulations for the Status and Transfer of Players. The player admitted that he had received ... 11,993.50 on 28 June 2005. However, the receipt submitted by the club documented nothing more than the compensation he had received corresponding to his salary for two months and 23 days. He said that this document did not absolve the club from any of its other contractual obligations and specifically, it did not affect the players right to take legal action against the club for unauthorised, unilateral termination of his contract.
5. On 23 March 2006, the Respondent submitted a response to the player's reply. It said once again that the contract had been terminated by mutual consent. Moreover, the Respondent alleged that even if it was found that the contractual relationship had not been terminated for an acceptable reason, the two parties had agreed upon the amount of compensation to be paid by the club. The club noted that such an arrangement is permitted under article 17 paragraph 2 of the Regulations for the Status and Transfer of Players.
6. As for the player's claim for ... 8,400 in rent payments that he had not received for the period from January 2005 to June 2005, the club explained that it had provided the player with accommodation up until 22 July 2005, which was one month after the termination of the contractual relationship. In addition, the Respondent asserted that it had always paid the medical costs that the player was entitled to claim. With regard to the claims for medical costs that the player made with his complaint, the club stressed that the player had neither specified nor substantiated any of them. In summary, the Respondent stated that it had terminated the contract in line with a legitimate clause that was specified in the addendum.

II. CONSIDERATIONS OF THE DISPUTE RESOLUTION CHAMBER

1. First of all, the Chamber analysed whether it was competent to deal with the matter at stake. In this respect, it referred to art. 18 par. 2 and 3 of the Rules Governing the Procedures of the Players' Status Committee and the Dispute Resolution Chamber. The present matter was submitted to FIFA on 26 October 2005. As a consequence, the Chamber concluded that the revised Rules Governing Procedures (edition 2005) on matters pending before the decisionmaking bodies of FIFA are applicable on the matter at hand.
2. With regard to the competence of the Chamber, art. 3 par. 1 of the abovementioned Rules states that the Dispute Resolution Chamber shall examine its jurisdiction in the light of articles 22 to 24 of the current version of the Regulations for the Status and Transfer of Players (edition 2005). In accordance with art. 24 par. 1 in connection with art. 22 (d) of the aforementioned Regulations, the Dispute Resolution Chamber shall adjudicate on employmentrelated disputes between a club and a player that have an international dimension.
3. As a consequence, the Dispute Resolution Chamber is the competent body to decide on the present litigation involving a club belonging to the country of the Respondent and a player with the Claimants nationality regarding contractual disputes in connection with an employment contract.
4. Subsequently, the members of the Chamber analyzed which edition of the Regulations for the Status and Transfer of Players should be applicable as to the substance of the matter. In this respect, the Chamber referred, on the one hand, to art. 26 par. 1 and 2 of the Regulations for the Status and Transfer of Players (edition 2005) and, on the other hand, to the fact that the relevant contract at the basis of the present dispute was signed in January 2005 and the claim was lodged at FIFA on

26 October 2005. In view of the aforementioned, the Chamber concluded that the current FIFA Regulations for the Status and Transfer of Players (edition 2005, hereinafter: the Regulations) are applicable to the case at hand as to the substance.

5. In continuation, and entering into the substance of the matter, the members of the Chamber started by acknowledging that, on the one hand, the Claimant maintains that the contractual relationship between the parties involved was illegally terminated by the Respondent, whereas the Respondent is of the opinion that the relevant relationship was terminated by mutual agreement and, in particular, in accordance with the valid addendum signed by the parties involved on 20 January 2005.
6. In view of the positions exposed by the parties in dispute, the Chamber deemed that, first of all, it has to establish whether, as maintained by the Respondent, the clause awarding the club Y the possibility to cancel the employment contract during any of the transfer windows and by paying a compensation in the amount of two months of the players monthly salary to the Claimant is valid or not.
7. In this respect, the Chamber acknowledged that art. 17 par. 2, set 3 of the Regulations clearly establishes that the parties to an employment contract can determine the compensation to be paid in case of an early termination of the contractual relationship wihtout just cause. The Chamber stressed that this provision does not establish whether such an arrangement must be made at a particular time. In other words, the Chamber unanimously came to the conclusion that such kind of mutual arrangements may be concluded at anytime, i.e. prior to, on the occasion of, or even after a premature termination of the contractual relationship.
8. In continuation, the Chamber acknowledged that the addendum to which the Respondent vicariously refers to in its submissions is duly signed by both parties. Consequently, the Chamber decided that the parties in dispute determined in advance, on 20 January 2005, the compensation to be paid by the Respondent to the Claimant in case of an early termination of the contractual relationship without just cause.
9. The Chamber highlighted that, in this specific case, the compensation to which the parties involved agreed upon in advance does not stand in a disproportion to the players whole contractual entitlements. In particular, the Chamber noted that, according to the addendum in question, the Claimant is entitled to compensation in the amount of two monthly salaries, in other words, to an amount that corresponds to approximately 22% of the players complete entitlement to remunerations in terms of the employment contract concluded by and between the parties in dispute. In addtition to that, the Chamber accentuated that according to the addendum in question, the Respondent was entitled to terminate the contractual relationship within a transfer window only, hence, foreseenable, at an assigned time and exlcusively at a time in which the player had the possibilty to be registered for another club of his choice.
10. On account of all of the foregoing, the Chamber decided that the clause in the addendum concluded by the parties involved according to which the Respondent is entitled to prematurly terminate the contractual relationship within a transfer window and by paying a compensation in the amount of two monthly salaries to the Claimant is legally binding.
11. Moreover, and with regard to the players argument that the Respondent only terminated the contractual relationship with the Claimant due to a knee injury that he had suffered in May 2005 while rendering his services for the Respondent, the Chamber considered that this allegation was never substantiated by the Claimant.
12. Once the Chamber had established that the addendum includes a valid option in favour of the Respondent to unilaterally terminate the relevant contractual relationship within a transfer window prior to 31 October 2005, it went on the scrutinise whether the player effectively received a compensation in the amount of two monthly salaries.
13. To that regard, the Chamber acknowledged that the Respondent presented a receipt dated 28 June 2005 which indicates that the Respondent paid to the Claimant monies in the amount of ... 14,110 gross, respectively ... 11,993.50 net. In this context, the Chamber took note that the Claimant never denied having received such amount. Effectively, the Claimant admitted having received a two months' salary from the club in compensation for the early termination of the contractual relationship on 7 June 2005. Additionally, the Chamber noted that the amount of ... 11,993.50 corresponds to a sum exceeding the value of the players two monthly gross salary, which would be ... 10,200 only. Recapitulatory, the Chamber decided that, obviously, the player received a compensation for the early termination of the contractual relationship in the amount foreseen in the respective addendum.

14. Finally, the Chamber acknowledged that it was never alleged by the player that the early termination of the contractual relationship was executed outside a transfer window. In other words, the player tacitly accepted the second precondition foreseen in the addendum authorising the Respondent to cancel the contractual relationship prior to the ordinary expiration date, i.e. prior to 31 October 2005.
15. Consequently, the Chamber decided that the early termination of the contractual relationship was even carried out in time which is the reason why the player has neither a claim for the values of the employment contract after the date of the early termination of the contractual relationship nor for any compensation.
16. With regard to the Claimants allegations that he did not receive monies for his accommodation, the Chamber stressed that according to the respective employment contract, the Respondent only had to make an accommodation available to the Claimant in the amount of, at most, ... 1,400 and not to pay him in addition to his monthly salary monies amounting to ... 1,400 for the rent of an accommodation. Moreover, the Chamber pointed out that the Respondent gave an accommodation to the Claimant even after the early termination of the contractual relationship. Therefore, the Chamber rejected the Claimants request for alleged outstanding accommodation costs in the total amount of ... 8,400 for the months of January to June 2005.
17. With regard to the Claimants requests for the reimbursement of medical costs in the amount of ... 1,000 and ... 4,000 respectively that he allegedly had due to his injury, the Chamber acknowledged that the Claimant did not present any written document substantiating such costs, which is the reason why, in accordance with its well-established jurisprudence, the Chamber also rejected these requests.
18. As a consequence of all of the above, the Dispute Resolution Chamber decided that the Claimants complaint is rejected.

III. DECISION OF THE DISPUTE RESOLUTION CHAMBER

1. The claim lodged by the Claimant, X, is rejected.
2. According to art. 61 par. 1 of the FIFA Statutes, this decision may be appealed against before the Court of Arbitration for Sport (CAS). The statement of appeal must be sent to the CAS directly within 21 days of receipt of notification of this decision and shall contain all the elements in accordance with point 2 of the directives issued by the CAS, a copy of which we enclose hereto. Within another 10 days following the expiry of the time limit for filing the statement of appeal, the appellant shall file a brief stating the facts and legal arguments giving rise to the appeal with the CAS (cf. point 4 of the directives).

86119

DECISION OF THE DISPUTE RESOLUTION CHAMBER

passed in Zurich, Switzerland, on 17 August 2006,
in the following composition:
Slim Aloulou (Tunisia), Chairman Jean-Marie Philips (Belgium), Member Zola Majavu (South Africa), Member Mick McGuire (England), Member Rinaldo Martorelli (Brazil), Member
On the claim presented by the Player X, XX, represented by Mr U, attorney at law as Claimant against the club, X, YY, represented by Mr O, attorney at law as Respondent
regarding a contractual dispute arisen between the parties involved.

I. FACTS OF THE CASE

1. On 18 November 2003, the XX player, (hereafter: the Claimant), and the YY club, X (hereafter: the Respondent), signed an employment contract valid from 1 December 2003 until 31 August 2006.
2. According to the employment contract, the Claimant was entitled to receive:
   - monthly salary of USD 15150
   - "signing fee" of USD 150000 (season 2003/2004), USD 100000.00 (season 2004/2005) and USD 100000 (season 2005/2006)
   - "official game bonus like all other players of the club, all other bonuses, championship and cup bonus"

- furnished apartment
- medium size car including insurance, premium and maintenance
- one economy class air ticket to his country of origin for him and his wife

3. On 22 August 2005, the Claimant lodged a formal claim in front of FIFA and requested that the Respondent has to pay to him the amount of EUR 20000 in connection with his transfer to K (KK) and, in addition, the amount of USD 396950 as compensation for breach of contract without just cause. The claimed amounts have been specified by the Claimant as follows:
   - EUR 20000: remuneration related to his transfer to the KK club
   - USD 296950: compensation for breach of contract (monthly salary of USD 15150 multiplied by thirteen [recte: 14] (July 2005 until August 2006) as well as the contractually foreseen signing fee of USD 100000
   - USD 50000: estimated value for the benefits during the execution of the employment contract
   - USD 50000: damage and interest for the breach of the employment contract
4. In this respect, the Claimant explained in particular that he moved for one season (season 2004/2005) to the KK club, K, with the option in favour of the latter to extend the employment contract by two years, whereby an agreement between him and the Respondent was signed on 11 August 2004 according to which the Respondent undertook to pay him EUR 20000 after the KK club would have paid this amount into the bank account of the Respondent.
5. According to the Claimant, at the end of the season 2004/2005, the KK club decided not to exercise the option for the extension of the employment contract. Therefore, he went back and presented himself at the Respondent in order to continue his contractual relationship with the latter. But the Respondent allegedly informed him that he was no longer under contract with it. Given that he had no revenue, he had to go back to XX.
6. In this respect, the Claimant maintained that, in order for him to play with the KK club in the season 2004/2005, his employment contract with the Respondent had been suspended on 3 August 2004 and on this occasion, he received the amount of USD 50000 as the remaining part of the signing fee. The Claimant remitted a duly signed declaration to the file, in which he, the Claimant, confirmed having received the amount of USD 50000.00 "as a full and final settlement" and not having "any outstanding amount or any financial obligation from Y (Respondent)". Furthermore, by means of the said declaration, the Claimant undertook "to declare that in the future ... (the Claimant) will not claim any amount from the said club (Respondent)". Hereinafter, this document, which bears the Claimants signature, is referred to as the Declaration.
7. In reply to the Claimants claim, the Respondent at first confirmed having received the amount of EUR 20000 from the KK club and informed that it would forward this amount to the Claimants bank account.
8. With regard to the employment contract between the parties involved, the Respondent rejected the Claimants allegation according to which the Respondent has breached the employment contract. In this respect, it referred to the Declaration the Claimant signed in August 2004 on the occasion of the Claimants transfer to KK. According to the Respondent, it agreed with the Claimant in the aforementioned agreement to terminate their contractual relationship for a lump sum of USD 50000 in accordance with the Declaration, the amount of which was paid to the bank account of the Claimant. The Respondent submitted a copy of the relevant payment voucher.
9. In reply thereto, the Claimant maintained that the Declaration signed by him concerns only the period during which he was engaged with K. In addition, the Claimant emphasized that by means of suspending the contractual relationship with the Respondent, he only renounced to perceive some advantage of his employment contract until his return.
10. Moreover, the Claimant stated that the amount of USD 50000 referred to by the Respondent only corresponded to the "premium" demanded by him for his "treatment" at the club FC K in addition to the payment of EUR 20000 as exposed under point I.4 and I.7 above.
11. Finally, the Claimant explained that he returned to the United Arab Emirates in July 2005 in order to continue with the execution of his employment contract with the Respondent. In this respect, he raised the question what his intentions would have been to return to the Respondent if the Declaration signified the termination of the employment contract with the Respondent. As a consequence, the Claimant deemed that his return to the Respondent after the period of time he spent with FC K in KK is sufficient proof that the Respondent acted in bad faith.

12. During the procedure, the Respondent transferred the amount of EUR 20000 to the bank account of the Claimant, the receipt of which was confirmed by the Claimant.
13. In its last position, the Respondent reiterated that the employment contract between the parties involved was terminated by mutual agreement and that it therefore paid to the Claimant the amount of USD 50000 as final settlement of their contractual relationship.
14. On 6 March 2006, the Claimant informed that he signed a new employment contract with the ZZ club, Z, commencing on 1 March 2006 and which lasts until 31 December 2006, a copy of which he has presented.
15. According to this employment contract, the Claimant is, inter alia, entitled to receive a monthly salary of USD 5000 as well as bonuses.
16. Furthermore, FIFA has been provided with a supplementary agreement to the employment contract concluded between the Claimant and the ZZ club, in accordance with which the Claimant shall receive a signing-on fee of USD 60000.

II. CONSIDERATIONS OF THE DISPUTE RESOLUTION CHAMBER

1. First of all, the Chamber analysed whether it was competent to deal with the matter at stake. In this respect, it referred to art. 18 par. 2 and 3 of the Rules Governing the Procedures of the Players' Status Committee and the Dispute Resolution Chamber. The present matter was submitted to FIFA on 22 August 2005, as a consequence the Chamber concluded that the revised Rules Governing Procedures (edition 2005) on matters pending before the decision making bodies of FIFA are applicable on the matter at hand.
2. With regard to the competence of the Chamber, art. 3 par. 1 of the abovementioned Rules states that the Dispute Resolution Chamber shall examine its jurisdiction in the light of articles 22 to 24 of the current version of the Regulations for the Status and Transfer of Players (edition 2005). In accordance with art. 24 par. 1 in connection with art. 22 (b) of the aforementioned Regulations, the Dispute Resolution Chamber shall adjudicate on employmentrelated disputes between a club and a player that have an international dimension.
3. As a consequence, the Dispute Resolution Chamber is the competent body to decide on the present litigation involving a XXian player and a club from the YY regarding the alleged breach of contract and allegedly outstanding compensation in connection with an employment contract.
4. Subsequently, the members of the Chamber analyzed which edition of the Regulations for the Status and Transfer of Players should be applicable as to the substance of the matter. In this respect, the Chamber referred, on the one hand, to art. 26 par. 1 and 2 of the Regulations for the Status and Transfer of Players (edition 2005) and, on the other hand, to the fact that the relevant contract at the basis of the present dispute was signed on 18 November 2003 and the claim was lodged at FIFA on 22 August 2005. In view of the aforementioned, the Chamber concluded that the current FIFA Regulations for the Status and Transfer of Players (edition 2005; hereafter; the Regulations) are applicable to the case at hand as to the substance.
5. In continuation, and entering into the substance of the matter, the members of the Chamber acknowledged the documentation contained in the file and took note that the Claimant and the Respondent signed an employment on 18 November 2003 contract valid from 1 December 2003 until 31 August 2006.
6. Moreover, in view of the circumstances of the case at stake, the members focussed on the question as to whether or not the contractual relationship between the Claimant and the Respondent had been terminated on the occasion of the Claimants transfer to KKy in the 2004/2005 season. Furthermore, the Chamber acknowledged that in the negative, i.e. the contractual relationship had not ended, it would have to address the question as to whether an unjustified breach of contract occurred and which party would be responsible for such breach of contract.
7. To this end, the members at first took note that it is uncontested that the Claimant went to KKy in 2004 and apparently entered into a contractual relationship with the KK club, K, in order to render his services to the latter in the season 2004/2005. Moreover, according to the statement of the Claimant, the KK club had an option to extend the duration of the contract for a maximum of two additional years.
8. In continuation, the Chamber took note that on the occasion of the said move of the Claimant to K, the Claimant maintains having received USD 50000 from the Respondent and the Claimant presented the aforementioned Declaration in this regard.

9. In this respect, the members of the Chamber noted that, while the Claimant maintained that the contractual relationship between the parties to the dispute was merely suspended, the Respondent is of the opinion that it clearly emanates from the Declaration that the employment contract between the parties signed on 18 November 2003 was terminated by mutual consent.
10. Furthermore, in accordance with the contents of the said Declaration, it was observed by the Chamber that the Claimant literally covenanted that the USD 50000 has to be considered as ".. a full and final settlement.." and and in particular that "I (the Claimant) discharge the club (Respondent) from all obligations".
11. Having duly studied this document, the deciding body reached the conclusion that after the Claimant had received the amount of USD 50000 before his move to KKy, he would leave the Respondent without claiming "in future ... any amount from the said club (the Respondent). The members of the Chamber agreed that this document must be considered as a waiver duly signed by the Claimant. That is, by signing the said Declaration, which refers explicitly to the employment contract the parties entered into, the Claimant waived all rights that he may have towards the Respondent on the basis of the relevant employment contract in future.
12. The Chamber could not grasp how the Claimant could have signed this Declaration should he have been convinced of the alleged fact that his employment contract with the Respondent would only be suspended on the occasion of his move to KK.
13. Moreover, the members noted that the Claimant could not corroborate with documentary evidence his statement that the employment contract he signed with the Respondent was merely suspended for the period of time he spent with the KK club and that his move to the KK club was on a loan basis.
14. In this respect, the deciding body noted that no loan agreement possibly concluded between the Respondent and the KK club was presented. Such loan agreement could possibly be an indication of a suspension of an employment contract, however, in such event, the suspension of an employment contract should be corroborated with additional documentary evidence. Furthermore, the members referred once again to the statement of the Claimant that the KK club had the option to extend the duration of the contract. Consequently, the Claimants argument that the contract he signed with the Respondent was suspended could not be supported by the Chamber either, since it was possible that he would have to stay in KK for a maximum of three years, i.e. until 2007, thus beyond the expiry date of his contract he signed with the Respondent.
15. On account of all the above, the members of the Chamber unanimously concluded that the employment contract signed between the Claimant and the Respondent on 18 November 2006 was terminated on the occasion of the Claimants transfer to KK in the 2004/2005 season.
16. As a consequence, the deciding body decided that the claim put forward by the Claimant has to be rejected.

III. DECISION OF THE DISPUTE RESOLUTION CHAMBER

1. The claim of the Claimant, Player X, is rejected.
2. According to art. 61 par. 1 of the FIFA Statutes this decision may be appealed before the Court of Arbitration for Sport (CAS). The statement of appeal must be sent to the CAS directly within 21 days of receiving notification of this decision and has to contain all elements in accordance with point 2 of the directives issued by the CAS, copy of which we enclose hereto. Within another 10 days following the expiry of the time limit for the filing of the statement of appeal, the appellant shall file with the CAS a brief stating the facts and legal arguments giving rise to the appeal (cf. point 4 of the directives).

⚽⚽⚽

86130 B
DECISION OF THE DISPUTE RESOLUTION CHAMBER
passed in Zurich, Switzerland, on 17 August 2006,
in the following composition:
Slim Aloulou (Tunisia), Chairman
Jean-Marie Philips (Belgium), member
Zola Malvern Percival Majavu (South Africa), member
Rinaldo Martorelli (Brazil), member

Mick McGuire (England), member
on the claim presented by the club, A, country X, as Claimant
against
the club, B, country Y, as Respondent
regarding training compensation for the player C

I. FACTS OF THE CASE

1. According to the confirmation of the Federation of the country X the player C (hereinafter: the player), born on 14 January 1983, was registered for the club A from the country X (hereinafter: the Claimant), from 22 October 1999 until 16 August 2001, the seasons of his 17th to his 18th birthday.
2. In July/August 2005 the player signed his first professional contract with the club B from the country Y (hereinafter: the Respondent), for which he was registered on 30 August 2005.
3. Subsequently, the player concluded a covenant with the Respondent accepting to assume completely the responsibility for possible claims related to transfer payments or training compensation. Furthermore, the said covenant contains a clause which stipulates that neither the player nor the training clubs are entitled to demand payment from the Respondent related to the aforementioned issues.
   Finally, it was agreed by the two parties concerned that no legal action would be taken against the Respondent.
4. On 5 December 2005, the Claimant lodged a claim in front of FIFA requesting the payment of training compensation as described in art. 20 and annex 4 of the FIFA Regulations for the Status and Transfer of Players (edition 2005) for the training and education of the player.
5. In its response to the claim, the Respondent refers to the aforementioned covenant denying any responsibility to pay the demanded training compensation.

II. CONSIDERATIONS OF THE DISPUTE RESOLUTION CHAMBER

1. First of all, the Chamber analysed whether it was competent to deal with the matter at stake. In this respect, it referred to art. 18 par. 2 and 3 of the Rules Governing the Procedures of the Players' Status Committee and the Dispute Resolution Chamber. The present matter was submitted to FIFA on 5 December 2005, as a consequence the Chamber concluded that the revised Rules Governing Procedures (edition 2005) on matters pending before the decision making bodies of FIFA are applicable to the matter at hand.
2. With regard to the competence of the Chamber, art. 3 par. 1 of the above mentioned Rules states that the Dispute Resolution Chamber shall examine its jurisdiction in the light of articles 22 to 24 of the current version of the Regulations for the Status and Transfer of Players (edition 2005). In accordance with art. 24 par. 1 in combination with art. 22 (d) of the aforementioned Regulations, the Dispute Resolution Chamber shall adjudicate on disputes between two clubs belonging to different Associations related to training compensation.
3. As a consequence, the Dispute Resolution Chamber is the competent body to decide on the present litigation concerning the training compensation claimed by the Claimant for the training of the player C.
4. Subsequently, the members of the Chamber analyzed which edition of the Regulations for the Status and Transfer of Players should be applicable as to the substance of the matter. In this respect, the Chamber referred to art. 26 par. 1 and 2 of the Regulations for the Status and Transfer of Players (edition 2005) in the modified version in accordance with the FIFA circular no. 995 dated 23 September 2005. Furthermore, it acknowledged that the player had been registered for the first time as a professional on 30 August 2005. Equally, the Chamber took note that the claim was lodged at FIFA on 5 December 2005. In view of the aforementioned, the Chamber concluded that the current FIFA Regulations for the Status and Transfer of Players (edition 2005, hereafter: the Regulations) are applicable to the case at hand as to the substance.
5. In continuation, and entering into the substance of the matter, the members of the Chamber acknowledged that on the one hand the Claimant requested training compensation based on the number of years of training and education of the player with the Claimant and that, on the other hand, the Respondent invoked that it is not responsible for paying the requested training compensation on the basis of the aforementioned covenant (cf. point I.3.).

6. In this respect, the members of the Chamber acknowledged that the argument put forward by the Respondent is a covenant, according to which the Respondent and the player agree that the latter completely assumes the responsibility for possible claims related to transfer payments and training compensation, that neither the player nor the training clubs are entitled to demand payments from the Respondent related to the aforementioned issues and that no legal action would be taken against the Respondent.
7. The deciding body went on to examine the relevant covenant, on the basis of which the Respondent refused to pay training compensation. In this respect, the Chamber noted in particular that the covenant was not signed by the Claimant.
Therefore, it was emphasised by the members of the Chamber that the Claimant was no party to the relevant covenant and that such covenant cannot be legally binding on the Claimant.
8. As a consequence, the members of the Chamber unanimously concluded that the argumentation of the Respondent cannot be supported since the covenant concluded between the Respondent and the player is not relevant to the present dispute between the Claimant and the Respondent and, thus, cannot in any sense deprive the Claimant of its entitlement to receive training compensation.
9. In continuation, the Dispute Resolution Chamber referred to art. 20 in combination with art. 1 par. 1 of annex 4 of the Regulations, and emphasised that, as a general rule, training compensation is payable to the players training club(s), for training incurred up to the age of 21, when a player signs his first contract as a professional up to the age of 23. In this respect, it was noted that at the time the player signed his first professional contract with the Respondent, the player was 22 years old.
10. As a result of the above, after having duly considered all the documentation on file, the members of the Dispute Resolution Chamber unanimously reached the conclusion that the Claimant is entitled to receive training compensation for the training and education of the player as established in annex 4 of the Regulations.
11. After having established the Respondents obligation to compensate the Claimant for the training and education of the player in question, the Chamber went on to deliberate on the proper calculation of this compensation, affirming that the amount due shall be calculated in accordance with the parameters provided for by the Regulations and the FIFA circular no. 959 dated 16 March 2005.
12. In accordance with art. 3 par. 1 and art. 5 par. 2 of annex 4 of the Regulations, the training period to be taken into account starts at the beginning of the season of the players 12th birthday and finishes at the end the season of the players 21st birthday.
13. In this respect, the Chamber acknowledged that, according to the confirmation of the Federation of the country X, the player, born on 14 January 1983, was registered for the Claimant as from 22 October 1999 until 16 August 2001, i.e. the seasons of his 17th to his 19th birthday.
14. In light of the above, the Chamber decided that the Claimant is entitled to training compensation for the period of 1 season and 9 months.
15. For the sake of good order, the Chamber stressed that art. 6 of annex 4 of the Regulations concerning special provisions for the EU/EEA does not apply to the present matter since the case at hand does no involve two clubs inside the territory of the EU/EEA.
16. In continuation, the Chamber stated that in accordance with art. 5 par. 1 of annex 4 of the Regulations, as a general rule, in order to calculate the training compensation due to the players former club(s), it is necessary to take the costs that would have been incurred by the new club if it had trained the player itself.
In this respect, in order to clarify the sense of the aforementioned clause, the Chamber referred to art. 5 par. 2 of annex 4 of the Regulations, according to which the first time a player registers as a professional the training compensation payable is calculated by taking the training costs of the new club multiplied by the number of years of training in principle from the season of the players 12th birthday to the season of his 21st birthday.
17. Then, the Chamber observed that in accordance with the FIFA circular no. 959 dated 16 March 2005, which regards the training costs and categorisation of the clubs, the Respondent belongs to category IV and, thus, the corresponding indicative amount for a category IV club belonging to the UEFA is EUR 10000.
18. Consequently, in application of art. 5 par. 2 of annex 4 of the Regulations, the indicative amount mentioned in the previous point of the present decision must be multiplied by the number of years that the player was trained and educated by the Claimant. In this regard, the Chamber referred to the point II.14. of the present decision, according to which the total relevant period of time to be taken into consideration corresponds to 1 season and 9 months.

19. On account of all the foregoing considerations, the Chamber concluded that the Respondent has to pay the amount of EUR 17500 to the Claimant as training compensation for the training of the player C.

III. DECISION OF THE DISPUTE RESOLUTION CHAMBER

1. The claim of the Claimant, A, is accepted.
2. The Respondent, B, shall pay the amount of EUR 17500 to the Claimant, A, within 30 days following the date of the notification of the present decision.
3. In the event that the above-mentioned amount is not paid within the stated deadline, an interest rate of 5% p.a. will apply as of expiry of the fixed time limit and the present matter shall be submitted to the FIFAs Disciplinary Committee, so that the necessary disciplinary sanctions may be imposed.
4. The Claimant, A, is instructed to inform the Respondent, B, immediately of the account number to which the remittance is to be made and to notify the Dispute Resolution Chamber of every payment received.
5. According to art. 61 par. 1 of the FIFA Statutes, this decision may be appealed against before the Court of Arbitration for Sport (CAS). The Statement of appeal must be sent to the CAS directly within 21 days of receipt of notification of this decision and shall contain all the elements in accordance with point 2 of the directives issued by the CAS, a copy of which we enclose hereto. Within another 10 days following the expiry of the time limit for filing the statement of appeal, the appellant shall file a brief stating the facts and legal arguments giving rise to the appeal with the CAS (cf. point 4 of the directives).

⚽⚽⚽

86137
DECISION OF THE DISPUTE RESOLUTION CHAMBER
passed in Zurich, Switzerland, on 17 August 2006,
in the following composition:
Slim Aloulou (Tunisia), Chairman
Jean-Marie Philips (Belgium), member
Zola Malvern Percival Majavu (South Africa), member
Rinaldo Martorelli (Brazil), member
Mick McGuire (England), member
on the claim presented by the club, X, as Claimant
against
the club, Y, as Respondent
regarding training compensation related to the transfer of the player

I. FACTS OF THE CASE

1. The player, Z, was born on 5 June 1987.
2. According to the Football Association of X, the player, Z, was registered with X from 1 November 2001 until 1 July 2003.
3. On 4 July 2003, the player in question and Y signed a “scholarship agreement” valid until 30 June 2006.
4. In accordance with this agreement, inter alia, Z is entitled to receive remuneration in the amount of GBP 80 per week as from 4 July 2003 until 30 June 2004, GBP 90 per week as from 1 July 2004 until 30 June 2005 and GBP 115 per week as from 1 July 2005 until 30 June 2006.
5. In addition, the club obliged itself to pay to Z legitimate travel expenses.
6. In July 2004, Z having signed the aforementioned agreement with Y, X turned to FIFA maintaining that it is entitled to receive from Y training compensation in the amount of EUR 70,833. X has presented its calculation of the said amount.
7. By letter dated 27 September 2004, Y informed X that whilst agreeing with the claimants calculation for compensation to the amount of EUR 70,833, Y did not consider itself obliged at that moment to pay training compensation to X given that Z was still registered as an amateur player on a scholarship with Y. The Respondent added that it would offer the player a professional contract on his 18th birthday in accordance with the agreement signed with the player.

8. In its claim, X stresses that according to article 2 of the Regulations for the Status and Transfer of Players the decisive point is whether the player has a written contract with the club and is paid more than the expenses he effectively incurs in return for his footballing activity. In this respect, X refers to a decision passed by the Dispute Resolution Chamber (DRC) in a similar case in which the DRC ruled that even though the Respondent claimed that the relevant contract was not a professional contract but rather a "aspirant contract", the Claimant was entitled to compensation since the financial obligations of the Respondent in accordance with the "aspirant contract" covered more than the expenses effectively incurred by the player. X has presented a copy of the said DRC decision.
9. In reply to the claim, Y vehemently refutes that it owes training compensation payments to X.
10. Y stresses that the player signed for Y as a scholar, not as a professional player. It adds that it has long been the practice of the Football Association of Y to reject any claims for compensation at the time a player signs on a scholarship agreement, on the basis that this does not constitute a first professional contract for the purpose of FIFAs Regulations, and that clubs on the territory of the country of Y have relied on that assurance.
11. Furthermore, Y points out that the player had agreed to sign a professional contract with Y on his 18th birthday and the club was disappointed that he decided to return to the country of Z instead. In the best interests of the player and to avoid any delay in his development, the club allowed Z to cancel his registration by mutual consent.
12. Y further emphasizes that it waived any rights to compensation from the players next club because it had understood that it would not have to pay any compensation to his former club following his refusal to sign a professional contract.
13. Without prejudice to its contention that training compensation is not due, if it should be found that it is, Y reserves the right to apply to the DRC under Annex 4, article 5.4 of the FIFA Regulations for the Status and Transfer of Players (edition 2005) for an adjustment of the amount due to zero.
14. According to the written confirmation of the Football Association of Y dated 6 July 2006, Y has always had the status of a category 1 club.
15. The Football Association of X confirmed in writing that its member club, X, was a category 3 club at the time of Zs registration with Y in 2003.
16. On 11 August 2006, after having been informed by FIFA on 4 August 2006 that the case at hand would be presented to the DRC on 17 August 2006, Y asked that the hearing of the matter be postponed in order for the club to make further representations. In addition, it asked that this matter is dealt with by way of a hearing at which the parties can attend and make further representations and submit further evidence in person.
17. In fact, according to Y it had not received any further correspondence from FIFA following its letter dated 14 December 2005 in which it allegedly requested the opportunity to present further submissions.
18. Therefore, Y deems that it has not had the right to be properly heard.

II. CONSIDERATIONS OF THE DISPUTE RESOLUTION CHAMBER

1. First of all, the Chamber analysed whether it was competent to deal with the matter at stake. In this respect, it referred to art. 18 par. 2 and 3 of the Rule Governing the Procedures of the Players' Status Committee and the Dispute Resolution Chamber. The present matter was submitted to FIFA in July 2004, as a consequence the Chamber concluded that the previous Procedural Rules (edition 2001) on matters pending before the decision making bodies of FIFA are applicable to the matter at hand.
3. With regard to the competence of the Chamber, article 42.1 lit. (b) (iv) of the FIFA Regulations for the Status and Transfer of Players (edition 2001) establishes that disputes concerning training compensation will be decided by the Dispute Resolution Chamber.
4. As a consequence, the Dispute Resolution Chamber is the competent body to decide on the present litigation concerning the training compensation claimed by the Claimant for the training and education of the player, Z.
5. Subsequently, the members of the Chamber analyzed which edition of the Regulations for the Status and Transfer of Players should be applicable as to the substance of the matter. In this respect, the Chamber referred to article 26.1 and 2 of the Regulations for the Status and Transfer of Players (edition 2005) in the modified version in accordance with the FIFA circular no. 995 dated 23 September 2005. Furthermore, it acknowledged that the player had been registered for his new club in the summer of 2003 (July or August) and that the claim was lodged in front of FIFA in July 2004.

In view of the aforementioned, the Chamber concluded that the former FIFA Regulations for the Status and TRansfer of Players (edition 2001, hereinafter: the Regulations) are applicable to the case at hand as to the substance.

6. Once its competence was thus established, the Chamber deemed it appropriate to firstly examine the allegation of Y (hereinafter referred to as the Respondent) that it has not had the right to be properly heard throughout the proceedings in the case at hand.
7. As it appears from the file, on 22 November 2005, the Respondent was invited to submit its response to the claim lodged by X (hereinafter referred to as the Claimant) within the following 15 days. In reply, on 5 December 2005, the Respondent provided a copy of the "scholarship agreement" while stressing that it was in the course of preparing a more detailed submission because it strongly resists the claim on the grounds that the player did not sign a professional contract with the Respondent.
8. On 15 December 2005, FIFA received further correspondence dated 14 December 2005 from the Respondent in which it refers to its fax of 5 December 2005 and via which it sets out more fully the basis on which the Respondent rejects the claim for training compensation put forward by the Claimant. In the final paragraph of its letter of 15 December 2005, the Respondent affirms that " ... and without prejudice to our contention that Training Compensation is not due, if it should be found that it is , Y ..., Y reserves all rights of appeal. Furthermore, Y in these circumstances reserves the right to apply to the Dispute Resolution Chamber under Annex 4, Article 5.4 of the FIFA Regulations for the Status and Transfer of Players, for an adjustment of the amount due to zero and we reserve our right to adduce further submissions on this point.
9. The Respondents response to the claim was sent by FIFA to the Claimant for information only and by fax dated 18 May 2006 FIFA informed the parties that the investigation into the case at hand was closed and that the matter would be submitted to the Dispute Resolution Chamber for a formal decision.
10. As stated above, on 4 August 2006, FIFA informed the parties, inter alia, that the case was to be submitted to the Dispute Resolution Chamber on 17 August 2006.
11. The members of the Chamber then referred to the procedure outlined in article 6 of the Rules Governing the Practice and Procedures of the Dispute Resolution Chamber (which, as explained above are applicable to the case at hand), in accordance with which only one exchange of correspondence shall be instituted. Taking into account the above-mentioned details, the members of the Chamber concluded that in line with the said Procedural Rules the Respondent has been given the opportunity to present its response to the claim and no second exchange of correspondence has taken place.
12. As far as the Respondents request for an oral hearing in the case at hand is concerned, from article 6.9 of the aforementioned Procedural Rules it can be noted that the DRC shall deal with the case on the basis of the documents submitted by the parties. The members of the Chamber confirmed that such is the standard procedure followed in cases submitted in front of it. Only in the event of the DRC requiring oral arguments or testimonies of any witnesses or experts, will the DRC invite the parties to an oral hearing.
13. Furthermore, the members of the DRC agreed that from the Respondents correspondence dated 14 December 2005 (under point II.8 above) it could not be noted that the Respondent asked for the opportunity to present further submissions. The Respondent apparently merely reserved its alleged right to present further positions.
14. For all these reasons, the Chamber unanimously concluded that the Respondents right to be heard has not been infringed upon in any way.
15. The members of the Chamber then turned to the substance of the present matter and duly noted from the facts of the file that the Claimant maintains being entitled to training compensation from the Respondent on the basis of the registration of the player, Z, with the Respondent and the "scholarship agreement" signed by and between the player in question and the Respondent.
    The Respondent, for its part, rejects the claim put forward by the Claimant alleging that the player, Z, was registered with amateur status and therefore no training compensation shall be payable to the Claimant.
16. The Chamber focussed on the crucial question to be answered in the case at hand, i.e. whether or not the Claimant is entitled to receive training compensation from the Respondent taking into consideration the status of the player while registered with the Respondent. To this end, the Chamber turned to an analysis of the said "scholarship agreement".

17. In accordance with the "scholarship agreement, Z is entitled to receive from the Respondent the following remuneration:
a. GBP 80 per week from 4 July 2003 to 30 June 2004; GBP 90 per week from 1 July 2004 to 30 June 2005; GBP 115 per week from 1 July 2005 to 30 June 2006
b. reimbursement of travel expenses
18. Thus, the player was entitled to receive approximately EUR 500 per month in addition to the reimbursement of travel expenses during the first season of the "scholarship agreement", which amount was due to increase during the subsequent seasons (approximately EUR 560 per month during the second season and EUR 710 per month during the third season).
19. In this context, the Chamber took into account article 2 of the Regulations, which states:
"1. Players who have never received any remuneration other than reimbursement of their actual expenses incurred during the course of their participation in any activity connected with association football are regarded as amateur.
2. Travel and hotel expenses incurred through involvement in a match and the costs of a players equipment, insurance and training may be reimbursed without jeopardising a players amateur status.
3. Any player who has ever received remuneration in excess of the expenses and costs described in par. 2 of this article in respect of participation in an activity connected with association football shall be regarded as non-amateur unless he has reacquired amateur status under the terms of Art. 26 par.1 below."
20. Taking into consideration the criteria set out in the stated article 2 and the monies payable to Z on the basis of the "scholarship agreement", the members of the Chamber concluded unanimously that the player evidently received remuneration in excess of the expenses and costs described in par. 2 of the said article.
21. In addition to reimbursement of travel expenses, the player received a weekly monetary compensation in return for his footballing activity at the club.
22. The Chamber considered it opportune to stress that a player's remuneration asper the criteria set out in above-mentioned article 2 of the Regulation constitutes the decisive factor in the determination of the status of the player and that the legal nature or the designation of the agreement is of no relevance in this regard.
23. This has been confirmed by the Court of Arbitration for Sport (CAS) in its decision TAS 2005/A/383.
24. Taking into consideration the above, the Chamber concurred that the relationship between the Respondent and the player, Z, must be regarded as non-amateur.
25. The members of the Chamber, consequently, decided that the Claimant is entitled to receive training compensation in accordance with Chapter VII of the Regulations and Chapter III of the Regulations governing the Application of the Regulations for the Status and Transfer of Players (hereinafter referred to as Application Regulations) as well as FIFA circular letter no. 826 dated 31 October 2002.
26. Having thus established the Respondents obligation to compensate the Claimant, the Chamber turned to the calculation of the amount of compensation, affirming that the amount due shall be calculated in accordance with the parameters provided by the Regulations and the Application Regulations as well as Circular nr. 826 dated 31 October 2002.
27. It was recalled that, within the EU/EEA area, training compensation is based on the training and education costs of the country in which the training club of the player was located (cf. article 7.4 of the Application Regulations) and that the calculation is the average of the training costs for the two categories if the player moves from a lower to a higher category (cf. article 7.4 (a) of the Application Regulations), i.e. EUR 60,000 (the average of EUR 30,000 for category 3 plus EUR 90,000 for category 1). In addition, the amount for players aged 12 to 15 shall be based on the training and education costs for category 4 (cf. article 7.2 of the Application Regulations), i.e. EUR 10,000.
28. In the case at hand, the period of registration in the country of X to be taken into consideration is from 1 November 2001 until 1 July 2003. It can be established that the player, Z, has been trained and developed by the Claimant during the seasons relating to the players age of 13 to 16.
29. Furthermore, the Respondent is a category 1 club and the Claimant is a category 3 club.
30. Taking into account point II.27 above, the amount payable by the Respondent for the training throughout the players age of 13 to 16 is calculated as follows. The player has been registered (a) 2

months in the season of the players age of 13-14 (EUR 1,666 pro rata temporis); (b) one full year in the season of the players age of 14-15 (EUR 10,000); and (c) half a year in the season of the players age of 15-16 (EUR 30,000 pro rata temporis).

31. Taking into account the above, the Chamber decided that the Respondent is liable to pay the amount of EUR 41,666 to the Claimant as compensation for the training and education of the player, Z.

III. DECISION OF THE DISPUTE RESOLUTION CHAMBER

1. The claim of the Claimant, X, is partially accepted.
2. The Respondent, Y, has to pay the amount of EUR 41,666 to the Claimant.
3. Any further claims of the Claimant are dismissed.
4. The amount due to the Claimant has to be paid by the Respondent within 30 days as from the date of notification of this decision.
5. If the sum of EUR 41,666 is not paid within the aforementioned deadline, an interest rate of 5% per year will apply as of expiry of the aforementioned time limit and the case will immediately be submitted to the FIFA Disciplinary Committee.
6. The Claimant is directed to inform the Respondent immediately of the account number to which the remittance is to be made and to notify the Dispute Resolution Chamber of every payment received.
7. According to art. 61 par. 1 of the FIFA Statutes, this decision may be appealed against before the Court of Arbitration for Sport (CAS). The statement of appeal must be sent to the CAS directly within 21 days of receipt of notification of this decision and shall contain all the elements in accordance with point 2 of the directives issued by the CAS, a copy of which we enclose hereto. Within another 10 days following the expiry of the time limit for filing the statement of appeal, the appellant shall file a brief stating the facts and legal arguments giving rise to the appeal with the CAS (cf. point 4 of the directives).

86558

DECISION OF THE DISPUTE RESOLUTION CHAMBER

passed in Zurich, Switzerland, on 17 August 2006,
in the following composition:
Slim Aloulou (Tunisia), Chairman
Rinaldo Martorelli (Brazil), Member
Mick McGuire (England), Member
Jean-Marie Philips (Belgium), Member
Zola Majavu (South Africa), Member
on a matter between the club, A, AA represented by Mr U, attorney at law
and the club, B, BB
and the club, C, CC as Intervening party
regarding the solidarity contribution related to the transfer of the player X

I. FACTS OF THE CASE:

1. The player X born on 18 May 1981.
2. According to the official confirmation received from the A Football Federation, the player was registered with the A club, for the football season 1998/1999 between the ages of 17 and 18.
3. On 20 June 2002, the player in question was transferred from the C club, to the B club, when the player was 21 years old.
4. The relevant transfer compensation amounted to EUR 5900000.00.
5. In accordance with the terms stipulated in the transfer contract, the B club undertook to pay to the C club the transfer amount in three installments as follows:
   - EUR 2000000.00 until 30 June 2002
   - EUR 1950000.00 until 30 June 2003
   - EUR 1950000.00 until 31 December 2003
6. On 8 April 2005, the A club, , lodged a claim in front of FIFA regarding its portion of the solidarity contribution concerning this transfer and claimed 10% of 5% of the transfer compensation paid by B , i.e. EUR 29500.00, and also late payment interest of 5%. Moreover, the A club requested that

the B club should pay it the costs of arbitration, i.e. reasonable travel expenses and costs of expert advices.

7. In addition to that, the A club informed that, as decided in other decisions passed by the Dispute Resolution Chamber, the solidarity contribution has only to be paid when the relevant installments of the transfer compensation are due. On account of these considerations, the A club deemed that, at least, the two installments of the transfer compensation, which were due on 30 June and 31 December 2003, have to be taken into account when establishing its entitlement to the solidarity contribution. Finally, the A club stated that in case the Dispute Resolution Chamber would find that its claim for solidarity contribution relating to the first installment of the transfer compensation has to be considered as prescribed, the B club shall then be urged to pay the solidarity contribution to the "National Association of Respondent" in accordance with Chapter 4 of the FIFA Circular nº 769.
8. The B club in its statements informed that it already paid the entire transfer compensation to the C club, C , and that it was surprised to receive the claim from the A club three years after the transfer of the player in question took place. It suggested that the A club should turn against the C club in order to collect its claimed amount.
9. The C club, C, mentioned in its statement that during the negotiations with B for the transfer of the player in question, it had never been agreed that the solidarity contribution should be on account of C. Therefore, it rejected any responsibility with regard to the payment of the solidarity contribution.

II. CONSIDERATIONS OF THE DISPUTE RESOLUTION CHAMBER:

1. First of all, the Chamber analysed whether it was competent to deal with the matter at stake. In this respect, it referred to art.18 par. 2 and 3 of the Rules Governing the Procedures of the Players' Status Committee and the Dispute Resolution Chamber. The present matter was submitted to FIFA on 8 April 2005, as a consequence the Chamber concluded that the previous Procedural Rules (edition 2001) on matters pending before the decision making bodies of FIFA are applicable to the matter at hand.
2. With regard to the competence of the Chamber, art. 25 par. 2 of the FIFA Regulations for the Status and Transfer of Players (edition 2001) establishes that, i falls within the purview of the Dispute Resolution Chamber to review disputes concerning the distribution of the solidarity contribution.
3. As a consequence, the Dispute Resolution Chamber is the competent body to decide on the present litigation concerning the distribution of the solidarity contribution claimed by the club, A, in connection with the transfer of the professional player X during the course of an employment contract.
4. Subsequently, the members of the Chamber analyzed which edition of the Regulations for the Status and Transfer of Players should be applicable as to the substance of the matter. In this respect, the Chamber referred to art. 26 par. 1 and 2 of the Regulations for the Status and Transfer of Players (edition 2005) in the modified version in accordance with the FIFA Circular no. 995 dated 23 September 2005. Furthermore, it acknowledged that the professional player in question had been registered for his new club, B, in June or July 2002. Equally, the Chamber took note that the claim was lodged at FIFA on 8 April 2005. In view of the aforementioned, the Chamber concluded that the former FIFA Regulations for the Status and Transfer of Players (edition 2001, hereinafter: the Regulations) are applicable to the case at hand as to the substance.
5. In continuation, the members took note of the B clubs objection that the claim of the A club should not be considered admissible on the grounds that the claim before FIFA had been filed out of time.
6. In this regard, the members underlined that it is actually the responsibility of the new club to calculate the amount of the solidarity contribution and the way in which it shall be distributed in accordance with the players career history. For that purpose, the new club may ask the player for his assistance in order to help in discharging its obligation (cf. art. 11 par. 2 of the Regulations governing the Application of the Regulations, hereinafter; the Application Regulations).
7. Furthermore, the Chamber referred to art. 44 of the Regulations in connection with art. 4 of the Rules Governing the Practice and Procedures of the Dispute Resolution Chamber (edition 2002), which state that the Chamber will not hear any case if more than two years have elapsed since the facts leading to the dispute arose. The members of the Chamber took note that, in the case at hand, the relevant transfer compensation paid by the B club to C for the transfer of the player in question was paid in three instalments.

8. In this respect, the Chamber deemed it appropriate to explain that, in order for it to duly consider the question whether the N clubs claim is admissible or not, it has to differ between the three instalments which were paid by B to C as transfer compensation pursuant to the transfer agreement the two clubs signed. In fact, such procedure appeared to be necessary since it was already an established jurisprudence of the Dispute Resolution Chamber under the former Regulations (edition 2001) that in case of contingent payments, the relevant solidarity contribution should be payable 30 days after the date of such payments. It is in fact on the basis of this jurisprudence that the revised Regulations (edition 2005) explicitly provide for this rule (cf. art. 2 par. 1 of Annex 5 of the revised Regulations for the Status and Transfer of Players).
9. In this connection, the members of the Chamber went on to examine the relevant transfer agreement signed between the two aforementioned clubs and noted that the first instalment agreed in the amount of EUR 2000000.00 was to be paid by the B club to the C club until 30 June 2002. On the other hand, the Chamber took note that the A club lodged its claim before FIFA on 8 April 2005.
10. In view of the above, the Chamber pointed out that between the moment the facts leading to the dispute arose and the moment the A club lodged its claim before FIFA, more than two years have elapsed. Therefore, the members of the Chamber concluded that this part of the A clubs claim for solidarity contribution in relation to the first instalment paid by B to C is not receivable due to prescription.
11. In continuation, the members of the Chamber took note of the A clubs position contained in its correspondence dated 15 October 2005, that in case the Dispute Resolution Chamber would find that its claim for solidarity contribution relating to the first instalment of the transfer compensation has to be considered as prescribed, the B club, pursuant to Chapter 4 of FIFA Circular nº 769, should then be held liable to pay the relevant part of the solidarity contribution to the "National Association of Respondent".
12. In this respect, the deciding body referred to the jurisprudence of the Dispute Resolution Chamber, which has been confirmed recently by the Court of Arbitration for Sport (CAS), according to which, as a general rule under the former Regulations (version 2001), associations are not entitled to receive a proportion of the solidarity contribution for years during which it was not possible to identify any clubs having trained a given player.
13. As a result of the above-mentioned considerations, the Chamber concluded that it has to reject the claim of the A club also in this respect.
14. Furthermore, with regard to the second and third instalment paid by B to C for the transfer of the player in question, the members noted that those payments were due on 30 June 2003 and 31 December 2003 respectively, whereas the A club lodged its claim for the solidarity contribution on 8 April 2005.
15. In view of the above, the members of the Chamber concluded that the claim for solidarity contribution put forward by the A club with regard to the second and third instalment paid by the B club to the C club had been lodged within the two- years prescription period and thus is to be considered receivable.
16. In continuation, and entering into the substance of the matter, the members of the Chamber carefully studied the facts outlined above and emphasized that, as established in art. 25 par. 1 of the Regulations in combination with art. 11 par. 1 of the Application Regulations, the new club to which a player is transferred, is the club responsible for the distribution of 5% of any compensation it paid to his former club, to the club(s) involved in the training and education of the player between the ages of 12 and 23.
17. In continuation, the Chamber duly noted that B (the players new club) asserts having paid the entire amount of EUR 5900000.00, agreed upon as transfer compensation, to C (the players previous club) and that A should thus turn to the aforementioned C club in order to collect the amount relating to its part of the 5% solidarity contribution. In other words, B omitted to deduct 5% of the relevant transfer compensation relating to the solidarity mechanism.
18. In this respect, the Chamber referred to its well-established jurisprudence applied in similar cases, in accordance with which the players new club is ordered to remit the relevant proportion(s) of the 5% solidarity contribution to the club(s) involved in the players training in strict application of art. 11 of the Application Regulations. At the same time, the players former club is ordered to reimburse the same proportion(s) of the 5% of the compensation that it received from the players new club.

19. In light of the aforementioned well-established jurisprudence, the members of the Dispute Resolution Chamber concluded that it is the responsibility of the new club, i.e. B, to pay the relevant proportion of the solidarity contribution to A , which was involved in the players training. Furthermore, and bearing in mind that the 5% solidarity contribution is to be deducted from the amount payable to the players former club, C will have to refund the same proportion to B.
20. After having established B's obligation to distribute the relevant proportion of the solidarity contribution to A , the Chamber went on to deliberate on the proper calculation of the said proportion due to A .
21. To that regard, the Chamber referred to art. 10 of the Application Regulations, which provides the figures for the distribution of the solidarity contribution, according to the time the player was effectively trained by a specific club.
22. In the present case, the Chamber outlined that according to the player passport submitted by the Hellenic Football Federation, the period to be taken into account is the football season 1998/1999 in AA , i.e. the time the player had been registered with A.
23. In light of all of the above, the Chamber decided that the period of effective training to be taken into account corresponds to 1 year, for the players registration between his ages of 17 to 18.
24. Therefore, the Chamber established that, in accordance with the breakdown provided for in art. 10 of the Application Regulations, A is entitled to receive 10% of 5% of the relevant, not prescribed, parts of the transfer compensation paid by B to C in relation to the transfer of the player X.
25. In this respect, the Chamber recalled that only the second and third instalment of the transfer compensation paid by the B club to the C club can be taken into consideration for the calculation of the solidarity contribution due to the A club.
    Therefore, the members stated that the relevant amount to be put at the basis of the calculation is EUR 3900000.00 (2x EUR 1950000.00).
26. Consequently, taking into account all the above, the Dispute Resolution Chamber decided that B must pay to A the amount of EUR 19500.00 (2 x EUR 9750.00 each for the second and the third instalment) as solidarity contribution for the training and education of the player X.
27. In this respect, the members of the Chamber made reference to art. 11 par. 1 of the Application Regulations, which reads, inter alia, that the amount due as a solidarity contribution shall be paid by the new club to the training clubs pursuant to the above provisions at the latest within 30 days of the players new registration. With regard to the case at stake, the members stated, however, that, as elucidated above, the second and third installments of the transfer compensation were due on 30 June 2003 and on 31 December 2003 respectively.
28. Consequently, in light of the fact that this payment were due at the latest since 1 July 2003 and 1 January 2004, the Chamber established that a default interest payment of 5% p.a. as of 1 July 2003 for the amount of EUR 9750.00 and from 1 January 2004 for the amount of EUR 9750.00 must be applied.
29. Turning its attention to the reimbursement of legal expenses claimed by the A club, the Chamber referred to its well established jurisprudence in accordance with which no procedural compensation shall be awarded in proceedings in front of the Dispute Resolution Chamber. Furthermore, the members stated that the N club did not quantify these compensations at all, nor provided FIFA with any proving document. Consequently, the Chamber decided not to award such claimed expenses.
30. Finally, in line with the above considerations, the previous club of the player that was involved in the transfer of the player in question to the B club, i.e. C, is liable to reimburse to B the relevant amount of EUR 19500.00.

III. DECISION OF THE DISPUTE RESOLUTION CHAMBER

1. The claim of A is partially accepted.
2. The B club, shall pay the total amount of EUR 19500.00 (2x EUR 9750.00) to A within 30 days as from the date of notification of this decision.
3. On the respective amounts of EUR 9750.00 each, a default interest payment of 5% p.a. as from 1 July 2003 and 1 January 2004 respectively, until the date of the payment is applied.
4. Any further claims lodged by A are rejected.
5. In the event that the above-mentioned amounts are not paid within the stated deadline, the present matter shall be submitted to FIFAs Disciplinary Committee, so that the necessary disciplinary sanctions may be imposed.

6. The Greek club, A , is instructed to inform the B club, B , directly and immediately of the account number to which the remittance is to be made and to notify the Dispute Resolution Chamber of every payment received.
7. The C club, C , has to reimburse to B the amount of EUR 19500.00 within 30 days as from the date of notification of this decision.
8. In the event that the above-mentioned amount is not paid within the stated deadline, the present matter shall be submitted to FIFAs Disciplinary Committee, so that the necessary disciplinary sanctions may be imposed.
9. The B club, B , is directed to inform the C club, C , directly and immediately of the account number to which the remittance is to be made and to notify the Dispute Resolution Chamber of every payment received.
10. According to art. 61 par. 1 of the FIFA Statutes this decision may be appealed before the Court of Arbitration for Sport (CAS). The statement of appeal must be sent to the CAS directly within 21 days of receiving notification of this decision and has to contain all elements in accordance with point 2 of the directives issued by the CAS, copy of which we enclose hereto. Within another 10 days following the expiry of the time limit for the filing of the statement of appeal, the appellant shall file with the CAS a brief stating the facts and legal arguments giving rise to the appeal (cf. point 4 of the directives).

86833
DECISION OF THE DISPUTE RESOLUTION CHAMBER
passed in Zurich, Switzerland, on 17 August 2006,
in the following composition:
Slim Aloulou (Tunisia), Chairman
Jean-Marie Philips (Belgium), member
Zola Malvern Percival Majavu (South Africa), member Rinaldo Martorelli (Brazil), member Mick McGuire (England), member
on the claim presented by
the player, X, as Claimant
against
the club, Y, as Respondent
regarding a contractual dispute between the player and the club,

I. FACTS OF THE CASE
1. On 9 March 2005, the Claimant and the Respondent signed an employment contract valid from 9 March 2005 until 9 June 2005 with an extension option to be exercised in accordance with article 9 of the same contract.
2. According to this employment contract, schedule A annexed to the contract outlines the salary payable to the Claimant. Schedule A, which was not signed by the parties, stipulates that the Claimant is entitled to receive a monthly salary of USD 1,000 during the season and of USD 500 at off season. The notion "off season" has been defined in the said annexe. The same annexe also stipulates that the Claimant's monthly "take home income" shall not exceed Y currency 20,000 during the season and Y currency 10,000 during off season.
3. Schedule B referred to in and annexed to the employment contract, which does not bear any signature either, includes other benefits due to the Claimant, including free medical benefits, housing, and transportation without any further indication.
4. According to article 11 of the same contract, all notices to the player shall be in writing and must be sent by registered post.
5. In accordance with its article 14, the player is subject to a 30-day probation period effective from the date the agreement was signed. At any time within the probation period the club may terminate the agreement if it is not satisfied with the performance of the player. Furthermore, it shall pay the player "a full monthly salary for the month the agreement was terminated and other compensation agreed by both the club and the player".

6. As regards the players performance, article 4 indicates that the player will be given a performance report in accordance with the guidelines issued by the Football Association of Y after every game played by him. If his performance is rated poor, he will be given a written warning in the first instance and a final warning in the second instance, after which he would be subject to disciplinary action.
7. In accordance with article 10 disputes are to be settled by the Players' Status Committee of the Football Association of Y or by an arbitrator (in country of Y) appointed by the parties involved in mutual agreement.
8. On 20 June 2005, the Claimant turned to FIFA maintaining that the Respondent abusively terminated his contract after having played one match only.
9. To this end, he submitted a copy of a document dated 26 March 2005 duly signed by the Respondent informing the Claimant that it terminates the contract as from 26 March 2005. According to this notice of termination, the Claimant "did not fit in well to the teams playing system."
10. In addition, the Claimant submitted a copy of his letter dated 8 April 2005 addressed to the club by means of which he protested against his dismissal and he gave notice to the club to settle his dues (salary and air fares), otherwise he would be obliged to refer the matter to the Players' Status Committee of the Football Association of Y.
11. The Claimant confirms that he has received the amount of USD 1,000 from the Respondent.
12. In the light of the above, the Claimant claims payment of the amount of USD 87,567 plus compensation for breach of contract.
13. In a first reaction to the Claimants claim, on 3 October 2005, the Footbal Association of Y informed FIFA, as per FIFAs request, that the Claimant never lodged an official claim in front of the Association against its member club.
14. The Football Association of Y however asks that the matter be referred to its Players' Status Committee.
15. In reply to FIFAs fax of 4 October 2005, the Claimant confirmed by fax dated 12 October 2005 that he wishes to proceed with his claim in front of FIFA.
16. Later on during the proceedings, the Football Association of Y, apparently acting on behalf of its member club, submitted a copy of a letter dated 15 April 2005 allegedly signed by the Claimant in which he acknowledges having received USD 1,000 as the final compensation for the termination of his contract with the club.
17. In the same letter, the Claimant confirms that he "would not hold X and/or X Holdings responsible for the contract termination or take any legal action to the said party(ies)".
18. The Respondent adds that there were witnesses present when the player signed this letter.
19. The Claimant asserts that he never signed the letter dated 15 April 2005 and affirms that the signature is forged.
20. FIFAs repeated requests to the Respondent to present the original version of the aforementioned letter dated 15 April 2005 remained unanswered by the Respondent.
21. The only reaction received was a fax from the Football Association of Y informing FIFA that the matter would be discussed at the next Players' Status Committee meeting of the Football Association of Y.
22. FIFA then asked the Football Association of Y twice to present further information on the claim which was apparently filed at the same Association, such as the date on which the claim was lodged and by whom as well as the contents of the claim.
23. This query has remained unanswered.
24. Later on during the proceedings, the Claimant modified his claim to contain the following:
    a) 2 remaining months' salary of Y currency 4,000;
    b) 50% of what was earned by the other players during their vacation;
    c) Referring to paragraph D of page 10 of the employment contract, the benefits relating to rent and transport;
    d) Payment of medical costs;
    e) Costs allegedly incurred for visa;
    f) Reimbursement of his air ticket and allocation of an air ticket to his wife.

II. CONSIDERATIONS OF THE DISPUTE RESOLUTION CHAMBER

1. First of all, the Chamber analysed whether it was competent to deal with the matter at stake. The Chamber referred to art. 18 par. 2 and 3 of the Rules Governing the Procedures of the Players' Status Committee and the Dispute Resolution Chamber. The present matter was submitted to FIFA on 20 June 2005, as a consequence the Chamber concluded that the previous Procedural Rules (edition 2001) on matters pending before the decision making bodies of FIFA are applicable to the matter at hand.
2. Taking into consideration the position of the Respondent that the matter should be referred to the Players' Status Committee of the Football Association of Y, the members of the Chamber agreed that in the absence of a national sports arbitration tribunal composed of members chosen in equal numbers by players and clubs as well as an independent chairman (cf. Article 42 of the Regulations for the Status and Transfer of Players, edition 2001), the Dispute Resolution Chamber of the FIFA Players' Status Committee is competent to deal with a dispute, even if written agreements signed between the parties involved in the dispute contain a clause by means of which the (exclusive) jurisdiction of another body is chosen.
3. With regard to the competence of the Chamber, art. 42 par. 1 lit. (b) (i) of the FIFA Regulations for the Status and Transfer of Players (edition 2001) establishes that the triggering elements of the employment-related dispute (i.e. whether a contract was breached, with or without just cause, or sporting just cause), will be decided by the Dispute Resolution Chamber.
4. If an employment contract is breached by a party, the Dispute Resolution Chamber is also responsible to verify whether a party is accountable for outstanding payments and/or compensation.
5. As a consequence, the Dispute Resolution Chamber is the competent body to decide on the present litigation involving a club from the country of Y and a player from the country of X regarding a dispute in connection with an employment contract.
6. Subsequently, the members of the Chamber analyzed which edition of the Regulations for the Status and Transfer of Players should be applicable as to the substance of the matter. In this respect, the Chamber referred, on the one hand, to art. 26 par. 1 and 2 of the Regulations for the Status and Transfer of Players (edition 2005) and, on the other hand, to the fact that the relevant contract at the basis of the present dispute was signed on 9 March 2005 and that the claim was lodged at FIFA on 20 June 2005. In view of the aforementioned, the Chamber concluded that the former FIFA Regulations for the Status and Transfer of Players (edition 2001, hereafter: the Regulations) are applicable to the case at hand as to the substance.
7. Once its competence was thus established, the Dispute Resolution Chamber went on to deal with the substance of the case acknowledging the abovementioned FACTS OF THE CASE, from which it can be noted that the Claimant was contractually bound to the Respondent as from 9 March 2005 until 9 June 2005.
8. On 26 March 2005, the Respondent prematurely terminated the employment contract in writing as the player allegedly did not fit in the teams playing system.
9. By letter dated 8 April 2005, the Claimant protested against the termination of his employment contract by the Respondent and he put the club in default of payment of his salary and air ticket.
10. Therefore, the Claimant initially claimed payment of the amount of USD 87,567 plus compensation for breach of contract. The Claimant, however, has failed to present a breakdown of this amount.
11. Later on during the proceedings, this claim was amended by the Claimant to comprise the details outlined in number I.24 above.
12. In reply to the claim, the Respondent, for its part, presented a document dated 15 April 2005 allegedly signed by the Claimant in which the Claimant acknowledges having received USD 1,000 as the final compensation for the termination of his contract with the club.
13. In the same letter, the Claimant would confirm that he "would not hold X and/or X Holdings responsible for the contract termination or take any legal action to the said party(ies)."
14. The Claimant, however, asserts that he never signed this letter dated 15 April 2005 and affirms that the signature is forged.
15. The Chamber noted that the Respondent failed to provide FIFA with the original version of this letter dated 15 April 2005 in spite of having been requested to do so on several occasions. Nor has the Respondent given any reasons explaining why it would possibly not be able to comply with such request.

16. Consequently, the members of the Chamber agreed that the faxed version of the said letter dated 15 April 2005 cannot be taken into consideration, since its authenticity is being contested by the Claimant and the Respondent has failed to corroborate its allegations in this respect, in particular, it failed to provide the requested original version.
17. The members of the Chamber then turned to the question as to whether the club had valid reasons to prematurely terminate the relevant employment contract.
18. In this context, firstly, the Chamber referred to article 14 of the employment contract, in accordance with which the player is subject to a 30-day probation period effective from the date on which the agreement was signed. In addition, according to the same article, at any time within the probation period the club may terminate the agreement if it is not satisfied with the performance of the player. The club shall pay the player "a full monthly salary for the month the agreement was terminated and other compensation agreed by both the club and the player".
19. After having discussed the issue at length, the members of the Chamber concurred that probation periods in football related employment contracts are unacceptable. Indeed, probation periods generally are solely in favour of the employer, i.e. the party that commonly has stronger bargaining power. What is more, by nature, probation periods principally go against one of the main pillars of both the previous and the current version of the FIFA Regulations for the Status and Transfer of Players, i.e. maintenance of contractual stability, and the rules related to contractual stability. Should, for instance, clubs and/or players have the possibility to put an end to an employment contract invoking a probation period, players in particular may have difficulty in finding another employment in the light of articles 5 and 6 of the Regulations for the Status and Transfer of Players (edition 2005). In addition, such termination of contract would be in violation of the main principle foreseen in article 13 of the said Regulations.
20. Regardless of the above, in the case at hand, the article relating to the probation period is undoubtedly potestative, the Respondent being the sole party able to terminate the employment contract during the probation period on the basis of the pertinent article.
21. In the light of the foregoing, the members of the Chamber agreed that the probation period inserted in the employment contract cannot justify the early termination of the relevant employment contract.
22. According to the notice of termination of the employment contract, the reason for the Respondent to terminate the contract was that the player "did not fit in well to the team's playing system. Although such phrase is rather ambiguous, the members of the Chamber agreed that this cannot be considered a valid reason to terminate an employment contract".
23. Consequently, and taking into consideration the above facts, the Chamber concluded that the Respondent had no just cause to terminate the relevant employment contract.
24. The members of the Chamber then turned to the financial claim put forward by the Claimant as described under point I.12. Taking into account that a) the Claimant has failed to provide a breakdown of and/or arguments for the amount of USD 87,567 plus compensation for breach of contract and that b) the Claimant modified his financial claim at a later stage of the proceedings (cf. point I.24), the Chamber decided to focus on the latter claim.
25. Under number I.24 a) the Claimant asks to be awarded two months' salary in the amount of Y currency 4,000. In the light of the termination by the club of the employment contract without just cause, the members of the Chamber decided that the Claimant is entitled to receive the remaining value of the employment contract. Consequently, and taking into consideration a monthly salary of USD 1,000, the Chamber decided that the Claimant is entitled to the amount of USD 2,000 pertaining to the two final months of the duration of his employment contract.
26. Referring to number I.24 f) the Claimant asks to be awarded the reimbursement of an air ticket and the allocation of an air ticket to his wife. In accordance with Schedule B of the relevant employment contract, the Claimant is entitled to "transportation" without any further indication as regards the type of transportation. The members of the Chamber considered that air tickets could not be excluded from the (international) players benefits pertaining to "transportation". Consequently, the Chamber decided that the Claimant is entitled to receive an amount of money corresponding to one air ticket country of X - country of Y - country of X in economy class, the price of which is to be determined by FIFAs travel agency. The Chamber decided, however, that no air ticket could be allocated to the Claimants wife on the basis of the relevant indications in the employment contract.
27. The price quoted by FIFAs travel agency for such ticket is USD 3,500.

28. With regard to the Claimants claim under number I.24 b) to e) the Chamber noted that the Claimant failed to indicate the relevant amounts of money and/or to present documentary evidence substantiating such claims.
29. Consequently, the Chamber decided to reject the Claimants claims pertaining to numbers I.24 b), I.24 c), I.24 d), and 1.24 e).
30. Taking into consideration the above numbers II.25, II.26 and II.27, the Chamber decided that the Respondent must pay to the Claimant the total amount of USD 5,500.

III. DECISION OF THE DISPUTE RESOLUTION CHAMBER

1. The claim of the Claimant, X, is partially accepted.
2. The Respondent, Y, shall pay the amount of USD 5,500 to the Claimant within 30 days of notification of the present decision.
3. Any further claims of the Claimant are rejected.
4. In the event that the amount of is not paid within the stated deadline, an interest rate of 5% per year will apply as of expiry of the aforementioned time limit and the case will immediately be presented to the FIFA Disciplinary Committee.
5. The Claimant is directed to inform the Respondent immediately of the account number to which the remittance is to be made and to notify the Dispute Resolution Chamber of every payment received.
6. According to art. 61 par. 1 of the FIFA Statutes, this decision may be appealed against before the Court of Arbitration for Sport (CAS). The statement of appeal must be sent to the CAS directly within 21 days of receipt of notification of this decision and shall contain all the elements in accordance with point 2 of the directives issued by the CAS, a copy of which we enclose hereto. Within another 10 days following the expiry of the time limit for filing the statement of appeal, the appellant shall file a brief stating the facts and legal arguments giving rise to the appeal with the CAS (cf. point 4 of the directives).

86999

DECISION OF THE DISPUTE RESOLUTION CHAMBER

passed in Zurich, Switzerland, on 17 August 2006,
in the following composition:
Slim Aloulou (Tunisia), Chairman
Jean-Marie Philips (Belgium), member
Zola Malvern Percival Majavu (South Africa), member
Rinaldo Martorelli (Brazil), member
Mick McGuire (England), member
on the claim presented by
the player, X, represented by Mr attorney at law as Claimant
against
the club, Y, represented by Mr attorney at law as Respondent
regarding an employment-related dispute between the player and the club

I. FACTS OF THE CASE

1. On 3 June 2003, the player, X, and the club, Y, signed an employment contract valid from 15 June 2003 until 15 June 2006.
2. According to art. 1.3 of this contract, the regulations of the Football League of Y and of the Football Federation of Y as well as the FIFA Regulations for the Status and Transfer of Players are applicable.
3. Art. 1.4 of the same contract stipulates that the player commits himself to refer any dispute arising from the relevant employment contract to the “Senate” of the Football League of Y.
4. In accordance with this contract the player is entitled to receive, inter alia, a net salary of EUR 135,000 per season.
5. On the same day, the parties signed a “side letter” which constitutes an integral part of the employment contract, in accordance with which, inter alia, X is entitled to receive EUR 25,000 net per year as a signing-on fee.

6. On 27 August 2004, the parties signed an agreement by means of which they terminated the employment contract by mutual consent taking effect as from 31 August 2004 (hereinafter also referred to as "termination agreement").
7. This agreement stipulates that the player, inter alia, is entitled to receive as compensation for the early termination of the employment contract the net amount of EUR 150,000 payable in three equal instalments of EUR 50,000 falling due on 1 September, 20 September, and 20 October 2004, respectively.
8. According to clause 4 of this agreement, should Y fail to remit one or more of the aforementioned instalments in a timely manner, the said agreement turns void and the player would be entitled to claim payment of all monies due to him in accordance with the employment contract in the period from August 2004 until June 2006. The same clause indicates that in such event any payment already made by the club to the player can be compensated.
9. By letter dated 19 November 2004, the player put the club in default of payment of all of the aforementioned instalments totalling EUR 150,000 net plus interest.
10. This default notice having remained without action on the part of the club, on 29 December 2004, the player sent a registered letter to the club claiming payment of the amount of EUR 291,875 invoking the aforementioned clause 4 of the termination agreement.
11. By fax dated 21 January 2005, referring to the players correspondence (without reference to a date) Y acknowledged in writing that it recognises the players claim and that a certain Mr. W already remitted EUR 50,000 as a first instalment.
12. In the same fax message, Y confirms that it would proceed with the payment of the remainder until 20 February 2005 due to lack of monetary funds.
13. On 4 July 2005, the player turned to FIFA claiming payment of the following monies on the basis of clause 4 of the termination agreement signed by the parties on 27 August 2004:
Signing-on fee of EUR 25,000 x 2 EUR 50,000
Net salary of EUR 135,000 per season / EUR 11,250 per month for the period from 01.09.04 - 15.06.06 (21,5 EUR 241,875 months)
10% interest as from 19.11.04 until date of full EUR 17,512.50 settlement
TOTAL EUR 309,387.50
+ Reimbursement of legal fees
14. In reply to the players claim, the club contends that FIFA, in particular its Players' Status Committee on the basis of article 34 of the FIFA Statutes, is not competent to deal with the present matter.
15. In addition, the present matter is a labour dispute between an employee who was employed in the country of Y and an employer from the country of Y, to which labour law of the country of Y is applicable. Therefore, FIFA would not be in the position to deal with this matter as to the substance.
16. According to the club, the player already lodged a claim in front of the "Senat 2" of the Football League of Y prior to having turned to FIFA, which allegedly is still pending.
17. Therefore, according to the club, regardless of the aforementioned non- competence of FIFA, FIFA cannot decide on the matter because there is no final and binding decision by the "Senat 2".
18. The club adds that the player having lodged his claim at a national deciding body he cannot turn to another deciding body with the same claim (ne bis in idem).
19. Furthermore, the club is of the opinion that the claim itself is not concrete.
20. In spite thereof, the club points out that in accordance with law of the country of Y the players earnings after the contract termination should be taken into consideration when deciding on the players financial claim.
21. According to Y, after their contract termination, the player signed on with another club.
22. In reaction to the clubs response, the player has presented documentary evidence showing that by letter dated 6 October 2005 he informed the Football League of Y of his withdrawal of his claim in front of the aforementioned "Senat 2" of the said Football League. Such withdrawal was confirmed by the "Senat 2" in writing on 9 November 2005.
23. Therefore, he rejects Ys position.
24. The player also points out that the respondent does not contest the players claim as to the substance. Moreover, he denies having received the instalment of EUR 50,000 referred to by the club in its fax dated 21 January 2005 and stresses that the club has not presented any documentary evidence of such payment.

25. Furthermore, the player argues that the Dispute Resolution Chamber is competent to deal with his claim in particular on the basis of article 22 of the Regulations for the Status and Transfer of Players.
26. In its final position dated 30 January 2006, Y maintains its position that FIFA is not competent to decide on the present case and presents a detailed argumentation which includes, inter alia, the following points:
The listing under the said article 22 is exhaustive and the present matter does not fall in any of the categories listed;
Should the matter at stake be deemed to fall in a category listed under article 22, then article 22.b would most probably be applied.
However, the present matter dealing with a dispute involving an employment contract of the country of Y and an employer from the country of Y, it lacks an international dimension;
Furthermore, the player has had the opportunity to claim in front of the national instance, the "Senat 2".
There is no arbitration clause in place between the player and the club which would entitle FIFA to deal with this matter.
27. In reply to FIFAs invitation to the club to present copies of the rules and regulations of the country of Y that it refers to in its defence, the club points out that the Football League of Y and the Football Federation of Y are no parties to the present matter and that it does not fall within the clubs responsibility to present such documentation.

II. CONSIDERATIONS OF THE DISPUTE RESOLUTION CHAMBER

1. First of all, and taking into consideration the Respondents position that FIFA is not competent to deal with the present claim, the Chamber analysed in detail whether it was competent to deal with the matter at stake. In this respect, it referred to art. 18 par. 2 and 3 of the Rules Governing the Procedures of the Players' Status Committee and the Dispute Resolution Chamber. The present matter was submitted to FIFA on 4 July 2005, as a consequence the Chamber concluded that the revised Rules Governing Procedures (edition 2005) on matters pending before the decision making bodies of FIFA are applicable to the matter at hand.
2. With regard to the competence of the Chamber, art. 3 par. 1 of the above- mentioned Rules states that the Dispute Resolution Chamber shall examine its jurisdiction in the light of articles 22 to 24 of the current version of the Regulations for the Status and Transfer of Players (edition 2005). In accordance with art. 24 par. 1 in combination with art. 22 (b) of the aforementioned Regulations, the Dispute Resolution Chamber shall adjudicate on employment- related disputes between a club and a player that have an international dimension.
3. According to the Respondent, the present matter lacks the international dimension referred to in the said art. 22 (b), the dispute involving an employment contract of the country of Y and an employer of the country of Y.
In this respect, the Chamber could not agree with the Respondent, since in order for an employment-related dispute between a player and a club to have an international dimension, it is sufficient, inter alia and under standard circumstances, that the Claimant and the Respondent do not have the same nationality. This position is confirmed by the jurisprudence of the Dispute Resolution Chamber, which is readily available by means of the publication of such jurisprudence on www.FIFA.com.
4. As regards the "independent arbitration tribunal" referred to in the said art. 22 (b), the Chamber emphasized that the Respondent has not presented any documentation to demonstrate that such independent arbitration tribunal guaranteeing fair proceedings and respecting the principle of equal representation of players and clubs has been established at national level within the framework of the Football Federation of Y.
5. In this respect, the members of the deciding body were eager to straighten out that the competence of such a national body would need to be explicitly stipulated by the parties in the relevant contract, at least with a clear reference to the national regulations providing for such competence. The members of the Chamber took particular note of the fact that the agreement by means of which the parties involved terminated their employment relation by mutual consent, thus the document which is at the basis of the present dispute, does not include any clause relating to competence as opposed to the employment contract that was terminated through the said agreement.

6. Notwithstanding the aforementioned and under the given circumstances (i.e. no clear choice of forum in the termination agreement), the members of the Chamber pointed out that the existence of such deciding body at national level (which was, however, not proven in the case at hand) does basically not exclude a players right to submit his claim against a club in front of the Dispute Resolution Chamber.
7. Furthermore, the members of the Chamber stated that in order for the Dispute Resolution Chamber to hear and decide on a dispute, it is not necessary for the parties to have a signed arbitration clause in place. This in particular in cases like the one at hand, in which the employment contract expressly refers to the FIFA Regulations for the Status and Transfer of Players (cf. art. 1.3 of the employment contract).
8. With respect to the Claimant having lodged his claim in front of the "Senat 2, the Chamber took into account that a) such claim was withdrawn by the Claimant, as a result of which no procedure appears to be pending any longer in front of a national deciding body and that b) no formal decision was yet passed by the said "Senat 2".
9. For the sake of good order, the Chamber also stressed that art. 34 of the FIFA Statutes to which the Respondent appears to be referring to has not been in force any longer since the coming into force of the 1 January 2004 edition of the Statutes. The facts that are at the basis of the present dispute occurred in August 2004. Therefore, the article referred to by the Respondent is not of any relevance.
10. For all of the above-mentioned reasons, the Chamber unanimously agreed that it is competent to decide on the present litigation involving a player from the country of Y and a club from the country of Y regarding an employment-related dispute.
11. Subsequently, the members of the Chamber analyzed which edition of the Regulations for the Status and Transfer of Players should be applicable as to the substance of the matter. In this respect, the Chamber referred, on the one hand, to art. 26 par. 1 and 2 of the Regulations for the Status and Transfer of Players (edition 2005) and, on the other hand, to the fact that the relevant employment contract was signed on 3 June 2003 and that the claim was lodged at FIFA on 4 July 2005. In view of the aforementioned, the Chamber concluded that the current FIFA Regulations for the Status and Transfers of Players (edition 2005, hereinafter: the Regulations) are applicable to the case at hand as to the substance.
12. In this respect, the Chamber deemed it appropriate to point out that in the employment contract signed on 3 June 2003 the parties had expressly agreed on the applicability of the FIFA Regulations for the Status and Transfer of Players.
13. Once its competence was thus established, the Dispute Resolution Chamber went on to deal with the substance of the matter acknowledging the above- mentioned Facts of the Case, from which it can be noted that the Claimant was bound to the Respondent by a contract signed between the parties on 3 June 2003.
    Such contract was prematurely terminated in writing and by mutual consent on 27 August 2004.
14. The relevant termination agreement stipulates that the Claimant, inter alia, is entitled to receive as compensation for the early termination of the employment contract the net amount of EUR 150,000 payable in three equal instalments of EUR 50,000 falling due on 1 September, 20 September, and 20 October 2004, respectively.
15. This agreement further sets forth in its clause 4 that should the Respondent fail to remit one or more of the aforementioned instalments in a timely manner, the said agreement turns void and the Claimant would be entitled to claim payment of all monies due to him in accordance with the employment contract in the period from August 2004 until June 2006.
16. The Claimants default notice addressed to the Respondent having remained non-executed by the Respondent, the Claimant invokes the above-mentioned clause 4 and claims payment of the amount of EUR 309,387.50 including signing-on fees and salaries for the period from 1 September 2004 until 15 June 2006 in accordance with the relevant employment contract as well as 10% interest. In addition, the Claimant claims that the Respondent shall reimburse his legal fees.
17. As to the substance of the present matter, the Chamber further noted that the Respondent has not rejected the players financial claim. The Respondent has merely stated that the players claim is not concrete and that in accordance with the law of the country of Y the players earnings after the contract termination should be taken into consideration when deciding on the players financial claim. According to the Respondent, after their contract termination, the Claimant signed on with another club.

18. The Chamber recalled that the Claimant presented a copy of the fax dated 21 January 2005 addressed by the Respondent to the Claimant and in which the Respondent acknowledges the players claim (cf. points I.11 and I.12).
19. In addition, according to the same correspondence, the Respondent asserts that a certain Mr. Jürgen Werner already remitted EUR 50,000 as a first instalment.
20. The Claimant, however, denies having received the said amount of EUR 50,000.
21. The Respondent, for its part, has not presented any documents demonstrating that indeed the amount of EUR 50,000 was paid by the Respondent to the Claimant in connection with the claim of the Claimant.
22. The Chamber disagreed with the Respondent that the Claimants earnings since the contract termination should be taken into consideration, given that the claim of the Claimant is based on a clause in the termination agreement duly signed by and between the parties involved specifying the amount payable to the Claimant for the early termination of the employment relationship and also specifying the financial consequences in the event of non-compliance by the Respondent of the terms relating to the amount agreed upon. The termination agreement does not stipulate that monies earned by the player after the termination of the employment contract shall be deductible from the amount relating to such financial consequences. Furthermore, the financial claim of the Claimant is not related to an amount of compensation for breach of contract.
    The Chamber agreed that under such circumstances no deduction of monies earned by the Claimant since the termination of the employment contract by mutual consent shall be legitimate.
23. For the above-mentioned reasons, the Chamber decided that the Claimant is entitled to receive the monies payable to him by the Respondent on the basis of clause 4 of the termination agreement.
24. According to the said clause 4 of the termination agreement, the player is entitled to receive all monies due to him in accordance with the employment contract relating to the period August 2004 until June 2006, i.e. the amount of EUR 291,875.
25. Furthermore, the Chamber decided that no monies shall be deductible from the amount to be received by the Claimant on the basis of clause 4 of the termination agreement. This relates to both the EUR 50,000 that the Respondent maintains having remitted to the Claimant, which allegation has not been substantiated with documentary evidence, and the monies earned by the Claimant since the termination of the employment contract by mutual consent.
26. Therefore, the Chamber decided that the Respondent is liable to pay to the Claimant the amount of EUR 291,875.
27. In addition, the Chamber decided that the Respondent shall pay default interest at a rate of 5% p.a. (and not 10% p.a. as requested by the Claimant) as from the date on which the Claimant put the club in default of payment, i.e. 19 November 2004, in accordance with the claim.
28. In accordance with its constant jurisprudence, the Chamber decided to reject the Claimants claim pertaining to reimbursement of legal expenses.

III. DECISION OF THE DISPUTE RESOLUTION CHAMBER

1. The claim of the Claimant, X, is partially accepted.
2. The Respondent, Y, shall pay to the Claimant the amount of EUR 291,875 plus 5% default interest applicable as from 19 November 2004 until the day on which payment is fully effected, within 30 days of notification of the present decision.
3. Any further claims of the Claimant are rejected.
4. In the event that the amount of EUR 291,875 plus the relevant interest is not paid within the stated deadline, the case will immediately be presented to the FIFA Disciplinary Committee.
5. The Claimant is directed to inform the Respondent immediately of the account number to which the remittance is to be made and to notify the Dispute Resolution Chamber of every payment received.
6. According to art. 61 par. 1 of the FIFA Statutes, this decision may be appealed against before the Court of Arbitration for Sport (CAS). The statement of appeal must be sent to the CAS directly within 21 days of receipt of notification of this decision and shall contain all the elements in accordance with point 2 of the directives issued by the CAS, a copy of which we enclose hereto. Within another 10 days following the expiry of the time limit for filing the statement of appeal, the appellant shall file a brief stating the facts and legal arguments giving rise to the appeal with the CAS (cf. point 4 of the directives).

861152
DECISION OF THE DISPUTE RESOLUTION CHAMBER
passed in Zurich, Switzerland, on 17 August 2006,
in the following composition:
Slim Aloulou (Tunisia), Chairman
Jean-Marie Philips (Belgium), member
Zola Majavu (South Africa), member
Rinaldo Martorelli (Brazil), member
Mick Mc Guire (England), member
on the claim presented by the club, X, as Claimant
against
the club, Y, as Respondent
regarding the solidarity contribution related to the transfer of the player

I. FACTS OF THE CASE

1. According to the player passport issued by the Football Association of the club X, the player Z, born on 27 January 1975, was registered as follows with the Claimant:
   - 25 February 1994 to 30 June 1994, i.e. for 4 months at the age of 19, loaned as an amateur player,
   - 31 January 1995 to 30 June 1995, i.e. for 5 months at the age of 20, loaned as an amateur player,
   - 1 January 1996 to 4 March 1996 as well as from 16 July 1996 to 4 January 1997, i.e. for approximately 7 months at the age of 21 as a non-amateur player.

   In total, the player was therefore registered with the Claimant for approximately 16 months.
2. Based on article 25 of the Regulations for the Status and Transfer of Players (2001 edition), the Claimant is claiming a solidarity contribution for a period of 16 months. This claim was lodged with FIFA on 5 September 2005.
3. In August 2003, the player Z was transferred from the club A to the Respondent for the sum of USD 1,300,000.
4. According to a letter of the Football Federation of the club Y, the player Z was registered for the Respondent on 15 August 2003.
5. Despite several requests either to pay to the Claimant any sum that may be due as solidarity contribution, or to present reasons for a possible refusal, the Respondent initially made no statement to FIFA. The Claimant, meanwhile, stated that it could not determine how much money it was owed, as it did not know how much the club A had received for the players transfer. Finally, in a letter dated 16 January 2006 and in response to FIFAs request for a copy of the transfer contract with the club A, the Respondent informed FIFA that it had been unable to locate the transfer contract concluded with the club A due to a recent reorganisation of its club in 2005.
6. On 14 February 2006, the Claimant stated that according to press reports, the Respondent had paid the club A the sum of USD 3,000,000 for the players transfer.
7. On 7 March 2006, the club Y stated that it did not have any written documentation that could confirm the Claimants complaint regarding a transfer compensation of USD 3,000,000.
8. In a letter dated 6 April 2006, the Respondent reiterated that it could neither provide a copy of the transfer contract concluded with the club A, nor confirm the claim made by the Claimant on the basis of press reports. At the same time, the club Y gave FIFA permission to contact the club A in order to obtain a copy of the relevant transfer agreement.
9. On 10 April 2006, the Claimant stated that as the transfer of the player in question had taken place in August 2003, it could not provide any copies of the press reports from which it had learnt that the transfer compensation had amounted to USD 3,000,000.
10. On 25 April 2006, FIFA contacted the Football Federation of the club A and the club A requesting a copy of the respective transfer contract.
11. On 3 May 2006, the Football Federation of the club A provided FIFA with a copy of the transfer contract concluded by and between the Respondent and the club A. Point 4 of this contract stipulates that the parties had agreed on a transfer compensation of USD 1,300,000 and that this compensation was "net of all taxes or contributions. At the same time, the Football Federation of the club A informed FIFA of the position of its affiliated club. The club A stated, in particular, that the player Z had been

transferred to Y on 14 August 2003, i.e. over two years ago. The club A therefore expressed its amazement at the fact that the Dispute Resolution Chamber had now been called upon to adjudicate on this matter.

12. On 15 May 2006, FIFA once again invited the Respondent to pay the corresponding solidarity contribution to the Claimant, or to state reasons for refusing to do so.
13. On 22 May 2006, the Respondent stated that it would not be making any payment to the Claimant. In its letter, the Respondent referred to art. 25 par. 5 of the Regulations for the Status and Transfer of Players (2005 edition) and stated that the player had been signed in August 2003. The club Y alleged that the Claimant had waited for more than two years before making its claim and, on the same occasion, stressed that it had not prevented the Claimant from making its claim earlier.

II. CONSIDERATIONS OF THE DISPUTE RESOLUTION CHAMBER

1. First of all, the Chamber analysed whether it was competent to deal with the matter at stake. In this respect, it referred to art. 18 par. 2 and 3 of the Rules Governing the Procedures of the Players' Status Committee and the Dispute Resolution Chamber. The present matter was submitted to FIFA on 5 September 2005. As a consequence, the Chamber concluded that the revised Rules Governing Procedures (edition 2005) on matters pending before the decision-making bodies of FIFA are applicable on the matter at hand. In this context, and by taking into account the circumstances of the present matter, the Chamber deemed it important to clarify that chapter VII of the Regulations for the Status and Transfer of Players (edition 2005) equally governs procedural issues which is the reason why the said chapter also applies to the present matter insofar as procedural questions are concerned.
2. With regard to the competence of the Chamber, art. 3 par. 1 of the above- mentioned Rules states that the Dispute Resolution Chamber shall examine its jurisdiction in the light of articles 22 to 24 of the current version of the Regulations for the Status and Transfer of Players (edition 2005). In accordance with art. 24 par. 1 in combination with art. 22 (d) of the aforementioned Regulations, the Dispute Resolution Chamber shall adjudicate on disputes between two clubs belonging to different Associations related to solidarity mechanism.
3. As a consequence, the Dispute Resolution Chamber is the competent body to decide on the present litigation concerning the distribution of the solidarity contribution claimed by the Claimant in connection with the transfer of the professional player Z during the course of a contract.
4. Subsequently, the members of the Chamber analyzed which edition of the Regulations for the Status and Transfer of Players should be applicable as to the substance of the matter. In this respect, the Chamber referred to art. 26 par. 1 and 2 of the Regulations for the Status and Transfer of Players (edition 2005) in the modified version in accordance with the FIFA circular no. 995 dated 23 September 2005. Furthermore, it acknowledged that the professional had been registered for the Respondent on 15 August 2003. In view of the aforementioned, the Chamber concluded that the former FIFA Regulations for the Status and Transfer of Players (edition 2001, hereinafter: the Regulations) are applicable to the case at hand as to the substance.
5. In continuation, and entering into the substance of the matter, the members of the Chamber started to carefully study the facts outlined above and, in this respect, first of all, referred to the latest argument of the Respondent according to which the latter disputed its obligation to distribute any amount as solidarity contribution to the Claimant by invoking prescription.
6. In this respect, the Chamber referred to art. 11 par. 1 of the Regulations governing the Application of the Regulations which clearly establishes that the players new club shall pay the amount due as solidarity contribution to the training club(s) no later than 30 days after the players registration. Consequently, the Chamber unanimously concluded that the clubs involved in the players training and education are entitled to bring an action in front of FIFA for the non- payment of the solidarity contribution against the players new club in cases in which such payment was not voluntarily made by the latter within the aforementioned time frame, i.e. within 30 days after the players registration for the new club. Prior to the expiry of this 30-day time limit, training clubs do not have any legal interest in starting legal action. In other words, the Chamber stressed that training clubs may start legal proceedings relating to the amount due as solidarity contribution in connection with the training and education of a player not earlier than 31 days after the players registration for the new club.
7. In this context, the Chamber acknowledged that the player in question was registered for the Respondent on 15 August 2003. Taking into account this fact as well as its foregoing conclusion,

the Chamber determined that the Claimant was entitled to claim for the relevant contribution of the solidarity mechanism in front of FIFA as from 16 September 2003 onwards.

8. In continuation, the Chamber referred to art. 25 par. 5 of the Regulations for the Status and Transfer of Players (edition 2005) which, in completion to the provisions foreseen in the revised Rules Governing the Procedures, establishes that no case shall be heard if more than two years have elapsed since the facts leading to the dispute arose. In the present matter, so the Chamber, the event leading to the dispute must be seen in the fact that the Respondent did not pay any amount as solidarity contribution to the Claimant until 15 September 2003, i.e. the aforementioned 30 days limit. In light of all of the above, the Chamber emphasised that the Claimants complaint for its proportion of the contribution of the solidarity mechanism was brought to FIFA on 5 September 2005, thus, 11 days prior to 16 September 2005, and, therefore, within the time limit set out in art. 25 par. 5 of the Regulations for the Status and Transfer of Players (edition 2005) in combination with art. 11 par. 1 of the Regulations governing the Application of the Regulations. Consequently, the Chamber concluded that the Respondents argument for prescription cannot be taken into consideration.
9. Once the issue regarding possible prescription had been clarified, the Dispute Resolution Chamber went on to evaluate whether or not the Claimant was entitled to any proportion of the solidarity mechanism foreseen in art. 25 ff. of the Regulations related to the transfer of the player concerned from the club A to the Respondent.
10. In this regard, the member of the Chamber carefully studied the facts outlined above and emphasised that, as further established in art. 25 of the Regulations, the new club, to which the player is transferred during the course of an employment contract with his previous club, is the club responsible for the distribution of 5% of the respective transfer compensation to the players training clubs.
11. Subsequently, the Chamber referred to art. 10 of the Regulations governing the Application of the Regulations, which provides the figures for the distribution of the solidarity contribution, taking into consideration the time the player was trained and educated by the club concerned.
12. Therefore, and considering that the player in question was born on 27 January 1975 and registered with the Claimant for the first time as from 25 February 1994 to 30 June 1994, later on as from 31 January 1995 to 30 June 1995 and from 1 January 1996 to 4 March 1996 as well as from 16 July 1996 to 4 January 1997, the Chamber concluded that 13% of the 5% solidarity contribution shall be apportioned to the Claimant.
13. Moreover, as it was ascertained that the amount paid by the Respondent to the players former club, A, for the definite transfer of the player Z was USD 1,300,000, the Chamber came to the conclusion that the Claimant is entitled to 13% of the 5% solidarity contribution, or, in other words to the amount of USD 8,450 (13% of 5% of USD 1,300,000).
14. In light of all of the above, the Chamber decided that the Respondent is liable to pay the amount of USD 8,450 as solidarity contribution to the Claimant.

III. DECISION OF THE DISPUTE RESOLUTION CHAMBER

1. The claim of the Claimant, club X, is accepted.
2. The Respondent, club Y, has to pay the amount of USD 8,450 to the Claimant, club X.
3. The amount due to the Claimant has to be paid by the Respondent within 30 days as from the date of notification of the present decision.
4. If the Respondent fails to comply with the above-mentioned deadline, an interest rate of 5% per year will apply and the case will immediately be presented to the FIFA Disciplinary Committee.
5. The Claimant is directed to inform the Respondent immediately of the account number to which the remittance is to be made and to notify the Dispute Resolution Chamber of every payment received.
6. According to art. 61 par. 1 of the FIFA Statutes, this decision may be appealed against before the Court of Arbitration for Sport (CAS). The statement of appeal must be sent to the CAS directly within 21 days of receipt of notification of this decision and shall contain all the elements in accordance with point 2 of the directives issued by the CAS, a copy of which we enclose hereto. Within another 10 days following the expiry of the time limit for filing the statement of appeal, the appellant shall file a brief stating the facts and legal arguments giving rise to the appeal with the CAS (cf. point 4 of the directives).

861174

DECISION OF THE DISPUTE RESOLUTION CHAMBER

passed in Zurich, Switzerland, on 17 August 2006,
in the following composition:
Slim Aloulou (Tunisia), Chairman, Jean-Marie Philips (Belgium), member, Zola Malvern Percival Majavu (South Africa), member Rinaldo Martorelli (Brazil), member Mick McGuire (England), member
On the claim presented by the player A, X, as Claimant/Counter-Respondent against the club B, Y, as Respondent/Counter-Claimant
regarding a contractual dispute between the player and the club.

I. FACTS OF THE CASE

1. On 27 October 2005, the player A from the country X, the Claimant, lodged a claim in front of FIFA against the club, B from the country Y, the Respondent, via the football association of the country of his origin. According to the player, on 17 June 2005 the parties had signed an employment contract for the period from 1 July 2005 to 30 June 2006. In this connection, the Claimant submitted a copy of the relevant employment contract to FIFA.
2. The player explained that he had injured himself during training after the contract had been signed on 1 July 2005. The club had sent him to his country of origin to recover on 13 July 2005. When the player tried to return to the club, neither he nor the football association of the country of his origin was able to establish contact with the respondent club. In this connection, the player sent FIFA a copy of a letter sent to the club, including a receipt of postage dated 20 September 2005.
3. The Respondent replied that the parties had agreed that the contract would be invalid if the player did not pass all of the medical examinations to its satisfaction. In support of its allegation, the club referred to clause 7 of the employment contract, stating: "it is understood that the player has to pass all the medical exams in the satisfaction of the club not later than the 31st of July 2005". (In other words, the player was obliged to take all of the medical examinations to the clubs satisfaction by 31 July 2005).
4. The club explained that, contrary to these requirements, the player had not undergone medical examinations after signing the contract but had gone to the first training session. Before training had begun, the player had run around the pitch and within five minutes had fallen over, claiming he had a pain in his knee. A visit to the doctor then confirmed that he had serious knee problems. The player had allegedly deceived the club by signing a statement in the player's certificate that he had no health problems before he signed the contract. He had done this although he had suffered from serious knee problems and had had a meniscus operation six months before signing the contract. The knee problems therefore did not derive from an injury in the first training session but originated from before he went to the respondent club. The club, the Respondent/the Counter-Claimant (hereinafter; the Respondent), is consequently demanding a refund of EUR 3,000 from the player, the Claimant/ Counter-Respondent (hereinafter; the Claimant), for the advance salary paid to him and that the player should also be sanctioned. In support of its statements, the Respondent sent FIFA copies of the medical report, the players certificate, the players receipt of the advance salary payment and a letter from the players agent regarding salary claims.
5. In reply, the Claimant stated that he had first warmed up, then played four against four and had finally played normal football before suffering a cruciate ligament injury. The knee specialist in the country of his origin had told him that he would be able to play again 60 days after the operation, which had cost him EUR 2,000. However, he had been unable to reach anyone at the club. As for previous injuries, the Claimant confirmed that he had had a meniscus operation in December 2004. The operation had been a success and he was able to play football again ten days later. This injury had nothing to do with the cruciate ligament injury suffered with the respondent club.
6. On 26 February 2006, the Respondent rejected the players statements entirely, commenting that after reading the Claimants reply, it would be necessary to ask its witnesses to make official statements in the district court. In the light of these statements, the Respondent had decided to take the case to the civil district court in Y. It had already begun proceedings. It claimed that FIFA was not competent for the case, as in clause 16 of the employment contract the parties had agreed to take any contractual disputes to the arbitration commission of the Y football association. The case in question was therefore to be decided by the Y football association and the Y civil court. Clause 16 of the contract stated: "Disputes in regard to this contract will be settled before arbitration commission of the Y football association".

7. In response to FIFAs request that it provide official confirmation from the Y district court that proceedings had been instituted, the Respondent explained the words “proceedings already begun” meant that statements from witnesses had been sought. In this connection, the club submitted a statement from a witness, confirmed by the acting registrar of the registry office of the district court that the witness had signed the statement concerned in his presence.
8. In response to FIFAs insistence that the above-mentioned confirmation regarding the institution of proceedings be submitted to it, the Respondent produced seven further witness statements of a similar nature and with similar contents. According to the witness statements, the Claimant had neither played nor trained with the respondent club.
9. The Claimant expressed his surprise at the news that proceedings had been instituted in the civil court. If he were a citizen of Y, it might be appropriate to take the case to a court in Y. As he was not, FIFA was the only body competent in his case, which was why he had contacted FIFA. As counterevidence to the abovementioned witness statements, the player sent FIFA two witness statements, claiming that the player had injured himself at the end of a training session. The Claimant also estimated his claims against the club as amounting to seven months' salary, i.e. he was claiming 7 x EUR 2,500 = EUR 17,500 from the respondent club in compensation.
10. The Respondent categorically rejects the players claims and adheres to the statements made so far.
11. In reply to a request from FIFA, the Claimant stated that he had not played for any other club since he had submitted his claim as he had a valid contract with the Respondent until May (recte: 30 June) 2006.

II. CONSIDERATIONS OF THE DISPUTE RESOLUTION CHAMBER

1. First of all, the Chamber referred to the argument of the Respondent according to which the latter disputed the competence of the Dispute Resolution Chamber (DRC) since clause 16 of the employment contract stipulates that “Disputes in regard to this contract will be settled before arbitration commission of the Y football association”.
2. In this respect, the members of the DRC referred to the well established jurisprudence of the Dispute Resolution Chamber according to which, in general, in employment-related disputes between a club and a player that have an international dimension, i.e. the parties do not belong to the same country, both parties were entitled to refer the dispute to FIFAs bodies, unless, if the parties have expressed a preference in a written agreement, or it is provided for by collective bargain agreement, an independent arbitration tribunal respecting the principle of equal representation of players and clubs with an independent chairman has been established at national level.
3. The DRC acknowledged that the Respondent was unable to prove that an independent arbitration tribunal in compliance with the requirements of the FIFAs regulations has been established in Y. In addition, the Chamber stated that the Respondent was unable to present an official confirmation proving that proceedings in front of the civil district court in Y had been instituted, either. As a consequence, the DRC established that the Respondent's objection to the competence of FIFA to deal with the matter has to be rejected and that the matter can be considered as to the substance.
4. In this respect, the Chamber referred to art. 18 par. 2 and 3 of the Rules Governing the Procedures of the Players' Status Committee and the Dispute Resolution Chamber. The present matter was submitted to FIFA on 27 October 2005, as a consequence the Chamber concluded that the revised Rules Governing Procedures (edition 2005) on matters pending before the decision making bodies of FIFA are applicable to the matter at hand.
5. With regard to the competence of the Chamber, art. 3 par. 1 of the abovementioned Rules states that the Dispute Resolution Chamber shall examine its jurisdiction in the light of articles 22 to 24 of the current version of the Regulations for the Status and Transfer of Players (edition 2005). In accordance with art. 24 par. 1 in combination with art. 22 (b) of the aforementioned Regulations, the Dispute Resolution Chamber shall adjudicate on employmentrelated disputes between a club and a player that have an international dimension.
6. As a consequence, the Dispute Resolution Chamber is the competent body to decide on the present litigation involving a player from the country X and a club from the country Y regarding a dispute in connection with an employment contract.

7. Subsequently, the members of the Chamber analyzed which edition of the Regulations for the Status and Transfer of Players should be applicable as to the substance of the matter. In this respect, the Chamber referred, on the one hand, to art. 26 par. 1 and 2 of the Regulations for the Status and Transfer of Players (edition 2005) and, on the other hand, to the fact that the relevant contract at the basis of the present dispute was signed on 17 June 2005 and the claim was lodged at FIFA on 27 October 2005. In view of the aforementioned, the Chamber concluded that the current FIFA Regulations for the Status and Transfer of Players (edition 2005, hereafter: the Regulations) are applicable to the case at hand as to the substance.
8. In continuation, the members of the Chamber acknowledged the abovementioned facts as well as all the further documentation contained in the file.
9. In this respect, the members took due note that the Claimant, on the one hand, asserts that he had injured himself during training after the contract had been signed, that the club did not let him join the club after his recovery and that the meniscus operation he had in December 2004 had nothing to do with the cruciate ligament injury he suffered with the respondent club on 1 July 2005. As a consequence, the Claimant ask compensation in the amount of EUR 17,500 from the Respondent.
10. At this point, the Chamber took note of the financial aspects provided for in the relevant employment-contract.
11. On the other hand, the members acknowledged that the respondent club is, in particular, convinced that the Claimant acted contrary to clause 7 "in fine" of the employment contract by not undergoing medical examinations after the signing of the contract, but having trained and injured himself. In addition, the Chamber acknowledged that according to the Respondent the positive medical examination established in the aforementioned clause 7 "in fine" of the employment contract is a condition for the validity of the said contract. Furthermore, the Chamber took due note that the Respondent asserts that the Claimant allegedly deceived it by signing a statement in the player's certificatethat he had no health problems before he signed the contract although he had allegedly suffered from serious knee problems before he came to the respondent club. Therefore, the Respondent asks the Claimant for reimbursing the sign-on fee in the amount of EUR 3,000.
12. Clause 7 "in fine" of the employment contract concluded between the parties involved on 17 June 2006 reads as follows:
"It is understood that the player has to pass all the medical exams in the satisfaction of the club not later than the 31st of July 2005".
13. In consideration of these positions, the members started their deliberations by verifying whether the above-mentioned clause 7 "in fine" of the employment contract, which establishes a contractual obligation of the player, respectively a condition for the validity of the present employment contract, is legally binding or not.
14. In this connection, the Chamber having established a valid employment contract has been entered into by and between the Claimant and the Respondent, art. 18 par. 4 of the Regulations is applicable to the case at hand.
15. This article clearly states that the validity of a contract between a professional and a club may not be made subject to a positive medical examination. Consequently, medical examinations shall be made by the players prospective new club prior to concluding the contract. In the case at hand, however, the medical examination was agreed being conducted prior to 31st of July 2005, i.e. after the parties signed the relevant employment contract.
16. In light of the above, the Chamber concluded that the above-mentioned clause 7 "in fine" of the employment contract violates the above-mentioned art. 18 par. 4 of the Regulations and is therefore not legally binding, respectively null and void.
17. As regards the argument of the Respondent, according to which the Claimant allegedly deceived the respondent club by signing a statement in the players certificate that he had no health problems before he signed the contract although he had allegedly suffered from serious knee problems already before he came to the country Y, the Chamber must refer the Respondent to the competent penal or criminal judicial bodies, since the basis of this claim is of penal nature (deceit).
18. As a consequence to all of the above, the Chamber deemed that the player did not breached the present employment contract by not undergoing medical examinations after the signing of the contract, but having trained and injured himself instead. Therefore, the Chamber rejected the Respondents counter-claim.

19. Subsequently, the Chamber proceeded to deliberate whether an unjustified breach of the employment contract had been committed by the Respondent and to verify and decide if sanctions for such possible breach of contract have to be applied.
20. In this respect, the Chamber recalled that the parties involved concluded a valid employment contract on 17 June 2005 valid until 30 June 2006. Furthermore, the DRC took note that it is uncontested by all parties that the player tried to join the respondent club after his recovery in his country of origin. In particular, the Respondent did not ask for the players return, but demanded the refund of its payment made to the Claimant and declared the present employment contract as invalid.
21. Taking into consideration the above, the members of the Chamber unanimously agreed that the "mutatis mutandis" unilateral cancellation of the employment contract by the Respondent constitutes a breach of contract without just cause.
22. On account of the above-mentioned conclusion, the DRC had to address the issue of possible financial sanctions against the Respondent for unjustified breach of contract, in accordance with art. 17 of the Regulations.
23. In this context, the DRC first of all pointed out that the employment contract between the Claimant and the Respondent was signed on 17 June 2005. Moreover, the DRC stated that the date to be considered as the date of the breach of the employment contract by the Respondent is at the end of September 2006, the date when the Claimant undisputedly failed to reintegrate the player in its team after having received the Claimants letter.
24. As to the amount of compensation for the unjustified breach of contract, and considering the objective criteria listed in art. 17 par. 1 of the Regulations the Chamber decided that the claimed compensation of EUR 17,500 by the Claimant is adequate in view of the short period of time remaining after the breach of contract (end of September 2005) until the end of the employment contract concluded between the Claimant and the Respondent.
25. As a consequence to the above, the Chamber fully accepted the players claim.
26. In light of the above, the Dispute Resolution Chamber decided that the employment relation between the Claimant and the Respondent has been terminated and that the Respondent has to pay to the Claimant the amount of EUR 17,500 as compensation for breach of contract.

III. DECISION OF THE DISPUTE RESOLUTION CHAMBER

1. The claim submitted by the Claimant/Counter-Respondent is accepted.
2. The Respondent/Counter-Claimant has to pay the amount of EUR 17,500 to the Claimant/Counter-Respondent.
3. The amount due to the Claimant/Counter-Respondent has to be paid by the Respondent/Counter-Claimant within 30 days as from the date of notification of this decision.
4. In the event that the debt of the Respondent is not paid within the stated deadline, an interest rate of 5% per year will apply as of expiry of the aforementioned deadline.
5. If the sum of EUR 17,500 is not paid within the aforementioned deadline, the present matter shall be submitted to the FIFA Disciplinary Committee, so that the necessary disciplinary sanctions may be imposed.
6. The Claimant is directed to inform the Respondent immediately of the account number to which the remittance is to be made and to notify the Dispute Resolution Chamber of every payment received.
7. The counter-claim submitted by the Respondent/Counter-Claimant is rejected.
8. According to art. 61 par. 1 of the FIFA Statutes, this decision may be appealed against before the Court of Arbitration for Sport (CAS). The statement of appeal must be sent to the CAS directly within 21 days of receipt of notification of this decision and shall contain all the elements in accordance with point 2 of the directives issued by the CAS, a copy of which we enclose hereto. Within another 10 days following the expiry of the time limit for filing the statement of appeal, the appellant shall file a brief stating the facts and legal arguments giving rise to the appeal with the CAS (cf. point 4 of the directives).

861307
DECISION OF THE DISPUTE RESOLUTION CHAMBER
passed in Zurich, Switzerland, on 17 August 2006,
in the following composition:
Slim Aloulou (Tunisia), Chairman
Jean-Marie Philips (Belgium), member
Zola Malvern Percival Majavu (South Africa), member
Rinaldo Martorelli (Brazil), member
Mick McGuire (England), member
on the claim presented by the player A, X, as Claimant/Counter-Respondent with the club B, Y, as Co-Counter-Respondent against the club C, Z, as Respondent/Counter-Claimant
regarding a contractual dispute between the club and the player and his new club.

I. FACTS OF THE CASE

1. In June 2004, the player A from the country X, the Claimant, and the club B from the country Z, the Respondent, signed an employment contract that was due to run until 1 July 2006.
2. On 1 August 2005, the above-mentioned parties signed a further document "Appendix" establishing the duration of the contract to be "one year and four months, namely until 1 July 2006".
3. On 20 January 2006, the Claimant, lodged a complaint against the club C. He requests FIFA to deem the contract terminated and declare him a free agent so that he can sign a contract with a new club. The Claimant cites the following grounds in support of his complaint:
    3.1. The Respondent intimidated him and threatened that he would not be allowed to play for the first team until he signed a new contract with them. Until 21 October 2005 he had played the full ninety minutes of every first team match, but after that date he had not been selected for a single match. Since then, the relationship between the Player and the club had deteriorated.
    3.2. At the beginning of January 2006 he signed a new employment contract with the club B from the country Y that was due to come into force on 1 July 2006. Since then, the Respondent has barred him from training with the first team and he has had to train with the third team in the mornings and on his own in the afternoons, as the third team only train once a day. He was barred from taking part in the respondent clubs training camp in mid-January 2006.
    3.3. The Claimant concludes that the Respondents conduct clearly shows that it was no longer interested in his services as a player.
4. In a supplementary submission dated 1 February 2006, the Claimant asserts that the Respondent was continuing to act in breach of points II.2 and II.3 of the contract (Provision of adequate training facilities and medical insurance) insofar as:
    4.1. It obliged him to train on unsafe football pitches;
    4.2. It obliged him to train with a third-string team with which the Respondent had no connection and to which he had no contractual obligations;
    4.3. Since 18 January 2006 it has only been obligatory for one coach to be present at training and at matches, i.e. no medical staff or other coaches. This was not the case prior to 18 January 2006;
    4.4. It obliged him on several occasions to warm up for training alone, i.e. without a coach;
    4.5. It obliged him to train in sub-zero temperatures.
5. The Claimant further submits that pursuant to point II.5 of the employment contract, he had the right to unilaterally terminate the contract with fifteen days' notice provided that he stated his reasons for doing so. He exercised this option on 20 January 2006, reserving the right to terminate the contract as of 4 February 2006 if the club did not release him from his contractual obligations.
6. Finally, the Claimant submitted extracts from his diary and photos of the frozen, snow-covered football pitch in support of his allegations.
7. In its response, the Respondent club denies all of the Claimants allegations. The Respondent is of the view that the Claimant was unable to put forward any valid reasons to justify his prematurely termination of the employment contract. The Respondent argues as follows:
    7.1. It dropped the Claimant from the first team because its management had decided to reduce its squad from 31 players to 20. The Claimant was one of those affected by this measure.
    7.2. The Claimant did not take part in the training camp because during negotiations with the club B, the possibility of the Player moving to said club as early as January 2006 had been discussed.

7.3. The Claimants training conditions were very good. He had trained exclusively at the clubs stadium on one of best football pitches in the country under the supervision of a category 1 trainer and UEFA licence holder. The Respondent submitted photos as proof of the good quality of their playing surface.

7.4. Contrary to the Claimants claims, he never trained with the third team. To support this assertion, the Respondent submitted to FIFA a statement from the president of the third team. At that time, February 2006, the Claimant was taking part in the club's second winter training camp, as the negotiations with the club B had broken down.

7.5. It is not true that the Claimant had not been allowed to play since 15 October 2005 (Note: the Respondents Football Association acknowledges that the match on 15 October 2005 was the last of the nine that the Player played for C). In fact, the Claimant refused to take part in subsequent matches because he did not want to be a substitute, he claimed to have stomach ache or he was out of the country. The Respondent has submitted statements from its sporting director and president to FIFA in support of the above claim.

7.6. The Claimant breached the terms of the contract by giving interviews that damaged the Respondents reputation.

8. The Respondent further argues that it was informed by the club B that the Claimant had signed a contract with said club that was due to come into force on 1 July 2006. Upon receiving this news, the Respondent informed the club B that its contract with the Claimant was not due to expire until 1 December 2006. As proof of this, the Respondent submitted to FIFA a copy of its letter to the club B of 3 February 2006. The Respondent further claims that Claimants Football Association website already indicates that he is registered with the club B.

9. On these grounds the Respondent requests FIFA to impose sanctions on the Player and the club B.

10. Subsequently, the Football Association of the country Z forwarded to FIFA a copy of a decision taken by its own Players' Status Committee on 14 February 2006. Said decision had found that the contractual relationship between the parties was not due to expire until 1 December 2006 (Note: the complainant club in that case, C, was represented in person by the president of its board of directors and a lawyer, whereas the respondent party, A (who was not present), was represented by the president of the Professional Footballers' Association of country Z, who is also a member of the aforementioned committee but withheld his vote).

11. 11.1. The Claimant disputes the legal effect of the decision taken by the Football Association of the country Zs Players' Status Committee, firstly because FIFA is the proper authority to decide on such issues and secondly because the composition of the said Committee did not respect the principle of equal representation and the Claimant could not exert any influence on the composition of the decision-making body.

11.2. In connection with the above-mentioned decision, the Claimant asserts that he signed a contract written in the language of country Z with the Respondent on around 30 June 2004. He subsequently received only an unsigned and undated English translation of said contract. On or about 1 August 2005 the Respondent requested him to sign a further document (the above-mentioned Appendix) following the clubs restructuring and change of name. However, at no time did he discuss or agree to a contract extension with the Respondent. The abovementioned document also indicates that the expiry date of the contract is 1 July 2006, yet the only relevant contract is the initial employment contract with an expiry date of 1 July 2006. The aforementioned Appendix is irrelevant because it contains no reference to the employment contract. Furthermore, it can be deduced from the clubs conduct that it understood the expiry date of the contract to be 1 July 2006, as the club proposed a contract extension from 1 July 2006 to 1 July 2007 to the Players agent. The Claimant has submitted to FIFA an email dated 17 January 2006 from the president of C to his agent.

12. 12.1. With regard to the decision taken by the Players' Status Committee of the Football Association of the country Z, the club C submits that the Player was adequately represented. The seven-day term for appealing against the decision was not used by either party, as a result of which the decision became binding and legally valid.

12.2. The Respondent informed FIFA that the members of the Players' Status Committee of the Football Association of the country Z are all independent persons, i.e. lawyers.

12.3. The Respondent argues that it is clear from the Appendix that the duration of the contract is one year and four months from 1 August 2005; that its expiry date is therefore 1 December

2006; and that the legal principle whereby the text takes precedence over numerals applies to this case.

13. In response to the position adopted by the Respondent, the Claimant argues that the word "July" in the contract is of more significance than the numeral 1.
14. Upon request the Claimant informed FIFA that the parties to the hearing before the Players' Status Committee of the Football Association of the country Z on 14 February 2006 received only a verbal summons. On 6 February 2006 the Claimant empowered president of the Professional Footballers' Association of country Z (see above) to represent him at said hearing. The Claimant has provided a copy of the president of the Professional Footballers' Association of country Zs submissions to the Players' Status Committee of 7 February 2006, in which he requests said body to determine the contracts expiry date to be 1 July 2006.
15. The Claimant has informed FIFA that following the above-mentioned decision by the Players' Status Committee, the Respondent filed a request with the Disciplinary Committee of the Football Association of the country Z to suspend the Claimant from 1 March to 1 September 2006. (Note: Both the Claimant and a representative of the respondent club took part in the hearing). The Disciplinary Committee rejected the Respondents request in a decision dated 8 March 2006. The Claimant further informed FIFA that the above-mentioned decision was appealed by the respondent club. The appeal was dismissed by the Appeals Committee of the Football Association of the country Z in a decision dated 10 April 2006. (Note: Both the Claimant and a representative of the respondent club took part in the hearing). The Claimant has submitted a copy of the relevant decisions to FIFA.
16. B informed FIFA on 2 March 2006 that it had declared its interest in the Player to the Respondent on 8 December 2005. The negotiations regarding the possible transfer of the Claimant in January 2006 were ultimately unsuccessful due to the Respondents high demands. The Claimant therefore entered into a contract with the club B that was due to come into force on 1 July 2006, i.e. after the expiry date of his contract with the respondent club.
17. The Claimant submits that the respondent club further breached the terms of the contract by:
    17.1. attempting to incite him to breach his contract with the club B and transfer him to P while fully aware that he had already signed a contract with the club B.
    17.2. threatening to suspend him without paying him any remuneration for nine months if he did not agree to be transferred to the above-mentioned club.
    17.3. threatening not to extend his work permit, which was due to expire on 23 March 2006, which could potentially lead to his arrest.
18. The Claimant further argues that he was entitled to sign a new contract with the club B because at the time of signing said contract he was in the last six months of his agreement with the Respondent. He therefore strongly rejects the Respondents request to impose any sanctions against him.
19. The Claimant rejects all the respondent club's claims, in particular the assertion that he refused to be selected as a substitute or to play. He stresses that he always made himself available to the club and he continues to do so.
20. The Respondent is adamant that it has never pressured, intimidated or threatened the Player.
21. The Respondent likewise insists that it informed the club B on 3 February that the Claimants contract was not due to expire until 1 December 2006 and that the club B ignored its comments by proceeding to sign a contract with the Claimant that was due to come into force on 1 July 2006. With regard to the email from the club president which the Claimant submitted to FIFA, the Respondent asserts that the club president did not purchase shares of the club until the summer of 2005 and therefore had no knowledge of the terms of the contract that the erstwhile president had agreed with the Claimant.
22. According to the Respondent, the above shows that the Claimant breached his contract at the instigation of the club B and damaged the interests of the Respondent. On this basis the respondent club, the Counter-Claimant (hereafter: the Respondent) has filed a counterclaim seeking EUR 1,500,000 in costs and damages from the Claimant/Counter-Respondent (hereafter: the Claimant) and the club B, Co-Counter-Respondent, and also requests the application of sanctions against said parties.
23. In response to the counterclaim, which the Claimant strongly rejects, he submits that the Respondent has not suffered any damage because he has always made himself available for duty. Finally, in the light of the particular circumstances of this case, the Claimant requests that no sporting sanctions be taken against him in the event that the Dispute Resolution Chamber were to find in favour of the respondent club. The Claimant further stands by his previous submissions.

24. In response to the counterclaim, the club B, the Co-Counter-Respondent, explained that the licensed players' agent provided them with a copy of the original contract, according to which the expiry date of the contract is 1 July 2006. The duration of the contract was confirmed to the players' agent by the respondent club in its fax of 18 January 2006. The Respondents statement that "by this summer you will have a more valuable player, not to mention that you can use him starting with January 2006" clearly gives the impression that the expiry date of the contract is 1 July 2006. B finds it surprising that C should wait almost an entire month from the date on which B informed it of its negotiations with the Claimant before notifying B that its contract with the Claimant was valid until December 2006. It is Bs opinion that when interpreting a contract, both the views of all the parties and custom should be taken into account. In the region in question, it is customary for contracts with footballers to be valid for at least one full season. In this sense, the Respondents allegation that the expiry date of the contact is 1 December 2006 is not logical.
25. In response to the counterclaim, the Respondent stands by its previous submissions.
26. In his response to the counterclaim, the Claimant argues that he only took part in the hearings in the country Z to contest the Respondents allegation that he had breached his contract through absence. Finally, the Claimant claims that the Respondent owes him his salary for the months of April, May and June 2006 (totalling USD 9,000) and a bonus payment of USD 1,735.
The above default on payment constitutes a breach of contract.
27. With regard to the Claimants allegation, according to which salaries and bonus are outstanding, the Respondent replied that the salaries for the months April and May 2006 were to be paid in cash to the Claimant on 29 June 2006 on the occasion of a meeting. Furthermore, the Respondent stated that the payment of the salary for June is to be made between 10 and 15 July 2006. Finally, the Respondent maintains that the Claimant did not come to the country Z after having been released for his national team on 21 May 2006. Moreover, the Respondent adds that the Claimant was not present at the meeting held on 29 June 2006, after summer holidays.
28. In reply to the above-mentioned, the Claimant asserts that the Respondent was not entitled to pay his April salary which was due on 10 May 2006 on 29 June 2006. The Claimant adds that the Respondent had the opportunity to pay him before his departure on 18 May 2006. Regarding the May and June salaries the Claimant refers to his previous statement. The Claimant carried on that the Respondent had his bank account details to directly deposit the money as it has regularly done for the previous two years. With regard to the Claimants returning to the respondent club, the Claimant asserts that the Respondent finished its season at the match on 7 June 2006, i.e. when the players were sent on summer holidays. The Claimant on his part, finished his national team commitments on 8 June 2006. Finally, the Claimant outlines that the Respondent has not made any effort to contact him or his Players' Agent to arrange the return flights to the Respondent as it has done during the last two years.
29. In a further submission, the Claimant informed FIFA that the Respondent still did not pay the salaries of April, May and June 2006, as well as the bonuses.
30. On 12 August 2006, the Respondent informed FIFA that it paid the players salaries until 30 June 2006. In this respect, the Respondent presented FIFA a bank transaction document, according to which it paid the amount of H USD 9,340 to the Claimant. Furthermore, the Respondent reported to FIFA that since the end of May, the player left the country Z an he did not come back until todays date. Finally, the Respondent alleges that it appears that the Claimant trained with the club B since July 2006.

II. CONSIDERATIONS OF THE DISPUTE RESOLUTION CHAMBER

1. First of all, the Chamber analysed whether it was competent to deal with the matter at stake. In this respect, it referred to art. 18 par. 2 and 3 of the Rules Governing the Procedures of the Players' Status Committee and the Dispute Resolution Chamber. The present matter was submitted to FIFA on 20 January 2006, as a consequence the Chamber concluded that the revised Rules Governing Procedures (edition 2005) on matters pending before the decision making bodies of FIFA are applicable to the matter at hand.
2. With regard to the competence of the Chamber, art. 3 par. 1 of the abovementioned Rules states that the Dispute Resolution Chamber shall examine its jurisdiction in the light of articles 22 to 24 of the current version of the Regulations for the Status and Transfer of Players (edition 2005). In accordance with art. 24 par. 1 in combination with art. 22 (b) of the aforementioned Regulations, the

Dispute Resolution Chamber shall adjudicate on employmentrelated disputes between a club and a player that have an international dimension.

3. As a consequence, the Dispute Resolution Chamber is the competent body to decide on the present litigation involving an player from X and a club from Z regarding a dispute in connection with an employment contract.
4. Subsequently, the members of the Chamber analyzed which edition of the Regulations for the Status and Transfer of Players should be applicable as to the substance of the matter. In this respect, the Chamber referred, on the one hand, to art. 26 par. 1 and 2 of the Regulations for the Status and Transfer of Players (edition 2005) and, on the other hand, to the fact that the relevant contract at the basis of the present dispute was signed in June 2004 and the claim was lodged at FIFA on 20 January 2006. In view of the aforementioned, the Chamber concluded that the current FIFA Regulations for the Status and Transfer of Players (edition 2005, hereafter: the Regulations) are applicable to the case at hand as to the substance.
5. In continuation, the members of the Chamber acknowledged the above mentioned facts as well as all the further documentation contained in the file.
6. To that regard, the members acknowledged that the player and the club C signed an employment contract in June 2004 that was due to run until 1 July 2006. Furthermore, the Chamber noticed that, the parties signed a further document "Appendix" establishing the duration of the contract to be "one year and four months, namely until 1 July 2006" on 1 August 2005. Finally, the Chamber took note of the fact that Players' Status Committee of the Football Association of the country Z passed a decision on 14 February 2006, according to which the contractual relationship between the parties was not due to expire until 1 December 2006.
7. In this respect, the members took due note that the Claimant demands for the above-mentioned decision regarding the contractual duration to be declared not binding, due to the lack of parity in the composition of the Players' Status Committee of the Football Association of the country Z and his impossibility to decide on the composition of the said body. As a consequence, and due to the fact that the player is of the firm opinion that the only valid contract is the initial employment contract with an expiry date of 1 July 2006, the player requests that it shall be established that he is not bound to the club C any longer and was free to sign a new employment contract with the club B. Finally, the Chamber acknowledged the fact that the player asserts that the club committed several breaches of contract and, in particular, demands from the Respondent the total amount of USD 10735 for alleged outstanding salaries (for the months April, May and June 2006) and bonuses.
8. On the other hand, the members acknowledged that the respondent club is, in particular, convinced that the above-mentioned decision taken by the Players' Status Committee of the Football Association of the country Z is binding, since the player was duly represented during this procedure, since the members of the said Committee are independent and since the player did not appeal against the relevant decision. Hence the club is of the opinion that the player is still bound by the employment contract it signed with him in June 2004 until 1 December 2006. The Chamber took note that, as a consequence to the aforementioned, the club is convinced that the player committed a breach of contract by signing a new employment contract with the club B, and hence is asking for compensation and the imposition of sanctions. Finally, the members of the Chamber acknowledged that the Respondent is of the firm opinion that it always fulfilled its contractual obligations.
9. In consideration of these positions, the members started their deliberations by verifying whether the relevant decision of the Players' Status Committee of the Football Association of the country Z, which declares the contractual relationship between the Claimant and the Respondent valid until 1 December 2006, is binding or not.
10. In this respect, the Chamber took note, in particular, that on 6 February 2006 the Claimant empowered the president of the Professional Footballers' Association of country Z to represent him at the hearing of the Players' Status Committee of the Football Association of the country Z of 7 February 2006. Furthermore, the members of the Dispute Resolution Chamber took note that the president of the Professional Footballers' Association of country Z duly represented the Claimant at the aforementioned hearing by submitting a statement, by means of which he requested the aforementioned deciding body to determine the contracts expiry date to be 1 July 2006.
11. On account of the foregoing, the Chamber decided unanimously that by presenting statements regarding the contractual duration, the Claimant manifested his position as to the substance of the present dispute with regard to the contractual duration and thus submitted himself to the jurisdiction

of the Players' Status Committee of the Football Association of the country Z, i.e. accepted the competence of the said decision-making body tacitly.

12. In light of the above, the Chamber concluded that the decision of the Players' Status Committee of the Football Association of the country Z is binding. In addition, the members stated that the fact that the Claimant did not appeal the aforementioned decision confirms this conclusion. Finally, the members of the Dispute Resolution Chamber outlined that in accordance with the general principle of res iudicata the DRC is not in a position to deal again with the substance of the present matter with regard to the duration of the employment contract and has to reject the Claimants allegations to that regard.
13. As a consequence to the above, the Chamber deemed that in accordance with the above-mentioned decision of the Players' Status Committee of the Football Association of the country Z of 14 February 2006, the Claimant is still contractually bound to the Respondent until 1 December 2006.
14. Subsequently, the Chamber proceeded to deliberate whether an unjustified breach of the employment contract between the club C and A had been committed and which party was responsible for such breach of contract and to verify and decide if sanctions for breach of contract have to be applied.
15. In this respect, the Chamber firstly took note that it is uncontested by all parties that the player and the club B (Co-Counter-Respondent) had signed an employment contract in January 2006 valid as of the season of 2006/07, i.e. 1 July 2006.
16. In continuation, the Chamber turned its attention to the responsibility of the Claimant regarding a possible breach of contract. To that regard, the members of the Chamber recalled that the above-mentioned decision of the Players' Status Committee of the of the Football Association of the country Z is binding. Furthermore, the Chamber referred to art. 5 par. 2 of the Regulations, according to which a player may only be registered for one club at a time. Taking into account the aforementioned, the Chamber deemed that the Claimant committed an unjustified breach of the employment contract he concluded with the Respondent.
17. On account of the above-mentioned conclusion, the DRC had to address the issue of possible financial or sporting sanctions against the Claimant for unjustified breach of contract, in accordance with art. 17 of the Regulations.
18. In this context, the DRC first of all pointed out that the employment contract between the Claimant and the Respondent was signed in June 2004. Moreover, the DRC stated that the date to be considered as the date of the breach of the employment contract by the player is at the end of June 2006, the date when the Claimant failed to return to the country Z after his permitted release for national duties.
19. Moreover, and with regard to the players allegations regarding the alleged outstanding salaries and bonuses, the Chamber took duly note that the Respondent provided the relevant documentary evidence, i.e. a bank transaction document dated 19 July 2006, according to which the Respondent paid the outstanding payments to the Claimant, even late. As a consequence to the aforementioned, the Chamber concluded that the Respondent fulfilled its contractual obligations towards the player and therefore decided to reject the players claim to that regard.
20. Subsequently, the Chamber considered all the other allegations of the Claimant regarding several breaches of contract allegedly committed by the Respondent as unfounded and therefore decided to reject the relevant complaints of the Claimant to that regard.
21. As to the amount of compensation for the unjustified breach of contract, and considering the objective criteria listed in art. 17 par. 1 of the Regulations the Chamber decided that a compensation of EUR 45,000 is adequate in view of the short period of time remaining after the breach of contract (end of June 2006) until the end of the employment contract concluded between the Claimant and the Respondent, i.e. 1 December 2006.
22. In light of the above, the Dispute Resolution Chamber decided that the employment relation between the Claimant and the Respondent has been terminated with immediate effect and that the Claimant has to pay to the Respondent the amount of EUR 45,000 as compensation for breach of contract.
23. The DRC then turned to the question of possible sporting sanctions to be imposed on the Claimant in accordance with art. 17 par. 3 of the Regulations. In this context, the Chamber considered that, per analogiam to the above-stated under point II.11., also the decision regarding the suspension of the player in question taken by the Disciplinary Committee of the Football Association of the country Z on 8 March 2006, which was confirmed by the Appeal Committee of the Football Association of the country Z on 10 April 2006, is binding. This is, since the involved parties by taking part in the respective hearings and submitting statements accepted the competence of the aforementioned

deciding bodies. The DRC therefore decided unanimously that in accordance with the general principle of res iudicata it is not in a position to deal again with the substance of the present matter, and therefore has to reject the Respondents demand for sporting sanctions.

24. Finally, and with regard to the due diligence of a club to verify that it does not take a player under contract who has still a valid contract with another club, the Chamber deemed that the club B was bona fide by concluding an employment contract with the Claimant. This is, due to the fact that the club B had been provided with a copy of the players current employment contract, which establishes the termination date 1 July 2006, and a copy of the appendix, which also establishes the termination date 1 July 2006 (even though not in a very clear way, since the contractual duration is also fixed by the wording (valid for 1-year and 4 months, since the 01.08.2005) as well as with a copy of the e-mail dated 17 January 2006 from the respondent clubs president directed to the players' agent, (cf. above), by means of which the said president offered to conclude a new 2years employment contract starting as of July 2006. Moreover, the Chamber took into account that B concluded the contract with the player prior to the letter of the club C sent in February 2006 as well as before the decision-making bodies in country Z passed their decisions regarding the duration of the contract.
25. On account of the above, the DRC decided unanimously that the Co-CounterRespondent was allowed to believe that the player was free of any contractual binding, thus free to sign a new contract valid as of 1 July 2006 and therefore, concluded that the club B did not induced the player to breach the contract and therefore neither financial nor sporting sanctions shall be imposed on the CoCounter-Respondent. However, in accordance with art. 17 par. 2 of the Regulations B is jointly liable for the compensation payable by the player to the respondent club.

III. DECISION OF THE DISPUTE RESOLUTION CHAMBER

1. The claim submitted by the Claimant/Counter-Respondent is rejected.
2. The counter-claim submitted by the Respondent/Counter-Claimant is partially accepted.
3. The Claimant/Counter-Respondent is ordered to pay EUR 45,000 to the club C within 30 days as of notification of the present decision.
4. The Co-Counter-Respondent is jointly and severally liable for the payment of the above-mentioned amount.
5. If the aforementioned amount is not paid within the stated deadline, an interest rate of 5% per year shall apply, as from expiry of the stated deadline.
6. In the event that the Claimant/Counter-Respondent does not comply with the present decision, the matter shall be submitted to FIFAs Disciplinary Committee, so that the necessary disciplinary sanctions may be imposed.
7. Any further claims of the club C are rejected.
8. The Respondent/Counter-Claimant is directed to inform the Claimant/Respondent directly and immediately of the account number to which the remittance is to be made, and to notify the Dispute Resolution Chamber about the receipt of the payment.
9. According to art. 60 par. 1 of the FIFA Statutes, this decision may be appealed against before the Court of Arbitration for Sport (CAS). The statement of appeal must be sent to the CAS directly within 21 days of receipt of notification of this decision and shall contain all the elements in accordance with point 2 of the directives issued by the CAS, a copy of which we enclose hereto. Within another 10 days following the expiry of the time limit for filing the statement of appeal, the appellant shall file a brief stating the facts and legal arguments giving rise to the appeal with the CAS (cf. point 4 of the directives).

28 SEPTEMBER 2006

96157
DECISION OF THE DISPUTE RESOLUTION CHAMBER
passed in Zurich, Switzerland, on 28 September 2006,
in the following composition:
Slim Aloulou (Tunisia), Chairman
Philippe Diallo (France), member

Essa M. Saleh Al-Housani (U.A.E.), member
Theo van Seggelen (the Netherlands), member
John Didulica (Australia), member
on the claim presented by the club X as Claimant
against the player Y as Respondent
regarding a contractual . dispute arisen on the basis of an employment contract concluded between the parties

I. FACTS OF THE CASE

1. On 28 September 2001, the Claimant and the Respondent, signed an employment contract valid as from the date of the signature until 28 September 2006. According to the copy of the employment contract remitted to FIFA, the Respondent was entitled to receive a monthly salary in the amount of 500 x.
2. On 26 February 2004, the Football Association xxxxx approached FIFA and maintained that despite having the Respondent an ongoing employment contract with its affiliated club valid until 28 September 2006, the said club found out that the Respondent was actually rendering his services to the club Z.

   Therefore, the Claimant asked for compensation for the breach of the employment contract as well as for the implementation of sanctions.
3. Furthermore, the Claimant informed FIFA that the Respondent had left on 15 November 2001 for vacations and had not resumed duties on 4 January 2002, but only six months later in June 2002. To this regard the Claimant emphasised that the Respondent argued that he had had difficulties with the relevant travelling documents. Moreover, the Claimant explained that due to the Respondent's insufficient physical condition, it instructed the Respondent to play with the reserve team. According to the Claimant, the Respondent disappeared again as from October 2002. Finally, the Claimant emphasised that it tried to transfer or loan the Respondent as from 1 November 2002 to another club, but no club was interested in obtaining the Respondent's services.
4. On 28 April 2004, FIFA suspended the Respondent from all football activities worldwide except for the Claimant, until further notice.
5. On 6 October 2004, the Respondent informed FIFA that he had no intentions to return to xxxxx due to the "inhuman treatments" imposed on him. Furthermore, the Respondent explained that he went to xxxxx during the Christmas break 2001/2002 and that on that occasion his residence permit for xxxxx, his passport as well as his return ticket were stolen. The Respondent maintained having spent six months organising these documents allowing him to resume duties with the Claimant.
6. On 12 November 2004, the Claimant maintained having fully complied with the employment contract at any time. Furthermore, the Claimant deemed it important to point out that short after signing the employment contract, i.e. in September 2001, the Respondent requested the advanced payment of all his future salaries in accordance with the employment contract. The Claimant affirmed having paid him the amount corresponding to all salaries until the expiry of the relevant employment contract, i.e. until 28 September 2006, namely the amount of USD 50,000 (according to the Claimant 1 USD = 6,5 xxxx).

   The Claimant provided FIFA with a receipt in the amount of 325,000 "rubles" bearing the signature of the player and the date of 28 September 2001. In addition, two receipts were provided dated 10 and 19 December 2001 titled as salary November 2001 and December 2001, whereby the amount of 432 "rubles" each was paid to the Respondent.
7. In view of the above and taking into account the player's unauthorized departure, the Claimant asks for the reimbursement of the sum 325,000 "rubles", according to it corresponding to USD 50,000, it has advanced to the Respondent.
8. On 7 December 2004, the Respondent explained that he never asked for any advance payment as affirmed by the Claimant. However, the Claimant confirmed that he had received the amount of 325,000 "rubles" as part of his signing-on fee, without knowing the value of the said amount in USD.
9. The Claimant agreed that the Respondent should be able to continue with his football career. However, it stressed that it was interested in directly negotiating the transfer of the Respondent with a potential new club in order to receive compensation. However, the Claimant did not at any time request that the Respondent should resume duties, although the relevant employment contract ran out in September 2006 only.

10. On 18 August 2005, FIFA advised the parties involved in this matter to consider their labour relationship as terminated and to focus on the financial aspects of the dispute. Furthermore, the parties were advised that should the Respondent enter into a new contractual relationship with a club and should the Association of this club ask for the issuance of the Respondent's International Transfer Certificate, the former Association is asked to comply with such a request, so as to not hinder the Respondent's career.
11. On 7 September 2005, the Claimant again affirmed that it paid the amount of USD 50,000 in advance to the Respondent shortly after signing the employment contract.
12. On 18 September 2005, the Respondent pointed out that he signed an employment contract with the Claimant in September 2001, based on which he was entitled to receive the amount of USD 100,000 as signing-on fee as well as the amount of USD 2,000 as monthly salary. However, the Respondent never provided FIFA with any employment contract establishing the amounts to which he referred.
13. The Respondent confirmed once again that he had received the amount of 325,000 "rubles", which, according to the Claimant, correspond to USD 50,000.
    Finally, the player explained that he rendered his services to the Claimant until August 2002, when he was forced to leave.
14. In its final submission, the Claimant referred to all its previous statements and pointed out that the only existing contract concluded between the parties stipulates that the Respondent was entitled to receive 500 "rubles".
15. According to the xxxxxx Football Association the player was registered for one of its affiliate s as from 30 January 2004 until the suspension pronounced by FIFA on 28 April 2004.

II. CONSIDERATIONS OF THE DISPUTE RESOLUTION CHAMBER

1. First of all, the Chamber analysed whether it was competent to deal with the matter at stake. In this respect, it referred to art. 18 par. 2 and 3 of the Rules Governing the Procedures of the Players' ' Status Committee and the Dispute Resolution Chamber. The present matter was submitted to FIFA on 26 February 2004, as a consequence the Chamber concluded that the previous procedural Rules (edition 2001) on matter pending before the decision making bodies of FIFA are applicable on the matter at hand.
2. With regard to the competence of the Chamber, art. 42 par. 1 lit. (b) (i) of the FIFA Regulations for the Status and Transfer of Players (edition 2001) establishes that, the triggering elements of the employment-related dispute (i.e. whether a contract was breached, with or without just cause, or sporting just cause), will be decided by the Dispute Resolution Chamber.
3. If an employment contract is breached by a party, the Dispute Resolution Chamber is also responsible to verify whether a party is accountable for outstanding payments and/or compensation. Equally, the Chamber shall decide whether sport sanctions shall be imposed.
4. As a consequence, the Dispute Resolution Chamber is the competent body to decide on the present litigation involving a club from xxxx and a xxxxx player regarding a claim in connection with an employment contract.
5. Subsequently, the members of the Chamber analyzed which edition of the Regulations for the Status and Transfer of Players should be applicable as to the substance of the matter. In this respect, the Chamber referred, on the one hand, to art. 26 par. 1 and 2 of the Regulations for the Status and Transfer of Players (edition 2005) and, on the other hand, to the fact that the relevant contract at the basis of the present dispute was signed on 28 September 2001 and the claim was lodged at FIFA on 26 February 2004. In view of the aforementioned, the Chamber concluded that the former FIFA Regulations for the Status and Transfer of Players (edition 2001, hereafter: the Regulations) are applicable to the case at hand as to the substance.
6. Entering into the substance of the matter, the members of the Chamber started their deliberations by acknowledging that the Claimant is of the opinion that the Respondent breached the employment contract signed on 28 September 2001. Therefore, the Claimant is requesting the reimbursement of the salary payment made in advance to the Respondent in the amount of 325,000 "rubles", according to the Claimant corresponding to USD 50,000. In particular, the Claimant explained that it had paid to the Respondent the amount corresponding to all salaries due until the expiry of the employment contract concluded between the parties to the present dispute, i.e. until 28 September 2006.
7. In continuation, the Chamber took due note that the parties are not contesting that the relevant employment contract was prematurely terminated. In particular, the Chamber remarked that, on the

one hand, the Claimant stated that the Respondent disappeared as from October 2002. On the other hand, the Respondent explained that he rendered his services to the Claimant until August 2002 when he was forced to leave the club.

8. Consequently, the Chamber established that the relevant employment contract at the basis of the present dispute was prematurely terminated within the first contractual year, respectively at the beginning of the second year of the contract.
9. Subsequently, the Chamber acknowledged that the Claimant stated that the Respondent had left on 15 November 2001 for vacations and had not resumed duties on 4 January 2002, but only six months later, in June 2002. Equally, the Claimant explained that the Respondent excused his late return by mentioning that he had had difficulties with the relevant travelling documents. Finally, the Chamber remarked that the Claimant stated that the Respondent disappeared again as from October 2002.
10. Turning its attention to the Respondent's position, the Chamber took due note that he maintained that he went to xxxxx during the Christmas break 2001/2002 and that on that occasion his residence permit for xxxxxxx, his passport as well as his return ticket were stolen. Furthermore, the Respondent claimed that six months elapsed before he could resume duties with the Claimant. Finally the Respondent explained that some months later he was forced to leave the club due to the "inhuman treatments" imposed on him.
11. In this context, the Dispute Resolution Chamber referred to the legal principle of the burden of proof, which is a basic principle in every legal system, according to which a party deriving a right from an asserted fact has the obligation to prove the relevant fact.
12. In view of the above mentioned principle, the Chamber pointed out that the Respondent never provided any documentary evidence together with his submissions in order to corroborate his allegations with regard to the reasons he might have had for his absence, in particular his prolonged absence of more than six months following the Christmas holidays, as well as with regard to the reasons he might have had to justify his premature leave of the club.
13. Moreover, the Chamber considered that based on all information at its disposal it could be established that the Respondent rendered his services to the Claimant for a period of time of maximum 5 ½ months only within the first year of the contractual relationship. In particular, for the months of October until 15 November 2001 and then from June 2002 until September 2002.
14. In view of the above as well as based on the submissions remitted by both parties, the Chamber concluded that the Respondent breached the employment contract concluded with the Claimant without just cause. In particular, the Chamber reiterated that the Respondent did not provide substantiated reasons which could justify his failure to fulfil his contractual obligations, particularly, with regard to his prolonged absence and his premature departure.
15. Subsequently, and having thus established that the Respondent had breached the relevant employment contract without just cause undoubtedly during the so-called protected period as provided for in art. 21 par. 1 of the Regulations, the Chamber stated that, in principle, compensation shall be payable by and sports sanctions shall be imposed on the Respondent (cf. art. 21 par. 1 (a) and (b) of the Regulations). For the sake of completeness, the Chamber reiterated that the breach of contract occurred within the first contractual year, respectively at the beginning of the second year of the contract.
16. Following the foregoing, the Chamber first focussed its analysis on the amount of compensation for the unjustified breach of contract due by the Respondent to the Claimant and in this respect referred to the non-exhaustive enumeration of objective criteria listed in article 22 of the Regulations.
17. To this regard, the Chamber took into account, in particular, the remuneration and other benefits under the existing contract, the length of time remaining on the existing contract as well as the specificities of the present case.
18. Subsequently, the Chamber considered that the Claimant stated that it had paid the entire value of the contract in advance to the Respondent, i.e. the amount of 325,000 "rubles". Equally, the Chamber stressed that the Respondent confirmed having received the aforementioned advance payment, however, he affirmed that he received the said amount as signing-on fee.
19. In this respect, the Chamber again referred to the aforementioned legal principle of the burden of proof (cf. point II.11.above) and emphasised that the Respondent did not provide any documentary evidence to corroborate his allegation that he was entitled to receive a signing-on fee. In particular, the deciding body emphasised that the contract concluded between the parties remitted to its attention did not provide for such payment. The Respondent had not presented any other contract or document with another contents.

20. In view of the above, the Chamber had no alternative but to conclude that the parties signed an employment contract in September 2001 valid until 28 September 2006 based on which the Respondent was entitled to receive a monthly salary in the amount of 500 xxx. Consequently, the total contractual value, according to the only employment contract remitted, corresponds to the amount of 30,000 xxxx.
21. For the sake of completeness, the Chamber pointed out that the payment receipts dated 10 and 19 December 2001 remitted by the Claimant along with its submissions and referring to the salaries for November and December 2001 also confirm the aforementioned monthly salary.
22. In continuation, the Chamber remarked that the Claimant had confirmed that the Respondent actually rendered his services during the period of 5 ½ months, i.e. October until 15 November 2001 as well as June until September 2002.
Consequently, the Chamber concluded that the Respondent was entitled to receive the amount of 2,750 xxxxxx (5 ½ times 500) as remuneration for the effective period of time he rendered his services to the Claimant.
23. As a result, the members of the Chamber concluded that the Respondent has in any case to refund to the Claimant the amount of 27,250 xxxxx, corresponding to the remainder contractual value of the relevant employment contract.
24. In continuation, the Chamber turned its attention to the contradictory positions of the parties to the present dispute with regard to the amount paid to the Respondent in advance, and in particular, the currency to which the advance payment refers. Particularly, the Chamber remarked that the Respondent confirmed the receipt of the advance payment in the amount of 325,000 "rubles".
25. In this respect, first and foremost, the members of the Chamber were of the unanimous opinion that the decisive and crucial currency to be taken into account, is the one to which the relevant employment contract at the basis of the present dispute refers to, i.e. xxxxxx.
26. Subsequently, the Chamber emphasised that it could not follow the relation between the amount paid in advance, i.e. 325,000 "rubles", corresponding according to the Claimant to the entire contractual value, and the actual total contractual value in accordance with the employment contract in question amounting to 30,000 xxxx, as previously exposed. Also, the Chamber underlined that it is rather very unusual that a club would pay the total value of a five-year contract in advance to a player.
27. In view of all of the above, the Chamber had to assume that some other arrangements had been concluded between the parties to the present dispute based on which the Respondent received an advance payment apart from the monthly salary agreed upon by the parties in the relevant employment contract signed on 28 September 2001.
28. Moreover, the Chamber considered that as from the moment of the breach until the original expiry of the employment contract, four contractual years remained. It was also stressed that the Claimant lodged its claim with FIFA almost 1½ years after the Respondent's departure only.
29. The Chamber also took into account that throughout the entire procedure the Claimant did not at any time request that the Respondent should resume duties with it, although the relevant employment contract was to run out in September 2006 only.
30. The Chamber also referred to the statement of the xxxxx Football Association which confirmed that the Respondent had been registered for one of its affiliates as from 30 January 2004 until the suspension pronounced by FIFA on 28 April 2004. In this context, the deciding body noted that following his departure from the Claimant the Respondent had been without employment for quite a long time. Equally, the Chamber pointed out that the Respondent had, de facto, been suspended for a considerable period of time and thus had not been able to work for a significant period. The Chamber deemed that, obviously by this fact his career had been heavily disturbed.
31. In view of all of the above as well as of the specificities of the present case, the Chamber concluded that under these circumstances an additional compensation in the amount of 13,000 xxxxx appears to be reasonable and justified.
32. As a result, the Chamber decided that the Respondent should pay compensation to the Claimant for breach of contract without just cause in the total amount of 40,250 xxxxx.
33. Finally, with regard to sports sanctions, which other than in exceptional circumstances should be applied in case a player breaches a contract without just cause within the first three respectively two years of the contract (cf. art. 21 par. 1 of the Regulations) in accordance with art. 23 par. 1 of the Regulations, the Chamber renounced to apply such sanctions in view of the fact that sports sanctions had already been imposed on the Respondent in connection with the present dispute.

III. DECISION OF THE DISPUTE RESOLUTION CHAMBER

1. The claim lodged by the Claimant is partially accepted.
2. The Respondent must pay the total amount of 40,250 xxxxx to the Claimant within 30 days as from the date of notification of this decision.
3. Any further claims lodged by the Claimant are rejected.
4. If the aforementioned sum is not paid within the aforementioned deadline an interest rate of 5% per year will apply as of expiring of the fixed time limit and the present matter shall be submitted to FIFA's Disciplinary Committee, so that the necessary disciplinary sanctions may be imposed.
5. The Claimant is directed to inform the Respondent directly and immediately of the account number to which the remittance is to be made and to notify the Dispute Resolution Chamber of every payment received.
6. According to art. 61 par. 1 of the FIFA Statutes, this decision may be appealed against before the Court of Arbitration for Sport (CAS). The statement of appeal must be sent to the CAS directly within 21 days of receipt of notification of this decision and shall contain all the elements in accordance with point 2 of the directives issued by the CAS, a copy of which we enclose hereto. Within another 10 days following the expiry of the time limit for filing the statement of appeal, the appellant shall file a brief stating the facts and legal arguments giving rise to the appeal with the CAS (cf. point 4 of the directives).

96338

DECISION OF THE DISPUTE RESOLUTION CHAMBER

passed in Zurich, Switzerland, on 28 September 2006,
in the following composition:
Slim Aloulou (Tunisia), Chairman
Theo van Seggelen (Netherlands), member
John Didulica (Australia), member
Philippe Diallo (France), member
Essa M. Saleh al-Housani (United Arab Emirates), member
on the claim presented by the club, X, as Claimant
against
the club, Y, as Respondent
regarding training compensation related to the transfer of the player

I. FACTS OF THE CASE

1. The player, Z, was born on 2 May 1985.
2. According to the players' passport issued by the Football Federation of X, Z was registered with X as follows:
   from the 1998-99 to the 2001-02 season as an amateur during the 2002-03 season as a non-amateur during the 2003-04 and the 2004-05 season as an amateur
3. On 31 August 2005, the Football Federation of X issued an International Transfer Certificate for the player on behalf of the Football Federation of Y and the Football Federation of Y confirmed that the player was registered with Y on 6 September 2005.
4. On 16 November 2005, X lodged a claim in front of FIFA against Y maintaining that the player, Z, signed his first professional contract with the Y during the summer of 2005 and that, therefore, X is entitled to training compensation for the period of time that it trained and educated the player on the basis of the FIFA Regulations for the Status and Transfer of Players.
5. In reply to the claim, Y asserts that the player, Z had a professional contract with X and that X did not offer a new contract to the player in question and allowed him to sign on with the club of his choice.
6. In this regard, Y refers to art. 6 of Annex 4 of the above-mentioned Regulations regarding special provisions for the EU/EEA area and points out that X had the right to offer to the player, Z, at least a contract of formation ("contrat de formation").
7. Therefore, Y rejects the claim put forward by X.
8. X confirms that during the entire period of time that the player was registered with X he only signed one contract ("contrat aspirant") during the 2002-03 season, when X had a professional status.

Thereafter, the player signed 2 "conventions de joueur en formation" for the 2003-04 and 2004-05 seasons, when the club had an amateur status.

9. A copy of these agreements has been provided to FIFA.
10. According to X, the decision passed by the Dispute Resolution Chamber (DRC) on 24 March 2004 in the case "W" is applicable to the present matter. X provided a copy of this decision, in accordance with which X was entitled to receive training compensation for the player W who signed on with another club after X's loss of its professional status at the end of the 2002-03 season and the communication by the Football Federation of X on 25 June 2003 that all players that had been under contract with X during the 2002-03 season would be free from their engagement as from 30 June 2003.
11. X points out that the situation of the player Z is identical to that of the player W and that the club's sportive and legal status has not changed either.
12. X asserts that its amateur status during the 2003-04 to 2005-06 seasons did not allow the club to sign professional contracts with players. In this regard, X also points out that the change of its sportive status does not affect its right to training compensation on the international level.
13. Therefore, the player having signed a professional contract with Y in the summer of 2005, X maintains being entitled to receive training compensation in accordance with the applicable -FIFA Regulations.
14. Y deems that the DRC decision passed in the case "W" is not applicable to the present matter, since the case at hand falls under the current FIFA Regulations for the Status and Transfer of Players (edition 2005) as opposed to the case "W" and the situation in this matter is different from when the club lost its professional status. Consequently, it re-affirms its rejection of the claim put forward by X.
15. The Football Federation of Y has confirmed that during the 1998-99 until 2000- 01 seasons Y was allocated category 4, during the 2001-02 to 2003-04 seasons category III, and the 2004-05 season category II.
16. The Football Federation of X has confirmed that during the 1998-99 and 1999- 00 seasons X was allocated category 1, during the 2000-01 and 2001-02 seasons category 2 and during the 2002-03 until the 2004-05 seasons X was allocated category 4 and had amateur status.
17. At the request of FIFA, the Football Federation of X provided the information that on account of the circumstance that X plays as an amateur club in the national championship (3rd level), AX has the possibility to have "federal contracts" ratified by the Football Federation of X, which, according to the Football Federation of X, are professional contracts limited in time (up to one or two seasons).

II. CONSIDERATIONS OF THE DISPUTE RESOLUTION CHAMBER

1. First of all, the Chamber analysed whether it was competent to deal with the matter at stake. In this respect, it referred to art. 18 par. 2 and 3 of the Rules Governing the Procedures of the Players' 7 Status Committee and the Dispute Resolution Chamber. The present matter was submitted to - FIFA on 16 November 2005, as a consequence the Chamber concluded that the Rules Governing the Procedures of the Players' Status Committee and the Dispute Resolution Chamber (edition 2005, hereinafter: the Rules) are applicable to the matter at hand.
2. With regard to the competence of the Chamber, art. 3 par. 1 of the above- mentioned Rules states that the Dispute Resolution Chamber shall examine its jurisdiction in the light of articles 22 to 24 of the current version of the Regulations for the Status and Transfer of Players (edition 2005). In accordance with art. 24 par. 1 in combination with art. 22 (d) of the aforementioned Regulations, the Dispute Resolution Chamber shall. adjudicate on disputes between two clubs belonging to different Associations related to training compensation.
3. As a consequence, the Dispute Resolution Chamber is the competent body to decide on the present litigation concerning training compensation claimed by the Claimant for the training and education of the player Z.
4. Subsequently, the members of the Chamber analyzed which edition of the Regulations for the Status and Transfer of Players should be applicable as to the substance of the matter. In this respect, the Chamber referred to art. 26 par. 1 and 2 of the Regulations for the Status and Transfer of Players (edition 2005) in the modified version in accordance with the FIFA circular no. 995 dated 23 September 2005.

   Furthermore, it acknowledged that the player had been registered for his new club on 6 September 2005.

Equally, the Chamber took note that the claim was lodged at FIFA on 16 November 2005.
In view of the aforementioned, the Chamber concluded that the current FIFA Regulations for the Status and Transfers of Players (edition 2005, hereinafter: the Regulations) are applicable to the case at hand as to the substance.

5. Once its competence and the applicable Regulations were thus established, the Chamber went on to deal with the substance of the case.
6. The members of the Chamber duly noted that the Claimant claims payment of training compensation for the training and education of the player, Z, between the ages of 13 and 20 maintaining that the player signed his first professional contract with Y in the summer of 2005.
7. The Respondent, for its part, contests the claim lodged by the Claimant maintaining that no training compensation is payable by it to X in the light of art. 6 of Annex 4 of the Regulations and the fact that the Claimant has not offered the player a contract while the Claimant allegedly could have offered the player at least a "contrat de formation".
8. This position is vehemently rejected by the Claimant, which asserts that due to its amateur status it was/is not in the position to offer professional contracts to its players and that this circumstance does not affect its alleged right to receive training compensation in the event of international transfers under the applicable rules. In support of its position, the Claimant invokes the decision passed by the Dispute Resolution Chamber in the case "W" in March 2004.
9. Taking into account the above, the Chamber concluded that it is undisputed that the Claimant has not offered a contract to the player, Z, prior to his move to Y in the summer of 2005.
In the light of the fact that the present dispute is between two clubs inside the territory of the EU/EEA and taking into account art. 6.3 of Annex 4 of the Regulations, the Chamber had thus to address the question as to whether the Claimant had the possibility to offer a contract to the player. In the negative, the Claimant could have a valid reason justifying that it is entitled to training compensation.
10. The members of the Chamber took note that the decision that it passed in the case "W" was based on facts that transpired during the transition of X from a professional club to an amateur club at the end of the 2002-03 season.
11. Furthermore, the members of the Chamber took into consideration that, in the interim, further information and documentation has been made available to it, including a decision passed by the Court of Arbitration for Sport (CAS) in another case in which the Claimant was involved (CAS 2004/A/…) and the information indicated under I.17 above.
12. In this context, the Chamber stressed that according to art. 12.4 of the Rules, the Dispute Resolution Chamber may also consider evidence not offered by the parties.
13. It was also duly noted that during the 2003-04 and the 2004-05 seasons the Claimant had amateur status.
14. With respect to art. 6 of Annex 4 of the Regulations, which is invoked by the Respondent, the members of the Chamber deemed that such article, in general, applies to circumstances under which a club is in the position to offer a professional contract to a player.
15. In the case at hand, it has been established that, in spite of its amateur status, the Claimant was in the position to offer a "federal contract" to the player, Z.
16. Moreover, it has been established that no such offer was made to Z by X.
17. Furthermore, the Chamber recalled that the 2005 edition of the Regulations for the Status and Transfer of Players and its art. 6 of Annex 4 apply to the present case.
18. On account of the above-mentioned facts, the Chamber decided that the Claimant, X, is not entitled to receive training compensation from the Respondent for the player in question.

III. DECISION OF THE DISPUTE RESOLUTION CHAMBER

1. The claim of the Claimant, X, is rejected.
2. According to art. 61 par. 1 of the FIFA Statutes, this decision may be appealed against before the Court of Arbitration for Sport (CAS). The statement of appeal must be sent to the CAS directly within 21 days of receipt of notification of this decision and shall contain all the elements in accordance with point 2 of the directives issued by the CAS, a copy of which we enclose hereto. Within another 10 days following the expiry of the time limit for filing the statement of appeal, the appellant shall file a brief stating the facts and legal arguments giving rise to the appeal with the CAS (cf. point 4 of the directives).

96391
DECISION OF THE DISPUTE RESOLUTION CHAMBER
passed in Zurich, Switzerland, on 28 September 2006,
in the following composition:
Slim Aloulou (Tunisia), Chairman
John Didulica (Australia), Member
Theo van Seggelen (Netherlands),Member
Essa M. Saleh Al Housani (United Arab Emirates), Member
Philippe Diallo (France), Member
on the claim presented by the Player X, XX, as Claimant
against the club, Y, YY, as Respondent
regarding a contractual dispute arisen between the parties involved

I. FACTS OF THE CASE

1. On 31 July 2005, the YY club, Y (hereinafter: the Respondent), and the U club, UU, entered into a loan agreement under which the player X (hereinafter: the Claimant) was loaned to the Respondent until 30 November 2006.
This loan agreement was co-signed by the Claimant.
2. Subsequently, the Claimant entered into an employment contract with the Respondent with a term as from 10 August 2005 to 30 November 2006.
3. Pursuant to said employment contract, which was submitted by the Claimant, a monthly salary of USD 15,000 was agreed for the year 2005.
A handwritten note was added to the employment contract, stating that the Claimant's monthly salary for 2006 would amount to USD 20,000.
The Claimant was also entitled to various bonuses payable by the Respondent according to the result (win, draw or defeat) and per game (league or cup).
4. On 12 April 2006, the Claimant filed his claim before FIFA against the Respondent.

Claim of the Claimant

5. On the one hand, the Claimant claims that the Respondent has yet to hand him an employment contract in his native language (UU), as he speaks neither YY nor English. On the other hand, he accuses the Respondent of having unilaterally terminated the employment contract without just cause.
6. In this respect, the Claimant submitted that the Respondent sent him a draft of a termination agreement for signature on 11 February 2006, with retrospective effect as from 1 January 2006.
The Claimant did, however, not sign this termination agreement, in particular because the loan agreement between U and the Respondent did not provide for a possibility to prematurely terminate this agreement and, in any case, such a dissolution of the loan agreement would only have been possible with the consent of all three parties involved. A short time later, he learnt from the management of the Respondent that the latter, according to an official statement, had terminated the employment contract with him on the grounds that he had not met the Respondent's sporting requirements and was therefore being released back to U. In this respect, the Claimant attached a letter from the Respondent to the UU club dated 6 December 2005, in which the former informed the UU club that it is terminating the employment contract with the Claimant and releasing him back to UU. The grounds given in the said letter were that the Claimant did not satisfy the Respondent's technical requirements and that therefore the contract for the season 2006 was not being extended. The UU club was requested by the Respondent to recommend another player with good technical ability.
7. The Claimant also maintained that during his spell with the YY club (from August to October 2005), no one from the Respondent ever found fault with his performances. In the aforementioned period, he played for the first team in every official game, scoring six goals in the process. The Claimant emphasised that these facts clearly demonstrate his ability as a player.
8. In addition, and irrespective of whether he had met the Respondent's requirements or not, the Claimant is of the opinion that the Respondent, in spite of a provision contained in the employment contract to this effect, had no right to unilaterally terminate the employment contract. The Respondent should have at least offered him an opportunity to play for the Respondent's reserve team first, as provided for by the employment contract.

9. The Claimant therefore demanded that the Respondent pay him USD 220,000 for the unilateral breach of contract, which corresponds to his salary of USD 20,000 for the remaining eleven months, i.e. until the end of November 2006, of the employment contract, and that appropriate sanctions be imposed on the Respondent for the unilateral contract termination.

Defence of the Respondent

10. In reply to the Claimant's claim, the Respondent submitted an employment contract that, except the financial provisions, clearly differs from the one remitted by the Claimant. This employment contract has been signed by both parties and by an agent whose name, however, could not be made out.
11. In this employment contract submitted by the Respondent, the Claimant's monthly salary is also fixed at USD 15,000.
A monthly salary of USD 20,000 is foreseen for the season 2006, should the Respondent be promoted to the CFA Premier League.
12. Article 8 par. 2 of this employment contract states the following:
"Party B (the Claimant) play in 2005 season must be no less than 85% of all the game time, and gave 7 goals, in 2006 season gave no less than 15 goals"
13. In addition, article 5 par. 7 of the employment contract states:
"During the contract period, if Party B (the Claimant) cannot implement obligation of contract or cannot finish the work because of health, Party A (the Respondent) has right to stop the contract. From the date when the contract is stopped, Party A will not pay salaries to Party B. Party B shouldn't put on forward the appeal of any kind or demand the compensation, in this time Party B must pay Party A 50,000 USD as penalty".
14. The Respondent is of the opinion that the Claimant did not fulfil the aforementioned obligations arising out of the employment contract, as during the season 2005, he played only 75% of all matches and scored just six goals.
For this reason, the Respondent deemed that the Claimant has to pay a contractual penalty amounting to USD 50,000.
15. As a consequence, the Respondent decided to return the Claimant to the UU club, U, and requested the latter to send it a new player.
16. Further, the Respondent submitted that the Claimant, like all the other players in the team, had gone on holiday at the end of October 2005, but had failed to return. This was the reason why it had wanted to terminate the employment contract with the Claimant and had informed him accordingly via fax (termination agreement) without, however, ever receiving any feedback from the Claimant. According to the employment contract, all players have to return on time after the holidays. If this obligation is violated, the players have to pay USD 10,000 per day. In addition, under the terms of the employment contract, i.e. art. 10 par. 5 and art. 17, the Respondent has the right in such a case to terminate the employment contract and demand compensation from the Claimant in the amount of USD 100,000.
17. In addition, the Respondent had discovered that the Claimant had been training on a trial basis with other clubs, in particular U, without its prior permission, which constituted another violation of the contract.
18. Due to the fact that the Claimant had not returned after the holidays and had already trained on a trial basis with other clubs, the Respondent took the view that the Claimant breached the employment contract.
19. In this respect, the Respondent stressed that it had still paid the Claimant's salaries for the months of November and December 2005.
20. With regard to the contract language, the Respondent explained that the contract had been drafted in both English and YY. When the contract was signed, an interpreter had allegedly been attending and had translated every single article of the employment contract for the Claimant.

Second statement of the Claimant

21. In his second submission, the Claimant emphasised that he had not signed the employment contract remitted to the file by the Respondent on every page and therefore it could easily have been forged. The Claimant stressed that he did not sign the employment contract submitted by the Respondent.
22. In this respect, the Claimant referred to the absurdly high compensation payments foreseen in the aforementioned contract that he would have to make in the event of a breach of contract and also the

fixed number of goals and matches that he would have to achieve. Were such contractual conditions translated exactly to him, he would never accept them and sign.

23. In addition, the Claimant submitted a letter dated 13 January 2006, in which he had requested the Respondent to inform him whether it still had any interest in him and by when he had to return from Russia.

Second statement of the Respondent

24. In its final submission, the Respondent again emphasised that it had translated every single article of the employment contract to the Claimant.
25. The Respondent also referred to the employment contract that the Claimant signed and according to which the Respondent had the right to terminate the employment contract if the Claimant fails to meet the obligations arising out of the contract. The Respondent noted that the Claimant's lack of ability was the principal reason for it to terminate the employment contract.
26. Finally, the Respondent pointed out once again that the Claimant had not returned to the club since 23 October 2005 and had trained at his previous club, U, on a trial basis during this period. The latter had then attempted to obtain the International Transfer Certificate from the YY Football Association of YY via the UU Football Association.

II. CONSIDERATIONS OF THE DISPUTE RESOLUTION CHAMBER

a) As to the competence of the Dispute Resolution Chamber

1. First of all, the Chamber analysed whether it was competent to deal with the matter at stake. In this respect, it referred to art. 18 par. 2 and 3 of the Rules Governing the Procedures of the Players' Status Committee and the Dispute Resolution Chamber. The present matter was submitted to FIFA on 12 April 2006, as a consequence the Chamber concluded that the revised Rules Governing Procedures (edition 2005) on matters pending before the decision making bodies of FIFA are applicable to the matter at hand.
2. With regard to the competence of the Chamber, art. 3 par. 1 of the above- mentioned Rules states that the Dispute Resolution Chamber shall examine its jurisdiction in the light of articles 22 to 24 of the current version of the Regulations for the Status and Transfer of Players (edition 2005). In accordance with art. 24 par. 1 in combination with art. 22 (b) of the aforementioned Regulations, the Dispute Resolution Chamber shall adjudicate on employment- related disputes between a club and a player that have an international dimension.
3. As a consequence, the Dispute Resolution Chamber is the competent body to decide on the present litigation involving a player from XX and a YY club in connection with an employment contract.
4. Subsequently, the members of the Chamber analyzed which edition of the Regulations for the Status and Transfer of Players should be applicable as to the substance of the matter. In this respect, the Chamber referred, on the one hand, to art. 26 par. 1 and 2 of the Regulations for the Status and Transfer of Players (edition 2005) and, on the other hand, to the fact that, independent of the version of employment contracts to be taken into account which have been remitted to the file from the player and the club respectively, the relevant contracts have been definitively signed after 31 July 2005.

   Moreover, taking into account the aforementioned and considering that the claim was lodged at FIFA on 12 April 2006, the Chamber concluded that the current FIFA Regulations for the Status and Transfer of Players (edition 2005, hereafter: the Regulations) are applicable to the case at hand as to the substance.

b) As to the substance of the present dispute

5. Entering into the substance of the matter the members of the Chamber acknowledged the documentation contained in the file, and in view of the circumstances of the matter at stake, focused on the question whether an unjustified breach of the employment contract between the Claimant and the Respondent occurred and which party is responsible for such breach of contract and to verify and decide if sanctions for breach of contract have to be imposed.

b1) Responsibility for the breach of contract

6. Firstly, the members of the Chamber acknowledged that two different employment contracts have been remitted to the file for the same period of time. The members noted that while the employment

contract submitted by the Claimant did neither contain the signatures of the parties to the contract nor a date, the relevant employment contract delivered by the Respondent, the same as the one remitted by the YY Football Association of YY, did bear the date of 8 August 2006 and the signatures of the Claimant and the Respondent as well as the signature of an agent apparently involved in concluding this contract.

7. In this respect, the Chamber took note that the Claimant objects having signed the employment contract remitted to the file by the Respondent, maintaining in particular that the said contract was not signed by him on every single page and therefore could have easily been falsified. Moreover, the Claimant referred to specific articles in the contract stipulating absurdly high compensation payments in case of breach of contract and also the fixed number of goals and matches that he would have to achieve. The Claimant stated that he would have never signed an employment contract containing such provisions.
8. Then, the Chamber pointed out that with regard to the alleged falsification of the employment contract, the present body is not competent to decide on the authenticity of a document. Moreover, the Chamber emphasized that each party is responsible to corroborate its allegations and that in respect with the alleged falsification, the Claimant abstained from providing the pertinent evidence.
9. For the sake of good order, the Chamber emphasized that in accordance with the legal principle of the burden of proof, which is a basic principle in every legal system, a party asserting a fact has the obligation to prove the same.
10. In accordance with the above-mentioned principle, the Claimant has the burden of proof regarding the falsification of the employment contract at the basis of the present dispute. However, the Claimant never provided FIFA with written evidence regarding the alleged falsification of the said contract.
11. In view of the above, the Chamber established that it could not uphold the Claimant's position with regard to the alleged falsification of the employment contract due to lack of evidence in this respect.
12. In view of the above, the deciding body evaluated that it has no alternative than to consider the signed and dated employment contract submitted by the Respondent as relevant. Such appreciation appeared to be justified given that the Claimant, despite failing to corroborate with documentary evidence his statement that the contract submitted by the Respondent is falsified, did not contest having signed an employment contract with the Respondent.
    Moreover, the version of the employment contract submitted by the Respondent is the same as the one which was deposited at the Football Association YY and which was also submitted to the file by the latter.
13. Notwithstanding the above, the members concurred that the financial terms of both contracts, the one remitted by the Claimant and the one remitted by the Respondent as well as the Football Association of YY, do not differ. In fact, both contracts stipulate that the Claimant is entitled to receive a salary of USD 15,000 for the year 2005 and for the year 2006 a salary of USD 20,000.
14. On the other hand, the Chamber acknowledged that the employment contract submitted by the Respondent, which was deposited at the Football Association of YY, bears superimposed obligations on the Claimant, the validity of which were questioned by the Claimant.
15. In continuation, the members of the Chamber continued by acknowledging that the Claimant maintained that the Respondent terminated the employment contract without just cause. In support of his allegations, the Claimant attached a letter dated 6 December 2005 from the Respondent addressed to U, the club which loaned him to the Respondent, by means of which the Respondent informed the aforementioned U club that it terminates the contract with the Claimant on the grounds that the latter did not met the Respondent's sporting requirements.
16. In this context, the Chamber took note of the Respondent's argument that it had just cause to terminate the employment contract since the Claimant did not fulfil the obligations arising out from the contract, in particular that the Claimant played only 75% of all matches and scored only six goals. Moreover, the Respondent deems that since the Claimant failed to achieve the targets provided for in the employment contract, he has to pay it a penalty of USD 50,000.
17. In this respect, the Chamber unanimously concluded that the application of the provision contained in art. 8 par. 2 of the employment contract, concerning the number of matches the Claimant has to play, is arbitrary since it is at the Respondent's sole discretion to decide how many matches the Claimant would have played. Moreover, the Chamber deemed it appropriate to underline in this respect that football is played in a team whereby success is only achievable when the members of

a team work together. The obligation imposed on a player in an employment contract that he has to obtain a certain number of goals within one season otherwise his employer may terminate the contract, clearly goes against the spirit of the game and contradicts the fundamental goal of team play.

18. Taking into account the above, the members concluded that the foregoing clauses in the employment contract, i.e. art. 8 par. 2 and art. 5 par. 7, are unacceptable and can certainly not be considered as valid reasons to terminate the employment contract.
19. In continuation, the Chamber took note that the Respondent's second argument to sustain its alleged valid reasons to terminate the employment contract was the Claimant's alleged late return from the holidays. The Respondent emphasized that for the Claimant's failure to return in time, according to the employment contract, he has to pay a fine of USD 10,000 per day. Moreover, the Respondent stressed that in application of art. 10 par. 5 and art. 17 of the employment contract, in case the Claimant violates the obligation to resume duty in time, it has the right to terminate the contract and ask compensation from the Claimant in the amount of USD 100,000.
20. In this context, the members of the Chamber at first stressed that with regard to the monthly income of the Claimant, i.e. USD 15,000 for the season 2005 and USD 20,000 for the season 2006 respectively, the penalty imposed on him is completely disproportionate and thus cannot be accepted.
21. Furthermore, the Chamber emphasized that it clearly emanates from the contents of the Respondent's letter dated 6 December 2005, addressed to the U club that the main reason for the Respondent to terminate the employment contract with the Claimant, was the latter's alleged failure to reach the skill and technical requirement of the Respondent. Furthermore, the aforementioned letter from the Respondent did neither include any request that the Claimant should resume duty with the Respondent nor that the Claimant breached the contract by failing to return in time after the holidays.
22. Thus, the Chamber reached the conclusion that the argument of the Respondent that it terminated the employment contract on the basis of the Claimant's alleged late return was not very credible. From the Chamber's point of view, such stance does not speak in favour of the Respondent's good faith either.
23. In view of all the above, the Chamber concluded that the reasons raised by the Respondent giving it allegedly just cause to terminate the employment contract with the Claimant have to be considered unjustified and non- considerable. Therefore, the Dispute Resolution Chamber concluded that the Respondent, by means of its correspondence dated 6 December 2006, terminated the employment contract it entered into with the Claimant without just cause.
24. In continuation, the Chamber observed, however, that from the respective positions presented by the Claimant and the Respondent concerned, it is uncontested that the Claimant was already absent from the Respondent at least as from the end of October 2005 and since then did not train or play with the latter, thus prior to the end of the validity of the employment contract.
25. In view of the above, the Chamber underlined that, as a general rule, a long- lasting absence of a player from his club without authorization and without other just cause is to be considered as an unjustified breach of the employment contract by the player.
26. In this respect, the members of the Chamber had to deliberate whether the Claimant was authorized or had just cause to be absent from the Respondent.
27. In this respect, it was noted by the Chamber that the Claimant, in support of his position, submitted a letter dated 13 January 2006, whereby he had requested the Respondent to inform him whether it is still interested in his services.
28. However, despite the fact that the Claimant could not prove with documentary evidence that the Respondent had received his letter dated 13 January 2006, the members took note that the Claimant stated, by means of his initial claim lodged at FIFA on 12 April 2006, that the Respondent sent him on 11 February 2006 a draft of a termination agreement, the proposal of which he rejected and did not sign. Moreover, according to the Claimant, he became aware later on, thus at least after 11 February 2006 when he received the draft of the termination agreement from the Respondent, that the latter apparently terminated the employment contract on the basis of his alleged failure to meet the Respondent's skill and technical requirements.
29. The deciding body deducted from the Claimant's statements that, until the time he offered his services to the Respondent in written by means of his letter dated 13 January 2006, he did not provide valid reasons justifying his absence from the Respondent.

30. Moreover, the members noted that the Respondent stressed having paid to the Claimant his salaries for the months of November and December 2005 although the Claimant did no longer render his services.
31. Yet, concerning in particular the financial aspect, the members of the Chamber concluded that the Respondent has complied with its financial obligations towards the Claimant, in particular, that, as not contested by the Claimant, it has paid to him all his salaries until December 2005, i.e. beyond the date of the Claimant's departure from YY. As a consequence, when the player left, not only were all his salaries paid but the Respondent also continued paying him his salaries even though he did not render his services to the Respondent.
32. After long deliberations and taking into account the above as well as all submissions made by both parties in this respect, the Chamber came to the conclusion that the conduct of both parties lead to the early termination of the relevant employment relation and that neither party can be held exclusively responsibly for the breach of the relevant employment contract.
33. As a result, the Chamber unanimously decided that the employment contract at the basis of the dispute has come to an end in December 2005 due to the reciprocally fault behaviour of both parties and that therefore, neither party can be held liable to pay compensation nor to be sanctioned.
34. In continuation, the Chamber turned its attention to the Claimant's claim with regard to the alleged outstanding remuneration in relation to his salaries for the year 2006 in the amount of USD 220,000.
    In this respect and first of all, the Chamber emphasized that based on the fact that the employment contract has to be considered as terminated as from December 2005 due to the reciprocally responsibility of both parties, the Claimant is not entitled to receive the salary for the said year.
35. To concluded with, and in view of all the above, the Dispute Resolution Chamber decided to reject the claim of the Claimant, as well as the counter-claim of the Respondent.

III. DECISION OF THE DISPUTE RESOLUTION CHAMBER

1. The claim of the Claimant, player X, is rejected.
2. The counter-claim of the Respondent, Y, is rejected.
3. According to art. 61 par. 1 of the FIFA Statutes this decision may be appealed before the Court of Arbitration for Sport (CAS). The statement of appeal must be sent to the CAS directly within 21 days of receiving notification of this decision and has to contain all elements in accordance with point 2 of the directives issued by the CAS, copy of which we enclose hereto. Within another 10 days following the expiry of the time limit for the filing of the statement of appeal, the appellant shall file with the CAS a brief stating the facts and legal arguments giving rise to the appeal (cf. point 4 of the directives).

⚽⚽⚽

96392

DECISION OF THE DISPUTE RESOLUTION CHAMBER

passed in Zurich, Switzerland, on 28 September 2006,
in the following composition:
Mr. Slim Aloulou (Tunisia), Chairman
Mr. Philippe Diallo (France), Member
Mr. Essa M. Saleh Al-Housani (U.A.E.), Member
Mr. Theo Van Seggelen (the Netherlands), Member
Mr. John Didulica (Australia), Member
on the claim presented by the Player A, X as Claimant
against the club G FC, XX as Respondent
regarding a contractual dispute between the parties involve

I. FACTS OF THE CASE

1. The player A was born on 1 July 1977.
2. On 1 September 2004, the player A and the club G FC signed an employment contract.
3. This contract does not expressly establish the commencement or conclusion dates but does contain a note of clarification as follows:
   (Note: the term of the contract shall be a minimum of one season and a maximum of five seasons).

4. On 14 March 2005, the player A requested the assistance of FIFA in order to claim unpaid salary and bonuses totalling ... 10,500. In this respect, the player appended a recognition of the debt signed by the club's authorities, dated 29 November 2004, which established that the said amount should be paid to the player by 15 January 2005.
5. FIFA contacted the respondent on 27 April, 17 June 2005, 14 September 2005 and 20 September 2006 but received no response.
6. On 8 June 2006, the player A informed FIFA that it was presumed that the club had changed its name to L FC in order to avoid its financial obligations and responsibilities.
7. The claimant requests FIFA for the payment of ... 10,500 on behalf of the respondent club.

II. CONSIDERATIONS OF THE DISPUTE RESOLUTION CHAMBER

1. First of all, the Chamber analysed whether it was competent to deal with the matter at stake. In this respect, it referred to art. 18 par. 2 and 3 of the Rules Governing the Procedures of the Players' ' Status Committee and the Dispute Resolution Chamber. The present matter was submitted to FIFA before 1 July 2005, more specifically on 14 March 2005, as a consequence the Chamber concluded that the previous Procedural Rules (edition 2001) on matters pending before the decision making bodies of FIFA are applicable to the matter at hand.
2. With regard to the competence of the Chamber, art. 42 par. 1 lit. (b) (i) of the FIFA Regulations for the Status and Transfer of Players (edition 2001) establishes that the triggering elements of the employment-related dispute will be decided by the Dispute Resolution Chamber.
3. If an employment contract is breached by a party, the Dispute Resolution Chamber (DRC) is also responsible to verify whether a party is accountable for outstanding payments and/or compensation.
4. As a consequence, the DRC is the competent body to decide on the present litigation involving a X player and a XX club regarding outstanding monies claimed by the player A in connection with an employment contract.
5. Subsequently, the members of the Chamber analyzed which edition of the Regulations for the Status and Transfer of Players should be applicable as to the substance of the matter. In this respect, the Chamber referred, on the one hand, to art. 26 par. 1 and 2 of the Regulations for the Status and Transfer of Players (edition 2005) and, on the other hand, to the fact that the relevant contract at the basis of the present dispute was signed on 1 September 2004 and the claim was lodged at FIFA on 14 March 2005. In view of the aforementioned, the Chamber concluded that the former FIFA Regulations for the Status and Transfer of Players (edition 2001, hereinafter: the Regulations) are applicable to the case at hand as to the substance.
6. In continuation, and entering into the substance of the matter, the members of the Chamber started by acknowledging that both parties signed an employment contract on 1 September 2004 with an undefined date of expiring.
7. Moreover, the Chamber noted that on 29 November 2004 both parties signed a private document by means of which the Respondent expressly recognized an outstanding amount of ... 10,500 to the Claimant. In this document it is expressly mentioned that this outstanding amount includes salaries and bonus in accordance with the relevant employment contract. Furthermore the members of the Chamber remarked that the Respondent compelled itself to make the payment of the entire amount (... 10,500) before 15 January 2005.
8. At this stage, the members of the Chamber pointed out that the Respondent failed four times to answer FIFA requests. In continuation, the Chamber then stated that as a general principle of procedure before the Dispute Resolution Chamber, if a Respondent does not reply to the claim, the case shall be decided by the Chamber only on the basis of the facts and proof provided by the Claimant, since with its conduct, the Respondent renounces to its right of defence and thus accepts the allegations of the Claimant.
9. On account of the above, the Chamber stated that because the Respondent never took position in the dispute, the Dispute Resolution Chamber has to pass a decision based only on the facts and evidence provided by the Claimant.
10. In this regard, the Chamber underlined that the Claimant is claiming outstanding remunerations and bonus, which amounts to ... 10,500 and that he provided FIFA with conclusive evidence in this respect.
11. Therefore, since this demand has remained uncontested by the Respondent, the Dispute Resolution Chamber decided that the Respondent has to pay the amount of ... 10,500 to the Claimant.

12. Finally the members of the Chamber remarked that in case G FC would have changed the name of its institution, as affirmed by the Claimant, this fact, in principle, would not affect the right of the player A to receive the acknowledged outstanding amount from the Respondent.

III. DECISION OF THE DISPUTE RESOLUTION CHAMBER

1. The claim of the Claimant, the player A, is accepted.
2. The Respondent, G FC, has to pay the amount of ... 10,500 to the Claimant.
3. The amount due to the Claimant has to be paid by the Respondent within 30 days as from the date of notification of this decision.
4. In the event that the debt of the Respondent is not paid within the stated deadline an interest rate of 5% per year will apply as of expiry of the said time limit and the file will be submitted to the Disciplinary Committee.
5. The Claimant is directed to inform the Respondent immediately of the account number to which the remittance is to be made and to notify the Dispute Resolution Chamber of every payment received.
6. According to art. 61 par. 1 of the FIFA Statutes, this decision may be appealed against before the Court of Arbitration for Sport (CAS). The statement of appeal must be sent to the CAS directly within 21 days of receipt of notification of this decision and shall contain all the elements in accordance with point 2 of the directives issued by the CAS, a copy of which we enclose hereto. Within another 10 days following the expiry of the time limit for filing the statement of appeal, the appellant shall file a brief stating the facts and legal arguments giving rise to the appeal with the CAS (cf. point 4 of the directives).

96633
DECISION OF THE DISPUTE RESOLUTION CHAMBER
passed in Zurich, Switzerland, on 28 September 2006,
in the following composition:
Slim Aloulou (Tunisia), Chairman
Theo van Seggelen (Netherlands), Member
John Didulica (Australia), Member
Philippe Diallo (France), Member
Essa M. Saleh Al Housani (United Arab Emirates), Member
on a matter between the club X, XX, represented by Mr U, attorney at law
and the club, Y, YY,
and the club, ZZ, XX, as Intervening party
regarding the solidarity contribution related to the
transfer of the player AB

I. FACTS OF THE CASE:

1. According to an official confirmation from the YY Football Federation, the player AB, born on 4 June 1979, was registered with the YYclub, X, from 25 September 1989 to 4 November 1998 and from 14 July 1999 to 18 July 2001. In between, i.e. from 5 November 1998 to 13 July 1999, the player was registered with another YY club, PP.
2. On 12 February 2005, ZZ and Y concluded a transfer agreement for the transfer of the player in question to the YY club by means of which they agreed on a transfer compensation of USD 1,000,000 payable in two instalments of USD 500,000 each, the first to be paid on 16 February 2005 and the second to be paid on 28 February 2005. Thereupon, on 18 February 2005, the player signed an employment contract with the said YY club, a copy of which has been presented.
3. On 19 April 2005, X contacted FIFA and lodged a claim against Y. At first, X was claiming the proportion of the solidarity contribution amounting to EUR 34,202.05 based on the information it had at that time, i.e. that the player had been permanently registered with X from 25 September 1989 to 18 July 2001 and an assumed transfer compensation amounting to EUR 750,000. During the course of the proceedings, after having taken knowledge of the actual transfer compensation, i.e. USD 1,000,000, X amended its claim and claimed the payment of USD 45,602.74.

4. On 3 May and 30 June 2005 Y informed FIFA, by referring to the transfer agreement it had entered into with ZZ, that it had paid the entire transfer compensation amount to the aforementioned YY club and that no further financial obligations on its part had been mentioned in the relevant transfer agreement. In addition, the YY club stated that it had received no official documents from the YY Football Federation, which had made it impossible for the YY club to know what it had to pay and to which club.
5. FIFA then informed the parties involved of the jurisprudence of the Dispute Resolution Chamber in similar cases, in accordance with which the player's new club is instructed to remit the relevant proportion(s) of the 5% solidarity contribution to the club(s) involved in the player's training as solidarity contribution and the player's former club is invited to reimburse the same proportion(s)to the player's new club.
6. On 27 September 2005, X informed FIFA that it agrees to FIFA's proposal for dealing with the matter in accordance with the jurisprudence of the Dispute Resolution Chamber.
7. The YY club informed FIFA that it had noted FIFA's proposal and accepted it in principle, but that it was attempting to resolve the matter with ZZ directly so that the latter would pay the solidarity contribution to X. In this respect, the YY club stated that international payment transactions always incur high additional charges that could be avoided if ZZ would pay the solidarity contribution straight to X.
8. On 10 October 2005, ZZ submitted its position, denying all responsibility for the payment of the solidarity contribution to X. According to ZZ, pursuant to the relevant applicable FIFA Regulations, such payment is the duty of the player's new club, i.e. Y.
9. On 17 October 2005, after it had become clear that no mutual agreement could be reached between ZZ and Y in this matter, X stated that it is now demanding payment of the solidarity contribution by Y in strict application of the FIFA Regulations. Should FIFA be required to pass a decision, X demanded a default interest on the due amount with effect as from 25 October 2005. For the period before this date, X accepted that Y had tried to resolve the matter by mutual agreement.
10. The YY club then expressed its concern that ZZ might fail to return the relevant proportion of the 5% of the transfer compensation, even if it would remit the relevant solidarity contribution to X. In this respect, the YY club demanded a guarantee that ZZ would reimburse the 5% of the transfer compensation. Finally, the YY club pointed out that it would incur 27,5% charges on the payment of the EUR 45,602.74, i.e. the relevant amount in dispute, and therefore asked that ZZ has to reimburse these charges as well.

II. CONSIDERATIONS OF THE DISPUTE RESOLUTION CHAMBER:

1. First of all, the Chamber analysed whether it was competent to deal with the matter at stake. In this respect, it referred to art.18 par. 2 and 3 of the Rules Governing the Procedures of the Players' ' Status Committee and the Dispute Resolution Chamber. The present matter was submitted to FIFA on 19 April 2005, as a consequence the Chamber concluded that the previous Procedural Rules (edition 2001) on matters pending before the decision making bodies of FIFA are applicable to the matter at hand.
2. With regard to the competence of the Chamber, art. 25 par. 2 of the FIFA Regulations for the Status and Transfer of Players (edition 2001) establishes that it falls within the purview of the Dispute Resolution Chamber to review disputes concerning the distribution of the solidarity contribution.
3. As a consequence, the Dispute Resolution Chamber is the competent body to decide on the present litigation concerning the distribution of the solidarity contribution claimed by the YY club, X, in connection with the transfer of the professional player AB to the YY club, Y, during the course of a contract.
4. Subsequently, the members of the Chamber analyzed which edition of the Regulations for the Status and Transfer of Players should be applicable as to the substance of the matter. In this respect, the Chamber referred to art. 26 par. 1 and 2 of the Regulations for the Status and Transfer of Players (edition 2005) in the modified version in accordance with the FIFA Circular no. 995 dated 23 September 2005. Furthermore, it acknowledged that the professional player in question had been registered for his new club in February 2005. Equally the Chamber took note that the claim was lodged at FIFA on 19 April 2005. In view of the aforementioned, the Chamber concluded that the former FIFA Regulations for the Status and Transfer of Players (edition 2001, hereafter: the Regulations) are applicable to the case at hand as to the substance.

5. In continuation, and entering into the substance of the matter, the members of the Chamber carefully studied the facts outlined above, which show that the player in question was transferred in February 2005 from ZZ to Y on a definite basis.
6. The Chamber took note that, to this end, a transfer agreement had been signed between ZZ and Y for the definitive transfer of the player AB to the aforementioned YY club.
7. At this point, the Chamber recalled that, as established in art. 25 of the Regulations in combination with art. 11 par. 1 of the Regulations governing the Application of the Regulations (hereafter: the Application Regulations), the new club to which a player is transferred, is the club responsible for the distribution of 5% of any compensation it paid to his former club, to the club(s) involved in the training and education of the player between the ages of 12 and 23.
8. In this respect, the members of the Chamber took into account that Y, after FIFA had informed the parties involved about the jurisprudence of the Dispute Resolution Chamber in similar cases, did not dispute X's apparent right to a proportion of the solidarity contribution. It was even noted by the Chamber that the parties made efforts to amicably settle the present affair without success.
9. The Chamber took particular note of the fact that ZZ has intervened in the present matter and that it maintained having no responsibility with regard to the payment of the solidarity contribution due to X, since, according to the Regulations, the new club shall pay the amount due as solidarity contribution.
10. In this respect, taking in particular into account the position of the intervening party, the Chamber referred to its well-established jurisprudence applied in similar cases, in accordance with which the player's new club is ordered to remit the relevant proportion(s) of the 5% solidarity contribution to the club(s) involved in the player's training in strict application of art. 11 of the Application Regulations. At the same time, the player's former club is ordered to reimburse the same proportion(s) of the 5% of the compensation that it received from the player's new club.
11. The said jurisprudence is based on the fact that there is no contractual link between the training club claiming for solidarity contribution and the player's former club. Therefore, such a claim would not find any contractual basis. Yet, the Regulations clearly establish that the distribution of the solidarity contribution is incumbent on the new club. As a consequence, the Regulations provide for a legal basis for the claim of the training club against the new club, yet not for a claim against the player's former club. Finally, the new club and the previous club are bound by a contractual agreement, which needs to be respected.
12. In addition, the members of the Chamber stressed that FIFA circular nr. 826 dated 31 October 2002, which deals with the interpretation of the FIFA Regulations for the Status and Transfer of Players (edition September 2001), elucidates that the 5% solidarity contribution is to be deducted from the amount payable to the player's former club.
13. In light of the above, in particular the aforementioned well-established jurisprudence of the Chamber, the members confirmed that it is the responsibility of the new club, Y, to pay the relevant proportion of the solidarity contribution to X, which was involved in the player's training and education.
14. In view of the above and referring to the objection raised by the YY club concerning additional charges that it allegedly incurs in case of international payment transactions, the members of the Chamber unanimously concluded that these alleged facts do not discharge a club from its obligation to pay the relevant proportion of the solidarity contribution to the clubs involved in the training and education of a player.
15. In addition, taking into account all of the above and, in particular, the aforementioned well-established jurisprudence of the Chamber, the members of the Chamber deemed that the arguments put forward by the intervening party, ZZ, cannot be accepted.
16. Therefore, ZZ, having unduly received the amount of money pertaining to solidarity contribution, is to be held liable for the reimbursement to Y of the relevant proportion(s) of the solidarity contribution payable by Y to the player's former training club, X.
17. The Chamber then went on to deliberate on the proper calculation of the said proportion due to X.
18. To that regard, the members of the Chamber referred to art. 10 of the Application Regulations, which provides the figures for the distribution of the solidarity contribution, according to the period of time that the player was trained by a specific club.
19. In the present case, the Chamber outlined that according to the player passport submitted by the YY Football Federation, the period to be taken into consideration went from the sporting season 1991/1992, when the player was 12 years old, until 4 November 1998 with respect to the first period

of time that the player was registered with X and from 14 July 1999 until 18 July 2001 for the second period of time that the player was registered with X. To that regard, the Chamber underlined that in accordance with art. 25 of the Regulations and art. 10 of the Application Regulations, the period of time during which the player had been registered with X before the player's age of 12 years cannot be taken into account.

20. In view of the above, taking in particular into account that the player AB, born on 4 June 1979, was registered for the club, X, for the period of times indicated above, the Chamber decided that 83,33% of 5% of the solidarity contribution shall be apportioned to X.
21. The Chamber noted that according to the transfer contract remitted to the file, the player AB was transferred from ZZ to Y for the amount of USD 1,000,000.
22. Based on all the foregoing considerations, the Dispute Resolution Chamber decided that Y has to pay the amount of USD 41,665 to X as solidarity contribution for the player AB.
23. Finally, the members of the Chamber made reference to art. 11 par. 1 of the Application Regulations, which reads that the amount due as a solidarity contribution shall be paid by the new club to the training clubs pursuant to the above provisions at the latest within 30 days of the player's new registration.
24. In this respect, the members noted, however, that X is asking a default interest payment only as from 25 October 2005.
25. Consequently, in light of the fact that the payment of the solidarity contribution is due since the thirty-first day after the registration of the player AB with the association of his new club and taking into account the relevant statement of X, the Chamber established that a default interest payment of 5% p.a. as from 25 October 2005 must be applied to the due amount of EUR 41,665.
26. Furthermore, in line with the above, the intervening party, ZZ, is liable to reimburse to Y the amount of EUR 41,665.

III. DECISION OF THE DISPUTE RESOLUTION CHAMBER

1. The claim of X is partially accepted.
2. The club, Y, has to pay the amount of USD 41,665 to X within 30 days as from the date of notification of this decision.
3. On the aforementioned amount, a default interest payment of 5% p.a. is applied as from 25 October 2005 until the day of execution of the present decision.
4. Any further claims lodged by X are rejected.
5. In the event that the above-mentioned amount is not paid within the stated deadline, the present matter shall be submitted to FIFA's Disciplinary Committee, so that the necessary disciplinary sanctions may be imposed.
6. X is directed to inform Y directly and immediately of the account number to which the remittance is to be made and to notify the Dispute Resolution Chamber of every payment received.
7. The intervening party, ZZ, has to reimburse to Y the amount of USD 41,665 within 30 days as from the date of notification of this decision.
8. If the aforementioned sum is not paid within the aforementioned deadline, an interest rate of 5% per year will apply as of expiry of the fixed time limit and th present matter shall be submitted to FIFA's Disciplinary Committee, so that the necessary disciplinary sanctions may be imposed.
9. Y is directed to inform the intervening party, ZZ, directly and immediately of the account number to which the remittance is to be made and to notify the Dispute Resolution Chamber of every payment received.
10. According to art. 61 par. 1 of the FIFA Statutes this decision may be appealed before the Court of Arbitration for Sport (CAS). The statement of appeal must be sent to the CAS directly within 21 days of receiving notification of this decision and has to contain all elements in accordance with point 2 of the directives issued by the CAS, copy of which we enclose hereto. Within another 10 days following the expiry of the time limit for the filing of the statement of appeal, the appellant shall file with the CAS a brief stating the facts and legal arguments giving rise to the appeal (cf. point 4 of the directives).

961007
DECISION OF THE DISPUTE RESOLUTION CHAMBER
passed in Zurich, Switzerland, on 28 September 2006,
in the following composition:
Slim Aloulou (Tunisia), Chairman
Philippe Diallo (France), member
Essa M. Saleh Al-Housani (U.A.E.), member
Theo van Seggelen (the Netherlands), member
John Didulica (Australia), member
on the claim presented by the player X as Claimant
against the club Y as Respondent
regarding outstanding remuneration on the basis of an employment contract concluded between the parties

I. FACTS OF THE CASE

1. On 1 December 2003,the Claimant, and the Respondent signed an employment contract valid until 1 December 2004.
2. According to the above-mentioned employment contract the Respondent agreed to pay to the Claimant a signing-on fee amounting to 60,000,000 and a monthly salary amounting to 12,000,000. Equally, the said employment contract provided for housing facilities amounting to 1,500,000, food facilities amounting to 1,500,000, transportation amounting to 1,500,000, international airplane tickets amounting to 30,000,000 and health treatment authorized by the club's doctor.
3. On 4 February 2005, the parties signed another employment contract valid until the end of the competitions (without a concrete specification as to the date) for a total amount of 300,000,000 payable over the period of 12 months (75,000,000 to be paid at the beginning of the contract, 27,858,000 monthly to be paid during seven months and 30,000,000 to be paid by the end of the contract). Besides paying to the Claimant administration, housing, transportation and food facilities, the Respondent agreed to pay to the Claimant health treatment and therapy authorized by the club's doctor.
4. On 27 September 2005, the Claimant contacted FIFA explaining that the Respondent owes him for the season 2004, the amount of 63,000,000 (3,000,000 for two months of transportation, 3,000,000 for two months of food facilities, 3,000,000 for two months of housing facilities, 30,000,000 for an airplane ticket Indonesia-Brazil dated 19 August 2005 (copy of ticket provided) as well as 24,000,000 for the salaries for the months of October and November 2004).
5. Moreover, the Claimant stated that during the season 2005, on 10 August 2005, during a match against the club xxxxxx he got injured. However, the Respondent neither paid him the treatment nor the surgery.
6. As a result, the Claimant requests the amount of 63,000,000 with regard to the first season plus 10% of the value of the contract for the second season as compensation, i.e. the amount of 30,000,000. In total the Claimant request the amount of 93,000,000.
7. On 11 November 2005, the Claimant provided several receipts of medical treatment in xxxx and xxxxx as well as a breakdown indicating the incurred costs in the total amount of USD 4,218.
8. On 17 April 2006, the Football Association of Indonesia informed FIFA that its affiliate was willing to solve the present matter by paying to the Claimant the amount of 30,000,000 only and not the amount of 63,000,000 as claimed by the Claimant. With regard to the airplane ticket and the compensation amounting to 10% of the value of the contract for the 2005 season, the Respondent said that it is not its responsibility to reimburse any ticket to the Claimant nor to pay him any compensation.
9. The Claimant rejected the Respondent's proposal and again requested the amount of 63,000,000 for the season 2004, the amount of 30,000,000 as compensation for the breach of contract and the amount of USD 4,218 for the costs incurred to him related to his injury.
10. The Respondent did not provide any further statement, despite having been granted the opportunity to do so.
11. The Dispute Resolution Chamber is asked to pass a formal decision on the present matter.

II. CONSIDERATIONS OF THE DISPUTE RESOLUTION CHAMBER

1. First of all, the Chamber analysed whether it was competent to deal with the matter at stake. In this respect, it referred to art. 18 par. 2 and 3 of the Rules Governing the Procedures of the Players' '

Status Committee and the Dispute Resolution Chamber. The present matter was submitted to FIFA on 27 September 2005, as a consequence the Chamber concluded that the revised Rules Governing Procedures (edition 2005) on matters pending before the decision making bodies of FIFA are applicable on the matter at hand.

2. With regard to the competence of the Chamber, art. 3 par. 1 of the above-mentioned Rules states that the Dispute Resolution Chamber shall examine its jurisdiction in the light of articles 22 to 24 of the current version of the Regulations for the Status and Transfer of Players (edition 2005). In accordance with art. 24 par. 1 in connection with art. 22 (b) of the aforementioned Regulations, the Dispute Resolution Chamber shall adjudicate on employment-related disputes between a club and a player that have an international dimension.
3. As a consequence, the Dispute Resolution Chamber is the competent body to decide on the present litigation involving a club from xxx and a xxxx player regarding a claim in connection with an employment contract.
4. Subsequently, the members of the Chamber analyzed which edition of the Regulations for the Status and Transfer of Players should be applicable as to the substance of the matter. In this respect, the Chamber referred, on the one hand, to art. 26 par. 1 and 2 of the Regulations for the Status and Transfer of Players (edition 2005) and, on the other hand, to the fact that the relevant contracts at the basis of the present dispute were signed on 1 December 2003 and 4 February 2005 respectively and the claim was lodged at FIFA on 27 September 2005. In view of the aforementioned, the Chamber concluded that the current FIFA Regulations for the Status and Transfer of Players (edition 2005, hereafter: the Regulations) are applicable to the case at hand as to the substance.
5. In continuation, and entering into the substance of the matter, the members of the Chamber started by acknowledging that on 1 December 2003 the Claimant and the Respondent signed an employment contract. According to the said employment contract the Claimant was entitled to receive a signing-on fee amounting to 60,000,000 and a monthly salary of 12,000,000. Equally, the Claimant was entitled to receive housing facilities amounting to 1,500,000 per month, food facilities amounting to 1,500,000 per month, transportation amounting to 1,500,000 per month, international airplane tickets amounting to 30,000,000 and health treatment authorized by the club's doctor.
6. Moreover, the Chamber acknowledged that on 4 February 2005, the Claimant and the Respondent signed another employment contract valid until the end of the competitions for a total amount of 300,000,000 payable over the period of 12 months. In particular, the aforementioned amount had to be paid to the Claimant as follows: 75,000,000 at the start of the contract, 27,858,000 monthly during seven months and 30,000,000 by the end of the contract. Furthermore, the Respondent agreed to pay to the Claimant administration, housing, transportation and food facilities as well as health treatment and therapy authorized by the club's doctor.
7. In this respect, the Chamber duly noted that, with regard to the contract for the season 2004, i.e. the first contract signed between the parties, the Claimant claims the amount of 63,000,000. In particular, the Claimant is requesting the amount of 3,000,000 for two months of transportation, 3,000,000 for two months of food facilities, 3,000,000 for two months of housing facilities, 30,000,000 for an airplane ticket dated 19 August 2005 as well as 24,000,000 for the salaries for the months of October and November 2004.
8. As far as the contract for the season 2005 is concerned, the Chamber remarked that the Claimant explained that on 10 August 2005, during an official match of the Respondent against the club xxxxxx he got injured. In this respect, the Claimant stressed that the Respondent neither paid his treatment nor his surgery. Therefore, the Claimant requests 10% of the value of the second contract, i.e. the amount of 30,000,000, as compensation as well as the incurred medical costs in the total amount of USD 4,218.
9. Subsequently, the Chamber pointed out that the Respondent offered to pay to the Claimant the amount of 30,000,000 only and not 63,000,000 as claimed by the Claimant in order to settle the case at stake. With regard to the claimed sum for the airplane ticket and the compensation amounting to 10% of the value of the contract for the 2005 season, the Respondent explained that it is not its responsibility to reimburse any ticket to the Claimant nor to pay any compensation. The Respondent neither referred to the Claimant's injury nor to the costs incurred in this respect.
10. The Chamber started its deliberations by emphasising that it is undisputed that the Claimant rendered his services to the Respondent during the season 2004. As a result, the Chamber underlined that the Respondent is liable to cancel all allegedly outstanding amounts contractually agreed upon by the parties for the relevant season.

11. In this context, the Chamber considered that all outstanding amounts requested by the Claimant in connection with the season 2004 in the total amount of 63,000,000 are foreseen in the relevant employment contract signed by and between the parties to the present dispute on 1 December 2003.
12. Yet, the Chamber noted that the copy of the flight ticket presented by the player in order to corroborate his claim of 30,000,000 related to this specific position dates 19 August 2005 and thus concerned the 2005 and not the 2004 season. Furthermore, the deciding body acknowledged that the second employment contract concluded between the parties on 4 February 2005 for the 2005 season does not comprise an obligation for the Respondent to pay any flight tickets to the player. Finally, it was remarked that the Respondent maintains that it is not its responsibility to reimburse any flight ticket to the Claimant.
13. Under these considerations, the Chamber concluded that it could not award the claimed amount of 30,000,000 to the Claimant related to the costs for the flight ticket.
14. Moreover, the Chamber took into account that the Respondent proposed to pay the amount of 130,000,000 only. Yet, the Respondent did not provide any documentary evidence to corroborate that it had fulfilled its financial obligations towards the Claimant with regard to the remaining amount of 3,000,000 also requested by the Claimant, after deduction of 30,000,00 related to the flight ticket.
15. In view of the above, the Chamber emphasized that in accordance with the legal principle of the burden of proof, which is a basic principle in every legal system, a party deriving a right from an asserted fact has the obligation to prove the relevant fact (cf. art. 12 par. 3 of the Rules Governing the Procedures of the Players' ' Status Committee and the Dispute Resolution Chamber (DRC)).
Therefore, due to the lack of proof with regard the Respondent's allegations related to the fulfilment of its financial obligations towards the Claimant for the season 2004 and bearing in mind its considerations in connection with the flight ticket the Dispute Resolution Chamber decided that the Respondent has to pay to the Claimant the amount of 33,000,000 in connection with the employment contract for the season 2004.
16. Turning its attention to the Claimant's request with regard to the employment contract signed in February 2005, the Chamber took due note that the Claimant explained that on 10 August 2005, during an official match of the Respondent against the club xxxxx he got injured. Equally, the Claimant pointed out that the Respondent neither paid his treatment nor his surgery.
Therefore, the Claimant requests 10% of the value of the second employment contract as compensation, i.e. the amount of 30,000,000, as well as the refund of the incurred medical costs in a total amount of USD 4,218.
17. In this context, the Chamber referred to the general principle according to which it comes under the club's obligations to be responsible for its players in case of injury occurred during the validity and performance of the employment contract, especially if, like in the case at hand, the injury is caused during a match played by the player for his club in fulfilment of his contractual obligations. This principle is essential within the scope of the provisions related to the maintenance of contractual stability between professionals and clubs as contained in art. 13 et seq. of the Regulations. Any conclusion establishing the contrary would mean to prejudice the weaker contracting party (the employee). As a result to this principle, it is in particular the club's obligation to continue to pay the salaries of an injured player during the latter's inability to work. The Chamber underlined that this principle is somehow reflected in the contract for the season 2005, which provides that the Respondent shall pay to the Claimant health treatment and therapy authorized by the club's doctor.
18. In continuation, the Chamber took due note of the fact that once again the Respondent did not provide any kind of documentary evidence in order to corroborate its allegations related to the player's injury. The Respondent basically explained that is not its responsibility to pay any compensation at all to the Claimant. In particular, the Chamber reiterated that the Respondent did not submit any evidence at all in order to show that it fulfilled the contractual obligations towards the Claimant in particular, as from the latter's injury.
Moreover, the Chamber observed that the Respondent in its submissions did not even refer to the Claimant's injury and his claim in this respect.
19. In the light of the above, the Chamber stated that based on all documentation at its disposal it has to be concluded that the Respondent ceased to fulfil its contractual obligations without justification. As a result, the Chamber was of the opinion that the Respondent breached the employment contract signed with the Claimant for the season 2005 without just cause.

20. In continuation, the Chamber turned its attention to the consequences in connection with the breach of the employment contract and concluded that in accordance with art. 17 par. 1 of the Regulations the Respondent is liable to pay compensation to the Claimant for the breach of contract.
21. In this context, the Chamber considered that the Claimant requests the amount of 30,000,000 as compensation for the breach of contract as well as the reimbursement of the incurred medical costs in the total amount of USD 4,218.
22. The Chamber referred to art. 17 par. 1 of the Regulations, in particular to the non-exhaustive enumeration of objective criteria, and took into account the remuneration due to the Claimant under the employment contract singed between the parties to the present dispute for the season 2005, i.e. the amount of 300,000,000 as well as the time remaining on the said employment contract as from the Claimant's injury. Equally, the Chamber considered that the Claimant got injured during the validity and performance of the relevant employment contract and did not receive any financial support from the Respondent.
23. Furthermore, the Chamber reiterated that in the employment contract in question the Respondent had committed itself to pay health treatment and therapy to the Claimant.
24. In view of all of the above, the Dispute Resolution Chamber concluded that the claimed amount of compensation appears to be reasonable and justified.
Therefore, the Respondent is liable to pay to the Claimant the compensation claimed in the amount of 30,000,000. Equally, the Respondent shall refund the medical costs of USD 4,218 satisfactory corroborated with documentary evidence.
25. As a result, the Chamber unanimously decided that the Respondent must pay to the Claimant the total amount of 63,000,000 as well as USD 4,218.
26. Finally and for the sake of good order the Chamber emphasised that the contractual relationship between the parties to the present dispute has come to an end.

III. DECISION OF THE DISPUTE RESOLUTION CHAMBER

1. The claim lodged by the Claimant is partially accepted.
2. The Respondent, must pay to the Claimant the total amount of 63,000,000 as well as USD 4,218 within 30 days as from the date of notification of this decision.
3. Any further claim lodged by the Claimant is rejected.
4. If the aforementioned sum is not paid within the aforementioned deadline an interest rate of 5% per year will apply as of expiring of the fixed time limit and the present matter shall be submitted to FIFA's Disciplinary Committee, so that the necessary disciplinary sanctions may be imposed.
5. The Claimant is directed to inform the Respondent directly and immediately of the account number to which the remittance is to be made and to notify the Dispute Resolution Chamber of every payment received.
6. According to art. 61 par. 1 of the FIFA Statutes, this decision may be appealed against before the Court of Arbitration for Sport (CAS). The statement of appeal must be sent to the CAS directly within 21 days of receipt of notification of this decision and shall contain all the elements in accordance with point 2 of the directives issued by the CAS, a copy of which we enclose hereto. Within another 10 days following the expiry of the time limit for filing the statement of appeal, the appellant shall file a brief stating the facts and legal arguments giving rise to the appeal with the CAS (cf. point 4 of the directives).

961202B

DECISION OF THE DISPUTE RESOLUTION CHAMBER

passed in Zurich, Switzerland, on 28 September 2006,
in the following composition:
Slim Aloulou (Tunisia), Chairman
Theo van Seggelen (Netherlands), member
John Didulica (Australia), member
Philippe Diallo (France), member
Essa M. Saleh al-Housani (United Arab Emirates), member
on the claim presented by the club, X represented by Mr. , attorney at law as Claimant

against
the club, Y, as Respondent
regarding solidarity contribution relate d to the transfer of the player

I. FACTS OF THE CASE

1. The player, Z, was born on 19 July 1973.
2. According to the player passport provided by the Football Federation of X, the player in question was formerly registered with X on loan from 22 April 1996 until 6 August 1996.
3. On 22 September 2005, X lodged a claim in front of the Dispute Resolution Chamber (DRC) against Y for payment of its proportion of the solidarity contribution on the basis of Annex 5 of the Regulations for the Status and Transfer of Players.
4. According to X, the player was transferred from the club V to Y in July 2005 and according to press reports the relevant transfer compensation amounts to EUR 3,500,000.
5. X maintains that the player was registered with its club from 22 April 1996 until 31 December 1996, 8 months and 13 days and that therefore it is entitled to receive 6,64% of the 5% solidarity contribution on the basis of article 1 of Annex 5 of the said Regulations.
6. In reply to the claim, Y asserts that it is negotiating a payment plan via its agent and that it would not fail to pay the solidarity contribution to X as soon as the parties would have agreed on the amount, terms and payment plan.
7. To date, no solidarity contribution was paid by Y to X.
8. The Dispute Resolution Chamber is asked to decide on the amount of solidarity contribution payable by the Respondent to the Claimant, if any.

II. CONSIDERATIONS OF THE DISPUTE RESOLUTION CHAMBER

1. First of all, the Chamber analysed whether it was competent to deal with the matter at stake. In this respect, it referred to art. 18 par. 2 and 3 of the Rules Governing the Procedures of the Players' Status Committee and the Dispute Resolution Chamber. The present matter was formally submitted to FIFA on 22 September 2005, as a consequence the Chamber concluded that the revised Rules Governing Procedures (edition 2005) on matters pending before the decision making bodies of FIFA are applicable to the matter at hand.
2. With regard to the competence of the Chamber, art. 3 par. 1 of the above- mentioned Rules states that the Dispute Resolution Chamber shall examine its jurisdiction in the light of articles 22 to 24 of the current version of the Regulations for the Status and Transfer of Players (edition 2005). In accordance with art. 24 par. 1 in combination with art. 22 (d) of the aforementioned Regulations, the Dispute Resolution Chamber shall adjudicate on disputes related to solidarity mechanism between clubs belonging to different Associations.
3. As a consequence, the Dispute Resolution Chamber is the competent body to decide on the present litigation concerning the distribution of the solidarity contribution claimed by the Claimant in connection with the transfer of the professional Z to the Respondent.
4. Subsequently, the members of the Chamber analyzed which edition of the Regulations for the Status and Transfer of Players should be applicable as to the substance of the matter. In this respect, the Chamber referred to art. 26 par. 1 and 2 of the Regulations for the Status and Transfer of Players (edition 2005) in the modified version in accordance with the FIFA circular no. 995 dated 23 September 2005. Furthermore, it acknowledged that according to the Claimant the professional had been registered for his new club in July 2005. This allegation has not been contested either by the Respondent or the Football Association of X. Equally, the Chamber took note that the claim was lodged at FIFA on 22 September 2005. In view of the aforementioned, the Chamber concluded that the current FIFA Regulations for the Status and Transfer of Players (edition 2005, hereafter: the Regulations) are applicable to the case at hand as to the substance.
5. Once its competence and the applicable Regulations were thus established, the Chamber went on to deal with the substance of the case.
6. The members of the Chamber duly noted that the Claimant claims payment of solidarity contribution for part of the season of the player's 23rd birthday (the 1996 season) on the basis of the transfer of the player, Z, from V to the Respondent in the summer of 2005.
7. The Respondent, for its part, has stated that it is negotiating a payment plan in order to pay the solidarity contribution to the Claimant. The Chamber took particular note of the fact that the Respondent, however, has not contested the allegations of the Claimant in its claim.

8. Taking into consideration the circumstance that the player was registered with the Claimant on a loan basis, the members of the Chamber deemed it opportune to refer to art. 10 of the Regulations, in accordance with which the loan of a professional "is subject to the same rules as apply to the transfer of players, including the provisions on training compensation and solidarity mechanism."
9. Taking into account the above-mentioned elements, the Chamber agreed that the Claimant is entitled to receive solidarity contribution in accordance with art. 1 of Annex 5 of the Regulations.
10. Consequently, the Chamber proceeded with the calculation of the amount of solidarity contribution payable by the Respondent to the Claimant.
11. The Chamber emphasized that, as established in art. 21 and art. 1 of Annex 5 of the Regulations, the new club, to which a player is transferred during the course of an employment contract, is responsible for the distribution of 5% of the compensation paid to the player's former club to the club(s) involved in the training and education of the player over the years. In the case at hand, and taking into account the statement and findings under points I.4 and II.7 above, respectively, the relevant transfer compensation amounts to EUR 3,500,000.
12. The said art. 1 of Annex 5 of the Regulations further provides the figures for the distribution of the solidarity contribution taking into consideration the number of years (calculated pro rata if less than one year) that the player was registered with the club(s) involved in his training and education between the seasons of his 12th and 23rd birthdays .
13. In the present case, the Chamber noticed that as regards the player's registration period with the Claimant there is a discrepancy between the statement of the Claimant and the player passport presented by the Football Federation of X. The Claimant has failed to present documentary evidence in support of its allegation that the player has remained registered with the Claimant until 31 December 1996. Therefore, the members of the Chamber concurred that the relevant registration period must be established on the basis of the documentary evidence presented by the Football . Federation of X, i.e. the player passport. In this context and bearing in mind article 7 of the Regulations, the Chamber pointed out that such player passport commonly constitutes the main documentary evidence pertaining to the period of registration of a player with a club.
14. Consequently, the Chamber concluded that the calculation of the solidarity contribution in the case at hand is to be made on a pro rata basis of the season of the player's 23rd birthday taking into consideration the registration period as from 22 April 1996 until 6 August 1996. Therefore, the Chamber concluded that 2,5% of the 5% solidarity contribution shall be apportioned to the Claimant.
15. Having ascertained that the amount agreed upon by and between the Respondent and V for the transfer of the player Z is EUR 3,500,000, 2,5% of the 5% solidarity contribution amounts to EUR 4,375.
16. In light of the above, the Chamber decided that the Respondent is liable to pay to the Claimant the amount of EUR 4,375 as solidarity contribution.

III. DECISION OF THE DISPUTE RESOLUTION CHAMBER

1. The claim of the Claimant, X, is partially accepted.
2. The Respondent, Y, must pay the amount of EUR 4,375 to the Claimant within 30 days of notification of the present decision.
3. Any further claims of the Claimant are rejected.
4. In the event that the amount of EUR 4,375 is not paid within the stated deadline, an interest rate of 5% per year will apply as of expiry of the aforementioned deadline and the case will immediately be presented to the FIFA Disciplinary Committee.
5. The Claimant is directed to inform the Respondent immediately of the account number to which the remittance is to be made and to notify the Dispute Resolution Chamber of every payment received.
6. According to art. 61 par. 1 of the FIFA Statutes, this decision may be appealed against before the Court of Arbitration for Sport (CAS). The statement of appeal must be sent to the CAS directly within 21 days of receipt of notification of this decision and shall contain all the elements in accordance with point 2 of the directives issued by the CAS, a copy of which we enclose hereto. Within another 10 days following the expiry of the time limit for filing the statement of appeal, the appellant shall file a brief stating the facts and legal arguments giving rise to the appeal with the CAS (cf. point 4 of the directives).

26 OCTOBER 2006

106176
DECISION OF THE DISPUTE RESOLUTION CHAMBER
passed in Zurich, Switzerland, on 26 October 2006,
in the following composition:
Slim Aloulou (Tunisia), Chairman
Mario Gallavotti (Italy), Member
Peter Friend (Australia), Member
Gerardo Movilla (Spain), Member
Joaquim Evangelista (Portugal), Member
on the claim presented by the club, X as Claimant
against the player, Y as Respondent
regarding a dispute about
the employment contract concluded between the parties

I. FACTS OF THE CASE

1. On 12 August 2003 the Player Y, born on 8 January 1979, was transferred from the club Z to the club. A five-year employment contract dated 11 August 2003 and expiring on 30 June 2008 was entered into between the player and the club.
2. On 1 October 2004 a targeted drug test was held on Mr Y by the X Football Association On 11 October 2004 the results of the drug test on the player were declared positive.
3. On 28 October 2004 the club notified a termination letter to the player with immediate effect.
4. On 4 November 2004 the X Football Association's Disciplinary Commission imposed a seven-month ban on the player commencing on 25 October 2004.
   The FIFA Disciplinary Committee extended the sanction to have worldwide effect by decision dated 12 November 2004.
5. On 10 November 2004 the player appealed against X's decision to terminate the employment contract.
6. By joint letter dated 26 January 2005 the parties agreed to refer the dispute to the Appeals Committee.
7. By letter dated 4 February 2005 X informed FIFA about the course it intended to give the proceedings in the matter involving the player Y. In this correspondence, the club suggested that FIFA acknowledged the filing of the claim, opened proceedings and then adjourned them pending receipt of the decision of the APPEALS COMMITTEE.
8. In particular, X suggested that the Dispute Resolution Chamber should, at a later stage, determine the consequences in terms of sporting sanctions and/or compensation following the decision on the substance of the contractual dispute that the APPEALS COMMITTEE would take in the meantime.
9. To this effect, the club referred to Article 42 of the 2001 edition of the FIFA Regulations for the Status and Transfer of Players (hereafter, the 2001 Regulations) then in force, whereby the triggering elements of the dispute (i.e. whether a contract was breached, with or without just cause, or sporting just cause), will be decided by the Dispute Resolution Chamber or, if the parties have expressed a preference in a written agreement, or it is provided for by collective bargain agreement, by a national sports arbitration tribunal composed of members chosen in equal numbers by players and clubs, as well as an independent chairman. If the decision reached under the aforementioned conditions is that a contract has been breached without just cause or sporting just cause, the Dispute Resolution Chamber shall decide within 30 days whether sports sanctions or disciplinary measures shall be imposed.
10. On 20 April 2005 the APPEALS COMMITTEE established that Mr Y had committed breach of contract without just cause within the Protected Period against the club X.
11. On 29 April 2005 Mr Y lodged an appeal with the Court of Arbitration for Sport (CAS) against the APPEALS COMMITTEE's decision. On 15 December 2005 CAS rendered its decision by dismissing the player's appeal.
12. On 12 May 2006 the club X contacted FIFA seeking an award of compensation against Mr Y, following the aforementioned decisions and consistently with their claim dated 4 February 2005.

13. To this effect, the club was eager to emphasise that, following their original claim dated 4 February 2005, there can be no doubt that the regulations applicable to this dispute are the 2001 Regulations.
14. In particular, X requested that the Dispute Resolution Chamber establishes an amount of compensation in favour of the club, following the established breach of contract committed by the player without just cause within the Protected Period, in accordance with Article 42 of the 2001 Regulations.
15. X maintained in their position that the aforementioned Article clearly distinguishes, for jurisdictional purposes, between the "triggering elements" and the "remedies" stage of a claim. The earlier may be decided either by the Dispute Resolution Chamber or by a national football arbitration tribunal, whereas the latter must be exclusively decided by the Dispute Resolution Chamber.
16. Consequently, and due to the fact that neither the APPEALS COMMITTEE, nor CAS, had jurisdiction to award damages to compensate the club following the player's contractual breach, the Dispute Resolution Chamber is the only authority that has jurisdiction to impose the appropriate measures.
17. The player, Mr Y, essentially addressed the issue of the applicable regulations.
18. In this regard, the player maintained that the club's letter of 4 February 2005 cannot be considered as a formal claim since it does not comply with the requirements of a claim, it does not establish any right of the club. Consequently, the procedure started on 12 May 2006, and referred to as "Application for an award of compensation" by X is to be considered as a completely new procedure and as the only one pending before FIFA.
19. In consequence, the FIFA Regulations for the Status and Transfer of Players of 2005 (hereafter, the Regulations) apply to this claim.
20. In particular, the player was eager to emphasise that, by letter dated 4 February 2005, the club only explained its self-constructed "two stages of the club's contractual claim" and proposed FIFA to acknowledge and endorse that uncommon course of procedure. The terminology used in that correspondence indicates the informative and suggestive nature of the letter.
21. The player further pointed out that the fact that X calls this document, i.e. the letter dated 4 February 2005, a claim does not change its legal nature. The way a party calls a document is irrelevant; it is only the contents and the substance of the document that establishes its legal nature. The letter of 4 February 2005 is not a claim.
22. According to Mr Y, the letter of 4 February 2005 does not comply with one single requirement of a formal claim and instead suggests the most convenient procedural path for the club (cf. the title "Proposed procedural course"). Notifying the intention to lodge a claim at a later stage before the Dispute Resolution Chamber is not sufficient to open a procedure before this body.
23. Furthermore, the proposed procedural path envisaged by the club does not respect the procedural rules and it is completely unknown by the FIFA proceedings. In fact, the FIFA procedure does not provide anywhere for the possibility to lodge a claim before the Dispute Resolution Chamber and ask for the adjournment of the proceedings pending the outcome of the decision to be reached by a national instance.
24. Since the procedure suggested by the club is neither established in the regulations nor in the procedural rules, nor has FIFA at any moment confirmed the conformity of such way of proceeding, the letter of 4 February 2005 has clearly a strict and exclusive informative character and nothing more. In particular it does not create any entitlement for the club to proceed as it has itself suggested.
25. The player further stated that the rule that applies to this dispute is clearly indicated under Article 22 lit. b) of the Regulations, whereby the competence of the Dispute Resolution Chamber is given unless an independent arbitration tribunal has been established at national level within the framework of the Association. This tribunal is compelled to decide on the entire matter, i.e. on the substance of the alleged breach and its consequences. Splitting the matter into two, i.e. the national arbitration tribunal establishing the breach of contract and the Dispute Resolution Chamber deciding on the consequences, is neither provided for by the Regulations nor by the procedural rules.
26. As a result, once the parties have agreed to refer the dispute to a national sports arbitration tribunal, this body will be required to decide on the entire matter. In the case at stake, the parties have agreed by joint letter dated 26 January 2005 to refer the dispute to the APPEALS COMMITTEE. As a result, the Dispute Resolution Chamber is unable to consider the claim lodged by X.
27. In the remote event that the 2001 Regulations applied to the matter, the Dispute Resolution Chamber would be anyway unable to consider any partial claim, which is the result of an existing decision passed by a different deciding body, like the claim at stake.

28. The player finally observed that the APPEALS COMMITTEE P, is not an arbitration tribunal as requested by the Regulations of both 2001 and 2005.
Any decision taken by this body is not an arbitral award. The procedure and the subsequent decision of APPEALS COMMITTEE are consequently not in conformity with the requirements of Art. 22 lit. b) of the Regulations as well as Art. 42 lit. b (i) of the 2001 Regulations and FIFA is hence not bound to it.
29. Since the decision of APPEALS COMMITTEE are final and binding and the CAS is not provided for as the body of appeal, the procedure before CAS is to be considered as an ad-hoc arbitration. It is not in conformity with the FIFA regulations to refer the dispute regarding the responsibilities for the breach of contract to CAS in an ad-hoc procedure and seize afterwards the Dispute Resolution Chamber in order to establish the financial compensation.
30. Mr Y concluded that, for all the reasons mentioned above, the Dispute Resolution Chamber is unable to consider the case and the claim shall not be entered into the substance.
31. In case the above was rejected, the player asked the Dispute Resolution Chamber to grant him a new deadline of four weeks for him to complete the considerations related to the quantification of the compensation due for breach of contract.
32. In response to the player's position, X reiterate that, when the claim was filed, i.e. on 4 February 2005, in force were the 2001 Regulations, which permitted the parties to agree that a domestic sports arbitration tribunal would determine the substance of the breach of contract, but reserved exclusive jurisdiction to the Dispute Resolution Chamber with respect to the applicable measures. This circumstance is further confirmed by the FIFA Circular Letter no. 769 dated 24 August 2001.
33. X further pointed out that the joint letter dated 26 January 2005 by means of which the parties agreed upon the course of the proceedings, is in full compliance with the aforementioned principles and the player never objected to it.
34. The club further maintained that the original claim dated 4 February 2005 was a proper and complete complaint ("in order formally to submit part of the club's contractual claim against the player to the Dispute Resolution Chamber") and fully consistent with the course of proceedings that the parties had agreed upon.
35. Furthermore, according to the club, the fact that FIFA never wrote back to dispute any respect of the club's claim should not be seen as FIFA's suggestion that the course of action was inappropriate. On the contrary, had FIFA intended to raise any objection with respect to the club's claim, it would have explicitly done so.
36. Also, the APPEALS COMMITTEE acknowledged that, when judging the triggering elements of the dispute at stake, it was sitting in loco of the Dispute Resolution Chamber, which fully justified the appeal lodged by the player before CAS. The APPEALS COMMITTEE is indeed a court of arbitration, whose features are in full compliance with Article 42 of the 2001 Regulations.
37. Both the APPEALS COMMITTEE and CAS decided the case on the grounds that they could only consider the triggering elements of the dispute, whereas the Dispute Resolution Chamber would have considered taking the appropriate measures at a later stage.
38. The club finally observed that, even if the Regulations of 2005 applied, quod non, the conclusion would be the same, as under Article 22 lit. b), similar to Article 42 of the 2001 Regulations, the Dispute Resolution Chamber continues to be competent to decide the remaining issues not resolved by the domestic arbitration tribunal.
39. In conclusion, X asked the Dispute Resolution Chamber to declare itself competent to deal with this dispute, and decide an amount of compensation in favour of the club, following the established breach of contract committed by the player without just cause within the Protected Period, in accordance with Articles 22 and 42 of the 2001 Regulations.
40. The player fully confirmed his initial position and requested the Dispute Resolution Chamber not to enter into the substance of the case or, in case their request was rejected, to grant him a new deadline of four weeks for him to complete the considerations related to the assessment of the compensation due for breach of contract.
41. The Dispute Resolution Chamber is asked to establish the regulations applicable to the case at stake and to decide whether or not to consider the substance.

II. CONSIDERATIONS OF THE DISPUTE RESOLUTION CHAMBER

1. First of all, and before considering the substance of the matter, the Dispute Resolution Chamber analysed whether it had jurisdiction to deal with the matter at stake and, on account of the parties'

respective positions, it emphasised that particular relevance had to be given to the question of the applicable regulations.

2. In this respect, the Chamber acknowledged that, by letter dated 4 February 2005, X informed FIFA about the course it intended to give the proceedings in the dispute opposing the club to the player Y. In this correspondence, the club suggested that FIFA acknowledged the filing of the claim, opened proceedings and then adjourned them pending receipt of the decision of the APPEALS COMMITTEE.
3. These submissions, referred to as "Application for an award of compensation", were filed "in order formally to submit part of the club's contractual claim against the player to the Dispute Resolution Chamber".
4. In this regard the Chamber deemed that, irrespective of any preliminary evaluation with respect to the relevant contents, by means of the aforementioned submission dated 4 February 2005 X unambiguously expressed their intention to lodge with FIFA, namely to the Dispute Resolution Chamber, though partly, a claim and the relevant proceedings concerning the dispute with the player.
5. According to the Chamber the above circumstances cannot be discounted and, therefore, the date of 4 February 2005 shall be regarded as the date on which X lodged their claim.
6. In continuation, the Chamber referred to Article 18 § 2 and § 3 of the Rules Governing the Procedures of the Players' Status Committee and the Dispute Resolution Chamber. As established earlier, this matter has to be considered as having been submitted to FIFA on 4 February 2005, as a consequence the Chamber concluded that the previous Procedural Rules (edition 2001) on matters pending before the decision making bodies of FIFA apply to the matter at hand.
7. Once the applicable regulations in respect of the proceedings were established, the Dispute Resolution Chamber focussed its attention on the contents of the club's submissions dated 4 February 2005 and referred to as "Application for an award of compensation".
8. In particular, the Chamber analysed X's claim in combination with Article 42 of the applicable 2001 Regulations, whereby the triggering elements of the dispute (i.e. whether a contract was breached, with or without just cause, or sporting just cause), will be decided by the Dispute Resolution Chamber or, if the parties have expressed a preference in a written agreement, or it is provided for by collective bargain agreement, by a national sports arbitration tribunal composed of members chosen in equal numbers by players and clubs, as well as an independent chairman. If the decision reached under the aforementioned conditions is that a contract has been breached without just cause or sporting just cause, the Dispute Resolution Chamber shall decide whether sports sanctions or disciplinary measures shall be imposed.
9. To this effect, the deciding body took note of the club's request that the Dispute Resolution Chamber only establish an amount of compensation in its favour, on the grounds of the aforementioned Article 42, in particular its paragraph 1 (b) (ii), and consistently with the course of the proceedings at stake, whereby X and Mr Y expressly agreed in writing to refer their dispute to the APPEALS COMMITTEE, which, on 20 April 2005, reached in favour of the club a decision, which was then confirmed by CAS on 15 December 2005.
10. In light of the above-mentioned facts, the members of the Chamber deeply considered the contents of Article 42 of the 2001 Regulations and firstly pointed out that, in spite of the wording of the provision, it was never the intention of the F'A' s legislator to split the jurisdiction on international football-related disputes between external (national) decision-making bodies and the Dispute Resolution Chamber.
11. The Chamber maintained that the above-mentioned interpretation would be contrary to the long-standing jurisprudence of the Chamber itself, whereby there can be found no trace of a decision distinguishing, for jurisdictional purposes, between the "triggering elements" and the "remedies" stage of a claim lodged with FIFA.
12. More crucially, it is imperative to emphasise that the football governing body launched its decision-making bodies in order to offer fair and qualified dispute resolution facilities in worldwide football-related disputes provided they have an international dimension. At the same time FIFA established that, under certain strict conditions, national sports arbitration tribunals may have jurisdiction to pass decisions on international football-related litigations.
13. The purpose of such a policy was to help enhance the level of dispute resolution remedies also at national level, and certainly not to have a hybrid solution between the FIFA's and the national decision-making bodies.

14. A football-related dispute, it was observed, is a multifaceted matter, whereby the stage of the cognition and that of the assessment of the specific consequences are inextricably interconnected trough a logical link. It is therefore of utmost importance that the implementation of a decision, including in particular the fixing of its consequences, is consistent with the facts that led to that decision. Incidentally, the Chamber observed that no such jurisdictional solution is envisaged in any of the civil law countries.
15. As a matter of fact, referring the substance of the litigation to a national sports arbitration tribunal and the assessment of the specific consequences as well as the implementation of the relevant decision to the Dispute Resolution Chamber does not help maintain the legal stability within the world of football.
16. The Dispute Resolution Chamber is anyhow by its own nature unable to consider any partial claim, which is the result of an existing decision passed by a different deciding body, like the claim at stake.
17. In other words, this Chamber can count on an enduring jurisdictional tradition in international football-related disputes and cannot confine itself to grant the exequatur to a decision passed by a different (national) body.
18. As a result it was emphasised that, following a teleological rather than a semantic interpretation of the relevant provisions, in compliance with the general legal principle whereby electa una via non datur recursus ad alteram, once the parties have agreed to refer their dispute to a certain decision-making body, this authority will be held to decide on the entire matter.
19. In the matter at stake, the parties have agreed in writing to refer the dispute to the APPEALS COMMITTEE, which therefore appears to be the body competent to decide every aspect of the dispute.
20. As a consequence, the Dispute Resolution Chamber is unable consider the claim lodged by X for an award of compensation following the decision reached by the APPEALS COMMITTEE and confirmed by CAS.
21. In conclusion, the Dispute Resolution Chamber decided that it does not have jurisdiction to pass a decision in the dispute between the club, X, and the player, Mr Y.

III. DECISION OF THE DISPUTE RESOLUTION CHAMBER

1. The claim of the club, X, is not admissible.
2. According to art. 61 par. 1 of the FIFA Statutes, this decision may be appealed against before the Court of Arbitration for Sport (CAS). The statement of appeal must be sent to the CAS directly within 21 days of receipt of notification of this decision and shall contain all the elements in accordance with point 2 of the directives issued by the CAS, a copy of which we enclose hereto. Within another 10 days following the expiry of the time limit for filing the statement of appeal, the appellant shall file a brief stating the facts and legal arguments giving rise to the appeal with the CAS (cf. point 4 of the directives).

⚽⚽⚽

106399
DÉCISION DE LA CHAMBRE DE RÉSOLUTION DES LITIGES
ayant siégé le 26 octobre 2006, à Zurich, Suisse
dans la composition suivante:
Slim Aloulou (Tunisie), Président
Gerardo Movilla (Espagne), membre
Joaquim Evangelista (Portugal), membre
Mario Gallavotti (Italie), membre
Peter Friend (Australie), membre
au sujet d'une plainte soumise par le
Joueur A, le demandeur
à l'encontre du Club B, le défendeur
concernant un litige contractuel survenu entre le demandeur et le défendeur.
le demandeur et le défendeur.

I. EN FAIT

1. Le 7 décembre 2003, le joueur A (ci-après ; le joueur) et le club B (ci-après ; le club) ont conclu un contrat de travail valide du 1 janvier au 30 juin 2004 et stipulant un salaire mensuel de $ 12 000.
2. Le 23 janvier 2006, le joueur a adressé une demande contre le club à la FIFA, parce que seul un mois de salaire lui avait été payé par le club.
3. Par conséquent, le joueur demande cinq mois de salaire pour le montant total de $ 60 000 de la part du club.
4. En support de sa demande, le joueur a présenté à la FIFA une lettre signée par le Directeur Général du club et datée du 21 janvier 2005, confirmant que le montant de $ 60 000 est toujours dû, et statuant que ce montant sera payé en cinq mensualités de $ 12 000, le 31 de chaque mois dès le 31 janvier 2005.
5. Le 14 juin 2006, le club a fait parvenir à la FIFA sa réponse à l'égard de la demande. Cette réponse est signée par le Directeur Général ayant signé aussi la lettre datée du 21 janvier 2005 présentée par le joueur.
6. Premièrement, le club a mentionné que le contrat de travail est contestable, puisque le Président de l'époque l'avait signé individuellement, alors que selon le registre officiel du commerce, le pouvoir de signature du Président était « collective à deux ».
7. En outre, le club a mentionné qu'aucune visite médicale n'avait été effectuée avec le joueur avant la conclusion du contrat. Ensuite, le joueur s'était blessé lors du premier match avec le club, et l'assureur du club avait refusé de prendre en charge l'incapacité de travail du joueur, argumentant avec des certificats médicaux à l'appui que le joueur était blessé déjà avant d'avoir signé le contrat avec le club.
8. Selon le club, le joueur avait refusé toute visite médicale et donc caché l'état de sa santé avant la signature du contrat de travail. Dès lors, le club était dans une erreur essentielle lors de la conclusion du contrat, ou même induit à contracter par un dol.
9. Finalement, le club a allégué qu'un accord avait été trouvé avec le joueur dans cette affaire, et à l'appui de cette allégation, a présenté la copie d'une facture sur le montant de $ 30,000 en faveur du joueur, adressé par un cabinet de conseil au club en date du 18 décembre 2005, concernant le « dossier joueur A » et portant la référence « selon convention tél. du 15.12.05, « honoraires » dus au 23.12.2005 ». Cette facture ne porte pas la signature du joueur.

II. CONSIDÉRANTS DE LA CHAMBRE DE RÉSOLUTION DES LITIGES

1. En premier lieu, la Chambre de Résolution des Litiges a analysé si sa compétence à traiter le présent litige était donnée. A cet égard, la Chambre s'est référée à l'article 18 alinéa 2 et 3 du Règlement de la Commission du Statut du Joueur et de la Chambre de Résolution des]Litiges. Le présent litige a été soumis à la FIFA le 23 janvier 2006.
   Par conséquent et en application de ce Règlement, la Chambre de Résolution des Litiges a conclus que le Règlement de la Commission du Statut du Joueur et de la Chambre de Résolution des Litiges (édition 2005), réglementation procédurale révisée, est applicable au présent litige.
2. En relation avec la compétence de la Chambre de Résolution des Litiges, l'article 3 alinéa 1 du Règlement susmentionné dispose que cette Chambre vérifie sa compétence en vertu des articles 22 à 24 de l'actuel Règlement du Statut et du Transfert des Joueurs (édition 2005) (ci-après: le Règlement). En application de l'article 24 alinéa 1 du Règlement, en relation avec l'article 22 litera b de ce même Règlement, la Chambre de Résolution des Litiges tranchera des litiges relatifs à la relation c contractuelle de travail entre un club et un joueur, qui présentent des éléments internationaux.
3. Par conséquent, la Chambre de Résolution des Litiges conclut qu'elle est l'organe décisionnel compétent pour trancher sur le présent cas opposant un club à un joueur avec des nationalités differents au sujet d'un litige relatif à la relation contractuelle de travail entre les parties.
4. Par la suite, la Chambre a analysé quelle édition du Règlement du Statut et du Transfert des Joueurs devrait être appliquée quant au droit matériel. A cet égard, la Chambre s'est référée, d'une part, à l'article 26 alinéa 1 et 2 du Règlement du Statut et du Transfert des Joueurs (édition 2005) et, d'autre part sur le fait que le contrat de travail objet du litige a été signé le 7 décembre 2003 et que la plainte a été déposée auprès de la FIFA le 23 janvier 2006.
   Au vu de ce qui précède, la Chambre a conclus que l'actuel Règlement du Statut et du Transfert des Joueurs (édition 2005) est applicable au présent litige quant au droit matériel.

5. Entrant dans la substance de l'affaire, la Chambre de Résolution des]Litiges a pris note des positions des parties et de la documentation contenue dans le dossier et, au vu des faits présentés, s'est concentrée sur les questions suivantes:
   1) Est-ce que le contrat de travail entre le joueur et le club a-t-il-été conclu validement ?
   2) Est-ce que des montants sont restés impayés par le club envers le joueur?
6. En ce qui concerne la première question, la Chambre a tout d'abord pris connaissance du fait que le joueur n'a exprimé aucun doute sur la validité du contrat de travail en question. Par contre, la Chambre a pris connaissance des deux arguments invoqués par le club selon lesquels le contrat ne devrait pas être considéré comme conclu validement, soit parce que a) le Président de l'époque avait signé le contrat de travail individuellement, alors que selon le registre officiel du commerce, le pouvoir de signature du Président était « collective à deux », et b) qu'aucune visite médicale n'avait été effectuée avec le joueur avant la conclusion du contrat. La Chambre a donc procédé à analyser ces deux arguments du club.
7. Concernant le pouvoir de signature du Président qui a signé le contrat de travail en question, la Chambre a déclaré que la question est de savoir si le contrat de travail du 7 décembre 2003, signé par le Président du club, est conclu validement, bien que le Président du club, selon le registre officiel du commerce, ne bénéficiait pas de la signature individuelle.
8. A cet égard, la Chambre a statué que, comme règle générale, si un tiers peut légitimement croire qu'un représentant agit au nom et pour le compte d'une autre personne, et qu'il existe des circonstances autorisant le tiers à raisonnablement et de bonne foi déduire des circonstances qu'à ce moment il existait un rapport de représentation ressortant des circonstances, cela constitue un rapport de représentation , avec la conséquence que la personne représentée est lié envers le tiers par les actes du représentant.
9. A l'égard du cas présent, la Chambre a statué que le fait que l'individu qui a agi pour le club en signant le contrat de travail en question détenait la fonction de Président du club, est un indice important pour le joueur de pouvoir légitimement croire que le Président du club était autorisé et avait les pouvoirs de représenter individuellement le club.
10. Le fait que selon le registre officiel du commerce, le Président n'avait pas bénéficié de la signature individuelle pour le club ne change pas la conclusion susmentionnée. Au vu des indices clairs, à la suite desquels le joueur pouvait raisonnablement et de bonne foi croire que le Président avait le pouvoir de signer individuellement pour le club.
11. Par conséquent, la Chambre a statué que le contrat de travail en question crée des obligations pour le club.
12. En outre, la Chambre a statué aussi que même si la conclusion ne susmentionnée était douteuse, ce qu'elle n'est pas dans le cas présent, le fait que le joueur a fait parti de l'équipe lors du premier match officiel du club en 2004 confirme que c'était l'intention du club de contracter avec le joueur, et que donc le contrat de travail était conclu validement et à quoiqu'il en soit été ratifié par la suite par le club.
13. Ensuite, en ce qui concerne l'allégation du club qu'aucune visite médicale n'avait été effectuée avec le joueur avant la conclusion du contrat, la Chambre a statué premièrement que cette allégation n'était pas prouvée par des preuves fournies par le club. Par conséquent, et en application du principe du fardeau de la preuve, qui est un principe de droit applicable, et selon lequel chaque partie doit prouver les faits qu'elle allègue pour en déduire son droit, cette allégation avancée par le club doit être rejetée.
14. En plus, selon la Chambre, comme règle générale, le manquement d'une visite médicale avant la conclusion d'un contrat de travail n'est dans aucun cas un manquement reprochable au joueur. Même si un joueur refuse une visite médicale et donc cache l'état de sa santé avant la signature du contrat de travail, la conclusion valide du contrat de travail, comme règle générale, n'est pas en question puisque le club n'est pas forcé de signer un contrat avec un joueur qui s'oppose à la visite médicale. Le club, au contraire, aurait la possibilité de ne pas entrer dans un contrat avec un joueur si le dernier ne coopère pas à l'égard de la visite médicale.
15. Le principe susmentionné est aussi confirmé par l'article 18 alinéa 4 du Règlement, selon lequel la validité d'un contrat de travail ne peut pas dépendre du résultat positif d'un examen médical.
16. Dans le cas présent, la Chambre a statué que le manquement allégué d'une visite médicale avant la conclusion du contrat de travail en question n'est pas reprochable au joueur. Même si une visite

médicale n'avait pas lieu avant la conclusion, ce qui est une allégation non prouvée du club, le contrat de travail entre le joueur et le club était validement conclu dans le cas présent.

17. En plus, la Chambre a maintenu que le club ne pouvait pas être dans une erreur essentielle au moment de la conclusion du contrat ou induite à contracter par un dol, puisque cela impliquerait que le joueur aurait activement caché l'état de sa santé. Dans le cas présent, pourtant, le joueur n'a pas activement caché l'état de sa santé, mais, selon les allégations du club, s'est seulement opposé à une visite médicale.
18. En conclusion, un contrat de travail a validement été conclu entre le joueur et le club.
19. Ensuite, la Chambre a constaté que le joueur, selon ce contrat de travail, avait droit a un salaire mensuel de $ 12 000, payable de janvier à juin 2004.
    Selon le joueur, seulement un mois de salaire avait été payé, donc cinq mois restaient dus, soit un montant total de $ 60 000.
20. Le club n'a jamais contesté que ce montant n'a pas été payé au joueur endéans les délais d'échéance. Cela est confirmé par la lettre du club daté du 21 janvier 2005, laquelle confirme que le montant de $ 60 000 est toujours dû au joueur. Pourtant, le club a présenté la copie d'une facture sur le montant de $ 30 000, adressé par un cabinet de conseil au club en date du 18 décembre 2005, concernant le « dossier joueur A » et portant la référence « selon convention tél. du 15.12.05, « honoraires » dûs au 23.12.2005 ».
21. Après avoir analysé ce document, la Chambre a conclu que rien n'indique sur ce document que les $ 30 000 étaient payé par le club au joueur au titre des salaires impayés. Le paiement d'une partie de la dette salariale du club envers le joueur n'est pas prouvé par le document concerné.
22. Au vu du susmentionné, la Chambre a conclu que le club n'a pas prouvé que le montant dû a été payé au joueur. Par conséquent, la Chambre a décidé que le club doit payer au joueur le montant de $ 60 000.

III. DÉCISION DE LA CHAMBRE DE RÉSOLUTION DES LITIGES

1. La demande du joueur A est admise.
2. Le club B doit payer au joueur A le montant de $ 60 000.
3. La somme due doit être payée par le club B dans les prochains 30 jours courants à compter de la date de notification de la présente décision.
4. Dans le cas où la somme due n'est pas payée dans le délai imparti, des intérêts à hauteur de 5% par année seront appliqués et ce à partir de l'échéance du délai imparti.
5. Dans le cas où la somme due n'est pas payée dans le délai imparti, le cas sera transmis à la Commission de Discipline de la FIFA, qui pourra infliger les sanctions disciplinaires nécessaires.
6. Le joueur A s'engage à communiquer au club B le numéro de compte bancaire auquel le joueur devra verser la somme allouée. De même, le joueur A s'engage à informer la Chambre de Résolution des Litiges sur les paiements effectués par le joueur.
7. Selon l'article 61 alinéa 1 des Statuts de la FIFA, cette décision peut fairel'objet d'un appel devant le Tribunal Arbitral du Sport (TAS). La déclaratio d'appel doit être soumise directement au TAS dans les 21 jours après notification de cette décision et doit contenir tous les éléments conformément au point 2 des directives émises par le TAS, dont copie est annexée. Dans les dix jours suivant l'expiration du délai d'appel, l'appelant doit soumettre au TAS un mémoire contenant une description des faits et des moyens de droit fondant l'appel (cf. point 4 des directives).

106419

DECISION OF THE DISPUTE RESOLUTION CHAMBER

passed in Zurich, Switzerland, on 26 October 2006, in the following composition:
in the following composition:
Slim Aloulou (Tunisia), Chairman
Gerardo Movilla (Spain), member
Joaquim Evangelista (Portugal), member
Mario Gallavotti (Italy), member
Peter Friend (Australia), member
on the claim presented by the club A, X, as Claimant

against the club B, Y as Respondent
regarding a solidarity mechanism dispute in connection with the transfer of the player C.

I. FACTS OF THE CASE

1. According to a written statement of the football association of the country X the player C, born on 20 May 1981, was registered for the club A from the country X, the Claimant, from 4 December 1999 to 3 March 2000 and from 8 May to 31 December 2002, from the age of 18 to the age of 19, respectively from the age of 20 to the age of 21, always as a professional player.
2. According to the copy of the International Transfer Certificate submitted by the football association of the country Y, the player was transferred internationally from the club D of the country X to the football association of the country Y on 29 July 2004.
3. On 28 July 2004, the company E of the country X and the alleged holder of the "federative rights" to the player in question and the club B of the country Y, the Respondent, concluded an agreement for the transfer of the player C. This aforementioned contract does not mention a transfer compensation. According to clause 6 of the said contract, E will be responsible to pay the relevant 5% of solidarity contribution.
4. On 10 February 2005, the Claimant contacted FIFA and demanded 8,33% of the 5% regarding the contribution to the solidarity mechanism.
5. In reply hereto, the Respondent rejected the claim. It maintained that according to the above-mentioned agreement E is responsible to pay the relevant solidarity contribution.
6. In the following, the Claimant insisted on receiving the relevant payment from the Respondent and asserted that the latter paid for the transfer of the player concerned the amount of USD 700,000.
7. Upon FIFA's request, the Respondent informed that it paid the amount of USD 325,000 as transfer compensation and 5% solidarity contribution to Mr F, who acts on behalf of E, providing a copy of the relevant payment order of the club to Mr F (note: drafted in language of country Y). The Respondent insisted that the aforementioned company is liable for the payment regarding the contribution to the solidarity mechanism.
8. In continuation, FIFA asked the Respondent to present a translation of the aforementioned payment order into one of the four official FIFA languages, without success.
9. Instead of a translation of the above-mentioned payment order, the Respondent presented a further position regarding the present matter.
   According to the Respondent, the claim has to be rejected because the player was registered with the Claimant on the basis of a loan. Furthermore, it asserted that in the case that FIFA decides that solidarity contribution is due, the calculation of such must follow on the basis of the compensation of USD 18,000, the amount the player paid to his former club D at the end of his employment.
   As a consequence to the aforementioned, the possible solidarity contribution would be 5% of USD 18,000 = USD 900, payable in 10 instalments.
10. In reply hereto, the Claimant maintained that the Respondent admitted having paid USD 325,000 for the transfer of the player. Therefore, the Claimant demanded that the amount of USD 16,250 (5%) should be distributed as solidarity mechanism. The Claimant finally added that considering that the player spent 11 months with the Claimant, it is entitled to receive 9,163%, i.e. USD 1,488.98.
11. The Respondent did not present a final statement.
12. Upon FIFA's request, the football association of the country X informed on 10 October 2006 that the employment contract concluded between the club D, i.e. the player's last club before his transfer to Y, and the player in question has been terminated on 12 August 2004 upon a Labour Court's decision.

II. CONSIDERATIONS OF THE DISPUTE RESOLUTION CHAMBER

1. First of all, the Dispute Resolution Chamber (DRC) analysed whether it was competent to deal with the matter at stake. In this respect, it referred to art. 18 par. 2 and 3 of the Rules Governing the Procedures of the Players' ' Status Committee and the Dispute Resolution Chamber. The present matter was submitted to FIFA on 10 February 2005, as a consequence the Chamber concluded that the previous Procedural Rules (edition 2001) on matters pending before the decision making bodies of FIFA are applicable on the matter at hand.
2. With regard to the competence of the Chamber, art. 25 par. 2 of the FIFA Regulations for the Status and Transfer of Players (edition 2001) establishes that, it falls within the purview of the Dispute Resolution Chamber to review disputes concerning the distribution of the solidarity contribution.

3. As a consequence, the Dispute Resolution Chamber is the competent body to decide on the present litigation concerning the distribution of the solidarity contribution claimed by the Claimant in connection with the transfer of the professional C.
4. Subsequently, the members of the Chamber analyzed which edition of the Regulations for the Status and Transfer of Players should be applicable as to the substance of the matter. In this respect, the Chamber referred to art. 26 par. 1 and 2 of the Regulations for the Status and Transfer of Players (edition 2005) in the modified version in accordance with the FIFA circular no. 995 dated 23 September 2005.
   Furthermore, it acknowledged that the professional had been registered for his new club on 29 July 2004.
   Equally the Chamber took note that the claim was lodged at FIFA on 10 February 2005.
   In view of the aforementioned, the Chamber concluded that the former FIFA Regulations for the Status and Transfer of Players (edition 2001, hereafter: the Regulations) are applicable on the case at hand as to the substance.
5. In continuation, and entering into the substance of the matter, the members of the Chamber started by acknowledging the above-mentioned facts as well as all the further documentation contained in the file.
6. In this respect, the Chamber duly noted that, on the one hand, the Claimant asserts being entitled to receive at least 9.163% of solidarity contribution in connection with the transfer of the player to the Respondent.
7. On the other hand, the Chamber observed that the Respondent is convinced that since it paid the amount of USD 325,000 as transfer compensation to the company E and since in accordance with the transfer agreement of 28 July 2004 concluded with the aforementioned company, the latter would be responsible for the payment of any further compensation to any possible party in connection with solidarity contribution. Furthermore, the Chamber took note that the Respondent is of the opinion that solidarity contribution is not due in case the player was registered with the relevant training club on a loan basis only. Finally, the DRC acknowledged that the Respondent asserts that in case the Chamber decides contrary to its position, the possible solidarity contribution has to be calculated on the basis of the compensation which the player paid to his former club D at the end of his employment and therefore the relevant amount would be USD 900.
8. In consideration of these positions, the Chamber referred to its well-established jurisprudence applied in similar cases, in accordance with which the player's new club is ordered to remit the relevant proportion(s) of the 5% solidarity contribution to the club(s) involved in the player's training in strict application of art. 11 of the Regulations governing the Application of the Regulations. At the same time, the player's former club is ordered to reimburse the same proportion(s) of the 5% of the compensation that it received from the player's new club.
9. In addition to the above-mentioned jurisprudence, the Chamber emphasised that in accordance with the ratio legis of the above-mentioned Regulations, the said jurisprudence applies independently of the fact if the new club paid the transfer compensation to the player's former club or to a company. In particular, the DRC stressed that the requirement which triggers the above- mentioned application of the said jurisprudence, is the fact that a transfer compensation has been paid in connection with the international transfer of the player concerned. Finally, the Chamber deemed that every contrary interpretation of the Regulations would violate the ratio legis of the above- mentioned Regulations.
10. Subsequently, the Dispute Resolution Chamber acknowledging that, as established in the art. 25 par.1 of the Regulations in connection with art. 11 par.1 of the Regulations governing the Application of the Regulations and according to the above-mentioned jurisprudence, the new club of the player is to distribute 5% of any compensation paid for the transfer of a player to the club(s) involved in the training and education of the player in proportion to the number of years the player has been registered with the relevant clubs between the ages of 12 and 23.
11. In addition, the Chamber referred to art. 10 of the Regulations governing the Application of the Regulations, which provides the figures for the distribution of the solidarity contribution, according to the time the player was effectively trained by the clubs involved.
12. Consequently of the above, the Chamber decided to reject the Respondent's allegation according to which solidarity contribution is not due since the player concerned was registered on a loan basis with the Claimant. This is, since according to the jurisprudence of the Dispute Resolution Chamber the solidarity contribution is payable to the club(s) which effectively trained and educated a player

independently of the basis on which the player was registered with a training club, i.e. on a loan or a definitive basis.

13. In light of the above, the Chamber outlined that, in the present case, according to the confirmation of the football association of the country X the period to be taken into consideration (period of registration of the player with the club A) went from 4 December 1999 to 3 March 2000 and from 8 May to 31 December 2002, from the age of 18 to the age of 19, respectively from the age of 20 to the age of 21.
    In this respect, the Chamber concluded that the period of effective training to be taken into account corresponds to 11 individual months.
14. Therefore, the Chamber established that, in accordance with the breakdown provided for in art. 10 of the Regulations governing the Application of the Regulations, the Claimant is entitled to receive 9.16% of the 5% of the compensation paid in relation to the transfer of the player C.
15. Consequently of the above, the DRC decided to reject the Respondent's allegation according to which the solidarity contribution shall be calculated on the basis of the compensation the player paid to his former club at the end of his employment contract.
16. The Chamber noted that the Respondent admitted having paid the amount of USD 325,000 in connection with the transfer of the player to its club.
17. Based on all of the above, the Dispute Resolution Chamber decided that the Respondent must pay to the Claimant 9.16% of the 5% of the transfer compensation paid in relation to the transfer of the player C, i.e. USD 1,488.50.

III. DECISION OF THE DISPUTE RESOLUTION CHAMBER

1. The claim of A is accepted.
2. The Respondent has to pay the amount of USD 1,488.50 to A within 30 days as from the date of notification of this decision.
3. If the aforementioned sum is not paid within the aforementioned deadline an interest rate of 5% per year will apply as of expiry of the fixed time limit and the present matter shall be submitted to FIFA's Disciplinary Committee, so that the necessary disciplinary sanctions may be imposed.
4. A is directed to inform B directly and immediately of the account number to which the remittance is to be made and to notify the Dispute Resolution Chamber of every payment received.
5. According to art. 61 par. 1 of the FIFA Statutes, this decision may be appealed against before the Court of Arbitration for Sport (CAS). The statement of appeal must be sent to the CAS directly within 21 days of receipt of notification of this decision and shall contain all the elements in accordance with point 2 of the directives issued by the CAS, a copy of which we enclose hereto. Within another 10 days following the expiry of the time limit for filing the statement of appeal, the appellant shall file a brief stating the facts and legal arguments giving rise to the appeal with the CAS (cf. point 4 of the directives).

106574
DECISION OF THE DISPUTE RESOLUTION CHAMBER
passed in Zurich, Switzerland, on 26 October 2006,
in the following composition:
Slim Aloulou (Tunisia), Chairman
Gerardo Movilla (Spain), member
Joaquim Evangelista (Portugal), member
Mario Gallavotti (Italy), member
Peter Friend (Australia), member
on the claim presented by the club, X, P, as Claimant
against the club, Y, Q, as Respondent
regarding a training compensation dispute related to the transfer of the player A

I. FACTS OF THE CASE

1. Confirmed by the Football Federation of P, the player A was born on 28 June 1982 and was registered with the club X from 7 April 1995 to 2 July 2003, first as an amateur and subsequently as a non-amateur player, that is, for a total of eight sporting seasons between the age of 12 to 21.

On 5 February 2004, the player was registered as a non-amateur for the club Y.

2. On 20 January 2006, the Football Federation of P approached FIFA and presented a complaint of its affiliate X against the club Y, by means of which the club X claimed the payment of EUR 240,000 as training compensation for the player A, corresponding to an amount of EUR 30,000 for each year of training.
3. In response to the claim of the club X, the club Y informed FIFA on 30 March 2006 that the player A had joined the club Y in January 2004, after his contract with the club X was terminated. It maintained that on the occasion of the transfer negotiations, the club X had waived its right to receive financial compensation of any kind, including training compensation, for the transfer of the player A. In this respect, the club Y presented a written confirmation, dated 30 January 2004 and signed by the president of the club X at that time, according to which "[X] confirms that it does not require any financial compensation for the footballer [A]". The club Y therefore deemed that no training compensation was payable to the club X.
4. By fax dated 6 June 2006, the Football Federation of P confirmed that its affiliate had not requested any compensation for the transfer of the player A, but maintained, with reference to arts. 2 and 3 of Annex 4 of the FIFA Regulations for the Status and Transfer of Players, that this agreement had no impact on X's right to receive training compensation from the Respondent.
Consequently, the Claimant was of the opinion that the club Y was obliged to pay training compensation for the player A.
5. On 25 July 2006, the Respondent referred to its previous position and declared that it did not recognize any claim from the club X in connection with the player in question.
6. By correspondence dated 18 August 2006, 9 October 2006, 18 October 2006 and 24 October 2006, the Football Federation of P explained that the player A had been registered for the club X as an amateur as from 7 April 1995 and that he had changed to scholarship status with the same club on 25 September 2000.
The scholarship agreement between the relevant player and Training Compensation for the player A 2 the club X, a copy of which was also submitted to PTA, had been concluded for the period from 25 September 2000 until 31 December 2002.
Furthermore, the Football Federation of P informed FIFA that on 2 July 2003, the player A had been cleared for an internal transfer since he had apparently intended to render his services for the club K, also affiliated to the Football Federation of P.
However, he had not played for this club since the relevant parties had not come to an agreement. Consequently, the club X had been the player's last club before his transfer to the club Y. The International Transfer Certificate for the player had been issued to the Football Federation of Q on 29 January 2004.
7. As regards the categorization of the clubs involved, in accordance with circular no. 826, dated 31 October 2002, the club X belongs to category 3 (indicative amount EUR 30,000 per year) whilst Y is a category 2 club (indicative amount EUR 60,000 per year). The categorization of the two clubs involved is confirmed by their respective Federations.

II. CONSIDERATIONS OF THE DISPUTE RESOLUTION CHAMBER

1. First of all, the Dispute Resolution Chamber analysed whether it was competent to deal with the matter at hand. In this respect, the Chamber referred to art. 18 paras. 2 and 3 of the Rules Governing the Procedures of the Players' ' Status Committee and the Dispute Resolution Chamber. The present matter was submitted to FIFA on 20 January 2006, thus after 1 July 2005.
Therefore, the Dispute Resolution Chamber concluded that the revised Rules Governing the Procedures (edition 2005) on matters pending before the decision making bodies of FIFA are applicable to the matter at hand.
2. With regard to the competence of the Dispute Resolution Chamber, art. 3 para. 1 of the above-mentioned Rules states that the Dispute Resolution Chamber shall examine its jurisdiction in the light of arts. 22 to 24 of the current version of the Regulations for the Status and Transfer of Players (edition 2005).
In accordance with art. 24 par. 1 in combination with art. 22 (d) of the aforementioned Regulations, the Dispute Resolution Chamber shall adjudicate on disputes between two clubs belonging to different Associations related to training compensation.

3. As a consequence, the Dispute Resolution Chamber is the competent body to decide on the present litigation concerning the training compensation claimed by the club X for the training and education of the player A.
4. Subsequently, the members of the Chamber analyzed which edition of the Regulations for the Status and Transfer of Players should be applicable as to Training Compensation for the player A 3 the substance of the matter. In this respect, the Chamber referred to art. 26 paras. 1 and 2 of the Regulations for the Status and Transfer of Players (edition 2005) in the modified version in accordance with the FIFA circular no. 995 dated 23 September 2005.
   Furthermore, it acknowledged that the player had been registered for the club Y on 5 February 2004.
   Equally the Chamber took note that the claim was lodged at FIFA on 20 January 2006.
   In view of the aforementioned, the Chamber concluded that the former FIFA Regulations for the Status and Transfer of Players (edition 2001, hereinafter: the Regulations) are applicable to the case at hand as to the substance.
5. Entering into the substance of the matter, the Dispute Resolution Chamber examined the documentation presented by the Claimant and took note that the player A had been registered for the club X as an amateur as from 7 April 1995, and that on 25 September 2000, the two parties had concluded a scholarship agreement valid until 31 December 2002.
   Furthermore, the members of the Chamber acknowledged that on 2 July 2003, the player had been cleared for an internal transfer and that he had been registered as an non-amateur for the club Y on 5 February 2004.
6. In this respect, the members of the Chamber carefully examined the written confirmation, dated 30 January 2004 and signed by the president of the club X at that time, according to which the club X waived its right to receive any "financial compensation" from the club Y for the player A. In this respect, the Dispute Resolution Chamber took note of the statement of the club X, according to which the waiver only referred to its alleged right to receive transfer compensation for the player in question, whereas the club Y was of the opinion that X had also renounced any right to receive training compensation. In this context, the members of the Chamber proceeded to deliberate whether the term "financial compensation" contained in the waiver of the club X also referred to its possible right to receive training compensation.
7. In this respect, the members of the Dispute Resolution Chamber stressed that the notion "financial compensation" was a general and unspecific term which, in principle, could not be understood to only include transfer compensation. The Dispute Resolution Chamber considered that the term rather encompassed any kind of monetary compensation which, in the case at hand, the club X could have possibly requested from the club Y in connection with the player A, thus also training compensation.
8. Furthermore, the Dispute Resolution Chamber took into account that at the time the player A joined the club Y, the player appeared to have been free to render his services for a club of his choice, since his scholarship agreement Training Compensation for the player A4 with the club X had expired on 31 December 2002 and he had been cleared for an internal transfer already on 2 July 2003.
   In view of the fact that, in principle, a club cannot request transfer compensation for a player who is free from contractual obligations towards that club, the Dispute Resolution Chamber had to assume that X's waiver dated 30 January 2004 referred to its possible right to receive training compensation for the training and education of the player in question.
9. On account of the above considerations, the members of the Dispute Resolution Chamber unanimously concluded that X's claim against the club Y for training compensation for the player A could not be admitted.

III. DECISION OF THE DISPUTE RESOLUTION CHAMBER

1. The claim lodged by the Claimant, the club X from P, is rejected.
2. According to art. 61 par. 1 of the FIFA Statutes, this decision may be appealed against before the Court of Arbitration for Sport (CAS). The statement of appeal must be sent to the CAS directly within 21 days of receipt of notification of this decision and shall contain all the elements in accordance with point 2 of the directives issued by the CAS, a copy of which we enclose hereto. Within another 10 days following the expiry of the time limit for filing the statement of appeal, the appellant shall file a brief stating the facts and legal arguments giving rise to the appeal with the CAS (cf. point 4 of the directives).

106672

DECISION OF THE DISPUTE RESOLUTION CHAMBER

passed in Zurich, Switzerland, on 26 October 2006,
in the following composition:
Slim Aloulou (Tunisia), Chairman
Gerardo Movilla (Spain), member
Joaquim Evangelista (Portugal), member
Mario Gallavotti (Italy), member
Peter Friend (Australia), member
on the claim presented by the player M., T., represented by players' ' agent K., C., as Claimant,
against the club O., R., represented by S., R.as Respondent,
regarding a contractual dispute arisen between the parties

I. FACTS OF THE CASE

1. On 5 June 2002, the player, M., and the club, O., signed an employment contract valid until 30 May 2004 (hereinafter: the "1st contract").
2. On 1 July 2003, the 1st contract was replaced by another employment contract valid until 31 May 2005 (hereinafter: the "2nd contract").
3. On 1 July 2004, the parties signed a third employment contract, valid until 31 May 2005 (hereinafter: the "3rd contract") and providing for a yearly salary of USD 50,000 to paid in 10 monthly .
4. Finally, on 22 July 2004, the player signed an agreement to alter the 3rd contract (hereinafter: the "alteration contract"). This agreement is not signed by the club but bears its stamp. Therein, the club confirmed that it owed the player for the second season the sum of USD 58,000, which would be paid in three separate instalments on the following dates: 30 September 2004 (USD 18,000), 31 October 2004 (USD 20,000) and 31 November 2004 (USD 20,000). Furthermore, in the alteration contract, the parties agreed on a salary of USD 101,000 for the 2004- 2005 season, payable in 10 monthly instalments of USD 10,100.
5. On 11 July 2005, the player contacted FIFA and stated that he had not received certain parts of his wages. The player is claiming the following amounts (amounts in national currency):

– Bonuses 2002-2003	... 5,000
– Flight ticket 2003-2004	... 1,148
– Flight ticket 2004-2005	... 932
– Car hire 2004-2005	... 1,300
– School 2004-2005	... 678
– Heating 2004-2005	... 380
– Total debt in accordance with alteration contract:	... 23,000
– Total debt in accordance with 2nd contract 2003-2004:	... 18,000
– Salary September 2004	... 2,300
– Salary October 2004	... 2,300
– Salary November 2004	... 2,300
– Salary December 2004	... 2,300
– Salary January 2005	... 2,300
– Salary February 2005	... 2,300
– Salary March 2005	... 2,300
– Subtotal	... 66,538
– Less down-payment -	... 4,400
– TOTAL	... 62,138

6. On 21 December 2005, the club responded and denied the player's claims. The club stated that the amounts specified in the 1st contract dated 5 July 2002 [recte: 5 June 2002] had been paid in their entirety. The club also added that the amounts specified in the 2nd contract dated 1 July 2003 had likewise been paid in their entirety. The club submitted a receipt for both of these claims.
   These receipts had been signed by the player, thereby confirming all payments for the duration of the contract for 2002-2003 and 2003-2004 seasons. With regard to the third year, the club stated that it had paid the player a total amount of ... 13,600 (receipts submitted). The club did admit, however, that it still owed the player ... 10,400.

7. Despite being invited to do so, the player has not submitted any further response to the club's position.

II. CONSIDERATIONS OF THE DISPUTE RESOLUTION CHAMBER

1. First of all, the Chamber analysed whether it was competent to deal with the matter at stake. In this respect, it referred to art. 18 par. 2 and 3 of the Rules Governing the Procedures of the Players' Status Committee and the Dispute Resolution Chamber. The present matter was submitted to FIFA on 11 July 2005, as a consequence the Chamber concluded that the revised Rules Governing Procedures (edition 2005) on matters pending before the decision making bodies of FIFA are applicable on the matter at hand.
2. With regard to the competence of the Chamber, art. 3 par. 1 of the above- mentioned Rules states that the Dispute Resolution Chamber shall examine its jurisdiction in the light of articles 22 to 24 of the current version of the Regulations for the Status and Transfer of Players (edition 2005). In accordance with art. 24 par. 1 in connection with art. 22 (b) of the aforementioned Regulations, the Dispute Resolution Chamber shall adjudicate on employment- related disputes between a club and a player that have an international dimension.
3. As a consequence, the Dispute Resolution Chamber is the competent body to decide on the present litigation involving a club from R. and player from T.regarding a contractual dispute in connection with an employment contract.
4. Subsequently, the members of the Chamber analysed which edition of the Regulations for the Status and Transfer of Players should be applicable as to the substance of the matter. In this respect, the Chamber referred, on the one hand, to art. 26 par. 1 and 2 of the Regulations for the Status and Transfer of Players (edition 2005) and, on the other hand, to the fact that the relevant contracts at the basis of the present dispute were signed on 5 June 2002, 1 July 2003, 1 July 2004 and 22 July 2004, respectively, and the claim was lodged at FIFA on 11 July 2005.
   In view of the aforementioned, the Chamber concluded that the current FIFA Regulations for the Status and Transfer of Players (edition 2005, hereinafter: the Regulations) are applicable on the case at hand as to the substance.
5. In continuation, and entering into the substance of the matter, the members of the Chamber started by acknowledging that the player M. and O. signed on 5 June 2002 an employment contract valid until 30 May 2004 and that on 1 July 2003, this contract was replaced by another employment contract valid until 31 May 2005 and subsequently, on 1 July 2004, by a third employment contract valid until 31 May 2005.
   Equally, the Chamber noted that the player signed an alteration contract on 22 July 2004 which is not signed by the club. The alteration contract bears, in fact, only the stamp of the club. Consequently, the Chamber concluded that this alteration contract cannot be taken into consideration. In this respect, and referring in particular to the amount of USD 58,000, according to the alteration contract still owed to the player for the 2003-2004 season, the Chamber emphasised that , in any case, the payment receipt presented by the club and signed by the player, by means of which the latter confirmed the settlement of all dies for the 2003-2004 seasons, had been issued after the date of the alteration contract, i.e. on 30 July 2004.
6. Furthermore, the Chamber took note that the club contested the allegations of the player and stated that the amounts specified in the 1st and the 2nd contract had been paid in their entirety. The Chamber then carefully examined the receipts forwarded by the club. The first payment receipt no. 03835 amounts to EUR 45,000 and contains the following sentence: "Settlement of Contract period 2002-2003". The second payment receipt no. 04286 amounts to … 28,000 and contains the sentence: "for full settlement of the contract for the football period 2003-2004". In this respect, the Chamber emphasised that both payment receipts had been signed by the player. Additionally, the Chamber stressed that the player never took position to nor contested the answer of the club. The Chamber pointed out that no reply having been received from the player to the answer to the claim and the receipts submitted, the player seems to renounce to his right to further substantiate his claims and thus accepts the allegations of the club. Therefore, the Chamber considered that the amounts specified in the 1st contract dated 5 June 2002 and in the 2nd contract dated 1 July 2003 had been paid in their entirety and decided to reject the respective claims of the player.
7. Subsequently, the Chamber drew its attention to the player's claims for the 3rd year of contract. According to the 3rd contract signed between the player and the club on 1 July 2004, the club agreed

to pay to the player for the period from 1 July 2004 to 31 May 2005 the total amount of USD 50,000 to be paid in ten monthly instalments, an amount which corresponds according to the club to ... 24,000.

The player, however, claimed for the last season monthly instalments in the amount of ...2,300. Therefore, the Chamber considered that the total salary for the season 2004-2005 to be taken into account amounts to ... 23,000.

8. The Chamber then carefully examined the payment receipts submitted by the club and signed by the player for the salaries paid in the season 2004-2005.
The Chamber took note that the club presented six payment receipts proving the payment of the following amounts: ... 2,400 (payment receipt no. 04512 dated 16 September 2004); ... 1,000 (payment receipt no. 01951 dated 14 January 2005); ... 500 (payment receipt no. 01844 dated 16 February 2005); ... 500 (payment receipt 02120 dated 1 March 2005); ... 2,000 (payment receipt no. 02057 dated 28 April 2005); ... 4,000 (payment receipt no. 02058 dated 28 April 2005). The Chamber therefore concluded that the club provided the evidence that the total amount of ... 10,400 had been paid to the player for the 2004- 2005 seasons. Consequently, the Chamber deemed that the calculation in the response of the club according to which it paid the player the amount of ... 13,600 is not sustained by evidence.
9. On account of the above, the Chamber considered that according to the 3rd contract, the player was entitled to receive an amount of USD 50,000 which corresponds, as mentioned above, to the amount of ... 23,000.
The club proved the payment of a total amount of ... 10,400.
Therefore, the Chamber concluded that the outstanding amount is of ... 12,600.
10. Subsequently, the Chamber turned to the question of the claimed reimbursement of two return flight tickets to T. The Chamber acknowledged that, on the one hand, the club did not contest this part of the claim and that, on the other hand, the 3rd contract stipulated that the player has the right to two return plane tickets R. - T. Therefore, the Chamber decided that the player is entitled to receive an amount of money corresponding to two tickets in economy class, the price of which, due to lack of receipts, is to be determined on the basis of the general market offers. The price on the market for two such tickets would average at least ... 1,100.
Therefore, the player is entitled to receive the claimed amount of ... 932.
11. In addition, the Chamber took note that the player claimed the car rent and the school fees as stipulated in the 3rd contract dated 1 July 2004.
However, the player failed to provide any evidence concerning these claims. Therefore, the Chamber decided to reject the relevant demands.
12. Concerning the claimed amount for the heating during the year 2004-2005, the Chamber pointed out that the 3rd contract dated 1 July 2004 does not stipulate any such obligation for the account of the club. Therefore, the Chamber concluded that the respective claim of the player has also to be rejected.
13. Taking into account the foregoing, and having analysed the financial aspects of the player's claims as well as the club's defence statements, the Dispute Resolution Chamber concluded its deliberations by announcing that the player's claims were partially accepted. Therefore, the Chamber decided that O. has to pay the amount of ... 13,532 (... 12,600 corresponding to outstanding salaries, ... 932 corresponding to two return flight tickets to T.) to the player M

III. DECISION OF THE DISPUTE RESOLUTION CHAMBER

1. The claim of the player M. is partially accepted.
2. O. has to pay the amount of ... 13,532 to the player M. within the next 30 days as from the date of notification of this decision.
3. Any further financial claim lodged by the player M. is rejected.
4. In the event that the above-mentioned amount is not paid within the stated deadline, an interest rate of 5% per year will apply and the present matter shall be submitted to FIFA's Disciplinary Committee, so that the necessary disciplinary sanctions may be imposed.
5. The player M. is instructed to inform O. immediately and directly of the account number to which the remittance is to be made and to notify the Dispute Resolution Chamber of every payment received.
6. According to art. 61 par. 1 of the FIFA Statutes, this decision may be appealed against before the Court of Arbitration for Sport (CAS). The statement of appeal must be sent to the CAS directly within

21 days of receipt of notification of this decision and shall contain all the elements in accordance with point 2 of the directives issued by the CAS, a copy of which we enclose hereto. Within another 10 days following the expiry of the time limit for filing the statement of appeal, the appellant shall file a brief stating the facts and legal arguments giving rise to the appeal with the CAS (cf. point 4 of the directives).

⚽⚽⚽

1061097
DECISION OF THE DISPUTE RESOLUTION CHAMBER
passed in Zurich, Switzerland, on 26 October 2006,
in the following composition:
Slim Aloulou (Tunisia), Chairman
Gerardo Movilla (Spain), member
Joaquim Evangelista (Portugal), member
Mario Gallavotti (Italy), member
Peter Friend (Australia), member
on the claim presented by
Player P, country x as Claimant/Counter-Respondent
against the club
Club C, country y as Respondent/Counter-Claimant
regarding a contractual dispute arisen between the player and the club

I. FACTS OF THE CASE

1. On 16 June 2005, the player P (hereinafter: the Claimant) and the club C (hereinafter: the Respondent) signed an agreement bearing the title "Promissory employment contract" (hereinafter: the contract), with the (translated) introductory sentence: "The club and the player hereby execute an individual job contract to be ruled by the following clauses:…"."
2. This contract which has been signed by the Claimant and a representative of the Respondent provides for a validity of one year, from 1 July 2005 until 30 June 2006.
   The contract provides, inter alia, for a basic yearly salary of EUR 50,000, payable in ten monthly instalments of EUR 5,000 net.
3. The following clauses are, inter alia, included in the contract:
   - Clause 6 of the (translated) contract reads: "If the athlete rescinds the contract unilaterally, he shall be automatically obliged to pay to Club C an indemnification of EUR 500,000."
   - Clause 9 of the (translated) contract reads: "The club declares that the player has an updated medical record with the club, …."
   - Clause 13 of the (translated) contract stipulates: "If, after medical exams, the Clinical Department of the Club C does not rate the athlete as capable beyond any limitations for the practice of professional football, this contract shall be considered null.
4. On 18 August 2005, the Claimant lodged a formal complaint at FIFA, claiming that it is to be declared that the Respondent had breached the contract with him without just cause and that he had duly terminated the contract on 1 August 2005.
   Furthermore, the Claimant requests payment of a total amount of EUR 50,000, taking into account the remaining period of the contract and that disciplinary sanctions are to be imposed on the Respondent.
5. The Claimant explains that after having signed the contract on 16 June 2005, for formal reasons he had signed another contract with the Respondent on 29 June 2005 before a notary public in Y. However, the Claimant affirms not having received a copy of the second contract. The Claimant asserts that after the signing the second contract, he was submitted to medical examination and then returned to X.
6. The Claimant continues that his agent, A (hereinafter: the agent of the player or the agent), became aware in the beginning of July 2005 through the Y press that the Respondent was no longer interested in him on the allegation of negative medical examination results. Some telephone conversations were carried out between the agent of the player and the Respondent whereby the latter insisted on its position of not wanting to hire the Claimant anymore. As a consequence of the breach of

contract allegedly committed by the Respondent, the Claimant explains having terminated the labour relationship with the Respondent on 1 August 2005.

7. In its response to the claim, the Respondent rejects the claim of the Claimant in full and explains that its president, V, had been contacted by the agent of the player and was presented by him three players and shown the DVDs of the players. The agent then invited the president and the coach of the Respondent to X in order to evaluate the three players in a live match. After arriving in X, the agent told the president and the coach that it was already publicly known that the Respondent was interested in the services of the Claimant and that it was best if the Claimant did not play the next day because the supporting fans would not like the situation if they knew that representatives of the Respondent were present at the match. Despite this fact, the agent proposed that a contract would be signed in order to end all speculations.
8. Furthermore, the Respondent explains that its president had informed the agent that in addition to his signature, the contract would have to be signed by two other board members of the Respondent in order for the contract to be valid and in order for the contract to be registered with the Professional Football League of Y and the Y Football Federation. The agent of the player affirmed that he understood the statement and that he perfectly knew the Y legislation as he had other players playing in Y.
9. The Respondent summarises that no valid contract had been signed between it and the Claimant but only a contract of promise with the commitment that a proper contract would be signed by three board members after the Claimant would have passed the medical examination. The Respondent affirms that the medical examination had shown that the Claimant suffered from serious injuries that were limiting his ability of playing. The Respondent explains that the injuries were so serious that the insurance company refused to insure the player. In support of this statement, the Respondent submitted a copy of the medical report and a copy of the report of the insurance company informing that the Claimant could not be insured by it.
10. The Respondent is of the opinion that only a promissory contract had been signed between the parties which did not have any legal effects. The Respondent furthermore states that the contract even had a clause stipulating that the passing of the medical test was a condition of the conclusion of the contract. Therefore, the Respondent considers not to have any financial obligations towards the Claimant and stresses that it had covered all travel and lodging expenses of the Claimant.
11. In his comments thereto, the Claimant maintains his position that a valid and binding employment contract had been concluded between him and the Respondent and not just a pre-contract as all the principal elements of a definite contract were contained in the contract: the duration, the salary, the bonus, a penalty clause and the choice of jurisdiction. Furthermore, the Claimant explains that the contract was not conditioned by the signature of another "definite" contract which means that the contract is final and binding.

    The Claimant furthermore refers to Clause 9 of the contract which states that he had all the required conditions for the practice of Football and which was in clear contradiction with Clause 13 which states that the contract shall be null in case he did not pass the medical tests. The Claimant alleges that the Respondent had named the contract "Promissory contract" with the bad intention to justify a possible invalidation of the contract if the Claimant did not pass the medical examination. In addition, the Claimant mentions that Clause 6 of the contract establishes a contractual penalty of EUR 500,000 in case he would breach the contract.
12. Moreover, the Claimant reiterates that he had not been submitted to any medical test before signing the contract and by that, the Respondent had taken the risk. According to the FIFA Regulations, the validity of a contract could not be made subject to a positive medical examination. Regarding the issue of the signatures, the Claimant comments that neither him nor his agent were told that more than one signature would be needed to validate the contract and that the Respondent had not submitted any documentary evidence. The Claimant reiterates that a second contract had been signed before a notary public in Y. He furthermore mentions that an agreement had been concluded between the Respondent and his agent by means of which the Respondent committed to pay EUR 24,200 to the agent as a commission fee for his transfer and the transfer of the players Q and R. The Claimant concludes that it is not reasonable for the Respondent to sign an agreement with his agent if it did not consider the contract to be final and binding.
13. In its comments thereto, the Respondent replies that the Claimant and the two other players (Q and R) had construed a strategy in order to damage it.

14. The Respondent recalls the FACTS OF THE CASE as follows: The agent of the player had entered into contact with it and had pictured all three players as top level professional players and had shown DVDs of them. On 16 June 2005, the president and the coach of the Respondent travelled to X to see the players performing live. The day before, the Respondent had expressly informed the Claimant and his agent that the medical examination would be an absolute condition prior to any binding agreement. Once arrived in X, the president and the coach of the Respondent had been prevented from seeing the Claimant and the two other players playing but the agent had proposed to sign a pre-contract immediately. The Respondent had informed each player and the agent that it was not a valid and definitive employment contract but only a promissory contract. The Respondent did not want to sign an employment contract before having conducted the medical test and the president had anyway not been empowered to validate the contract with his sole signature.
The signature of two other board members would have been needed. The players and the agent had fully understood the situation. Later, the medical exam showed that the Claimant was suffering from serious injuries and so the club decided not to enter into a definitive employment contract.
15. The Respondent emphasizes once again that the parties had only signed a pre- contract which was named "promise of contract". This contract was subject to positive medical results which is, according to the Respondent, a fully legitimate condition. The Respondent mentions that as a small size club, it would never sign an employment contract with unknown players whom it had never really seen playing but only seen them on DVD. According to the Respondent, it was the intention of both parties to sign a definitive employment contract only after the positive outcome of the medical examination. The Respondent also stresses that the contract is printed on white paper without any official heading of the Respondent. Also, the contract provides for space for three signatures as it contains three lines for the signatures. In order to corroborate its statement, the Respondent submitted a sample of a standard employment contract, provided by the Y Football Federation, on official paper of the club. In addition to that, the Respondent mentions that Art. 48 of its Statutes rules that documents which create obligations for the Respondent need to be furnished at least with the signature of the President and one of the Vice Presidents or the Delegate President. The Respondent reiterates that the parties had not signed any contract before a public notary in Y. Regarding the agreement concluded between it and the agent, the Respondent explains that it had entered into the agreement for the event that a definitive employment contract would be signed with the Claimant.
16. The Respondent claims that the Claimant and his agent were hiding information on the physical problems of the Claimant such as his serious alcohol problems which and that the agent did everything to prevent the representatives of the Respondent from seeing the players playing. Therefore, the Respondent should be compensated for the damage it had suffered. By means of a counter-claim, the Respondent requests to be reimbursed for all expenses which it had covered for the Claimant such as the flight expenses from X to Y, the hotel expenses in X and Y as well as the medical expenses in the total amount of EUR 60,000.
The Respondent adds that the Claimant was jointly and severally liable with the players Q and R to reimburse the amount of EUR 60,000.
17. In his comments, the Claimant rejects the counter-claim of the Respondent and all allegations made by the Respondent. He mentions that it is hard to believe that the president of the Respondent would travel to X for negotiations but that his signature would not be sufficient to bind the Respondent. Just after the representatives went to X, the Respondent had organised the travel of the Claimant to Y in order to present him to the club. The Claimant adds that all expenses had indeed been paid by the Respondent which acted as an employer but that the Respondent had acted at its own risk by going to X to hire the players. The Claimant remarks that the Respondent had not submitted any evidence to prove the allegation that he and his agent where fully aware of the situation when signing the contract.
18. The Respondent rejects the claim of the player and is claiming the amount of EUR 60,000 for the damage it suffered.

II. CONSIDERATIONS OF THE DISPUTE RESOLUTION CHAMBER

1. First of all, the Chamber analysed whether it was competent to deal with the matter at stake. In this respect, it referred to art. 18 par. 2 and 3 of the Rules Governing the Procedures of the Players' Status Committee and the Dispute Resolution Chamber (DRC). The present matter was submitted to FIFA on 18 August 2005, as a consequence the Chamber concluded that the revised Rules Governing

Procedures (edition 2005) on matters pending before the decision making bodies of FIFA are applicable to the matter at hand.

2. With regard to the competence of the Chamber, art. 3 par. 1 of the above- mentioned Rules states that the Dispute Resolution Chamber shall examine its jurisdiction in the light of articles 22 to 24 of the current version of the Regulations for the Status and Transfer of Players (edition 2005). In accordance with art. 24 par. 1 in combination with art. 22 (b) of the aforementioned Regulations, the Dispute Resolution Chamber shall adjudicate on employment-related disputes between a club and a player that have an international dimension.
3. As a consequence, the Dispute Resolution Chamber is the competent body to decide on the present litigation involving a Xian player and a Portuguese club regarding a dispute arisen in connection with an employment contract.
4. Subsequently, the members of the Chamber analyzed which edition of the Regulations for the Status and Transfer of Players should be applicable as to the substance of the matter. In this respect, the Chamber referred, on the one hand, to art. 26 par. 1 and 2 of the Regulations for the Status and Transfer of Players (edition 2005) and, on the other hand, to the fact that the relevant contract at the basis of the present dispute was signed on 16 June 2005 and the claim was lodged at FIFA on 18 August 2005.

   In view of the aforementioned, the Chamber concluded that the current FIFA Regulations for the Status and Transfer of Players (edition 2005, hereinafter: the Regulations) are applicable to the case at hand as to the substance.
5. In continuation, and entering into the substance of the matter, the members of the Chamber started by acknowledging the above mentioned facts and all further documentation contained in the file. In particular, they took note that a contract called "promissory contract" had been signed by the Claimant and the president of the Respondent which provided for a period of validity from 1 July 2005 until 30 June 2006.
6. Furthermore, the Chamber noted that the Claimant claims that a valid and binding employment contract had been concluded between him and the Respondent and that the contract had been breached by the Respondent wherefore he claims payment of compensation in the amount of EUR 50,000 equal to the salaries of the whole contractual period.
7. On the other hand, the members of the Chamber acknowledged that the Respondent claims that no valid contract had been signed between it and the Claimant and that by means of a counter-claim, the Respondent claims payment in the amount of EUR 60,000 from the Claimant (joint and several liability with the players R and Q) for sustained damages as the Claimant had allegedly been hiding information about his physical problems.
8. The Chamber stated that it first had to analyse whether a valid and binding employment contract had been concluded between the parties and, in a second step, to determine whether any party is accountable for compensation and/or sporting sanctions.
9. The Chamber stated that a contract has to be signed by both parties in order to be valid and binding. In this respect, the Chamber noted that the contract had been signed by the Claimant and one representative of the Respondent, namely the club's president, therefore it had been signed by both parties.
10. The Chamber drew its attention to the argument of the Respondent that two other board members would have had to sign the contract in order for the contract to become valid. The Respondent further alleged that the Claimant had been informed that the sole signature of the club's president was not sufficient for the validity of the contract. The Chamber took note of the fact that this allegation was contested by the Claimant.
11. In this regard, the Chamber stated that the alleged necessity of three signatures for the validity of an employment contract is a club-internal proxy rule which is not known to third parties and therefore does not have any legal effects on the validity of the present contract unless the contracting partner, in casu the Claimant, is clearly informed about the respective rule. The Chamber noted that the Respondent had failed to provide any kind of evidence in order to corroborate its allegation that the Claimant had indeed been informed that the signature of the president of the Respondent was not sufficient for the validity of the contract. The Chamber also stated that the Claimant did not have the obligation to verify whether or not the president of the Respondent was empowered to solely sign a contract. As in the present case the signature of the club's president is concerned, the Claimant could assume that as the highest possible representative of the club, he is authorised to sign individually.

12. Furthermore, the DRC turned its attention to the argument of the Respondent that the contract provides for three lines, i.e. allegedly space for three signatures. The Chamber stated by simply providing space for three signatures, it could not be concluded that the Respondent had informed the Claimant about the necessity of three signatures from the club.
13. In conclusion of the aforementioned, the Chamber stated that the Respondent's argument that the contract is not valid due to the missing of two signatures, has to be rejected and that the contract has therefore been duly signed by both parties.
14. In continuation, the Chamber stated that in order to determine whether or not a valid and binding employment contract was concluded between the parties, it furthermore has to verify whether all principle elements ("essentialia negotii") were contained in the relevant document.
15. After analysing the contract, the Chamber concluded that the parties had agreed in the contract upon all principle elements such as the place of work,the period of validity, the salary, a penalty clause etc., and therefore decided that the contract is valid and binding.
16. For the sake of good order, the Chamber added that for the interpretation of a contract its content is relevant and not its title (in casu "promissory employment contract").
17. Furthermore, the Chamber took note of the Respondent's allegation that the player had been hiding information on his physical condition. In this respect, the members of the Chamber stated that the Respondent had not provided any evidence in this respect. Furthermore, it added that in order for a club to be informed about a player's physical condition, it usually conducts a medical examination prior to the signing of the employment contract. Therefore, the Chamber rejected the argument of the Respondent that the Claimant had been hiding information on his physical condition.
18. The Chamber furthermore took note of the fact that the contract is only conditioned by one Clause, namely Clause 13, which states that if, after medical exams, the athlete is not rated as capable for the practice of professional football, the contract shall be considered null. The Chamber noted that this Clause was in contradiction with Clause 9 of the contract which states that "the club declares that the player has an updated medical record with the club, ...".
19. In this respect, the Chamber referred to art. 18 par. 4 of the Regulations which stipulates that the validity of a contract may not be made subject to a positive medical examination. The Chamber stated that the condition in Clause 13 of the contract clearly contravenes art. 18 par. 4 of the Regulations and therefore, has to be considered null and void, i.e. not legally binding.
20. The Chamber noted that it was an undisputed fact that the Claimant had not undergone the medical examination until after the signing of the contract and that the results were not positive. The members of the DRC stated that by not conducting the medical examination before the signing of the contract, the Respondent had taken the risk of a possible negative outcome of the examination as negative examination results do not constitute a valid reason for unilaterally terminating an employment contract.
21. In view of all the above, the Chamber concluded that by not implementing the employment contract concluded with the Claimant due to the negative outcome of his medical examination, the Respondent had breached the relevant employment contract without valid reason.
22. In conclusion of the fact that the Respondent had breached the contract without just cause, the Chamber decided that the Claimant is entitled to receive compensation from the Respondent for breach of contract committed by the club.
23. In this respect, the Chamber, however, added that the Respondent apparently had believed that it had only concluded a "promissory contract" with the Claimant and not a final contract. The Chamber deemed that this should have a mitigating effect on the compensation which is to be paid by the Respondent.
24. The Chamber took into consideration that the employment contract concluded between the parties provided for a period of validity of one year.
25. With regard to the compensation due for breach of contract without just cause committed by the Respondent, the Chamber decided that taking into account all the aforementioned considerations (points II.20 to II.24), the Respondent has to pay to the Claimant the lump sum of EUR 20,000.

III. DECISION OF THE DISPUTE RESOLUTION CHAMBER

1. The claim of the player is partially accepted.
2. The Respondent has to pay the total amount of EUR 20,000 as compensation to the player within 30 days following the date of the communication of the present decision.

3. In the event that the above-mentioned amount is not paid within the stated deadline, an interest rate of 5% per year will apply as of expiry of the relevant time-frame and the present matter shall be submitted to FIFA's Disciplinary Committee, so that the necessary disciplinary sanctions may be imposed.
4. Any further claims submitted by the Claimant are rejected.
5. The Claimant is directed to inform the Respondent directly and immediately of the account number to which the remittance is to be made and to notify the Dispute Resolution Chamber of every payment received.
6. The counter-claim submitted by the Respondent is fully rejected.
7. According to art. 61 par. 1 of the FIFA Statutes, this decision may be appealed against before the Court of Arbitration for Sport (CAS). The statement of appeal must be sent to the CAS directly within 21 days of receipt of notification of this decision and shall contain all the elements in accordance with point 2 of the directives issued by the CAS, a copy of which we enclose hereto. Within another 10 days following the expiry of the time limit for filing the statement of appeal, the appellant shall file a brief stating the facts and legal arguments giving rise to the appeal with the CAS (cf. point 4 of the directives).

1061118
DECISION OF THE DISPUTE RESOLUTION CHAMBER
passed in Zurich, Switzerland, on 26 October 2006,
in the following composition:
Slim Aloulou (Tunisia), Chairman
Gerardo Movilla (Spain), member
Joaquim Evangelista (Portugal), member
Mario Gallavotti (Italy), member
Peter Friend (Australia), member
on the claim presented by the player P, country x as Claimant/Counter-Respondent
against the club
C, country Y as Respondent/Counter-Claimant
regarding a contractual dispute arisen between the player and the club

I. FACTS OF THE CASE

1. On 16 June 2005, the player P (hereinafter: the Claimant) and the club C (hereinafter: the Respondent) signed an agreement with the title "Promissory contract" (hereinafter: the contract), with the (translated) introductory sentence: "The club and the player hereby execute an individual job contract to be ruled by the following clauses:…"."
2. The aforementioned contract which has been signed by the Claimant and a representative of the Respondent provides for a validity of one year, from 1 July 2005 until 30 June 2006.
   Inter alia, the contract provides for a basic yearly salary of EUR 37,000, payable in ten monthly instalments of EUR 3,700.
3. The following clauses are, inter alia, contained in the contract:
   - Clause 6 of the (translated) contract reads: "If the athlete rescinds the contract unilaterally, he shall be automatically obliged to pay to the club C an indemnification of EUR 500,000."
   - Clause 9 of the (translated) contract reads: "The club declares that the player has an updated medical record with the club, …."
   - Clause 13 of the (translated) contract stipulates: "If, after medical exams, the Clinical Department of the club C does not rate the athlete as capable beyond any limitations for the practice of professional football, this contract shall be considered null."
4. On 23 August 2005, the Claimant lodged a formal complaint at FIFA, claiming that it is to be declared that the Respondent had breached the contract with him without just cause and that the Respondent is to be obliged to pay him the total amount of EUR 37,000, taking into account the remaining period of the contract. He furthermore claims that disciplinary sanctions are to be imposed on the Respondent.

5. The Claimant explains that after having signed the contract on 16 June 2005, for formal reasons he had signed another contract with the Respondent on 29 June 2005 before a notary public in X which established exactly the same terms as the first contract. However, the Claimant affirms not having received a copy of the second contract. The Claimant asserts that after the signing of both contracts, he was submitted to medical examination and then returned to X.
6. The Claimant continues that his agent A (hereinafter: the agent of the player or the agent), became aware in the beginning of July 2005 through the Y press that the Respondent was no longer interested in him because he had allegedly not played for the X club which the agent had indicated to the Respondent.
However, the Claimant affirms having been part of the squad of club M and, as he was contacted by the club E, he was playing for the club, G (2nd division of the local championship of U). Some telephone conversations were carried out between the agent of the player and the Respondent in which the latter insisted on its position that it did not accept to hire the Claimant anymore. As a consequence of the alleged breach of contract committed by the Respondent, the Claimant explains having terminated the labour relationship with the Respondent on 2 August 2005.
7. In his reply, the Respondent rejects the claim of the Claimant in full and explains that its President had been contacted by the agent of the player and was presented three players by him. The agent had invited the President and the coach of the Respondent to X in order to evaluate all three players in a live match. The agent had informed the representatives of the Respondent that the Claimant was playing for the club M and suggested that an employment contract should be signed between the Claimant and the Respondent.
8. Furthermore, the Respondent explained that its President informed the agent that in addition to his signature, the contract would have to be signed by two other board members of the Respondent in order for the contract to be valid and in order for the contract to be registered with the Professional Football League of Y and the Y Football Federation. The agent of the player affirmed that he understood the statement and that he perfectly knew the Y legislation as he had other players playing in Y.
9. The Respondent summarises that no valid contract had been signed between it and the Claimant but only a contract of promise which was not binding. The Respondent states that the contract even had a clause that the passing of the medical examination was a condition to the contract. Therefore, the Respondent is of the opinion that it does not have any financial obligations towards the Claimant and stressed that it had covered all travel and lodging expenses for the Claimant. The Respondent adds that the Claimant had not played for the club M as indicated by the agent of the player but instead for the club G. In support of its statement, the Respondent enclosed a listing of the club G.
10. In his comments thereto, the Claimant maintains his position that a valid and binding employment contract and not just a pre-contract had been concluded between him and the Respondent as all the principal elements of a definite contract were contained in the contract: The duration, the salary, the bonus, a penalty clause and the choice of jurisdiction. F, urthermore, the Claimant explains that the contract was not conditioned by the signature of another "definite" contract which means that the contract was final and binding. The Claimant furthermore refers to Clause 9 of the contract which states that he had all the required conditions for the practice of Football which was in clear contradiction with clause 13 which states that the contract shall be null in case he did not pass the medical tests. The Claimant alleges that the Respondent had named the contract "promissory employment contract" with the bad intention to justify a possible invalidation of the contract if he did not pass the medical examination.
In addition, the Claimant mentions that Clause 6 established a contractual penalty of EUR 500,000 in case he would breach the contract.
11. The Claimant states that the only excuse that the Respondent had used to justify its breach of contract was the fact that in 2005, he had not played for the club M but instead for the club G but that this was not a valid reason for a premature termination of the contract. The Claimant explains that his agent had informed the President of the Respondent that he had played for the club M in the 1st division of the U championship until the end in March 2005 and afterwards has joined the squad of the club G in April 2005.
12. Moreover, the Claimant affirms that his medical examination had a positive outcome and that the insurance company was ready to insure him. In support of his allegation, the Claimant enclosed a copy of the medical report in y.

13. Regarding the issue of the signatures, the Claimant comments that neither him nor his agent were told that more than one signature would have been needed to validate the contract and that the Respondent had not submitted any documentary evidence in this respect. The Claimant reiterates that a second contract was signed before a notary public in Y.
14. The Claimant furthermore mentions that an agreement had been concluded between his agent and the Respondent by means of which the latter committed to pay EUR 24,200 to the agent as a commission for his transfer and the transfer of the players Q and R. In support of this statement, the Claimant submitted a copy of the agreement. The Claimant concludes that it is not reasonable that the Respondent signs an agreement with his agent if it did not consider the contract to be final and binding.
15. In its comments thereto, the Respondent replied that the Claimant and the two other players (Q and R) had construed a strategy in order to damage the Respondent.
16. The Respondent recalls the FACTS OF THE CASE as follows: The agent of the player had entered into contact with it and had described all three players as top level professional players and had shown DVDs of them. The agent had assured that the Claimant was registered with a first division club. Once arrived in X, the President and the coach of the Respondent had been prevented from seeing the players playing and the agent had proposed to sign a pre-contract immediately. If the representatives of the Respondent had seen the Claimant playing, they would have noticed that he was not registered with a first division club as they would have noticed his physical deficiencies. The Respondent had informed each player and also the agent that it was not a valid and definitive employment contract but only a promissory contract. The Respondent did not want to sign an employment contract before the conducting of the medical examination and because the President was anyway not empowered to validate the contract with his sole signature. The signature of two other board members would be needed. The players and the agent had fully understood the situation. The Respondent asserts that at no point in time, an employment contract had been signed before a notary public and that the burden of proof rests with the Claimant. The Respondent continues that with his assertion, the Claimant recognises that the signed document of 16 June 2005 was not a binding employment contract.
17. The Respondent explains that once it found out that the Claimant had been registered with a second division club instead of with a first division club, it decided not to enter into a definitive employment contract. The Respondent affirms that the category in which a player is playing, is capital for the taking of a decision about a player and that it was a fact that at the moment of the conclusion of the pre-contract, the Claimant had been playing with the second division club, G.
18. The Respondent claims that the Claimant and his agent had been hiding information from the beginning and that the Respondent would never sign an employment contract with unknown players which it had never seen playing.
The Respondent reiterates that it had seen the Claimant playing only on DVD.
Furthermore, the Respondent stresses that the contract is printed on white paper without any official heading of the Respondent. Also, the contract provides for space for three signatures as it provides for three lines. In support of this statement, the Respondent enclosed a sample of an ordinary employment contract which is printed on official paper of the club.
19. In addition to that, the Respondent mentions that according to art. 48 of its Statutes, each document which creates obligations for the club needs to be furnished at least with the signature of the club's President as well as with the signature of either one of the Vice Presidents or the delegate President. In order to corroborate its statement, the Respondent submitted a copy of an extract of its Statutes. Regarding the agreement concluded between the Respondent and the agent of the player, the Respondent explains that it had entered into the agreement for the event that a definitive employment contract would be signed with the Claimant.
20. The Respondent claims that the misleading acts and the misconduct of the Claimant and his agent during the negotiations were a clear case of "culpa in contrahendo" which means the lack of loyal and honest behaviour during negotiations and that therefore, the Respondent should be compensated for sustained damages. By means of a counter-claim, the Respondent requests to be reimbursed for all expenses which it had incurred such as the expenses for the flight of the Claimant from X to Y, the expenses for the hotel in x and y as well as the medical expenses in the total amount of EUR 60,000.
The club adds that the Claimant is jointly and severally liable with the players Q and R to reimburse the amount of EUR 60,000.

21. In his comments, the Claimant rejects the counter-claim of the Respondent and all allegations produced by the Respondent. Regarding the submitted standard employment contracts, the Claimant considers it to be common practice to have a private agreement besides the "federative" one. He mentions that the only reason why the contract had been called pre-contract was due its subjection to medical examination. The arguments that the representatives of the Respondent did not have the opportunity to watch him playing had not prevented the Respondent from signing the contract and from taking him to Y.He adds that all expenses had been paid by the Respondent but that the latte had acted at its own risk by going to X to hire him and the two other players. The Claimant adds that he had remained unemployed until January 2006.
22. The Claimant informed FIFA that he had signed new employment contracts with the club M from 21 February 2006 until 30 August 2006 and with the club V from 1 August 2006 until 30 December 2006.
23. The Respondent rejects the claim of the player and is claiming the amount of EUR 60,000 for the damage it had suffered.

II. CONSIDERATIONS OF THE DISPUTE RESOLUTION CHAMBER

1. First of all, the Chamber analysed whether it was competent to deal with the matter at stake. In this respect, it referred to art. 18 par. 2 and 3 of the Rules Governing the Procedures of the Players' ' Status Committee and the Dispute Resolution Chamber (DRC). The present matter was submitted to FIFA on 23 August 2005, as a consequence the Chamber concluded that the revised Rules Governing Procedures (edition 2005) on matters pending before the decision making bodies of FIFA are applicable to the matter at hand.
2. With regard to the competence of the Chamber, art. 3 par. 1 of the above- mentioned Rules states that the Dispute Resolution Chamber shall examine its jurisdiction in the light of articles 22 to 24 of the current version of the Regulations for the Status and Transfer of Players (edition 2005). In accordance with art. 24 par. 1 in combination with art. 22 (b) of the aforementioned Regulations, the Dispute Resolution Chamber shall adjudicate on employment-related disputes between a club and a player that have an international dimension.
3. As a consequence, the Dispute Resolution Chamber is the competent body to decide on the present litigation involving a X player and a Y club regarding a dispute arisen in connection with an employment contract.
4. Subsequently, the members of the Chamber analyzed which edition of the Regulations for the Status and Transfer of Players should be applicable as to the substance of the matter. In this respect, the Chamber referred, on the one hand, to art. 26 par. 1 and 2 of the Regulations for the Status and Transfer of Players (edition 2005) and, on the other hand, to the fact that the relevant contract at the basis of the present dispute was signed on 16 June 2005 and the claim was lodged at FIFA on 23 August 2005.
   In view of the aforementioned, the Chamber concluded that the current FIFA Regulations for the Status and Transfer of Players (edition 2005, hereinafter: the Regulations) are applicable to the case at hand as to the substance.
5. In continuation, and entering into the substance of the matter, the members of the Chamber started by acknowledging the above mentioned facts and all further documentation contained in the file. In particular, they took note that a contract called "promissory employment contract" had been signed by the Claimant and the President of the Respondent which provided for a period of validity from 1 July 2005 until 30 June 2006.
6. Furthermore, the Chamber noted that the Claimant claims that a valid and binding employment contract had been concluded between him and the Respondent and that the contract had been breached by the Respondent wherefore he claims payment of compensation in the amount of EUR 37,000 equal to the salaries of the whole contractual period.
7. On the other hand, the members of the Chamber acknowledged that the Respondent claims that no valid contract had been signed between it and the Claimant and that by means of a counter-claim, the Respondent claims payment in the amount of EUR 60,000 from the Claimant (joint and several liability with the players Q and R) for sustained damages as the Claimant had provided the Respondent with wrong information on his former club.
8. The Chamber stated that it first had to analyse whether a valid and binding employment contract had been concluded between the parties and, in a second step, to determine whether any party is accountable for compensation and/or sporting sanctions.

9. The Chamber stated that a contract has to be signed by both parties in order to be valid and binding. In this respect, the Chamber noted that the contract had been signed by the Claimant and one representative of the Respondent, namely the club's President, therefore it had been signed by both parties.
10. The Chamber drew its attention to the argument of the Respondent that two other board members would have had to sign the contract in order for the contract to become valid. The Respondent further alleged that the Claimant had been informed that the sole signature of the club's President was not sufficient for the validity of the contract. The Chamber took note of the fact that this allegation was contested by the Claimant.
11. In this regard, the Chamber stated that the alleged necessity of three signatures for the validity of this employment contract is a club-internal proxy rule which is not known to third parties and therefore does not have any legal effects on the validity of this contract unless the contracting partner, in casu the Claimant, is clearly informed about the respective rule. The Chamber noted that the Respondent had failed to provide any kind of evidence in order to corroborate its allegation that the Claimant had indeed been informed that the signature of the President of the Respondent was not sufficient for the validity of the contract. The Chamber also stated that the Claimant did not have the obligation to verify whether the President of the Respondent was empowered to solely sign a contract. As in the present case the signature of the club's President is concerned, the Claimant could assume that as the highest possible representative of the club, the President is authorised to sign individually.
12. Furthermore, the DRC turned its attention to the argument of the Respondent that the contract provides for three lines, i.e. allegedly for space for three signatures. The Chamber stated by simply providing space for three signatures, it could not be concluded that the Respondent had informed the Claimant about the necessity of three signatures from the club.
13. In conclusion of the aforementioned, the Chamber stated that the Respondent's argument that the contract is not valid due to the lack of two more signatures, has to be rejected and therefore, the Chamber considered that the contract has been duly signed by both parties concerned.
14. In continuation, the Chamber stated that in order to determine whether or not a valid and binding employment contract had been concluded between the parties, it furthermore had to verify whether all principle elements ("essentialia negotii") were contained in the relevant document.
15. After analysing the contract, the Chamber concluded that in the contract, the parties had agreed upon all principle elements such as the place of work, the period of validity, the salary and a penalty clause. Therefore, it decided that the contract is valid and binding.
16. For the sake of good order, the Chamber added that for the interpretation of a contract its content is relevant but not its title (in casu "promissory employment contract").
17. Furthermore, the Chamber took note of the Respondent's allegation that it had been provided with inaccurate information on the Claimant's former club by the agent of the Claimant by being informed that the Claimant had played for the first division club M at the time of the contract negotiations whereas he was playing for the second division club G.
18. In this respect, the members of the DRC remarked that if a club is interested in signing an employment contract with a new player, it is the responsibility of the new club to inform itself about the player's career, before signing an employment contract.
19. Furthermore, the Chamber added that the contract concluded between the parties does not contain any clause stipulating the condition that the Claimant had previously played for a first division club.
20. On account of the aforementioned considerations, the Chamber stated that by not verifying the relevant facts concerning the Claimant, the Respondent had taken the risk of not being accurately informed about the Claimant's career and that being provided with inaccurate information on the Claimant's former club, does not constitute a valid reason for the unilateral termination of the contract.
21. For the sake of good order, the Chamber added that the Respondent's argument that it was prevented from seeing the Claimant playing live, is irrelevant in the case at hand as it is the Respondent's responsibility to take the necessary steps to verify if the player fulfils the conditions for being hired prior to the signing of any contract, in particular to verify his skills and fitness level.
22. In view of all the above, the Chamber concluded that by not implementing the employment contract concluded with the Claimant due to the alleged inaccurate information on the Claimant's previous club, the Respondent had breached the relevant employment contract without valid reason.

23. In conclusion of the fact that the Respondent had breached the contract without just cause, the Chamber decided that the Claimant is entitled to receive compensation from the Respondent for breach of contract committed by the Respondent.
24. In this respect, the Chamber, however, added that the Respondent apparently had believed that it had only concluded a "promissory contract" with the Claimant and not a final contract and deemed that this should have a mitigating effect on the compensation which is to be paid by the Respondent.
25. The Chamber took into consideration that the employment contract concluded between the parties provided for a period of validity of one year.
26. Furthermore, and still with respect to the amount of compensation payable to the Claimant, the Chamber took note of the fact that the Claimant had signed a new employment contract with the club M from 21 February 2006 until 30 August 2006.
27. With regard to the compensation due for breach of contract without just cause committed by the Respondent, the Chamber decided that taking into account all the aforementioned considerations (points II.23 to II.26), the Respondent has to pay to the Claimant the lump sum of EUR 15,000.

III. DECISION OF THE DISPUTE RESOLUTION CHAMBER

1. The claim of the player P is partially accepted.
2. The Respondent, Club C, has to pay the total amount of EUR 15,000 as compensation to the player P, within 30 days following the date of the communication of the present decision.
3. In the event that the above-mentioned amount is not paid within the stated deadline, an interest rate of 5% per year will apply as of expiry of the relevant time-frame and the present matter shall be submitted to FIFA's Disciplinary Committee, so that the necessary disciplinary sanctions may be imposed.
4. Any further claims submitted by the Claimant are rejected.
5. The Claimant is directed to inform the Respondent directly and immediately of the account number to which the remittance is to be made and to notify the Dispute Resolution Chamber of every payment received.
6. The counter-claim submitted by Club C is fully rejected.
7. According to art. 61 par. 1 of the FIFA Statutes, this decision may be appealed against before the Court of Arbitration for Sport (CAS). The statement of appeal must be sent to the CAS directly within 21 days of receipt of notification of this decision and shall contain all the elements in accordance with point 2 of the directives issued by the CAS, a copy of which we enclose hereto. Within another 10 days following the expiry of the time limit for filing the statement of appeal, the appellant shall file a brief stating the facts and legal arguments giving rise to the appeal with the CAS (cf. point 4 of the directives).

1061207
DECISION OF THE DISPUTE RESOLUTION CHAMBER
passed in Zurich, Switzerland, on 26 October 2006,
in the following composition:
Slim Aloulou (Tunisia), Chairman
Gerardo Movilla (Spain), member
Joaquim Evangelista (Portugal), member
Mario Gallavotti (Italy), member
Peter Friend (Australia), member
on the claim presented by the Player P, Country X as Claimant
against the club C, Country Y as Respondent
regarding a contractual dispute arisen between the player and the club

I. FACTS OF THE CASE

1. In July 2004, the player P (hereinafter: the Claimant) and the club C (hereinafter: the Respondent) concluded an employment contract which does not stipulate the period of validity. In addition to this contract, the parties concluded an Annex on 14 July 2004 stipulating the financial conditions for the period from 20 June 2004 until 21 June 2006 (hereinafter: Annex 1) and a second Annex on

25 July 2005 stipulating the financial conditions for the period from 20 July 2005 until 20 July 2007 (hereinafter: Annex 2).

2. Annex 1 provides for the first year an allowance of USD 20,000 for the Claimant plus monthly wages of USD 4,000.
   Annex 2 provides for the same remuneration for the first year: a net allowance of USD 20,000 for the costs of moving and USD 4,000 as monthly wages. Both Annexes left out the remuneration for the second year.
3. On 10 October 2005, the Claimant lodged a formal complaint at FIFA against the Respondent, claiming that the latter had breached the employment contract. He asserts that salaries in the amount of USD 6,000 net are outstanding for the first season (2004/2005) for the following months:
   - USD 2,000 for October 2004 (he was paid only USD 2,000)
   - USD 2,000 for November 2004 (he was paid only USD 2,000)
   - USD 2,000 for June 2005 (he was paid only USD 2,000).
4. The Claimant affirms not having received any salary with respect to Annex 2 (2005/2006) in which the terms were identical to the first one and claims the amount of USD 68.000 net (USD 20,000 plus 12xUSD 4,000). The Claimant requests the total net amount of USD 74,000 from the Respondent.
5. The Claimant furthermore states that after the game of Z against C, the coach of the Respondent had physically attacked him, insulted him in front of the other players and had forbidden him to participate in the trainings. In support of his statement, the Claimant submitted a translation of a certificate dated 1 September 2005 from a community health center attesting that the Claimant suffered from anxiety, fear and unsteady sleep. The Claimant also stated that he had asked the Y Football Federation for protection but that he had never received any reply from it.
6. In its statement of defence, the Respondent asserts that even though the employment contract concluded between the parties was valid until 20 July 2007, the Claimant left the club on 1 August 2005 without permission. The Respondent affirms having held a council meeting on 10 August and 30 August 2005 regarding the Claimant's violation of the contract. At the council meeting, it was decided that financial sanctions were to be imposed on the Claimant and that the Professional Football League of Y would be informed about the problems with the Claimant. The Respondent states that it does not have any financial obligations towards the Claimant as the latter had breached the employment contract.
7. The Respondent alleged that the employment contract submitted by the Claimant was not identical with the one in its possession and the one deposited at the Professional Football League of Y as the registration number is missing. The Respondent hereto enclosed a copy of the employment contract in its possession. In addition to that, the Respondent asserts that the Annex to the employment contract submitted by the Claimant is forged which could be seen from the stamp of the Respondent. The Respondent did not specify which Annex it was referring to and did not present the alleged authentic Annex. The Respondent enclosed extracts of the minutes of its council meetings of 10 August and 30 August 2005, witness statements that the Claimant had left the Respondent on 1 August 2005 without authorisation, a copy of the order of the Respondent dated 31 August 2005 which rules that salary would be stopped being paid to the Claimant as of 1 September 2005 and that a fine would be imposed on the Claimant for the unauthorised leaving from it.
8. In his comments thereto, the Claimant confirmed that he had played for the Respondent until 1 August 2005 and that he had left the Respondent after having been exposed to verbal and physical violence by the head coach. He adds that all statements made by the Respondent were attempts of faking the facts in order to avoid to be held liable for its contractual obligations. The Claimant furthermore refers to his declarations contained in his statement of claim.
9. Upon FIFA's invitation to submit its closing arguments, in particular with respect to the allegation of the Claimant that he was verbally and physically exposed to violence of the head coach and that the salaries of October 2004, November 2004 and June 2005 were outstanding and to submit documentary evidence on the effected salary payments, the Respondent rejected all allegations regarding the alleged violent acts committed against the Claimant and affirms having paid the Claimant all the salaries until 1 August 2005.
   The Respondent asked for an extension of the deadline until 31 August 2006 to submit evidence of salary payments but has actually not submitted any evidence.
10. With respect to the allegation of the Respondent that the Annexes to the contract were forged by the Claimant, FIFA invited the Respondent to submit the original Annex to the contract. However, the Respondent has not submitted any such document.

II. CONSIDERATIONS OF THE DISPUTE RESOLUTION CHAMBER

1. First of all, the Chamber analysed whether it was competent to deal with the matter at stake. In this respect, it referred to art. 18 par. 2 and 3 of the Rules Governing the Procedures of the Players' ' Status Committee and the Dispute Resolution Chamber. The present matter was submitted to FIFA on 10 October 2005, as a consequence the Chamber concluded that the revised Rules Governing Procedures (edition 2005) on matters pending before the decision making bodies of FIFA are applicable to the matter at hand.
2. With regard to the competence of the Chamber, art. 3 par. 1 of the above- mentioned Rules states that the Dispute Resolution Chamber (DRC) shall examine its jurisdiction in the light of articles 22 to 24 of the current version of the Regulations for the Status and Transfer of Players (edition 2005). In accordance with art. 24 par. 1 in combination with art. 22 (b) of the aforementioned Regulations, the Dispute Resolution Chamber shall adjudicate on employment- related disputes between a club and a player that have an international dimension.
3. As a consequence, the Dispute Resolution Chamber is the competent body to decide on the present litigation involving a Y club and a X player regarding the dispute arisen in connection with an employment contract.
4. Subsequently, the members of the Chamber analyzed which edition of the Regulations for the Status and Transfer of Players should be applicable as to the substance of the matter. In this respect, the Chamber referred, on the one hand, to art. 26 par. 1 and 2 of the Regulations for the Status and Transfer of Players (edition 2005) and, on the other hand, to the fact that the relevant contract at the basis of the present dispute was signed in July 2004 and the claim was lodged at FIFA on 10 October 2005.
   In view of the aforementioned, the Chamber concluded that the current FIFA Regulations for the Status and Transfer of Players (edition 2005, hereinafter: the Regulations) are applicable to the case at hand as to the substance.
5. In continuation, and entering into the substance of the matter, the members of the Chamber started by acknowledging the above mentioned facts and all further correspondence contained in the file. In particular, they took note that the two parties had signed an employment contract for the period from 20 June 2004 until 20 July 2007, which can be established in accordance with the documents contained in the file.
6. Equally, the Chamber noted that it is uncontested that the Claimant had left the Respondent on 1 August 2005, i.e. prior to the end of the validity of the employment contract, without permission and without giving any notice to the Respondent.
7. Furthermore, the Chamber took note that on the one hand the Claimant is of the opinion of having left the Respondent with a valid reason as allegedly half of three monthly salaries were outstanding and as he allegedly was assaulted by the coach of the Respondent and prevented from4 participating in the trainings. The members of the DRC noted that the Claimant requests payment of USD 6,000 for outstanding salaries and USD 68,000 as compensation for the contractual value of the second year of the employment contract.
8. On the other hand, the Chamber acknowledged that the Respondent considers that the Claimant had breached the employment contract by leaving it prematurely. The members noted that the Respondent had affirmed to have paid all salaries to the Claimant until 1 August 2005 and that it rejected the allegation of the Claimant that he had been exposed to violent acts committed by the coach.
9. In continuation, the Chamber first drew its attention to the alleged outstanding salaries of October and November 2004 und June 2005 in the total amount of USD 6,000.
   According to the Claimant, he had only received half of the salaries for the aforementioned months, i.e. for each month USD 2,000 instead of USD 4,000.
   The Chamber acknowledged the fact that this allegation was contested by the Respondent.
10. The members added that the alleged outstanding amount of USD 6,000 which equals to one and a half months of the Claimant's salary, could not be considered, in the present case, as substantial enough to justify a premature termination of an employment contract. In this respect, the Chamber concluded that the relevant alleged outstanding salaries did not constitute a just cause for the unilateral termination of the employment contract.
11. In continuation, the members drew their attention to the allegation of the Claimant that he had been physically assaulted by the coach of the Respondent and noted that this allegation was contested by the Respondent. The Chamber acknowledged that the Claimant had submitted a medical certificate

attesting anxiety, fear and unsteady sleep. The Chamber stated that the medical certificate had been issued on 1 September 2005, i.e. one month after the Claimant's leaving from the Respondent. The members considered that from the aforementioned medical certificate, it could not be drawn any conclusion as to why the Claimant suffered anxiety and fear and - in the case of a possible assault - as to the time of the assault and the aggressor.

12. In view of the above, the Chamber concluded that the Claimant had not been able to provide FIFA with evidence with respect to the alleged assault committed by the coach of the Respondent and that the allegation of the Claimant therefore has to be rejected.
13. As a result of the above mentioned deliberations, the Chamber concluded that there was no just cause for the Claimant to leave the Respondent prior to the expiry of the employment contract. As a consequence, the Chamber decided that the Claimant had breached the relevant employment contract by leaving the Respondent without just cause on 1 August 2005.
14. However, the Chamber added that the Respondent bears a considerable part of the responsibility for the early termination of the employment contract as it had not contested the assertion of the Claimant that he was prevented from participating in the trainings of the Respondent.
15. The Chamber continued that notwithstanding the abovementioned breach of contract committed by the Claimant, it had to verify the allegation of the latter that he had not received half of his salaries for October and November 2004 as well as for June 2005 in the total amount of USD 6,000.
    In this respect, the Chamber noted that the Respondent had asserted having paid the Claimant all due salaries until 1 August 2005, however, without submitting any documentary evidence in support of its allegation. The members stated that as it is the responsibility of the employer to submit evidence on effected salary payments and as the Respondent has failed to provide evidence in this respect, the Respondent has to pay the Claimant the outstanding and claimed salaries in the amount of USD 6,000.
    The Chamber added that for the period from 20 July 2005 until 1 August 2005, in accordance with Annex 2 of the relevant employment contract, the Claimant was additionally entitled to receive the proportionate salary in the amount of USD 1,330 which leads to a total of USD 7,330 which the Respondent has to pay to the Claimant.

III. DECISION OF THE DISPUTE RESOLUTION CHAMBER

1. The claim of the player is partially accepted.
2. The Respondent has to pay the total amount of USD 7,330 as outstanding salaries to the player within 30 days following the date of the communication of the present decision.
3. In the event that the above-mentioned amount is not paid within the stated deadline, an interest rate of 5% per year will apply as of expiry of the relevant time-frame and the present matter shall be submitted to FIFA's Disciplinary Committee, so that the necessary disciplinary sanctions may be imposed.
4. Any further claims submitted by the Claimant are rejected.
5. The Claimant is directed to inform the Respondent directly and immediately of the account number to which the remittance is to be made and to notify the Dispute Resolution Chamber of every payment received.
6. According to art. 61 par. 1 of the FIFA Statutes, this decision may be appealed against before the Court of Arbitration for Sport (CAS). The statement of appeal must be sent to the CAS directly within 21 days of receipt of notification of this decision and shall contain all the elements in accordance with point 2 of the directives issued by the CAS, a copy of which we enclose hereto. Within another 10 days following the expiry of the time limit for filing the statement of appeal, the appellant shall file a brief stating the facts and legal arguments giving rise to the appeal with the CAS (cf. point 4 of the directives).

1061318
DECISION OF THE DISPUTE RESOLUTION CHAMBER
passed in Zurich, Switzerland, on 26 October 2006,
in the following composition:
Slim Aloulou (Tunisia), Chairman

Gerardo Movilla (Spain), member
Joaquim Evangelista (Portugal), member
Mario Gallavotti (Italy), member
Peter Friend (Australia), member
on the claim presented by the player P, country X as Claimant
against the club C, country Y as Respondent
regarding a contractual dispute arisen between the player and the club

I. FACTS OF THE CASE

1. On 20 December 2005, the player P (hereinafter: the Claimant) lodged a formal complaint at FIFA, requesting that it be declared that a valid employment contract had been concluded between him and the club C (hereinafter: the Respondent), and that the latter is to be obliged to pay him the following amounts:
   - EUR 1,680.43 for incurred travel costs of the Claimant and his wife
   - USD 200,000 as net salaries for two years (yearly salary of USD 100,000)
   - USD 12,000 payment of commission by the Respondent to "Z" (Z is an agency founded by Mr F, assignee of the Claimant)
   - CHF 25,000 as court fees
   - EUR 1,500 as lawyer fees
2. The Claimant describes the FACTS OF THE CASE as follows: On 16 October 2005 an oral agreement had been concluded between the Respondent and him at the presence of the following persons:
   - Mr G, board manager of the Respondent
   - Mr H, manager of the Respondent
   - The Claimant and his wife
   - Mr F and Mr V, both assignees of the Claimant
3. According to the Claimant, the oral agreement provided, inter alia, for the following terms:
   - The Claimant would be hired by the Respondent for two years
   - The basic yearly salary amounts to USD 100,000 net
   - The Claimant will be provided with a furnished apartment and a car will be put at his disposal
   - The Claimant would receive a return flight ticket for himself and his wif to his city of origins
   - The Claimant would receive the usual premiums from the Respondent and the goal premiums for championships
   - The Respondent would pay a commission of USD 12,000 to Mr F and Mr V (both assignees of the Claimant)
   - A maximal transfer compensation of EUR 50,000 would be paid by the Respondent to the Claimant's previous club in X, club L, with which the Claimant was under contract until 31 December 2006
   - The Claimant would travel to the training camp of the Respondent in D on 9 November 2005 and would subsequently fly to E with the team of the Respondent.
4. On 27 October 2005, the Claimant agreed with his club, L, that the transfer compensation would amount to EUR 33,000.

   However, there was not yet an agreement regarding the date of the payment. By means of an email dated 28 October 2005, Mr F (assignee of the Claimant) informed Mr G (board manager of the Respondent) about the transfer amount of EUR 33,000 agreed upon with L and confirmed the terms and conditions of the employment contract as earlier agreed upon orally (employment contract for two years, yearly salary of USD 100,000 to be paid in 12 monthly rates, free apartment and free car, match bonuses and USD 12,000 as commission payable to Mr F's agency). He also confirmed that the Claimant would participate in the training camp of the Respondent.
5. On the same day, by means of an email, Mr G (board manager of the Respondent) confirmed that they agreed on a two year contract on condition that the Claimant's age would not exceed 33 in October 2007.

   Equally, Mr G confirmed that he personally agreed on a yearly salary of USD 100,000 and a transfer compensation of EUR 33,000 payable to the Claimant's former club but that he had to discuss this with his colleagues from the club. In his email, Mr G offered that a Memorandum of Understanding (hereinafter: MOU) would be signed in the training camp in D. Mr G described the MOU as a "simplified version of the contract and a legally binding document". He furthermore mentioned that the signing of the final contract would take place in E. (The exact wording of the email reads: "We agree on a two-year contract on condition P's age does not exceed thirty three years in October 2007").

6. By means of an email dated 2 November 2005, Mr G asked the Claimant's former club, L, about the date of payment of the transfer compensation, the bank details and the date on which the Claimant would be free. In an email dated 6 November 2005, L confirmed the details of the transfer compensation.
7. As agreed, the Claimant participated in the daily trainings of the Respondent in D from 9 November until 13 November 2005.
   On 11 November 2005, the MOU and the employment contract, both signed by a representative of the Respondent, were handed out to the Claimant.
8. The MOU provided, inter alia, for the following:
   - A two-year contract
   - Monthly salary of USD 8,000 and an additional "appearance fee" of 500 (in local currency) per game
   - A three bedroom apartment free of rent
   - Providing of a car for the Claimant's use
   - Flight tickets
   - Hospital expenses and medical treatment in case of illness or injury
9. The employment contract provided, inter alia, for the following:
   - Contract period from 10 November 2005 until 31 October 2007
   - Salary according to schedule A which provides for a monthly salary of USD 2,500 for the first year (Note: There is no indication of the salary for the second year).
   - Bonus at the discretion of the Respondent
   - Benefits according to Schedule B
10. Still following the FACTS OF THE CASE as outlined by the Claimant, on 16 November 2005, the Respondent told the Claimant orally that a three bedroom apartment had been organised for the Claimant in E. Further details were discussed between the Claimant and the Respondent on the same day regarding the employment contract and both parties agreed in all the discussed points.
11. On 14 November and 21 November 2005, the Claimant participated in trainings and three preparatory matches of the Respondent. On 20 November 2005, Mr G contacted Mr F (assignee of the Claimant) and complained about the Claimant's performance. A day later, Mr G spoke to the team and criticised the Claimant and the coach. By means of a sms of 22 November 2005, Mr G told Mr F that the Claimant was not worth the amounts agreed upon and that the final signing of the employment contract would only take place if the Claimant showed excellent performances.
12. Mr F communicated the new situation to L. The latter club mentioned that it had not received the arranged transfer compensation from the Respondent within the agreed deadline and that therefore, the Claimant did not have its permission anymore to participate in trainings or test matches of the Respondent. Mr F explained the situation to Mr G by sms and mentioned that the Claimant had no interest in going back to X since he had already moved to Y and therefore, the player insisted on the execution of the contract.
13. Via sms, Mr G told Mr F that he had to respect the decision of L and that the Claimant would not participate in any matches or trainings of the Respondent anymore. He mentioned that he would remunerate the Claimant for the period from 8 November 2005 until 30 November 2005 and that he would also cover the expenses of his flight. L invited the Respondent by fax to pay the agreed transfer compensation otherwise the Claimant had to return to X. According to the Claimant, however, the transfer compensation was never paid to L.
14. The Claimant is of the opinion that by handing out the MOU and the employment contract to him, both signed by a representative of the Respondent, the latter had made him a valid employment offer which contained all essentialia negotii and that he had accepted all the terms and conditions as stipulated in the MOU and in the employment contract .
15. In response to the claim of the Claimant, the Football Association of Y informed FIFA that it intended to submit the present matter to the next meeting of its Players' Status Committee.
16. FIFA invited the FA of Y to inform about the claim apparently pending at it, in particular as to by whom and on which date the claim was lodged.
    Furthermore, clarification was demanded as to the precise request of the claim.

FIFA also invited the Respondent to submit its response to the claim with respect to the substance of the matter. However, FIFA did not get any reply from neither the Respondent nor the FA of Y, despite numerous reminders.

17. Being asked about his position with regard to the challenged issue of the jurisdiction, the Claimant responded that he insisted that the competent body of FIFA renders a decision in the matter at hand. The Claimant enclosed two witness statements of Mr V and Mr F by means of which they confirmed that the statements of the Claimant submitted to FIFA were true and that an employment contract had been concluded with the Respondent.
18. Upon FIFA's invitation to the Football Federation of X to inform if an International Transfer Certificate (ITC) had been issued for the Claimant in favour of FA of Y, the FA of X replied on 13 July 2006 that no ITC had been issued for the Claimant and that the latter was still registered with its affiliated club L.

II. CONSIDERATIONS OF THE DISPUTE RESOLUTION CHAMBER

1. First of all, the Dispute Resolution Chamber (DRC) referred to the argument of the Respondent respectively the Football Association of Y that "the matter will be discussed at the next Players Status' Committee meeting of the Football Association of Y by means of which the competence of FIFA was implicitly disputed.
2. In this respect, the Chamber referred to its well established jurisprudence according to which, in general, in employment-related disputes between a club and a player that have an international dimension, i.e. the parties do not belong to the same country, both parties were entitled to refer the dispute to FIFA's bodies, unless an independent arbitration tribunal respecting the principle of equal representation of players and clubs with an independent chairman has been established at national level.
3. The members of the DRC acknowledged that the Respondent respectively the of Y had not provided FIFA with any evidence to prove that an independent arbitration tribunal in compliance with the requirements of the FIFA regulations of Y nor the Respondent had presented evidence showing that proceedings regarding the present case had actually been initiated in order to bring the case at hand before the deciding body of the FA of Y on the request of any of the two parties. As a consequence, the Chamber established that the Respondent's objection to the competence of FIFA to deal with the matter has be rejected and that, in principle, the matter can be considered as to the substance.
4. In continuation, the Chamber referred to art. 18 par. 2 and 3 of the Rules Governing the Procedures of the Players' ' Status Committee and the Dispute Resolution Chamber. The present matter was submitted to FIFA on 20 December 2005, as a consequence the Chamber concluded that the revised Rules Governing Procedures (edition 2005) on matters pending before the decision making bodies of FIFA are applicable to the matter at hand.
5. With regard to the competence of the Chamber, art. 3 par. 1 of the above- mentioned Rules states that the DRC shall examine its jurisdiction in the light of articles 22 to 24 of the current version of the Regulations for the Status and Transfer of Players (edition 2005). In accordance with art. 24 par. 1 in combination with art. 22b) of the aforementioned Regulations, the DRC shall adjudicate on employment-related disputes between a club and a player that have an international dimension.
6. As a consequence, the DRC is the competent body to decide on the present litigation involving a X player and a Y club regarding a dispute pertaining to an employment contract.
7. Subsequently, the members of the Chamber analyzed which edition of the Regulations for the Status and Transfer of Players should be applicable as to the substance of the matter. In this respect, the Chamber referred, on the one hand, to art. 26 par. 1 and 2 of the Regulations for the Status and Transfer of Players (edition 2005) and, on the other hand, to the fact that the relevant contract negotiations between the two parties at the basis of which the present dispute arose, were mainly held in the period from 16 October 2005 until 16 November 2005 and the claim was lodged before FIFA on 20 December 2005.

   In view of the aforementioned, the Chamber concluded that the current FIFA Regulations for the Status and Transfer of Players (edition 2005, hereinafter: the Regulations) are applicable to the case at hand as to the substance.
8. Once its competence and the applicable regulations were thus established, the Chamber went on to deal with the substance of the matter. The Chamber carefully studied the facts outlined above and all the documents contained in the file. In particular, the members took note that the Claimant considers

that a valid employment contract had been concluded between him and the Respondent, and that he is entitled to receive compensation for breach of contract.

9. On the other hand, the Chamber acknowledged the fact that despite numerous reminders of FIFA, the Respondent had not submitted its position in the substance of the matter. The Chamber stated that by not submitting any response to the claim, the Respondent had renounced its right to be heard and had left the statements of the Claimant uncontested. Therefore, the Chamber exposed that its considerations and its decision shall be based on the information and documentation contained in the file. In other words, the decision shall be taken upon the basis of the documents on file (cf. art. 9 par. 3 of the Rules Governing the Procedures of the Players' ' Status Committee and the Dispute Resolution Chamber).
10. The Chamber pointed out that it first had to analyse whether or not a valid employment contract had been concluded between the two parties concerned and that it had to do so by perusing the relevant incidents which had occurred in the course of the contract negotiations between the Claimant and the Respondent.
11. In this respect and referring to art. 2 par. 2 of the Regulations, according to which employment contracts between a professional player and a club shall be concluded in writing, the Chamber examined whether in the case at stake a written contract had actually been concluded between the two relevant parties.
12. In this regard, the Chamber acknowledged that the Respondent had handed out a MOU and an employment contract to the Claimant on 11 November 2005, both documents being signed by a representative of the Respondent.
13. After having examined the two aforementioned documents, copies of which were remitted to the file, the Chamber noted that the two documents had not been signed by the Claimant. Referring to the general principle that every contract requests an offer and the acceptance of the offer, the Chamber concluded that the offer of the Respondent for employment had not been followed by an acceptance of the offer by the Claimant. The deciding authority deemed that this was somehow understandable since the financial terms of the employment contract significantly differed from those contained in the MOU, the latter being closer to the alleged previous negotiations. Therefore, the Chamber considered that no valid employment contract had been concluded between the parties.
14. For the sake of good order, the Chamber added that the contract negotiations conducted between the two parties prior to the handing over of the two aforementioned documents, did not have a binding character as they had to be regarded as mere statements of intention showing the general willingness to enter into a contractual relationship.
15. After having elaborated that no formal and valid written employment contract had been concluded between the parties, the Chamber acknowledged that the Claimant had actually joined the Respondent, had moved to Y and had taken part in the daily trainings and three preparatory matches with the Respondent from 9 until 14 November 2005 and on 21 November 2005.
16. The Chamber went on to state that the aforementioned actual circumstances of the present matter, in particular the participation of the Claimant in three preparatory matches with the Respondent, lead to the conclusion that a factual employment relationship had been established between the parties and that this factual relationship was to be taken into consideration.
17. Furthermore, the Chamber drew its attention to the ending of the factual employment relationship established between the two parties, respectively the reasons for the non-finalisation of a formal employment contract. In this respect, the Chamber recalled that in cases like the one at stake in which a player who is still under contract with his former club, is supposed to be transferred to a new club, the consent of three parties is necessary, namely the one of the player, the one of his former club as well as the one of his new club. The Chamber emphasised that in the present matter, the Respondent had failed to pay any transfer compensation to the Claimant's former club, L, and that therefore, the latter did not accept to free the Claimant. The Chamber was of the opinion that for these reasons, which did not lie in the Claimant's scope of influence, the factual employment relationship did not get finalised even though the Claimant had the serious intention of executing the envisaged employment contract.
18. Given that a factual employment relationship had been established between the Claimant and the Respondent in which the Claimant had rendered services to the Respondent and given the fact that the Claimant did not bear any responsibility for the actual ending of the aforementioned factual employment relationship, respectively the non-finalisation of a formal employment contract, the

Chamber deemed that the Claimant was entitled to receive compensation from the Respondent. This despite the fact that no formal and valid written employment contract had been concluded between the parties to the dispute. The Chamber deemed that on account of its stance, the Respondent had to be called to account for its responsibilities pertaining to the failure of the envisaged transaction.

19. On a side note, the members of the DRC present at the meeting, added that the aforementioned interpretation of the relationship between the Claimant and the Respondent and the conclusion that compensation had to be awarded to the Claimant was corroborated by the statement of Mr G that the Claimant would also be remunerated for the services rendered in the period from 8 November until 30 November 2005 and would also be compensated for his flight expenses.
20. In continuation, and with respect to the amount of compensation to be paid to the Claimant, the Chamber took into consideration that the MOU and the employment contract handed out to the Claimant both provided for a period of validity of two years. Yet, as already indicated, the financial terms of the two documents considerably differ one from the other.
21. Comparing the two aforementioned documents, the Chamber noted that the date of issue of the MOU was the 11 November 2005 whereas the employment contract handed out to the Claimant was issued on 10 November 2005.
    Following a general legal principle according to which a more recent agreement prevails over a previous one, the Chamber concluded that the MOU was to be considered as the decisive document being the more recent document. Furthermore it was pointed out that its content was more consistent with the substance of the contract negotiations.
22. Equally, and still with respect to the amount of compensation to be paid to the Claimant, the Chamber referred to the information provided to FIFA by the FA of X on 13 July 2006 that no ITC had been issued for the Claimant and that the latter was still registered with the club L. On this basis, the Chamber concluded that after having left the Respondent, the Claimant had apparently rejoined his previous club and continued to play for the club L, with which he had a valid employment contract until 31 December 2006.
    As a consequence, the earnings resulting from the latter contract also needed to be considered. In this respect, the DRC remarked in particular, that the existing contract with the X club covered 14 of the 24 months of the envisaged contractual relationship with the Respondent.
23. On account of all the above, the Chamber decided that taking into account the aforementioned considerations, a lump sum compensation of USD 35,000 to be paid by the Respondent to the Claimant appears to be reasonable and appropriate.
24. Finally, and referring to the Claimant's request pertaining to court fees and lawyer fees, the Chamber stated that according to art. 15 par. 2 of the Rules Governing the Procedures of the Players' ' Status Committee and the Dispute Resolution Chamber, DRC proceedings are free of charge. Moreover, par. 3 of the said provision establishes that no procedural compensation shall be awarded in proceedings of the DRC. The relevant requests had thus to be rejected.

III. DECISION OF THE DISPUTE RESOLUTION CHAMBER

1. The claim of the player P is partially accepted.
2. The Respondent, club C, has to pay the amount of USD 35,000 to the Claimant, within 30 days following the date of the notification of the present decision.
3. In the event that the above-mentioned amount is not paid within the stated deadline, an interest rate of 5% per year will apply as of expiry of the aforementioned deadline and the present matter shall be submitted to the FIFA Disciplinary Committee, so that the necessary disciplinary sanctions may be imposed.
4. Any further claims submitted by the Claimant are rejected.
5. The Claimant is instructed to inform the Respondent immediately and directly of the account number to which the remittance is to be made and to notify the Dispute Resolution Chamber of every payment received.
6. According to art. 61 par. 1 of the FIFA Statutes, this decision may be appealed against before the Court of Arbitration for Sport (CAS). The statement of appeal must be sent to the CAS directly within 21 days of receipt of notification of this decision and shall contain all the elements in accordance with point 2 of the directives issued by the CAS, a copy of which we enclose hereto. Within another 10 days following the expiry of the time limit for filing the statement of appeal, the appellant shall file a brief stating the facts and legal arguments giving rise to the appeal with the CAS (cf. point 4 of the directives).

21 NOVEMBER 2006

116132
DECISION OF THE DISPUTE RESOLUTION CHAMBER
passed in Zurich, Switzerland, on 21 November 2006,
in the following composition:
Slim Aloulou (Tunisia), Chairman
Paulo Rogerio Amoretty Souza (Brazil), member
Ivan Gazidis (USA), member
Carlos Soto (Chile), member
John Didulica (Australia), member
on a claim presented by the club, D, X represented by Mr. , Lawyer as "Claimant"
against the club, I, XX as "Respondent"
regarding the solidarity contribution related to the transfer of the player, C

I. FACTS OF THE CASE

1. The X Football Association has confirmed that the player C was born on 26 December 1979 and was registered with its affiliated club D from 11 January 1993 until 14 December 2000, i.e. between the ages of 13 and 20.
2. On 31 August 2004, the player C was transferred from the XX club J to the fellow XX club I.
3. On 15 October 2004, the X club D lodged a complaint with FIFA against the XX club I regarding the payment of a solidarity contribution. D alleged that I paid to J. the sum of ... 10,000,000 in connection with the transfer of the player C.
4. FIFA referred the X club D to the jurisprudence of the Dispute Resolution Chamber (in particular in a decision passed on 22 July 2004) in similar cases, in accordance with which the principle regarding the solidarity mechanism contained in the Regulations for the Status and Transfer of Players (edition September 2001) is not applicable to national transfers, not even in cases where the club claiming the payment of the relevant contribution is affiliated to another association. The said jurisprudence particularly refers to par. 1 of the Preamble of the aforementioned Regulations which establishes that the Regulations deal with the status and eligibility of players, as well as with the rules applicable whenever players move between clubs belonging to different associations. Equally, in its relevant jurisprudence, the Chamber points out that the principle of the solidarity mechanism is not binding at national level (cf. par. 2 of the Preamble of the said Regulations).
5. D responded to FIFA that it was in total disagreement with the invoked jurisprudence of the Dispute Resolution Chamber (DRC), in essence basing its position on the following arguments: The DRC is competent to hear this matter because it concerns clubs from different associations (X and XX) and therefore, the case is of an international nature. In support of the above, the X club referred to the decision of the DRC no. 55102 dated 13 May 2005, in which the DRC confirmed the international nature of the dispute on the basis of the parties" nationality. Consequently, the international nature that justifies the application of FIFA's regulations and the intervention of its deciding bodies arises from the different nationalities of the parties to a dispute. This ensures that the aims pursued in the regulations are met.

   In its decision of 22 July 2004 cited by FIFA, the DRC expressly recognised its competence to hear solidarity contribution claims.

   It is evident that the purpose of establishing the solidarity mechanism is to benefit the training clubs (cf. FIFA circular no. 769 dated 24 August 2001), irrespective of whether the transfer at the basis of a specific claim for the relevant contribution was between two clubs that belong to the same association or not, as the most important factor is that the claimant club belongs to a different association than the respondent club.

   If FIFA is not competent, it becomes impossible for training clubs to exercise the right to receive a solidarity contribution in cases of transfers between clubs that belong to the same association.

   The Preamble of the Regulations for the Status and Transfer of Players (edition September 2001) establishes that the associations have to draw up their own regulations to govern the domestic transfer system. However, very few associations have done so. In the absence of any such regulations, the pertinent FIFA regulations need to be directly applicable. The XX FootballFederation should have drawn up such regulations, which would have bee the applicable legislation in this case. However,

since the XX Federation has not done so, the DRC must be the competent body to deal with the present matter and apply its regulations. The negligence or passivity of an association should not prevail over the legitimate right of a training club to profit from a system established by FIFA for its benefit.
Even in the event that the XX Federation had drawn up its own regulations on domestic transfers, it would be virtually impossible to admit a foreign club (i.e. a non-member of the XX Federation) as a claimant. This situation leaves D with no legal redress and makes it impossible for the club to enforce any possible decision.
FIFA's regulations provide for differential treatment for certain transfers within the European Union (EU) (e.g. protection of minors and training compensation).
The jurisprudence of the DRC infringes principles of European Community Law and discriminates international transfers inside the territory of the EU in favour of domestic transfers. In fact, if the transfer of the player had been to a club belonging to a European association other than the XX Federation, D would have received the solidarity contribution.
The principles of European law do not permit differential treatment depending on whether the transfer of a player takes place within a single member state or not. In particular, in the present case the Italian club would have an additional incentive to transfer a player to another XX club instead of to a club from another association, because it would save itself from having to pay the solidarity contribution. From the standpoint of European law it is illegal not to treat the transfer of players within the EU on an equal basis irrespective of whether they are between clubs from the same association or two different associations.
The Claimant submitted a detailed report on the European laws that have allegedly been infringed. In particular, it points out that failure to apply the solidarity mechanism to domestic transfers constitutes a decision by a business association (FIFA) and that said decision distorts the competition between clubs and players. The Claimant particularly considers arts. 81 and 82 of the European Community Treaty to have been infringed by FIFA's jurisprudence.

6. In view of the above, D requests the Dispute Resolution Chamber to reconsider the jurisprudence laid down in its decision of 22 July 2004 and to recognise the club´s right to receive the corresponding solidarity contribution related to the transfer of the player C.
7. For its part, Inter informed FIFA that they categorically rejected the X club's claim, on the basis that the FIFA regulations are not applicable to transfers between two clubs that belong to the same association, and also cited the Decision of the Dispute Resolution Chamber of 22 July 2004.

II. CONSIDERATIONS OF THE DISPUTE RESOLUTION CHAMBER

1. First of all, the Chamber analysed whether it was competent to deal with the matter at stake. In this respect, it referred to art. 18 par. 2 and 3 of the Rules Governing the Procedures of the Players' ' Status Committee and the Dispute Resolution Chamber. The present matter was submitted to FIFA on 15 October 2004, as a consequence the Chamber concluded that the previous Procedural Rules (edition 2001) on matters pending before the decision making bodies of FIFA are applicable to the matter at hand.
2. With regard to the competence of the Chamber, art. 25 par. 2 of the FIFA Regulations for the Status and Transfer of Players (edition September 2001) establishes that, it falls within the purview of the Dispute Resolution Chamber to review disputes concerning the distribution of the solidarity contribution.
3. As a consequence, the Dispute Resolution Chamber is the competent body to decide on the present litigation concerning the distribution of the solidarity contribution claimed by the Claimant in connection with the transfer of the non-amateur player C during the course of a contract.
4. Subsequently, the members of the Chamber analyzed which edition of the Regulations for the Status and Transfer of Players should be applicable as to the substance of the matter. In this respect, the Chamber referred to art. 26 par. 1 and 2 of the Regulations for the Status and Transfer of Players (edition 2005) in the modified version in accordance with the FIFA circular no. 995 dated 23 September 2005.
Furthermore, it acknowledged that the non-amateur had been registered for his new club on 31 August 2004.
Equally the Chamber took note that the claim was lodged at FIFA on 15 October 2004.
In view of the aforementioned, the Chamber concluded that the former FIFA Regulations for the

Status and Transfer of Players (edition September 2001, hereinafter: the Regulations) are applicable on the case at hand as to the substance.

5. In continuation, and entering into the substance of the matter, the Chamber acknowledged that, for the case at hand, it was essential to establish whether an internal transfer, this means a move of a player from one club to another, both affiliated to the same association, could be the basis for a claim for solidarity contribution or not. In other words, the Dispute Resolution Chamber recognised that in view of D´s disagreement with the existing jurisprudence, first of all, it would once again have to address a matter of principle. If it were to follow its own jurisprudence, which it had previously answered in a certain way within the scope of its appreciation of similar cases. In its submissions regarding the application of the Regulations, to which also the Respondent referred to, no solidarity contribution would be due whenever a player is transferred from one club to another both affiliated to the same association. This principle would apply regardless of whether the claiming club is affiliated to a different association, like in the case at issue, or to the same association as that of the two clubs directly involved in the relevant transfer at the basis of the claim.
6. The members of the deciding authority stressed that the answer to the central question related to the case at stake needs, first and foremost to be sought in the wording and systematics of the Regulations. In this respect, the Chamber referred to the contents of the Preamble of the Regulations and in particular to its par. 1 which establishes that the Regulations deal with the status and eligibility of players, as well as with the rules applicable whenever players move between clubs belonging to different associations. Like in previous decisions, the deciding body lent emphasis to the wording of the last part of the aforementioned clause and reiterated that, in fact, the Regulations are not applicable to transfers of players between two clubs affiliated to the same association. The deciding body did not see any reason which would justify the departure from this understanding, which as it was emphasised, is the result of the clear wording of the Regulations.
7. In continuation, the Chamber pointed out once again that the principle of the solidarity mechanism is not included in par. 2 of the Preamble of the Regulations and therefore, it is not binding at national level.
8. In view of the above, the members of the Chamber unanimously concluded that, in confirmation of the jurisprudence of the Dispute Resolution Chamber, the principle regarding the solidarity mechanism contained in the Regulations is not applicable to national transfers, not even in cases, like in the one at issue, where the club claiming the payment of the relevant contribution is affiliated to another association.
9. As a result, the Chamber confirmed its established jurisprudence applied in cases in which the basis of the claim for solidarity contribution was, like in the case at hand, the transfer of a player between two clubs affiliated to the same association.
10. Referring to certain points of the Claimant's submission, for the sake of good order and so as to avoid misunderstandings the Chamber deemed it important to point out that, contrary to what the Claimant appears to have understood, the Dispute Resolution Chamber never objected to its competence to deal with disputes regarding solidarity mechanism where the claiming and the responding club belong to different associations. This principle has always been applied even in the case where the transfer of a player at the basis of the claim occurred between two clubs belonging to the same association. However, in the latter case (domestic transfer) under the light of the Regulations (Preamble, par.1 and 2) and the aforementioned established jurisprudence the principle of the Regulations regarding the solidarity mechanism is not applicable.
11. Moreover, and for the sake of completeness, the Chamber stressed that par. 3 of the Preamble of the Regulations, and also the current Regulations (edition July 2005) in its art. 1 par. 2 state that the specific regulations governing national transfers issued by the association concerned should also foresee a system to reward the clubs investing in the training and education of young players. Yet, the Chamber underlined that the member associations are free to decide on the kind of system they would like to introduce to reward the clubs investing in the training and education of players. In other words, they do not necessarily have to provide a solidarity mechanism which follows the role model of the Regulations.
12. In this respect, the Chamber explained that in case an association would decide to implement at national level in its own regulations a solidarity mechanism, like the one contained in the relevant FIFA regulations, the pertinent system would obviously also have to be applied to training clubs belonging to different associations. The Dispute Resolution Chamber would thus be in a position to

protect the rights of such foreign clubs, even in cases where the transfer at the basis of a claim would be an internal one.

13. Finally, the Chamber pointed out that art. 26 par. 3 of the current Regulations (edition July 2005), establishes a deadline on 30 June 2007 for the member associations to submit their own regulations to FIFA for its approval.
14. On account of all the above, the Dispute Resolution Chamber decided that the claim of the D against I for payment of solidarity contribution has to be rejected.

III. DECISION OF THE DISPUTE RESOLUTION CHAMBER

1. The claim of the X club, D, is rejected.
2. According to the art. 61 par. 1 of the FIFA Statutes, this decision may be appealed against before the Court of Arbitration for Sport (CAS). The statement of appeal must be sent to the CAS directly within 21 days of receipt of notification of this decision and shall contain all the elements in accordance with point 2 of the directives issued by the CAS, a copy of which we enclose hereto.
   Within another 10 days following the expiry of the time limit for filing the statement of appeal, the appellant shall file a brief stating the facts and legal arguments giving rise to the appeal with the CAS (cf. point 4 of the directives).

116218
DECISION OF THE DISPUTE RESOLUTION CHAMBER

passed in Zurich, Switzerland, on 21 November 2006,
in the following composition:
Slim Aloulou (Tunisia), Chairman
Paulo Amoretty Souza (Brazil), member
Ivan Gazidis (USA), member
Carlos Soto (Chile), member
John Didulica (Australia), member
on the claim presented by the player
A, xxx, as Claimant
against the club B, xxx, as Respondent
regarding a contractual dispute between the parties

I. FACTS OF THE CASE

1. On 31 August 2004, the xxx player, A (hereinafter: the Claimant), and the xxx club, B (hereinafter: the Respondent), signed an employment contract valid from 1 September 2004 until 30 June 2005.
2. The above-mentioned employment contract provided for a signing-on fee of USD 140,000 payable within 2 weeks upon signing the contract. Furthermore, the contract provided for an additional payment of USD 140,000 as salary, payable in ten monthly instalments in the amount of USD 14,000.
   The remuneration is set forth in an amendment to the employment contract signed by both parties.
3. Art. 3.4 of the said employment contract stipulates textually that "Both parties have the right to terminate this contract upon written notice of One Month.
   The financial conditions for the termination of contract shall be: In the case that Club terminates the contract, the player shall keep all the money that he received as sign-on amount, the salary he received so far the date of termination and One Month Salary for the notice period.
   In the case that Player terminates the contract, the player must return the sign-on amount to Club in appropriation of the actual time of the player worked. The amount will be calculated as the sign-on amount dividing into one year period.
   The Club and the Player also agree on immediate termination of the contract in cases of Breach of Obligations by either party".
4. In a letter dated 4 January 2005, the Respondent informed the Claimant that the relevant employment contract would be terminated due to unsatisfactory performances and in application of clause 3.4 of the contract.

5. On 28 November 2005, the Claimant filed a complaint with FIFA against the Respondent. The Claimant stated that the contract had been terminated unilaterally and without just cause, and that the termination could therefore not be enforced under the FIFA Regulations. As a consequence, the Claimant stated that the contract was still valid, and the Respondent owed him his salary for the months of January, February, March, April, May and June 2005, totalling the amount of USD 84,000 plus interest.
6. In its statement regarding the Claimant's complaint, on 22 March 2006, the Respondent noted that the Claimant had no right to claim salary payments for February to June 2005, as the contract had been terminated in application of clause 3.4 at the end of January 2005 after conclusion of the notice period.
The Respondent stated that the Claimant had actually breached his own contract, as after the Respondent had terminated the contract on 4 January 2005, the player had not continued to play for the Respondent until the end of the notice period, i.e. until the end of January 2005, choosing instead to leave the country immediately. The player had also failed to claim the salary due to him for January 2005, and after he closed his bank account in xxx, he had failed to notify the Respondent of a new account abroad. Consequently, the Claimant had not received his salary for the duration of the one-month notice period in January 2005.
The Respondent stated that as a result, the Claimant had lost his right to a monthly salary for January 2005, and the complaint should be rejected in its entirety for these reasons.
7. In his reply to the Respondent's response, the Claimant claimed that clause 3.4 of the employment contract, to which the Respondent had made reference when terminating the contract, was illegal, i.e. not in line with the FIFA Regulations, and that it consequently could not be enforced. This clause could therefore not be used to justify the termination of the contract.
Furthermore, clause 3.4 stated that the contract could only be terminated if the one-month notice period was observed. Consequently, this contractual termination only came into force one month after its notification on 4 January 2005, i.e. on 4 February 2005.
In addition, the Claimant stated that the Respondent's allegation that he had not fulfilled his contractual obligations during the one-month notice period was absurd. As a matter of fact, the Respondent had prevented him returning to the club's premises. The Claimant noted that if these claims needed to be proven, he could call upon two named witnesses. Finally, he stated that in view of the above, his termination had not been lawful.
8. In its subsequent submission, the Respondent reiterated its previous statement that the contractual termination in accordance with clause 3.4 had been in line with the law and that it was therefore legally valid. Furthermore, the Respondent stressed that through his conduct during the notice period, the Claimant had breached his own contract. The Respondent also stated that in the hypothetical event of the Respondent being found to have unilaterally terminated the contract without just cause, the Respondent's payment of the signing-on fee in the amount of USD 140,000 should be taken into account when determining any compensation due. The Respondent also noted that it was not yet clear whether the Claimant had found a new club after leaving xxx, and stated that FIFA should investigate in this regard. Finally, the Respondent expressed doubts regarding the veracity of the witnesses.
9. According to the Claimant himself, he only found a new club, xxx, in July 2005.

II. CONSIDERATIONS OF THE DISPUTE RESOLUTION CHAMBER

1. First of all, the Dispute Resolution Chamber had to analyze whether it was competent to deal with the matter at stake. In this respect, it referred to art. 18 par. 2 and 3 of the Rules Governing the Procedures of the Players' Status Committee and the Dispute Resolution Chamber. The present matter was submitted to FIFA on 28 November 2005, as a consequence the Chamber concluded that the revised Rules Governing Procedures (edition 2005) to matters pending before the decision making bodies of FIFA are applicable to the matter at hand.
2. With regard to the competence of the Chamber, art. 3 par. 1 of the above- mentioned Rules states that the Dispute Resolution Chamber shall examine its jurisdiction in the light of articles 22 to 24 of the current version of the Regulations for the Status and Transfer of Players (edition 2005). In accordance with art. 24 par. 1 in combination with art. 22 b) of the aforementioned Regulations, the Dispute Resolution Chamber shall adjudicate on employment-related disputes between a club and a player that have an international dimension.

3. As a consequence, the Dispute Resolution Chamber is the competent body to decide on the present litigation involving a xxx player and a xxx club regarding a dispute in connection with an employment contract.
4. Subsequently, the members of the Chamber analyzed which edition of the Regulations for the Status and Transfer of Players should be applicable as to the substance of the matter. In this respect, the Chamber referred, on the one hand, to art. 26 par. 1 and 2 of the Regulations for the Status and Transfer of Players (edition 2005) and, on the other hand, to the fact that the relevant contract at the basis of the present dispute was signed on 31 August 2004 and the claim was lodged at FIFA on 28 November 2005.
   In view of the aforementioned, the Chamber concluded that the current FIFA Regulations for the Status and Transfer of Players (edition 2005, hereafter: the Regulations) are applicable to the case at hand as to the substance.
5. Entering into the substance of the matter, the members of the Chamber started by analysing the relevant employment contract and noted that the Claimant and the Respondent had signed an employment contract valid from 1 September 2004 until 30 June 2005.
6. Furthermore, the Dispute Resolution Chamber noted that the mentioned employment contract had been unilaterally terminated by the Respondent.
7. In this regard, the members of the Chamber acknowledged that the Respondent had unilaterally terminated the employment contract based on clause 3.4 of the relevant employment contract at the basis of the present dispute. Furthermore, the Chamber noted that the above-mentioned clause provides for both parties the right to terminate the employment contract upon a written notice of one month, that in the event of the contract being terminated by the Respondent, the Claimant could retain the signing-on fee in the amount of USD 140,000 as well as all monthly salary payments in the amount of USD 14,000 that had been made up to that point and that the Claimant would also be entitled to a further monthly salary of USD 14,000 for the time covered by the notice period.
8. In continuation, the Dispute Resolution Chamber acknowledged, on the one hand, that the Claimant argued that the Respondent had terminated the employment contract without just cause and, on the other hand, that the Respondent maintained that the employment contract had been terminated in accordance with clause 3.4 of the relevant employment contract. In this respect, the Chamber noted that such clause was agreed between the Claimant and the Respondent.
9. As a consequence of the above, the members of the Chamber considered that the question at the basis of the present dispute is to analyse the validity of clause 3.4 of the relevant employment contract and, consequently, to determine whether the said contract was terminated without just cause by the Respondent.
10. The Dispute Resolution Chamber duly analysed clause 3.4 of the relevant employment contract concerning the termination of the contract. In this respect, the members of the Dispute Resolution Chamber took note that the above-mentioned contractual termination clause provides for the right to terminate the relevant contract for both parties, the Claimant and the Respondent. Furthermore, the Chamber acknowledged that the aforementioned clause grants, in case of termination of the contract by either party, a compensation payable to the other party. Finally, the Chamber took note that the said clause contains a one month notice period to be respected by the respective terminating party.
11. On account of the above, the Dispute Resolution Chamber concluded that clause 3.4 of the relevant employment contract has to be considered as totally valid and legally binding. As a consequence, the members of the Chamber decided that the Respondent did not breach the relevant employment contract without just cause but in accordance with clause 3.4 of the relevant contract, which was signed and approved by both parties.
12. In continuation, the Chamber concluded that no compensation for breach of contract without just cause (cf. art. 17 of the Regulations) is due. In other words, the members of the Chamber decided that the Claimant, in view of the legally valid termination of the employment contract, has no right to claim the salary for the following months February, March, April, May and June 2005.
13. As a consequence, the Chamber remarked that the remaining financial aspect of the present dispute concerns the salary for the month of January 2005 in the amount of USD 14,000, i.e. the question whether the Claimant is entitled to receive, in accordance with clause 3.4 of the relevant employment contract, the allegedly outstanding monthly salary for the notice-period January 2005.
14. In this regard, the Chamber acknowledged, on the one hand, that according to the Respondent, the Claimant, after having been notified about the termination of the relevant contract on 4 January

2005, did not continue to play for the Respondent until the end of the notice period, i.e. until the end of January 2005, choosing instead to leave the country immediately and, thus, failed to fulfil his contractual obligations during the one-month notice period.
On the other hand, the Chamber took note that according to the Claimant, the Respondent had prevented him from returning to the club's premises.

15. In this respect, the members of the Chamber referred to art. 12 par. 3 of the Rules Governing the Procedures of the Players' Status Committee and the Dispute Resolution Chamber, in accordance with which a party deriving a right from an alleged fact shall carry the burden of proof.
16. In view of the above, the Chamber decided that the Claimant was not able to prove that he returned to the Respondent after having been notified about the termination of the relevant contract on 4 January 2005, respectively, that he was prevented by the Respondent to return to the Respondent during the notice-period in January 2005.
Consequently, the Chamber determined that the Claimant has not fulfilled his contractual obligation towards the Respondent during the relevant notice-period.
17. On account of the above, the Dispute Resolution Chamber concluded one the Claimant is also not entitled to receive the salary for the notice-period January 2005.
18. As a result, the Chamber decided to fully reject the Claimant's claim.'

III. DECISION OF THE DISPUTE RESOLUTION CHAMBER

1. The claim lodged by the Claimant, A, is rejected.
2. According to art. 61 par. 1 of the FIFA Statutes this decision may be appealed against before the Court of Arbitration for Sport (CAS). The statement of appeal must be sent to the CAS directly within 21 days of receit of notification of this decision and shall contain all the elements in accordance with point 2 of the directives issued by the CAS, a copy of which we enclose hereto. Within another 10 days following the expiry of the time limit for filing the statement of appeal, the appellant shall file a brief stating the facts and legal arguments giving rise to the appeal with the CAS (cf. point 4 of the directives).

116336

DECISION OF THE DISPUTE RESOLUTION CHAMBER

passed in Zurich, Switzerland, on 21 November 2006,
in the following composition:
Slim Aloulou (Tunisia), Chairman
Paulo Amoretty Souza (Brazil), member
Ivan Gazidis (USA), member
Carlos Soto (Chile), member
John Didulica (Australia), member
on the claim presented by the player A, xxx, as Claimant
against the club B, xxx, as Respondent
regarding a contractual dispute between the parties

I. FACTS OF THE CASE

1. On 1 September 2003, the xxx player, A (hereinafter: the Claimant), and the xxx club, B (hereinafter: the Respondent), signed an employment contract, valid from 1 August 2004 until 30 June 2005.
2. On 17 July 2004, the parties involved concluded a supplement to the above- mentioned employment contract specifying bonuses. This supplement provides for bonuses in the amount of USD 5,000 for each goal scored or assisted by the Claimant in winning games completed by the Respondent in official matches of the xxx League, the xxx Cup or the xxx Cup.
3. On 10 January 2006, the Claimant, based on the relevant employment contract respectively the relevant supplement and a non-official document indicating goals scored and assisted as well as penalties provoked by the Claimant, lodged a claim against the Respondent for allegedly outstanding bonuses amounting to USD 60,000 with FIFA. In this respect, the Claimant affirms having scored 8 goals and assisted 4 goals in winning games played for the Respondent.
4. In its reply, the Respondent maintains that bonuses per goal scored or assisted had to be paid for winning games disputed during internal competitions only, i.e. the xxx League, the xxx Cup and

the xxx Cup. As a consequence, the Respondent is of the opinion that the player is not entitled to receive bonuses of USD 5,000 for each goal scored or assisted during matches of any other official football competition including the–.–League. On account of the above, the Respondent, in accordance with the official statistics, i.e. the player's official "match history 2004/2005" issued by the xxx Football Association, argues that the Claimant scored only five goals in official games of the above-mentioned competitions and that the latter did not provide with any assists to goals. Furthermore, the Respondent emphasises that a foul committed on the Claimant provoking a penalty does not count as a goal scored or an assist provided. In this sense, according to the Respondent the Claimant is only entitled to receive bonuses in the amount of USD 25,000.
Finally, the Respondent alleged that bonuses in the amount of USD 25,000 have not been paid yet to the Claimant due to the fact that the latter allegedly always refused to accept this amount as bonus payment.

5. In his replica, the Claimant states that the translation of the allegedly official statistics into xxx is not legally binding. He insists on having scored 8 goals and assisted 4 goals. Furthermore, the Claimant refers to an allegedly official declaration made by the Respondent by means of which the latter acknowledged its debt in the amount of USD 60,000 towards him. On account of all the aforesaid, the Claimant insists on his claim for allegedly outstanding bonuses in the amount of USD 60,000.
6. In its final statement, the Respondent emphasises that the player's "match history 2004/2005" as well as the relevant translation into xxx constitute official documents issued by the xxx Football Association and, therefore, they shall be considered as absolutely reliable. Furthermore, with regard to the Claimant's allegation that it has acknowledged its debt in the amount of USD 60,000, the Respondent declares that it has never been provided with the pertinent document and, as a consequence, it is not able to express any comments referring to this. On account of the above, the Respondent requests that the Claimant is only entitled to receive the amount of USD 25,000, i.e. that the claim is partially rejected.

II. CONSIDERATIONS OF THE DISPUTE RESOLUTION CHAMBER

1. First of all, the Dispute Resolution Chamber had to analyze whether it was competent to deal with the matter at stake. In this respect, it referred to art. 18 par. 2 and 3 of the Rules Governing the Procedures of the Players' ' Status Committee and the Dispute Resolution Chamber. The present matter was submitted to FIFA on 10 January 2006, as a consequence the Chamber concluded that the revised Rules Governing Procedures (edition 2005) to matters pending before the decision making bodies of FIFA are applicable to the matter at hand.
2. With regard to the competence of the Chamber, art. 3 par. 1 of the above- mentioned Rules states that the Dispute Resolution Chamber shall examine its jurisdiction in the light of articles 22 to 24 of the current version of the Regulations for the Status and Transfer of Players (edition 2005). In accordance with art. 24 par. 1 in combination with art. 22 b) of the aforementioned Regulations, the Dispute Resolution Chamber shall adjudicate on employment-related disputes between a club and a player that have an international dimension.
3. As a consequence, the Dispute Resolution Chamber is the competent body to decide on the present litigation involving a xxx player and a xxx club regarding a dispute in connection with an employment contract.
4. Subsequently, and entering into the substance of the matter, the Chamber acknowledged that, on 17 July 2004, the parties signed the supplement to the employment contract dated 1 September 2003, valid from 1 August 2004 until 30 June 2005.
5. Furthermore, the Chamber noticed that according to the relevant supplement to the employment contract, the Claimant is entitled to receive a bonus in the amount of USD 5,000 for each goal scored or assisted by him, but that the said entitlement to bonuses is applicable to winning games Player Carlos Pedro Silva Morais, Cape Verde Island / Al Ahly Sports Club, Qatar3 completed by the Respondent in official matches of the xxx League, the xxx Cup or the xxx Cup only.
6. In this regard, the Chamber considered that the official statistics issued by the xxx Football Association, i.e. the player's official "match history 2004/2005" that was translated into xxx by the same xxx Football. Association, constitute the basis for the establishment of the number of goals scored and assists to goals provided by the Claimant in official matches of the above-mentioned competitions. Furthermore, the Chamber stated that the Claimant failed to provide FIFA with any adequate documentary evidence regarding the number of goals scored and assisted by him.

7. In continuation, the Chamber acknowledged that the Claimant in accordance with the applicable statistics issued by the xxx Football Association scored five goals in winning games completed by the Respondent in official matches of the relevant competitions. In particular, the Chamber determined that the relevant prerequisites for receiving bonuses are met by the Claimant on the following occasions: the 3:2 victory of the Respondent in the match of 21 January 2005 of the xxx League against the club xxx by scoring 2 goals the 1:0 victory of the Respondent in the match of 15 February 2005 of the xxx League against the club xxx by scoring 1 goal the 1:0 victory of the Respondent in the match of 19 February 2005 of the xxx League against the club xxx by scoring one 1 goal the 3:2 victory of the Respondent in the match of 14 April 2005 of the xxx League against the club xxx by scoring 1 goal
8. Furthermore, the Chamber acknowledged that no assists to goals provided by the Claimant are listed in the relevant statistics issued by the xxx FootballAssociation. Consequently, the Chamber concluded that the Claimant provided with no assists to goals.
9. In view of the above, and taking into account that the number of goals scored and assists to goals provided has to be established on the basis of the relevant statistics issued by the xxx Football Association, the Chamber decided that the Claimant is entitled to receive bonuses for having scored 5 goals.
10. In this sense, the Dispute Resolution Chamber decided that the Respondent must pay the amount of USD 25,000 to the Claimant.

III. DECISION OF THE DISPUTE RESOLUTION CHAMBER

1. The claim of the Claimant, A, is partially accepted.
2. The Respondent, B, has to pay the amount of USD 25,000 to the Claimant, A, within 30 days as from the date of notification of this decision.
3. In the event that the above-mentioned amount is not paid within the stated deadline, an interest rate of 5% per year will apply as of expiry of the aforementioned deadline and the present matter shall be submitted to FIFA's Disciplinary Committee, so that the necessary disciplinary sanctions may be imposed.
4. Any further claim of the Claimant, A, is rejected.
5. The Claimant, A, is instructed to inform the Respondent, B, immediately and directly of the account number to which the remittance is to be made and to notify the Dispute Resolution Chamber of every payment received.
6. According to art. 61 par. 1 of the FIFA Statutes this decision may be appealed against before the Court of Arbitration for Sport (CAS). The statement of appeal must be sent to the CAS directly within 21 days of receipt of notification of this decision and shall contain all the elements in accordance with point 2 of the directives issued by the CAS, a copy of which we enclose hereto. Within another 10 days following the expiry of the time limit for filing the statement of appeal, the appellant shall file a brief stating the facts and legal arguments giving rise to the appeal with the CAS (cf. point 4 of the directives).

116338

DECISION OF THE DISPUTE RESOLUTION CHAMBER

passed in Zurich, Switzerland, on 21 November 2006,
in the following composition:
Slim Aloulou (Tunisia), Chairman
Paulo Rogerio Amoretty Souza (Brazil), member
Ivan Gazidis (USA), member
Carlos Soto (Chile), member
John Didulica (Australia), member
on the claim presented by Player O, X
Represented by Mrs. , attorney at law, as Claimant
against
Club P, XX as Respondent
regarding a contractual dispute between the parties involve

I. FACTS OF THE CASE

1. The player O was born on 22 September 1976.
2. On 2 September 2002, the player O and the club P signed an employment contract valid until 31 August 2003.
   The relevant employment contract establishes a monthly salary of ... 26,610,000 in favour of the player O.
3. On 26 November 2004, the player O requested the assistance of FIFA claiming 3 monthly salaries owed by the club totalling ... 79,830,000.
4. The player states that he fulfilled his obligations towards the club until 23 April 2003 when the club P asked him to sign a termination agreement.
5. On 26 May 2003, due to the club's pressure as well as the club's threat to retain his personal documents allowing him to leave Indonesia the player was forced to sign a letter of termination. In the article 2 of the aforementioned letter the club agreed to pay a compensation of ... 6,000 to the player O.
6. On 27 May 2003 the player O together with two other X players went to the X Embassy and filed a protest.
7. FIFA contacted the club P on 7 September 2005, 13 March 2006 and 20 September 2006 but received no response.
8. The player O requests FIFA to condemn the club P to pay the amount of ... 79,830,000.

II. CONSIDERATIONS OF THE DISPUTE RESOLUTION CHAMBER

1. First of all, the Chamber analysed whether it was competent to deal with the matter at stake. In this respect, it referred to art. 18 par. 2 and 3 of the Rules Governing the Procedures of the Players' ' Status Committee and the Dispute Resolution Chamber. The present matter was submitted to FIFA on 26 May 2003, as a consequence the Chamber concluded that the previous Procedural Rules (edition 2001) on matter pending before the decision making bodies of FIFA are applicable on the matter at hand.
2. With regard to the competence of the Chamber, art. 42 par. 1 lit. (b) (i) of the FIFA Regulations for the Status and Transfer of Players (edition 2001) establishes that, the triggering elements of the employment-related dispute (i.e. whether a contract was breached, with or without just cause, or sporting just cause), will be decided by the Dispute Resolution Chamber.
3. If an employment contract is breached by a party, the Dispute Resolution Chamber (DRC) is also responsible to verify whether a party is accountable for outstanding payments and/or compensation.
4. As a consequence, the DRC is the competent body to decide on the present litigation involving a X player and an XX club regarding outstanding salaries claimed by the player O in connection with an employment contract.
5. Subsequently, the members of the Chamber analyzed which edition of the Regulations for the Status and Transfer of Players should be applicable as to the substance of the matter. In this respect, the Chamber referred, on the one hand, to art. 26 par. 1 and 2 of the Regulations for the Status and Transfer of Players (edition 2005) and, on the other hand, to the fact that the relevant contract at the basis of the present dispute was signed on 2 September 2002 and the claim was lodged at FIFA before 1 July 2005.
   In view of the aforementioned, the Chamber concluded that the former FIFA Regulations for the Status and Transfer of Players (edition 2001, hereinafter: the Regulations) are applicable on the case at hand as to the substance.
6. In continuation, and entering into the substance of the matter, the members of the Chamber started by acknowledging that both parties signed an employment contract on 2 September 2002 expiring on 31 August 2003.
   Moreover, the DRC took note that on 26 May 2003 both parties concluded a document called "Termination Letter of Contract", by means of which, the relevant parties finished their contractual relationship.
7. At this stage, the DRC deemed appropriate to focus its attention to the claimant's allegation stating that he signed the termination agreement under pressure and forced by the XX club.
8. In this respect the Chamber pointed out that a document signed by the relevant parties, is in principle a written proof of a valid contract and cannot be declare invalid for a simple allegation. Moreover the DRC remarked that the party that makes an allegation has the burden of proof to sustain it reasonably in order to preserve the legal principle of legal security.

9. After a thorough analysis of the termination agreement, the DRC was of the opinion that this document dated 26 May 2003 contains, in principle, all requisites and legal elements in order to be valid.
10. The DRC took note, that the claimant provide FIFA with a document "Protest" filed by the claimant on 27 May 2003 together with another two X players at the Embassy, in order to prove that the respondent forced him to sign the termination agreement. In this respect, the members of the Chamber analyzed carefully the relevant document, concluding that this document is an unilateral declaration made by the player and it does not constitute an evidence able to justify the alleged pressure exerted on the claimant by the respondent.
11. In view of the foregoing, the members of the Chamber concluded that the claimant's allegation about the invalidity of the termination agreement was not sufficiently proved. Consequently, the player's position with regard that the termination agreement is invalid cannot be upheld by the Chamber.
12. In continuation the DRC considered appropriate to focus on the amounts mentioned in the matter at stake. In this respect the Chamber noted that, on the one hand, the claimant requests the payment of a compensation equivalent to three month salaries i.e. ... 79,830,000 and on the other hand, the DRC acknowledge that the respondent undertook, in the clause 2 of the termination agreement, to pay to the claimant the amount of ... 6,000 as compensation for the premature compensation of the employment contract.
13. At this stage, the Chamber turned its attention to the respondent's behaviour.
First of all, the DRC remarked that from the allegations and documents provided by the claimant during the process of the matter at stake, it appears that the respondent did not owe salaries to the player O since the termination of the employment contract was agreed on 26 May 2003 and the player O claims the payment of the months of June, July and August 2003.
Secondly, the DRC reiterated that in the letter of termination the respondent undertook to pay the amount of ... 6,000 as a compensation to the player. Finally, the members of the Chamber remarked that the respondent failed to answered FIFA's requests in three opportunities. In this way the respondent renounced to its right to defence.
14. In view of all the above, the Chamber concluded that the termination agreement dated 26 May 2003 is legally valid and binding between the relevant parties. Therefore an based on the terms agreed by the player O and the club P in the referred termination agreement, the claimant is entitled to perceive the amount of ... 6,000 as compensation.

III. DECISION OF THE DISPUTE RESOLUTION CHAMBER

1. The claim of the player O is partially accepted.
2. The respondent P has to pay the amount of ... 6,000 to the claimant.
3. The amount due to the claimant has to be paid by the respondent within 30 days as from the date of notification of this decision.
4. In the event that the debt of the respondent is not paid within the stated deadline an interest rate of 5% per year will apply as of expiring of the above fixed time limit. Furthermore, the FIFA will be entitled to submit the file to the Disciplinary Committee.
5. The claimant is directed to inform the respondent immediately of the account number to which the remittance is to be made and to notify the Dispute Resolution Chamber of every payment received.
6. According to art. 61 par. 1 of the FIFA Statutes, this decision may be appealed against before the Court of Arbitration for Sport (CAS). The statement of appeal must be sent to the CAS directly within 21 days of receiving notification of this decision and shall contain all the elements in accordance with point 2 of the directives issued by the CAS, a copy of which we enclose hereto. Within another 10 days following the expiry of the time limit for filing the statement of appeal, the appellant shall file a brief stating the facts and legal arguments giving rise to the appeal with the CAS (cf. point 4 of the directives).

116339

DECISION OF THE DISPUTE RESOLUTION CHAMBER

passed in Zurich, Switzerland, on 21 November 2006,
in the following composition:

Slim Aloulou (Tunisia), Chairman
Paulo Rogerio Amoretty Souza (Brazil), member
Ivan Gazidis (USA), member
Carlos Soto (Chile), member
John Didulica (Australia), member
on the claim presented by Player D, X
Represented by Mrs. , attorney at law,as Claimant
against Club P, XX as Respondent
regarding a contractual . dispute between the parties involve

I. FACTS OF THE CASE

1. The player D was born on 22 January 1975.
2. On 2 September 2002, the player D and the club P signed an employment contract valid until 31 August 2003.
   The relevant employment contract establishes a monthly salary of ... 24,836,000 in favour of the player D.
3. On 26 November 2004, the player D requested the assistance of FIFA claiming 3 monthly salaries owed by the club totalling ... 74,508,000.
4. The player states that he fulfilled his obligations towards the club until 23 April 2003 when the club P asked him to sign a termination agreement.
5. On 26 May 2003, due to the club's pressure as well as the club's threat to retain his personal documents allowing him to leave Indonesia the player was forced to sign a letter of termination. In the article 2 of the aforementioned letter the club agreed to pay a compensation of ... 5,600 to the player D.
6. On 27 May 2003 the player D together with two other X players went to the X Embassy and filed a protest.
7. FIFA contacted the XX club P on 7 September 2005, 13 March 2006 and 20 September 2006 but received no response.
8. The player D requests FIFA to condemn the club P to pay the amount of ... 74,508,000.

II. CONSIDERATIONS OF THE DISPUTE RESOLUTION CHAMBER

1. First of all, the Chamber analysed whether it was competent to deal with the matter at stake. In this respect, it referred to art. 18 par. 2 and 3 of the Rules Governing the Procedures of the Players' ' Status Committee and the Dispute Resolution Chamber. The present matter was submitted to FIFA on 26 May 2003, as a consequence the Chamber concluded that the previous Procedural Rules (edition 2001) on matter pending before the decision making bodies of FIFA are applicable on the matter at hand.
2. With regard to the competence of the Chamber, art. 42 par. 1 lit. (b) (i) of the FIFA Regulations for the Status and Transfer of Players (edition 2001) establishes that, the triggering elements of the employment-related dispute (i.e. whether a contract was breached, with or without just cause, or sporting just cause), will be decided by the Dispute Resolution Chamber.
3. If an employment contract is breached by a party, the Dispute Resolution Chamber (DRC) is also responsible to verify whether a party is accountable for outstanding payments and/or compensation.
4. As a consequence, the DRC is the competent body to decide on the present litigation involving a X player and an XX club regarding outstanding salaries claimed by the player D in connection with an employment contract.
5. Subsequently, the members of the Chamber analyzed which edition of the Regulations for the Status and Transfer of Players should be applicable as to the substance of the matter. In this respect, the Chamber referred, on the one hand, to art. 26 par. 1 and 2 of the Regulations for the Status and Transfer of Players (edition 2005) and, on the other hand, to the fact that the relevant contract at the basis of the present dispute was signed on 2 September 2002 and the claim was lodged at FIFA before 1 July 2005.
   In view of the aforementioned, the Chamber concluded that the former FIFA Regulations for the Status and Transfer of Players (edition 2001, hereinafter: the Regulations) are applicable on the case at hand as to the substance.

6. In continuation, and entering into the substance of the matter, the members of the Chamber started by acknowledging that both parties signed an employment contract on 2 September 2002 expiring on 31 August 2003.
   Moreover, the DRC took note that on 26 May 2003 both parties concluded a document called "Termination Letter of Contract", by means of which, the relevant parties finished their contractual relationship.
7. At this stage, the DRC deemed appropriate to focus its attention to the claimant's allegation stating that he signed the termination agreement under pressure and forced by the XX club.
8. In this respect the Chamber pointed out that a document signed by the relevant parties, is in principle a written proof of a valid contract and cannot be declare invalid for a simple allegation. Moreover the DRC remarked that the party that makes an allegation has the burden of proof to sustain it reasonably in order to preserve the legal principle of legal security.
9. After a thorough analysis of the termination agreement, the DRC was of the opinion that this document dated 26 May 2003 contains, in principle, all requisites and legal elements in order to be valid.
10. The DRC took note, that the claimant provide FIFA with a document "Protest" filed by the claimant on 27 May 2003 together with another two X players at the X Embassy, in order to prove that the respondent forced him to sign the termination agreement. In this respect, the members of the Chamber analyzed carefully the relevant document, concluding that this document is an unilateral declaration made by the player and it does not constitute an evidence able to justify the alleged pressure exerted on the claimant by the respondent.
11. In view of the foregoing, the members of the Chamber concluded that the claimant's allegation about the invalidity of the termination agreement was not sufficiently proved. Consequently, the player's position with regard that the termination agreement is invalid cannot be upheld by the Chamber.
12. In continuation the DRC considered appropriate to focus on the amounts mentioned in the matter at stake. In this respect the Chamber noted that, on the one hand, the claimant requests the payment of a compensation equivalent to three month salaries i.e. ... 79,830,000 and on the other hand, the DRC acknowledge that the respondent undertook, in the clause 2 of the termination agreement, to pay to the claimant the amount of ... 5,600 as compensation for the premature termination of the employment contract.
13. At this stage, the Chamber turned its attention to the respondent's behaviour.
    First of all, the DRC remarked that from the allegations and documents provided by the claimant during the process of the matter at stake, it appears that the respondent did not owe salaries to the player D since the termination of the employment contract was agreed on 26 May 2003 and the player D claims the payment of the months of June, July and August 2003.
    Secondly, the DRC reiterated that in the letter of termination the respondent undertook to pay the amount of ... 5,600 as a compensation to the player. Finally, the members of the Chamber remarked that the respondent failed to answered FIFA's requests in three opportunities. In this way the respondent renounced to its right to defence.
14. In view of all the above, the Chamber concluded that the termination agreement dated 26 May 2003 is legally valid and binding between the relevant parties. Therefore an based on the terms agreed by the player D and the club P in the referred termination agreement, the claimant is entitled to perceive the amount of ... 5,600 as compensation.

III. DECISION OF THE DISPUTE RESOLUTION CHAMBER

1. The claim of the player D is partially accepted.
2. The respondent P has to pay the amount of ... 5,600 to the claimant.
3. The amount due to the claimant has to be paid by the respondent within 30 days as from the date of notification of this decision.
4. In the event that the debt of the respondent is not paid within the stated deadline an interest rate of 5% per year will apply as of expiring of the above fixed time limit. Furthermore, the FIFA will be entitled to submit the file to the Disciplinary Committee.
5. The claimant is directed to inform the respondent immediately of the account number to which the remittance is to be made and to notify the Dispute Resolution Chamber of every payment received.
6. According to art. 61 par. 1 of the FIFA Statutes, this decision may be appealed against before the Court of Arbitration for Sport (CAS). The statement of appeal must be sent to the CAS directly within

21 days of receiving notification of this decision and shall contain all the elements in accordance with point 2 of the directives issued by the CAS, a copy of which we enclose hereto. Within another 10 days following the expiry of the time limit for filing the statement of appeal, the appellant shall file a brief stating the facts and legal arguments giving rise to the appeal with the CAS (cf. point 4 of the directives).

611727
DECISION OF THE DISPUTE RESOLUTION CHAMBER
passed in Zurich, Switzerland, on 21 November 2006,
in the following composition:
Slim Aloulou (Tunisia), Chairman
Carlos Soto (Chile), Member
John Didulica (Australia), Member
Paulo Amoretty Souza (Brazil), Member
Ivan Gazidis (USA), Member
on the claim presented by the club, X, XX as Claimant / Counter-Respondent
against the player, Y, YY, represented by Mr AA, attorney at law as player / Counter-Claimant
and the club, Z, ZZ as second Respondent
regarding a dispute about the breach of contract and the inducement to breach of contract arisen between the parties involved

I. FACTS OF THE CASE

1. The YY player, Y (hereafter: the player) and the XX club, X (hereafter: the Claimant) signed the following contracts:
   a) 1st standard employment contract (hereafter contract) valid as from 3 August 2004 until 31 May 2009, according to which the player would receive a minimum wage (not specified) as well as TRL (XX Lira) 250 Mrd payable in 5 instalments of TRL 50 Mrd, whereby 20% of each instalment are guaranteed and the remaining amount would be divided into 34 league matches.
   b) 1st Annex to contract (hereafter Annex), signed on 2 August 2004 valid for the season 2004/2005 until 2 August 2005, according to which the player was entitled to receive USD 15,000 on the signing date, USD 15,000 on 30 October 2004, 10 instalment of USD 4,620 as from August 2004, as well as payments per match (USD 23,800 would be paid as per match payment for each league match, if the player is in 18 he should receive USD 700).
   c) 2nd Annex to contract (hereafter: Annex) signed on 29 July 2005 for the season 2005/2006, according to which the player was entitled to receive the total amount of USD 150,000.
   d) Copy of the original and of a translation of the termination agreement dated 3 February 2006, by means of which the parties declared that due to the necessity they mutually agree to terminate the contract and that both parties discharge each other from any debt.
   e) 2nd standard employment contract (hereafter: contract) dated 10 February 2006 valid until 31 May 2009, according to which the player would receive a minimum wage as well as TRY (new XX Lira) 250,000 for the whole term of the contractual duration, payable in 4 instalments, whereby, for the first season 2005/2006, a payment of TRY 25,000 was agreed and which was divided into 15 league matches.
2. In the file at hand, a copy of an undated confirmation of the XX Customs authorities stating that the player arrived in XX on 21 January 2006, left XX on 7 February 2006, re-entry XX on 9 February 2006 and again left XX on 22 February 2006.
3. Moreover, a copy of a termination letter sent by the player to the Claimant and the XX Football Federation dated 19 April 2006 was submitted to the file.
   By means of this letter, the player terminated the employment contract he signed with the Claimant dated 10 February 2006 on the grounds that the Claimant had apparently not fulfilled its financial obligations.
4. Furthermore, a copy of a document dated 20 July 2006 was submitted, by means of which the XX Football Federation confirmed to the player that it had registered the termination of the employment

contract dated 10 February 2006 and that the player, with regard to his financial requests, should contact FIFA.

5. In the meantime, on 22 May 2006, the Claimant lodged a claim with FIFA against the player for breach of contract arguing that the player had left the club without prior notice and without valid reasons on 22 February 2006.
6. The Claimant remitted copies of decisions passed by its competent authority dated 28 February and 15 March 2006 by means of which fines where imposed on the player for having missed, without justifications, the training and the official match on 21 February 2006, fines for each training missed between the 23 and 28 February 2006 and a fine for having unauthorizedly left XX on 22 February 2006.
   The total fines imposed on the player amounted to TRY 140,000.00.
7. The Claimant affirmed that it paid the amount of USD 100,000 to the player for the season 2004/2005 as well as the extra amount of USD 10,000 due to his excellent performance.
8. Moreover, the Claimant affirmed very vague that in January 2006, the player desired to leave the Claimant, since from a sporting point of view, it would be better for him to go on loan to another club in order to be more regularly fielded. Moreover, the Claimant maintains that "due to the fact that the Claimant could not participate in the official games and player desires to leave the club, parties decided not to continue together". Therefore, on 3 February 2006, the parties mutually terminated the contract and the player apparently went to France to another club (no documentary evidence with regard to the player's transfer to France). However, the player returned to XX and signed a new employment contract on 10 February 2006 valid until 31 May 2009.
   To this regard, the Claimant provided a copy of a payment receipt in the amount of USD 30,000 dated 10 February 2006 and signed by the player. The Claimant affirmed that this payment was paid to the player in advance due to the signature of the contract and that this amount would be deducted from the game payments (bonus) that the player would receive in future.
9. The Claimant affirmed that until the player's departure, he was entitled to receive the total amount of USD 98,500 (USD 50,000 as "guarantee payments", USD 16,000 corresponding to 5 monthly salaries [September 2005 until January 2006], bonuses amounting to USD 28,000 [14 matches played] and USD 4,500 [3 matches in February 2006 as substitute]). In this respect, the Claimant maintains having fully complied with its financial obligations towards the player and regularly paid all the remuneration due to the player.
10. On account of its statements, the Claimant deemed that the player breached the contract without, however, specifying which contract, and requested payment of the amount of USD 500,000 as compensation for breach of contract, TRY 140,000 corresponding to the fines imposed on the player and a restriction of four months on the player's eligibility to play in official matches. Finally, it emphasized that the new club of the player shall be jointly and severally liable for the payment of the claimed compensation.
11. On 25 September 2006, the player presented FIFA his position and lodged a counter-claim against the Claimant. The player/Counter-Claimant (hereinafter: the player) contested the arguments put forward by the Claimant/Counter-Respondent (hereinafter: the Claimant) and argued that in fact, the Claimant breached the contract and the Annex to the contract. In particular, the player contested that the Claimant had paid him all his money due for the season 2004/2005.
    In this respect, he presented a detailed schedule and maintained that for the season 2004/2005, he was entitled to receive on the basis of the contract TRL 41,76 Mrd and on the basis of the Annex USD 100,000, but the Claimant paid him only the amount of USD 79,735 (amount for which he signed receipts), thus an amount of USD 20,265 and TRL 41,76 Mrd remained outstanding.
12. In this respect, he explained that the Claimant paid him very irregular and that therefore, the outstanding amounts can only be calculated ale on a yearly basis. Furthermore, he argued that for each payment received, he signed a receipt, but the Claimant refused, however, to provide him with a copy.
13. In continuation, the player, on the one hand, acknowledged receipt of the amount of USD 98,500 which were due to him under the Annex for the term until 3 February 2006.
    However, he explains that a part of this amount was covered by the payment of USD 30,000.
    In this respect, he emphasized that this payment of USD 30,000 was given to him in connection with the termination agreement dated 3 February 2006, signed between the parties, and not as affirmed by the Claimant, as an advanced payment for signing the contract dated 10 February 2006.

On the other hand, the player stressed that the Claimant failed to pay him for the season 2005/2006 the amount of TRL 25 Mrd on the basis of the contract still in force.

14. In view of the above, the player maintained that the Claimant owed him, on 3 February 2006, the date the contract was breached by the Claimant, the amount of TRL 66,76 Mrd and USD 20,265.
15. With regard to the developments until the termination agreement was signed, the player contested the arguments of the Claimant and emphasized that he was not looking for a new club. In particular, he stressed that he played regularly for the Claimant and therefore had no intention, from a sporting point of view, to change the club.
16. Moreover, he argued that the Claimant would certainly had asked to be compensated from a new club, but did, however, not specify the real circumstances and even could not provide any evidences. Moreover, the player pointed out that the Claimant itself stated that he showed excellent performances and in view that the contractual relationship between the parties lasted until 2009, the story of the Claimant does clearly not convince
17. The player maintained that, since he repeatedly asked for the payment of the outstanding monies, the Claimant assured to pay him his outstanding debts on condition that he signs a termination agreement in order to terminate the contract in force and that the parties thereupon would sign a new employment contract. The player argued having had no alternative than to agree, otherwise he would have lost his chance to get his money and the Claimant would have not allowed him to play in future which meant to face less remuneration due to the fact that a great part of his wages depend on his bonus.
18. To this end, a meeting was held on 3 February 2006 on the occasion of which the player signed with the Claimant the termination agreement. However, the player maintains that the Claimant abused the situation. In this respect, he stressed that his agent was not allowed to take part in the relevant meeting and that the document was written only in XX, a language that he does not understand and no translation was provided to him. Therefore, the player affirmed having not been aware of the contents of the termination agreement. In contrast, the Claimant did pay him on the occasion of the meeting only the amount of USD 30,000 for the outstanding amounts instead of the allegedly due amounts of TRL 66,76 Mrd and USD 20,265.

    In respect of his statements, the player maintained that the Claimant breached the contract and the Annex and therefore requested compensation amounting to TRL 177 Mrd and USD 440,000 calculated as the financial damage for the remaining period of the contractual duration (i.e. 3 February 2006 until 31 May 2009) as well as disciplinary sanctions against the Claimant.
19. With regard to the period of time between 3 February and 22 February 2006, the player explained that he went to YY in order to wait for the signature of a new contract as ordered by the President of the Claimant. After having been notified by the Claimant to return, he came back on 9 February 2006 and played for the Claimant in three official matches, believing that the contract was still in force, given that the Claimant told him that the termination of the contract was not yet notified to the XX Football Federation (no evidence provided). In continuation, upon his insistence, a meeting between the parties was held on 21 February 2006 on which he was told that no new contract would be signed. However, on the same day, he found out that on 10 February 2006, the contract was signed on his behalf, the validity of which he firmly rejected. In order to support his position, he maintained that the falsification is evident since there were several different signatures under his name. Moreover, the total remuneration agreed in the contract appears to be ridicule compared to the remuneration agreed in the first contract. After he informed the Claimant that under such circumstances he cannot continue playing for the Claimant, he was threaten with a gun, thus he had no alternative than to leave XX on 22 February 2006.
20. The player signed an employment contract with the ZZ club, Z (hereinafter: the Respondent), for the term as from 28 July 2006 until May 2007 on the basis of which the player is entitled to receive the amount of EUR 55,000.

    The Single Judge of the FIFA Players' Status Committee authorized the ZZ Football Federation on 22 September 2006 to provisionally register the player for th Respondent at its Federation on, considering, inter alia, that the player had terminated the employment contract and that Claimant did not appear to be interested in the services of the player any longer but was merely seeking for financial compensation.
21. Having been confronted with the claim of the Claimant, the Respondent explained in particular that it had contact with the player only in August 2006.

It was told that the player had no contractual relationship with another club. In this respect, it maintained having been furnished with a copy of the letter dated 24 July 2006 from the XX Football Federation in which it informed the player that the contract between the Claimant and the player has been terminated. Finally, it mentioned that it clearly emanates from the player's passport that the player had not been registered with the Claimant for a long period of time.

II. CONSIDERATIONS OF THE DISPUTE RESOLUTION CHAMBER

a) As to the competence of the Dispute Resolution Chamber

1. First of all, the Chamber analysed whether it was competent to deal with the matter at stake. In this respect, it referred to art. 18 par. 2 and 3 of the Rules Governing the Procedures of the Players' ' Status Committee and the Dispute Resolution Chamber. The present matter was submitted to FIFA on 22 May 2006, as a consequence the Chamber concluded that the revised Rules Governing Procedures (edition 2005) on matters pending before the decision making bodies of FIFA are applicable to the matter at hand.
2. With regard to the competence of the Chamber, art. 3 par. 1 of the above- mentioned Rules states that the Dispute Resolution Chamber shall examine its jurisdiction in the light of articles 22 to 24 of the current version of the Regulations for the Status and Transfer of Players (edition 2005). In accordance with art. 24 par. 1 in connection with art. 22 (b) of the aforementioned Regulations, the Dispute Resolution Chamber shall adjudicate on employment- related disputes between a club and a player that have an international dimension.
3. As a consequence, the Dispute Resolution Chamber is the competent body to decide on the present litigation involving a YYian player and a XX club regarding the alleged breach of contract and allegedly outstanding salaries and compensation in connection with an employment contract.
4. Subsequently, the members of the Chamber analyzed which edition of the Regulations for the Status and Transfer of Players should be applicable as to the substance of the matter. In this respect, the Chamber referred, on the one hand, to art. 26 par. 1 and 2 of the Regulations for the Status and Transfer of Players (edition 2005) and, on the other hand, to the fact that the relevant contracts at the basis of the present dispute were signed on 3 August 2004 and 10 February 2006 respectively and the claim was lodged at FIFA on 22 May 2006.

   In view of the aforementioned, the Chamber concluded that the current FIFA Regulations for the Status and Transfer of Players (edition 2005; hereafter; the Regulations) are applicable to the case at hand as to the substance.

b) As to the substance of the present dispute

5. Entering into the substance of the matter the members of the Chamber acknowledged the documentation contained in the file, and in view of the circumstances of the matter at stake, focused its considerations on the question whether an unjustified breach of the first and/or second employment contract signed between the Claimant and the player occurred and, in the affirmative, which party is responsible for such breach of contract, whether inducement to breach of contract occurred and to verify and decide if sanctions for breach of contract and inducement to breach of contract have to be applied.

b1) Responsibility for breach of the employment contract

6. In continuation, the Chamber started its deliberations by acknowledging that the Claimant and the player signed on 3 August 2004 a first standard employment contract (hereafter: the contract) valid until 31 May 2009 and two Annexes (hereafter: and Annex) to the contract, signed on 2 August 2004 and 29 July 2005 respectively and valid for the seasons 2004/2005 and 2005/2006 respectively.
7. With regard to the contract and its and Annex, it was observed by the members of the Chamber that on the one hand the Claimant maintains having fulfilled all its financial obligations towards the player. Moreover, the members of the Chamber noted that the Claimant referred to the termination agreement it signed with the player on 3 February 2006 by means of which the parties agreed to discharge each other from any debt.
8. On the other hand, the Chamber took note of the player's allegations that the Claimant had failed to meet its financial obligations and remained outstanding the payment of USD 20,265 and TRL 41,76 Mrd on the basis of the contract and the Annex to the contract covering the season 2004/2005. and TRL 25 Mrd on the basis of the contract and its corresponding Annex to the contract related to the season 2005/2006.

As regards the termination agreement signed between the parties, the player argued having been not aware about the contents of the said agreement since his agent, who was normally present in the negotiations with the Claimant, was apparently not allowed to take part in the relevant meeting and that the document was only written in XX without a translation having been provided to him.

9. In view of the above, the deciding body went on to examine the relevant agreement signed between the Claimant and the player on 3 February 2006.
In this context, in accordance with the contents of the translation of the said termination agreement, it was observed by the Chamber that the Claimant and the player literally covenanted that "from now on the mentioned contract is null and due to this fact we hereby declared once again that both parties discharge each other from debt".

10. In this respect, the members of the Chamber noted that, as uncontested by the parties concerned, the player received on the occasion of the meeting dated 3 February 2006 the amount of USD 30,000. Yet, the Claimant and the player provided divergent statements with regard to the background and the reason of this payment.

11. Having duly studied this document, the deciding body reached the conclusion that the player and the Claimant agreed to terminate their contractual relationship and that no party can request any payment from the other party.
The members of the Chamber agreed that this document must be considered as a waiver duly signed by the Claimant and the player. That is, by signing the said agreement, which explicitly refers to contract the parties entered into, the player waived all rights that the may have towards the Claimant on the basis of the relevant contract in future.

12. Thereupon, the members turned to the player's argument that the agreement dated 3 February 2006 was only written in XX, a language which he does not understand, and without having been provided with a translation of the said agreement, he could not understand the meaning and the contents of it.

13. In this respect, the Chamber concluded that since the agreement mentioned above was indeed signed by the player, which the latter does not deny, the player thus gave his consent to such termination.

14. Moreover, the Chamber could not grasp how the player could have signed this agreement should he not have been aware of the significance of this agreement. In addition to that, the members of the Chamber recalled that, on the occasion of signing the relevant termination agreement, the player received the amount of USD 30,000 from the Claimant. The receipt of such payment by the player and the conclusion of the termination agreement on the same date, strengthens the Chamber in its conviction that the player must have been aware about the situation and the relevant contents of the agreement he did not deny having signed.

15. Taking into account all of the above, the Dispute Resolution Chamber decided that it has to reject the player's claim for outstanding payments on the basis of the contract and its corresponding Annexes.

b2) Responsibility for breach of the employment contract

16. With regard to the contract, the members of the Chamber noted that according to the Claimant, the player breached the employment contract the parties signed on 10 February 2006 (hereafter: the contract) by leaving the club without prior notice and without its authorization. On the other hand, the player contested having signed the contract. From the player's point of view, it is obvious that the said contract was falsified given the several different signatures under his name and considering that the remuneration agreed in the contract is ridicule compared to the one he signed with the Claimant on 3 August 2004.

17. In this respect, at first, the members of the Chamber deemed it important to underline that the contract stipulated a remuneration due to the player in new XX Lira (TRY) and the contract a remuneration in the former currency, i.e. the XX Lira (TRL). As a general information, the Chamber explained that according to the information in its possession, the new currency in XX (TRY) was implemented as of 1 January 2005.
To that regard, the Chamber calculated that the remuneration agreed in the contract, i.e. TRY 250,000 equates to approximately USD 171,069, which corresponds to the amount which had been agreed for by and between the Claimant and the player in the contract.

18. On account of the above, the Chamber concluded that this argumentation put forward by the player does not supply evidence that the contract was forged.

19. Nevertheless, in continuation, the Chamber emphasized that, as a general rule, it is not the competent body to decide upon matters of criminal law, such as the alleged falsified signature or document, but that such affairs fall into the jurisdiction of the competent national criminal authority.
20. In continuation the Dispute Resolution Chamber recalled that alldocumentation remitted shall be considered with free discretion and therefore focused its attention to the contract as well as the other documents containing the player's signature. After a thorough analysis of the aforementioned documents, in particular, comparing the relevant signatures of the player, the DRC had no alternative than to conclude that for a layman the signatures do clearly not seem to be alike. In fact, considering the signatures of the player on the copy of the contract initially remitted to the file by the Claimant by means of its communication dated 22 May 2006 and sent through the XX Football Federation, compared to his signature on the original of the contract delivered directly by the XX Football Federation, the deciding body ascertained that the signatures do not seem to correspond.
21. In view of the all of the above, and based on the documentation currently at its disposal, the Chamber unanimously came to the conclusion that, unless proven otherwise by a neutral expertise or a decision of the competent national criminal authority, for the moment, the claim of the Claimant has to be rejected since the relevant contract dated 10 February 2006 seems not to have been signed by the player in question.
22. In conclusion, the Dispute Resolution Chamber decided that no employment contract appears to have been signed between the Claimant and the player on 10 February 2006, thus no ongoing contractual relationship between the Claimant and the player exists any longer.

b3) Consequences against the Respondent

23. In continuation, the Chamber went on to deliberate whether it has to pass a decision on the request made by the Claimant against the player's new club, i.e. the Respondent, for inducement to breach of contract.
24. In this context, the Chamber pointed out that, in order to apply possible sanctions on the Respondent for inducement to breach of contract, as a condition sine que non, a breach of contract must have actually occurred.
25. In this respect, the deciding body referred to its precedent considerations and recalled that, as established above, no breach of contract was committed by none of the parties involved.
26. As a consequence, the Dispute Resolution Chamber decided that this part of the Claimant's claim directed against the Respondent has to be rejected.

III. DECISION OF THE DISPUTE RESOLUTION CHAMBER

1. The claim of the Claimant/Counter-Respondent, X, is fully rejected.
2. The counter-claim of the player/Counter-Claimant is fully rejected.
3. According to art. 61 par. 1 of the FIFA Statutes this decision may be appealed before the Court of Arbitration for Sport (CAS). The statement of appeal must be sent to the CAS directly within 21 days of receiving notification of this decision and has to contain all elements in accordance with point 2 of the directives issued by the CAS, copy of which we enclose hereto. Within another 10 days following the expiry of the time limit for the filing of the statement of appeal, the appellant shall file with the CAS a brief stating the facts and legal arguments giving rise to the appeal (cf. point 4 of the directives).

⚽⚽⚽

611814

DECISION OF THE DISPUTE RESOLUTION CHAMBER

passed in Zurich, Switzerland, on 21 November 2006,
in the following composition:
Slim Aloulou (Tunisia), Chairman
Carlos Soto (Chile), Member
John Didulica (Australia),Member
Paulo Amoretty Souza (Brazil), Member
Ivan Gazidis (USA), Member
on the claim presented by the

Player X, XX, as Claimant
against the club, Y, YY, as Respondent
regarding a contractual dispute arisen between the parties involved

I. FACTS OF THE CASE

1. On 5 June 2005, the XXn player, X (hereinafter: the Claimant), born on 1 July 1977, signed an employment contract, valid from 5 June 2005 to 25 October 2005, with the YY club, Y (hereinafter: the Respondent). The parties also signed an employment contract for the period from 8 April 2006 to 8 June 2006, without indicating the exact date of signature.
2. According to the first employment contract for the 2005 season, the parties agreed on a monthly salary of USD 5,000 for the Claimant. Furthermore, the Claimant was entitled to a bonus depending on the team's results as well as payment of a return trip to visit his family.
3. According to the second employment contract concluded for part of the 2006 season, it is not clear from the employment contract submitted by the Claimant whether he was entitled to a monthly salary of RMB (YY Yuan Renminbi) 40,000 or USD 40,000. No indications were made with regard to the bonuses to be paid to the Claimant in the second employment contract. However, according to the second employment contract, the Claimant was likewise entitled to receive a payment from the Respondent for a round trip to XX.
4. The Claimant's undated claim against the Respondent was received by FIFA on 14 June 2006.
5. The Claimant maintained in his written claim that the Respondent still owes him a total of USD 29,500 based on the two employment contracts.
6. The Claimant is claiming RMB 127,500 from the Respondent for the 2005 season.
   In this connection, the Claimant remitted a document to the file bearing the Respondent's stamp but the date of the Respondent's signature appeared only in YY characters. According to a translation of the document submitted by the Claimant, the Respondent stated therein that it still owes the Claimant salary in the amount of RMB 127,500 for the 2005 season.
7. For the 2006 season, the Claimant is claiming two outstanding salary payments amounting to a total of USD 8,000, two bonuses for draws totalling USD 2,000 and USD 3,500 for a return trip to XX.
8. On 27 July and 22 August 2006, the Respondent was requested in writing to comment on the Claimant's claim.
9. The Respondent has to date not replied.

II. CONSIDERATIONS OF THE DISPUTE RESOLUTION CHAMBER

1. First of all, the Chamber analysed whether it was competent to deal with the matter at stake. In this respect, it referred to art. 18 par. 2 and 3 of the Rules Governing the Procedures of the Players' ' Status Committee and the Dispute Resolution Chamber. The present matter was submitted to FIFA on 14 June 2006, as a consequence the Chamber concluded that the revised Rules Governing Procedures (edition 2005) on matters pending before the decision making bodies of FIFA are applicable to the matter at hand.
2. With regard to the competence of the Chamber, art. 3 par. 1 of the above- mentioned Rules states that the Dispute Resolution Chamber shall examine its jurisdiction in the light of articles 22 to 24 of the current version of the Regulations for the Status and Transfer of Players (edition 2005). In accordance with art. 24 par. 1 in combination with art. 22 (b) of the aforementioned Regulations, the Dispute Resolution Chamber shall adjudicate on employment- related disputes between a club and a player that have an international dimension.
3. As a consequence, the Dispute Resolution Chamber is the competent body to decide on the present litigation involving a XXn player and a YY club in connection with an employment contract.
4. Subsequently, the members of the Chamber analyzed which edition of the Regulations for the Status and Transfer of Players should be applicable as to the substance of the matter. In this respect, the Chamber referred to art. 26 par. 1 and 2 of the Regulations for the Status and Transfer of Players (edition 2005) and to the fact that the claim was lodged at FIFA on 14 June 2006. In view of the aforementioned, the Chamber concluded that the current FIFA Regulations for the Status and Transfer of Players (edition 2005, hereafter: the Regulations) are applicable to the case at hand as to the substance.
5. In continuation, and entering into the substance of the matter, the members of the Chamber started by acknowledging the above-mentioned facts and documentation contained in the file and took note

that the Claimant and the Respondent signed a first employment contract dated 5 June 2005 valid from the date of signature of the contract until 25 October 2005. Moreover, the members took note that for the period lasting from 8 April 2006 until 8 June 2006, the parties signed a second contract.

6. Furthermore, the members acknowledged that according to the first employment contract at stake, the Claimant was entitled to receive a monthly salary of USD 5,000, a bonus depending on the Respondent's result as well as the payment of a return trip to XX. Moreover, the members noted that the Claimant was, according to the second employment contract he concluded with the Respondent, entitled to receive either a monthly salary of RMB 40,000 or USD 40,000 as well as the payment of his return flight ticket to XX.
7. Subsequently, the Chamber took note that, according to the breakdown provided by the Claimant, he alleges having not received from the Respondent for the 2005 season the amount of RMB 127,500 on the basis of a document signed by the Respondent. Moreover, on the basis of the employment contract concerning the 2006 season, the Claimant maintains having not received two salary payments amounting to USD 8,000, two bonus for draws totaling to USD 2,000 and finally, USD 3,500 for flight tickets to XX.
8. Turning its attention to the Respondent, the members of the Chamber took note of the fact that the Respondent never provided FIFA with its position in the present proceeding, despite having been asked by FIFA to do so on several occasions.
9. Consequently, the Respondent renounced to its right of defence.
10. In continuation, the Chamber then stated that as a general principle of procedure before the Dispute Resolution Chamber, if a Respondent does not reply to the claim of the Claimant, the case shall be decided by the Chamber only on the basis of the facts and documentary evidences provided by the Claimant.
11. On account of the above, the deciding body stated that due to the Respondent's failure to reply to the claim of the Claimant, it has to pass a decision only on the facts and evidences provided by the Claimant.
12. Therefore, with respect to the amount of RMB 127,500, claimed by the Claimant for the 2005 season, the Chamber noted the contents of the undated document submitted by the Claimant and bearing the Respondent's stamp and stating that the Respondent owes the Claimant the amount of RMB 127,500.
13. The members of the Chamber concluded at first that the said letter unquestionably indicated that the Respondent owes the amount of RMB 127,500 to the Claimant.
14. The Chamber noted that the translation of the documents outlined under I.6d was not contested by the Respondent
15. As a consequence, the members initially concluded that the Respondent has in any case to pay the amount of RMB 127,500 to the Claimant.
16. With regard to the two salary payments amounting to USD 8,000 and the flight tickets in the amount of USD 3,500, the Chamber concluded that the Respondent, by failing to respond to the claim of the Claimant, admitted having failed to pay the latter the two salary payments and the flight tickets.
17. In light of the above, the Dispute Resolution Chamber decided that the Respondent has to pay also the amount of USD 11,500 to the Claimant.
18. Finally, with regard to the bonus of USD 2,000 claimed by the Claimant, the deciding body referred to the contents of the second employment contract concluded by the parties concerned and emphasized that no indications were given in the said contract about the bonus that the Claimant should receive depending on the Respondent's results.
19. Therefore, the members of the Chamber concluded that this part of the claim of the Claimant concerning the bonus has to be rejected.
20. In view of all the above, the Dispute Resolution Chamber decided that the Respondent must pay the Claimant the amounts of RMB 127,500 and USD 11,500.

III. DECISION OF THE DISPUTE RESOLUTION CHAMBER

1. The claim of the Claimant, player X, is partially accepted.
2. The Respondent, Y, has to pay the amounts of RMB 127,500 and USD 11,500 to the Claimant, player X, within 30 days as from the date of notification of this decision.
3. Any further claim of the Claimant, player X, has to be rejected.
4. In the event that the due amounts are not paid within the stated deadline, an interest rate of 5% p.a. will apply as of expiry of the fixed time limit.

5. If the aforementioned sums are not paid within the aforementioned deadline, the present matter shall be submitted to FIFA's Disciplinary Committee, so that the necessary disciplinary sanctions may be imposed.
6. The Claimant, player X, is directed to inform the Respondent, Y, immediately of the account number to which the remittance is to be made and to notify the Dispute Resolution Chamber of every payment received.
7. According to art. 61 par. 1 of the FIFA Statutes this decision may be appealed before the Court of Arbitration for Sport (CAS). The statement of appeal must be sent to the CAS directly within 21 days of receiving notification of this decision and has to contain all elements in accordance with point 2 of the directives issued by the CAS, copy of which we enclose hereto. Within another 10 days following the expiry of the time limit for the filing of the statement of appeal, the appellant shall file with the CAS a brief stating the facts and legal arguments giving rise to the appeal (cf. point 4 of the directives).

1161241
DECISION OF THE DISPUTE RESOLUTION CHAMBER
passed in Zurich, Switzerland, on 21 November 2006,
in the following composition:
Slim Aloulou (Tunisia), Chairman
Paulo Amoretty Souza (Brazil), member
Ivan Gazidis (USA), member
Carlos Soto (Chile), member
John Didulica (Australia), member
on the claim presented by the club X, as Claimant
against the
Player Y and the club Z as Respondents
regarding a contractual dispute arisen on the basis of an employment contract signed between the Claimant and the player

I. FACTS OF THE CASE

1. On 18 January 2004, the player X (hereafter: the player), born on 20 May 1981, and Y, (hereafter: the Claimant) signed an employment contract valid until 31 December 2004.
   The aforementioned employment contract foresaw that the Claimant would pay to the player a monthly salary amounting to ... 350.
2. In addition, the above-mentioned two parties signed an annex to the said employment contract, also on 18 January 2004, with the following content: " PENAL CLAUSE: The party who does not comply with, breaches, or unilaterally terminates this agreement, will bear the fine of ... 450,000.00 (four hundred and fifty thousand), according to the terms of 3rd 1 paragraph of article 28, Law 9,615/98.
   (2) If the non-compliance is motivated by an international transfer, the fine will be freely negotiated.
   (3) In case of assignment of the rights of this agreement by xxxx to any team in xxxxx or abroad, the player hereon waives any fine set forth in article (01) and (02) above, as well as the remaining of the contract pro rata. (4) As jointly agreed, upon the liberation of the comply of the employment agreement balance, the rescission can be observed with the waive of the agreed penal clauses, as well the waive of the indemnifications foreseen in sections 479, 480 of the Consolidation of the Labor Laws (CLT). (5) It is herein between the parties that, in case of sale of the Federative Rights (pass) of the athlete for any team abroad, xxxx pledges to liberate the same by means of payment of 30% (thirty percent) of the liquid value of the negotiations.
   (6) The player hereon grants preference to xxxx. for the extension/renewal of this agreement." (translation from the Portuguese provided by the Claimant).
   Both, the contract and the annex dated 18 January 2004 were registered with the xxxxx.
3. Moreover, the Claimant provided along with its submission a copy of an amendment to the relevant employment contract dated 18 January 2004, according to which on 1 July 2004 the Claimant and the player, apparently, agreed that the employment contract would be extended until 18 January 2009 and that the player would receive a monthly salary amounting to ... 2,500.

4. Equally, the annex dated 18 January 2004 was, apparently, amended on 1 July 2004 as follows: "PENAL CLAUSE: The party that does not comply, breaches or unilaterally terminates this agreement, shall bear the fine of ... 3.000.000.00 million), according to the terms of 3rd paragraph of article 28, Law 9,615/98.
(2) If the non-compliance is motivated by an international transfer, the fine will shall be of US$ 1.500.000.00 (one million, five hundred thousand American dollars) in the terms of 5th § of section 28 of the Law 9,615/98.
(3) It is herein agreed that xxxxx will pay ... 20,000 (twenty thousand) for the transfer at the end of the agreement. (4) In case the rights of this instrument are assigned by xxxxx to any team in xxxx or abroad, the player hereon WAIVES his right on fines established in clauses (01) and (2) and also the remaining amounts of the agreement. (5) It is herein mutually agreed that upon the release concerning the compliance with the balance of the labour agreement, the termination can be observed with a waive to the agreed penal clauses, a waive to section 479 and 480 of the Consolidation of the Labor Laws- CLT. (6) The player irrevocably and permanently grants the preference to xxxx for this agreement renewal. (7) The parties agree that xxxx, on July 26, 2004 will make available to the player the amount of ... 150.000.00 (one hundred and fifty thousand xxx) as payment for 100% (hundred per cent) of his federative rights.
(8) Section 05 of the agreement in force will be effective where it is read 30% of the federative rights, read 100% of the federative rights, being the former agreement revoked."
5. According to the copies of the files of the xxxx, provided by the Claimant along with its submissions, the employment contract signed on 18 January 2004 and its annex also dated 18 January 2004 were registered with the xxxx on 30 January 2004.
However, the amendments dated 1 July 2004 were not registered.
6. On 12 August 2004, the termination of the employment contract (released by order) and the international transfer of the player concerned to xxxx were registered by the xxxxx. Equally, on 31 August 2004, the xxxxx registered that a labour court granted by preliminary order the authorization to transfer the player concerned to xxxxx. The final and last entry in the xxxxxx's files is dated 9 September 2004 and refers to the labour court decision by means of which the player was released from his employment contract (no further specification is made). No further entries are contained in the copies of the registers of the xxxxx remitted by the Claimant along with its submissions.
7. On 11 July 2005, FIFA received the compliant of the Claimant. Basically, the Claimant explained that upon receiving an offer from the club, Z on 15 June 2004, the player went to xxxx by the end of June 2004.
However, the player returned to xxxx, the exact date was not specified, and, apparently, the Claimant was informed by phone that the Z club was no longer interested in the player's services. Yet, according to the Claimant the player left again without notice on 24 July 2004.
8. The Claimant further stated that on 16 July 2004 and in view of the player's departure it brought a lawsuit against the player before a national court in xxxx postulating the recognition of the extension of the employment contract until January 2009.
Moreover, the Claimant apparently deposited the amount of ... 150,000 in virtue of clause (7) of the relevant amendment dated 1 July 2004.
9. On 4 August 2004, the player also brought a lawsuit before a labour court in xxxx seeking the declaration of the termination of the employment contract signed with the Claimant on 18 January 2004 and originally valid until 31 December 2004.
10. The Claimant explained that according to a decision of a xxxx labour court passed on 13 September 2004 the player's claim in connection with the termination of the employment contract signed with the Claimant on 18 January 2004 was extinct due to the player's failure to appear at the relevant hearing. The Claimant further stated that the aforementioned decision dated 13 September 2004 revoked the preliminary decision taken by a xxxxx court, by means of which the player's transfer to xxxx was authorized. The Claimant quoted the following paragraph of the decision dated 13 September 2004: "By the fundaments above exposed, this labour Court declares extinct without the appreciation of its merit the non-nominated preventive measure proposed by the xxxx. in face of xxxxx judges in favour to the payment consignation lawsuit involving the same litigator to declare extinct the obligation represented by the deposit of page 27 corresponding to the title pointed at clause 7th of document 19" (translation from the Portuguese provided by the Claimant).

11. In view of all of the above, the Claimant is of the opinion that the player breached the employment contract concluded between the parties on 1 July 2004 valid until January 2009 and should therefore be liable to pay compensation.
12. In particular, the Claimant requests compensation from the player in the amount of USD 1,500,000 (plus 5% default interest as from the date of the decision) in accordance with clause (2) of the amendment dated 1 July 2004.
Or alternatively, the Claimant requests compensation in the amount of USD 1,000,000 (plus 5% default interest as from the date of the decision). The Claimant calculated the aforementioned amount as follows: offer made by the Z club USD 300,000, plus 40% of any future transfer, plus 40% as compensation.
Furthermore, the Claimant requests that the player be sanctioned with a restriction of his eligibility to play for a period of six months. Equally, the Claimant demands compensation in the same amount payable by the Z club, being the latter jointly liable for the payment of compensation for the breach of contract.
In addition, the Claimant requests that the Z club also be sanctioned.
13. On 23 February 2006, the Z club vehemently contested the Claimant's claim arguing that no legally binding contractual relationship exists between the two clubs. Moreover, the Z club explained that it had signed an employment contract with the player concerned only after being informed that the player had properly terminated the employment contract signed with the Claimant by means of his claim with the labour courts.
14. In addition, the Z club emphasised that it had always acted in accordance with the FIFA regulations since by the time it had started negotiations with the player his contract with the Claimant was expected to expire within the next 6 months, i.e. in December 2004.
15. Furthermore, the Z club pointed out that the player had told them that the alleged extension of the employment contract until January 2009, which is at the basis of the Claimant's claim, cannot be considered valid since his signature was fake.
16. Finally, the Z club stressed that the relevant International Transfer Certificate (ITC) had been issued by the xxxx, which, in the Z club's opinion, would not have been the case if there had been any irregularity with regard to the player's contractual situation with the Claimant.
17. The xxxxxx Football Association provided a copy of the relevant ITC issued by the xxxxxx on 29 July 2004, based on which it had registered the player concerned for its affiliate.
On 27 March 2006, also the player vehemently contested the Claimant's claim.
First of all, the player emphasised that his signature on the alleged amendments dated 1 July 2004 submitted by the Claimant along with its claim was fake.
19. Moreover, the player contested FIFA's jurisdiction on the present affair, arguing that the present dispute involves a club and a player from xxxx and that the matter had already been dealt with by the competent xxxxx labour courts. In this respect, the player presented along with his submission a copy of a preliminary decision of a xxxx labour court dated 10 August 2004, by means of which it had been concluded and decided that he could be transferred to ...
20. Furthermore, the player explained that he had been originally bound to the Claimant until 31 December 2004.
However, the relevant employment contract signed on 18 January 2004 had been terminated by means of the labour court's decision.
21. In particular, the player pointed out that based on the aforementioned employment contract originally valid until 31 December 2004, respectively its annex also dated 18 January 2004, he was entitled to unilaterally terminate the relevant contract by paying compensation for the premature termination of the employment contract to the Claimant. In this respect, the player referred to clause (5) of the relevant annex according to which upon payment of 30% of the value of any possible negotiation, the Claimant committed itself to "liberate" him. In this context, the player maintained having fully complied with the aforementioned clause (5) since he allegedly paid 30% of USD 55,000 to the Claimant.
22. Finally, the player stressed that also the labour court in xxxx had established that his alleged signatures on the relevant amendments dated 1 July 2004, on which the Claimant is basing its claim, are different from his signature on all other documents containing his signature provided to the court.

23. The Claimant contested the positions of the Z club and the player and basically referred to his previous correspondence. As a result, the Claimant asks for compensation amounting to USD 1,500,000, plus 5% default interest as from the date of the decision, from the player and the Z club as well as that the player be sanctioned with a restriction on his eligibility to play for 6 months.
24. The player and the Z club referred to their previous submissions.

II. CONSIDERATIONS OF THE DISPUTE RESOLUTION CHAMBER

1. First of all, the Chamber analysed whether it was competent to deal with the matter at stake. In this respect, it referred to art. 18 par. 2 and 3 of the Rules Governing the Procedures of the Players' Status Committee and the Dispute Resolution Chamber. The present matter was submitted to FIFA on 11 July 2005, as a consequence the Chamber concluded that the revised Rules Governing Procedures (edition 2005) on matters pending before the decision making bodies of FIFA are applicable to the matter at hand.
2. With regard to the competence of the Chamber, art. 3 par. 1 of the above- mentioned Rules states that the Dispute Resolution Chamber shall examine its jurisdiction in the light of articles 22 to 24 of the current version of the Regulations for the Status and Transfers of Players (edition 2005). In accordance with art. 24 par. 1 in combination with art. 22 (a) of the aforementioned Regulations, the Dispute Resolution Chamber shall adjudicate on disputes between clubs and players in relation to the maintenance of contractual stability if there has been a request for the issuance of an International Transfer Certificate (ITC) and if there is a claim from an interested party in relation to such ITC request, in particular regarding its issuance, regarding sporting sanctions or regarding compensation for breach of contract.
3. As a consequence, as a first step, it was concluded that, in principle, the Dispute Resolution Chamber was the competent body to decide on the present litigation involving a xxx club, a xxxx player and a xxxx club related to the maintenance of contractual stability in connection with an international transfer of the player concerned.
4. Subsequently, and before entering into the substance of the present matter, the Chamber deemed it, however, of utmost importance to consider the following chronological crucial facts which are at the basis of the present litigation:
5. On 15 June 2004, the Claimant, apparently, received an offer for the acquisition of the services of the player from the Z club. Therefore, by the end of June 2004, the player went to xxxxx. However, it appears that the relevant negotiations were not successful and the player returned to xxxxx. Subsequently, or even before the player went to xxxx, the Claimant and the player, apparently, agreed on 1 July 2004 that the duration of the original employment contract would be extended and would thus be valid until 18 January 2009.
The Chamber deemed it important to underline that such proceedings appear to be rather unusual and that the chronological order of the aforementioned events cannot be exactly followed or reconstructed.
6. Equally, the Chamber took into account that on 16 July 2004, the Claimant lodged an action for declaratory judgment before a labour court postulating the recognition of the extension of the employment contract. On 29 July 2004 the relevant ITC for the player was issued by the xxxx to the xxxxxx Football Association. Moreover, on 4 August 2004, also the player brought a lawsuit before a labour court in xxxx seeking the declaration of the termination of the employment contract signed with the Claimant on 18 January 2004.
7. Subsequently, the Chamber considered that on 10 August 2004, a xxxxx labour court passed a preliminary decision according to which the player could be transferred to xxxx and that on 12 August 2004, the termination of the employment contract (released by order) and the international transfer of the player to xxxx were registered by the xxxxx.
8. Moreover, the Chamber stated that it appears that both claims lodged by the player and the Claimant before the civil courts were joined. In this context, the Chamber acknowledged that the Claimant maintained that by a decision dated 13 September 2004 the preliminary authorization for the player's transfer to xxxx had been revoked. In this respect, the Claimant quoted the following paragraph of the relevant decision dated 13 September 2004: "By the fundaments above exposed, this labour Court declares extinct without the appreciation of its merit the non-nominated preventive measure proposed by the xxxxxx. in face of xxxxx and judges in favour to the payment consignation lawsuit involving the same litigator to declare extinct the obligation represented by the deposit of page 27

corresponding to the title pointed at clause 7th of document 19" (translation from the Portuguese provided by the Claimant).

9. With regard to the above-mentioned decision and the Claimant's comments in this respect the Chamber first and foremost emphasized that the translation provided is rather difficult to understand.

10. Yet, the Chamber underlined that, in any case, the above-mentioned decision appears not to be a decision as to the substance of the matter, i.e. the labour dispute arisen between the player and the Claimant. Based on the statements of the Claimant, which are confirmed by the official documentation of the relevant labour court, the Chamber also remarked that the player was not present at the pertinent meeting of the decision-making body. In fact, this appears to be the main reason for the conclusions reached by the relevant labour court.

11. In continuation, the Chamber reiterated that, in principle, the Dispute Resolution Chamber is competent to deal with disputes between players and clubs that have an international dimension (cf. art. 24 par. 1 in connection with art. 22 (a) of the Regulations for the Status and Transfer of Players, edition 2005). Yet, the Chamber also emphasised that players and clubs have the right to seek redress before a civil court for employment-related disputes (cf. art. 22 of the aforementioned Regulations).

12. In view of the foregoing, the Chamber duly considered that the Claimant made use of the above-mentioned right and primarily lodged its claim before a civil court for employment-related disputes, although it could have lodged its claim related to the contractual relationship with the player directly with FIFA.

13. For the sake of completeness, the Chamber also underlined that at the latest when the relevant ITC was issued by the xxxxx in favour of the xxxxx Football Association, on 29 July 2004, the present matter acquired an international dimension (cf. point II. 2. above), and the Claimant could have withdrawn its claim lodged before a xxxxx civil court for employment-related disputes and referred the matter to FIFA.

14. In continuation, and for the sake of good order, the Chamber was equally eager to emphasise that, irrespective of the fact whether or not a decision- making body would have pronounced itself on the validity of the extension of the contractual relationship until January 2009, the player and the Claimant appear to have been contractually bound at least until December 2004 based on the original employment contract signed on 18 January 2004.

    In other words, the Chamber deemed that the establishment of the validity of the extension appears not to have been a prerequisite to entitle the Claimant to lodge a complaint before the competent decision-making bodies of sports authorities.

    Therefore, this argument cannot be used by the Claimant in order to justify its initial decision to refer its claim to an ordinary court instead of to FIFA.

15. Yet, the Claimant adhered to its claim, already lodged in July 2004, before a civil court for employment-related disputes. The Chamber emphasised that the Claimant's adherence to seek redress before a civil court is also corroborated by the fact that based on the decision of the competent court dated 13 September 2004, the Claimant, contrary to the player, attended the relevant hearing.

16. Bearing in mind the above-mentioned considerations, the Chamber underlined that only in July 2005, almost a year after having the Claimant lodged its claim before a civil court and 10 months after the player's transfer to xxxxxx, the Claimant decided to seek redress before FIFA after the proceedings before the civil courts were apparently suspended or (temporarily) dismissed. For the sake of completeness, the Chamber underlined in this respect that based on the documentation at its disposal it cannot clearly be established whether the proceedings before the civil courts were suspended or (temporarily) dismissed.

17. The Chamber reiterated that players and clubs are entitled to seek redress before a civil court for employment-related disputes, since, for such issues, the choice of judge is a fundamental right that cannot be denied. Parties may, however, decide to divert from the choice of judge and instead refer the matter to sports arbitration. Yet, according to the principle of "litispendency", a case pending in front of civil courts cannot be dealt with by the decision- making bodies of sports arbitration.

18. In view of all of the above, the Chamber deemed it of utmost importance to underline that the practice of parties to have their legal cases heard by several decision-making bodies with the aim to get the most favourable judgment, known as "forum shopping", cannot be upheld at all by the Chamber.

19. On the basis of all these considerations the members of the Chamber unanimously concluded that if a player or a club, by using their right according to the regulations seek redress before an ordinary court in connection with employment-related disputes, and the competence of the ordinary court is not contested by the other party, as a general rule, the addressed civil court, which was first contacted by a party, shall deal with the matter in its entirety. For the sake of completeness, the Chamber underlined that contrary to the former version of the Regulations for the Status and Transfer of Players (edition 2001), the current version does not leave space for possible interpretation related to a possible split-up in the sense that two different decision-making bodies pass separate decisions, one, taken by a first body, related to the potential breach, and another, taken by a second body, related to the consequences of such a breach.
20. In view of the above, the Chamber emphasized that if an ordinary court expresses itself on the liability of a party in connection with a possible contractual breach, it should also decide as to the relevant consequences implied by such a potential breach of the contract.
21. Finally, and for the sake of good order, the Chamber emphasized that, in principle, the Dispute Resolution Chamber could deal with the question of a possible inducement to breach of contract by a third party, in casu, the Z club, however, only after the competent ordinary court renders its final decision with respect to the substance of the labour dispute arisen between the player and his former club, in casu, the Claimant and the player.
22. The Chamber thus concluded that the Claimant would have to seek for the protection of its alleged rights towards the player in front of the ordinary court, as it had originally chosen to do.
23. On account of all the foregoing considerations, the Chamber decided that it is not competent to deal with the claim lodged by the Claimant.

III. DECISION OF THE DISPUTE RESOLUTION CHAMBER

1. The claim of the club X is not admissible.
2. According to art. 61 par. 1 of the FIFA Statutes, this decision may be appealed against before the Court of Arbitration for Sport (CAS). The statement of appeal must be sent to the CAS directly within 21 days of receipt of notification of this decision and shall contain all the elements in accordance with point 2 of the directives issued by the CAS, a copy of which we enclose hereto. Within another 10 days following the expiry of the time limit for filing the statement of appeal, the appellant shall file a brief stating the facts and legal arguments giving rise to the appeal with the CAS (cf. point 4 of the directives).

6111183 A
DECISION OF THE DISPUTE RESOLUTION CHAMBER

passed in Zurich, Switzerland, on 21 November 2006,
in the following composition:
Slim Aloulou (Tunisia), Chairman
Paulo Rogerio Amoretty Souza (Brazil), member
Ivan Gazidis (USA), member
Carlos Soto (Chile), member
John Didulica (Australia), member
on a matter between
the club, X represented by Mr., attorney-at-law
and the club, Y
and the club, Z as Intervening party
regarding the distribution of solidarity contribution in connection with the player, V

I. FACTS OF THE CASE

1. The player, V, was born on 15 April 1983.
2. On 3 March 2005, Y and Z signed an agreement in accordance with which the player, V, was transferred to Y involving the payment of a transfer compensation of USD 4,500,000.
3. According to an additional agreement signed by and between the same parties on the same day, which agreement is an integral part of the transfer agreement, Y and Z agreed that Z would be responsible

for solidarity contribution payments to the maximum amount of USD 50,000. Furthermore, Y would be responsible for any solidarity contribution payments exceeding the said amount of USD 50,000.
4. Y confirmed that the player in question was registered with it on 10 March 2005.
5. On 6 September 2005, X lodged a claim in front of the Dispute Resolution Chamber against Y for payment of its proportion of the solidarity contribution relating to the above-mentioned transfer.
6. According to the player's playing passport issued by the Football Federation of X, the player was formerly registered with X as from 7 April 1999 until 22 January 2004.
7. X has presented the following calculation of its alleged part of the solidarity contribution on the basis of article 1 of Annex 5 of the current Regulations for the Status and Transfer of Players:
   a. the player was allegedly registered with X from 25 January 1999 until 22 January 2004, i.e. from the season of the player's age of 15 years and 9 months until 20 years and 9 months.
   b. therefore, X claims being entitled to 2.427% of the transfer compensation equalling the amount of USD 97,480.
8. In reply to the claim, Y refers to the transfer agreement that it signed with Z, in accordance with which Z would be responsible for solidarity contribution payments to an amount not exceeding USD 50,000. In addition, Y refers to the obligation allegedly undertaken by ".... Agency" in ... to pay part of the amount of solidarity contribution according to the agency's letter of guarantee of 28 February 2005.
9. In addition, Y points out that there is a contradiction in the period of registration of the player with X and that the calculation put forward by X is thus wrong. Y accepts the period of registration as confirmed by the Football Federation of X.
10. On 13 January 2006, FIFA suggested to the parties that Y distributes the relevant proportion relating to the 5% solidarity contribution of the transfer compensation to X and that Z reimburses to Y the relevant proportion in line with the jurisprudence of the DRC.
11. The parties have not been able to settle the matter in this way.
12. On 18 January 2006, Y lodged a claim in front of the Players' Status Committee against Z maintaining that Z has not proceeded with the payment of the relevant solidarity contribution in spite of having been asked by X to do so in view of the claim presented by X.
13. Z has intervened in this matter explaining that it would proceed with a payment of up to USD 50,000 to X.
14. During the proceedings in the present matter, Z paid the amount of USD 50,000 to X, receipt of which was confirmed by X.
15. Y thereafter informed FIFA that "*the parties involved in this situation*" are carrying on negotiations with each other.
16. Having received the amount of USD 50,000 only, X insists that Y pays the remainder of USD 47,480, which remains unpaid to date.

II. CONSIDERATIONS OF THE DISPUTE RESOLUTION CHAMBER

1. First of all, the Dispute Resolution Chamber analysed whether it was competent to deal with the matter at stake. In this respect, it referred to art. 18 par. 2 and 3 of the Rules Governing the Procedures of the Players' Status Committee and the Dispute Resolution Chamber. The present matter was submitted to FIFA on 6 September 2005, as a consequence the Chamber concluded that the revised Rules Governing Procedures (edition 2005) on matters pending before the decision making bodies of FIFA are applicable to the matter at hand.
2. With regard to the competence of the Chamber, art. 3 par. 1 of the above-mentioned Rules states that the Dispute Resolution Chamber shall examine its jurisdiction in the light of articles 22 to 24 of the current version of the Regulations for the Status and Transfer of Players (edition 2005). In accordance with art. 24 par. 1 in combination with art. 22 (d) of the aforementioned Regulations, the Dispute Resolution Chamber shall adjudicate on disputes between two clubs belonging to different Associations related to solidarity mechanism.
3. As a consequence, the Dispute Resolution Chamber is the competent body to decide on the present litigation concerning the distribution of the solidarity contribution claimed by X in connection with the transfer of the professional V during the course of a contract.
4. Subsequently, the members of the Chamber analyzed which edition of the Regulations for the Status and Transfer of Players should be applicable as to the substance of the matter. In this respect, the Chamber referred to art. 26 par. 1 and 2 of the Regulations for the Status and Transfer of Players

(edition 2005) in the modified version in accordance with the FIFA circular no. 995 dated 23 September 2005. Furthermore, it acknowledged that the professional had been registered for his new club on 10 March 2005. Equally, the Chamber took note that the claim was lodged at FIFA on 6 September 2005. In view of the aforementioned, the Chamber concluded that the former FIFA Regulations for the Status and Transfer of Players (edition 2001, hereinafter: the Regulations) are applicable to the case at hand as to the substance.

5. Once its competence and the applicable Regulations were thus established, the DRC went on to deal with the substance of the case. The members of the Chamber carefully studied the facts outlined above, which show that the player, V, was transferred from Z (hereinafter also referred to as: Intervening party) to Y on a definitive basis in March 2005.
6. To this end, Z and Y signed a transfer agreement in accordance with which the Y was obliged to pay to the Intervening party a transfer compensation to the amount of USD 4,500,000.
7. At this point, the Chamber recalled that, as established in article 10 in conjunction with article 11 of the Regulations governing the Application of the Regulations (edition September 2001), the new club to which a player is transferred during the course of an employment contract with his previous club is responsible for the distribution of 5% of the compensation payable to the player's former club to the club(s) involved in the training and education of the player between the ages of 12 and 23.
8. The Chamber took into account that Y, i.e. the player's new club, rejects the claim put forward by X maintaining that X should turn to the Intervening party, i.e. the player's former club, in order to obtain its proportion of the 5% solidarity contribution payment, given that Z committed itself to paying solidarity contribution up to the maximum amount of USD 50,000.
9. In this respect, the Chamber once more referred to paragraph 1 of the above-mentioned article 11 of the Regulations governing the Application of the Regulations (edition September 2001) which clearly states that the new club shall pay the amount due as a solidarity contribution to the training clubs.
10. However, the Chamber noted that, during the proceedings in the case at stake, the Intervening party remitted USD 50,000 to X in accordance with the relevant transfer agreement (cf. point I.3 above).
11. In addition, X has acknowledged receipt of the same amount of USD 50,000. Referring to point I.7.b. above, the Chamber noted that, as a consequence, X insists that Y pays the remainder of USD 47,480.
12. In its defence, Y equally refers to the obligation allegedly undertaken by " ..Agency" in ... to pay part of the amount of solidarity contribution according to the alleged agency's letter of guarantee of 28 February 2005.
13. The Chamber noticed that Y failed to submit documentary evidence in this regard. However, irrespective of such fact, the Chamber pointed out that any such "guarantee" issued by an agency or private company could not be taken into consideration and that should it have been possible to take such document into account it would not preclude the Y's obligation to pay solidarity contribution in the light of points II.7 and II.9 above.
14. In light of all the above, the Chamber concluded that in application of article 11 of the Regulations Governing the Application of the Regulations (edition September 2001) it is the responsibility of Y, i.e. the new club, to pay the relevant proportion of the solidarity contribution to the club(s) involved in the player's training, i.e. X
15. Having established that the transfer of the player in question was on a definitive basis and that a transfer compensation was agreed upon between the player's former club and new club, the Chamber then turned to the calculation of the relevant proportion due to X on the basis of the period of time that the player was trained and educated by X.
16. The Chamber subsequently referred to art. 10 of the Regulations governing the Application of the Regulations, which provides the figures for the distribution of the solidarity contribution.
17. The members of the Chamber underlined that the player passport issued by the Football Federation of X is to be the basis on which the amount of solidarity contribution must be calculated.
18. Considering that the player, V, born on 15 April 1983, was registered with X as from 7 April 1999 until 22 January 2004, i.e. from the age of 16 until the age of almost 21, 48.3% of the 5% solidarity contribution shall be apportioned to this club.
19. The members of the Chamber, however, recalled that X demands payment of the total amount of USD 97,480. Departing from the principle that the amount awarded shall not exceed the claimed amount, the Chamber concluded that X shall be entitled to the total amount of solidarity contribution of USD 97,480.

20. Bearing in mind that X has already received USD 50,000 and, as a consequence, X reduced its claim to the amount of USD 47,480 (cf. points I.16 and II.11 above), the Chamber decided that X is entitled to receive the amount of USD 47,480 from Y.
21. Therefore, the Chamber decided that Y is liable to pay the amount of USD 47,480 as solidarity contribution to X.

III. DECISION OF THE DISPUTE RESOLUTION CHAMBER

1. The claim lodged by X is accepted.
2. Y has to pay the amount of USD 47,480 to X within 30 days as from the date of notification of this decision.
4. If the sum of USD 47,480 is not paid within the aforementioned deadline by Y, an interest rate of 5% per year will apply and the matter shall be submitted to the FIFA Disciplinary Committee for its consideration and decision.
5. X is directed to inform Y immediately of the account number to which the remittance is to be made and to notify the Dispute Resolution Chamber of every payment received.
6. According to art. 61 par. 1 of the FIFA Statutes, this decision may be appealed against before the Court of Arbitration for Sport (CAS). The statement of appeal must be sent to the CAS directly within 21 days of receipt of notification of this decision and shall contain all the elements in accordance with point 2 of the directives issued by the CAS, a copy of which we enclose hereto. Within another 10 days following the expiry of the time limit for filing the statement of appeal, the appellant shall file a brief stating the facts and legal arguments giving rise to the appeal with the CAS (cf. point 4 of the directives).

12 JANUARY 2007

DECISION OF THE DISPUTE RESOLUTION CHAMBER
passed in Zurich, Switzerland, on 12 January 2007,
in the following composition:
Slim Aloulou (Tunisia), Chairman
Phllippe Piat (France), Member
Rinaldo Martorelli (Brazil), Member
Jean-Marie Philips (Belgium), Member
Mohamed Mecherara (Algeria), Member
on the claim presented by the
Player X, XX, as Claimant
against
the Club Y FC, YY, as Respondent
regarding a contractual dispute arisen between the Claimant and the Respondent

I. FACTS OF THE CASE

1. On 14 July 2003, the Romanian player Lucian X (hereinafter; the player) and the YY club Y FC (hereinafter: the club) concluded an employment contract (hereinafter: the private agreement).
2. According to section 2 of the private agreement, the duration of the latter is *"five (5 years (3+1+1)"*. The private agreement starts on 15 July 2003 and ends on 30 June 2006. At the end of the third and the fourth year of the private agreement, the club has the option to renew it unilaterally, each time for one year. The private agreement does not contain formal rules regarding the procedure of unilateral renewal.
3. According to section 3 of the private agreement, the salary for the first year of the contract is USD 180,000 (for the entire year). This amount increases by USD 20,000 per year, so that for the possible fifth year of the contract, the salary would be USD 260,000.
4. Finally, section 9 stipulates that the private agreement has priority over all other contracts, especially over league or club contracts.
5. On the same date, the parties signed a standard employment contract of the YY Football Federation (hereinafter; the standard agreement) with the same duration and the same financial obligations for

the club as stipulated in the private agreement.

6. According to the standard agreement, the potential renewal has to be notified by a court bailiff to the player, the YY Players' Union and the YY Football League five days before the opening of the registration period.
7. The last section of the standard agreement, just above the signatures, mentions that Mrs. Q is appointed as the player's proxy.
8. On 14 November 2006, the player submitted a claim with FIFA against the club, and thereby requested for a declaration that the labour relationship between him and the club is terminated.
9. At the end of the season 05/06, the player wanted to leave the club, as during the entire season, he had neither played for the club, nor had he been elected as a substitute. However, as the player was of the opinion that the labour relationship would end any way at the end of the said season, he did not invoke sporting just cause within due course.
10. On 2 June 2006, the player's agent informed the club in writing that the labour relationship would be terminated as of 1 July 2006, and that the player would be free to transfer to the club of his choice (copy of the relevant document is in the file.
11. On 28 June, according to the player, the YY Football Federation informed the player's lawyer via phone that the club had reported to it that it had unilaterally renewed the labour relationship with the player.
12. In this respect, the player is of the opinion that the notification of the unilateral renewal to a third party does not constitute a renewal of the employment contract with the contracting party.
13. On 6 July 2006, the player's lawyer requested a confirmation from the club that the labour relationship with the player had ended. (Copy of the relevant document is in the file). The club did not react to such request, and did not, in any other way, notify the player directly of the unilateral renewal.
14. Moreover, the player claims not having received his salaries from the club as of July 2006.
15. Therefore, the player is of the opinion that the labour relationship ended on 30 June 2006.
16. Subsidiary, in case the renewal should be considered as valid by the Dispute Resolution Chamber, the player is of the opinion that the renewal is not based on a reasonable and fair motive, as it appears that the club only renewed the labour relationship in order to possibly receive transfer compensation for the player, but that it had no sportive interest in the player.
17. Furthermore, to strengthen his position, the player invoked the decision of the Court of Arbitration for Sport (CAS) in the matter *TAS 2005/A/983&984 Peñarol vs. Bueno Suarez, Rodriguez Barrotti and Paris Saint-Germain.*
18. On 22 November 2006, the club provided its answer to the player's claim, and thereby requested that the player's claim be rejected, the agreements between the player and the club be recognised as valid, and that the player be urged to fulfil his obligations with the club as stipulated in the agreements
19. In this respect, the club maintained having validly exercised the right to unilateral renewal. In particular, the club mentioned that the renewal was filed with the competent process server on 21 June 2006 and, as proven by the stamp of the latter, notified by the process server to the YY Football League, the YY Football Federation, the YY Players' Union, and to the player's proxy on 23 June 2006 (copy of the relevant document is in the file).
20. According to the club after the notification of the renewal, the payer did not object to the unilateral renewal before the competent committees in accordance with the applicable sport legislation. Therefore, the renewal had become final.
21. In view of the above, the player would have been obliged to rejoin the club on 3 July 2006 . However, the player failed to do so.
22. Therefore, the club asked the player in writing for his explanations for not having resumed duty with the club. Such correspondence was also sent to Mrs. Q. As the player did not provide his position, the board of directors of the club decided to suspend him for four months. After the four months had passed, the player again failed to resume duty. Therefore, he was again requested to provide his position, and such correspondence was again also notified to Mrs. Q. As the player again did not respond to the club's correspondence, he was suspended for another four months.
23. According to the club, in case of suspension of an employment contract, the contract term shall be extended for a period equal to the period of suspension. Therefore, the labour relationship between the player and the club must currently be extended for eight months.

24. Furthermore, the club invoked that the letters allegedly sent by the player to the club were sent to a fax number that does not belong to the club. Therefore, it may not be deemed that the club did not respond to the player's correspondence, since it was not aware of its existence.
25. With respect to the player's remarks regarding sporting just cause, the club emphasised that the period to invoke such sporting just cause, i.e. 15 days following the last official match of the season, had expired long before the player filed his present claim.
26. Finally, to strengthen its position, the club invoked the decision of the CAS in the matter *CAS 2005/A/973 Panathinaikos FC v/ Sotirios Kyrgiakos*.
27. On 7 December 2006, the player provided his position with regard to the answer of the club.
28. Thereby, the player mentioned that he did not understand the standard agreement when he signed it, as it is written in YY. Moreover. he does not know Mrs. Q. but the latter appears to be a colleague of the club's lawyer. Had he known that a proxy is appointed for him, he would have appointed someone who really would have taken care of his interests, and not just a third party that did not even bother to notify him of the documents the club apparently tried to send him.
29. Furthermore, the player emphasised that the existence of Mrs. Q was not mentioned in the private agreement. In this respect, the player invokes section 9 of the private agreement, according to which the latter has priority over all other contracts, especially over league or club contracts. Therefore the appointment of Mrs. Q as the player's proxy must be considered as void.
30. Moreover, the player underlined that he had left Greece after the team's last match of the season 05/06, on 14 May 2006 and therefore had not received any correspondence that had possibly been sent to his address in Greece after that date.
31. The player further explained that his agents were also not notified about the renewal of the labour relationship
32. Finally the player emphasised that the fax number to which he used to send correspondence to the club was the fax number of the person in charge of the club's transfers of players. The said person would be reporting directly to the president of the club.
33. With regard to the suspensions mentioned by the club, the player stated that such suspensions are void, as on the one hand, he never received the relevant correspondence from the club, and on the other hand, no contractual relation exists between the parties as of 1 July 2006.
34. On 3 January 2007, the club filed its final position, thereby entirely referring to its former submission and without making any further comment on the matter

II. CONSIDERATIONS OF THE DISPUTE RESOLUTION CHAMBER

1. First of all, the Chamber analysed whether it was competent to deal with the matter at stake. In this respect, it referred to art. 18 par. 2 and 3 of the Rules Governing the Procedures of the Players' Status Committee and the Dispute Resolution Chamber. The present matter was submitted to FIFA on 14 November 2006, as a consequence the Chamber concluded that the revised Rules Governing Procedures (edition 2005) on matters pending before the decision making bodies of FIFA are applicable to the matter at hand.
2. With regard to the competence of the Chamber, art. 3 par. 1 of the above-mentioned Rules states that the Dispute Resolution Chamber shall examine its jurisdiction in the light of articles 22 to 24 of the current version of the Regulations for the Status and Transfer of Players (edition 2005). In accordance with art. 24 par. 1 in combination with art. 22 (b) of the aforementioned Regulations the Dispute Resolution Chamber shall adjudicate on employment-related disputes between a club and a player that have an international dimension.
3. As a consequence, the Dispute Resolution Chamber is the competent body to decide on the present litigation involving a YY club and a Romanian player regarding a contractual dispute in connection with an employment contract.
4. Subsequently, the members of the Chamber analyzed which edition of the Regulations for the Status and Transfer of Players should be applicable as to the substance of the matter. In this respect the Chamber referred, on the one hand, to art. 6 par. 1 and 2 of the Regulations for the Status and Transfer of Players (edition 2005) and, on the other hand, to the fact that the relevant contract at the base of the present dispute was signed on 14 July 2003 and the claim was lodged at FIFA on 14 November 2006. In view of the aforementioned, the Chamber concluded that the current FIFA Regulations for the Status and Transfer of Players (edition 2005, hereinafter: the Regulations) are applicable to the case at hand as to the substance.

5. In continuation and entering into the substance of the matter, the members of the Chamber took note of the parties' statements and submissions as well as of the documents on file and in view of this, deemed that the following questions have to be considered:
   1) Is the unilateral option in favour of the club to renew the employment contract with the player valid?
   2) Was the option rightfully exercised by the club?
   3) What are the consequences of the fact that the player left the club at the end of the season 2005/06?
6. As far as the validity of the club's option to unilaterally renew the employment contract is concerned, the Chamber made, first of all, reference to the decision of the Court of Arbitration for Sport (CAS) in the matter *TAS 2005/A/983&984 Peñaro vs. Bueno Suarez, Rodriguez Barrotti and Paris Saint-Germain*, which was invoked by the player, and which is considered as a leading case within the subject of unilateral options for the extension of employment contracts signed between players and clubs.
7. In this respect, the Chamber first of all noted that according to the abovementioned decision of the CAS, the system of unilateral renewal of a contract is, as a principle, not compatible with the juridical frame which the new Regulations of FIFA aimed to establish (cf. pt. 127 of the decision in question).
8. Considering such clear conclusion of the CAS, the members present explained that the option for the unilateral renewal of the employment contract in the present case should be declared invalid by the Chamber since, as a matter of principle, the entire system of unilateral renewal is not in compliance with the juridical frame of the applicable Regulations of FIFA.
9. However, the Chamber also acknowledged that, in pt. 110 of the said decision of the CAS, five elements were established which were to be analysed in order to decide upon the validity of a club's option to unilaterally renew an employment contract, if at all. The elements are the following:
   1) The potential maximal duration of the labour relationship shall not be excessive.
   2) The option shall be exercised within an acceptable deadline before the expiry of the current contract.
   3) The salary reward deriving from the option right has to be defined in the original contract.
   4) One party shall not be at the mercy of the other party with regard to the contents of the employment contract.
   5) The option shall be clearly established and emphasised in the original contract to that the player is conscious of it at the moment of signing the contract.
10. In the present case, the maximal duration of the labour relationship is five years. According to art. 18 par. 2 of the Regulations, the maximum length of an employment contract between a player and a club shaal be five years. Therefore the Chamber deemed that the maximal duration of the labour relationship in the case at stake is not to be considered as excessive. In other words, the duration of the employment contract concerned does not affect the validity of the unilateral option in the present case.
11. With regard to the deadline for the exercise of the option, the Chamber noted that according to the standard agreement in question, the renewal has to be notified to the player (*inter alia*) five days before the opening of the registration period.
12. As the main registration period in Greece in 2006 started on 1 July 2006 and the employment relationship in question expired on 30 June 2006, the dates of the opening of the registration period and of the expiry of the contract coincide. The option in question had thus to be exercised five days before the originally agreed expiry of the employment contract in question.
13. The decision of the CAS in the matter *TAS 2005A/983&984* does not contain any specific considerations with regard to the question within which deadline the relevant option shall be exercised so that such deadline is acceptable. In fact as explained before, the CAS came to the conclusion that unilateral renewal options are not to be considered as a matter of principle. The Chamber, however referred to the decision of the CAS in the matter *CAS 2005/A/973 Panathinaikos FC v/ Sotirios Kyrgiakos*, which was invoked by the club, and in which an unilateral option for the renewal of a contract in favour of the club was considered as valid. In that case, the club concerned had to notify the player of the exercise of the option right two weeks before thoe end of the intermediate contractual renewal. Unfortunately, the decision in question does also not contain any considerations with regard to the criteria that is applicable in order to establish whether such a deadline is acceptable or not. Therefore,

the Chamber was of the opinion that it had to analyse whether a deadline of five days before the expiry of the contract is an acceptable deadline for the notification of a unilateral renewal, and also had to establish the relevant criteria for such analysis.

14. In this regard, the Chamber stated that a deadline of five days before the expiry of the employment contract appears to be extremely short. Considering the player's situation, it is to be concluded that the player is left in an uncertain employment situation until a very late moment. Until five days before the opening of the registration period, the player does not know whether he will continue to be employed by his current club or if he will have to find a new club. Therefore, he is not in a position to plan his future career. This is an important disadvantage for a player concerned compared to other players who precisely know about their contractual situation and therefore can undertake the necessary steps to find a new club already at an earlier stage, within the limits set by art. 18 par. 3 of the Regulations. In particular, after the end of the relevant season on 14 May 2006 and the deadline for the exercise of the option, the player was left with no choice but to wait in incertitude.
15. In view of the above, the Chamber deemed that a deadline of only five days before the expiry of the employment contract for the relevant option to be exercised cannot be considered as acceptable.
16. In continuation, the Chamber had to analyse whether the salary reward deriving form the option right was defined in the original contract and in this respect, confirmed that such salary reward was indeed defined in the original contract.
17. Concerning the condition that no party shall be at the mercy of the other party with regard to the contents of the employment contract, the Chamber stated that in particular, the increase of the salary after the exercise of the option is the most important indication to establish if a party is at the mercy of the other party with regard to the contractual contents.
18. In this respect the Chamber referred, once again, to the decision *CAS 2005/A/973* invoked by the club. From the respective decision of the CAS, the Chamber noted that according to the employment contract at the basis of the relevant affair, if the first option had been exercised the yearly remuneration, excluding bonuses, would have increased from EUR 58,694 to EUR 73,668 and if the second option would be exercised, to EUR 146,734. The increase of the remuneration was thus 25% with the exercise of the first option, and 100% with the second option.
19. In the present case the yearly salary of the player would increase from USD 220,000 to USD 240,000 with the exercise of the first option and from USD 240,000 to USD 260,000 with the exercise of the second option, thus for 9% respectively 8,33%. In consequence, the increase of remuneration is not comparable at all to the increase stipulated in the contract analysed in the case *CAS 2005/A/973.* Furthermore, and contrary to the contract considered by the CAS in the aforementioned decision, in the case at stake, the increase is not directly linked to the exercise of the option. In fact, in absolute figures the increase is the same every year, i.e. during the first three fixed years of the contract and for each of the possible additional ones. Percentages, the increase is even decreasing.
20. The Chamber therefore concluded that the bargaining power between the player and the club was unequal and that the player had no apparent gain from the unilateral extension of the contract. Thus it is to be considered that the player was at the mercy of the club with regard to the contents of the employment contract.
21. Finally, the Chamber had to analyse whether the option right was clearly established and emphasized in the original employment contract and if it is to be presumed that the player was conscious of the club's option right at the moment of signing the relevant contract. In this respect, the Chamber acknowledged that the relevant clause was indeed established in the employment contract. However, in both the private and the standard agreement the clause is mentioned in the middle of the contractual text, i.e. not at the end, and is not emphasized.
22. Therefore the Chamber was of the opinion that the relevant clause had rot been included in such a way in the relevant agreements as to ensure that the player was fully conscious of it.
23. As a first conclusion of the aforementioned analysis, the Chamber stated that on one side, in the present case, the potential maximal duration of the labour relationship is not excessive and the salary reward deriving from the option right was defined in the original contract. On the other side, the option was not to be exercised within an acceptable deadline before the expiry of the originally agreed duration of the contract, and, in view of the increase of remuneration provided by the contract it is to be concluded that the player was al the mercy of the club with regard to the contents of the employment contract. Furthermore, the option had not been included in the employment contract in such a way as to ensure that, presumably, the player was fully conscious of the option right at the

moment of signing the employment contract. Thus, only two out of the five analysed points were fulfilled.

24. In view of the above, and since the condition that a party shall not be at the mercy of the other party with regard to the contents of the employment contract is of predominant importance, the Chamber decided that the renewal option in the present case must be considered as not valid. Consequently, the player is not contractually bound to the club anymore, and the labour relationship between the player and the club terminated with effect as of 1 July 2006.
25. In continuation, the Chamber also pointed to the fact that in the case *CAS 2005/A/973*, the player had explicitly stated that he knew that he had entered into a five year contract, and moreover, had even accepted the first unilateral renewal, but only opposed to the club's exercise of the second option for renewal of the employment contract. Considering that these facts certainly contributed to the decision of the CAS that the clause for unilateral renewal was valid, the Chamber emphasised that such facts did not occur in the present case. Therefore, the decision of the CAS in the case *CAS 2005/A/973* can be considered even less as a prejudice for the present case.
26. Equally the Chamber emphasised that, as already mentioned, in the case *TAS 2005/A/983 & 984* the CAS had denied the system of unilateral renewal of a contract as a matter of principle. In the subsequent case (*CAS 2005/A/973*), the relevant panel had passed the award by considering that no jurisprudence declares such options as absolutely void under all circumstances (cf. pt 9 of the decision in question.) Therefore, it has to be concluded that the relevant decision was taken without considering CAS' previous jurisprudence, a fact that again leads to the conclusion that the decision in the case *CAS 2005/A/973* cannot be considered as precedence for the case at stake.
27. Finally, the Chamber stated that in view of its conclusions reached on the basis of the previous considerations, the other questions outlined above, i.e. whether the option was rightfully exercised by the club, and which are the consequences of the fact that the player left the club at the end of the season 2005/2006, have not to be examined since they are not of any relevance anymore.

III. DECISION OF THE DISPUTE RESOLUTION CHAMBER

1. The claim of the Romanian player X is accepted.
2. The labour relationship between the player X and the YY club Y FC terminated with effect as of 1 July 2006.
3. The requests of the YY club Y FC are rejected.
4. According to art. 61 par. 1 of the FIFA Statutes this decision may be appealed before the Court of Arbitration for Sport (CAS). The statement of appeal must be sent to the CAS directly within 21 days of receiving notification of this decision and has to contain all elements in accordance with point 2 of the directives issued by the CAS, copy of which we enclose hereto. Within another 10 days following the expiry of the time limit for the filing of the statement of appeal, the appellant shall file with the CAS a brief stating the facts and legal arguments giving rise to the appeal (cf. point 4 of the directives).

⚽⚽⚽

4 APRIL 2007

47936

DECISION OF THE DISPUTE RESOLUTION CHAMBER

passed in Zurich, Switzerland, on 4 April 2007,
in the following composition:
Slim Aloulou (Tunisia), Chairman
Mario Gallavotti (Italy), Member
Ivan Gazidis (USA), Member
Theo van Seggelen (Netherlands), Member
Carlos Soto (Chile), Member
on the claim presented by
the club, B, as Claimant
against
the player, A, and the club, C as Respondents
regarding compensation for contractual breach and inducement to contractual breach

I. FACTS OF THE CASE

1. The player A, born on 23April 1982, signed an employment contract with the club B on 31 March 2001 and due to expire on 30 June 2005 which, on 1 July 2003, was renewed until 30 June 2007.
2. The above-mentioned employment contract also provides, *inter alia*, that in the event of an intentional failure of the club to fulfil the terms of the contract, the player is entitled to give 14 days written notice to the club to terminate the agreement.
3. A transfer compensation of 75,000 had been paid by B to the club Arbroath for A's transfer.
4. On 9 August 2006 the player A signed a three-year employment contract with the club, C, whereby a basic weekly wage of 10,000 is foreseen in favour of the player for the season 2006/2007. A bonus of 3,000 or 1,500 would be paid to the player in case he was named in the starting eleven or as a substitute, respectively.
5. The weekly salary would rise up to 11,000 in case the player was named in the starting eleven in 12 league games. Should this be the case, a bonus of 4,000 or 2,000 would be paid to the player in case he was named in the starting eleven or as a substitute, respectively.
6. If the player was named in the starting eleven in 20 league games, a bonus of 5,000 or 2,000 would be paid to him in case he was named in the starting eleven or as a substitute, respectively.
7. The weekly salary would rise up to 12,000 as of 1 July 2007 in case the player was named in the starting eleven in 25 league games.
8. On 9 August 2006 the C Football Association requested the international transfer certificate (ITC) from the B Football Association for the player in question.
9. The Football Association replied in writing to this request stating that they cannot issue the requested ITC since the player A is still under contract with their affiliated club, B.
10. On 18 August 2006 the C Football Association turned to FIFA asking for the authorisation to provisionally register the player concerned for its member club, C.
11. On 28 August 2006, at the request of FIFA, the B Football Association stated that it was not in a position to comply with the ITC request, since the player A was still under contract with their affiliated club, B.
12. On 31 August 2006 the Single Judge of the Players' Status Committee authorised the C Football Association to provisionally register A with its affiliated club C with immediate effect.
13. Whereas the matter of the player's provisional registration has been decided upon, the dispute at stake lies on the substance of the contractual dispute between the player and the club and, in particular, on the conditions of the contractual termination.
14. In January 2007 A was transferred to the club Y on a loan basis until the end of the season.

B's position:

15. In November 2006 B contacted FIFA claiming compensation for breach of contract in the amount of 5,037,311 against Mr A as well as against C, for having induced the aforementioned breach.
16. The claimant also asks for the player to be ineligible to take part in any official matches for a period of two months, in compliance with Article 17.3 of the FIFA Regulations for the Status and Transfer of Players (hereafter, *the Regulations*), and for C to be banned from registering any new player for one registration period, in compliance with Article 17.4 of the FIFA Regulations.
17. According to the club, the relationship with A, until then one of the team's bedrocks, deteriorated when the player refused to extend the contract eighteen months before its expiry. It is clear, in the club's view, that Mr A was already then seeking a more lucrative contract and, to this effect, planning to walk out of his contract.
18. Subsequently, Mr A first notified B that lie would terminate his contract for just cause with a 14-day notice from 4 May 2006 under clause 18 of the employment contract. Such termination notice would then be withdrawn by the player on 7 July 2006.
19. Then, the player notified the club in writing on 26 May 2006 of his intention to terminate the employment contract in accordance with the provision contained in Article 17.3 of the Regulations, i.e. allegedly outside of the Protected Period and within 15 days following the last match of the Season.
20. After having rejected B's proposals for an extension of the contract, Mr A addressed, through his agent, Mr ..., a fax to approximately fifty clubs, stating that the player had terminated his contract with the club, that no sanctions would apply as a result of this termination and that compensation would be fixed by FIFA at 200,000.

21. It is clear that Mr A breached the contract without just cause utterly disregarding the principles set out in the Regulations for the maintenance of the contractual stability, but whereas the first notice of termination will not be taken into account, the second notice of termination raises the most relevant issues.
22. To this effect, the club asserts that, according to point 9) of the Definitions of the Regulations, the Season ends with the last Official Match of the relevant national league championship. As the last match of the national league championship, i.e. the Premier League, for the Season 2005/2006 was on 7 May 2006, the notice of termination dated 26 May 2006 was not issued within 15 days following the last match of the Season under the purpose of Article 17.3 of the Regulations.
23. In all cases, as the player breached the employment contract without just cause, he shall pay compensation. The latter should be calculated in accordance with the criteria established by Article 17 of the Regulations, yet bearing in mind that the relevant list is not exhaustive, as already pointed out by the Dispute Resolution Chamber itself in its previous decisions.
24. In particular, national law, *in casu* National Law, should also assist in the calculation of the amount due as compensation by the player and/or the new club. This is confirmed by the parties' intention, expressed in clause 26 of the employment contract, to have the rules of the Football Association and of the Premier League govern any issue pertaining to the suspension and termination of the contract. The rules of the Football Association and of the Premier League are governed by the law of, where the contract was performed and where both parties were domiciled.
25. According to National Law, remedies for the breach of contract are based on the *restitutio in integrum,* which attempts to return the injured party to the same position it would have been in had the breach not occurred. Hence, B request to be awarded an amount, which would return the club in the position it would have been in had A not committed breach of contract without just cause.
26. According to National Law, it should also be taken into account the *lucrum cessans* suffered by the club, insomuch as Mr A and C should be condemned to pay 1% default interest until such time as B receive the full payment of the amount due as compensation.
27. As regards the loss of opportunity to receive a transfer compensation (*lucrum cessans*) for the transfer of the player, the claimant requests that the Chamber apply the same principle that it applied in one of their precedents (Auxerre Football Club, France v Player Philippe Mexes, France and AS Roma, Italy), the damage suffered by the club being analogous to the one for which the French dub was appropriately restored.
28. Mr A was in fact one of the best players for the club, and a leading player for the national team. B would have received at least 3 million for the player's transfer, had he not unilaterally terminated the contract. The second division club X made an offer of 1.5 million on 21 June 2006, which was rejected since it was deemed considerably below the player's real value. A number of top division clubs would have been ready to pay significantly more for the player's transfer and some of them, Blackburn Rovers among the others, expressed their genuine interest in the player.
29. This would be corroborated by the fact that in the top division the amount paid for the transfer of a player of a similar pedigree to A would have been between 3 million and 5 million. The claimant further resorts to an expertise according to which, in comparison with a number of players sharing the same age and ability with A, the latter's market value at the last transfer window would be of 5 million.
30. The club invested a lot of money and resources in the player's training and education. Between salary, appearance bonuses, other bonuses and sign-on fee, B as from 1 July 2003 invested on A the amount total of 709,137, also taking into account the amount that the player would have earned for the last season of contract.
31. By means of a further submission received by FIFA after the investigation was officially closed, B amended the above-mentioned figure, through the witness statement of the club's secretary, whereby the total amount paid to the player in the five years spent with the club as from 31 March 2001 is of 1,004,346.
32. On account of the fact that the compensation should also take into consideration the remuneration and other benefits due to the player under the new contract, the claimant reckons that the difference between the bast season of contract with them and the first season of contract with C amounts to 717,335.
33. The costs of a replacement player to be paid by the claimant should also be taken into account by the Chamber, in accordance with its previous jurisprudence. Yet again, the price for a player of A's calibre would be between 3 million and 5 million.

34. Mr A's unilateral termination of contract deprived the claimant of a very valuable player and, as a consequence, the club suffered a competitive and commercial loss, the player being very popular among the supporters. The shirt sales and other commercial revenues, which could have been generated are quantified by the claimant in 70,000.
35. B further maintain that they should be entitled to receive a reimbursement of 50,000 incurred in as legal expenses.
36. The claimant, B, request the Dispute Resolution Chamber to condemn Mr A and C to pay the total amount of 5,037,311 corresponding to 4 million as loss of opportunity to receive a transfer compensation (*lucrum cessans*) for the transfer of the player, 199,976 as the remaining value of the player's employment contract with the claimant, 717,335 as the difference between the last season of contract with the claimant and the first season of contract with C, 50,000 as legal expenses, 70,000 as commercial loss following the player's unilateral termination.
37. Finally, B request that Mr A be declared ineligible to take part in any official matches for a period of two months, in compliance with Article 17.3 of the Regulations, for having breached the contract without just cause and failed to give notice in due time. The fact that the player attempted to breach the contract twice should be taken into account by the Chamber as an aggravating circumstance.
38. B also request that C be banned from registering any new player for one registration period, in compliance with Article 17.4 of the Regulations, for having induced the contractual breach and failed to contact the claimant with regard to the player's contractual position before signing him.

Mr A's position:

39. Mr A firstly states that he was an ever present in the B's first team in seasons 2003/04, 2004/05 and until 7 February 2006 of the 2005/06 season. He was widely acknowledged as one of B's best and most consistent players. Despite having approximately one and a half years left to run on the contract, he was being pressured by B into entering into a new playing contract to extend his term at the club, on terms that were not acceptable to him. Following his refusal to enter into a new playing contract on such terms, on 7 February 2006, he was dropped from the side for which he had featured in every minute of every match from the start of the 2005/06 season. This began a course of non-selection by B of Mr A.
40. Mr A considers that he was dropped from the B's team due to his refusal to sign a new contract and that the decision taken to consistently drop him was based on non-sporting reasons, and taken by the majority shareholder, Vladimir Romanov, rather than by the manager of B.
41. Mr A sought legal advice from the Professional Footballers Association ("SPFA"), which advised him that the course of unfair treatment, culminating in the very public and unwarranted criticism of him and his family constituted a complete breakdown of mutual trust and confidence and thus gave him a legal right to terminate the contract for just cause.
42. It was also considered that Mr A could terminate the contract under the Regulations on the grounds of sporting just cause due to his sudden non-selection from the team after having been an ever present for purely non-sporting reasons. This non-selection also resulted in him losing his place in the national team. The SPFA considered that such a situation should fail within the definition of sporting just cause under Article 15 of the Regulations, particularly as Mr A had been told that he would not play again for the remainder of the contract (i.e. that this non-selection would continue throughout the 2006/07 season).
43. Mr A therefore served notice on B to terminate his contract for just cause with a 14-day notice from 4 May 2006 under clause 18 of the employment contract. The SPFA advised Mr A that this process may take some time as the procedure and possible appeals process that may follow, could be lengthy This could damage his prospects of securing a contract with another club before the end of the next registration period in August. The SPFA therefore also advised Mr A of his rights to terminate the contract under Article 17.3 of the Regulations which would present a more expedient route.
44. Mr A resolved to proceed with a termination under Article 173 of the Regulations and served a notice on B to this effect on 26 May 2006. This decision was based on procedural reasons to ensure a swift resolution to his contractual relationship with the club and was not an acceptance that he did not have grounds to terminate for just cause.
45. Mr A therefore reiterates his right to terminate the contract for just cause and sporting just cause as well as under Article 17.3 of the Regulations and requests that the Dispute Resolution Chamber make a pronouncement on these grounds before considering the termination under Article 17.3 and the issues of compensation and sanctions.

46. Mr A contends that he should not be liable for any sanctions or compensation in this case as he had just cause and sporting just cause to terminate the contract. If this is not accepted, then Mr A makes the following points with regard to any sanctions and compensation that the Dispute Resolution Chamber decides to award.
47. Mr A, unlike B, has acted properly throughout this process and in principle, It is the club that should be liable to pay damages to Mr A. Mr A was badly treated due to the simple fact that he would not extend his contract with B. He was dropped from the team for non playing reasons and then suffered the ultimate punishment when lie was left out of the team for the Cup Final.
48. However, to reduce the damages that B would have otherwise been liable to pay, Mr A did his utmost to find a new club in due time. As he was successful in obtaining a new job at C, there is no direct financial damage for the player and there was no need for him to claim damages from B.
49. The misconduct of B leading to this conflict could instead justify a referral to the FIFA Disciplinary Committee.
50. The contract was terminated in accordance with Article 17.3 of the Regulations outside of the Protected Period by the unilateral action of the player. Mr A signed the contract at the age of 21 and served 3 full seasons under it and was thus entitled to utilise "the Article 17.3 procedure". The fact that Mr A has been allowed to play for his new club underlines this, and no sporting sanctions can be applied to Mr A in this case.
51. Mr A wants to emphasise that it was his own decision to terminate the contract. There was no club involved that induced this termination, nor did his agent. Mr A refers the Dispute Resolution Chamber to the witness statement of the agent which confirms that Mr A's new club, C, only became involved in this case on 10 July 2006 following receipt of a fax from Mr A's agent. C therefore had no involvement in the contract termination. As such, there is no justifiable reason to hold his new club, C, responsible for the consequences of his termination.
52. Mr A also wishes to state that he terminated the contract within 15 days of the last game of the season that his club played, i.e. the Cup Final on 13 May 2006 which is the premier cup competition in and is organised and controlled by the Football Association. The winner of this trophy gains automatic entry into the UEFA Cup for the following season.
53. Mr A notes that the Cup Final is an "Official Match" under the Regulations and he therefore understood that the 15 day notice period would run from this game. In this respect, it is noted that under Article 15 of the Regulations when terminating for sporting just cause, the notice is to be sent within 15 days of the last "Official Match".
54. It is therefore contended that Mr A's actions of sending the letter under Article 17.3 of the Regulations, which was aimed at avoiding disruption to B before the Cup Final, are justifiable and in line with the principle behind the notice period of Article 17.3 of the Regulations.
55. Even if the Dispute Resolution Chamber does not accept that the end of the season was the Cup Final on 13 May 2006, then Mr A would state that his notice to terminate on 26 May 2006 was only 4 days outside the 15-day period after the last league fixture (7 May 2006) and therefore caused no prejudice to B.
56. In the circumstances, and for the reasons set out, Mr A respectfully requests that he should not face any disciplinary measures under Article 17.3 of the Regulations. It is also dear that there can be no 'sporting sanctions' in this case as the termination came outside the Protected Period.
57. In this regard, Mr A would request the Dispute Resolution Chamber to note that lie has already been out of football for some time due to his non-selection at B and subsequent lack of match fitness whereby lie did not play during the period from April to October 2006 at either club or international level.
58. In the event that Mr A is held liable for damages to B he would like to point out that these damages must be limited to the residual value of the contract.
59. As the termination of contract occurred outside of the Protected Period there is no factor available to increase the amount of this residual value although B uses a lot of paperwork to state otherwise. In the view of the player It is not possible that the breach of a contract between two parties with a certain value (the salary of the player) would lead to a compensation that exceeds this amount many times. In previous Dispute Resolution Chamber cases the residual value of the contract has been the guideline for the settlement of the compensation. In this case there is no justified reason to deviate from that guideline.

60. The residual value of the contract is in fact the only applicable factor for calculating the compensation as it is obvious that the said value represents the value of the contract between the two parties. The fact that the termination of the contract took place outside of the stability period is a mitigating factor.
61. In the Regulations and Dispute Resolution Chamber's jurisprudence there is no foundation for the position of B that the compensation shall be calculated on the basis of an alleged "market value" of a player. In any case B failed to substantiate this.
62. Of course it is possible that parties come to a mutual agreement that exceeds the residual value of the contract, but this is not the position here.
63. Moreover, from the submission of B can be learnt that an offer of 1.5 million (10 times the residual value of the contract) was turned down. It should be noted that this bid came after A had terminated the contract. So even if B were minded to accept the bid it was not in a position to do so as A had already terminated the contract.
64. Furthermore, B seem to forget that at the end of the contract on 1 July 2007 – if it were not terminated – A could have left the club without any compensation at all.
65. To this effect, Mr A has also noted the details response of C to B's claim for compensation and confirms that he fully concurs with these submissions and requests that the Dispute Resolution Chamber also take them into account when assessing any compensation that may be payable by him in this case.
66. Finally, and as far as B's latest submission is concerned, whereby they propose a calculation of the amount paid to the player during the course of his contract, Mr A maintains that the club has had two previous opportunities to submit any evidence regarding this case. Therefore, according to the procedures set out by FIFA to govern the manner in which these proceedings are conducted, any evidence produced by the club within its latest submission is out of time and cannot be relied upon. In any case the evidence produced does not offer any new insight into the case and is not relevant to the facts of the case.
67. However, if the Dispute Resolution Chamber does choose to allow this new evidence, Mr A would like to state that the club has chosen to outline salary figures it maintains were paid to him for a period of five seasons from 2001 until 2006. These figures cannot contribute to the calculation of any compensation that may be payable to B, as it can only be the residual value of the contract that can be taken into consideration by the Chamber.
68. Furthermore, within the club's own schedule of payments the amounts for the seasons 2001/02 and 2002/03 relate to a previous contract concluded between the parties and are therefore completely irrelevant, whereas for the seasons 2003/04, 2004/05 and 2005/06 the club has of course had a return for these payments by way of having Mr A play for them during this period. Again these figures are irrelevant to the case.
69. It is interesting however to note that B, in submitting this as evidence, are clearly acknowledging that the player's contract is indeed the only relevant factor with regard to the calculation of any compensation. This is a change from the club's previous submissions where its position was based around purely subjective views of the player's transfer market value.
70. A would like to stress once more that it can only be the residual value of the final year of his contract that can be taken as relevant, and the club appears indeed to agree with this view by means of its latest submission. The new evidence does not in any case contribute to the facts of the matter.
71. For the reasons set out above, Mr A hereby request the dismissal of the claims of B against him. Mr A submits he had just cause and sporting just cause to terminate the contract. Furthermore, the player acted entirely properly in terminating the contract under Article 17.3 of the Regulations and no sporting sanctions or disciplinary measures can be imposed against him. Finally, any compensation deemed payable to B, must be limited to the residual value of the contract.

C's position:

72. C's recollection of the facts reflect that of the player.
73. C maintain in their position that the employment contract between the player, Mr A, and B was unilaterally terminated by the earlier outside the Protected Period. The employment contract at stake was in fact concluded on 1 July 2003 and is due to expire on 30 June 2007. Therefore, the Protected Period has come to an end with the end of the third season, i.e. on 7 May 2006.
74. To this effect, C are eager to point out that the player gave the club even two notices of termination, one on 4 May 2006 on the grounds of just cause, and the second on 26 May 2006, in compliance

with the provision contained in Article 17 of the Regulations, i.e. outside of the Protected Period and within 15 days following the last match of the Season. This second notice was not, however, a withdrawal of the underlying allegations that support the player's right to terminate the contract for just cause.

75. According to the club, the first contact between Mr A and C occurred on 10 July 2006, i.e. six weeks after the termination of contract performed by the player. As a matter of law, there is no causative link between C and the termination of the contract, as a consequence of which, the club cannot be deemed liable for any damage arising from such a breach.
76. As regards B's request to be awarded an amount, which would return the club in the position it would have been in had A not committed breach of contract without just cause, It is not so obvious that the club is the damaged party in this case, especially taking into account that their behaviour led the player to terminate the contract.
77. Furthermore, the club appears to request a *"transfer fee"* which not only is not provided for in the Regulations, but what is more is not included in the criteria listed in Article 17 of the Regulations to assess the amount of compensation due for breach of contract.
78. The club also points out that the offer made by X occurred after the player had terminated the contract and, therefore, cannot be taken into consideration as loss of opportunity, apart from the fact that the evaluation X give of the player is subjective and cannot be regarded as a proof of the player's actual value. In fact, all the club's allegation with respect to the player's value are entirely arbitrary and hypothetical.
79. As regards B's calculation of the compensation due, when it comes to the remaining value of the contract, only the salary and sign-on fee and no other bonuses should be taken into account. Therefore, the residual value of Mr A's contract with B should not exceed 149,976.
80. Also the projection for the player's future salary made by the claimant is totally ungrounded, since no sign-on fee is provided for under the new contract and, taking into account that the player earns 10,000 per week, a likely figure as yearly salary is 450,000 plus approximately 33,000 as appearance bonus.
81. For the record, the player only featured in a small number of matches for C and is now on ban to the club Y.
82. As far as B's request for A to be imposed disciplinary sanctions is concerned, C's position reflects that of the player.
83. Finally, and as far as B's latest submission concerning the player's salaries is concerned, C's position again reflects that of the player, especially under the procedural point of view, i.e. the latest evidence was produced out of time and should not be taken into consideration.
84. However, It the Dispute Resolution Chamber does choose to allow this new evidence, it has to be noted that the amounts for the seasons 2001/02 and 2002/03 are completely irrelevant, since they relate to a previous different contract, which was superseded by the one signed on 1 July 2003.
85. In any case, Article 17.1 of the Regulations refers to "benefits due to the player under the existing contract", i.e. the sums that have not yet been paid to him. Therefore, what has been paid by the club is totally irrelevant. Plus, that club has largely benefited from the services of the player, who played 239 games with them.
86. It is also worth emphasising that the figures of the latest submission are greater than those presented by means of the claimant's submission.
87. To conclude with, C request the Dispute Resolution Chamber that all requests filed by B be rejected.
88. The Dispute Resolution Chamber is asked to rule upon the breach of contract, as well as on the possible consequences.

Players' Agent:

89. The Dispute Resolution Chamber is also asked to pronounce itself on the relevance of the role played by Mr A's agent in the affair at stake.

II. CONSIDERATIONS OF THE DISPUTE RESOLUTION CHAMBER

1. First of all, the Dispute Resolution Chamber analysed whether It was competent to deal with the matter at stake. In this respect, it referred to art. 18 par. 2 and 3 of the Rules Governing the Procedures of the Players' Status Committee and the Dispute Resolution Chamber. The present matter was submitted to FIFA in November 2006, as a consequence the Chamber concluded that the revised

Rules Governing Procedures (edition 2005) on matters pending before the decision making bodies of FIFA apply to the matter at hand.

2. With regard to the competence of the Chamber, art. 3 par. 1 of the abovementioned Rules states that the Dispute Resolution Chamber shall examine its jurisdiction in the light of articles 22 to 24 of the current version of the Regulations (edition 2005). In accordance with art. 24 par. 1 in connection with art. 22 (a) of the aforementioned Regulations, the Dispute Resolution Chamber shall adjudicate on employment-related disputes between a club and a player in relation to the maintenance of contractual stability if there has been an ITC request and if there is a claim trom an interested party in relation to such ITC request, in particular regarding its issuance, regarding sporting sanctions or regarding compensation for breach of contract.
3. As a consequence, the Dispute Resolution Chamber is the competent body to decide on the present litigation regarding a dispute in relation to the maintenance of contractual stability arisen following the issuance of an ITC regarding compensation for breach of contract.
4. Subsequently, the members of the Chamber analysed which edition of the Regulations should be applicable as to the substance of the matter. In this respect, the Chamber referred, on the one hand, to art. 26 par. 1 and 2 of the Regulations (edition 2005) and, on the other hand, to the fact that the relevant contract at the basis of this dispute was signed on 1 July 2003 and that this claim was lodged at FIFA by B in November 2006. In view of the aforementioned circumstances, the Chamber concluded that the current FIFA Regulations for the Status and Transfer of Players apply to the case at hand as to the substance.
5. Before entering the substance of the matter, the Chairman of the Dispute Resolution Chamber addressed the issue raised by B, that challenged one of the members, Mr Theo van Seggelen, and asked the Chamber to reconsider the constitution of the panel.
6. In this context, B drew FIFA's attention to the article that appeared on the website of FIFPro, the General Secretary of which is Mr Theo van Seggelen himself, under the title: *"A case, step forwards in the freedom of players"*. This report contained some statements suggestive of the decision that the Dispute Resolution Chamber would have reached in the case at hand.
7. The club therefore questioned the presence of a FIFPro member (what is more, its General Secretary) in the case at stake and, in particular, challenged Mr Theo van Seggelen and sought its replacement on the grounds of lack of impartiality.
8. In this respect, Mr Theo van Seggelen pointed out that the above-said article represents an independent opinion expressed by an individual operating outside FIFPro and that, either in this one or in any other case in which he has been involved in his quality of member of the Dispute Resolution Chamber, he has never made any comment either before or after a decision, abways abiding by the duty of confidentiality.
9. The Chairman was then eager to emphasise that the Chamber is an impartial deciding authority composed by an equal number of members chosen amongst representatives of clubs and representatives of players, of which FIFPro is the leading organisation at international level. It was also underlined that the aforementioned composition has always allowed a fair resolution of the football-related disputes.
10. None of the members, the Chairman assured, has ever represented the interests of either the players or the clubs, but always taken care of the exclusive interest of the Dispute Resolution Chamber itself.
11. Consequently, and in view of the concerned person's above explanations, the Chairman along with all the remaining members concluded that the request for the dismissal of Mr Theo van Seggelen shall be rejected.
12. In continuation, and entering into the substance of the matter, the Chamber acknowledged the documentation contained in the file and focussed its attention on the fact that the player A and the club B signed an employment contract on 31 March 2001 due to expire on 30 June 2005 which, on 1 July 2003, was renewed until 30 June 2007.
13. The Chamber also noted that, on 9 August 2006, A signed a three-year employment contract with the club, C and that, whereas the subsequent matter of the player's provisional registration had been decided upon by the FIFA competent authority, the dispute at stake lay on the substance of the contractual dispute between the player and the club and, in particular, on the conditions of the contractual termination.

14. To this effect, the Chamber took note of the fact that, on 26 May 2006, Mr A served notice of termination on B and, in this regard, the members had to ascertain whether or not the said notice of termination, and the subsequent unilateral termination of the contract, occurred in compliance with the provisions established under Article 17.3 of the Regulations, i.e. outside of the Protected Period and within 15 days following the last match of the Season.
15. It was observed that, on account of the fact that the employment contract between the player and the club was concluded on 1 July 2003 and due to expire on 30 June 2007, the unilateral termination undeniably occurred after three seasons, i.e. outside of the Protected Period, as indicated under point 7) of the Definitions section of the Regulations.
16. This being established, the Chamber stated that it had to assess the unavoidable consequences of this unilateral termination, in accordance with the provisions provided for by Articles 13 ff. of the Regulations.
17. The deciding authority incidentally noticed that Mr A had firstly served notice on B to terminate his contract for just cause with a 14-day notice from 4 May 2006 under clause 18 of the employment contract whereby, in the event of an intentional failure of the club to fulfil the terms of the contract, the player would be entitled to give a 14-day written notice to the club to terminate the agreement.
18. However, it was also noted that Mr A had been advised that this process may have taken some time as the procedure and possible appeals process that may have followed, could have been lengthy and that this could have damaged his prospects of securing a contract with another club before the end of the next registration period in August. Mr A then resolved to proceed with a termination under Article 17.3 of the Regulations and served a further notice on B to this effect on 26 May 2006. This decision was based on procedural reasons to ensure a swift resolution to his contractual relationship with the club and, according to the player, was not an acceptance that he did not have grounds to terminate for just cause.
19. In this context, and whilst not discounting the difficulties that the player and the club may have been faced with in the final part of their contractual relationship, the Chamber was left with no other choice than to regard the termination that the player actually performed on 26 May 2006, on the basis of Article 17.3 of the Regulations as the only valid one, for the purpose of this procedure.
20. In continuation, and for the sake of good order, the Chamber deemed it essential to state that also the termination of the contract for sporting just cause, which the player appears to invoke, at least on a subsidiary basis, could not be further considered. In fact, a player intending to make use of this possibility, would have to proceed by serving notice on the club that he is registered with and call upon the relevant sporting just cause in the fifteen days following the last Official Match of the Season (cf. Article 15 of the Regulations). Undisputedly, the player had never served such a notice. Yet, on 7 July 2006 the player withdrew his first termination notice.
21. However, as far as the timeliness of the notice of termination of 26 May 2006 is concerned, It has to be noted that according to point 9) of the Definitions section of the Regulations, the Season ends with the last Official Match of the relevant national league championship. As the last match of the national league championship, i.e. the Premier League, for the Season 2005/2006 occurred on 7 May 2006, the notice of termination dated 26 May 2006 does not appear to have been issued within 15 days following the last match of the Season for the purpose of Article 17.3 of the Regulations.
22. In this respect, the members of the Chamber understood that Mr A terminated the contract within 15 days of the last game of the season that his club actually played, i.e. the Cup Final on 13 May 2006, and that such a match is to be regarded as an Official Match" under the FIFA Statutes and Regulations (cf., in particular, point 5) of the Definitions section of the Regulations) and he therefore understood that the 15-day notice period would run from this game.
23. However, point 9) of the Definitions section of the Regulations is unambiguous in stating that the Season ends with the last Official Match of the relevant *national league championship* and, therefore, any notice of termination served after fifteen days of the last Official Match of the Season may result in the application of disciplinary measures, in accordance with Article 17.3 of the Regulations.
24. The deciding authority emphasised the relevance of the strict implementation of this rule, and of the consequent adoption of disciplinary measures, so as to enhance the legal certainty in the contractual relationships between players and clubs.
25. Nonetheless, the Chamber took also into consideration that, in any case, the notice was notified nineteen days after the last Official Match of the Season, i.e. four days only beyond the fifteen days required by Article 17.3 of the Regulations.

26. In light of the above, the Dispute Resolution Chamber decided that Mr A failed to give B due notice of termination on time as provided for under Article 17.3 of the Regulations, and, as a consequence, the player will not be eligible to participate in any official football match for a period of two weeks as from the beginning of the next national league championship of the club for which he will be registered.
27. After the consequences of the failure to give B due notice of termination on time were thus established, the Chamber went on to consider the consequences of terminating the employment contract without just cause.
28. In this respect, the deciding body first and foremost laid emphasis on the primacy of the principle of the maintenance of contractual stability, which represents the backbone of the agreement between FIFA/UEFA and the European Commission signed in March 2001. This agreement and its pillars represent the core of the former (edition 2001) as well as of the current version of the Regulations.
29. In particular, the Chamber was eager to point out that the measures provided for by the above Regulations concerning compensation for breach of contract without just cause serve as a deterrent and that a back of a firm response by the competent deciding authorities would represent an inappropriate example towards all the football actors, especially in view of the particular attention that this case arouses in the world of football.
30. Above all, it was underscored that the criteria contained in Article 17 of the Regulations are applied on the principle of reciprocity for clubs and players, signifying that both clubs and professionals who are seen to have committed a breach of contract without just cause will in all cases be subject to pay compensation and, under specific circumstances, also subject to the imposition of sporting sanctions.
31. In this respect, awarding compensation in favour of the damaged party (either the player or the club, as the case may be) has proven to be an efficient means and has always found a widespread acceptance since it guarantees that the fundamental principle of the respect of the contracts is duly taken care of.
32. As it was observed, Article 17 of the Regulations, far from stipulating the right of a contractual party to terminate the employment contract, affirms that in all cases the party in breach of contract shall pay compensation.
33. This notwithstanding, the members of the Chamber were also unanimously keen to emphasise that the breach of contract without just cause committed by Mr A outside of the Protected Period cannot result in the imposition of sporting sanctions, in compliance with the applicable Regulations (cf. Article 17 of the Regulations).
34. Consistently with the above, and in conformity with the relevant Regulations, the player's new club, the C, shall not suffer sporting sanctions for inducing the contractual breach and its responsibility shall be limited to being jointly and severally liable for the payment of any amount of compensation for breach of contract that Mr A will be ordered to pay (cf. Article 17.3 and 17.2 of the Regulations). In this respect, the Chamber was eager to point out that the joint liability of the player's new club is independent from the question of a possible inducement to contractual breach.
35. Moreover, and with respect to a possible responsibility of the club for having entered into negotiations with A during the course of his contract and for having failed to inform B in writing in accordance with Article 18.3 of the Regulations, the Dispute Resolution Chamber underlined that there is no evidence in support of the fact that the club contacted the player any time before the unilateral termination of the contract with the club.
36. On the contrary, the time elapsed between the notice of termination, dated 26 May 2006, and the conclusion of the contract between C and A on 9 August 2006 led the Chamber to conclude that there is no causative link between C and the termination of the contract by the player and, therefore, to rule out any wrongdoing by the club.
37. In continuation, according to the members of the Chamber a careful reading of the applicable provision, i.e. Article 17.1 of the Regulations, provides the key to assess the amount of compensation due by the player to the club.
38. The Chamber stated that the criteria listed therein are, however, not exhaustive and that each request for compensation for breach of contract has to be assessed on a case-by-case basis, leaving to the deciding body the faculty to decide *ex aequo et bono,* where appropriate.
39. The members thus stated that it falls under their responsibility to estimate the prejudice suffered by B in the case at hand, not only in accordance with the above-stated criteria, but also with their specific

knowledge of the world of football, as well as with the experience the Chamber itself has gained throughout the years.

40. In the calculation of the amount of compensation due by A, at first the Chamber turned its attention on the remuneration and other benefits due to the player under the existing contract and under the new contract.
41. According to the documentation provided by B to FIFA, it appears that the remaining value of the player's employment contract with the club can be calculated in the amount of 199,976.
42. As regards the financial conditions of the employment contract concluded between A and C, the Chamber acknowledged the fact that the player would receive a basic weekly wage of 10,000 for the season 2006/2007, plus a number of appearance bonuses.
43. In addition to that, transfer compensation of 75,000 had also been paid by B to the club Arbroath for A's transfer. According to Article 17.1 of the Regulations, this amount shall be amortised over the term of the relevant employment contract.
44. The deciding body concluded its analysis of the objective criteria listed in Article 17.1 of the Regulations, by recalling that the contractual breach occurred outside the Protected Period and pointing out that, at the time when the contract was breached, A was still bound to B by one further year of contract only.
45. As a matter of fact, the five seasons A spent with B shall also play a chief role in determining the amount of compensation due for contractual breach.
46. Likewise, the deciding authority observed that another crucial factor to be taken into account is the way B have greatly contributed to the steady improvement of a player, A, who joined the club at the age of nineteen and, throughout the course of his spell with the side, has become a high-profile footballer, deserving a constant presence in the national team and arousing the interest of top-flight clubs both in the and in the Premiership, as the events revealed. According to the Chamber, such a stance demonstrates the real interest the club had always had in the services of the player.
47. Once again, emphasis was placed on the tact that Article 17.1, while listing certain factors to be included in the Chamber's consideration in the calculation of the amount of compensation payable, does not purport to limit the factors that may be considered by the Chamber in any individual case. These factors may include, in addition to local law and the specificity of sport, "any other objective criteria", including those specifically listed in Article 17.1.
48. The aforementioned considerations led the deciding authority to the conclusion that limiting the compensation for breach of contract to the residual value of the contract not only is not in line with the jurisprudence of the Dispute Resolution Chamber, but would also undermine the principle of maintenance of contractual stability, reducing to a mere formula the legitimate right of the damaged party to receive compensation.
49. In this respect, it was declared that as a general rule, a player cannot, at any time and under any circumstances, "buy out" an employment contract by simply paying to his club the remaining value of his contract.
50. In light of all the above-exposed circumstances, and after a careful analysis of the documentation at its disposal, the specificities of the case at hand, as well as of all the parties' respective positions, the Chamber decided that A must pay the amount of 625,000 to B as compensation for breach of contract.
51. To conclude with, the members of the Dispute Resolution Chamber were of the unanimous opinion that, under the light of the facts of this dispute, the role played by the players' agent in the breach of contract requires further investigation by the competent authorities.
52. Therefore, in compliance with Article 21.1 in connection with Article 14 c) of the Players' Agents Regulations and 17.5 of the Regulations, the matter will be forwarded to the Players' Status Committee for investigation and decision.

III. DECISION OF THE DISPUTE RESOLUTION CHAMBER

1. The claim of the club, B, is partially accepted.
2. The player, A, has unilaterally breached the employment contract with S without just cause outside the Protected Period.
3. Mr A has to pay the amount of 625,000 to B within 30 days of notification of this decision.
4. If this amount is not paid within the aforementioned deadline, a 5% interest rate *per annum* as from the expiry of the aforementioned deadline will apply, and the present matter will be submitted to the FIFA's Disciplinary Committee, so that the necessary disciplinary sanctions may be imposed.

5. The club C is jointly and severally liable for the aforementioned payment.
6. Any other request filed by B is rejected.
7. B is directed to inform Mr A and C immediately of the account number to which the remittance is to be made, and to notify the Dispute Resolution Chamber of any payment received.
8. Mr A failed to give B due notice of termination.
9. Mr A is not eligible to participate in any official football match for a period of two weeks as from the beginning of the next national league championship for which he will be registered.
10. The matter concerning the role played by the players' agent in the breach of contract, will be forwarded to the Players' Status Committee for investigation and decision.
11. According to art. 61 par. 1 of the FIFA Statutes, this decision may be appealed against before the Court of Arbitration for Sport (CAS). The statement of appeal must be sent to the CAS directly within 21 days of receipt of notification of this decision and shall contain all the elements in accordance with point 2 of the directives issued by the CAS, a copy of which we enclose hereto. Within another 10 days following the expiry of the time limit for filing the statement of appeal, the appellant shall file a brief stating the facts and legal arguments giving rise to the appeal with the CAS (cf. point 4 of the directives).

AUTHOR'S NOTE

On 30 January 2008, the Court of Arbitration for Sport (CAS) rendered its judgment in what is commonly referred to as the "Webster case." This case revolves around the question of the amount of the compensation that the player Webster must pay to his former club, Heart of Midlothian F.C. (hereinafter "Hearts") for breaching his contract with that Scottish club prematurely and unilaterally after the expiry of the Protected Period.

In an extensively argued decision, CAS reached the conclusion that Webster must pay the residual value of the contract (between Webster and Hearts) as compensation. The judgment stated that in the course of the session, the parties reached agreement on the amount of that residual value: £ 150,000.

Principally, CAS considered that Article 17 of the FIFA Regulations for the Status and Transfer of Players (hereinafter the "FIFA Regulations"), under which Webster breached his contract, is not an exception to the main rule that contracts may not be unilaterally terminated, and therefore cannot be seen as a provision allowing a club or a player to unilaterally terminate a contract, without grounds, whether during or after the Protected Period. Termination of a contract under Article 17 can be seen as wrongful breach of contract, and as such Webster must pay compensation to Hearts.

On the issue of the determination of the amount of the compensation for breach of contract, CAS considers that priority must be given to the provisions in that area in the contract in question. If the contract has no provisions in that area (which was the case with Webster's contract), the amount of the compensation must be determined based on the criteria in Article 17 of the FIFA Regulations, which refer to the law of the country in question, the specificity of the sport and other criteria, with the most important factors being the player's remaining salary under the existing contract, the transfer sum that the player's old club may have to pay (spread out over the entire term of the contract) and whether the breach of contract was within or after the Protected Period.

CAS considers that which of these aspects must be considered in the specific case in the determination of the amount of the compensation to be paid depends on the circumstances of the breach (during or after the Protected Period, breach by club or by player).

CAS is of the opinion that the protection that clubs enjoy during the Protected Period (severe penalties on breach by the players) entitles the players to some degree of protection after the Protected Period. In CAS's view, if the compensation for breach to be paid after the Protected Period were to be punitive in nature or result in a financial benefit to the club, this would be a violation of that protection. The compensation for breach after the Protected Period must be the same for both players and clubs, and must be set on the basis of criteria that lead to this equality of compensation.

With this in mind, CAS considers that the determination of the amount of the compensation to be paid by Webster cannot be based on any hypothetical value of the player on the transfer market (club's loss of

profit), nor can it take into account the player's substitution value, for the reason that either one would enrich the club and express a punitive measure against the player. In its judgment CAS determines that independently of such considerations there is no economic, moral or legal justification for a club to demand the market value of the player as loss of profit.
Finally, CAS considers that the value of the contract between Webster and his new club (Wigan Athletic) is irrelevant to the determination of the amount of the compensation to be paid, being that the only relevant factor is the value of the contract breached by Webster.
CAS concludes by determining that the compensation to be paid by Webster to Hearts must be the remaining value of Webster's contract with Hearts. If a club prematurely terminates a temporary contract with a player, it must generally pay that player the remaining salary under that contract, and so in view of the consideration that after the Protected Period the compensation upon breach must be the same for both club and player, this rule must be applied in the event of termination by a player.

27 APRIL 2007

47585
DECISION OF THE DISPUTE RESOLUTION CHAMBER
passed in Zurich, Switzerland, on 27 April 2007,
in the following composition:
Slim Aloulou (Tunisia), chairman
Wilfried Straub (Germany), Member
Mario Gallavotti (Italy), Member
Joaquim Evangelista (Portugal), Member
Gerardo Movilla (Spain), Member
on the claim presented by the club,
X, XX, represented by Mr 00, attorney at law, as "Claimant"
against the club, Y, YY, as "Respondent"
regarding a training compensation dispute related to the transfer of the player Z.

FACTS OF THE CASE

1. According to the official confirmation from the XX Football Association, the player Z born on 8 September 1983, was registered as a professional player with the XX club, X (hereinafter: *the Claimant*), from 6 July 2002 until 21 August 2005, i.e. between the ages of 18 and 21. The player in question had signed an employment contract with the Claimant on 4 July 2002 which ran until 30 June 2005.
2. A copy of the said employment contract was remitted to the Dispute Resolution Chamber.
3. On 3 July 2005, the player signed an employment contract as a professional with the YY club, Y (hereinafter: *the Respondent*), and, according to the official confirmation from the YY Football Federation, was registered with the Respondent at the YY Football Federation on 23 August 2005.
4. By means of its letter dated 25 April 2006, the Claimant submitted a complaint with FIFA against the Respondent in which It requested training compensation of EUR 180,000 plus five per cent interest accrued since 1 October 2005, in accordance with FIFA circular no. 826, dated 31 October 2002. The Claimant based its complaint on the allocation of the Respondent, a YY first-division club, to Category 2, which corresponds to an amount of EUR 60,000 per year of training. With regard to the interest charged, the Claimant asserted that it had requested the Respondent to pay the training compensation in a letter dated 13 September 2005, setting a deadline until 30 September 2005.
5. The Claimant also asserted that the Respondent had so far refused to pay training compensation, objecting that the Claimant had not offered the player a new contract with at lest equivalent terms than his previous contract with the Claimant. In this connection, the Claimant submitted a contract offer dated 29 April 2005 signed by the Claimant, which It had apparently sent to the player by registered post with recorded delivery. The Claimant added that the contract offer was delivered to the player on 3 May 2005. According to the Claimant, the player was informed beforehand that such an offer would be forthcoming. In this regard, the Claimant is of the view that the FIFA Regulations for the Status and Transfer of Players (edition 2005), in particular art. 6 par. 3 of Annex 4 of the

Regulations, do not stipulate that the 60-day term is only deemed to have been met when the relevant letter reaches the player within the said term.

6. Finally, the Claimant is of the view that the former edition of the Regulations (edition 2001) is applicable on the case at hand and not the revised edition of the Regulations (edition 2005). In this connection, the Claimant emphasized that its obligation to make a contract offer to the player, the breach of which the Respondent asserts, had to be fulfilled by April 2005 at the latest, at which point in time the old Regulations were unquestionably still in force. The Claimant further asserts that the old Regulations set no term within which the relevant contract offer had to be made to the player concerned.
7. The Claimant further points out that in the FIFA circular no. 995, dated 23 September 2005, It is clearly stated that due to the transition from the former to the revised edition of the Regulations, there should be no negative effect on facts of a particular case that had already arisen before the entry into force of the revised Regulations, as this would otherwise contravene the general legal principle prohibiting retroactive effect.
8. The Claimant further underlines that even if, contrary to its expectations, art. 6 par. 3 of Annex 4 of the revised Regulations should be considered applicable on the case at stake and thus its letter dated 29 April 2005 would 1w deemed not to have met the relevant deadline, it would still be entitled to training compensation. The aforementioned article provides that the corresponding amount of compensation is payable if the former club, i.e. the Claimant, can justify that it is entitled to. In this regard, the Claimant has submitted a list of its alleged expenditure on the player during the training period, i.e. from 4 July 2002 to 30 June 2005. According to this list, the Claimant had spent around EUR 520,000 on the player in salary, bonuses and social security contributions. Commission in the amount of EUR 45,600 were allegedly also paid to the player's agent at the time of his transfer to the respondent as well as transfer compensation amounting to EUR 150,000 to the player's former club. Finally, the Claimant also submitted a list of the general costs per year of its second team, where the player in question mainly played. According to this list, EUR 87,707.64 per year and player is spent on the team's operational costs.
9. On 5 July 2006, the Respondent informed FIFA that in its opinion, the Claimant had no right to receive training compensation. The Respondent further indicated that, according to the information provided by the player at the time of his transfer to the Respondent, the Claimant had not offered the player a new contract within the 60-day term. The Respondent further indicated that the Claimant did not raise any objections to his transfer to the Respondent at the time of the issuance of the International Transfer Certificate for the player Z.
10. The Respondent further pointed out that it had only signed an employment contract with the player because he was not contractually bound to any other club. In this respect, the Respondent alleges that it was suffering financial problems at that time and that it would not have been able to afford to pay transfer compensation.
11. The Respondent underlined that according to art. 26 par. 2 of the revised Regulations, said regulations are applicable to cases brought after their entry into force.
12. In its second statement, the Claimant particularly confirmed its statements made in its initial complaint. It also reiterated that even if the Respondent had been under the impression that the player was a free agent, this would not affect the Claimant's entitlement to training compensation.
13. In its second statement, the Respondent reiterated the position it had previously adopted, i.e. that the new Regulations are applicable on the case at stake and that the Claimant, having failed to offer the player a new contract within the 60-day term, has no right to training compensation.

II. CONSIDERATIONS OF THE DISPUTE RESOLUTION CHAMBER

1. First of all, the Chamber analysed whether it was competent to deal with the matter at stake. In this respect. it referred to art. 18 par. 2 and 3 of the Rules Governing the Procedures of the Players' Status Committee and the Dispute Resolution Chamber. The present matter was submitted to FIFA on 26 April 2006, as a consequence the Chamber concluded that the revised Rules Governing Procedures (edition 2005) on matters pending before the decision making bodies of FIFA are applicable to the matter at hand.
2. With regard to the competence of the Chamber, art. 3 par. 1 of the abovementioned Rules states that the Dispute Resolution Chamber shall examine its jurisdiction in the light of art. 22 to 24 of the current version of the Regulations for the Status and Transfer of Players (edition 2005). In accordance

with art. 24 par. 1 in combination with art. 22 (d) of the Regulations 2005, the Dispute Resolution Chamber shall adjudicate on disputes between two clubs belonging to different Associations related to training compensation.

3. As a consequence, the Dispute Resolution Chamber is the competent body to decide on the present litigation concerning the training compensation claimed by the Claimant for the training and education of the player Z.
4. Subsequently, the members of the Chamber analyzed which edition of the Regulations for the Status and Transfer of Players should be applicable as to the substance of the matter. In this respect, the Chamber referred to art. 26 par. 1 and 2 of the Regulations for the Status and Transfer of Players (edition 2005) in the modified version in accordance with the FIFA circular no. 995, dated 23 September 2005. Furthermore, it acknowledged that the professional had been registered for his new club on 23 August 2005. Equally the Chamber took note that the claim of the Claimant was lodged at FIFA on 26 April 2006. In view of the aforementioned, the Chamber concluded that the current FIFA Regulations for the Status and Transfer of Players (edition 2005, hereafter: *the Regulations)* are applicable on the case at hand as to the substance.
5. In continuation, and entering into the substance of the matter, the members of the Chamber started by acknowledging the above-mentioned facts of the case as well as all the documentation contained in the file. In particular, the Chamber acknowledged that on the one hand, the Claimant requested training compensation amounting to EUR 180,000 based on the number of years the player spent training with the Claimant plus 5% interest accrued since 1 October 2005 and, on the other hand, the Respondent mainly invoked that the Claimant is not entitled to receive any training compensation by means of not having offered the player a contract of at least an equivalent value to his existing one within the deadline of 60 days as provided for by art. 6 par. 3 of Annex 4 of the Regulations (edition 2005).
6. In this respect, the members of the Chamber acknowledged that the Claimant offered, by means of its letter dated 29 April 2005, the player Z a better contract than the existing one (in the sense of the value of the contract) in writing. The Chamber took note that the Claimant provided a copy of the said letter as well of its enclosures, containing a new contract offer for the season 2005/2006.
7. In continuation, and taking into account that as established above under point 11.4. the revised Regulations are applicable on the matter at stake, the members of the Chamber referred to art. 6 of Annex 3 of the said Regulations, which contains special provisions regarding players moving from one Association to another inside the territory of the EU/EEA. According to par. 3 of the mentioned provision, training compensation is only payable if the former club does offer the player a contract of at least an equivalent value to the current contract in writing via registered mail at least 60 days before the expiry of his current contract or if it can justify that it is entitled to training compensation.
8. At this point, the Chamber underlined that, considering the divergent statements of the Claimant and the Respondent, the core issue between the parties to the present dispute is therefore whether the Claimant had to satisfy the formal criteria of art. 6 par. 3 of Annex 4 of the Regulations in order to be entitled to training compensation. i.e. to offer the player an employment contract of at least an equivalent value to the current contract and, in particular that such offer has to be made at least 60 days before the expiry of the player's current contract.
9. Subsequently, considering the fact that the player moved between two EU/EEA countries, the Chamber took into consideration the Regulations 2001 (cf. art. 5 par. 5 of the Regulations governing the Application of the Regulations 2001 and FIFA circular no. 769, dated 24 August 2001) and the Regulations 2005 (cf. art. 6 per. 3 of Annex 4 of the Regulations). in case a player moves within the territory of the EU/EEA.
10. In this context, the Chamber deemed It appropriate to emphasize that due to the often experience difficulties by the relevant parties concerned to demonstrate that they have proceeded to offer a player a new Contract, the revised Regulations (edition 2005) integrate some formal requirements in order to facilitate the evidence that a contract offer was effectively made.
11. In the present case, the Chamber emphasized, however, that at the time the Claimant should have made the contractual offer to the player in question, the formal requirements provided for by the Regulations (edition 2005) were not yet in farce. In fact, the player's contract he signed with the Claimant on 4 July 2002 was valid until 30 June 2005. Thus, even by assuming that the Claimant would have to comply with the term of 60 days as established by art. 6 par. 3 of Annex 4, the relevant decisive date for the proposal of a contract would unquestionably had been before the entry into force

of the Regulations (edition 2005), i.e. on 1 July 2005. To require that the Claimant should have had to comply with the formal requirements of the Regulations (edition 2005) before their entry into force would constitute a retroactive application of the said formal requirements.

12. In view of the above, the deciding body concluded that these formal requirements of 60 days do not apply on the case at hand. Therefore, the entitlement of the Claimant to training compensation was not subject to the formal time limit requirement established by art. 6 par. 3 of Annex 4 of the Regulations.
13. Furthermore, the members of the Chamber observed the argument raised by the Respondent according to which, at the time of the player's transfer from the Claimant to the Respondent, the Claimant did not make any objections against such a transfer of the player. Moreover, the Respondent pointed out that it only signed a contract with the player in question because the latter was not contractually bound to any other club.
14. To this regard, the Chamber stressed, however, that such a possible and, by the way not evidenced, renouncement of the Claimant to claim for transfer compensation from the Respondent does not affect or include the Claimant's entitlement to receive *training compensation* in accordance with the relevant Regulations (it is us who emphasize). In this connection, the Chamber underlined that the right of a club to claim transfer compensation from the player's new club is clearly to be distinguished from a club's entitlement to training compensation for the contribution of training and development it provided to a specific player.
15. The Dispute Resolution Chamber then referred to art. 20 and art. 2 of Annex 4 of the Regulations and emphasized that, as a general rule, training compensation is payable up to the age of 23. In this respect, It was noted that at the time of his move to the Respondent, the player Z was 21 years old.
16. As a result of all the above, and after having duly considered all the documentation provided by both parties as well as their respective positions, the members unanimously concluded that the Claimant offered a new employment contract to the relevant player and is entitled to receive training compensation for the training and education of the player Z.
17. After having established the Respondent's obligation to compensate the Claimant for the training of the player in question, the members went on to deliberate on the proper calculation of this compensation.
18. In accordance with art. 1 par. 1 of Annex 4 in combination with art. 2 of Annex 4 of the Regulations, training compensation is payable, as a general rule, for training incurred between the ages of 12 and 21, when the player concerned is registered for the first time as a Professional, or when a Professional is transferred between two clubs of two different Associations, before the end of the season of the player's 23 birthday.
19. In this respect, the Chamber acknowledged that, according to the relevant player passport remitted by the XX Football Association, the player Z, born on 8 September 1983, was registered with the Claimant as a Professional from 6 July 2002 until 21 August 2005.
20. In light of all of the above, the Chamber decided that the Claimant is entitled to training compensation for the period of 3 seasons (season 2002/2003, season 2003/2004 and season 2004/2005).
21. The Chamber amplified that the player was moving between two Associations inside the territory of the EU/EEA. Moreover, the Chamber took note of the fact that the player was moving from a higher category club (the Claimant classified in category 1) to a lower category club (the Respondent classified in category 2).
22. Taking into account the above and in accordance with art. 6 lit. par. 1 lit. b) of Annex 4 of the Regulations, as a general rule, in order to calculate training compensation due to the player's former club, i.e. the Claimant, the calculation shall be based on the training costs of the lower category dub. The established lower amount is, according to the general rule of art. 5 par. 2 of Annex 4 of the Regulations, to be multiplied by the number of years of training by the player's training club.
23. According to the FIFA circular no. 959, dated 16 March 2005, which regards the categorisation of clubs, the Claimant belongs to category 1, thus the corresponding indicative amount for a first category club in Europe is EUR 90,000 and the Respondent belongs to category 2, for which the corresponding indicated amount is EUR 60,000.
24. Consequently, as mentioned above, the relevant amount of training costs of the lower category is EUR 60,000, an amount which must be multiplied by the number of years the player spent training with the Claimant, i.e. 3 seasons as established under point II.20.

25. Based on all the foregoing considerations, the Chamber concluded that the Respondent has to pay the amount of EUR 180,000 to the Claimant as training compensation for the training and education of the player Z.
26. Consequently, in light of the fact that this payment is due since the thirty-first day after the registration of the player Z with the Association of his new club, i.e. 23 August 2005, and considering that the Claimant asks application of interest as from 1 October 2005, the Chamber established that a default interest payment of 5% *p.a.* as from 1 October 2005 must be applied on the due amount.

III. DECISION OF THE DISPUTE RESOLUTION CHAMBER

1. The claim lodged by the Claimant, X, is accepted.
2. The Respondent. Y, shall pay the amount of EUR 180,000 to the Claimant, X, within 30 days following the date of the notification of the present decision.
3. On the aforementioned amount, a default interest payment of 5% p.a. as from 1 October 2005 until the date of the payment is applied.
4. In the event that the above-mentioned amount is not paid within the stated deadline, the present matter shall be submitted to FIFA's Disciplinary Committee, so that the necessary disciplinary sanctions may be imposed.
5. The Claimant, X, is instructed to inform the Respondent, Y, directly and immediately of the account number to which the remittance is to be made and to notify the Dispute Resolution Chamber of every payment received.
6. According to art. 61 par. 1 of the FIFA Statutes this decision may be appealed before the Court of Arbitration for Sport (CAS). The statement of appeal must be sent to the CAS directly within 21 days of receiving notification of this decision and has to contain all elements in accordance with point 2 of the directives issued by the CAS, copy of which we enclose hereto. Within another 10 days following the expiry of the time limit for the filing of the statement of appeal, the appellant shall file with the CAS a brief stating the facts and legal arguments giving rise to the appeal (cf. point 4 of the directives).

REGULATIONS

TABLE OF CASES

FIFA DISPUTE RESOLUTION CHAMBER*

* Italics: cases *in extenso*

COURT OF ARBITRATION FOR SPORT (CAS)

EUROPEAN COURT OF JUSTICE

SUBJECT INDEX

ASSER INTERNATIONAL SPORTS LAW SERIES

Editors
Robert C.R. Siekmann and Janwillem Soek

ISSN 1874–6926

Basic Documents of International Sports Organisations, R.C.R. Siekmann and J.W. Soek, eds. (The Hague/Boston/London, Kluwer Law International 1998)

Doping Rules of International Sports Organisations, R.C.R. Siekmann, J.W. Soek and A. Bellani, eds. (The Hague, T.M.C.ASSER PRESS 1999)

Arbitral and Disciplinary Rules of International Sports Organisations, R.C.R. Siekmann and J.W. Soek, eds. (The Hague, T.M.C.ASSER PRESS 2001)

Professional Sport in the European Union: Regulation and Re-regulation, A. Caiger and S. Gardiner, eds. (The Hague, T.M.C.ASSER PRESS 2001)

Mediating Sports Disputes: National and International Perspectives, I.S. Blackshaw (The Hague, T.M.C.ASSER PRESS 2002)

The European Union and Sport: Legal and Policy Documents, R.C.R. Siekmann and J.W. Soek, eds. (The Hague, T.M.C.ASSER PRESS 2005)

Sports Image Rights in Europe, I.S. Blackshaw and R.C.R. Siekmann, eds. (The Hague, T.M.C.ASSER PRESS 2005)

The Court of Arbitration for Sport 1984–2004, I.S. Blackshaw, R.C.R. Siekmann and J.W. Soek, eds. (The Hague, T.M.C.ASSER PRESS 2006)

The Strict Liability Principle and the Human Rights of Athletes in Doping Cases, J.W. Soek (The Hague, T.M.C.ASSER PRESS 2006)

The Council of Europe and Sport: Basic Documents, R.C.R. Siekmann and J.W. Soek, eds. (The Hague, T.M.C.ASSER PRESS 2007)

European Sports Law: Collected Papers, S. Weatherill (The Hague, T.M.C.ASSER PRESS 2007)

Players' Agents Worldwide: Legal Aspects, R.C.R. Siekmann, R. Parrish, R. Branco Martins and J.W. Soek, eds. (The Hague, T.M.C.ASSER PRESS 2008)

The Sporting Exception in European Union Law, R. Parrish and S. Miettinen (The Hague, T.M.C.ASSER PRESS 2008)

GPSR Compliance

The European Union's (EU) General Product Safety Regulation (GPSR) is a set of rules that requires consumer products to be safe and our obligations to ensure this.

If you have any concerns about our products, you can contact us on ProductSafety@springernature.com

In case Publisher is established outside the EU, the EU authorized representative is:

Springer Nature Customer Service Center GmbH
Europaplatz 3
69115 Heidelberg, Germany

Batch number: 10682177

Printed by Printforce, the Netherlands